FEDERAL
TAX
ACCOUNTING

SECOND EDITION

STEPHEN F. GERTZMAN

STUDENT EDITION

WARREN GORHAM LAMONT

This publication is designed to provide accurate and
authoritative information in regard to the subject matter
covered. In publishing this book, neither the author nor
the publisher is engaged in rendering legal, accounting, or
other professional service. If legal advice or other expert
assistance is required, the services of a competent
professional should be sought.

*Still dedicated with love to
Alice, Casey, Lauren,
Sylvia, and Milton*

About the Author

Stephen F. Gertzman is a partner in the law firm of Sutherland, Asbill & Brennan. An honors graduate in accounting and law from the University of Florida (B.S.B.A., M.A., and J.D.), Mr. Gertzman has chaired the Subcommittee on Inventories and the Committee on Tax Accounting Problems of the Tax Section of the American Bar Association and has served on a number of task forces on tax accounting. He is also a member of the adjunct faculty of the Emory University School of Law, a Fellow of the American College of Tax Counsel, and a Trustee of the Southern Federal Tax Institute and the Georgia Federal Tax Conference. He has written and lectured frequently and conducts an active practice in the area of tax accounting.

Preface

When the first edition of *Federal Tax Accounting* was published, tax accounting had only begun to emerge as one of the more important areas of tax law. In large part, this emergence was due to the relatively high rates of inflation and interest experienced during the late 1970s and early 1980s. Since publication of the first edition, the significance of tax accounting has increased steadily. Many law schools and schools of accounting have given it substantially more attention, and several schools now provide courses on the topic. Also, to an increasing extent, tax literature regularly includes relevant discussions of tax accounting issues.

The recognized importance of tax accounting and the attention given to it are expected to continue to grow for several reasons. First, it has become clear that tax accounting changes and policies can generate significant tax revenues for the government—with concurrent liabilities for taxpayers—or they can create significant benefits for taxpayers. As a consequence, tax accounting is receiving considerably more attention today than in the past: from Congress in legislation; from the IRS on audit and in rulings; from the courts in litigation; and, of course, from taxpayers and practitioners in planning and compliance. Second, the inherent complexity of tax accounting is being dealt with in various, sometimes inconsistent, ways. On one hand, more and more courses are offered on the topic and IRS agents are receiving improved training. On the other hand, tax accounting affords the IRS considerable discretion, and many agents and others within government sometimes seek to ignore sound principles of tax accounting and instead support their positions on the basis of the Service's inherent discretion in the area, thereby sometimes creating anomalous results and inconsistent applications of principle and effectively precluding a uniform administration of the tax law. Such results can be prevented only with a more thorough understanding of proper tax accounting. *Federal Tax Accounting* is directed towards this end.

This book acquaints both the taxpayer and the tax practitioner with tax accounting. Further, and more importantly, it provides the taxpayer (whether a sole practitioner or a multinational corporation) and tax practitioner with the information, analyses, and insights necessary to plan for, and comply with, this increasingly important area of tax law. It provides both sophisticated analyses as well as clear and understandable explanations of the complexities inherent in this area of tax law. It apprises the taxpayer, tax practitioner, and others of the applicable legal principles, rules, and authorities governing tax accounting issues. It also advises the taxpayer and tax practitioner how to respond to issues that may be raised on audit, as well as how to respond to tax laws when the business in question lacks the accounting sophistication and capacity for literal compliance with all applicable rules and regulations.

This book is divided into 12 chapters. Chapter 1 defines tax accounting and discusses the complexity of the topic, including the political, economic, and fiscal considerations that resulted in the tax accounting laws that are in force today. Chapter 2 identifies and analyzes the requirements governing all methods of tax accounting. Chapters 3, 4, and 5 cover the cash method, accrual methods, and the installment method, respectively. Chapters 6 and 7 cover methods of accounting for inventories. Chapters 8 and 9 cover changes in methods of accounting and techniques for obtaining the most beneficial methods of accounting. Chapter 10 covers taxable periods. Chapter 11 covers the rules affecting so-called time value of money issues. Chapter 12 identifies and analyzes overriding principles affecting all tax accounting.

In addressing the various topics, the taxpayer is referred to as "it" if the authority or topic under discussion involves, or is most likely to be of interest to, a corporation, partnership, or other nonindividual. The taxpayer is referred to as "he" or "she" according to whether the taxpayer in a particular discussion is a man or woman or if the taxpayers most likely to be affected by the particular issue are individuals. The National Office of the IRS is referred to whenever the discussion focuses on policy decisions of the IRS or rulings, revenue procedures, or other pronouncements by the National Office of the IRS.

Acknowledgments

I would like to acknowledge and thank several people whose contributions and assistance in preparing this treatise were invaluable: first, my secretary, Deborah Branter, who worked tirelessly in typing and checking drafts, in preparing the voluminous tables and index, and in sacrificing much of her personal time to see this work through to timely completion; next, my colleague, Daniel R. McKeithen, a fine lawyer who specializes, among other topics, in issues involving the time value of money and who worked many hours to ensure that this topic was accurately and adequately addressed; finally, my book editor at Warren Gorham Lamont, Lynne Marsala, whose wonderful approach to completing this revision made the entire process so enjoyable.

I would also like to thank my partners, Randolph W. Thrower, Mac Asbill, Jr., and N. Jerold Cohen, who have provided me with so many opportunities to practice in this area of tax law. I consider myself fortunate to have worked with these fine attorneys for so many years and to have learned so much from them. I also wish to express my gratitude to all of my other partners and associates in Sutherland, Asbill & Brennan for the comradery and quality of practice that has made my professional expertise so fulfilling.

Finally, and most importantly, I thank my family: my daughters, Casey and Lauren, for understanding my all too frequent inattention and absence; and my wife, Alice, for her assistance in reading drafts and checking on matters of style and grammar, for her (usually) positive suggestions, and for all her patience, support, and encouragement.

STEPHEN F. GERTZMAN

Atlanta, Georgia
October 1993

Summary of Contents

1 Tax Accounting—What Is It? 1-1

2 Methods of Accounting 2-1

3 The Cash Receipts and Disbursements Method 3-1

4 Accrual Methods 4-1

5 The Installment Method 5-1

6 Inventories 6-1

7 LIFO 7-1

8 Changes in Methods of Accounting 8-1

9 Accounting Changes Not Requiring IRS Approval 9-1

10 Accounting Periods 10-1

11 Time Value of Money 11-1

12 Annual Accounting and Transactional Concepts 12-1

TABLE OF IRC SECTIONS T-1

TABLE OF TREASURY REGULATIONS T-11

TABLE OF REVENUE RULINGS AND REVENUE PROCEDURES T-19

TABLE OF CASES T-23

INDEX I-1

Table of Contents

1 Tax Accounting—What Is It?

¶ 1.01 What Is Tax Accounting? 1-1
    [1] Originally Considered of Little Importance 1-2
    [2] Change in Attitude 1-2
    [3] Legislative Activity 1-4
    [4] Financial Accounting Impact 1-5

¶ 1.02 Tax Accounting Topics 1-6
    [1] Methods of Accounting 1-6
    [2] Cash and Accrual Methods 1-7
    [3] Installment Reporting 1-7
    [4] Inventories 1-8
    [5] Changes in Accounting Practices and Methods 1-8
    [6] Accounting Periods 1-9
    [7] Time Value of Money 1-9
    [8] Annual Accounting and Transactional Concepts 1-10

¶ 1.03 Difficulties Facing Taxpayers and Tax Advisors 1-10
    [1] Complexity 1-10
    [2] Political, Fiscal, and Economic Considerations 1-12
    [3] Compliance and Application 1-13

¶ 1.04 Constant Change 1-14

2 Methods of Accounting

¶ 2.01 Scope and Definition of "Method of Accounting" 2-2
    [1] Timing 2-2
    [2] Consistency 2-3
    [3] Certainty and Predictability 2-4
    [4] Overall Methods and Methods for Individual Items 2-4

¶ 2.02 Requirements Governing All Methods of Accounting 2-5
    [1] Book Conformity 2-6
        [a] Origin of Requirement 2-7
        [b] Does Information on Different Bases Violate
            Requirement? 2-9

        [c] Conversion Workpapers Reconcile Different Methods ...   2-13
        [d] Consistency Favored Over Conformity   2-17
        [e] Financial Statements Do Not Determine Method   2-19
    [2] Clear Reflection of Income   2-22
        [a] Method Must Be Correctly Applied   2-24
        [b] Is Authorization by Code or Regulations Enough? 2-25
        [c] Effcct of Consistent Use of GAAP   2-27
        [d] Nature of Business Transactions, Manipulation, and
            Abuse   2-29
        [e] Effect of Consistency   2-30
        [f] Mismatching (Virtually Identical Results) 2-31
        [g] Relevance of Size of Taxpayer's Business 2-37
        [h] To Reflect Income More Clearly   2-38
        [i] Use of Method by Others   2-39
        [j] Judicial Application of Requirement   2-40
            [i] Fair and honest reporting standard 2-40
            [ii] Accuracy standard   2-43
        [k] Reconciliation of Authorities   2-46

¶ 2.03 Taxpayer's Discretion in Choice of Method 2-47
    [1] Use of More Than One Method   2-48
        [a] Use of Different Methods for Separate Trades or
            Businesses   2-48
        [b] Combination (Hybrid) Method   2-53
    [2] Incorrect Initial Choice   2-54
    [3] Application of Correct Choice to Incorrect Year 2-55

¶ 2.04 Commissioner's Discretion in Determining Method   2-55
    [1] Proper Exercise of Discretion   2-58
    [2] Abuse of Discretion   2-60
    [3] Impact of IRS Actions on Commissioner's Discretion 2-60
        [a] Acceptance of Returns Without Notice   2-60
        [b] Acceptance of Returns Giving Notice   2-62
        [c] IRS Nonacceptance Despite Agent's Actions 2-65
        [d] Acceptance Because of Agent's Actions 2-67
        [e] Change Approved or Directed by Commissioner   2-70

3 The Cash Receipts and Disbursements Method

¶ 3.01 Definition   3-2
    [1] Characteristics   3-3
    [2] Users   3-3
    [3] Issues   3-4

¶ 3.02 History and Development   3-4
    [1] Cash-Flow Principles   3-8
        [a] Items of Income   3-8
        [b] Items of Expense   3-9
        [c] Ability to Pay   3-10
    [2] Benefits of Cash Method   3-10

	[3] Attitude of IRS	3-11
¶ 3.03	Reporting Items of Income	3-12
	[1] Cash Equivalence	3-13
	[a] Items of Income	3-13
	[b] Time for Recognition	3-14
	[c] Problem of Intangible Property	3-14
	[d] Alternative Resolutions of Problem	3-15
	[i] Traditional cash equivalence	3-16
	[ii] Fair market value	3-17
	[iii] Subsequent cases	3-18
	[iv] Position of Treasury	3-19
	[v] Present status	3-20
	[2] Constructive Receipt	3-22
	[a] Purpose	3-22
	[b] Restrictions and Limitations	3-23
	[3] Particular Items of Income	3-25
	[a] Interest	3-25
	[b] Dividends	3-28
	[c] Compensation	3-29
	[d] Rent and Royalty Income	3-30
	[e] Other Items	3-31
¶ 3.04	Reporting Items of Expense	3-31
	[1] Payment by or on Behalf of Taxpayer	3-31
	[2] Constructive Payment	3-32
	[3] Form of Payment	3-33
	[a] Payment With Borrowed Funds or Third-Party Obligation	3-33
	[b] Payee	3-34
	[4] Payment by Taxpayer's Check or Note	3-35
	[a] Checks	3-35
	[b] Notes or Other Evidences of Taxpayer's Indebtedness	3-36
	[5] Particular Items of Expense	3-36
	[a] Interest	3-37
	[b] Insurance Premiums	3-41
	[c] Taxes	3-41
¶ 3.05	Prepayments	3-42
	[1] Basic Issues	3-42
	[a] Character of Payment	3-43
	[b] Capitalization and the One-Year Rule	3-43
	[2] Prepaid Expenses of Cash Basis Tax Shelters	3-45
	[a] Section 461(i) Prior to 1986 Act	3-45
	[b] The 90-Day Exception	3-46
	[i] Deduction limited to cash basis	3-46
	[ii] Drilling costs	3-46
¶ 3.06	Availability of Cash Method	3-47
	[1] Limitations Under the 1986 Act	3-49
	[a] Gross Receipts Test	3-49
	[b] Qualified Personal Service Corporations	3-51
	[i] Permitted activities: function test	3-51
	[ii] Ownership test	3-53

　　　[c] Farming Business 3-53
　　　[d] Effective Date and Required Change From Cash
　　　　　Method 3-54
　　[2] Transactions Involving Merchandise 3-55
　　[3] Termination of Business 3-57

¶ 3.07　Required Use of Cash Method 3-58

¶ 3.08　Clear Reflection of Income 3-59
　　[1] Amount of Deferral 3-60
　　[2] Existence of Accrual Basis Information 3-61
　　[3] Accrual Basis Financial Reporting 3-62
　　[4] Generally Accepted Accounting Principles 3-64
　　[5] Mismatching of Income and Expense 3-64
　　[6] Consolidated Group 3-67
　　[7] IRS Difficulty With Cash Method 3-68

4　Accrual Methods

¶ 4.01　Definition 4-2
　　[1] Requirements for Recognizing Income and Expense 4-2
　　[2] Differences Between Accrual Tax Accounting and Accrual
　　　　Financial Accounting 4-3
　　[3] IRS View 4-4
　　[4] Users 4-4
　　[5] Characteristics 4-5

¶ 4.02　History and Development 4-6
　　[1] Early History 4-6
　　[2] Acceptance of Financial Accounting 4-6
　　[3] Divergence Between Book and Tax Accounting 4-7
　　[4] *Thor Power Tool Co.* 4-8

¶ 4.03　Reporting Items of Income 4-10
　　[1] All Events Test 4-10
　　　[a] Fixed Right to Receive 4-10
　　　　[i] Conditions precedent, conditions subsequent, and
　　　　　　disputes 4-11
　　　　[ii] Taxpayer's knowledge of right or amount 4-13
　　　　[iii] Flexibility to determine right to receive 4-14
　　　[b] Determination of Amount With Reasonable Accuracy .. 4-15
　　[2] Items of Doubtful Collectibility 4-17
　　　[a] Level of Uncertainty 4-18
　　　[b] Time of Uncertainty 4-19
　　　[c] Accrual of Item Whose Collection Was Previously in
　　　　　Doubt 4-20
　　　[d] Nonaccrual of Service Income 4-20
　　[3] Prepaid Income 4-24
　　　[a] Pretrilogy Treatment 4-24
　　　[b] The Trilogy 4-26
　　　[c] Post-Trilogy Decisions 4-29
　　　[d] Length of Deferral 4-32

　　　　　　　[e] Provisions Permitting Deferral 4-32
　　　　　　　　　[i] Congressional 4-32
　　　　　　　　　[ii] Treasury and IRS 4-33

¶ 4.04　Reporting Items of Expense 4-40
　　　　[1] Fact of Liability Must Be Fixed 4-42
　　　　　　　[a] Identification of Liability 4-42
　　　　　　　　　[i] Identification of payee 4-44
　　　　　　　　　[ii] Likelihood of performance and conditions
　　　　　　　　　　　subsequent 4-45
　　　　　　　　　[iii] Conditions precedent 4-48
　　　　　　　[b] Matching 4-49
　　　　　　　[c] Contested Liabilities 4-52
　　　　　　　　　[i] Payment of contested liability 4-54
　　　　　　　　　[ii] Resolution of contest 4-55
　　　　[2] Determination of Amount With Reasonable Accuracy 4-55
　　　　　　　[a] Certainty of Amount 4-56
　　　　　　　[b] Possibility of Adjustment 4-58
　　　　　　　[c] Timing of Facts on Which Amount Is Based 4-58
　　　　[3] Economic Performance 4-58
　　　　　　　[a] Section 461(h) 4-59
　　　　　　　[b] Time When Economic Performance Occurs 4-61
　　　　　　　　　[i] Services and property provided to taxpayer 4-62
　　　　　　　　　[ii] Services and property provided by taxpayer 4-63
　　　　　　　　　[iii] Workers' compensation and tort liabilities 4-63
　　　　　　　　　[iv] Other items 4-64
　　　　　　　[c] "As Provided" Requirement 4-65
　　　　　　　　　[i] General rules and questions arising prior to issuance
　　　　　　　　　　　of regulations 4-65
　　　　　　　　　[ii] Applicable Treasury regulations 4-67
　　　　　　　[d] Proof of Compliance With Economic Performance Test 4-75
　　　　　　　[e] Impact on Other Than Current Deductions 4-75
　　　　　　　[f] Exception for Certain Recurring Items 4-77
　　　　　　　　　[i] Timely return or eight and one half months 4-78
　　　　　　　　　[ii] Recurring nature 4-79
　　　　　　　　　[iii] Not a material item or a more proper match 4-80
　　　　　　　　　[iv] Adopting recurring item exception 4-82
　　　　[4] Items Where Payment Is Doubtful 4-83

5   The Installment Method

¶ 5.01　Overview: Problem, Resolution, and Change 5-3
　　　　[1] Problem 5-3
　　　　[2] Resolution 5-4
　　　　[3] Legislative Change and Structure 5-5

¶ 5.02　Benefits and Burdens 5-5
　　　　[1] Deferral in Recognition of Gain 5-5
　　　　[2] Increase in Cash Flow 5-6
　　　　[3] Lowering Effective Tax Rate 5-7
　　　　[4] Flexibility in Time of Recognition 5-7

[5] Investment of Deferred Tax Liability 5-8
[6] Risk of Loss 5-9
[7] Changes in Tax Rates and Laws 5-9

¶ 5.03 Requirements and Conditions 5-9

¶ 5.04 Dealers in Personal Property 5-10
[1] History and Development 5-10
[2] Issues 5-13
    [a] Who Is a Dealer? 5-14
    [b] Is Personal Property Involved? 5-15
    [c] Do Sales Occur Regularly? 5-16
        [i] Definition of "regularly" 5-17
        [ii] Portion of total sales 5-17
        [iii] Continuous vs. periodic sales 5-19
    [d] Sales on Installment Plan 5-20
        [i] Traditional installment plans 5-20
        [ii] Revolving credit plans 5-25
[3] Installment Computations by Dealers 5-27
    [a] By Year 5-28
    [b] By Type of Sale 5-29
    [c] By Type of Goods 5-30
[4] Disposition of Dealer Installment Obligations 5-30
[5] Defaults, Repossessions, and Bad Debts 5-31
[6] Disposition to Member of Consolidated Return Group 5-32
[7] Election of Installment Method 5-34

¶ 5.05 Installment Sales of Property Other Than Inventory 5-35
[1] History and Development 5-35
    [a] Prior Conditions to Use of Installment Method 5-35
    [b] Statutory Format and Perceived Inadequacy 5-37
    [c] 1980 Act 5-38
    [d] 1986 Act 5-38
    [e] 1987 Act 5-39
[2] Installment Sale 5-39
[3] Installment Method 5-40
[4] What Is a Payment? 5-41
[5] What Is Not a Payment? 5-41
[6] Proportionate Disallowance Rule 5-42
[7] Issues Regarding Payments 5-46
    [a] Payments Prior to Year of Sale 5-47
    [b] Right to Prepay 5-47
    [c] Payment or Assumption of Seller's Qualifying
        Indebtedness 5-48
    [d] Third-Party Indebtedness 5-49
    [e] Third-Party Guarantees 5-50
    [f] Purchaser Debt Payable on Demand or Readily
        Tradable 5-51
[8] Computation of Installment Income 5-51
    [a] Selling Price 5-51
    [b] Selling Expenses 5-52
    [c] Contract Price 5-53
    [d] Sale of Multiple Assets 5-55
[9] Recapture Under Sections 1245 and 1250 5-56

[10] Wraparound Mortgages 5-57
    [a] Reasons for Use 5-57
    [b] Law Prior to 1980 Act 5-58
    [c] Regulations Under 1980 Act 5-59
    [d] Potential Benefit From New Regulations 5-61
[11] Related-Party Sales 5-65
    [a] Installment Obligations Received in Corporate
        Liquidations 5-67
    [b] Related-Party Rules 5-68
        [i] Marketable securities 5-69
        [ii] Property other than marketable securities 5-71
        [iii] Exceptions to application of related-party rules 5-71
        [iv] Extension of statute of limitations 5-72
    [c] Sales of Depreciable Property to Controlled Entity 5-72
[12] Contingent Price Rules 5-73
    [a] Maximum Sales Price Stated 5-74
    [b] No Maximum Price, but Fixed Payment Period 5-74
    [c] Both Selling Price and Payment Period Indefinite 5-76
    [d] Alternatives 5-76
        [i] Income forecast method 5-76
        [ii] Avoiding inappropriate basis deferral or
            acceleration 5-77
    [e] Private Annuities 5-78
[13] Like-Kind Exchanges 5-79
[14] Defaults and Repossessions 5-80
[15] Elections Out 5-81
    [a] Fixed Amount Obligations 5-83
    [b] Contingent Payment Obligations 5-84

¶ 5.06 Disposition of Installment Obligations 5-84
    [1] At Death 5-85
    [2] Cancellation or Unenforceability 5-86
    [3] To and From Corporations and Other Entities 5-87
        [a] Transfers to Controlled Entities 5-87
        [b] Certain Liquidations 5-88
        [c] To Life Insurance Companies 5-88
    [4] Modifications, Substitutions, and Other Changes 5-89
    [5] Using Installment Obligations as Collateral 5-91

¶ 5.07 The 1987 Act: Repeal and Revision 5-92
    [1] Repeal of Installment Method for Dealers 5-92
    [2] Repeal of Proportionate Disallowance Rule 5-93
    [3] Special Rules for Nondealers of Real Property 5-94
    [4] Pledges of Installment Obligations Treated as Payments 5-94
    [5] Minimum Tax 5-95

6   Inventories

¶ 6.01 Significance of Inventories 6-3
    [1] Primary Issues 6-3
    [2] Consequences of Having Inventories 6-3

¶ 6.02 Need for Inventories 6-4
    [1] To Determine Gross Income 6-4
    [2] To Determine Cost of Goods Sold 6-5
    [3] Use of Accrual Method 6-6

¶ 6.03 History 6-7

¶ 6.04 Basic Requirements 6-8
    [1] Statutory Provisions 6-9
       [a] Section 471 6-9
          [i] Best accounting practice 6-9
          [ii] Most clearly reflecting income 6-10
       [b] Section 263A 6-10
    [2] Regulatory Provisions 6-11

¶ 6.05 Merchandise, Supplies, and Other Inventories 6-12
    [1] Merchandise 6-13
       [a] Definition 6-13
       [b] Ownership 6-14
       [c] Acquired for Sale 6-16
       [d] Sale of Goods and Services 6-18
       [e] Dual-Use Property or Change in Use 6-22
       [f] Ordinary Course of Business 6-23
          [i] Profit element 6-23
          [ii] Regular business activity 6-24
       [g] Taxpayer Intent 6-25
    [2] Supplies Under Section 162 6-26
       [a] Business Expense or Inventoriable Cost 6-27
       [b] Supplies Inventories Required 6-29
       [c] Supplies Inventories Not Required 6-30
          [i] Records of consumption and physical inventories ... 6-31
          [ii] Incidental supplies 6-31
          [iii] Clear reflection of income 6-32
    [3] Other Inventories—Ability to Trace Costs 6-32
       [a] Real Estate 6-33
       [b] Special Order Merchandise 6-33

¶ 6.06 Inventoriable Costs 6-34
    [1] Wholesalers, Retailers, and Other Nonmanufacturers 6-35
       [a] Discounts 6-37
          [i] Trade discounts 6-37
          [ii] Cash discounts 6-37
       [b] Excessive Costs 6-38
       [c] Impact of 1986 Act 6-38
          [i] General method 6-39
          [ii] Simplified resale methods 6-39
    [2] Manufacturers 6-47
       [a] Direct Material Costs 6-48
       [b] Direct Labor Costs 6-48
       [c] Indirect Production Costs 6-49
          [i] Full absorption costing rules 6-50
          [ii] Uniform capitalization costing rules 6-57

¶ 6.07 Allocation of Inventoriable Costs to Items Produced 6-72
    [1] Manufacturing Burden Rate Method 6-74

[2] Standard Cost Method 6-76
[3] Practical Capacity 6-76
[4] Simplified Production Method 6-78
[5] Simplified Method for Allocating Mixed Service Cost 6-80

¶ 6.08 Allocation of Inventoriable Costs to Ending Inventory 6-83
[1] Cost-Flow Assumptions 6-83
[2] FIFO and LIFO 6-84
    [a] Record Keeping 6-85
    [b] Proscribed Methods 6-87
[3] Average Cost 6-87
    [a] IRS Position 6-88
    [b] Judicial Review 6-91

¶ 6.09 Inventory Write-Downs to Market 6-92
[1] Evolution of Rule 6-92
[2] Abnormal Goods 6-94
[3] Normal Goods 6-95
    [a] Definition of "Market for Purchased Goods" 6-97
    [b] Definition of "Market for Manufactured Goods" 6-98
        [i] No open market or nominal quotations 6-100
        [ii] Goods offered for sale 6-101
        [iii] Impact of GAAP on market write-downs 6-104
        [iv] Taxpayer response to *Thor Power Tool* 6-104

¶ 6.10 Special Inventory Costing Rules 6-105
[1] Dealers in Securities 6-106
[2] Inventories of Livestock Raisers and Other Farmers 6-106
[3] By-Products 6-107
[4] Inventories of Retail Merchants 6-107

¶ 6.11 Nontraditional Inventory Methods 6-109

7 LIFO

¶ 7.01 Reason for Cost-Flow Assumptions 7-2

¶ 7.02 LIFO Concept 7-3
[1] Objective 7-4
[2] History and Development 7-6

¶ 7.03 Requirements for Adoption and Use of LIFO 7-8
[1] Adoption 7-9
    [a] Application or Other Statement 7-9
    [b] Selective Use of LIFO 7-10
    [c] Subsidiary Elections 7-12
    [d] Commissioner's Discretion in Terminating LIFO 7-13
[2] Conformity Requirement 7-14
    [a] Rationale for Requirement 7-15
    [b] Application of Requirement 7-16
        [i] Supplementary or explanatory information 7-17
        [ii] Reporting on non-LIFO basis on a balance sheet ... 7-18
        [iii] Internal management reports 7-19

        [iv] Reports covering less than entire taxable year 7-19
        [v] Lower of LIFO cost or market 7-19
        [vi] Use of different costing procedures 7-20
        [vii] Reconciliations 7-22
        [viii] Controlled groups 7-22
        [ix] Financial forecasts and projections 7-23
    [3] Cost Requirement 7-24
      [a] Rationale for Requirement 7-25
      [b] Requirement's Impact on Timing of Adoption of LIFO .. 7-25
      [c] Restored and Prohibited Write-Downs 7-26
      [d] How Restoration Is Made 7-27
    [4] Books and Records 7-27
    [5] Statutory Periods of Limitation 7-29

¶ 7.04 LIFO Systems 7-29
    [1] Essentials 7-30
    [2] Specific Goods LIFO 7-30
      [a] Pooling 7-33
      [b] Quantitative Measure 7-34
      [c] Valuing Increments 7-34
    [3] Dollar-Value LIFO 7-35
      [a] Pooling 7-38
        [i] Natural-business-unit pools 7-38
        [ii] Other pools 7-43
        [iii] Single pool for certain small businesses 7-44
      [b] Base Costs and Alternative Measurement Procedures ... 7-44
        [i] Double-extension method 7-45
        [ii] Index method 7-48
        [iii] Link-chain method 7-49
        [iv] Reconstruction techniques 7-50
      [c] Valuing Increments 7-51
      [d] New or Revised Base Year 7-52
      [e] Product Costing Versus Component Costing 7-53
    [4] Retail LIFO 7-64
    [5] Simplified LIFO Methods 7-64
      [a] Price Index Method 7-65
        [i] Operation of method 7-65
        [ii] Adoption of price index method 7-70
        [iii] Changing to price index method 7-71
      [b] Simplified Dollar-Value LIFO: Section 474 7-72

¶ 7.05 Termination of LIFO 7-73
    [1] Judicial Attitude 7-75
      [a] In General 7-75
      [b] Regarding Proposed Terminations 7-77
    [2] IRS Attitude 7-78

¶ 7.06 Change From LIFO and Readoption of LIFO 7-79
    [1] Change Requiring Consent 7-80
    [2] Change Pursuant to Automatic Consent Provisions 7-80
    [3] Readoption of LIFO 7-82

¶ 7.07 Liquidations of LIFO Inventory 7-82
    [1] The Problem 7-82

[2] Taxpayer Response	....	7-83
[3] Statutory Relief	....	7-84
¶ 7.08 Acquisition and Transfer of LIFO Inventory	....	7-85
[1] Section 351 Transfer	....	7-85
[a] Impact on Transferor	....	7-85
[b] Impact on Transferee	....	7-87
[2] Acquisition at Bargain Price	....	7-88
[3] Section 381 Transaction	....	7-90
[a] Acquired Business and Acquirer on Same Method	.....	7-90
[b] Businesses to Remain Separate	....	7-92
[c] Businesses to Be Integrated	....	7-92
¶ 7.09 Adoption of S Corporation Status	....	7-92

8   Changes in Methods of Accounting

¶ 8.01 Governing Rules	....	8-3
¶ 8.02 What Constitutes a "Change in Method of Accounting"	....	8-4
¶ 8.03 Requirement of Prior Approval	....	8-5
¶ 8.04 Section 481 Adjustment Required	....	8-7
[1] Amount of Adjustment	....	8-11
[2] Limitations on Tax: Spread-Back of Adjustment	....	8-14
[a] Three-Year Allocation	....	8-14
[b] Consecutive Prior Years Allocation	....	8-15
[c] Special Rules	....	8-16
[d] Character of Taxpayer	....	8-17
[3] Spread-Forward of Adjustment	....	8-18
[4] Spread of Adjustment Under Revenue Procedure 84-74	.....	8-23
[a] General Rule	....	8-23
[b] Exceptions to General Rule	....	8-24
[i] Prior-year rule	....	8-24
[ii] Disproportionate build-up rule	....	8-24
[iii] Spread period for Category A methods	....	8-26
[iv] Spread period for Category B methods	....	8-27
[5] Acceleration of Adjustment Balance Under Revenue Procedure 84-74	....	8-28
[a] Cessation of Trade or Business	....	8-28
[b] Substantial Reduction in Inventory	....	8-31
[c] Change to LIFO Inventory Method	....	8-32
[d] Termination of LIFO Inventory Method	....	8-33
[e] Other Circumstances	....	8-33
[6] Spread of Adjustments Required by 1986 Act	....	8-33
[a] Change From Cash Method	....	8-34
[b] Change From Installment Method for Revolving Credit Sales	....	8-35
[c] Inventory Capitalization Rules	....	8-36
[d] Repeal of Reserve Method for Bad Debts	....	8-37
[7] Spread of Adjustment Under Revenue Procedure 92-20	.....	8-38

[8] Cut-off Method for LIFO Changes Under Revenue Procedure 92-20 8-38

¶ 8.05 Earnings and Profits 8-39

¶ 8.06 Application to Change Method of Accounting 8-39
        [1] General Rule 8-39
        [2] Governing Procedures Under Revenue Procedure 84-74 8-40
            [a] IRS Change of Erroneous Method in First Year Method Used 8-41
            [b] Change From Category A Method Following Contact by IRS 8-41
                [i] Definition of "Category A method" 8-41
                [ii] Contact by IRS 8-43
                [iii] Taxpayers subject to continuous audit 8-44
            [c] Return Under Review When Form 3115 Filed 8-44
            [d] Proposed LIFO Termination 8-46
            [e] Criminal Investigation 8-46
            [f] IRS Decision Not to Process Application 8-46
        [3] Governing Procedures Under Revenue Procedure 92-20 8-47
            [a] Categorization and Definition of "Accounting Methods" 8-47
                [i] Definition of "Category A method" 8-48
                [ii] Definition of "Designated A method" 8-49
                [iii] Definition of "Category B method" 8-50
                [iv] Definition of "Designated B method" 8-50
            [b] Terms and Conditions of Change 8-50
                [i] Taxpayers not under examination (timely, early, and late applications) 8-52
                [ii] Taxpayers under examination 8-57
                [iii] Special rules regarding Designated A methods 8-64
                [iv] Exceptions to Section 481 adjustment spread periods 8-67
                [v] Special rules for LIFO taxpayers 8-70
            [c] General Procedures Under Revenue Procedure 92-20 ... 8-72
                [i] IRS discretion not to apply revenue procedure or to modify other provisions 8-72
                [ii] Compliance with provisions 8-72
                [iii] Effect of particular facts and circumstances 8-73
            [d] Incomplete Forms 3115: Forty-Five-Day Rule 8-74
            [e] Two or More Trades or Businesses 8-74
            [f] Particular Filing Details 8-75
                [i] Where to file 8-75
                [ii] Copy to District Director 8-75
                [iii] Signature requirements 8-75
            [g] Consent Agreement Requirements 8-76
            [h] Protection for Years Prior to the Year of Change 8-77
            [i] Request for Conference the National Office 8-77
            [j] Effect of Revenue Procedure 92-20 on Appeals Office and Others 8-77
            [k] Effective Date 8-78
        [4] Year of Change 8-78
        [5] Application Pending at Time Return Is Due 8-78

¶ 8.07 Commissioner's Discretion in Approving Request for Change 8-80

        [1] Change From One Acceptable Method to Another 8-80
        [2] Change From Improper to Proper Method 8-82
           [a] IRS Consent Required on Change From Incorrect
                Method 8-84
           [b] IRS Consent Not Required on Change From Incorrect
                Method 8-85
        [3] Automatic Changes and Changes Deemed Approved 8-87

¶ 8.08 Obligation of Taxpayer to Change From Incorrect Method 8-88

¶ 8.09 Imposition of Penalties 8-88

9 Accounting Changes Not Requiring IRS Approval

¶ 9.01 Opportunities for Taxpayers 9-2
        [1] When There Is a Change in Method of Accounting 9-2
        [2] When There Is No Change in Method of Accounting 9-3
        [3] Planning 9-4

¶ 9.02 Definition of "Change in Method of Accounting" 9-6
        [1] What Is Included? 9-6
        [2] What Is Excluded? 9-7
        [3] Factors to Consider 9-8

¶ 9.03 Material Item 9-9
        [1] Development of Regulations 9-9
           [a] 1939 Code Regulations 9-9
           [b] Legislative History 9-9
           [c] Regulatory Definition Evolves 9-10
        [2] Pre-1970 Regulation Cases 9-11
           [a] Absolute Materiality 9-12
           [b] Relative Materiality 9-13
               [i] Material item of gross income 9-13
               [ii] Comparison to gross amount of item, taxable income,
                    or gross income 9-14
        [3] Post-1970 Regulation Cases 9-16

¶ 9.04 Consistent Treatment 9-20
        [1] Adoption of Method in Initial Year 9-21
           [a] Change of Correct Method 9-21
           [b] Change of Incorrect Method 9-22
        [2] Consistent Use of Arbitrary Procedures 9-25
           [a] Problem Confronting Taxpayers 9-25
           [b] Alternatives Available to Taxpayers 9-27
               [i] Treat existing practice as a method of accounting
                    and request change 9-27
               [ii] Elect method not requiring prior approval 9-27
               [iii] Make "do-it-yourself" correction 9-28
               [iv] Continue past practice 9-28
           [c] Recommendation 9-29

¶ 9.05   Correction of Errors   9-30
         [1] United States Court of Federal Claims   9-31
         [2] Tax Court   9-33
         [3] Courts of Appeals for Fifth and Tenth Circuits   9-35
         [4] Other Forums   9-37
         [5] Challenging Commissioner's Denial of Change   9-37

¶ 9.06   Change in Underlying Facts   9-38
         [1] Regulations   9-38
         [2] Judicial Development   9-40
              [a] Change in Contract, Business Practice, or Economic
                   Consequences   9-40
              [b] Significant Consequences to Parties   9-43
         [3] Importance of Defining "Method"   9-46
         [4] Change in Fact vs. Adoption of Method for New "Item" ...   9-48
         [5] Expansion of Existing Business   9-51

¶ 9.07   Change in Character of the Item   9-52

¶ 9.08   Techniques for Changes Without Prior Approval   9-56
         [1] The Drop-Down   9-57
              [a] Section 351 Transfers   9-58
              [b] Section 368 Reorganizations   9-58
              [c] Section 269 Acquisitions   9-60
         [2] Carryover Tax Attributes in Certain Corporate Acquisitions   9-62
         [3] Transfers of Business Growth   9-64

10   Accounting Periods

¶ 10.01   Need for Accounting Periods   10-3

¶ 10.02   Taxable Year   10-4
          [1] Annual Accounting Period   10-4
               [a] General Definition   10-4
               [b] Significance of Books   10-5
          [2] 52–53 Week Year   10-6
          [3] Short Periods   10-7
               [a] Change in Accounting Periods   10-7
                    [i]   Change in year requested and approved   10-8
                    [ii] Change in year required—Joining or leaving
                          consolidated group   10-8
                    [iii] Change in year required—Joining or leaving
                          partnership   10-9
               [b] Taxpayer in Existence for Less Than Entire Year   10-9
               [c] Jeopardy Assessments   10-10
          [4] FSCs and DISCs   10-11

¶ 10.03   Selection of Taxable Year   10-11
          [1] Business Considerations—Natural Business Year   10-12
          [2] Tax Considerations   10-13

¶ 10.04   Adoption of Taxable Year   10-14
          [1] Taxpayer Choice   10-14

[2] Time of Adoption 10-15
[3] Means of Adoption 10-16
[4] Rules Affecting Particular Taxpayers 10-16
     [a] Individuals 10-16
     [b] Regular Corporations 10-17
          [i] General rules 10-17
          [ii] First taxable year—New corporation 10-17
          [iii] First taxable year—Successor corporation 10-18
          [iv] First taxable year—Reactivated dormant
                corporation 10-19
     [c] Partnerships and Partners 10-19
          [i] Ordering rules under 1986 Act 10-19
          [ii] Sufficient business purpose rules 10-20
          [iii] Required change in year 10-22
          [iv] Effect of 1986 Act on business decisions 10-23
     [d] S Corporations and Shareholders 10-24
     [e] Personal Service Corporations 10-25
     [f] Other Entities 10-26
          [i] Trusts and estates 10-26
          [ii] Members of an affiliated group 10-27
          [iii] Real estate investment trusts 10-27
[5] Adoption of 52–53 Week Taxable Year 10-27

¶ 10.05 Change in Taxable Year 10-29
[1] Reasons for Change in Taxable Year 10-29
[2] Requirements for Change in Taxable Year 10-30
     [a] Substantial Business Purpose 10-30
     [b] Conform to Natural Business Year 10-30
     [c] Circumstances Not Amounting to Substantial Business
          Purpose 10-31
     [d] Request for Change Within 10 Years of Prior Change ... 10-32
     [e] Deferral or Distortion of Income Resulting From
          Change 10-32
     [f] Change to Conform to Annual Accounting Period 10-34
     [g] Change to or From 52–53 Week Taxable Year 10-34
          [i] Without prior approval 10-34
          [ii] With prior approval 10-35
[3] Applications for Change in Taxable Year 10-36
     [a] Form 1128 10-36
     [b] Taxpayer Acceptance of IRS Approval 10-37
     [c] Return Due Before IRS Determination 10-37
[4] Requests for Change Affected by Nature of Taxpayer 10-38
     [a] Individuals 10-38
     [b] Corporations 10-39
          [i] Automatic change per regulations 10-39
          [ii] Automatic change per revenue procedure 10-40
          [iii] Special rules 10-42
     [c] Partnerships, S Corporations, and Personal Service
          Corporations 10-43
          [i] Deferral of three months or less 10-43
          [ii] Change to natural business year 10-45
          [iii] Corporate partners 10-46
     [d] Other Entities 10-46

             [i] Exempt organizations 10-46
             [ii] Taxpayer with no prior accounting period 10-47
        [5] Computation of Taxable Income for Short Period 10-47
             [a] Normal Annualization 10-48
             [b] Alternative Method of Annualization 10-50

¶ 10.06 Special Requirements Affecting 52–53 Week Taxable Years 10-52
        [1] General 10-52
        [2] Effective Dates 10-52

¶ 10.07 1987 Act: Use of Fiscal Year 10-53
        [1] Section 444 Election by Partnerships, S Corporations, and
             Personal Service Corporations 10-54
             [a] Background 10-54
             [b] Conditions for Making Section 444 Election 10-55
        [2] Termination of Section 444 Election 10-55
        [3] Tiered Structures 10-55
             [a] De Minimis Rules 10-56
             [b] Same-Taxable-Year Exception 10-57
        [4] Limitations on Deferral Period 10-57
        [5] Section 444 Election Procedures 10-58
             [a] Corporation Electing S Corporation Status 10-58
             [b] Back-Up Section 444 Election 10-59
        [6] Required Payment by Partnership or S Corporation 10-59
             [a] Amount of Payment 10-59
                  [i] Net base year income 10-60
                  [ii] Base year, deferral ratio, and applicable payment ... 10-60
                  [iii] Special rule for base years of less than 12 months ... 10-61
                  [iv] Special rules for certain applicable election years ... 10-61
             [b] Payment of Required Payments 10-61
             [c] Refunds of Required Payments 10-61
        [7] Returns Under Section 7519 10-62
        [8] Distributions or Reduced Deductions by Personal Service
             Corporations 10-62
             [a] Applicable Amount 10-62
             [b] Minimum Distribution Requirement 10-63
                  [i] Preceding-year test 10-63
                  [ii] Three-year-average test 10-63
             [c] Adjusted Taxable Income 10-64
             [d] Maximum Deductible Amount 10-64
             [e] Disallowance of Operating Loss Carry-Backs 10-64

11 Time Value of Money

¶ 11.01 Definition of "Time Value of Money" 11-3
        [1] The Problem—A Failure to Consider 11-3
             [a] Different Character of Income 11-4
             [b] Different Methods of Accounting 11-5
        [2] Congressional Response 11-5
             [a] Before 1984 Act 11-5
                  [i] Original Section 483 11-5

                [ii] Section 163(b) 11-6
                [iii] Early OID provisions 11-7
                [iv] IRS position 11-7
          [b] 1984 Act 11-8

¶ 11.02 Original Issue Discount 11-9
     [1] Debt Instruments 11-11
     [2] Amounts Received for Debt Instruments: Section 1271 11-12
          [a] Effect of Intent to Call Before Maturity 11-13
          [b] Short-Term Obligations 11-15
          [c] Exceptions 11-16
     [3] Current Inclusion of OID: Section 1272 11-16
          [a] Obligations Issued After July 1, 1982 11-17
                [i] Definitions and terms 11-18
                [ii] Exceptions 11-22
                [iii] Subsequent holders of debt obligation 11-24
          [b] Corporate Obligations Issued Before July 2, 1982 11-25
     [4] Amount of OID: Section 1273 11-26
          [a] Stated Redemption Price at Maturity 11-26
                [i] Qualified stated interest 11-26
                [ii] Loans with indefinite maturities 11-28
                [iii] Installment obligations 11-28
                [iv] Puts, calls, and other options 11-31
          [b] Issue Price 11-31
                [i] Publicly offered debt instruments issued for cash ... 11-31
                [ii] Non–publicly offered debt instruments issued for
                     cash 11-32
                [iii] Debt instruments issued for property with public
                     trading 11-33
                [iv] Investment units; convertible debt 11-34
                [v] Other cases 11-35
          [c] De Minimis Rule 11-35
     [5] Issue Price in Certain Cases Involving Property: Section
          1274 11-37
          [a] Imputation of Interest 11-38
                [i] General rules—applicable federal rates 11-38
                [ii] Potentially abusive situations 11-40
                [iii] Use of special 9 percent discount rate 11-42
                [iv] Sale-leaseback transactions 11-42
          [b] Exceptions 11-42
                [i] Sale of certain farms for $1 million or less 11-42
                [ii] Sale of principal residence 11-43
                [iii] Sale or exchange of property for $250,000 or less ... 11-43
                [iv] Sale of patent 11-43
                [v] Sale or exchange to which Section 483(e) applies ... 11-44
                [vi] Debt instruments due in six months or less 11-44
                [vii] Personal use property 11-44
          [c] Election to Use Cash Method 11-44

¶ 11.03 Contingent Payments 11-45
     [1] Definition 11-46
     [2] Market-Based Contingent Payments 11-47
          [3] Small Issues 11-49

       [4] Other Contingent Debt Instruments   11-51

¶ 11.04 Certain Deferred Payments: Section 483   11-53
       [1] History and Development   11-53
       [2] Application of Section 483   11-55
           [a] Due Dates of Payments   11-55
           [b] Unstated Interest   11-56
               [i] General rules   11-56
               [ii] Special rules on sale of land to related party   11-57
           [c] Periods When Unstated Interest Is Recognized   11-57
           [d] Exceptions to Application of Section 483   11-57

¶ 11.05 Market Discount: Sections 1276–1278   11-58
       [1] Definitions   11-58
       [2] Treatment of Market Discount Income   11-59
       [3] Deferral of Interest Deductions Allocable to Accrued Market
           Discount   11-60

¶ 11.06 Short-Term Obligations: Sections 1281–1283   11-61
       [1] Current Inclusion of Acquisition Discount   11-61
       [2] Deferral of Interest Deduction   11-62

¶ 11.07 Tax Treatment of Stripped Bonds: Section 1286   11-62
       [1] Treatment of Stripper   11-62
       [2] Treatment of Purchaser   11-63

¶ 11.08 Gains on Certain Obligations: Section 1287   11-63

¶ 11.09 OID on Tax-Exempt Obligations: Section 1288   11-64

¶ 11.10 Use of Property or Services: Section 467   11-64
       [1] Section 467 Rental Agreement   11-64
           [a] Deferred Payments of Rent   11-65
           [b] Stepped Rents   11-65
       [2] Treatment of Section 467 Rental Agreements   11-66
       [3] Agreements Pertaining to Deferred Payments for Services . . .   11-67

¶ 11.11 Below-Market Loans: Section 7872   11-67
       [1] Definition of "Below-Market Loan"   11-68
       [2] Below-Market Loans Subject to Section 7872   11-68
       [3] Treatment of Below-Market Loans   11-69
           [a] Demand Loans   11-69
           [b] Term Loans   11-71
           [c] Special Rules for Gift Loans   11-72

12   Annual Accounting and Transactional Concepts

¶ 12.01 Goal of Tax Accounting   12-2

¶ 12.02 Annual Accounting Concept   12-3
       [1] Codification of Concept   12-5
       [2] Application of Concept   12-5
           [a] Deduction Proper in Year Claimed   12-5

        [b] Deduction Improper in Year Claimed 12-6
        [c] Deduction Not Taken in Year Originally Available 12-6
        [d] Income Erroneously Reported Before Proper Year 12-8
        [e] Income Not Reported in Proper Year 12-9
        [f] Influential Events After Year of Reporting 12-9
            [i] Change in law 12-10
            [ii] Additional income 12-11
            [iii] Tax retroactively imposed 12-11
            [iv] Taxpayer attempts to change facts retroactively 12-12
            [v] State court attempts to alter nature of earlier
                payments 12-12
    [3] Legislative and Judicial Ameliorations of Annual Accounting
    Concept 12-13

¶ 12.03   Claim-of-Right doctrine 12-14
    [1] Origin 12-14
    [2] Requirements for Application 12-16
        [a] Receipt of Income 12-16
        [b] Unlimited Control 12-17
        [c] Asserted Claim of Right 12-19
    [3] Prevailing Issues Under Claim-Of-Right Doctrine 12-19
        [a] Characterization of Receipts as Income 12-19
            [i] Prepaid income 12-20
            [ii] Illegal income 12-21
            [iii] Amounts received under mistaken claim 12-22
            [iv] Agreements to refund 12-22
            [v] Conduits and trustees 12-23
            [vi] Deposits 12-24
        [b] Availability of Deduction for Repaid Amounts 12-26
    [4] Statutory Relief: Section 1341 12-26
        [a] General Requirements 12-26
        [b] Unrestricted Right vs. Claim of Right 12-27
        [c] Connection Between Receipt and Repayment 12-27

¶ 12.04   *Arrowsmith* Doctrine 12-28
    [1] Scope 12-29
    [2] Applications 12-31
        [a] Initial Gain—Later Loss 12-32
        [b] Initial Loss—Later Gain 12-33
        [c] Initial Gain—Later Gain 12-33
        [d] Initial Loss—Later Loss 12-34
    [3] Inapplicability of Doctrine 12-35
    [4] Statutory Relief: Section 1341 12-35

¶ 12.05   Tax Benefit Rule 12-36
    [1] History and Rationale 12-36
    [2] Definition of "Recovery" 12-38
    [3] Amount of Recovery 12-39
    [4] Established Applications of Rule 12-40
        [a] Judicial Applications 12-40
            [i] Previously expensed items 12-40
            [ii] Charitable contributions returned 12-41
            [iii] Casualty losses 12-42
            [iv] Reimbursed losses 12-42

　　　　[v]　Unpaid accrued expenses 12-43
　　　　[vi]　Accrued liabilities abandoned by creditor 12-43
　　　　[vii]　Bad debt reserves 12-43
　　　　[viii]　Transfer of accounts receivable or other assets to
　　　　　　　controlled corporation 12-44
　　　　[ix]　Corporate liquidations 12-45
　　　　[x]　Contributions to capital 12-47
　　　　[xi]　Cancellation of indebtedness 12-48
　　　[b]　Legislative Applications 12-48
　　　　[i]　Section 111 12-48
　　　　[ii]　Depreciation recapture including ACRS 12-49
　　　　[iii]　Damage recoveries 12-49
　　　　[iv]　Foreign expropriation losses 12-50
　　　　[v]　LIFO recapture provisions 12-51
　　　[c]　Exceptions to Tax Benefit Rule 12-52
　　　　[i]　Erroneous deductions 12-52
　　　　[ii]　Absence of "deduction" 12-54

TABLE OF IRC SECTIONS T-1

TABLE OF TREASURY REGULATIONS T-11

TABLE OF REVENUE RULINGS AND REVENUE PROCEDURES T-19

TABLE OF CASES T-23

INDEX I-1

CHAPTER 1

Tax Accounting
—What Is It?

¶ 1.01 What Is Tax Accounting? 1-1
        [1] Originally Considered of Little Importance 1-2
        [2] Change in Attitude 1-2
        [3] Legislative Activity 1-4
        [4] Financial Accounting Impact 1-5

¶ 1.02 Tax Accounting Topics 1-6
        [1] Methods of Accounting 1-6
        [2] Cash and Accrual Methods 1-7
        [3] Installment Reporting 1-7
        [4] Inventories 1-8
        [5] Changes in Accounting Practices and Methods 1-8
        [6] Accounting Periods 1-9
        [7] Time Value of Money 1-9
        [8] Annual Accounting and Transactional Concepts 1-10

¶ 1.03 Difficulties Facing Taxpayers and Tax Advisors 1-10
        [1] Complexity 1-10
        [2] Political, Fiscal, and Economic Considerations 1-12
        [3] Compliance and Application 1-13

¶ 1.04 Constant Change 1-14

¶ 1.01 WHAT IS TAX ACCOUNTING?

The tax law essentially deals with only two major issues—character and timing. Character issues generally relate to whether items are includable in income or deductible as an expense.[1] Timing issues relate to when items of

---

[1] More particularly, character issues include whether items are taxable, nontaxable, or tax exempt, whether income is ordinary or capital, and whether expenditures are deductible or must be capitalized.

income and expense should be recognized. Tax accounting addresses the question of timing. In general, tax accounting is not concerned with whether an item is includable in income or deductible as an expense.

Tax accounting issues are among the most important in the tax field. Frequently, the amounts of money involved in these issues significantly exceed the amounts involved in whether a particular item is includable in income or deductible as an expense. Today, Congress, the Treasury, and the Internal Revenue Service are paying significant attention to tax accounting issues in legislation, in regulations, and on audit. Taxpayers and their tax advisors must therefore be more sensitive to these issues and considerably more familiar with them than in prior years. This book addresses in detail the most important of the tax accounting issues.

[1] Originally Considered of Little Importance

Prior to the high rates of inflation and interest experienced during the late 1970s and early 1980s, tax accounting issues were not considered of major importance either by taxpayers and their tax advisors or by the IRS. In most cases, taxpayers, their tax advisors, and the IRS instead focused their attention on what items were subject to the income tax and what items were deductible.

Issues as to when items would be recognized as income or expense were considered of less significance because of two principal factors. First, rates of inflation and interest were not considered high enough to cause the value of a deduction to be worth significantly more in one year than another, nor was the cost of recognizing income in an early year considered significantly greater than recognizing it in a later year. Simply stated, although economists, accountants, and financial analysts might have disagreed, most taxpayers, tax advisors, and IRS representatives were not concerned about timing issues because these issues were not considered to involve much money.

Second, because timing issues were considered to be relatively unimportant, they were often resolved administratively with either side, taxpayers or the IRS, willing to concede them. When controversies did include both timing issues and the includability of items as income or the deductibility of items as expense, the timing issues were often given short shrift. Tax advisors and the IRS frequently resolved their differences on tax accounting issues with the salutary statement that the issue involved only a matter of timing and should not stand in the way of a settlement of other, more important issues.

[2] Change in Attitude

Coincident with the high rates of inflation and interest during the late 1970s and early 1980s, considerable attention began to be focused on the time value of money. Taxpayers and their advisors became more sophisticated in these matters and soon learned that a deferral in the recognition of income or an acceleration in the deduction of an expense could produce significant financial advantages. Although many taxpayers and tax advisors had believed that these timing issues involved merely the benefit derived from the use of money for one year, the true benefit when a recurring item was involved was significantly in excess of the mere use of the funds for a short period.

> **EXAMPLE:** If an item of income were reported in year 2 rather than year 1, the taxpayer would obtain the financial benefit of delaying the payment of tax on that item for one year. If the tax amounted to $1,000 and the taxpayer could earn 10 percent on its funds, the benefit of the one-year deferral would be $100 before tax or $70 after tax, assuming a 30 percent tax rate. However, if the item of income being deferred was of a recurring nature, the financial benefit of the one-year deferral would be the entire $1,000.
>
> To illustrate further, assume (1) that a taxpayer who has been in business for three years receives $2,500 each year for services to be rendered in the immediately succeeding year; (2) that the taxpayer has recognized this amount in income in the year of receipt; (3) that the effective rate of tax on this income is 40 percent; and (4) that the taxpayer is considering a change in its method of reporting this item from the year of receipt to the year in which the services are rendered. If the taxpayer does not make the change, its income and tax for the first six years of operation will be as follows:

Year	Income	Tax (40 percent)
1	$2,500	$1,000
2	2,500	1,000
3	2,500	1,000
4	2,500	1,000
5	2,500	1,000
6	2,500	1,000

However, if the taxpayer changes its method of reporting income, beginning with year 4, from the year of receipt to the year in which the services are rendered, taxable income and tax will be as follows:

Year	Income	Tax (40 percent)
1	$2,500	$1,000
2	2,500	1,000
3	2,500	1,000
4	0	0
5	2,500	1,000
6	2,500	1,000

As this simple example demonstrates, the one-year deferral in the recognition of a recurring item of income can produce an economic benefit substantially greater than the mere use of funds for one year. The actual benefit is equivalent to excluding the item from tax for one full year.

In addition, taxpayers and tax advisors learned that a taxpayer often could obtain a greater financial benefit when it resolved a controversy by agreeing to include the entire amount of an item in income if the time of its recognition could be deferred than by agreeing to include immediately in income even a portion of the amount at issue. For instance, a taxpayer who had been in business for 10 years might be involved in a controversy over the includability of an item in income in year 5. The taxpayer could often obtain a greater financial benefit by agreeing to include the entire amount of the item in income in year 10 than by agreeing to include only a portion of the item in income in year 5. In the latter case, the taxpayer would have to pay not only the deficiency in tax but also the several years of interest that would be associated with that deficiency.

Of course, the IRS also learned the importance of the time value of money and began focusing on these issues. It began challenging methods of accounting more frequently, and for issues that it lost, it often sought to have the Treasury promulgate regulations or to have Congress enact legislation to reduce or eliminate the benefits that the IRS perceived were being realized by taxpayers through their methods of accounting.

[3] Legislative Activity

In recent years, Congress also has become more aware of tax accounting issues and the significant revenues associated with these issues. Accordingly, it has become considerably more active than in prior years in legislating tax accounting rules. This activity has been both a response to the efforts of the IRS and the Treasury to curb perceived taxpayer abuse and an effort to increase revenues in ways that cause less adverse political consequences than other areas or subjects of increased taxation.

Following the periods of high inflation and high interest rates during the late 1970s and early 1980s, the first major legislative enactment to address broad issues of tax accounting was the Tax Reform Act of 1984 (the 1984 Act). It made significant changes to the use of accrual methods of tax accounting by requiring that new conditions be satisfied before deductions would be allowed.[2] In addition, the 1984 Act made major changes to rules involving the characterization of deferred payments as principal or interest and to rules specifying the time when the interest would be recognized.[3]

A second major piece of tax legislation, the Tax Reform Act of 1986 (the 1986 Act), made additional significant changes in tax accounting rules.

---

[2] See IRC § 461(h) and discussion at ¶ 4.04[3]. All references to "IRC" are to the Internal Revenue Code of 1986, as amended (the Code).

[3] See, e.g., IRC §§ 467, 1271–1275, and discussion at ¶¶ 11.10, 11.02.

The 1986 Act imposed limitations on the use of the cash method of accounting, substantially revised the treatment of costs incurred in connection with the acquisition or production of inventory, eliminated the use of bad debt reserves in many instances, and significantly revised the use of the installment method of reporting.

In addition to these major pieces of legislation, it is now commonplace for most legislation to have tax accounting implications. For example, in late 1987, Congress passed H.R. 3545, the Revenue Act of 1987 (the 1987 Act). Among other provisions, the 1987 Act significantly limited continued use of the installment method and afforded S corporations, partnerships, and personal service corporations the opportunity to elect to retain a fiscal year by making advance payments of tax.[4]

Taxpayers and tax advisors should expect continued legislation in the tax accounting area for two principal reasons: (1) the financial importance of tax accounting issues and (2) the relatively minor adverse political reaction that legislation in this area provokes. It is therefore essential that taxpayers and tax practitioners be aware of both pending legislation and new regulations in this area.

[4] Financial Accounting Impact

At the outset, it must be recognized that financial accounting and tax accounting are not the same. They have different objectives, are subject to different rules, and serve different purposes.[5] Nevertheless, tax accounting affects financial accounting in many important ways, and financial accounting affects tax accounting in similarly important ways.

For example, items of income or expense may be recognized in different periods for tax and financial reporting purposes. Income may be reported in one period for financial reporting purposes and in an earlier or later period for tax reporting purposes. Consequently, the liability for federal income taxes is generally broken down into current and deferred portions. Where income is reported for financial and tax purposes in the same period, the associated tax liability that is reported on the financial statements is identified as a current liability. Where the income reported for financial reporting purposes will not be reported for tax purposes until a later period, the tax liability that is reported on the financial statement on account of that income is identified as a deferred liability and not as a current liability.

The rules governing the manner in which an entity's tax liability should

---

[4] See discussion at ¶ 5.07, regarding the 1987 Act's effect on installment reporting, and ¶ 10.07, regarding the Act's effect on the use of fiscal years by S corporations, partnerships, and personal service corporations.

[5] See discussion at ¶ 2.02[2][c], regarding generally accepted accounting principles.

be reported on its financial statements had for many years been the subject of opinions and interpretations of the Accounting Principles Board of the American Institute of Certified Public Accountants.[6] However, in response to various criticisms of these opinions and interpretations, the Financial Accounting Standards Board (FASB) reviewed the situation and in December 1987, issued Statement of Financial Accounting Standards (SFAS) No. 96, "Accounting for Income Taxes," which was to supersede or modify the prior rules and to be effective for fiscal years beginning after December 15, 1988. However, owing to comments received from practitioners and others about the complexity of the new rules and how they would be applied, the FASB agreed on December 6, 1989, to defer the implementation of SFAS 96 to fiscal years beginning after December 15, 1991. Accountants must remain alert to developments in this area. This area is but one example of the manner in which tax accounting affects financial accounting.

Conversely, financial accounting affects tax accounting in equally important ways. For example, under present law, some taxpayers are subject to the imposition of an alternative minimum tax (AMT) in circumstances where it produces a tax liability that is in excess of the taxpayer's regular tax for the year.[7] The AMT is imposed on "alternative minimum taxable income" (AMTI). Among the items that must be taken into account in determining a taxpayer's AMTI is the difference between the income reported by the taxpayer for financial reporting purposes and income reported for tax reporting purposes.

The application of SFAS 96 and the rules governing AMTI are beyond the scope of this treatise. However, the effect of the tax accounting methods discussed in this treatise on both the current and deferred portions of the tax liability shown on financial statements and in the computation of AMTI are most significant and must be kept in mind.

¶ 1.02 TAX ACCOUNTING TOPICS

This book addresses the most important tax accounting topics, which are summarized in the following paragraphs.

[1] Methods of Accounting

Chapter 2 focuses on methods of accounting. It defines the term "method of accounting" and analyzes the requirements governing the use of all methods

---

[6] See, e.g., APB Opinion No. 11, Accounting for Income Taxes (1967); APB Opinion No. 23, Accounting for Income Taxes—Special Areas (1972).

[7] See IRC §§ 55–59.

of accounting, including the requirements that tax methods (1) conform to the taxpayer's book methods and (2) clearly reflect income. Chapter 2 also discusses the discretion of both the taxpayer and the Commissioner in selecting methods of accounting and in determining whether the selected methods clearly reflect income.

The IRS almost always takes the position that it has virtually unlimited discretion in the area of tax accounting. However, as Chapter 2 describes, although the IRS does have considerable discretion, its discretion is not unlimited. In fact, there are significant restraints on the IRS's discretion and significant planning opportunities available to taxpayers. Taxpayers and their tax advisors should be familiar with both the limitations on the Commissioner's discretion and the opportunities available to taxpayers. Tax advisors should no longer assume (1) that the Commissioner can prevail on accounting issues merely by asserting that the resolution of the issue involves a matter of his discretion or (2) that the taxpayer has virtually no chance of overcoming the Commissioner's exercise of discretion.

[2] Cash and Accrual Methods

Chapters 3 and 4 cover the two most widely used overall methods of accounting. Chapter 3 covers the cash method, and Chapter 4 covers accrual methods.

Chapter 3 describes the manner in which items of income and expense are recognized under the cash method, the availability of the cash method to taxpayers, limitations on the use of the cash method (both before and after the 1986 Act), and circumstances in which the cash method is deemed to reflect income clearly. In typical tax practice today, there is a great deal of uncertainty and misunderstanding about the use of the cash method and its availability to taxpayers. Taxpayers and their tax advisors will find Chapter 3 most helpful in clarifying these matters.

Chapter 4 provides the rules for recognizing items of income and items of expense under accrual methods of accounting. It distinguishes accrual tax accounting from accrual financial accounting and discusses the fact that under the law today, accrual methods of tax accounting often have many more elements in common with cash method accounting than with accrual methods of financial accounting. Chapter 4 describes the treatment of accrued income that is unlikely to be collected and the treatment of income received prior to the time it is earned (so-called prepaid income). This chapter also covers the economic performance test that was enacted as part of the 1984 Act, and U.S. Supreme Court decisions affecting the proper time for accruing items of expense.

[3] Installment Reporting

Chapter 5 covers the installment method of reporting income from sales of property. It describes the benefits and burdens associated with the use of the method and the requirements for use of the method. It addresses virtually all issues that may be raised by the IRS in connection with the use of the installment method. In addition, it discusses the special rules governing application of the method to transactions between related parties and transactions where the amount of the sales price is contingent on subsequent events. This chapter also covers transactions involving like-kind exchanges, defaults and repossessions, and dispositions of installment obligations. Finally, it includes a discussion of the rules enacted as part of the 1986 Act and the changes made and limitations imposed by the 1987 Act.

[4] Inventories

Chapters 6 and 7 cover inventories. Chapter 6 deals with inventories in general. It addresses (1) the basic requirements governing all inventories; (2) distinctions between merchandise inventories and supply inventories, including differences in their treatment; (3) the costing of inventories by manufacturers, retailers, wholesalers, and others; and (4) write-downs of inventories from cost to market.

Chapter 6 also discusses nontraditional inventory methods that have been allowed by the IRS and the courts. It addresses practical problems facing taxpayers and tax advisors when the method of inventory costing used is one that is not expressly approved by the Code or Treasury regulations; in particular, when the taxpayer's record-keeping capacity, cost accounting system, and financial condition do not permit it to make precise calculations under an authorized method.

Chapter 7 covers the last-in, first-out (LIFO) method of inventory accounting. It discusses all requirements associated with the adoption and use of LIFO. In addition, Chapter 7 describes the various LIFO systems that are available to taxpayers, including specific goods LIFO, dollar-value LIFO, and simplified dollar-value LIFO, which was enacted as part of the 1986 Act. Chapter 7 also discusses the termination of LIFO, changes from LIFO, liquidations of LIFO inventories, the use of so-called LIFO component costing, the acquisition or transfer of LIFO inventories in both taxable and nontaxable transactions, and the acquisition of LIFO inventory in a bargain purchase.

[5] Changes in Accounting Practices and Methods

Chapters 8 and 9 cover changes in accounting methods and practices. Chapter 8 focuses on changes in accounting methods, requirements for those changes, and the tax treatment of those changes. It includes a discussion of Section 481, which governs the adjustments required on changes in methods of accounting, the applications to be filed, and the procedures to be used.

Further, the chapter analyzes the discretion of the Commissioner to approve requests for changes in methods of accounting, the obligations of taxpayers to change from incorrect to correct methods of accounting, and the imposition of penalties for use of improper methods of accounting. These topics generally have not received much attention in the past. However, as the importance of tax accounting methods and changes in methods have increased, these topics have become extremely significant.

As a companion to Chapter 8, Chapter 9 focuses on accounting changes that are not considered changes in accounting methods and, hence, do not require IRS approval. Among the included topics are the definition of "change in method of accounting," whether the item involved in the change is a material item, and whether the accounting method has been used consistently. The chapter also addresses the issue of whether a change in tax reporting is actually a change in underlying facts, the correction of an error, or a change in the character of an item instead of a change in accounting method.

In addition, Chapter 9 describes various techniques for changing methods of accounting without the need for prior IRS approval. These involve various corporate and business restructuring techniques that are generally known by the IRS and the Treasury but have received very little attention from taxpayers and their tax advisors, considering the significant benefits that may be derived from their use.

[6] Accounting Periods

Chapter 10 covers accounting periods. It defines "taxable year" and provides the rules regarding both the adoption of, or change in, a taxable year. The chapter focuses on all forms of business, including partnerships, S corporations, and so-called personal service corporations. It also describes the significant changes made by the 1986 and 1987 Acts and the use of fiscal years by each of these forms of business.

[7] Time Value of Money

Chapter 11 covers the time value of money provisions of the Code, particularly those focusing on the treatment of so-called original issue discount. Most of these provisions were enacted as part of the 1984 Act. They are extremely complex, and they are uncertain in scope. Moreover, it is not yet known to what extent examining agents will seek to apply these provisions to the transactions they cover. This relatively new area of tax law is most important. It covers virtually every transaction involving deferred payments, including sales, loans, leases, and even contracts for personal services. Chapter 11 also identifies basic rules and seeks to familiarize readers with both the general concepts and their various applications.

[8] Annual Accounting and Transactional Concepts

Chapter 12 covers fundamental concepts and principles that underlie all matters of tax accounting. The topics covered include the annual-accounting concept, claim-of-right doctrine, Arrowsmith doctrine, and the tax benefit rule. One or more of these concepts affects almost every transaction or series of transactions in which a taxpayer may become involved. Consequently, it is important for taxpayers and tax advisors to be aware of them and their possible applications. Application of these concepts frequently overrides what would otherwise be contrary statutory or regulatory treatment.

¶ 1.03 DIFFICULTIES FACING TAXPAYERS AND TAX ADVISORS

Tax accounting issues often arise from the coalescence of a number of unique factors: (1) the overall complexity of this area of tax law and the general unfamiliarity of so many tax practitioners with it; (2) the fact that so many of the laws in the area are more the product of political, fiscal, and economic considerations than an overall legal framework based on logic, reason, practicality, and common sense; (3) the difficulty experienced by taxpayers in complying with the applicable rules; and (4) the problems encountered by IRS representatives in attempting to apply these rules uniformly and fairly to all taxpayers.

These factors often result in inexplicable and illogical rules. Taxpayers and tax advisors who expect tax accounting rules to have the same symmetry and foundation as financial accounting rules will be sorely disappointed.

The discussion of these difficulties is not intended to take issue with or criticize Congress, the Treasury, or the IRS. The tax accounting laws and regulations in effect today are the result of the practical aspects of obtaining the revenue necessary to provide for the functions and responsibilities of government, combined with the existing nature of our political process. Thus, this discussion is intended only to identify problems that exist and to alert taxpayers and their tax advisors to those problems.

[1] Complexity

The Code sections, Treasury regulations, and IRS rulings and procedures applicable to tax accounting matters are often among the most complex and technical of all tax law. Yet, because so few schools provide courses or training in tax accounting, members of Congress, their staffs, judges, lawyers, and other tax practitioners often are unfamiliar with tax accounting topics and ill-equipped to deal with them. Even trained accountants or others who have had numerous accounting and business courses find themselves at a loss in handling tax accounting matters because tax accounting principles are often so different from, and inconsistent with, financial accounting principles.

Congress often deals with these topics by going to extremes--either by enacting detailed, complex provisions[8] or by enacting only the most general of rules in the Code.[9] In either case, Congress generally delegates significant discretion to the Treasury to promulgate rules and regulations to carry out the intent of Congress. Taxpayers and their tax advisors should be aware that, in many cases, the regulations or other rules designed to provide guidance to taxpayers as to how the law applies are not promulgated or issued for many months, even years, after the statute is enacted.[10] Moreover, after the Treasury issues proposed or temporary regulations, they are often changed when comments have been received, but until that time, temporary regulations remain in full force and effect.[11] Despite these difficulties, in only rare instances has Congress even implicitly delayed the effective date of the statutory provision until regulations are promulgated.[12] Congress has even gone so far as to suggest that new legislation could be amended effectively by later promulgated, inconsistent regulations.[13]

The courts are also troubled by tax accounting concepts and have great difficulty in applying them. Consequently, decisions are often inconsistent

---

[8] See, e.g., IRC §§ 453A–453C, 263A, 1271–1275.

[9] See, e.g., IRC §§ 446, 471.

[10] See, e.g., the regulations governing many aspects of installment reporting and the application of the original issue discount rules. The temporary regulations affecting installment sales apply to Code provisions enacted in 1980. The original issue discount regulations were first proposed in 1986, although the applicable Code sections were enacted in 1984. Section 461(h), pertaining to economic performance, was enacted in 1984; yet, final regulations were not issued effective until April 10, 1992. Many of the provisions affecting the 1986 Act are already in force; yet, final regulations have to be issued.

[11] See, e.g., Temp. Reg. §§ 1.263A-1T, which pertains to the application of the uniform capitalization rules; 1.448-1T, which pertains to application of the limitations on use of the cash method; 1.441-3T, 1.442-2T, and 1.442-3T, which pertain to the rules governing fiscal years.

[12] See, e.g., Section 467(g), pertaining to time value of money concepts applied to deferred payments for services. The provision indicates that rules comparable to those affecting deferred payments of rent will apply to deferred payments for services under regulations prescribed by the Treasury. Because no such regulations have yet been issued, practitioners have generally ignored the potential impact of these concepts on deferred payments for services.

[13] See Section 461(h)(2), where Congress set forth the principles to be applied in determining when economic performance occurs for purposes of obtaining deductions under accrual methods of accounting, but added the caveat that these principles apply except to the extent they are inconsistent with subsequently issued Treasury regulations. The Treasury has not been reluctant to issue such regulations. See discussion at ¶ 4.04[3].

and irreconcilable.[14] Courts often defer to the Commissioner's discretion, because of their desire to avoid becoming the final arbiter of these matters. Yet, these matters are likely to consume an increasing amount of judicial time in the future.

Taxpayers, tax advisors, IRS examining agents, and even those at the National Office of the IRS and the Treasury are often at a loss to understand exactly what rules should apply in a given circumstance and how to apply them. These people often have inadequate training, experience, or expertise in applying the general principles or formulating positions about them. All of these factors greatly affect the ability of taxpayers to comply with the law and the ability of their tax advisors to provide guidance.

[2] Political, Fiscal, and Economic Considerations

As previously stated, another major reason for the difficulty and complexity in this area is that fact the tax accounting rules are often enacted more for the purpose of obtaining revenues with minimum adverse political reaction than for the purpose of codifying a rational system of tax accounting. For example, significant effort was made to make the 1986 Act revenue neutral, i.e., to make certain that reductions in rates and other reductions in tax would be offset by increases in revenue so that the net result of the 1986 Act would be to maintain the level of total revenues, not to increase or decrease it. Towards this end, the Treasury has made it clear that in drafting regulations, the effects on revenue are just as important as a fair interpretation of the law.[15] To the extent that two approaches are appropriate, the Treasury is likely to choose the one that generates the greater revenue.

The tax accounting changes of the 1986 Act were among the major producers of revenue. Yet, to a great extent, the changes made were so complex that many taxpayers did not understand them or fully appreciate the financial impact they would have. Hence, there was relatively little initial objection to them. For example, many of the inventory costing rules, which in the aggregate are expected to provide a large percentage of the total increase in revenue under the 1986 Act,[16] represent a significant change from an approach that had been working well and that had tied in to cost accounting concepts

---

[14] See, e.g., Mooney Aircraft, Inc. v. United States, 420 F2d 400 (5th Cir. 1969), where deductions were disallowed on the basis that the time between the existence of the liability and its payment was so great that deductions should not be permitted; Ohio River Collieries Co., 77 TC 1369 (1981), where deductions were permitted even though payment of the liability would not take place for many years.

[15] See, e.g., "Treasury's effort to 'hold revenue' in implementing tax overhaul brings tax administration role into question," Bureau of National Affairs, Daily Report for Executives, No. 84, p. K-1 (May 4, 1987).

[16] See revenue effects of 1986 Act as provided in the General Explanation of the Tax Reform Act of 1986, at 1354–1379 (May 4, 1987).

of financial accounting. Under the 1986 Act, taxpayers are now required to inventory costs that had never previously been treated as costs of producing inventory in any financial accounting or economic sense. Although the legislative tax-writing committees asserted that these changes were needed to make the tax system fair and to compute income accurately, it is difficult to believe that those charged with the collection of tax revenue have found a fundamental flaw in the costing of inventories that economists and financial accountants have consistently missed.

Finally, the lack of symmetry between the rules for recognizing income on one hand and expense on the other is often troubling to taxpayers and their tax advisors. For example, a taxpayer must include in income under the cash method all income that has actually or constructively been received. However, deductions are permitted for expenses actually paid. No deductions are allowed under a concept of constructive payment. Similarly, items of income that are of doubtful collection need not be accrued under an accrual method. However, the uncertainty of payment does not prohibit the deduction of an expense under an accrual method. As a further example, income must be recognized under accrual methods pursuant to the controlling all events test, without regard to whether the performance that gives rise to the income has occurred. Yet, deductions are no longer permitted until the economic performance associated with the liability has occurred.

[3] Compliance and Application

Frequently, the drafters of the law and regulations have little familiarity with practical aspects of business record-keeping systems. Consequently, the drafters often fail to appreciate the difficulty taxpayers will have in accumulating the information necessary to comply with new laws and regulations. Correlatively, taxpayers are frequently at a loss to understand why they must incur significant accounting and data processing costs to comply, particularly when the additional tax generated by the new rules is slight in comparison to the cost of developing systems and obtaining information. A primary example of this is the application of the new uniform capitalization rules to the inventories of many taxpayers. It may be expected that many taxpayers will simply ignore the new rules, estimate what the results would be if the new rules could be followed precisely, and hope to resolve in a practical manner any issues that arise on audit.

Similarly, examining agents may also have very little understanding of how to apply the new rules. The treatment of original issue discount and its broad applicability is a case in point. Many agents simply do not understand these rules or how to apply them. Similar problems may be anticipated in connection with application of the new uniform capitalization costing rules.[17]

The Treasury has issued lengthy regulations pertaining to a wide variety of tax accounting subjects in an effort to provide guidance. Frequently, these regulations have the effect of reducing the judgment and discretion that otherwise would be required of agents applying the law to particular circumstances. The regulations are helpful in some cases, but produce unfortunate and unintended results in other circumstances. To the extent that the results produced are inconsistent with the controlling statute, the validity of the regulations is subject to challenge.[18]

¶ 1.04 CONSTANT CHANGE

Taxpayers and their tax advisors must remain alert to the ever-changing nature of tax accounting rules. Because even slight changes in these rules can generate significant amounts of revenue without significant adverse political repercussions, these rules are ripe for change whenever there is a need to increase revenue. It may be expected that these rules will also be targeted for change whenever there is the desire to spur investment or to otherwise stimulate the economy.

Major changes in the tax accounting rules occurred in the 1984 Act. Even greater changes occurred in the 1986 Act, and still further changes were made by the 1987 Act and later acts. Many regulations have been issued in temporary form; others have only been issued in proposed form. In addition, numerous revenue rulings and revenue procedures are issued throughout the year affecting tax accounting issues. Taxpayers and tax advisors must remain alert to these pronouncements and must always seek to obtain the most currently applicable law governing their particular issues.

As a consequence of the rapidity of this change (and as a practical matter in light of the time it takes to produce a book of this scope), every aspect of every issue covered may not represent the most current state of affairs affecting that issue. Accordingly, taxpayers and their tax advisors are encouraged to keep abreast of all current developments. In many cases, in an attempt to be as up-to-date as possible, citations are given to new developments but, to avoid delay in publication, analyses of these developments must be deferred until forthcoming supplements.

---

[17] See IRC § 263A.

[18] See, e.g., Temp. Reg. § 1.448-2T, pertaining to application of the nonaccrual-experience method. The regulatory formula for determining the amount that may be excluded from income based on the taxpayer's experience is deficient. Its application will require many taxpayers to include in income amounts that the statute prohibits the taxpayer from being required to include. See discussion at ¶ 4.03[2][d].

Finally, many of the conclusions in the book are presented in the form of what might be the law, of what should be the law, or of what might ultimately prove to be the law. This equivocation is, in many cases, mere habit, the typical behavior of the ever-cautious attorney. However, in other cases, it is the recognition that notwithstanding the seemingly incontrovertible nature of the authority pertaining to a problem, it is often the case in practice that this authority is just not interpreted as requiring literal compliance with the controlling Code or regulatory provisions. Taxpayers and their tax advisors should never automatically assume that everything means what it says, nor should they assume that there are no exceptions to what is stated. Creativity and imagination in handling the needs of clients are often the hallmark of good practice in the area of tax accounting. Yet, because of the risks, complexities, and uncertainties inherent in this area of tax practice, most tax practitioners are reluctant to engage in the issues that arise from tax accounting questions. They should not be. Indeed, in light of the significant revenues affected by tax accounting issues and the potential advantage to taxpayers, they cannot afford to be.

CHAPTER 2

Methods of Accounting

¶ 2.01 Scope and Definition of "Method of Accounting"   2-2
    [1] Timing   2-2
    [2] Consistency   2-3
    [3] Certainty and Predictability   2-4
    [4] Overall Methods and Methods for Individual Items   2-4

¶ 2.02 Requirements Governing All Methods of Accounting   2-5
    [1] Book Conformity   2-6
        [a] Origin of Requirement   2-7
        [b] Does Information on Different Bases Violate
             Requirement?   2-9
        [c] Conversion Workpapers Reconcile Different Methods . . .   2-13
        [d] Consistency Favored Over Conformity   2-17
        [e] Financial Statements Do Not Determine Method   2-19
    [2] Clear Reflection of Income   2-22
        [a] Method Must Be Correctly Applied   2-24
        [b] Is Authorization by Code or Regulations Enough?   2-25
        [c] Effect of Consistent Use of GAAP   2-27
        [d] Nature of Business Transactions, Manipulation, and
             Abuse   2-29
        [e] Effect of Consistency   2-30
        [f] Mismatching (Virtually Identical Results)   2-31
        [g] Relevance of Size of Taxpayer's Business   2-37
        [h] To Reflect Income More Clearly   2-38
        [i] Use of Method by Others   2-39
        [j] Judicial Application of Requirement   2-40
             [i] Fair and honest reporting standard   2-40
             [ii] Accuracy standard   2-43
        [k] Reconciliation of Authorities   2-46

¶ 2.03 Taxpayer's Discretion in Choice of Method   2-47
    [1] Use of More Than One Method   2-48
        [a] Use of Different Methods for Separate Trades or
             Businesses   2-48
        [b] Combination (Hybrid) Method   2-53
    [2] Incorrect Initial Choice   2-54
    [3] Application of Correct Choice to Incorrect Year   2-55

¶ 2.04   Commissioner's Discretion in Determining Method   2-55
         [1] Proper Exercise of Discretion   2-58
         [2] Abuse of Discretion   2-60
         [3] Impact of IRS Actions on Commissioner's Discretion   2-60
              [a] Acceptance of Returns Without Notice   2-60
              [b] Acceptance of Returns Giving Notice   2-62
              [c] IRS Nonacceptance Despite Agent's Actions   2-65
              [d] Acceptance Because of Agent's Actions   2-67
              [e] Change Approved or Directed by Commissioner   2-70

¶ 2.01 SCOPE AND DEFINITION OF "METHOD OF ACCOUNTING"

This chapter defines and examines the phrase "method of accounting" and covers the requirements governing all methods of accounting, both overall methods and methods used for individual items of income and expense. The chapter also covers the discretion of the taxpayer in choosing and applying methods of accounting and the discretion of the Commissioner in accepting, rejecting, or changing methods of accounting. Later chapters focus on particular overall methods of accounting (Chapter 3 on the cash method and Chapter 4 on accrual methods), special methods of accounting (Chapter 5 on the installment method and Chapters 6 and 7 on inventory methods), and changes in methods of accounting (Chapters 8 and 9).

The phrase "method of accounting" is not defined by either the Internal Revenue Code (the Code)[1] or the Treasury regulations. Congress and the Treasury apparently assume that a method of accounting is an understood concept of financial accounting and that ascertaining its definition will not be unduly difficult for taxpayers. On the whole, this assumption is correct. A method of accounting is generally understood to refer to any regularized practice or procedure for determining when to recognize items of income and expense. However, applying this general understanding to particular situations is not always easy, and, as discussed in the following sections, certain elements are critical in defining a method of accounting: timing, consistency, certainty, and predictability.

[1] Timing

Financial accounting is generally concerned with the means by which financial activities are recorded, classified, and summarized.[2] Methods of

---

[1] Unless otherwise specified, all references to "Code" or to "IRC" are to the Internal Revenue Code of 1986, as amended.

[2] American Institute of Certified Public Accountants (AICPA), Accounting Terminology Bulletin No. 1 (1953) states: "Accounting is the art of recording, classifying, and summarizing in a significant manner and in terms of money,

accounting are the particular means for determining when to recognize assets, liabilities, and items of income and expense. Consistently, the underlying assumption of tax accounting is that a method of accounting determines the time when an item of income or expense is to be recognized or reported for tax purposes.[3] It does not determine the aggregate amount of income or expense to be recognized from any particular transaction or series of transactions, which should be the same under any method of accounting.

Nevertheless, different methods may require income and expense to be recognized at different times. For example, accrual methods (see Chapter 4) generally require income and expense to be recognized at earlier times than the cash method (see Chapter 3).[4] For businesses that are stable in size or growing, the use of one method of accounting over another may often result in such a long deferral in the time when income will be recognized that the result is economically equivalent to a reduction in the aggregate income reported. This deferred income will be recognized only as the business declines in size.

To illustrate, if a business has $100 of accounts receivable at the end of its initial year and expects to have at least $100 of accounts receivable at the end of each succeeding tax year, its aggregate reported income will always be at least $100 less under the cash method than under an accrual method. As long as the level of year-end receivables is not reduced, that level of income will not be taxed.

[2] Consistency

Once a method of tax accounting has been adopted, it is assumed that the method will be consistently applied to a taxpayer's activities. Otherwise, there is no "method," only arbitrary procedures whose inconsistent application

---

transactions and events which are, in part at least, of a financial character, and interpreting the results thereof."

[3] (See ¶ 9.03 for discussion of "items" that may be the subject of changes in accounting methods.

[4] Under the cash receipts and disbursements method (the cash method), income is recognized in the year of actual or constructive receipt, and deductions are recognized in the year of actual payment. Under an accrual method, income is recognized in the year in which all events have occurred that fix the taxpayer's right to receive the income, and the amount of the income can be determined with reasonable accuracy. Deductions are recognized in the year in which all events have occurred that fix the fact of liability, the amount of the liability can be determined with reasonable accuracy, and economic performance has occurred.

makes the logical determination of income and expense during any particular period impossible.[5]

[3] Certainty and Predictability

The use of a method of accounting lends certainty and predictability to the recognition and recording of financial transactions and events. Thus, any particular method of accounting, as opposed to an arbitrary practice, should be so defined that any person applying that method to a particular set of facts will reach the same result. For example, one retailer may value each item in inventory at $1, while another values each item at whatever price he thinks it will sell for. Neither approach is correct, [6] but the former is a method of accounting.[7] The latter is not.

[4] Overall Methods and Methods for Individual Items

The Code makes it clear that the concept of a method of accounting includes not only overall methods of accounting, such as the cash receipts and disbursements method and accrual methods, but also the method of accounting used for each individual item of income or expense.[8] Thus, while it is important to determine a taxpayer's overall method of accounting, it is often just as important to determine the method used in reporting any particular item of income or expense.[9] The propriety of both overall methods and

---

[5] See, e.g., Walter H. Potter, 44 TC 159 (1965), acq. 1966-1 CB 3, where the taxpayer's practices were "regularly inconsistent throughout the years"; Holt Co. v. United States, 368 F2d 311 (5th Cir. 1966), regarding the taxpayer's seemingly arbitrary practice of charging off debts that were not worthless.

[6] See discussion at ¶ 6.08.

[7] See L.R. Gustafson, 55 TCM 250 (1988), where the taxpayer-lawyer's deduction of expenses when paid and recognition of income when all client work was completed was found to be an improper "method of accounting."

[8] Section 446(c) includes the following among permissible methods of accounting: "(1) the cash receipts and disbursements method; (2) an accrual method; (3) any other method permitted by this chapter; or (4) any combination of the foregoing methods permitted under regulations prescribed by the Secretary." By including categories (3) and (4), Congress effectively recognized that permissible overall methods of accounting include hybrid methods under which some items of income and expense may be accounted for under one method while other items of income and expense are accounted for under a different method. Moreover, Treas. Reg. § 1.446-1(a)(1) expressly provides that the "term 'method of accounting' includes not only the overall method of accounting of the taxpayer but also the accounting treatment of any item."

[9] Prior to the enactment of Section 446(c) as part of the 1954 Code, only two overall methods were permitted, the cash method and the accrual method. If a taxpayer's treatment of any particular item of income or expense departed from its

methods used for individual items is to be determined on the basis of the same standards. There is no general requirement of conformity between the overall method and the method used for individual items, except as affected by the clear reflection of income requirement.[10]

The Code also makes it clear that every method of accounting must satisfy certain requirements to be accepted for federal income tax purposes. These requirements apply to overall methods of accounting and to the method of accounting selected for each particular item of income or expense. In addition, once a method of accounting has been adopted for a particular item of income or expense, that method must generally be continued until changed on audit by the Internal Revenue Service or until permission to change has been received from the IRS.[11] (For further discussion of changes in accounting methods, see Chapters 8 and 9.)

¶ 2.02 REQUIREMENTS GOVERNING ALL METHODS OF ACCOUNTING

The general rules governing methods of accounting are set forth in Section 446, which establishes three requirements applicable to all methods of accounting.

1. The method must conform to the taxpayer's method of computing income in keeping its books.[12] This is known as the book conformity requirement.

2. The method must clearly reflect the income of the taxpayer.[13]

3. Except with the permission of the Commissioner (or as might otherwise be provided by the Code, Treasury regulation, or published revenue ruling or revenue procedure), a taxpayer must use its method of accounting consistently and without change.[14]

The first two requirements are discussed in the following two sections. The third requirement is the subject of Chapters 8 and 9.

---

initially chosen overall method, the taxpayer risked having that treatment changed on audit to the overall method. (See, e.g., cases cited infra note 39.) As a result of the enactment of Section 446(c), which permits taxpayers to use an overall method that consists of a combination of methods, departures from the overall method are not prohibited. Rather, they merely suggest that the overall method is a hybrid method rather than a pure cash or accrual method.

[10] See discussion infra ¶ 2.02[2].

[11] IRC § 446(e).

[12] IRC § 446(a).

[13] IRC § 446(b).

[14] IRC § 446(e).

[1] Book Conformity

The book conformity requirement is set forth in Section 446(a) as follows: "Taxable income shall be computed under the method of accounting on the basis of which the taxpayer regularly computes his income in keeping his books."

The regulations under Section 446 provide little guidance as to the scope of this provision. They point out that (1) the requirement does not preclude a taxpayer from using a nonbook method for reporting particular items of income or expense if such nonconforming method is otherwise required or permitted;[15] (2) a taxpayer whose sole source of income is wages does not need to keep formal books;[16] and (3) a taxpayer "who changes the method of accounting employed in keeping his books shall, before computing his income upon such new method for purposes of taxation, secure the consent of the Commissioner."[17]

On the surface, the book conformity requirement is rather straightforward. A taxpayer must compute income for tax purposes on the same basis it computes income for book purposes. Consequently, if a taxpayer wishes to use a particular method or methods for tax purposes, the taxpayer needs only to adopt those methods for book purposes. Unfortunately, decisions as to book accounting methods are generally made at the beginning of the business, well before preparation of the initial tax return. By the time the taxpayer's attention has turned to tax reporting opportunities, book methods have already been established, and much flexibility has been lost. For this reason, tax advisors should encourage taxpayers to consider tax reporting methods at the outset of business activities. The book methods may thereafter be changed to conform to the demands of financial record keeping and decision making, but the tax methods will have been properly established.

---

[15] Treas. Reg. § 1.446-1(a)(1). This conclusion not only is explicitly provided in the regulations, but it also seems obvious from the fact that many methods of accounting for tax purposes are not generally acceptable for financial accounting and reporting purposes (e.g., the cash and installment methods) or were established solely for tax purposes (e.g., methods of tax depreciation). See, e.g., First Fed. Sav. & Loan Ass'n v. United States, 694 F. Supp. 230 (WD Tex. 1988). Indeed, accrual methods of tax accounting are subject to different standards than accrual methods of financial accounting (see Chapter 4). See, e.g., Challenge Publications, Inc. v. Comm'r, 845 F2d 1541 (9th Cir. 1988), where the court made it clear that the book conformity requirement of Section 446(a) does not permit accrual basis taxpayers to take deductions that otherwise fail to satisfy the all events test of accrual tax accounting. See discussion of all events test at ¶ 4.03[1].

[16] Treas. Reg. § 1.446-1(b)(2). In these cases, the returns themselves "or other records may be sufficient to establish the use of the method of accounting used in the preparation of the taxpayer's income tax returns."

[17] Treas. Reg. § 1.446-1(e)(2)(i).

This is important, since, as discussed later,[18] a change in book methods generally does not require a change in tax methods.

Notwithstanding its surface simplicity, numerous issues arise as a consequence of the book conformity requirement. These issues generally arise as a result of computing book income on more than one basis, making adjustments to convert from one method of book accounting to another, and reporting to creditors and shareholders on a basis other than that used for tax purposes. Each of these circumstances is discussed in the following sections.[19] First, however, to have a sound basis for interpreting the manner in which these issues should be resolved, it is essential to understand the evolution of the book conformity requirement.

[a] Origin of Requirement

Initially, all taxpayers were required to compute income on the basis of cash receipts and disbursements (the cash method).[20] The required use of the cash method for tax purposes proved inconvenient to many businesses, particularly large enterprises that kept books on accrual methods. To ameliorate this burden, concessions were made by the Treasury, which announced the following:

> [N]o particular system of bookkeeping or accounting will be required by the Department. However, the business transacted by corporations, etc., must be so recorded that each and every item therein set forth may be readily verified by an examination of the books and accounts where such examination is deemed necessary.[21]

By virtue of this statement, the Treasury indicated that an important aspect of tax accounting was the verifiability of the taxpayer's computation of income on audit. Assuming this objective was satisfied, the Treasury did not seem unduly concerned by the use of some method other than the cash method.

Later, the Revenue Act of 1916 provided that subject to certain limitations, a taxpayer keeping books on a basis other than that of actual receipts and disbursements could make its returns on the basis on which its accounts were kept.[22] Thus, taxpayers were permitted to conform their tax methods to their book methods, but this was not required. The Revenue Act of 1918 was the first revenue act to impose the requirement that taxable income be

---

[18] See discussion infra ¶ 2.02[1][c]. See also discussion at ¶ 8.03.

[19] See discussion infra ¶¶ 2.02[1][b]–2.02[1][e].

[20] See discussion at ¶ 3.02.

[21] TD 1675 (Feb. 14, 1911).

[22] Revenue Act of 1916, §§ 13(d) (pertaining to corporations), 8(g) (pertaining to individuals).

computed in accordance with "the method of accounting regularly employed in keeping the books. . . ."[23] This language remained unaltered until the adoption of the 1954 Code.[24] The language was then changed to its present form, but there was apparently no intent to change the substance of the requirement.[25]

Thus, the book conformity requirement has stood as a standard requirement of tax accounting for more than 70 years. Its genesis was the practical realization that, in determining taxable income, it was appropriate and convenient for a taxpayer to use the methods of accounting that it used for financial purposes. This conformity enabled the taxpayer to maintain a single set of books and records for both tax and financial reporting purposes, while at the same time providing the government with the knowledge that the method used for book purposes would generally serve to offset the taxpayer's normal desire to reduce taxable income.[26] The requirement also provided for ready verification of reported income on examination by the IRS.

Over the years, a number of issues have arisen in connection with the book conformity requirement, generally as the result of attempts by revenue agents to require a taxpayer to conform its method of tax accounting to the method assertedly used for financial accounting.[27] In large part, these issues are attributable to increased accounting sophistication and capacity as a result of the advent of computers. The issues relate to the maintenance and use of accounting information generated under more than one method, the use of adjusting entries to convert the method used for book purposes to the method used for tax purposes, and the impact of financial reporting to

---

[23] Revenue Act of 1918, § 212(b).

[24] See § 41 of the 1939 Code.

[25] The earlier language focused broadly on the book method, while the current language focuses on the book method *of computing income.*

[26] See United States v. Anderson, 269 US 422 (1926).

[27] In First Fed. Sav. & Loan Ass'n v. United States, 694 F. Supp. 230 (WD Tex. 1988), the government argued that the book conformity requirement requires taxpayers to use for tax purposes the same methods of accounting that they use for book purposes in all cases except those where the Commissioner has expressly approved a deviation on the basis that the financial accounting method does not clearly reflect income. The court rejected this argument and concluded instead that a more reasonable and consistent interpretation of the requirement is that a taxpayer should use for tax purposes the same method that it uses for book purposes unless the tax accounting method or treatment is specifically authorized or controlled by another section of the Code. The court stated that this implicit exception to the book conformity requirement is necessary to prevent taxpayers from having to obtain the consent of the Commissioner merely to depart from use of the financial accounting method in circumstances where they are expressly required or authorized to do so by other provisions of the Code. The court noted that the government's position was in direct conflict with those provisions of the Code requiring or permitting the use of nonbook methods in particular instances.

shareholders, creditors, and others on the basis of generally accepted accounting principles (GAAP).[28]

[b] Does Information on Different Bases Violate Requirement?

Virtually every taxpayer maintains information that is consistent with more than one method of accounting. For example, every taxpayer has at least some information in documentary form that reflects what it receives, what it pays, what it owes, and what it is owed. Thus, a taxpayer using one method of accounting for tax purposes may have information available that is consistent with the use of another method (or information from which returns could be prepared on such other method).

Generally, the mere existence of that information does not pose a problem. Nevertheless, the question often arises as to whether the existence of such information permits either the taxpayer or the IRS to assert a violation of the book conformity requirement and, as a consequence, permit or require a change in the method of tax accounting.[29] The issue frequently arises in the context of a cash method taxpayer that maintains book information on an accrual basis. The IRS sometimes seeks to use that circumstance to require the taxpayer to change to an accrual method. In addressing this issue, the courts have generally considered the following:

- Whether the accrual information in question is primary or merely supplementary
- The purpose of the information
- The intent of the taxpayer
- Whether the additional information is in a form acceptable for tax purposes
- The comparative significance in the use of the two methods

The maintenance of supplementary or auxiliary information or memorandum accounts on a nontax basis for management, credit, or other nontax

---

[28] Issues have also arisen due to the different objectives of financial and tax accounting. For instance, accrual tax accounting is substantially different from accrual financial accounting. Neither would be acceptable for purposes of the other, absent considerable adjustment. (See Chapter 4 for discussion of accrual methods.)

[29] Section 446(a) is not worded in terms of maintaining information but, rather, in terms of computing income. It is implicit from this wording that the mere existence of information and records on one basis does not mean income is computed on that basis for book purposes. However, it may be argued that Congress did not intend the present language, which incorporates the reference to computing income, to have a meaning different from the meaning of the predecessor language, which did not contain such a reference, and therefore, that the present language should not be interpreted to support the above interpretation.

reporting purposes does not mean that a taxpayer uses that nontax method in computing income for book purposes or that its use violates the book conformity requirement. For example, in *Cosmopolitan Bond & Mortgage Co.*,[30] the taxpayer reported on a cash basis for book and tax purposes but maintained an accrual account showing commissions due. The Commissioner sought to include these commissions in the taxpayer's income. The Board of Tax Appeals (the Board) held for the taxpayer, finding that the commissions account was "at most a memorandum account kept for purposes of information."[31] As this discussion suggests, taxpayers who develop and use information on a basis different from that used for tax purposes should label those records "supplementary," "auxiliary," or "memorandum" to distinguish them from primary records. The primary records should be maintained on the method used for tax purposes. Although this labeling may seem silly, it often serves as a practical deterrent to a book conformity challenge by the IRS.[32]

The purpose for which information is accumulated may also be important. For example, in *Michael Drazen*,[33] a cash method partnership began to use an accrual method for tax purposes (without having obtained the prior approval of the IRS) following a request by lenders that the partnership maintain accrual basis records in connection with certain financing. The court found that "the books contained sufficient information to report income on either the cash or accrual basis,"[34] but the court concluded: "There is no question that the partnership kept its books and reported income on a cash basis. A memorandum of accounts receivable was kept and inventory value was taken from the spread sheets. These were subsidiary records kept to provide the partners and banks with 'accrual' information."[35] Accordingly, where a taxpayer must accumulate and report data on a nontax basis for a particular purpose, it may be helpful to identify that purpose and, again, to label reports as supplementary to the primary records and reports.

The fact that the information maintained on a nontax basis would not be accepted for tax purposes is also important. For example, in *Estate of Paul*

---

[30] Cosmopolitan Bond & Mortgage Co., 30 BTA 717 (1934), acq. as to method of accounting issue XIV-1 CB 5.

[31] Id. at 720. It should be noted that the parties in this case had in fact stipulated that the taxpayer was on the cash basis. See also Great Bear Spring Co., 12 BTA 383 (1928), nonacq. as to method of accounting issue VIII-1 CB 54, where the maintenance of customer account information in "auxiliary ledgers" was found not to be inconsistent with maintaining books on the cash method; Daily Record Co., 13 BTA 458 (1928), nonacq. VIII-2 CB 61, where use of an accounts receivable account without a corresponding income account did not prevent the court from finding use of the cash method for book purposes.

[32] See also discussion at ¶ 7.03[2][c], pertaining to the labeling necessary to prevent violation of the LIFO conformity requirement.

[33] Michael Drazen, 34 TC 1070 (1960).

[34] Id. at 1073.

[35] Id. at 1077.

Hansen,[36] the Commissioner asserted that the books of an engineering partnership were kept on an accrual basis because accounts were maintained for "services billed" and "work in progress." However, the Board held that the amounts entered in these accounts were mere estimates or impressions of the value of the services rendered rather than accruable rights to income.[37] Similarly, in *Ocean Accident & Guaranty Co.,*[38] an insurance company taxpayer estimated its probable liability when an accident or injury occurred. These estimates were not entered on the books as a liability. Nevertheless, they were "considered necessary to determine the financial condition of the company and to fix premium rates."[39] The taxpayer sought to deduct certain losses accrued, but not paid, during the taxable year at issue. The evidence established that what was described as the taxpayer's "books of account" were intended to be kept on a cash basis and that its "records," consisting of certain reserves and estimates, were intended to be maintained on an accrual basis. The Board held that the maintenance of those records did not mean that the taxpayer kept its books on the accrual method.[40]

Another group of cases holds that relatively minor departures from an otherwise consistent method of book accounting do not prevent a taxpayer from reporting its income in accordance with the generally applied method.[41]

---

[36] Estate of Paul Hansen, 4 TCM 264 (1945).

[37] Under an accrual method, income accrues when all the events have occurred that fix the right to receive the income and the amount thereof can be determined with reasonable accuracy. See discussion at ¶ 4.03[1].

[38] Ocean Accident & Guar. Co., 13 BTA 1057 (1928).

[39] Id. at 1060.

[40] The Board stated as follows:

We seriously doubt whether these estimates can be said to be a part of petitioner's accounting records for the purpose of determining income, the evidence being to the effect that the estimates were made and summarized for statistical purposes, for the purpose of determining the financial condition of the company, and to determine premium rates. Neither the estimates on individual cases nor the summaries were ever entered on the ledger or other books of account. It may well be that the scope of petitioner's business required the maintenance of records of the different phases of its business for various purposes, for example, such as making reports to the States in which incorporated and in which it operates, for advertising purposes, for the information of its solicitors; but it does not follow that all such records are parts of the accounting system maintained for the purpose of determining income.

Id. at 1063. See also Boca Ceiga Dev. Co., 25 BTA 941 (1932), nonacq. XI-1 CB 8, rev'd on other grounds, 66 F2d 1004 (3d Cir. 1933) (memorandum entries of mortgages and notes receivable and payable did not require finding that taxpayer used accrual method).

[41] See M.D. Rowe, 7 BTA 903 (1927), acq. as to method of accounting issue IX-1 CB 47, where the existence of a few accounts receivable did not justify a change from the cash to an accrual method; Thomas W. Briggs, 15 TCM 440 (1956), where the taxpayer showed that it was on the cash basis, since its most substantial items of

These decisions generally consist of older cases, which arose prior to the permitted use of hybrid methods, that is, at a time when the cash and accrual methods were the only overall methods expressly recognized. Nevertheless, these cases are instructive in that they demonstrate that maintenance of information for book purposes on a basis different from that used for tax purposes does not necessarily violate the book conformity requirement. They also point up a number of additional factors. For example, the book conformity requirement is concerned with the taxpayer's method of computing income. Thus, the presence of accrual accounts that do not have an effect on income is not significant.

The cases discussed in the preceding paragraphs also suggest the significant, if not determinative, importance of form rather than substance. A taxpayer who pays close attention to establishing cash basis books and records with its accrual data recorded or maintained in supplementary, auxiliary, memorandum, or other such accounts may be found to be on the cash method for keeping books, whereas the contrary may be found (or asserted by the IRS) for a taxpayer who has the identical accounts as part of its general ledger.

These matters of form remain significant, despite the impact of computerized data processing for accounting. Although it might be concluded that the form of a computerized printout should be irrelevant, examining agents continue to stress its importance.[42] In addition, the National Office has indicated in a conference on a ruling request that was subsequently withdrawn that, where a taxpayer had been granted permission to change to a cash method on the condition that it change its financial books to a cash basis, a change from its originally established cash basis computer system to

---

income and expense were accounted for on that method; Glenn v. Kentucky Color & Chem. Co., 186 F2d 975 (6th Cir. 1951), where the court held that because the taxpayer kept its books, "with only minor deviations," on the cash method, the Commissioner could not change it to an accrual method; Hiram W. Evans, 5 TCM 336 (1946), where the taxpayer's listing of accrued expenses on a balance sheet was not a basis for finding that the taxpayer was on an accrual method; Estate of L.W. Mallory, 44 BTA 249 (1941), acq. 1941-2 CB 9, where interest was the only accrued item, the taxpayer was held to be on the cash basis; John F. Cook, 4 BTA 916 (1926), acq. VI-1 CB 2, where a partnership was found to keep its books on an accrual method, based on the number of accrued items shown; Bartles-Scott Oil Co., 2 BTA 16, 18 (1925), where the mere fact that some items were not reported on an accrual method did not prevent use of an accrual method. See also Nibley-Mimnaugh Lumber Co., 32 BTA 791 (1935), acq. XIV-2 CB 16; Schram v. United States, 118 F2d 541 (6th Cir. 1941); James J. Standing, 28 TC 789 (1957), acq. as to method of accounting issue 1958-1 CB 6, aff'd, 259 F2d 450 (4th Cir. 1958).

[42] See, e.g., Tech. Adv. Mem. 8029008 (Apr. 10, 1980), where the examining agent took the position that the ability of the taxpayer to generate accrual basis information indicated a violation of the book conformity requirement. Although the IRS National Office (the National Office) rejected this contention in the circumstances, such arguments continue to be made by agents.

an accrual basis computer system would permit the IRS to terminate use of the cash method.

[c] Conversion Workpapers Reconcile Different Methods

Taxpayers and their tax advisors have often assumed that a taxpayer's right to choose its method of tax accounting[43] allows it to use one method (e.g., an accrual method) in keeping books but a different method (e.g., the cash method) for reporting taxes, as long as sufficient workpapers reconciling the different methods are available. This view is widely shared and has apparently been accepted by both the tax-writing committees of Congress and, on occasion, the National Office.[44] Nevertheless, as discussed in the following paragraphs, there appears to be no direct judicial support for such a position, and examining agents continue to assert a violation of the book conformity requirement when that conformity is based only on conversion workpapers. Consequently, taxpayers who want to adopt particular methods of accounting for tax purposes should also adopt those methods for book purposes. The book method may thereafter be changed without changing the tax method.

The cases and other authorities generally cited by taxpayers in support of a position that book conformity is satisfied merely by means of reconciling data pertained to unique situations. For example, the leading case in the area is *Patchen v. Commissioner*,[45] where the taxpayer initially adopted and used the cash method for both book and tax reporting purposes. In 1948, the taxpayer changed to an accrual method for book purposes but continued to file tax returns on the cash method. In preparing the tax returns, the taxpayer's accountants prepared memorandum journal entries that converted all elements of income and expense to the cash method. These entries were not entered on the partnership's books but were kept by the accountants as a permanent part of their records. The papers were furnished to the revenue agents in the course of their examination of the taxpayer's returns.

---

[43] See discussion infra ¶ 2.03, regarding a taxpayer's right to choose its methods of accounting.

[44] See, e.g., S. Rep. No. 99-313, 99th Cong., 2d Sess. 118 (1986), on the Tax Reform Act of 1986 (the 1986 Act), where the Finance Committee stated:

> Under present law, a taxpayer generally may elect (on its first income tax return) to use any method of accounting for Federal income tax purposes that clearly reflects income and that is regularly used in keeping the taxpayer's books and records (sec. 446). The latter requirement is considered satisfied where the taxpayer maintains sufficient records to allow reconciliation of the results obtained under the method regularly used in keeping its books and the method used for Federal income tax purpose[s].

In some cases, the National Office itself has accepted this view. See, e.g., Tech. Adv. Mem. 8029008 (Apr. 10, 1980); and withdrawal of prior nonacquiescence on this point, 1991-7 IRB 5.

[45] Patchen v. Comm'r, 258 F2d 544 (5th Cir. 1958).

The IRS asserted that the taxpayer should have prepared its returns on an accrual method beginning in 1948, since its books were changed to an accrual method beginning in that year. The IRS argued that, where there is a conflict between the requirements of conformity to the book method and consistency in application of the tax method, the IRS has an option as to which should control. The Tax Court upheld the position of the IRS,[46] but the court of appeals reversed.[47] The IRS thereafter followed the decision of the appeals court in *Patchen* in several rulings involving taxpayers converting from the cash method to an accrual method for book purposes but remaining on the cash method for tax purposes.[48]

The *Patchen* conclusion appears consistent with regulations that provide that the accounting records of a taxpayer "include the taxpayer's regular books of account and such other records and data as may be necessary to support the entries on his books of account and on his return, as for example, a reconciliation of any differences between such books and his return."[49] This provision was effective prior to the decision in *Patchen*,[50] but it is not clear

---

[46] Josef C. Patchen, 27 TC 592 (1956). The Tax Court found that Section 41 of the 1939 Code clearly required the accounting method used for income tax purposes to conform to the method employed in the taxpayer's books. The court held that the joint effect of this conformity requirement and the requirement that the Commissioner give prior consent to a change in method for tax purposes was that the Commissioner had the option of accepting cash basis returns, which were consistent with those filed in earlier years, or of requiring the use of an accrual method that conformed with the method then used in the firm's books if that method proved to be more accurate.

[47] In Patchen v. Comm'r, 258 F2d 544, 549 (5th Cir. 1958), the court stated:

The partnership started out with the Cash method of bookkeeping. Its returns were in conformity with that. Returns for subsequent years were consistent with the prior returns. For its own internal purposes it installed an Accrual system. But this was to supplement, not supplant, the Cash method. An integral part of the 1948 system was the recognized necessity for accounting adjustments which were to be made by the partnership's accountants in accordance with accepted professional concepts in order that the books would show income on the Cash method so that, in turn, tax returns could be computed both in conformity with such books and consistent with prior returns.

That this system called for adjustments or that mechanical evidences of the results of them were kept in the physical possession of the partnership's regular accountants is of no significance.

[48] See, e.g., Rev. Rul. 68-35, 1968-1 CB 190, Rev. Rul. 68-83, 1968-1 CB 190, and Rev. Rul. 74-383, 1974-2 CB 146, where, in each case, the taxpayer changed its book method from cash to accrual but was permitted to continue to file its tax returns on the cash method, provided that proper reconciling entries were maintained. See also Rev. Rul. 67-147, 1967-1 CB 105, where the taxpayer changed from the installment method to an accrual method for book purposes but was permitted to retain the installment method for tax purposes as long as it maintained reconciling records.

[49] Treas. Reg. § 1.446-1(a)(4).

[50] TD 6282, 1958-1 CB 215 (Dec. 24, 1957).

that the regulation was intended to apply to a *Patchen*-type situation. It may have been intended only to cover general differences existing between financial and tax accounting. Nevertheless, the rulings that have followed *Patchen* support the position that, when a taxpayer changes its method of book accounting but continues to use its original method for tax accounting, the maintenance of reconciling records is sufficient to comply with the book conformity requirement of Section 446(a).

Neither *Patchen* nor the rulings that followed addressed specifically the issue of whether a taxpayer could, in its initial year, establish and use an accrual method for book and financial reporting purposes but convert to the cash method for tax reporting purposes. This precise issue has still not been addressed, and the result is not certain. For example, consider *Yates v. United States*,[51] a case somewhat similar to *Patchen*, but with a different result. In *Yates*, an individual had engaged in the coal business for years prior to 1947. His records consisted only of a list of expenditures, and tax returns had consistently been filed on a cash basis. In late 1946, the taxpayer established a double-entry accrual set of books showing cash receipts, cash disbursements, and accounts receivable. On audit, the Commissioner asserted that the taxpayer should have filed its 1949 return on an accrual basis. The 1949 return included a statement that the accrual method book income had been converted to cash method income. The district court agreed with the Commissioner, requiring the taxpayer to use the accrual method for tax purposes because the taxpayer had adopted that method when it established a formal bookkeeping system in 1947.[52] The court rejected the taxpayer's contention, based on *Patchen*, that the adjustments converting accrual book income to a cash computation were themselves a part of its books. The court also found unpersuasive the taxpayer's argument that it had to continue to use the cash basis to report income, since the prior consent of the Commissioner to change to the accrual method had not been obtained.[53]

The court distinguished *Patchen* on the ground that the taxpayer there had used the cash method of bookkeeping and that its returns conformed to

---

[51] Yates v. United States, 205 F. Supp. 738 (ED Ky. 1962).

[52] In *Yates*, the court said that it was

of the opinion that prior to 1947 the method of bookkeeping was inconsequential and the basis of reporting income for tax purposes was necessarily on a cash basis. With the beginning of the partnership and later the corporation and the setting up of a formal system of bookkeeping, the method of keeping the books and reporting the income of the business must be uniform as required by the statute above quoted. Taxpayer has kept his books of accounting on the accrual basis but has filed his income tax returns on the cash basis. Since the accrual basis of accounting clearly reflected the net income of taxpayer, the income should have been computed and reported in accordance with the bookkeeping methods.

Id. at 740.

[53] The court stated the following:

that method. The court in *Yates* found that prior to adoption of accrual books, the taxpayer had no method of accounting. Thus, the court found that once a method was adopted for the first time, the taxpayer was required to report taxable income using that method. Also, unlike *Patchen* and the rulings previously discussed, the taxpayer in *Yates* did not maintain any reconciliation records apart from the statement filed with the return.

Another leading case in the area is *St. Luke's Hospital Inc.,*[54] which involved a hospital that had consistently used an accrual method for both book and tax purposes. Later, following an application for a change in method, the Commissioner granted the taxpayer permission to change to the cash method for tax purposes. The taxpayer retained the accrual method for book purposes. The court noted that although the taxpayer's bookkeeping system was "basically unchanged from the accrual system previously used, [its] books contained complete and full information from which an accountant could determine net income on a cash basis."[55]

The IRS thereafter argued that the taxpayer's income for the years in question should have been computed under the accrual method used with respect to its books. The taxpayer contended that it had complied with the conditions set forth in the IRS letter granting permission to change its method of accounting for tax purposes. The taxpayer conceded that it retained basically an accrual system of accounting but argued that its books and records properly reflected cash income upon the making of certain adjustments. It contended that the reconciliation between book and taxable income was revealed in the accountant's work papers and audit reports, which, if necessary, should be considered a part of its books and records.

Rejecting the Commissioner's contention that "the general rule [the conformity requirement] set forth in the statute is mandatory," the Tax Court held that the taxpayer was entitled to report income on the cash basis for the taxable years at issue. The court relied primarily on the language of the Commissioner's 1953 letter granting a change in method, which "did not expressly make the discontinuance of the accrual method of accounting a condition precedent to the granting of the permission to change the method of reporting income." As a result of the decision in *St. Luke's*, the IRS often

---

Such an interpretation would nullify the salutary effects of the statute and leave the determination of how the books were to be kept and how the income was to be reported entirely in the hands of the taxpayer, thereby permitting him to change back and forth at will upon the two methods of reporting his income. The court sees no point in giving a tortured construction to a statute which has a primary objective of avoiding confusion by requiring that bookkeeping and the reporting of income shall be by the same method.

Id. at 740–741.

[54] St. Luke's Hosp., 35 TC 236 (1960), nonacq. as to method of accounting issue, 1963-2 CB 6, withdrawal of nonacquiescence, 1991-7 IRB 5.

[55] Id. at 242.

requires as a condition to allowing a change in method of accounting that the taxpayer use the new method for book purposes.[56]

While *Patchen* and *St. Luke's* demonstrate that conversion entries may be relied on to justify compliance with the book conformity requirement, each involved rather unique circumstances. The courts in these cases did not give, or purport to give, blanket approval to such a conversion in all cases. Nevertheless, the legislative history drafted in connection with the Tax Reform Act of 1986 (the 1986 Act) clearly suggested that the book conformity requirement is satisfied where appropriate reconciliations are maintained between book income and taxable income.[57] Consequently, it would appear unduly harsh and inequitable for the IRS to continue to press this issue. Indeed, the IRS began accepting this point in recent years,[58] although some agents continue to assert a violation of the book conformity requirement in such circumstances.

[d] Consistency Favored Over Conformity

Although the precise scope of the cases discussed in the previous section is still evolving, those cases did make it clear that the consistent use of a method of accounting for tax purposes is more important than conformity between the taxpayer's book and tax methods. This conclusion has been accepted by the courts in other cases as well. For example, in *Geometric Stamping Co.*,[59] the IRS initially had accepted the use of one accounting method for tax purposes, although a different method was used for book purposes. In a later year, the IRS attempted to change the taxpayer's tax method on the basis of a violation of the conformity requirement. The Tax Court held for the taxpayer, pointing out that the book conformity requirement was not absolute and that in any event, consistency was more important than conformity.[60]

---

[56] See discussion at ¶ 8.07[1].

[57] See, e.g., S. Rep. No. 99-313, 99th Cong., 2d Sess. 118 (1986), on the 1986 Act, where the Finance Committee stated: "This [book conformity] requirement is considered satisfied where the taxpayer maintains sufficient records to allow reconciliation of the results obtained under the method regularly used in keeping its books and the method used for Federal income tax purpose[s]."

[58] See 1991-7 IRB 5, where the IRS withdrew its prior nonacquiescence on this point, and Tech. Adv. Mem. 9103001 (June 19, 1990), in which the National Office concluded that there was no violation of the book conformity requirement where the taxpayer used the cash method for tax purposes and an accrual method for book purposes but maintained appropriate reconciliations between the two methods.

[59] Geometric Stamping Co., 26 TC 301 (1956), acq. in result 1958-2 CB 5.

[60] The court said:

It has been held, however, that such a [conformity] requirement is not absolute. . . . And we should be most hesitant to say that [the Commissioner],

Consistency also took precedence over conformity in *National Airlines*,[61] where, prior to 1944, an accrual basis taxpayer included ticket sales in income whether or not the transportation had been furnished. In early 1944, the Civil Aeronautics Board (CAB) directed the use of a different book method under which income from transportation not yet furnished would be placed in a deferred account. The taxpayer sought the Commissioner's permission to change its tax method of reporting income to that required by the CAB. This request was denied. The taxpayer nevertheless filed its returns for its 1943, 1944, and 1945 taxable years using the CAB-prescribed method of accounting. The Tax Court held that the Commissioner did not abuse his discretion in refusing to allow the taxpayer to change its method of accounting for tax purposes.[62] Similarly, in *R.G. Bent Co.*,[63] a contractor and builder had consistently reported income from contract work only as the work was completed. The Commissioner determined that income should have included profits on work in process because the taxpayer's books were kept on a strict accrual basis. In finding that the taxpayer had properly computed its income, the Board held the taxpayer was entitled to report under the long-term contracts provision of the regulations under the Revenue Act of 1928. These regulations permitted the taxpayer to report its income either on the percentage-of-completion basis or the completed contract basis. The Board noted that the only condition imposed by the regulations was that the method used clearly reflect income, and pointed out that no mention was made of bookkeeping methods. The court thus held that the conformity requirement did not apply.[64]

---

where he feels that the method of reporting clearly reflects income, must withhold his approval because such a method is not precisely reflected in the taxpayer's books. There is in fact a tacit assumption that variances between books and returns are bound to occur. Otherwise there would be no reason for the elaborate provision for reconciliation between book entries and return items, which is a part of every corporate return. At any rate, where as here the choice must be made between conformity to a bookkeeping system on the one hand and consistency of reporting on the other, and where [the Commissioner's] task is not rendered impossible by the complete absence of the figures from the taxpayer's accounting records, we think it more fundamental that the method of reporting be consistent.

26 TC at 306.

[61] National Airlines, 9 TC 159 (1947).

[62] Therefore, while a request for change in method of accounting may be premised on a desire for book conformity, that reason alone may not be sufficient to support the change. See discussion at ¶ 8.07[1], regarding reasons for a requested change in method.

[63] R.G. Bent Co., 26 BTA 1369 (1932), acq. XII-1 CB 2.

[64] The Board stated as follows:

It seems to us that under the law and the regulations the method regularly employed in making the returns is a more important consideration than the

[e] Financial Statements Do Not Determine Method

Taxpayers are frequently required by creditors, shareholders, the government, or others to prepare financial statements on a specified method of accounting, most often on an accrual method in conformity with GAAP. Examining agents sometimes take the position that the preparation of statements on such a basis demonstrates that a taxpayer uses the financial statement method in computing book income and, as a consequence, that it must use that method for tax purposes. Although the financial statement method may often be the method used for book purposes, this is not always the case. Where the two methods differ, such as where adjustments must be made to the book method to prepare the financial statements, the book method is the more important method for tax reporting purposes.

There is no general requirement of financial statement conformity under Section 446(a). This has been recognized by both Congress and the Treasury. For example, in Section 472, Congress provided a requirement of financial statement conformity as a condition to the use of the last-in, first-out (LIFO) inventory method.[65] Section 472(c) provides that LIFO may be used only if the taxpayer establishes to the satisfaction of the Secretary that the taxpayer has used no procedure other than LIFO in preparing financial statements and reports to shareholders, partners, other proprietors, or to beneficiaries, or for credit purposes. The legislative history of this section makes it clear that this financial statement conformity requirement is separate and distinct from the general book conformity requirement embodied in Section 446(a).[66] The applicable committee report explained that the right to use the LIFO method for tax purposes was subject not only to the general book conformity requirement but also to the added requirement that no other method could be used in reports to shareholders, partners, or other proprietors, or to beneficiaries, or for credit purposes.

The regulations governing the costing of inventories under the so-called full absorption method (as in effect prior to the 1986 Act) also imposed a requirement of financial statement conformity.[67] These regulations provided that the inclusion or exclusion of certain indirect production costs from the inventoriable costs taken into account for financial reporting purposes determined whether those costs had to be included in or excluded from the computation of inventoriable costs for tax purposes.

---

method of keeping the books, and that where a taxpayer has for any year filed a return, consistent with its method in prior years, which clearly reflects its net income as readily ascertainable from its books and records, it should neither be required nor permitted to change the return to show a different taxable income computed by some other method which is said more nearly to conform to the book income.

26 BTA at 1374.

[65] See discussion at ¶ 7.03[2].

[66] H.R. Rep. No. 2333, 77th Cong., 1st Sess. 372 (1942).

[67] Treas. Reg. § 1.471-11(c)(2)(iii). See discussion at ¶ 6.06.

As the preceding discussion indicates, the book conformity requirement of Section 446(a) does not require conformity between a taxpayer's tax method and the method used for financial reporting purposes. Consequently, to satisfy the book conformity requirement, the taxpayer should establish as its book method the method it desires to use for tax purposes. The taxpayer may then adjust the book method to whatever method is otherwise required or desired for nontax reporting purposes.[68] Thus, if a taxpayer desires to use the cash method for tax purposes but an accrual method for financial reporting purposes, it should establish its books on a cash basis and then make adjustments to those books, by means of subsidiary records, to prepare its financial statements.

This approach in establishing the book method should be acceptable. For example, in *Wolf Bakery & Cafeteria Co.*,[69] a cash basis taxpayer prepared financial statements for credit purposes on an accrual basis. In doing so, a list of accounts receivable and accounts payable was prepared. These accounts were prepared for financial statement purposes only. The taxpayer did not use them in computing taxable income, nor did the taxpayer maintain an accounts receivable or accounts payable ledger. The IRS determined deficiencies in the taxpayer's income tax by use of the accrual method. However, the court found that the taxpayer had used the cash method in keeping its books. The court did not give any recognition in its analysis to the taxpayer's preparation of financial statements that included accrual information.[70]

On the other hand, the IRS may impose a requirement of financial statement conformity in approving requests for changes in accounting methods.[71] The imposition of financial statement conformity in these cases is based on the Commissioner's authority under the regulations to prescribe conditions to the approval of a taxpayer's request to change its method of accounting, not on any independent statutory provision concerning the proper method of reporting income.[72]

The importance of this authority is illustrated by a situation that occurred in the late 1970s. The situation involved a taxpayer that had

---

[68] In Rev. Ruls. 68-83, 1968-1 CB 190, and 74-383, 1974-2 CB 146, the IRS permitted taxpayers to report income on the cash method despite the fact that they were required by governmental agencies to prepare financial statements on an accrual basis.

[69] Wolf Bakery & Cafeteria Co., 5 TCM 389 (1946).

[70] See also Patchen v. Comm'r, 258 F2d 544 (5th Cir. 1958), and discussion supra ¶ 2.02[1][c].

[71] See, e.g., IRS News Release No. 1125 (Apr. 14, 1971), where the IRS stated its intent to impose just such a requirement. The IRS later discontinued this condition as a general requirement. Nevertheless, it may still be imposed in many instances, such as where the requested change is from one proper method of accounting to another proper method. See also discussion at ¶ 8.07.

[72] Treas. Reg. § 1.446-1(e)(3)(ii). See discussion at ¶ 8.07.

received IRS permission to change from the cash method to an accrual method on condition that the accrual method be used for all financial reports to shareholders and creditors.[73] The taxpayer complied with the condition for its 1973 and 1974 tax years, but, in 1975, the taxpayer retained a new accounting firm that was not informed of the ruling letter. The new firm prepared the taxpayer's financial statements using the percentage-of-completion method in accordance with GAAP, but it employed the accrual method in preparing the tax return.

On a request for technical advice, the following questions were addressed by the National Office:

1. Whether the balance of the Section 481 adjustment arising from the original change in tax method must be included in income for the 1975 tax year[74]

2. Whether future financial statements could be prepared on the percentage-of-completion method, while taxes were computed in accordance with the accrual method

The National Office first noted the applicable requirements, including the book conformity requirement, the requirement of Section 446(e) that the consent of the Commissioner be obtained prior to a change in method of accounting, the Commissioner's authority to prescribe conditions to changes in methods,[75] and the then-applicable provisions of Revenue Procedure 70-27,[76] which provided that a taxpayer could take the adjustment resulting from a change in accounting method into account ratably over a 10-year period. The National Office then stated that under the facts presented, the IRS District Office would have the discretion to accelerate the balance of the Section 481 adjustment and to hold that the letter granting the change in accounting method was void as of the year of violation. Nevertheless, the National Office concluded that, because the accrual method more clearly reflected income than the percentage-of-completion method, the IRS should waive the violation of the financial statement conformity requirement, but the conditions of the 1973 letter would have to be complied with in future years in the absence of a ruling to the contrary.[77] As this technical advice memorandum demonstrates, taxpayers must be sensitive to all conditions

---

[73] Tech. Adv. Mem. 7752008 (Sept. 26, 1977).

[74] See discussion at ¶ 8.04, regarding Section 481 adjustments.

[75] Treas. Reg. § 1.446-1(e)(3)(ii).

[76] Rev. Proc. 70-27, 1970-2 CB 509. For the current rules governing the periods over which Section 481 adjustments may be taken into account, see discussion at ¶ 8.04.

[77] The issue of whether future financial statements could be prepared on a different method than the method used in preparing tax returns was held not to be a proper subject for technical advice because it did not involve a tax year under audit.

imposed in connection with IRS-approved changes in accounting methods. A failure to do so may result in disallowance of the new method. (See Chapter 8 for further discussion of changes in accounting methods.)

[2] Clear Reflection of Income

Section 446(b) provides, "If no method of accounting has been regularly used by the taxpayer, or if the method used does not clearly reflect income, the computation of taxable income shall be made under such method as, in the opinion of the Secretary, does clearly reflect income."[78]

Neither the Code nor the regulations define the phrase "clearly reflect income," although the regulations provide, "A method of accounting which reflects the consistent application of generally accepted accounting principles in a particular trade or business will ordinarily be regarded as clearly reflecting income, provided all items of gross income and expense are treated consistently from year to year."[79]

The clear reflection of income requirement is one of the most perplexing of all tax accounting requirements. Its definition seems to vary as the facts and circumstances of each case vary.[80] For example, methods that are deemed to reflect clearly the income of one type of business (e.g., a service business) are often deemed not to reflect clearly the income of other types of businesses (e.g., the business of a retailer, wholesaler, or manufacturer).[81] In addition, various statutory or regulatory rules may make a method that is proper for one size or form of business improper for the same type of business if it has higher revenues or operates in a different form.[82]

Clearly reflecting income is both a requirement to be met by the taxpayer and a discretionary club to be wielded by the Commissioner whenever he believes income would more appropriately be reflected on some basis other than that being used by the taxpayer. The discretion of the Commissioner is very great with respect to whether a method clearly reflects income. However, his discretion is not unlimited.[83]

Finally, as Congress becomes more active in the area of tax accounting, it would seem appropriate for courts to consider subsequent congressional

---

[78] See infra ¶ 2.04 for a discussion of the Commissioner's right to determine, as a preliminary matter, whether the method selected by the taxpayer clearly reflects income.

[79] Treas. Reg. § 1.446-1(a)(2). See also Treas. Reg. § 1.446-1(c)(1)(ii)(C).

[80] As the Tax Court stated in Sam W. Emerson Co., 37 TC 1063, 1067 (1962), acq. in result 1964-2 CB 5, "In essence, the crux of the problem is the language 'clearly reflects income,' and while the revenue Acts do not define the phrase, it is evident that what method will or will not clearly reflect income must vary greatly from business to business and from factual situation to factual situation."

[81] See Treas. Reg. § 1.446-1(c)(2)(i), and discussion at ¶ 3.06[2].

[82] See, e.g., discussion at ¶ 3.06[1].

[83] See discussion infra ¶ 2.04.

action (as well as prior congressional action) in determining whether a particular method of accounting clearly reflects income. However, such consideration does not occur automatically. For example, in *Buckeye International, Inc.*,[84] the Tax Court took note of a congressional amendment to Section 461 in the Tax Reform Act of 1984 in concluding that, prior to the effective date of that Act, the law had been to the contrary. In effect, the court noted that the subsequent action of Congress confirmed the position of the taxpayer as to the proper interpretation of the prior law. Similarly, in *Cal-Maine Foods, Inc.*,[85] the Tax Court determined that the taxpayer qualified for use of the cash method as a "family corporation" under Section 447 despite the fact that the taxpayer's gross receipts were in the hundreds of millions of dollars. The IRS had asserted that "family corporation" should be defined as a small business. The court rejected this argument, noting among other things the subsequent action of Congress (in the Omnibus Budget Reconciliation Act of 1987), which limited the benefits available to family corporations (for years beginning after December 31, 1985) to those family corporations not having gross receipts in excess of $25 million. The court recognized that this subsequent action of Congress necessarily meant that prior to that action, there had been no limitation on the benefits available to family corporations based on the taxpayer's level of gross receipts.[86] On the other hand, in *Applied Communications, Inc.*,[87] the Tax Court made no mention whatsoever of the limitations imposed by Congress on the use of the cash method in the 1986 Act in holding that a particular taxpayer's use of the cash method in pre-1986 Act years did not clearly reflect income. The court's analysis lacked clarity, indicated confusion about the relevant principles of law, had the effect of ignoring basic, well-established principles of law, and for the most part seemed inconsistent with the subsequent action of Congress in enacting Section 448.[88] Consequently, taxpayers and their counsel would be well advised to make sure that any subsequent congressional, Treasury, or IRS action is put before the court so that such action may be taken into account by the court in evaluating whether a particular method of accounting clearly reflects income.[89]

---

[84] Buckeye Int'l, Inc., 49 TCM 376 (1984).

[85] Cal-Maine Foods, Inc., 93 TC 181 (1989).

[86] See also Lloyd Williams, Jr., 94 TC 464 (1990), where, in holding that neither Section 446(b) nor Section 461(g) limited the amount of the taxpayer's deduction for interest determined under Section 483 to the amount of interest that had economically accrued, the court noted that Section 483 was *subsequently* amended to provide such a limitation.

[87] Applied Communications, Inc., 57 TCM 1473 (1989).

[88] See also In re BKW Sys., Inc., 90-1 USTC ¶ 50,139 (Bankr. DNH 1989), for a similarly confused analysis.

[89] For example, in RLC Indus. Co., 98 TC 457 (1992), where the taxpayer argued that its method of accounting was consistent with applicable regulations and

Set forth in the following sections[90] is a discussion of a number of factors that have a bearing on whether a particular method of accounting clearly reflects income. This discussion is followed by an analysis of two widely cited, but seemingly quite different, judicial standards of clear reflection of income that have evolved over the years, each of which continues to be cited by the courts.

[a] Method Must Be Correctly Applied

Obviously, to clearly reflect income under the method adopted, the taxpayer must adhere to the requirements of that particular method. A failure to apply the method accurately or in accordance with all applicable requirements governing the use of the method may be corrected by the IRS on audit (or by the filing of an amended return by the taxpayer) on the basis of the clear reflection of income standard. If an erroneous application of the taxpayer's method is not susceptible to correction (e.g., because of a lack of necessary data), the method may presumably be changed.[91]

The question that frequently arises on audit is whether an incorrectly applied method is subject only to correction or, instead, to change. For example, assume a taxpayer is improperly applying the percentage-of-completion method. May the IRS use the incorrect application to require a change from the percentage-of-completion method to an accrual method, or may the taxpayer limit any proposed IRS adjustment to a correction of the application of the percentage-of-completion method? Although this precise issue has not been decided, it would seem proper for the correction to be made, if possible, prior to consideration of any change in method. This approach would preserve the taxpayer's right to choose its accounting methods.[92]

---

therefore clearly reflected income, the same judge who issued the opinion in *Applied Communications Inc.* stated first that the court was asked to decide whether compliance with a regulation would result in a clear reflection of income even though the results under that method were much different than the results desired by the Commissioner. The court then responded: "In essence, we are asked by respondent to decide that the regulation may produce results which do not clearly reflect income. We suggest that the Secretary should seek to correct any perceived defects in the [applicable] regulations . . . by appropriate amendment or modification." This statement suggests the potential benefit of making sure the effects of subsequent legislation are put before the court.

[90] See discussion infra ¶¶ 2.02[2][a]–2.02[2][i].

[91] See American Fletcher Corp. v. United States, 86-1 USTC ¶ 9283 (SD Ind. 1986), aff'd, 832 F2d 436 (7th Cir. 1987), where use of the cash method was denied to a taxpayer who could not accurately compute income under the cash method, the court finding that cash method income had been determined on the basis of "estimates, business experience, opinions and statistical data."

[92] See discussion infra ¶ 2.03.

As this discussion suggests, the proper issue is whether the practice in question may properly be characterized as (1) the incorrect application of a correct method or, instead, (2) the application of an incorrect method. Although this may seem an issue of semantics, as a practical matter, it often determines the method to be used. For example, if a taxpayer uses an acceptable method of accounting (such as a lower-of-cost-or-market method of accounting for inventory)[93] and has all the data necessary to apply this method correctly, an error in application should be correctible. However, if the taxpayer's inventory method is not an acceptable method (because it is based on arbitrary write-downs to market), that method may be changed.[94]

[b] Is Authorization by Code or Regulations Enough?

All methods of tax accounting are subject to the clear reflection of income requirement. Since the Code and the Treasury regulations authorize the use of various methods of accounting, it is logical to conclude that the correct use of any such method per se clearly reflects income[95] even though that method is otherwise not accepted for financial accounting purposes or not in accordance with GAAP. Examples of these latter methods include many accelerated methods of depreciation, use of the installment method, the cash method, and tax accrual methods.

Correlatively, the Code and the regulations may expressly limit the methods of accounting available to some taxpayers or may proscribe the use

---

[93] See discussion at ¶ 6.09.

[94] See discussion at ¶¶ 6.08[2][b] (regarding proscribed methods of inventory accounting), 9.06[3] (regarding the importance of defining the taxpayer's method).

[95] See, e.g., Hallmark Cards, Inc., 90 TC 26, 31 (1988), where the court stated that the Commissioner's

broad authority to determine whether a taxpayer's accounting method clearly reflects income is limited, in that he may not reject, as not providing a clear reflection of income, a method of accounting employed by the taxpayer which is specifically authorized in the Code or regulations and has been applied on a consistent basis.

See also So. California Sav. & Loan Ass'n, 95 TC 35 (1990), where the court stated: "We have held that respondent may not reject, as not providing a clear reflection of income, a method of accounting employed by the taxpayer which is specifically authorized in the code and has been applied on a consistent basis"; Marcor, Inc., 89 TC 181, 194 (1987), where, in responding to the Commissioner's contention that income was not clearly reflected under the taxpayer's installment method because certain noninventoriable costs associated with the preparation and installation of goods sold on an installment basis were deducted currently while the income from sales was deferred, the court rejected the Commissioner's contention, stating: "The 'clear reflection of income' doctrine implements, and does not contradict, well-established statutory and case law."

of certain methods in certain circumstances.[96] Similarly, the courts may find that a particular method will not clearly reflect income in certain circumstances[97] even though that method may otherwise be considered the best method of accounting for financial accounting purposes.[98]

This per se acceptance or prohibition has often been recognized by the courts. For example, in *Kenneth H. Van Raden*,[99] the issue was whether a cash method limited partnership could deduct the cost of a one-year supply of cattle feed in the year of purchase. With respect to whether the deduction would materially distort income,[100] the Tax Court held that a method expressly set forth in the regulations clearly reflects income.[101] If this were not the case, virtually no permitted method could be used with confidence because each reflects tax accounting requirements and objectives that are not

---

[96] See, e.g., IRC § 448, denying use of the cash method to certain corporate taxpayers with revenues above a specified level (see discussion at ¶ 3.06[1]); Treas. Reg. § 1.446-1(c)(2)(i), denying use of the cash method in accounting for purchases and sales of inventory (see discussion at ¶ 3.06[2]); IRC § 453, limiting use of the installment method to sales of property and denying it to "sales" of services (see discussion at ¶ 5.03).

[97] For example, the cash method is generally deemed not to clearly reflect income in the year in which a business is terminated. See discussion at ¶ 3.06[3].

[98] For example, numerous cases exist where the courts have found the use of proper accrual methods of financial accounting not to clearly reflect income for tax purposes. See discussion at ¶¶ 4.02[3], 4.02[4].

[99] Kenneth H. Van Raden, 71 TC 1083 (1979), aff'd, 650 F2d 1046 (9th Cir. 1981). See also Hallmark Cards, Inc., 90 TC 26 (1988); So. California Sav. & Loan Ass'n, 95 TC 35 (1990).

[100] See Rev. Rul. 79-229, 1979-2 CB 210, which provided that a cash method farmer could deduct in the year of payment the cost of feed that was consumed in the following taxable year only when (1) the expenditure for the feed was a payment rather than a mere deposit; (2) the payment was made for a business purpose and not for tax avoidance; and (3) the deduction of such cost in the year of payment did not result in a material distortion of income. See also Tech. Adv. Mem. 8641002 (June 26, 1986), in which the National Office stated that so long as a taxpayer complies with the requirements of Section 464 (pertaining to limitations on the deduction of certain farming expenses), the taxpayer's use of the cash method may not be challenged as not clearly reflecting income under Section 446.

[101] The Tax Court stated the following:

> If an accounting method is in accord with generally accepted accounting principles and is consistently used, then it will be regarded as clearly reflecting income for tax purposes, . . . unless the generally accepted accounting principle conflicts with the tax regulations. *Thor Power Tool Co. v. Commissioner*. . . . Here, the cash method of accounting without the use of inventories for farmers was countenanced by the income tax regulations. [Commissioner] does not contend that his own regulations prescribed an optional accounting system that does not clearly reflect income.

Kenneth H. Van Raden, 71 TC 1083, 1105 (1979).

identical with financial accounting requirements and objectives or with economic concepts of income determination.[102]

[c] Effect of Consistent Use of GAAP

The regulations under Section 446 provide that the consistent use of GAAP may also be important in determining whether a method of accounting clearly reflects income. The regulations provide that if a method of accounting reflects the consistent application of GAAP in accordance with accepted conditions or practices in the taxpayer's particular trade or business, that method will ordinarily be regarded as clearly reflecting income, as long as all items of income and expense are treated consistently from year to year.[103]

Taxpayers traditionally have defended the use of a particular method on the basis of the foregoing regulation and on their adherence to GAAP. Nevertheless, those arguments have not been persuasive in and of themselves. In

---

[102] See, e.g., Marcor, Inc., 89 TC 181 (1987), which involved the taxpayer's use of the installment method. The taxpayer sold certain goods that required preparation and installation. The costs of such preparation and installation were deducted currently while the income from the sales was deferred under the installment method. The Commissioner sought to have the court deny the current deduction on the basis that the resulting mismatching of interrelated items of income and expense did not clearly reflect income. The court rejected the Commissioner's contention, pointing out that the cost of such installation and preparation were not required to be treated as inventoriable costs under the then-applicable law (i.e., the law in effect prior to the enactment of Section 263A), that the taxpayer complied with all requirements relating to inventory costing and use of the installment method, and, finally, that the clear reflection of income "doctrine" implements, and does not contradict, well-established statutory and case law. Id. at 194. By this statement, the court suggests that the Commissioner does not have the discretion to deny to a taxpayer the use of methods of accounting expressly authorized by the Code when the taxpayer satisfies applicable explicit requirements for use of the method, if any, and otherwise is not expressly precluded from use of the method. See also RLC Indus. Co., 98 TC 457 (1992), where the court reviewed the Commissioner's assertion that the method of accounting in question did not clearly reflect income even though the method might comply with the applicable regulations. The court stated that it would be justified in holding that compliance with the regulations should suffice, but the court nevertheless decided to review the matter fully in light of the Commissioner's wide authority in matters of tax accounting. However, in doing so, the court noted that "[u]sually, courts have found a taxpayer's method to clearly reflect income where the method is in compliance with the regulations. [citations omitted.] This should be especially so here, where we consider legislative regulations to which we pay greater deference [citations omitted], and which have been held to have the force and effect of law [citations omitted]."

[103] Treas. Reg. § 1.446-1(a)(2). Treas. Reg. § 1.446-1(c)(1)(ii)(C) provides the same basic rule, although it did not contain any qualifier such as "ordinarily" prior to its amendment, effective April 10, 1992, when the qualifier "generally" was added.

fact, the courts and the IRS have made it clear that compliance with GAAP is frequently of little significance, particularly where GAAP is inconsistent with the objectives of tax accounting.

The relationship between GAAP and the clear reflection standard was directly addressed by the U.S. Supreme Court in *Thor Power Tool Co. v Commissioner*.[104] In affirming the lower court's disallowance of certain write-downs of inventory, the Court noted that Section 471, pertaining to methods of accounting for inventories, "establishes two distinct tests to which an inventory must conform": (1) it must comply as closely as possible with the "best accounting practice" and (2) it must "clearly reflect income." The Court held that the first requirement was synonymous with a requirement that the method be in accordance with GAAP. The Court held that the taxpayer's method satisfied this requirement. The Court therefore framed the remaining issue as whether the Commissioner had abused his discretion in determining that the write-down failed to clearly reflect income. By its interpretation of the first requirement and by framing the issue as it did, the Court made it clear that compliance with GAAP would not, in and of itself, satisfy the clear reflection of income requirement. Similarly, compliance with GAAP was not a necessary condition for satisfaction of the requirement.

The Court rejected the taxpayer's arguments that (1) since the write-down conformed to GAAP, there was a presumption that it clearly reflected income and (2) this presumption could be overcome only by the Commissioner's showing that the method failed to clearly reflect income or was adopted for tax avoidance purposes. The Court noted first that even if the Code and regulations provided for such a presumption, it would be of little assistance to the taxpayer because the method used was inconsistent with the regulations. However, the Court went further and held that no such presumption exists.

The Court also noted that methods of accounting that were approved for financial accounting purposes and in accordance with GAAP did not necessarily clearly reflect income for tax purposes. In a frequently cited passage, the Court stated the following:

> The primary goal of financial accounting is to provide useful information to management, shareholders, creditors, and others properly interested; the major responsibility of the accountant is to protect these parties from being misled. The primary goal of the income tax system, in contrast, is the equitable collection of revenue; the major responsibility of the Internal Revenue Service is to protect the public fisc. Consistently with its goals and responsibilities, financial accounting has as its foundation the principle of conservatism, with its corollary that "possible errors in measurement [should] be in the direction of understatement rather than overstatement of net income and net assets." In view of the

---

[104] Thor Power Tool Co. v. Comm'r, 439 US 522 (1979).

Treasury's markedly different goals and responsibilities, understatement of income is not destined to be its guiding light. Given this diversity, even contrariety, of objective, any presumptive equivalency between tax and financial accounting would be unacceptable.[105]

Finally, the Court stated that any such presumption would create vast difficulties in tax administration because the use of generally accepted accounting principles tolerates a wide range of alternative approaches and would not necessarily result in identical tax treatment for identical transactions. Thus, while compliance with GAAP is often influential, it is not determinative.[106] Moreover, meeting GAAP is certainly not required for compliance with the clear reflection of income requirement. Consequently, taxpayers should not assume that their GAAP methods will automatically be accepted for tax purposes, nor should they concede, if challenged on audit, that any method that does not meet GAAP fails to clearly reflect income.

[d] Nature of Business Transactions, Manipulation, and Abuse

The courts sometimes find a link between the clear reflection of income requirement and the business transactions of the taxpayer. Where the taxpayer attempts to manipulate the timing of transactions solely to take advantage of its method of tax accounting (e.g., where a cash basis taxpayer pays in advance to accelerate deductions, or delays billing and collection to defer income), issues of clear reflection may be raised. On the other hand, where the tax accounting method is applied to transactions that occur in the ordinary course of business or that are motivated by business, not tax, reasons, the results produced are generally held to reflect income clearly.[107]

The Tax Court reached this conclusion in *Kenneth H. Van Raden*.[108] In

---

[105] Id. at 542–543.

[106] See American Fletcher Corp. v. United States, 832 F2d 436 (7th Cir. 1987), for an analysis of the relevance of the failure of the taxpayer's method to comply with GAAP.

[107] See Tech. Adv. Mem. 8029008 (Apr. 10, 1980), where the National Office suggested that the manipulation of business transactions for tax reasons might cause the IRS to conclude that the taxpayer's method of accounting fails to reflect income clearly.

[108] In Kenneth H. Van Raden, 71 TC 1083, 1105–1106 (1979), the court stated the following:

Because the method of accounting and the nature of a trade or business are so interdependent, we conclude that the distortion of income must not be examined in a vacuum but in light of the business practice or business activities which give rise to the transaction which the Commissioner had determined must be accorded a different accounting treatment. For example, material distortions of income may occur if the sales force of a business is more successful in December than in January, yet such a distortion would not require adjustment to clearly reflect income because the distortion resulted from the business

this case, the court noted that the hazardous and seasonal nature of the taxpayer's farming business brought about the cyclical feed prices on which the success of farmers greatly depends. Thus, the court concluded that the Commissioner had abused his discretion under Section 446(b) in disallowing the deduction for feed purchased.[109]

This case suggests that any perceived distortion in levels of taxable income arising from transactions occurring in the normal course of a business (or from normal transactions in the particular circumstances of the business) is not the sort of distortion that gives rise to a failure to clearly reflect income. Rather, it is the proper reporting of income arising from a combination of the normal course of the business and the normal application of the taxpayer's chosen method of accounting.

The impact of the type or nature of the business on the clear reflection test is also evidenced by the IRS's audit practices. For example, use of the cash method by small service businesses and by individuals is considered to clearly reflect income based on convenience to the taxpayers, simplicity of the method, its certainty in application, the nature of their business activities, and similar concerns.[110] A certain degree of accelerated payments or deferred billing is usually tolerated. The level of tolerance decreases markedly as the size of the business grows.

[e] Effect of Consistency

Consistency in application of a method of accounting is often regarded as one of the most important hallmarks of whether a method clearly reflects income.[111] The importance of consistency is based on the fact that over the

---

activity itself. Should the result be different if the taxpayer purchases a year's supply of its primary cost item at its lowest cost consistently from year to year? We do not think so. In short, a substantial legitimate business purpose satisfies the distortion of income test.

[109] A similar analysis was employed by the Tax Court in a memorandum decision overturning the Commissioner's disallowance of a cattle feeding partnership's deduction of the cost of cattle feed purchased during its short initial taxable year. James F. Haynes, 38 TCM 950 (1979). See also Sierracin Corp., 90 TC 341 (1988), where the court concluded that the Commissioner had abused his discretion in rejecting the taxpayer's application of the completed contract method. The court was strongly influenced by the business activities of the taxpayer.

[110] See discussion infra ¶ 2.02[2][g].

[111] See, e.g., Koebig & Koebig, Inc., 23 TCM 170 (1964). The consistency factor has been accorded particular weight in inventory valuation cases as a result of the following regulation:

In order clearly to reflect income, the inventory practice of a taxpayer should be consistent from year to year, and greater weight is to be given to consistency than to any particular method of inventorying or basis of valuation so long as the method or basis used is in accord with §§ 1.471-1 through 1.471-11.

life of the taxpayer, the same amount of aggregate income will be reported under any method of accounting. Consequently, any under- or over-reporting of income in one year (as between one method and another) will be offset in other years.

Notwithstanding the importance of consistency, it has been held that consistency of use, standing alone, is not a sufficient basis for rejecting the Commissioner's determination that a method of accounting does not clearly reflect income.[112] This is especially true where the method at issue is otherwise not permitted.[113]

Moreover, where operation of a particular method does not permit the offsetting previously referred to, consistency may be of relatively little importance. This is particularly true in the costing of inventories where such costs are taken into account on either a LIFO basis or a first-in, first-out (FIFO) basis. Under LIFO, the cost of the last goods acquired or produced is matched against sales revenue to determine gain. Under FIFO, the cost of the earliest goods acquired or produced is matched against sales revenue to determine gain.[114] Consequently, under FIFO, any incorrect costing of inventory will flow through to cost of goods sold quite quickly. Thus, a correction in costing procedures will result in a relatively quick correction in both the aggregate and current amounts of reported income. On the other hand, under LIFO, incorrect costs may permanently be included in inventory and may affect LIFO computations in subsequent years. Moreover, correction may not have a complete or immediate effect on aggregate or currently reported income.

[f] Mismatching (Virtually Identical Results)

The fact that one method of accounting results in a different matching of income and expense than would occur under some other method does not

---

Treas. Reg. § 1.471-2(b). See also Geometric Stamping Co., 26 TC 301 (1956), acq. in result 1958-2 CB 5.

[112] See Fort Howard Paper Co., 49 TC 275 (1967), and cases cited therein.

[113] See, e.g., William K. Coors, 60 TC 368, 395 (1973), aff'd sub. nom., Adolph Coors Co. v. Comm'r, 519 F2d 1280 (10th Cir. 1975), cert. denied, 423 US 1087 (1975) (stating that "consistency does not make it right. A failure to clearly reflect income over many years cannot be justified on the grounds of tenure"); Photo-Sonics, Inc., 42 TC 926, 935 (1964), acq. 1965-2 CB 6, aff'd, 357 F2d 656 (9th Cir. 1966) ("An erroneous method does not become acceptable solely upon the consistent use over an extended period of time"); L.R. Gustafson, 55 TCM 250 (1988) ("consistent use of an erroneous method for more than 40 years does not make the method acceptable"); Ralston Dev. Corp. v. United States, 937 F2d 510 (10th Cir. 1991) (consistent use of cash method with inventories does not make the cash method acceptable even though use of that method had previously been approved on audit).

[114] See discussion at ¶ 6.08.

require a finding that the first method fails to clearly reflect income. Nor is such a finding required by the fact that two or more taxpayers involved in a particular transaction report the transaction under different methods of accounting. These conclusions are evident from the fact that Section 446(c) provides several alternative overall methods of accounting to each taxpayer, and other provisions of the Code and regulations provide each taxpayer with numerous alternative methods of accounting for particular items of income or expense.[115]

Notwithstanding the foregoing, a recurring issue on audit is whether related items of income and expense must be matched, as under an accrual method of tax accounting or even an accrual method of financial accounting. The question is most often raised during the audit of a cash method taxpayer or an accrual method taxpayer whose accrual tax method differs from its accrual financial method. Generally, the answer is no.[116]

The failure of a taxpayer's method to precisely match related items of income and expense as they would be matched for financial accounting purposes is not fatal. This is the case regardless of whether the taxpayer uses

---

[115] See James V. Cole, 64 TC 1091, 1110 (1975), aff'd, 586 F2d 747 (9th Cir. 1978), cert. denied, 441 US 924 (1979), where, in a concurring opinion, Judge Hall correctly noted, "If the cash method [or, presumably, any authorized method] is properly used, the disparity [between the results under the method used and any other method] is not a *distortion* of income but merely the consequences of proper use of a permissible method of *measuring* income." (Emphasis by court.)

[116] See, e.g., Michael Drazen, 34 TC 1070 (1960), where the taxpayer sought to file an amended return on the accrual basis by contending that the cash method used in the initial return did not clearly reflect income because it did not match related items of income and expense. In finding against the taxpayer, the court noted:

While it is theoretically desirable to match expenses with income earned in incurring those expenses, it must be remembered that exact and precise matching is seldom, if ever, achieved with either method of accounting. We pointed this out in *H.G. Irby, Jr.,* 30 T.C. 1166, *modified* 274 F2d 208 (C.A. 5), when we stated (at p. 1175): "Under either the cash or the accrual method, it is possible that expenses, paid or accruable, may be deductible in a year that is either prior or subsequent to the year in which income related to such expenses is includible. . . . This is simply the result of the facts, that taxable income must be computed on an annual basis, and that the computation of taxable income does not necessarily follow business accounting practices. . . ."

Id. at 1077–1078; Marquardt Corp., 39 TC 443 (1962), acq. as to this issue 1965-2 CB 6, where the Tax Court, in deciding whether a particular item of income had accrued in the taxable year at issue, stated:

Accrual of an item as income in a particular year is not required merely because the expenses attributable to that item were deducted from gross income in that year. . . . As a practical matter, the income tax laws must operate on an annual basis, and there is no assurance under either an accrual or cash basis of accounting that there will be complete correlation between items of income and deductions pertinent thereto.

39 TC at 453.

an accrual method or the cash method. For example, in *Koebig & Koebig, Inc.*,[117] an engineering firm accrued as income only the amounts billed during the taxable year, but it deducted expenses actually incurred, even when such expenses were incurred after the last billing date. The use of this accrual method was challenged by the IRS on the basis of mismatching, the IRS seeking to disallow the deduction of expenses incurred after the period to which the bill related. In finding that the taxpayer's income had been reflected clearly, the Tax Court rejected any requirement of precise matching.[118]

The cash method, of course, does not match items of income and expense in the same way as an accrual method. The courts have acknowledged that this mismatching (as compared to accrual accounting) is inherent in the cash method and does not result in a failure of the method to reflect income clearly.[119]

Similarly, use of the installment method may not result in matching in the same tax year related items of income and expense. For example, in *Marcor, Inc.*,[120] the taxpayer reported sales of certain items on an installment method. Some of the items sold on this method required that the taxpayer

---

[117] Koebig & Koebig, Inc., 23 TCM 170 (1964).

[118] The Tax Court stated the following:

The fact that an accrual method of reporting income does not always give a precise matching of income and expenses does not mean that it does not clearly reflect the income of [taxpayer]; the vital point is consistency. Since [taxpayer's] books and accrual method of reporting income clearly reflected its income, the [Commissioner] is not empowered to reconstruct [taxpayer's] income on some other system to secure more favorable tax results. . . . It is immaterial that the method used by the [Commissioner] in recomputing [taxpayer's] taxable income for 1959 . . . would also clearly reflect [taxpayer's] income or would result in a more precise matching of income with expenses. It is not within the province of the court to weigh and determine the relative merits of methods of accounting.

Id. at 181–182.

[119] See, e.g., Maurice W. Simon, 6 TCM 57, 58 (1947), aff'd, 176 F2d 230 (2d Cir. 1949), where the court stated:

Defects of this kind are inherent in the cash receipts and disbursements method. It is not perfect. Nearly always some accounts due a taxpayer will remain uncollected at the end of the year, and some of his own obligations may remain unpaid, but if the method is consistently applied, it will bring about a reasonably fair reflection of income. Certainly it was not contemplated that all taxpayers could be forced to use an accrual method or one which perfectly reflects income.

See also RLC Indus. Co., 98 TC 457 (1992), where the court stated:

By definition, the cash method may result in mismatching between expenses and income where expenses are paid in a year prior to the receipt of related income. Generally, the cash method is not permitted under accounting standards, whereas the cash method is permitted (for the years under consideration) for tax purposes.

[120] Marcor, Inc., 89 TC 181 (1987).

incur preparation and installation expenses. The taxpayer deducted these expenses in the year incurred, although the income from the sale was recognized in later years under the installment method. The Commissioner argued that the failure to match these related items of income and expense in the same year resulted in a failure to reflect income clearly. The court rejected that contention, pointing out that although the tax rules could have been written to require such matching, they were not so written. Moreover, since the taxpayer had followed all requirements for use of the method, the government could not use the clear reflection of income doctrine as a means of denying the taxpayer the right to adopt expressly authorized methods for which the taxpayer was otherwise eligible.

The IRS has accepted these principles. For example, it has permitted the use of the cash method despite the fact that the method does not precisely match related items of income and expense with the accuracy of an accrual method. On the other hand, the IRS reserves the right to disallow use of the cash method where transactions are taken out of the ordinary course of business or the chosen method is otherwise abused or manipulated to the taxpayer's benefit.[121]

The Tax Court has indicated that even though a method operates in the ordinary course without deliberate abuse, the distortion that results from the particular method may be so exceptional that the Commissioner is allowed to change that method on the basis that it fails to clearly reflect income.[122] Similarly, where an accrual method taxpayer deducts a liability whose payment will be delayed for a substantial period, the Commissioner has been permitted, in at least one case, to disallow the deduction on the basis of the clear reflection of income standard.[123] However, these cases are the exceptions rather than the rule. Moreover, as Congress has become more active in the area of tax accounting (e.g., by enacting the economic performance rules in

---

[121] See, e.g., Tech. Adv. Mem. 8029008 (Apr. 10, 1980).

[122] See, e.g., William J. Silberman, 47 TCM 778 (1983), involving an entity engaged in the production of a motion picture film where costs would be incurred in early years and revenue would be derived in later years. The court indicated that the mismatching that would arise in that circumstance would be sufficient to permit the Commissioner to disallow use of the cash method. It is not clear whether the court actually intended to go this far or, instead, merely intended to hold that in the particular circumstances, the taxpayer should be treated as having an ownership interest in the film being produced and, for that reason, should be required either to capitalize its cost or to use an accrual method. (Of course, use of the accrual method without capitalization would also not achieve the matching discussed by the court. Thus, the real concern appeared to be one of capitalization.)

[123] See Mooney Aircraft, Inc. v. United States, 420 F2d 400 (5th Cir. 1970), where deductions were disallowed because they would not be paid for 15, 20, or even 30 years. Although the court did not require the taxpayer to convert from an accrual method to the cash method, it effectively placed the taxpayer on the cash basis with respect to the deductions at issue.

1984 and the limitations on the availability of the cash method in 1986,[124]) courts may find it more difficult to find new exceptions.[125]

Finally, several cases have noted (or suggested) that the use of a particular method of accounting will (or may) be deemed to reflect income clearly only if the results produced under that method are virtually identical to the results produced under the method sought by the Commissioner.[126] This conclusion is warranted in the context of a taxpayer engaged in the purchase and sale of merchandise. In such a circumstance, unless the method used by the taxpayer appropriately matches related items of sales price and cost of goods sold, gross profit will not be computed accurately or correctly.[127] Hence, the courts have suggested that where a taxpayer does not use a traditional accrual method for the reporting of those items, the taxpayer's method may be sustainable only if it achieves results that are virtually identical to the results that would be achieved under an accrual method.[128] Consequently, a requirement of virtually identical results makes sense in any case where the taxpayer uses a method of accounting other than the method that is expressly required by the Code or regulations. In this sense, the test operates as a relief provision for taxpayers, i.e., a taxpayer may use a method other than an authorized method where virtually identical results are obtained. However, a requirement of virtual identity in results to reflect income clearly would not make sense where more than one method is authorized, and the taxpayer uses one of the authorized methods. To impose the test as a condition or requirement in situations where more than one method is authorized would

---

[124] See ¶¶ 4.04[3], 3.06, respectively, for discussion of the economic performance rules and limitations on the availability of the cash method.

[125] Under the doctrine of legislative reenactment, the force of law is given to administrative interpretations of statutory provisions that have been reenacted by Congress without substantial change. See e.g., Mass. Mutual Life Ins. Co. v. United States, 288 US 269 (1933); Helvering v. Winmill, 305 US 79 (1938).

[126] See, e.g., Caldwell v. Comm'r, 202 F2d 112 (2d Cir. 1953); Wilkinson-Beane, Inc. v. Comm'r, 420 F2d 352 (1st Cir. 1970); Knight-Ridder Newspapers, Inc. v. United States, 743 F2d 781 (11th Cir. 1984).

[127] See, e.g., Louis S. Rotolo, 88 TC 1500 (1987), which involved a taxpayer whose inclusion in income of advance payments on long-term contracts was held proper but whose corresponding deduction of the cost of inventory attributable to those contracts was denied by the Commissioner. The court held for the taxpayer and allowed the deduction, stating that the Commissioner's disallowance of the offset (deduction) would amount to and result in a tax on gross income. The court stated that the Commissioner's method would not properly reflect income, was unreasonable, and would result in a tax on gross receipts; a result that repeatedly has been rejected.

[128] Caldwell v. Comm'r, 202 F2d 112 (2d Cir. 1953). See discussion infra ¶ 2.02[j][ii].

have the effect of destroying the opportunity granted to taxpayers to choose from among any of several available methods.[129]

The preceding analysis was implicitly accepted by the court in *Ralston Development Corp. v. United States*.[130] In *Ralston*, a taxpayer using inventories, which constituted a material income-producing factor, sought to preclude the Commissioner from changing it from the cash method to an accrual method. The appeals court allowed the Commissioner to make the change and noted the fact that the taxpayer's use of the cash method in its circumstances did not produce results substantially identical to the results produced under an accrual method. In so noting, the court cited the preceding analysis and quoted it in part.[131]

---

[129] In American Fletcher Corp. v. United States, 86-1 USTC ¶ 9283 (SD Ind. 1986), aff'd, 832 F2d 436 (7th Cir. 1987), the district court suggested that the virtual identity or substantial identity test could be applied to a service business to disallow use of the cash method on the basis that the cash method did not produce results consistent with an accrual method. However, in that case the taxpayer was unable to compute accurately its income under a cash method. It remains to be seen whether the virtual identity test will be applied where the assertedly improper method complies with all applicable requirements for use of that method but does not produce results identical to those produced under the method desired by the IRS. The appeals court recognized that the virtual identity (or substantial identity) test had generally been applied under Section 471, which pertains to inventories, and the appeals court added that this test was equally applicable to cases under Section 446(b). This conclusion makes sense if the taxpayer is using an impermissible method or a method expressly made unavailable to a particular taxpayer or to particular transactions. However, the conclusion is not appropriate as a general principle.

Nevertheless, in Applied Communications, Inc., 57 TCM 1473 (1989), a case involving the use of the cash method by a company whose business was changing from a service-oriented business to a product-oriented business, the court noted the Commissioner's argument that his proposed change in method would not amount to an abuse of discretion because among other things, the taxpayer's method produced a different result than the Commissioner's method. The court indicated that this factor, together with other factors, demonstrated that the Commissioner had not abused his discretion in denying continued use of the cash method. It is troubling that the court suggests that the Commissioner should have the discretion to require a change from one authorized method to another on the basis of differences in results when it is so obvious that the use of different methods necessarily produces differences in results. See also In re BKW Sys., Inc., 90-1 USTC ¶ 50,139 (Bankr. DNH 1989).

[130] Ralston Dev. Corp. v. United States, 937 F2d 510 (10th Cir. 1991).

[131] See also RLC Indus. Co., 98 TC 457 (1992), where the court stated that the disparity in results between the method of accounting sought by the Commissioner and the method used by the taxpayer was not a sufficient reason for the imposition of the method preferred by the Commissioner. The court stated that "[t]he best method is not necessarily the one which produces the most tax in a particular year. If, as here, a taxpayer's method is consistently applied and clearly reflects income, we will not sustain respondent's determination merely because it produces more income tax for the taxable year under consideration." The court went on to say that "[d]isparity in amount is not, per se, necessarily indicative of a failure to clearly reflect income."

Notwithstanding the foregoing discussion, it is appropriate to consider whether each party to a transaction is characterizing the facts consistently. To the extent each is characterizing the facts differently, such "mismatching" of characterizations may be inappropriate, unless the mismatching is justifiable in the circumstances or otherwise authorized under applicable law. Such consideration of each side's characterization occurred, for example, in *Bell Federal Savings & Loan Association*,[132] where the factual issue was whether agreements between the taxpayer and its borrowers required points in the nature of interest to be withheld from the proceeds of the loans or, instead, to be paid by the borrowers from their separate funds at the time of the loan closings. In deciding that the taxpayer had not discounted the points from the proceeds of the loans, the court pointed to the fact that borrowers were viewed as having paid the points from their separate funds at the time of the loan closings.

[g] Relevance of Size of Taxpayer's Business

Examining agents sometimes assert that the size of the taxpayer's business (in terms of its level of revenues or taxable income, or the deferral in income under the method used as compared to the method desired by the agents) is relevant in determining whether the method used reflects income clearly. Typically, this assertion has been made when the IRS is, on audit, challenging use of the cash method by a large business or even large deductions by an accrual method business. Such assertions have not generally been successful before either the courts or the National Office.[133]

The irrelevance of size on the issue of clear reflection of income was seemingly first confirmed by enactment of the economic performance rules,

---

Moreover, the court suggested earlier in its opinion that in evaluating equivalency of results, such results should be considered over a period of years, not in any particular year.

[132] Bell Fed. Sav. & Loan Ass'n, 62 TCM 376 (1991).

[133] See, e.g., William H. White, Sr., 12 TCM 996, 997 (1953), where the court stated:

The argument of the Commissioner in effect is that although the cash receipts and disbursements method of accounting clearly reflected the income of the [taxpayer] when its business income resulted from small contracts, that system can not clearly reflect its income consisting largely of income from large contracts. He cites no authority for any such proposition. The tax should be computed on the cash method.

See also TAM 8029008 (Apr. 10, 1980), where the National Office held that the cash method could be used by a large international accounting firm. In so holding, the National Office stated that, "historically, the Service has not by regulations or otherwise denied the use of the cash method to a service business having substantial receivables and payables, even in cases where substantial mismatching of income and expense has occurred."

which delayed the timing of accrual method deductions but did not otherwise suggest limitations on current deductions because of the size of the amount deducted.[134] The lack of any size limitation on use of the cash method was effectively confirmed both by the permitted use of such method by very large businesses prior to the 1986 Act and by the 1986 Act itself, which for the first time imposed size limitations on use of the cash method.[135] On the other hand, some cases do exist in which the propriety of the use of a particular method seems to be predicated on the materiality of the difference in income under the method used by the taxpayer and the method preferred by the IRS. These cases, which generally involve taxpayers with income derived from the purchase and sale of inventory, hold that although an accrual method of accounting must be used with respect to the purchase and sale of merchandise, the IRS has the discretion to accept another method if the level of inventories, purchases, and sales is immaterial. In this sense, the lack of materiality may permit an exception to the regulatory requirement of an accrual method.[136] The size of the difference is therefore not relevant as to whether an available method clearly reflects income, but as to whether any method may be used other than an expressly required method.

[h] To Reflect Income More Clearly

If the taxpayer's method of accounting clearly reflects income, the Commissioner may not require the taxpayer to change to a method that, in the Commissioner's view, more clearly reflects income.[137] In other words, the

---

[134] See ¶ 4.04[3] for discussion of economic performance rules.

[135] See discussion at ¶ 3.06[1].

[136] See discussion at ¶ 3.06[2].

[137] See, e.g., W.P. Garth, 56 TC 610, 618 (1971), acq. 1975-1 CB 1, where the court stated:

It is well settled that the Commissioner has broad powers in determining whether the accounting method used by a taxpayer does clearly reflect income . . . but this is not to say that the Commissioner has authority to force a taxpayer to change from a method of accounting which does "clearly reflect income" to a method which in the Commissioner's opinion more clearly reflects income.

Maloney v. Hammond, 176 F2d 780, 781 (9th Cir. 1949), where the court stated:

If appellant's position is that, having granted permission to a taxpayer to use a certain method of accounting and the taxpayer having in good faith followed the allowed method, the Commissioner may subsequently determine that some other method would be more advantageous to the government in the amount of taxes to be collected and substitute the second method for the first, we say the Commissioner has no such right. To do so would be most unfair to the taxpayer.

Capitol Fed. Sav. & Loan Ass'n, 96 TC 204 (1991), where the court stated, "Where, however, a taxpayer does demonstrate that his method of accounting clearly reflects income, the Commissioner cannot require him to change to a different method of

Commissioner does not have the right to rank acceptable methods of accounting and then to require the taxpayer to use the method with the highest rank. Courts have expressed this long-standing rule by stating that "[i]t is not the province of the court[s] to weigh and determine the relative merits of systems of accounting."[138] Consequently, courts have held that if the taxpayer's method clearly reflects income, but not as clearly as the method preferred by the IRS (because, for example, it does not precisely match related items of income and expense), the taxpayer's method must nevertheless be accepted as long as it is used on a consistent basis.[139] The IRS itself has seemingly accepted this analysis.[140]

On the other hand, in *Fort Howard Paper Co.*,[141] a case in which an accrual basis taxpayer's treatment of overhead expenses connected with self-constructed assets was approved, the Tax Court stated that "we neither hold nor imply that, under all circumstances, a taxpayer has a right to choose between alternative generally accepted methods of accounting or that [Commissioner] may not, under some circumstances, require a taxpayer to accept his determination as to a preferred selection among such alternatives."[142] Nevertheless, there has been no decision expressly permitting the IRS to change a taxpayer from a method that clearly reflects income to a method that, in the view of the IRS, more clearly reflects income.

[i] Use of Method by Others

The use of a method of accounting by others in the same business or profession is sometimes cited as a factor in the determination of whether a particular method clearly reflects income. For example, in *V.T.H. Bien*,[143] the Tax Court found that the taxpayer, an architect, used a hybrid method of accounting that did not clearly reflect income. Among the reasons cited by the court was that the taxpayer "failed to show that his books of account relating to his profession have been kept on the same basis as other archi-

---

accounting, even if such different method, in the Commissioner's view, more clearly reflects income."

[138] See Brown v. Helvering, 291 US 193, 205 (1963); Auburn Packing Co., 60 TC 794 (1973), acq. 1974-2 CB 1.

[139] Auburn Packing Co., 60 TC 794, 799 (1973), acq. 1974-2 CB 1; accord W.P. Garth, 56 TC 610 (1971), acq. 1975-1 CB 1 (taxpayer's use of farm price method of inventory valuation clearly reflected its income).

[140] See Gen. Couns. Mem. 38852 (May 17, 1982), revoked for other reasons by Gen. Couns. Mem. 38912 (Oct. 26, 1982).

[141] Fort Howard Paper Co., 49 TC 275 (1967).

[142] Id. at 286.

[143] V.T.H. Bien, 20 TC 49 (1953), acq. 1953-2 CB 3.

tects."[144] Similar reasoning has been applied in the case of taxpayers who practice many of the recognized professions and taxpayers who are contractors.[145] Of course, a taxpayer desiring to rely on the practices of others in the industry to show that its method clearly reflects income has the burden of demonstrating that its business and accounting practices are the same as those with which it wants to be compared.[146]

[j] Judicial Application of Requirement

Although the courts have applied the requirement of clear reflection of income in numerous circumstances, only two general standards of clear reflection have emerged from those cases. The earlier of the two standards is based on fair and honest reporting. It provides the Commissioner with the opportunity to monitor taxpayer conduct, and it raises the possibility that application of a particular method may be denied on the basis of the clear reflection requirement if results produced under the method are due to the taxpayer's manipulation of its transactions to achieve desired tax results. The second standard is more mechanical and is based on the proper, accurate computation of income under the method selected. Taxpayers, the IRS, and the courts have frequently assumed that these standards are not consistent and, hence, that only one of these two standards may be applied to a given set of circumstances. Actually, the two standards are not inconsistent, and the courts are beginning to recognize this, as explained in the following paragraphs.

[i] **Fair and honest reporting standard.** This standard, the earlier of the two, was first announced in 1930 by the Ninth Circuit in *Osterloh v. Lucas*.[147] The issue was the taxpayer's deduction of a loss that had neither

---

[144] Id. at 55. See also Seas Shipping Co., 1 TC 30 (1942), where the court, in finding that the completed voyage basis of accounting used by a taxpayer that operated steamships clearly reflected income, noted that "numerous other" taxpayers in the business used the same method; American Fletcher Corp. v. United States, 832 F2d 436 (7th Cir. 1987), where the court found the failure of others in the taxpayer's industry to use the cash method (for either financial or tax reporting purposes) to be relevant in determining whether the method clearly reflected income.

[145] See Gen. Couns. Mem. 38288 (Feb. 21, 1980), where it was recognized that, in certain circumstances, professionals should be permitted to use the cash method despite the furnishing of products as part of their service; Rayman D. Magnon, 73 TC 980, 1004 (1980), acq. 1981-2 CB 2, where, in allowing use of the cash method, the court stated, "The cash method of accounting has been widely used throughout the contracting industry and accepted by the respondent since time immemorial."

[146] See Applied Communications, Inc., 57 TCM 1473 (1989), where the court made these points clear while recognizing the relevance of industry practices.

[147] Osterloh v. Lucas, 37 F2d 277 (9th Cir. 1930).

been paid nor reflected on his cash basis books.[148] In disallowing the loss, the court stated that the case turned on what was meant by the requirement that an accounting method clearly reflect income. The court pointed out that the cash method rarely, if ever, reflects true income because, at the end of the tax year, there are almost always accounts receivable and accounts payable. However, the court added that in its opinion, all that is meant by the requirement is that the taxpayer's books be kept fairly and honestly, without any attempt to evade tax. The court recognized that this construction of the requirement could work to the disadvantage of the taxpayer or the government at times, but if followed consistently and honestly year after year, would approximate equality as nearly as could be hoped for in the administration of the tax law.[149]

The fair and honest standard of *Osterloh* conveys certain points about the clear reflection requirement. First, the requirement does not necessitate application of the most economically sound method of computing income or the most precise concepts and principles of financial accounting. If it did, there would be no right to use any of the several authorized methods, each of which results in a different computation of income.[150] Second, taxpayers have a responsibility not to abuse or manipulate their chosen method so as to cause unfair results. For example, if a taxpayer were to manipulate transactions or prevent transactions from occurring in the ordinary course of business to generate certain tax results (i.e., to accelerate expenses or to defer income), such activity might cause the method used not to reflect income clearly.

The *Osterloh* standard was initially followed in a number of instances,[151]

---

[148] Section 212 of the Revenue Act of 1921 required that taxable income be computed in accordance with the method of accounting used by the taxpayer in keeping his books, which was the cash method, unless that method did not clearly reflect income.

[149] Osterloh v. Lucas, 37 F2d 277, at 278–279 (9th Cir. 1930).

[150] Of course, because of the different objectives of financial and tax accounting, the *Osterloh* court recognized implicitly that tax accounting could not be controlled by financial accounting. See also Thor Power Tool Co. v. Comm'r, 439 US 522 (1979).

[151] See, e.g., Glenn v. Kentucky Color & Chem. Co., 186 F2d 975, 977 (6th Cir. 1951) (stating, "The statute requires only that the taxpayer's books shall be kept fairly and honestly, without any attempt to evade the tax. . . . It does not require absolute precision.") The *Osterloh* definition was also cited by the courts in the following cases: Towers Warehouses, Inc., 6 TCM 59 (1947) (accrual basis taxpayer allowed deduction for estimated labor charges); William H. White, Sr., 12 TCM 996 (1953) (cash method clearly reflected income); Estate of James H. Post, 8 BTAM 311 (1939) (accrual method clearly reflected income); Cedar Rapids Eng'g Co., 86 F. Supp. 577 (ND Iowa 1949) (proper time for accrual basis taxpayer to accrue capital stock liability resulting from an increased declared value of its capital stock); Koebig & Koebig, Inc., 23 TCM 170 (1964) (accrual method clearly reflected income); Welch v. DeBlois, 94 F2d 842 (1st Cir. 1938) (cash basis taxpayer allowed deduction for full cost of multiyear insurance policies in year of purchase); Wolf Bakery & Cafeteria

including inventory valuation cases, which are governed by both the standards of Section 446 and the even stricter standards of Section 471.[152] For example, in *Huntington Securities Corp. v. Busey*,[153] the court stated that, in construing tax statutes, the natural and ordinary meaning of the words used should be applied unless Congress has indicated otherwise. The court then stated that "clearly," as used in the statute, "means plainly, honestly, straightforwardly and frankly, but does not mean 'accurately' which, in its ordinary use, means precisely, exactly, correctly, without error or defect."[154]

In *C.A. Hunt Engineering Co.*,[155] the issue involved application of the clear reflection of income requirement to the use of the cash method in reporting income from long-term contracts. Citing the *Osterloh* standard, the Tax Court held that the deferral in the recognition of income from contracts until payments were received did not mean that the cash method failed to clearly reflect income.[156]

As the evolution of the *Osterloh* principle continued over time, taxpayers sometimes attempted to rely on it in support of a position that even an erroneous method, or a method producing inaccurate results, could clearly reflect income if applied fairly, honestly, and consistently. In effect, these taxpayers argued that fair and honest reporting took precedence over

---

Co., 5 TCM 389 (1946) (cash method clearly reflected income); International Cigar Mach. Co., 36 BTA 124 (1937), acq. 1937-2 CB 15 (accrual basis taxpayer's treatment of royalty payments clearly reflected income).

[152] Section 471 provides that where the use of inventories is necessary to clearly determine a taxpayer's income, "inventories shall be taken by such taxpayer on such basis as the Secretary may prescribe as conforming as nearly as may be to the best accounting practice in the trade or business and as *most* clearly reflecting the income" (emphasis added). See also Treas. Reg. § 1.471-2, and discussion at ¶ 6.04.

[153] Huntington Sec. Corp. v. Busey, 112 F2d 368 (6th Cir. 1940).

[154] Id. at 370–371. Similarly, in S. Weisbart & Co., 23 TCM 788 (1964), the court found that the taxpayer's use of a modified FIFO method of inventory accounting was reasonable, in accordance with the best inventory accounting practices, and clearly reflected income. Citing *Huntington Sec. Corp.*, the court stated, "It is not necessary that [taxpayer's] inventories be absolutely accurate or correct. As used in the pertinent Code sections, 'clearly' to reflect income means plainly, honestly, straightforwardly and frankly, not accurately, precisely, exactly, correctly or without error or defect." Id. at 798.

[155] C.A. Hunt Eng'g Co., 15 TCM 1269 (1956).

[156] The Tax Court stated the following:

> Any distortion in income which may have resulted from delayed payments on account by related companies . . . does not, standing alone, convince us that the cash receipts and disbursements method of accounting used by the [taxpayer] did not clearly reflect its income. . . . We are convinced that the [taxpayer] kept his books fairly, honestly, and in good faith under the cash receipts and disbursements method of accounting and without any attempt to evade taxes.

Id. at 1274.

so-called accurate reporting. Of course, *Osterloh* did not so hold. The emphasis placed by *Osterloh* and its progeny on fairness and honesty over accuracy was in the context of recognizing that a method of accounting could clearly reflect income even if it was not the most precise, exact, or error-free method.

[ii] Accuracy standard. The efforts of taxpayers to take advantage of *Osterloh* came to a head in *Caldwell v. Commissioner*,[157] where the Second Circuit announced what has subsequently become the other most frequently cited standard for clear reflection of income. In *Caldwell*, a taxpayer, who used the cash method to account for the purchase and sale of merchandise, contested the validity of the regulation that required use of an accrual method in such circumstances.[158] The taxpayer argued that Section 41 of the 1939 Code (the predecessor to Section 446) required only that a method of accounting clearly, not accurately, reflect income. The Second Circuit upheld the regulation on the ground that where inventories were used and expenses were stated in terms of the cost of goods actually sold during the year, profit from sales could be reflected accurately only if the income from all sales made during the year were taken into account. The court found that this could be accomplished only by use of an accrual method.[159] The court also referred to the taxpayer's argument that "clearly" merely meant fairly and honestly, but concluded that if clearly meant fairly and honestly in lieu of accurately, such an interpretation should be rejected. The court then stated: "While taxpayer's honesty and good faith have not been in the slightest impugned in the present case, we read 'clearly reflect the income' in I.R.C. § 41 to mean rather that income should be reflected with as much accuracy as standard methods of accounting practice permit."[160]

Two important points should be noted about *Caldwell*. First, the court did not reject the *Osterloh* standard per se. Rather, the court said that if that standard were deemed to connote good faith over accuracy, it would not be acceptable in the present context. The context involved the treatment of

---

[157] Caldwell v. Comm'r, 202 F2d 112 (2d Cir. 1953).

[158] Reg. 111, 29.41-2.

[159] This is the reason for the regulation. See discussion at ¶ 3.06[2].

[160] Caldwell v. Comm'r, 202 F2d 112, 115 (2d Cir. 1953). It should be noted that although the Second Circuit suggested that *Osterloh* had been discredited by the Ninth Circuit in Herberger v. Comm'r, 195 F2d 293 (9th Cir. 1952), cert. denied, 344 US 820 (1952), the Ninth Circuit did not in that decision explicitly reject *Osterloh*. The taxpayers in *Herberger* were engaged in the business of processing and selling pickles. They maintained their books and filed their income tax returns on the cash method. The Commissioner redetermined income on an accrual method. In upholding the Commissioner's determination, the court noted that only the accrual method of accounting for purchases and sales would "correctly" reflect their income. The Ninth Circuit did not otherwise refer to any standard of clear reflection, nor did it expressly reject the fair and honest language of *Osterloh*.

inventories and the matching of sales and related cost of goods sold. Profit from the sale of inventory (i.e., the profit that is included within taxable income under Section 61) could not be stated accurately unless the sales revenue was reported in the same period as the related cost of goods sold.[161]

Second, the court was referring to accuracy in the context of responding to the taxpayer's argument, not in the context of suggesting a need for precision or exactitude. It emphasized that the clear reflection of income requirement should be construed to mean with as much accuracy as standard methods of accounting practice permit. By focusing on the plural, "methods," the court implied that the method that computed income with the greatest degree of accuracy in the context of economic theory or financial accounting was not the only method that could clearly reflect income. The Second Circuit itself had previously held that the clear reflection of income requirement did not contemplate that taxpayers could be forced to use either an accrual method or any other method that perfectly reflects income.[162]

Nevertheless, several cases interpreted *Caldwell* as announcing a new standard to be applied in lieu of the *Osterloh* standard. In virtually every such case, the issue involved a taxpayer's attempt to use the cash method to account for purchases and sales of inventory.[163]

It would appear that the proper interpretation of *Caldwell* is that where

---

[161] See discussion at ¶ 3.06[2]. The IRS acknowledged this very point in Tech. Adv. Mem. 7405291610B (May 29, 1974), where, in confirming the taxpayer's use of the cash method for a service business, it distinguished a service business from a business involving the sale of inventory:

> The rationale, of course, in the foregoing provision of the regulations (limiting methods of accounting for purchases and sales of inventory) is easily understood since expenditures with respect to the purchase or manufacture of inventory items must be correlated with the income from sales of such items, otherwise gross income would be substantially distorted if the cash method was employed. Nevertheless, the specific requirement in the foregoing section of the regulations regarding the accrual method refers only to purchases and sales, the so-called "above the line" (gross income) items. Presumably, miscellaneous expenses which are deductible "below the line" from gross income in determining net income may be deducted on the cash method without materially distorting income. In a service type of business where inventories are not an income-producing factor, all expenses are of the type which would normally be deducted "below the line."

[162] Maurice W. Simon, 176 F2d 230 (2d Cir. 1949), aff'g 6 TCM 57 (1947).

[163] See, e.g., Boynton v. Pedrick, 136 F. Supp. 888 (SDNY 1954), aff'd on other grounds, 228 F2d 745 (2d Cir. 1955), cert. denied, 351 US 938 (1956), where the court rejected the taxpayer's attempt to rely on *Osterloh*, stating:

> [T]he Caldwell case interprets Section 41 to require that income be reflected "with as much accuracy as standard methods of accounting practice permit." In a business which consists of entirely the purchase, processing and sale of a commodity, in which the overwhelming number of purchases and sales are made on credit, an accrual method to reflect income is the standard method of accounting.

a taxpayer is required to maintain inventories, the taxpayer may only avoid the general requirement that it use the accrual method with respect to purchases and sales if it can show a substantially identical result between its method and the required accrual method. Such a showing might be achieved by a cash basis taxpayer who maintains inventories and defers the deduction for cost of sales until the revenue from the sales is recognized, such as under the installment method.[164] This, of course, would impose a very rigid standard that the taxpayer would have to meet to use the cash method. The *Caldwell* standard has also been cited by the courts in many other cases.[165]

As indicated by the preceding discussion, the *Osterloh* standard has been relied on by courts to uphold the use of both cash and accrual methods of accounting. On the other hand, the *Caldwell* standard has usually been relied on by the courts in cases involving taxpayers required to use the accrual method due to the presence of inventories. *Caldwell* tends to be cited somewhat more frequently than *Osterloh* in determining whether a method of accounting clearly reflects income, but each decision remains viable. Although this evolution suggests that courts construe the *Caldwell* and *Osterloh* standards as if they were inconsistent, if not mutually exclusive, this is not

---

136 F. Supp. at 891; Wilkinson-Beane, Inc. v. Comm'r, 420 F2d 352 (1st Cir. 1970), where the court stated with respect to the taxpayer's contention that the use of inventories did not necessarily mean that the cash method of accounting failed to clearly reflect income:

> The standard we apply is whether the taxpayer's method of accounting reflects his income with as much accuracy as standard methods of accounting permit. In our view, this means that the taxpayer must demonstrate substantial identity of results between his method and the method selected by the Commissioner. This he has failed to do. . . .
>
> The application of this rigorous standard may occasionally work a harsh result, as may be true here. However, it must be borne in mind that regardless of the accuracy of taxpayer's cash method in the past, there is no guarantee that the stability of sales, costs, collections and other factors which make for that result will continue in the future. Hence, even if the taxpayer may avoid the imposition of the full accrual system, despite the presence of § 471 inventories, by showing that his method reflects income clearly, the standard it must satisfy is extremely high.

Id. at 356–357.

[164] See discussion at ¶ 5.04.

[165] See, e.g., Peterson Produce Co. v. United States, 205 F. Supp. 229 (WD Ark. 1962), aff'd, 313 F2d 609 (8th Cir. 1963) (taxpayer could not use cash method for broiler division, since it did not constitute a separate trade or business; use of accrual method for this division would clearly reflect taxpayer's income, since inventories would be used); Fort Howard Paper Co., 49 TC 275 (1967) (accrual basis taxpayer's method of treating overhead expenses in determining cost of self-constructed assets upheld); Electric & Neon, Inc., 56 TC 1324 (1971), acq. 1973-1 CB 1, aff'd per curiam, 496 F2d 876 (5th Cir. 1974) (accrual basis taxpayer could not treat costs of constructing signs that it leased as currently deductible business expenses).

the case. As explained in the following section, the two standards should work together, and each should be required.[166]

[k] Reconciliation of Authorities

To reconcile the foregoing authorities in applying the chosen accounting method, the taxpayer and the IRS must take into account the following factors:

- The differences between tax and financial accounting as set forth by the Supreme Court in *Thor Power Tool*
- The fact that the choice among different methods is given to taxpayers
- The requirements imposed and authorizations provided by the applicable statutory and regulatory provisions
- All other circumstances (including taxpayer conduct)

Assuming this is done, it would appear that for a method to clearly reflect income, the method must be available to the taxpayer and applied consistently, accurately, fairly, honestly, and without manipulation.[167] That definition would preclude a taxpayer from applying an available method in an erroneous fashion and would also preclude a taxpayer from arranging its business transactions out of the ordinary course (or for nonbusiness reasons) solely to achieve a distortion in reported income. Satisfaction of such a test should, of itself, satisfy the clear reflection of income standard. Failure to satisfy the test should merely provide the IRS with the discretion to determine what, if any, change should be required.[168] In *RLC Industries Co.*,[169] the Tax Court seemed to recognize these very factors in considering a reconciliation of applicable authorities. The court first pointed out that, "[i]n general, a method of accounting clearly reflects income when it results in accurately reported taxable income under a recognized method of account-

---

[166] This very point was seemingly recognized by the Tax Court in RLC Indus. Co., 98 TC 457 (1992).

[167] See Jerry Fong, 48 TCM 689, 716 (1984), aff'd in unpublished opinion (9th Cir. 1987), where the Tax Court specifically recognized the compatibility of the *Caldwell* and *Osterloh* standards, stating, "An accounting method clearly reflects income if income is stated with as much accuracy as standard methods of accounting practices permit [citing *Caldwell*], and the books are kept fairly and honestly [citing *Osterloh*]."

[168] See Asphalt Prods. Co. v. Comm'r, 796 F2d 843 (6th Cir. 1986), where the court concluded that the clear reflection of income requirement imposes a need for both accuracy and fair and honest reporting.

[169] RLC Indus. Co., 98 TC 457 (1992).

ing."[170] The court then noted the differing positions of the parties on *Osterloh* and *Caldwell*, pointing out that too much reliance was placed on these cases because they predated a substantial body of law, including the Supreme Court's decision in *Thor Power Tool Co.*[171] Nevertheless, the court recognized that the two standards were not really that different when all relevant factors were taken into account.

¶ 2.03 TAXPAYER'S DISCRETION IN CHOICE OF METHOD

Section 446(a) provides, "Taxable income shall be computed under the method of accounting on the basis of which the taxpayer regularly computes his income in keeping his books." There is no requirement as to which method the taxpayer uses in computing its income in keeping its books. Consequently, the taxpayer's methods of tax accounting are determined by his own choice, subject only to the requirement that the method clearly reflect income and not otherwise expressly be denied to the taxpayer. This element of choice and discretion is clearly recognized by the courts.[172] Should there be any question about the taxpayer's choice of accounting method, the courts and the IRS will examine carefully all relevant facts and circumstances, including the manner in which items have been reported on relevant tax returns.[173]

In evaluating the taxpayer's chosen method, the Commissioner should not have carte blanche to assert a failure to reflect income clearly and, thereby, cause the taxpayer to change to a different method of accounting. If the Commissioner had too much discretion, the element of choice inherent in this basic accounting provision would have little meaning.

---

[170] Id. at 490.

[171] Id. at 493.

[172] See, e.g., Morris-Poston Coal Co. v. Comm'r, 42 F2d 620, 621 (6th Cir. 1930) ("The law plainly recognizes that the selection of the system or method of keeping his books is primarily for the taxpayer"); Huntington Sec. Corp. v. Busey, 112 F2d 368, 370 (6th Cir. 1940) ("The selection of a system of accounting is lodged exclusively in the taxpayer provided it is within the statutory limits of clearly reflecting income . . ."). See also Ronnie L. Barber, 64 TC 314 (1975), where the court noted that a taxpayer may unilaterally change his method of accounting for the first year for which the method is elected if the amended return is filed prior to the due date of the original return. See also discussion at ¶ 9.04[1].

[173] See, e.g., First Nat'l Bank of Gainesville, 88 TC 1069 (1987), which involved a taxpayer's adoption of the LIFO method of inventory accounting; Tech. Adv. Mem. 9132001 (Jan. 9, 1991), where the IRS evaluated applicable facts and circumstances in determining the scope of a taxpayer's election to capitalize interest expense under Section 266. Citing Kentucky Utils. Co. v. Glenn, 394 F2d 631 (6th Cir. 1968), the IRS stated correctly the principle that where a taxpayer's choice is not clear, it is appropriate to examine the taxpayer's established method of accounting for such items and the reporting of relevant items on applicable returns in order to determine the taxpayer's intent with respect to its election.

The issues that generally arise in connection with the choice of a method involve the use of more than one method by the taxpayer and the consequences that arise if the initially chosen method is later determined to be incorrect.

[1] Use of More Than One Method

A taxpayer may use more than one method of accounting in either of two circumstances: (1) when it conducts more than one trade or business and elects a different method for each or (2) when it elects to use a combination of methods (sometimes known as a hybrid method) for the operation of a single business. Prior to the enactment of Section 446(c) as part of the 1954 Code, a combination of methods for a single business was not expressly permitted. Accordingly, the use of a combination of methods was generally proscribed unless the taxpayer could demonstrate that the separate methods were used for separate and distinct trades or businesses. Following enactment of Section 446(c), the separate trade or business issue has diminished in significance. This result has also been achieved because of increased sophistication by taxpayers and their legal, tax, and accounting advisors, who often recommend avoiding the issue by separately incorporating each of the various trades or businesses. Each corporation is then able to adopt its own methods of accounting. The issue that arises more frequently today is whether the use of a combination of methods properly reports all related items of income and expense under the same method so that income may clearly be reflected.

[a] Use of Different Methods for Separate Trades or Businesses

Section 446(d) provides, "A taxpayer engaged in more than one trade or business may, in computing taxable income, use a different method of accounting for each trade or business." For this purpose, the regulations require that the businesses be "separate and distinct" and give as an example of the proper application of Section 446(d) a taxpayer that uses the cash method in accounting for the operations of a service business and an accrual method in accounting for the operations of a manufacturing business.[174]

The regulations provide little guidance for determining whether various business activities constitute separate and distinct trades or businesses. A trade or business is not considered separate and distinct unless a "complete and separable" set of books and records is maintained for that trade or business. Furthermore, trades or businesses are not considered separate and distinct if, as a result of the use of different methods, there is a "creation or shifting of profits and losses" between the trades or businesses so that the

---

[174] Treas. Reg. § 1.446-1(d)(1).

income of the taxpayer is not clearly reflected.[175] The regulations also require the method of accounting used for each business to clearly reflect the income of that business and the method first used by the taxpayer in connection with a business to be consistently followed thereafter.[176]

The separate-trade-or-business rule was not a part of the statutory language until the 1954 Code. However, prior case law had recognized that a taxpayer engaged in two or more separate businesses could use different accounting methods for each business. The legislative history confirms that the statutory provision was intended to codify the then-existing case law.[177]

The separateness of the two businesses was especially important under pre–1954 Code law because there was no express authorization of the use of an overall hybrid method. Consequently, where a taxpayer departed from the use of its overall method for particular items of income or expense, the departure could be corrected by the IRS unless the particular items constituted items associated with a new, separate and distinct business.

Under present law, such a departure may be acceptable under either the separate-trade-or-business rule or the use of a hybrid method. Moreover, taxpayers that desire to use different methods of accounting for different trades or businesses may find it less cumbersome and less subject to challenge on audit to incorporate separately each trade or business. Thus, each corporation is a separate taxpayer that may elect its own methods of accounting. The issue of separateness generally does not arise unless the IRS asserts that the corporation is a sham that may be disregarded for tax purposes. That assertion may frequently be avoided by making sure the corporation has employees and bank accounts, conducts activities in its own name, and serves a legitimate nontax business purpose.

An extended analysis of the separate-trade-or-business rule is contained in two cases, *Peterson Produce Co. v. United States*[178] and *Burgess Poultry Market Inc. v. United States*.[179] Each case dealt with a taxpayer engaged in poultry farming operations.

In *Peterson*, the taxpayer's initial business was the sale of feed for livestock and poultry. The taxpayer later entered the hatchery business and, in 1958, entered the broiler farming business. The creation of the broiler division arose from dissatisfaction with the taxpayer's then-existing agreements with growers under which the taxpayer had no direct control over the growing of chicks. Upon organization of the broiler division, the taxpayer began using a

---

[175] Treas. Reg. §§ 1.446-1(d)(2), 1.446-1(d)(3).

[176] Treas. Reg. § 1.446-1(d)(1).

[177] See H.R. Rep. No. 1337, 83d Cong., 2d Sess. 4073 (1954).

[178] Peterson Produce Co. v. United States, 205 F. Supp. 229 (WD Ark. 1962), aff'd, 313 F2d 609 (8th Cir. 1963).

[179] Burgess Poultry Mkt. Inc. v. United States, 64-2 USTC ¶ 9515 (ED Tex. 1964).

new form of contract, under which the taxpayer retained title to the chicks and complete control over their care, feeding, and marketing.

Prior to the creation of the broiler division, the taxpayer had used an accrual method for its feed and hatchery businesses. However, the broiler division used a cash method. Each of the taxpayer's three divisions kept its own journal and, at the end of each month, the journal entries were posted to a single general ledger. The taxpayer continued to have a single bank account. Administrative costs were shared by the three divisions on a pro rata basis, and a separate determination of profit and loss for each of the divisions was made for tax purposes.

The case arose out of the taxpayer's attempt to obtain a refund for 1956 by use of a net operating loss carry-back from 1959. The loss resulted from the use of the cash method of accounting with respect to the broiler division. The government argued that the broiler division was not a new and separate business, since it carried on substantially the same activity that the taxpayer had conducted prior to its formation and its operations were fully integrated with those of the feed and hatchery divisions.

The district court held that once a taxpayer adopts an accounting method, it must continue to use the same method in the same business until it either obtains permission from the Commissioner to change methods or enters a new, separate and distinct business. The court found that the taxpayer had not substantially changed its overall operations by the creation of the broiler division.[180] Moreover, the court noted that even if the broiler division amounted to a new business, the regulations require that the broiler operations be separate and distinct.[181] The court held that the broiler division did not constitute a separate business of the corporation because the three divisions were functionally integrated and interdependent.[182] Although the general ledger accounts of the three divisions could be physically separated,

---

[180] The court stated the following:

The "new" division was created within an existing corporate entity which at all times previous to and subsequent to September 1, 1958, has remained the same taxable entity. The creation of the new division was a convenience and perhaps an economic necessity to the plaintiff, and by concurrent utilization of the new form of contracts with the farmers, the plaintiff acquired more control over the growing and marketing of the chickens, but the fact remains that as a farming or nonfarming enterprise the plaintiffs over-all operation for the past ten years or more was the growing and marketing of broilers.

Peterson Produce Co. v. United States, 205 F. Supp. 229, 239 (WD Ark. 1962).

[181] Treas. Reg. § 1.446-1(d).

[182] The court stated the following:

There is no doubt but that [the taxpayer] functions as a corporate entity made up of three well-integrated departments, not as a loose confederation made up of autonomous divisions. Whatever internal arrangements have been worked out over the years have not altered its corporate image in dealing with growers or in entering the chicken market as a seller.

the court also held that the taxpayer had not met the complete-and-separable-books requirement imposed by the regulations, because the books of original entries, such as daily journals, were not physically separable.[183] (The basis of the court's holding on this point is not clear, since its statement of facts indicated that each division kept its own journal and that entries from these journals were posted to a single ledger.)

The court further held that even if the taxpayer were engaged in two or more separate and distinct businesses, the hybrid method of accounting used did not clearly reflect its income. The court noted that although the corporation was a farmer, it had chosen to use an accrual method that used inventories to account for its feed and hatchery divisions. Under the practice of transferring chicks and feed at cost, an inventory reduction in these two departments was accompanied by the creation of an immediate business expense in the broiler division without the establishment of any offsetting inventory. The court stated that this method did not clearly reflect income and also created an opportunity to shift profits and losses between divisions.

In *Burgess*, an accrual method taxpayer had engaged in the business of processing and selling broiler chickens since its formation in 1953. In 1960, the taxpayer's board of directors established a separate farm operation to grow broilers. The board specified that the farm would use a new and distinct trade name and would maintain separate accounts and records. The broilers were charged to the market division at prevailing prices, and the operations of the farm did not interfere with the normal activities of the market division. The books of the farm division, which consisted of a cash disbursement journal, payroll journal, and general ledger, were kept on a cash basis and maintained separately from the books of the market division.

When the farm began its operations, new employees were hired, and each division had its own separate employees, including bookkeepers. Each division had its own bank account, out of which it paid its employees. The principal shareholder of the taxpayer acted as general manager of the taxpayer's entire business operations, including the farm. The taxpayer's office manager supervised the bookkeeping and accounting of both divisions. However, neither the shareholder nor the office manager devoted a substantial amount of time to the operations of the farm division. The activities of the farm division were also geographically separated from the processing operations.

The district court found, as a fact, that the operations of the farm division were separate and distinct from the processing activities of the corporation. The opinion is in memorandum form and does not specify the

---

Peterson Produce Co. v. United States, 205 F. Supp. 229, 240 (WD Ark. 1962). See also Gold-Pak Meat Co., 30 TCM 337 (1971), remanded on other grounds, 522 F2d 1055 (9th Cir. 1975).

[183] Peterson Produce Co. v. United States, 205 F. Supp. 229, 240 (WD Ark. 1962).

basis of the court's conclusion on this issue. The court did not discuss or cite the *Peterson* decision.

These cases suggest that the degree of separateness is quite important, as is the potential for shifting income or distorting reported income. Again, the well-advised taxpayer should consider incorporating separately the divisions for which it desires to use different accounting methods.[184]

The other cases that have addressed the applicability of Section 446(d) have dealt with the issue in a conclusively manner, focusing on the nature of the activities asserted to be separate and distinct trades or businesses. For example, sufficient separateness was found where the two businesses were of completely different characters.[185] The different character of the businesses may also be cited by the IRS as the basis for limiting any proposed adjustment to one business only. For example, in *Loyd L. Parker*,[186] a husband and wife bought and sold both automobiles and residential real estate. A hybrid system of accounting was used to report the taxpayers' income from both businesses. The Commissioner determined that the taxpayers' income from the sale of automobiles should be changed to an accrual basis, but no change in method was proposed for the sale of real estate. The taxpayers conceded that their hybrid method of accounting did not clearly reflect income from the sale of automobiles, but they argued that the Commissioner should also have computed income from their real estate transactions on an accrual basis. The Tax Court upheld the Commissioner's finding that the taxpayers were engaged in two separate businesses and therefore could have elected to use a different method of accounting for each

---

[184] See Rocco Inc., 72 TC 140 (1979), where the issue involved the use of different methods of accounting by corporations joining in the filing of a consolidated tax return. The IRS attempted to rely on *Peterson Produce* to prohibit use of the different methods, but the court held that *Peterson* was concerned with Section 446(d), which was not applicable to the present case, because the broiler and turkey subsidiaries were separate corporations, each entitled to elect its own methods of accounting regardless of whether its businesses were separate and distinct from those of its parent.

[185] See, e.g., Joseph Stern, 14 BTA 838 (1928), acq. VIII-2 CB 50, where the taxpayer operated retail stores that used an accrual method, and bought and sold coal lands, using a cash method; Bennett Properties Co., 45 BTA 696 (1941), where the Board approved use of the cash method for one business and a hybrid method for a newly acquired business, stating:

> The [new] operation was unlike its established business and activities, and it had the right to keep its accounts relating to such new operations without regard to the method of keeping its accounts for the earlier business, so long as it maintained a clean separation which prevented confusion and resulted in a clear reflection of its entire income.

45 BTA at 698. See also Rev. Rul. 74-270, 1974-1 CB 109, and Rev. Rul. 74-280, 1974-1 CB 121, each of which concerned the use of different methods of accounting for different departments within a bank.

[186] Loyd L. Parker, 37 TC 331 (1961).

business. Thus, there was nothing that prevented the Commissioner from determining that the method used in one of the separate businesses did not clearly reflect income without making the same determination with respect to the other business. Additionally, the receipt of income from a source other than the taxpayer's principal source does not, by itself, constitute a separate trade or business under Section 446(d). For example, in *J.F. Stevenhagen Co.*,[187] the Tax Court held that the "receipt of interest did not constitute a separate trade or business."

[b] Combination (Hybrid) Method

Taxpayers are expressly permitted under Section 446(c) to use a combination of the cash method, accrual method, and other methods expressly provided by the Code and regulations.[188] The use of a combination of methods is generally referred to as an overall hybrid method.

Hybrid methods are permitted as long as income is clearly reflected. For income to be clearly reflected, however, it is essential that all related items of revenue and expense be reported under the same method. In other words, it is not appropriate for items of income to be reported under one method and corresponding items of expense to be reported under another method.[189] This principle has been recognized in case law. For example, in *Birch Ranch & Oil Co.*,[190] a corporation owned a ranch, an interest in an oil partnership, a citrus grove, and various rental properties. A separate set of books on the cash method was kept for the ranch operations. However, the corporation sought to accrue and deduct certain interest on bonds that were treated by the taxpayer as operating expenses of the ranch. In upholding the Commissioner's disallowance of the interest deduction, the court noted that even if the taxpayer's contention was true that the books that it kept for its nonranching operations used an accrual method, the taxpayer would not prevail because books for separate businesses could be kept on different methods. Since the interest expense was found to relate solely to the ranching business, which kept its books on the cash basis, the court refused to allow a deduction for any interest not actually paid.

---

[187] J.F. Stevenhagen Co., 34 TCM 852, 859 (1975), aff'd, 551 F2d 106 (6th Cir. 1977).

[188] See discussion supra ¶ 2.01[4].

[189] Treas. Reg. § 1.446-1(c)(1)(iv).

[190] Birch Ranch & Oil Co., 3 TCM 378 (1944), aff'd, 152 F2d 874 (9th Cir. 1946), cert. denied, 328 US 863 (1946). See also W.W. Enters., 50 TCM 237 (1985), where an accrual method taxpayer was denied the opportunity to account for employee loans on a cash basis because the loans were considered to be connected with the operation of the accrual method business.

[2] Incorrect Initial Choice

An unresolved question is whether a taxpayer that finds its initially chosen method to be incorrect may select the correct method to which it must change.[191] Although there is virtually no authority on this precise question, revenue agents sometimes have asserted that where the taxpayer's method is incorrect, the IRS may select the method to which the taxpayer must change.

The IRS position may be sound where the use of the incorrect method is challenged by the IRS on audit.[192] However, this same position has sometimes been taken even where the change in method is requested by the taxpayer prior to the commencement of an audit. In effect, the IRS position is that once an incorrect method is identified, all discretion over the new method shifts to the IRS. The IRS apparently believes that it may deny a request to change from an incorrect method to a correct method unless the correct method is one desired by the IRS. Such a contention seems incorrect.[193]

---

[191] For rules applicable to a change from an incorrect method by the timely filing of an amended return for the year in which the incorrect method was first used, see discussion at ¶ 9.04[1].

[192] See, e.g., Payne E.L. Thomas, 92 TC 206 (1989), where the court stated, in connection with an IRS determination on audit, that the taxpayer's method of accounting did not clearly reflect income and that the taxpayer's income was then "to be computed under a method of accounting that respondent chooses that does clearly reflect the taxpayer's income ... including a proper method of accounting for inventories. . . ."

[193] See discussion infra ¶ 2.04, and ¶ 8.07. See also Mamula v. United States, 346 F2d 1016 (9th Cir. 1965), where the court permitted the taxpayer, on finding its initially chosen method to be incorrect, to use the installment method rather than the accrual method preferred by the IRS. The court stated:

> We are not here concerned with a taxpayer who uses hindsight to learn that the method he had chosen, though proper, was not the most advantageous to him. We are rather concerned with an instance where the method chosen by the taxpayer is advanced in good faith, and later conceded to have been improper. At the insistence of the government, not the taxpayer, the prior calculations which adopted the improper method must now be set aside, and new calculations, *of necessity*, must be undertaken. The taxpayer has not been accused of any fraudulent activities nor any criminal violations; he rather has been found to have adopted, in good faith, an incorrect method of income recognition. *No forfeiture or penalty is assessed by law for such a mistake.* The only methods subsequently available to him were the installment method, which he now seeks to utilize, and the closed transaction basis, which would have recognized all the profit in 1959, the year of the sales. Taxpayer wishes to recalculate by using the former method, but the respondent and Tax Court have insisted that he recalculate using the latter method.

Id. at 1018–1019 (emphasis by court). The appeals court then reversed the Tax Court and held for the taxpayer. But see Joseph H. Gibson, 89 TC 1177 (1987), where the court held that the so-called binding-election rule prevented a taxpayer who reported all gain on a 1979 transaction in 1980 from electing the installment method after

[3] Application of Correct Choice to Incorrect Year

Where the taxpayer selects an acceptable method of accounting but applies that method to the wrong year, the question is whether the taxpayer's choice of method is binding. This issue was addressed in *Joseph H. Gibson*,[194] which involved a taxpayer who had sold property in 1979 for deferred payments. The transaction was not reported at all in 1979. Instead, the transaction was reported as a completed transaction in 1980. Thereafter, the taxpayer sought to elect the installment method of reporting for the transaction. The court, after an extensive analysis of the applicable rules, refused to permit the taxpayer to change to the installment method. The Tax Court noted that the taxpayer had chosen a correct method of accounting. The court held that the mere fact that the method chosen was initially applied to an incorrect year did not prevent the choice from being valid and binding on the taxpayer.[195]

¶ 2.04 COMMISSIONER'S DISCRETION IN DETERMINING METHOD

Section 446(b) provides the basic authority for the Commissioner's exercise of discretion with respect to accounting methods: "If no method of accounting has been regularly used by the taxpayer, or if the method used does not clearly reflect income, the computation of taxable income shall be made under such method as, in the opinion of the Secretary, does clearly reflect income."

This language fails to identify the party who is to make the initial determination of whether a taxpayer's present method clearly reflects income. Early legislative history supported an interpretation that this initial determination was for the courts.[196] However, when regulations were first promul-

---

learning that the transaction should have been reported in 1979. See discussion infra ¶ 2.03[3].

[194] Joseph H. Gibson, 89 TC 1177 (1987).

[195] The court discussed the so-called binding election rule of Pacific Nat'l Co. v. Welch, 304 US 191 (1938), and many of the cases that have interpreted that rule.

[196] The requirement that a method clearly reflect income first appeared in the Revenue Act of 1916. It provided that a corporation could use a method other than the cash method "unless such other basis [did] not clearly reflect its income. . . ."Revenue Act of 1916, ch. 463, § 13(d), 39 Stat. 756, 771 (repealed 1918). Cf. id. § 8(g) (similar language applied to individuals). Although neither the legislative history of present Section 446(b) nor earlier committee reports considered who was to make the initial determination, the 1916 Act, as originally introduced, read, "unless the Commissioner of Internal Revenue finds that such other basis does not clearly reflect his income." H.R. 16763, 64th Cong., 1st Sess., *reprinted in* S. Doc. No. 531, 64th Cong., 1st Sess. 35 (1916). This language was dropped in the final bill. The only inference that can be drawn from this change works against the existence of discretion

gated under Section 446(b),[197] they contained the provision that "no method of accounting is acceptable unless, in the opinion of the Commissioner, it clearly reflects income." This formulation of the rule suggested that the Commissioner had the discretion of making the initial determination. In light of the legislative history of this matter, legitimate questions were raised as to the validity of the statement in the regulations.[198]

The issue remained confused in practice. In cases involving an alleged abuse of discretion or a proposed change of tax accounting by the Commissioner, the courts vacillated. Frequently, when the courts wanted to rule against the Commissioner, they found that the present method clearly reflected income and, hence, it was an abuse of discretion for the Commissioner to change the method. When the courts desired to uphold the Commissioner, they often stated that the Commissioner had the discretion to determine that a method did not clearly reflect income and that the court's review of that issue was limited to whether there was a reasonable basis for the Commissioner's determination.

However, the issue was apparently settled by the Supreme Court in *Thor Power Tool Co. v. Commissioner.*[199] In that case the Court, citing numerous other cases,[200] concluded on the facts before it that the Commissioner does

---

in the Commissioner to make the initial determination whether income is clearly reflected. However, the conference committee report referred to the deletion of this language as "clerical" and did not discuss it. H.R. Rep. No. 1200, 64th Cong., 1st Sess. 28 (1916). See 1 J.S. Seidman, Seidman's Legislative History of Federal Income Tax and Excess Profits Tax Laws 1953-1939, (1954), at 974.

The corresponding section of the Revenue Act of 1918 read as follows:

> The net income shall be computed . . . in accordance with the method of accounting regularly employed in keeping the books of such taxpayer; but if no such method of accounting has been so employed, or if the method employed does not clearly reflect the income, the computation shall be made upon such basis and in such manner as in the opinion of the Commissioner does clearly reflect the income.

Revenue Act of 1918, ch. 18, § 212(b), 40 Stat. 1057, 1064, 1065 (repealed 1921). The Code of 1939 adopted the 1918 language without any comment in the applicable committee reports. IRC of 1939, ch. 2, § 41, 53 Stat. 1, 24 (repealed 1954). See 1 J.S. Seidman, supra, at 1460.

[197] Treas. Reg. § 1.446-1, TD 6282, 1958-1 CB 215, 217 (1957).

[198] See Graves, Limitations on Commissioner's Power to Require Accounting Changes, 19 NYU Tax Inst. 1209, 1212 (1961), stating, "Unless the Commissioner can demonstrate that the method he seeks to change does not reflect income clearly, he has substantially no basis on which to proceed."

[199] Thor Power Tool Co. v. Comm'r, 439 US 522 (1979).

[200] See, e.g., Comm'r v. Hansen, 360 US 446, 467 (1959); Lucas v. American Code Co., 280 US 445, 449 (1930); United States v. Catto, 384 US 102, 114 (1966); Schlude v. Comm'r, 372 US 128, 133–134 (1963); American Auto. Ass'n. v. United States, 367 US 687, 697–698 (1961); Automobile Club of Mich. v. Comm'r, 353 US 180, 189–190 (1957); Brown v. Helvering, 291 US 193, 203 (1934).

have the discretion to make the initial determination.[201] The Court stated that Sections 446 and 471 vest the Commissioner with wide discretion in determining whether a particular method should be disallowed as not clearly reflecting income and that his interpretation of the statute's clear reflection standard should not be interfered with unless clearly unlawful.

Many practitioners anticipated that *Thor Power Tool* would be construed quite broadly, and, in *RCA Corp. v. United States*,[202] the Court of Appeals for the Second Circuit gave *Thor Power Tool* a very broad reading. The issue before the court in *RCA* was whether an accrual basis taxpayer could defer prepayments of income and yet clearly reflect income for tax purposes. The trial court had entered judgment for the taxpayer, but the court of appeals reversed. Citing *Thor Power Tool*, the appeals court stated that the case highlighted the fundamentally different perspective that courts must adopt when reviewing the propriety of administrative discretion rather than substantive law. The court concluded that the district court did not give sufficient weight to the objectives of tax accounting and to the Commissioner's wide discretion in implementing those objectives. The court added that the Commissioner's exercise of his discretion must be upheld unless it is clearly unlawful.

> The task of a reviewing court, therefore, is not to determine whether in its own opinion RCA's method of accounting for prepaid service contract income "clearly reflect[ed] income," but to determine whether there is an adequate basis in law for the Commissioner's conclusion that it did not.[203]

Although this language is quite broad, it oversimplifies the matter. To determine whether there is an adequate basis for the Commissioner's determination, the courts must necessarily evaluate the substantive issue. Otherwise, the Commissioner's discretion could be used to change virtually every method of accounting used by taxpayers to the method that would generate the most taxable income to the government.[204] This very point was recognized

---

[201] See Asphalt Prods. Co. v. Comm'r, 796 F2d 843 (6th Cir. 1986), to the same effect.

[202] RCA Corp. v. United States, 664 F2d 881 (2d Cir. 1981), cert. denied, 457 US 1133 (1982).

[203] RCA Corp. v. United States, 664 F2d at 886. See also American Fletcher Corp. v. United States, 832 F2d 436 (7th Cir. 1987), where the court of appeals affirmed the decision of the district court to reject the taxpayer's use of the cash method based on (1) its lack of use by others in the taxpayer's industry; (2) the fact that its computation was based on estimates; and (3) the fact that it did not produce results substantially identical to the results produced by the method required by the Commissioner.

[204] See Applied Communications, Inc., 57 TCM 1473 (1989), where the court gave the Commissioner broad discretion to change a taxpayer's method of accounting. Although the court noted that the taxpayer's business was changing from a service-

by the claims court in *Mulholland v. United States.*[205] In evaluating whether the court was limited to reviewing whether the Commissioner abused her discretion in finding that a method did not clearly reflect income, the court disagreed with the government's contention that the court's review was so limited based on the Supreme Court's decision in *Thor.* Instead, the court concluded on the basis of its evaluation of relevant cases that the proper standard of review is for the court to conduct a de novo review, i.e., the court may review the precise issue of whether the method in question clearly reflects income. Moreover, in conducting that review the court stated that it is not limited to reviewing only those facts that were administratively before the Commissioner, but, instead, may look to and consider all other relevant facts.

[1] Proper Exercise of Discretion

The Commissioner is generally successful in using his discretion to require a taxpayer to comply with tax accounting regulations. For example, the Commissioner can require a taxpayer that has changed its method of accounting without obtaining the prior approval of the Commissioner to revert back to the method from which it had changed.[206] Similarly, the

---

oriented business to a product-oriented business, the court did not specify that this change was the principal reason for its conclusion. Instead, the language employed by the court suggested that the Commissioner had broad discretion to require a change whenever the Commissioner believed that sufficient factors demonstrated that the taxpayer's present method did not clearly reflect income. Although this position would not be troubling by itself, the factors relied on by the court were essentially the very same factors that would prohibit the use of the cash method by taxpayers in virtually every case. These factors included such circumstances as the fact that (1) the cash method was not used for financial reporting purposes; (2) the results under the cash method differed from results under the accrual method; (3) the cash method was not consistent with GAAP; and (4) the deferrals of revenue under the cash method are substantial. In effect, the court appeared to conclude that the Commissioner had not abused his discretion on the basis of the number of factors cited without any evaluation or analysis of those factors. The court seems to have given far more discretion to the Commissioner than would be logical considering the fact that the factors cited, principally those relating to methods of accounting used for various financial purposes, would also cause accrual methods of tax accounting not to be acceptable for tax purposes. See In re BKW Sys., Inc., 90-1 USTC ¶ 50,139 (Bankr. DNH 1989), and discussion at ¶ 4.01[2].

[205] Mulholland v. United States, 92-1 USTC ¶ 50,267 (Cl. Ct. 1992).

[206] See Comm'r v. O. Liquidating Corp., 292 F2d 225 (3d Cir. 1961), cert. denied, 368 US 898 (1961) (to make certain that changes in accounting methods are treated in the appropriate fashion, the Commissioner has the power to require his prior approval); Advertisers Exch. Inc., 25 TC 1086 (1956), aff'd per curiam, 240 F2d 958 (2d Cir. 1957) (Commissioner may reject any change in accounting that is made without his prior consent and approval to ensure that distortions arising therefrom

Commissioner can require use of an accrual method of accounting for purchases and sales of inventory.[207] The Commissioner also has discretion to allow a retroactive change in method.[208]

Where the method used does not clearly reflect income because it is not an authorized method or is an expressly prohibited method, the Commissioner has the discretion to change the taxpayer's method of accounting.[209] The Commissioner also has authority to require a taxpayer to report income on the basis of the same accounting method used for bookkeeping purposes,[210] or to choose a method of accounting where the taxpayer has not consistently used a method. However, the Commissioner does not have the discretion to require a taxpayer to change from one incorrect method of accounting to another incorrect method.[211]

Of course, as the preceding discussion implies, the Commissioner also has the discretion in these circumstances not to require a change in method. A difficult issue for the Commissioner is whether it amounts to an abuse of discretion for him to allow the use of a particular unauthorized method to some taxpayers but not to others. Another question is whether it amounts to an abuse of discretion for the Commissioner to challenge a taxpayer's use of a particular method for certain years, while approving other taxpayers' changes to the same method for those years. For example, during the 1981 period, the National Office was routinely approving changes by taxpayers to

---

are not at the expense of the government); Woodward Iron Co. v. United States, 396 F2d 552 (5th Cir. 1968); Hackensack Water Co. v. United States, 352 F2d 807 (Ct. Cl. 1965). See also Diebold, Inc. v. United States, 89-1 USTC ¶ 9141 (Cl. Ct. 1989), where the court held that it was not an abuse of discretion for the Commissioner to deny a taxpayer's retroactive change in method of accounting by the filing of an amended return for the initial year in which the accounting method was adopted, if the taxpayer's action to change its method arose from actions of the IRS during an audit of returns.

[207] See, e.g., Caldwell v. Comm'r, 202 F2d 112 (2d Cir. 1953); Wilkinson-Beane, Inc. v. Comm'r, 420 F2d 352 (1st Cir. 1970); Knight-Ridder Newspapers, Inc. v. United States, 743 F2d 781 (11th Cir. 1984).

[208] See, e.g., Ronnie L. Barber, 64 TC 314, 318 (1975), where the court stated in a case involving a retroactive change from one permissible method to another permissible method that "the overwhelming weight of cases found by us either state or strongly imply that, where the respondent is not prohibited by statute, he may in his discretion either accept or reject a request for retroactive change in choice between two permissible accounting methods."

[209] See, e.g., Wilkinson-Beane, Inc. v. Comm'r, 420 F2d 352 (1st Cir. 1970); Standard Paving Co. v. Comm'r, 190 F2d 330 (10th Cir. 1951), cert. denied, 342 US 860 (1951).

[210] Charles E. Yates, 205 F. Supp. 738 (ED Ky. 1962); Charles D. Mifflin, 24 TC 973 (1955).

[211] See, e.g., Capitol Fed. Sav. & Loan Assoc., 96 TC 204 (1991). See discussion at ¶ 8.07[2].

the cash method. Thereafter, agents in the field attempted to deny use of the cash method to other taxpayers for 1981.[212]

[2] Abuse of Discretion

The Commissioner has been found to have abused his discretion in cases where (1) the court finds that the taxpayer's method does clearly reflect income; (2) the Commissioner purports to deny a taxpayer the opportunity to change from an incorrect method to a correct method of reporting; and (3) the Commissioner seeks to deny the taxpayer's use of a method that is expressly sanctioned by the Code or applicable regulations.

In effect, where the taxpayer shows that it has complied with all applicable requirements for adopting a method of accounting, and the use of that method is not otherwise expressly denied to the taxpayer, the Commissioner's discretion to change the taxpayer's method is extremely limited.[213] Specifically, the Commissioner abuses his discretion by changing a taxpayer from a method that clearly reflects income to a method that in the Commissioner's view more clearly reflects income.[214] On the other hand, if the taxpayer uses a method that is otherwise denied to it, the Commissioner has substantial discretion to terminate the taxpayer's use of that method. The only opportunity for the taxpayer to overcome the Commissioner's decision to terminate is to show that the decision is unwarranted due to the immaterial effect on income of the use of the method or, alternatively, that similarly situated taxpayers also use the method and, hence, the taxpayer should not be singled out for such a change.[215]

The point of these rules is that all accounting methods emanate from Code section, Treasury regulation, judicial decision, or the exercise of IRS discretion. If the method selected by the taxpayer can be shown to fit within any of these four categories and is not otherwise denied to the taxpayer or manipulated or abused by it, the Commissioner should not be permitted to deny use of the method on the basis of a failure to reflect income clearly. Correlatively, where the taxpayer cannot show that the method it has chosen emanates from one of these four categories, the Commissioner's discretion in changing the taxpayer from that method will be upheld in virtually all cases.

[3] Impact of IRS Actions on Commissioner's Discretion

[a] Acceptance of Returns Without Notice

As a general rule, the failure of the IRS to object to a method of accounting or to the continued use of an incorrect method for a number of

---

[212] See also discussion at ¶ 9.04[1][b].

[213] See, e.g., Sierracin Corp., 90 TC 341 (1988), where the court found the Commissioner to have abused his discretion in rejecting the taxpayer's application of the completed contract method.

[214] See discussion supra ¶ 2.02[2][h].

[215] See discussion supra ¶ 2.02[2][f], regarding the virtual-identity-in-results test.

years does not constitute approval of the method or otherwise prevent the Commissioner from changing the method on audit.[216] This is true where the method used by the taxpayer is not disclosed on the return or, if disclosed, is disclosed in an ambiguous manner.[217] It is also true even where it is the IRS that is asserting that it has approved the method in question.[218] In

---

[216] See, e.g., Electric & Neon, Inc., 56 TC 1324 (1971), acq. 1973-2 CB 1, aff'd per curiam, 496 F2d 876 (1974); Holt v. United States, 368 F2d 311 (5th Cir. 1966).

[217] See, e.g., Ed Smithback Plumbing, Inc. v. United States, 76-1 USTC ¶ 9139 (Ct. Cl. 1975), opinion of trial judge adopted, 76-1 USTC ¶ 9373 (Ct. Cl. 1976), where the question was whether the taxpayer's president was a cash or accrual basis taxpayer. The president filed returns through 1962 on the cash basis. In late 1963, after learning that he had failed to account properly for inventory, he filed an amended return for 1962 that stated (on Schedule C, Form 1040) that he used the accrual method. The only change made from the original return was the inclusion of inventory data. Thus, it could not be ascertained from the return whether the accrual designation was applicable only to inventory or to the entire return. The court rejected the taxpayer's claim that the amended 1962 return served to notify the Commissioner of a change in accounting method, and that his acceptance of the return amounted to implied consent to such change:

> The amended return itself was ambiguous at best. It was not audited by the Internal Revenue Service. Under the hybrid method of accounting, both accrual- and cash-basis methods can be utilized on the federal income tax return. . . . Accordingly, it would be impossible for anyone to determine on the basis of the return alone that the taxpayer was either an accrual- or a cash-basis taxpayer and that said taxpayer was changing from one method to another. It is true in some circumstances the courts have implied from the Commissioner's actions in accepting a return a consent to change accounting methods. However in those cases the Commissioner was fully aware of the change in accounting methods, *Fowler Bros. & Cox v. Commissioner*, 138 F2d 774 (6th Cir. 1943), or played some part in initiating said change in accounting methods, *Lindner v. United States*, 7 AFTR (2d) 1224 (D. Utah 1961). Here the Commissioner was unaware of any change in accounting methods, assuming that such change did occur, nor did the Commissioner initiate any such change. There is certainly no basis on this record to conclude that the Commissioner by implication consented to any such change in accounting methods.

76-1 USTC ¶ 9139, at 83, 144.

[218] In Alexander H. Kerr & Co. v. United States, 97 F. Supp. 796 (SD Cal. 1951), the Commissioner contended that he had consented to the taxpayer's change in method or had waived any requirement of prior consent. This contention was based on his acceptance of returns using the new method. The court held to the contrary, stating:

> The requirement of advance consent for changing from one basis to another is clearly mandatory. [Citation omitted.] However, it has been held that this requirement may be satisfied by the Commissioner's acceptance of returns prepared on the new basis, *provided that the return gives notice* to the Commissioner that the method originally adopted has been changed. [Citation omitted.]
>
> As seen in the *Fowler Bros. & Co., Inc.* case, the court held that a waiver would result *if* the return gave notice to the Commissioner that there had been a change. There is nothing in the record to show that [taxpayer's] returns gave

addition, where a taxpayer has improperly switched methods of accounting, the Commissioner may not use his acceptance of some of the returns to show approval of a particular method.[219] On the other hand, the continued acquiescence of the IRS to a particular method of accounting that is clearly reflected by the taxpayer's books may prohibit the IRS from imposing a penalty on the taxpayer for use of that method.[220]

[b] Acceptance of Returns Giving Notice

In contrast to the cases discussed in the preceding section, there are a number of cases that hold that the Commissioner impliedly consents to a change in method of accounting where information contained in the taxpayer's return is found to have placed the Commissioner on notice that a partic-

---

such notice. Therefore, even though it be assumed that the change made by the taxpayer required the Commissioner's consent, there was neither consent nor waiver of the requirement.
Id. at 798–799 (emphasis by court).

[219] In Jones v. Comm'r, 306 F2d 292 (5th Cir. 1962), the taxpayer's books were maintained on a cash basis in 1948, 1949, and 1950, but the taxpayer filed no returns for these years. For 1951, the taxpayer kept his books and reported his income on an accrual basis. In 1953, the taxpayer kept his books and reported his income on the cash method. The Commissioner determined that certain sums should have been included in the taxpayer's 1951 income, since the taxpayer had used the accrual method for 1951, and the sum was properly accrued on books during such year. The Tax Court agreed with the Commissioner, stating:

> [Taxpayer] here has made a change in 1951 in his accounting method voluntarily and without consent of [Commissioner]. In making his determination [Commissioner] has sought to impose consistency upon [taxpayer] under the accounting method of [taxpayer's] choice, thereby accepting the change and implying consent.

A. Raymond Jones, 19 TCM 611, 614 (1960). The Court of Appeals for the Fifth Circuit reversed, stating:

> In the circumstances of this case we conclude that the only just and proper conclusion is to require reporting of income in 1951 on a cash basis, consistent with the other years involved. It does not seem appropriate to hold that the taxpayer is bound by the asserted conclusion that he changed from cash to accrual in 1951 without the express permission of the Commissioner and therefore he is bound by it under the theory of implied consent; while in the same decision holding that he must report in 1953 on the accrual basis because he had not followed the regulations requiring permission to change back to the cash basis. It does not appear that to permit the taxpayer to report on the cash basis for all the years involved (including 1951) would result in any substantial distortion of taxable income. The cash basis for all years would certainly achieve greater consistency.

Jones v. Comm'r, 306 F2d 292, 304 (5th Cir. 1962). See also Korn Indus., Inc. v. United States, 532 F2d 1352 (Ct. Cl. 1976), and discussion at ¶ 9.05[1].

[220] See Lynn Haynes, 59 TCM 107 (1990).

ular method is being used. The courts in these cases have found that such notice, coupled with the Commissioner's acceptance of the return, provides a basis for holding that the Commissioner has approved the use of the accounting method and has excused compliance with any procedural requirements relating to its adoption.

In *Fowler Bros. & Cox, Inc. v. Commissioner*,[221] the Commissioner argued that he had impliedly consented to a change in method. The taxpayer had reported from 1920 to 1932 on an accrual basis and from 1933 to 1937 on the cash method. Returns for these later years included a notation that income was reported on the cash basis. In 1937, the taxpayer sought to deduct certain salaries on an accrual basis. The Commissioner disallowed this deduction on the ground that the taxpayer used the cash method. The taxpayer contended that it had never obtained approval to use the cash basis and therefore was entitled to report on the accrual method. The Commissioner countered that his consent to the change in method could be implied from his acceptance of the taxpayer's returns using the cash basis.

In sustaining the Commissioner's denial of the deduction, the Sixth Circuit stated:

> [I]t is held that such requirement [of prior approval] may be satisfied by the Commissioner's acceptance of returns which give notice to him that the method originally adopted has been changed; and the situation then stands as though the Commissioner had given express permission to allow the change in method of accounting.[222]

This ruling worked against the IRS in *Tampa Tribune Publishing Co. v. Tomlinson*,[223] where the taxpayer kept its books and filed its returns prior to 1932 on an accrual method but changed to the cash method for book and tax purposes in 1932. The IRS assessed deficiencies in 1954 for the taxpayer's 1947 to 1950 fiscal years by disallowing certain deductions on the cash basis on the ground that the Commissioner had not consented to the change to the cash method in 1932.

The taxpayer did not request permission from the Commissioner to institute the change in method, and it was stated by the Tax Court that "the only evidence of the change outside the specific items within the tax return was the statement on the tax returns, beginning with the return for the fiscal year ending June 30, 1932 through 1950, to the question: 'Is this Return Made on the Basis of Cash Receipts and Disbursements. Yes.'"[224] It was also stated that a schedule in the taxpayer's 1932 return reflected a change from

---

[221] Fowler Bros. & Cox, Inc. v. Comm'r, 138 F2d 774 (6th Cir. 1943).

[222] Id. at 776.

[223] Tampa Tribune Publishing Co. v. Tomlinson, 57-1 USTC ¶ 9421 (SD Fla. 1957).

[224] Id. at 56, 755.

the accrual to the cash method. The taxpayer's returns from 1932 to 1948 were marked "reviewed" by the IRS, and the returns from 1942 to 1947 were marked "accepted." "Partial examinations" of the taxpayer's returns from 1940 to 1946 years were made in 1945 and 1948. In these circumstances, the court found that the Commissioner was estopped, by 1954, from objecting to the use of the cash method by virtue of his implied consent to the taxpayer's actions.[225]

These same principles have been applied in cases involving changes of annual accounting periods. In *Clark Brown Grain Co.*,[226] the taxpayer filed its first three income tax returns on the basis of a fiscal year ending October 31. The taxpayer then changed to a June 30 fiscal year without the prior approval of the Commissioner. Returns for the 1919 and 1920 years were also filed on the basis of a June 30 year. In determining a deficiency for the fiscal year ended June 30, 1918, the Commissioner refused to allow as a deduction a loss that was sustained after the close of that year. The taxpayer contended that the return for the period ending June 30, 1918, which covered only the eight months from November 1, 1917, was not lawfully made because approval of the Commissioner to the change in accounting periods was not obtained. In rejecting the taxpayer's reasoning, the court stated that the return (for the period ended June 30, 1918) disclosed to the Commissioner the change in accounting period. The return was timely filed with respect to the new period and well in advance of the due date for a return filed on the basis of the old fiscal year, in case the Commissioner wanted to disapprove the new year. The court stated that in these circumstances, the timely filing

---

[225] The Tax Court stated the following:

   It is the conclusion of the Court that the filing of returns by the [taxpayer] on a cash basis from 1932 to the present time, where prior thereto same had been filed on an accrual basis, ipso facto gave the Commissioner notice of the change in accounting methods; that the acceptance of such returns by the Commissioner on said changed basis of reporting for the years 1932 through 1947, his acquiescence therein without objection or question, is tantamount to approval of such change and the Commissioner must be deemed to have impliedly consented to the change, so as to be estopped, by 1947, to assert that he has not consented to the change and that therefore, [taxpayer] was entitled to report for the years 1947 through 1950 on a cash basis, and to deduct during those years the cash items of interest disallowed by the defendant.

Id. at 56, 755. See also Lawrence L. Rector, 4 TCM 1013 (1945), where, prior to 1937, the taxpayer prepared his returns on the cash basis but, beginning in 1938, reported on an accrual method. The returns for 1938 to 1940 contained statements that they were prepared on an accrual basis. In 1943, an amended return was filed for 1941 reporting income on a cash basis. The court held that the income had been properly accrued in 1941. The fact that the taxpayer had changed previously from the cash to the accrual method without the Commissioner's prior consent did not prevent this holding, since "[w]here the change has been made and adhered to without objection . . . approval will be presumed." Id. at 1020.

[226] Clark Brown Grain Co., 18 BTA 937 (1930).

of the return on the basis of the new year constituted sufficient notice of the change of accounting period. The acceptance of the initial return and of subsequent returns with income computed on the basis of the June 30 fiscal year demonstrated either Commissioner approval of the change or waiver of the notice required by the regulations.[227] Thus, the court concluded that the taxpayer had met the technical requirements of changing accounting periods. The court also indicated that absent such a determination, it would have found the Commissioner's acceptance of returns that provided notice of the change to have constituted a waiver of these procedural requirements.[228]

It is important to distinguish cases holding that the Commissioner, by accepting returns, waives compliance with procedural requirements for adoption of a method from cases holding that the Commissioner's long-standing acceptance of returns using a particular method of accounting does not estop him from subsequently challenging that method on substantive grounds. For example, the Commissioner may determine that a method of accounting that has been used for a number of years without challenge from the IRS does not clearly reflect income.[229] Similarly, the Commissioner may require a taxpayer that has improperly reported income on the basis of a method of accounting different from that used on its books to change to its book method despite the fact that prior returns using the improper method have been accepted without question.[230] In effect, these cases demonstrate that taxpayers may be able to use the Commissioner's acceptance of returns giving notice of the method to obtain implied approval of a change to a correct method, but the taxpayers cannot rely on that principle to continue use of an incorrect method.

[c] IRS Nonacceptance Despite Agent's Actions

The two preceding sections focused on the mere acceptance of returns by the IRS. When the return is examined on audit, the issue of IRS approval of a change becomes more difficult. Nevertheless, it is clear that the mere suggestion by a revenue agent that a taxpayer use a certain method of accounting is not a sufficient basis for the taxpayer to begin reporting income

---

[227] Id. at 941–942.

[228] Accord Jonas-Cadillac Co., 16 BTA 932 (1929), aff'd, 41 F2d 141 (7th Cir. 1930) (Commissioner's determination of overassessments and deficiencies on basis of a changed taxable year constituted approval of the change).

[229] See, e.g., Caldwell v. Comm'r, 202 F2d 112 (2d Cir. 1953); Travis v. Comm'r, 406 F2d 987 (6th Cir. 1969).

[230] See, e.g., Charles D. Mifflin, 24 TC 973 (1955), where Commissioner was permitted to require change to book method despite prior acceptance of returns without question. See also Leon W. Perry, 19 TCM 540 (1960), where, despite prior accrual of item in issue, Commissioner could require change to cash method for taxpayer who kept no books.

on that method. For example, in *Michael Drazen*,[231] the taxpayers were members of a partnership that reported its income on the cash method until 1954, when it changed to the accrual method without having obtained prior permission from the Commissioner. The taxpayers formally requested permission to change to the accrual method in 1955. Thereafter, an IRS agent audited the partnership books. He advised the taxpayers that income should have been reported on an accrual basis from 1952 to 1953 as well as 1954, but he did not order the taxpayers to file amended returns for these years. Nevertheless, the taxpayers filed amended partnership returns for 1952 and 1953 on an accrual method. The Commissioner rejected these amended returns, and, using the cash method, determined small deficiencies in the taxpayer's income taxes for 1953. The issue before the Tax Court was whether the Commissioner had erred in denying the taxpayers permission to report income on an accrual basis of accounting for 1953. The court found that the partnership had maintained its books and records on the cash method for 1953 and that the taxpayer had failed to show that such method did not clearly reflect income. In these circumstances, the court concluded that use of the cash method was required despite the suggestion of the agent.

Similarly, in *Brooks-Massey Dodge, Inc.*,[232] a retail automobile dealer valued its inventory of used cars at 80 percent of their average wholesale value. One of several contentions offered by the taxpayer in an attempt to justify its use of this method was that the practice had been suggested to it by a revenue agent in the 1940s. In dismissing this argument, the Tax Court stated that the recommendations of revenue agents are not binding on the IRS and do not justify the continuance of an erroneous accounting practice, even where that practice has been followed for a number of years.[233]

In addition, the fact that agents examined the returns and were aware of (or even consented to) an erroneous method does not, by itself, sanction the continued use of the method.[234] For example, in *Ross B. Hammond, Inc. v. Commissioner*,[235] the court found that the Commissioner had not given his implied consent to a change in method of accounting from the completed contract basis to a percentage-of-completion basis. It so found despite the fact that the return in question was audited by an agent who became aware of the use of the percentage-of-completion basis and informed the taxpayer

---

[231] Michael Drazen, 34 TC 1070 (1960).

[232] Brooks-Massey Dodge, Inc., 60 TC 884 (1973).

[233] Id. at 895–896.

[234] See, e.g., Ezo Prods. Co., 37 TC 385 (1961). See also Ralston Dev. Corp. v. United States, 937 F2d 510 (10th Cir. 1991), where the Commissioner was not precluded from changing the taxpayer from the cash method to an accrual method because of the existence of inventories despite the fact that the use of the cash method had been approved by agents during the examination of returns for several prior years.

[235] Ross B. Hammond, Inc. v. Comm'r, 97 F2d 545 (9th Cir. 1938).

that his office was recommending to the Commissioner that the returns be accepted as correct, although he pointed out that this action was subject to approval in Washington. The court refused to find any implied consent or waiver on the part of the Commissioner because no approval was ever expressly given. The fact that the IRS remained silent and took no action for a period of two years following the taxpayer's receipt of the agent's letter did not by itself indicate approval by the Commissioner.[236]

It has also been held that where the Commissioner accepts on audit the use of an improper inventory valuation method, he is not estopped from subsequently forcing the taxpayer to abandon the use of this method. The court in *Fruehauf Trailer Co.*[237] came to that conclusion where the taxpayer had for many years valued its inventory of used trailers at $1 each without objection from the Commissioner.

The court concluded that, while an estoppel argument may be appropriate with respect to taxable years that had been examined and for which the taxpayer's inventory method had been accepted, this prior acceptance could not bar a challenge to the method in later years.[238] However, the court suggested that its holding might have been different if the Commissioner had required the use of the $1 method in these prior years rather than merely acquiescing to it.[239]

[d] Acceptance Because of Agent's Actions

There are several cases in which the courts have found that the Commissioner's consent to a change should be implied from the circumstances even though the taxpayer had not formally sought and obtained the approval of the Commissioner to the change. In effect, the courts find that

---

[236] Id. at 547. See also Cyrus W. Scott Mfg. Co., 37 BTA 726 (1938), where the Commissioner was found not to have acquiesced to a change in method, the Board being influenced by the fact that no field examination had been made.

[237] Fruehauf Trailer Co., 42 TC 83 (1964), acq. 1965-2 CB 5, aff'd, 356 F2d 975 (6th Cir. 1966), cert. denied, 385 US 822 (1966).

[238] See Payne E.L. Thomas, 92 TC 206 (1989), where the court held that acceptance of a taxpayer's improper method of valuing inventories for a period of eleven years did not bar a change to a correct method in a succeeding year despite the fact that agents had initially determined that the taxpayer's method appeared reasonable and substantially correct. In effect, this prior approval by the agents on audit was not binding on the IRS because the taxpayers method did not comply with the applicable Treasury regulations. See also Tog Shop, Inc. v. United States, 721 F. Supp. 300 (MD Ga. 1989), where the court found that the Commissioner had the right to deny the taxpayer's method of writing down inventory from cost to a lower market value on the basis that the write-down did not comply with the applicable regulations, even though the court was impressed by the fact that the IRS had approved the use of that method during two prior audits.

[239] See discussion infra ¶ 2.04[3][e].

because of circumstances occurring in connection with the audit of a taxpayer, the Commissioner will lack the discretion to change a taxpayer to the previously used method.

For example, courts have found the Commissioner to have impliedly consented to a change in method where the IRS examined a return using a new method and either made adjustments on the basis of this method or otherwise accepted the use of the method. In *Geometric Stamping Co.*,[240] the taxpayer had for many years used a direct costing method in costing inventory for tax purposes but a full absorption method in costing inventory for book purposes. The use of the direct costing method subsequently came to the attention of the IRS during an audit of the taxpayer's 1946 and 1947 years. Following their review, the examining agents proposed to disallow the direct costing method. The taxpayer thereafter filed a petition in the Tax Court to litigate this and other issues. While the issues pertaining to 1946 and 1947 were pending, an examination was made of the 1948 year, and the use of the direct costing method was again challenged.

Ultimately, in 1951, a settlement was reached on the several issues affecting the 1946 and 1947 years. As part of the settlement, the IRS allowed the use of the direct costing method. Following the settlement, adjustments were made to the agent's report for the 1948 year to allow the direct costing method for that year. Later, on examination of the 1949 and 1950 years, the IRS again challenged the use of the direct costing method.

The taxpayer argued that its use of the direct costing method had been accepted by the IRS and that the method's continued use should be permitted. The court agreed. The court noted that the actions of the IRS were more than mere passive acceptance. Rather, the actions "would be the equivalent and have the effect of a formal request on the part of the petitioner to change its method of reporting and a formal approval by the Commissioner of that change."[241]

---

[240] Geometric Stamping Co., 26 TC 301 (1956), acq. in result 1958-2 CB 5.

[241] According to the Tax Court:

The year as to which respondent's acquiescence in petitioner's changed method of reporting is the clearest is 1948. In that year, which was the third under the new system, a large refund would have been due petitioner had the other method of reporting been adopted. An over-assessment was, in fact, first determined by respondent on this theory but when he subsequently refunded only a small part of the overpayment, so as to reach a tax computation in accordance with the new reporting system, petitioner maintained its consistent position, made no protest to the reduced amount of the refund and accepted the determination. It follows that respondent was given the opportunity to make any necessary adjustment in that year and evidently made the only one that was required, which was to reduce the over-assessment earlier determined. While we agree with respondent that no such clear-cut situation existed in the years 1946 and 1947, when claimed deficiencies were apparently settled in Tax Court proceedings prior to hearing, we think the conclusion inescapable that as to 1948

The *Geometric Stamping Co.* principle was followed in *Klein Chocolate Co.*,[242] a case involving the number of inventory pools to be used by a LIFO taxpayer. At the first hearing of the case,[243] the Tax Court held that the taxpayer was required to change from the use of a single pool to the use of separate pools for raw materials, goods in process, and finished goods. A rehearing was subsequently granted as to the applicability of the *Geometric Stamping* principle. On the production of new evidence, the court found that the taxpayer had consistently used a single pool for LIFO purposes and that sufficient information of this use had been disclosed to, and reviewed by, an examining agent during his audit of earlier years so that the Commissioner should be considered as having given his approval to the taxpayer's pooling method.[244] Of course, as these cases demonstrate, the court has the authority not only to determine whether approval has been given to a change to a new method of accounting or to continued use of a particular current method, but

---

respondent's approval was tacitly requested and effectively given for the change in reporting methods.

26 TC at 305. See McPike Inc. v. United States, 90-1 USTC ¶ 50,092 (Cl. Ct. 1988), where the court recognized that the acceptance of methods of reporting as part of the settlement of an issue may not carry as much weight as determinations made by the IRS on audit.

[242] Klein Chocolate Co., 36 TC 142 (1961), acq. 1961-2 CB 4.

[243] Klein Chocolate Co., 32 TC 437 (1959).

[244] According to the Tax Court:

Whatever may have been the shortcomings of the application which accompanied the 1942 return, or the shortcomings of the accountants with respect to the completeness of the [taxpayer's] records. . . . , we are satisfied that full and complete disclosure of all of the facts . . . was made known to the revenue agent in his examination of the taxpayer's returns and records for the years 1942, 1943, and 1944. . . . [and] there seems to be no question that the results of the adjustment of the inventories to a single-pool basis are reflected by the books even though the worksheets covering the adjustments were kept by the accountants. . . . The [Commissioner's] agent in his report declared to his superiors that . . . the taxpayer had strictly adhered to the provisions of section 22(d) . . . and he neither made nor proposed any changes therein. That his superiors accepted this conclusion as to the facts and the law is indicated by the further fact that the years covered were closed according to the recommendation of the agent.

Klein Chocolate Co., 36 TC 142, 145–156 (1961). See also S. Rossin & Sons, Inc. v. Comm'r, 113 F2d 652 (2d Cir. 1940); accord Home Ice Cream & Ice Co., 19 BTA 762, 765 (1930), nonacq. IX-2 CB 75:

The Commissioner accepted the [taxpayer's] return for 1923 and computed and settled tax liability on the facts set forth therein, which included a deduction from gross income on account of a net addition to a reserve for bad debts. We think such acceptance was sufficient permission to this [taxpayer] to make its subsequent returns on the reserve basis.

Ganahl Lumber Co., 21 BTA 118, (1930), nonacq. X-1 CB 80, to the same effect.

also to interpret the terms and scope of any settlement entered into between the taxpayer and the Commissioner.[245]

[e] Change Approved or Directed by Commissioner

There is support for the position that even the Commissioner's power to object to the use of a method on substantive grounds may be limited where the Commissioner himself has directed that a taxpayer use a particular method of accounting. For example, in *Maloney v. Hammond*,[246] the court found that the Commissioner had given the taxpayer express permission to use the accrual method of accounting. In rejecting the Commissioner's argument that the method used did not clearly reflect income, even assuming the taxpayer had received such permission, the court stated:

> If [Commissioner's] position is that, having granted permission to a taxpayer to use a certain method of accounting and the taxpayer having in good faith followed the allowed method, the Commissioner may subsequently determine that some other method would be more advantageous to the government in the amount of taxes to be collected and substitute the second method for the first, we say the Commissioner has no such right. To do so would be most unfair to the taxpayer.[247]

The court went on to note, however, that it may have been "more accurate" to state that the Commissioner's position was that the method used by the taxpayer was not strictly in accordance with "generally accepted accrual methods of accounting." The court held that, since the taxpayer had used the accrual method in a proper manner, it could not be forced to change from this method.

Where the Commissioner requires the use of a particular method, the need for the taxpayer to obtain formal approval to use that method may be obviated. In *Gus Blass Co.*,[248] the taxpayer had filed its returns on an accrual basis, except with respect to income from installment sales made in its retail department store. From 1918 through the years at issue (1940 to 1942), the taxpayer had consistently deferred 50 percent of its outstanding year-end installment receivables. On its returns, income would be increased or decreased each year by the amount of any increase or decrease in the account during the year. The Commissioner disallowed use of the installment method for the taxable years involved on the basis that the taxpayer did not

---

[245] See, e.g., Nelson Brothers, Inc., 61 TCM 1865 (1991), where the Tax Court reiterated these points in determining the terms and scope of a particular settlement agreement.

[246] Maloney v. Hammond, 176 F2d 780 (9th Cir. 1949).

[247] Id. at 781.

[248] Gus Blass Co., 9 TC 15 (1947), acq. as to this issue 1948-1 CB 1.

maintain its books in a manner that enabled an accurate computation of income on the installment basis.

In the Tax Court, the taxpayer argued that, since the Commissioner had required a change to an accrual method, he should have included in the taxpayer's 1940 income the 1939 balance in the unrealized profit account. The contention was based on a regulation that required such inclusion on changes from the installment method to an accrual method.[249] The taxpayer's motive for this argument was that inclusion of this sum would increase its base income for purposes of determining the excess profits taxes for the 1941 and 1942 years.

At trial, the Commissioner asserted that he had erred in requiring the taxpayer to account for its installment sales on an accrual basis. He asserted that this admission thereby removed from the court's consideration any issue of change in accounting method. In rejecting the Commissioner's argument, the court noted that despite the Commissioner's admission of error, his computations of deficiencies for the taxable years in question used the accrual method and disallowed deductions for annual increases in the taxpayer's unrealized profit account. It was held that whether or not the Commissioner had made a mistake, it was clear that the taxpayer's method of accounting had been changed. The court then dismissed the Commissioner's argument based on the failure of the taxpayer to obtain approval for a change in method:

> The regulation requiring consent of the Commissioner to a change in method does not limit the right to change to cases where the consent is given upon formal application of the taxpayer. The [Commissioner's] consent can be implied from his acceptance of a changed method of reporting, without rejection or other indication of his nonacquiescence. . . . And where, as here, the change is directed by the Commissioner in the first instance, it cannot be soundly argued that the taxpayer must secure formal permission to change in order to comply with the regulations.[250]

In *Reynolds Cattle Co.*,[251] the taxpayer had consistently used an inventory system under which it divided livestock into classes and placed arbitrary values on each class. In 1929, the Internal Revenue Bureau examined the returns for 1926 to 1928 and objected to the use of the inventory method on the ground that it did not clearly reflect income. The Bureau's representatives ordered that the returns for those years be made on the cash method. The

---

[249] Reg. 103 § 19.41-2, states, "The taxpayer will be required to return as additional income for the taxable year in which the change is made all the profit not theretofore returned as income pertaining to the payments due on installment sales contracts as of the close of the preceding taxable year."

[250] Gus Blass Co., 9 TC 15, 35 (1947).

[251] Reynolds Cattle Co., 31 BTA 206 (1934), acq. XIII-2 CB 16.

taxpayer protested the change to the revenue agent in charge of the Dallas office, who upheld the field representatives and ordered that the cash basis be used. The returns for the years at issue were subsequently prepared on the cash basis, and the Commissioner proposed a deficiency for these three years. The taxpayer claimed that it was entitled to a refund of about the same amount as the proposed deficiency if it used the cash method. In 1931, the Commissioner closed the case by accepting the use of the inventory method and making a refund to the taxpayer.

While the dispute with respect to the 1926 to 1928 years was pending, the taxpayer prepared and filed its returns for 1929 and 1930 on the cash method in accordance with instructions by the field examiner and revenue agent in Dallas. The Commissioner held that these returns should have been made according to the inventory system, since it had not granted permission for the taxpayer to change his method of accounting. The permission was subsequently granted for 1932 and the following years. The taxpayer contended that although it did not obtain the formal approval of the Commissioner to change its method, the actions of the field examiner and revenue agent were tantamount to consent by the Commissioner to that change, and that in any event, the inventory system previously used did not clearly reflect its income.

In holding for the taxpayer, the Board first found that the inventory method of accounting employed by the taxpayer did not clearly reflect its income and that the taxpayer was entitled to use the cash basis to report its income in 1929 and 1930. The Board stated that this was the decision reached by the field agent after his examination of the taxpayer's books and, on review, by the agent in charge. The court added that the making of an audit and the approval of an accounting method are administrative acts and that the regulation requiring the Commissioner's consent to any change is purely administrative in character. Consequently, if the IRS directs that a change in method must be made, "it could hardly be argued that the taxpayer must secure formal permission to change in order to comply with the regulations. This would be requiring the doing of a vain thing, which the law does not require."[252] The Board went on to hold that the Commissioner had abused his discretion in refusing to approve the use of the cash method for the years at issue.

This same principle was followed in *Koebig & Koebig, Inc.*,[253] where an engineering firm performed services under contracts that often covered periods in excess of one year. From the time of its organization in 1948 to 1951, the taxpayer reported its income on the completed contract method. In March 1951, the taxpayer sought permission from the Commissioner to change its method of accounting to the percentage-of-completion method.

---

[252] Reynolds Cattle Co., 31 BTA at 211.

[253] Koebig & Koebig, Inc., 23 TCM 170 (1964).

The Commissioner denied this application in May 1951, and also advised the taxpayer that it was not entitled to report its income on either of the long-term contract methods of accounting, i.e., the completed contract method or the percentage-of-completion method. The taxpayer was instructed to employ an authorized method of accounting in computing its income. In response to this letter, the taxpayer requested an audit of its returns for 1949, 1950, and 1951 so that certain adjustments might be made in connection with the change in its accounting method.

The revenue agent's final report of this audit, dated April 22, 1953, and received by the taxpayer on May 1, 1953, determined deficiencies in the 1949 to 1951 years through the use of an "actual billings" method of accounting. Under this method, the amounts billed to clients under contracts during the taxable year were included in income for the year whether or not the taxpayer had received payment for the amounts billed. Expenses incurred under a contract prior to the date of the last bill submitted to the client during the taxable year were treated as deductions for such year. The taxpayer prepared its 1952 return on the same billings method used by the agent. This return was filed in March 1953, however, before the agent's final report was approved by the IRS and received by the taxpayer.

In 1953, the taxpayer hired a new accounting firm, which, although aware of the fact that the taxpayer's returns had been filed on the billings basis in 1952, prepared the taxpayer's returns for 1953 and subsequent years using a standard accrual method of accounting. The amount of income from contracts included in any taxable year under the accrual method was the same as would have been reported under the billings method, since the contracts used by the taxpayer provided that the taxpayer only had the right to bill for services at certain dates. The treatment of expenses under the accrual method differed in that expenses actually incurred were deducted even though they had accrued after the last billing date.

The use of the accrual method was not questioned by the Commissioner until 1959, when the taxpayer reported a net operating loss. The Commissioner disallowed the deduction of certain accrued expenses in this year on the ground that the billings method, which it was asserted the taxpayer had adopted for income tax purposes, required the deferral of certain costs. However, in computing the amount of expenses to be deferred, the Commissioner used a different type of billings method than had been used by the agent in 1952.

In rejecting the Commissioner's determinations, the Tax Court found that the use of the billings method in the taxpayer's 1952 return did not constitute the adoption of that method for income tax purposes:

> [Taxpayer's] return for 1952 necessarily was filed prior to its receipt of the Commissioner's letter of April 29, 1953, advising it as to the final disposition of his audit of the returns for 1949, 1950 and 1951. In the circumstances, the only logical thing the [taxpayer] could do, pending

receipt of such final notification, was to prepare and file its 1952 return under the same billings method of accounting and reporting income that had been used by [the] agent . . . in auditing the returns for the 3 prior years. It is concluded that the filing of the 1952 return under the billings method was a mere interim measure, and that [taxpayer] did not thereby intend to adopt and did not adopt that method as its permanent method of accounting and reporting income.[254]

The court also noted that the billings method was, in effect, a type of long-term contract accounting method that could not be used under the terms of the Commissioner's May 1951 letter. The court thus found that the taxpayer was not required to obtain any further consent from the Commissioner to adopt the accrual method in 1953 because the Commissioner had required it to change to an authorized method of accounting. The court noted that there was some ambiguity concerning the relationship of this ruling and the agent's subsequent audit of the taxpayer's 1949 to 1951 returns. In view of the failure of the Commissioner to establish that the ruling was not controlling or was superseded by the agent's report employing the billings method, the court resolved the uncertainty surrounding this issue in the taxpayer's favor.

As the previous discussion demonstrates, if the Commissioner knowingly permits a taxpayer to report on a basis that is not expressly denied by the Code, Treasury regulation or decision of the U.S. Supreme Court, the Commissioner may be bound to that method of reporting.

---

[254] Id. at 178.

CHAPTER 3

The Cash Receipts and Disbursements Method

¶ 3.01 Definition 3-2
    [1] Characteristics 3-3
    [2] Users 3-3
    [3] Issues 3-4

¶ 3.02 History and Development 3-4
    [1] Cash-Flow Principles 3-8
        [a] Items of Income 3-8
        [b] Items of Expense 3-9
        [c] Ability to Pay 3-10
    [2] Benefits of Cash Method 3-10
    [3] Attitude of IRS 3-11

¶ 3.03 Reporting Items of Income 3-12
    [1] Cash Equivalence 3-13
        [a] Items of Income 3-13
        [b] Time for Recognition 3-14
        [c] Problem of Intangible Property 3-14
        [d] Alternative Resolutions of Problem 3-15
            [i] Traditional cash equivalence 3-16
            [ii] Fair market value 3-17
            [iii] Subsequent cases 3-18
            [iv] Position of Treasury 3-19
            [v] Present status 3-20
    [2] Constructive Receipt 3-22
        [a] Purpose 3-22
        [b] Restrictions and Limitations 3-23
    [3] Particular Items of Income 3-25
        [a] Interest 3-25
        [b] Dividends 3-28
        [c] Compensation 3-29
        [d] Rent and Royalty Income 3-30
        [e] Other Items 3-31

¶ 3.04 Reporting Items of Expense 3-31

[1] Payment by or on Behalf of Taxpayer 3-31
[2] Constructive Payment 3-32
[3] Form of Payment 3-33
   [a] Payment With Borrowed Funds or Third-Party
      Obligation 3-33
   [b] Payee 3-34
[4] Payment by Taxpayer's Check or Note 3-35
   [a] Checks 3-35
   [b] Notes or Other Evidences of Taxpayer's Indebtedness ... 3-36
[5] Particular Items of Expense 3-36
   [a] Interest 3-37
   [b] Insurance Premiums 3-41
   [c] Taxes 3-41

¶ 3.05 Prepayments 3-42
[1] Basic Issues 3-42
   [a] Character of Payment 3-43
   [b] Capitalization and the One-Year Rule 3-43
[2] Prepaid Expenses of Cash Basis Tax Shelters 3-45
   [a] Section 461(i) Prior to 1986 Act 3-45
   [b] The 90-Day Exception 3-46
      [i] Deduction limited to cash basis 3-46
      [ii] Drilling costs 3-46

¶ 3.06 Availability of Cash Method 3-47
[1] Limitations Under the 1986 Act 3-49
   [a] Gross Receipts Test 3-49
   [b] Qualified Personal Service Corporations 3-51
      [i] Permitted activities: function test 3-51
      [ii] Ownership test 3-53
   [c] Farming Business 3-53
   [d] Effective Date and Required Change From Cash
      Method 3-54
[2] Transactions Involving Merchandise 3-55
[3] Termination of Business 3-57

¶ 3.07 Required Use of Cash Method 3-58

¶ 3.08 Clear Reflection of Income 3-59
[1] Amount of Deferral 3-60
[2] Existence of Accrual Basis Information 3-61
[3] Accrual Basis Financial Reporting 3-62
[4] Generally Accepted Accounting Principles 3-64
[5] Mismatching of Income and Expense 3-64
[6] Consolidated Group 3-67
[7] IRS Difficulty With Cash Method 3-68

¶ 3.01 DEFINITION

Under the cash receipts and disbursements method (the cash method),
income is generally recognized in the year of actual or constructive receipt,

and expenses are deductible in the year of actual payment.[1] The year in which the income is earned or the expense is incurred is not determinative of the year in which recognition is to occur for federal income tax purposes.[2]

[1] Characteristics

The cash method is not in accordance with generally accepted accounting principles (GAAP); therefore, it is not widely used or accepted for financial reporting purposes.[3] Nevertheless, the cash method has characteristics that often make it desirable for tax reporting purposes: (1) It is comparatively simple to use and easy to audit; (2) it is imbued with certainty as to the actual realization of income and expense;[4] and (3) it provides for payment of the tax at the time when the taxpayer is most likely to have the ability to pay. For these reasons, the cash method is often the most appropriate method to use and the one most likely to reflect taxable income clearly.

[2] Users

The cash method is predominantly used by individuals and by small businesses that are not engaged in the acquisition and sale of merchandise.[5] Users include lawyers, accountants, doctors, dentists, engineers, architects, consultants, contractors, electricians, plumbers, banks and other financial institutions, providers of credit and other business information, claims

---

[1] Treas. Reg. § 1.446-1(c)(1)(i).

[2] Despite the general cash basis rules for recognizing items of income and expense, there are numerous instances where cash basis taxpayers must recognize income or expense without regard to the year of receipt or payment. Examples include the rules governing discharge of indebtedness income, depreciation, and similar expenses. See also IRC §§ 467 (pertaining to certain payments for use of property or services), 483 (pertaining to interest on certain deferred payments), 1271–1274 (pertaining to original issue discount).

[3] R. Wixon, Accountants' Handbook 5.11 (1965).

[4] See Willcuts v. Gradwohl, 58 F2d 587, 589 (8th Cir. 1932), cert. denied, 287 US 637 (1932), where the court stated:

> There were and are two accepted methods of such accounting resting on different bases. One was based on the theory of actual receipts and disbursements during the year. The other—called accrual basis—was based on liabilities to and against the taxpayer contracted for during the year. Since the former basis dealt with realizations, it probably was a truer measure, yet the latter was not unacceptable. Therefore, both were recognized as proper methods to use in ascertaining true income.

[5] Treas. Reg. § 1.446-1(c)(2)(i) provides, "In any case in which it is necessary to use an inventory the accrual method of accounting must be used with regard to purchases and sales unless otherwise authorized. . . ."

adjusters, television and radio broadcasters, hospitals and other health care providers, advertisers, trucking companies, leasing companies, and virtually every other segment of the service sector of the economy.

Prior to the Tax Reform Act of 1986 (the 1986 Act), use of the cash method was not limited to individuals or small businesses. Some of the country's largest corporations and partnerships reported for tax purposes on the cash method. This use of the cash method by large businesses often frustrated the Internal Revenue Service, which believed that such use permitted inappropriate deferrals in the recognition of income. In response, Congress imposed various limitations on the use of the cash method by some but not all large businesses for taxable years beginning after December 31, 1986.[6] Subsequent to enactment of the 1986 Act, consideration has sometimes been given to requiring the use of an accrual method by certain professionals such as lawyers and accountants. Generally, such efforts have been perceived by practitioners and taxpayers as attempts to increase tax revenues without an appropriate justification in terms of sound tax policy.[7] These actions implicitly confirm the appropriateness of the use of the cash method under present law by such professionals.

[3] Issues

The issues associated with use of the cash method, while not difficult to grasp intellectually, are sometimes among the most frustrating and esoteric of the tax law. Primary issues include (1) whether income has been received; (2) whether such income is in a form that warrants taxation at the time of receipt; (3) whether use of the cash method is available to the taxpayer; and (4) if such method is available, whether its use clearly reflects income in the particular circumstances.

¶ 3.02 HISTORY AND DEVELOPMENT

Originally, the cash method was the only correct method for computing taxable income. The Excise Tax Act of 1909 (the 1909 Act) defined "net income" as "income received within the year from all sources," less "ordinary and necessary expenses actually paid within the year," certain "losses actually sustained within the year," and interest on indebtedness "actually

---

[6] IRC § 448. Unless otherwise indicated, all references to "IRC" or to "Code" are to the Internal Revenue Code of 1986, as amended. See infra ¶ 3.06[1] for discussion of the limitations imposed by new Section 448.

[7] See, e.g., the reference to a General Accounting Office report on whether legal and accounting firms should be required to use an accrual method, Daily Tax Rep. (BNA) No. 172, at G-5 (Sept. 5, 1991).

paid within the year."[8] This language, with its focus on income received and expenses paid, rather than income earned and expenses incurred, established the cash method as the only permissible method.

The required use of the cash method under the 1909 Act presented an administrative burden to businesses that used accrual methods of accounting for financial reporting purposes. As a consequence, accountants objected to the required use of the cash method, arguing that it ignored the accounting practices actually employed by mercantile and manufacturing businesses. These accountants sought permission from the Attorney General for such businesses to compute taxable income on an accrual basis, i.e., reporting income when earned and expenses when incurred. However, the Attorney General denied the request, replying that the intent of the statute was to impose a tax on corporate income calculated on a cash basis; that such language was employed advisedly; and that "[t]he theory of the framers of the bill in this respect differs from that which you advocate."[9]

The Treasury was more receptive. It recognized the merit of the accountants' position and attempted to provide the relief sought by requiring inventory accounting for mercantile and manufacturing companies and by providing that income reported under the 1909 Act could be the same "as [that] shown by the entities on [their] books."[10] The Treasury later decided as follows:

> No particular system of bookkeeping or accounting will be required by the Department. However, the business transacted by corporations, etc., must be so recorded that each and every item therein set forth may be readily verified by an examination of the books and accounts where such examination is deemed necessary.[11]

Although these efforts by the Treasury were intended to provide the relief sought, considerable doubt remained within the Internal Revenue Bureau (IRB) as to the acceptability of accrual basis reporting for tax purposes. For instance, the IRB reported that "the records of the Bureau show that the accrual method of accounting was not recognized [by the Excise Tax Act of 1909]. . . ."[12]

The Revenue Act of 1913 (the 1913 Act) imposed the first direct income tax on individuals after passage of the Sixteenth Amendment. In imposing the tax, the 1913 Act used the phrase "net income arising or accruing,"

---

[8] 1909 Act, § 38(2)(d). This act imposed a tax on the privilege of doing business in the corporate form. The tax was equal to one percent of annual net corporate income above $5,000.

[9] T. Adams, "When Is Income Realized?" The Fed. Income Tax 29, 31 (R. Haig ed. 1921).

[10] Reg. 31, art. 2 (Dec. 3, 1909).

[11] TD 1675 (Feb. 14, 1911).

[12] Appeals and Review Recommendations (ARR) 915, 1-2 CB 44, 46.

instead of "income received," the phrase used in the 1909 Act.[13] Although this change in language suggested the acceptability of accrual accounting, the Supreme Court held that the tax should be levied on income "received" during the year, and that no change from the cash flow standard mandated by the 1909 Act was intended by the language of the 1913 Act.[14]

The Revenue Act of 1916 (the 1916 Act) was the first revenue act that expressly permitted tax accounting on a basis other than that of cash receipts and disbursements. It provided that

> a corporation ... keeping accounts upon any basis other than that of actual receipts and disbursements, unless such other basis does not clearly reflect its income, may, subject to regulations made by the Commissioner of Internal Revenue ... make its return upon the basis upon which its accounts are kept, in which case the tax shall be computed upon its income as so returned.[15]

This provision upheld the cash method as presumptively correct and applied the "clear reflection of income" test only when the taxpayer sought to keep its books and compute its taxable income on some basis other than the cash method. Thus, taxpayers were permitted to deviate from the cash method only when the other method (e.g., an accrual method) clearly reflected income.

The Revenue Act of 1918 (the 1918 Act) continued the trend of permitting added flexibility to taxpayers and, for the first time, imposed the clear reflection of income requirement on the use of the cash method. The 1918 Act authorized the computation of net income in accordance with:

> the method of accounting regularly employed in keeping the books of such taxpayer; but if no such method of accounting has been so employed, or if the method employed does not clearly reflect the income, the computation shall be made upon such basis and in such manner as in the opinion of the Commissioner does clearly reflect the income.[16]

Notwithstanding imposition of the clear reflection of income requirement, there was nothing in the 1918 Act that suggested that Congress

---

[13] 1913 Act, § II(6)(a). The 1913 Act permitted expense deductions only when such items were paid. Id. at § II B.

[14] Maryland Casualty Co. v. United States, 251 US 342 (1920). The court rejected the government's claim that premiums due on insurance policies written during the year were income, whether or not collected.

[15] 1916 Act, § 13(d) (pertaining to corporations). Section 8(g) was essentially the same, but applicable to individuals.

[16] 1918 Act, § 212(b).

believed that the cash method did not clearly reflect income or that its use should be discouraged.

The method of accounting provisions in the 1918 Act remained essentially unchanged through the Internal Revenue Code of 1939 (the 1939 Code),[17] and they formed the basis of current Sections 446(a) and 446(b). Thus, throughout this period of statutory development, it was the cash method that was initially preferred by the government. The accrual method won only gradual congressional acceptance as an alternative method of accounting.[18]

Despite the gradual acceptance of the accrual method, neither Congress nor the IRS intended that concepts of accrual financial accounting should control accrual tax accounting.[19] Nevertheless, beginning in the late 1960s, the cash method sometimes came under attack from the IRS, which often viewed its use as abusive and not clearly reflecting income, particularly when used by large businesses that maintained accrual basis data for nontax purposes. IRS agents contended that use of the cash method did not clearly reflect income, citing the size of the deferral income arising from use of the cash method, the existence of accrual basis information, and other factors.[20] The position of the agents was frequently rejected by the IRS National Office (the National Office).[21] However, the efforts of agents to deny use of the cash method continued as did the IRS view that the method should not be used by large businesses.

---

[17] 1939 Code, § 41.

[18] In Henry Reubel, 1 BTA 676, 678 (1925), the Board of Tax Appeals (the Board) stated:

> We thus see the steady development, through the acts passed by Congress from 1909 to 1918, of the concept of measuring income either upon a cash receipts and disbursements basis or upon the accrual basis. We see how slowly Congress moved away from the cash receipts and disbursements basis unequivocally laid down in the Act of 1909 through the grudging admission of the alternative accrual basis in 1916 and 1917 to the absolute requirement of [conforming tax and book accounting] as set forth in the Act of 1918.

For a somewhat different view, which suggests that initial use of the cash method was limited in scope, see B. Bittker & L. Lokken, Federal Taxation of Income, Estates and Gifts ¶ 105.3.1 n.9 (Warren Gorham Lamont, 2d ed. 1992) [hereinafter Bittker & Lokken].

[19] As part of the 1954 Code, Congress enacted Sections 452 (pertaining to prepaid income) and 462 (pertaining to estimated expenses) to bring about greater conformity between accrual tax accounting and accrual financial accounting. However, these sections were repealed retroactively by Pub. L. No. 74, 84th Cong. (June 15, 1955). See Thor Power Tool Co. v. Comm'r, 439 US 522 (1979); discussion infra ¶ 3.08[4].

[20] See discussion infra ¶ 3.08.

[21] See, e.g., Tech. Adv. Mem. 7405291610B (1974); Priv. Ltr. Rul. 8029008 (Apr. 10, 1980).

Finally, in response to these views, Congress enacted Section 448 as part of the 1986 Act in order to deny use of the cash method to certain large businesses.[22] Although this legislation prevents many large businesses from using the cash method, it does not preclude partnerships, S corporations, or qualified personal service corporations from using the method, regardless of the size of their business. In these circumstances, taxpayers and tax practitioners expected that the IRS would accept the use of the cash method by qualifying businesses that achieved substantial deferrals but whose use of the method was not expressly denied by Section 448. However, this expectation has not been borne out by subsequent events. The IRS continues to challenge use of the cash basis by large businesses, citing the same factors that were routinely rejected by courts in the past and that gave rise to Section 448.[23]

[1] Cash-Flow Principles

The predominant concept of tax accounting has always been cash flow. Notwithstanding the general authorization in Section 446(a) and its predecessors for taxpayers to compute taxable income by the same method they use for book purposes, the method that is used for tax purposes is often controlled by Code provisions and judicial doctrines that require cash-flow accounting.

[a] Items of Income

With respect to the recognition of income, Section 451 and corresponding provisions in earlier acts set forth the general rule that payments are to be included in taxable income in the year of receipt unless, under the method of accounting used in computing taxable income, such amounts are to be properly accounted for as of a different period. Although this rule (when considered in light of the book conformity requirement of Section 446(a)) might suggest that accrual financial accounting principles will be accepted for purposes of accrual tax accounting, such a result is often not the case.[24] For tax purposes, these principles of accrual financial accounting are often overridden by cash-flow principles.

---

[22] Section 448 is discussed infra ¶ 3.06[1].

[23] See ¶ 2.02[2] for a discussion of cases suggesting that the IRS should not ignore the enactment of Section 448 in evaluating whether use of the cash method clearly reflects income in circumstances where its use is not otherwise denied.

[24] Principles of accrual financial accounting are not acceptable, per se, for accrual tax accounting. The history of Sections 452 and 462 (see ¶ 4.02[3]) illustrates the deliberateness and care taken by the Treasury when altering the principles of cash-flow accounting found throughout the Code. See also Thor Power Tool Co. v. Comm'r, 439 US 522 (1979); discussion at ¶ 2.02[2][c].

The predominance of cash-flow principles for tax accounting is illustrated by the following Code provisions and judicial doctrines:

1. Section 453 requires (and, prior to the Revenue Act of 1987 (the 1987 Act), Section 453A permitted) taxpayers making installment sales (including sales of inventory) to report gain in the taxable periods in which payments are received, notwithstanding the fact that the taxpayer maintains inventories or is otherwise on an accrual method of tax accounting.

2. Sections 351 (transfers to controlled corporations), 354–368 (corporate reorganizations), and 1031 (like-kind exchanges) exemplify sections of the Code that permit taxpayers to defer the recognition of gain until the receipt of (1) cash; (2) other property readily convertible into cash; or (3) property that is dissimilar to the property transferred by the taxpayer.

3. The Claim-of-Right Doctrine requires amounts received under a claim of right and without restriction to be taxed in the year received, even though the taxpayer may have to repay such amounts.[25]

4. Under judicially established principles, income received by a taxpayer as a prepayment for future goods or services may be taxable in the year received without regard to the taxpayer's method of accounting.[26]

[b] Items of Expense

Principles of accrual financial accounting do not control the timing of deductions for purposes of accrual tax accounting. Accrual basis taxpayers have long been denied the opportunity to accrue liabilities for tax purposes in accordance with GAAP. Thus, the use of reserves and the deduction of estimated expenses, which reduce income for financial accounting purposes, are generally not permitted for tax purposes.[27] In addition, in 1984, Congress became concerned with the deduction of even fixed liabilities by accrual basis taxpayers. Accordingly, it enacted the so-called economic performance rules to (1) defer the deduction of fixed liabilities beyond the year in which they

---

[25] See, e.g., North Am. Oil Consol. v. Burnet, 286 US 417 (1932). For a full discussion of the claim-of-right doctrine, see ¶ 12.03.

[26] See, e.g., Schlude v. Comm'r, 372 US 128 (1963); and American Auto. Ass'n v. United States, 367 US 687 (1961). For a full discussion of the application of this rule to accrual method taxpayers, see ¶ 4.03[3].

[27] See, e.g., Brown v. Helvering, 291 US 193 (1934), and discussion at ¶ 4.04.

would be deducted for financial accounting purposes and (2) deny the deductions in certain cases until the year in which the liability is paid.[28]

[c] Ability to Pay

Cash-flow principles of tax accounting are also grounded in the equitable principle that in some cases permits (and in other cases requires) taxpayers to recognize income and pay tax after they have received the cash with which to pay, but not before or after that time. For example, Congress has recognized that "the installment method alleviates possible liquidity problems which might arise from the bunching of gain in the year of sale when a portion of the selling price has not been actually received."[29] Similarly, the underlying assumption of many of the tax-free exchange provisions, such as Sections 354–368 and 1031, is that the continuation of an investment, albeit in a different form, should not result in taxation until the investment is liquidated.[30]

[2] Benefits of Cash Method

As compared to an accrual method, the cash method benefits taxpayers by permitting them to defer taxation until payments are received. This benefit assumes that payments are received after the performance of services and that there is no increase in applicable tax rates. This deferral tends to be permanent in nature, lasting as long as the taxpayer remains in business and varying in amount as net accounts receivable (accounts receivable less accounts payable) increase or decrease.

On the other hand, the cash method may benefit the Treasury by accelerating taxation. This can occur where payments are received in advance of the rendition of services or are otherwise received prior to the time when the taxpayer would recognize income under an accrual method.[31]

The cash method is beneficial to both taxpayers and the Treasury in that it fosters the orderly collection of governmental revenues at the time when the taxpayer is best able to pay. This method is certain in result, practical to administer, and much simpler to apply than an accrual method, which is subject to complex statutory and regulatory rules and is based on fixed rights

---

[28] IRC § 461(h), added by the Revenue Provisions of the Deficit Reduction Act of 1984. See discussion at ¶ 4.04[3].

[29] S. Rep. No. 96-1000, 96th Cong., 2d Sess. 4701 (1980).

[30] See B. Bittker & J. Eustice, Federal Income Taxation of Corporations and Shareholders ¶ 14.01 (Warren Gorham Lamont, 5th ed. 1987).

[31] See ¶ 4.03[3] for the treatment of "prepaid income" under an accrual method of tax reporting and for available opportunities for deferring the recognition of such income beyond the year of receipt.

that emanate, for example, from contracts and business customs. See Chapter 4 for discussion of accrual methods.

The cash method is also beneficial to the Treasury in that it is less subject to abuse and manipulation than is an accrual method. Although cash method taxpayers may seek to defer collection of income or accelerate the payment of expense in order to benefit from use of the method, this opportunity is available principally to individuals and small businesses. By reason of the very size of their operations, larger businesses cannot as a practical matter delay billing and collection or accelerate the payment of expense. On the other hand, because accrual methods are based on contracts and business customs, it is often possible for accrual basis taxpayers to achieve substantial tax benefits through relatively slight changes in applicable contracts or business practices.

[3] Attitude of IRS

Over the years, the IRS's view on the appropriateness of the cash method has been highly inconsistent. Prior to 1971, the IRS generally considered requests for changes to the cash method on their merits. However, in 1971, the IRS announced that it would not approve method changes unless the new method would be used for financial reporting purposes.[32] Since the cash method does not satisfy GAAP, this new policy had the practical effect of precluding changes to the cash method.

This policy was dropped in 1980, when the IRS began to approve requests for changes to the cash method, even where the taxpayers filing the requests were going to continue to compute income for all other purposes on an accrual basis. However, by 1981, the IRS had again changed its mind. It considered adoption and use of the cash method abusive, denied virtually every request for change to that method, and stepped up challenges to its use.[33]

The IRS also supported legislation to curb perceived abuse from the availability of the cash method to the largest taxpayers. Its efforts, together with other factors, led to the enactment of Section 448 as part of the 1986 Act. Section 448 denies the availability of the cash method to specified taxpayers.[34] Notwithstanding the clear intent of Congress for use of the cash method not to be denied to other taxpayers, revenue agents have sometimes sought to deny use of the cash basis to such other taxpayers merely because

---

[32] Internal Revenue News Release 1125 (Apr. 14, 1971). For the reasons behind the 1971 announcement, see Nolan, "The Merit in Conformity of Tax to Financial Accounting," 50 Taxes 761 (1972).

[33] See remarks of then Associate Chief Counsel Gerald Portney, Daily Tax Rep. (BNA) No. 97, at G-5 (May 18, 1983).

[34] See discussion infra ¶ 3.06[1].

use of the cash method produces results that differ from use of the method preferred by the agents. Such actions by revenue agents are wrong, and taxpayers and their advisors should be willing to challenge such actions.

Typically, the primary concern of the IRS during periods of disapproval is the deferral of income inherent in the cash method and the consequent loss in revenue associated with its use. The IRS frequently takes the position that the cash method is not based on economic concepts of wealth accumulation or income realization. It therefore argues that accrual methods should be used, at least by larger businesses and others who have accrual information available. While such arguments have surface appeal, they fail to address the key issue, which is to determine when income should be recognized for tax purposes under existing law, not whether income has been realized in an economic sense.

All of these circumstances have left taxpayers and tax practitioners in confusion and distress. They have also resulted in a dissimilar and sometimes inequitable administration of the tax laws, permitting some taxpayers to use the cash method while denying it to others in the same industry.

Although the limitations on use of the cash method imposed by Section 448 may have been expected to lessen the antagonism of the IRS to the method, it has not, and inequities among taxpayers remain both in the law and in its administration. For example, taxpayer organizations that are of comparable size may now be required to use different methods of accounting solely on the basis of their form of business. Under the provisions of Section 448, a partnership or an S corporation with large revenues may continue to use the cash method, while C corporations with much smaller revenues will be denied use of the method.[35] Similarly, some taxpayers may find their use of the cash method challenged, while other taxpayers, operating in the same form of organization and using the same practices and procedures but located in a different part of the country, are not challenged. Such inequities are likely to continue.

¶ 3.03 REPORTING ITEMS OF INCOME

Section 451 sets forth this general rule: "The amount of any item of gross income shall be included in the gross income for the taxable year in which received by the taxpayer, unless, under the method of accounting used in computing taxable income, such amount is to be properly accounted for as of a different period."

Under the cash method, an "item" of gross income is to be recognized

---

[35] See infra ¶ 3.06[1] for discussion of Section 448.

in the year in which "actually or constructively received."[36] Two basic issues arise in connection with the application of the cash method. The first is whether the item of income in question is in such a form (or is of such a type or a character) that its receipt should trigger its recognition for tax purposes. The second is whether the item of income has in fact been received. These two issues are discussed respectively under the doctrines of cash equivalence and constructive receipt.

[1] Cash Equivalence

The doctrine of cash equivalence pertains to the issue of whether income is in such a form (or is of such a character) that its receipt should trigger its recognition for tax purposes. To illustrate, assume a cash method taxpayer renders services valued at $100 and receives $100 of property as compensation. Should he be taxed on receipt of the property? Assume that a second cash method taxpayer also renders services valued at $100 but has only an account receivable to show for it. Should he be taxed on receipt of the receivable?

Although each item of income (the property and the account) was received, the recognition of each on receipt would eliminate the distinction between the cash method and accrual methods. Under the cash method, income is recognized when actually or constructively received. Under accrual methods, income is recognized when the right to the income becomes fixed and the amount of the income can be determined with reasonable accuracy. See Chapter 4 for discussion of accrual methods.

The foregoing rules and considerations have caused the IRS and the courts to recognize that under the cash method, not all items of income should be recognized on receipt. However, uncertainty and confusion exists as to where to draw the line. This uncertainty and confusion arises from (1) a desire to achieve the benefits of the cash method and (2) the fact that certain provisions of the Code and Treasury regulations attempt to delineate "items" of income while other provisions attempt to regulate when those items should be recognized.

[a] Items of Income

Section 61 provides that unless otherwise excluded by law, items of gross income include income from "whatever source derived." The regulations under Sections 61 and 446 add that items of income may be "realized" in any form, whether in money, property, or services.[37] Although these authorities

---

[36] Treas. Reg. §§ 1.446-1(c)(1)(i), 1.451-1(a).

[37] Treas. Reg. §§ 1.61-1(a), 1.446-1(c)(1)(i).

make it clear that income may be realized in virtually any form, the question still remains as to when such realized items of income should be recognized for tax purposes.

[b] Time for Recognition

The regulations under Section 446 provide that under the cash method, "all items which constitute gross income (whether in the form of cash, property, or services) are to be included for the taxable year in which actually or constructively received."[38] Similarly, the regulations under Section 451 provide that "[g]ains, profits, and income are to be included in gross income for the taxable year in which they are actually or constructively received by the taxpayer. . . ."[39] These provisions literally suggest that if an item of income is received, the character or form of the item is irrelevant; the item must be included in income in the year of receipt.

Support for such an interpretation is provided by Section 1001 and the regulations thereunder, which provide for the recognition of gain or loss on the sale or other disposition of property. The amount of gain or loss is the difference between the amount realized on the sale (or other disposition) and the taxpayer's basis in the property. The amount realized is the sum of any money received plus the fair market value (FMV) of any property (other than money) received. Congress has indicated for purposes of Section 1001 (and its predecessors) that property is taxable to the extent of its FMV and that no gain or loss is recognized unless the property received has a readily realizable market value.[40] Thus, for purposes of Section 1001, the time for recognition is dependent on market value, not on the character or form of the income received.

[c] Problem of Intangible Property

The foregoing statutory and regulatory provisions (together with those authorizing use of the cash method) did not fully answer the question as to when items of income, including gains from the sale or exchange of property, should be included in taxable income. On one hand, if property were

---

[38] Treas. Reg. § 1.446-1(c)(1)(i). See Tech. Adv. Mem. 8952061 (Oct. 3, 1989), applying these principles to conclude that a real estate brokerage business's receipt of a second mortgage, which provided it with a 20 percent interest in real estate in lieu of cash commissions, was not only "realized" income but also income to be "recognized" in the year of receipt.

[39] Treas. Reg. § 1.451-1(a).

[40] The 1918 Act, § 202(b); Reg. 45, art. 1563 (1919); Revenue Act of 1921, § 202(c); and Revenue Act of 1924, § 203, which is the source of the present statutory language. For a discussion of this legislative development, see "Rept. of Committee on Sales, Exchanges and Basis," 31 Tax Law. 1481 (1978).

received and had an ascertainable FMV, authority existed for the proposition that the FMV of the property should be recognized as income in the year of receipt, regardless of its character. On the other hand, if the authorities were interpreted in this manner, there frequently would be no discernible difference between the cash method and accrual methods, particularly where the items received consisted of intangible property, such as contract rights, accounts receivable, and promissory notes. If receipt of such items triggered the recognition of income, the very cash-flow problems that the cash method was intended to alleviate would arise. Tax would be due at a time when the taxpayer had not yet received the cash with which to pay. Such an interpretation would also cause seemingly unnecessary complexity to taxpayers, such as individuals, whose record-keeping systems are generally insufficient to record the receipt of such intangible items of property. Such an interpretation would eliminate the general simplicity of the cash method and would lose the certainty associated with systems that recognize income and expense on ultimate receipt or payment (i.e., on ultimate completion of the transaction).

In response to these concerns, the courts have interpreted the applicable Code sections and Treasury regulations to exclude the receipt of certain intangible property from the requirement that income be recognized under the cash method on receipt. The intangible property whose receipt is to be excluded is that property whose character is such that it should not be deemed the "equivalent of cash" and whose recognition should therefore be delayed until cash or an equivalent of cash is, in fact, received.[41] In effect, the doctrine that has emerged is that an item of realized income need not be recognized for tax purposes until that item has become, or has been converted to, cash or an equivalent of cash.

In the formulation and evolution of this cash equivalence doctrine, a basic tension has arisen between the desire to tax the actual or constructive receipt of property (which has an ascertainable FMV) and the desire not to impose a tax on cash method taxpayers until actual cash or its equivalent has been received. This tension does not arise where the property received consists of services or tangible property rather than rights to receive cash in the future. In the former cases, the receipt of tangible property or services is all that will be received by the taxpayer. The transaction is complete. Thus, assuming the property or service represents income and has an ascertainable FMV, it is appropriate to impose the tax for the year of receipt.

[d] Alternative Resolutions of Problem

As to items of intangible property, three different approaches have evolved. The first, or traditional approach, is that a mere right to receive

---

[41] A full discussion of the applicable rules is contained infra ¶ 3.03[1][d].

cash (as evidenced by a contract, note, or other written instrument) should not be taxed until such right is converted into cash or into property rights that are essentially equivalent to cash, without regard to whether the initial right to receive cash has an ascertainable FMV or is in any particular form. The second approach is based on the concept of ascertainable FMV. If property has an FMV (and there is a market for such property), its receipt should be taxed even though it is not essentially equivalent to cash. The third approach is that the mere existence of an FMV (without regard to the existence of a market for the property) eliminates the need to consider cash equivalency at all. The Treasury seems to favor this third approach.

[i] **Traditional cash equivalence.** The traditional view of the cash equivalence doctrine is represented by the 1961 decision of the Court of Appeals for the Fifth Circuit in *Cowden v. Commissioner.*[42] The issue in *Cowden* was the proper time for recognizing income evidenced by contractual rights to receive payments of cash in the future. The *Cowden* court first noted that courts in prior cases had looked to the form of the contract right in order to determine whether a cash equivalent had been received.[43] However, the *Cowden* court held that form alone should not answer the question; nor should the existence of an ascertainable FMV. The court then stated:

> A promissory note, negotiable in form, is not necessarily the equivalent of cash. Such an instrument may have been issued by a maker of doubtful solvency or for other reasons such paper might be denied a ready acceptance in the marketplace. We think the converse of this principle ought to be applicable. We are convinced that if a promise to pay of a solvent obligor is unconditional and assignable, not subject to set-offs, and is of a kind that is frequently transferred to lenders or investors at a discount not substantially greater than the generally prevailing premium for the use of money, such promise is the equivalent of cash and taxable in like manner as cash would have been taxable had

---

[42] Cowden v. Comm'r, 289 F2d 20 (5th Cir. 1961).

[43] See, e.g., Alice G.K. Kleberg, 43 BTA 277 (1941), and Harry L. Barnsley, 31 TC 1260 (1959), which had suggested the simple rule that cash equivalence did not exist with respect to mere contract rights but did exist when such rights were embodied in negotiable notes. In addition, consider Treas. Reg. § 1.61-2(d)(4), which provides:

Notes or other evidences of indebtedness received in payment for services constitute income in the amount of their fair market value at the time of the transfer. A taxpayer receiving as compensation a note regarded as good for its face value at maturity, but not bearing interest, shall treat as income as of the time of receipt its fair discounted value computed at the prevailing rate. As payments are received on such a note, there shall be included in income that portion of each payment which represents the proportionate part of the discount originally taken on the entire note.

it been received by the taxpayer rather than the obligation. The principle that negotiability is not the test of taxability in an equivalent of cash case such as is before us, is consistent with the rule that men may, if they can, so order their affairs as to minimize taxes, and points up the doctrine that substance and not form should control in the application of the income tax laws.[44]

The court made it clear that cash equivalence is not dependent on the form of the obligation but rather on its substance. If the instrument in question is (1) issued by a solvent obligor; (2) unconditional and transferable; (3) of a kind for which there is a market; and (4) of a type that trades at a discount based only on the prevailing time value of money, then there is no reason to treat its receipt differently from a receipt of cash. Indeed, since the obligor or obligee could easily have obtained cash, the holding of the instrument is essentially the same as a receipt of cash followed by an investment of that cash in the particular instrument. Thus, there is no reason to defer the taxpayer's recognition of income beyond the year of receipt.

However, if any of these conditions is not present, such treatment is inappropriate. In such a case, taxation on receipt would impose unnecessary complexity and undue hardship on the taxpayer or otherwise would be inconsistent with the use of the cash method. The mere fact that the item received has an FMV does not mean that it is the equivalent of cash. *Cowden* is recognized as a leading case in this area[45] and is widely cited by commentators.[46]

[ii] **Fair market value.** In 1975, in *Warren Jones Co. v. Commissioner*,[47] the Court of Appeals for the Ninth Circuit announced a different view of cash equivalence. In *Warren Jones*, a cash basis taxpayer sold an apartment building, and received as consideration cash plus the buyer's obligation to pay the balance of the sales price. The buyer's obligation was evidenced by a standard-form real estate contract of a type that was frequently bought and sold in the area in which the taxpayer conducted its business. Although there was a market for such obligations, the prices at which the obligations sold reflected substantial discounts from the face amounts of the obligations. Following *Cowden*, the Tax Court found that the contract was not includable in income on receipt because it was not the equivalent of cash.

However, after a lengthy review of the history of Section 1001, the Court

---

[44] Cowden v. Comm'r, 289 F2d 20, 24 (5th Cir. 1961).

[45] "Rept. of Committee on Sales, Exchanges and Basis," supra note 40, at 1484.

[46] See, e.g., Surrey, Warren, McDaniel & Ault, 1 Federal Income Taxation 793, 795 (1972); Bittker & Lokken, ¶ 105.3.2 n.13.

[47] Warren Jones Co. v. Comm'r, 524 F2d 788 (9th Cir. 1975), rev'g 60 TC 663 (1973).

of Appeals reversed the Tax Court, concluding that if property received in an exchange has an FMV, then that FMV must be included in the "amount realized" on the transaction, and gain must be recognized at that time.[48] Thus, as a consequence of *Warren Jones*, at least in the Ninth Circuit, the doctrine of cash equivalency is apparently conditioned on an absence of FMV in a transaction governed by Section 1001. However, since the basis of the *Warren Jones* decision was Section 1001, which pertains to gain on a sale or other disposition of property, it is not clear that *Warren Jones* would (or should) be applied to transactions not involving a sale or exchange of property.

The court in *Warren Jones* recognized that its conclusion might cause hardship to some taxpayers. However, the court believed that any such hardship was ameliorated by the availability of installment reporting under Section 453. Since Section 453 applies only to sales of property for deferred payments, this conclusion by the court further suggests that *Warren Jones* should not be applied to transactions not involving a sale or an exchange of property.

Should a taxpayer who sells property elect out of the installment method, *Warren Jones* may impose a major problem as to the character of the gain recognized. For example, if a note with a face amount of $100 and an FMV of $70 is received on a sale of a capital asset with a basis of $40, only $30 of capital gain will be recognized at the time of sale. The difference between the face amount of the note ($100) and its FMV ($70) will constitute ordinary income, to be recognized by a cash basis taxpayer ratably as payments are received. If installment reporting were used or if the obligation were not a cash equivalent, then the capital gain on the sale would be the difference between the face amount of the note and the basis of the property sold, unless such gain was recharacterized by other sections of the Code, such as Section 483 (interest on certain deferred payments) or Section 1274 (original issue discount).

[iii] **Subsequent cases.** In *Watson v. Commissioner,*[49] a 1980 decision of the Court of Appeals for the Fifth Circuit, the issue was whether a letter of credit received by the taxpayer as a result of his sale of cotton was taxable in the year of receipt or in the following year when the letter of credit was paid. Applying the *Cowden* standards, the court found the letter of credit to be taxable in the year of receipt. The court did not refer to *Warren Jones*, but the court did refer to Section 1001(a) and stated that the issue for decision was whether the letter of credit "was 'property' with an ascertainable

---

[48] For a summary of the applicable legislative history, see "Rept. of Committee on Sales, Exchanges and Basis," supra note 40, at 1481.

[49] Watson v. Comm'r, 613 F2d 594 (5th Cir. 1980).

'fair market value.'"[50] Thus, the court appeared to adopt the *Warren Jones* approach.

However, rather than concluding that the existence of an FMV was determinative of the existence of property for purposes of Section 1001, the court applied the *Cowden* standard to determine whether the letter of credit was, in fact, property. The court implied that had the *Cowden* standard not been satisfied, the recognition of income would have been deferred until the year the letter of credit was paid. The deferral would have been based, not on an absence of FMV, but on a finding that "property" had not been received.

On the other hand, in *Campbell v. United States,*[51] a court of claims decision involving the availability of the cost recovery method of accounting,[52] the court cited *Warren Jones* for the proposition that where the FMV of an obligation can be ascertained, that amount must be included as an amount realized in the year of receipt under Section 1001(b). No mention was made of *Cowden*, and no issue was raised as to the existence of property.

Subsequently, in *Bright v. United States,*[53] the taxpayer asserted that a large check received from a sale of stock at the end of the year was not the equivalent of cash because it failed the readily-marketable and immediately-convertible tests established in *Cowden.* However, the court responded that actual cash was available to the taxpayer on the same day the check was received. Thus, the court said the taxpayer's argument was "bootless." The court then added that the large amount for which the check was drawn did not ultimately affect its ready marketability. This discussion suggests the continuing viability of the *Cowden* standards even when a sale of property takes place, at least in the Fifth Circuit.

[iv] Position of Treasury. For many years, the IRS has been plagued by the deferral available under the cash method. This has been particularly irritating to the IRS where taxpayers received intangible property with an FMV but were nonetheless able to defer the recognition of income on the basis of the cash equivalence doctrine. *Warren Jones* was therefore a significant victory for the IRS.

The Treasury sought to improve on this victory when it promulgated

---

[50] Id. at 597.

[51] Campbell v. United States, 661 F2d 209, 215 (Ct. Cl. 1981).

[52] Under the cost recovery method, which is also known as the open transaction method, gain is not recognized at the time of the transaction because of an inability to value the amounts due to the taxpayer, i.e., the obligation received by the taxpayer from the other party to the transaction does not have an ascertainable FMV. In such a case, payments received by the taxpayer are first applied against the taxpayer's basis in the property sold (to the extent thereof) and thereafter are treated as gain. See Burnet v. Logan, 283 US 404 (1931).

[53] Bright v. United States, 91-1 USTC ¶ 50,142 (5th Cir. 1991).

temporary regulations under Section 453 following enactment of the Installment Sales Revision Act of 1980 (the 1980 Act). This 1980 Act provides for automatic installment reporting on deferred payment sales of real property and casual sales of personal property unless the taxpayer elects out from its provisions. With respect to elections out, the regulations provide:

> A taxpayer who elects not to report an installment sale on the installment method must recognize gain on the sale in accordance with the taxpayer's method of accounting. The FMV of an installment obligation shall be determined in accordance with paragraph[s] (d)(2)(ii) and (iii) of this section [which pertain to fixed amount and contingent payment obligations, respectively]. In making such determination, any provision of contract or local law restricting the transferability of the installment obligation shall be disregarded. Receipt of an installment obligation shall be treated as a receipt of property, in an amount equal to the FMV of the installment obligation, whether or not such obligation is the equivalent of cash. An installment obligation is considered to be property and is subject to valuation, as provided in paragraph (d)(2)(ii) and (iii) of this section, without regard to whether the obligation is embodied in a note, an executory contract, or any other instrument, or is an oral promise enforceable under local law.[54]

Consequently, with respect to sales of real property and casual sales of personal property, the Treasury has taken the position that the doctrine of cash equivalence is neither applicable nor relevant. If an obligation has an ascertainable FMV, its year of actual or constructive receipt determines the existence of property and the year of income recognition (without regard to the nature, quality or character of the item received). Since it is quite possible for an obligation to have an ascertainable FMV without there being an existing or active market for such obligations, application of the Treasury's position could pose a dilemma for cash basis taxpayers. For example, it is likely that even an oral promise to pay in the near future by a solvent obligor would be susceptible of ready valuation.

[v] **Present status.** The present status of the cash equivalence doctrine depends in large part on (1) the jurisdiction in which the transaction takes place and (2) whether the obligation received is for a sale or other disposition of property. If the obligation does arise from a disposition of property, the further issue arises as to whether the regulatory requirements quoted in the preceding section[55] are lawful and would be upheld as valid if challenged (assuming, of course, that the taxpayer has elected out of the installment method).

---

[54] Temp. Reg. § 15A.453-1(d)(2)(i).
[55] See supra ¶ 3.03[1][d][iv].

If the transaction occurs in the Fifth Circuit (or the Eleventh Circuit), it seems reasonable to conclude that a court would follow *Cowden* without regard to whether the transaction involved an obligation received for property or services.

If the transaction occurs in the Ninth Circuit (and possibly the United States Court of Federal Claims) and involves a sale or other disposition of property, the court would probably follow *Warren Jones*. If the obligation is received for services (or for an item that otherwise is not property), it is unclear whether *Warren Jones* would be applied.

Until cases have been decided in other jurisdictions, it seems reasonable to conclude that *Cowden* would be applied with respect to a sale of services. However, there would be substantial support for application of *Warren Jones* to a sale or a disposition of property.

In any event, it appears that the cash equivalence issue may arise in the future only with respect to obligations received for services rendered. Because of the wide application of the installment method to sales or other dispositions of property, the fact that such method is mandatory unless an election out is made, and the fact that it is unlikely that the IRS would challenge an election out if the gain were reported entirely in the year of sale, there is less potential today than in earlier years for cash equivalent issues to arise in connection with sales of property.

With respect to services, the ultimate outcome of the issue is uncertain. However, it seems more appropriate to apply *Cowden* in such cases than *Warren Jones*. If *Warren Jones* were applicable, it would effectively destroy use of the cash method for most service businesses. Taxpayers hoping to benefit from *Cowden* should evidence the obligations due them in a manner that would limit the marketability of the obligation. If notes must be used for nontax reasons, the notes should be accepted only as evidence of the obligation, not as payment. That is, the taking of the note should not extinguish the taxpayer's obligation but, rather, should confirm it.[56] In addition, the note should not be negotiable or assignable.

---

[56] Compare Robert J. Dial, 24 TC 117, 123, (1955), acq. 1955-2 CB 5, where the court stated, "The notes were never meant to be anything more than additional security for the principal debts, for nobody intended them to be payment thereof," with Rev. Rul. 76-135, 1976-1 CB 114, where the IRS ruled that the FMV of the note constituted income where the note was received as payment. See also Ray E. Omholt, 60 TC 541, 549 (1973) (stating, "Since both the debt and the notes were payable on demand it cannot be said that the notes were more than the evidence of the debt"); Jay A. Williams, 28 TC 1000, 1002 (1957), acq. 1958-1 CB 6 (stating, "A note received only as security, or as an evidence of indebtedness, and not as a payment, may not be regarded as income at the time of receipt"); Mellinger v. United States, 21 F. Supp. 964, 967 (1938) (stating, "The rule in most jurisdictions, including the federal courts, is that in the absence of agreement or consent to receive it as such, a promissory note of the debtor, although accepted by the creditor, does not in itself constitute payment or amount to a discharge of the debt"). In Tech. Adv. Mem. 8952061 (Oct. 3, 1989), a real estate brokerage

[2] Constructive Receipt

An item of income is to be recognized by a cash basis taxpayer on actual or constructive receipt. The doctrine of constructive receipt is set forth in the Treasury regulations as follows:

> Income although not actually reduced to a taxpayer's possession is constructively received by him in the taxable year during which it is credited to his account, set apart for him, or otherwise made available so that he may draw upon it at any time, or so that he could have drawn upon it during the taxable year if notice of intention to withdraw had been given. However, income is not constructively received if the taxpayer's control of its receipt is subject to substantial limitations or restrictions.[57]

[a] Purpose

The purpose of the doctrine is to include in the taxable income of a cash basis taxpayer that money or other property (1) that is subject to the taxpayer's unfettered will and control;[58] (2) that the taxpayer is free to enjoy at his own option; (3) that exists and is available to taxpayer; and (4) that, except for taxpayer's own volition, can immediately be reduced to his possession.[59] The doctrine's objective is to preclude a taxpayer from deferring the recognition of income for tax purposes when the only thing preventing its earlier actual receipt is the taxpayer's own will. However, application of the doctrine is not limited to the IRS. It may be invoked by taxpayers to

---

business's receipt of a second mortgage interest in real estate sold, in lieu of cash commissions, was required to be recognized in the year of receipt.

[57] Treas. Reg. § 1.451-2(a).

[58] Income received by the taxpayer's agent may be constructively received by the taxpayer. See, e.g., Leo A. Woodbury, 49 TC 180 (1967), acq. 1969-2 CB xxv; Bratton v. Comm'r, 283 F2d 257 (6th Cir. 1960), cert. denied, 366 US 911 (1961). However, where an agent acts for two or more principals, neither under the control of the other, constructive receipt may be delayed until funds due each principal are available and under the control of each. United States v. Unger, 159 F. Supp. 850 (DNJ 1958). Similarly, where proceeds of a sale are deposited into an escrow account, the seller is not deemed to have constructively received those proceeds where the escrow account was set up pursuant to a bona fide agreement between the parties, which was entered into before the seller had any right to the funds; where the seller was not entitled to receive any economic benefits from the fund prior to its scheduled disbursement; and where the escrowee was not the seller's agent. Reed v. Comm'r, 723 F2d 138 (1st Cir. 1983), rev'g 45 TCM 398 (1982).

[59] Fetzer Refrigerator Co. v. United States, 437 F2d 577 (6th Cir. 1971); W.C. Leonard & Co. v. United States, 324 F. Supp. 422 (ED Miss. 1971); Rosenberg v. United States, 295 F. Supp. 820 (ED Mo. 1969), aff'd, 422 F2d 341 (8th Cir. 1953). The doctrine also applies with respect to the "receipt" of advance payments of income by accrual method taxpayers.

show that income was received in a year prior to the year of actual receipt,[60] even where that prior year is closed by the running of the applicable period of limitations.[61]

If the income is not unqualifiedly subject to the taxpayer's demand, it cannot be deemed to have been constructively received by him. In addition, even though the taxpayer may have the power to compel conditions to occur so as to permit a distribution of cash or other property, the mere existence of that power will not give rise to a constructive receipt as long as such power has not been exercised.[62] In accordance with this strict conceptual framework, the courts have repeatedly and uniformly held that the doctrine of constructive receipt is to be applied sparingly, only in situations where clearly justified.[63]

[b] Restrictions and Limitations

In most situations, the issue is whether there are any restrictions or limitations that preclude the taxpayer from exercising his own free, unfettered will to obtain immediately the items of income at issue.[64] To prevent

---

[60] See, e.g., Hyland v. Comm'r, 175 F2d 422 (2d Cir. 1949); Fetzer Refrigerator Co. v. United States, 437 F2d 577 (6th Cir. 1971).

[61] Ross v. Comm'r, 169 F2d 483 (1st Cir. 1948). To overcome such a consequence, the IRS may seek to apply the mitigation provisions of Sections 1311–1314, if applicable. Alternatively, the IRS might assert that a consistent practice of recognizing income in year of actual receipt establishes a method of accounting from which the taxpayer cannot depart without prior approval. See Moran v. Comm'r, 67 F2d 601 (1st Cir. 1933); Chapter 8.

[62] Hyland v. Comm'r, 175 F2d 422 (2d Cir. 1949).

[63] See, e.g., Lacy Contracting Co., 56 TC 464 (1971); R.E. Hughes, Jr., 42 TC 1005 (1964), acq. 1965-2 CB 5; John A. Brander, 3 BTA 231 (1925).

[64] If a check is paid on presentment, it is deemed received in the year of receipt by the taxpayer. See, e.g., Lavery v. Comm'r, 158 F2d 859 (7th Cir. 1946). The year of receipt controls, even if the check is received after banking hours. Charles F. Kahler, 18 TC 31 (1952). However, if the taxpayer refuses the check for legitimate reasons, such as to avoid the possibility of an accord and satisfaction, no constructive receipt exists. See Walter I. Bones, 4 TC 415 (1944), acq. 1945 CB 2. Contra, Nathan Fogle, 25 TCM 785 (1966), where constructive receipt was found even though the taxpayers refused checks representing their share of proceeds from a judicial sale in the belief that acceptance would prejudice their right to attack the sale. See also L.M. Fischer, 14 TC 792 (1950), acq. 1950-2 CB 2, where no constructive receipt was found, the taxpayer having agreed to hold the check until the following year because the obligor did not presently have sufficient funds to cover the check. See also Baxter v. Comm'r, 816 F2d 493 (9th Cir. 1987), where the court held that the mere availability of a check to the taxpayer did not amount to constructive receipt, because the taxpayer would have needed to make an 80-mile round trip on a Saturday to pick it up and, even then, could not have received credit from the bank until the next year; Priv. Ltr. Rul. 8606012 (Nov. 5, 1985), where the IRS held that checks are not constructively received when the bank on which they are drawn returns them unpaid.

constructive receipt, the restriction or limitation must exist prior to the time the right to receive comes into fruition. Moreover, the restriction or limitation must not be one imposed by the taxpayer itself or an agent of the taxpayer.[65]

The courts have identified numerous factors that are relevant in determining whether sufficient restrictions and limitations exist to prevent application of the constructive receipt doctrine. These factors include the explicit and tacit policies of the obligor,[66] oral or informal understandings among shareholders, officers, or creditors as to when and under what circumstances amounts due the taxpayer may be withdrawn or received,[67] and the fact that the consent of another is required before a taxpayer may obtain funds.[68]

The authority of a taxpayer to draw funds from a corporation's depository on his own signature (without cosignature) is always highly influential with respect to a finding of constructive receipt.[69] Conversely, where a taxpayer cannot obtain funds on his signature alone or where countersignature is required, the courts have repeatedly found the doctrine's application inappropriate.[70] This is so even where the taxpayer, by reason of being the majority stockholder, could easily have obtained the funds by exercising the power he possessed.[71]

---

[65] Bright v. United States, 91-1 USTC ¶ 50,142 (5th Cir. 1991).

[66] See, e.g., Lacy Contracting Co., 56 TC 464 (1971), where obligor's consistent practice of paying bonuses at same time each year indicated absence of constructive receipt at earlier time; W.W. Slaughter, 2 TCM 528 (1943), where practice of frequent withdrawals at irregular intervals suggested constructive receipt as to amounts available for such withdrawal.

[67] See, e.g., George W. Johnson, 25 TC 499 (1955), acq. 1956-1 CB 4; Oliver v. United States, 193 F. Supp. 930 (ED Ark. 1961); L.M. Fischer, 14 TC 792 (1950), acq. 1950-2 CB 2; Walter L. Hopkins, 2 BTA 549 (1925), acq. 1925 IV-2 CB 3, where the taxpayer orally agreed with three other officers to withdraw certain authorized bonuses "only as funds were actually available therefor." This agreement and the corporation's inadequate cash balance caused the Board to find that there had been no constructive receipt. See also Richard M. Evans, 55 TCM 902 (1988), to the same effect, the payment of bonuses being subject to the availability of adequate working capital.

[68] Elmer J. Benes, 42 TC 358 (1964), aff'd, 355 F2d 929 (6th Cir. 1966), cert. denied, 384 US 961 (1966); Estate of Pratt, 7 BTA 621 (1927), acq. 1927 VII-1 CB 26; Wolder v. Comm'r, 493 F2d 608 (2d Cir. 1974), cert. denied, 419 US 828 (1974).

[69] Fetzer Refrigerator Co. v. United States, 437 F2d 577 (6th Cir. 1971); W.C. Leonard & Co. v. United States, 324 F. Supp. 422 (ND Miss. 1971); C.D. Fountain, 59 TC 696 (1973), acq. 1973-2 CB 2; Robert B. White, 61 TC 763 (1974); Raleigh v. United States, 5 F. Supp. 622 (Ct. Cl. 1934); Rev. Rul. 72-317, 1972-1 CB 128.

[70] Radom & Neidorff Inc. v. United States, 281 F2d 461 (Ct. Cl. 1960), cert. denied, 365 US 815 (1961); Bullock's Dep't Store, Inc., 32 TCM 1168 (1973); George J. Kolowich, 1 TCM 416 (1943).

[71] Bullock's Dep't Store, Inc., 32 TCM 1168 (1973); Hyland v. Comm'r, 175 F2d 422 (2d Cir. 1949); Lacy Contracting Co., 56 TC 464 (1971). See also Richard M. Evans, 55 TCM 902 (1988), where no constructive receipt of bonuses was found even though the taxpayers controlled the corporation that was to pay the bonuses.

Practical considerations are also important. For example, a mandatory prerequisite to a finding of constructive receipt is that the obligor must have the financial ability to pay the amounts in question.[72] A shortage of cash, or a showing that the obligor otherwise lacked the funds to pay the amounts in question, will preclude the doctrine's application.[73] Similarly, a controversy between the principals of a company or the particular history and nature of their relationship may preclude authorized amounts from being paid or constructively received.[74]

Constructive receipt also does not exist where the taxpayer has an unqualified right to funds but would have to give up a valuable or substantial property right to obtain the funds. For example, where the annual increment to the cash surrender value of a life insurance policy reflects interest, no constructive receipt is deemed to occur in the year the increment is credited to the policy if the taxpayer is forced to surrender his entire investment to realize the income.[75] Similarly, there is no constructive receipt where employees have to give up past service credits to obtain their prior contributions to a retirement plan that is being terminated[76] or where a taxpayer has to give up rights of appeal under local law.[77]

[3] Particular Items of Income

[a] Interest

Except as otherwise required by Code section or Treasury regulation,[78] interest income is recognized by cash method taxpayers in the year of actual or constructive receipt. The regulations point out that income is deemed

---

The court held that the bonuses were to be paid only as working capital was available, the taxpayers had a fiduciary responsibility to determine the adequacy of working capital before paying the bonuses, and a determination of adequate working capital could not have been made during the tax year at issue.

[72] Basil F. Basila, 36 TC 111 (1961), acq. 1962-1 CB 3; Raleigh v. United States, 5 F. Supp. 622 (Ct. Cl. 1934); C.E. Gullett, 31 BTA 1067 (1935).

[73] Rosenberg v. United States, 295 F. Supp. 820 (ED Mo. 1969), aff'd, 422 F2d 341 (8th Cir. 1953); Walter L. Hopkins, 2 BTA 549 (1925), acq. 1925 IV-2 CB 3.

[74] Radom & Neidorff, Inc. v. United States, 281 F2d 461 (Ct. Cl. 1960), cert. denied, 365 US 815 (1961); George J. Kolowich, 1 TCM 416 (1943).

[75] Theodore H. Cohen, 39 TC 1055 (1963), acq. 1964-1 CB 4 (pt. 1); see also Blum v. Higgins, 150 F2d 471 (2d Cir. 1945).

[76] Rev. Rul. 55-317, 1955-1 CB 329.

[77] See General Baking Co., 48 TC 201 (1967), involving an accrual method taxpayer.

[78] See, e.g., IRC §§ 483 (interest on certain deferred payments), 1272–1274 (original issue discount). See also Prop. Reg. § 1.446-2 (method of accounting for interest on certain transactions).

constructively received in the taxable year in which it is credited to the recipient's account, set apart for him or otherwise made available so that he may draw on it at any time or could have drawn on it during the taxable year if notice of intention to withdraw had been given.[79] Thus, the amount of interest credited on accounts with banks, savings and loan associations, and other financial institutions is income in the year credited.[80] The recognition of interest income cannot be deferred by directing that accrued interest be accumulated for payment at a later date.[81] Nor may interest income be deferred by having it received by an agent on behalf of the taxpayer.[82]

Constructive receipt of interest income does not exist where the receipt is subject to substantial limitations or restrictions. Thus, if any portion of the interest that is credited to an account is not subject to withdrawal at the time credited, that portion is not constructively received until the year in which it may be withdrawn.[83] Additionally, if interest may not be withdrawn under a particular plan until maturity of the plan, the crediting of interest during the period of the plan is not constructively received and does not become constructively received until maturity.[84] Similarly, amounts payable with respect to matured interest coupons are received in the year of maturity unless it can be shown that there were no funds available for payment of the interest within that year.[85]

The regulations provide that the following are not substantial limitations or restrictions: (1) a requirement that the deposit or account, and the earnings thereon, be withdrawn in multiples of even amounts; (2) the fact that the taxpayer would receive not substantially less earnings by early withdrawal than he would receive at maturity (a forfeiture of three months interest on withdrawal or redemption before maturity of a certificate of one year or less is substantially less); (3) a requirement that earnings be withdrawn only on a withdrawal of all or part of the deposit or account; and (4) a requirement that notice of intention to withdraw be given in advance of the actual withdrawal.[86]

A more frequent question is when to recognize interest on a certificate of deposit (CD) whose term spans two or more taxable years. If the CD provides for a substantial penalty for withdrawal of interest prior to maturi-

---

[79] Treas. Reg. § 1.451-2(a).

[80] Treas. Reg. §§ 1.451-2(a), 1.451-2(b).

[81] Theodore R. Bayard, 16 TC 1345 (1951).

[82] See, e.g., Capitol Fed. Sav. & Loan Assoc., 96 TC 204 (1991).

[83] Elizabeth W. Bates, 4 BTA 1079 (1926); Rev. Rul. 64-215, 1964-2 CB 19.

[84] Treas. Reg. § 1.451-2(b). But see Priv. Ltr. Rul. 8830004 (Apr. 22, 1988), where the National Office made it clear that even where interest is not constructively received within a particular year, it nevertheless may have to be recognized in that year under the original issue discount provisions of Sections 1272–1278.

[85] Treas. Reg. § 1.451-2(b).

[86] Treas. Reg. § 1.451-2(a).

ty, no constructive receipt occurs until maturity. Moreover, it is not necessary to recognize prior to maturity the income that would have been available on the early termination of the CD. In effect, the penalty itself is a substantial limitation on the availability of the funds. However, if the amount is not substantial, then the withdrawable earnings are included in income.[87] If there is no penalty for a withdrawal of interest but only a penalty on an early withdrawal of principal, then income is received in the year in which the interest is credited to the taxpayer's account or otherwise made available to him without regard to maturity of the certificate.[88]

Cash method lenders sometimes obtain interest through charges such as points, loan origination fees, and commissions. The interest represented by these charges must be recognized in the year of actual or constructive receipt.

Absent agreement to the contrary, when a note is acquired at a discount (the discount representing interest) or where the face amount of the note includes both principal and interest, the interest will be deemed received by the lender ratably as the note is repaid.[89] This rule has consistently been followed by the courts and the IRS.[90] (However, see Chapter 11 for discussion of rules governing original issue discount.)

On the other hand, the lender and borrower may agree as to when interest will be paid or what portion of each payment will be deemed interest and what portion will be deemed principal. Absent application of Section 483 (interest or certain deferred payments) or Sections 1272–1274 (original issue discount), such an agreement will control.[91] Where an agreement does not

---

[87] Treas. Reg. § 1.451-2(a)(2). This provision reflects a 1980 amendment to the regulations (TD 7663, 1980-1 CB 101) as a result of the prior issuance of Rev. Rul. 71-72, 1971-1 CB 278, in which the IRS held that holders of a six-month, nonnegotiable certificate constructively received at the end of the year the amount of interest they would have received if the certificate had been redeemed at that time.

[88] Rev. Rul. 80-157, 1980-1 CB 186.

[89] Blair v. First Trust & Sav. Bank, 39 F2d 462 (5th Cir. 1930), cert. denied, 282 US 851 (1930).

[90] See, e.g., Helvering v. Martin-Stubblefield, Inc., 71 F2d 944 (8th Cir. 1934); Comm'r v. Central Republic Trust, 75 F2d 708 (7th Cir. 1935); Great Southern Life Ins. Co., 33 BTA 512 (1935), acq. 1936 XV-1 CB 10, aff'd, 89 F2d 54 (5th Cir. 1937), cert. denied, 302 US 698; Rev. Rul. 65-95, 1965-1 CB 208, relating to seller's points; Rev. Rul. 70-540, 1970-2 CB 101, relating to buyer's points; Rev. Rul. 74-607, 1974-2 CB 149, relating to points charged by accrual basis construction lender. See also Bell Federal Savings & Loan Ass'n, 62 TCM 376 (1991), where the Tax Court recognized that the time for reporting interest income by an accrual method taxpayer would differ depending on whether points, which were in the nature of interest, were discounted from the proceeds of the loan or were paid by the borrower from its own funds. The court recognized the rules set forth in the text but demonstrated how a careful analysis must be made to determine whether the points, in fact, were discounted at the time of closing or, instead, were paid by the borrower.

[91] Rev. Rul. 63-57, 1963-1 CB 103; Internal Revenue Manual 222(2)(a)(ii) (Jan. 8, 1981).

specify the character of each payment or how each payment is to be allocated between principal and interest, the payment usually is considered first applicable to accrued interest (to the extent thereof) and thereafter to principal.[92] However, applicable state or federal laws pertaining to these matters might require a different application.

For many years, lenders used the Rule of 78's method of computing the interest and principal portions of short-term consumer installment obligations.[93] The Rule of 78's method was also used by some tax shelters in connection with long-term debt obligations as a means of accelerating the deduction of interest as compared to an economic accrual of that interest. In response, the IRS issued a series of revenue rulings and revenue procedures during 1983 and 1984 in which it disallowed or modified the use of the Rule of 78's method.[94] These rulings and procedures made clear that the IRS would object to the recognition of interest income or expense through use of the Rule of 78's method and, instead, would require a form of economic accrual. An exception was provided in the case of self-amortizing consumer loans over a period not in excess of five years.

These rulings and procedures evidenced a growing concern within the IRS and the Treasury as to the use of any means for computing, determining, characterizing, and recognizing interest other than on a basis consistent with concepts of economic accrual. These concerns ultimately resulted in substantial revisions to the rules governing original issue discount. These revisions, which were enacted in 1984, are discussed in Chapter 11.

[b] Dividends

The treatment of dividends is very similar to the treatment of interest, i.e., the same rules of constructive receipt apply.[95] Thus, a dividend on corporate stock is constructively received when it is unqualifiedly made

---

[92] John B. Ferenc, 33 TCM 136 (1974).

[93] Under the Rule of 78's (or sum-of-the-months digits) method of allocation, the amount to be allocated is multiplied by a fraction, the numerator of which is the remaining number of months to maturity and the denominator of which is the sum of the number of months in the original term. For example, interest on a one-year note would be allocated $12/78$ to the first month, $11/78$ to the second, and so forth.

[94] See Rev. Rul. 83-84, 1983-1 CB 97, modifying and superseding Rev. Rul. 72-100, 1972-1 CB 122; Rev. Proc. 83-40, 1983-1 CB 774. See also Rev. Procs. 84-27–84-30, 1984-1 CB 469. See Tech. Adv. Mem. 8752007 (Sept. 10, 1987), where the use of the straight-line method of computing interest was found inappropriate even though the interest to which the taxpayer was entitled on a default by the borrower was the amount computed on a straight-line basis rather than a Rule of 78's basis. (Rev. Rul. 83-84 was not applicable because of the exception provided by Rev. Proc. 83-40.) See also discussion infra ¶ 3.04[5][a] regarding the impact of these rules on interest deductions by cash method taxpayers.

[95] Avery v. Comm'r, 292 US 210 (1934).

subject to the demand of the shareholder.[96] The fact that the taxpayer does not cash a dividend check,[97] or that he has an available dividend mailed so as to delay possession,[98] will not defer the time for recognition. However, if a dividend is declared payable on the last day of the taxable year and the corporation follows a practice of mailing dividend checks so that shareholders will not receive the checks until the following year, the dividends are deemed received in the following year.[99]

It is not necessary that a dividend be formally declared in order for it to be includable in income. Thus, distributions of property or cash may be characterized as dividends and included in income in the year of receipt in the absence of a formal declaration.[100]

[c] Compensation

Generally, compensation must be included in the year of actual or constructive receipt, without regard to the time when services are rendered.[101] Therefore, payments for services rendered in the past or payments for services to be rendered in the future are taxable when actually or constructively received.[102]

When compensation for services is due and payable, a taxpayer cannot defer recognition of the income by requesting the employer, customer, or client to delay payment or to place the funds in an escrow or other account to be paid out at a later time.[103] However, where the submission of a bill is a condition precedent to the other party's obligation to pay, the taxpayer's delay in billing is ordinarily effective to preclude constructive receipt.[104]

A taxpayer who controls a close corporation cannot avoid compensation by failing to credit his account for salary if in fact the salary has been autho-

---

[96] See Cecil Q. Adams 20 BTA 243 (1930), aff'd, 54 F2d 228 (1st Cir. 1931); Mary M. Braxton 22 BTA 128 (1931). The rules for recognizing dividend income are essentially the same for accrual method taxpayers. See Treas. Reg. § 1.301-1(b); Rev. Rul. 78-117, 1978-1 CB 214; Bay Ridge Operating Co., 29 TCM 58 (1970); and discussion at ¶ 4.03[1].

[97] Abram Nesbitt, 43 TC 629 (1965).

[98] Kunze v. Comm'r, 203 F2d 957 (2d Cir. 1953), aff'g per curiam, 19 TC 29 (1952).

[99] Treas. Reg. § 1.451-2(b).

[100] Dawkins v. Comm'r, 238 F2d 174 (8th Cir. 1956).

[101] See Section 83 for additional rules governing property received in connection with the performance of services.

[102] In contrast, service providers on an accrual method have the opportunity of deferring prepayments until the year in which the service is rendered. See Rev. Proc. 71-21, 1971-2 CB 549; discussion at ¶ 4.03[3].

[103] See Rev. Rul. 60-31, 1960-1 CB 174, which contains an analysis of several fact patterns.

[104] Bittker & Lokken, ¶ 105.33.

rized and may be withdrawn at any time.[105] However, if there is no authorization of salary for withdrawal, the mere possession of the power to cause the authorization will not result in constructive receipt.[106]

Taxpayers who have received compensation must report it in the year received even though they may have a contingent liability to refund all or a portion of the compensation.[107] For example, the fact that future policy cancellations may require an insurance agent to refund commissions does not reduce the amount of commission to be reported in the year of receipt.[108] However, if compensation is received under a fixed obligation to repay it, this preexisting obligation may prevent the amount received from being income. For example, if an agreement requires the employee to loan back to the corporation the very compensation it paid to him, the employee is deemed not to have had actual or constructive receipt of the funds and, therefore, is not required to report the funds as income.[109]

When an employee and employer agree to a deferred payment arrangement prior to the rendition of services or prior to the employee otherwise becoming entitled to the compensation, the employee need not recognize the compensation until the deferred payments are actually or constructively received.[110]

[d] Rent and Royalty Income

Except as expressly provided by other sections of the Code,[111] rent and royalty payments are included in income in the year of actual or constructive receipt, without regard to the period to which the rent or the royalty relates.[112] Thus, advance rentals and other lump-sum payments made on the execution of a lease are includable in the year of actual or constructive receipt

---

[105] Elmer J. Benes, 42 TC 358 (1964), aff'd, 355 F2d 929 (6th Cir. 1966), cert. denied, 384 US 961 (1966); Jacobus v. United States, 9 F. Supp. 41 (Ct. Cl. 1934).

[106] Hyland v. Comm'r, 175 F2d 422 (2d Cir. 1949).

[107] Rev. Rul. 83-12, 1983-1 CB 99.

[108] See Brown v. Helvering, 291 US 193 (1934), which involved an accrual method taxpayer.

[109] Eakins v. United States, 36 F2d 961 (EDNY 1930); Welker J. Smucker, 6 TCM 1054 (1947), aff'd, 170 F2d 147 (6th Cir. 1948).

[110] Deferred compensation arrangements are subject to numerous Code sections. For a discussion of various arrangements, see Bittker & Lokken, ch. 60.

[111] See, e.g., IRC § 467 (pertaining to certain payments for use of property), discussed at ¶ 11.10.

[112] As to rents, see Morris-Poston Coal Co. v. Comm'r, 42 F2d 620 (6th Cir. 1930); United States v. Boston & Providence R.R., 37 F2d 670 (1st Cir. 1930). As to royalties, see Joe S. Ray, 32 TC 1244 (1959), aff'd, 283 F2d 337 (5th Cir. 1960); Perfumers Mfg. Corp., 33 TC 532 (1959), acq. 1960-2 CB 6.

rather than apportioned over the term of the lease.[113] As with other forms of income, a contingent obligation to repay amounts does not reduce or otherwise prevent amounts from being actually or constructively received.[114]

[e] Other Items

The Code contains numerous provisions focusing on particular items of income and expense. Taxpayers must always be aware of the existence of these provisions and must consider their impact. Some of these special rules are generally known to tax practitioners. Examples include the rules governing original issue discount under Sections 1272 through 1274. In other cases, the existence of these rules may not be so widely known. For example, special rules are provided for the recognition of employee tips,[115] crop insurance proceeds,[116] and proceeds from the sale of livestock on account of drought conditions.[117] In addition, payments to be received on a sale of marketable securities must be treated as received in the year of the sale.[118]

¶ 3.04 REPORTING ITEMS OF EXPENSE

[1] Payment by or on Behalf of Taxpayer

Section 461 provides the general rule that deductions are permitted for the taxable year, "which is the proper taxable year under the method of accounting used in computing taxable income." The regulations provide the following:

> Under the cash receipts and disbursements method of accounting, amounts representing allowable deductions shall, as a general rule, be taken into account for the taxable year in which paid. Further, a

---

[113] Treas. Reg. § 1.61-8(b); Crile v. Comm'r, 55 F2d 804 (6th Cir. 1932), aff'g 18 BTA 588 (1929), cert. denied, 287 US 60 (1932); Jennings & Co. v. Comm'r, 59 F2d 32 (9th Cir. 1932), aff'g 21 BTA 381; Hyde Park Realty, Inc., 20 TC 43, aff'd, 211 F2d 462 (2d Cir. 1954); Harry L. Barnsley, 31 TC 1260 (1959).

[114] See ¶ 12.03 for discussion of the claim-of-right doctrine.

[115] Treas. Reg. § 1.451-1(c).

[116] See Section 451(d) and Treas. Reg. § 1.451-6, which permit insurance proceeds from the destruction of (or damage to) crops to be reported in the year following the year of destruction if income from the crops would have been reported in that year.

[117] Section 451(e) permits farmers to recognize income from the sale of certain livestock (in excess of the number that would have been sold if the taxpayer had followed his usual practice) in the year following the year of sale, if the sale would not have occurred but for drought conditions.

[118] See IRC § 453(k).

taxpayer using this method may also be entitled to certain deductions in the computation of taxable income which do not involve cash disbursements during the taxable year, such as the deductions for depreciation, depletion, and losses under sections 167, 611, and 165, respectively. If an expenditure results in the creation of an asset having a useful life which extends substantially beyond the close of the taxable year, such an expenditure may not be deductible, or may be deductible only in part, for the taxable year in which made. An example is an expenditure for the construction of improvements by the lessee on leased property where the estimated life of improvements is in excess of the remaining period of the lease. In such a case, in lieu of the allowance for depreciation provided by section 167, the basis shall be amortized ratably over the remaining period of the lease.[119]

As these regulations make clear, merely because a taxpayer is using the cash method does not mean that each payment of cash results in a deduction. Obviously, the item with respect to which payment has been made must represent an otherwise deductible expense. Correlatively, deductions are not in all cases denied in the absence of concurrent payment. For example, should the acquired property have a useful life extending substantially beyond the close of the year, the cost of the item must be capitalized and depreciated (or deferred and amortized) over the appropriate period.[120]

[2] Constructive Payment

Although the doctrine of constructive receipt is applicable to items of income, there is no corresponding doctrine of constructive payment with respect to items of expense.[121] This frequently results in a trap for the unwary and illustrates the lack of symmetry within the tax system. For example, the situation may arise, particularly between related taxpayers, where the related employee is treated as having constructively received an amount due him from his corporation. Despite the fact that the employee must recognize the amount in income under principles of constructive receipt, the corporation is not entitled to a deduction under a principle of constructive payment.[122]

---

[119] Treas. Reg. § 1.461-1(a)(1).

[120] See infra ¶ 3.05[1][b].

[121] See, e.g., Vander Poel, Francis & Co., 8 TC 407 (1947).

[122] See Section 267, which pertains to deductions on transactions between related parties.

[3] Form of Payment

For purposes of claiming a deduction, payment may be made in cash, property, or services or by offset of an amount due the debtor from the creditor.[123] If made in property or services, the amount of the deduction is generally the FMV of the property or services. However, the transfer of the property or the rendition of the service may itself give rise to an additional taxable event. For example, if the FMV of the property being transferred differs in amount from the transferor's basis in that property, the transferor will generally be required to recognize gain or loss, as may be appropriate, in the amount of the difference. Similarly, a taxpayer who makes a payment through the rendition of services is normally treated as receiving compensation to the extent of the FMV of the services rendered. If payment is effected by offset, the taxpayer must be able to demonstrate that such offset has, in fact, been made.[124]

[a] Payment With Borrowed Funds or Third-Party Obligation

Payment may be made with borrowed funds.[125] Thus, the source of the funds (or property) used to make payment generally is not relevant. As long as the funds used to make the payment were obtained from a third-party lender (i.e., one who is unrelated to the creditor to whom the liability is owed), the payment will be deemed made, and the deduction will be allowed.[126]

The third-party lender may make payment directly to the creditor on behalf of the taxpayer. It is not necessary for the lender to distribute the funds to the taxpayer so that the taxpayer can make the payment.[127] If the third-party lender issues funds directly to the taxpayer's creditor in payment

---

[123] See, e.g., Saverio Eboli, 93 TC 123 (1989).

[124] See, e.g., TSI, Inc. v. United States, 91-2 USTC ¶ 50,524, aff'd, 977 F2d 424 (8th Cir. 1992), where in the context of reviewing asserted payments of commissions by a domestic international sales corporation, the court concluded that the elimination of offsetting items of income and expense in accountant's work papers did not constitute payment, because the eliminations had not been made in the actual books and records of the affected corporations.

[125] See, e.g., William J. Granan, 55 TC 753 (1971).

[126] See, e.g., Crain v. Comm'r, 75 F2d 962 (8th Cir. 1935); McAdams v. Comm'r, 198 F2d 54 (5th Cir. 1952); William J. Granan, 55 TC 753 (1971).

[127] See, e.g., Rev. Rul. 78-173, 1978-1 CB 73, where taxpayer was permitted to deduct medical payments made by his parent on his behalf, taxpayer then issuing a note to his parent to evidence the obligation; Rev. Rul. 78-38, 1978-1 CB 67, and Rev. Rul. 78-39, 1978-1 CB 73, where use of credit cards was deemed equivalent of payment of liability with borrowed funds. See also Commercial Sec. Bank, 77 TC 145 (1981), acq. 1986-1 CB 1, where Tax Court, in allowing liabilities for unpaid expenses to be deducted by cash basis taxpayer in year in which it sold all its assets subject to its liabilities, stated that taxpayer effectively paid liabilities at time of sale by

of the taxpayer's obligation, the lender, in effect, has acted as a paying agent for the taxpayer.

In addition, the fact that the taxpayer's creditor is not paid by the third-party lender until some later time should not deny the taxpayer's deduction, assuming the taxpayer's creditor has accepted the third-party lender's obligation to pay as satisfaction of the taxpayer's debt. In other words, if a taxpayer who is liable to a creditor can satisfy that liability by delivering to the creditor (or causing to be delivered to the creditor) the obligation of a third party to make payment, payment will be deemed to have been made at that time by the taxpayer.[128]

[b] Payee

Where a payment has been made, the person to whom the payment is made (and the purpose of the payment) must be considered before a deduction is permitted. Questions may be raised whether the payment was (1) made to the creditor; (2) intended to satisfy the liability giving rise to the expense; or (3) intended for some other purpose.

To illustrate, generally a taxpayer may not deduct a transfer of funds to his agent because that transfer is not a completed payment for tax purposes. Thus, if a taxpayer incurs a liability for property taxes and makes payments to the mortgagee who is to transfer the funds at some later time to the taxing authority, payment of the taxes would not normally occur until the mortgagee has actually paid over the funds.

A transfer of property as security for a debt or to guarantee collection of the debt also does not amount to payment. Assuming the item in question is deductible, the deduction is appropriate in the year the property is taken (or accepted) by the creditor in satisfaction of all or part of the debt.[129]

The fact that the taxpayer pays under protest or contests the liability

---

accepting less cash for its assets in consideration of purchaser's assumption of liabilities. The applicability of this conclusion is questionable in most circumstances because, absent a novation, the original debtor continues to remain liable even after the assumption. In Priv. Ltr. Rul. 8804056 (Nov. 4, 1987), the IRS recognized that with regard to an accrual method taxpayer, the expenses of one entity within a controlled group can be paid by another entity within that same controlled group and allocated back to the first entity, the first entity being treated as incurring the liability even though all payments to its creditors were made by the second entity. But see Rev. Rul. 78-30, 1978-1 CB 133, which makes it clear that no deduction will be permitted where, in substance, the loan is not a liability of the taxpayer. See discussion infra ¶ 3.06[3].

[128] See Rev. Rul. 78-38, 1978-1 CB 67, and Rev. Rul. 78-39, 1978-1 CB 73, allowing deductions at the time a credit card was used to pay a party unrelated to the issuer of the card.

[129] Richard D. Lord, 29 TCM 653 (1970).

after payment does not preclude deduction.[130] However, a deduction will not be permitted where the payment is not accepted.[131]

[4] Payment by Taxpayer's Check or Note

[a] Checks

It has long been accepted that a check constitutes payment at the time of delivery (e.g., at the time of mailing) even though the check will not be received or deposited by the payee or otherwise presented to the maker's bank for payment until some later time.[132] In addition, it is irrelevant that the maker can (1) stop payment of the check; (2) issue the check at a time when there are insufficient funds in the account; or (3) withdraw funds that are available at the time the check is written and divert them to a different use. As long as the check is paid in the normal course after presentation by the recipient, the deduction will be permitted.[133]

On the other hand, if the check is not honored when presented to the bank for payment, the question arises as to whether the deduction should be permitted. It appears that the correct result should depend on the circumstances and that no blanket general rule should be applied. If conditions are imposed on the payee on or before the time of delivery (or if agreements or other arrangements are made, any or all of which are designed to delay the consummation of the payment until some time in the future), a present deduction should be denied.[134]

The important issue is whether the check was intended as an immediate payment and was so honored or whether the check was intended as evidence of an obligation to make payment at some point in the future. In the former case, the deduction should be allowed. In the latter case, the deduction should be denied. These rules are consistent with the practical business need for permitting cash basis taxpayers to claim deductions in the year in which the check is delivered (i.e., mailed) just as if the check were cash. Otherwise,

---

[130] Compare United States v. Consolidated Edison Co. of N.Y., Inc., 366 US 380 (1961), where an accrual method taxpayer was not entitled to deduction for taxes paid under protest.

[131] Joseph C. Weber, 70 TC 52 (1978).

[132] Modie J. Spiegel Estate, 12 TC 524 (1949), acq. 1949-2 CB 3; Estate of Witt v. Fahs, 160 F. Supp. 521 (SD Fla. 1956); Rev. Rul. 73-99, 1973-1 CB 412.

[133] Gabriel Field, 15 TCM 631 (1956); Modie J. Spiegel Estate, 12 TC 524 (1949), acq. 1949-2 CB 3; Comm'r v. Bradley, 56 F2d 728 (6th Cir. 1932).

[134] See, e.g., L.M. Fischer, 14 TC 792 (1950), acq. 1950-2 CB 2, where payee agreed not to cash check until subsequent year; Hubbell's Estate, 10 TC 1207 (1948), where check was not intended as absolute payment but rather as conditional payment; Brooks Griffin, 49 TC 253 (1967), where check was postdated until the subsequent year.

significant hardships would be imposed on cash method taxpayers in the conduct of their business transactions.

[b] Notes or Other Evidences of Taxpayer's Indebtedness

The issuance of a note by a cash basis taxpayer has long been treated as no more than an acknowledgment by the taxpayer that his debt must be "paid" at some later time. The issuance of the note does not occasion a deduction.[135] This is the rule even though the note (1) is negotiable; (2) is secured by adequate collateral; or (3) is includable in the income of a cash basis payee. It is irrelevant that the taxpayer could have obtained funds from a third-party lender (through the issuance of a similar note) and then have used those funds to pay the obligation and thereby obtain the deduction.[136]

The taxpayer may not avoid the treatment afforded notes by going through the form of obtaining funds from its creditor and then using those funds to make payment to that very creditor. In that case, the general rule is that no deduction is allowed.[137] The disallowance is premised on the fact that, in substance, all that has happened is that the taxpayer has acknowledged a larger indebtedness to its lender. It is usually the case that the taxpayer does not have unrestricted use or control over the funds that were obtained from the lender and used to make the payment in question. Where this is not the case, deduction may be appropriate. For example, if the taxpayer has unrestricted control over newly borrowed funds and, by exercise of its own volition, decides to use those funds to pay a liability to the same creditor, the reason for denying the deduction (i.e., lack of control) is not present. To illustrate, if a taxpayer has a bank line of credit that may be used in any manner in which the taxpayer sees fit and if the taxpayer uses that line of credit to pay interest incurred to that bank on a different, independent loan, there may be no justification for denying the deduction. However, until such a conclusion is reached by the IRS or the courts, prudence would suggest that the payment be made with other funds.

[5] Particular Items of Expense

Assuming (1) the item paid is a deductible expense and (2) the payment does not result in the creation of an asset having a useful life substantially beyond

---

[135] Helvering v. Price, 309 US 409 (1940); Eckert v. Burnet, 283 US 140 (1931); John B. Howard, 36 TCM 1140 (1977); Rev. Rul. 77-257, 1977-2 CB 174.

[136] See, e.g., Rev. Rul. 76-135, 1976-1 CB 114.

[137] Battelstein v. IRS, 631 F2d 1182 (5th Cir. 1980), cert. denied, 451 US 938 (1981); Alan A. Rubnitz, 67 TC 621 (1977); William M. Roberts, 53 TCM 787 (1987).

the close of the year of payment, a deduction is generally permitted in the year of actual payment.[138]

[a] Interest

Except as otherwise provided by Code section or Treasury regulation,[139] a cash basis taxpayer may deduct interest only in the year of actual payment.[140] As a general rule, the agreement of the parties controls as to the time when interest is due and payable and, if paid, deductible.[141] In the absence of an agreement or a law to the contrary, partial payments are allocable first to interest and thereafter to principal.[142]

Interest may be paid by cash, by other property, or by rendering services.[143] Interest due from a taxpayer may also be paid by offset of a taxpayer's overpayment of tax or by refund of tax due to the taxpayer. In such a case, the interest due from the taxpayer is deemed paid in the year in which the IRS applies the credit, refund, or offset to the interest that is due.[144] The taxpayer may designate that his payment is intended as a payment of interest assertedly due, and his designation will be respected.[145] However, a cash basis taxpayer cannot obtain a deduction (i.e., is deemed not to make payment) by issuing its own note (or other obligation to pay) even though the obligation is adequately secured.[146] Similarly, increasing the principal balance of an existing obligation by the amount of interest owed does not provide a deduction,[147] nor does withholding interest from the proceeds of the loan (the borrower receiving less than the principal amount).[148] In addition, actual payments in cash will be scrutinized to determine (1) whether the cash came

---

[138] See infra ¶ 3.05[1][b] regarding the question of whether assets have a useful life extending substantially beyond the close of the year of payment.

[139] See, e.g., IRC §§ 483, 467, 1272–1274, and the regulations thereunder.

[140] James W. England, Jr., 34 TC 617 (1960).

[141] Rev. Rul. 63-57, 1963-1 CB 103.

[142] Story v. Livingston, 38 US 359 (1839).

[143] If paid by property or services, the taxpayer may realize income on the transaction to the extent of the difference between the interest paid and the taxpayer's basis in the property, or to the extent of the FMV of the services. See supra ¶ 3.04[3].

[144] See, e.g., Saverio Eboli, 93 TC 123 (1989).

[145] See James W. Perkins, 92 TC 749 (1989), where a cash basis taxpayer was permitted a deduction for interest paid where, in response to a notice of deficiency, the taxpayer forwarded a check to the Commissioner with the designation that the remittance be credited to interest that had theretofor accrued on a previously asserted deficiency.

[146] Helvering v. Price, 309 US 409 (1940).

[147] James W. England, Jr., 34 TC 617 (1960); Rev. Rul. 70-647, 1970-2 CB 38.

[148] Cleaver v. Comm'r, 158 F2d 342 (7th Cir. 1946), cert. denied, 330 US 849 (1947); Robert E. Stewart, 41 TCM 318 (1980).

from the taxpayer's own property or property obtained from someone other than the creditor and (2) whether the cash was otherwise subject to the taxpayer's control. If, in fact, the cash was made available by the creditor so that the taxpayer could then pay the creditor to obtain a tax deduction, the deduction will be denied.[149]

In addition to the foregoing, prepayments of interest may not be deductible by a cash basis taxpayer in the year of actual payment. Section 461(g) provides that interest, which is paid by a cash method taxpayer and properly allocable to a period after the close of the taxable year in which paid, is deductible only in the period to which it is allocable. This is the case even where the prepaid interest is not refundable.[150] This is also the case whether the interest is incurred under a loan or in connection with an installment sale of property (i.e., a so-called time-price differential).[151]

However, an exception is provided in the case of points paid with respect to an indebtedness (1) that is incurred in connection with the purchase or improvement of a principal residence of the taxpayer and (2) that is secured by the principal residence, as long as the payment of points is an established business practice in the area in which the indebtedness occurred.[152] Of course, factual issues may arise over whether there has been an actual payment of points and whether the loan was incurred in connection with the purchase or the improvement of a principal residence.[153] In *James Richard Huntsman*,[154] the full Tax Court concluded that the exception

---

[149] See discussion supra ¶ 3.04[4][b].

[150] Joseph A. Zidanic, 79 TC 651 (1982).

[151] See, e.g., Beek v. Comm'r, 85-1 USTC ¶ 9236 (9th Cir. 1985).

[152] IRC § 461(g)(2).

[153] See, e.g., Rev. Rul. 70-540, 1970-2 CB 101, with respect to payment; Rev. Rul. 87-22, 1987 1 CB 146, with respect to the purpose of the loan, the IRS ruling that points incurred in the refinancing of a home mortgage did not qualify for immediate deduction. See also Rev. Proc. 87-15, 1987-1 CB 624, regarding the amount of points allocable to and deductible in years subsequent to the year of payment; Tech. Adv. Mem. 8707001 (June 30, 1986), for a recent application of Rev. Rul. 70-540; Bell Fed. Sav. & Loan Ass'n, 62 TCM 376 (1991), where the issue was whether an accrual method lender discounted points owed to it by borrowers, in which case the income associated with the points would be recognized ratably over the life of the loans, or received payment of the points in the year of the loan closing, in which case the full amount of the points would be recognized in income in that year. In reviewing the situation, the court noted that the transactions had been structured so that the borrowers could deduct the full amount of the points in the year of the loan closing. This fact influenced the court in finding that under the particular agreements between the lender and the borrower, there had been no discounting but, instead, full payment. The agreements did not require a discounting of the points from the proceeds of the loans, but instead required the borrowers to bring separate funds to the closing in amounts sufficient to pay the points.

[154] James Richard Huntsman, 91 TC 917 (1988), rev'd, 90-2 USTC ¶ 50,340 (8th Cir. 1990).

provided by Section 461(g)(2) is not available to points paid in connection with the refinancing of a principal residence. The court concluded that the exception must be construed narrowly. However, the Tax Court was reversed by the Court of Appeals for the Eighth Circuit, the appeals court noting that the language contained in the exception—the words "in connection with"— had been construed broadly when used in other code sections, and there was no indication that congress had intended for the use of that language in this section to have a different meaning.[155] Moreover, the court noted that the refinancing in question "was merely an integrated step in securing the permanent financing to purchase the home," the taxpayer having purchased the home with short-term interim financing that had to be replaced. Consequently, although the exception may hereafter be construed more broadly than in the past, taxpayers may be required to demonstrate that the refinancing was an integral part of the original purchase or improvement to the home. In order to minimize the potential for disputes regarding the application of Section 461(g)(2), the IRS has announced that it will treat as deductible points any amounts paid by a cash basis taxpayer during a taxable year in which the following requirements are satisfied:[156]

- The amounts in question must clearly be designated as points incurred in connection with the indebtedness, i.e., as loan origination fees, loan discount, discount points, points, or similar designations.

- The amounts must be computed as a percentage of the stated principal amount of the debt incurred by the taxpayer.

- The payments in question must result from charges under an established business practice of charging points for loans in the geographical area in which the residence is located, and the amount must not exceed the amount generally charged in that area. Moreover, the amounts designated as points must not be payments in lieu of amounts that are ordinarily stated separately on a settlement statement for such items as appraisal fees, inspection fees, title fees, attorney fees, property taxes, and mortgage insurance premiums.

- The amounts must be paid in connection with the acquisition of the taxpayer's principal residence, and the loan must be secured by the residence. However, the revenue procedure does not apply to points paid in connection with an acquisition to the extent the points are allocable to an amount of principal in excess of the aggregate amount treated as acquisition indebtedness under Section 163(h)(3)(B)(ii), points paid for loans to be used for improvement rather than for acquisition, points paid for loans to purchase a residence that is not the taxpayer's principal residence (e.g., a second home, vacation

---

[155] Huntsman v. Comm'r, 90-2 USTC ¶ 50,340 (8th Cir. 1990).
[156] Rev. Proc. 92-12, 1992-1 CB 663.

property, investment property, or trade or business property), and points paid on a refinancing of the loan, home equity loan, or line of credit, even though such loan is secured by the principal residence.[157]

- The points must be paid directly by the taxpayer from his own funds and not from funds that were themselves borrowed as part of the overall transaction. Such funds must at least equal the amount required to be applied as points at the closing. The amount provided may include down payments, escrow deposits, earnest money applied at a closing, and other funds actually paid over at the closing.

The revenue procedure is effective for points paid by cash basis taxpayers during taxable years beginning after December 31, 1990. Although the revenue procedure clarifies many points and is quite helpful in this regard, it remains to be seen whether it will be applied in a helpful manner by agents. For example, if the settlement documents do not specify the use of the particular down payment, will the agents treat the down payment as applicable to the payment of points, or will they instead treat the down payment as being paid directly to the seller with no payment of points to the lender? To obtain maximum protection, the provisions of applicable settlement agreements should be reviewed carefully to ensure consistency with the benefits provided under the revenue procedure.

To limit deductions for interest to the amount of interest economically accrued, the IRS has disallowed use of the Rule of 78's method of allocating payments between principal and interest (or of determining the amount of interest).[158] However, an exception has been provided for certain consumer installment loans of a duration of five years or less.[159] The full impact of these revenue rulings and their correctness are not yet known.[160] In *Don P. Setliff*,[161] the Tax Court upheld the Commissioner's disallowance of the Rule of 78's method of allocating interest and denied the deduction of accrued interest in excess of the amount that had accrued economically. However, the court made it clear that the facts did not support the actual use of the Rule of 78's, and the court expressly declined to determine what the result would have been if the parties had actually intended to follow the Rule of 78's. The court concluded that the use of the Rule of 78's in the case before it was merely a gimmick. Although the case involved the use of an accrual method, it sheds light on the willingness of the court to tax a transaction according to its substance and, therefore, suggests that the use of the Rule of 78's may not be an incorrect method of allocating interest in all cases. This point was

---

[157] But see Huntsman v. Comm'r, 90-2 USTC ¶ 50,340 (8th Cir. 1990).

[158] See supra ¶ 3.03[3][a].

[159] Id.

[160] See General Explanation of the Revenue Provisions of the Deficit Reduction Act of 1984, at 110.

[161] Don P. Setliff, 53 TCM 1295 (1987).

recognized in *Mulholland v. United States*,[162] where the court denied the government's motion for summary judgment and indicated that genuine issues of fact existed regarding whether use of the Rule of 78's method clearly reflected income. Nevertheless, in two other cases, *Bruce A. Prabel*,[163] and *Allen J. Levy*,[164] the court made it clear that where the use of the Rule of 78's method provides deductions for accrual method taxpayers materially in excess of both the amount that otherwise would be accrued on an economic accrual basis and the amount actually paid, the Commissioner has the discretion to deny the excessive deductions determined under the Rule of 78's method.[165]

[b] Insurance Premiums

Generally, insurance premiums are deductible in the year paid even though some portion of the payment might be refunded in the future.[166] However, if the amount paid covers premiums not only for the current year but also for subsequent years, the deduction attributable to the subsequent years may be deferred until such years. The cases vary on this issue.[167] The IRS takes the position that only the pro rata portion of a premium applicable to more than one taxable year is deductible in the year of payment.[168]

[c] Taxes

Taxes are generally deductible when paid without regard to whether the taxes are attributable (1) to an earlier or later year or (2) to the year in which the return is actually filed.[169] However, no deduction is allowed unless the tax is determinable as to amount and fact of assessment. Taxpayers are not permitted to pick arbitrary sums, pay them, and claim deductions.[170]

---

[162] Mulholland v. United States, 92-1 USTC ¶ 50,267 (Cl. Ct. 1992).

[163] Bruce A. Prabel, 91 TC 1101 (1988), aff'd, 882 F2d 820 (3d Cir. 1989).

[164] Allen J. Levy, 92 TC 1360 (1989).

[165] See discussion at ¶ 4.04[3][c].

[166] Rev. Rul. 83-66, 1983-1 CB 43.

[167] Compare Comm'r v. Boylston Market Ass'n, 131 F2d 966 (1st Cir. 1942), where the court approved proration of prepaid insurance premiums over the life of a three-year policy, with Waldheim Realty & Inv. Co. v. Comm'r, 245 F2d 823 (8th Cir. 1957), where deduction of multiyear prepaid insurance premium was allowed in year of payment, and Kauai Terminal, Ltd., 36 BTA 893 (1937), acq. 1939-2 CB 20, where deduction of one-year prepaid insurance premium was allowed in year of payment even though it covered two taxable years. See also Comm'r v. Lincoln Sav. & Loan Ass'n, 403 US 345 (1971).

[168] Rev. Rul. 70-413, 1970-2 CB 103.

[169] Lewis Mitchell, 45 TCM 1058 (1983); Rev. Rul. 71-190, 1971-1 CB 70.

[170] Edward Hagelin, 37 BTA 8 (1938); Rev. Rul. 82-208, 1982-2 CB 58.

To be deductible, the payment must be made to the appropriate taxing authority. Payment of funds to a taxpayer's agent does not entitle the taxpayer to a deduction. The deduction is denied until the funds are paid over to the proper authority.[171] Thus, a mortgagor who pays taxes to an escrow account maintained by the mortgagee is not entitled to a deduction until the mortgagee makes the payment.[172]

Special rules apply to real estate taxes. When real property is sold, the deduction for real estate taxes must be apportioned between the buyer and the seller based on the number of days that each owned the property and without regard (1) to the manner in which they actually apportioned the tax or (2) to their methods of tax accounting.[173] Examples are provided in the regulations.[174]

¶ 3.05 PREPAYMENTS

One of the most troublesome issues affecting use of the cash method is the payment and deduction of items prior to the time when the items accrue in an economic sense. In these cases, the taxpayer may be perceived as obtaining an early deduction through the mechanism of payment. Since the taxpayer may borrow the funds or other property with which to make the payment, the opportunities for significant tax reduction through the use of the cash method in this manner has long troubled the IRS and the courts. Nevertheless, as long as the cash method remains an authorized method, deductions for such prepayments are not inappropriate or incorrect per se.

[1] Basic Issues

Two issues generally arise in connection with prepayments. The first is the character of the payment. Was the payment intended as payment of the expense or was it intended as security, a mere deposit, or otherwise as something other than actual payment of the expense? The second issue is whether the payment resulted in the acquisition or creation of property (or property rights) having a useful life extending substantially beyond the close of the taxable year. In such a case, capitalization may be required. If it is, the initial deduction is limited to an appropriate portion of the total payment, with the balance deducted over time by way of depreciation or amortization.

---

[171] Fitzhugh L. Odom, 44 TCM 1132 (1982); George L. Schultz, 50 TC 688 (1968), aff'd, 420 F2d 490 (3d Cir. 1970).

[172] Hradesky v. Comm'r, 540 F2d 821 (5th Cir. 1976); Rev. Rul. 78-103, 1978-1 CB 58.

[173] See IRC § 164 and the regulations thereunder.

[174] Treas. Reg. § 1.164-6(d)(4).

[a] Character of Payment

As with items of income, the deduction of payments depends initially on the character or purpose of the payment. Was the payment made to satisfy the taxpayer's liability for an expense or was it made for some other purpose, such as a loan, or repayment of a loan, or a deposit? All too frequently, taxpayers and their advisors ignore or pay only scant attention to this very important issue of character.[175]

[b] Capitalization and the One-Year Rule

When long-lived assets, such as buildings and major pieces of equipment, are acquired, their cost is expensed pursuant to the various provisions for cost recovery, depreciation, or amortization. Issues that arise with respect to these assets are not unique to cash method taxpayers.

However, where payments are made for regularly recurring items of expense and these payments result in the creation of an asset having a life extending substantially beyond the year of payment, difficult questions arise, and there is a lack of symmetry in approach. On one hand, where expenses attributable to several periods are paid in the last period to which the expenses relate, deduction is allowed only in the year of payment. The IRS does not seek to accelerate the deduction to reflect income clearly. On the other hand, where the payment is made in the first of the several periods to which the expense relates, a deferral in the deduction of all or some portion of the expense may be required to reflect income clearly. In striking a balance between use of cash basis accounting and prevention of abuse, practical rules have evolved.

Except as otherwise specified by Code provision, Treasury regulation, or particular case, deduction of prepaid expenses is generally permitted where the period to which the payment relates covers a period of less than one year from the time of payment. This is known as the one-year rule and has been discussed in connection with many types of expenses.[176]

---

[175] See discussion at ¶ 12.03[3].

[176] See, e.g., Jack's Cookie Co. v. United States, 597 F2d 395, 405 (4th Cir. 1979), cert. denied, 444 US 899 (1979) (pertaining to rental payments, where the court stated, "The one-year rule is useful because it serves to segregate from all business costs those which cannot possibly be considered capital in nature because of their transitory utility to the taxpayer"); Bilar Tool & Die Corp. v. Comm'r, 530 F2d 708 (6th Cir. 1976) (attorney fees); Colorado Springs Nat'l Bank v. United States, 505 F2d 1185 (10th Cir. 1974) (costs incurred in participating in credit card system); Briarcliff Candy Corp. v. Comm'r, 475 F2d 775 (2d Cir. 1973) (costs of acquiring business entity); American Dispenser Co. v. Comm'r, 396 F2d 137 (2d Cir. 1968) (payments to competitor in exchange for covenant not to manufacture); Fall River Gas Appliance Co. v. Comm'r, 349 F2d 515 (1st Cir. 1965) (installation costs for leased gas appliances); United States v. Akin, 248 F2d 742 (10th Cir. 1957), cert.

Although commentators and the courts frequently refer to the one-year rule as if it were widely applicable, it has in fact not been applied to all expenses. The particular circumstances affecting each type of expense must be considered independently. For example, cash basis (and accrual basis) taxpayers may be able to deduct prepaid supplies under Treasury Regulation § 1.162-3 (or may have the deduction denied) without regard to the period over which the supplies may be consumed.[177] Prepaid interest (except for the payment of points in certain circumstances) may be deducted only in the period to which the interest relates.[178] The treatment of prepaid insurance has varied,[179] and taxes are deductible when paid even if it is ultimately determined that too much tax was paid for the year in question.[180]

One of the potentially more significant cases regarding the one-year rule is *Zaninovich v. Commissioner*,[181] in which the court approved the deduction of 11 months prepaid rent by a cash basis taxpayer. In considering the application of the one-year rule, the court made it clear that whatever approach is ultimately taken, that approach must be consistent with the inherent benefits and burdens of the cash method. The approach should be simple to apply and avoid unnecessary complexity in record keeping. It should also seek to strike the proper balance between accepting cash method principles and preventing abuse and distortion. The court emphasized, however, that the one-year rule is merely a guidepost and should not be regarded as rigid and automatic in every case.

Although there is significant support for the one-year rule, as illustrated by *Zaninovich*, the scope of the rule is still evolving. In *Hillsboro National Bank v. Commissioner*,[182] the Supreme Court indicated support for the *Zaninovich* formulation of the one-year rule, but the dissent recognized that the scope of that one-year rule is still being debated and has not been

---

denied, 355 US 956 (1958) (sums paid by farmers); Waldheim Realty & Inv. Co. v. Comm'r, 245 F2d 823 (8th Cir. 1957) (pertaining to insurance premiums). See also Section 263 and Treas. Reg. § 1.263(a)-(2)(a), which include within capital expenditures assets having a "useful life substantially beyond the taxable year."

[177] See discussion at ¶ 6.05[3].

[178] IRC § 461(g). The IRS applies this rule even where interest is allocated under the provisions of Section 483 as it existed prior to the 1986 Act. Tech. Adv. Mem. 8830002 (Apr. 18, 1988).

[179] Compare Waldheim Realty & Inv. Co. v. Comm'r, 245 F2d 823 (8th Cir. 1957), with Comm'r v. Lincoln Sav. & Loan Ass'n, 403 US 345 (1971), and Comm'r v. Boylston Market Ass'n, 131 F2d 966 (1st Cir. 1942).

[180] See Estate of Aaron Lowenstein, 12 TC 694 (1949), aff'd sub nom. First Nat'l Bank of Mobile v. Comm'r, 183 F2d 172 (5th Cir. 1950), cert. denied, 340 US 911 (1951), where taxes were paid in good faith belief that they were owing. But see Rev. Rul. 82-208, 1982-2 CB 58, where deduction of an overpayment was denied where there was no reasonable basis for concluding that additional tax was due.

[181] Zaninovich v. Comm'r, 616 F2d 429 (9th Cir. 1980).

[182] Hillsboro Nat'l Bank v. Comm'r 460 US 370 (1983).

endorsed by either the Commissioner or the Tax Court.[183] Thus, taxpayers should not blindly assume that all prepayments covering periods of one year or less will be permitted,[184] nor should accrual method taxpayers expect to receive the same flexibility as cash basis taxpayers on this issue.[185] Also, it should be noted that *Zaninovich* involved a prepayment that was required under the agreement and, arguably, may be read as applying the one-year rule only with respect to such prepayments.[186]

[2] Prepaid Expenses of Cash Basis Tax Shelters

[a] Section 461(i) Prior to 1986 Act

Under Section 448(a), enacted in 1986, the use of the cash method is denied to tax shelters.[187] Prior to the 1986 Act, the use of the cash method by tax shelters had been limited by Section 461(i),[188] which was enacted in 1984 and provided that a cash basis tax shelter would not be permitted a deduction unless the item in question had been paid and economic perfor-

---

[183] *Zaninovich* was followed by the Tax Court in Herschel H. Hoopengarner, 80 TC 538 (1983), but apparently only because the decision was appealable to the Ninth Circuit. Id. at 544. In Gordon S. Sorrell, 53 TCM 1362 (1987), the Tax Court refrained from applying (or even commenting on the application of) the one-year rule to the facts before it, merely noting that it was not required to adopt the one-year rule, because its decision was not appealable to the Ninth Circuit.

[184] Character of the payment and motive for the payment may also be important. See, e.g., Rev. Rul. 79-229, 1979-2 CB 210, pertaining to prepaid feed expenses.

[185] For example, the cost of merchandise inventories may not be deducted even though the asset may be disposed of shortly after the end of the year.

[186] See Harry W. Williamson, 37 TC 941 (1962); Bonaire Dev. Co. v. Comm'r, 679 F2d 159 (9th Cir. 1982).

[187] See discussion infra ¶ 3.06[1].

[188] Section 91(a) of the Tax Reform Act of 1984 (the 1984 Act). For purposes of Section 461(i), the term "tax shelter" was defined as (1) a partnership or other enterprise (other than a C corporation) in which interests were offered for sale, at any time, in an offering required to be registered with a federal or state agency; (2) a partnership or other enterprise (other than a corporation that is not an S corporation) where more than 35 percent of the losses during the taxable year were allocable to limited partners or limited entrepreneurs (generally investors who did not actively participate in the management of the enterprise); or (3) any partnership, entity, plan, or arrangement that was a tax shelter within the meaning of Section 6661(b)(2)(C)(iii) (i.e., the principal purpose of which was the avoidance or evasion of federal income tax). The General Explanation of the 1984 Act prepared by the Joint Committee on Taxation provided that with respect to farming activities, marketed arrangements in which individuals use the assistance of a common managerial or administrative service may be presumed under certain circumstances to have the principal purpose of tax avoidance. Id. at 280. The Explanation further indicated that such a presumption would generally apply when the taxpayer prepaid a substantial portion of his farming expense with borrowed funds. Id. at 281.

mance had occurred.[189] Thus, cash basis tax shelters would have to meet requirements pertaining to both accrual and cash basis taxpayers in order to deduct prepayments.

[b] The 90-Day Exception

Under Section 461(i), a cash basis tax shelter could deduct an item paid in the taxable year if economic performance with respect to that item occurred within 90 days after the close of that year.[190] However, neither the Code nor the applicable legislative history explained the proper treatment if economic performance commenced either within the year of the prepayment or within 90 days thereafter but was not completed within that period. Would the taxpayer be entitled to deduct the amount attributable to the economic performance that had occurred within the 90-day period, or would the deduction be deferred until the year in which economic performance was completed? Presumably, total or complete performance would not be required, but this raised questions as to how the amount of the prepayment was to be allocated.

[i] **Deduction limited to cash basis.** Even if the 90-day exception were applicable, the amount that could be deducted was limited to the taxpayer's cash basis in the tax shelter.[191] A partner's cash basis in the partnership was equal to his adjusted basis in the partnership, determined without regard to (1) the liabilities of the partnership and (2) any amount borrowed by the partner with respect to the partnership, but only if such borrowing was arranged by the partnership, the general partner, or the promoter, or was secured by assets of the partnership.[192]

[ii] **Drilling costs.** For purposes of determining whether economic performance had occurred within the 90-day exception with respect to the drilling of a well, complete economic performance would be treated as having occurred when drilling was commenced.[193] If drilling was commenced in the

---

[189] The time when economic performance occurs is governed by Section 461(h)(2). Hence, the issues that could arise in connection with the application of paragraph (h) were also likely to arise with respect to Section 461(i) as it existed prior to amendment by the 1986 Act.

[190] Section 461(i)(2), as it existed prior to amendment by the 1986 Act.

[191] Section 461(i)(2)(B), as it existed prior to amendment by 1986 Act. Section 461(i)(2)(B)(ii), as it existed prior to amendment by 1986 Act, authorized the Treasury to promulgate regulations similarly limiting the aggregate amount of deductions allowable to tax shelters other than a partnership. These tax shelters would include entities, plans, and arrangements under Section 6661(b)(2)(C)(ii).

[192] Section 461(i)(2)(C), as it existed prior to amendment by 1986 Act.

[193] Section 461(i)(2)(D), as it existed prior to amendment by 1986 Act.

taxable year of prepayment rather than within the 90-day period following the year of prepayment, the statute suggested that only that portion of the payment attributable to drilling costs prior to the end of the year (and incurred during the first 90 days of the following year) would be deductible in the year of payment.

¶ 3.06 AVAILABILITY OF CASH METHOD

Prior to the 1986 Act, there were virtually no conditions or restrictions on the adoption and use of the cash method. Assuming that the taxpayer satisfied the book conformity requirement of Section 446(a),[194] the method was available to all taxpayers and without regard to the size of their business. However, there were particular transactions for which the cash method could not be used and particular circumstances under which use of the method was prohibited. In 1986, following years of IRS frustration caused by its inability to deny use of the cash method to taxpayers conducting large businesses,[195] the IRS succeeded in having Congress enact as part of the 1986 Act various limitations on the use of the cash method based on the size and character of the taxpayer. These limitations as well as the transactions and circumstances for which the cash method has always been denied are described in the following sections.

Many taxpayers believed the enactment of Section 448 would eliminate issues affecting their use of the cash method in years prior to the effective date of that section. However, this has not been the case. The temporary regulations issued under Section 448 made it clear that examining agents could question on audit the propriety of a taxpayer's use of the cash method in both post and pre 1986 Act years,[196] and agents have been doing so.[197] In

---

[194] See discussion at ¶ 2.02[1].

[195] See discussion infra ¶ 3.08[7].

[196] Temp. Reg. § 1.448-1T(c) provides that nothing in Section 448 shall have any effect on the application of other provisions of law, which otherwise might limit use of the cash method, and no inference is to be drawn from Section 448 with respect to the application of such other provisions.

[197] See Tech. Adv. Mem. 8939003 (June 20, 1989), where the National Office concluded that a taxpayer's use of the cash method could be evaluated for years prior to the effective date of Section 448 to determine whether its use clearly reflected income, but the National Office did not conclude whether that particular taxpayer's use of the cash method clearly reflected income. See also Tech. Adv. Mem. 9113001 (July 25, 1990), where the National Office concluded that the taxpayer's use of the cash method in years prior to the effective date of Section 448 could be challenged even though the taxpayer had already changed to an accrual method pursuant to Section 448. Moreover, the National Office stated that the procedures and relief pro-

addition, agents have sometimes concluded that the operation of Revenue Procedure 84-74 to proposed changes from the cash method in pre–1986 Act years would not produce a deficiency, because the applicable year of change would be delayed to the first 1986 Act year; the very year in which the change had already been made by the taxpayer. In those cases, agents have sought to get around this result by breaking down the taxpayer's overall cash method into component methods (e.g., the taxpayer's method of deducting some or all expenses) and then proposing a change in the treatment of only those expenses that when viewed in isolation, would not be eligible for the delay in the year of change provided by Revenue Procedure 84-74. Such an approach is arbitrary, seemingly inconsistent with the principles of Revenue Procedure 92-20,[198] and should not be sustained.

On the other hand, it would seem illogical for certain challenges to the use of the cash method during pre–1986 Act years to be continued. For example, it would seem to make no sense to deny use of the cash method in prior years on the basis of the level of the taxpayer's revenues and resulting deferral in the recognition of income as compared to an accrual method. If the mere level of these revenues and resulting deferrals could have caused the cash method not to reflect income clearly, there would have been no need for, or effect of, the gross receipts limitation of Section 448.[199] Similarly, there would seem to be no need to challenge use of the cash method for particular reasons if such reasons would have the effect of denying all taxpayers use of the cash method. Such reasons would include that the cash method produces a result that differs from the result produced under an accrual method, the cash method fails to conform to GAAP, and the cash method is not used for financial reporting purposes. Yet, challenges to the cash method based on such reasons continue. In effect, agents have taken the position that the congressional denial of the cash basis to C corporations with a specified level of revenues, which is to be effective prospectively, is in reality nothing more than a confirmation of prior law even though the congressional enactment would not have been necessary if that had been the case.[200]

---

visions of Rev. Proc. 84-74, 1984-2 CB 736, did not apply to changes in methods of accounting pursuant to Section 448, but only to changes made pursuant to Section 446. See ¶ 8.06[6] for discussion of present rules governing changes pursuant to Section 448.

[198] Rev. Proc. 92-20, 1992-1 CB 685, § 10.12.

[199] See discussion infra ¶ 3.08[1].

[200] See ¶ 2.02[2] for a discussion of cases recognizing the importance of subsequent legislation in determining whether a method of accounting clearly reflects income.

[1] Limitations Under the 1986 Act

Under Section 448, which was enacted as part of the 1986 Act, the cash method is denied to the following three entities:[201]

1. C corporations (other than farming businesses and qualified personal service corporations) with average annual gross receipts of more than $5 million[202]
2. Partnerships (other than farming businesses) that have (1) a C corporation (other than a qualified personal service corporation) as a partner and (2) average annual gross receipts of more than $5 million
3. Tax shelters[203]

As this list makes clear, use of the cash method is not per se improper or unavailable because of the level of the taxpayer's revenues. C corporations that are qualified personal service corporations, S corporations, and partnerships (whose partners do not include an entity not permitted to use the cash method) may use the cash method without regard to the level of their revenues. Simply put, Congress decided not to deny their use of the cash method for this reason. Consequently, where agents seek to disallow use of the cash basis for failing to reflect income clearly, the agent's reasons for so concluding should be based on factors other than the level of the taxpayer's revenues or factors necessarily attributable to the level of those revenues.

[a] Gross Receipts Test

For purposes of applying these limitations, a C corporation or a partnership does not violate the gross receipts test if its average annual gross receipts for the three-taxable-year period ending with the year prior to the taxable year does not exceed $5 million.[204] In applying this test, gross receipts for any particular year are reduced by returns and allowances of that year.[205] In addition, the National Office has concluded that amounts received by a

---

[201] IRC §§ 448(a), 448(b). See Temp. Reg. § 1.448-1T.

[202] For this purpose, a trust subject to tax under Section 511(b) is treated as a C corporation with respect to its unrelated trade or business activities. IRC § 448(d)(6).

[203] For this purpose the term "tax shelters" is defined by the same meaning it has under Section 461(c)(3). See also Temp. Reg. § 1.448-1T(b). In Priv. Ltr. Rul. 8837068 (June 22, 1988), the National Office concluded that "partnership" was a tax shelter required to use an accrual method of accounting, because interests of the partnership had been offered for sale in an offering required to be registered with a federal or state agency. Had the interests not been offered for sale, the tax shelter rule would not have applied. See Priv. Ltr. Rul. 8753032 (Oct. 5, 1987).

[204] IRC § 448(c)(1). See Temp. Reg. § 1.448-1T(f).

[205] IRC § 448(c)(3)(C).

taxpayer as agent for others are not included in the taxpayer's gross receipts.[206]

Aggregation rules are provided to prevent this limitation from being circumvented by dividing a single entity into several related entities. Towards this end, all corporations or partnerships that are treated as a single employer under paragraph (a) or paragraph (b) of Section 52 (pertaining to computation of the targeted jobs credit) or Section 414(m) or Section 414(o) (pertaining to employees of members of affiliated groups) are treated as a single taxpayer.[207]

In addition, if an entity was not in existence for all years within the applicable three-year period, then the shorter period of actual existence will be used.[208] Gross receipts for a prior taxable year of less than 12 months must be annualized by multiplying gross receipts for the short period by a fraction, the numerator of which is 12 and the denominator of which is the number of months in the short period.[209] For example, if a taxpayer's first applicable year consisted of only three months during which gross receipts aggregated $800,000, annualized gross receipts would be $3,200,000 ($800,000 x $12/3$). The IRS National Office has concluded that the annualization rule must be applied to a short period even though the rule's application may distort annual income and thereby prevent the taxpayer from satisfying the gross receipts test.[210]

The $5 million gross receipts test is likely to affect the business decisions of many corporations and partnerships. Entities approaching the $5 million threshold may seek to delay receipts (or arrange the timing of receipts) to avoid exceeding that threshold. Others that fail to monitor their receipts on an ongoing basis run the risk that an otherwise inconsequential transaction may push them above the threshold and, consequently, cause them to lose their use of the cash method.

The taxpayer may not return to the cash method, once lost by reason of the $5 million limitation, without the prior approval of the IRS, even if the taxpayer's average gross receipts decline below the $5 million level. Thus, businesses may find that it is not in their best interest to grow, unless they are confident that the benefits of that growth will outweigh the disadvantages of losing the continued use of the cash method.

Similarly, cash method partnerships with average gross receipts in excess of $5 million must be careful to exclude C corporations as partners. Cash method partnerships with average gross receipts of $5 million or less should consider provisions in the partnership agreement that will allow them to

---

[206] Priv. Ltr. Rul. 8746013 (Aug. 13, 1987).

[207] IRC § 448(c)(2); Temp. Reg. § 1.448-1T(f)(2)(ii).

[208] Temp. Reg. § 1.448-1T(f)(2)(i).

[209] Temp. Reg. § 1.448-1T(f)(2)(iii).

[210] See Priv. Ltr. Rul. 8820058 (Feb. 22, 1988).

remove C corporations as partners if the partnership appears likely to exceed the gross receipts limitation.

Cash method C corporations that appear likely to exceed the $5 million threshold should consider election of S corporation status. S corporations are permitted to continue use of the cash method regardless of the amounts of their gross receipts. Similarly, partnerships without C corporations as partners are permitted to use the cash method regardless of the amounts of their gross receipts.

[b] Qualified Personal Service Corporations

The limitations do not apply to "qualified personal service corporations."[211] These corporations are defined as including any corporation that satisfies two tests. The first test relates to the particular activity of the corporation. The second test relates to the ownership of the corporation.

[i] Permitted activities: function test. For a corporation to be a qualified personal service corporation, substantially all its activities must involve the performance of services in the fields of health, law, engineering, architecture, accounting, actuarial science, performing arts, or consulting.[212] Although it seems illogical to exclude other service-oriented businesses, apparently such businesses are excluded. Excluded businesses include those involved in providing plumbing, electric, construction, real estate, and insurance services. Thus, any of these businesses whose gross receipts exceed the $5 million threshold will be unable to use the cash method, unless they can be found to be engaged in the activity of consulting.

The temporary regulations provide a number of explanatory rules and procedures. For example, they provide that "substantially all" the corporation's activities means that 95 percent or more of the time spent by the corporation's employees must be devoted to services in a qualifying field. For this purpose, qualifying services include the supervision of employees who engage directly in the provision of the qualifying services, the performance of related administrative and support services, and the rendition of other services incident to the actual performance of services in the qualifying field.[213]

The temporary regulations also provide guidance as to what types of activities will be considered within a particular qualifying field. For instance, they specify that the performance of services in the field of health means the provision of medical services by physicians, nurses, dentists, and similar health care professionals but does not include services not directly related to the medical field even though such services might purportedly relate to the

---

[211] IRC § 448(b)(2).

[212] IRC § 448(d)(2)(A).

[213] Temp. Reg. § 1.448-1T(e)(4)(i).

health of the recipient of the services. Examples of the latter type of service include the operation of health clubs, spas, or other businesses that provide physical exercise or conditioning to customers.[214] An example of the former type of service includes the services rendered by veterinarians.[215]

The temporary regulations provide that "performance of services in the field of performing arts" means the provision of services by actors, actresses, singers, musicians, entertainers, and similar artists in their capacity as an artist but does not include services by persons who themselves are not performing artists.[216] This latter category includes those who manage or promote such artists and those who are in a trade or business that relates to the performing arts. In addition, the performance of services in the performing arts does not include services rendered by persons who broadcast or otherwise disseminate performances of artists to members of the public (e.g., employees of a radio or a television station), nor does it include services provided by athletes.[217]

The temporary regulations also discuss the meaning of services performed in the field of consulting.[218] The regulations specify that the performance of services in the consulting field means the provision of advice and counsel, but not the performance of services in addition to advice and counsel, such as typical brokerage services or economically similar services. Generally, the line drawn by the temporary regulations is the manner of compensation to the provider of the asserted services. If the provider of the services is compensated without regard to whether a sale or purchase occurs or to whether a similar transaction is closed, the provider may be within the field of providing advice and counsel. However, to the extent that the asserted provider of services is compensated only if a purchase, sale, or similar transaction occurs, the service will not be considered within the scope of the consulting field.[219] For example, the performance of services in the consulting field includes the services of those who provide economic analyses and forecasts of business prospects to clients and those whose services consist of determining a client's electronic data processing needs and making recommendations about them. However, consulting services do not include making recommendations to a client regarding the design and implementation of data processing systems if the taxpayer's compensation for this service is based on equipment orders made by the clients. In other words, if the services are

---

[214] Temp. Reg. § 1.448-1T(e)(4)(ii).

[215] Rev. Rul. 91-30, 1991-1 CB 61.

[216] Temp. Reg. § 1.448-1T(e)(4)(iii).

[217] Id.

[218] Temp. Reg. § 1.448-1T(e)(4)(iv).

[219] Temp. Reg. § 1.448-1T(e)(4)(iv)(A).

incidental to the making of sales, the services will not be deemed within the consulting field.[220]

[ii] Ownership test.   The second test for status as a qualified personal service corporation is that substantially all the corporation's stock must be held directly or indirectly by (1) employees who perform the specified services; (2) retired employees who had performed such services in the past; (3) the estate of such an individual; or (4) any other person who acquired his stock by reason of the death of a current or retired employee, but this permitted ownership lasts only for a period of two years beginning on the date of the death of such individual.[221] The temporary regulations specify that for purposes of the ownership test, substantially all the stock is considered owned by the qualifying persons only if the amount held is 95 percent or more of the value of all such stock.[222] These regulations also make it clear that a person is not considered an employee of a corporation unless the services performed for the corporation are more than de minimis services.[223] Thus, the ownership test cannot be satisfied by having an owner perform only minor services.

For the purpose of applying these rules, community property laws are disregarded.[224] In addition, stock held by a Section 401(a) plan that is exempt from tax under Section 501(a) is treated as held by an employee who performs the requisite services.[225] Finally, at the election of the common parent of an affiliated group, all members of the group may be treated as one taxpayer if substantially all the activities of the members involve the performance of services in the same field of activity.[226] The temporary regulations contain numerous examples of how these principles are to be applied.[227]

[c] Farming Business

The new limitations on use of the cash method are not applicable to a farming business.[228] For this purpose, the term "farming business" is defined as including the trade or business of (1) farming; (2) operating a nursery or

---

[220] See Temp. Reg. § 1.448-1T(e)(4)(iv)(B) for these and numerous other examples.

[221] IRC § 448(d)(2)(B).

[222] Temp. Reg. § 1.448-1T(e)(5).

[223] Temp. Reg. § 1.448-1T(e)(5)(ii).

[224] Temp. Reg. § 1.448-1T(e)(5)(iv).

[225] Temp. Reg. § 1.448-1T(e)(5)(v).

[226] Temp. Reg. § 1.448-1T(e)(5)(vi).

[227] Temp. Reg. § 1.448-1T(e)(5)(vii).

[228] A farming business that uses the cash method of accounting for purchases and sales of livestock may not, for purposes of Treas. Reg. § 1.61-4(a), determine the cost of livestock as if the business used an inventory method. Rev. Rul. 88-60, 1988-2

subfarm; or (3) raising or harvesting trees bearing fruit, nuts, or other crops, or ornamental trees under Section 263A(e)(4).[229] In addition, the term includes the raising, harvesting, or growing of trees to which IRC 263A(e)(5) applies.[230]

[d] Effective Date and Required Change From Cash Method

The limitations provided by Section 448 are applicable to tax years beginning after December 31, 1986.[231] Section 448(d)(7) provides that if any taxpayer is required under the new limitations to change its method of accounting, such change will be treated as a change initiated by the taxpayer with the consent of the Secretary. In general, the required adjustment under Section 481 may be taken into account over a period of up to four years in accordance with the principles of Revenue Procedure 84-74.[232] However, hospitals are required to take the adjustment into account over a fixed period of 10 years without regard to the principles of Revenue Procedure 84-74.

In addition to the foregoing general rule, three special transition rules are provided.[233] One is for the benefit of a taxpayer engaged in the performance of engineering services. This rule expressly permits the taxpayer to continue its use of the cash method. It is doubtful that this rule will benefit any other taxpayer.

The other two transition rules provide means by which the full application of the new limitations can be delayed. The first rule allows taxpayers to elect not to have the new rules apply to transactions with related parties that accrued on or before September 25, 1985. The second rule specifies that the new rules do not apply to contracts for the acquisition or transfer of real property (or for services related to the acquisition or development of real property), but apply only if such contracts were entered into on or before September 25, 1985, and the sole element of the contract not performed as of that date was payment.

CB 30. This ruling is a designated ruling under Section 5.12.2 of Rev. Proc. 84-74, 1984-2 CB 736. Designated rulings are discussed at ¶ 8.04[4][b][iv].

[229] IRC § 448(d)(1). See Tech. Adv. Mem. 9009003 (Nov. 8, 1989) for an illustration of circumstances in which the IRS would approve a taxpayer's use of the cash method of accounting (because its activities constituted farming activities), but the IRS cautioned against interpreting its conclusion to mean that all farmers who used the cash method before the enactment of Section 448 would be allowed to continue use of that method in the future.

[230] IRC § 448(d)(1)(B).

[231] 1986 Act, § 801(a).

[232] Rev. Rul. 84-74, 1984-2 CB 736. See discussion at ¶ 8.06[2].

[233] 1986 Act, § 801(d)(2)–801(d)(4).

[2] Transactions Involving Merchandise

Applicable regulations prohibit use of the cash method in accounting for purchases and sales of merchandise where such purchases and sales constitute a material income-producing factor.[234] The reason for this requirement is relatively simple. Gross income under Section 61 includes income from whatever source derived, including gain from the sale of property. To determine that gain, the amounts realized on the sale must be matched with the basis of the property sold. Where taxpayers acquire items of property that are not held for sale in the ordinary course of business (i.e., not merchandise under Section 471), it is relatively easy to maintain records permitting basis to be matched against amounts realized on the sale (because there are relatively few such transactions) and use of the cash method is permitted.

However, where taxpayers maintain inventories for sale in the ordinary course of business (and, as a consequence, adopt an assumption as to the flow of costs, such as first-in, first-out (FIFO) or last-in, first-out (LIFO)), the use of the cash method is not appropriate for two reasons. First, if deductions were permitted as payments were made for merchandise and if income were recognized as payments were received, such reporting would amount to (1) the deduction of the basis of nondepreciable assets prior to sale and (2) the inclusion in taxable income of gross sales prices rather than gain from the sale. Neither the deduction nor the inclusion would be appropriate. Second, in order to tax only gain from the sale, it would be necessary for a cash method taxpayer to maintain even more detailed records than are necessary under an accrual method. Thus, it is often neither practical nor convenient to use the cash method.[235]

On the other hand, when the taxpayer's inventories are of supplies only, use of the cash method is permitted. These items are not inventories under Section 471.[236] They are not held for sale in the ordinary course of business. Thus, there is no potential mismatching of sales price with basis, and the inherent reason for the requirement of accrual method reporting is not present.[237]

The courts have sometimes held that where the inventories in question

---

[234] Treas. Reg. § 1.446-1(c)(2)(i).

[235] For example, it might be possible for a cash basis taxpayer to accumulate payments for merchandise in an inventory account and then to offset amounts in that account against sales proceeds, thereby achieving the requisite matching. This approach was permitted, in effect, under the installment method, as it existed prior to the 1987 Act. See Section 453A, as in effect before the 1987 Act, and discussion at ¶ 5.04.

[236] See Treas. Reg. § 1.162-3.

[237] Although the installment method permitted a cash-flow concept in the recognition of income from installment sales of inventory prior to the 1987 Act, the gross profit percentage that was used to determine the amount of installment income

are insignificant, use of the cash method will not be denied.[238] However, it is often difficult for a taxpayer to convince the IRS that inventories, which are held for sale in the ordinary course of business, are so insignificant that use of the cash method should be acceptable. Most courts, although recognizing that services may be the major element of the taxpayer's business, prohibit use of the cash method in connection with such sales unless the taxpayer's records are sufficient to demonstrate clearly what portion of the sale price is attributable to the item sold and what portion is attributable to the service rendered.[239] In the absence of those records, the taxpayer may only hope that the IRS will apply its discretion to permit use of the cash method.[240]

On the other hand, if the taxpayer can demonstrate that the results achieved under its use of the cash method are virtually identical to the results that would have been achieved under an accrual method, the IRS and the courts may permit use of the cash method to continue.[241] Although no court has squarely held that a taxpayer would have the right to use the cash method with inventories in such circumstances, the courts have implied that it might be an abuse of discretion for the Commissioner to change a taxpayer from use of the cash method to an accrual method where there would be virtually no difference in results produced. Of course, this acceptance of the cash method may only be of limited significance to taxpayers in that such acceptance may be short-lived. Once a material difference in results arises, a change to an accrual method may be required.

The IRS and taxpayers frequently fail to recognize that use of an accrual method is required only with respect to purchases and sales of merchandise.[242] Hybrid methods of accounting are permitted. The regulations expressly permit use of an accrual method in accounting for the purchases and sales of a business and the cash method in accounting for all other items of

---

arising from installment sales was a percentage that appropriately took into account and matched sales price with the cost of the items sold (see Chapter 5).

[238] See, e.g., Michael Drazen, 34 TC 1070, 1079 (1960), stating that "the mere presence of inventory does not necessarily mean that the cash method did not correctly reflect income"; Ezo Prods. Co., 37 TC 385, 392 (1961), where, although requiring accrual method, the court stated: "In a number of cases we have recognized as petitioner argues that where inventories are so small as to be of no consequence or consist primarily of labor, the presence of inventories is not necessarily sufficient to require a change in petitioner's method of accounting."

[239] See Applied Communications, Inc., 57 TCM 1473 (1989), where the Tax Court upheld the Commissioner's rejection of the taxpayer's use of the cash method, noting among other things that the taxpayer's business had changed from a service-oriented business to a product-oriented business.

[240] For discussion of IRS discretion, see ¶ 2.04.

[241] See discussion of virtual identity test at ¶ 2.02[2][f].

[242] Treas. Reg. § 1.446-1(c)(2)(i).

income and expense of that same business.[243] Other regulations provide for the use of an accrual method for a taxpayer's manufacturing or merchandising business and use of the cash method for its service business.[244] Thus, use of the cash method in connection with purchases and sales of merchandise should be denied only with respect to those purchases and sales. It is neither necessary nor appropriate for the IRS to propose a termination of the cash method for the taxpayer's entire business or for that portion of its business that consists of the rendition of services. To the extent that it is not possible to delineate the service and sale activities, a record-keeping problem may arise, and it may be within the discretion of the IRS to terminate the use of the cash method for the entire business rather than to accept or make arbitrary judgments about what portion of the total charge for the transaction is for goods and what portion is for services.[245] However, it may be a relatively easy matter for many taxpayers to generate the records necessary to segregate the inventory aspects of the business from the service elements of the business. If this is done, the cash method may be preserved for the service elements.

[3] Termination of Business

The use of the cash method is also inappropriate for certain significant events in the life of a business, such as a dissolution, liquidation, or sale of assets. In effect, an accrual method may be required in such circumstances to ensure that income is taxed to the taxpayer who earned it.[246]

Many of the cases that have focused on this issue have relied on the "assignment of income" doctrine in denying use of the cash method. Under this doctrine, income is taxed to the person who earned it. Other cases have relied on the requirement that income be clearly reflected in denying use of the cash method. A third group of cases has viewed the act of distributing

---

[243] Treas. Reg. § 1.446-1(c)(1)(iv)(A).

[244] Treas. Reg. § 1.446-1(d)(1).

[245] See, e.g., Wilkinson-Beane, Inc. v. Comm'r, 420 F2d 352 (1st Cir. 1970), aff'g 28 TCM 450 (1969), where sales and services portions of transactions made in connection with funerals were so interrelated that an accrual method was required for the entire transaction, the Tax Court having noted that the use of a hybrid method had not been put in issue. This same result occurs even where the inventories arise from temporary conditions in the industry. Asphalt Prods. Co. v. Comm'r, 796 F2d 843 (6th Cir. 1986), rev'd per curiam on other grounds, 482 US 117 (1987).

[246] See, e.g., Susan J. Carter, 9 TC 364 (1947), acq. 1958-2 CB 4, aff'd, 170 F2d 911 (2d Cir. 1948); Jud Plumbing & Heating, Inc., 5 TC 127 (1945), aff'd. 153 F2d 681 (5th Cir. 1946); Guy M. Shelley, 2 TC 62 (1943); Williamson v. United States, 292 F2d 524 (Ct. Cl. 1961); Floyd v. Scofield, 193 F2d 594 (5th Cir. 1952), Comm'r v. Kuckenberg, 309 F2d 202 (9th Cir. 1962), cert. denied, 373 US 909 (1963); Standard Paving Co. v. Comm'r, 190 F2d 330 (10th Cir. 1951), cert. denied, 342 US 860 (1951).

the receivables to shareholders as a taxable event, i.e., the distribution represents an economic benefit just as if collection itself had occurred. In any event, it is clear that in the absence of judicial interpretations such as these, use of the cash method would provide an opportunity for tax avoidance.

In applying the principle that on termination or dissolution of a cash basis business, an accrual method should be used, several points should be noted. First, if a right to income has not become fixed at the time of liquidation or dissolution, it is not includable by the cash method entity, i.e., normal accrual accounting rules are applied in determining whether an item has accrued.[247] Second, although effectively placing the entity on an accrual method, the taxpayer has not technically been subject to a change in accounting method and therefore may not be entitled to the benefits (and limitations on tax) under Section 481.[248] Third, the IRS may take the position that expenses should continue to be deducted only when paid, even if paid in years after the termination of the business,[249] but if an expense is directly associated with the particular items of income that must be accrued, that expense should also be accrued.[250]

¶ 3.07   REQUIRED USE OF CASH METHOD

It is frequently stated that where a taxpayer has no formal books and records, he may be required to use the cash method.[251] This is both logical and

---

[247] Williamson v. United States, 292 F2d 524, 529 (Ct. Cl. 1961).

[248] Id. at 531; Susan J. Carter, 9 TC 364, 374 (1947), acq. 1958-2 CB 4, aff'd, 170 F2d 911 (2d Cir. 1948). See discussion of Section 481 at ¶ 8.04.

[249] Rev. Rul. 67-12, 1967-1 CB 29. See also Commercial Sec. Bank, 77 TC 145 (1981), acq. 1986-1 CB 1, where the IRS sought to deny deductions to a cash basis taxpayer even though the corresponding liabilities were assumed by the purchaser as of the date of the sale of the taxpayer's assets. The court disagreed with the IRS and allowed the deductions.

[250] Susan J. Carter, 9 TC 364, 374 (1947), acq. 1958-2 CB 4, aff'd, 170 F2d 911 (2d Cir. 1948), where the court stated:

> Next, as to the deduction claimed because of salary payable to Harvey D. Carter: Such amount was never actually paid to him, but we agree with the petitioner that, since the effort here is to reflect clearly the corporate income, we should consider any liability . . . to which the [income] is subject, for, since we are considering, contrary to fact, that the corporation received the income, we should consider also the proper deductions to which it would have been subject had it been received.

See also Commercial Sec. Bank, 77 TC 145 (1981), acq. 1986-1 CB 1.

[251] See, e.g., James W. England, Jr., 34 TC 617 (1960), where taxpayers kept no books or records and prepared their tax returns solely on the basis of routine notices and statements furnished by the bank to all its customers, the court rejected their contention that they were on the accrual basis; George V. Williams, 25 TCM 767, 770

reasonable. Section 446(a) imposes on the taxpayer responsibility for computing income for tax purposes on the same basis as income is computed in keeping books. Absent the maintaining of books on an accrual or other noncash basis, the cash basis would be the method of reporting most consistent with the actual practice of the taxpayer. For example, although a taxpayer may not have formal books on a cash method, he is much more likely to have cash basis records available than accrual basis records. These records give the IRS an opportunity to audit the taxpayer and to use records that are available to determine income.

Of course, just as an accrual method is generally required where the cash method is found not to reflect income clearly under the circumstances, the IRS is not reluctant to assert that the cash method should be used when the accrual method is deemed not to reflect income clearly. Circumstances in which this argument has been made by the IRS include those where an accrual method taxpayer (1) has received prepayments of income or (2) has deducted a significant expense that is unlikely to be paid (or may not be paid for a long time).[252]

¶ 3.08 CLEAR REFLECTION OF INCOME

Over the years, the IRS has frequently challenged a taxpayer's use of the cash method as not clearly reflecting income in particular circumstances. In virtually every case, the circumstances cited included the size of the taxpayer's business (and, consequently, the magnitude of the deferral created by use of the cash method), the existence and use of accrual basis information by the taxpayer for internal and external reporting purposes, the failure of the cash method to satisfy GAAP, and the asserted distortion and mismatching associated with the use of the cash method. Although it remains to be seen how the enactment of Section 448 as part of the 1986 Act ultimately will affect the attitude of the IRS toward use of the cash method by those to

---

(1966), where court found cash basis proper for taxpayer who determined his taxable income based solely on "bank statements, invoices, cancelled checks, check stubs and duplicates of deposit slips" and "conducted his business on a purely cash basis without using accounts receivable, accounts payable or inventory"; Bellevue Mfg. Co. 16 TCM 390, 391–392 (1957), stating, "Where books and records are not in existence, and absent any other satisfactory evidence as to method of accounting, this Court has approved the determination . . . that the cash receipts and disbursement method should be used." Compare American Fletcher Corp. v. United States, 86-1 USTC ¶ 9283 (SD Ind. 1986), aff'd, 832 F2d 436 (7th Cir. 1987), where taxpayer was denied use of cash method where it could not accurately compute cash basis income but maintained accurate accrual basis information.

[252] See, e.g., Mooney Aircraft, Inc. v. United States, 420 F2d 400 (5th Cir. 1970), and cases cited therein.

whom it has not expressly been denied,[253] agents have not been reluctant to challenge use of the cash method in pre–1986 Act years to those expressly covered by the 1986 Act.[254]

[1] Amount of Deferral

The IRS and the Treasury often cite the amount of the deferral in income that has arisen from use of the cash method (as compared to an accrual method) as an indication that the cash method does not clearly reflect income. Nevertheless, both the actions of the IRS (on audit and otherwise) and the decisions of the courts and the National Office (when the issue has been presented to it) make it clear that prior to the 1986 Act, the amount of the deferral was not relevant. For example, the continued use of the cash method by many very large taxpayers (in terms of assets, revenues, or income) year after year without challenge belied the assertion that size was relevant. In addition, despite the continued requirement of clear reflection of income, the National Office had, over the years, permitted some very large taxpayers to change their methods of accounting to the cash method.

In the rare case where an argument based on size had been made to the courts, it had not been persuasive. In *William H. White*,[255] the government was concerned with the potential distortion in reporting income under the cash method as a business grew rapidly in size. The court responded that the rapid growth of the business was not relevant:

> The argument of the Commissioner in effect is that although the cash receipts and disbursements method of accounting clearly reflected the income of the petitioner when its business income resulted from small contracts, that system cannot clearly reflect its income consisting largely of income from large contracts. He cites no authority for any such proposition. The tax should be computed on a cash method.[256]

The National Office itself had generally indicated that size was not rel-

---

[253] In Applied Communications, Inc., 57 TCM 1473 (1989), the Tax Court concluded that the Commissioner had the discretion to require a change from the taxpayer's use of the cash method. The court referred to the above factors as well as to the change in the nature of the taxpayer's business from a service-oriented business to a product-oriented business. No mention was made of Section 448. See also BKW Sys., Inc., 90-1 USTC ¶ 50,139 (Bankr. DNH 1989).

[254] For example, agents have challenged the use of the cash method by hospitals in pre–1986 Act years, even though Congress grants special transition rules to hospitals in Section 448(d)(7)(C)(ii). The agents position, in effect, is that no hospitals are entitled to the benefits of the special transition rules.

[255] William H. White, 12 TCM 996 (1953).

[256] Id. at 997.

evant for determining whether the cash method clearly reflected income.[257] The irrelevance of size under pre–1986 Act law was recognized most directly by the enactment of Section 448, which for the first time imposed limitations on the use of the cash method by some but not all taxpayers based on the level of their gross receipts.[258] Accordingly, for years prior to the effective date of the 1986 Act, size of revenues or of the deferral in income should not be relevant. For years to which the 1986 Act is applicable, size in revenues is relevant to the extent affected by Section 448.[259]

Notwithstanding the foregoing analysis, the actions of revenue agents since the enactment of the 1986 Act have not been consistent. In some instances, agents have advised taxpayers that pre–1986 Act cases involving their use of the cash method, that were initiated because of their substantial revenues, would not be pursued. In other instances, the agents are continuing to press such cases, even though the asserted principal basis for terminating the cash method is the size of the deferral in income that has resulted from its use. This latter approach appears wholly inappropriate and at odds with the 1986 Act.[260]

[2] Existence of Accrual Basis Information

The IRS is often troubled by the fact that accrual basis information is maintained and used by taxpayers, although such taxpayers report for tax

---

[257] See Tech. Adv. Mem. 7405291610B (1974), where the National Office stated, "The growth of the [taxpayer], standing alone, is not a basis for the Service to now hold that the cash receipts and disbursements method does not clearly reflect income." See also Priv. Ltr. Rul. 8029008 (Apr. 10, 1980), where the National Office pointed out that historically it had not, by regulations or otherwise, denied use of the cash method to a service business even in cases where there were substantial receivables and payables and a substantial mismatching of income and expense, absent evidence of manipulative abuse with resultant gross distortion.

[258] See discussion supra ¶ 3.06[1].

[259] Id.

[260] Cf. Cal-Maine Foods, Inc., 93 TC 181 (1989), where the Tax Court rejected a contention that the benefits then available under Section 447, which permitted "family corporations" engaged in farming to use the cash method, were available only to family corporations with relatively low gross receipts, the court noting the subsequent enactment in 1987 of present Section 447(d)(2)(A), which for years beginning after December 31, 1985, limits the benefits available to family corporations to those corporations with gross receipts of $25 million or less; and Lloyd Williams, Jr., 94 TC No. 27 (1990), where the court refused to limit the interest deductible under Section 483 to the amount of interest that had economically accrued, the court noting that Section 483 was later amended to reduce the available deduction to such amount. On the other hand, in Applied Communications, Inc., 57 TCM 1473 (1989), the Tax Court found the Commissioner had not abused his discretion in rejecting continued use of the cash method, citing the large accounts receivable and deferral in revenues as factors to be considered. No reference was made to the limitations imposed by the 1986 Act on the availability of the cash method.

purposes on a cash basis and purport to maintain books and records on a cash basis. Although it is understandably frustrating to the IRS to find the cash method coexisting with the widespread use of accrual information, virtually every business, regardless of size, character, or method of accounting, must maintain accrual basis information. This is a necessity of conducting business. Indeed, even individuals and taxpayers with the simplest of businesses generally maintain records showing what they owe and what is owed to them. Assuming no violation of the conformity requirement of Section 446(a),[261] the existence of such information and the format in which it is recorded does not preclude use of the cash method,[262] a fact that has been recognized by the National Office.[263]

It must be emphasized, however, that the maintenance and use of accrual basis information must not be inconsistent with the requirement of book conformity under Section 446(a). It would be a mistake for taxpayers to conclude that use of the cash method for tax purposes is permitted without regard to the method employed by the taxpayer in computing income in keeping its books.[264]

[3] Accrual Basis Financial Reporting

Many companies, including credit reporting companies, trucking companies, hospital management companies, and other service organizations, use the cash basis for tax purposes but an accrual method in their published financial statements. The use of the accrual method is frequently necessary to satisfy both GAAP and the requirements of various state and federal regulatory agencies. Although there does not appear to be a single litigated case in which the IRS has even argued that the lack of conformity between the method used for tax purposes and the method used for financial statement purposes

---

[261] See discussion at ¶ 2.02[1].

[262] See Michael Drazen, 34 TC 1070, 1077 (1960), stating, "There is no question that the partnership kept its books and reported income on the cash basis. A memorandum of accounts receivable was kept and inventory value was taken from the spread sheets. These were subsidiary records kept to provide the partners and banks with 'accrual' information"; Estate of Paul Hansen, 4 TCM 264, 267 (1945), stating, "Since substantially all accounts were kept on a cash basis, it was a simple matter for [the taxpayer] to report income on that basis from the books of account disregarding the memorandum accounts called services billed and work in progress"; Cosmopolitan Bond & Mortgage Co., 30 BTA 717, 720 (1934), acq. as to method of accounting issue XIII-2 CB 5 (taxpayer held to use cash method even though memorandum accrual accounts were maintained for management purposes).

[263] See, e.g., Priv. Ltr. Rul. 8029008 (Apr. 10, 1980).

[264] See discussion at ¶ 2.02[1].

disqualifies a taxpayer from using the cash method for tax purposes,[265] such a circumstance is nevertheless frequently cited by agents who propose to terminate a taxpayer's use of the cash method.

The agents are wrong. There is no general requirement of financial statement conformity in the Code,[266] and facts presented in cases addressing other issues of tax accounting have made it clear that such a conformity requirement is not to be inferred.[267] The National Office has also recognized that the method of accounting used in the preparation of financial statements has no bearing on the correctness of the use of the cash method by a taxpayer.[268] Nevertheless, the preparation of financial statements on an accrual basis has been cited as a factor to be considered when evaluating whether use of the cash method clearly reflects income.[269] The citation to this factor should have little bearing, however, particularly since accrual tax accounting does not comply with accrual financial reporting.[270]

---

[265] In fact, in Patchen v. Comm'r, 258 F2d 544 (5th Cir. 1958) and St. Luke's Hosp., Inc., 35 TC 236 (1960), the two cases most squarely confronting the conformity requirement of Section 446(a), there was no suggestion whatsoever of any financial statement conformity requirement.

[266] In contrast, Section 472(c), which pertains to the LIFO method of accounting for inventories, does contain a requirement of financial statement conformity. Congress recognized that the conformity requirement of Section 472(c) is different from, and in addition to, the requirement of Section 446 that a taxpayer report its income on the same method of accounting used in keeping its books. In a legislative report accompanying the Revenue Act of 1942, which amended Section 22(d) of the 1939 Code, the predecessor of Section 472(c), it was noted that the use of LIFO for tax purposes was subject

> not only to the *general requirement* of Section 41 that it be in conformity with the method of accounting regularly employed by the taxpayer in keeping his books, but also the *added requirement*, among others, that no other procedure be used in reports to shareholders, partners, or other proprietors, or to beneficiaries, or for credit purposes.

H.R. Rep. No. 2333, 77th Cong. 2d Sess. 71 (1942) (emphasis added)

[267] See, e.g., Wolf Bakery & Cafeteria Co., 5 TCM 389 (1946), where taxpayer kept its books on the cash basis for tax purposes and was required to continue to report its income on that basis, even though it prepared financial statements on an accrual basis for credit purposes; Michael Drazen, 34 TC 1070 (1960), where cash basis taxpayer provided creditors with reports containing accrual basis information; Ocean Accident & Guar. Co., 13 BTA 1057 (1928), where cash basis taxpayer prepared accrual basis reports for management and governmental regulatory purposes.

[268] See Rev. Rul. 68-35, 1968-1 CB 190; Rev. Rul. 68-83, 1968-1 CB 190; Rev. Rul. 74-383, 1974-2 CB 146; Priv. Ltr. Rul. 7750024 (Sept. 14, 1977), where the IRS permitted taxpayers to report their income on the cash method despite the fact that they prepared financial statements on an accrual basis for management or regulatory purposes.

[269] See Applied Communications, Inc., 57 TCM 1473 (1989).

[270] See discussion at ¶ 4.01[2].

[4] Generally Accepted Accounting Principles

Historically, the use of the cash method has not been deemed in accordance with GAAP. Yet, it has been permitted over the years for tax purposes. Similarly, for tax purposes, other methods have been used, although not permitted for financial reporting purposes and not in accordance with GAAP. An example is the installment method under which accrual method taxpayers were permitted (prior to the 1987 Act) to report income from the sale of merchandise as payments were received. Thus, common sense and past practice indicate that the use of the cash method cannot be deemed to violate the clear reflection of income requirement on the basis that it departs from GAAP. Nevertheless, courts sometimes refer to the cash method's failure to satisfy GAAP when concluding that use of the cash method fails to clearly reflect income.[271]

Such references may be more the result of specific points not having been brought to the court's attention than to the court actually suggesting that a failure to satisfy GAAP precludes use of the cash method. For example, in *RLC Industries Co.*,[272] the very judge who decided *Applied Communications*, stated: "Generally, we cannot look to financial accounting standards alone to determine if a taxpayer is appropriately reporting and in compliance with the Internal Revenue Code. This is so because reporting for tax purposes is ultimately governed by the statutes, regulations, and case law interpretations and not by the financial accounting standards."[273] The court also stated specifically that "the cash method is not permitted under accounting standards, whereas the cash method is permitted (for the years under consideration) for tax purposes."[274] Finally, the court noted that any application of the clear reflection standard that would prohibit the authorized use of the cash method would not be appropriate. These clarifying points by this particular judge are quite helpful in properly gauging the application of the clear-reflection-of-income standard to cash method taxpayers.

[5] Mismatching of Income and Expense

IRS agents frequently assert that the cash method's mismatching of related items of income and expense results in distortion of income and a failure to

---

[271] See, e.g., Applied Communications, Inc., 57 TCM 1473 (1989); and BKW Sys., Inc., 90-1 USTC ¶ 50,139 (Bankr. DNH 1989); but see Capitol Fed. Sav. & Loan Ass'n, 96 TC No. 11 (1991), where a change was made in the taxpayer's use of the cash method; yet there was no suggestion at all that the overall cash method failed to clearly reflect income.

[272] RLC Indus. Co., 98 TC 457 (1992).

[273] Id. at 489.

[274] Id. at 493, n.29.

reflect income clearly. This argument has not generally been accepted by the courts or the National Office.

The history and development of the cash method (as well as its explicit sanction by the Code) make it clear that the method's failure to result in a precise matching of income and expense in an economic or financial accounting sense does not mean that it fails to reflect income clearly for tax purposes. If precise matching were required, the cash method would not have been made available to taxpayers in the first place.

The inherent mismatching of related items of income and expense under the cash method (as contrasted with an accrual method) is acknowledged and accepted.[275] It is not a basis for denial of the cash method.[276] Technical

---

[275] See, e.g., Koebig & Koebig, Inc., 23 TCM 170, 181 (1964). The courts have accepted the fact that even under an accrual method, there will frequently be some form of mismatching in the computation of taxable income. Marquardt Corp., 39 TC 443, 453 (1962), acq. as to this issue 1965-2 CB 6:

> Accrual of an item as income in a particular year is not required merely because the expenses attributable to that item were deducted from gross income in that year. [Citations omitted.] As a practical matter, the income tax laws must operate on an annual basis, and there is no assurance under either an accrual or cash basis of accounting that there will be complete correlation between items of income and deductions pertinent thereto.

[276] Kenneth H. Van Raden, 71 TC 1083, 1104 (1979), aff'd, 650 F2d 1046 (9th Cir. 1981):

> The cash method of accounting will usually result in some distortion of income because the benefits derived from payments for expenses or materials extend to varying degrees into more than one annual accounting period. If the cash method is consistently utilized and no attempt is made to unreasonably prepay expenses or purchase supplies in advance, the distortion is not material and over a period of years the distortions will tend to cancel out each other.

Michael Drazen, 34 TC 1070, 1077–1078 (1960), stating, "While it is theoretically desirable to match expenses with income earned in incurring those expenses, it must be remembered that exact and precise matching is seldom, if ever, achieved with either method of accounting"; H.G. Irby, Jr., 30 TC 1166, 1175 (1958), corrected and aff'd, 274 F2d 208 (5th Cir. 1960), stating:

> Under either the cash or the accrual method, it is possible that expenses, paid or accruable, may be deductible in a year that is either prior to or subsequent to the year in which income related to such expenses is includable. [Citation omitted.] This is simply the result of the facts, that taxable income must be computed on an annual basis, and that the computation of taxable income does not necessarily follow business accounting practices.

Maurice W. Simon, 6 TCM 57, 58 (1947), aff'd, 176 F2d 230 (2d Cir. 1949), stating:

> Defects of this kind are inherent in the cash receipts and disbursements method. It is not perfect. Nearly always some accounts due a taxpayer will remain uncollected at the end of the year, and some of his own obligations may remain unpaid, but if the method is consistently applied, it will bring about a reasonably fair reflection of income. Certainly it was not contemplated that all taxpayers could be forced to use an accrual method or one which perfectly reflects income.

accounting precision is simply not required.[277] Thus, any inherent mismatching, which is due to the normal application of the cash method to the transactions of a taxpayer as they occur in the ordinary course of business, should not be a basis for asserting that the cash method fails to reflect income clearly.[278]

However, where manipulation occurs in the use of the cash method (e.g., by accelerating deductions or by deferring the receipt of income), a valid question exists as to whether the method clearly reflects income. On one hand, it is not illogical to argue that such manipulation prevents the method from clearly reflecting income. On the other hand, it may reasonably be argued that if a taxpayer runs the business risks associated with deferring collections or accelerating payments, the cash method does clearly reflect the income associated with such transactions as they actually occurred. As an alternative, it may be argued that the IRS should accept use of the cash method, but should consider more carefully possible application of the doctrines of constructive receipt (as to deferred collections) and capitalization or other deferral of deductions (as to prepaid expenses). In any event, the IRS clearly reserves the right to challenge use of the cash method where manipulation is observed.[279] However, it should be understood that this type of manipulation (i.e., arranging transactions so as to benefit from application of the chosen method) affects all methods of accounting, not just the cash method.

In 1983, the Tax Court showed some receptivity to the government's position that even the inherent mismatching of the cash method may result in a failure to reflect income clearly, at least in certain situations.[280] In *William J. Silberman*, the Commissioner successfully challenged the adoption of the cash method by a partnership formed to produce a motion picture. The partnership completed production of the motion picture during its initial taxable year when expenses were paid and deducted, but no revenues were

---

[277] Section 471, pertaining to inventories, offers a direct contrast. In that section, Congress authorized the Secretary to prescribe that inventories be taken on a basis "conforming as nearly as may be to the best accounting practice in the trade or business and as most clearly reflecting the income." Even then, Congress recognized that different methods of inventory accounting would be acceptable for tax purposes. See, e.g., IRC § 472.

[278] In James V. Cole, 64 TC 1091, 1110 (1975), aff'd, 586 F2d 747 (9th Cir. 1978), cert. denied, 441 US 924 (1979), Judge Hall correctly pointed out in a concurring opinion, "If the cash method is properly used, the disparity [between cash and accrual income] is not a *distortion* of income but merely the consequences of proper use of a permissible method of *measuring* income." (Emphasis by court.) See also RLC Indus. Co., 98 TC 457 (1992), where the court noted: "By definition, the cash method may result in mismatching between expenses and income where expenses are paid in a year prior to the receipt of related income. Generally, the cash method is not permitted under accounting standards, whereas the cash method is permitted (for the years under consideration) for tax purposes."

[279] See, e.g., Priv. Ltr. Rul. 8029008 (Apr. 10, 1980).

[280] William J. Silberman, 47 TCM 778 (1983).

to be received until succeeding taxable years. With respect to this mismatching, the court stated:

> The predicted delay between expenditures and receipts creates a mismatching of funds and a distortion of income of the type which section 446(b) intends to avoid. Under these circumstances, the cash receipts and disbursements method of accounting does not clearly reflect income, and the respondent's denial of its use is proper.[281]

Although *Silberman* focused on a one-shot activity of the partnership, the willingness of the court to deny the use of the cash method was nevertheless an important victory for the IRS.

[6] Consolidated Group

Members of an affiliated group filing consolidated returns are entitled to select their own methods of accounting.[282] However, they may not be permitted to select methods and employ business practices so as to distort income of the group.[283] In *Epic Metals Corp.*,[284] an accrual method manufacturer created a cash method sales subsidiary. The adoption of the cash method by the subsidiary produced a deferral of almost $1.4 million of income in the subsidiary's initial year of operations. This deferral would not have been available under the parent's accrual method. The Commissioner challenged the subsidiary's adoption of the cash method of accounting on the ground that it did not clearly reflect the consolidated income of the group.[285]

Although the Tax Court concluded that the subsidiary was required to maintain inventories and, hence, was required to use an accrual method of accounting,[286] the court also considered whether use of the cash method by the sales subsidiary clearly reflected the consolidated income of the group. After noting that the adoption of the cash method created a substantial deferral of income that could not have been achieved but for the creation of the subsidiary, the court stated:

---

[281] Id. at 785.

[282] Treas. Reg. § 1.1502-17.

[283] See, e.g., Treas. Reg. § 1.1502-13.

[284] Epic Metals Corp., 48 TCM 357 (1984). See also Thomas Nelson, Inc. v. United States, No. 3-86-0671 (ND Tenn. 1988).

[285] In Priv. Ltr. Rul. 8430008 (Apr. 16, 1984), the IRS acknowledged that members of an affiliated group filing consolidated returns may adopt different methods of accounting, but it noted that use of the cash method was permissible only if it clearly reflected income.

[286] Epic Metals Corp., 48 TCM 357, 362 (1984) (citing Treas. Reg. § 1.446-1(c)(2)(i)). See Thomas Nelson, Inc. v. United States, No. 3-86-0671 (ND Tenn. 1988).

The creation of [the subsidiary] to handle certain of the sales . . . and its use of the cash method of accounting for tax purposes would result in the deferral of substantial income, and such circumstances provide a sound basis for the Commissioner's position that the deferral of such income would be a failure to clearly reflect income within the meaning of section 446(b).[287]

The subsidiary argued that its method of accounting had been consistently used since incorporation and that its method had been used by similarly situated taxpayers engaged in the same line of business. The court dismissed these arguments as "irrelevant," noting that the challenge by the Commissioner to the adoption of the cash method of accounting in the taxpayer's *initial* year of operation precluded reliance on the consistency argument. Industry practice regarding methods of accounting was described as merely one factor to be considered in determining whether a method of accounting clearly reflects income, but it was not determinative of the issue.

[7] IRS Difficulty With Cash Method

In challenging use of the cash method on the basis of some or all of the foregoing factors, the IRS was often frustrated by the following circumstances. The cash method was expressly sanctioned by the Code. Except for the clear-reflection-of-income requirement (and certain other specified requirements), there was no general limitation on adoption and use of the cash method prior to the 1986 Act. Use of the cash method had gone far beyond the class of individual and small taxpayers for whom the IRS believed the method to be suitable and appropriate, in terms of convenience and simplicity. When used by larger taxpayers, its use frequently coexisted with the use of accrual data for virtually all internal and external financial reporting purposes.

The book conformity requirement of Section 446(a) permitted taxpayers to use their methods of book accounting for tax reporting purposes. This was viewed as convenient and economical for taxpayers; in addition, it provided a measure of assurance to the government that, since taxpayers would always be faced with countervailing considerations concerning their use of accounting methods for nontax purposes, the government would receive a fair determination of income subject to tax.

Over the years, however, without any deliberate thought being given to it, technology and ingenuity had permitted taxpayers to maintain different records for different reporting purposes. Thus, major organizations began reporting to the government on a cash basis while, as a practical matter, using such information for almost no other financial reporting purpose. To

---

[287] Epic Metals Corp., 48 TCM 357, 362 (1984).

require those taxpayers to report on an accrual method for federal income tax purposes was thought by the IRS to occasion no hardship in terms of the accumulation of the necessary information, as that information already existed. Moreover, the government believed it had been taken advantage of, since these taxpayers obtained the benefits of the cash method, and the countervailing considerations simply did not come into play. However, as time went on, accrual tax accounting departed to an increasing extent from accrual financial accounting.[288] Consequently, the very points made by the IRS with respect to the cash method could also be made by taxpayers with respect to accrual tax methods.

Although the 1986 Act now prevents use of the cash method by certain large organizations, it does not deny use of that method to all large organizations. Consequently, despite the above-stated concerns of the IRS, use of the cash method should remain appropriate except where expressly prohibited by the Code, Treasury regulation, or special circumstance associated with the termination of the business.[289]

---

[288] See discussion at ¶ 4.02[3].

[289] See Roy C. Kennedy, 89 TC 98 (1987), where the Tax Court held that the IRS challenge to the taxpayers' use of the cash method was unreasonable and awarded attorney fees. The court noted that the position of the IRS was contrary to regulations and applicable case law and was without factual support.

CHAPTER 4

Accrual Methods

¶ 4.01 Definition 4-2
    [1] Requirements for Recognizing Income and Expense 4-2
    [2] Differences Between Accrual Tax Accounting and Accrual
        Financial Accounting 4-3
    [3] IRS View 4-4
    [4] Users 4-4
    [5] Characteristics 4-5

¶ 4.02 History and Development 4-6
    [1] Early History 4-6
    [2] Acceptance of Financial Accounting 4-6
    [3] Divergence Between Book and Tax Accounting 4-7
    [4] *Thor Power Tool Co.* 4-8

¶ 4.03 Reporting Items of Income 4-10
    [1] All Events Test 4-10
        [a] Fixed Right to Receive 4-10
            [i] Conditions precedent, conditions subsequent, and
                disputes 4-11
            [ii] Taxpayer's knowledge of right or amount 4-13
            [iii] Flexibility to determine right to receive 4-14
        [b] Determination of Amount With Reasonable Accuracy .. 4-15
    [2] Items of Doubtful Collectibility 4-17
        [a] Level of Uncertainty 4-18
        [b] Time of Uncertainty 4-19
        [c] Accrual of Item Whose Collection Was Previously in
            Doubt 4-20
        [d] Nonaccrual of Service Income 4-20
    [3] Prepaid Income 4-24
        [a] Pretrilogy Treatment 4-24
        [b] The Trilogy 4-26
        [c] Post-Trilogy Decisions 4-29
        [d] Length of Deferral 4-32
        [e] Provisions Permitting Deferral 4-32
            [i] Congressional 4-32
            [ii] Treasury and IRS 4-33

¶ 4.04 Reporting Items of Expense 4-40

[1] Fact of Liability Must Be Fixed 4-42
    [a] Identification of Liability 4-42
        [i] Identification of payee 4-44
        [ii] Likelihood of performance and conditions
             subsequent 4-45
        [iii] Conditions precedent 4-48
    [b] Matching 4-49
    [c] Contested Liabilities 4-52
        [i] Payment of contested liability 4-54
        [ii] Resolution of contest 4-55
[2] Determination of Amount With Reasonable Accuracy 4-55
    [a] Certainty of Amount 4-56
    [b] Possibility of Adjustment 4-58
    [c] Timing of Facts on Which Amount Is Based 4-58
[3] Economic Performance 4-58
    [a] Section 461(h) 4-59
    [b] Time When Economic Performance Occurs 4-61
        [i] Services and property provided to taxpayer 4-62
        [ii] Services and property provided by taxpayer 4-63
        [iii] Workers' compensation and tort liabilities 4-63
        [iv] Other items 4-64
    [c] "As Provided" Requirement 4-65
        [i] General rules and questions arising prior to issuance
             of regulations 4-65
        [ii] Applicable Treasury regulations 4-67
    [d] Proof of Compliance With Economic Performance Test 4-75
    [e] Impact on Other Than Current Deductions 4-75
    [f] Exception for Certain Recurring Items 4-77
        [i] Timely return or eight and one half months 4-78
        [ii] Recurring nature 4-79
        [iii] Not a material item or a more proper match 4-80
        [iv] Adopting recurring item exception 4-82
[4] Items Where Payment Is Doubtful 4-83

¶ 4.01 DEFINITION

Section 446(c) sets forth permissible methods of accounting.[1] It lists first *the* cash receipts and disbursements method (the cash method) and second *an* accrual method. As the use of the article *an* suggests, no particular accrual method is required, and far greater flexibility and variation in reporting exists under accrual methods than under the cash method. (See Chapter 3 for discussion of the cash method.)

[1] Requirements for Recognizing Income and Expense

Under an accrual method, income is generally recognized in the year in which (1) all the events have occurred that fix the taxpayer's right to receive

---

[1] Unless otherwise indicated, all IRC references are to the Internal Revenue Code of 1986, as amended (the Code).

the income and (2) the amount of the income can be determined with reasonable accuracy.[2] All events that fix the right to receive income need not occur in the same year. If relevant events occur over two or more years, the right to receive becomes fixed in the year in which the last event occurs.

Expenses are generally deductible in the year in which (1) all events have occurred that establish the fact of liability; (2) the amount of the liability can be determined with reasonable accuracy; and (3) economic performance has occurred.[3] Just as in the case of items of income, all events that establish the fact of liability and economic performance need not occur in the same year. However, a deduction is available only in the first year by which all three conditions have been satisfied.

As these general rules indicate, the requirements for recognizing income and expense are not symmetrical. The recognition of income is subject to a two-pronged test, while the recognition of expense is subject to a three-pronged test.

In addition to these general rules, accrual methods are often subject to requirements that have the effect of treating accrual-basis taxpayers as if they were on the cash method. For example, in certain situations, income must be recognized on receipt, even though all events that fix the taxpayer's right to the income have not occurred,[4] and deductions may be denied until payment has been made, even though the fact of liability had been established in an earlier year.[5]

[2] Differences Between Accrual Tax Accounting and Accrual Financial Accounting

Accrual methods for tax reporting purposes differ from accrual methods for financial reporting purposes.[6] In many cases, tax accrual accounting results in an earlier reporting of income and a later reporting of expense than accrual financial accounting.[7] In other cases, accrual tax accounting allows the use of special rules to defer the recognition of income as compared to accrual financial accounting. (See Chapter 5 for a discussion of the installment method of reporting pursuant to Section 453.) For reasons such as these, accrual

---

[2] Treas. Reg. §§ 1.446-1(c)(1)(ii), 1.451-1(a). See discussion infra ¶ 4.03.

[3] Treas. Reg. §§ 1.446-1(c)(1)(ii), 1.461-1(a)(2); IRC § 461(h). See discussion infra ¶ 4.04.

[4] See discussion infra ¶ 4.03[3].

[5] See discussion infra ¶ 4.04[3].

[6] See Thor Power Tool Co. v. Comm'r, 439 US 522 (1979), and discussion infra ¶ 4.02[4].

[7] See, e.g., discussion infra ¶¶ 4.03[3] (regarding the treatment of prepaid income), 4.04[3] (regarding satisfaction of the economic performance requirement for deductions under accrual tax accounting).

tax accounting is often not consistent with generally accepted accounting principles (GAAP).[8]

[3] IRS View

Accrual methods are generally regarded by the Internal Revenue Service as the most accurate methods of tax accounting in the sense that they more closely approximate a true economic determination of income, at least prior to enactment of the economic performance test.[9] In some cases, use of accrual methods has attained an almost revered status in the eyes of the IRS and the Treasury. The IRS frequently challenges a taxpayer's use of the cash method on the basis that it is not as sound or as accurate as accrual methods. Considering the significant differences between accrual tax accounting and accrual financial accounting and the different objectives of each,[10] this status is not deserved. Indeed, in many cases, results under the cash method of tax accounting more closely approximate the results under accrual financial accounting than do the results produced under accrual methods of tax accounting.

[4] Users

Accrual methods are generally used by large corporate and other business taxpayers who already maintain accrual information for nontax purposes and, with certain exceptions, must be used (1) by C corporations (or partnerships that have a C corporation as a partner) if their average gross

---

[8] On the other hand, compliance with GAAP may be sufficient to show that an accrual method clearly reflects income. For example, Treas. Reg. § 1.446-1(c)(1)(ii)(C) provides with respect to accrual methods: "The method used by the taxpayer in determining when income is to be accounted for will generally be acceptable if it accords with generally accepted accounting principles, is consistently used by the taxpayer from year to year, and is consistent with the Income Tax Regulations." Prior to its amendment, effective April 10, 1992, the above regulation did not include the word "generally." It is understood that inclusion of this word was in recognition of the fact that the economic performance test is *so* contrary to GAAP accrual accounting. On the other hand, some representatives of the IRS stated in various speeches given after enactment of the final economic performance regulations that the word "generally" was inadvertently omitted from earlier regulations. This assertion seems incorrect. The more likely reason for inclusion of the word "generally" was to attempt to limit taxpayers' ability to argue that if their tax method satisfied the prior regulatory standard, their method *per se* clearly reflected income. See ¶ 2.02[2] for a discussion of the clear reflection of income standard.

[9] See discussion infra ¶ 4.04[3].

[10] See discussion infra ¶ 4.02[4].

receipts exceed $5 million;[11] (2) by all taxpayers in connection with the purchase and sale of merchandise;[12] (3) by certain corporations engaged in farming;[13] and (4) on the termination of businesses not already on an accrual method.[14]

[5] Characteristics

Accrual methods generally require more record keeping than the cash method, are more complex, and, in some cases, are less certain in result than the cash method.[15] Accrual methods are also less concerned with the taxpayer's ability to pay than is the cash method. Moreover, because of special rules allowing or requiring accrual method taxpayers to recognize certain items of income as payments are received (e.g., under the installment method or when certain "advance payments" or "prepayments" are received, respectively) and to defer the recognition of other items of income beyond the year of receipt, accrual tax accounting closely approximates use of the cash method in some cases, while in other cases it provides a deferral in the recognition of income as compared to the cash method.[16]

Finally, accrual tax accounting is often more susceptible to abuse and manipulation by large businesses than is the cash method.[17] Because of the very size of their operations and the volume of their transactions, large businesses cannot as a practical matter accelerate payments or delay billings or collections. Thus, they are not able to manipulate regularly recurring business transactions and thereby abuse the cash method. However, because items of income and expense are recognized under accrual methods on the basis of, for example, contract rights and business practices, it is often comparatively

---

[11] See IRC §§ 448(b)(3), 448(c), and discussion at ¶ 3.06[1][a].

[12] Treas. Reg. § 1.446-1(c)(2)(i). See discussion at ¶¶ 3.06[2], and 6.02[3].

[13] Section 447 requires use of an accrual method by corporations (or partnerships in which a corporation is a partner) engaged in the trade or business of farming. An exception is provided for small business corporations and family corporations. See Cal-Maine Foods, Inc., 93 TC 181 (1989), where the court concluded that a taxpayer could qualify as a "family corporation" under Section 447 regardless of its level of gross receipts during years prior to the effective date of Section 447(d)(2). This section imposed a gross receipt limit of $25 million for years beginning after December 31, 1985. As a separate matter, in Rev. Rul. 88-60, 1988-2 CB 30, the IRS ruled that when the taxpayer adopts use of the cash method in accounting for purchases and sales of livestock, the cost of the livestock sold is its actual cost. The taxpayer may not determine this cost on the basis of inventory methods.

[14] See discussion at ¶ 3.06[3].

[15] See discussion at ¶ 3.01.

[16] See discussion infra ¶ 4.03[3].

[17] See discussion at ¶ 3.06[1] regarding limitations on the use of the cash method by certain large businesses.

easy to rearrange these contracts or practices to accelerate deductions or to defer the recognition of income as compared to the cash method.[18]

¶ 4.02 HISTORY AND DEVELOPMENT

[1] Early History

Initially, the cash method was the only acceptable method of accounting for tax purposes. However, many taxpayers used accrual methods for financial reporting purposes. Because of the inconvenience of requiring these taxpayers to convert their accrual records to the cash basis for tax purposes, efforts were made by the accounting profession and taxpayers to obtain Treasury approval of accrual methods for tax purposes. Eventually, the government acquiesced, and accrual methods were permitted, but only on condition that they clearly reflected income.[19]

In the early years of tax reporting, accrual methods were not subject to all the technical restrictions and conditions that have evolved over time. In effect, except as might otherwise be required by express statutory or regulatory provision, it appeared that the rules of financial accrual accounting would be applicable to tax accrual accounting.[20] This conclusion was consistent with the early justification for permitting accrual methods of tax accounting, a justification that was to permit taxpayers to compute income for tax purposes on the basis on which they computed income for book purposes.[21]

[2] Acceptance of Financial Accounting

In *United States v. Anderson*,[22] the seminal case involving use of an accrual method, the Supreme Court suggested that unless the method did not clearly reflect income, an accrual method used for financial reporting purposes would be acceptable for tax reporting purposes. The Court stated that the initial allowance of accrual methods

was to enable taxpayers to keep their books and make their returns according to scientific accounting principles, by charging against income

---

[18] Such accelerations or deferrals can often be achieved without the need for filing an application for a change in accounting method. See discussion at ¶ 9.06.

[19] See discussion at ¶ 3.02 for a full development of the early history of cash and accrual methods.

[20] See discussion infra ¶ 4.02[2].

[21] See discussion at ¶ 3.02.

[22] United States v. Anderson, 269 US 422 (1926).

earned during the taxable period, the expenses incurred in and properly attributable to the process of earning income during that period; and indeed, to require the tax return to be made on that basis, if the taxpayer failed or was unable to make the return on a strict receipts and disbursements basis.[23]

Later in its opinion, the Court stated that while the particular deduction at issue in the case (a deduction for munitions taxes) may not have accrued in a technical legal sense,

> it is also true that in advance of the assessment of a tax, all the events may occur which fix the amount of the tax and determine the liability of the taxpayer to pay it. In this respect, for purposes of accounting and of ascertaining true income for a given accounting period, the munitions tax here in question did not stand on any different footing than other accrued expenses appearing on appellee's books. In the economic and bookkeeping sense with which the statute and Treasury decision were concerned, the taxes had accrued.[24]

As this language suggests, use of an accrual method for tax purposes was initially predicated on the use of an accrual method for financial accounting purposes. The purpose of accrual methods for tax purposes was to allow taxpayers to make their returns according to scientific accounting principles, and the words in the applicable statute ("accrue" and "accrual") were intended to allow a determination of income in the economic and bookkeeping sense.[25]

[3] Divergence Between Book and Tax Accounting

Over time, this reliance on financial accounting computations and economic concepts of income gave way to concern for particular attributes normally associated with tax accounting, including ability to pay, the need for certainty, and protection of the public treasury. Various aspects of accrual accounting for tax purposes began to depart from principles of accrual financial accounting (generally on a case-by-case basis), and while general references to economic theory and accounting precision were still made by

---

[23] Id. at 440.

[24] Id. at 441.

[25] Id. at 440–441. Although focusing on economic and bookkeeping concepts, the Supreme Court did refer to the fact that "all the events may occur which fix the amount ... and determine the liability. ..." Because of this language, *United States v. Anderson* is generally regarded as the source of the present all events test. However, it is doubtful that the Court anticipated that the technicalities of the present all events test would control over economic and bookkeeping concepts of computing income to the extent they do today.

courts, decisions on when various items of income and expense should be recognized were more often than not based on the ever-changing principles of applicable tax policy.

As an example, consider the treatment of prepaid income and estimated expenses for accrual tax accounting and accrual financial accounting purposes. For tax purposes, prepaid income was often recognized in the year of receipt, and deductions for estimated expenses (such as warranty claims) were generally denied. The opposite treatment was required for accrual financial accounting purposes. To narrow these differences and to reduce disputes over the proper tax treatment, Congress enacted Sections 452 and 462 as part of the 1954 Code. Section 452 permitted a deferral in the recognition of prepaid income, and Section 462 permitted a deduction for certain estimated expenses. However, because of a fear of substantial revenue loss, these provisions were repealed retroactively in 1955.

[4] Thor Power Tool Co.

The relationship of accrual tax accounting and accrual financial accounting was directly focused on by the Supreme Court in 1979 in *Thor Power Tool Co. v. Commissioner.*[26] There, the taxpayer sought to deduct certain write-downs in the value of its inventory on the basis that the write-downs were appropriate under concepts of financial accrual accounting.[27] The Court responded with one of the most often-cited and articulate descriptions of the differences between tax and financial accounting:

> The primary goal of financial accounting is to provide useful information to management, shareholders, creditors, and others properly interested; the major responsibility of the accountant is to protect these parties from being misled. The primary goal of the income tax system, in contrast, is the equitable collection of revenue; the major responsibility of the Internal Revenue Service is to protect the public fisc. Consistent with its goals and responsibilities, financial accounting has as its foundation the principle of conservatism, with its corollary that "possible errors in measurement [should] be in the direction of understatement rather than overstatement of net income and net assets." In view of the Treasury's markedly different goals and responsibilities, understatement of income is not destined to be its guiding light. Given this diversity, even contrariety, of objectives, any presumptive equivalency between tax and financial accounting would be unacceptable.
>
> This difference in objectives is mirrored in numerous differences of treatment. Where the tax law requires that a deduction be deferred until

---

[26] Thor Power Tool Co. v. Comm'r, 439 US 522 (1979).

[27] See ¶ 6.09 for discussion of write-downs of inventory from its cost to a lower market value.

"all the events" have occurred that will make it fixed and certain . . . accounting principles typically require that a liability be accrued as soon as it can reasonably be estimated. Conversely, where the tax law requires that income be recognized currently under "claim of right," "ability to pay," and "control" rationales, accounting principles may defer accrual until a later year so that revenues and expenses may be better matched. Financial accounting, in short, is hospitable to estimates, probabilities, and reasonable certainties; the tax law, with its mandate to preserve the revenue, can give no quarter to uncertainty. This is as it should be. Reasonable estimates may be useful, even essential, in giving shareholders and creditors an accurate picture of a firm's overall financial health; but the accountant's conservatism cannot bind the Commissioner in his efforts to collect taxes.[28]

The evolution of accrual tax accounting led to distinctions between accrual financial accounting and accrual tax accounting. These distinctions arose as tax law concepts of fixed rights and fixed obligations on one hand came into conflict with economic and financial accounting concepts of income earned and expense incurred on the other. The distinctions between the two accounting concepts are not always clear, and some courts have used the words "earned" and "fixed right to receive" (or "incurred" and "fixed obligation to pay") interchangeably. This usage suggests that the terms are synonymous or that their application will result in the recognition of items of income and expense in the same year.[29] However, as the Supreme Court made clear in *Thor Power Tool*, this is not always the case.[30]

The distinctions between (and the different objectives of) tax and financial accrual accounting are also important as they affect evaluation of the cash method (see Chapter 3). The IRS often asserts that the cash method does not clearly reflect income because of its failure to satisfy GAAP. This is disingenuous. It is misleading to suggest that use of the cash method should be denied because it is not consistent with GAAP, while failing to point out that the accrual tax method (to which cash method taxpayers would be changed) also is not consistent with GAAP.[31]

---

[28] Thor Power Tool Co. v. Comm'r, 439 US 522, 542–543 (1979).

[29] See, e.g., Beacon Publishing Co. v. Comm'r, 218 F2d 697, 699 (10th Cir. 1955), "Where a taxpayer keeps his books and files his returns on an accrual basis, income is accounted for in the year in which the amount is earned or becomes fixed, irrespective of when the payment is ultimately received."

[30] Enactment of the economic performance test for deductions under an accrual method of tax accounting greatly increased the differences between accrual tax and accrual financial accounting. See discussion infra ¶ 4.04[3].

[31] See discussion at ¶ 3.08. See also Consumers Power Co., 89 TC 710 (1987), where the court held that the taxpayer's particular meter reading and billing cycle method of accounting for utility income qualified as a correct method in years prior to the effective date of Section 451(f), which requires use of a full accrual method. In its opinion, the court noted that the audit of the taxpayer resulted from the taxpayer's

¶ 4.03 REPORTING ITEMS OF INCOME

Section 451 sets forth the general rule that items of income must be recognized in the year of receipt "unless, under the method of accounting used in computing taxable income, such amount is to be properly accounted for as of a different period." Under accrual methods of tax accounting, income and expense are recognized pursuant to the so-called all events test, a test whose origin was the Supreme Court's 1926 decision in *United States v. Anderson.*[32]

[1] All Events Test

In 1957, the present all events test, which governs the recognition of income under an accrual method, was incorporated in regulations promulgated by the Treasury as follows: "Under an accrual method of accounting, income is includable in gross income when all the events have occurred which fix the right to receive such income and the amount thereof can be determined with reasonable accuracy."[33]

This regulation sets forth a two-pronged test for the recognition of income under an accrual method. First, all events must occur that fix the taxpayer's right to receive the income, and, second, the amount of that income must be determinable with reasonable accuracy. As this test indicates, economic concepts of determining income and financial concepts of accrual accounting are not intended to determine proper tax accrual accounting. However, as discussed in the succeeding sections,[34] this conclusion has not always been followed or accepted by the courts.

[a] Fixed Right to Receive

Under an accrual method, "it is the *right* to receive and not the actual receipt that determines the inclusion of the amount in gross income. When the right to receive an amount becomes fixed, the right accrues."[35] It is not

---

adoption of the full accrual method for financial reporting purposes while at the same time retaining a different accrual method for tax purposes. This case illustrates the audit risk that arises when there is a change in financial reporting without a commensurate change in tax reporting.

[32] United States v. Anderson, 269 US 422 (1926). See discussion supra ¶ 4.02[2].

[33] Treas. Reg. § 1.451-1(a).

[34] See discussions infra ¶¶ 4.03[1][a], 4.03[1][b].

[35] Spring City Foundry Co. v. Comm'r, 292 US 182, 184 (1934) (emphasis by Court). However, see discussion infra ¶ 4.03[3] regarding the treatment of prepaid income.

necessary in all circumstances that the right to receive be legally enforceable.[36] Enforceability of the right often pertains more to whether a debt may be collected than to whether the right to receive exists. For practical purposes (including protection of the public treasury), the IRS takes the position that a right to receive income becomes fixed at the earliest of (1) required performance; (2) the date a payment becomes due; or (3) the date the payment is made.[37]

In determining whether the right to receive has become fixed, consideration must be given to a number of factors. These include the substance of the transaction, the agreement of the parties, the time when services are rendered or property delivered, the existence of contingencies or conditions precedent or subsequent, and whether the liability is acknowledged or disputed.[38] The character of the item of income is also important.[39]

[i] **Conditions precedent, conditions subsequent, and disputes.** Under the first prong of the all events test (i.e., that there be a fixed right to receive income), income arising from the rendition of services or the sale of goods is not accruable for tax purposes if the right to receive that income is subject

---

[36] See, e.g., Flamingo Resort, Inc. v. United States, 485 F. Supp. 926 (D. Nev. 1980), aff'd, 664 F2d 1387 (9th Cir. 1982), cert. denied, 459 US 1036 (1982) (reasonable expectancy is all that is necessary); Desert Palace Inc. v. Comm'r, 698 F2d 1229 (9th Cir. 1982), rev'g 72 TC 1033 (1979), cert. denied, 464 US 816 (1983).

[37] See, e.g., Rev. Rul. 74-607, 1974-2 CB 149. Although this position may be consistent with the result required by regulation for some items (see, e.g., Treas. Reg. § 1.61-8(b), which provides that advance payments of rent must be included in income in the year of receipt without regard to the method of accounting employed by the taxpayer; Treas. Reg. § 1.301-1(b), which pertains to dividends and other distributions of property by a corporation; and the discussion of dividend income at ¶ 3.03[3][b]), the position of the IRS is overly broad and is not consistent with Treasury regulations and revenue procedures issued with regard to other items. See discussion infra ¶ 4.03[3][e][ii].

[38] See North Am. Oil Consol. v. Burnet, 286 US 417 (1932), and discussion at ¶ 12.03. See Bell Fed. Sav. & Loan Assoc., 62 TCM 376 (1991), where just such a consideration of applicable facts and circumstances was made in determining whether an accrual method lender had discounted from the proceeds of the loans the points owed it by borrowers or, instead, whether the full amount of the points had been paid at the time of the loan closings. See also Tech. Adv. Mem. 9143083 (Aug. 1, 1991), where the IRS National Office (the National Office) made such an analysis in the context of determining whether the taxpayer had acquired a fixed right to receive a reimbursement of costs incurred pursuant to a cooperative advertising arrangement.

[39] See, e.g., Resale Mobile Homes, Inc., 91 TC 1085 (1988), where the court held that a fixed right to receive so-called participation interest (i.e., the difference between the interest charged by the seller of property and the interest charged by the finance company to which the customer's paper was sold) arose in the year in which the customer's paper was sold. Apparently, the differential was not viewed as interest with respect to which a fixed right to receive would arise only as time passed, but instead, the differential was treated as part of the proceeds of the sale of the paper.

to conditions precedent or other contingencies. Thus, if a purchaser is not yet committed under the agreement to purchase the goods, accrual is not required or permitted.[40] If the obligor disputes the right of the taxpayer to the amount in question, accrual is not proper until the dispute is resolved.[41] The dispute is generally resolved when the obligor acknowledges liability or when liability is finally determined by the courts or other body and is not subject to further appeal or contest.[42] If the taxpayer's right to receive is conditioned on an approval of a third party, such as a government agency, income is not accruable for tax purposes until that approval is obtained.[43] However, if any required approval is reasonably certain to occur so that lack of approval is only an extremely remote and speculative possibility, accrual may be required despite the requirement of such approval.[44]

---

[40] See, e.g., Ringmaster, Inc., 21 TCM 1024 (1962), dismissed per curiam, 319 F2d 860 (8th Cir. 1963) (income was not accruable where the buyer was not committed to purchase goods until he approved them as meeting specifications); Webb Press Co. Ltd., 3 BTA 247 (1925), acq. VI-1 CB 6 (no accrual where buyer was committed only on acceptance following a period of testing); Florence Mills, Inc., 9 BTA 579 (1927), acq. VII-1 CB 11 (no accrual where goods rejected); Rev. Rul. 70-68, 1970-1 CB 122 (no accrual until payment when goods sold COD). See also Hallmark Cards, Inc., 90 TC 26 (1988), where the court held as follows with respect to the issue of when a sale occurs:

> At what point in time a sale takes place is to be determined from the totality of the circumstances. While no single factor is controlling, passage of title is perhaps the most significant factor to be considered, although the transfer of the possession is also significant. [Citations omitted.] The objective is to determine at what point in time the seller acquired an unconditional right to receive payment under the contract.

The court then concluded that the sales in question had not occurred until January 1 of the year following the year in which the goods were transferred to the purchaser.

[41] See, e.g., Continental Tie & Lumber Co. v. United States, 286 US 290 (1932); Breeze Corps. v. United States, 117 F. Supp. 404 (Ct. Cl. 1954); The Cold Metal Process Co., 17 TC 916 (1951), aff'd, 1953-1 USTC ¶ 9135 (6th Cir. 1952); Rev. Rul. 60-237, 1960-2 CB 164; Rev. Rul. 73-385, 1973-2 CB 151.

[42] United States v. Safety Car Heating and Lighting Co., 297 US 88 (1936); Snyder Air Prods., Inc., 71 TC 709 (1979); Breeze Corps. v. United States, 117 F. Supp. 404 (Ct. Cl. 1954); H. Liebes & Co. v. Comm'r, 90 F2d 932 (9th Cir. 1937); Thomas A. Ryan, 54 TCM 1503 (1988).

[43] See, e.g., Mutual Tel. Co. v. United States, 204 F2d 160 (9th Cir. 1953); Daniel Rosenthal, 32 TC 225 (1959).

[44] See Tech. Adv. Mem. 9143083 (Aug. 1, 1991), where the National Office held that a taxpayer had a fixed right to receive income (i.e., a reimbursement of certain costs incurred) pursuant to a cooperative advertising arrangement at the time the taxpayer placed the required advertising, even though the taxpayer had not yet submitted the various forms for reimbursement to the vendors who had made the offers of reimbursement. The National Office emphasized that the arrangements with the vendor were relatively simple, problems of interpretation and evaluation were not anticipated, the filing of the forms was only ministerial in nature, and the nature of the relationship with the vendor was such that the very essence of the contract was

On the other hand, accrual is not prevented by the fact that some condition subsequent may occur; that is, a condition that (1) may require the taxpayer to return any amounts he might receive or (2) may cause the taxpayer to lose a right to receive income that had previously become fixed.[45] In each case, the right to the income has become fixed and should be recognized. Any return of that income (or loss of the right to it) must be taken into account for tax purposes as a separate transaction.[46]

The application of the foregoing rules to the accrual of interest income has involved some interesting circumstances. For example, in *Continental Illinois Corp.*,[47] a lender made loans based on a floating interest rate. This rate was usually a percentage of the lender's prime rate or its prime rate plus a specified number of points. The loan agreements also provided that if the borrower paid an amount of interest in excess of an amount based on a specified fixed rate (and assuming the borrower neither prepaid nor defaulted on the loan), the amount of this excess would be returned to the borrower at maturity of the loan or shortly thereafter. The issue was whether the lender had to accrue all interest earned at the floating rate or, when the floating rate exceeded the specified fixed rate, only interest earned based on the fixed rate. The court held that all interest earned under the floating rate had to be accrued. The court recognized that all conditions precedent to the lender's right to accrue income at the floating rate occurred as time passed, while the obligation of the lender to repay any excess interest was subject to various contingencies in the nature of conditions subsequent.[48]

[ii] Taxpayer's knowledge of right or amount. The existence of a fixed right to receive income is not nullified by a showing that the taxpayer was not aware of the right until after the year in which it arose. For instance, many rights to receive income become fixed on the approval of some party, such as the debtor. The taxpayer's unawareness of the fixed right (i.e., the debtor's approval) is generally not a basis for deferring the recognition of

---

to induce the taxpayer to undertake the advertising, all of which made it unlikely that issues would be raised about the requests for reimbursement.

[45] See, e.g., J.J. Little & Ives Co., 25 TCM 372 (1966), where income accrued at time of sale even though buyer might have right to return goods; George Herberger, 9 TCM 546 (1950), aff'd on related issue, 195 F2d 293 (9th Cir. 1952), cert. denied, 344 US 820 (1952), where amount charged in excess of lawful ceiling price had to be accrued even though obligor would have opportunity to assert a defense with respect to such excess.

[46] See discussion at ¶ 12.03 regarding the claim-of-right doctrine.

[47] Continental Ill. Corp., 58 TCM 790 (1989).

[48] See also Fourth Fin. Corp., 49 TCM 1485 (1985), where the court held with respect to a similar loan that the borrower was entitled to deduct its full liability for floating interest; and discussion infra ¶ 4.04[1][a][iii].

income.[49] This interpretation seems sound; it generally imposes no significant hardship on taxpayers, and, if not applied, it might otherwise result in a never-ending series of controversies over whether the taxpayer had become aware of the right within the year in question. However, a more difficult (and still open) question exists if the obligor may retract its acceptance of liability before that acceptance has been communicated to the taxpayer. In such a case, accrual may not be appropriate. Also, where the amount of income to which the taxpayer has a fixed right is not known or, as a practical matter, knowable, within the taxable year and is not acknowledged as owed within that year, accrual of that amount has not been required.[50]

[iii] Flexibility to determine right to receive.   In many cases, the right to receive income will occur as the taxpayer renders services or transfers property. However, this is not always the case. If the parties agree that the right to receive is to become fixed prior to the rendition of services or the transfer of property, accrual may be required at the earlier time.[51]

For example, in *Decision, Inc.,*[52] the taxpayer provided recruiting services and sold advertising space in various publications. Under its agreement with customers, noncancellable orders were sometimes obtained in one year with the services to be rendered (or advertising to be provided) and the payment to be received in the succeeding year. The taxpayer sought to defer recognition of the income until the later year in which the services were rendered (or the advertising provided), but the court disagreed, finding that all events fixing the right to receive the amount had occurred in the earlier year. To avoid the effect of this decision, the taxpayer later changed its contracts to provide that it would not obtain any right to receive the income in question until the year in which the service was rendered (or the

---

[49] See Harrisburg Steel Corp. v. United States, 142 F. Supp. 626, 630 (MD Pa. 1956), where the taxpayer had no knowledge that insurance company had issued a refund check, but this fact did not prevent the required accrual of income. The court stated that it did "not feel that knowledge is a necessary ingredient in the ascertainment of the time of income accrual for tax purposes."

[50] See Camilla Cotton Oil Co., 31 TC 560, 568 (1958), acq. 1959-1 CB 3, where no accrual was required of a landlord who "did not know of the existence, much less the amount, of any additional [previously unacknowledged rental] income due it from [its tenant] at the close of its taxable year." See also discussion infra ¶ 4.03[1][b] regarding the rule that no accrual is required before the relevant amount can be determined with reasonable accuracy.

[51] See, e.g., Bell Fed. Sav. & Loan Assoc., 62 TCM 376 (1991), where a lender was found to have received a fixed right to points, which were in the nature of interest, at the time of the loan closings rather than ratably over the life of the loans, the court so finding because of particular provisions in the taxpayer's agreements with its borrowers. But see infra ¶ 4.03[3][e] for a discussion of circumstances in which a taxpayer may defer the recognition of income associated with certain accrued rights to the year in which services are rendered or property is transferred.

[52] Decision, Inc., 47 TC 58 (1966), acq. 1967-2 CB 2.

advertising provided). The court found that this change in the contract (and the resulting change in the time income was recognized) did not require the prior approval of the Commissioner.[53]

The principles referred to in *Decision, Inc.* point up one of the significant advantages of using an accrual method. Because agreements and business customs and practices are among the circumstances that affect when rights to income become fixed, it is often possible for taxpayers to make relatively minor modifications in their agreements, customs, or practices to delay the time when the right becomes fixed and, thus, the time when income must be recognized. Frequently, these modifications do not adversely affect their businesses or relations with customers. Of course, should any of the agreed on requirements be regarded as certain to occur and, not bona fide, or as purely ministerial in nature, they may not be regarded by the IRS as conditions precedent that prevent the accrual of income.[54]

[b] Determination of Amount With Reasonable Accuracy

Treasury Regulation § 1.451-1(a) precludes the recognition of income unless its amount can be determined with reasonable accuracy. Where an amount is properly accrued on the basis of a reasonable estimate, any difference between that amount and the precise amount, as later determined, must be taken into account in the year in which the precise determination is made.[55] This rule indicates that the difference should be taken into account only in that later year. Nevertheless, the taxpayer may have the option of taking the difference into account by filing an amended return for the year of initial accrual.[56]

In deciding whether an amount can be determined with reasonable accuracy, all relevant facts and circumstances must be considered.[57] Thus,

---

[53] See discussion at ¶ 9.06.

[54] See, e.g., Tech. Adv. Mem. 9143083 (Aug. 1, 1991), where the National Office required the accrual of income by a taxpayer who had performed certain advertising services but had not yet submitted the necessary forms for reimbursement, because the submission of the forms was purely ministerial in nature and it could not reasonably be anticipated that any dispute would arise regarding the right of the taxpayer to reimbursement.

[55] Treas. Reg. § 1.451-1(a). Kollsman Instruments Corp. v. Comm'r, 870 F2d 89 (2d Cir. 1989).

[56] See Continental Tie & Lumber Co. v. United States, 286 US 290, 298–299 (1932), where the Court stated, "Any necessary adjustment of [petitioner's] tax [due to a final determination of an Interstate Commerce Commission award] could readily have been accomplished by an amended return, claim for refund, or additional assessment, as the final award of the Commission might warrant."

[57] In Resale Mobile Homes, Inc., 91 TC 1085 (1988), the amount of a taxpayer's right to obtain so-called participation interest on the sale of its consumer paper to a finance company was found to be subject to reasonable estimate despite the fact that

where determination of the amount is itself subject to conditions precedent or contingencies, it is not possible to determine the amount with reasonable accuracy. Accordingly, although transactions may already have occurred, no accrual is necessary if the consideration to be paid is subject to later determination by the parties[58] or to resolution of a dispute over the amount.[59] However, the mere fact that the parties have not yet computed an amount that is otherwise determinable will not prevent accrual.[60]

Although there seems to be no express authority, accrual apparently is not required if the full amount cannot be determined with reasonable accuracy. Thus, where it is obvious that some amount will be paid to the taxpayer as a result of a transaction, but the full amount has yet to be determined, accrual of some arbitrarily determined amount is not required. For example, if an accrual method taxpayer using a calendar year provides services to his client during December and January, with the charge to be determined after all services have been rendered, no amount of income will be accrued at the end of the first year even though it is obvious that the December services alone entitle the taxpayer to some amount of income.

On the other hand, if it is certain that a fixed amount is due and only the excess above that amount is in question, the fixed amount should be accrued. Thus, if the taxpayer in the preceding example charged $100 per hour plus an additional amount to be determined at the conclusion of matter, then the amount of income to be accrued in the first year will be $100 times the number of hours worked in that year. The balance of the income, if any, will be reported in the following year.

The amount that is relevant is the amount that the taxpayer has a fixed right to receive. Therefore, if an obligation of the taxpayer's client or customer has an FMV that differs from its face amount, it is the face amount that is subject to accrual.[61] The IRS has taken this position even where

---

the precise amounts would be dependent on the actual dates of payment by consumers, including possible prepayments and defaults. The court was influenced by the fact that the calculation sought by the Commissioner was used by the taxpayer in its financial statements.

[58] Globe Corp. v. Comm'r, 20 TC 299 (1953), acq. 1953-2 CB 4.

[59] See, e.g., US Cartridge Co. v. United States, 284 US 511 (1932), where amounts to be received on cancellation of contract were not to be taken into account until allowed or otherwise definitely determined; Henry Hess Co., 16 TC 1363 (1951), aff'd, 210 F2d 553 (9th Cir. 1954), where the accrual was questioned because of a conflict over the value of a ship requisitioned by the War Shipping Administration.

[60] Frost Lumber Indus. Inc. v. Comm'r, 128 F2d 693 (5th Cir. 1942). An amount was determinable with reasonable accuracy where the price per acre was fixed and the number of acres could reasonably be estimated.

[61] See, e.g., First Sav. & Loan Ass'n, 40 TC 474, 487 (1963), where the court stated that "[a]n accrual-basis taxpayer does not treat an unconditional right to receive money as property received, but rather as money received to the full extent of the face value of the right." See also Western Oaks Bldg. Corp., 49 TC 365 (1968).

applicable statutory language indicates to the contrary.[62] Such a position by the IRS is seemingly wrong and clearly subject to challenge.[63]

Indeed, in *Nestle Holdings, Inc.*,[64] the court held that the IRS position was unfounded in the particular circumstance before it, one which involved the receipt of preferred stock under Section 1001. The court explained that it was appropriate for the face amount of a purchaser's obligation to pay money to be taken into account by an accrual basis taxpayer because the face amount was treated as money received for purposes of Section 1001 and not because of any theory that Section 1001 was subject to accrual method rules. The court thereupon held that only the FMV of preferred stock received by the taxpayer on the sale of certain inventory had to be included in the amount realized because the preferred stock was more in the nature of property received than money received.

[2] Items of Doubtful Collectibility

Even though a right to receive income has become fixed within a particular year and the amount thereof can be determined with reasonable accuracy,[65] an accrual basis taxpayer need not include that amount in income if there is a reasonable doubt as to its collectibility.[66] This doubt may be established by reason of the financial condition, insolvency, or other circumstances affecting the debtor or the obligation. In essence, the courts have determined that it is inappropriate to tax an individual on amounts whose collection is reasonably in doubt, even though those amounts are unquestionably due the taxpayer.[67]

Three main issues arise from this principle: (1) What level of uncertainty of collection must exist before accrual becomes unnecessary? (2) When must

---

[62] See Rev. Rul. 79-292, 1979-2 CB 287, where the amount realized by an accrual method taxpayer on a sale of property was held to be the face amount of the purchaser's obligation, not its FMV, notwithstanding the requirement of Section 1001(b), which defines the amount realized on a sale of property to include the FMV of property other than money. But see Nestle Holdings, Inc., 94 TC 803 (1990).

[63] See, e.g., Treas. Reg. § 1.461-1(a)(2)(iii)(A) providing so-called alternative timing rules and specifying that where any provision of the Code requires a liability to be taken into account in a taxable year that is later than the taxable year provided under the normal accrual rules, the liability must be taken into account as prescribed by that Code provision.

[64] Nestle Holdings, Inc., 94 TC 803 (1990).

[65] See discussion supra ¶ 4.03[1].

[66] See European Am. Bank & Trust Co. v. United States, 90-2 USTC ¶ 50,333 (Cl. Ct. 1990), where the court stated, "The 'all events' test is subject to an exception. A fixed right to a determinable amount does not require accrual if the item is uncollectible when the right to receive the income item arises. Accrual of income is not required when a fixed right to receive arises if there is not a reasonable expectancy that the claim will ever be paid." Clifton Mfg. Co. v. Comm'r, 137 F2d 290 (4th Cir. 1943). See also Commercial Solvents Corp., 42 TC 455 (1964), acq. 1965-1 CB 4.

[67] See Corn Exch. Bank v. United States, 37 F2d 34 (2d Cir. 1930), where the theory was expressed by the court as follows:

the uncertainty arise: at the time of the transaction, at the time of accrual, or merely prior to the end of the taxable year? (3) When should items whose collection was previously in doubt be accrued? In addition, consideration must be given to recently enacted provisions of the Tax Reform Act of 1986 (the 1986 Act) that permit accrual method service providers to exclude a portion of their accounts receivable from income.[68]

[a] Level of Uncertainty

Very few cases have focused on the level of uncertainty that is necessary to prevent an accrual of income by a taxpayer who otherwise has a fixed right to receive the income. The issue is the likelihood of ultimate payment, not whether the obligor is able to pay either at the time of entering into the agreement or at the time the amount is otherwise due.[69] Generally, the level of uncertainty must be significant.[70] Mere financial difficulty or hardship is insufficient.[71]

When a tax is lawfully imposed on income not actually received, it is upon the basis of reasonable expectancy of its receipt, but a taxpayer should not be required to pay a tax when it is reasonably certain that such alleged accrued income will not be received and when, in point of fact, it never was received. A taxpayer, even though keeping his books on an accrual basis, should not be required to pay a tax on an accrual income unless it is good and collectable, and, when it is of doubtful collectability or it is reasonably certain it will not be collected, it would be an injustice to the taxpayer to insist upon taxation.

[68] See IRC § 448(d)(5); Temp. Reg. § 1.448-2T. See also discussion infra ¶ 4.03[2][d].

[69] Corn Exch. Bank v. United States, 37 F2d 34 (2d Cir. 1930); Harmont Plaza, Inc., 64 TC 632 (1975), aff'd, 549 F2d 414 (6th Cir.), cert. denied, 434 US 955 (1977).

[70] In Jones Lumber Co. v. Comm'r, 404 F2d 764, 766 (6th Cir. 1968), the court stated:

In all of the cases cited in briefs and those found by our research which have held an item non-accruable because of doubtful collectibility, substantial evidence had been presented as to the financial instability or even the insolvency of the debtor. In fact, it has been said that to prevent accrual because of doubtful collectibility there must be a definite showing that the insolvency of the debtor makes receipt improbable. [Citations omitted.] It is not necessary for us now to decide whether the rule goes so far.

Although finding that the income in question had to be accrued, the court suggested that insolvency of the debtor is not required in order to show a reasonable doubt and that the course of dealings between the parties and any irregularity of payments are factors to be considered. See European Am. Bank & Trust Co. v. United States, 90-2 USTC ¶ 50,333 (Cl. Ct. 1990), the court stating that the uncertainty must be substantial and not simply technical and that substantial evidence must be presented to establish that there was no reasonable expectancy of payment.

[71] See Koehring Co. v. United States, 421 F2d 715 (Ct. Cl. 1970), where temporary financial difficulties were insufficient to prevent accrual; Georgia School-Book Depository, Inc., 1 TC 463 (1943), where the likelihood of legislative

The uncertainty of payment need not be related to financial circumstances only. Any other circumstance that brings ultimate collectibility into serious question may prevent accrual. For example, where collection depended on political action being taken by a governmental body that was not reasonably certain to take such action, accrual was unnecessary.[72]

Of course, the mere fact that the taxpayer enters into the transaction with the debtor suggests there is not at that time a sufficient level of uncertainty of collection to prevent accrual. Otherwise, presumably, the taxpayer would not have entered into the transaction.[73] Thus, to prevent accrual, the taxpayer must be able to show sufficient business reasons to warrant the transaction, notwithstanding the unlikelihood of collection. These reasons might include adverse publicity if the transaction does not occur, favorable publicity if it does occur, and beneficial effects of the transaction on other transactions.

[b] Time of Uncertainty

In *Spring City Foundry Co. v. United States*,[74] the Supreme Court held that the uncertainty of collection must exist at the time of accrual, i.e., at the time the right becomes fixed and the amount thereof can be determined with reasonable accuracy.[75] *Spring City Foundry* involved a sale of merchandise to a purchaser whose financial condition subsequently deteriorated. According to the Court, the gain on the sale accrued at the time of sale and prior to the deterioration of the purchaser's financial condition. The Court then held that the gain in question had to be recognized because its collection was not reasonably in doubt at the time of sale. The Court pointed out that the taxpayer's only relief was through the Code's bad debt provisions.[76]

---

appropriation of funds warranted accrual, although sufficient funds were not then available.

[72] Cuba R.R., 9 TC 211 (1947), acq. 1947-2 CB 2.

[73] See Jerry C. Moore, 45 TCM 557, 562 (1983): "Undoubtedly, if petitioners had real doubt as to collecting any amount whatsoever, they would have refused to extend credit to the prospective customers." See discussion infra ¶ 4.03[2][b] regarding the requisite time of uncertainty to prevent accrual.

[74] Spring City Foundry Co. v. United States, 292 US 182 (1934).

[75] European Am. Bank & Trust Co. v. United States, 90-2 USTC ¶ 50,333 (Cl. Ct. 1990).

[76] Accord Clifton Mfg. Co. v. Comm'r, 137 F2d 290 (4th Cir. 1943), involving interest on debt during period debtor was in receivership. See Credit Life Ins. Co. v. United States, 948 F2d 723 (Fed. Cir. 1991), where the taxpayer attempted to support its exclusion of an item from income on the basis of Treas. Reg. § 1.166-2(d), which provides a conclusive presumption of worthlessness for certain bad debts that regulatory agencies had required taxpayers to charge off. In that case, the taxpayer had been advised by a regulatory agency that a particular receivable shown on its books should either be written off or the correlative amount excluded from income.

[c] Accrual of Item Whose Collection Was Previously in Doubt

If accrual is not required owing to uncertainty of collection, when should accrual be required—when the uncertainty is removed or when the income is received? The better reasoned answer is when the uncertainty is removed,[77] although there is support for the latter view.[78]

[d] Nonaccrual of Service Income

In connection with the 1986 Act's limitations on the use of the cash method and the 1986 Act's repeal of the bad debt reserve method,[79] Congress enacted a special exclusionary method of accounting (the so-called nonaccrual-experience method) for accrual method service providers. Section 448(d)(5) provides that an accrual method taxpayer is not required to accrue that portion of amounts due for services rendered that, on the basis of the taxpayer's past experience, is unlikely to be collected.[80]

This special method is not available for accounts on which interest is charged or on which a penalty is imposed for the customer's or the client's failure to pay timely.[81] For this purpose, the offering of a discount for early

---

The taxpayer chose the latter course and also reported on that basis for tax purposes. The court denied the taxpayer the benefit of the conclusive presumption in the regulation, because the regulation pertained to writeoffs and the taxpayer did not write off the receivable on its return but, instead, excluded the same amount from income. The facts of the case suggested that the worthlessness occurred after the fixed right to receive had been obtained. See also Rev. Rul. 80-361, 1980-2 CB 164, where IRS ruled that taxpayer-creditor should accrue interest up to time of debtor's insolvency. But see Corn Exch. Bank v. United States, 37 F2d 34 (2d Cir. 1930), where interest income attributable to the taxable year 1918 had accrued during the year. The obligor went into receivership on December 31, 1918, and the issue was the accruability by the taxpayer of the interest income attributable to the period that ended on that date. The court did not require accrual of the income. This result suggests that the uncertainty of collection may exist at any time prior to the close of the taxable year.

The economic problem facing the taxpayer in *Spring City Foundry* was the fact that there was no statutory authority at the time permitting a deduction for partial worthlessness of a debt or use of a bad debt reserve. Following *Spring City Foundry*, Congress enacted provisions for both. However, because the 1986 Act repealed the use of bad debt reserves (see discussion infra ¶ 4.03[2][d] and at ¶ 8.04[6][d]), issues of collectibility are likely to increase.

[77] See Clifton Mfg. Co. v. Comm'r, 137 F2d 290 (4th Cir. 1943).

[78] See Corn Exch. Bank v. United States, 37 F2d 34 (2d Cir. 1930).

[79] See IRC § 448. See also discussion at ¶¶ 3.06[1] regarding the 1986 Act's limitations on use of the cash method, and 8.04[6][a] and 8.04[6][d], respectively, regarding adjustments required by reason of changes from the cash method and the bad debt reserve method.

[80] See also Temp. Reg. § 1.448-2T.

[81] IRC § 448(d)(5).

payment will not be regarded as a charging of interest or a penalty for late payment if (1) the full amount due the taxpayer is otherwise accrued as the services are provided and (2) the discount for early payment is treated as an adjustment to income in the year of payment (assuming the discount is allowed).[82]

The temporary regulations make it clear that the method is available to all accrual method service providers, not merely to those who were required to change to an accrual method by reason of the 1986 Act.[83] The method is not available to activities involving the lending of money, the selling of goods, or the acquiring of receivables from other persons, regardless of whether those other persons earned the receivables through the rendition of services.[84] The method is a method of accounting and, hence, once adopted, may not be departed from without the prior approval of the Commissioner. (See Chapters 8 and 9 regarding changes in accounting methods.

Under the temporary regulations, the method is deemed to apply to each affected receivable.[85] The uncollectible portion of the receivable is the portion that is equal to the ratio of (1) total bad debts actually sustained during a moving six-year period (or, with the approval of the IRS, a shorter period) ending with the taxable year and adjusted for recoveries of bad debts during the period to (2) the total of all accounts receivable earned throughout the entire period of six (or fewer) taxable years. In making this computation, accounts receivable on which interest is charged or for which a penalty is imposed for late payments must be disregarded.[86] According to the temporary regulations, no other method or formula may be used.[87] It remains to be seen whether this prohibition on other approaches will be accepted by the courts in their interpretation of the applicable statutory provision.

This particular formula produces erroneous results in certain circumstances and, hence, is inconsistent with the statutory mandate that a taxpayer shall not be required to include amounts which, based on experience, are unlikely to be collected. Where the average age of the taxpayer's debt at the time it is written off exceeds a relatively short period, application of the present formula may produce too low an exclusion.

EXAMPLE: Assume that X uses the nonaccrual-experience method in 1987 and that its total accounts receivable (i.e., credit charges for the

---

[82] Temp. Reg. § 1.448-2T(c)(1).

[83] Temp. Reg. § 1.448-2T(a).

[84] Temp. Reg. § 1.448-2T(d).

[85] Alternatively, in Notice 88-51 1988-1 CB 535, the IRS allowed taxpayers to make their nonaccrual-experience method calculations under a so-called periodic system, which, while different in form, operates substantially very much like the previously repealed bad debt reserve method.

[86] Temp. Reg. § 1.448-2T(e)(2).

[87] Temp. Reg. § 1.448-2T(e)(1).

year), year-end accounts receivable balances, and bad debts (adjusted for recoveries) are as follows:

Years	Total accounts receivable	Year-end accounts receivable	Bad debts adjusted for recoveries
1982	$ 30,000	$ 18,488	$ 5,700
1983	40,000	24,650	7,200
1984	50,000	30,813	11,000
1985	60,000	36,975	10,200
1986	70,000	43,138	14,000
1987	80,000	49,300	16,800
	$330,000	$203,364	$64,900

This information shows that just under 20 percent of X's annual credit charges are not collected ($64,900 ÷ $330,000 = 19.67 percent). Thus, based on experience, an aggregate of $15,736 (19.67 percent of the $80,000 of 1987 credit charges) should be uncollectible and, therefore, should be written off during the year or excluded. Since $49,300 of the total $80,000 of accounts receivable was outstanding at the end of the year, the remaining $30,700 of charges ($80,000 − $49,300) was either collected or written off during the year. Using the regulatory formula, X is entitled to exclude $9,697.31 from income ($49,300 × 19.67 percent). Thus, there is an additional $6,038.69 ($15,736 − $9,697.31) to be accounted for. If this amount of current year charges was written off during 1987, X received the proper exclusion from year-end receivables. However, if less than this amount was written off during the year, X will be required by the formula to include in income amounts which (based on experience) it will not collect, a result expressly prohibited by the statute.

The Treasury has informally recognized the defects inherent in the present formula and is considering alternative formulae. However, until a new formula is announced, taxpayers should consider carefully whether they should follow the present formula or depart from it on the basis that it is inconsistent with the statute and therefore invalid.

The temporary regulations specify that a period of fewer than six years may be used only if the taxpayer receives the approval of the Commissioner to use a shorter period. That approval will be available if the taxpayer is able to demonstrate that a change in the economic conditions of the area in which the taxpayer's business is conducted has made the taxpayer's experience in earlier years not comparable to its current years. However, a mere increase in the taxpayer's bad debt experience will not justify the use of fewer than six years. The request for use of a shorter period must be sent to the Commissioner at least 30 days before the close of the year for which the approval is requested. The request is made just as a request for any other ruling.[88]

For a new taxpayer who has been in business fewer than five years preceding the tax year, only actual years of experience are taken into account. However, if the taxpayer is the successor to another trade or business, the experience of the predecessor trade or business may be used in making the computations. This appears to be permissive rather than mandatory.[89]

The temporary regulations provide that on collection of any particular account receivable, any income received in excess of the amount originally included in income must be taken into account in the year received. Similarly, any subsequent bad debt deduction must be reduced by the amount previously excluded from income. In addition, the exclusion from income of a portion of each affected amount receivable is to be made only once. In other words, once a receivable is taken into account for purposes of the exclusion, it is not taken into account in the succeeding tax year and is not to be the basis for a further exclusion.[90] The temporary regulations provide a number of examples illustrating the computations to be made.[91]

As a result of the new nonaccrual-experience method, taxpayers whose business includes both the sale of goods and the sale of services may be advantaged by segregating their charges for the sales and service portions of their business. This segregation should permit taxpayers to use the nonaccrual-experience method for that portion of total receivables associated with the rendition of services. Absent this segregation, it is likely that the IRS will take the position that the entire charge relates to a sale of goods and, hence, that no portion of it is subject to reduction by virtue of the nonaccrual-experience method.[92] Similarly, taxpayers who use supplies in rendering services are eligible to use the nonaccrual-experience method. However, if the supplies used are actually merchandise sold, the charges will not be subject to reduction under the nonaccrual-experience method.[93]

Finally, use of the nonaccrual-experience method for accrual method service providers does not preclude application of the normal accrual rules. Consequently, accrual of amounts which, at the time of accrual, are unlikely to be collected is not required, regardless of the origin of the receivable, whether it relates to a sale of merchandise or services, or whether interest or a penalty is charged for late payment.[94] Taxpayers and their advisors should remain alert to this point.

---

[88] Temp. Reg. § 1.448-2T(e)(2)(ii).

[89] Temp. Reg. § 1.448-2T(e)(2)(iii).

[90] Temp. Reg. § 1.448-2T(e)(3).

[91] Temp. Reg. § 1.448-2T(e)(4).

[92] See discussion at ¶ 6.05[1][d].

[93] See discussion at ¶ 6.05[2][a].

[94] See discussion supra ¶ 4.03[2][d].

[3] Prepaid Income

The focus of the previous discussion was the recognition of income by accrual method taxpayers prior to their receipt of payment. When payment precedes satisfaction of the all events test, numerous questions arise. Foremost among them is (1) whether tax considerations (such as protection of the public treasury and ability to pay) warrant taxation on receipt (actual or constructive)[95] or (2) whether characteristics of accrual accounting (such as assertedly more accurate matching of income and expense than other methods)[96] warrant deferral until some later year when all events have occurred that fix the taxpayer's right to the income.

The answer to this question has varied over time and still varies today. However, in general, the judicial, congressional, and administrative treatment of prepaid income by accrual method taxpayers may be broken down into three distinct approaches centering on the Supreme Court's decisions in a trilogy of cases: *Automobile Club of Michigan v. Commissioner*,[97] *American Automobile Association v. United States*,[98] and *Schlude v. Commissioner*.[99]

Unfortunately, the trilogy serves only as a chronological reference point to answering the question of proper tax accounting for prepaid income. The trilogy and the cases that have preceded and followed it do not provide clear guidance as to the correct result. Depending on the particular facts, pretrilogy cases may be just as applicable today as both the trilogy and post-trilogy cases. Moreover, following the trilogy, there have been congressional enactments, Treasury regulations, and revenue procedures providing varying opportunities for deferral in the recognition of particular prepayments. Thus, taxpayers who seek deferrals must gauge their particular circumstances against a host of judicial, legislative, and administrative pronouncements, most of which have emanated from political or practical considerations.

[a] Pretrilogy Treatment

The leading pretrilogy case was *Beacon Publishing Co. v. Commissioner*,[100] which involved the proper treatment of prepaid newspaper subscriptions. The Commissioner sought to include the prepayments in income in the year of receipt, while the taxpayer sought to include them over the subscription periods to which they related. The Court of Appeals for the Tenth Circuit held for the taxpayer, citing a number of factors in support of

---

[95] See ¶ 3.03[2] for discussion of constructive receipt.

[96] See ¶ 2.02[2][f] regarding the effect of matching related items of income and expense on the clear reflection of income standard.

[97] Automobile Club of Mich. v. Comm'r, 353 US 180 (1957).

[98] American Auto. Ass'n v. United States, 367 US 687 (1961).

[99] Schlude v. Comm'r, 372 US 128 (1963).

[100] Beacon Publishing Co. v. Comm'r, 218 F2d 697 (10th Cir. 1955).

its decision. First, the court noted the applicable Code provisions,[101] which expressly permitted an accrual method of accounting and required that items of income be included in the year of receipt unless those amounts were properly accounted for in a different period. The court pointed out that if accrual-basis taxpayers were required to recognize prepaid income in the year of receipt (if earlier than the year in which the items would otherwise be recognized), accrual methods would be limited to cases "where money has been earned and the right to it has been fixed, but the receipt is delayed to a subsequent taxable period. The application of [such a] doctrine would in most cases result in a distortion of an accrual taxpayer's true income."[102]

The court also held that the so-called claim-of-right doctrine was not relevant or applicable to the issue because there was no dispute over the ownership of the funds in question (and, if applicable, it would have the practical effect of placing all accrual method taxpayers on the cash basis with respect to prepayments).[103] The court noted that the recognition of prepaid income in the year of receipt would result in a mismatching of related items of income and expense that, in turn, would cause a distortion of income. According to the court, Congress's enactment of Section 452 as part of the 1954 Code indicated the appropriateness of applying an accrual method for tax purposes as it would be applied for financial accounting purposes. The court viewed the enactment of Section 452 as an expression of congressional preference for greater conformity between book and tax accounting as well as a rejection of judicial decisions and IRS rulings that had resulted in many divergences between book and tax reporting.

Following *Beacon Publishing*, a related issue was considered by the

---

[101] Sections 41 and 42 of the 1939 Code, the predecessors to Sections 446(a) and 451.

[102] Beacon Publishing Co. v. Comm'r, 218 F2d 697, 700 (10th Cir. 1955). The court added:

To a large extent, [inclusion of prepayments in the year of receipt] destroys the principle inherent in the accrual method of accounting. Plainly, Section 42 contemplates that prepaid sums can be returned in a year other than when received. It says that income shall be included in the taxable year received, 'unless, under methods of accounting permitted under section 41, any such amounts are to be properly accounted for as of a different period.' This is not a case where the Commissioner has exercised his broad discretion to require a taxpayer to adopt an accounting method which will clearly reflect income, but is one in which he has improperly implied a legal principle.

Id. at 701. The preceding analysis appears to be reinforced by Treas. Reg. § 1.61-8(b), where the Treasury made it clear that in certain cases, prepaid rent would be taxable in the year of receipt without regard to the taxpayer's method of accounting. Since rent is generally associated with precisely determinable periods, it would appear that absent such regulatory provision, deferral would be appropriate.

[103] The claim-of-right doctrine was first announced in North Am. Oil Consol. v. Burnet, 286 US 417 (1931). For discussion of the claim of right doctrine, see ¶ 12.03.

Court of Appeals for the Fifth Circuit in *Schuessler v. Commissioner.*[104] The issue was whether the taxpayer should be permitted to deduct, in the year of its sales, a reserve for the estimated costs of carrying out its obligations under guarantees made with respect to the items sold. The evidence established both the cost of the taxpayer's obligation under the guarantee and the fact that the taxpayer generally charged more for his product because of the guarantee. Deduction of the reserve had the effect of reducing (or deferring) income equal in amount to the cost of satisfying the guarantee. To this extent, the issue was similar to that involving prepaid income. The Court expressed a preference for the reasoning of *Beacon Publishing* and allowed the deduction, although Sections 452 and 462, whose enactment had been relied on by the court in *Beacon Publishing,* had since been repealed.

[b] The Trilogy

Notwithstanding the analyses in *Beacon Publishing* and *Schuessler,* the three cases comprising the trilogy established that in particular circumstances, it was not an abuse of discretion for the IRS to require advance payments to be included in income in the year of receipt without regard to satisfaction of the all events test. Because the trilogy focused on the particular circumstances then before the Court, *Beacon Publishing* and *Schuessler* may remain viable authorities when evaluating other circumstances.

In the first case in the trilogy, *Automobile Club of Michigan v. Commissioner,*[105] the taxpayer received advance payments of one year's membership dues, which entitled its customers to receive certain services during the ensuing 12 months on an "as needed" basis. The taxpayer took $1/12$ of the annual dues into income each month. The IRS sought to require inclusion of the entire amount in income in the year of receipt on the basis of the claim-of-right doctrine.[106] The Supreme Court held for the IRS, but not on the basis of claim of right. Rather, the Court reasoned that, since the inclusion of the prepayment on a pro rata basis was "purely artificial and [bore] no relation to the services which petitioner may in fact be called upon to render,"[107] the Commissioner had the discretion to require the advance payments to be recognized in income in the year of receipt. The basis for the Court's decision was the failure of the taxpayer's method to reflect income clearly.[108]

---

[104] Schuessler v. Comm'r, 230 F2d 722 (5th Cir. 1956).

[105] Automobile Club of Mich. v. Comm'r, 353 US 180 (1957).

[106] The claim-of-right doctrine is discussed at ¶ 12.03.

[107] Automobile Club of Mich. v. Comm'r, 353 US 180, 189 (1957).

[108] See ¶¶ 2.02[2] regarding the clear reflection of income standard and 12.03 regarding the claim-of-right doctrine. It was clear that the Supreme Court did not accept the claim-of-right argument inasmuch as it referred to *Beacon Publishing* and

Following *Automobile Club of Michigan*, the IRS asserted that all prepayments should be taxed in the year of receipt. A conflict in decisions soon developed. In *Bressner Radio Inc. v. Commissioner*,[109] the Court of Appeals for the Second Circuit allowed a seller of television sets to defer the recognition of prepaid income attributable to one-year service contracts. The court permitted the taxpayer to include the prepayments in income ratably over the one-year period. It found that such recognition was not "purely artificial" but reasonable, taking into account aggregate service contracts. However, in *American Automobile Association v. United States*,[110] the Court of Claims held to the contrary in circumstances involving association members, who prepaid annual dues in exchange for certain travel-related services to be rendered solely on a member's demand. The court disapproved the association's practice of recognizing the dues ratably over the 12-month membership period.

To resolve this conflict, the Supreme Court granted certiorari, and *American Automobile Association*[111] became the second case in the trilogy. The Supreme Court affirmed the decision of the Court of Claims and, hence, the position of the Commissioner. The Court again based its decision on the artificiality of the taxpayer's approach. It viewed as insufficient certain statistical evidence, which was based on aggregate data and which suggested that the taxpayer's method of recognizing income had been appropriate. The Court stated:

> [F]indings merely reflecting statistical computations of average monthly cost per member on a group or pool basis are without determinate significance to our decision that the federal revenue cannot, without legislative consent and over objection of the Commissioner, be made to depend upon average experience in rendering performance and turning a profit.[112]

The Court stated that its finding of artificiality was based on the fact that

---

Schuessler and stated that each was distinguishable. (The deferral provided in *Beacon* lasted only until specified publication dates, and the services to be rendered in *Scheussler* were also to be rendered at specified times in the future.) Had the Court chosen to accept the government's claim-of-right argument, it necessarily would have determined that the courts of appeals had erred in *Beacon* and *Scheussler*. The claim-of-right argument had been successful in earlier cases. See, e.g., Curtis R. Andrews, 23 TC 1026 (1955); South Dade Farms v. Comm'r, 138 F2d 818 (5th Cir. 1943); Clay Sewer Pipe Ass'n v. Comm'r, 139 F2d 130 (3d Cir. 1943); see also the dissent of J. Stewart in *Schlude*.

[109] Bressner Radio Inc. v. Comm'r, 267 F2d 520 (2d Cir. 1959).

[110] American Auto. Ass'n v. United States, 181 F. Supp. 255 (Ct. Cl. 1960).

[111] American Auto. Ass'n v. United States, 367 US 687 (1961).

[112] Id. at 693.

services were rendered only on demand and not according to or relating to fixed dates.[113] The Court also placed significance on the congressional decision to repeal Sections 452 and 462, which would have allowed the deferral sought by the taxpayer.[114]

The final case in the trilogy, *Schlude*,[115] involved the treatment of prepaid dance lessons. The dance contracts guaranteed students a certain number of lesson hours and, in some cases, provided a lifetime entitlement to lessons and dance parties.[116] The contracts designated the period over which the lessons had to be taken, but there was no schedule of specific dates on which the lessons would be provided. Income was reported on the basis of the number of hours of lessons taught within the year multiplied by a designated rate per hour. In addition, if there were no activity on a contract for over a year or if the number of lessons in the course were reduced, prepayments attributable to the untaught portions of the contract would at that time be recognized in income. The Commissioner sought to include the prepayments in income in the year received. Relying on the reasoning of its earlier cases, the Court determined that the method used by the taxpayer did not clearly reflect income and could be changed.

In each of the cases in the trilogy, the Court regarded as significant the fact that services would be performed only on customer demand. Thus, there was no certainty as to when those services would be performed and when the advance payments would be included in income. It was therefore possible under the taxpayers' methods that all required services might be performed in one year, but some portion of the income would be deferred until a later year. In each case, the taxpayer's method of estimating performance over time was found to be purely artificial.

The Court's analysis in these cases was consistent with sound tax policy. Since the method of recognition was arbitrary and possibly unrelated to when or if services would be rendered, it was appropriate for concepts of ability to pay, certainty, and protection of the public treasury to require that the income be recognized on its receipt. Otherwise, either uncertainty in the time of recognition or artificiality in the amount of recognition would result.

---

[113] For this reason, the Court again distinguished *Beacon Publishing* and *Schuessler*. Id. at 691, n.4.

[114] Id. at 695–696.

[115] Schlude v. Comm'r, 372 US 128 (1963).

[116] The dance lessons were offered under two contracts. Under one, the entire down payment was paid in cash on the execution of the contract with the balance due in installments. Under the other, only a portion of the down payment was paid in cash. The remainder of the down payment was due in stated installments with the customer's obligation for the balance of the contract evidenced by a negotiable note.

[c] Post-Trilogy Decisions

Following the trilogy, the IRS took the position that accrual method taxpayers were required to report income in the year in which the all events test was satisfied or, if earlier, the year of receipt.[117] Initially, the courts agreed. In some cases, their conclusion was set forth as if the particular circumstances of the case were irrelevant.[118] In other cases, the decisions to deny deferral were not stated as broadly but, rather, were in line with the circumstances and principles espoused in the trilogy.[119]

Over time, however, decisions were forthcoming in which deferrals in the recognition of prepaid income were allowed, the courts concluding that

---

[117] The IRS position was that except as might otherwise be permitted under applicable regulations or revenue procedures, income must be recognized by an accrual method taxpayer on the earliest of (1) performance; (2) when payment is due; or (3) when payment is received. See, e.g., Rev. Rul. 74-607, 1974-2 CB 149; Rev. Rul. 80-308, 1980-2 CB 162; Rev. Rul. 83-106, 1983-2 CB 77; Rev. Rul. 84-31, 1984-1 CB 127. See also Rev. Rul. 75-195, 1979-1 CB 177, where the IRS ruled that the right to receive income from the performance of severable acts occurs as each severable act is completed, even though all performance under the contract has not then been completed; Tech. Adv. Mem. 8744005 (July 22, 1987), for an illustration of the manner in which Rev. Proc. 79-195 is applied by the IRS.

[118] See Gillis v. United States, 402 F2d 501, 506 (5th Cir. 1968), where the court stated: "The theory behind the accrual system is not complicated. Income items are reported in the year in which the right to receive them becomes fixed even though such items are not immediately receivable. At no time, however, are such items reportable later than the year of actual receipt." Similarly, in E. Morris Cox, 43 TC 448 (1965), acq. 1965-2 CB 4, the taxpayer was not permitted to defer the recognition of prepaid fees for financial advisory services even though performance of the services was to occur regularly over specified periods and was not to be subject to client demand. See also Hagen Advertising Displays, Inc. v. Comm'r, 407 F2d 1105 (6th Cir. 1969), where the court denied a deferral of prepaid income attributable to a sale of goods, the court giving great import to the congressional repeal of Sections 452 and 462, as interpreted in *Schlude*.

[119] See, e.g., Angelus Funeral Home, 47 TC 391 (1967), acq. 1969-2 CB xxiii, aff'd, 407 F2d 210 (9th Cir. 1969), cert. denied, 396 US 824 (1969) (prepaid funeral services taxable on receipt); Standard Television Tube Corp., 64 TC 238 (1975) (prepaid warranty services not deferrable where deferral was based on the taxpayer's experience, judgment, and statistical data); Allied Fidelity Corp., 66 TC 1068 (1976), aff'd, 572 F2d 1190 (7th Cir. 1978), cert. denied, 439 US 835 (1978) (prepaid insurance premiums, while related to particular periods, were actually obligations incurred by the taxpayer to pay money on certain conditions, and were neither fixed nor definite); T.F.H. Publications, Inc., 72 TC 623 (1979), aff'd in unpublished opinion, 622 F2d 579 (3d Cir. 1980), cert. denied, 449 US 921 (1980) (Tax Court unwilling to permit deferral unless facts show a certainty of performance or fixed dates); Chesapeake Fin. Corp., 78 TC 869 (1982) (not only must the requisite certainty exist but the requested deferral must result in a matching of related items of income and expense); see also Modernaire Interiors, Inc., 27 TCM 1334 (1968).

the Supreme Court had left open the possibility that particular methods of deferring advance payments could clearly reflect income under certain circumstances, and that the Commissioner's rejection of those methods would constitute an abuse of discretion.[120]

In *Artnell Co. v. Commissioner*,[121] the issue was the treatment of advance ticket sales for Chicago White Sox baseball games. The taxpayer deferred the inclusion of the sales in income until the year in which the games were played. The Court of Appeals for the Seventh Circuit found that none of the infirmities of the cases in the trilogy were present. The time of performance was fixed, and related items of income and expense would be matched. The court pointed out that in certain cases,

> the extent and time of future performance [may be] so certain, and related items properly accounted for with such clarity, that a system of accounting involving deferral of prepaid income [may be] found clearly to reflect income, and the Commissioner's rejection [of that system would be] deemed an abuse of discretion.[122]

On remand, the Tax Court determined that the taxpayer's method "clearly reflected" income, and the deferral was permitted.[123] However, the Tax Court did not enthusiastically follow the reasoning of the appeals court.[124]

Eight years after *Artnell*, the Court of Claims concluded in *Boise Cascade Corp. v. United States*[125] that the method of accounting employed by an engineering services company, under which the recognition of advance payments of income was deferred until the related services were performed, clearly reflected income. The obligation to perform was definite and not subject to the demands of clients. Although performance was to occur within the year following receipt of payment, there were no fixed dates for perfor-

---

[120] It must be remembered that the Supreme Court did not reject *Beacon Publishing* and *Schuessler* (discussed supra ¶ 4.03[3][a]) but, instead, had distinguished them in both *Automobile Club of Michigan* and *American Automobile Association*. This action also suggested that the Court had not intended to prevent deferral in the recognition of every prepayment.

[121] Artnell Co. v. Comm'r, 400 F2d 981 (7th Cir. 1968).

[122] Id. at 984.

[123] Artnell Co. v. Comm'r, 29 TCM 403 (1970).

[124] For example, in Collegiate Cap and Gown Co., 37 TCM 960 (1978), the Tax Court applied the principles established in *Artnell* because the case before it was appealable to the Seventh Circuit. The court held that the taxpayer's method clearly reflected income, but made it clear that it was so holding "without necessarily implying that [it would] accept the Seventh Circuit's approach [in *Artnell*] in comparable cases not appealable to that Circuit." Id. at 965.

[125] Boise Cascade Corp. v. United States, 530 F2d 1367 (Ct. Cl. 1976), cert. denied, 429 US 867 (1976).

mance.[126] Similarly, in *Morgan Guaranty Trust Co. v. United States*,[127] the Court of Claims concluded that prepaid interest income could be deferred until the time it was earned by the passage of time, where (1) the date it would be earned could be determined precisely; (2) the deferral method was required by the Federal Reserve Board; (3) the method had been used consistently for many years; (4) the amounts involved were insignificant compared with the total interest income ($166,000 compared with $126 million); and (5) the prepayments were not required as a condition of the loan. In conclusion, the Court of Appeals for the Seventh Circuit and the Claims Court have permitted deferral of advance payments in situations where both the fact and the year of performance were certain, although in *Boise Cascade* the specific time of performance was not certain.

Although other courts of appeals have not yet applied the rationale of *Artnell* and *Boise Cascade* following the trilogy, it is not clear that they would reject that rationale. For example, the pretrilogy decisions of *Beacon Publishing* and *Scheussler* suggest that the Courts of Appeals for the Tenth and Fifth Circuits might be receptive.[128]

Despite the apparent willingness of the Claims Court, the Seventh Circuit, and perhaps other circuits to distinguish the trilogy and thereby limit its impact, other courts have been less inclined to allow deferrals, although not ruling them out in all cases. For example, the Court of Appeals for the Second Circuit rejected an extension of the *Artnell* principle to services rendered on demand, notwithstanding statistical evidence indicating the appropriateness of the deferral.[129] However, the court suggested that if certainty as to the time of performance had been present, it might have been inclined to follow the *Artnell* rationale.[130] The Tax Court, too, has rejected attempts by taxpayers to defer income on the basis of *Artnell*, indicating that it is not generally inclined to follow that decision, but nevertheless implying that it might do so in appropriate circumstances.[131]

---

[126] Compare E. Morris Cox, 43 TC 448, 451 (1963), acq. 1965-2 CB 4, where the court held that billings had to be included in income in the year received, even though the billings reflected quarterly fees paid in advance by clients "for the 3-month period commencing with the day on which the corporation's services are engaged and the corresponding day of every third month thereafter."

[127] Morgan Guar. Trust Co. v. United States, 585 F2d 988 (Ct. Cl. 1978).

[128] However, the receptivity of the Fifth Circuit is somewhat suspect in light of Mooney Aircraft, Inc. v. United States, 420 F2d 400 (5th Cir. 1969), discussed infra ¶ 4.04[4].

[129] RCA Corp. v. United States, 664 F2d 881 (2d Cir. 1981), cert. denied, 457 US 1133 (1982).

[130] RCA Corp. v. United States, 664 F2d at 888–889.

[131] See Collegiate Cap and Gown Co., 37 TCM 960 (1978), discussed supra ¶ 4.03[3][c], note 110; see also Handy Andy T.V. & Appliances, Inc., 47 TCM 478, 487 (1983):

[d] Length of Deferral

An important remaining issue, even in jurisdictions that have permitted a deferral of prepaid income, is the length of any permitted deferral. *Artnell* involved a deferral of a relatively short period of one year. *Boise Cascade*, although not as definite, clearly indicated that all services attributable to the prepaid income would be rendered in the year following the receipt of the prepayment.[132]

Courts have not limited the deferral to one year, however. For example, in *Automated Marketing Systems, Inc. v. United States*,[133] the court, without analysis, permitted a deferral of up to 30 months. Similarly, in *Beacon Publishing* and *Schuessler*, pretrilogy cases, the deferrals were for periods well in excess of one year.[134] Additionally, as discussed in the following section, statutory and regulatory provisions also permit deferrals in excess of one year.

[e] Provisions Permitting Deferral

[i] **Congressional.** Following repeal of Sections 452 and 462, the IRS adopted an approach that all items of prepaid income were taxable in the year of receipt. Numerous cases arose, resulting in the trilogy and other cases discussed in the preceding sections.[135]

Sections 455 and 456 were enacted in response to many of the issues that arose. Section 455 pertains to prepaid subscription income and permits that income to be recognized over the period covered by the subscription. For this purpose, the taxpayer is permitted to determine the subscription period on the basis of its experience, taking into account aggregate transactions.[136]

[P]etitioner failed to show that, based either upon the terms of its existing service policy contracts or upon historical data as related to services previously rendered to individual payees, it actually would perform its claimed estimated future services within a specific period with reasonable certainty. Without such a showing, under the principles set forth by the trilogy of the Supreme Court decisions and followed by the Second Circuit, we must conclude that petitioner's method of reporting its prepaid service policy contract income during the years in issue did not clearly reflect its income.

[132] See also Petroleum Heat & Power Co., Inc. v. United States, 405 F2d 1300 (Ct. Cl. 1969), where the court noted the fact that the deferral would be for a relatively short period.

[133] Automated Mktg. Sys., Inc. v. United States, 1974-2 USTC ¶ 9711 (ND Ill. 1974), aff'd, No. 74-1678 (7th Cir. 1975).

[134] The deferrals were for periods up to five years in both *Beacon* and *Scheussler*, discussed supra ¶ 4.03[3][a].

[135] See discussion supra ¶¶ 4.03[3][b]–4.03[3][d].

[136] Treas. Reg. § 1.455-3.

Section 456 pertains to prepaid dues income of certain membership organizations and permits a similar deferral of prepayments.

In 1970, the President's Task Force on Business Taxation concluded that increasing divergence between the computation of income for financial and tax purposes resulted in unnecessary complexity and controversy. It recommended that steps be taken by regulation and legislation to achieve greater conformity.[137] As a consequence, regulations and rulings were issued that provide a deferral in the recognition of certain prepayments by accrual method taxpayers.[138]

[ii] **Treasury and IRS.**　Beginning in the early 1970s, the Treasury and the IRS responded to the 1970 recommendation of the President's Task Force. They recognized the appropriateness of permitting limited deferrals in the recognition of income arising from prepayments for services and goods. In part, the decision to allow these deferrals may have stemmed from the reasoning of the court in *Artnell* and the recognition that without such permitted deferrals, the IRS would engage in a never-ending series of disputes with taxpayers.[139]

Advance payment for services.　Revenue Procedure 71-21[140] sets forth the circumstances under which the IRS will permit a one-year deferral in the recognition of certain prepaid income. In effect, the revenue procedure permits taxpayers to defer payments received in one year for services to be rendered in the next succeeding year. The ruling applies both to actual payments and to amounts that are due and payable. Thus, when the all events test otherwise requires the inclusion of items in income, this procedure may permit a deferral until the next year when the service is rendered.[141]

In general, the ruling permits an accrual method taxpayer who, pursuant to an agreement, receives a payment in one taxable year for services to be performed before the end of the next succeeding taxable year to include those amounts in income in the year the services are rendered. The agreement may be written or oral. However, the agreement must provide that all services required by it must be performed before the end of the next succeeding

---

[137] Report of the President's Task Force on Business Taxation 60 (Sept. 1970).

[138] See discussion infra ¶ 4.03[3][e][ii].

[139] See Rev. Proc. 70-21, 1970-2 CB 501, 502, where the IRS stated that "many problems [had] arisen in connection with the tax accounting treatment of payments received by accrual method taxpayers in one taxable year for services to be performed by them in the next succeeding taxable year."

[140] Rev. Proc. 71-21, 1971-2 CB 549. This revenue procedure superseded Rev. Proc. 70-21, 1970-2 CB 501.

[141] Had this revenue procedure been issued earlier, the taxpayer in *Decision, Inc.*, discussed supra ¶ 4.03[1][a][iii], might not have found it necessary to change its agreements with customers in order to defer the recognition of income until services were provided.

year. If the agreement requires that a portion of the services relating to the prepayment are to be rendered in the second year following receipt or later (or if any portion of the services may be performed at an unspecified date that may be after the year following the year of prepayment), the benefits of the revenue ruling are not available to any portion of the prepayment. On the other hand, if the services to be rendered in the year following prepayment are not rendered in that year for any reason, the amount allocated to those services must nevertheless be included in income in the year following the year of prepayment. Thus, the one-year deferral will not be denied because of the failure to render the services when required.[142]

One question that has plagued taxpayers under this procedure is whether it applies to agreements for the rendition of services over a period of several years where, pursuant to the agreement, a series of prepayments will be made with the services relating to each prepayment always performed in the year succeeding the year of prepayment. For example, an agreement might provide for prepayments to be made in years 1, 2, 3, and 4 with the corresponding services to be rendered in years 2, 3, 4, and 5, respectively. The IRS has been reluctant to apply Revenue Procedure 71-21 in these circumstances. However, application of the procedure may be warranted. Since the ruling would clearly apply if four separate contracts had been entered into, it is illogical to deny application of the procedure where the agreements are contained in a single document. In either case, the prepayment is for services that must be rendered in the year following receipt of the prepayment.

In the case of advance payments for bus or streetcar tokens or transportation tickets, Revenue Procedure 71-21 permits these amounts to be included in income in accordance with generally accepted industry accounting practices, provided that the recognition of income occurs no later than the taxable year subsequent to the year of receipt. Somewhat similar rules are provided for "mailers, certificates or other evidence of a prepaid obligation to process photographic film, prints or other photographic materials."

Where an agreement requires a taxpayer to perform contingent services with respect to property that has been sold, leased, built, installed, or constructed by the taxpayer (or by a "related person"),[143] Revenue Procedure 71-21 permits the one-year deferral, but only if, in the ordinary course of business, the taxpayer offers to sell, lease, build, install, or construct the property without a related contingent service agreement. The revenue procedure does not otherwise apply to (1) amounts received under guarantee or

---

[142] Application of this revenue procedure would have benefited the taxpayer in E. Morris Cox, 43 TC 448 (1965), discussed supra ¶ 4.03[3][c].

[143] Rev. Proc. 71-21, 1971-2 CB 549, 550, provides that "a person is related to the taxpayer if the taxpayer and such other person are owned or controlled directly or indirectly by the same interests within the meaning of section 482 of the Code and section 1.482-1(a) of the regulations."

warranty contracts; (2) prepaid rent; or (3) prepaid interest.[144] For this purpose, rent does not include payments for the use or occupancy of rooms or other space where significant services are also rendered to the occupant. Examples include the use or occupancy of rooms or other quarters in hotels, motels, and boarding houses.[145]

Where the procedure applies to contingent services such as those described above, the amount of the advance payment to be included in income in a particular year may be determined (1) on the basis of adequate statistical data; (2) on a straight-line ratable basis (if reasonable); or (3) on any other basis that in the opinion of the Commissioner, will result in a clear reflection of income. Allowing the amounts to be determined in this fashion indicates an IRS departure from the Supreme Court's earlier refusal to accept such determinations.[146]

The revenue procedure also provides certain general rules applicable to each of the situations covered by it. For example, in no event may the amount included in taxable income in the year of receipt be less than the amount included in income of that year for book and financial reporting purposes. If, in any year, a taxpayer using Revenue Procedure 71-21 should die (if an individual), cease to exist by reason of a transaction other than one to which Section 381(a) applies,[147] or cease to have liability to perform services, then all payments not previously included in income must be included in that year. The deferral method of Revenue Procedure 71-21 must be used consistently, unless or until approval to make a change in method is received from the

---

[144] See Continental Ill. Corp., 58 TCM 790 (1989), confirming that Rev. Proc. 71-21 does not apply to contracts for the payment of interest. See also Tech. Adv. Mem. 8537002 (May 22, 1985), where the IRS held that Rev. Proc. 71-21 was not applicable to annual membership fees charged by a credit institution to holders of its credit cards; the IRS concluded that the membership fee was in the nature of a loan commitment fee resulting in the acquisition of a property right and not a right to the performance of future services.

[145] In Tech. Adv. Mem. 8639006 (June 5, 1986), the IRS concluded that amounts due on the sale of so-called vacation licenses, pursuant to which the customer/purchaser makes deferred payments, plus interest, for the right to use a room, involved the performance of services and, hence, under an accrual method, no amounts were includable in income until the earlier of the payment of the installments, the due date of the installments, or the actual rendition of services (i.e., the occupancy has occurred or the right to use the room during the year has expired). See Rev. Rul. 74-607, 1974-2 CB 149, discussed supra ¶ 4.03[3][c], note 103. See also Priv. Ltr. Rul. 8909002 (Oct. 28, 1988), where the IRS ruled that advance payments for the storage of grain could be deferred under Rev. Proc. 71-21, because significant services were to be performed, including inspection, fumigation, testing, and other services for maintaining the quality of the grain.

[146] See discussion supra ¶ 4.03[3][b].

[147] Section 381 pertains to carryovers of corporate tax attributes (from a transferor corporation to a transferee corporation) in certain corporate reorganizations and liquidations of subsidiaries. See discussion at ¶ 9.08[2].

Commissioner. The taxpayer must maintain adequate books and records to permit verification of the use of the deferral method of Revenue Procedure 71-21.

Finally, a change to this deferral method is a change of accounting method to which Sections 446 and 481 apply. (See Chapter 8 for discussion of changes in accounting methods.) Thus, a proper application for change must be made. Application must also be made if similar services were performed by a "related person" (or predecessor thereof) during the five taxable years preceding the taxable year for which the Revenue Procedure 71-21 method is adopted. The benefits of Revenue Procedure 71-21 apparently apply automatically and without need for formal adoption if the taxpayer is already using that method, assuming its initial adoption of, or earlier change to, such method was appropriate.

Revenue Procedure 71-21 identifies circumstances in which the IRS will permit the limited one-year deferral. This is not to say that courts will deny deferrals in circumstances to which Revenue Procedure 71-21 is not applicable.[148]

Advance payment for goods. Treasury Regulation § 1.451-5 sets forth the circumstances under which the Treasury will permit a deferral in the recognition of income arising from advance payments for goods. The regulation is available to accrual method taxpayers and to taxpayers who use a long-term contract method of accounting.[149] The regulation applies both to amounts received and to amounts that are due and payable within the year. The amounts so received (or so due and payable) must be made pursuant to (and must be applied against) an agreement (1) for the sale in a future taxable year of goods held primarily for sale in the ordinary course of the taxpayer's business or (2) for the building, installation, construction, or manufacture of items when the contract is not completed within that taxable year.[150] For

---

[148] See discussion supra ¶ 4.03[3][c]. See also Standard Television Tube Corp., 64 TC 238 (1975), where the court refused to allow a deferral in the recognition of amounts paid to the taxpayer for services to be rendered under warranty contracts. The court found that Rev. Proc. 71-21 was, by its terms, inapplicable, and that the principles of existing case law did not warrant a deferral.

[149] See Treas. Reg. § 1.451-3 regarding long-term contract methods.

[150] For this purpose, the term "agreement" includes (1) a gift certificate that can be redeemed for goods and (2) an agreement that obligates a taxpayer to perform activities pertaining to the sale of goods and that also contains an obligation to perform services, which are to be performed as an integral part of such sale activities. If a taxpayer receives an advance payment pursuant to an agreement that obligates the taxpayer to perform not only integral services but also non-integral services, the amount allocated to the non-integral services is not covered by the regulation. However, if the amount not so allocable is less than 5 percent of the total contract price, such amount will be treated as so allocable except that such treatment cannot result in delaying the time at which the taxpayer would otherwise accrue the amounts attributable to the sale of goods. Treas. Reg. §§ 1.451-5(a)(2), 1.451-5(a)(3). The

purposes of this regulation, it has been held that an agreement may exist in the absence of a formal contract and that even implicit understandings may suffice.[151]

In general, advance payments for the sale of goods must be reported in (1) the year of receipt or (2) the earlier of (a) the year when the amounts would otherwise be reported for tax purposes or (b) the year when the amounts would be reported for financial accounting purposes.[152] For example, if a taxpayer received advance payments in year 1 for goods that were shipped in year 3 but delivered to and received by the purchaser in year 4, and if the taxpayer otherwise recognizes income from these sales for financial purposes in the year shipped but for tax purposes in the year delivered, then the advance payments must be reported in year 3, the year shipped. However, this financial reporting conformity requirement did not bar the taxpayer from using the installment method of accounting.[153]

Under the general rule just described, it is possible for a taxpayer to obtain a deferral of several years. However, to limit the deferral period to some extent, a special rule applies where (1) the advance payment is substantial and (2) the taxpayer has on hand in the year of payment (or has available to it in such year through its normal source of supply) goods of a kind and quantity sufficient to satisfy the agreement.[154] In these circumstances, all advance payments received with respect to the agreement by the last day of the second taxable year following the year of receipt and not previously included in income in accordance with the taxpayer's normal accrual method of tax accounting must be included in income in that second taxable year.

A taxpayer will be considered to have received substantial advance payments if all advance payments received through the end of the current taxable year (including advance payments received in prior taxable years) equal or exceed the total cost of expenditures reasonably estimated as includable in inventory with respect to the agreement.[155] In other words, the Treasury will not impose the two-year deferral limitation unless it is reasonably clear that the advance payments already received are sufficient to prevent the taxpayer from realizing a loss on the transaction, i.e., the

---

benefits of Treas. Reg. § 1.451-5 are not available to agreements for the payment of interest. Continental Ill. Corp., 58 TCM 790 (1989).

[151] City Gas Co. of Fla., 47 TCM 971 (1984).

[152] Treas. Reg. § 1.451-5(b)(1).

[153] Treas. Reg. § 1.451-5(b)(4). See also ¶ 5.04 for discussion of the installment method as it applied to sales of inventory prior to the Revenue Act of 1987.

[154] Treas. Reg. § 1.451-5(c).

[155] Treas. Reg. § 1.451-5(c)(3) states: "Advance payments received in a taxable year with respect to an agreement (such as a gift certificate) under which the goods or type of goods to be sold are not identifiable in such year shall be treated as 'substantial advance payments' when received."

amounts already received are equal to or in excess of the reasonably estimated costs and expenses to be incurred by the taxpayer.[156]

Where the two-year limitation rule applies, the taxpayer must take into account in the taxable year the costs and expenditures included in inventory at the end of that year with respect to those goods (or substantially similar goods). If necessary, the taxpayer may estimate the costs involved. No such estimate is permitted, however, where the goods with respect to which the advance payment is received are not identifiable in the year the advance payment is required to be taken into income, e.g., where the amount is received for a gift certificate.

Finally, if advance payments are received subsequent to the second taxable year, the costs associated with the goods that were previously taken into account may not be taken into account again. However, any difference between the costs or estimated costs previously taken into account and the costs actually incurred in fulfilling the taxpayer's obligations under the agreement must be taken into account as adjustments to the cost of goods sold in the year the taxpayer completes its obligations under the agreement.

EXAMPLE: Assume in year 1, X, a calendar-year accrual method taxpayer, enters into a contract for the sale of goods with a total contract price of $100. X estimates that its total inventoriable costs and expenditures for the goods will be $50. X receives the following advance payments with respect to the contract:

Year	Amount
1	$35
2	20
3	15
4	10
5	10
6	10

The goods are delivered pursuant to the customer's request in year 7. X's closing inventory for year 2 of the type of goods involved in the contract is sufficient to satisfy the contract. Since advance payments received by the end of year 2 exceed the inventoriable costs X estimates it will incur, those payments constitute "substantial advance payments." Accordingly, all payments received by the end of year 4, the end of the second taxable year following the taxable year during which "substantial advance payments" are received, are includable in gross income for year 4. Therefore, for taxable year 4, X must include $80 in gross income. X

---

[156] This approach is consistent with Hagen Advertising Displays, Inc. v. Comm'r, 407 F2d 1105 (6th Cir. 1969), where the court recognized that only prepayments in excess of the basis of property represent income, but concluded that the burden is on the taxpayer to support its determination of basis (or cost of goods sold).

must include in cost of goods sold for year 4 the cost of those goods (or similar goods) on hand or, if no such goods are on hand, the estimated inventoriable cost necessary to satisfy the contract. Since no further deferral is available on this contract, X must include in gross income for the remaining years of the contract the advance payment received each year. Any variance between X's estimated costs and the costs actually incurred in fulfilling the contract is taken into account in year 7, when the goods are delivered.[157]

In the preceding example, the advance payments amounted to "substantial advance payments" by the end of year 2, because the $55 that had been received equaled or exceeded the estimated cost of $50. If the taxpayer had arranged with the purchaser for less than $50 to be received through year 2 (e.g., if the payment in year 2 had been $10 rather than $20), then year 3 would have been the first year in which substantial advance payments would have been received, and an additional one-year deferral could have been obtained. This is another indication of how accrual method taxpayers may benefit from careful attention to the details of arrangements with customers and others.

In *City Gas Co. of Florida*,[158] a gas company was held to have received advance payments for gas to be delivered in a later year. The taxpayer's practice was to credit the advance payment against the customer's final bill. The taxpayer asserted that the advance payments were not substantial because they were less than the anticipated costs of gas to be delivered from the time of receipt of the payment through the end of the period of service, whenever that might be. The IRS argued that the payments were substantial because the advance payment was, in effect, a payment for a specified amount of gas pursuant to rates set at levels intended to cover all costs. In other words, if an advance payment of $15 were made, the inventory cost of the gas to which the $15 relates would necessarily be less than $15. The court accepted the IRS view. However, the lack of detail specifying the nature of the agreement on this point allowed the court flexibility to make this determination. An agreement that specifies the goods to which the advance payment relates could produce a different result.

If a taxpayer wants to report in accordance with Treasury Regulation § 1.451-5, it must attach an information schedule to its return for each taxable year, specifying (1) the total amount of advance payments received in the current year; (2) the total amount of advance payments received in prior years and not included in income before the current year; and (3) the total amount of payments received in prior years and included in income for the current year. The taxpayer must also apply for a change in method of

---

[157] See Treas. Reg. § 1.451-5(c)(4) for the example on which this example is based.

[158] City Gas Co. of Fla., 47 TCM 971 (1984).

accounting in accordance with the normal rules governing applications for changes in accounting methods (see Chapter 8). If the taxpayer is already reporting in accordance with the regulatory method, it need not obtain the consent of the Commissioner to continue use of the method, but it must comply with all requirements associated with the use of that method. Finally, if a taxpayer has adopted the method and then dies (if an individual), or ceases to exist in a transaction other than one to which Section 381(1) applies, or if its liability under the agreement otherwise ends, then the amount of the advance payment (that was not includable in gross income in preceding taxable years) must be included in income in that year.

¶ 4.04   REPORTING ITEMS OF EXPENSE

Section 461(a) provides that the amount of any deduction must be taken in the taxable year that is the proper year under the taxpayer's method of accounting used in computing taxable income. This requirement precludes the taxpayer from accelerating or deferring a deduction beyond the appropriate tax year in order to gain a tax advantage, conform to its financial accounting treatment, or achieve a more precise matching of related items of income and expense.[159]

For accrual method taxpayers, there is a three-pronged all events test for determining when the deduction is appropriate. Under this test, a deduction is appropriate in the first year in which three requirements have been satisfied: (1) all events have occurred that fix the fact of liability; (2) the amount of the liability can be determined with reasonable accuracy; and (3) economic performance has occurred. Each of these requirements is independent of the other. No deduction is permitted until the year by which each has been satisfied.

These three requirements are contained in the following Treasury regulation:

---

[159] Treas. Reg. § 1.461-1(a)(3) provides that a "taxpayer may not take into account in a return for a subsequent taxable year liabilities that, under the taxpayer's method of accounting, should have been taken into account in a prior taxable year. If a taxpayer ascertains that a liability should have been taken into account in a prior taxable year, the taxpayer should, if within the period of limitation, file a claim or credit or refund of any overpayment of tax arising therefrom. Similarly, if a taxpayer ascertains that a liability was improperly taken into account in a prior taxable year, the taxpayer should, if within the period of limitation, file an amended return and pay any additional tax due." See discussion at ¶ 2.02[2][f] regarding matching and the clear reflection of income requirement. See also Treas. Reg. § 1.461-1(a)(2)(iii), pointing out that the above general rule is subject to the provisions of any Code section requiring a liability to be taken into account in a taxable year later than the taxable year provided in this regulation.

Taxpayer using an accrual method. Under an accrual method of accounting, a liability ... is incurred, and generally taken into account for Federal income tax purposes, in the taxable year in which all the events have occurred that establish the fact of liability, the amount of the liability can be determined with reasonable accuracy, and economic performance has occurred with respect to the liability.[160]

Before 1984, satisfaction of the first two requirements was all that was necessary to permit the accrual and deduction of the relevant expense. Deduction was proper even though the liability of the taxpayer might consist only of an obligation to perform services in the future (or to incur further obligations in the future).[161] This construction of the test allowed taxpayers to obtain the tax benefit of a deduction before performance or payment was required.

In 1984, Congress became concerned that this construction permitted abuse and created too great a benefit for taxpayers in light of the time value of money. (See Chapter 11 for discussion of other time value of money concepts.) Consequently, Congress enacted an ameliorating provision, generally effective for amounts that otherwise would have been allowable as deductions after July 18, 1984.[162] This provision, Section 461(h), added the third requirement for deduction by providing that the all events test would not be satisfied prior to the time that economic performance occurs with respect to the item at issue. This third requirement was added to the regulations

---

[160] Treas. Reg. § 1.461-1(a)(2)(i). Of course, the amount is deductible only if it is an otherwise deductible expense. If the liability results in the creation of an asset with a life substantially beyond the close of the year, the amount should be capitalized (or otherwise deferred) and amortized, depreciated, or expensed over the appropriate period to which it relates in accordance with applicable rules governing, e.g., cost recovery and depreciation. See, e.g., Section 461(c) regarding taxes; Shelby Salesbook Co. v. United States, 104 F. Supp. 237 (ND Ohio 1952); Ohmer Register Co. v. Comm'r, 131 F2d 682 (6th Cir. 1942), regarding sales commissions.

[161] See, e.g., Harrold v. Comm'r, 192 F2d 1002 (4th Cir. 1951) (taxpayer entitled to deduction for mining reclamation costs in year of mining rather than in subsequent year when actual reclamation would occur); Crescent Wharf & Warehouse Co. v. Comm'r, 518 F2d 772 (9th Cir. 1975) (taxpayer permitted to deduct uncontested liability under workers' compensation law even though medical service would not be provided to employee until a later year); Pacific Grape Prods. Co. v. Comm'r, 219 F2d 862 (9th Cir. 1955) (taxpayer permitted to deduct in current year anticipated costs of labeling, packaging, and shipping goods already sold); Ohio River Collieries Co., 77 TC 1369 (1981) (strip miner allowed deduction for estimated costs of required reclamation work prior to time such work performed).

[162] As an alternative to this prospective only or so-called cut-off approach, the taxpayer could elect to comply with the law by a change in accounting method, effective as of either (1) July 19, 1984 or (2) the first day of the taxable year that included July 19, 1984. See Temp. Reg. § 1.461-3T, which was redesignated as Treas. Reg. § 1.461-7T by the final economic performance regulations, effective April 10, 1992.

when they become effective on April 10, 1992. These three requirements are discussed in ensuing sections.[163]

[1] Fact of Liability Must Be Fixed

For an expense to be deductible, all events must have occurred that fix the fact of liability for that expense. If existence of the liability is subject to any conditions precedent, contingencies, or other circumstances, which prevent the taxpayer from having a recognized, acknowledged, and existing liability, deduction is premature and will be denied.[164] Determination of the fact of liability must be made on the basis of facts actually known or reasonably knowable as of the close of the year.[165]

In interpreting this requirement, the courts have tried to strike a balance between the hardship imposed by a literal reading of the requirement and the practical necessity of having a workable test that achieves a clear reflection of income. The courts have most often been concerned with (1) identifying the relevant liability; (2) considering whether related items of income and expense will be matched in the same year; and (3) determining whether the liability is in any way contingent or contested. The cases frequently discuss all these points without necessarily focusing on any specific point.

As a final matter, the following cases[166] generally focus on whether the fact of the liability has been fixed and, hence, whether a deduction will be permitted. While these cases are still relevant for purposes of determining the fact of liability, it must be remembered that many predate enactment of the economic performance requirement and, consequently, do not address economic performance. Under present law, a deduction will not be permitted unless economic performance has occurred. This relatively new condition for deduction must not be ignored.

[a] Identification of Liability

Identifying the relevant liability has often been one of the more difficult issues pertaining to the fact of liability. Taxpayers frequently enter into

---

[163] See infra ¶¶ 4.04[1]–4.04[3].

[164] United States v. Hughes Properties, Inc., 476 US 593 (1986). See Fong Venture Capital Corp., 53 TCM 647 (1987), where the court denied a deduction for interest paid on an asserted liability for a personal guarantee provided by an individual, because the amount to be paid for the guarantee was payable only at the "financial convenience" of the obligor. This case involved the issue of whether an asserted obligation was, in fact, a valid indebtedness. See also Hitachi Sales Corp., 64 TCM 634 (1992), where the court denied a deduction for liabilities to be incurred in the future, because such liabilities were not fixed within the year of deduction.

[165] The Baltimore Transfer Co., 8 TC 1 (1947), acq. 1947-2 CB 1.

[166] See discussion infra ¶¶ 4.04[1][a]–4.04[1][c].

transactions that obligate them to perform services, transfer property, or take other action in the future. To satisfy their initial obligation (the first liability), taxpayers are sometimes required to incur obligations to others in the future (the second liability). For example, if a taxpayer's board of directors agrees to take certain action that will result in a deductible expense, the issue regarding fixed liability is whether the board's action itself obligated the company or, instead, merely authorized the company to incur liability at a later time. The question is whether the first "liability" actually establishes a fixed liability or merely authorizes the taxpayer to incur a liability (a second liability) in the future.[167]

In early cases, the courts often found that the first liability was not fixed (and, therefore, denied the deduction) until services were rendered, property was transferred, or second liabilities were incurred in carrying out the obligations required under the first liability.[168] Subsequently, however, courts began finding a fixed obligation at the time of the first liability even though the taxpayer had not yet incurred the second liability associated with carrying out the performance required under the first liability. Many cases involved the obligation of taxpayers to restore or reclaim land used for mining purposes. Deductions were permitted in the year in which the taxpayer's obligation under state or other applicable law became fixed, notwithstanding the fact that the taxpayer would not incur liabilities for performance of these obligations until later years.[169]

Similar questions arose in a number of other business contexts. For example, in *Gillis v. United States*,[170] a partnership bought and sold cotton pursuant to contracts with the Commodity Credit Corporation. Under these contracts, the taxpayer was permitted to acquire and sell cotton domestically

---

[167] Compare Comm'r v. Champion Spark Plug Co., 266 F2d 347 (6th Cir. 1959), where the obligation of the company to pay an annuity was fixed upon the Board's action, with Comm'r v. H.B. Ives Co., 297 F2d 229 (2d Cir. 1961), cert. denied, 370 US 904 (1962), where the Board's initial action, which merely authorized the company to purchase an annuity, did not itself result in a fixed liability.

[168] See, e.g., William J. Ostheimer, 1 BTA 18 (1924), (deductions for existing obligation to restore leased chattels denied in year prior to year in which actual expenses incurred in restoring such chattels); Amalgamated Hous. Corp. 37 BTA 817 (1938), aff'd per curiam, 108 F2d 1010 (2d Cir. 1940) (deductions with respect to existing obligation to renovate the real property denied until those required to perform the renovation actually rendered services); Spencer, White & Prentis, Inc. v. Comm'r, 144 F2d 45 (2d Cir. 1944), cert. denied, 323 US 780 (1944) (deduction was denied with respect to obligation to restore property damaged during course of taxpayer's work until expense was incurred by those who were to make restorations); National Bread Wrapping Mach. Co., 30 TC 550 (1958) (deductions denied for obligation to furnish installation services with respect to property sold until such services were performed).

[169] See Harrold v. Comm'r, 192 F2d 1002 (4th Cir. 1951); Denise Coal Co. v. Comm'r, 271 F2d 930 (3d Cir. 1959); Ohio River Collieries Co., 77 TC 1369 (1981).

[170] Gillis v. United States, 402 F2d 501 (5th Cir. 1968).

at a gain only if it agreed to acquire and sell domestic cotton in foreign transactions at a loss. In general, any gain derived from the domestic sale would be offset by the loss incurred on the subsequent foreign sale. Where the sale resulting in the gain occurred during one taxable year, the taxpayer reported the gain in the year of the domestic sale and, at that time, estimated and accrued as a deduction the loss that would arise on the foreign sale in a later year. A question arose as to the propriety of these deductions. The court held for the taxpayer. "There is no way this export obligation could be viewed as being contingent. The transactions in question were designed to be offsetting transactions."[171] The court also relied on the fact that the taxpayer's accounting treatment was "so much in line with plain common sense that [the court is] at a loss to understand what could have prompted the Commissioner to disapprove it."[172]

[i] **Identification of payee.** As the previous discussion indicates, an obligation may constitute a fixed liability even though the ultimate payee is not yet identified. In *Washington Post Co. v. United States*,[173] the taxpayer established a deferred compensation plan for its independent circulation dealers under which it promised to accrue certain amounts on its books each year for the benefit of the dealers. The taxpayer reserved the right to discontinue or alter the plan at any time but was obligated to distribute all amounts accrued as of the time of discontinuance. However, under the plan, the accrued amounts did not fully vest in an individual dealer unless and until that dealer either changed his status from that of independent contractor to an employee of the taxpayer, died, became disabled, or reached age 55. The Commissioner disallowed deduction of that portion of the amount accrued that was not immediately vested in the individual on the grounds that the liability was contingent. The Claims Court rejected this contention, observing that the "one overriding reality" in the case was that the taxpayer was "irrevocably bound to pay whatever it accrued to the Fund."[174] The court pointed out that although the ultimate recipients and time of actual payment could not be determined at the time, such uncertainty "does not make the liability any less real, or any less fixed."[175]

---

[171] Id. at 508. This statement by the court also illustrates the practical importance to the court of matching interrelated items in the same year as well as the need for the liability to be certain and not contingent.

[172] Id. at 507.

[173] Washington Post Co. v. United States, 405 F2d 1279 (Ct. Cl. 1969).

[174] Id. at 1283.

[175] Id. See also Lukens Steel Co. v. Comm'r, 442 F2d 1131 (3d Cir. 1971); Keebey's Inc. v. Paschal, 188 F2d 113 (8th Cir. 1951); Clark v. Woodward Constr. Co., 179 F2d 176 (10th Cir. 1950); United Control Corp., 38 TC 957 (1962), acq. 1966-1 CB 3. But see Rev. Rul. 72-34, 1972-1 CB 132, and Rev. Rul. 76-345, 1976-2 CB 134, where the IRS announced that it would not follow *Lukens Steel* and

Similarly, in *United States v. Hughes Properties, Inc.*,[176] the Supreme Court allowed the taxpayer, a gambling casino, to accrue and deduct each year the annual increase in amounts shown on its progressive slot machines even though the ultimate recipient of such amounts would not be known until a winning combination was pulled. The Court stated that the identification of the winning player was irrelevant to the existence of the basic liability.

On the other hand, the inability to identify the persons who will receive the economic benefits at issue may suggest that there is no fixed liability at all, a circumstance which precludes deduction. For example, in *Iowa Southern Utilities Co. v. United States*,[177] the state regulatory commission permitted the taxpayer utility company to increase its rates (by means of a surcharge) subject to a required reduction in rates to be charged in later years. The increase was intended to provide funds for the utility to use in meeting various construction financing costs. The utility argued first that the surcharge was, in fact, a loan, but this argument was rejected by the court. The utility argued next that its obligation to reduce rates in the future amounted to a fixed liability for which it should be able to take an immediate and corresponding deduction. The court rejected this proposition, noting among other factors that the identities of the persons to whom the payments would be made were unknown, therefore negating the concept of loan and demonstrating that the future reductions would be price adjustments only, not fixed liabilities deductible at the time of the agreement. The court emphasized the distinction between a deduction from income and a reduction in income.[178]

[ii] Likelihood of performance and conditions subsequent. In some cases, courts have found the likelihood of performance an important practical consideration. For instance, in *Helvering v. Russian Finance & Construction Corp.*,[179] a taxpayer had purchased and mined minerals in the Soviet Union and, as a result, had a contractual liability to pay royalties at a future date.

Washington Post, respectively. These IRS rulings should be of less concern today in light of the Supreme Court's opinion in United States v. Hughes Properties, Inc., 476 US 593 (1986). Yet, examining agents still sometimes disallow deductions on the basis of these revenue rulings. Such disallowances are usually inconsistent with controlling cases and should not be sustained.

[176] United States v. Hughes Properties, Inc., 86-1 USTC ¶ 9440 (1986).

[177] Iowa S. Utils. Co. v. United States, 87-1 USTC ¶ 9217 (Cl. Ct. 1987), aff'd, 841 F2d 1108 (Fed. Cir. 1988).

[178] See Roanoke Gas Co. v. United States, 92-2 USTC ¶ 50,496 (4th Cir. 1992), for this same point; but see Illinois Power Co. v. Comm'r, 792 F2d 683 (7th Cir. 1986), where the original receipt of excess rates was held not to constitute income because the subsequent refunds of the excess rates would be in the form of a credit on the bills of particular customers, interest would be paid, and the utility would function more in the nature of a custodian of the funds than in some other capacity.

[179] Helvering v. Russian Fin. & Constr. Corp., 77 F2d 324 (2d Cir. 1935).

However, pursuant to the terms of the controlling agreement, this liability would be extinguished for certain reasons, e.g., if a strike occurred, if certain parties breached the agreement, or by an agreement of the parties to terminate the contract. The court of appeals held that the liability was accruable because the "taxpayer had a reasonable expectance at the time it accrued this liability on its books that its liability would be enforced."[180] The court stated that "the test is whether a taxpayer is justified in entertaining a reasonable expectation that an expense will be incurred."[181] The court went on to say: "When books are kept on an accrual basis, a presently existing obligation which, in the normal course of events, the taxpayer is justified in believing he must fulfill, may be accrued. The existence of an absolute liability is necessary; absolute certainty that it will be discharged is not."[182] The court seemed to base its decision, in part, on the practical realization that if an expense or a liability that is attributable to a transaction is not accrued in the same taxable year as the income from that transaction, the result would be a distortion of the taxpayer's income for both the year in which the income is accrued and the year in which the expense or liability is actually paid. The court's decision also reflects the principle that once a liability has arisen and is fixed, the fact that conditions may later arise and eliminate the liability does not preclude accrual and deduction.[183]

Although this principle is well established, it has not yet been applied to the deduction of interest on convertible debentures.[184] The typical fact pattern in these cases is that interest on the convertible debentures is paid

---

[180] Id. at 327.

[181] Id.

[182] Id.

[183] See also United States v. Hughes Properties, Inc., 476 US 593 (1986) (fact that liability could be extinguished by certain actions of taxpayer, such as its termination of business, bankruptcy, or the like, does not prevent accrual); Lawyers' Title Guar. Fund v. United States, 508 F2d 1 (5th Cir. 1975) (commissions accrued even though they could be reduced by subsequent events before actual payment); Consolidated Foods Corp., 66 TC 436 (1976) (rent accrued even though it could be reduced or eliminated by subsequent events); Geo. K. Herman Chevrolet. Inc., 39 TC 846, 853 (1963) ("An otherwise proper deduction should not be disallowed in the year it was paid or incurred because of the existence of a possibility that at some future date the taxpayer might receive a reimbursement therefor"); The Electric Tachometer Corp., 37 TC 158 (1961) (moving expenses accrued, although they could be reduced by subsequent reimbursement); Alleghany Corp., 28 TC 298 (1957), acq. 1957-2 CB 3 (possibility of reimbursement does not preclude deduction); Midwest Motor Express, Inc., 27 TC 167 (1956), aff'd on other grounds, 251 F2d 405 (8th Cir.), cert. denied, 358 US 875 (1958) (retrospective adjustment deductible in year prior to actual assessment); Burnham Corp., 90 TC 953 (1988), aff'd, 878 F2d 86 (2d Cir. 1989) (liability fixed even though payments would terminate upon death of party to whom liability owed).

[184] See, e.g., Scott Paper Co., 74 TC 137 (1980); Tandy Corp. v. United States, 626 F2d 1186 (5th Cir. 1980); Rev. Rul. 74-127, 1974-1 CB 47.

semi-annually on dates that do not coincide with the end of the taxpayer's year. The issue is whether the interest that accrues economically from the last payment date to the end of the taxable year should be allowed as a deduction. The bond indenture generally provides that if a conversion occurs between interest payment dates, no interest will be payable for the period from the last payment date through the date of the conversion. The IRS and the courts have denied the deduction in these cases even though the conversion results in the extinguishment or elimination of a previously established liability and, in this sense, clearly is a condition subsequent.[185] In light of the Supreme Court's decision in *United States v. Hughes Properties, Inc.*,[186] it is uncertain whether these decisions will be followed in the future.

In addition to the foregoing cases, there may be cases where the "existence of liability is so highly probable that the reasonableness of the expectancy [of that liability] should govern its accrual."[187] For example, in *Eastman Kodak Co. v. United States*,[188] the issue involved the deduction of a liability for payroll taxes on wages accrued in the last week of one taxable year. Legal liability for the tax would not actually arise until the succeeding taxable year when the wages were paid. Nevertheless, the court stated, "[W]e cannot say . . . that the remote possibility of the plaintiff's bankruptcy injects an element of uncertainty sufficient to deny a deduction. . . . [S]uch reasoning would totally destroy accrual tax accounting. . . ."[189]

These cases suggest that the crucial question is whether all operative facts have occurred that establish the liability. The operative facts are those that make it clear that the taxpayer has incurred an obligation to pay money, render services, deliver property, or take some other action, which obligation, although not yet fulfilled, is nevertheless fixed. However, it is often difficult to distinguish cases that focus on "reasonable expectancy" from other cases that have denied the deduction of a seemingly similar expectancy.[190]

---

[185] See, e.g., Scott Paper Co., 74 TC 137 (1980); Tandy Corp. v. United States, 626 F2d 1186 (5th Cir. 1980); Rev. Rul. 74-127, 1974-1 CB 47.

[186] United States v. Hughes Properties, Inc., 476 US 593 (1986).

[187] United States v. Texas Mexican Ry., 263 F2d 31, 35 (5th Cir. 1959).

[188] Eastman Kodak Co. v. United States, 534 F2d 252 (Ct. Cl. 1976). However, consider the impact of the economic performance test. If economic performance were deemed to occur only as payments are made, the deduction might be denied until the year of payment unless an exception to the economic performance test were applicable. See discussion infra ¶ 4.04[3].

[189] Id. at 260, n.12. See also United States v. Hughes Properties, Inc., 476 US 593 (1986); Burlington N. R.R., 82 TC 143 (1984).

[190] See, e.g., Hollingsworth v. United States, 568 F2d 192 (Ct. Cl. 1977), where taxpayer asserted that because income was accrued for federal tax purposes, he should receive a deduction for the state tax that would be attributable to and payable on account of that accrued income, despite the fact that he was on a cash method for

[iii] **Conditions precedent.** If the existence of the liability is subject to a condition precedent, the obligation is not fixed until the condition has occurred or is satisfied.[191] For example, if an obligation does not arise unless demands are made for the rendition of services by customers, a deduction prior to the demand will be denied. In *Simplified Tax Records, Inc.*,[192] the Tax Court denied the deduction for an obligation to render services that did not need to be rendered until demands were made by customers of the taxpayer. The fact that the demand could be estimated and prudent business would require that a reserve be established for it did not justify the deduction.[193] Although there is considerable merit in the analysis made by the courts in these matters, few, if any, taxpayers have argued that income

state tax purposes and was in the process of contesting a proposed change to an accrual method for state tax purposes. The taxpayer argued that the contest with the state was over *when* the income accrued for federal tax purposes would be reported to the state, not *if* that income would be subject to tax. The court nevertheless held that the state tax was contingent and not deductible until the contest was resolved. See discussion infra ¶ 4.04[1][c] regarding the impact on accrual of an existing dispute or contest.

[191] See, e.g., United States v. Hughes Properties, Inc., 476 US 593 (1986); United States v. General Dynamics Corp., 481 US 239 (1987); Fourth Fin. Corp., 49 TCM 1485 (1985). See also Tech. Adv. Mem. 9143083 (Aug. 1, 1991), where in the course of determining whether a taxpayer had obtained a fixed right to receive income (i.e., reimbursements for certain costs incurred), the National Office concluded that the filing of the forms requesting reimbursement was not a condition precedent that would prevent accrual because the filing of the forms was ministerial in nature and the likelihood of any challenge to the requests was extremely remote and speculative. Presumably, a similar analysis would be made by the IRS for items of expense.

[192] Simplified Tax Records, Inc., 41 TC 75 (1963).

[193] See United States v. General Dynamics Corp., 481 US 239 (1987), estimate of future liability, no matter how accurate, is not the equivalent of a presently fixed liability; Bell Elec. Co., 45 TC 158 (1965), acq. 1966-2 CB 4, where deduction was denied for the estimated future cost of servicing appliances sold under warranty agreements; Juniata Farmers Coop. Ass'n, 43 TC 836 (1965), where deduction was denied for estimated spoilage and damage to stored grain. See also Challenge Publications, Inc. v. Comm'r, 845 F2d 1541 (9th Cir. 1988); Dana Distribs., Inc., 56 TCM 569 (1988), aff'd, 874 F2d 120 (2d Cir. 1989). *Challenge* involved a magazine publisher contractually obligated to credit its customers for unsold copies of its magazines. The publisher was denied a deduction from income (or a reduction in income) for its estimate of unsold copies. The court found that the taxpayer was not under a fixed obligation to make refunds until it received evidence of the unsold copies from its customers. *Dana Distributors* involved a beverage distributor who charged a container deposit on all beverages sold in nonrefillable containers. The taxpayer argued that if the deposit were treated as income, the taxpayer should be entitled to an offsetting deduction for its liability to pay refunds when the containers were returned. The court disagreed, pointing out that no liability for any such refund would become fixed until the container was returned by a customer. See generally Stanger, Vander Kam & Polifka, "Prepaid Income and Estimated Expenses; Financial Accounting Versus Tax Accounting Dichotomy," 33 Tax Law. 403 (1980).

should not be accrued in the first instance because of its doubtful collectibility.[194]

[b] Matching

Under GAAP, costs and expenses are generally required to be deducted in the same period as the revenues to which those costs and expenses relate.[195] In many cases, this economic and financial accounting objective of matching requires (1) that costs and expenses directly identifiable with particular revenues be deducted in the same period or periods in which those revenues are recognized and (2) that other expenses, which relate to particular periods of time, be deducted in or over the periods to which they relate.

Initially, courts adopted a test very similar to that used for financial reporting purposes, i.e., that expenses should be deducted in the same year or years in which related items of income are recognized. For example, the Supreme Court stated in *United States v. Anderson*:

> [Accrual accounting] enable[s] taxpayers to keep their books and make their returns according to scientific accounting principles, by charging against income earned during the taxable period, the expenses incurred in and properly attributable to the process of earning income during that period; and indeed, to require the tax return to be made on that basis. . . .[196]

Similar statements were made by courts in a number of other contexts. For example, in *Ohmer Register Co. v. Commissioner*,[197] an accrual-basis taxpayer was in the business of selling cash registers and other products. Its sales agents were compensated through commissions on monies received by the company from the sale of its products. The arrangement provided for "advance commissions" on consummation of a sale and initial payment by the purchaser. The remainder of the sales commission was also credited to the salesman at that time, pending full payment by the customer. If full payment was not received on the sale, the salesman would lose part or all of his deferred commission. When the merchandise was shipped, the taxpayer reported the full amount of the sale price as income, whether the sale was for

---

[194] See, e.g., Challenge Publications, Inc. v. Comm'r, 845 F2d 1541 (9th Cir. 1988), where the taxpayer was denied the opportunity to reduce income by amounts estimated to be uncollectible, but the taxpayer based its argument to the court on an asserted right to deduct the anticipated uncollectibles rather than on a right to exclude the amounts from income. See also discussion of items of doubtful collectibility supra ¶ 4.03[2].

[195] R. Wixon, Accountants' Handbook 1.17 (4th ed. 1965).

[196] United States v. Anderson, 269 US 422, 440 (1926).

[197] Ohmer Register Co. v. Comm'r, 131 F2d 682 (6th Cir. 1942). See also Shelby Salesbook Co. v. United States, 104 F. Supp. 237 (ND Ohio 1952).

cash or on credit. At the same time, it claimed a deduction for the full amount of the salesman's commission. The Board of Tax Appeals denied the taxpayer's deduction on the ground that, when taken, the liability was "contingent," but the court of appeals reversed, holding that denial of the deduction for the accrued commission would distort income, i.e., the sales income and related sales commission had to be recognized in the same period.[198]

In *Dravo Corp. v. United States*,[199] the court summarized the need for matching by stating:

> The question of when items accrue for Federal income tax purposes has been the subject of extensive litigation and many decisions. From

---

[198] The *Ohmer* court stated:

> To divide the sales transactions here involved so as to treat them upon an accrual basis with respect to income and upon a cash basis with respect to expense in commissions in making sales from which the income was derived would be . . . objectionable. . . . [T]he net income . . . could not have been correctly determined upon the accrual basis, without deducting the commission expense from gross income.

Id. at 686. See also Pacific Grape Prods. Co. v. Comm'r, 219 F2d 862 (9th Cir. 1955) (seller of food products permitted to deduct in year of sale the costs of packaging and shipping the products sold, even though such activities had not yet occurred); Consolidated Edison Co. of N.Y. v. United States, 135 F. Supp. 881, 884 (Ct. Cl. 1955), cert. denied, 351 US 909 (1956): "Under the accrual system of accounting revenues are accrued as nearly as practicable to the period earned and expenses, which include taxes, are accrued in the period and against the revenues they helped to produce." The particular issue in *Consolidated Edison* was whether an asserted liability was deductible in the year of payment, if later contested. The Court of Claims answered in the affirmative. Later, because of a conflict among jurisdictions, the Supreme Court considered the issue in a related case and held to the contrary. United States v. Consolidated Edison Co. of N.Y., 366 US 380 (1961). In response, Congress overturned the result of the decision of the Supreme Court by enacting Section 461(f). See discussion infra ¶ 4.04[1][c][i].

[199] Dravo Corp. v. United states, 348 F2d 542 (Ct. Cl. 1965). See also Helvering v. Russian Fin. & Constr. Corp., 77 F2d 324, 328 (2d Cir. 1935), where the court stated:

> The fundamental requirement is that the return reflects true income, and expenses must be set off against the income to which they are attributable. United States v. Anderson, supra; Miller & Vidor Lumber Co. v. Comm'r, 39 F.(2d) 890, 892 (C.C.A.5). In the latter case, the court said: "We think these cases and the regulations clearly establish the rule that, as to taxpayers making their returns on the accrual basis, deductions attributable to the business of a particular year must be applied against the income they help to create from the business of that year, and not against that of a subsequent year in which payment was made."

In Beacon Publishing Co. v. Comm'r, 218 F2d 697, 699 (10th Cir. 1955), the court stated: "An important feature of the accrual system is that income shall be reported at such a time that it will, so far as possible, be offset by expenditures incident to earning it, rather than expenditures related to earning other income."

them emerge a series of simple propositions which determine the appropriate period for reflecting items of income and expense. We start with the admonition that in order for tax accrual accounting to provide a meaningful picture of operations, the expense items or deductions must be included in the same period as the income items they help to produce. In other words, interrelated items of expense and income must be "matched" in some particular period.[200]

Although these cases might suggest that the matching principle of financial accounting (i.e., that related items of income and expense *must* be recorded in the same taxable year) is a dominant element of accrual tax accounting in order for income to be reflected clearly, this is not the case.[201] The matching principle is certainly relevant in testing whether a particular method clearly reflects income for tax purposes, but matching is not of itself the determinative test for finding a fixed liability or for permitting a deduction. Certainty of liability and, since 1984, economic performance are by far the more dominant concerns. Thus, deduction will generally be denied where an expense is not yet certain (or where economic performance has not occurred) even though the item to be deducted is related to a recognized item of income.[202]

In 1954, Congress attempted to alleviate some of the confusion in the area by enacting Sections 452 and 462, which were intended to conform accrual tax accounting to accrual financial accounting in certain instances. However, these provisions were repealed retroactively in 1955 because of the Treasury's fear that their application might generate a huge loss in revenue. As a result of their repeal, confusion continued as to the importance of matching revenues and expenses through concepts of deferral in income or recognition of expense at a time that might otherwise be inconsistent with the all events test.[203] However, because of the economic performance requirement of the all events test, matching should be of less significance in the future than it has been in the past.

---

[200] Dravo Corp. v. United States, 348 F2d 542, 544 (Ct. Cl. 1965).

[201] See ¶¶ 2.02[2] generally and 2.02[2][f] for discussions of the clear reflection of income standard and the effect on it of any particular matching of related items of income and expense.

[202] See, e.g., Brown v. Helvering, 291 US 193 (1934) (no deduction for commission refunds due insurance companies by taxpayer-agent even though it was likely that a portion of commission income recognized in one year would be refunded in later years); Northwestern States Portland Cement Co. v. Huston, 126 F2d 196 (8th Cir. 1942); Readers' Publishing Corp. v. United States, 40 F2d 145 (Ct. Cl. 1930).

[203] See Gunn, "Matching of Costs and Revenues as a Goal of Tax Accounting," 4 Va. Tax Rev. 1 (1984).

[c] Contested Liabilities

The requirement of a fixed liability for the obligation in question prevents a deduction where the liability is contested by the taxpayer.[204] The term "contest" is defined by the applicable regulations as follows:

> A contest arises when there is a bona fide dispute as to the proper evaluation of the law or the facts necessary to determine the existence or correctness of the amount of an asserted liability. It is not necessary to institute suit in a court of law in order to contest an asserted liability. An affirmative act denying the validity or accuracy, or both, of an asserted liability to the person who is asserting such liability, such as including a written protest with payment of the asserted liability, is sufficient to commence a contest. Thus, lodging a protest in accordance with local law is sufficient to contest an asserted liability for taxes. It is not necessary that the affirmative act denying the validity or accuracy, or both, of an asserted liability be in writing if, upon examination of all the facts and circumstances, it can be established to the satisfaction of the Commissioner that a liability has been asserted and contested.[205]

It is apparent from this regulation that determination of whether a contest has occurred cannot be made merely on the basis of words used to describe an action. Rather, it requires an appraisal of all the facts and circumstances to determine the true significance of the purported dispute.[206]

Since a finding of contest involves a departure from traditional concepts of accrual tax accounting, the concept of contest is to be narrowly construed. For example, in *Dravo Corp. v. United States*,[207] which is often cited and widely recognized as one of the leading cases in this area, the court noted a "[c]ongressional intent to restrict the effect of the concept of 'contest' in tax cases."

A finding of contest must be predicated on a genuine, bona fide dispute directed by the taxpayer toward the substance of an asserted liability.[208] Such

---

[204] Dixie Pine Prods. Co. v. Comm'r, 320 US 516 (1944).

[205] Treas. Reg. § 1.461-2(b)(2).

[206] See, e.g., Hitachi Sales Corp., 64 TCM 634 (1992), where deduction of a purported liability to terminated employees was denied because, from all the facts and circumstances, there had been no clear admission of liability by the taxpayer.

[207] Dravo Corp. v. United States, 348 F2d 542, 46 n.1 (Ct. Cl. 1965). In *Dravo*, the court held that the mere filing of return showing a specified amount of tax is not a contest of a later asserted and accepted deficiency. See also Lutz v. Comm'r, 396 F2d 412, 415 (9th Cir. 1968), where the Court of Appeals for the Ninth Circuit held: "[A]s the Court of Claims indicated in *Dravo*, adoption of a narrow interpretation of 'contest' within the meaning of *Dixie Pine Products* will lead to a more accurate and equitable determination of net income for the purposes of taxation."

[208] Lutz v. Comm'r, 396 F2d 412 (9th Cir. 1968); See Harry Gordon, 63 TC 501 (1975), aff'd in part and rev'd in part on other issues, 572 F2d 193 (9th Cir. 1977), cert. denied, 435 US 924 (1978); Hollingsworth v. United States, 568 F2d 192 (Ct.

a dispute must be actively and vigorously asserted. Insubstantial questioning of, or resistance to, a proposed liability will not amount to a contest.[209] On the other hand, it is not necessary that the dispute be explicit; it may be found from a consideration of all the relevant facts and circumstances.[210]

Woodmont Terrace, Inc. v. United States,[211] is illustrative of these principles. The taxpayer in *Woodmont* had taken issue with the basis on which a state tax had been computed. Nevertheless, no contest was found. The court held that "in the absence of any type of formal proceedings or a more obvious lack of acquiescence, ... the meeting ... [to discuss the deficiencies] did not constitute the type of 'contest' contemplated by *Dixie Pine Products.*"[212]

Similarly, in *Gillis v. United States,*[213] a partnership shipped cotton overseas that unavoidably was inferior to what was called for in the contract. Payments were promptly made on the basis of the contract price and claims were made for proper adjustment. In accordance with standard practice in the international cotton trade, the contract provided that these claims could be subjected to arbitration. Because the partnership was able to estimate very closely what would eventually be due on these claims, it included in its tax return for the year of sale both the gross receipts and an amount representing anticipated claims of foreign buyers. When the claims were made, several were submitted to arbitration. Because of this, the Commissioner denied the deduction, and his determination was upheld by the district court. However, the court of appeals reversed, pointing out that liability, within a narrow range, was acknowledged and that "arbitration in the international trade is not as adversarial as usual litigation" and should not be viewed "as the handmaiden of contingency."[214] The court pointed out that it would be unacceptable to penalize the partnership, as urged by the government, for using

---

Cl. 1977) (because dispute must be bona fide, fraudulent acts designed to avoid liability will not be deemed a contest of that liability assuming such fraud could be proved). See also Bear Film Co., 18 TC 354 (1952), acq. 1955-1 CB 3, aff'd on other grounds, 219 F2d 231 (9th Cir. 1955) (capricious failure to pay liability is not a contest).

[209] Woodmont Terrace, Inc. v. United States, 261 F. Supp. 789 (MD Tenn. 1966).

[210] See Fox v. Comm'r, 874 F2d 560 (8th Cir. 1989), aff'g 53 TCM 651 (1987), where the court concluded that the taxpayer's position in certain litigation (involving the taxpayer's denial of liability under certain obligations), when taken as a whole and in concert with the relevant documents and other applicable testimony, caused the taxpayer to be treated as contesting any and all possible obligations that were inherently associated with the obligations he explicitly contested.

[211] Woodmont Terrace, Inc. v. United States, 261 F. Supp. 789 (MD Tenn. 1966).

[212] Id. at 793.

[213] Gillis v. United States, 402 F2d 501 (5th Cir. 1968).

[214] Id. at 509.

the arbitration procedure.[215] The court added that the procedure "is not the same as contesting liability in a judicial proceeding, and we will not treat it as if it were."[216]

[i] **Payment of contested liability.**   As a result of the application of the all events test to contested liabilities, accrual method taxpayers who had, in fact, paid the contested liability and were seeking a refund of the amount paid were not treated as favorably as cash method taxpayers. Since the liability was in dispute, the deduction would not be permitted for accrual method taxpayers even though payment had been made.[217]

As a consequence, Congress enacted Section 461(f), which permits an accrual method taxpayer to deduct a contested liability if (1) the taxpayer transfers money or other property to provide for the satisfaction of the asserted liability; (2) the contest exists after the time of transfer; and (3) but for the fact of contest, the deduction would have been allowed in the year of transfer or in an earlier year.

The transfer of money or other property that must be made in satisfaction of the asserted liability must be made to the person asserting the liability or to an escrowee or a trustee. The transfer must be pursuant to a written agreement between the taxpayer and the person asserting the liability (and the escrowee or trustee, if applicable), and the agreement must provide that the money or other property will be retained (or delivered) in accordance with the settlement of the contest. Alternatively, the transfer may be made pursuant to an order of the United States, any state or political subdivision, or any agency or instrumentality of the foregoing. The key point is that the money or property be transferred beyond the control of the taxpayer. Any transfer that permits the taxpayer to maintain control over the cash or other property is not a sufficient transfer.[218]

---

[215] Id. at 510.

[216] Id.

[217] United States v. Consolidated Edison Co. of N.Y., 366 US 380 (1961).

[218] Although Section 461(f) was intended to alleviate the problems experienced by accrual method taxpayers, Treas. Reg. § 1.461-2(e) suggests that the section is also applicable to cash method taxpayers, because it states that the existence of a contest must be the only factor preventing a deduction for the year of transfer or "in the case of an accrual method taxpayer, for an earlier taxable year. . . . This language suggests that the section covers taxpayers other than those on an accrual method. However, the section provides that the sole reason for the denial of the deduction must be the existence of the contest. For a cash method taxpayer, existence of a contest does not prevent deduction if payment is made to the person asserting the liability. (See discussion at ¶ 3.04.) If a cash method taxpayer pays someone other than the person asserting the liability, then, arguably, the deduction should be denied for failing to pay the correct person, not because of the contest. However, that result seems unsound. A more principled analysis would permit the cash basis taxpayer to pay someone other than the person asserting the liability, albeit an appropriate entity,

Assuming other requirements are met, the taxpayer's transfer may be made to an escrow account if there is an agreement among the escrowee, the taxpayer, and the party asserting the liability as to the transfer of funds from escrow at the time the liability is resolved.[219] The courts have made it clear that unilateral transfers (by the taxpayer to an escrow account) that are unknown to the person asserting the liability will not satisfy the regulatory requirement and, hence, a deduction will not be permitted.[220] On the other hand, the regulatory provision does not require that the person asserting the claim know the amount transferred to the escrow account, only of the account's existence.

The economic performance test of Section 461(h) applies to contested liabilities.[221] Thus, an amount transferred to a Section 461(f) trust with respect to a contested liability may not be deducted earlier than when economic performance occurs. In the case of workers' compensation or tort liabilities, economic performance occurs only as payments are made to the claimant. Because payment to a Section 461(f) trust is not a payment to the claimant, it may not satisfy the economic performance test.

An important question, as yet not fully addressed, is the treatment of income earned on amounts transferred to an escrow account or a trustee. The Treasury has not yet provided its position on this matter.[222]

[ii] **Resolution of contest.** Resolution of the contest establishes the fixed liability required under the all events test. The contest is deemed resolved when a final determination has been made by a court and the issue is no longer subject to appeal, or, in other cases, when the relevant party has acknowledged the liability.[223]

[2] Determination of Amount With Reasonable Accuracy

The requirement that the amount of the liability must be determinable with reasonable accuracy is set forth in the Treasury regulations as follows:

---

such as an escrowee or trustee, and still obtain the deduction. In James W. Perkins, 92 TC 749 (1989), the Tax Court allowed interest paid on an asserted federal income tax deficiency to be deducted in the year of payment, noting the applicability of Section 461(f). See also Wallace Preble, 57 TCM 295 (1989), to the same effect.

[219] Treas. Reg. § 1.461-2(c)(1)(ii).

[220] See, e.g., Poirier & McLane Corp., 547 F2d 161 (2d Cir. 1976), rev'g 63 TC 570 (1975); Rosenthal v. United States, 86-2 USTC ¶ 9776 (Ct. Cl. 1986).

[221] For a discussion of the economic performance test, see infra ¶ 4.04[3].

[222] Treas. Reg. § 1.461-2(f) has been reserved by the Treasury for rules governing this issue as well as overall rules governing the treatment of money or property transferred to an escrowee, trustee, or a court.

[223] See, e.g., Comm'r v. Fifth Ave. Coach Lines, Inc., 281 F2d 556 (2d Cir. 1960), cert. denied, 366 US 964 (1961). See also discussion supra ¶ 4.03[1][a][i].

While no liability shall be taken into account before economic performance and all of the events that fix the liability have occurred, the fact that the exact amount of the liability cannot be determined does not prevent a taxpayer from taking into account that portion of the amount of the liability which can be computed with reasonable accuracy within the taxable year.[224]

The regulations later provide that where a deduction is properly accrued on the basis of a computation made with reasonable accuracy and the exact amount is subsequently determined in a later taxable year, the difference, if any, between such amounts should be taken into account in the later taxable year in which exact determination is made.[225]

Once the amount of the liability has been determined, it is that full amount that is subject to accrual. In other words, the amount of the deduction is not limited to the present value of the amount to be paid in the future.[226]

The following questions have been raised in considering whether an amount can be determined with reasonable accuracy: (1) Must the amount itself be certain? (2) Will the fact that the amount is subject to later adjustment preclude accrual and deduction? (3) If all facts affecting computation of the amount have not occurred within the taxable year, will the deduction be denied?

[a] Certainty of Amount

The regulation requires only that the amount be determined with reasonable accuracy, not that it be certain. Thus, if services are rendered to a taxpayer for which the taxpayer is charged $10,000, but the taxpayer admits liability for $6,000 only and contests the remainder, the taxpayer may take

---

[224] Treas. Reg. § 1.461-1(a)(2)(ii). The regulation provides the following example. Assume A renders services to B during the taxable year for which A charges $10,000. B admits a liability to A for $6,000 but contests the remainder. According to the regulations, B may take into account only $6,000 as an expense for the taxable year in which the services were rendered.

[225] Treas. Reg. § 1.461-1(a)(3). Although this regulation suggests the possibility that a taxpayer might shift some deductible expense from one year to another on the basis of erroneous estimates, that possibility is limited by Treas. Reg. § 1.461-1(a)(3), which points out that each year's return must be complete and based on the facts and circumstances of that year. A taxpayer may not take advantage in a subsequent year of his failure to claim a deduction in the earlier year if it was appropriate to claim the deduction in such earlier year. In other words, if errors were made in computation of the amount because of a failure to consider all applicable facts and circumstances, the appropriate procedure may be to file an amended return rather than merely correcting the amount of the deduction in the subsequent year.

[226] See Burnham Corp., 90 TC 953 (1988), aff'd, 878 F2d 86 (2d Cir. 1989).

into account only the $6,000.[227] The balance may not be deducted because the amount is contingent and cannot then be ascertained with reasonable accuracy.[228] In focusing on the need to determine the amount with reasonable accuracy, taxpayers sometimes forget to deduct that portion of an asserted liability to which they agree. Taxpayers inadvertently defer deduction of the entire liability even though only a portion of the liability may be uncertain in amount. Correlatively, examining agents rarely challenge a deduction in one tax year on the basis that some portion of it should have been accrued and deducted in an earlier year. Of course, while such a position may not be in the government's interest in most cases, situations do arise where such a position by the agents will benefit the government.

The rules regarding the determination of an amount with reasonable accuracy and the fact that the amount need not be certain are fairly clear. Nevertheless, some cases contain language that has suggested a need for certainty. For example, the Supreme Court has said that for the expense to be deductible, all events must occur within the year that fix the "amount" of the taxpayer's liability.[229] It is probable that this language was inadvertent and not intended to alter the regulatory standard.

As to the precise basis for making computations, the courts have been more liberal than the IRS. "Generally, estimates based on industry-wide experience or the experience of the taxpayer have been accepted by the courts as reasonable."[230] For example, the Ninth Circuit has permitted liabilities to be estimated on an aggregate basis rather than on an individual claim basis as had been required in earlier cases.[231]

In *ESCO Corp. v. United States*,[232] the court considered the impact of actual experience and hindsight on the amounts estimated on the basis of facts and circumstances available to the taxpayer at the end of the year of deduction. The district court found that an average error rate of 10.17 percent was not sufficiently accurate for tax accounting purposes to permit the deduction.[233] However, the appeals court pointed out that while such

---

[227] Treas. Reg. § 1.461-1(a)(2)(ii).

[228] But see discussion supra ¶ 4.04[1][c] regarding contested liabilities.

[229] See, e.g., Dixie Pine Prods. Co. v. Comm'r, 320 US 516, 519 (1944).

[230] See Joint Comm. on Taxation, General Explanation of the Revenue Provisions of the Deficit Reduction Act of 1984 (Dec. 31, 1984) (hereafter Blue Book), at 259. Note that this same type of evidence has not been sufficient to permit a deferral in the recognition of prepaid income. See discussion infra ¶ 4.03[3].

[231] Kaiser Steel Corp. v. United States, 717 F2d 1304 (9th Cir. 1983). See also Crescent Wharf & Warehouse Co. v. Comm'r, 518 F2d 772 (9th Cir. 1975), rev'g 59 TC 598 (1973). But see Wien Consol. Airlines v. Comm'r, 528 F2d 735 (9th Cir. 1976); Milwaukee & Suburban Transp. Corp. v. Comm'r, 367 US 906 (1961), vacating and remanding 283 F2d 279 (7th Cir. 1960).

[232] ESCO Corp. v. United States, 750 F2d 1466 (9th Cir. 1985).

[233] ESCO Corp. v. United States, 578 F. Supp. 738 (D. Or. 1983).

hindsight considerations are important, they are not dispositive. The court held that it was more important that the estimates be based on reasonable, commercially accepted standards. The court added that statistical testing is appropriate for the purpose of making the estimate.

[b] Possibility of Adjustment

The possibility of later adjustment of the amount does not prevent accrual and deduction. Frequently, the adjustment arises from a condition subsequent, i.e., a fact or circumstance that occurs after the existence of a liability that may terminate or modify the liability itself or cause an adjustment in the amount of the liability.[234] Of course, an adjustment may also arise where the original amount is estimated.[235]

[c] Timing of Facts on Which Amount Is Based

A further question is whether all facts (on which the computation is based) must occur within the year in which the deduction is claimed. The courts and the IRS appear to have somewhat different views of this. Generally, the mere willingness of courts prior to the 1984 Act to permit taxpayers to deduct a liability for obligations associated with future performance demonstrates that the amount of the deduction need not be based on facts occurring wholly within the year of deduction.[236] If this were not the case, deductions would not have been permitted until performance had occurred because, until then, it would not have been possible to determine the amount of liability.

Nevertheless, the IRS has indicated in a private letter ruling that the exact amount of the liability must be "determinable by a mere computation based on presently known or knowable factors."[237] The position of the IRS in the private letter ruling appeared to be that all facts on which the computation is based must occur within the year of deduction, although the taxpayer may not learn of them until the subsequent year. If the private letter ruling correctly reflects the IRS view, it does not appear to be adequately supported.

[3] Economic Performance

For several years prior to 1984, the trend of court decisions was to permit deductions for liabilities to perform (or to incur expenses in connection with

---

[234] See discussion infra ¶ 4.04[1][a][ii].

[235] Treas. Reg. §§ 1.451-1(a), 1.461-1(a)(3).

[236] See discussion infra ¶ 4.04[3] regarding the economic performance requirement.

[237] Priv. Ltr. Rul. 7831003 (Apr. 13, 1978).

performing) obligations in the future. This, combined with opportunities for estimating the amounts of the liabilities in question, was perceived by the Treasury as leading to abuse. In many cases, taxpayers were able to obtain large deductions and then use the tax savings arising from the deductions to fund payment of the liability itself. For example, in the case of the so-called structured settlement, a taxpayer with a tort obligation might settle with the plaintiff by agreeing to pay some amount in the future. The taxpayer would obtain a present deduction that, in turn, would create tax savings that could be invested. The tax savings plus the after-tax earnings from investment of these savings provided the amount necessary to pay the plaintiff. In such a case, the government bears the economic cost of paying the taxpayer's obligation. In general, this was part of the so-called time value of money problem, i.e., permitting present deductions without taking into account the time delay in the payment of the amounts at issue.[238]

Congress believed that these opportunities necessitated a change in the rules governing application of accrual method reporting to deductions. Not only was Congress concerned about the potential loss of revenue from deductions, which did not take into account the time value of money, but also it was concerned about the potential for abuse.[239] Congress responded to these concerns by enacting Section 461(h). Following that section's enactment in 1984, revenue agents and taxpayers were generally uncertain as to how the rules should be applied in all but the most obvious circumstances. However, on June 6, 1990, approximately six years after the enactment of Section 461(h), the Treasury issued proposed regulations.[240] Corresponding amendments were proposed for other related provisions in the regulations. Ultimately, final regulations were promulgated, effective April 10, 1992.[241]

[a]　Section 461(h)

Under Section 461(h), a taxpayer incurring an obligation for an item of expense will not be entitled to a deduction until economic performance has occurred with respect to that item.[242] As a general rule, where a taxpayer's

---

[238] See, e.g., McGowan, "Structured Settlements: Deduct Now and Pay Later," 60 Taxes 251 (1982).

[239] Blue Book, supra note 230, at 260–261.

[240] Prop. Reg. § 1.461-4.

[241] Treas. Reg. § 1.461-4.

[242] Section 461(h) is effective for amounts that would be allowable as a deduction after July 18, 1984. Under the temporary regulations (Temp. Reg. § 1.461-3T, which was later redesignated by the final regulations, effective April 10, 1992, as § 1.461-7T), taxpayers are to apply the new rules to deductions that otherwise would have occurred after July 18, 1984. Alternatively, taxpayers may elect to treat the application of Section 461(h) as a change in accounting method effective for the first taxable year that includes July 19, 1984. In addition, a taxpayer making that election may

obligation consists of promising to pay for services or property provided to him or providing services or property to another, economic performance occurs only as these services or property are provided. Under this section, a taxpayer may no longer obtain a tax deduction prior to the time of performance. Thus, this provision has the effect of resolving many of the issues that had arisen in the past with respect to identification of the relevant liability.[243]

Although intended to prevent tax abuse, Section 461(h) applies to all taxpayers using an accrual method of accounting. It is not limited in scope to particular categories of taxpayers or to particular transactions. It applies even where payment has already been made, i.e., except in certain designated instances,[244] payment is not economic performance. The provision thus produces an anomalous result. It was, in large part, intended to correct the problem of permitting a deduction to be taken substantially in advance of payment; yet, it may deny a deduction even where payment has been made.

Perhaps in recognition of this anomaly, the Treasury has adopted a special rule to permit economic performance to occur as payments are made in particular circumstances.[245] For example, under the special rule, a taxpayer may treat property or services provided to it as satisfying economic performance at the time payment is made, if the taxpayer can reasonably expect the person who is to provide the property or services to provide them within three and one half months after the date of payment. This special provision is interesting in several respects. First, the property or services apparently do not actually need to be provided within three and one half months of payment as long as the taxpayer can reasonably expect the person who is to provide the property or services to provide them within three and one half months after payment. Consequently, a failure to provide the property or services within the specified time frame should not prevent the occurrence of economic performance at the time of payment, if the failure was not reasonably expected. Second, although the time of payment normally does not accelerate a deduction by an accrual method taxpayer, this special rule allows accrual method taxpayers the opportunity for accelerating deductions merely by making payment. Thus, accrual method taxpayers should consider their tax postures as they near the end of each taxable year. If deductions are desired, they may be able to accelerate certain deductions merely by making payment and taking advantage of this special three-and-one-half-month rule. Alternatively, if they wish to defer a deduction until a later year, they may do so

---

further elect to treat the change in accounting method as effective for the entire taxable year or for only that part of the taxable year that begins with July 19, 1984. The temporary regulations are set forth in question-and-answer style, and numerous examples are provided.

[243] See discussion supra ¶ 4.04[1][a].

[244] See discussion infra ¶ 4.04[3][b].

[245] Treas. Reg. § 1.461-4(d)(5)(ii).

simply by deferring payment. Finally, it would appear that eligibility for this special rule does not in any way depend on satisfaction of the requirements pertaining to applicability of the recurring item exception.[246]

Although an exception is provided for certain recurring items,[247] the Section 461(h) rules otherwise apply to everyday business transactions as well as to transactions motivated wholly by tax considerations. With certain exceptions,[248] the section applies for all purposes of the Code, not just to deductions under Section 461.[249] Small and large businesses as well as tax shelter transactions and transactions not associated with tax shelters are subject to this new requirement of the all events test.

In many cases, economic performance will occur in the same taxable year in which the old requirements of the all events test would be satisfied and, therefore, will not cause a deferral in the timing of deductions. When economic performance does not occur in the same year, the recurring item exception may apply.[250] Nevertheless, every transaction of every accrual basis taxpayer must now be examined in light of this relatively new requirement.

[b] Time When Economic Performance Occurs

Section 461(h) provides rules for determining when economic performance occurs and exceptions to those rules. In addition, Congress has provided the Treasury with the authority to alter these statutory provisions.[251]

---

[246] See discussion infra ¶ 4.04[3][f].

[247] Id.

[248] Section 461(h) will not apply to items covered by Section 166(c) or Section 166(f), which relate to reserves for bad debts, by Section 463, which relates to vacation pay, by Section 466, which relates to discount coupons, or by any other provision that expressly provides for the deduction of a reserve for estimated expenses. IRC § 461(h)(5). In addition, Treas. Reg. § 1.461-1(a)(2)(iii) provides that if any provision of the Code requires a liability to be taken into account in a taxable year later than the taxable year provided under Section 461, the liability must be taken into account in accordance with that Code provision. Similarly, these same regulations make it clear that Section 461 does not govern the timing of a deduction for liabilities attributable to Sections 165, 170, 192, 194A, 468, or Section 468A. Nor do the regulations apply to any amount that the Code allows as a deduction for a reserve for estimated expenses. Finally, these regulations make it clear that except as otherwise provided by regulation, revenue procedure, or revenue ruling, the requirements of Section 461(h) and the regulations promulgated thereunder are satisfied to the extent that any amount is allowable as a deduction under Sections 404, 404A, or 419.

[249] See, e.g., Joseph W. La Rue, 90 TC 465 (1988), where the Tax Court held that the time for including a liability in the basis of a partnership interest is controlled by the time the liability has satisfied the all events test for deductions under an accrual method.

[250] See discussion infra ¶ 4.04[3][f].

[251] Section 461(h)(2) provides, "Except as provided in regulations prescribed by the Secretary, the time when economic performance occurs shall be determined under [rules provided in IRC Sections 461(h)(2)(A)–461(h)(2)(D)]."

Until regulations were finally adopted, effective April 10, 1992, the precise manner in which the general rules would apply was necessarily speculative. This was especially troublesome where, as here, the new test was already effective.[252] Nevertheless, general rules are provided by the statute, and on June 6, 1990, comprehensive regulations were proposed.[253] Although the proposed regulations were subject to change before adoption (and they had been the subject of numerous comments by practitioners and taxpayers), they provided significant additional guidance as to when economic performance would occur.

Ultimately, final regulations were adopted. Together with the statutory provisions, these regulations cover numerous circumstances including where services or property are provided to the taxpayer, where services or property are provided by the taxpayer, and where workers' compensation or tort liability is involved.[254] The regulations also provide that in any case where the statutory or regulatory rules do not provide the time when economic performance occurs, economic performance will be deemed to occur only as payment is made to the person to which the liability is owed.[255] It is anticipated that such instances will occur rarely and only in situations where the liability cannot properly be characterized as one covered by other economic performance rules.[256]

[i] **Services and property provided to taxpayer.** If a taxpayer's liability arises from its promise to pay for services or property provided by another, economic performance is deemed to occur as such services or property are provided.[257] For example, if a taxpayer enters into a contract in year 1, which unconditionally obligates it to pay for services to be rendered to it in year 2, then unless an exception is applicable, the taxpayer will be entitled to the deduction only in year 2, as the services are rendered. If a portion of the services is rendered in year 2 and the balance is rendered in year 3, then economic performance will occur in years 2 and 3. Guidelines have not yet been provided as to how the cost of the total services should be allocated between the two years.[258]

If the taxpayer's liability arises out of its use of property, economic performance occurs only as the taxpayer uses the property. The use requirement initially raised a troubling interpretive question. If the taxpayer leased a

---

[252] Section 461(h) is applicable to all amounts that would be deductible after July 18, 1984, the date of enactment.

[253] Prop. Reg. § 1.461-4.

[254] See discussion infra ¶ 4.04[3][b][iv].

[255] Treas. Reg. § 1.461-4(g)(7).

[256] Id.

[257] IRC § 461(h)(2)(A).

[258] See discussion infra ¶ 4.04[3][c].

building for a period of 12 months beginning December 1 of year 1, would the taxpayer be entitled to a deduction for one month's rent in year 1 if it did not actually occupy or otherwise use the leased premises during that month? Would availability for use constitute use? It was feared that the IRS might take the position that the deduction for that rent should be deferred until the period of actual use.[259]

Ultimately, this question, together with others, was answered by the Treasury. On June 7, 1990, the Treasury issued proposed regulations providing guidance as to how the economic performance rules would operate.[260] Final regulations were adopted, effective April 10, 1992.[261] These regulations are discussed below.[262]

[ii] Services and property provided by taxpayer. If the taxpayer's obligation is to provide property or services to another, economic performance occurs as the taxpayer provides such property or services.[263] For example, if the taxpayer is obligated to repair or maintain property that it sells, economic performance occurs only as those repairs are made or as the maintenance is performed. Thus, absent an exception, taxpayers would not be entitled to deduct in the year of sale the estimated cost of carrying out warranty or similar obligations in the future. This also appears to have the effect of legislatively overruling the decisions in a number of other cases.[264]

On June 7, 1990, the Treasury issued proposed regulations providing guidance as to how the economic performance rule would operate.[265] Final regulations were adopted, effective April 10, 1992.[266] These regulations are discussed below.[267]

[iii] Workers' compensation and tort liabilities. If the taxpayer's obligation requires a payment to another as a result of any workers' compensation act or tort liability, economic performance occurs only as the payments

---

[259] Although this might seem a strained interpretation, it is one that has been suggested by Treasury officials in panel discussions with members of the American Bar Association.

[260] Prop. Reg. § 1.461-4.

[261] Treas. Reg. § 1.461-4.

[262] See discussion infra ¶ 4.04[3][c][ii].

[263] IRC § 461(h)(2)(B).

[264] See, e.g., Gillis v. United States, 402 F2d 501 (5th Cir. 1968), where taxpayer allowed to accrue in current year loss on sale that must occur in subsequent year; Pacific Grape Prods. v. Comm'r, 219 F2d 862 (9th Cir. 1955), where taxpayer was allowed to deduct in one year anticipated expenses of shipping goods in subsequent year.

[265] Prop. Reg. § 1.461-4.

[266] Treas. Reg. § 1.461-4.

[267] See discussion infra ¶ 4.04[3][c][ii].

are made.[268] Thus, the taxpayer is effectively placed on the cash method with respect to such obligations. However, the taxpayer is not actually on the cash method because satisfaction of the economic performance test does not, of itself, permit a deduction. The liability to which the payment relates must be fixed. If payment precedes existence of a fixed liability, a deduction will not be allowed merely because of the payment.

However, if a taxpayer takes out insurance to cover such liabilities, economic performance will occur with respect to the taxpayer's liability to the insurance company as payments are made.[269] Thus, the taxpayer's deduction will not be postponed until the insurance company itself makes payment to the injured person.

If the taxpayer satisfies its tort liability by purchasing an annuity for the benefit of the claimant, a question arises as to the time of economic performance. If the taxpayer delivers the annuity contract to the claimant in satisfaction of the taxpayer's obligation, should economic performance be deemed to occur on delivery? If so, the amount of the deduction presumably should be limited to the amount of the claim satisfied at the time of delivery of the annuity, and gain or loss might arise to the extent of the difference between the amount of the claim satisfied and the taxpayer's basis in the annuity contract.

On June 7, 1990, the Treasury issued proposed regulations providing guidance as to how the economic performance rules would operate.[270] Final regulations were adopted, effective April 10, 1992.[271] These regulations are discussed below.[272]

[iv] **Other items.** Section 461(h) sets forth the principles governing when economic performance occurs only in certain specified instances.[273] The Code provides that, in all other instances, economic performance will be deemed to occur only as determined under Treasury regulations.[274] Thus, a taxpayer incurring an obligation that requires economic performance in a

---

[268] IRC § 461(h)(2)(C).

[269] See Treas. Reg. § 1.461-4(g)(5). See infra ¶ 4.04[3][c][ii].

[270] Prop. Reg. § 1.461-4.

[271] Treas. Reg. § 1.461-4.

[272] See discussion infra ¶ 4.04[3][c][ii].

[273] See discussion ¶¶ 4.04[3][b][i]–4.04[3][b][iii].

[274] IRC § 461(h)(2)(D). Nevertheless, the report of the Conference Committee indicates that (1) with respect to disposal of nuclear wastes, the regulations should provide that economic performance occurs as payments are made to the federal government and (2) with respect to deduction of refunds made to customers by natural gas utility companies of refunds it receives from its suppliers, the deduction should be made in the year in which the refund is received if the refunds are passed through to the utilities customers within a reasonable period following the year of receipt and adequate interest is paid to customers and includable in their incomes.

manner other than as specifically set forth in the Code had no ascertainable standard for determining the period in which the deduction should be recognized prior to the issuance of Treasury regulations.

On June 7, 1990, the Treasury issued proposed regulations providing guidance as to how the economic performance rules would operate.[275] Final regulations were adopted, effective April 10, 1992.[276] These regulations are discussed below.[277]

[c] "As Provided" Requirement

[i] **General rules and questions arising prior to issuance of regulations.** Taxpayers generally satisfy the economic performance requirement only as property or services are provided. Consequently, the requirement is not satisfied at the commencement of the rendition of services or the delivery of property. Rather, assuming the other requirements of the all events test are satisfied, the taxpayer is entitled to a deduction in any particular year for only that portion of the total liability that may be attributable to the services or property actually provided in that taxable year. Because the "as provided" requirement is a facts-and-circumstances test, there is a considerable likelihood of disputes and controversies.

In many instances, it should be comparatively easy to apportion the liability to the activities performed in a particular year. For example, with respect to many liabilities, economic performance would most likely be found to occur ratably over time, e.g., rent and insurance.[278]

In other instances, an appropriate apportionment may be more difficult to make, if not virtually impossible. For example, if a taxpayer becomes obligated to pay a fixed amount for certain services (such as legal, accounting, and engineering), the services may be of little value to the taxpayer until their completion. Alternatively, the obligation of the professional may be the preparation of an opinion, report, or other document. Until the document is delivered, the taxpayer may believe it has received no service. In this sense, the question may be raised as to whether the taxpayer should be viewed as requesting a product.

Several questions arise in circumstances where the services result in the creation of such an intangible product. Should the taxpayer get a deduction as services are rendered (and payments made), or only on completion of the services or delivery of the document? If deductions are permitted as the services are rendered, should apportionment be made on some possibly arbitrary standard (such as time lapsed or hours spent) or on some other basis?

---

[275] Prop. Reg. § 1.461-4.

[276] Treas. Reg. § 1.461-4.

[277] See discussion infra ¶ 4.04[3][c][ii].

[278] But see Section 461(h)(2)(A)(iii) regarding rent.

EXAMPLE: Assume a 10,000-foot well is to be dug for the taxpayer at a total cost of $80,000. If 2,000 feet are dug in year 1 and the remaining 8,000 feet are dug in year 2, what portion of the $80,000 liability is attributable to the 2,000 feet dug in year 1? Is it determined simply on a pro rata basis, in which event it would be $16,000 (2,000/10,000 x $80,000), or should recognition be given to the fact that the cost of digging each foot may not be the same, i.e., the deeper footage may cost more than the shallow footage?

The treatment of interest also poses interesting questions. The Joint Committee Explanation of the rules indicates that economic performance with respect to interest occurs with the passage of time rather than as payments are made. It suggests that interest incurred by accrual method taxpayers should be deductible on a so-called constant interest basis.[279] Although this seems reasonable if the agreement of the parties provides for an economic accrual of interest on a constant rate basis, it would seem illogical and inappropriate to apply a constant rate approach if the agreement calls for interest that varies according to a fixed standard, such as a prime rate or other rate tied to an accepted index. A constant rate approach would also appear inappropriate if the applicable agreement calls for different fixed interest rates (1) for different periods of time or (2) on the basis of different levels of security. For example, if it is anticipated that the holder of the note may be secured by a first mortgage on property during some periods and by a second mortgage during other periods, it would seem appropriate that the applicable interest rate vary in accordance with the relative risks during the relevant periods of the loan. Similarly, use of a constant rate, while perhaps consistent with some economic analyses, may be inconsistent with the agreement of the parties, applicable nontax laws, or other factors. These circumstances should not be ignored in applying the economic performance requirement.[280]

---

[279] Blue Book, supra note 230, at 265.

[280] See Don P. Setliff, 53 TCM 1295 (1987), where the court, in finding the Rule of 78's method of allocating interest to be inappropriate in the particular circumstances, nevertheless indicated that circumstances might exist where the use of that method (or, arguably, any other method agreed on by the parties) would clearly reflect income. This holding calls into question the validity of the position expressed by the IRS in Rev. Rul. 83-84, 1983-1 CB 97. See discussion at ¶ 3.03[3][a]. However, in Bruce A. Prabel, 91 TC 1101 (1988), aff'd, 882 F2d 820 (3d Cir. 1989), the full Tax Court concluded that the Commissioner did not abuse his discretion in disallowing that portion of interest deductions determined under the Rule of 78's method that were in excess of the amounts determined under an economic accrual method. The court noted that use of the Rule of 78's produced interest significantly in excess of both the economically accrued interest and the amounts of interest to be paid in most years. The court also noted that under the particular agreement, the Rule of 78's method of allocation would not have been used unless there were a prepayment. Subsequently, in Allen J. Levy, 92 TC 1360 (1989), the Tax Court again denied a taxpayer the right to accrue and deduct interest on a Rule of 78's basis even though

In some cases, questions may arise over the character of the item to which the liability relates. To illustrate, assume that in year 1, a taxpayer purchases season tickets for sporting events, concerts, or similar events to be performed in year 2. An initial question is whether the taxpayer has purchased services or property. If the tickets represent a right to services to be rendered in the future, will the taxpayer's deduction be deferred until the year in which the performance occurs? If the tickets are property, will the taxpayer be entitled to a deduction in the year the tickets are acquired? What law will be applied in determining whether the taxpayer has obtained property or a right to receive services? Will the year of deduction be affected by whether the taxpayer acquires the tickets for itself, gives them to its employees, or provides them to customers or clients? To what extent will the taxpayer's intent be relevant? Until clarifying regulations or other authorities address these questions, taxpayers can only speculate as to the ultimate answer. Presumably, taxpayers will characterize the item in the manner most favorable to them and await a challenge on audit.

[ii] **Applicable Treasury regulations.** The Treasury adopted final regulations, effective April 10, 1992, providing guidance on the manner in which the economic performance rules would apply.[281] These regulations focus on how the "as-provided" requirements of the economic performance rules will be interpreted.

Services and property provided to the taxpayer. The regulations confirm the principle established in Section 461(h)(2)(B) that if the liability of a taxpayer arises out of the provision of property or services by another, economic performance occurs as the property or services are provided to the taxpayer or to another person at the taxpayer's direction.[282] However, the regulations provide two exceptions that may accelerate the time when economic performance will be deemed to occur from the time the property or services are provided to the time payment is made by the taxpayer.

---

the Rule of 78's method would be applied in determining the amount of interest accrued and earned by the lender in all cases and not merely in the event of prepayment. The court stated that the key point in *Prabel* was that where interest accruals calculated under the Rule of 78's method materially exceed both the interest determined under an economic accrual method and the amount of interest the taxpayer is required to pay under the applicable payment schedule, the Commissioner has the authority to remedy the resulting distortion in income. In light of these cases, it would appear that the only remaining issue is whether accrual under a Rule of 78's method would be allowed where the difference between the Rule of 78's method and an economic accrual method is material but the interest required under the Rule of 78's method actually is paid. On the other hand, the Claims Court recognized that whether use of the Rule of 78's method clearly reflects income is a question of fact for consideration by the court. Mulholland v. United States, 92-1 USTC ¶ 50,267 (Cl. Ct. 1992).

[281] Treas. Reg. § 1.461-4.

[282] Treas. Reg. § 1.461-4(d)(6)(i).

First, if the expense incurred by the taxpayer is attributable to a long-term contract with respect to which the taxpayer uses the percentage-of-completion method, economic performance will occur at the earlier of the time the property or services are provided or the time the taxpayer makes payment in satisfaction of the liability to the person providing the property or services.[283] This provision, although suggesting an acceleration in the time when liability is taken into account, actually has the effect of accelerating the taxpayer's recognition of income. Simply stated, by accelerating the time when the expenses are taken into account, the provision accelerates the time when the corresponding income will be recognized under the percentage-of-completion method.

Second, a special rule is provided allowing the taxpayer to treat property or services as being provided at the time that the taxpayer makes payment for the property or services, if the taxpayer can reasonably expect the person who is to provide the property or services to provide them within three and one half months after the time of payment.[284] Literally, this rule does not require that the property or services actually be provided within three and one half months; only that the taxpayer reasonably expect property or services to be provided within three and one half months after payment. This provision is a special rule, separate and apart from the recurring item exception.[285]

Each of these special rules requires taxpayers to consider carefully the timing of their payments. Moreover, the wording of these rules raises various interpretive questions. For example, the first special rule appears to be mandatory whereas the second rule appears to be permissive. If the second rule is permissive, the taxpayer's initial decision to treat economic performance as occurring at the time of payment (or not to treat payment as the term of economic performance) may constitute the adoption of a method of accounting. Thus, if a taxpayer treats payments as constituting economic performance where services or property are reasonably expected to be delivered within three and one half months of payment, the taxpayer may not thereafter have the option of ignoring payments in determining when economic performance occurs. On the other hand, the taxpayer can take these rules into account on an ongoing basis in deciding whether to make a payment.

Use of property by taxpayer. If the liability of the taxpayer arises out of the use of property, economic performance occurs ratably over the period that the taxpayer is entitled to use the property.[286] By clarifying that the economic performance occurs over the period the taxpayer is entitled to use the property rather than over the period of actual use, the regulation clarifies

---

[283] Treas. Reg. § 1.461-4(d)(2)(ii).

[284] Treas. Reg. § 1.461-4(d)(6)(ii).

[285] See discussion of recurring item exception infra ¶ 4.04[3][f].

[286] Treas. Reg. § 1.461-4(d)(3).

the fact that it is the right to use the property and not the actual use that controls. Thus, if a taxpayer enters into a lease to occupy property beginning December 1 of year 1 but does not occupy the property until January of year 2, economic performance would be deemed to accrue ratably beginning December 1 of year 1 even though the taxpayer did not actually use the property during that month.

By making economic performance occur ratably as the property is used, taxpayers are apparently precluded from arbitrarily structuring lease payments in such a way as to accelerate the amount of deduction for which economic performance will be deemed to have accrued. In other words, the taxpayer may not be able to pay a premium for the first month's rent and declining amounts of rent thereafter and thereby accelerate deductions disproportionately to earlier portions of the lease term. On the other hand, if a multi-year lease agreement provides for annual or less frequent adjustments to the rent, based on changes in underlying costs and similar factors normally giving rise to such changes, the resulting changes in rent should be taken into account ratably over the period to which they relate. Bona fide changes occurring more frequently than annually should be examined carefully to determine how and when they should be taken into account.

Special rule regarding purchases of property or purchases of multiple items of property or services. The regulations permit a taxpayer to treat property as provided when the property is delivered to the taxpayer, accepted by the taxpayer, or when title to the property has passed to the taxpayer. Whichever method is used by the taxpayer to determine when property is provided constitutes a method of accounting from which the taxpayer may not change without the prior approval of the Commissioner.[287] This rule may be somewhat inconsistent with normal principles governing when a sale occurs and when property is acquired by a taxpayer.[288] It is not yet known whether the Treasury proposes to apply this rule without regard to changes in facts and circumstances so that any approach used must be used in all cases. Such an interpretation, if made, would be inconsistent with normal interpretations of methods of accounting.[289]

Under a second special rule, if a taxpayer is to receive different services or items of property under a single contract, economic performance generally occurs over time as each service is provided or as each item of property is provided. However, if such service or property is incidental to other services or property to be provided under the agreement, the taxpayer is not required to allocate any portion of the total contract price to such incidental services or property. For this purpose, property or services are treated as incidental only if (1) the cost of the property or services is treated on the taxpayer's

---

[287] Treas. Reg. § 1.461-4(d)(6)(iii).

[288] See discussion supra ¶ 4.03[1][a], and ¶ 6.05[1][b].

[289] See discussion at ¶ 9.06.

books and records as part of the cost of the other property or services provided under the contract and (2) the aggregate cost of the property or services does not exceed 10 percent of the total contract price.[290] Consequently, the regulation implies that in the cases not covered by this special rule, an allocation of the contract price must be made among the various items of property and services to be provided. Such a requirement may give rise to numerous controversies involving both the allocations made and the time when economic performance occurs for each particular item of service or property.

Services and property provided by the taxpayer. Section 461(h)(2)(B) provides the general rule that if the taxpayer's obligation is to provide property or services to another, economic performance occurs as the taxpayer provides such property or services. The regulations clarify this statutory provision by providing that economic performance in such cases will occur as the taxpayer incurs costs in connection with the satisfaction of the liability.[291] In determining whether the taxpayer has incurred costs, the regulations refer to the general rules for accrual method taxpayers as set forth in Treasury Regulation § 1.446-1(c)(1)(ii). As a result, taxpayers would be deemed to incur costs when all the events had occurred that established the fact of liability, when the amount could be determined with reasonable accuracy, and when economic performance had occurred with respect to that liability.

This rule requires an evaluation of two separate liabilities, the liability of the taxpayer to provide property or services to another (the first liability) and the liability of the taxpayer to those who provide property or services to the taxpayer so that the taxpayer will be able to satisfy the first liability. To illustrate, assume that a calendar year, accrual method taxpayer sells property under a warranty. Assume that the property is sold in year 1, that a defect, which requires the taxpayer to replace certain parts, occurs in year 2, that the taxpayer incurs costs to its own employees during year 3 as they manufacture the replacement parts, and that the actual replacement occurs in year 4. In these circumstances, economic performance with respect to the taxpayer's obligation to its customer (the first liability) begins to occur in year 3 as the taxpayer incurs costs associated with the property to be provided to the customer.[292]

Barter transactions. If the taxpayer is required to provide services or property or the use of property as a result of the taxpayer's use or receipt of property or services from another, economic performance occurs to the

---

[290] Treas. Reg. § 1.461-4(d)(6)(iv).

[291] Treas. Reg. § 1.461-4(d)(4).

[292] See examples 2, 3, and 4 under Treas. Reg. § 1.461-4(d)(7). See also Section 263A and the regulations thereunder for rules relating to the capitalization and inclusion in inventory of such incurred costs.

extent of the lesser of two amounts.[293] The first amount is the cumulative extent to which the taxpayer incurs costs in connection with its liability to provide property or services, and the second amount is the cumulative extent to which the property or services are provided to the taxpayer. To illustrate, assume a taxpayer agrees to pay a worker $20 per hour to provide services to another person in consideration for that other person providing the taxpayer with property worth $20 per unit. If the taxpayer incurs $40 of liability to the worker during year 1 for services provided to the other person and the other person had provided the taxpayer with only one unit or $20 of property during year 1, economic performance has occurred during year 1 to the extent of the $20 of property received, the lesser amount. If the situation were reversed and two units of property had been received but only one hour of the worker's time had been spent, economic performance would have occurred to the extent of the $20 of services. This rule may result in a taxpayer not having a basis in the property acquired until the taxpayer itself has provided property or services. To illustrate, assume that the taxpayer does not provide property or services until after it has disposed of the property it received, the taxpayer presumably would recognize gain in connection with the disposition of property for which it has no basis. This could pose serious financial difficulty where this rule applies and none of the exceptions for accelerating the time of economic performance are otherwise applicable.

Payment as economic performance. The regulations specify that except where economic performance is deemed to occur in some other fashion, economic performance will arise as payments are made. In other words, unless the taxpayer can identify a particular provision providing for a different time for economic performance, economic performance will occur as payments are made in satisfaction of the particular liability. Thus, payment is a catchall rule for economic performance where no other rule applies.[294] Of course, the regulations provide specific rules governing when economic performance occurs in the majority of cases, such as when the liability arises out of the use or receipt of the property or services. Thus, the Treasury anticipates that this catchall provision will not apply in that many circumstances.

The regulations nevertheless identify five specific instances that will be covered by the payment rule. First, economic performance occurs as payment is made in the case of any liability arising under a worker's compensation act or out of any tort, breach of contract, or violation of law.[295] For a liability to pay for services, property, or other consideration provided under a contract, the liability is not considered a liability arising out of a breach of that contract unless the payments made are in the nature of incidental, consequen-

---

[293] Treas. Reg. § 1.461-4(d)(4)(ii).
[294] Treas. Reg. § 1.461-4(g)(7).
[295] Treas. Reg. § 1.461-4(g)(2).

tial, or liquidated damages.[296] However, a liability arising out of a tort, breach of contract, or violation of law includes a liability arising out of the settlement of a dispute in which a tort, breach of contract, or violation of law is alleged.[297] These various categories of liabilities are much broader than those identified in the Section 461(h), itself, which pertained only to worker's compensation and tort liabilities. The regulations also provide that none of the liabilities coming within this category is eligible for the recurring item exception.[298]

Second, economic performance occurs as payment is made in the case of liabilities to pay a rebate or refund to another person (without regard to whether the liability is paid in property, money, or a reduction in the price of goods or services to be provided in the future).[299] This rule applies to all rebates, refunds, and payments or transfers in the nature of the rebate or refund regardless of whether they are characterized as a deduction from gross income, an adjustment to gross receipts or total sales, or an adjustment or addition to cost of goods sold. In the case of a rebate or refund taking the form of a reduced price for goods or services to be provided in the future, payment is deemed to occur at the time the taxpayer otherwise would be required to recognize income resulting from the provision of services or the providing of goods. The recurring item exception is available for this type of liability.

Third, economic performance occurs as payment is made if the liability of a taxpayer is to provide an award, prize, jackpot, or similar payment.[300] The recurring item exception is available for this type of liability.

Fourth, economic performance occurs as payment is made in the case of a liability arising out of the provision to the taxpayer of insurance or a warranty or service contract.[301] "Warranty" or "service contract" is defined as a contract entered into in connection with property purchased or leased by the taxpayer pursuant to which the other party promises to replace or repair property under specified circumstances. The term "insurance" has the same meaning as it has under Section 162. The recurring item exception is available for this type of liability.

Fifth, economic performance occurs as payments are made in the case of a liability to pay a tax.[302] (The only exceptions to this rule are for foreign

---

[296] Treas. Reg. § 1.461-4(g)(2)(i).

[297] Treas. Reg. § 1.461-4(g)(2)(ii).

[298] Treas. Reg. § 1.461-5(c). The recurring item exception is discussed infra ¶ 4.04[3][f].

[299] Treas. Reg. § 1.461-4(g)(3).

[300] Treas. Reg. § 1.461-4(g)(4).

[301] Treas. Reg. § 1.461-4(g)(5).

[302] Treas. Reg. § 1.461-4(g)(6).

taxes and real estate taxes subject to the election under Section 461(c)).[303] For purposes of this rule, a tax does not include a charge collected by a governmental authority for specific extraordinary property or services provided to a taxpayer by the governmental authority, including for example charges for land sold to the taxpayer or for the labor of government employees who improved the land. The recurring item exception is available for these liabilities.

In applying these various payment rules, a number of principles of cash basis accounting are adopted.[304] In general, the term "payment" has the same meaning as it has in applying the cash method.[305] Consequently, payment includes the furnishing of cash or a cash equivalent. Payment should also include the providing of property for services. However, payment will not include the furnishing of a note or other evidence of indebtedness of the taxpayer, whether or not that note or other evidence of indebtedness is guaranteed by a third person or by some other instrument, including a standby letter of credit. Payment also will not include an amount transferred in a fashion other than as payment (e.g., as a loan, refundable deposit, or a contingent payment that may be refunded or otherwise credited back to the taxpayer).[306]

Although satisfaction of the foregoing rules generally would determine whether a payment has been made for cash basis taxpayers, the regulations apparently impose an additional requirement in order for the taxpayer to be treated as having made payment. Under the regulations, payment is accomplished by satisfaction of the principles set forth in the preceding paragraph and by showing that, if the person to whom the payment is made were a cash basis taxpayer, the payment would be treated as having actually or constructively been received by that person so that the amount of the payment would be includable in that person's gross income.[307] To illustrate, if the taxpayer

---

[303] Treas. Reg. § 1.461-4(g)(6)(iii). In Ann. 91-89, 1991-25 IRB 48, the IRS announced guidance regarding the election under Section 461(c) for ratably accruing real property taxes. The IRS stated that the final Section 461(h) regulations would provide rules allowing taxpayers automatically to make or to revoke an election under Section 461(c) without regard to the 180-day limitation period provided in Treas. Reg. §§ 1.461-1(c)(3)(ii), 1.461-1(c)(3)(iv), 1.446-1(e)(3); and Rev. Proc. 83-77, 1983-2 CB 594. The automatic election or revocation would be available for the first taxable year in which the payment rule of then Prop. Reg. § 1.461-4(g)(6) was effective. At the time of its adoption of final regulations, the Treasury announced that applicable rules governing these elections would be provided in Rev. Proc. 92-28, 1992-1 CB 745.

[304] Treas. Reg. § 1.461-4(g)(1).

[305] Id., but see Treas. Reg. § 1.461-6 providing certain circumstances in which certain liabilities are assigned or are extinguished by the establishment of a particular type of fund. See Chapter 3 for a discussion of the cash method.

[306] Treas. Reg. § 1.461-4(g)(1)(ii)(A).

[307] Treas. Reg. § 1.461-4(g)(1)(ii)(B).

were to purchase an annuity contract or other asset, that purchase would not be regarded as a payment to the person to whom the liability is owed unless the ownership of the contract or other asset was transferred to that person.[308] It is not known whether the constructive receipt rules will be deemed to preclude economic performance from having occurred in other situations where a payment may have been made directly to the person to whom the liability is owed, but where, because of unusual circumstances, that person is not deemed to have actually or constructively received the payment in the same year.[309]

The regulations also specify when payment will be deemed to have occurred in the case of liabilities that are assumed in connection with the sale of a trade or business. In general, if the purchaser expressly assumes a liability arising out of the trade or business and the seller would have been entitled to accrue that liability as of the date of sale (but for the economic performance requirement), then the taxpayer-seller will be deemed to have made payment with respect to the liability as the amount of the liability is included in the amount realized from the sale by the taxpayer.[310] For purposes of this provision, "trade or business" is defined as a specific group of activities carried on by the taxpayer for the purpose of earning income or profit if every operation that is necessary to the process of earning that income or profit is included in such group, e.g., the group of activities generally must include the collection of income and the payment of expenses.[311] However, to further complicate matters, the special rules regarding payment in the case of liability assumed in connection with the sale of a trade or business will not apply if the District Director determines that tax avoidance was one of the taxpayer's principal purposes for the sale of the trade or business.[312]

Effective dates. As a general rule, the regulations apply to liabilities that would, under the law in effect before the enactment of Section 461(h), be allowable as a deduction or otherwise be incurred after July 18, 1984.[313]

However, the rules governing liabilities for which payment constitutes economic performance (other than liabilities arising under a worker's compensation act or out of any tort) generally apply to liabilities that would be allowable as a deduction or otherwise be incurred for tax years beginning after December 31, 1991.[314] Thus, there is no Section 481 adjustment with re-

---

[308] Id.

[309] See discussion of constructive receipt at ¶ 3.03[2].

[310] Treas. Reg. § 1.461-4(g)(1)(ii)(C). See also Treas. Reg. § 1.461-4(d)(5).

[311] Treas. Reg. §§ 1.461-4(d)(5)(ii), 1.461-4(g)(1)(ii)(C)(2).

[312] Treas. Reg. § 1.461-4(g)(1)(ii)(C)(3), as further revised by Ann. 92-30, 1992-9 IRB 38.

[313] Treas. Reg. § 1.461-4(k)(1).

[314] Treas. Reg. § 1.461-4(k)(2).

spect to the application of this effective date and, instead, a cutoff approach is used. However, the regulations provide an alternative permitting a taxpayer to elect to treat the change as a full-year change in method of accounting pursuant to the procedures of Temporary Regulation § 1.461-7T, subject to the conditions of Section 4 of Revenue Procedure 84-74.[315]

[d] Proof of Compliance With Economic Performance Test

An obvious concern among taxpayers is the degree of additional record keeping that the economic performance test entails. Some guidance is provided in the legislative history of the provision, which states that enforcement of compliance with the economic performance standard should be carried out in a manner that does not impose substantial additional record-keeping burdens on the taxpayers.[316] Nevertheless, taxpayers must be able to demonstrate when economic performance actually occurred with respect to an obligation.

The legislative history indicates that except in unusual circumstances, a taxpayer may establish the fact of economic performance at a particular time by reference to a valid contract that requires economic performance at that time. Although the contract apparently is not required to be in writing, a taxpayer may be well advised to reduce the contract to writing to establish proof of compliance. A contract should be valid for these purposes if the fact of the liability is fixed under applicable state law. The legislative history refers only to the valid contract rule for services or property to be provided to the taxpayer. However, the rule should be equally available in the case of a taxpayer whose obligation is to provide services or property.

The legislative history also indicates that a more lenient compliance standard may be applied where the item at issue involves a foreign corporation.[317] Because information regarding economic performance may need to come from third parties, it may be difficult for a U.S. taxpayer to obtain that information, particularly when the U.S. taxpayer owns only a minority interest in the foreign corporation. Of course, it may be equally difficult for U.S. taxpayers to obtain information from other U.S. taxpayers.

[e] Impact on Other Than Current Deductions

Section 461(h) provides that for all purposes of the income tax laws, an item is not incurred (or taken into account) until economic performance has occurred. As a result, this provision may affect other sections of the Code where it is important to determine when an item has been incurred. The

---

[315] See discussion at ¶¶ 8.04[4], 8.06[2].

[316] Blue Book, supra note 230, at 266.

[317] Id.

intended broad application of Section 461(h) was confirmed in regulations proposed by the Treasury on June 7, 1990, and adopted, effective April 10, 1992. These regulations include an amendment to the general rules governing application of accrual methods under Section 446 and provide that the term "liability" includes any item allowable as a deduction, cost, or expense for federal income tax purposes.[318] Thus, the regulations would affect any amount that would be allowable as a capitalized cost, a cost to be taken into account in computing cost of goods sold, a cost allocable to a long-term contract, or any other cost or expense including, for example, any amount that the taxpayer spends or will spend for capital improvements to property where the amount must be incurred before the taxpayer may take it into account in computing the basis of property.[319] Thus, the regulations answer a number of questions. For example, assume a taxpayer incurs start-up costs in connection with a new trade or business and that certain of these costs involve obligations for which economic performance will not occur until after the trade or business has commenced. Should the taxpayer capitalize the expense and amortize it over 60 months as a start-up cost under Section 195? Section 461(h)(1) may require that the amount be treated as incurred only when performance occurs, which in this case would be after the trade or business has commenced. The regulations suggest that this result is exactly what is required.

Assume that a taxpayer subdivides real property and begins selling lots and that he is contractually obligated to make future improvements to lots that have already been sold. Under Revenue Procedure 75-25, he would have been permitted to add the estimated costs of the future improvements to the basis of the property in determining gain or loss from sales.[320] However, pursuant to Section 461(h), these costs should apparently be taken into account only after the improvements have been made. The regulations address these and other troubling questions. For example, the regulations make it clear that because economic performance must occur in order for a liability to be taken into account, the estimated cost of future improvements to subdivided real estate may not be added to the basis of lots sold if economic performance has not occurred with respect to these costs. Therefore, the regulations make it clear that Section 461(h) overrules Revenue Procedure 75-25. However, pursuant to its authority under Section 7805(b), the Treasury initially made this result effective prospectively only for taxable years beginning after December 31, 1989.[321]

Following the issuance of this proposed regulation, the IRS decided that it needed to study further the special circumstances of subdividers of real

---

[318] Treas. Reg. § 1.446-1(c)(1)(ii)(B).

[319] Id.

[320] Rev. Proc. 75-25, 1975-1 CB 720.

[321] Prop. Reg. § 1.461-4 (Preamble).

estate. Accordingly, the IRS issued Notice 91-4,[322] in which it announced that Revenue Procedure 75-25 would remain in effect until the issuance of further rules. As a result, subdividers of real estate were permitted to continue to request permission from the District Director to add to the cost or other basis of property sold the estimated cost of future improvements in accordance with that revenue procedure. For sales of property after December 31, 1990, subdividers who did not obtain such permission pursuant to Revenue Procedure 75-25 were bound by the economic performance rules. For sales of property prior to January 1, 1991, the IRS would not apply the economic performance rules to prevent the inclusion in the actual cost or other basis of property sold any estimated cost for future improvements to the extent those costs would have been included in basis under the law as it existed prior to the enactment of the economic performance rules. At the time the final regulations were adopted, the IRS notified taxpayers that special rules would be provided in a forthcoming revenue procedure.[323]

[f] Exception for Certain Recurring Items

Section 461(h)(3) provides an exception under which certain expenses will be treated as incurred (and, hence, will be deductible in the taxable year in which the all events test is otherwise satisfied) without regard to whether economic performance has occurred. This exception is not applicable to liabilities arising as a result of workers' compensation or tort claims.[324]

The exception applies and the deduction is required if the following criteria are satisfied:[325]

- The all events test is otherwise satisfied without regard to economic performance.
- Economic performance with respect to the obligation in question occurs on or before the earlier of (1) the date the taxpayer files a timely return (including extensions) for the taxable year or (2) eight and one half months after the close of such taxable year.
- The item is recurring in nature.
- Either (1) the item is not a material item or (2) the accrual of such item in the taxable year in which the all events test is otherwise met results in a more proper match against income than accruing the item in the taxable year in which economic performance occurs.

The recurring item exception is mandatory, not permissive or elective.

---

[322] Notice 91-4, 1991-4 IRB 19.

[323] These rules were provided in Rev. Proc. 92-29, 1992-1 CB 748.

[324] IRC § 461(h)(3)(C).

[325] IRC § 461(h)(3)(A). See also Treas. Reg. § 1.461-5.

Thus, a taxpayer who fails to claim a deduction in the year permitted under the exception will be denied the deduction in a later year.

[i] **Timely return or eight and one half months.** Section 461(h)(3)(A)(ii) sets forth the rule that the recurring item exception applies if economic performance occurs within the shorter of a reasonable period or eight and one half months after the close of the taxable year. The term "reasonable period" is not defined in the statute or the legislative history. It was reasonable to assume that a facts-and-circumstances test would be employed. However, recognizing that application of such a test would create numerous practical problems, the Treasury promulgated a different rule in its regulations, which is discussed below.

The eight-and-one-half-month period in the Section 461(h)(3) requirements presumably was chosen because it is the same as the maximum period for which extensions of time may be obtained within which to file returns.[326] Assuming these extensions are filed, Congress apparently believed that taxpayers would be able to determine whether economic performance had occurred within the eight-and-one-half-month period. This assumption is not accurate in many cases. Assuming economic performance occurs near the end of the eight-and-one-half-month period, many businesses (or the persons responsible for preparing the return) will not know of the economic performance until after the period for filing returns has expired.

Effect of regulations. In an effort to simplify the application of this requirement, the regulations have made a number of changes to the statutory rule. First, economic performance must occur on or before the earlier of (1) the date the taxpayer files a timely (including extensions) return for that taxable year or (2) eight and one half months after the close of that taxable year.[327] Moreover, if the taxpayer files a return before the running of the eight and one half month period and economic performance occurs thereafter but within the eight-and-one-half-month period, an amended return may be filed for the year claiming the benefit of the recurring item exception.[328]

As a result of this simplification, taxpayers do not need to focus on whether the liability has occurred within a reasonable period after the close of the taxable year. The application of this rule may cause taxpayers to delay filing the return until the end of the eight-and-one-half-month period and thereby avoid the need to consider the filing of amended returns.

On the other hand, literally, the language governing the filing of an amended return is discretionary. Therefore, even though use of the recurring item exception constitutes a method of accounting, taxpayers may be able to have the exception apply or not based on the time the original return is filed.

---

[326] See IRC § 6081.

[327] Treas. Reg. § 1.461-5(b)(1)(ii).

[328] Treas. Reg. § 1.461-5(b)(2).

For example, if the taxpayer expects economic performance to occur within eight and one half months but would prefer to delay the deduction, the taxpayer apparently may do so merely by filing the original return before economic performance has occurred and not thereafter filing an amended return.

[ii] **Recurring nature.** The exception is available only for items that are recurring in nature. Section 461(h)(3)(A)(iii) includes within the criteria for application of the recurring item exception that the items must not only be recurring in nature but also that they must be treated consistently with similar items. However, the regulations dropped the consistency portion of this requirement.[329]

Recurrence. The legislative history does not describe the type of items that are considered to be recurring. Two immediate questions that arise are (1) whether the item must recur every year or virtually every year and (2) whether the dollar amount (or fluctuations in the dollar amount) of the item is relevant. As to the first question, the legislative history provides that in determining whether an item is recurring, consideration must be given to the frequency with which that item or similar items are incurred or expected to be incurred.[330] However, the legislative history also provides that an expense that does not recur every year should not necessarily be excluded from the exception.[331] As explained below, the regulations follow this approach.

As to the second question, no guidance is provided. Thus, a taxpayer who regularly incurs routine legal or accounting services each year has no guidance as to whether an extraordinary expense incurred for an unusual legal or accounting service will be treated as recurring in nature.

Consistency. Under the statute, a taxpayer could not satisfy the consistency test solely by reference to the treatment of a specific item. Rather, the taxpayer had to treat consistently all items of such kind as incurred in the year the all events test was otherwise satisfied without regard to economic performance. The phrase "items of such kind" was not defined by the legislative history.

Effect of regulations. The regulations provide some guidance on whether liabilities are recurring in nature.[332] They specify that a liability is recurring in nature if it generally can be expected to be incurred from one taxable year to the next. However, a taxpayer may treat a liability as recurring even if it is not incurred by the taxpayer in each taxable year. In addition, a liability that has not previously been incurred by a taxpayer may be treated as recurring in nature if it is reasonable to expect the liability to be incurred on a recurring basis in the future.

---

[329] Treas. Reg. §§ 1.461-5(b)(2), 1.461-5(b)(3).

[330] Blue Book, supra note 230, at 263.

[331] Id.

[332] Treas. Reg. § 1.461-5(b)(3).

[iii] Not a material item or a more proper match. For the exception to apply, either the item must not be a material item or its deduction in the earlier year must result in a more proper matching of income and expense.

Materiality . In determining the materiality of a particular item, the IRS is to consider the size of the item, both in absolute terms and in relation to the taxpayer's income and other expenses.[333] The IRS is also to consider the treatment of the item on the taxpayer's financial statements. An item is considered material for tax purposes if it is considered material for financial statement purposes.[334] However, the converse is not true. An item that is not considered material for financial statement purposes may nevertheless be considered material for tax purposes.[335]

The materiality of an item is to be determined separately with respect to each activity. For items that are not directly related to an activity (such as overhead items that may be related to several activities), the items of expense are to be tested against the aggregate of the activities. This determination of materiality requires the taxpayer to identify each activity separately. Thereafter, the taxpayer must apportion its direct income and expense between the various activities. Neither the legislation nor its history addresses how items of income and expense are to be apportioned among activities and whether similar activities are to be aggregated. The legislative history is also unclear regarding whether materiality is to be tested with respect to each item of expense or whether all items of similar expense are to be aggregated before applying the materiality test. Presumably, all expenses of the same type or similar items should be aggregated; otherwise, it would be easy to avoid this requirement.

The legislative history provides that in appropriate circumstances and to the extent provided in regulations, an item is to be considered immaterial only if it is not material when analyzed at both the partnership and the partner level, the trust or estate and beneficiary level, or the S corporation and shareholder level, as the case may be.[336] Until regulations are promulgated with respect to this issue, the test of materiality should be made in each case at both the entity level and the partner or beneficiary level. Congress provided little guidance in determining when the test is not required to be applied at both levels. The sole illustration provided in the legislative history pertains to the situation in which an accrual basis partnership specially allocates to a partner an item that is not material to the partnership but is material to the partner.[337] Whether this situation is in fact an appropriate one in which to test materiality at both levels would seem to depend on other

---

[333] Treas. Reg. § 1.461-5(b)(4)(i).

[334] Treas. Reg. § 1.461-5(b)(4)(ii).

[335] Treas. Reg. § 1.461-5(b)(4)(iii).

[336] Blue Book, supra note 230, at 263.

[337] Id. at 264.

factors. For example, it would not appear to be appropriate to apply the materiality test at both the partner and partnership level if the special allocation had been a part of the partnership agreement from the outset and the item had unanticipatedly increased in that year owing to business exigencies.

The legislative history further provides that this rule is not intended to impose significant additional reporting requirements on pass-through entities in nonabusive situations. In that regard, many partnerships allocate net income or loss rather than each specific item of income, deduction, loss, or credit. As a result, it would appear to be extremely difficult for a partner to identify each particular item that must be tested for materiality. Also, it is important to note that the focus is on nonabusive situations, not tax shelters. Therefore, in determining whether an abusive situation exists, taxpayers apparently must look at each transaction independently rather than at the overall operation of the activity. Several unanswered questions remain. Is the determination of a transaction as abusive or nonabusive to be tested at the partner level or the partnership level? Is the term "abusive," to be defined by reference to the intent of the partner or partnership or is it an objective determination made by reference to the result of the transaction?

More proper match. Even if the item is material, the exception provided in Section 461(h)(3) may nevertheless be available if the deduction of the item in a taxable year prior to the year of economic performance results in a more proper match against income than deducting the item in the later year in which economic performance occurs.

GAAP is to be an important factor, although not necessarily a conclusive factor, in determining whether the accrual of an item in a particular year results in a better matching of the item with the income to which it relates. Thus, a strong presumption may be given to GAAP for this purpose. This standard appears to be significantly different than the presumption given GAAP in determining materiality. This difference appears only in the legislative history, not in the legislation itself.[338] Section 461(h)(3)(B) provides only that in making the determination of materiality and matching, the treatment of the item on the financial statement of the taxpayer must be taken into account.

Congress recognized that certain items (e.g., rent and insurance) are inherently period costs. For example, the rent attributable to a 12-month lease entered into on December 1 of year 1 by a calendar-year taxpayer normally would be allocated $1/12$ to year 1 and $11/12$ to year 2. Other costs (e.g., advertising costs) cannot practically be associated with the income in a particular period but under GAAP are assigned to the period in which the costs are incurred. With respect to these costs, the matching requirement is

---

[338] Id.

to be satisfied if the period to which the expenses are assigned for tax and financial reporting purposes are the same.

Effect of regulations. The regulations provide that in determining whether a liability is material, consideration should be given both to the amount of the liability in absolute terms and the amount of the liability as related to other items of income and expense attributable to the same activity.[339] Moreover, the proposed regulations specify that a liability will be treated as material if it is material for financial statement purposes under GAAP, but a liability that is immaterial for financial statement purposes under GAAP may nevertheless be material for purposes of recurring item exception.

With respect to the matching requirement, the regulations specify that the matching principle of financial accounting is an important but not dispositive factor. However, the regulations go on to specify that in the case of rebates and refunds, awards, prizes and jackpots, insurance, warranty and service contracts, and taxes, all of which require payment for determination of economic performance, the matching requirement will be deemed satisfied.[340]

In conclusion, accrual method taxpayers must now satisfy three independent requirements before deduction of an expense will be permitted. Cases that have permitted particular deductions in the past may now serve as precedent in determining whether the first two requirements have been satisfied. Satisfaction of the third requirement, economic performance, involves an entirely new analysis and increases the divergence between accrual accounting for financial and tax purposes.

[iv] Adopting the recurring item exception. The proposed regulations provided a number of rules regarding the time and manner of adopting the recurring item exception.[341] If a taxpayer had never incurred a particular type of liability prior to the first taxable year beginning after December 31, 1989, the taxpayer could adopt the recurring item exception for that type of liability but only for the taxpayer's first year beginning after December 31, 1989, in which that type of liability had been incurred. If a particular type of liability

[339] Treas. Reg. § 1.461-5(b)(4).

[340] Treas. Reg. § 1.461-5(b)(5).

[341] Prop. Reg. § 1.461-5(d), as revised by Notice 91-10, 1991-11 IRB 9. Notice 91-10 delayed the proposed effective date of these rules for one year. Ann. 92-30, 1992-9 IRB 38, provided that the final regulations would be delayed for one more year. Accordingly, the IRS stated that the final regulations would substitute "December 31, 1991," for "December 31, 1989." The IRS added that the final regulations also would permit a taxpayer to change to the recurring item exception for the first taxable year beginning after December 31, 1989, or December 31, 1990, on either the original return for the taxable year or an amended return for the taxable year. The IRS recognized that this would amount to allowing a retroactive change. The manner of making the change was to be prescribed in the final regulations.

had been incurred prior to December 31, 1991, the taxpayer was granted the consent of the Commissioner to change to the recurring item exception for that type of liability beginning with the taxpayer's first taxable year beginning after December 31, 1991. In either of these cases the recurring item exception had to be adopted as prescribed in Q&A-7(b) of Temporary Regulation § 1.461-7T, applied by substituting the appropriate taxable year described above for "the taxable year that includes July 19, 1984" and any resulting Section 481 adjustment had to be taken into account ratably over a three-year period. In all other cases, any change to or from the recurring item exception was a method of accounting subject to the normal rules governing changes in methods of accounting. Ultimately, final rules for adopting the recurring item exception were promulgated.[342] In general, these new rules provide that a taxpayer may adopt the recurring item exception merely by accounting for applicable items under the recurring item method. There will be no need to file a written statement.

Although the use of the recurring item exception constitutes a method of accounting, it should be noted that the statutory language governing the recurring item exception is mandatory, i.e., it provides that an item shall be treated as incurred if the recurring item exception is met. Consequently, the possibility arises that a failure to use the recurring item exception where a taxpayer is eligible for it constitutes the use of an improper method of accounting.

[4] Items Where Payment Is Doubtful

An accrual method taxpayer is not obligated to accrue and include in income items whose collection is reasonably in doubt.[343] On the other hand, the courts have made it clear that with limited exceptions, the inability of a taxpayer to pay an expense is not a reason for denying deduction of that expense. Some courts hold this to be a firm rule.[344] Other courts appear less willing to adopt an absolute rule, suggesting by their decisions that inability to pay is irrelevant as long as a reasonable belief existed at the time the obligation was incurred that it would be paid.[345] In at least one case, the

---

[342] Treas. Reg. § 1.461-5(d).

[343] See discussion supra ¶ 4.03[2].

[344] See Fahs v. Martin, 224 F2d 387 (5th Cir. 1955); Keebey's, Inc. v. Paschal, 188 F2d 113 (8th Cir. 1951); Zimmerman Steel Co. v. Comm'r, 130 F2d 1011 (8th Cir. 1942).

[345] Helvering v. Russian Fin. & Constr. Corp., 77 F2d 324 (2d Cir. 1935); United Control Corp., 38 TC 957 (1962), acq. 1966-1 CB 3.

court concluded that the liability was deductible even though it was certain at the time of deduction that the liability would not be paid.[346]

Although the IRS has challenged deductions in various circumstances on the basis that the amounts accrued and deducted could not reasonably be expected to be paid, it too has recognized that inability to pay is generally not relevant.[347] Thus, although questions can certainly be raised about particular circumstances, it seems quite clear that inability to pay does not preclude accrual and deduction of the liability. This is appropriate. Since the tax is imposed on income, it would be illogical to approve a deduction to those who can pay but deny a deduction to (and, hence, increase the income of) those who cannot pay.

Nevertheless, in particular circumstances, some courts have denied the accrual and deduction of a liability. This denial is appropriate, for example, where the liability is itself contingent on an ability to pay. Thus, where payment is in doubt, deduction may be denied.[348]

Also, a denial may be appropriate because of the relationship of the parties. For example, in *Tampa & Gulf Coast Railroad v. Commissioner*,[349] a subsidiary had accrued interest on a debt owed to its parent. The subsidiary argued that its inability to pay the accrued interest should not bar its ability to take an interest deduction. However, the court held that in the context of

---

[346] In SEC v. HJH, Inc., No. CA3-76-1611-F (D. Tex. 1979), an unreported decision, the district court found that a taxpayer that was then in receivership and did not have sufficient funds to pay the liability in question nor any prospect of obtaining such funds was nevertheless entitled to a deduction.

[347] The IRS has distinguished (1) a fixed liability to pay an expense and (2) the accrual method taxpayer's ultimate ability to pay that expense in three revenue rulings. In Rev. Rul. 70-367, 1970-2 CB 37, the IRS discussed deduction-of-interest obligations by a taxpayer undergoing a bankruptcy reorganization "when the financial condition of the corporation is such that there is no reasonable expectancy that it will pay the accrued interest in full." The IRS ruled that "[t]he doubt as to the payment of such interest is not a contingency of a kind that postpones the accrual of the liability until the contingency is resolved." Id. This ruling may be read in the context of a deferral of payment rather than ultimate nonpayment, but the IRS's presentation of facts was not this restrictive. In Rev. Rul. 72-34, 1972-1 CB 132, 133, the IRS stated that "where there exists a contingency as to payment of an obligation, and such contingency relates to other than the ability of the obligor to pay, it cannot be said that the obligation is fixed within the meaning of section 1.461-1(a)(2) of the regulations." This implies that doubt as to the taxpayer's ability to pay does not bar a deduction if the obligation is otherwise fixed. Finally, in Rev. Rul. 77-266, 1977-2 CB 236, the IRS permitted a deduction, noting that "[a]lthough a loss year might reduce the company's assets and thus delay the availability to members of payments otherwise maturing, this event would relate to the company's ability to pay rather than to the amount of the company's liability to the member."

[348] If existence or fruition of the liability itself is contingent upon ability to pay, the deduction may be denied. See, e.g., Putoma Corp. v. Comm'r, 601 F2d 734 (5th Cir. 1979); see also ABKCO Indus. Inc. v. Comm'r, 482 F2d 150 (3d Cir. 1973).

[349] Tampa & Gulf Coast R.R. v. Comm'r, 469 F2d 263 (5th Cir. 1972).

the parent-subsidiary relationship (when the same party is on both sides of the transaction and thus able to control payment of the debt) the general rule should not apply.[350]

One of the most troubling cases is *Mooney Aircraft, Inc. v. United States*,[351] where the taxpayer issued a $1,000 bond to customers when they purchased a plane. The bonds were payable on retirement of the planes, which could be 15, 20, or 30 years after purchase. The court could have found that the liability did not become fixed until the plane was retired, but it did not so conclude. Rather, it denied the deduction for what it held to be a clearly fixed liability whose amount could be determined with reasonable accuracy. Denial of the deduction was based on the fact that the time for payment was to be delayed for so long a time that deduction would be inappropriate and not clearly reflect income.[352] This case has always posed a problem for courts and commentators because it denied a deduction even though it found the all events test to have been satisfied.[353]

If a liability is not paid and is ultimately forgiven, compromised, discharged in bankruptcy, or terminated by the running of the applicable period of limitations, income may be recognized by application of the tax benefit rule.[354]

---

[350] "Tampa also refers to the general principle that an accrual method taxpayer's inability to pay interest obligations does not prevent deductibility. [citing *Fahs*] We believe the principle gives away to the extreme circumstances in this case." 469 F2d at 264. See also In re Continental Vending Mach. Corp., 77-1 USTC ¶ 9121 (EDNY 1976) (denial of deduction for interest by taxpayer undergoing bankruptcy reorganization).

[351] Mooney Aircraft, Inc. v. United States, 420 F2d 400 (5th Cir. 1969).

[352] See Raymond W. Hodge, 32 TCM 277 (1973), where so-called bond warranty expenses were not deductible in the year the bonds were issued to aircraft purchasers, because warranty bond was to be paid only when aircraft was removed from service. But see Denise Coal Co. v. Comm'r, 271 F2d 930 (3d Cir. 1959), where deduction was allowed even though payments were made 11 years after accrual; Reynolds Metals, Inc., 68 TC 943 (1977), where deduction was allowed for liability to fund a trust even though funding would not be completed for 13 years; John Ferenc, 33 TCM 136 (1974), where the court concluded that if the all events test were satisfied, deduction would be permitted.

[353] For example, in Burnham Corp., 90 TC 953 (1988), aff'd, 878 F2d 86 (2d Cir. 1989), the court allowed the taxpayer to deduct the full amount of payments to be made over an estimated period of 16 years. The Commissioner argued that the deduction should be denied on the basis of *Mooney Aircraft*. However, the court distinguished that case on the basis that the payments in *Mooney Aircraft* were not to begin for a substantial period of time, while the payments in *Burnham Corp.* were to begin shortly after accrual of the deduction.

[354] See discussion of the tax benefit rule at ¶ 12.05.

CHAPTER 5

The Installment Method

¶ 5.01 Overview: Problem, Resolution, and Change 5-3
    [1] Problem 5-3
    [2] Resolution 5-4
    [3] Legislative Change and Structure 5-5

¶ 5.02 Benefits and Burdens 5-5
    [1] Deferral in Recognition of Gain 5-5
    [2] Increase in Cash Flow 5-6
    [3] Lowering Effective Tax Rate 5-7
    [4] Flexibility in Time of Recognition 5-7
    [5] Investment of Deferred Tax Liability 5-8
    [6] Risk of Loss 5-9
    [7] Changes in Tax Rates and Laws 5-9

¶ 5.03 Requirements and Conditions 5-9

¶ 5.04 Dealers in Personal Property 5-10
    [1] History and Development 5-10
    [2] Issues 5-13
        [a] Who Is a Dealer? 5-14
        [b] Is Personal Property Involved? 5-15
        [c] Do Sales Occur Regularly? 5-16
            [i] Definition of "regularly" 5-17
            [ii] Portion of total sales 5-17
            [iii] Continuous vs. periodic sales 5-19
        [d] Sales on Installment Plan 5-20
            [i] Traditional installment plans 5-20
            [ii] Revolving credit plans 5-25
    [3] Installment Computations by Dealers 5-27
        [a] By Year 5-28
        [b] By Type of Sale 5-29
        [c] By Type of Goods 5-30
    [4] Disposition of Dealer Installment Obligations 5-30
    [5] Defaults, Repossessions, and Bad Debts 5-31
    [6] Disposition to Member of Consolidated Return Group 5-32
    [7] Election of Installment Method 5-34

¶ 5.05 Installment Sales of Property Other Than Inventory 5-35

[1] History and Development 5-35
    [a] Prior Conditions to Use of Installment Method 5-35
    [b] Statutory Format and Perceived Inadequacy 5-37
    [c] 1980 Act 5-38
    [d] 1986 Act 5-38
    [e] 1987 Act 5-39
[2] Installment Sale 5-39
[3] Installment Method 5-40
[4] What Is a Payment? 5-41
[5] What Is Not a Payment? 5-41
[6] Proportionate Disallowance Rule 5-42
[7] Issues Regarding Payments 5-46
    [a] Payments Prior to Year of Sale 5-47
    [b] Right to Prepay 5-47
    [c] Payment or Assumption of Seller's Qualifying
        Indebtedness 5-48
    [d] Third-Party Indebtedness 5-49
    [e] Third-Party Guarantees 5-50
    [f] Purchaser Debt Payable on Demand or Readily
        Tradable 5-51
[8] Computation of Installment Income 5-51
    [a] Selling Price 5-51
    [b] Selling Expenses 5-52
    [c] Contract Price 5-53
    [d] Sale of Multiple Assets 5-55
[9] Recapture Under Sections 1245 and 1250 5-56
[10] Wraparound Mortgages 5-57
    [a] Reasons for Use 5-57
    [b] Law Prior to 1980 Act 5-58
    [c] Regulations Under 1980 Act 5-59
    [d] Potential Benefit From New Regulations 5-61
[11] Related-Party Sales 5-65
    [a] Installment Obligations Received in Corporate
        Liquidations 5-67
    [b] Related-Party Rules 5-68
        [i] Marketable securities 5-69
        [ii] Property other than marketable securities 5-71
        [iii] Exceptions to application of related-party rules 5-71
        [iv] Extension of statute of limitations 5-72
    [c] Sales of Depreciable Property to Controlled Entity 5-72
[12] Contingent Price Rules 5-73
    [a] Maximum Sales Price Stated 5-74
    [b] No Maximum Price, but Fixed Payment Period 5-74
    [c] Both Selling Price and Payment Period Indefinite 5-76
    [d] Alternatives 5-76
        [i] Income forecast method 5-76
        [ii] Avoiding inappropriate basis deferral or
            acceleration 5-77
    [e] Private Annuities 5-78
[13] Like-Kind Exchanges 5-79
[14] Defaults and Repossessions 5-80
[15] Elections Out 5-81
    [a] Fixed Amount Obligations 5-83

	[b] Contingent Payment Obligations	5-84
¶ 5.06	Disposition of Installment Obligations	5-84
	[1] At Death	5-85
	[2] Cancellation or Unenforceability	5-86
	[3] To and From Corporations and Other Entities	5-87
	[a] Transfers to Controlled Entities	5-87
	[b] Certain Liquidations	5-88
	[c] To Life Insurance Companies	5-88
	[4] Modifications, Substitutions, and Other Changes	5-89
	[5] Using Installment Obligations as Collateral	5-91
¶ 5.07	The 1987 Act: Repeal and Revision	5-92
	[1] Repeal of Installment Method for Dealers	5-92
	[2] Repeal of Proportionate Disallowance Rule	5-93
	[3] Special Rules for Nondealers of Real Property	5-94
	[4] Pledges of Installment Obligations Treated as Payments	5-94
	[5] Minimum Tax	5-95

¶ 5.01 OVERVIEW: PROBLEM, RESOLUTION, AND CHANGE

[1] Problem

As a general rule, gain or loss on the sale or exchange of property is recognized in the year in which the transaction occurs. Gain is measured by the excess of the amount realized over the adjusted basis of the property.[1] Under the cash receipts and disbursements method (the cash method), the amount realized is the sum of any money received and the fair market value (FMV) of any property received (including any note or other evidence of indebtedness of the purchaser).[2] Under an accrual method, the amount realized is the same as under the cash method except that it includes the face amount of the purchaser's note or other evidence of indebtedness rather than its FMV.[3]

Application of the cash and accrual methods to transactions in which the purchase price is to be paid over a number of years often causes practical problems to the taxpayer. Gain is recognized in the year of sale, and, thus, liability for tax arises in that year; yet, by year-end, the taxpayer might have received none or only a small portion of the purchase price in cash. This result poses especially serious problems for taxpayers who might have to sell or dispose of other property in order to obtain the cash with which to pay the tax, or who are unable without great inconvenience or cost to borrow the funds necessary to pay the tax.

---

[1] IRC § 1001. Unless otherwise noted, all IRC references are to the Internal Revenue Code of 1986, as amended.

[2] See discussion at ¶ 3.03.

[3] See Rev. Rul. 79-292, 1979-2 CB 287, and discussion at ¶ 4.03.

[2] Resolution

Congress and the Treasury have long been aware of the inequity of applying the general rules of cash or accrual accounting to deferred payment transactions. In order to ameliorate the harsh effects of these general rules to certain transactions, without any apparent loss of the Treasury's ability to protect the public treasury, provision has been made to allow both cash and accrual method taxpayers to defer the recognition of gain on the sale or exchange of property until payments are actually or constructively received. The gain is then recognized proportionately as payments are made. Receipt of the purchaser's note or other evidence of his indebtedness is generally not treated as a payment. This method of recognizing gain is known as the installment method.[4]

> EXAMPLE: Assume that property with a basis of $30,000 is sold for $100,000 to be paid at the rate of $10,000 per year for 10 years beginning with the year of sale. Assume further that the buyer issues a note for the $100,000, bearing a market rate of interest so that its face amount is equal to its FMV. Under the cash and accrual methods, the seller will recognize $70,000 of gain in the year of sale ($100,000 − $30,000). Under the installment method, the seller will recognize 70 percent of each payment as gain in the year received ($70,000 of gain to be recognized ÷ $100,000 of payments to be received).

By accepting the installment method, Congress recognized that in effect, the tax system makes government a partner in every business enterprise. Consequently, it would be harsh and inequitable to require taxpayers to distribute to the government its share of the income in cash before such cash became available to taxpayers themselves.[5]

---

[4] Installment reporting was first permitted by regulation in 1918 (Regulation 33, Articles 116, 117); impliedly by statute in 1921 (Revenue Act of 1921, § 202(f)); and explicitly by statute in 1926 (Revenue Act of 1926, § 212(d)). See discussion infra ¶¶ 5.04[1], 5.05[1].

[5] See Comm'r v. South Tex. Lumber Co., 333 US 496, 503 (1948), where the Supreme Court stated as follows:

> The installment basis of reporting was enacted . . . to relieve taxpayers who adopted it from having to pay an income tax in the year of sale based on the full amount of anticipated profits when in fact they had received in cash only a small portion of the sales price. Another reason was the difficult and time-consuming effort of appraising the uncertain market value of installment obligations.

See also Thomas F. Prendergast, 22 BTA 1259, 1262 (1931), where the Tax Court stated that the "chief idea which motivated Congress . . . was to enable a merchant to actually realize the profit arising out of each installment before the tax was paid . . . [in order that] the tax could be paid from the proceeds collected rather than be advanced by the taxpayer.

[3] Legislative Change and Structure

Early in the history of installment reporting, the method was available to virtually all taxpayers, both dealers and nondealers.[6] Changes were made throughout the years with a major simplification effort taking place in the Installment Sales Revision Act of 1980 (the 1980 Act). However, by the time of the Tax Reform Act of 1986 (the 1986 Act), economic conditions had created a need to generate revenues, and the installment method was one of the chosen targets. From that time to the present, limitations have been imposed on the availability of the installment method, and its availability and benefits have been greatly reduced.

Although installment reporting is required for many dispositions of property where all or some portion of the consideration will be received after the year of disposition,[7] with certain exceptions it is no longer available to many transactions, including dispositions of inventory, dispositions of publicly traded property, dispositions of real or personal property by dealers, and dispositions of certain property to related parties.[8] Moreover, even where the method is still available, special rules applicable to certain transactions limit the benefit of installment reporting.[9]

The number and structure of the Code sections pertaining to installment sales have varied over the years. Initially, all applicable rules were set forth in a single set of rules—Section 453.[10] However, during the 1980s, there were several restructurings of the installment provisions. The installment method rules currently are contained in three separate sections. Section 453 provides the general rules governing application of the installment method. Section 453A provides special rules governing the disposition of property by nondealers. Section 453B provides rules pertaining to the recognition of gain or loss on the disposition of installment obligations.[11]

¶ 5.02 BENEFITS AND BURDENS

[1] Deferral in Recognition of Gain

The installment method permits gain (but not loss) on a transaction to be recognized in the year in which a payment is received rather than in the year

---

[6] See discussion infra ¶¶ 5.04[1] (regarding the history of the method for dealers in personal property), 5.05[1] (regarding the history of the method for others).

[7] IRC § 453(a).

[8] See discussion infra ¶¶ 5.04, 5.05[11], 5.07.

[9] IRC § 453A.

[10] IRC § 453 as in effect prior to the 1980 Act.

[11] See discussion infra ¶¶ 5.05 with regard to IRC § 453, 5.07[3] with regard to IRC § 453A, and 5.06 with regard to IRC § 453B.

in which the transaction occurs. Thus, the most obvious benefit of the installment method is the ability to defer the recognition of income (and, hence, the imposition of tax) until payment is received. This deferral in the time of recognition permits the tax to be paid from the proceeds of the sale itself and avoids the need for the taxpayer to dispose of other assets, to borrow, or to take other action in order to obtain the funds with which to pay the tax. On the other hand, as a result of recent changes in the rules governing installment sales, the deferral available for certain transactions by nondealers—dispositions where the sales price exceeds $150,000, the relevant obligation is outstanding as of the close of the year, and the face amount of all such obligations of the taxpayer as of the close of the year exceeds $5 million—is not interest free. Taxpayers may use the installment method in such circumstances but only if they pay interest on the deferred tax liability.[12] Consequently, taxpayers affected by these rules must determine whether the interest imposed by the government will be higher or lower than the cost of other borrowing. If the cost of borrowing from others is less than the cost of borrowing from the government, use of the installment method may not be beneficial.[13]

[2] Increase in Cash Flow

When used by a taxpayer who regularly sells property for deferred payments, the installment method has the effect of generating cash in an amount equal to the deferred tax.

> EXAMPLE: Assume that property costing $5 per unit is sold for $8 per unit, with $4 paid in the year of sale and $4 paid in the following year. If 100 units are sold each year under an accrual method, $300 of income is recognized each year (100 x ($8 − $5)) and, at a 34 percent rate, $102 of tax will be paid (34 percent of $300). In the year the installment method is elected, gain on sales of that year is reduced to $150 (($3 profit ÷ $8 selling price) x $400 of payments received), and tax is $51 (34 percent of $150) for a savings (or increase) in after-tax cash of $51 ($102 − $51). Thereafter, each year's income and tax will be the same as before the election.[14]

A taxpayer may estimate this potential benefit merely by multiplying its

---

[12] See IRC § 453A and discussion infra ¶ 5.07[3].

[13] See discussion infra ¶ 5.05[15] regarding elections not to use the installment method.

[14] See discussion infra ¶¶ 5.04[3] and 5.05[8] with respect to computations of installment income. But see discussion infra ¶ 5.07 with respect to the impact of the 1987 Act on the use of the installment method for dispositions of inventory and dealer dispositions of real or personal property.

anticipated accounts or notes receivable at the end of the year by its anticipated gross profit percentage and then multiplying that product by its anticipated tax rate. Of course, taxpayers who regularly sell property for deferred payments must make sure that they are eligible for use of an installment method. The availability of the method to such taxpayers has been greatly curtailed in recent years.[15]

[3] Lowering Effective Tax Rate

To the extent that gain on the sale would place the taxpayer in a higher tax bracket under the progressive rate structure of the U.S. tax system, spreading the gain over a period of years enables the taxpayer to avoid a bunching of income and to be taxed at the lowest possible rates. For example, if a taxpayer averages $40,000 of taxable income and is subject to an effective federal income tax rate of 15 percent on income up to $50,000, the taxpayer may increase taxable income by $10,000 without being subject to a higher tax rate. If the taxpayer sells property at a gain of $50,000, the taxpayer may seek to have payments deferred so that no more than $10,000 of gain per year is recognized in any year in order to avoid having any of the gain taxed at higher rates. Similarly, if the taxpayer is subject to other provisions of the tax law that impose adverse tax consequences on income in excess of a certain level (e.g., provisions for alternative minimum tax),[16] use of the installment method may permit the taxpayer to avoid or minimize those adverse consequences.

[4] Flexibility in Time of Recognition

The installment method also provides the taxpayer with flexibility in picking the year in which to recognize gain, such as a year in which an offsetting loss is expected or years in which the taxpayer expects to be in a lower tax bracket.[17] Of course, the degree of any such flexibility is subject to negotiation with the other parties to the transaction.

---

[15] See discussion infra ¶ 5.04.

[16] Section 55 may subject to the alternative minimum tax "alternative minimum taxable income" in excess of certain specified amounts. Limitations on the use of the installment method to avoid application of the alternative minimum tax were imposed by the 1986 Act. See Section 56(a)(6), which disregards the installment method in determining the amount of income subject to the alternative minimum tax (i.e., treats all gain as occurring in the year of sale), thereby eliminating the prior advantage obtained from use of the installment method. The new limitations apply to dispositions of certain property after March 1, 1986. But see discussion infra ¶ 5.07 with respect to the impact of the 1987 Act.

[17] The installment method is a method of reporting income. It is not available for deferring the recognition of loss. Thus, if a taxpayer sells for $80 property with a

During periods when there is uncertainty as to the applicable tax rates (or tax rules), such as when new tax proposals have been announced but not yet acted on by Congress, parties to a transaction may seek to take into account any uncertainties associated with the proposed legislation by providing in their agreement contingent or alternative payment scenarios depending on what, if any, action is taken by Congress. Such provisions should provide the parties with great flexibility, particularly since the installment method is available for such contingent payment agreements.[18]

[5] Investment of Deferred Tax Liability

Assuming that the taxpayer enters into an economically sound transaction (i.e., one in which adequate interest is charged to the purchaser on the unpaid portion of the sales price), use of the installment method allows the taxpayer to earn interest on the unpaid tax liability. For example, assume (1) that property with a basis of $0 is sold for $1,000 to be paid in 10 years and (2) that gain on the sale is subject to tax at a 20 percent tax rate. Under the cash or accrual methods, $1,000 of gain would be recognized in the year of sale, tax of $200 would be due, and the taxpayer would have the balance of $800 to invest. However, under the installment method, the taxpayer would not recognize income or pay tax until payment is received. Prior to that time, the taxpayer would effectively have the full $1,000 to invest. Alternatively, the taxpayer may sell on the installment method, then borrow against the installment obligation. This would permit him to obtain cash immediately, yet defer the recognition of income and the payment of tax.[19] Even in circumstances where taxpayers using the installment method are required to pay interest on any deferred tax liability, the benefit of deferring payment and investing the deferred tax liability may exist, assuming that the expected return on investment is greater than the cost associated with the interest on the deferred tax liability.[20] Of course, to the extent the taxpayer is able to borrow at a rate approximating (or less than) the rate on the deferred tax liability, there may be no particular benefit associated with deferring the applicable tax liability.

---

basis of $100, the $20 of loss must be recognized in the year of sale even though the $80 is to be paid in later years. On the other hand, the basis allocation rules of Temp. Reg. § 15a.453-1(c) may result in a loss being created through use of the installment method. See discussion infra ¶ 5.05[12].

[18] See Temp. Reg. § 15a.453-1(c) and discussion infra ¶ 5.05[12].

[19] But see discussion infra ¶¶ 5.05[6] for rules treating taxpayer debt as a payment on installment obligations, 5.06[5] regarding the use of installment obligations as collateral, 5.07 regarding the impact of the 1987 Act.

[20] See discussion infra ¶ 5.07[3].

[6] Risk of Loss

There may also be disadvantages to using the installment method. Most importantly, by deferring collection of the sales price, the taxpayer incurs all risks associated with deferred payments as opposed to immediate payment. Taxpayers must evaluate carefully the creditworthiness of their purchasers and obtain adequate security before agreeing to a deferred payment arrangement. Of course, as explained in the next section, the taxpayer also risks paying taxes at a higher rate, if applicable tax rates or laws change. In such a situation, taxpayers must compare the benefits of deferring the tax liability, even if it is an increased tax liability, and the use of funds for the period prior to the time when actual payment of the tax liability is required.

[7] Changes in Tax Rates and Laws

If the taxpayer's effective tax rate increases over the years or if unfavorable tax laws are enacted, deferral in the recognition of income may place the taxpayer in a higher tax bracket (with respect to the deferred amounts) or cause him otherwise to be in a less favorable tax posture than he would have been if all gain had been recognized in the year of the transaction.[21] Similarly, if the taxpayer has a status in the year of sale that precludes taxation (e.g., as a nonresident alien), a later change in that status may cause subsequent payments to become taxable.[22] Finally, because installment reporting is not permitted in determining income subject to the alternative minimum tax, the potential application of that tax must be considered in determining whether to use the installment method.[23]

¶ 5.03 REQUIREMENTS AND CONDITIONS

Prior to the 1987 Act, use of the installment method generally was available to all taxpayers who sold property where one or more payments would be received in later years. However, the requirements and conditions for use of the method varied, depending on whether the taxpayer was a dealer (i.e., one who regularly sold such property as part of its business) and whether the property was real property, personal property, or inventory. The 1987 Act

---

[21] See Zola Klein, 42 TC 1000 (1964). See also Stewart Perry, 59 TCM 533 (1990).

[22] But see Tech. Adv. Mem. 8708002 (Oct. 29, 1986), discussed infra note 114.

[23] See IRC § 56(a)(6). See also Stewart Perry, 59 TCM 533 (1990), where the court denied the taxpayer's attempt, through the filing of amended returns, to retroactively revoke an earlier installment sale election. The taxpayer filed the amended returns because he had not anticipated subsequently enacted changes to the alternative minimum tax, which made his earlier election too costly.

and later tax acts have modified many of the applicable rules and have significantly restricted the general availability of the installment method. The various requirements and conditions for use of the installment method, together with the effects of the 1987 Act and later tax acts, are described in the remainder of this chapter.

¶ 5.04 DEALERS IN PERSONAL PROPERTY

As a general rule, the installment method is not available to dealers in either personal or real property. Section 453(b) expressly excludes from the definition of "installment sale" "any dealer disposition." Dealer dispositions generally include any disposition of personal property by a person who regularly sells or otherwise disposes of such property on an installment plan and any disposition of real property that is held for sale in the ordinary course of a taxpayer's trade or business.[24] Nevertheless, there are certain exceptions from the definition of "dealer disposition." These exceptions include the disposition of property used or produced in the trade or business of farming,[25] any disposition of so-called timeshares or residential lots,[26] and certain qualifying dispositions by manufacturers.[27]

Although use of the installment method by dealers in personal property (as well as by dealers in real property) has been greatly curtailed, there nevertheless are a number of issues that affect the use of the installment method by such taxpayers in previous years. Accordingly, set forth in succeeding sections are discussions of relevant issues, code sections, and Treasury regulations affecting the use of the installment method by dealers in such previous years. Cases and issues are still arising as audits of such years occur. Of course, to the extent similar issues arise with respect to those transactions and for those taxpayers still eligible for use of the installment method, prior decisions will remain applicable.

[1] History and Development

Section 453A (as applicable to dispositions prior to the 1987 Act)[28] governed use of the installment method by dealers in personal property, i.e., those who

---

[24] IRC § 453(l)(1).

[25] IRC § 453(l)(2)(A).

[26] IRC § 453(l)(2)(B).

[27] See Temp. Reg. 1.453C-10T.

[28] The 1987 Act repealed the use of the installment method by dealers. See discussion infra ¶ 5.07. Consequently, the discussion and analysis in this Section is of primary interest with respect to dispositions prior to the 1987 Act and remains important as long as pre–1987 Act dispositions remain subject to IRS audit.

sold inventory. Section 453A provided that any taxpayer who regularly sold personal property on an installment plan could elect to report income from such sales on the installment method.[29]

The use of the installment method by dealers in personal property was first permitted administratively in 1918. The only condition was that title remain in the vendor until the property was fully paid for.[30] In 1921, the regulatory requirement that title remain in the vendor was eliminated, and a provision was made to allow computation of installment income on the basis of an aggregate gross profit percentage.[31]

The first congressional recognition of the installment method for dealers was only implicit. The Revenue Act of 1921 (the 1921 Act) provided that in the case of property that was sold under a contract providing for installment payments, nothing in the law prohibited the reporting of gain under the installment method.[32] Nevertheless, courts subsequently held that this statute was not a sufficient basis to permit use of the installment method of reporting income.[33]

Thereafter, Congress explicitly sanctioned installment reporting for dealers in the Revenue Act of 1926 (the 1926 Act).[34] This sanction remained

---

[29] Section 453A(1) (as applicable to dispositions prior to the 1987 Act) provided as follows:

Under regulations prescribed by the Secretary, a person who regularly sells or otherwise disposes of personal property on the installment plan may return as income therefrom in any taxable year that proportion of the installment payments actually received in that year which the gross profit, realized or to be realized when payment is completed, bears to the total contract price.

In mid-1986, the Treasury proposed new regulations to conform to the restructuring of Code sections that occurred in connection with the 1980 Act. See discussion infra ¶ 5.07 for impact of 1987 Act.

[30] Reg. 33 (Rev.), art. 117 (Jan. 2, 1918), provided as follows:

In the case of a contract to sell real estate or other property on the installment plan, title remaining in the vendor until the property is fully paid for, the income to be returned by the vendor will be that proportion of each installment payment which the gross profit to be realized when the property is paid for bears to the gross contract price.

[31] Reg. 45, art. 42 (Jan. 28, 1921) provided as follows:

Such income may be ascertained by taking as profit that proportion of the total cash collections received in the taxable year from installment sales (such collections being allocated to the year against the sales of which they apply), which the annual gross profit to be realized on the total installment sales made during each year bears to the gross contract price of all such sales made during that respective year.

[32] 1921 Act, § 202(f).

[33] See Appeal of Blum's Inc., 7 BTA 737, 751–758 (1927), acq. and nonacq. IX-1 CB 6, for a discussion of the early history of installment reporting by dealers.

[34] 1926 Act, § 212(d). See S. Rep. No. 52, 69th Cong. 1st Sess. 19 (1926), reprinted in 1939-1 CB 346, 347 (pt. 2). The 1926 Act, § 212(d) provided:

virtually unchanged from its enactment through the 1986 Act. The only exception was the manner in which a change to the installment method was effected. The 1926 Act applied the installment method to all payments received subsequent to the method's election. This caused a double tax with respect to payments received after the election on account of sales made before the election and, hence, already reported on an accrual method.[35]

EXAMPLE: Assume that (1) personal property with a basis of $150 was sold by a dealer for $250; (2) the sale was made and reported on an accrual method in year 1, when the taxpayer was subject to tax at a 30 percent rate; (3) the taxpayer elected installment-method reporting beginning with year 2; and (4) payments aggregating the $250 attributable to the earlier sale were received in year 2, when the taxpayer was subject to tax at a 40 percent rate. A total tax of $70 would be paid with respect to $100 of gain (30 percent of the $100 gain reported on an accrual method in year 1 plus 40 percent of the same $100 gain reported on the installment method in year 2, when all payments were received).

This hardship of double taxation was alleviated somewhat by the enactment of Section 453(c)(2) as part of the 1954 Code. Although the requirement continued that payments received after election of the installment method must be subject to taxation, this new provision permitted the taxpayer to reduce the double tax to the higher single tax, i.e., to pay the higher of the tax attributable to use of accrual method or the installment method.[36] Thus, the taxpayer in the preceding example would pay $40 of tax, which is the tax associated with installment reporting.

To avoid the effect of an increasing tax rate, some taxpayers would sell their installment receivables prior to election of the installment method.[37] For instance, the taxpayer in the preceding example would sell the installment receivables in year 1 and thereby subject the income to the 30 percent tax

---

Under regulations prescribed by the Commissioner with the approval of the Secretary, a person who regularly sells or otherwise disposes of personal property on the installment plan may return as income therefrom in any taxable year that proportion of the installment payments actually received in that year which the total profit realized or to be realized when the payment is completed, bears to the total contract price.

[35] Unless installment reporting is elected, the taxpayer must use an accrual method to report gain on the sale of inventory. See Treas. Reg. § 1.446-1(c)(2)(i) and discussion at ¶ 3.06[2]. But see discussion infra ¶ 5.07 for the impact of the 1987 Act.

[36] IRC § 453(c)(2), repealed by the 1980 Act.

[37] An issue under this prior law was whether the sale was bona fide. Compare City Stores Co. v. Smith, 154 F. Supp. 348 (ED Pa. 1957), and Rev. Rul. 59-343, 1959-2 CB 136, where the transfers were held to be bona fide sales, with Reed's Jewelers, Inc. v. United States, 78-2 USTC ¶ 9732 (EDNC 1978), where the transfer was found not to be a bona fide sale.

rate. This would permit the taxpayer to accelerate the gain to the earlier year, to avoid the impact of higher taxes, and to have the election effective only for sales made after the election.

In the 1980 Act, Congress repealed this adjustment procedure. The legislative history to the 1980 Act provided that the installment method should only apply to installments received on sales made after the election.[38] Thus, the taxpayer in the preceding example would pay only $30 in tax and would not be penalized by having this method apply to payments that had already been reported in income. This was the only provision in the 1980 Act pertaining to dealers.[39]

Changes in use of the installment method by dealers also occurred in the 1986 Act. The 1986 Act denied use of the installment method to revolving credit sales and imposed rules to treat certain borrowings by the taxpayer as if they were payments on its installment receivables.[40]

The most significant changes occurred in the 1987 Act. With certain exceptions,[41] the 1987 Act repealed use of the installment method by dealers.[42] Consequently, except for those who are excepted from the prohibition on use of the installment method by dealers, the installment method for dealers is largely important only to the extent of transactions in prior years.[43]

[2] Issues

The basic issues that arose with respect to use of the installment method by dealers in personal property were as follows:[44]

- Who was a dealer in personal property?
- How was "personal property" defined for installment sale purposes?

---

[38] S. Rep. No. 1000, 96th Cong., 2d Sess. 8, reprinted in 1980-2 CB 494 (hereinafter 1980 Senate Report). See also Prop. Reg. § 453A-3(d), which provides that an election to adopt the installment method is applicable to sales made on or after the first day of the year of election.

[39] The 1980 Senate Report stated, "Except for an amendment relating to the election of the installment method by an accrual basis dealer, the substantive changes under the bill relate only to sales of realty and casual sales of personal property." 1980-2 CB 494, 497–498.

[40] See discussion infra ¶¶ 5.04[2][d][ii] with respect to limitations on use of the method by dealers, 5.05[6] with respect to the treatment of debt as payment.

[41] See discussion supra ¶ 5.04 and infra ¶ 5.07[1].

[42] See discussion infra ¶ 5.07.

[43] See infra ¶ 5.07[1] for discussion of current rules governing dealer dispositions for which the installment method is still available.

[44] See discussion infra ¶ 5.07 regarding the 1987 Act's repeal of the installment method for most dealers.

- What did "regularly" mean with respect to the requirement that sales or other dispositions of personal property be made regularly on an installment plan?
- How was "installment plan" defined for this purpose?
- How were the computations to be made?
- How was the use of the method to be elected?
- How were repossessions and defaults to be treated?

These questions are considered in the succeeding sections. Again, these questions may remain relevant to transactions excepted from the prohibition on the use of the installment method by dealers.[45]

[a] Who Is a Dealer?

To have qualified for the installment method under Section 453A (as applicable to dispositions prior to the 1987 Act), the selling party must have been a dealer in personal property. The term "dealer" was not expressly defined in either the Code or the Treasury regulations, but by virtue of the applicable statutory and regulatory language,[46] it was clear that a person who regularly sold or otherwise disposed of property would be regarded as a dealer. As one court had stated, a dealer is one who is engaged in the business of selling personal property, i.e., an activity that continues or is anticipated to continue for a substantial period and that includes or is expected to include numerous transactions.[47]

When evaluating a particular arrangement to determine if the taxpayer was a dealer, attention was given to all the facts and circumstances, including whether the taxpayer owned the property being sold. For example, Revenue Ruling 73-5 focused on a manufacturer that sold its products through franchised dealers operating on a consignment basis.[48] The manufacturer was found to qualify as a dealer eligible to report on the installment method, but the franchised dealers were found to act principally as sales agents and, hence, did not qualify as dealers.

Because the installment method is generally not available to "dealer dispositions," efforts may be made by taxpayers to avoid characterization as a dealer. Section 453(l)(1) provides that dealer dispositions of personal property consist of those dispositions "by a person who regularly sells or otherwise disposes of personal property of the same type on the installment

---

[45] See discussion infra ¶ 5.07[1].

[46] Treas. Reg. § 1.453-2(a).

[47] See 50 East 75th St. Corp. v. Comm'r, 78 F2d 158 (2d Cir. 1935).

[48] Rev. Rul. 73-5, 1973-1 CB 212.

plan."[49] Dealer dispositions of real property consist of dispositions of property "held by the taxpayer for sale to customers in the ordinary course of the taxpayer's trade or business."[50] Determination of whether a taxpayer's activities would cause its sales to constitute dealer dispositions will be most important on an ongoing basis.

[b] Is Personal Property Involved?

The subject of the transaction must have been personal property. If the transaction involved real property, different rules were applicable.[51] If the transaction involved services as opposed to property, installment reporting was not available.[52] Similarly, if the transaction involved a financing of property, installment reporting was not available.[53] However, since a sale of property was not involved in these cases, the taxpayer might have been able to

---

[49] IRC § 453(l)(1)(A).

[50] IRC § 453(l)(1)(B).

[51] See discussion infra ¶¶ 5.05, 5.07.

[52] See, e.g., Rev. Rul. 73-438, 1973-2 CB 157 (building contractor who constructed custom-built homes on purchaser's property using purchaser's material not considered a dealer even though such person might qualify as a dealer under state law); Rev. Rul. 73-437, 1973-2 CB 156 (taxpayer selling standardized homes on purchaser's land using precut materials furnished by him is a dealer); see also W.W. Pope, 24 TCM 1096 (1965); Jones Lumber Co., Inc., 404 F2d 764 (1968); Rev. Rul. 73-436, 1973-2 CB 155; Town and Country Food Co., 51 TC 1049, 1055 (1969), acq. 1969-2 CB xxv, where the court found that "[t]he sale of a life membership [entitling the purchaser to warranty protection and discounts on subsequent purchases] did not itself effect the sale by petitioner of any property whatsoever"; Cappel House Furnishing Co. v. United States, 244 F2d 525 (6th Cir. 1957), where installment reporting was denied to the proceeds of business interruption insurance even though the business sold its goods on an installment plan; Priv. Ltr. Rul. 8019009 (Jan. 24, 1980), where portion of "sales" price attributable to breeding services was found not to be eligible for installment reporting.

[53] See Iowa Guar. Mortgage Co., 28 BTA 213 (1933), aff'd, 73 F2d 217 (8th Cir. 1934), where the court held that the taxpayer was engaged in financing automobile sales and was not a dealer within the meaning of Section 212(d) of the 1926 Act and Section 705(a)(2) of the Revenue Act of 1928 (statutory predecessors to Section 453A as it existed prior to the 1987 Act). The court pointed out that the seller of the automobile assigned the contract to the taxpayer and that the taxpayer's rights under the contract were those of a mortgagee with security for money loaned. See also Rev. Rul. 85-133, 1985-2 CB 192, where a corporate retailer was found not to sell on an installment basis, because sales were financed by its banking subsidiary that was the original holder of the installment obligations and bore all risks with respect to them. See also Benjamin D. Hyman, 53 TCM 727 (1987), where the court recharacterized a purported sale of property as a part-loan, part-sale. The part attributable to the sale was eligible for the installment method, assuming other applicable conditions for its use were satisfied.

adopt (or to change to) the cash method, and thereby use that method of accounting to defer the recognition of income until payment was received.[54]

Where a transaction consisted of providing both goods and services, the availability of the installment method was in doubt. For example, it was understood that in the case of a taxpayer engaged in the business of providing property and services on an installment payment basis, the National Office of the Internal Revenue Service (the National Office) had argued that use of the cash method was inappropriate because the taxpayer's business involves the sale of inventory, but that use of the installment method was also inappropriate because the taxpayer was essentially providing services and not goods. This result seems unduly harsh. A more appropriate result (and one consistent with the requirement that purchases and sales of inventory be accounted for on an accrual method) would have been to treat the transaction as one involving a sale of goods, unless (1) the sale of goods component was so negligible that the taxpayer would have been eligible for the cash method or (2) the taxpayer could demonstrate what portion of the total charge was allocable to the sale of goods and what portion was allocable to the rendition of services.[55]

[c] Do Sales Occur Regularly?

Under Section 453A (as applicable to dispositions prior to the 1987 Act),[56] sales pursuant to an installment payment plan must have occurred "regularly." In other words, use of the installment method was not available to isolated sales of inventory. This rule prevented use of the method for bulk sales.

The Treasury regulations do not set out the circumstances under which a taxpayer may be found to be selling regularly on an installment plan,[57] nor is there any instructive case law. In addition, applicable legislative history does not contain any insight as to the meaning of the term. Thus, resort must be made to the general definition of "regularly,"[58] and the definition given the word in other contexts of the tax law.[59]

---

[54] See discussion at ¶ 3.06 regarding the availability of the cash method.

[55] See discussion at ¶ 3.06[2].

[56] See discussion infra ¶ 5.07 regarding the 1987 Act.

[57] See Treas. Reg. § 1.453-2(a).

[58] See National Muffler Dealers Assoc. v. United States, 440 US 472 (1979), and 1 J. Mertens, Law of Federal Income Taxation § 3.14 (1985), for the proposition that it is appropriate to consult dictionaries to determine the ordinary meaning of words. This proposition has been followed in an installment sales context. See, e.g., Thomas F. Prendergast, 22 BTA 1259 (1931).

[59] In one case, the court said: "Identical words used in different parts of the same statute must be construed to mean the same thing unless a contrary meaning is clearly shown." Estate of Robert J. Cuddihy, 32 TC 1171, 1176 (1959); see also

[i] Definition of "regularly." The term "regularly" was generally defined to mean at "fixed and certain intervals, regular in point of time,"[60] and "in a regular, orderly, lawful, or methodical way."[61] It had not been defined to mean continuously throughout a period.[62] For tax purposes, "regularly" has been defined in other contexts. For example, the definition of "regularly" is important with regard to the taxation of the unrelated business income of tax-exempt organizations under Section 512(*l*)(1), which states that the term "unrelated business taxable income" means the net gross income derived by any exempt organization from any unrelated trade or business "regularly" carried on by it. The regulations under Section 513(a) provide that to determine whether a trade or a business is "regularly carried on," one must look to the frequency and continuity of the income-producing activity and the manner in which it is pursued.[63] Two rulings, which have interpreted the term "regularly" for this purpose, involved the solicitation of advertising for yearbooks during a period of three to four months each year.[64] In each ruling, the IRS determined that the advertising revenue was unrelated business income from trades or businesses regularly carried on by the tax-exempt entities.[65] These rulings and the general definitions suggest that important considerations were the number of sales made on an installment plan and whether such sales occurred continuously or only periodically throughout the year. These considerations are discussed in the two succeeding sections.

[ii] Portion of total sales. In the context of installment sales, whether transactions occur regularly is often influenced by the number of such sales, the ratio of such sales to total sales (in both number and dollar amount), and

---

United States v. Olympic Radio & Television, Inc., 349 US 232 (1955); Helvering v. Stockholms Enskilda Bank, 293 US 84 (1934).

[60] Black's Law Dictionary 1156 (5th ed. 1979). The second edition of Black's Law Dictionary, which was published in 1910 and represented the most recent edition at the time the 1926 Act was enacted, did not define the term "regularly."

[61] Webster's Third New International Dictionary of the English Language 1913 (unabridged, 1963).

[62] Anderson, A Dictionary of Law 869 (1893), a dictionary in existence at the time of the enactment of the 1926 Act. The pertinent definition of the term "regular" in the edition of a standard dictionary, which existed at the time of the drafting of the 1926 Act, was "steady or uniform in course, practice, or occurrence; not subject to unexplained or irrational variation; returning or recurring at stated or fixed times or uniform intervals . . . orderly; methodical; . . . operating at proper intervals. . . ." Webster's New International Dictionary of the English Language 1797 (1923).

[63] Treas. Reg. § 1.513-1(c)(1).

[64] Rev. Rul. 75-200, 1975-1 CB 163; Rev. Rul. 73-424, 1973-2 CB 190.

[65] See also Suffolk County Patrolmen's Benevolent Assoc., 77 TC 1314 (1981), where exempt organization's annual fund-raising show was found an intermittent activity not constituting an unrelated trade or business regularly carried on.

whether the taxpayer generally holds itself out to its customers as making sales on an installment basis.[66] Although there are comparatively few decisions, the Tax Court had held that the number and relative dollar amount of installment sales did not need to be high in order for the taxpayer to be regularly engaged in making installment sales.[67]

It was also clear that a dealer in personal property could have different terms of payment during the year and still be allowed to use installment sales reporting for those sales that were, in fact, sold under installment terms.[68] For example, a dealer could sell equipment under two plans, one calling for a single specified payment of the selling price and one calling for installment payments over a period of months or years. The customer could choose whichever payment plan it desired, and if the installment plan were chosen, the installment method could have been used. The dealer could report income from such sales on the installment method, even though the remainder of its credit sales were reported on an accrual method.[69]

---

[66] See generally Marshall Bros. Lumber Co., 13 BTA 1111, 1116–1117 (1928), rev'd and remanded without opinion, 51 F2d 1081 (6th Cir. 1931); Louis Greenspon, 23 TC 138, 153 (1954), acq. 1955-1 CB 4, aff'd in part and rev'd in part, 229 F2d 947 (8th Cir. 1956), where the decision turned on the fact that "[i]t was generally known in the trade and among its customers that the company would sell on the installment basis. . . ."; Davenport Mach. & Foundry Co., 18 TC 39, 43 (1952), acq. 1952-2 CB 1, where the court was impressed with the fact that the taxpayer "held itself out as willing to sell . . . on a credit basis, and it was generally known throughout the trade that it would do so"; Rev. Rul. 85-133, 1985-2 CB 192, where the IRS ruled as follows:

> Whether a dealer is regularly selling on the installment basis is determined by several factors, such as the number and frequency of installment sales made throughout the year, the ratio or proportion between installment sales and total sales, the period over which the installment sales are made and the general holding out to the public that such arrangements could be made.

[67] Davenport Mach. & Foundry Co., 18 TC 39 (1952), acq. 1952-2 CB 1. The taxpayer made one installment sale during the taxable year constituting approximately 8 percent of its total sales and made only 11 installment sales in 13 years. Yet, the taxpayer qualified as being "regularly" engaged in selling on the installment basis. In Louis Greenspon, 23 TC 138 (1954), acq. 1955-1 CB 4, aff'd in part and rev'd in part, 229 F2d 947 (8th Cir. 1956), the taxpayer was found to be regularly engaged in the sale of personal property on the installment plan even though only four installment sales, constituting 22 percent of total sales, were made during that taxable year. In Marshall Bros. Lumber Co., 13 BTA 1111 (1928), rev'd and remanded without opinion, 51 F2d 1081 (6th Cir. 1931), installment reporting was allowed, even though installment sales were made in 10 months of each year and constituted only 14 to 17 percent of total sales during the years in question.

[68] Rev. Rul. 71-595, 1971-2 CB 223. A similar principle was noted in Priv. Ltr. Rul. 8208087 (Nov. 27, 1981) and Priv. Ltr. Rul. 8117111 (Jan. 29, 1981).

[69] In John Wanamaker Philadelphia, 22 BTA 487 (1931), acq. and nonacq. X-2 CB 74, aff'd, 62 F2d 401 (3d Cir. 1932), cert. denied, 289 US 738 (1933), the Board of Tax Appeals (the Board) held that a taxpayer could adopt the installment method

[iii] Continuous vs. periodic sales. An important question was whether the phrase "regularly selling on the installment plan" required that installment arrangements be available throughout the year. For example, many businesses make credit sales throughout the year under arrangements calling for a single payment within 30 days from the date of sale. Under an accrual method (discussed in Chapter 4), gain on such sales is recognized at the time of sale, and the taxpayer may have 30 days worth of accounts receivable as of the end of its year. If sales made during the last month of the year were under an installment plan,[70] the taxpayer was able to defer the recognition of such income until the year of payment. The question was whether such a plan would be accepted if offered only during the last month of each year. The reasons for offering the plan only at that time might include a desire to spur the sale of new products, to reduce inventory to the fullest extent possible, to increase sales, and to reduce taxes.

To date, no authority has focused directly on this question. However, the definition of "regularly" indicates that no requirement of year-round sales existed,[71] and in Revenue Ruling 71-595,[72] although this precise issue was not discussed, the IRS ruled that the taxpayer was regularly selling on the installment plan, even though it did so during only six months of each taxable year.

Nevertheless, the IRS had been reluctant to approve installment reporting where the sales in question were to be made during only a portion of each year, and there are two cases that suggested, although implicitly, that continuous (i.e., year-round) selling was necessary in order to qualify as regularly selling on the installment plan.[73] Each case held that a taxpayer was not engaged in regularly selling personal property (corporate stock) on the installment plan in a situation in which the taxpayer was not a dealer in personal property because it was not the taxpayer's normal course of business to sell such personal property. In both cases, the Board determined that persons had to engage continuously in the sale of personal property to constitute in personal property and that persons were required to be "dealers in personal property" in order to qualify as regularly selling such personal property on the installment plan. Nevertheless, the precise issue had not been

---

of reporting for installment sales and an accrual method of reporting for sales on open account.

[70] Installment plans are discussed infra ¶ 5.04[2][d]. But see discussion infra ¶ 5.07 for impact of 1987 Act.

[71] See discussion supra ¶ 5.04[2][c][i].

[72] Rev. Rul. 71-595, 1971-2 CB 223; see also Priv. Ltr. Rul. 8208087 (Nov. 27, 1981) (installment sales during last two months of each year); and Priv. Ltr. Rul. 8117111 (Jan. 29, 1981), subsequently amended regarding another issue in Priv. Ltr. Rul. 8129036 (Apr. 22, 1981), installment sales during last month of each year. Each private letter ruling cited Rev. Rul. 71-595, but neither discussed the fact that taxpayer was "regularly" selling on the installment plan only in a seasonal context.

[73] 50 East 75th St. Corp., 29 BTA 277 (1933), rev'd, 78 F2d 158 (2d Cir. 1935); E.P. Greenwood, 34 BTA 1209 (1936), acq. 1937-1 CB 11.

focused on, and the better view appeared to be that the availability of year-round installment arrangements was not required as long as such arrangements were available at sufficiently recurring intervals.[74] Although a nontax business reason for offering installment payment plans during only a limited period each year should have pleased the IRS and made challenge less likely, there was no requirement for such a reason. If sales were made under an installment plan at regularly recurring intervals, installment reporting should have been available even if motivated solely by tax reasons.[75]

[d] Sales on Installment Plan

To qualify for use of the installment method, sales must have occurred on an installment plan. Prior to the 1986 Act, installment plans included traditional installment plans and, to a limited extent, revolving credit plans. The 1986 Act eliminated use of the installment method for sales made under a revolving credit plan.[76] The 1987 Act eliminated use of the method for virtually all dealers.[77]

Assuming sales were made under an installment plan, there was no limitation on the amount of any down payment; nor was there any requirement that payments be received in the year of sale. No requirement existed as to the amount of the sales price, the form of sale, or the length of time over which the dealer could receive payments.

[i] Traditional installment plans. Traditional installment plans were usually characterized by (1) the execution of a separate installment contract for each sale of personal property and (2) the retention by the dealer of some type of security interest in that property.[78] However, these characteristics

---

[74] See Emory, "The Installment Method of Reporting Income: Its Election, Use and Effect," 53 Cornell L. Rev. 181, 267 (1968), where the commentator concluded that "while a lone sale of inventory property will not qualify, a pattern involving only slightly more would likely pass judicial muster." See also Giljum, "Installment Sales," Tax Mgmt. (BNA) 48-6th, A-11 (1987). "Presumably sales are made regularly under the installment plan if they are made under such a plan with some degree of consistency and regularity."

[75] See, e.g., Decision, Inc., 47 TC 58 (1966), acq. 1967-2 CB 2, where a taxpayer's change in its applicable agreements with customers to achieve certain tax benefits was approved by the court. See also discussion at ¶ 9.06[2][a], for changes in tax reporting as a result of changes in applicable contracts, business practices, or economic consequences.

[76] IRC § 453(k). Because revolving credit sales were afforded installment sale treatment prior to the 1986 Act, the pre–1986 Act law is discussed infra ¶ 5.04[2][d][ii].

[77] See infra ¶ 5.07[1] for discussion of the repeal of installment reporting by dealers and limited exceptions to that repeal.

[78] Treas. Reg. § 1.453-1(a)(1).

were merely typical and illustrative, not mandatory. Neither the execution of a separate contract for each sale nor the retention of a security interest was required.[79]

If the dealer did retain a security interest, he usually did so by means of (1) retaining title to the goods until the purchaser had fully paid for them; (2) conveying title but subjecting the property to a lien; (3) conveying title but taking back a chattel mortgage; or (4) conveying property to a trustee pending full performance by the buyer. However, in the latter case, the seller had to make sure that a sale had occurred for tax purposes. If the applicable benefits and burdens of ownership had not passed to the buyer on transfer of the property, a question could have been raised as to whether a sale had actually taken place. Again, these means of retaining a security interest were optional with the seller. Other means were not precluded.[80]

Number of payments. The applicable regulations provide that the phrase a "sale under a traditional installment plan" means:

> (1) A sale of personal property by the taxpayer under any plan for the sale or other disposition of personal property which plan, by its terms and conditions, contemplates that each sale under the plan will be paid for in two or more payments, or
> (2) A sale of personal property by the taxpayer under any plan for the sale or other disposition of personal property—
> (i) Which plan, by its terms and conditions, contemplates that such sale will be paid for in two or more payments, and,
> (ii) Which sale is in fact paid for in two or more payments.[81]

Under these regulations, installment plans were of two types. The first type consisted of plans where it was contemplated, but not required, that each sale under the plan would be paid for in two or more payments. The second type consisted of plans that contemplated that particular (but not all) sales would be paid for in two or more installments, and such sales were actually paid for in two or more payments. Taxpayers making sales under this second type of plan must not only have been paid in two or more payments, but they must have contemplated that two payments would be made. Thus, if a purchaser actually made two or more payments on a sale for which only a single payment had been contemplated, installment reporting would not have been available.

---

[79] In Gen. Couns. Mem. 38938 (Dec. 14, 1982), the IRS focused on a dealer who sold garment labels used in various types of clothing but who retained no security interest in products shipped. The IRS held, "The retention of a security interest is not a requirement of an installment sale under I.R.C. § 453A [repealed by 1987 Act]. It is merely a permissible characteristic of an installment sale."

[80] Treas. Reg. § 1.453-2(a).

[81] Treas. Reg. § 1.453-2(b).

The distinction between the two plans was most significant. Under the first type of plan (a so-called paragraph (b)(1) plan), it was contemplated that each sale made under the plan would be paid for in two or more payments. If this expectation existed, the use of the installment method was available for all sales made under the plan, including those which were actually paid by a single payment.[82] To illustrate, assume that sales were made under a plan requiring two equal payments with no interest charge, one due 30 days after the date of sale and one due 180 days after the date of sale. Since it was reasonable to conclude that customers would take advantage of these terms and pay the purchase price in two payments, the income from the sales would be recognized only as payments were received. This rule applied even if a customer, for whatever reason, paid the entire selling price in a single payment made 30 days after the date of sale.

On the other hand, if it was not reasonable to conclude that each sale under a plan would be paid in two or more payments (e.g., where the plan was the same as that previously described except that interest was charged, thereby making it reasonable to conclude that some customers would make a single payment to avoid the interest charge), then the second type of plan would have been in place (a so-called paragraph (b)(2) plan), and installment reporting would have been available only for sales actually paid for in two or more payments.

As to whether a plan contemplated that each sale would be paid in two or more payments, the IRS concluded in Revenue Ruling 71-595 that a payment plan that gave customers a discount if they paid in a single accelerated payment did not contemplate that each sale would be paid for in two or more payments. Accordingly, the plan did not qualify under paragraph (b)(1), but did under paragraph (b)(2). Thus, only those sales actually paid for in two or more payments were eligible for installment reporting.[83]

Following enactment of the 1980 Act, the National Office became quite liberal in ruling that proposed installment sale plans were of the (b)(1) type.[84]

---

[82] See, e.g., Priv. Ltr. Ruls. 8439009 (June 21, 1984) and 8439017 (June 25, 1984), where no terms were offered that would encourage a single payment of the entire price.

[83] See, e.g., Priv. Ltr. Rul. 8318092 (Feb. 3, 1983), where 90 percent of price was due in 25 days after the invoice date and balance was due 10 days later. The sales were found to come under Treas. Reg. § 1.453-2(b)(1) because no discount was provided for prepayment, and no interest was charged on either payment unless it was not made when due. See also Priv. Ltr. Ruls. 8208087 (Nov. 27, 1981), and 8117111 (Jan. 29, 1981).

[84] See, e.g., Priv. Ltr. Ruls. 8439009 (June 21, 1984) and 8538020 (June 19, 1985), where the plan called for 90 percent of the sales price in 30 days and the balance 10 days later.

These rulings were issued even though the second payment's financial benefit to the purchaser and the financial detriment to the seller might have been insignificant, and a large portion of actual sales might be paid with a single payment.[85] Ultimately, the IRS concluded that its liberal policy should be terminated and, in 1987, ruled that a (b)(1) plan would be found only if the contemplation of two or more payments was reasonable in light of all relevant facts and circumstances, including the financial benefit to customers of making two or more payments, whether a single payment violated the sales contract, the length of time between the scheduled payments, and the taxpayer's actual experience under the plan.[86] Recognizing that this ruling could be viewed as a change from its prior position, the IRS made the ruling prospective only, applying to tax years beginning after June 21, 1987.[87] The IRS issued a companion revenue procedure providing automatic changes from a (b)(1) plan where the plan was similar to the plan described in the revenue ruling.[88] The IRS also announced that it would no longer issue advance rulings on whether a particular plan contemplated two or more payments, i.e., whether it would qualify as a (b)(1) plan.[89] After promulgating this revenue ruling and companion revenue procedure, the IRS did not treat uniformly those taxpayers subject to the ruling who did not qualify for or otherwise accept the benefits of the revenue procedure. Some revenue agents did not disallow use of installment methods in circumstances similar to those set forth in the revenue ruling. These agents apparently concluded that such action was unnecessary in light of the 1987 Act's disallowance of the installment method for dealers.[90] On the other hand, other agents vigorously pursued taxpayers in similar circumstances, even where the existence of net operating losses (carry-backs or carry-forwards) was of such magnitude that the adjustments were of little consequence in light of the 1987 Act.

It should be noted that the two-payment rule was eliminated by the 1980 Act for casual sales of personal property and sales of real property but not for dealer sales of personal property.[91] However, the Senate Finance Committee indicated that the Treasury would promulgate a similar rule for deferred

---

[85] On the other hand, the National Office was not reluctant to issue technical advice supporting an agent's disallowance of a (b)(1) plan, where actual experience and other facts suggested that it had been unreasonable to conclude that all sales would be paid in two or more payments. See, e.g., Tech. Adv. Mem. 8610007 (Nov. 20, 1985).

[86] Rev. Rul. 87-48, 1987-1 CB 145.

[87] Id.

[88] Rev. Proc. 87-29, 1987-1 CB 771.

[89] Rev. Proc. 87-30, 1987-1 CB 774.

[90] See discussion infra ¶ 5.07[1].

[91] IRC § 453(b)(1).

payment sales by dealers in personal property.[92] However, no such rule was ever promulgated.[93] It was understood that the Treasury believed that elimination of the two-payment rule would result in too great a revenue loss.[94] Concerns with revenue eventually prompted elimination of installment method reporting for most dealers.[95]

Dollar amount of payments. No requirement existed in the Code or regulations regarding the dollar amount of any contemplated installment payment. Case law indicated that whether payment terms qualified as installment sales was a question to be resolved on the basis of all the facts and circumstances relevant to the sale.[96] Numerous private rulings indicated that installment sales calling for a second payment of as little as 10 percent of the selling price would qualify for installment reporting.[97] Logically, as long as a payment was actually made, its amount should not have been relevant.

---

[92] 1980 S. Rep., supra note 34, at 499.

[93] On December 10, 1980, Donald C. Lubick, then Assistant Secretary of the Treasury for Tax Policy, wrote to Senator Russell B. Long, then Chairman of the Senate Finance Committee, as follows:

> [T]he Report of the Committee on Finance refers to the possibility of a change in regulations extending to dealers something analogous to the provision deleting the two-payment rule for casual sales. Neither the Treasury nor any of the professional groups involved in the development of the legislation had any intention to eliminate the requirement that the installment method be limited to dealers selling on the installment plan. In fact, the Committee Report clearly disavowed any intent to make substantive changes as to dealers except for the elimination of a double tax problem which occurred when accrual basis dealers elected to change to the installment method. What we do understand the Finance Committee expected us to do, and what we will do, is review the regulations defining installment plans for dealers to determine whether the two-payment rule is in all cases a necessary criterion to distinguish installment plan sales from ordinary sales on account.

Cong. Rec. 33,959 (daily ed. Dec. 13, 1980). A similar comment was then made by Senator Long in his report to the Senate regarding the 1980 Act. Cong. Rec. 33,958 (daily ed. Dec. 13, 1980).

[94] See "Washington Item No. 1," Tax Mgmt. (BNA) Mem. 80-26 (Dec. 29, 1980), which stated: "Tax Management understands that the Treasury considers the language in the Committee Report to be advisory, and not directory. Moreover, because of the potential revenue loss, the Treasury currently has no plans to promulgate regulations which would extend the 'one-payment' rule to dealers."

[95] See discussion infra ¶ 5.07[1].

[96] See, e.g., Marshall Bros. Lumber Co., 13 BTA 1111 (1928), rev'd and remanded without opinion, 51 F2d 1081 (6th Cir. 1931); Davenport Mach. & Foundry Co., 18 TC 39 (1952), acq. 1952-2 CB 1; Louis Greenspon, 23 TC 138 (1954), acq. 1955-1 CB 4, aff'd in part and rev'd in part, 229 F2d 947 (8th Cir. 1956).

[97] See, e.g., Priv. Ltr. Rul. 8318092 (Feb. 3, 1983) (installment plan called for 90 percent of selling price to be paid 25 days after the invoice was rendered and the remaining 10 percent to be paid 10 days later); Priv. Ltr. Ruls. 8316034 (Jan. 14, 1983), 8313061 (Dec. 29, 1982), 8313011 (Dec. 21, 1982), and 8251027 (Sept. 16, 1982) (90 percent to be paid 30 days after invoice rendered and the remaining 10

Two-year rule. The regulations did not address the issue of whether the purchase price must have been paid over a period of two or more taxable years, and, prior to 1969, it did not appear the issue had ever been raised. However, in 1969 the IRS held in the case of a sale of real property in a deferred payment transaction that the installment method was available only where the terms and conditions of the sale provided for two or more payments in two or more taxable years.[98] This ruling, which pertained to a sale of real property, did not mention whether the two-taxable-year rule should also be applied to installment sales of personal property by dealers.

In order to resolve uncertainty over this matter, the IRS issued Revenue Ruling 71-595, which stated that the two-or-more-taxable-year rule was "satisfied if the total contract price (viewed in the aggregate) of all the sales made during the taxable year which otherwise would qualify for installment method treatment is to be paid in two or more taxable years."[99] Despite this analysis by the IRS, there seemed to have been no requirement of payments being made over two taxable years.

[ii] Revolving credit plans. The opportunity to use the installment method for revolving credit sales was eliminated by the 1986 Act.[100] Congress believed that revolving credit sales were akin to the provision of a flexible line of credit accompanied by cash sales. Hence, Congress considered continued use of the installment method to be inappropriate.[101] Nevertheless, prior to the 1986 Act, the regulations provided the means by which a portion of the sales made under a revolving credit plan could be treated as sales made

---

percent to be paid 10 days later); Priv. Ltr. Rul. 8149058 (Sept. 11, 1981) (90 percent to be paid on the tenth day of the second month after the month in which the invoice is rendered, and the remaining 10 percent to be paid 10 days later); Priv. Ltr. Rul. 8125060 (Mar. 25, 1981) (90 percent to be paid at the time of sale and the remaining 10 percent to be paid 30 days later); see also Priv. Ltr. Rul. 8208087 (Nov. 27, 1981) (first installment payment could be as little as 2 percent).

[98] Rev. Rul. 69-462, 1969-2 CB 107. This IRS requirement of two or more payments over two or more taxable years for casual sales of personal property and sales of real property was eliminated by the 1980 Act. See discussion infra ¶ 5.05[2].

[99] Rev. Rul. 71-595, 1971-2 CB 223, amplifying Rev. Rul. 69-462, 1969-2 CB 107; see also Priv. Ltr. Ruls. 8318092 (Feb. 3, 1983), 8316034 (Jan. 14, 1982), 8314024 (Dec. 30, 1982).

[100] IRC § 453(k). For taxpayers that had been reporting revolving credit sales under the installment method, Section 812(c)(2) of the 1986 Act provides that the change from that method will be treated as initiated by the taxpayer with the consent of the IRS. The Section 481 adjustment arising from the change may be taken into account over a period not to exceed four years. The General Explanation of the Tax Reform Act of 1986, at 500 (May 4, 1987) (hereinafter Blue Book), provides that where the adjustment is taken into account over a period of four years, it would be taken into account 15 percent in the first year, 25 percent in the second year, and 30 percent in each of the two succeeding years. See also discussion at ¶ 8.04[6][b].

[101] See Blue Book, supra note 100, at 490.

on an installment plan.[102] For this reason, application of the installment method to revolving credit sales remains important as long as pre–1986 Act years remain subject to IRS audit.

Revolving credit plans were arrangements for the sale of property under which the customer agreed to pay a portion of the outstanding balance of his account each month (or other billing period) as statements were rendered. Such plans included so-called cycle budget accounts, flexible budget accounts, and continuous budget accounts. Virtually every retailer who made sales on account was making sales under either a revolving credit plan or a traditional installment plan.

Typically, sales under a revolving credit plan did not constitute sales under traditional installment plans. This was because revolving credit plans did not contemplate that each sale made under the plan would be paid in two or more payments. In addition, payments could not generally be applied to particular sales to determine whether such sales were, in fact, paid for in two or more installments.

The rules for using the installment method for revolving credit sales before the 1986 Act often seemed complex, but they actually involved relatively simple concepts. First, using generally accepted probability sampling techniques, a sample of year-end account balances would be selected for examination.[103] Those portions of the account balances representing charges for services or any other items not involving personal property would be excluded. Similarly, all accounts on which no payments were made from the time of the sale through the first billing period of the succeeding year would be excluded.

Two tests were then applied to the remaining account balances. All account balances that passed these two tests were treated as sales on an installment plan. Under the first test, the aggregate dollar amount of sales made during the billing period had to exceed the required monthly payment. Under the second test, the amount of the first payment made in the first month of the next year had to be less than the customer's account balance.[104] In other words, if sales made during the month were less than the required monthly payment, or if the first payment made in the new year exceeded the account balance at the beginning of the year, it was reasonable to conclude that the balances of such accounts would not be paid in two or more payments and therefore should not be treated as installment sales. Numerous examples of how these computations were made are contained in the regulations.[105]

After determining the percentage of the total account balances that satisfied these tests, that percentage was applied to the ending accounts to

---

[102] Treas. Reg. § 1.453-2(d).

[103] With respect to determining the sample, see Rev. Proc. 64-4, 1964-1 (Part 1) 644, modified and amplified by Rev. Proc. 65-5, 1965-1 CB 720.

[104] Treas. Reg. §§ 1.453-2(d)(3)(i), 1.453-2(d)(3)(ii).

[105] Treas. Reg. §§ 1.453-2(d)(3), 1.453-2(d)(4).

determine the portion of the total balance of accounts receivable that would be treated as sales on an installment plan.

[3] Installment Computations by Dealers

This discussion of installment computations by dealers pertains to installment dispositions by all dealers in personal property prior to the 1987 Act[106] and by those few dealers of real or personal property who are still permitted to use the installment method.[107]

Eligible dealers (both in the past and presently) often fail to avail themselves of the advantages of installment reporting, frequently because neither they nor their tax advisors have focused on the method's availability and benefits. In other cases, use of the method may have been focused on, but taxpayers and their advisors often concluded that the computational requirements (discussed in the example below) were too complex. Such conclusions were often the result of quick judgment. In light of the possible savings available, full consideration was (and remains) warranted. Incurring the cost of increased accounting capacity to handle the computational requirements of installment reporting may be one of the best investments a business can make.

With respect to the computations, all dealers in goods are subject to the inventory-costing requirements of Sections 263A and 471.[108] These rules, together with those provided by Section 472 for last-in, first-out (LIFO) taxpayers, set the framework for determining cost of goods sold and, hence, gross profit on sales. The general inventory costing requirements are discussed in Chapter 6, while the LIFO requirements are the subject of Chapter 7.

The use of the installment method required more record keeping than was required for use of an accrual method. Installment-method use was predicated on being able to trace payments received from customers to both the year of sale and the particular goods that were sold. This tracing was necessary so that the applicable gross profit percentage could be applied to each payment to determine the correct amount of installment income to be reported.

> **EXAMPLE:** Assume two items, *A* and *B*, are sold to the same customer; that item *A* cost $10 and was sold for $16 in year 1, and that item *B* cost $8 and was sold for $16 in year 2. Assume each sale calls for installment payments of $1 per month until paid in full. Under an accrual method, $6 of gain would be recognized on the sale of *A* and $8 of gain would be recognized on the sale of *B*. Under an installment method, the taxpayer must be able to trace each payment to the sale to

---

[106] See discussion infra ¶ 5.07 for impact of 1987 Act.

[107] See discussion infra ¶ 5.07[1].

[108] See, e.g., Marcor, Inc., 89 TC 181 (1987).

which it relates to know whether to apply a gross profit percentage of 37.5 percent ($6 ÷ $16) or 50 percent ($8 ÷ $16).

The computational requirements are discussed in more detail in the succeeding sections.

[a] By Year

The regulations require application of the following formula to determine the amount of installment income to be recognized by dealers in any particular year.[109]

$$\text{Payments received in the taxable year on account of installment sales made in a particular year} \times \frac{\text{Gross profit realized on account of installment sales made in that particular year}}{\text{Total contract price of all installment sales in that particular year}}$$

For the purpose of making this computation, "gross profit" means sales price less cost of goods sold (see Chapters 6 and 7).[110] Contract price is the selling price, including applicable carrying charges (or interest) that are determined at the time of sale and added to (and treated on the seller's books as part of) the selling price.[111] If the applicable carrying charges or interest are not added to the contract price at the time of sale, then payments are applied first to carrying charges or interest that has accrued, with the balance of the payments applied to the sales price.[112] For pre–1986 Act years, such carrying charges or interest were not to be treated as part of the contract price for sales on a revolving credit plan.

The selling price also includes state and local taxes that are imposed on the dealer[113] but not state and local taxes that are imposed on the customer and collected by the dealer.[114] In addition, selling and other distribution expenses are deducted in accordance with the taxpayer's normal method of

---

[109] Treas. Reg. § 1.453-2(c).

[110] Treas. Reg. § 1.453-1(b)(1). See also Marcor, Inc., 89 TC 181 (1987). See IRC §§ 263A, 471, 472, and the regulations thereunder for determining cost of goods sold. Use of the installment method in conjunction with the LIFO inventory method could be particularly advantageous. It is surprising how infrequently the two methods were used in concert.

[111] Treas. Reg. § 1.453-2(c)(2).

[112] Treas. Reg. § 1.453-2(c)(3).

[113] See Rev. Rul. 60-53, 1960-1 CB 185, and Rev. Rul. 68-163, 1968-1 CB 201, each amplified by Rev. Rul. 79-196, 1979-1 CB 181. Where state and local taxes are not included in sales price, payments are applied to such taxes first and only thereafter to the sales price.

[114] Rev. Rul. 79-196, 1979-1 CB 181. See Marcor, Inc., 89 TC 181 (1987).

accounting.[115] These expenses need not be deferred and deducted proportionately as payments of the selling price are received.[116]

[b] By Type of Sale

To reflect income clearly, it was generally necessary for the gross profit computations to be made for the installment sales only. Cash sales and credit sales not made on an installment basis generally were to be excluded.

However, recognizing that such record keeping could prove quite burdensome, the Treasury provided that taxpayers could use the gross profit percentage realized on all credit sales of the particular year or on all sales of the year, cash and credit, if the District Director of the IRS could be satisfied that income from installment sales would be clearly reflected.[117]

In addition to the foregoing, case authority exists for the use of averages and estimates in calculating gross profit on installment sales. In *Appeal of Blum's Inc.*,[118] where the percentage of profit on cash sales could not accurately be determined separately from sales on the installment plan, the use of a composite gross-profit percentage to determine the taxable portion of payments received for goods sold on the installment plan was determined to be proper.[119] Use of a composite gross-profit percentage was also found to

---

[115] See A. Finkenberg's Sons, Inc., 17 TC 973 (1951), acq. 1952-1 CB 2, and Chapter 6, pertaining to inventory costing. See also Marcor, Inc., 89 TC 181 (1987).

[116] See Marcor, Inc., 89 TC 181 (1987).

[117] Treas. Reg. § 1.453-2(c)(1).

[118] Appeal of Blum's Inc., 7 BTA 737 (1927), nonacq. on other installment-sales-related issues IX-1 CB 6 (1930).

[119] In *Appeal of Blum's, Inc.*, the court stated the following:

[T]he petitioner is in no position to make an accurate determination of the gross profits from installment sales; and the proportion of the installment payments to be returned as income is not susceptible of accurate ascertainment. This deficiency in accounting records undoubtedly exists in a large majority of installment businesses, rendering it impracticable when they follow the installment sales method for them to make a meticulously exact return of income. . . . [I]t was the intent of Congress in permitting the installment sales method of returning income to authorize the use of a method which would as nearly as practicable clearly reflect income, and if a workable and reasonable rule for computing income by the use of the installment sales method can be found under which taxpayers employing this method will ultimately return all of the profits from installment sales—nothing more or nothing less—we believe such a rule should be followed. . . . The entire plan of income taxation recognizes the fact that income is a matter, at best, of estimate, and can never be reduced to absolutely definite terms in the case of a large modern business institution. . . . [W]here, as in this case, the percentage of profit on cash sales, which certainly was not uniform in respect of all such sales, is not known, no other course appears proper than to treat all sales, cash and installment, on the same basis

be appropriate in *Mayer & Co.*[120] However, almost 30 years later, the Tax Court distinguished *Blum's Inc.* and found a composite gross-profit percentage to be inappropriate where the inclusion of noninstallment sales (on which no profit was realized) with installment sales (on which a significant profit was realized) was determined to cause a material distortion of the percentage.[121] *Blum's Inc.* was also distinguished in a case where only a small portion (6 percent) of the taxpayer's sales was on the installment plan, and the taxpayer could not support the gross-profit percentage claimed for installment sales.[122]

[c] By Type of Goods

Separate gross-profit calculations were generally to be made for each different class of property sold on an installment plan. Early in the history of installment reporting, the Internal Revenue Bureau (IRB) stated:

> If books have been so kept that the cost of each article sold was not shown, gross profit may be determined by taking the average percentage of gross profit on gross sales. If several different lines of merchandise are handled, on which the average percentages of profit differ, the gross profit on total sales of each different class of merchandise should be computed separately.[123]

Of course, consistent with the intent of Congress as expressed in *Blum's Inc.*, a reasonable approach to accomplish this computation of gross profit percentages should be accepted if adequate records are not otherwise available. However, if the taxpayer were unable to demonstrate that its approach was reasonable and clearly reflected income, its use of that approach might be denied.

[4] Disposition of Dealer Installment Obligations

Section 453B provides that unless specifically excepted, any disposition of an installment obligation is a taxable event for which gain or loss is recognized. In pertinent part, it provides:

---

and to determine a composite percentage of profit on the total sales which will represent the proportion of the cash collections to be returned as income. Id. at 757–758, 765.

[120] Mayer & Co., 9 BTA 815 (1927).

[121] Kay-Jones Furniture Co., Inc., 14 TCM 944 (1955).

[122] Estate of Walter Tillman, 10 BTA 4 (1928).

[123] OD 25, 1 CB 75 (1919), (declared obsolete in Rev. Rul. 68-575, 1968-2 CB 603, 604).

If an installment obligation is satisfied at other than its face value or distributed, transmitted, sold, or otherwise disposed of, gain or loss shall result to the extent of the difference between the basis of the obligation and—

(1) the amount realized in the case of satisfaction at other than face value or a sale or exchange, or

(2) the FMV of the obligation at the time of distribution, transmission, or disposition, in the case of the distribution, transmission, or disposition otherwise than by sale or exchange.

Any gain or loss so resulting shall be considered as resulting from the sale or exchange of the property in respect of which the installment obligation was received.[124]

Section 453B(b) adds that the basis of an installment obligation is the excess of the unpaid face value of the obligation over an amount equal to the income that would be reported if the obligation were satisfied in full. For example, if property with a basis of $60 were sold for $100 to be paid at the rate of $10 per year beginning with the year of sale, the basis of the obligation before any payments are made is $60 (the face value of $100 less the gain of $40 to be recognized). After two payments are made, the seller's basis in the note would be $48 (remaining face value of $80 less remaining gain to be recognized of $32).

The present Code provisions are identical to the provisions of old Sections 453(d)(1) and 453(d)(2), which set forth the rules for gain or loss on dispositions of installment obligations prior to the passage of the 1980 Act. Therefore, it follows that existing Treasury regulations, which were promulgated under old Section 453(d), remain applicable.[125]

[5] Defaults, Repossessions, and Bad Debts

If the purchaser defaults in the making of any installment payments and the seller repossesses the property, gain or loss occurs on the repossession. The gain or loss is measured by the difference between the FMV of the repossessed property (at the time of repossession) and the basis of the installment obligations that are satisfied, discharged, or applied, with adjustment for other amounts realized or costs incurred, as a result of the repossession.[126]

EXAMPLE: Assume property with a basis of $60 is sold in year 1 for

---

[124] IRC § 453B(a).

[125] See infra ¶ 5.06 for a discussion of dispositions of installment obligations.

[126] Treas. Reg. § 1.453-1(d).

$100, to be paid $50 in year 2 and $50 in year 3. Assume further that the purchaser defaults before making the first payment, and the property is repossessed. If the property is worth $80 at the time of repossession, the taxpayer will recognize $20 of gain ($80 − $60 of basis). The basis of the property to the taxpayer will be $80, its FMV. If the default occurs after the first payment is made, then gain of $20 would have been recognized on receipt of the first payment (40 percent of $50) and gain of $50 will be recognized on the default ($80 FMV of repossessed property − $30 of remaining basis of installment obligation ($50 unpaid face amount − $20 of remaining gain on original sale)).

If the purchaser has no further liability to the seller as a result of the repossession, no deduction for a bad debt will be permitted. If the purchaser remains liable after the repossession (or if property is not repossessed), then the seller may be entitled to a deduction for a bad debt. For instance, if the dealer is on the specific charge-off method, it is permitted to deduct the basis of any unpaid or unsatisfied obligations in the year it is determined that such unpaid obligations are uncollectible in accordance with the rules regarding deductions for bad debts. However, in no event is the deduction to exceed the dealer's basis in the installment obligation. Thus, if the FMV of the repossessed property had been $40 in the preceding example (rather than $80) and had the purchaser remained liable for $20 after repossession, the bad debt deduction would be limited to $20.

As a result of the 1986 Act, use of the reserve method of accounting for bad debts is no longer permitted. Prior to the 1986 Act, dealers were permitted to use the reserve method. However, if a dealer made sales under an installment plan and also made other credit sales that were not on an installment plan, a separate reserve had to be maintained for the installment plan sales.[127]

[6] Disposition to Member of Consolidated Return Group

The consolidated return regulations define a "deferred intercompany transaction" as the sale or exchange of property during a consolidated return year between corporations that are members of the same group immediately after the transaction.[128] To the extent gain or loss on a deferred intercompany transaction arises from a disposition of an installment obligation, recognition of the gain or loss is deferred by the selling member.[129] The regulation makes no distinction between installment obligations of dealers and nondealers.

The regulations also provide for the holder of the installment obligation

---

[127] Rev. Rul. 70-139, 1970-1 CB 39.

[128] Treas. Reg. § 1.1502-13(a).

[129] Treas. Reg. § 1.1502-13(c).

to recognize any deferred gain proportionately as payments of the obligation are made by the debtor.[130]

> EXAMPLE: Assume that corporations P and S file consolidated returns on a calendar-year basis. On January 15, 1966, P sells an installment obligation, with a basis of $48, to S for $60. At the time of the sale, the debtor is obligated to pay three annual installments of $20 on each July 1. The sale by P to S is a deferred intercompany transaction. Consequently, P defers the $12 gain ($60 − $48) on the sale of the obligation to S. If the debtor makes all required payments, P will report $4 of its deferred gain each year, computed as follows: $12 deferred gain x ($20 payment ÷ $60 aggregate amount to be paid).[131]

In Revenue Ruling 85-133,[132] the IRS considered an arrangement under which a parent company/retailer sold items to customers whose purchases were financed by a bank that was a subsidiary of the parent. The installment obligations of customers were issued directly to the banking subsidiary. The question was whether the sales could be reported under the installment method. The parent took the position that since it could have structured the transactions to be installment sales followed by a sale of the installment paper to the subsidiary in a deferred payment transaction, application of the installment method should not be denied. Although ruling that the taxpayer was not able to use the installment method, the IRS indicated that if the sales themselves had been on an installment basis, the taxpayer's analysis of the manner in which Sections 453A (as it existed prior to the 1987 Act), 453B

---

[130] Treas. Reg. § 1.1502-13(e) reads as follows:

Restoration of deferred gain or loss for installment obligations and sales—

(1) Installment obligations. If an installment obligation (within the meaning of section 453(d)) is transferred in a deferred intercompany transaction, then on each date on which the obligation is satisfied the selling member shall take into account an amount equal to the deferred gain or loss on such transfer, multiplied by a fraction, the numerator of which is the portion of such obligation satisfied on such date, and the denominator of which is the aggregate unpaid installments immediately after the deferred intercompany transaction.

(2) Installment sales. If—(i) Property acquired in a deferred intercompany transaction is disposed of outside the group, and (ii) The purchasing member-vendor reports its income on the installment method under section 453, then on each date on which the purchasing member-vendor receives an installment payment the selling member shall take into account an amount equal to the deferred gain or loss attributable to such property (after taking into account any prior reductions under paragraph (d)(3) of this section) multiplied by a fraction, the numerator of which is the installment payment received and the denominator of which is the total contract price. . . .

[131] Treas. Reg. § 1.1502-13(h), Example (11).

[132] Rev. Rul. 85-133, 1985-2 CB 192.

and Treasury Regulation §§ 1.453(2)(b)(1) and 1.1502-13 interrelated would have been accurate.[133]

[7] Election of Installment Method

This discussion (of the election of the installment method by dealers) pertains to installment dispositions prior to the 1987 Act.[134] Proposed regulations detailing the manner in which adoption of the installment method should be made were issued in 1986.[135] The proposed regulations pointed out that the election to adopt the installment method was to be made on the taxpayer's income tax return for the first year for which the election was to be effective. The return had to be timely filed, taking into account available extensions of time for filing.

The taxpayer was to specify on a statement attached to the return that the installment method was being adopted. The statement was to show the method of accounting previously used and was to identify the particular types of sales to be included within the election. Consequently, if a taxpayer adopted the method in a year during which only a particular type of installment sale was made, extension of the installment method to other types of sales would require separate elections. Notwithstanding the foregoing, a dealer in personal property, including any person who was a dealer as a result of his transaction being recharacterized as sales as opposed to some other type of transaction (e.g., leases), was deemed to have elected the installment method if the dealer failed to report the full amount of gain in the year of sale.

The use of the installment method did not require the prior approval of the IRS. However, a change from the installment method to some other method could not be made without prior IRS approval.

Once the election had been made, the installment method applied only to gain on sales made on or after the first day of the year of election. Thus,

---

[133] See also Priv. Ltr. Ruls. 7831026 (May 4, 1978), 7932041 (May 9, 1979).

[134] See discussion infra ¶ 5.07 for impact of 1987 Act.

[135] Prop. Reg. § 1.453A-3. The proposed regulations are consistent with the 1980 Senate Report, which also provided the following:

> It is intended that, under Treasury regulations, a failure to report the full amount of gain from sales may be treated as an election of the installment method. For example, it is intended that a dealer, who treats a transaction as a lease of personal property and only reports the payments received as rental income, may be eligible for installment reporting under the regulations if the transaction is recharacterized as a sale rather than a lease in an audit by the Internal Revenue Service. However, it is intended that no taxpayer who has reported sales under the accrual method will be required to change from that method under the regulations.

1980-2 CB 494, 507.

payments received on account of sales made in prior years were not to be taken into account in computing installment income for the year of election or for any subsequent year.[136]

¶ 5.05 INSTALLMENT SALES OF PROPERTY OTHER THAN INVENTORY

Sections 453 and 453A (as enacted by the 1987 Act) set forth the applicable requirements for use of the installment method in connection with all sales or other dispositions of property other than inventory, most dealer dispositions of real or personal property, and dispositions of publicly traded property. Prior to the 1987 Act, installment sales included all deferred payment sales of realty and all casual (i.e., nondealer) deferred payment sales of personal property. The 1987 Act and later acts repealed use of the installment method by dealers in real property and imposed new conditions on use of the installment method for certain dispositions of real and personal property by nondealers.[137] Where available, installment reporting is automatic and, unless the taxpayer elects not to use the installment method, is mandatory for nondealer dispositions of property where at least one payment is to be received after the close of the taxable year in which the disposition occurs.[138]

[1] History and Development

[a] Prior Conditions to Use of Installment Method

Prior to the 1980 Act, the installment method was not available for casual sales of personalty or for sales of realty unless certain conditions were satisfied. First, payments in the year of sale could not exceed 30 percent of the sales price. This condition was premised on two assumptions: (1) if a taxpayer received a sufficiently large payment in the year of sale, he would have the resources to pay the tax and would not need the benefits of the installment method and (2) because of the size of the initial payment, the obligation of the buyer was so secured (i.e., so likely to be paid) that it should

---

[136] However, where a taxpayer was not subject to U.S. tax law in the year of sale, installment payments received by him in later years, after he had become subject to U.S. laws, were found not to be subject to tax. Tech. Adv. Mem. 8708002 (Oct. 29, 1986).

[137] See IRC §§ 453, 453A, and discussion infra ¶ 5.07.

[138] IRC §§ 453(a), 453(b). For rules applying to dispositions of inventories or personal property by dealers prior to the 1987 Act, see discussion supra ¶ 5.04. For impact of 1987 Act, see discussion infra ¶ 5.07. The installment method remains applicable for sales of property only, not for other types of transactions. See discussion supra ¶ 5.04[2][b].

be regarded as the equivalent of cash and recognized as income in the year of receipt.[139] Over the years, the applicable percentage varied—from a low of 25 percent in the early regulations (and, later, in the first statutory provision in the 1926 Act) to a high of 40 percent in the Revenue Act of 1928.[140] Although initially perceived as a logical condition to use of the installment method, this requirement unduly complicated business transactions, fostered an inordinate amount of litigation and confusion, and operated as a trap for those not aware of it.[141]

A second condition for use of the installment method was that there be two or more payments. The method was not available for deferred payment sales where the contract called for only a single deferred payment.[142] This so-called two-payment rule arose from the definition of the word "installment," which contemplated more than one payment. The rule resulted in incongruity and hardship. For example, a taxpayer who sold property for a single payment due 10 years in the future was subject to tax in the year of sale, but a taxpayer who received up to 30 percent of the selling price in the year of sale could use the method and thereby delay the recognition of the balance of the income until payments were received.[143]

Third, use of the installment method for casual sales of personalty was denied where the sales price did not exceed $1,000.[144] Although apparently intended as a de minimis rule, this requirement was sometimes difficult to apply, particularly where several items were sold for an aggregate price of more than $1,000. The difficulty stemmed from the rule that where two or more items are sold, the purchase price is to be allocated among the items sold on the basis of their relative FMVs.[145]

Finally, use of the installment method was subject to an election by the taxpayer.[146] This presented many problems for both taxpayers and the IRS.[147]

---

[139] See discussion of the cash equivalent doctrine at ¶ 3.03[1].

[140] See 2 J. Mertens, Law of Federal Income Taxation § 15.02; J.S. Seidman, Seidman's Legislative History of Federal Income Tax Laws 1938-1861, at 590–593 (1938).

[141] See 1980 S. Rep., supra note 28, at 498.

[142] Rev. Rul. 69-462, 1969-2 CB 107, amplified by Rev. Rul. 71-595, 1971-2 CB 223; Baltimore Baseball Club, Inc. v. United States, 481 F2d 1283 (Ct. Cl. 1973); 10-42 Corp., 55 TC 593 (1971), acq. 1979-1 CB 1.

[143] Initially, it was thought by some in the IRS that the method should be unavailable unless a payment was received in the year of sale. Gen. Couns. Mem. 12148, XII-2 CB 57, declared obsolete by Rev. Rul. 68-674, 1968-2 CB 609.

[144] IRC § 453(b)(1)(B) as it existed prior to the 1980 Act. The $1,000 requirement had remained virtually unchanged since the 1926 Act.

[145] See discussion infra ¶ 5.05[8][d].

[146] Once made, the taxpayer is subject to the consequences of the election. See, e.g., Stewart Perry, 59 TCM 533 (1990), where the court refused to permit a taxpayer to file amended returns retroactively revoking his earlier election of the installment

For taxpayers, the requirement of election became a trap for the unwary.[146] For the IRS, it provided a potential whipsaw. For example, a taxpayer could take the position on its initial return that it was reporting under a cost recovery method pursuant to which payments are applied first to basis with the excess of payments over basis taken into account in the year received. If use of this method were later challenged by the IRS, the taxpayer could retroactively elect the installment method or, if the year of sale were closed by the running of the applicable statutory period of limitation, take the position that no tax was due.[149]

[b] Statutory Format and Perceived Inadequacy

From the inception of installment reporting to the 1980 Act, the applicable Code provisions remained relatively simple.[150] They (1) set forth the conditions for eligibility previously discussed; (2) gave substantial discretion to the Treasury to promulgate regulations; and (3) excepted from the benefits of installment reporting obligations of the purchaser that were payable on demand or readily tradable in an established securities market. Over the years, numerous issues and problems arose in the application of the

---

method. The taxpayer filed the amended returns in order to reduce his overall tax liability, which was higher than anticipated because of subsequent changes in the law governing alternative minimum taxable income.

[147] See, e.g., Mamula v. United States, 346 F2d 1016 (9th Cir. 1965) and Joseph H. Gibson, 89 TC 1177 (1987), respectively, for analysis of circumstances in which a taxpayer may be allowed to elect the installment method retroactively, because its initial reporting was not inconsistent with such a later election and circumstances in which the taxpayer's initial election of a noninstallment method may preclude a later election of the installment method. See also ¶¶ 2.03[2] and 2.03[3], and accompanying notes, for further discussion of these two cases.

[148] See, e.g., W.R. Royster, 48 TCM 1594 (1985), aff'd per curiam, 820 F2d 1156 (11th Cir. 1987), where the Tax Court imputed income from a sale of property away from children and to their parents but denied use of the installment method to the parents, because the parents had themselves not elected use of the installment method.

[149] See 1980 S. Rep., supra note 34, at 499–500, which provided in pertinent part:

[P]resent law [i.e., law prior to the 1980 Act] creates a whip-saw problem for the Internal Revenue Service, e.g., where the taxpayer does not report gain from a sale for the year of sale but later attempts to retroactively elect installment treatment if the omission is discovered on audit, or, if the statute of limitations has run, contends that the full amount of gain should have been reported for the year of sale.

See also Joseph H. Gibson, 89 TC 1177 (1987), for an identification of issues that arose under prior law because of the election requirement and a discussion of the manner in which the courts resolved those issues.

[150] See IRC § 453(b) as it existed prior to the 1980 Act.

installment method, but there was no legislative guidance for taxpayers or the IRS. Techniques were developed by tax practitioners to avoid limitations or otherwise benefit from installment reporting in unintended ways. The IRS often regarded these techniques as abusive, but the IRS believed that it lacked the authority to respond to the abuse.[151]

[c] 1980 Act

The 1980 Act was passed to achieve many goals, including (1) simplifying and modernizing the law by removing unnecessary conditions of eligibility and (2) adding provisions to correct prior deficiencies in the law or to curb perceived abuse. The 1980 Act was unique in that it was the product of a joint effort by tax practitioners, the Treasury, and Congress to work together in ameliorating problems and correcting abuse.[152]

As a result of the 1980 Act, the prior conditions for use of the installment method were eliminated. Taxpayers no longer have to worry about the amount of the payment received in the year of sale, the number of payments to be made under the agreement, the amount to be paid for small or incidental items of personalty, or the making of a formal election.

In order to respond to the problems and perceived abuses under prior law, the 1980 Act restructured the installment sales provisions and included a number of provisions that focused on particular topics.[153]

[d] 1986 Act

The 1986 Act imposed several limitations on the use of the installment method. These limitations included (1) the so-called proportionate disallowance rule, pursuant to which a portion of the taxpayer's outstanding indebtedness at the end of each year was treated as a payment on certain installment obligations of the taxpayer; (2) a denial of the use of the installment method to revolving credit sales; and (3) a denial of the use of the installment method to sales of marketable securities or other property regularly traded on an established market.[154]

---

[151] See 1980 S. Rep., supra note 34.

[152] M.D. Ginsburg, "Future Payment Sales After the 1980 Revision Act," 39 NYU Tax Inst. 43-1, 43-70 n.130 (1981).

[153] These provisions are discussed in succeeding sections of ¶ 5.05.

[154] See IRC § 453C (prior to its repeal by the 1987 Act) and discussion infra ¶¶ 5.05[6] and 5.07 regarding the proportionate disallowance rule and its repeal by the 1987 Act, respectively; § 453(k)(1) and discussion supra ¶ 5.04[2][d][ii] regarding revolving credit sales; Section § 453(k)(2) regarding marketable securities and other property regularly traded on an established market. Section 453(k) specifies that all payments to be received on account of a disposition of personal property under a revolving credit plan or on a sale of marketable securities shall be treated as received

Congress justified each of these new limitations on the basis that the taxpayer had economically received (or was in a position to economically receive) cash resulting from the transaction. As a result, Congress believed that the benefits of the installment method should not be available, since the taxpayer did not have the liquidity problems that the installment method was designed to alleviate.[155] It is doubtful that this justification, although plausible, was the actual genesis for the limitations. The method had been available to taxpayers in those circumstances for such a long time that it is hard to imagine that the rationale only just came to the attention of Congress. Moreover, in connection with the 1980 Act, Congress had suggested easing the rules to make installment method reporting more readily available to dealers in inventory. Congress seemed unconcerned about the ability of such taxpayers to finance receivables and obtain cash in that fashion. Thus, the real impetus for the limitations appears to be the additional tax revenue they would generate.

[e] 1987 Act

The Revenue Act of 1987 was signed into law on December 22, 1987. It, together with the Technical and Miscellaneous Revenue Act of 1988 (the 1988 Act), made a number of changes to the law. The effect of these Acts is discussed in the last section of this Chapter.[156]

[2] Installment Sale

Under Section 453, income from an installment sale must be reported under the installment method, unless the taxpayer elects not to report on that method.[157] With certain exceptions,[158] "installment sale" is defined as any disposition of property where at least one payment is to be received after the close of the taxable year in which the disposition occurs.[159] Thus, there is no requirement that the purchase price be paid in more than one payment or that the payments be received in any particular year or over any particular number of years. There is no requirement that a minimum price be charged for the property that is sold, nor is there any prohibition against more than a specified maximum amount being received in the year of sale.

---

in the year of disposition. This rule may come as a surprise to cash basis sellers of marketable securities, who might expect to delay recognition of gain until cash is received.

[155] See Blue Book, supra note 100, at 489–491.

[156] See discussion infra ¶ 5.07.

[157] See IRC § 453(d) and discussion infra ¶ 5.05[15] regarding so-called elections out.

[158] IRC § 453(b)(2).

[159] IRC § 453(b)(1).

Prior to the 1987 Act, the only deferred payment dispositions that were excluded from the definition of "installment sales" were deferred payment dispositions of (1) inventory; (2) personal property by a dealer; and (3) stock or securities that were traded on an established securities market or, to the extent provided by regulations, other property regularly traded on an established market.[160] Deferred payment dispositions of real property by dealers in real property were included within the definition of "installment sales." However, in order to prevent perceived tax abuse, certain limitations were provided on the use of the installment method in transactions involving transfers of depreciable property between or among related persons.[161] The 1987 Act continues the prior exclusions and limitations. In addition, the 1987 Act excludes dealer dispositions of real property from installment reporting and adds certain new conditions to the use of the installment method for certain nondealer dispositions of real or personal property.[162]

The exclusion of sales and other dispositions of marketable securities and other publicly traded property from installment method reporting that was part of the 1986 Act[163] was explained on the basis that, since the taxpayer could "easily sell such property for cash in the public market," liquidity problems arose only at the taxpayer's option.[164] Although this reasoning may be sound for many sales, it is not sound for all sales of marketable securities or other publicly traded property. In many circumstances, where a taxpayer owns a substantial block of publicly traded shares or other securities, it is often not possible to readily dispose of those shares in the marketplace. Instead, purchasers must be found. Deferred payment transactions with such persons are often the result of arm's-length bargaining and do not result merely from the taxpayer's desire to defer payment. For taxpayers who have such shares, the 1986 Act limitations impose a substantial economic burden.

[3] Installment Method

The term "installment method" means "a method under which the income recognized for any taxable year from a disposition is that proportion of the payments received in that year which the gross profit (realized or to be real-

---

[160] See Section 453(b)(2), as it existed prior to the 1987 Act, which excluded sales of inventory and dealer sales of personal property from the definition of installment sales. But see Section 453A, as it existed prior to the 1987 Act, which provided installment sale treatment for such sales. See Section 453(k) regarding denial of the installment method to stock, securities, and other property traded on an established market.

[161] See discussion infra ¶¶ 5.05[11][b][ii], 5.05[11][c].

[162] See discussion infra ¶ 5.07.

[163] IRC § 453(k).

[164] See Blue Book, supra note 100, at 490–491.

ized when payment is completed) bears to the total contract price."[165] In other words, under the installment method, gain is recognized proportionately as payments are received.

[4] What Is a Payment?

Since income is recognized under the installment method as payments are received, it is most important to consider the scope of the term "payment." The Code itself does not define the term, but the regulations provide that "payments may be received in cash or other property, including foreign currency, marketable securities, and evidences of indebtedness which are payable on demand or readily tradable."[166] Therefore, absent an exception, virtually any item received from the purchaser or on the purchaser's behalf will be treated as a payment in the year in which actually or constructively received.[167]

In addition, as a result of rules imposed by the 1987 Act, amounts borrowed by the taxpayer are treated as payments on an installment obligation if the taxpayer's obligation to repay such borrowed amounts is secured by that very installment obligation.[168] The obligations subject to this special rule are those arising from the disposition of property under the installment method, but only if the sales price exceeds $150,000.[169] Where the borrowings are treated as payments, the borrowed amounts are treated as payments received as of the later of (1) the time the relevant debt is secured by the installment obligation or (2) the time the proceeds are received by the taxpayer.[170] The details of these rules are discussed below.[171]

Prior to its repeal by the 1987 Act, the 1986 Act provided a rule causing certain indebtedness of a taxpayer to be treated as a payment on installment obligations held by the taxpayer. This rule was referred to as the proportionate disallowance rule.[172]

[5] What Is Not a Payment?

Although the Code does not precisely specify what is included within the concept of payment, it does specify certain exclusions. With certain excep-

---

[165] IRC § 453(c). See infra ¶ 5.05[8] for discussion of installment sale computations.

[166] Temp. Reg. § 15a.453-1(b)(3)(i).

[167] See Tech. Adv. Mem. 8622002 (Feb. 20, 1986), where IRS found installment method not available to purchaser who used funds to purchase nonredeemable certificates of deposits for seller. See also ¶ 3.03[2] for a discussion of constructive receipt.

[168] IRC § 453A(d)(1).

[169] IRC §§ 453A(b)(1), 453A(d)(1).

[170] IRC § 453A(d)(1).

[171] See discussion infra ¶ 5.07[4].

[172] See IRC § 453C, repealed by the 1987 Act, and discussion infra ¶ 5.05[6].

tions, the term "payment" does not include "evidences of indebtedness of the person acquiring the property (whether or not payment of such indebtedness is guaranteed by another person)."[173] However, payment does include a purchaser's evidence of indebtedness if such evidence of indebtedness (1) is payable on demand or (2) is issued by a corporation or a government or political subdivision thereof and is readily tradable.[174] To be considered readily tradable, the evidence of indebtedness must be issued with interest coupons attached or in registered form or in any other form designed to render such evidence of indebtedness readily tradable in an established securities market.[175] The rationale for this limitation is that if the obligation of the purchaser is in such form that the seller can demand payment in cash or other property at any time he so desires, or if the obligation is in a form which makes it readily convertible into cash, then there is no need to provide the benefit of installment reporting. If installment reporting were available in these circumstances, it would permit unintended tax benefits.

In addition, except for purposes of determining whether an installment sale has been made, the term "payment" will not include any property permitted to be received without the recognition of gain under a like-kind exchange described in Section 1031(b).[176] Similar rules apply in the case of an exchange, which is described in Section 356(a) and which is not treated as a dividend.[177] Thus, gain that would be reported in connection with a tax-free transaction may be deferred until the year payment is received even though gain on the balance of the transaction is not to be recognized.

[6] Proportionate Disallowance Rule

This discussion (of the proportionate disallowance rule) pertains to the law prior to the 1987 Act. The proportionate disallowance rule was repealed by the 1987 Act.[178]

Prior to the 1986 Act, taxpayers could defer the recognition of income through use of an installment method but nevertheless obtain cash immediately by borrowing against the installment obligations.[179] Congress tolerated this practice for many years but ultimately concluded (to keep the 1986 Act as revenue neutral as possible) that this practice should be stopped in the case of dealers and sales of certain business or rental property. Accordingly, to achieve this objective, Section 453C was enacted to treat a portion of the taxpayer's indebtedness as payments on covered installment obligations.

---

[173] IRC § 453(f)(3). See discussion infra ¶ 5.05[7][e].

[174] IRC § 453(f)(3).

[175] IRC §§ 453(f)(3), 453(f)(4), 453(f)(5). See discussion infra ¶ 5.05[7][e].

[176] IRC § 453(f)(6). See discussion infra ¶ 5.05[13].

[177] IRC § 453(f)(6)(C).

[178] See discussion infra ¶ 5.07.

[179] See discussion infra ¶ 5.06[5].

The obligations that were covered by these rules (i.e., the so-called proportionate disallowance rules) consisted of those obligations that were held by the taxpayer at the end of the year (or by a member of the same affiliated group as the seller)[180] and that arose from any of the three following categories:[181]

1. Dispositions after February 28, 1986, of personal property on an installment plan by dealers

2. Dispositions after February 28, 1986, of real property by taxpayers who hold such property for sale to customers in the ordinary course of business

3. Dispositions after August 16, 1986, of real property by taxpayers, if such property was used in the taxpayer's trade or business or held for the production of rental income and the sales price exceeds $150,000[182]

The increase in tax for dealers in personal property who were subject to application of this new rule could be spread over a period of years. The increase in tax arising in the first year for which the section was applicable was spread ratably over that year and the succeeding two years. The increase in tax arising in the second year could be allocated ratably over that year and the succeeding year.[183] For dealer sales of real property, the rule was the same, except that it was the gain that was spread, not the liability for tax.[184]

Unless the taxpayer or its sales fit within one of the foregoing three categories, neither the taxpayer nor the sale was subject to the proportionate disallowance rule. Accordingly, the rule did not apply to casual sales of personal property or sales of real property held for rental or used in trade or business if the sale price was $150,000 or less.[185] The Code expressly excluded personal use property (as defined in Section 1275(b)(3)) and property used or produced in a farming business (as defined in Sections 2032A(e)(4) and 2032A(e)(5)).[186] Also, sales of so-called timeshare interests in residential real property or unimproved residential lots were excluded if the seller so elected

---

[180] For this purpose, the affiliated group has the same meaning as in Section 1504(a), but without regard to Section 1504(b). See IRC § 453C(e)(1)(A)(ii).

[181] IRC § 453C(e)(1)(A), prior to repeal by 1987 Act. See discussion infra ¶ 5.07.

[182] Section 1274(c)(3)(A)(ii) applies in order to prevent fragmentation of a sale in an attempt to reduce the price to the $150,000 amount or less.

[183] 1986 Act, § 811(c)(7).

[184] 1986 Act, § 811(c)(6).

[185] Some members of Congress had indicated a desire to exclude nondealer sales from the proportionate disallowance rules. See 44 BNA Daily Tax Rep. G-1 (Mar. 9, 1987).

[186] IRC § 453C(e)(1)(B), prior to repeal by 1987 Act.

and agreed to pay interest on the deferred tax liability.[187] Finally, sales by manufacturers to dealers were excluded if the manufacturer had the right to reacquire the property if the purchaser/dealer failed to resell the property within nine months of its acquisition.[188]

The installment obligations covered by the proportionate disallowance rule were called applicable installment obligations. To determine what portion of the taxpayer's indebtedness would be treated as a payment on these applicable installment obligations, the taxpayer first determined what portion of its assets were represented by applicable installment obligations. The taxpayer determined this portion by dividing the outstanding face amount of its applicable installment obligations at the end of the year by the sum of the outstanding face amount of all installment obligations and the adjusted basis of all other assets. To illustrate, if the taxpayer had $10 million of applicable installment obligations, $5 million of other installment obligations, and an aggregate adjusted basis of $10 million in its remaining assets, the applicable portion of its applicable installment obligations were 40 percent (($10 million) ÷ ($10 million +$5 million +$10 million)).

To determine what portion of the taxpayer's indebtedness would be treated as a payment on the applicable installment obligations each year, the taxpayer first multiplied the percentage just determined by its average quarterly indebtedness during the year and then subtracted the amount treated as a payment on such applicable installment obligations arising in prior years.

A number of special rules and computational procedures could be applicable. For example, in determining the adjusted basis of its assets, a taxpayer could elect to compute basis using straight-line depreciation.[189] In computing the amount of all installment obligations and all other assets, personal use property was excluded.[190] In computing allocable installment indebtedness, if the taxpayer had no installment obligation attributable to dealer sales, then debt at the end of the year was to be used in lieu of average quarterly debt.[191]

The foregoing procedures may be illustrated by the following example, which assumes that the taxpayer was a dealer in real property, used the calendar year as its taxable year, began its operations in 1987, and that all the taxpayer's sales were made at a profit and were accounted for under the installment method.[192]

---

[187] IRC § 453C(e)(4), prior to repeal by 1987 Act.

[188] 1986 Act, § 811(c)(2).

[189] IRC § 453C(b)(2), prior to repeal by 1987 Act.

[190] IRC § 453C(b)(3)(A), prior to repeal by 1987 Act.

[191] IRC § 453C(b)(4), prior to repeal by 1987 Act.

[192] This example was set forth in the Blue Book, at 495–496.

EXAMPLE: *Calendar year 1987.*—During 1987, the taxpayer sells one property for $90,000, taking back the purchaser's note for the entire purchase price. No payments are received on the obligation in 1987.

The aggregate adjusted basis of the taxpayer's assets, other than the installment obligation, is $310,000 as of the end of 1987. The taxpayer's average quarterly indebtedness for 1987 is $200,000.

The taxpayer's allocable installment indebtedness for 1987 would be $45,000. This amount is computed by multiplying (1) the taxpayer's average quarterly indebtedness for 1987 ($200,000) by (2) the quotient of (a) the total face amount of taxpayer's outstanding applicable installment obligations ($90,000) and (b) the sum of (i) the total face amount of the taxpayer's installment obligations ($90,000) and (ii) the adjusted basis of its other assets as of the end of 1987 ($310,000). The taxpayer would be treated as receiving a payment of $45,000 on the outstanding installment obligation as of the close of 1987.

Calendar year 1988.—During 1988, the taxpayer sells another property for $110,000, taking back the purchaser's note for the entire purchase price. No payments are received in 1988 on either the 1987 or 1988 installment obligations held by the taxpayer.

The aggregate adjusted basis of the taxpayer's assets, other than the installment obligations, is $400,000 as of the end of 1988. The taxpayer's average quarterly indebtedness for 1988 is $300,000.

The taxpayer's allocable installment indebtedness for 1988 would be $55,000. This amount is computed by multiplying (1) the taxpayer's average quarterly indebtedness for 1988 ($300,000) by (2) the quotient of (a) the total face amount of the taxpayer's outstanding applicable installment obligations ($200,000) and (b) the sum of (i) the total face amount of the taxpayer's installment obligations ($200,000) and (ii) the adjusted basis of its other assets as of the end of 1988 ($400,000) and (3) subtracting the amount of allocable installment indebtedness allocated to applicable installment obligations that arose prior to 1988 ($45,000). The taxpayer would be treated as having received a payment of $55,000 on the installment obligation that arose in 1988, as of the close of 1988.

Calendar year 1989.—In 1989, the taxpayer sells a third property for $130,000. Also in 1989, the installment obligation that the taxpayer received in 1987 is paid in full. No payments are received on either the obligation that was received in 1988 or the one received in 1989.

The aggregate adjusted basis of the taxpayer's assets, other than its installment obligations, is $360,000 as of the end of 1989. The taxpayer's average quarterly indebtedness for 1989 is $500,000.

With respect to the $90,000 payment that was received on the installment obligation that arose in 1987, the first $45,000 of the payment would not result in the recognition of any additional gain with respect to the obligation and would reduce the amount of allocable installment indebtedness that is treated as allocated to that obligation.

The next $45,000 would be treated as an additional payment on the obligation that results in the recognition of additional gain under the installment method.

Taking into account the payment of the 1987 installment obligation, the allocable installment indebtedness allocated to taxable years before 1989, for purposes of computing allocable installment indebtedness for 1989, would be $55,000 ($45,000 of allocable installment indebtedness from 1987 plus $55,000 of allocable installment indebtedness from 1988 minus $45,000 of allocable installment indebtedness from 1987 returned in 1989).

The taxpayer's allocable installment indebtedness for 1989 would be $145,000. This amount is computed by multiplying (1) the taxpayer's average quarterly indebtedness for 1989 ($500,000) by (2) the quotient of (a) the total face amount of the taxpayer's outstanding applicable installment obligations as of the end of 1989 ($110,000 plus $130,000, or $240,000) and (b) the sum of (i) the total face amount of the taxpayer's installment obligations ($240,000) and (ii) the adjusted basis of its other assets as of the end of 1989 ($360,000) and (3) subtracting the amount of allocable installment indebtedness allocated as of the close of 1989 to applicable installment obligations that arose prior to 1989 ($55,000).

Since the taxpayer's allocable installment indebtedness for 1989 ($145,000) exceeds the amount of applicable installment obligations arising in 1989 and outstanding at the end of the year ($130,000), the taxpayer is treated as having received a payment, as of the close of 1989, of $130,000 on the installment obligation that arose in 1989, and a payment of $15,000 (i.e., the excess of $145,000 over $130,000) on the installment obligation that arose in 1988.

Although the proportionate disallowance rules were subsequently repealed, they may remain applicable to certain installment obligations arising from certain dispositions occurring after August 16, 1986, but in taxable years beginning before January 1, 1988.[193]

[7] Issues Regarding Payments

Issues involving payments often focus on the effect of (1) payments received prior to the year of disposition; (2) the existence in the buyer of a right to prepay; (3) the buyer's payment or assumption of the seller's indebtedness; (4) whether a purchaser's indebtedness is (or should be treated as being) payable on demand or in a form readily tradable in an established securities market; and (5) whether particular arrangements (especially those involving a guarantee) constitute a payment.

---

[193] See also discussion infra ¶ 5.07[2].

[a] Payments Prior to Year of Sale

A payment may be received on account of property prior to the year in which the property is sold. In such a case, the payment generally is treated as a payment in the year of sale. Thus, if a deposit or an option payment on property is received in year 1 with the sale taking place in year 2, the payments received in year 1 will be treated as a payment on the purchase price in year 2, the year of sale.[194]

When determining the year of sale, it is important to analyze the intent of the parties, to determine whether all conditions precedent to consummation of the transaction have been satisfied, and to determine whether all benefits and burdens of ownership have passed.[195] The mere recitation in the agreement of an effective, or "as if," date of sale will not be controlling.

[b] Right to Prepay

Section 453 specifies that at least one payment must be received after the close of the year of sale.[196] If the agreement provides that a payment is to be received in a subsequent year, the mere fact that the purchaser accelerates payment (or has the right to prepay) does not preclude use of the installment method. Such an election would be in the nature of a condition subsequent, which is not taken into account for tax purposes until it occurs.[197] (Of course, if the purchaser does accelerate all payments into the year of sale, there will be no deferred payments, and, in effect, no installment sale.)

By way of contrast, if the purchaser is obligated to make all payments in the year of sale but thereafter fails to make payments when due, the IRS might argue that the installment method is not available because the original agreement did not provide for a payment to be made after the close of the taxable year. Although that position seems silly and, as a practical matter, would arise only infrequently if at all, a taxpayer may avoid the issue by requiring at least one payment in the year following the year of sale. That provision will ensure that the sale will be an installment sale, and gain will be recognized as payments are received.

EXAMPLE: If *A* sells property to *B* for $100, with payment to be made

---

[194] See, e.g., Waukesha Malleable Iron Co. v. Comm'r, 67 F2d 368 (7th Cir. 1933); John F. Westrom, 25 TCM 1019 (1966); Rev. Rul. 73-369, 1973-2 CB 155.

[195] Fletcher v. United States, 303 F. Supp. 583 (ND Ind. 1967), aff'd per curiam, 436 F2d 413 (7th Cir. 1971); Bradford v. United States, 444 F2d 1133 (Ct. Cl. 1971); Ted F. Merrill, 40 TC 66 (1963), aff'd per curiam, 336 F2d 771 (9th Cir. 1964); Karl R. Martin, 44 TC 731 (1965), aff'd on this ground, 379 F2d 282 (6th Cir. 1967); Pacific Coast Music Jobbers, Inc., 55 TC 866 (1971), aff'd, 457 F2d 1165 (5th Cir. 1972).

[196] IRC § 453(b)(1).

[197] See ¶ 4.03[1][a][i] for discussion of conditions subsequent.

in year 1, all gain might have to be recognized in year 1 even if payment is not made until year 2. However, if the agreement provides that $10 of the $100 selling price is due in year 2, gain will be recognized only as payments are received. Thus, if *B* pays the entire $100 in year 2, all gain will be recognized in year 2.

Alternatively, if such a planned deferred payment is not advisable for business reasons, similar protection may be available by modifying the agreement after the determination has been made that a payment will be deferred into the succeeding year. Although questions may then be raised as to whether the initial obligation has been so modified or changed to constitute a taxable exchange for a different obligation, such a conclusion seems unduly harsh and inappropriate.[198]

[c] Payment or Assumption of Seller's Qualifying Indebtedness

It is not unusual for a purchaser to pay (or to agree to pay) various obligations of the seller as part of the consideration for the property acquired. These obligations may include (1) expenses of the seller in connection with the sale itself; (2) existing obligations of the seller secured by the property that is the subject of the sale; or (3) other obligations of the seller unrelated to the transaction or the property.

Does the purchaser's payment or assumption of these obligations of the seller represent payments to the seller for installment sale purposes? For many years, the proper resolution of this question was in doubt.[199] To bring clarity to this area of law, the regulations issued under the 1980 Act provide a new term, "qualifying indebtedness."

If the seller's obligation that is to be paid, assumed, or taken subject to by the purchaser is a qualifying indebtedness, then the amount of that qualifying indebtedness will be treated as a payment only to the extent that amount exceeds the seller's basis in the property (determined after adjustment to include selling expenses). Thus, the amount of the indebtedness that is equal to or less than the seller's basis is not treated as a payment.

If debts of the seller are paid, assumed, or taken subject to by the acquirer and do not qualify as qualifying indebtedness, then the amounts of the debts are treated as payments to the seller in the year of sale. "Qualifying indebtedness" is defined as follows:

> "[Q]ualifying indebtedness" means a mortgage or other indebtedness encumbering the property and indebtedness, not secured by the property but incurred or assumed by the purchaser incident to the purchaser's acquisition, holding, or operation in the ordinary course of

---

[198] See discussion infra ¶ 5.06[4].

[199] See 1980 S. Rep., 1980-2 CB 494, 498–499.

business or investment, of the property. The term "qualifying indebtedness" does not include an obligation of the taxpayer incurred incident to the disposition of the property (*e.g.*, legal fees relating to the taxpayer's sale of the property) or an obligation functionally unrelated to the acquisition, holding, or operating of the property (*e.g.*, the taxpayer's medical bill). Any obligation created subsequent to the taxpayer's acquisition of the property and incurred or assumed by the taxpayer or placed as an encumbrance on the property in contemplation of disposition of the property is not qualifying indebtedness if the arrangement results in accelerating recovery of the taxpayer's basis in the installment sale.[200]

As this definition makes clear, only indebtedness encumbering the property or functionally related to the purchaser's acquisition, holding, or operation of the property may qualify as qualifying indebtedness. Expenses incurred incident to the disposition of the property itself or functionally unrelated to the property will not so qualify. In addition, any indebtedness incurred by the taxpayer after his acquisition of the property and placed on the property in anticipation of its disposition will not so qualify, but only if the arrangement results in accelerating recovery of basis (i.e., deferring the recognition of gain).

For purposes of determining qualifying indebtedness, an assumption is deemed to include any arrangement under which the taxpayer's liability for qualifying indebtedness is eliminated incident to the disposition (e.g., by a novation that involves the release of the original debtor from liability). If the taxpayer sells the property to a creditor and the indebtedness of the taxpayer is canceled as a result, the cancellation amounts to a payment. However, if the cancellation is not consideration for the sale, then it is not treated as a payment but is subject to provisions regarding discharge of indebtedness. If the taxpayer sells encumbered property for which he is not personally liable and the person acquiring the property is the obligee, the taxpayer is treated as having received payment in the amount of such indebtedness.

[d] Third-Party Indebtedness

A purchaser may make payment by transferring to the seller an obligation of another person, i.e., a person other than the purchaser. Such a transfer constitutes a payment for installment sale purposes. However, an exception to this rule exists in the case of third-party indebtedness received by a shareholder in connection with certain corporate liquidations.

For example, Section 453(h) provides that in a liquidation to which Section 331 applies, if a shareholder receives an installment obligation in

---

[200] Temp. Reg. § 15a.453-1(b)(2)(iv).

exchange for its stock and if the liquidating corporation acquired that obligation in connection with its sale or exchange of property during a 12-month period beginning on the date the plan of liquidation was adopted, then the payments received on that obligation are treated as payments received on the exchange of stock. In other words, the taxpayer/shareholder is permitted to use installment reporting even though these are third-party installment obligations. This rule does not extend to obligations arising from a sale of inventory by the corporation unless that sale of inventory was a bulk sale, i.e., a sale to one person involving substantially all the inventory.[201] Special rules are provided to make sure that these nonrecognition rules are not abused where the obligor and the shareholder are related parties.[202] These rules correspond to the rules that were available to transactions under Section 337, as such rules existed prior to the 1986 Act.[203]

[e] Third-Party Guarantees

Since third-party obligations are generally treated as payments, the question arises as to the impact of a third-party guarantee (including a standby letter of credit) of the purchaser's obligation. The key question is whether the purchaser or the guarantor is expected to make the payments. If the guarantor is, in fact, only a guarantor of the purchaser's obligation with the burden of making payment on default by the purchaser, then the third-party guarantee is not to be treated as a payment even though (1) the guarantor may be a government agency or (2) the guarantee may be embodied in a standby letter of credit.[204]

"Standby letter of credit" means a nonnegotiable, nontransferable (except together with the evidence of indebtedness which it secures) letter of credit, which is issued by a bank or other financial institution and serves as a guarantee of the evidence of indebtedness secured by the letter of credit. Applicable local law will control whether the letter of credit is nonnegotiable and nontransferable. The mere right of the secured party under applicable local law to transfer the proceeds of the letter of credit is to be disregarded. A letter of credit is not a standby letter of credit if it may be drawn on in the absence of a default in payment of the underlying evidence of indebtedness.

The use of an escrow or similar security arrangement does not per se amount to a payment, but the substance of such an arrangement will be scrutinized closely. If it appears that the escrowed property is to provide the source of payments, or if the seller has the right to control the escrowed

---

[201] IRC § 453(h)(1)(B).

[202] IRC §§ 453(h)(1)(C)–453(h)(1)(E).

[203] See discussion infra ¶ 5.05[11][a].

[204] Temp. Reg. § 15a.453-1(b)(3)(i).

property (or to reap all benefits from it) during the period it is in escrow, the taxpayer may be treated as having actually received payment under the doctrine of constructive receipt.

The regulations expressly provide that where the purchaser's obligation is secured directly or indirectly by cash or a cash equivalent, such as a bank certificate of deposit or a Treasury note, receipt of the obligation will be treated as receipt of a payment.[205]

[f] Purchaser Debt Payable on Demand or Readily Tradable

The obligation of a purchaser is treated as a payment in the year of its actual or constructive receipt if the obligation (1) is evidenced by an indebtedness that is payable on demand or (2) is issued by a corporation or a governmental or political subdivision thereof and is readily tradable.[206] For this purpose, the term "readily tradable" means an indebtedness issued with interest coupons attached or in registered form or in any other form designed to render such indebtedness readily tradable in an established securities market.[207] An obligation that is issued in registered form will not be treated as a payment in the year of receipt if the taxpayer establishes that the obligation will not be readily tradable in an established securities market.[208]

[8] Computation of Installment Income

The amount of installment income to be recognized each year is that portion of each payment that the gross profit realized (or to be realized) bears to the total contract price. "Gross profit" is defined as the selling price less the adjusted basis of the property as defined in Section 1011. For example, if property with a basis of $60 is sold for $100, the gross profit is $40. The selling price and the contract price are defined in the following sections. The ratio of gross profit to contract price is known as the gross-profit ratio. Each payment received is multiplied by the gross-profit ratio to determine the amount of installment income to be recognized.

[a] Selling Price

The term "selling price" means the gross selling price without reduction to reflect any existing mortgage or other encumbrance on the property and

---

[205] Id.

[206] IRC §§ 453(f)(3), 453(f)(4).

[207] IRC § 453(f)(5). See Priv. Ltr. Rul. 8533004 (May 13, 1985), where a general obligation bond issued by a city to the seller of an electric utility company was found not to be payable on demand or readily tradable.

[208] IRC § 453(f)(5)(A).

without reduction for selling expenses.[209] However, neither stated nor unstated interest original issue discount is considered part of the selling price. Consequently, provisions of the agreement itself or other Code sections that would recharacterize part of the principal as interest must be taken into account.[210]

[b] Selling Expenses

In the case of sales of either real property by a person other than a dealer or casual sales of personal property, commissions and other selling expenses must be added to basis for purposes of determining gross profit and the extent to which qualifying indebtedness exceeds basis. These additions to basis will not affect the holding period of the property.[211]

For dealers (prior to the 1987 Act's repeal of the installment method for most dealers), commissions and other selling expenses were treated as ordinary and necessary business expenses deductible under Section 162 rather than as additions to the basis of the property sold. Thus, use of the installment method by a dealer accelerated the deduction of selling and other expenses as compared to use of the method by a nondealer.[212]

Prior to the 1980 Act, a question existed as to the appropriate treatment of selling expenses.[213] The issue was whether such expenses should be treated (1) as a reduction in the amount realized on the sale or (2) as an addition to the basis of the property. Under the then-applicable regulations, commissions and other selling expenses were taken into account as an offset to selling price for purposes of determining gross profit from a sale by a nondealer but otherwise did not reduce the amount of any payments received, the total contract price, or the selling price.[214] However, in *Kirschenmann v. United States*,[215] the Ninth Circuit held that selling expenses were to be added to the basis of the property. This rule had the effect of reducing the amount by

---

[209] Temp. Reg. § 15a.453-1(b)(2)(ii).

[210] Temp. Reg. §§ 15a.453-1(c)(2)(ii) and 15a.453-1(c)(2)(iii) provide rules and examples, respectively, governing the manner in which the selling price, contract price, and gross profit should be calculated when a portion of the selling price of a contingent price sale may be recharacterized as interest. See also Chapter 11 pertaining to the time value of money.

[211] Temp. Reg. §§ 15a.453-1(b)(2)(v), 15a.453-1(b)(3)(i).

[212] In Tech. Adv. Mem. 8531008 (Apr. 19, 1985), the National Office rejected the position of the examining agent that the deduction of selling expenses in years prior to the years in which gain would be recognized distorted income and resulted in a failure to reflect income clearly. For a discussion of the clear reflection of income standard, see ¶ 2.02[2].

[213] Selling expenses include sales commissions, advertising expenses, attorney fees, other legal fees, and similar expenses.

[214] Treas. Reg. § 1.453-1(b), as in effect prior to 1980 Act.

[215] Kirschenmann v. United States, 488 F2d 270 (9th Cir. 1973).

which debt might exceed basis, which in turn reduced the size of the payment in the year of sale and lessened the risk of a violation of the former 30 percent test. The IRS announced that it would not follow the decision of the Ninth Circuit,[216] but following the 1980 Act, the Treasury promulgated regulations that adopted the position of the Ninth Circuit.

[c] Contract Price

The contract price is equal to the selling price less any qualifying indebtedness that is assumed (or taken subject to) to the extent the qualifying indebtedness does not exceed the seller's basis in the property.[217] To the extent the qualifying indebtedness does exceed the seller's basis in the property, the excess is treated as a payment in the year of sale and does not reduce selling price in determining contract price. Also, to the extent that indebtedness secured by the property is not qualifying indebtedness, the indebtedness is treated as a payment in the year of sale and is ignored for purposes of determining contract price.

The use of the contract price (rather than the selling price) to determine the gross-profit ratio is a rule of administrative convenience. It was designed to deal with the problem of recognizing gain on installment payments when at least some of the payments would be made to the holder of the mortgage rather than to the seller. The explanation for the contract price rule was set forth by the United States Supreme Court in *Burnet v. S.&L. Building Corp.*:[218]

> The method suggested by the respondent [*i.e.*, to compute the installment income on the basis of all payments made by the purchaser without regard to the fact that some of those payments would be made directly to the holder of the existing indebtedness] would inevitably lead to many practical difficulties; might postpone collection far beyond the time when the vendor would receive any direct payments; and probably would render impossible determination from the taxpayer's books of what he should account for.

Later in *J. Carl Horneff*,[219] the Tax Court had occasion to review the history of the rule and the reasons for its use. The court stated:

> The rationale behind the early regulation [setting forth the contract price rule], and the reason why the term "contract price" is to this day

---

[216] Rev. Rul. 74-384, 1974-2 CB 152.

[217] "Qualifying indebtedness" is defined and discussed supra ¶ 5.05[7][c].

[218] Burnet v. S.&L. Bldg. Corp., 288 US 406, 414 (1933).

[219] J. Carl Horneff, 50 TC 63 (1968).

given an artificial meaning in applying the installment sales provisions in mortgage situations, was explained by the Supreme Court in *Burnet v. S. & L. Bldg. Corp., supra.* The installment method of reporting requires a *portion* of every payment made by the buyer to be taxed as gain to the seller. If the buyer assumes a mortgage or other liability of the seller, in all cases in which the regulation does not apply, recognition of gain is spread over not only the payments made by the buyer to the seller but also over payments made by the buyer to creditors of the seller. Thus, each time the buyer makes a payment to a creditor of the seller, the seller must report some income. This application of the installment method results from including liabilities assumed in the "contract price," the denominator in the fraction which produces the gross-profit percent by definition of section 453(a). If these assumed liabilities are included in the denominator, it is easy to see that in order to tax the entire net gain it is necessary to apply the gross-profit percent to the payment of the assumed liabilities, even though these payments are not made to the seller but to some third party.

In order to eliminate the administrative inconvenience of imposing and collecting a tax from the seller every time the buyer made a payment to the third party mortgagee, the original version of article 44, Regs. 69, was promulgated by the Commissioner. By defining "contract price," the term used in the statute to describe the denominator in the gross-profit percent fraction, as not including the amount of an assumed mortgage, the regulation has the effect of raising the gross-profit percent, thereby permitting a recognition of all the gain solely upon payments made directly to the seller. As the Supreme Court said in *Burnet v. S. & L. Bldg. Corp., supra*, in the case of an assumption of a mortgage, if the installment method were not applied in a manner prescribed in the regulation, it "would inevitably lead to many practical difficulties, might postpone collection far beyond the time when the vendor would receive any direct payments, and probably would render impossible determination from the taxpayer's books of what he should account for."[220]

This judicial analysis makes the following points clear. First, the contract rule is a departure from the normal rule of installment reporting that a portion of every payment made by the buyer should be taxed as a gain to the seller. Second, the normal rule would be difficult to apply in circumstances involving an assumption of the underlying debt and might postpone the recognition of income by the seller far beyond the time when he would be receiving payments from the buyer with which he could pay the tax.[221] Third, the contract price rule was a rule of administrative convenience designed to deal with "unusual circumstances"; the "unusual circumstances" being that some payments by the buyer would go to a third party rather than

---

[220] Id. at 71–72.

[221] Of course, the reason for installment reporting in the first place was to permit the seller to pay the tax as he received payments with which he could pay the tax. Burnet v. S.&L. Bldg. Corp., 288 US 406, 413 (1933). See discussion supra ¶ 5.01.

to the seller. Fourth, if all payments by the buyer went directly to the seller, the rule would be unnecessary.

[d] Sale of Multiple Assets

In some cases, a taxpayer may sell or exchange several items of property for an aggregate price. If the purchaser and seller are dealing at arm's length and allocate the total purchase price among the properties being sold, that allocation generally will be respected by the IRS and the courts.[222] On the other hand, if the sales agreement does not allocate the purchase price among the assets (or if it is determined that the parties did not act at arm's length and, hence, that their allocation should be disregarded), then the purchase price must be allocated among the assets on the basis of their relative FMVs.[223]

It is frequently helpful to taxpayers to allocate among the properties being sold both the aggregate purchase price and the particular installment payments to be made. For example, the agreement could specify that early payments are to be allocated (1) to items of inventory that may have a high basis; (2) to assets on which losses will be recognized; and (3) to other items for which installment reporting is not available. In this way, by allocating the later payments to items for which installment reporting is available, the maximum deferral of gain may be achieved.

Similarly, taxpayers may sell property that could easily be the subject of separate sales. For example, a taxpayer selling several acres of land may sell all the land for an aggregate price or, depending on the intent of the parties, may engage in a series of sales of separate parcels consisting of specified acres. Careful consideration should be given to the best way of structuring such sales. If the different parcels have different tax bases, the taxpayer may benefit from precise allocations or from a series of separate sales. Separate sales may be particularly appropriate where the property will serve as security for the purchaser's obligation and where parcels will be released for development only as payments are received. Such taxpayers and their advisors will need to consider carefully whether the sales constitute "dealer dispositions" for which installment reporting may not be available, or dispositions for which special rules requiring the payment of interest on deferred payments are applicable.[224]

---

[222] Williams v. McGowan, 152 F2d 570 (2d Cir. 1945); Rev. Rul. 55-79, 1955-1 CB 370; Rev. Rul. 68-13, 1968-1 CB 195.

[223] Williams v. McGowan, 152 F2d 570 (2d Cir. 1945); Rev. Rul. 55-79, 1955-1 CB 370; Rev. Rul. 68-13, 1968-1 CB 195.

[224] See IRC §§ 453(b)(2), 453A, and discussion infra ¶¶ 5.07[1], 5.07[3].

[9] Recapture Under Sections 1245 and 1250

On any deferred payment sale or other disposition, all income to be recaptured (i.e., treated as ordinary income rather than capital gain) under Sections 1245 and 1250 as well as property expensed pursuant to Section 179 must be recognized in the year of sale or other disposition without regard to when payments are received.[225] This requirement of immediate recapture was added to the Code in 1984.[226]

Prior to the 1984 Act, the applicable rule required the recognition of recapture only as payments were received. Thus, the 1984 Act provides a potential trap for those who are not aware of it. As illustrated later in this section, a taxpayer with substantial recapture income to be recognized may have a substantial tax liability in the year of sale even though he may not receive payments in that year that would provide him with the cash to pay the tax.

Although regulations have not yet been promulgated setting forth the manner in which the gain in excess of the recapture will be recognized, the report of the Senate Finance Committee suggested that the gross-profit ratio should be computed on the basis of the ratio of (1) gain in excess of recapture to (2) contract price.[227] In other words, the amount of the recapture income will be added to basis with the difference between the amount realized and the newly adjusted basis as the gross profit for this purpose.

EXAMPLE: Assume property with an adjusted basis of $30 is sold for $100, to be paid at the rate of $10 per year for each of 10 years. If depreciation, subject to recapture of $40, had been taken on the property, the $70 of gain will be reported as follows: $40 will be reported in the year of sale; the balance of $30 will be reported ratably as payments are made.

As this illustration demonstrates, under the depreciation recapture requirement, not only will the depreciation recapture income be accelerated as compared to prior law, but also recognition of the balance of the gain will be accelerated as compared to prior law. Under prior law, gain in the previous example would have been recognized at the rate of $7 per year for each of 10 years. The gain would have been applied first to depreciation recapture to the extent thereof with the balance treated as capital gain.

---

[225] IRC § 453(i).

[226] IRC § 453(i), added by the Tax Reform Act of 1984 (the 1984 Act), § 112. This provision was effective for dispositions made after June 6, 1984, except for sales pursuant to a contract that was binding on March 22, 1984, and thereafter.

[227] General Explanation of the Revenue Provisions of the Deficit Reduction Act of 1984, at 333–335 (Dec. 31, 1984).

[10] Wraparound Mortgages

Where encumbered property is sold subject to an underlying indebtedness (or the purchaser assumes the indebtedness), it is typically contemplated that payment of the underlying obligation thereafter will be made by the purchaser and that payments from the purchaser to the seller will represent the seller's equity in the property. However, in some cases, the transaction is structured so that the seller will be expected to pay the underlying indebtedness, with all payments by the purchaser made directly to the seller. In this latter case, the obligation of the purchaser to the seller is said to "wrap" the underlying obligation and, if secured by the property, is referred to as a wraparound mortgage.

[a] Reasons for Use

Apart from the tax benefits discussed in this section, there are several nontax reasons for the use of a wraparound mortgage. First, there may be economic benefits to the seller in retaining the underlying indebtedness. The underlying indebtedness may be at a favorable interest rate. By using a wraparound mortgage, the seller is able to earn interest at the current rate from the buyer and yet pay a lower rate on the underlying indebtedness thereby achieving an economic gain equal to the difference between the rates. For example, if an underlying indebtedness were $1 million requiring interest at a rate of 10 percent per annum and the wraparound indebtedness were $2 million earning interest at a rate of 12 percent per annum, then, assuming no principal amortization, the yield on the seller's equity investment would be 14 percent per annum, 12 percent on equity of $1 million plus 2 percent on the underlying indebtedness of $1 million. If the rate of principal amortization of the underlying indebtedness is faster than the rate of principal amortization of the wraparound indebtedness, the overall economic return to the seller will be increased through the use of the wraparound. In other words, the seller's equity in the property is increasing more rapidly than the buyer's equity in the property and, to use the preceding example, the seller will be earning 12 percent on a larger amount and 2 percent on a smaller amount.

In some cases, a wraparound mortgage is used to protect the seller. For example, it is often the case that for a significant period, the seller's equity in the property will be greater than that of the buyer. Through the use of the wraparound mortgage, the seller is able to make certain that payments will be made to the holder of the underlying indebtedness and that no events will occur that would trigger the right of the holder to accelerate the underlying indebtedness, foreclose on it, or otherwise take action that could have an adverse economic effect on either the seller or the property.

In other cases, the holder of the underlying indebtedness may prefer to continue to look to the seller rather than to the purchaser for making all payments on the underlying indebtedness. In that case, the holder will prefer or will require the use of a wraparound mortgage before it will approve a transfer of the property.

[b] Law Prior to 1980 Act

Although the Treasury promulgated proposed/temporary regulations governing the treatment of wraparound mortgages subsequent to the 1980 Act, substantial questions were raised as to the validity of these regulations,[228] and in July 1987, the Tax Court held the regulations invalid.[229] For this reason, the cases and their authorities that predated the 1980 Act remain relevant.[230]

Cases decided under the law prior to the 1980 Act suggested that a sale of property using a "true" wraparound mortgage did not involve a transfer of property where the purchaser either (1) assumed the existing mortgage or (2) took the property subject to the existing mortgage. Hence, the contract price was not reduced, and gain was recognized as payments (including payments on the wraparound indebtedness) were made to the seller. The IRS initially took the position that all sales of encumbered property should be treated alike. This position was soundly rejected by the Tax Court:[231]

> While the regulation first refers broadly to "the sale of mortgaged property," the language following this broad reference describes the two types of sales of mortgaged property to which the regulation applies: (a) where a buyer takes property subject to mortgage, or (b) assumes the mortgage. These expressions we take to have the meaning customarily attributed to them in transactions concerned with the transfer of mortgaged property. *Crane v. Commissioner*, 331 U.S. 1, 6 (1947). Taking property subject to a mortgage means that the buyer pays the seller for the latter's redemption interest, i.e., the difference between the amount of the mortgage debt and the total amount for which the property is being sold, but the buyer does not assume a personal obligation to pay the mortgage debt. The buyer agrees that as between him and the seller, the latter has no obligation to satisfy the mortgage debt, and that the debt is to be satisfied out of the property. Although he is not obliged to, the buyer will ordinarily make the payments on the mortgage debt

---

[228] See discussion infra ¶ 5.05[10][c].

[229] Professional Equities Inc., 89 TC No. 165 (1987). See also Vincent E. Webb, 54 TCM 443 (1987).

[230] In 1988, the IRS acquiesced to the decision in *Professional Equities.* See 1988-2 CB 1. However, the regulations have not yet been withdrawn or modified. Consequently, taxpayers who desire to follow the regulations apparently may do so.

[231] Stonecrest Corp., 24 TC 659, 666 (1955), nonacq., 1956-1 CB 6; see also United Pac. Corp., 39 TC 721 (1963); R.A. Waldrep, 52 TC 640 (1969), aff'd per curiam, 428 F2d 1216 (5th Cir. 1970); Frank Hutchison, 42 TCM 1089 (1981); D.A. Hunt, 80 TC 1126 (1983).

in order to protect his interest in the property. Where a buyer assumes a mortgage on property, he pays the seller for the latter's redemption interest, and in addition promises the seller to pay off the mortgage debt. This promise of the buyer can ordinarily be enforced by the mortgagee. 5 Tiffany, The Law of Real Property, secs. 1435, 1436 (3d ed. 1939); IV American Law of Property, secs. 16.125, 16.127, 12.128-16.132 (1952).

Thereafter, the IRS challenged particular transactions on the basis that they did not involve true wraparound mortgages but, rather, assumptions of a mortgage or the taking of property subject to it. The IRS was often successful with this approach.[232]

Although wraparound mortgages were used for nontax reasons, they also were perceived to have a potential for tax abuse. Taxpayers could "mortgage out" property prior to a sale and then sell the property under a wraparound mortgage. This procedure would avoid the impact of the rules governing mortgages in excess of basis, i.e., under wraparound treatment, the excess of debt over basis would not be treated as a payment in the year of sale.

EXAMPLE: Assume that property has a basis of $100 and an FMV of $200. If the taxpayer wanted to defer the recognition of gain on a sale of the property, yet receive all the cash immediately, he could mortgage the property for $200, then sell the property for a $200 wraparound mortgage. Gain would be recognized only as payments were made on the wraparound obligation.[233]

[c] Regulations Under 1980 Act

Neither the 1980 Act nor its legislative history suggested a congressional desire to change the treatment of wraparound mortgages. Indeed, the relevant Committee Report recognized the use of the wraparound technique in connection with the congressional decision to eliminate the 30 percent rule.[234] Interestingly, Congress sought only to eliminate the 30 percent

---

[232] See, e.g., R.A. Waldrep, 52 TC 640 (1969), aff'd per curiam, 428 F2d 1216 (5th Cir. 1970); Floyd J. Voight, 68 TC 99 (1977), aff'd per curiam, 614 F2d 94 (5th Cir. 1980); Republic Petroleum Corp. v. United States, 613 F2d 518 (5th Cir. 1980); William J. Goodman, 74 TC 684 (1980), nonacq. 1981-2 CB 3; Orville C. Wacker, 40 TCM 1009 (1980); Frank Hutchison, 42 TCM 1089 (1981).

[233] But see Temp. Reg. § 15a.453-1(b)(2)(iv) defining "qualifying indebtedness," and discussion supra ¶ 5.05[7][c] for rules that may preclude such mortgaging out notwithstanding the use of wraparound mortgages or the validity of the temporary regulations governing such mortgages. See also the impact of the 1987 Act, discussed infra ¶ 5.07.

[234] The 1980 Senate Report, 1980-2 CB 494, 498, stated:

requirement. It did not suggest any problem with the use of wraparound mortgages and even suggested that their use was appropriate under prior law as a means of avoiding the 30 percent test.

Notwithstanding the foregoing, the Treasury promulgated regulations setting forth new rules governing the use of wraparound mortgages in connection with installment reporting. The new rules seek to adopt the prior position of the IRS, but in some key respects they differ from that position.

Under the temporary regulations, the wrapped indebtedness will be deemed to have been taken subject to the underlying indebtedness,[235] even if title to the property does not pass in the year of sale and even if the seller remains liable for payments on the wrapped indebtedness. Gain will be recognized on payments made in the year of sale as if the property had been sold subject to the underlying indebtedness. Remaining gain will be recognized proportionately over time as payments are made on the wraparound obligation.[236]

Substantial adverse reaction has focused on the Treasury's authority to promulgate such regulations, as well as the soundness of those regulations. A principal problem is that where payments are made in the year of sale, use

---

The problem arising from this treatment [i.e., treatment of mortgage in excess of basis as payment in the year of sale] does not involve its correctness but rather the inadvertent disqualification of the sale for installment method reporting for failing to take the amount of the mortgage in excess of basis into account for the 30-percent initial payment requirement. Where the taxpayers are cognizant of problems of this type, the 30-percent requirement has fostered ingenious 'wrap-around' mortgage arrangements to qualify for installment method reporting.

Under the wrap-around arrangement, the buyer does not assume the mortgage and agrees not to make direct payments to the mortgagee but agrees to make the payments to the seller who will continue to pay the mortgage debt. In one case, the wrap-around technique was used by having the seller retain title to the property for a period of years so there would be no transfer of property "subject to" the existing mortgage. If title passes in the year of sale, the Internal Revenue Service will treat the mortgage debt in excess of basis as a payment received in the year of sale. This issue is said to be another instance of the 30-percent initial payment rule fostering uncertainty and litigation.

[235] See discussion supra ¶ 5.05[10][b] for a description of what is meant by taking property subject to an indebtedness.

[236] Temp. Reg. § 15a.453-1(b)(3)(ii) provides that for this purpose, the gross-profit ratio shall be a fraction, the numerator of which is the face value of the obligation less the taxpayer's basis in the obligation and the denominator of which is the face value of the obligation. The taxpayer's basis in the wraparound obligation is the taxpayer's basis in the property that was sold, increased by any gain recognized in the year of sale, and decreased by the amount of any cash and the FMV of any payments received in the year of sale. The rules described in the text are illustrated by the examples set forth infra ¶ 5.05[10][d].

of the new regulations requires the use of different gross-profit percentages, one in the year of sale and another for all subsequent years.[237]

[d] Potential Benefit From New Regulations

Assuming the regulations are followed (or are ultimately found valid or are repromulgated in a similar form that is found to be valid), they open the door to interesting planning possibilities for taxpayers. Because at least part of the gain will be recognized over the term of the wraparound obligation, the treatment prescribed in the temporary regulations will not be identical to the treatment prescribed under the normal subject-to rules. Where the payout of the seller's equity is over a term that is shorter than the remaining term of the wrapped indebtedness, the temporary regulations will defer the reporting of income as compared to the treatment accorded to a typical subject-to transaction (see Example 1 below). On the other hand, when the terms of the wraparound provide for a payout of the seller's equity over a term that is longer than the remaining term of the underlying indebtedness, the prescribed regulatory treatment will accelerate the reporting of income as compared to normal subject-to reporting (see Example 2 below). Where the initial payment will not be made in the year of sale, the temporary regulations treat wraparounds just as they were treated under prior law—with one exception. Under prior law, such treatment was available only if the sale involved a true wraparound mortgage. The temporary regulations prescribe such treatment even for purported wraparounds (see Example 3 below), i.e., those that are wraparound mortgages only in form, but are substantively more in the nature of a transaction where the purchaser takes the property subject to the underlying indebtedness.

---

[237] Under Section 453(a), the installment method is based on recognizing a proportionate portion of each payment received by the seller. It has been held that the predecessor to this provision required the use of an unchanging percentage or ratio to all payments received by the seller. See Estate of E.P. Lamberth, 31 TC 302, 318 (1958), nonacq. 1959-1 CB 6, in which the court said:

> [I]t was the purpose of section 44 [the predecessor to section 453] that a constant proportion, determined by a fixed ratio of gross profit to total contract price, of each installment payment be returned as income. It was not intended that the first payments be taxed completely to the extent of gain and that the latter payments represent recovery of cost and be tax-free.

It was understood that the IRS was troubled by this problem and that thought was given to changing the temporary regulations to provide for the use of a fixed percentage. However, no change was ever promulgated. This very problem was also focused on by the Tax Court in Professional Equities, Inc., 89 TC No. 165 (1987), where the court held the temporary regulations governing wraparound mortgages to be invalid. See also Vincent E. Webb, 54 TCM 443 (1987).

EXAMPLE 1: *Seller's equity paid out more rapidly than underlying indebtedness.*

Assume that property has an FMV of $2,000, a basis of $1,200, and is encumbered by an indebtedness of $1,000 to be paid over a period of 20 years at the rate of $50 per year, beginning with the year following the year of sale. Assume further that the seller's $1,000 of equity in the property (the difference between the value of the property and the existing debt) will be paid off with a down payment of $200 in the year of sale and $100 per year for each of the next eight years. Under prior law and the temporary regulations, the recognition of income will be as follows:

Income	If sale of property is subject to debt	If property is sold using wrap Under prior law	If property is sold using wrap Under temporary regulations
Year of sale	$160	$ 80	$160
Subsequent years 1–8	80 each	60 each	53. each
Subsequent years 9–20	—	20 each	18 each
Total	$800	$800	$800

If the sale is subject to the underlying debt, the contract price is $1,000 (selling price of $2,000 less existing debt of $1,000). The gross profit is $800 (selling price of $2,000 less basis of $1,200). The gross-profit percentage is 80 percent ($800 ÷ $1,000). Installment income in the year of sale is $160 (80 percent of $200). Installment income in each of the subsequent years 1 through 8 is $80 (80 percent of each $100 of equity paid to the seller). No payments of the underlying indebtedness are received by the seller.

If the property is sold using a wraparound indebtedness, then under old law, the contract price is $2,000, the gross profit is $800, and the gross-profit percentage is 40 percent ($800 ÷ $2,000). Under the agreement, the buyer will pay the seller $200 in the year of sale. The wraparound mortgage will have a face amount of $1,800 and call for payments of $150 for subsequent years 1 through 8 and $50 for subsequent years 9 through 20. Installment income in the year of sale is $80 (40 percent of $200). Installment income in each of the subsequent years 1 through 8 is $60 (40 percent of $150). Installment income in each of the subsequent years 9 through 20 is $20 (40 percent of $50).

Under the temporary regulations, the wraparound indebtedness has the same terms as in the preceding paragraph. However, the contract price is $1,000 ($2,000 − $1,000). The gross profit is $800, and the gross-profit percentage in the year of sale is 80 percent ($800 ÷ $1,000). For subsequent years, the gross-profit percentage will be 35.56 percent, computed as follows: basis of wraparound indebtedness = $1,200 (basis of property sold) + $160 (gain recognized in year of sale) − $200 (cash received in year of sale) = $1,160; gross profit percentage = ($1,800 face amount − $1,160 basis) ÷ $1,800 = 35.56 percent. Installment income in the year of sale is $160 (80 percent of $200), just as if the property had been sold with the purchaser taking the property subject to the underlying debt. Installment income in each of the subsequent years 1 through 8 and 9 through 20, respectively, is $53 (35.56 percent of $150) and $18 (35.56 percent of $50).

EXAMPLE 2: *Underlying indebtedness paid off more rapidly than seller's equity.*

Assume the same facts as in Example 1, except that the underlying mortgage calls for remaining payments of $200 per year for five years, with the first payment due in the year following the year of sale. In that case, the reporting of income would be as follows:

| | If sale of | If property is sold using wrap | |
| | property is | Under | Under |
Income	subject to debt	prior law	temporary regulations
Year of sale	$160	$ 80	$160
Subsequent years 1–5	80	120 each	107 each
Subsequent years 6–8	80 each	40 each	35 each
Subsequent years 9–20	—	—	—
Total	$800	$800	$800

As in the preceding example, where the property is sold subject to the underlying debt, the contract price, the gross profit, and the gross-profit percentage are as follows: contract price = $2,000 − $1,000 = $1,000; gross profit = $2,000 − $1,200 = $800; gross-profit percent = $800 ÷ $1,000 = 80 percent.

Where a wraparound indebtedness is used, then under prior law, these three items would be computed as follows: contract price = $2,000; gross profit = $800; gross-profit percentage = $800 ÷ $2,000 = 40 percent. Installment income in the year of sale is $80 (40 percent of $200). Installment income in each of the subsequent years 1 through 5 and 6 through 8, respectively, is $120 (40 percent of ($100 payout of equity plus $200 of underlying debt)) and $40 (40 percent of remaining $100 payout of equity).

Under the temporary regulations, these three items would be computed as follows in the year of sale: contract price = $2,000 − $1,000 = $1,000; gross profit = $800; gross-profit percentage in year of sale = $800 ÷ $1,000 = 80 percent. For subsequent years, the gross-profit percentage will be 35.56 percent, computed as follows: basis of wraparound indebtedness = $1,200 + $160 − $200 = $1,160; gross-profit percentage = ($1,800 − $1,160) ÷ $1,800 = 35.56 percent. Installment income in the year of sale is the same as if the property had been sold subject to the underlying debt. Installment income in each subsequent year is simply 35.56 percent of the payment received ($300 in each of the subsequent years 1 through 5 and $100 in each of the subsequent years 6 through 8).

EXAMPLE 3: *No payments in year of sale.*

Assume the same facts as in Example 1, except that the initial payment of $200 will be deferred until the first year following the year of sale. The recognition of income would be as follows:

Income	If sale of property is subject to debt	If property is sold using wrap — Under prior law	If property is sold using wrap — Under temporary regulations
Year of sale	$ 0	$ 0	$ 0
Subsequent year 1	240	140	140
Subsequent years 2–8	80 each	60 each	60 each
Subsequent years 9–20	—	20 each	20 each
Total	$800	$800	$800

When the sale is subject to the underlying debt, the contract price, gross profit, and gross-profit percentage are computed as follows: contract price = $2,000 − $1,000 = $1,000; gross profit = $2,000 − $1,200 = $800; gross-profit percentage = $800 ÷ $1,000 = 80 percent.

If a wraparound mortgage is used, then under prior law these three items would be computed as follows: contract price = $2,000; gross profit = $800; gross-profit percentage = $800 ÷ $2,000 = 40 percent.

Under the temporary regulations, in the year of sale, these items would be computed as follows: contract price = $2,000 − $1,000 = $1,000; gross profit = $800; gross-profit percentage in year of sale = 80 percent. For subsequent years, the gross-profit percentage will be 40 percent, computed as follows: basis of wraparound = $1,200; gross-profit percentage = ($2,000 − $1,200) ÷ $2,000 = 40 percent. In each case, installment income is determined merely by multiplying the applicable gross-profit percentage times the payment received.

The foregoing examples point up that in particular circumstances, the use of a wraparound mortgage (in concert with the present temporary regulations) will provide a deferral in the recognition of income as compared to normal subject-to reporting. Under the regulations, this deferral is available even where the wraparound mortgage is not a true wraparound but only a purported wraparound. Taxpayers may be expected to take advantage of this possibly unintended consequence of the temporary regulations. The Treasury was advised of this consequence soon after the issuance of the temporary regulations but, to date, has not responded.

The potential for abuse inherent in these regulations (by causing taxpayers to benefit by arranging transactions in a form that differs from their substance) highlights the difficulty of employing additional, complex rules to attack other perceived abuse. In this case the abuse the Treasury perceived was in allowing taxpayers to use wraparound mortgages to avoid the rules governing debt in excess of basis.[238] If the initially perceived abuse is not significant, it is often less costly to accept it rather than to attempt to close it and in the process open new opportunities for abuse.

[11] Related-Party Sales

Prior to the 1980 Act, the installment method was available for sales between related parties even though a subsequent resale might accelerate the realization of cash within the related-party group without a concurrent recognition of gain. For example, A could sell property to B, a related party, for an amount equal to the property's FMV. A would elect to report the gain on the installment method. B would thereafter resell the property at its FMV for cash or other property. On resale, the related-party group would have received all the cash (or other property), but gain would be recognized only over time as payments were received on the original sale.

> EXAMPLE: Assume that property with a basis of $40,000 and an FMV of $100,000 was sold by A to related party B for a $100,000 note to be paid at the rate of $5,000 per year for 20 years. Under prior law, A would recognize the gain of $60,000 at the rate of only $3,000 per year (60 percent of each payment of $5,000). If B resold the property for its FMV of $100,000, there would be no taxable gain to B on the transaction, because the amount realized ($100,000) would not exceed B's basis in the property (also $100,000). Yet, all the gain would have been received within the related-party group.

The IRS often sought to disallow the tax benefits arising from these related-party transactions. In some cases, it was successful, such as where the related-party buyer was found to be the agent of the seller, or the original seller was found to be in constructive receipt of the proceeds of the second sale, or the original sale was found not to be a bona fide sale.[239] However, in other cases, the IRS was not successful.[240] Frequently, in these other cases,

---

[238] See discussion supra ¶¶ 5.05[8][c], 5.05[10][b].

[239] See, e.g., Paul G. Lustgarten, 71 TC 303 (1978), aff'd per curiam, 639 F2d 1208 (5th Cir. 1981), sale to son; and Philip W. Wrenn, 67 TC 576 (1976), sale to spouse. For a discussion of constructive receipt, see ¶ 3.03[2].

[240] See, e.g., W.B. Rushing, 441 F2d 593 (5th Cir. 1971), aff'g, 52 TC 888 (1969); James H. Weaver, 71 TC 443 (1978), aff'd per curiam, 647 F2d 690 (6th Cir. 1981); William D. Pityo, 70 TC 225 (1978); Nye v. United States, 407 F. Supp. 1345 (MDNC 1975); Stewart v. United States, 739 F2d 411 (9th Cir. 1984); Lorraine T. Fink, 43 TCM 1452 (1982); Robert R. Bowen, 78 TC 55 (1982), acq. 1982-2 CB 1, aff'd on other issues, 706 F2d 1087 (11th Cir. 1983).

the use of related-party transactions was seen by the court, not as abuse, but as taxpayer self-help.

For example, prior to the 1980 Act, the installment method had not been available to the sale of a business in a transaction involving the application of then-applicable Section 337 pursuant to which no gain or loss would be recognized by a corporation on certain sales of property made pursuant to a plan of liquidation. Consequently, if a taxpayer sold shares of stock in his corporation for an installment obligation, he could recognize the gain over time under the installment method. However, if the corporation's assets were sold for an installment obligation under then-applicable Section 337 and the installment obligation was then distributed to the taxpayer in complete liquidation of the selling corporation, the installment method would not be available to the shareholder, and recognition of the gain could not be deferred. The problem was attributable to the fact that on liquidation, the taxpayer received third-party notes.[241]

To prevent this disparity in treatment and to achieve installment reporting, the seller might sell his stock to a related party under the installment method; then the related-party buyer would cause the corporation to sell its assets under Section 337 and liquidate. Gain would be recognized by the original seller of stock only as payments were made by the related-party buyer. The liquidation itself would cause little, if any, gain or loss.

In the 1980 Act, Congress decided that shareholders in Section 337 transactions such as that previously described should be treated similarly to shareholders who sell stock to an unrelated purchaser on the installment method. Congress also decided to eliminate the otherwise perceived tax avoidance attributable to allowing the realization of appreciation within a related-party group without the concurrent recognition of gain and payment of tax.

Although the 1980 Act has seemingly resolved the prior problems for both taxpayers and the IRS, situations may still arise where a taxpayer benefits from a sale to a related party followed by a resale. Where the original seller would recognize capital gain (such as on a sale of raw land that is to be developed and sold in units that generate ordinary income) or where the original seller is in a high tax bracket relative to the related party, such a sale/resale transaction may still be attractive and available, as long as the rules in the following sections are not violated.[242]

---

[241] See, e.g., West Shore Fuel, Inc. v. United States, 598 F2d 1236 (2d Cir. 1979). For a discussion of the receipt of third-party notes being treated as the receipt of a payment, see supra ¶ 5.05[7][d].

[242] See Bradshaw v. United States, 683 F2d 365 (Ct. Cl. 1982), involving an exchange of land to a controlled corporation. See also the impact of the 1987 Act, discussed infra ¶ 5.07.

[a] Installment Obligations Received in Corporate Liquidations

Prior to the 1986 Act, which repealed Section 337, Section 453(h) had permitted installment reporting in connection with Section 337 transactions. Hence, installment obligations would not be treated as a payment received by the shareholder for his stock if the obligations were (1) acquired as a result of a sale or exchange of property by a corporation pursuant to the nonrecognition provisions of Section 337 and (2) distributed to a shareholder on a liquidation to which Section 331 applied.[243] Rather, the payments received pursuant to the obligation would be treated as payments for the stock. To obtain similar treatment with respect to obligations arising from the corporation's sale of inventory, the sale of inventory had to constitute a bulk sale.[244]

Although the 1986 Act repealed Section 337, use of the installment method with respect to installment obligations distributed to shareholders in connection with liquidations under Section 331 is still available.[245] The special provisions that permit installment reporting in the context of these liquidations will not apply if (1) the installment obligation arose from a sale of depreciable property by the corporation and (2) the issuer of the installment obligation and the shareholder who receives the obligation on liquidation are either husband and wife or are related within the meaning of Section 1239(b).[246] Under these circumstances, all payments to be received under the installment obligation will be treated as received in the year the shareholder receives the obligation.[247] Thus, for this purpose, the obligation is to be taken into account not at its FMV but at its face amount.

The installment sales rules regarding a "second disposition by related persons"[248] also may apply in the context of a Section 453(h) transaction.

---

[243] The 1980 Senate Report, 1980-2 CB 494, 505, n.27, provides as follows:

This treatment will apply to the target company in an acquisition if it is treated as having liquidated under [then-applicable] Code section 337 (Rev. Rul. 69-6, 1969-1 CB 104). Further, in the case of a corporate acquisition involving the use of a "transitory" or "phantom" company, the obligations issued by the acquiring parent company would be considered issued by the "purchaser," although the assets of the acquired company are technically transferred to the transitory company set up to effect the acquisition, if that company is disregarded for Federal tax purposes under present law.

[244] IRC § 337(b)(2)(B).

[245] IRC § 453(h) as amended by the 1986 Act.

[246] IRC § 453(h)(1)(C). Section 1239(b) defines the term "related persons" to mean a corporation or a partnership and a shareholder or a partner, respectively, who owns more than 50 percent of the value of the outstanding stock or interest in capital and profits, an entity that is related to a person under certain provisions of Section 267(b), and (with certain exceptions) a person and any trust in which the taxpayer or his spouse is the beneficiary.

[247] IRC § 453(h)(1)(C)(ii).

[248] See discussion infra ¶ 5.05[11][b].

Under these rules, if a person disposes of property to a related person on the installment method and, before all the installment payments are received, the related person disposes of the property, the amount received by the related party on the second disposition is deemed to have been received by the party making the original installment sale. This result prevents related parties from engaging in an installment sale in order to step up the basis of property without immediate recognition of gain and then selling the property to a third party to obtain cash within the related-party group.[249] For purposes of this provision, the shareholder who receives the installment obligation is deemed to have made the original disposition of property, i.e., the shareholder is deemed to have made the sale.[250]

> **EXAMPLE:** Assume that a taxpayer owns stock with a basis of $200,000 and that the corporation sells property for $1 million, of which $250,000 is received in cash and $750,000 is evidenced by an installment note. The gain on the sale is $800,000. If the corporation is liquidated and the cash and note are distributed to the taxpayer at the same time, 80 percent of the cash and 80 percent of each payment on the note will be recognized as installment income by the taxpayer in the year of receipt. If the $250,000 of cash is distributed in year 1 and the note is distributed in year 2, then $50,000 of gain will be recognized in year 1 ($250,000 received less basis of $200,000); in year 2, on distribution of the note, the overall gross-profit percentage will be determined and applied against the cash received and payments under the note. An amended return must be filed for year 1 in which an additional $150,000 of gain will be reported (80 percent of $250,000 less $50,000 originally recognized), and 80 percent of each payment thereafter received under the note must be reported as gain.[251]

[b] Related-Party Rules

To prevent the abuse that had been perceived in connection with certain related-party transactions, special rules have been provided. These rules cover the situation where property is sold to a related party who then disposes of the property before the original seller has recognized all the gain on the first installment sale. The rules are designed to ensure that gain on the original installment sale is recognized as cash is received within the related-party group.

Separate rules were initially promulgated for each of three categories of transactions. The first category consists of sales or other dispositions of mar-

---

[249] IRC § 453(e).
[250] IRC § 453(h)(1)(D).
[251] 1980 S. Rep., 1980-2 CB 494, 505.

ketable securities to related parties. These rules have been abrogated to a great extent by provisions of the 1986 Act that deny installment reporting to sales of stock or securities traded on an established securities market.[252] The second category consists of sales or other dispositions of depreciable or nondepreciable property (other than marketable securities) to related parties, and the third category consists of sales of depreciable property to controlled entities. So-called safe haven provisions (designed to prevent application of these rules) have been provided for certain sales and dispositions of property in these latter two categories. There are also exceptions to the application of the related-party rules and definitions.

[i] **Marketable securities.**   "Marketable security" is defined as "any security for which, as of the date of the disposition, there was a market on an established securities market or otherwise."[253] The Senate Finance Committee Report for the 1986 Act states that marketable securities would include (1) securities listed on any city, regional, or national exchange where quotations appear on a daily basis; (2) securities regularly traded in the national or a regional over-the-counter market for which quotations are published; (3) securities traded locally for which quotations can be obtained readily from established brokerage firms; (4) units in a common trust fund; and (5) mutual fund shares for which redemption prices are published. Although it is not yet clear what issues will arise as a result of this definition, it is likely that they will involve closely held corporations, partnerships, or other private entities whose shares or ownership interests are either not traded or traded only among related parties, but whose assets consist, at least in part, of marketable securities.

Definition of "related party."   For the purpose of this provision, the term "related party" was defined prior to the 1986 Act to mean "a person whose stock would be attributed under Section 318(a) (other than paragraph (4) thereof) to the person first disposing of the property."[254] Thus, related parties included a spouse, children, grandchildren, and parents; trusts, estates, partnerships, and 50-percent-or-more owned corporations, but they did not include siblings.[255] The definition of "related party" was amended by the 1986 Act to include persons having any of the relationships described in Section 267(b).[256] Thus, siblings are now treated as related parties, but not in-laws.[257]

General rule.   Prior to the 1986 Act, which denied installment report-

---

[252] IRC § 453(k)(2).

[253] IRC § 453(f)(2).

[254] IRC § 453(f)(1).

[255] IRC § 318(a).

[256] See IRC § 453(f), as amended by 1986 Act.

[257] IRC § 267(b).

ing to sales of marketable securities,[258] if marketable securities were sold or otherwise disposed of on an installment basis to a related party and the related-party buyer thereafter sold or otherwise disposed of the property anytime prior to the time the original seller had recognized all the gain from his transfer, the amount realized on the related party's resale (or the FMV of the marketable securities if the securities are not disposed of by sale or exchange) would be treated as a payment received by the original seller. Special rules were provided to make sure the original seller did not report more than the total gain to be realized on the first sale and that he received credit for all payments that had already been received or had been treated as having been received.[259] The foregoing rule may be illustrated by a simple example.

EXAMPLE: Assume A had marketable securities with a basis of $40 and an FMV of $100. Assume A sold these securities to B, a related party, for a $100 note payable at the rate of $5 a year for each of 20 years. Under the installment method, the $60 of gain on the sale would be recognized proportionately as payments were received by A. Consequently, 60 percent of each payment received would be treated as installment income. If, after five payments were received by A, B resold the securities for $80, A was treated as receiving $55 as a result of B's resale (B's resale price of $80 less payments already received by A of $25). Thus, at this point, A would have been treated as having received payments aggregating $80 (the deemed payment of $55 plus the $25 already received), he would have reported gain of $48 (60 percent of $80), and he would have actually received payments of $25. (B of course retained the $80 received on his sale and was not required actually to pay any portion of it to A.) B would have recognized a loss of $20 in the year of his resale.

To prevent both double taxation to A and too great an acceleration in the recognition of income by A, no subsequent payments would have been taxable to A until the amount of the "deemed" payment of $55 was fully recovered. Hence, in the example, A would not have recognized any gain on the next 11 payments made to him by B under the note. After 11 payments, the "deemed" payment would have been fully recovered and the twelfth and subsequent payments would again produce installment income.

If B had resold the stock for $120 rather than $80, B would have recognized gain of $20 and A would have been treated as receiving a payment of $75 (the full unpaid balance of the installment obligation); no subsequent payments to A under the note would be taxable to him.

---

[258] IRC § 453(k)(2). This prohibition on the use of the installment method for sales of marketable securities was generally applicable to sales occurring after December 31, 1986, in taxable year ending after that date.

[259] IRC § 453(e)(3).

In taking into account the excess of any amount realized from resales over payments received on the first sale, determinations were made as of the end of the taxable year. Thus, the tax treatment did not turn on a strict chronological order in which resales or payments were made.

[ii] Property other than marketable securities. The same rules applicable to marketable securities prior to the 1986 Act still apply to sales of other property, but only if the resale occurs within two years from the date of the original sale.[260] If the resale occurs more than two years from the date of the first sale, the related-party rules do not apply, and the resale does not affect the reporting of gain by the original seller.

The running of the two-year safe haven period is tolled where the risk of loss on the related-party buyer is substantially diminished.[261] This would be the case where the related-party buyer held a put, had an option, or otherwise had entered into a transaction whose effect was to diminish substantially the risk of loss to the related-party buyer. However, the legislative history indicates that a typical close corporation's shareholder agreement is not the type of arrangement that will toll the running of the two-year period. Similarly, if the put, option, or other arrangement merely provides the related-party buyer with the opportunity of disposing of the property at its then FMV (i.e., at the time the option is exercised), the running of the period will not be tolled.[262]

[iii] Exceptions to application of related-party rules. The related-party rules are not applicable to certain transactions or in certain circumstances:[263]

- To the original sale of stock, where the related-party buyer is the issuer of the stock
- Where there is a compulsory or involuntary conversion under Section 1033 that causes the resale, if the original sale occurred before the "threat or imminence" of conversion
- Where the resale occurs after the death of either the original seller or related-party buyer
- In any case where it is established to the satisfaction of the Secretary that neither the first nor the second disposition had as one of its principal purposes the avoidance of tax

The preceding exceptions illustrate the circumstances where tax abuse is not evident and, hence, where related-party transactions should not be subject to the related-party limitations. However, with respect to the last circum-

---

[260] IRC § 453(e)(2)(A).

[261] IRC § 453(e)(2)(B).

[262] 1980 S. Rep., 1980-2 CB 494, 501–502.

[263] IRC §§ 453(e)(6), 453(e)(7).

stance listed above, the legislative history indicates that it will be the exceptional case in which the nontax avoidance exception is available.[264] The legislative history adds that regulations should be provided setting forth definitive rules so as to eliminate the need for further legislation in this area. It is anticipated that tax-free transfers (e.g., charitable transfers, like-kind exchanges, gift transfers, and transfers to a controlled corporation or a partnership) will not be treated as a second disposition of property for purposes of the related-party rules. It is also anticipated that if the second disposition is of an involuntary nature (e.g., foreclosure by a creditor or bankruptcy of the purchaser), the nontax avoidance exception will be available. Similarly, where the second disposition is itself an installment sale with terms essentially similar to those of the first sale, the exception should be available. The overall point is that the nontax avoidance exception should be applied in situations where the abuse that the related-party rules were intended to eliminate is not present. The nontax avoidance exception should not be applied as a club by which the IRS may obtain additional revenue.

[iv] **Extension of statute of limitations.** To ensure a mechanism for compliance with the related-party rules, Congress has provided that the applicable period of limitations for assessing a deficiency with respect to the recognition of gain on the first disposition (where the gain is attributable to application of the related-party rules) will not expire before two years after the person who made the first disposition has notified the IRS of the second disposition.[265] This places an obligation on the person who made the first disposition to monitor the activities of the related-party acquirer. This was especially burdensome (and constituted a potential trap) in the case of deferred payment dispositions of marketable securities, since the related-party rules applied to all subsequent dispositions, not merely to those occurring within two years of the first disposition.

[c] **Sales of Depreciable Property to Controlled Entity**

Unless it is established to the satisfaction of the IRS that a disposition did not have tax avoidance as a principal purpose, the installment method is not applicable to a sale of depreciable property between related parties.[266] Instead, all payments to be received shall be treated as if received in the year of sale. Thus, in effect, an accrual method will be required.

In determining whether a person is a "closely-related party," the definition of "related person" under Section 1239 is used. Section 1239 defines "related persons" to include:

---

[264] 1980 S. Rep., 1980-2 CB 494, 502.

[265] IRC § 453(e)(8).

[266] IRC § 453(g).

- A person and any corporation of which that person owns (directly or indirectly) more than 50 percent of the value of its outstanding stock
- A person and a partnership of which that person owns (directly or indirectly) more than 50 percent of the overall interest in capital and profits of the partnership
- Two corporations that are members of the same controlled group
- A corporation and a partnership if the same persons own more than 50 percent in value of the outstanding stock of the corporation and more than 50 percent of the overall interest capital and profits of the partnership
- An S corporation and another S corporation if the same persons own more than 50 percent in value of the outstanding stock of each corporation
- An S corporation and a C corporation if the same persons own more than 50 percent of the value of the outstanding stock of each corporation

The foregoing rules apply to sales made after October 22, 1986, the date of enactment of the 1986 Act. However, these rules are not applicable to sales made after August 14, 1986, if the sales were made pursuant to binding contracts that were in effect at all times on and after August 14, 1986. Prior to the 1986 Act changes, the related-party rules governing transfers of depreciable property were applicable only if the entities were 80 percent owned as opposed to 50 percent owned. Because of the various amendments to the Code that have taken place, taxpayers and their tax advisors must exercise care in determining the applicable rules.

[12] Contingent Price Rules

In many instances, the parties to a purchase and sale desire to consummate the transaction but are unable to determine a fixed purchase price. The parties may conclude that the value of the property depends on future productivity, sales, income, or on some other variable. As a consequence, the selling price may be set at a fixed or varying percentage of one of these factors.

Prior to the 1980 Act, the installment method was generally not available where all or a portion of the selling price was subject to a contingency.[267] The principal reason for this rule was, simply, the inability to make the necessary computations. Because the selling price was not certain, neither the contract price nor the gross profit could be determined.

---

[267] Gralapp v. United States, 458 F2d 1158 (10th Cir. 1972); In re Steen, 509 F2d 1398 (9th Cir. 1975). See also Rev. Rul. 77-56, 1977-1 CB 135 (purchaser's obligation to pay is fixed even though the obligation may be satisfied by offset of an obligation of the seller to the purchaser).

To broaden the availability of the installment method and thereby reduce use of the cost recovery method (under which the purchaser's payments are applied first to reduce basis, and gain is recognized by the seller only as payments are received in excess of basis), the 1980 Act authorized the Treasury to provide rules for use of the installment method in contingent price transactions.[268] The Treasury has issued temporary regulations providing for such use where the sales price cannot readily be ascertained, i.e., where the sales price is subject to a contingency.[269]

[a] Maximum Sales Price Stated

Where the applicable contract provides for a maximum purchase price subject to reduction, the maximum price is used to determine the gross-profit percentage. If a contingency occurs (or becomes certain to occur) and the maximum price is thereby reduced (or is certain to be reduced), the gross-profit percentage will be reduced for that year and subsequent years so that no more than total realized gain will be recognized. If, because of the occurrence of a contingency, the maximum price is reduced to a point where the actual gain to be realized is less than the aggregate gain already recognized, the seller will be permitted to recognize a loss.[270]

EXAMPLE: Assume a taxpayer owns stock with a basis of $15,000. He sells the stock for 15 annual payments, each payment to be equal to 5 percent of the net profits of the corporation for the year. However, in no event is more than $60,000 aggregate consideration (exclusive of interest) to be paid. In these circumstances, the selling price is $60,000; the gross profit is $45,000 ($60,000 − $15,000), and the appropriate gross profit percentage is 75 percent ($45,000 ÷ $60,000). Assuming that the first 12 payments were made on time and that they aggregated $45,000, A would have recognized $33,750 of income (75 percent of $45,000). If, at that time, the corporation goes out of business so that no further payments will be made, A's actual gain on the transaction will only have been $30,000 ($45,000 − $15,000). Assuming the stock was a capital asset, A will then be entitled to a capital loss of $3,750 ($33,750 − $30,000).

[b] No Maximum Price, but Fixed Payment Period

Where a maximum sales price is not provided in the agreement, but the obligation is to be paid over a fixed period, the basis of the property sold is

---

[268] IRC § 453(j).

[269] Temp. Reg. § 15a.453-1(c).

[270] Temp. Reg. § 15a.453-1(c)(2).

to be recovered in equal annual increments over the period during which payments may be received.[271] However, if the agreement provides for consideration based on a variable component, the recovery of basis will be proportionate to the payments to be received. In this regard, all payment terms will be considered. Of course, because the installment method is available only for the reporting of gain, these rules on deferred payment transactions are not applicable to transactions when it is reasonable to conclude that no gain will be realized.[272]

If the basis recovered in any particular year exceeds the payments received in that year, the excess is not deducted at that time but, rather, is carried over to the next succeeding year. This rule does not apply to a taxable year that is the final scheduled year of payment or to the year in which the unpaid obligation has become worthless.

> **EXAMPLE:** Assume that A has stock with a basis of $20,000 that he sells to B for 5 percent of the corporation's profit for each of the five years following the year of sale. Basis will be recovered at the rate of $4,000 per year. Gain in any particular year will be the excess of the amount received over $4,000. If only $3,000 is received in the first year and $6,000 is received in the second year, then the $1,000 excess of basis recovery over payments in the first year will be carried over to the second year, and a total of $5,000 ($4,000 regular basis recovery $1,000 carryover) will be offset against the $6,000 received in year 2, thereby producing no gain in year 1 and a gain of $1,000 in year 2.
>
> Alternatively, if the selling price were 40 percent of the corporation's profit in year 1, 30 percent in year 2, and 10 percent in each of the years 3, 4, and 5, the basis of the stock would be recovered on a basis that was proportionate to these payments. Thus, 40 percent of basis would be allocated to year 1, 30 percent to year 2, and 10 percent to each of the subsequent three years. However, merely because the percentage varies does not mean that the basis allocated to each year should vary. For instance, if the circumstances indicated that the varying percentages were designed to produce relatively equal payments (i.e., to offset or smooth out anticipated fluctuations in profit or any other factor on which the payments will be based), it may be appropriate for basis to be recovered equally over the period of years.

If basis is fully recovered over the designated period but, as a result of delays in payment or modifications of the sales agreement, payments are received after the designated period, the question arises as to whether amend-

---

[271] Temp. Reg. § 15a.453-1(c)(3).

[272] See, e.g., Priv. Ltr. Rul. 8533008 (May 17, 1985), where contingent payments over a fixed period were not subject to the installment rules, because it was unlikely that gain would be realized by the selling taxpayers.

ed returns should be filed (adjusting basis) or whether the entire payment should be included in income in the year of receipt. Absent manipulative purpose by the taxpayer, the latter position should be acceptable.[273]

[c] Both Selling Price and Payment Period Indefinite

If both the selling price and payment period are indefinite (and assuming the transaction qualifies as a sale for tax purposes), basis will be recovered in equal annual increments over a period of 15 years beginning with the year of sale.[274] The excess of basis recovered over payments received in any year will be reallocated in equal amounts to the remainder of the 15-year period. Any remaining unrecovered basis at the expiration of the 15-year period will continue to be carried over until all basis has been recovered or the future payment obligation has become worthless, in which case a loss will be allowed in such year.[275]

[d] Alternatives

[i] **Income forecast method.** In circumstances where the property sold is depreciable property of a type normally eligible for depreciation on the income forecast method, basis may be recovered using the income forecast method. This method may also be used where the property sold is depletable property of a type normally eligible for cost depletion in which total future production must be estimated, and payments under the contingent selling price agreement are based on receipts or units produced by or from this property.[276]

Under the income forecast method, the amount of basis to be recovered each year is determined by multiplying total basis by a fraction, the numerator of which is the payments (exclusive of interest) received in the year and the denominator of which is total estimated payments (exclusive of interest). For example, if the property sold is expected to produce aggregate revenue to the seller of $100 and if $10 is received by the seller in the year of sale, 10 percent of the seller's basis will be recovered in the year of sale.

The regulations identify mineral properties, motion picture and television films, and television shows as property that may qualify for use of the income forecast method. In addition, a taxpayer may seek a ruling from the

---

[273] See Stewart v. United States, 739 F2d 411 (9th Cir. 1984), where adjustments were made to prevent deduction of more than 100 percent of basis.

[274] Temp. Reg. § 15a.453-1(c)(4). Transactions assertedly coming within this paragraph of the regulations will be closely scrutinized to make sure the transaction actually involves a sale.

[275] Temp. Reg. § 15a.453-1(c)(4).

[276] Temp. Reg. § 15a.453-1(c)(6).

IRS as to whether the character of specific property qualifies for use of income forecast recovery of basis.

[ii] Avoiding inappropriate basis deferral or acceleration. In particular circumstances, the taxpayer or the IRS may find that the operation of the "normal basis recovery rules" will substantially and inappropriately defer or accelerate the recovery of basis, thereby distorting income. In such a case, an alternative to the normal-basis-recovery-rules may be used.[277]

A taxpayer who desires to show that the operation of the normal-basis-recovery rule will substantially and inappropriately defer recovery of basis must demonstrate that (1) his proposed alternative is a reasonable method of ratably recovering basis and (2) under his proposed method, it is reasonable to conclude that over time, he will likely recover basis at a rate twice as fast as the rate that basis otherwise would have been recovered under the normal rule.[278]

At first glance, this rule might seem unduly harsh. It would require a taxpayer to use the normal-basis-recovery rule unless he can demonstrate both that his alternative is reasonable and that unless his alternative is used, it will take at least twice as long to recover basis than it reasonably should. To illustrate, assume that a taxpayer sells a widget-making machine to X for an amount equal to 10 percent of the selling price of all widgets sold by X. Assuming that the transaction amounts to a true sale, the normal rule would require the taxpayer to allocate and recover basis ratably over a 15-year period. If the taxpayer can demonstrate that the widget-making machine will have an economic useful life of fewer than 15 years, it would seem reasonable for the basis to be recovered over that economic life. However, under the test described in the preceding paragraph, such an alternative could not be used unless the machine's useful life were less than eight years. A life of eight years or more would not satisfy the "twice as fast" rule.

To guard against that result, the taxpayer might specify the period over which payments must be made and use a period of fewer than 15 years. Although this solution involves a risk that the purchaser would minimize use of the widget-making machine during the specified period in order to reduce the aggregate purchase price from what it otherwise would be, the seller might be able to negotiate various warranties or other obligations of the purchaser to prevent this. If these protections are not feasible, then the normal-basis-recovery rule might indeed be unfair. However, it seems just as reasonable to conclude that ultimate risk for such matters should be placed on the taxpayer rather than the IRS. On the other hand, there may be circumstances that demonstrate that the IRS position is so clearly unreasonable that the twice-as-fast rule should not be applied.

---

[277] Temp. Reg. § 15a.453-1(c)(7).
[278] Temp. Reg. § 15a.453-1(c)(7)(ii).

If the IRS determines that the normal-basis-recovery rules will substantially and inappropriately accelerate a recovery of basis, it may require an alternative method of recovery. The taxpayer may avoid use of the alternative if he is able to demonstrate either that (1) the method of basis recovery required by the IRS is not a reasonable method of ratable recovery or (2) it is not reasonable to conclude that the taxpayer is likely to recover basis at a rate twice as fast under the normal rule as under the method proposed by the IRS.

The preceding paragraph relates to an IRS attempt to avoid application of the normal rules. The taxpayer may defeat this attempt by demonstrating that either of the two conditions apply; it is not necessary for the taxpayer to demonstrate both.

The taxpayer must receive permission from the IRS before using the proposed alternative method.[279] The request for permission is made by filing a ruling request with the Commissioner prior to the due date of the return, including extensions.[280]

The National Office has approved the use of alternative-basis recoveries where the consideration to be received on a sale contained both fixed and contingent portions and the taxpayer sought to allocate basis between the fixed and contingent portions, resulting in a recovery of basis in the first year alone of almost four times as fast as otherwise would be the case.[281] Similarly, an alternative-basis-recovery method has been approved where payments due under the agreement were contingent but subject to reasonable estimation, thus allowing basis to be recovered proportionate to anticipated payments,[282] and where the time of the payments was uncertain but experience showed that all payments would be made within three to four years after the sale.[283]

[e] Private Annuities

In some circumstances, property may be transferred in exchange for the purchaser's obligation to pay the transferor a life annuity, i.e., a series of payments for the remainder of the transferor's life. The amount to be paid each year may be a specified amount or an amount that is contingent on sales, earnings, or some similar factor. Over the years, various rules have governed the manner in which the annuity payments will be characterized as a recovery of basis, gain, and interest.[284]

---

[279] Id.

[280] Id.

[281] See, e.g., Priv. Ltr. Rul. 8707025 (Nov. 14, 1986), Priv. Rul. Ltr. Rul. 8728026 (Apr. 10, 1987).

[282] See, e.g., Priv. Ltr. Rul. 8537049 (June 17, 1985).

[283] See, e.g., Priv. Ltr. Rul. 8621023 (Feb. 19, 1986).

[284] See IRC § 72 pertaining to annuities; Rev. Rul. 69-74, 1969-1 CB 43.

Technically, a private annuity may fit within the definition of a contingent price installment sale. As such, a private annuity may be subject to the contingent price installment sale regulations. However, this is not certain. In the background statement to the temporary regulations under Section 453, the Treasury stated: "It is anticipated that regulations will be issued in the near future explaining the relationship among section 72, 453, 453B, and 1001 for purposes of reporting a disposition of property in exchange for an annuity obligation."[285]

To date, regulations have not been promulgated. Since the application of the installment sales rules is mandatory unless a taxpayer elects out from those rules, it is recommended that taxpayers who desire to report deferred payment dispositions of properties in accordance with the private annuity rules expressly elect out from the installment method to the method consistent with the private annuity rules. Otherwise, it would appear that these taxpayers may be subject to the installment sales rules.[286]

[13] Like-Kind Exchanges

The installment method may be used in conjunction with a like-kind exchange under Section 1031, pursuant to which no gain or loss is recognized on an exchange of property used in a trade or business or for investment if such property is exchanged for property of a like kind. However, if a taxpayer is to receive cash or other property on the exchange (in addition to receiving like-kind property), gain realized on the exchange will be recognized to the extent of the cash received and the FMV of any non-like-kind property received.[287] Use of the installment method permits the recognition of this gain to be deferred until the cash or other property is received.

In making the necessary computations, the value of like-kind property is excluded from the contract price and is not, itself, treated as a payment that has been received.[288]

EXAMPLE: Assume that property with a basis of $400,000 an an FMV of $1 million is exchanged for property with an FMV of $200,000 plus an installment note of $800,000 of which $100,000 is paid in the year of sale. The proper computations are as follows:

---

[285] TD 7768, 1981-1 CB 296, 298.

[286] See Rev. Rul. 86-72, 1986-1 CB 253, and Gen. Couns. Mem. 39503 (May 7, 1986), pertaining to the relationship of private annuities and installment sales where the installment obligation is canceled on the death of the seller. See also discussion infra ¶ 5.06[2].

[287] IRC § 1031(b).

[288] 1980 S. Rep., 1980-2 CB 494 at 504.

Contract price	$800,000
Gross profit	$600,000
Gross profit percentage	75%
Payments received:	$100,000
Year of exchange	
Thereafter	700,000
Gain recognized:	$ 75,000
Year of exchange	
Thereafter	525,000
Total gain	$600,000

The basis of the property received by the taxpayer in the preceding example will be determined as follows. First, the basis of the property transferred by the taxpayer (i.e., property with a basis of $400,000) is allocated to the like-kind property to the extent of its FMV ($200,000). Thus, the basis of the property received will be $200,000. The $200,000 balance of the basis of the transferred property ($400,000 − $200,000) is allocated to the installment obligation received by the taxpayer.[289]

[14] Defaults and Repossessions

As a general rule, a seller who repossesses property on default by the buyer must recognize gain or loss measured by the difference between the FMV of the property at the time of repossession and the taxpayer's basis in the obligation satisfied as a result of the repossession.[290] This rule can produce particularly harsh results in the case of deferred payment transactions involving high valued property, such as real property, where payments are often deferred over a substantial period of years. This rule can cause a taxpayer who has sold property with a relatively low basis, to recognize a substantial amount of gain on the repossession even though the taxpayer ends up with little cash and owning the very property that he had sold. To alleviate this burden, Section 1038 was enacted in 1964.

Section 1038 provides that where real property is reacquired in partial or total satisfaction of the purchaser's indebtedness, (1) gain or loss resulting from the reacquisition will be limited and (2) the debt will not be treated as worthless or partially worthless as a result of the reacquisition. The gain is limited to the lesser of:

1. The excess of the sum of the money and FMV of other property received prior to the reacquisition over (b) the amount of gain recognized prior to the reacquisition; or

2. The gain to be realized as a result of the original sale reduced by the

---

[289] See Prop. Reg. § 1.453-1(f).

[290] See discussion supra ¶ 5.04[5].

sum of the gain already reported and the amount of money and the FMV of other property paid or transferred by the seller in connection with its reacquisition of the property.

In other words, the gain will be limited to an amount that is no greater than the cash and FMV of the property that has already been received by the seller, but in no event will the gain be more than the gain still to be recognized on the original sale less the additional cash and property that the taxpayer must pay the purchaser to reacquire the property.

EXAMPLE: Assume real property with a basis of $40 and an FMV of $100 is sold for $20 cash and the purchaser's obligation to pay $40 in year 4 and $40 in year 5. Assume further that the purchaser defaults on his obligation in year 4, prior to the first $40 payment, that the property then has an FMV of $90, and that the seller pays $10 to the purchaser ($90 FMV less $80 owed to the seller) and takes back the property. In the absence of Section 1038, the seller would recognize $48 of gain on the reacquisition ($90 value of property received over the sum of the $10 cash paid and the $32 of basis in the unpaid installment obligation). Under Section 1038, the seller will recognize $8 of gain, the lesser of $8 computed under alternative (1), above ($20 received prior to the reacquisition over $12 of gain recognized), and $38 computed under alternative (2), above ($60 of originally computed gain less the sum of the $12 of gain recognized and the $10 of cash paid in connection with the reacquisition).

The basis of the reacquired property will be the adjusted basis of the indebtedness secured by the property increased by the sum of (1) the amount of gain recognized under Section 1038 and (2) the amount paid to the seller in connection with the reacquisition.

If the seller had previously treated part of the indebtedness as worthless, then at the time of reacquisition the seller will be treated as having received an amount equal to the amount previously treated as worthless and the adjusted basis of the indebtedness will be increased by that amount.[291]

[15] Elections Out

In certain circumstances, a taxpayer may prefer not to report on an installment basis. For example, acceleration in the recognition of gain through use of another method may permit the taxpayer to take advantage of expiring loss carryovers, to be taxed at a then-favorable tax rate, or

---

[291] See Section 1038(e) for additional rules governing principal residences.

otherwise to avoid the risks and uncertainties of changes in tax rates and laws.[292]

The rules regarding elections not to use the installment method are set forth in the regulations.[293] They provide that the election must be made on or before the due date for filing the taxpayer's return (including extensions) for the taxable year in which the installment sale occurred. Notwithstanding the availability of forms that can be used for this purpose, the regulations point out that a taxpayer who reports the full amount of the gain on the return for the year in which the sale occurred will be considered to have made a proper election out.[294] The fact that the taxpayer or its accountant failed to realize that installment reporting was available and, hence, reported the entire gain in error rather than as the consequence of a deliberate decision may be irrelevant.[295]

Should a taxpayer fail to elect out from the installment method within the time frame specified, it generally will not be able to do so subsequently.[296] However, the regulations provide that such later elections may be available, but "only in those rare circumstances when the Internal Revenue Service concludes that a taxpayer had good cause for failing to make a timely election."[297] The regulations also provide that a recharacterization of a transaction, e.g., the recharacterization of a lease to a sale, will not justify a later election.[298] In addition, conditional elections will not be permitted.[299]

Once made, an election may be revoked only with the consent of the IRS. However, no revocation will be permitted when one of its purposes is the avoidance of federal income tax or when the taxable year in which any payment was received has closed.[300]

---

[292] See, e.g., Stewart Perry, 59 TCM 533 (1990), where the taxpayer's election of the installment method under pre–1980 Act law resulted in unanticipated additional taxes due to subsequent changes in the alternative minimum tax.

[293] Temp. Reg. § 15a.453-1(d).

[294] Temp. Reg. § 15a.453-1(d)(3)(i). The regulations add that "[a] cash method taxpayer receiving an obligation the fair market value of which is less than the face value must make the election in the manner prescribed by appropriate instructions for the return filed for the taxable year of the sale."

[295] See Cornelius Wierschem, 82 TC 718 (1984).

[296] See Stewart Perry, 59 TCM 533 (1990), where under pre–1980 Act law, the court upheld the Commissioner's disallowance of a taxpayer's attempted revocation of an earlier election. The taxpayer sought to revoke the earlier election in order to avoid an unanticipated increase in tax liability due to post-election amendments to the rules governing alternative minimum taxable income.

[297] Temp. Reg. § 15a.453-1(d)(3)(ii).

[298] Id.

[299] Id. Compare Warren Jones Co. v. Comm'r, 524 F2d 788 (9th Cir. 1975), where the IRS conceded the right of the taxpayer under prior law to make conditional elections in certain circumstances.

[300] Temp. Reg. § 15a.453-1(d)(4). See Priv. Ltr. Rul. 8530096 (Apr. 30, 1985), where taxpayer being out of the country and unable to advise the accountant not to

In addition to the foregoing, assuming a taxpayer has elected out of the installment method, the regulations purport to alter the manner in which other methods of accounting will be applied. For example, the regulations provide that the FMV of the installment obligation will be treated as property received by the taxpayer without regard to whether the obligation is "the equivalent of cash."[301] In effect, the Treasury is attempting by administrative fiat to eliminate the cash equivalence doctrine.[302] The regulations add that FMV is to be determined without regard to whether any provisions of the contract or local law restrict the transferability of the obligation, and without regard to whether the obligation is embodied in a note, an executory contract, or any other instrument, or is an oral promise enforceable under local law. Thus, the Treasury is attempting to reduce the opportunities for use of the cost recovery method of accounting. Apparently, the Treasury is also seeking to discourage taxpayers from electing out. It remains to be seen whether these regulations will be deemed lawful.[303]

In determining the FMV of the obligation for purposes of determining gain following an election out, the regulations provide additional rules covering fixed amount obligations and contingent payment obligations.

[a] Fixed Amount Obligations

"Fixed amount obligation" is an installment obligation under which the amount payable is fixed. For purposes of determining whether the amount is fixed, the provisions of Section 483 and any payment recharacterization arrangements must be disregarded.[304] Fixed obligations include obligations payable in fungible units or foreign currency that may be measured in terms of U.S. dollars even though the value of those units may vary over time in relation to the dollar. The fixed amount of the obligation is its value in U.S. dollars on the date of the installment sale.

Under the regulations, a cash method taxpayer must treat as the amount realized in the year of sale the FMV of the installment obligation. In no event

---

elect out was insufficient to cause the IRS to permit a revocation of the election out. But see Priv. Ltr. Rul. 8639020 (June 25, 1986), where IRS permitted the filing of amended returns on an installment basis to correct the erroneous election out made by the taxpayer's former director of taxes, who had been dismissed for numerous tax errors. See also Priv. Ltr. Rul. 8519010 (date not given), where taxpayer elected out because he had not yet received permission to use an alternative method of basis recovery on a contingent price sale. After getting permission, IRS permitted taxpayer to revoke his prior election out.

[301] Temp. Reg. § 15a.453-1(d)(2)(i).

[302] See discussion at ¶ 3.03[1].

[303] There is no suggestion in the legislative history that Congress intended for the Treasury to include within its regulations any modifications to the operation of other methods of accounting.

[304] Temp. Reg. § 15a.453-1(d)(2)(ii).

is the FMV of the obligation to be considered less than the FMV of the property sold. For example, if property with an FMV of $100 is sold for an installment obligation in the amount of $100 payable 10 years from the date of sale and bearing an appropriate market rate of interest, the amount realized by the taxpayer in the year of sale will be $100, the FMV of the installment obligation. If the interest rate in the obligation is higher than a market rate so that the FMV of the obligation is in excess of the $100 face amount, the higher FMV is the amount realized. However, if the interest rate is less than the then-applicable current market rate so that the FMV of the obligation is less than $100, the amount realized would still be $100, because the amount realized may not be less than the FMV of the property sold.

An accrual method taxpayer follows essentially the same rules as the cash method taxpayer, except that the accrual method taxpayer must treat the total amount payable under the obligation (rather than its FMV) as the amount realized on the sale. For this purpose, both stated and unstated interest are excluded from the amount realized.

[b] Contingent Payment Obligations

Any installment obligation that is not a fixed amount obligation is considered a contingent-payment obligation. In determining the amount realized on a sale, if an obligation has both fixed and contingent components, the fixed component is subject to the rules governing fixed amount obligations.

The FMV of the contingent payment obligation is determined by disregarding restrictions imposed under the agreement or applicable local law. As with fixed amount obligations, the FMV of the contingent payment obligation must not be less than the FMV of the property sold (less other consideration transferred for the property). The value of the property transferred to the purchaser may be used as the basis for deriving the value of the contingent payment obligation. The regulations warn that only in rare and extraordinary cases will the taxpayer be entitled to assert that there is no reasonably ascertainable FMV and, hence, use the open transaction or cost recovery method of recognizing income.[305]

¶ 5.06 DISPOSITION OF INSTALLMENT OBLIGATIONS

Under the installment method, the recognition of gain is deferred until such time as payment is received. Typically, the purchaser's obligation to make payment is evidenced by a note or some other form of written obligation. The

---

[305] Temp. Reg. § 15a.453-1(d)(2)(iii).

disposal of that obligation by a taxpayer results in a taxable event, either accelerating the recognition of gain or occasioning the recognition of a loss.

The rules governing the treatment of dispositions of installment obligations are set forth in Section 453B. It provides as follows:

> If an installment obligation is satisfied at other than its face value or distributed, transmitted, sold, or otherwise disposed of, gain or loss shall result to the extent of the difference between the basis of the obligation and—
>
> (1) the amount realized, in the case of satisfaction at other than face value or a sale or exchange, or
>
> (2) the FMV of the obligation at the time of distribution, transmission, or disposition, in the case of the distribution, transmission, or disposition otherwise than by sale or exchange.
>
> Any gain or loss so resulting shall be considered as resulting from the sale or exchange of the property in respect of which the installment obligation was received.

For purposes of determining gain or loss on the disposition of an installment obligation, the basis of the installment obligation is the excess of the face value of the obligation over the amount that would be returnable as income if the obligation were satisfied in full.[306] In other words, if property with the basis of $40 were sold for $100, with the seller receiving the purchaser's obligation to pay $100 at the rate of $10 per year for a period of 10 years, the seller's basis in the purchaser's obligation would be $40 at the time of sale ($100 face value less $60 of gain to be realized). After three payments had been made, the seller's basis in the obligation would be $28 ($70 of remaining face value less $42 of gain still to be realized).

The key issues that arise in connection with dispositions of installment obligations are whether particular transactions will be treated as dispositions for purposes of these rules. In some cases, the rules are relatively clear. For example, gifts, distributions in the form of dividends, and certain liquidation distributions are taxable dispositions.[307] A transfer from one spouse to another incident to a divorce is not a taxable disposition.[308] In other cases, the rules are not as clear. The various circumstances that have generally been troublesome for taxpayers are discussed in the following sections.[309]

[1] At Death

On the death of the holder of an installment obligation, the obligation passes to the decedent's estate, either to be collected by the estate, with the proceeds

---

[306] IRC § 453B(b).

[307] IRC § 453B.

[308] IRC § 453B(g).

[309] See infra ¶¶ 5.06[1]–5.06[5].

distributed to the decedent's beneficiaries, or with the obligation itself distributed to the beneficiaries. As a general rule, the transmission of the obligation from the decedent to his estate does not result in a taxable disposition of the installment obligation.[310]

The tax consequences of the subsequent payments are covered by Section 691, pertaining to income in respect of a decedent.[311] Payments received on the installment obligation by the estate will be treated as income of the estate in the same amount and character as would have been reported by the decedent.[312] The IRS has concluded that this rule applies, notwithstanding the fact that the note is valued at a substantial discount for estate tax purposes.[313]

Similarly, if the estate transfers the obligation to the beneficiaries, that transfer does not amount to a taxable disposition.[314] However, if the estate sells or exchanges the obligation (even if the sale or exchange is to a beneficiary), a taxable disposition has occurred.[315]

Amounts received by the beneficiary/transferee of the installment obligation will be reported just as it would have been reported by the decedent.[316] Prior to the 1980 Act, a question remained as to the application of these rules where the beneficiary who received the installment obligation from the decedent's estate was also the obligor on the obligation. Some taxpayers had argued that as a consequence of the applicable rules, the gain would never be reported. The 1980 Act clarified this to provide that the transfer of the installment obligation on the death of the holder to the obligor of that obligation would be treated as a cancellation of the obligation and, hence, as a taxable disposition.[317]

Where the installment obligation is held as a joint tenancy with right of survivorship, the transfer that is effected as a result of the death of one of the joint tenants does not result in a taxable disposition.[318] The surviving joint tenant reports all the income and gain as it would have been reported in the aggregate had the deceased joint tenant survived.

[2] Cancellation or Unenforceability

If an installment obligation is canceled or otherwise becomes unenforceable, the obligation is treated as if it were disposed of in a transaction other than

---

[310] IRC § 453B(c).

[311] Generally, except for that portion of the obligation that constitutes income in respect of a decedent, the obligation will have a step-up in basis. IRC § 2031(a).

[312] IRC §§ 691(a)(3), 691(a)(4).

[313] See Tech. Adv. Mem. 8702004 (Sept. 24, 1986).

[314] IRC §§ 691(a)(2), 691(a)(4).

[315] IRC § 691(a)(2).

[316] IRC § 691.

[317] IRC § 453B(f). See discussion infra ¶ 5.06[2].

[318] See Rev. Rul. 267, 1953-2 CB 32; Rev. Rul. 76-100, 1976-1 CB 123.

a sale or exchange. If the obligor and obligee are related persons within the meaning of Section 453(f)(1), the FMV shall be treated as not less than the face amount of the obligation.[319]

The rule embodied in the present law emanates from tax avoidance possibilities that existed under prior law. Prior to the 1980 Act, individuals who desired to make a gift of property could use the installment method to make the gift. In form, they would sell the property on an installment basis. This sale would permit the donee/purchaser to obtain a step-up in basis and thereby avoid the carry-over basis rules that otherwise would apply. To illustrate, assume that A wanted to make a gift of property with a value of $100 and a basis of $40. If A were to give the property to B, A would not recognize any taxable gain on the transaction, and B would have a basis of $40. However, if A sold the property to B for $100, B would obtain a basis of $100. If thereafter, but prior to receipt of any payment on the obligation, A were to cancel the obligation, some courts took the position that although a gift may have been made, there was no income tax to the transferor.[320] By taking advantage of annual and other exclusions from gift tax or by use of available credits, substantial income tax and gift tax could be avoided.

[3] To and From Corporations and Other Entities

In certain cases, the transfer of an installment obligation to or from a corporation will not be treated as a disposition that results in taxable gain.

[a] Transfers to Controlled Entities

The regulations provide that a transfer of an installment obligation to a controlled corporation under Section 351 is not a taxable disposition of that obligation.[321] Similarly, transfers under Section 361 pertaining to certain exchanges in connection with corporate reorganizations and contributions of property to a partnership by a partner under Section 721 or by a partnership to a partner under Section 731 (except as provided by Sections 736 and 751) are not taxable dispositions.[322] In the case of such transfers, the obligation will have the same basis and character in the hands of the acquiring entity

---

[319] IRC § 453B(f). See Rev. Rul. 86-72, 1986-1 CB 253.

[320] See, e.g., Miller v. Usry, 160 F. Supp. 368 (WD La. 1958), where a father's cancellation of his son's obligations under an installment note was found not to be a taxable disposition. See also Estate of Moss, 74 TC 1239 (1980), acq. in result only 1981-1 CB 2, for same result where the installment obligation was of the so-called self-cancelling type, i.e., one that was canceled automatically in the case of the seller's death.

[321] Treas. Reg. § 1.453-9(c)(2).

[322] Id.

as it had in the hands of the transferor.[323] However, if the transferee of the installment obligation is the obligor under that obligation, the disposition will be treated as a cancellation and, hence, will be taxable.[324]

[b] Certain Liquidations

If an installment obligation is distributed in a liquidation to which Section 332 applies and the basis of the obligation in the hands of the transferee is determined under Section 334(b)(1), then the disposition is not treated as a taxable disposition.[325] This is the same rule that was in effect prior to the 1986 Act. However, other provisions did not survive the 1986 Act. For example, prior to the 1986 Act, distributions of installment obligations in liquidations following sales under then-applicable Section 337 did not amount to taxable dispositions.[326] However, gain had to be recognized to the extent it would have been recognized under Sections 341(f), pertaining to collapsible corporations, 617(d)(1), pertaining to disposition of certain mining property, 1245(a) and 1250(a), pertaining to recapture, 1252(a), pertaining to dispositions of farm land, and 1254(a), pertaining to dispositions of interests in oil, gas, and geothermal property.[327]

[c] To Life Insurance Companies

Prior to the 1980 Act, a special rule prevented transfers of installment obligations to a life insurance company from being eligible for the nonrecognition treatment otherwise available in tax-free transfers.[328] The legislative history of the 1980 Act indicated that Congress believed this restriction should be lifted if the insurance companies were willing to take into account any remaining gain arising on the obligation as taxable investment income. Accordingly, the 1980 Act provides that the special disposition rules will not apply if the company elects to report remaining gain as investment income as payments are received.[329]

---

[323] Advance Aluminum Castings Corp. v. Harrison, 158 F2d 922 (7th Cir. 1946); Treas. Reg. § 1.453-9(c)(3).

[324] IRC § 453B(f)(2). See discussion supra ¶ 5.06[2].

[325] IRC § 453B(d).

[326] IRC § 453B(d)(2), repealed by 1986 Act.

[327] Id. Section 1006(e)(22) of the 1988 Tax Act amended Section 453B to permit liquidating distributions of installment obligations by S corporations not to be treated as dispositions triggering the recognition of gain or loss.

[328] IRC § 453(d)(5) as it existed prior to 1980 Act. See also 1980 S. Rep., 1980-2 CB 494, 507.

[329] IRC § 453B(e).

[4] Modifications, Substitutions, and Other Changes

Business exigencies often necessitate the modification of obligations, the substitution of collateral, or other adjustments to take into account changed circumstances. In addition, it is not uncommon for the original purchaser to resell the property before making all payments on his installment obligation. The purchaser in such a case often asks the original seller to accept the obligation of the new purchaser in lieu of the remaining obligation of the original purchaser. The question arises as to whether these modifications and adjustments are taxable dispositions of the original installment obligation. In answering the question, the courts have tried to strike a balance between the need to prevent a taxpayer from abusing the installment method rules and the need to allow for business exigencies.

The central issue is whether the changes in the installment obligation are of such import that they should be treated as if the original installment obligation were liquidated or otherwise disposed of, with the proceeds of such liquidation or disposition invested in a different obligation. In responding to this issue, the IRS has issued a number of rulings that have generally been favorable to the taxpayer. For example, where a mortgage contract was substituted for a land contract with substantially the same terms and conditions, a disposition was not found.[330] Similarly, the IRS held that no taxable disposition had occurred where the holder of the obligation permitted the obligor to defer payments but charged him a somewhat higher interest rate,[331] where two installment obligations secured by separate security instruments were substituted for a single obligation secured by a single instrument,[332] and where the holder of the obligation permitted the obligation to be assumed by a new obligor.[333]

However, where the original obligor is replaced by a new obligor, the circumstances must be scrutinized carefully to determine whether the original obligor has, in fact, paid the obligation with the obligation of a third party.[334] An important factor is whether it was contemplated at the time of the original installment sale that the original obligor would be replaced at some point in the future. If so, it might appear that the original obligation was intended to be exchanged for, or paid by, the new third-party obligation. Conversely, if there were no such contemplation and the original obligor has

---

[330] Rev. Rul. 55-5, 1955-1 CB 331.

[331] Rev. Rul. 68-419, 1968-2 CB 196.

[332] Rev. Rul. 74-157, 1974-1 CB 115.

[333] Rev. Rul. 75-457, 1975-2 CB 196, amplified by Rev. Rul. 82-122, 1982-1 CB 80.

[334] See discussion supra ¶ 5.05[7][d].

merely disposed of property with the request that a new obligor assume the existing obligation, no taxable disposition should be found.[335]

The circumstances in some cases have suggested that the holder of the obligation has liquidated one obligation for another and that a taxable disposition has occurred. For example, in *Burrell Groves, Inc.*,[336] a corporation sold property to its shareholders. The shareholders thereafter sold the property. At the time of the shareholders' sale, the corporation surrendered the notes and mortgage of its shareholders and accepted in exchange the installment obligations of the new purchaser. These obligations differed in both maturity date and interest rate. The court held that the new purchaser did not step into the shoes of the old purchaser (or merely assume the obligation of the old purchaser), but instead, that the corporation exchanged one obligation for another independent, different obligation. Similarly, in Revenue Ruling 82-188,[337] the taxpayer held a corporate installment obligation that was convertible into stock of the corporation. A disposition was found to occur when this obligation was exchanged for a new obligation reflecting a substantial increase in the face amount of the obligation and eliminating the holder's right to convert the obligation into stock.

Generally, where the obligor has difficulty in meeting the payments or where, as a consequence of various factors, an adjustment is made in the purchase price, any renegotiations or other similar adjustments do not amount to a disposition. This result is evidenced not only by earlier cases and rulings,[338] but also by the promulgation of the contingent payment rules.[339] The contingent payment rule makes it clear that Congress intends for deferred payment transactions to be reported under an installment method even though the purchase price may be adjusted or the timing of payments changed owing to various contingencies. Since this is the case with obligations that are contingent at the outset, no more restrictive rule should apply where the parties intend for the obligation to be definite and certain but subsequent economic or business circumstances generate a need for the modification.[340]

---

[335] See, e.g., John I. Cunningham, 44 TC 103 (1965), acq. 1966-2 CB 4.

[336] Burrell Groves, Inc., 22 TC 1134 (1954), aff'd, 223 F2d 526 (5th Cir. 1955).

[337] Rev. Rul. 82-188, 1982-2 CB 90.

[338] See, e.g., J.P. Jerpe, 45 BTA 199 (1941), acq. 1942-1 CB 9; Rev. Rul. 72-570, 1972-2 CB 241.

[339] See discussion supra ¶ 5.05[12].

[340] See Akira Kutsunai, 45 TCM 1179 (1983), where no taxable disposition was found where, as the result of the settlement of a breach of contract suit, the obligor substituted a new obligation for the original obligation.

[5] Using Installment Obligations as Collateral

One of the most difficult issues for the IRS and taxpayers arises when a seller pledges an installment obligation or otherwise uses it as collateral to secure a loan. Of course, this problem is not unique to installment sales. Whenever a taxpayer is able to borrow sums in a nontaxable transaction, he is able to obtain the proceeds of the borrowing without income tax consequences. For example, in the context of installment sales, the courts had permitted (and may permit in the future) taxpayers to borrow against the property and then to sell the property under a wraparound mortgage, thereby obtaining cash but deferring the recognition of gain.[341]

To answer the question whether there has been a nontaxable borrowing or a taxable disposition, all the facts and circumstances must be evaluated. If the obligations are, in substance, sold or discounted, with the acquirer assuming risk of nonpayment, a disposition will be deemed to have occurred. On the other hand, if the obligations serve only as security for a financing arrangement with the holder of the obligations, the holder being responsible in full for the amount of the loan without regard to payment of the obligations by customers of the holder, a true borrowing is generally found.[342] As a consequence of the opportunities arising from borrowing, Congress enacted new rules in the 1986 Act that were designed to treat a portion of the proceeds of borrowing as a payment on certain installment obligations.[343] These rules were then repealed by the 1987 Act and replaced with new, more limited rules.[344]

---

[341] See discussion supra ¶ 5.05[10].

[342] See, e.g., Rev. Rul. 65-185, 1965-2 CB 153, where a transaction that was in the form of a pledge was found, in substance, to be a sale. But see Tech. Adv. Mem. 8711002 (Nov. 13, 1986), where the IRS seemed to back away from Rev. Rul. 65-185. See also Joe D. Branham, 51 TC 175 (1968), where a sale was found; Yancey Bros. Co. v. United States, 319 F. Supp. 441 (ND Ga. 1970); Town & Country Food Co., 51 TC 1049 (1969), acq. 1969-2 CB xxv; United Surgical Steel Co., 54 TC 1215 (1970), acq. 1971-2 CB 3, where, in each case, a true pledge was found. See also Sprague v. United States, 627 F2d 1044 (10th Cir. 1980); William B. Korstad, 45 TCM 1032 (1983); Gen. Couns. Mems. 39584 (Oct. 10, 1985) and 37848 (Feb. 5, 1979), for numerous factors to be considered in determining whether a pledge is a true borrowing or a taxable disposition. These factors include who collects the payments and bears the expenses of collection, who is liable for property, excise, sales, and other taxes arising from ownership of the obligations, whether an agency relationship was created between the taxpayer and the lender, whether the obligor was notified of a change in ownership, whether the lender reserved all rights of a lender (e.g., examining the books and records of the taxpayer), whether the secured loan mirrored the terms and conditions of the obligation, whether there was a right to substitute collateral and what were the economic reasons for the pledge.

[343] See discussion supra ¶ 5.05[6].

[344] See discussion infra ¶ 5.07.

¶ 5.07　THE 1987 ACT: REPEAL AND REVISION

The 1987 Act made significant changes in the availability and application of the installment method. Its rules were generally applicable to dispositions in taxable years beginning after December 31, 1987, although different effective dates applied to particular matters.[345]

[1]　Repeal of Installment Method for Dealers

The 1987 Act repealed Section 453A as it existed prior to the Act.[346] The 1987 Act also revised Section 453(b)(2)(A) to exclude from the definition of "installment sale" all so-called dealer dispositions of real or personal property.[347] The repeal was applicable to installment obligations arising from dispositions after December 31, 1987.[348] The treatment of installment obligations arising from dispositions before March 1, 1986, was not affected by the 1987 Act. The treatment of installment obligations arising from dispositions between February 28, 1986, and January 1, 1988, was subject to special rules.[349]

As a consequence of this repeal and revision, the installment method of reporting may no longer be used in connection with sales of inventory or for most dealer dispositions of real or personal property. For these purposes, "dealer disposition" is defined to mean "[a]ny disposition of personal property by a person who regularly sells or otherwise disposes of personal property on the installment plan" and "[a]ny disposition of real property which is held by the taxpayer for sale to customers in the ordinary course of the taxpayer's trade or business."[350]

However, the term "dealer disposition" does not include "the disposition on an installment plan of any property used in the trade or business of farming."[351] Nor does the term include any disposition of (1) certain time

---

[345] 1987 Act, 10202(e). In addition, certain relief provisions in the Tax Reform Act of 1986 are continued. For example, Section 10202(e)(5) of the 1987 Act provides, "The amendments made by this section shall not apply to any installment obligation or to any taxpayer during any period to the extent the amendments made by section 811 of the Tax Reform Act of 1986 do not apply to such obligation or during such period."

[346] 1987 Act § 10202(c).

[347] See the 1987 Act, § 10202(b)(1) and IRC § 453(b)(2)(A), as amended.

[348] 1987 Act, § 10202(e)(2).

[349] See discussion infra ¶ 5.07[2].

[350] IRC § 453(*l*), as enacted by 1987 Act, § 10202(b).

[351] For this purpose, "farming" has the same meaning as it has in Section 2032A(e)(4) or Section 2032A(e)(5), essentially the operation of any stock, dairy, poultry, fruit, fur-bearing animal, or truck farm; any plantation, ranch, nursery, range, greenhouse, or similar structure used for raising agricultural or horticultural

share rights in residential real property or (2) residential lots, but only if (in either case) the taxpayer elects to pay interest on the deferred tax liability.[352] In addition, the term "dealer disposition" does not include certain dispositions of tangible personal property by a manufacturer or an affiliate to a dealer for a resale or for leasing by the dealer.[353] To be eligible for this special rule, the dealer must not be obligated to make payments on its installment obligation to the manufacturer/seller until the dealer resells (or rents) the property. Moreover, the manufacturer must have the right to repurchase the property at a fixed or ascertainable price, exercisable on any day within the first nine months after the date of sale.[354]

[2] Repeal of Proportionate Disallowance Rule

The 1987 Act repealed Section 453C, which pertained to the treatment of certain indebtedness as a payment on installment obligations—the so-called proportionate disallowance rule.[355] However, installment obligations arising from dealer dispositions between February 28, 1986, and January 1, 1988, remain subject to the proportionate disallowance rule for taxable years ending after December 31, 1986, and beginning before January 1, 1988.[356] The applicable committee report points out that any gain from such obligations that remains to be recognized as of the first day of the first taxable year beginning after December 31, 1987, is not to be recognized as payments are received (or treated as received under the proportionate disallowance rule). Instead, the gain remaining to be recognized is to be taken into account as a Section 481 adjustment over a period of up to four years, starting with the first taxable year that begins after December 31, 1987, and in accordance with the principles of Revenue Procedure 84-74.[357]

For nondealer dispositions of real property, the proportionate disallowance rule is repealed for obligations arising from dispositions in taxable years beginning after December 31, 1987. Nondealer dispositions of real property

---

commodities; and any orchard or woodland. It also includes the activity of cultivating the soil; raising or harvesting agricultural or horticultural commodities; handling, drying, packing, grading, or storing agricultural or horticultural commodities in their unmanufactured state by a person regularly producing more than one half of that commodity; and the planting, cultivating, caring for, or cutting of trees, or the preparation (other than milling) of trees for market.

[352] IRC §§ 453(l)(2), 453(l)(3), as enacted by 1987 Act, § 10202(b).

[353] See Temp. Reg. § 1.453C-10T.

[354] Id.

[355] 1987 Act, § 10202(a). See supra ¶ 5.05[6] for discussion of this rule.

[356] 1987 Act, § 10202(e)(2)(B).

[357] See Conf. Rep. No. 100-495, 100th Cong., 1st Sess. 926–931 (Dec. 21, 1987) (hereinafter Conference Report). See also ¶¶ 8.04 regarding Section 481 adjustments and 8.06[2] regarding Rev. Proc. 84-74.

after August 16, 1986 (in taxable years beginning before January 1, 1988), are subject to the proportionate disallowance rule in later years in which the taxpayer has so-called allocable installment indebtedness.[358] However, a taxpayer may elect for years ending after December 31, 1986, to apply the new interest rules and the new "pledge rules" to dispositions and pledges occurring after August 16, 1986.[359] If the taxpayer makes that election, the proportionate disallowance rule will not apply to obligations arising from dispositions after August 16, 1986.

[3] Special Rules for Nondealers of Real Property

The 1987 Act enacted new Section 453A, which provides special rules for nondealers of real property. The special rules require that if a taxpayer uses the installment method for dispositions of either (1) real property used in the taxpayer's trade or business or (2) property held for the production of rental income (but only if sold for a price in excess of $150,000), the taxpayer must pay interest on the deferred tax liability.[360] However, the rules apply only if installment obligations from dispositions of such property exist as of the end of the year and have an aggregate face amount exceeding $5 million.[361] In addition, special exceptions from (and modifications of) these rules are provided for installment obligations that arise from a disposition of personal use property, farm property, time-shares, and residential lots.[362] Congress thereafter enacted the 1988 Act, which includes technical corrections to the 1986 and 1987 Tax Acts. Among the provisions of the 1988 Act was an extension of the special rules for nondealers to installment sales of any personal use property where the sales price exceeds $150,000, other than farm property, time-shares, and presidential lots.

[4] Pledges of Installment Obligations Treated as Payments

The 1987 Act repealed the proportionate disallowance rule, but it did not abandon the principle of treating borrowing by the taxpayer as a payment received on an installment obligation.[363] New Section 453A(d) covers any indebtedness of a taxpayer that is secured by an installment obligation that arose from a disposition of real property used in the taxpayer's trade or busi-

---

[358] See Conference Report, supra note 357, at 926–931, and discussion supra ¶ 5.05[6] regarding allocable installment indebtedness.

[359] See infra ¶ 5.07[4] for discussion of the new pledge rules.

[360] IRC § 453A, as enacted by 1987 Act, § 10202(c).

[361] IRC §§ 453A(b)(1), 453A(b)(2), as enacted by 1987 Act, § 10202(c).

[362] IRC §§ 453A(b)(3), 453A(b)(4), as enacted by 1987 Act, § 10202(c).

[363] See discussion supra ¶ 5.05[6] regarding the proportionate disallowance rule.

ness or held by him for the production of rental income. In that situation, the net proceeds of the borrowing are treated as payments received on the installment obligations that serve as security. Although this is another form of proportionate disallowance rule, it applies only to borrowings secured by particular obligations. Thus, compliance with this provision should prove easier than prior compliance with the proportionate disallowance rule.[364]

[5] Minimum Tax

Section 56(a)(6) relating to the minimum tax was amended by the 1987 Act so that the installment method could be used in determining alternative minimum taxable income attributable to nondealer dispositions of property.[365] This amendment took effect with respect to dispositions in taxable years beginning after December 31, 1986.[366]

---

[364] The property affected by this provision is the same property as described supra ¶ 5.07[3].

[365] 1987 Act, 10202(d).

[366] 1987 Act, 10202(e)(4).

CHAPTER 6

Inventories

¶ 6.01 Significance of Inventories 6-3
    [1] Primary Issues 6-3
    [2] Consequences of Having Inventories 6-3

¶ 6.02 Need for Inventories 6-4
    [1] To Determine Gross Income 6-4
    [2] To Determine Cost of Goods Sold 6-5
    [3] Use of Accrual Method 6-6

¶ 6.03 History 6-7

¶ 6.04 Basic Requirements 6-8
    [1] Statutory Provisions 6-9
        [a] Section 471 6-9
            [i] Best accounting practice 6-9
            [ii] Most clearly reflecting income 6-10
        [b] Section 263A 6-10
    [2] Regulatory Provisions 6-11

¶ 6.05 Merchandise, Supplies, and Other Inventories 6-12
    [1] Merchandise 6-13
        [a] Definition 6-13
        [b] Ownership 6-14
        [c] Acquired for Sale 6-16
        [d] Sale of Goods and Services 6-18
        [e] Dual-Use Property or Change in Use 6-22
        [f] Ordinary Course of Business 6-23
            [i] Profit element 6-23
            [ii] Regular business activity 6-24
        [g] Taxpayer Intent 6-25
    [2] Supplies Under Section 162 6-26
        [a] Business Expense or Inventoriable Cost 6-27
        [b] Supplies Inventories Required 6-29
        [c] Supplies Inventories Not Required 6-30
            [i] Records of consumption and physical inventories ... 6-31
            [ii] Incidental supplies 6-31
            [iii] Clear reflection of income 6-32
    [3] Other Inventories—Ability to Trace Costs 6-32
        [a] Real Estate 6-33

　　　　　　　[b] Special Order Merchandise 6-33

¶ 6.06　Inventoriable Costs 6-34
　　　　[1] Wholesalers, Retailers, and Other Nonmanufacturers 6-35
　　　　　　　[a] Discounts 6-37
　　　　　　　　　　[i] Trade discounts 6-37
　　　　　　　　　　[ii] Cash discounts 6-37
　　　　　　　[b] Excessive Costs 6-38
　　　　　　　[c] Impact of 1986 Act 6-38
　　　　　　　　　　[i] General method 6-39
　　　　　　　　　　[ii] Simplified resale methods 6-39
　　　　[2] Manufacturers 6-47
　　　　　　　[a] Direct Material Costs 6-48
　　　　　　　[b] Direct Labor Costs 6-48
　　　　　　　[c] Indirect Production Costs 6-49
　　　　　　　　　　[i] Full absorption costing rules 6-50
　　　　　　　　　　[ii] Uniform capitalization costing rules 6-57

¶ 6.07　Allocation of Inventoriable Costs to Items Produced 6-72
　　　　[1] Manufacturing Burden Rate Method 6-74
　　　　[2] Standard Cost Method 6-76
　　　　[3] Practical Capacity 6-76
　　　　[4] Simplified Production Method 6-78
　　　　[5] Simplified Method for Allocating Mixed Service Cost 6-80

¶ 6.08　Allocation of Inventoriable Costs to Ending Inventory 6-83
　　　　[1] Cost-Flow Assumptions 6-83
　　　　[2] FIFO and LIFO 6-84
　　　　　　　[a] Record Keeping 6-85
　　　　　　　[b] Proscribed Methods 6-87
　　　　[3] Average Cost 6-87
　　　　　　　[a] IRS Position 6-88
　　　　　　　[b] Judicial Review 6-91

¶ 6.09　Inventory Write-Downs to Market 6-92
　　　　[1] Evolution of Rule 6-92
　　　　[2] Abnormal Goods 6-94
　　　　[3] Normal Goods 6-95
　　　　　　　[a] Definition of "Market for Purchased Goods" 6-97
　　　　　　　[b] Definition of "Market for Manufactured Goods" 6-98
　　　　　　　　　　[i] No open market or nominal quotations 6-100
　　　　　　　　　　[ii] Goods offered for sale 6-101
　　　　　　　　　　[iii] Impact of GAAP on market write-downs 6-104
　　　　　　　　　　[iv] Taxpayer response to *Thor Power Tool* 6-104

¶ 6.10　Special Inventory Costing Rules 6-105
　　　　[1] Dealers in Securities 6-106

As this edition was going to press, the Treasury issued new proposed and final inventory costing regulations under Section 263A. These new regulations will generally be effective for years beginning after December 31, 1993. The prior, present regulations will continue to be effective for years beginning prior to January 1, 1994. In addition, transition rules regarding implementation of the new regulations have not yet been promulgated. These rules are expected to be promulgated within the next several months. An analysis of the new final and proposed regulations, together with the rules that will be published for implementation of these regulations, will be addressed in the first supplement to this second edition.

    [2] Inventories of Livestock Raisers and Other Farmers 6-106
    [3] By-Products 6-107
    [4] Inventories of Retail Merchants 6-107

¶ 6.11 Nontraditional Inventory Methods 6-109

¶ 6.01 SIGNIFICANCE OF INVENTORIES

For businesses engaged in manufacturing, wholesaling, or retailing goods, the tax treatment of inventories is without question the most significant tax aspect of their business. The cost of the goods acquired or manufactured is the largest cost of their business. The revenue derived from the sale of such goods constitutes the bulk of their revenues and, hence, is the most significant determinant of profit or loss.

Despite the overwhelming significance of inventories to taxpayers engaged in manufacturing, wholesaling, and retailing activities, the number of taxpayers and tax advisors familiar with the intricacies of tax accounting for inventories is surprisingly small. The tax treatment of inventories is frequently viewed as inherently complex, technical, esoteric, and perhaps boring. Yet, the decisions made regarding the tax treatment of inventories are often the most significant.

This chapter covers all aspects of inventory tax accounting other than the use of the last-in, first-out (LIFO) method. The LIFO method is the subject of Chapter 7.

[1] Primary Issues

The primary issues associated with inventories are relatively simple. In essence, they consist of no more than identifying the merchandise inventories of the business, determining what those inventories cost, and determining when those costs should be offset against revenues to determine gain. Virtually every question that arises in connection with inventory tax accounting relates to one or more of these three basic issues.

[2] Consequences of Having Inventories

If a business incurs costs in acquiring or manufacturing merchandise inventories, four basic consequences result. First, the costs incurred in acquiring or manufacturing the inventory (so-called inventoriable costs) do not reduce or offset revenues until the inventory is sold. Thus, deduction of an inventoriable cost may be deferred beyond the year in which the cost is incurred. If the cost is not an inventoriable cost but is otherwise deductible under the Code,[1] the cost may be deducted in the year in which it is incurred or paid, depending on the taxpayer's method of accounting. (See Chapter 3

---

[1] Unless otherwise indicated, all references to "IRC" or the "Code" are to the Internal Revenue Code of 1986, as amended.

on the cash-receipts-and-disbursements method (the cash method), Chapter 4 on accrual methods, and Chapter 5 on the installment method.)

Second, in particular cases, if the fair market value (FMV) of the inventory declines below its cost, the amount of the decline may be deducted in the year in which it occurs even though the inventory is not sold until a later year.[2]

Third, the costs incurred in purchasing or producing merchandise inventory, and the income from selling that inventory, must be accounted for under an accrual method.[3] The cash method generally may not be used.[4]

Fourth, the inventory costing rules of Section 263A, which was enacted as part of the Tax Reform Act of 1986 (the 1986 Act), apply to merchandise inventories.[5] However, pursuant to Section 263A itself, Section 471 and the costing regulations thereunder will continue to apply in many instances.[6] Also, and regardless of which rules apply (Section 263A or Section 471), inventoriable costs are not to be taken into account until the economic performance rules of Section 461(h) have been satisfied.[7]

As the rules set forth in the preceding paragraphs suggest, taxpayers are generally advantaged if items are not characterized as merchandise inventories or if related costs are not treated as inventoriable costs. This is because supply inventories (i.e., inventories that are not merchandise inventories) are generally not subject to the foregoing rules,[8] noninventoriable costs are generally deductible in the year incurred rather than deferred until the year of sale, and use of the cash method of accounting may be available. (See Chapter 3 for rules governing use of the cash method.)

¶ 6.02　NEED FOR INVENTORIES

[1]　To Determine Gross Income

Section 61 and the regulations thereunder make it clear that the amount realized on the sale of property is not itself an item of taxable income. Only that portion of the amount realized that represents gain is subject to tax.[9] For

---

[2] See discussion infra ¶ 6.09.

[3] Nevertheless, prior to the Revenue Act of 1987 (the 1987 Act) if sales qualified for installment reporting, the recognition of gain could have been deferred until payment was received. However, even under installment reporting, the cost of the inventory was not deducted in the year paid or incurred but, in effect, was deducted proportionately as payments were received. See Chapter 5.

[4] See discussion of substantial identity test at ¶ 2.02[2][f].

[5] See discussion infra ¶ 6.06[2][c][ii].

[6] See Treas. Reg. § 1.471.11 and discussion infra ¶ 6.06[2][c][i].

[7] See discussion of economic performance test at ¶ 4.04[3].

[8] See discussion infra ¶ 6.05.

[9] See, e.g., Heinz Molsen, Jr., 85 TC 485, 502 (1985) where the court pointed out:

Although purchases are an "expense" in the colloquial sense, it is well settled that they are not a "deduction" within the meaning of section 461 and that they

example, Section 61(a) provides that "gross income means all income from whatever source derived, including . . . gross income derived from business [and] gains derived from dealings in property." The regulations reiterate this point by providing that for manufacturing, merchandising, and mining businesses, gross income is total sales less cost of goods sold plus income from other sources.[10]

To determine gross income (i.e., gain on the sale of property), it is essential that the cost of the goods sold be matched against the amounts realized on sales.[11] For unique items of property, or where only a few items of property are sold each year, it is a comparatively simple matter for both cash and accrual method taxpayers to match cost against sales price to determine taxable gain. For example, all taxpayers are required to determine gain on the sale of real property or capital assets by matching amounts realized with the cost (or adjusted basis) of the property sold. The associated record-keeping responsibilities have not proved unduly burdensome or impractical.

[2] To Determine Cost of Goods Sold

For businesses that sell a large number of essentially similar or fungible items, it is neither practical nor reasonable to require that the actual cost of each item sold be matched against its selling price. As a consequence, other, more practical means have evolved for determining the cost of the items sold and for matching such cost against sales revenue.

These other means involve the use of inventories,[12] an accrual method

---

are not subject to the rules governing deductions under such section. Purchases are taken into account in computing the cost of goods sold, which is an offset, or exclusion, employed in the computation of gross profit and gross income [citations omitted]; whereas, throughout the Code, the term "deduction" is used to refer to amounts subtracted from gross income to arrive at taxable income.

[10] Treas. Reg. § 1.61-3. The regulation also provides that "[t]he cost of goods sold should be determined in accordance with the method of accounting consistently used by the taxpayer."

[11] See Louis S. Rotolo, 88 TC 1500 (1987), where the court noted that a failure to allow the costs of inventory to offset gross receipts would be unreasonable, would result in an improper reporting of income, and would impose an inappropriate tax on gross receipts.

[12] Treas. Reg. § 1.471-1 states:

In order to reflect taxable income correctly, inventories at the beginning and end of each taxable year are necessary in every case in which the production, purchase or sale of merchandise is an income producing factor. The inventory should include all finished or partly finished goods and, in the case of raw materials and supplies, only those which have been acquired for sale or which will physically become a part of merchandise intended for sale. . . .

Should the taxpayer's inventory records be susceptible to two or more interpretations as to the quantity of inventory present, the taxpayer must be prepared to accept the counts determined from those records by the IRS unless the taxpayer can demonof accounting[13] (see Chapter 4 on accrual methods of accounting), and various assumptions as to the manner in which the actual costs incurred in acquiring or producing items of inventory are allocated among the items so acquired or produced. Using these means, applicable costs of items acquired or produced during the year are first aggregated. This total is then combined with the aggregate cost of the items on hand at the beginning of the year to produce the total cost of goods available for sale during the year. This latter total is then allocated among items on hand at the end of the year and items sold during the year. The formula is essentially as follows.[14]

> Beginning inventory
> + Purchases and other acquisition or production costs
> = Cost of goods available for sale
> − Ending inventory
> = Cost of goods sold

This formula demonstrates the manner in which inventories are used to simplify the determination of cost of goods sold so that gain from the sale of goods may be determined in a reasonable and expedient manner. The use of inventories permits the aggregation of inventory-related costs and avoids the need to determine or trace the actual cost of each item sold during the year.

[3] Use of Accrual Method

Use of an accrual method in recording purchases and sales of inventory is also an instrumental part of the process. To compute gain or loss on a sale, it is necessary for the cost of the goods sold to be matched against the revenues arising from such sales. By recording purchases and sales as they occur, accrual methods achieve a reasonably accurate matching of costs and revenues.[15] (See Chapter 4 for a discussion of accrual methods of accounting.) In contrast, under the cash method, transactions are recorded only as payments are made and received. Application of this method often results in a mismatching of related purchases and sales. For example, assume a taxpayer buys four units of a product for $3 per unit and sells these units for

---

strate that those counts are not correct. See Coastal Expanded Metal Co., 55 TCM 101 (1988), where the IRS determination of the taxpayer's inventory was found reasonable, because it was based on documented physical counts and corroborated by other records of the taxpayer, notwithstanding that it was much higher than the inventory value claimed by the taxpayer.

[13] Treas. Reg. § 1.446-1(c)(2)(i) states, "In any case in which it is necessary to use an inventory the accrual method of accounting must be used with regard to purchases and sales unless otherwise authorized. . . ."

[14] See infra ¶ 6.08 for applications of this formula.

[15] The matching achieved for tax purposes is not necessarily identical to the matching required for financial accounting purposes. See discussion of matching at ¶ 2.02[2][f] and of the economic performance rules at ¶ 4.04[3].

$5 per unit, all purchases and sales occurring within the same year. To compute gain correctly, it is essential that the $3 cost of each unit be matched against the $5 sales price. If the $3 cost were deducted when paid and the $5 sales price were reported when received, proper matching would occur only if those payments and receipts occurred in the same year.

To avoid such mismatching, cash method taxpayers could capitalize the cost of goods acquired or produced by them and defer the deduction of that cost until payments are received on account of sales, but this would often require costly and cumbersome record keeping. Moreover, the cost of property acquired or held for sale is ordinarily not a deductible expense. Rather, it is taken into account in determining the basis of property under Sections 471 and 1013. Prior to the 1987 Act, the installment method provided a mechanism for allowing the sellers of goods to report gain from the sale of goods on a cash basis. However, the installment method was only available for qualifying sales and often involved significantly more record keeping than even an accrual method. (See Chapter 5 for discussion of the installment method.)

¶ 6.03 HISTORY

The original revenue acts following adoption of the Sixteenth Amendment did not expressly provide for inventories. Nevertheless, the need for inventories was recognized at an early date by the Treasury. For example, following enactment of the Excise Tax Act of 1909, which imposed a tax on doing business in a corporate form and based the tax on income computed on the cash method, the Treasury promulgated regulations allowing mercantile and manufacturing businesses to use inventories and to compute income in accordance with accrual methods.[16] These inventory regulations were amended in 1917 to permit inventories to be valued at cost or at the lower of cost or market.[17] These amended regulations followed established financial accounting practice and allowed taxpayers to treat a decline in the value of their inventories as a deductible expense in the year of the decline.[18]

The first statutory income tax provision regarding inventories was Section 203 of the Revenue Act of 1918. It recognized the need for inventories and authorized them to be computed on a basis that conformed to sound financial accounting and also clearly reflected income in the opinion

---

[16] Reg. 33 Article 161. See also discussion at ¶ 3.02 pertaining to the history of the cash method.

[17] TD 2609 (Dec. 19, 1917).

[18] See discussion infra ¶ 6.09 pertaining to write-downs of inventory from cost to market.

of the Treasury.[19] This provision allowed a great variety of approaches to be used in valuing inventory and has remained essentially intact through the present.[20]

Other broad statutory and regulatory developments in the area of inventory tax accounting have been comparatively few. They have addressed the LIFO method of inventory accounting and the particular costs that must be treated as inventoriable costs.

The LIFO method was first permitted in 1938, but it was made available only to certain taxpayers.[21] In 1939, the LIFO method was made available to all taxpayers.[22] In 1981, provisions for a simplified form of LIFO were enacted so that use of the method could be extended to even more taxpayers who had previously declined its use because of its perceived complexity. These provisions were then changed by the 1986 Act.[23] (The LIFO method is discussed in Chapter 7.)

The particular costs that should be included in and excluded from the computation of inventories have always been a continuing source of questions. Prior to 1973, most of these questions were resolved on a case-by-case basis, resulting in confusion and a lack of uniformity. Finally, in 1973, to clarify this area of inventory accounting, regulations were promulgated setting forth detailed rules.[24] These rules, known as the full absorption rules, worked quite well, but they were substantially revised by the uniform capitalization costing rules of Section 263A, which was enacted as part of the 1986 Act.[25]

¶ 6.04　BASIC REQUIREMENTS

The basic requirements governing inventories differ, depending on whether the inventory consists of merchandise, which is generally defined as items that are acquired or produced for sale at a profit in the ordinary course of

---

[19] Section 203 of the Revenue Act of 1918 provided:

[W]henever, in the opinion of the Commissioner, the use of inventories is necessary in order clearly to determine the income of any taxpayer inventories shall be taken by such taxpayer upon such basis as the Commissioner, with the approval of the Secretary, may prescribe as conforming as nearly as may be to the best accounting practice in the trade or business and as most clearly reflecting the income.

[20] See Section 22(c) of the 1939 Code and present Section 471.

[21] Section 22(d) of the Revenue Act of 1938 permitted the use of LIFO by tanners and the producers and processors of nonferrous metals.

[22] Revenue Act of 1939, § 22(d).

[23] IRC §§ 472(f), 474 (prior to and after the 1986 Act).

[24] Treas. Reg. § 1.471-11. See discussion infra ¶ 6.06[2][c][i].

[25] See discussion infra ¶¶ 6.06[1][c], 6.06[2][c][ii].

business,[26] or of supplies, which are generally items that are used by taxpayers in rendering services or in manufacturing merchandise.[27] Except for use of the LIFO method, the basic requirements governing merchandise inventories are set forth in Sections 471 and 263A and their accompanying regulations. The basic requirements governing supply inventories are set forth in the regulations under Sections 162, pertaining to the deduction of ordinary and necessary business expenses, and 471 and 263A to the extent that supplies are used in the manufacture of merchandise inventory.[28] The classification of inventory items as merchandise or supplies is quite important in that the applicable rules and requirements differ depending on this classification.[29]

[1] Statutory Provisions

[a] Section 471

Section 471 sets forth the following basic rules governing all merchandise inventories:

> Whenever in the opinion of the Secretary the use of inventories is necessary in order clearly to determine the income of any taxpayer, inventories shall be taken by such taxpayer on such basis as the Secretary may prescribe as conforming as nearly as may be to the best accounting practice in the trade or business and as most clearly reflecting the income.

This provision first gives wide discretion to the Secretary of the Treasury to require the use of inventories and then sets forth the following two bases on which the Secretary may require that inventories be computed. The first is that the inventory conform as much as possible to the best accounting practice in the trade or business; the second is that the inventory be taken on a basis that most clearly reflects income.

[i] **Best accounting practice.** The U.S. Supreme Court has held that the first requirement (that the inventory "conform as nearly as may be to the best accounting practice") is synonymous with a requirement that the inventory conform to generally accepted accounting principles (GAAP).[30]

---

[26] See discussion infra ¶ 6.05[1].

[27] See discussion infra ¶ 6.05[2].

[28] See Treas. Reg. § 1.162-3 regarding all supply inventories; Treas. Reg. § 1.471-11(c)(2)(i)(F) and Temp. Reg. § 1.263A-1T(b)(2)(iii)(F) regarding supplies used in the manufacture of merchandise inventories.

[29] See discussion supra ¶ 6.01[2] and infra ¶¶ 6.05[1], 6.05[2].

[30] Thor Power Tool Co. v. Comm'r, 439 US 522, 532 (1979). The "best accounting practice" conformity requirement should be satisfied as long as the

This GAAP provision necessarily implies that great flexibility exists in inventory practices.[31] This flexibility is also recognized by the regulations that add that "inventory rules cannot be uniform but must give effect to trade customs" and that "greater weight is to be given to consistency than to any particular method of inventorying" as long as the approach used conforms with the regulations.[32] This broad-based reliance on business custom and GAAP accounting sets the framework for all inventory tax accounting not otherwise expressly covered by the Code or Treasury regulations.[33]

[ii] **Most clearly reflecting income.** An inventory method is also subject to the clear reflection of income requirement.[34] The Supreme Court emphasized the importance of this requirement in *Thor Power Tool* when it stated that even if an inventory method conforms to GAAP, it is still subject to the requirement that no method of accounting is acceptable unless, in the opinion of the Commissioner, it clearly reflects income. In other words, compliance with GAAP does not ensure that the method is proper for tax purposes. Moreover, unlike the general requirement of clear reflection of income under Section 446(b), the inventory must be on a basis that *most* clearly reflects the income. This requirement gives considerable discretion to the Commissioner, but, as discussed later, this discretion is not unlimited.[35] Moreover, the cases discussing this requirement seem to ignore the word "most," as they have interpreted the requirement as not permitting the Commissioner to change the taxpayer from one method that clearly reflects income to another method that in the Commissioner's opinion "more clearly" reflects income.[36]

[b] Section 263A

Section 263A was enacted as part of the 1986 Act. It provides rules governing the costs that must be treated as inventoriable costs by taxpayers

---

taxpayer's method conforms to GAAP. The taxpayer should not be required to demonstrate that its method is the best of all available GAAP methods.

[31] In *Thor Power Tool*, the Supreme Court pointed out that "[a]ccountants have long recognized that 'generally accepted accounting principles' are far from being a canonical set of rules that will ensure identical accounting treatment of identical transactions. 'Generally accepted accounting principles,' rather, tolerate a range of reasonable treatments, leaving the choice among alternatives to management." Id. at 544.

[32] Treas. Reg. § 1.471-2(b).

[33] Thor Power Tool Co. v. Comm'r, 439 US 522 (1979). See infra ¶ 6.11 for discussion of nontraditional inventory methods.

[34] See ¶ 2.02[2] for discussion of the clear reflection of income requirement.

[35] See discussion infra ¶ 6.11 on nontraditional inventory methods and discussions at ¶¶ 2.02–2.04 regarding the requirements governing all methods of accounting and the discretion of the taxpayer and Commissioner with respect to these requirements.

[36] See discussion at ¶ 2.02[2][h].

who purchase or manufacture merchandise inventory. Section 263A does not apply to supply inventories, except to the extent those supplies may be used in the acquisition or manufacture of merchandise inventories.[37] Pursuant to special rules, Section 263A does not apply to the merchandise inventories of retailers or wholesalers whose average annual gross receipts do not exceed $10 million.[38] In essence, Section 263A requires the cost of all covered merchandise inventory to include all direct costs of the property as well as all indirect costs allocable to the property.[39] The provision is quite complex, containing a number of special rules authorizing the Treasury to promulgate regulations to carry out the purpose of the section.[40]

[2] Regulatory Provisions

The regulations under Sections 446, 471, 263A, and 162 provide detailed, often complex rules governing the costing and computation of merchandise inventories and supplies. These rules are described in succeeding sections. However, at the outset, it should be noted that these regulations also specify when inventories must be taken, and what items are subject to the inventory requirements.

The regulations under Sections 446 and 471 provide that in all cases in which the production, purchase, or sale of merchandise is an income-producing factor, merchandise on hand at the beginning and end of the year must be taken into account in computing the taxable income of that year.[41] For this purpose, merchandise includes all finished goods, work in process, raw materials, and supplies used in the manufacturing process.

The regulations under Section 471 add that merchandise inventory includes only those raw materials and supplies that have been acquired for sale or that will physically become a part of the goods intended for sale.[42] These raw materials and supplies include containers, such as kegs, bottles, and cases, whether returnable or not, if title to the container passes to the purchaser of the product.[43]

In addition to these requirements pertaining to the use of merchandise inventories under Sections 446, 471, and 263A, the regulations under Section 162 provide rules pertaining to inventories of supplies. Although merchandise

---

[37] IRC § 263A(b). But see Notice 88-86, 1988-2 CB 401 (1988) and discussion infra ¶ 6.05[2][a].

[38] IRC § 263A(b)(2)(B). The application of Section 263A to wholesalers and retailers is discussed infra ¶ 6.06[1][c].

[39] IRC § 263A(a)(2). See discussion infra ¶ 6.06[1][c].

[40] IRC § 263A(h).

[41] Treas. Reg. §§ 1.446-1(a)(4)(i), 1.471-1.

[42] Treas. Reg. § 1.471-1.

[43] Id.

inventories are subject to the requirements of Sections 446, 471, and 263A, supplies inventories are subject to the requirements of Sections 471 and 263A only to the extent they are used or consumed in manufacturing merchandise inventory.[44] To the extent the supplies inventories are not used or consumed in the production of merchandise inventory, the cost of those supplies is determined without regard to Section 263A and is deductible under Section 162.[45]

¶ 6.05　MERCHANDISE, SUPPLIES, AND OTHER INVENTORIES

As indicated previously, the existence of merchandise inventories is quite significant.[46] Among the major reasons for this is that an accrual method must be used to account for purchases and sales of merchandise.[47] This required use of an accrual method is premised on the existence of purchases and sales and not on the existence of merchandise inventory at the end of the year. Thus, taxpayers cannot avoid the required use of an accrual method on the grounds that they do not have inventories on hand at the beginning and end of the taxable year.[48] Nor may taxpayers avoid the required use of an accrual method on the ground that inventory is acquired only on an "as needed" basis with any excess inventory returned to the supplier for credit.[49] (See Chapter 5 for discussion of the installment method.)

Taxpayers with merchandise inventories may elect to value these inventories on the basis of the lower-of-cost-or-market method under which taxpayers may deduct a decline in the value of merchandise that remains unsold at the end of the year.[50] These deductions (or write-downs) are not permitted for supply inventories or other nonmerchandise inventories.

Taxpayers with merchandise inventories must account for such property in accordance with the rules governing inventories. They may not depreciate the property as if it were property used in a trade or business or

---

[44] Treas. Reg. § 1.471-11(c)(2)(i)(F); Temp. Reg. § 1.263A-1T(b)(2)(iii)(F). But consider Notice 88-86, 1988-2 CB 401 (1988) and infra ¶ 6.05[2][a] regarding supplies.

[45] See discussion infra ¶ 6.05[2]. But see Notice 88-86, 1988-2 CB 401 (1988) and discussion infra ¶ 6.05[2][a].

[46] See discussion supra ¶ 6.01[2].

[47] Treas. Reg. § 1.446-1(c)(2)(i); Thomas Nelson, Inc. v. United States, 88-1 USTC ¶ 9339 (ND Tenn. 1988).

[48] See Epic Metals Corp., 48 TCM 357 (1984).

[49] J.P. Sheahan Assocs., Inc., 63 TCM 2842 (1992).

[50] See infra ¶ 6.09 for discussion of the lower of cost or market method.

held for the production of income and, hence, subject to depreciation under Section 167.[51]

Finally, merchandise inventories are subject to the new inventory costing rules of Section 263A. Although these rules cover certain other property, they are not applicable to supply inventories.[52]

For these reasons, it is important to focus on the particular characteristics of merchandise and supply inventories, the issues normally associated with these inventories, and the treatment accorded them.

[1] Merchandise

[a] Definition

The regulations make it clear that merchandise consists only of items that have been produced or acquired for sale in the ordinary course of business, or will physically become a part of the goods that are intended for sale.[53] Merchandise includes both finished goods and partly finished goods. It also includes raw materials and supplies that will become part of the goods held for sale or will be used or consumed in producing such goods.[54]

Numerous questions arise in defining "merchandise inventory." Generally, these questions pertain to (1) whether the taxpayer is the owner of the goods; (2) whether the items were acquired for sale; (3) the effect of a combined sale of goods and services; (4) the treatment of so-called dual-use property (or the effect of a change in the use of property); (5) whether any sale of goods was intended to be at a profit and in the ordinary course of business; and (6) the intent of the parties and, more particularly, whether they intended for the transaction to be treated as a sale of inventory.[55]

---

[51] See Honeywell, Inc., 64 TCM 437 (1992), where the court held that the taxpayer's supply of so-called ratable parts were not merchandise inventory but, instead, depreciable property.

[52] But see Notice 88-86, 1988-34 IRB 10 (1988), where the Treasury implicitly suggested that some supplies may be subject to the uniform capitalization costing rules of Section 263A. See also discussion infra ¶ 6.05[2][a].

[53] Treas. Reg. § 1.471-1.

[54] Id. See also discussion infra ¶ 6.05[2][a].

[55] Under the so-called Corn Products doctrine, certain transactions, such as those involving trading in commodity futures and investments in companies to ensure a source of supply, which are integral parts of an inventory acquisition system, may give rise to ordinary gains and losses rather than to capital gains and losses. See, e.g., Corn Prods. Ref. Co. v. Comm'r, 350 US 46 (1955); Arkansas Best Corp. v. Comm'r, 485 US 212 (1988); Circle K Corp. v. United States, 91-1 USTC ¶ 50,383 (Cl. Ct. 1991).

[b] Ownership

The regulations provide that merchandise should be included in inventory only if its title has vested in or passed to the taxpayer.[56] Although stated in terms of title, the objective of this regulation is to include in inventory only items that are owned by the taxpayer. Formalistic considerations of title do not control. Rather, the concept of ownership is based on a consideration of relevant facts and circumstances, including the intent of the parties, who has the benefits and burdens of ownership, and who bears the risk of loss, all in accordance with applicable provisions of the Uniform Commercial Code or corresponding provisions of applicable local law.[57]

The requisite ownership must also be considered in light of the taxpayer's method of accounting for purchases and sales. For example, if a taxpayer has established a method of accounting that recognizes purchases or sales at the time of order, shipment, or delivery, that time determines when items will be included in or excluded from inventory, notwithstanding the technicalities of title or the legal transfer of ownership. In other words, although the correct time for recording the inclusion and exclusion of items of inventory may be tied to ownership, the adoption and use of methods of accounting for purchases and sales may take precedence over actual ownership.[58] However, if the taxpayer's method does not coincide with the time ownership passes, the taxpayer should be able to obtain the Commissioner's approval for a change from that method to one that does coincide with the change in ownership.[59]

As a result of the foregoing principles, circumstances can arise where the same goods are included in or excluded from the inventories of both the

---

[56] See Treas. Reg. § 1.471-1, which adds:

[T]he seller should include in his inventory goods under contract for sale but not yet segregated and applied to the contract and goods out upon consignment, but should exclude from inventory goods sold (including containers), title to which has passed to the purchaser. A purchaser should include in inventory merchandise purchased (including containers), title to which has passed to him, although such merchandise is in transit or for other reasons has not been reduced to physical possession, but should not include goods ordered for future delivery, transfer of title to which has not yet been effected.

[57] See, e.g., Pacific Grape Prods. Co. v. Comm'r, 219 F2d 862 (9th Cir. 1955); Consolidated-Hammer Dry Plate & Film Co. v. Comm'r, 317 F2d 829 (7th Cir. 1963); United States v. Amalgamated Sugar Co., 72 F2d 755 (10th Cir. 1934); Dana Distribs., Inc., 56 TCM 569 (1988), aff'd, 874 F2d 120 (2d Cir. 1989); Tech. Adv. Mem. 8718003 (Jan. 7, 1987).

[58] This is recognized by Treas. Reg. § 1.446-1(c)(1)(ii), which states:

[A] taxpayer engaged in manufacturing may account for the sale of an item when the item is shipped, when the item is delivered, when the item is accepted, or when title to the item passes to the purchaser, whether or not billed, depending upon the method regularly employed in keeping the taxpayer's books.

[59] See Chapter 8 regarding changes in methods of accounting.

seller and the buyer. For example, if the seller recognizes sales on delivery and the buyer recognizes purchases on shipment, goods in transit may be included in the inventories of both the buyer and the seller. Although the Internal Revenue Service might argue that the methods of the seller or buyer should be changed to conform to the ownership requirements of the regulations, these changes are rarely proposed. Moreover, in light of the Treasury regulation expressly authorizing methods of recognizing sales that may not coincide with the transfer of ownership,[60] it is uncertain whether such a proposal would be approved by the courts.

Notwithstanding the foregoing discussion, where a taxpayer seeks to acquire inventory outside of its normal or routine practice, the transfer of ownership should be the paramount consideration. For example, if a purchaser normally records purchases on shipment but nevertheless acquires goods (in an atypical transaction) that are to be held by the seller for later shipment, the time of transfer of ownership should determine the time of inclusion in inventory. Goods may be acquired in this manner to take advantage of favorable prices, to ensure a continued supply, or for other business reasons. Goods may also be acquired in this manner to increase inventories for financial or tax accounting purposes, such as to avoid a liquidation of LIFO inventory.[61]

Determining the proper time for recognition of income or loss may prove difficult in particular circumstances. For example, some manufacturing entities that take orders for products prior to their manufacture may follow bookkeeping and accounting practices that result in sales being recorded as products emerge from an assembly line. In effect, these taxpayers do not have a finished goods inventory. Increases in their inventory could only arise from the accumulation of raw materials and work in process. This could be most important to a taxpayer seeking to avoid a liquidation of LIFO inventory.[62]

As the previous discussion indicates, it is important for the taxpayer to review the particularities of its agreements with suppliers and customers to determine when ownership is transferred. The nature of the transaction is also important in this regard. For example, COD sales are generally not recorded until the goods have been accepted and paid for by the purchaser.[63] Consigned goods must be included in the inventory of the consignor until those goods have been sold to the consignee or have otherwise been transferred to the consignee's inventory in accordance with its agreement

---

[60] See Treas. Reg. § 1.446-1(c)(1)(ii).

[61] See ¶ 7.07 for discussion of the effects of liquidations of LIFO inventory.

[62] Id.

[63] See Rev. Rul. 70-68, 1970-1 CB 122, and Rev. Rul. 75-96, 1975-1 CB 139 (ownership of goods shipped COD does not pass until payment).

with the consignor.[64] Goods sold on approval or subject to acceptance by the purchaser are not included in the purchaser's inventory until they have been accepted and, correlatively, are not excluded from the seller's inventory until they have been accepted.[65]

On the other hand, goods may be sold under a so-called sale or return contract. Under this type of arrangement, the buyer intends to resell the goods, but, if he is unable to do so, he may resell the goods to the original seller. In this situation, the initial sale is treated as a true sale.[66]

In certain instances, taxpayers have attempted to use cash basis reporting in connection with sales of inventory by forming a subsidiary to act as a sales agent. The subsidiary solicits orders for its parent corporation (typically a manufacturer) who then ships the goods directly to the purchaser. If the subsidiary acts as a true agent, it generally is regarded as not engaged in the purchase or sale of inventory and, hence, may use the cash method, thereby deferring the recognition of commission income until payment is received.[67] However, if the parent and subsidiary attempt to defer more than a reasonable commission, or if the subsidiary does more than act as a mere agent, the subsidiary may be required to use inventories and an accrual method.[68]

[c] Acquired for Sale

The classification of items as merchandise requires that the items be acquired for sale.[69] If items are not acquired and held for sale, they are not considered merchandise and, thus, are not subject to the requirements of the

---

[64] See, e.g., Treas. Reg. § 1.471-1 (inventory of taxpayer/consignor includes "goods out upon consignment"); Floyd L. Musgrove, 27 BTA 554 (1933), acq. XII-1 CB 9 (1933) (goods shipped on consignment and not paid for by end of year are included in consignor's inventory).

[65] See, e.g., Ringmaster, Inc., 21 TCM 1024 (1962); Cleveland Woolen Mills, 8 BTA 49 (1927), acq. VII-1 CB 7; Monroe Cotton Mills, 6 BTA 172 (1927), acq. VII-1 CB 22; Morrison Woolen Co., 10 BTA 8 (1928), acq. VIII-1 CB 32.

[66] See J.J. Little & Ives Co., Inc., 25 TCM 372 (1966); Ertegun v. Comm'r, 531 F2d 1156 (2d Cir. 1976).

[67] Cf. Simon v. Comm'r, 176 F2d 230 (2d Cir. 1949), where the agent was an individual.

[68] See Epic Metals Corp., 48 TCM 357 (1984); Thomas Nelson, Inc. v. United States, 88-1 USTC ¶ 9339 (ND Tenn. 1988).

[69] See, e.g., Wilkinson-Beane, Inc. v. Comm'r, 420 F2d 352, 354–355 (1st Cir. 1970), where the court stated that definitions of "merchandise" include

"goods purchased in condition for sale," "goods awaiting sale," "articles of commerce held for sale," and "all classes of commodities held for sale." Clearly, the meaning of the term must be gathered from the context and the subject. . . . The common denominator, however, seems to be that the items in question are merchandise if held for sale.

regulations under Sections 446 and 471 governing merchandise or to the inventory costing requirements of Section 263A. Consequently, when analyzing the character of particular items, it is necessary to determine whether they are acquired and held for sale or are acquired and held for some other purpose.[70]

Supply items that are acquired and used by the taxpayer in the course of rendering services are not acquired for sale and, hence, are not merchandise. Examples include paper, binders, folders, and mats used by taxpayers who render professional services (e.g., lawyers and accountants). Although these items may be delivered to clients, customers, and others in the course of rendering opinions, conveying information, or otherwise providing services, these items are not acquired for sale and, therefore, are not merchandise. Examples of other taxpayers who use or consume supplies in providing services are mechanics who use oil, grease, and other items in maintaining or repairing equipment, and bootblacks, hair stylists, and others who use supplies in providing personal care services. Each of these service providers uses or consumes supplies in rendering services, but the supplies themselves are not treated as having been sold, or acquired for sale, to customers. Although the cost of these supply items is traditionally taken into account by the taxpayer when setting the price for the services, and the items may, in fact, be transferred to customers, there is no sale in the sense of goods having been acquired for sale.

This same analysis is applicable to replacement parts and other items used in a business and possibly conveyed to customers but not thought of as merchandise inventories. For example, the Tax Court has held that spare parts used by a seller of computers to replace defective parts in computers previously sold (the replacement being pursuant to obligations under a maintenance agreement) were more in the nature of depreciable property than merchandise inventory.[71] Similarly, the Claims Court has concluded that gas contained in a gas pipeline, which is necessary to provide sufficient pressure for gas to be shipped through the pipeline, so-called line pack gas, was depreciable property even though substantively identical to gas actually sold.[72]

---

[70] See, e.g., Kermit M. DeHaai, 56 TCM 1549 (1989), where the court made a careful evaluation of all relevant facts in determining that certain property produced by the taxpayer was more in the nature of equipment than merchandise and, consequently, was depreciable property and eligible for applicable investment tax credit. See also Honeywell, Inc., 64 TCM 437 (1992), where the court held that parts, which were maintained by a seller of computers to carry out its responsibilities under a maintenance agreement to replace defective parts in computers previously sold to customers, were more in the nature of depreciable property than merchandise inventory.

[71] Honeywell, Inc., 64 TCM 437 (1992).

[72] Transwestern Pipeline Co. v. United States, 639 F2d 679 (Cl. Ct. 1980).

[d] Sale of Goods and Services

In some circumstances, taxpayers may provide (or sell) both goods and services. If separate charges are made for the services and the goods, respectively, the taxpayer may be able to report income from services in accordance with accounting methods available for services (e.g., cash or accrual), and the income from sales in accordance with methods available for sales (e.g., accrual methods or, prior to the 1987 Act, the installment method).[73] Thus, a plumber who sells and installs sinks, or a carpenter who sells and installs doors and cabinets, might report the sales on an accrual method and the services on the cash method.[74] This tax planning opportunity is available for all mixed sales and service businesses.

On the other hand, business practice or custom often dictates that a single charge be made for the combined service and sale. For example, a carpenter, painter, or plumber might make a single charge that covers both the services rendered and the washers, nuts, bolts, nails, caulking, and paint used. Because these items are of little value compared to the service, the entire charge is traditionally treated as a charge for services.[75]

However, as the relative value of the "goods" component becomes more significant, the issue arises as to whether there is a sale of goods and services or whether the entire transaction should be treated as a sale of goods rather than a sale of services. Typical activities where the issue has been raised include the provider of yard care and maintenance services (who uses various sprays and chemicals) and pest control businesses that protect the home and office against insect infestation. Should the application of weed killer or bug spray be treated as a sale of goods?

Taxpayers in these businesses generally argue that the sales component is immaterial and should be ignored. The IRS often argues to the contrary and has sometimes been upheld in treating the entire amount as attributable to a sale as opposed to a service. Two examples are *Wilkinson-Beane* and

---

[73] See Treas. Reg. § 1.446-1(d). See also discussion at ¶ 2.03.

[74] Compare, e.g., Cornelius J. Sullivan, 22 TCM 1331 (1963), where the court recognized the right of a roofing contractor to use an accrual method for purchases and sales and the cash method for the remainder of his income and expenses, with J.P. Sheahan Assocs., Inc., 63 TCM 2842 (1992), where a similar taxpayer's specific identification of materials sold in connection with the job (the materials being sold at a price equal to cost plus a 25 percent markup) indicated that the full amount associated with that charge should be treated as income from the sale of goods and not income from services.

[75] See, e.g., Honeywell, Inc., 64 TCM 437 (1992), where a single charge for maintenance and repair services, which services included the installation of new parts pursuant to a maintenance agreement, was nevertheless considered a charge for services and not for a sale of merchandise, the parts being treated as depreciable equipment used in the taxpayer's business.

Knight-Ridder.[76] In *Wilkinson-Beane*, the taxpayer operated a funeral home whose business consisted of providing a complete package of funeral services including the casket. Customers could purchase only complete funeral services. They could not purchase a casket separately. The taxpayer made a single unitemized charge for the complete service, which included the casket, and sought to report on a cash basis. The court held for the government, treating the transaction as a sale, because the caskets played a central role in the business of the taxpayer. In *Knight-Ridder*, the taxpayer published a newspaper. The taxpayer argued that its income came principally from advertising and that the sale of newspapers was rather small and should not be treated as a sale of merchandise. Again, the contrary position of the Commissioner was upheld by the court.

No cases have yet been decided on whether the IRS must permit a breakdown of a single charge into service and sale components, where the sales component is only an incidental aspect of a service business. In some cases, taxpayers were permitted to ignore the sales component where it was minor, but it is not clear that these decisions would be followed today or where the line should be drawn.[77]

One of the most difficult issues in this context concerns the treatment of items used in providing health care services. On the one hand, where it is clear that the primary transaction involves the sale of an item of property to be used and controlled by patients, inventories and use of an accrual method have been required.[78] However, where the delivery of items to patients is less the conveyance of property and more the delivery of service, the character-

---

[76] Wilkinson-Beane, Inc. v. Comm'r, 420 F2d 352 (1st Cir. 1970); Knight-Ridder Newspapers, Inc. v. United States, 743 F2d 781 (11th Cir. 1984).

[77] See, e.g., Michael Drazen, 34 TC 1070, 1079 (1960), where the court stated that "the mere presence of inventory does not necessarily mean that the cash method did not correctly reflect income"; EZO Prods. Co., 37 TC 385, 392 (1961), where the court stated, "In a number of cases we have recognized as petitioner argues that where inventories are so small as to be of no consequence or consist primarily of labor, the presence of inventories is not necessarily sufficient to require a change in petitioner's method of accounting." See also Honeywell, Inc., 64 TCM 437 (1992), where a charge made by the taxpayer for maintenance services to purchasers of its computers was treated as a charge for services, even though the taxpayer substituted new parts for defective ones as part of its maintenance activity, the court refusing to break down the single charge for the maintenance agreement into a service component and a component representing the charge for a sale of goods. The taxpayer was an accrual method taxpayer, but the court's logic should be applicable to a cash method taxpayer also.

[78] See Rev. Rul. 73-485, 1973-2 CB 150, where cash method taxpayer selling artificial limbs and orthopedic braces to physically handicapped persons was required to use inventories and an accrual method even though a substantial portion of the charge was for services rendered in instructing patients in the use of those items; Rev. Rul. 74-279, 1974-1 CB 110, where an optometrist was required to use inventories and an accrual method with respect to the sale of eyeglasses and frames even though the charge included the significant services rendered in preparing those items.

ization of the items in question is not as clear. For example, in *St. Luke's Hospital*,[79] the court stated with respect to a hospital rendering typical hospital services:

> Petitioner owns and operates a hospital in Bluefield. Its business is the customary hospital service business. It is not a merchandising business, and petitioner has no merchandise inventories which would require the use of an accrual method in keeping its books or reporting its income. Its income is derived from providing hospital and professional care to the sick.[80]

Despite this precedent, the IRS has often sought to have hospitals report charges for the administration of drugs and other pharmacy items, IV solutions, and bandages on an accrual method, even though the service portion of the charge is clearly the more significant. Hospitals have sometimes acquiesced and agreed to use a hybrid method.[81]

When evaluating the appropriate treatment of charges for items such as these, it may be helpful to determine whether there actually has been a "sale."[82] Generally, if an item is not sold or if the item asserted to have been sold is not available for subsequent sale or disposition by the recipient, the item should be treated as a supply used in providing services rather than as an item of merchandise. For example, in the ordinary sense of the word, a sale involves the transfer of title to property so that the seller has actually relinquished and transferred his entire bundle of ownership rights.[83] Included

---

[79] St. Luke's Hosp., Inc., 35 TC 236 (1960).

[80] Id. at 238. In the normal operations of a hospital, where drugs, IV solutions, bandages, blood, gases, and other items are administered directly to patients, patients acquire no ownership rights over those items. To the extent any portion of those items remain after use, they generally remain within the possession and control of the hospital.

[81] Interestingly, in Tech. Adv. Mem. 9103002 (Aug. 20, 1990), the IRS National Office (the National Office) stated, in conjunction with an evaluation of the book conformity requirement (see discussion at ¶ 2.02[1]), that the Tax Court in *St. Luke's* "held for the taxpayer and pointed out that the hospital had proven that its books and records were sufficient to correctly reflect cash basis income and did clearly reflect such income although the adjustments and closing entries had to be made." By this statement, the National Office strongly suggests that use of the cash method by the hospital satisfied the clear reflection of income requirement. This is an important point, because some examining agents had previously taken the position that *St. Luke's* did not address the clear reflection of income argument, although none of the conclusions in *St. Luke's* would have been appropriate had the court not determined, at least implicitly if not explicitly, that use of the cash method was appropriate for hospital operations.

[82] See discussion infra ¶ 6.05[1][g].

[83] See Frank Lyon Co. v. United States, 435 US 561 (1978); Comm'r v. Sunnen, 333 US 591 (1948); Helvering v. Clifford, 309 US 331 (1940); Rev. Rul. 83-59, 1983-1 CB 103.

within the applicable "bundle of rights" is the right to use and enjoy the property, to control it, and to dispose of it in any manner not contrary to law.[84]

Thus, where services and property are provided and the recipient obtains something over which he has full ownership rights, it would appear that an actual sale has occurred and that the seller acquired the items for sale. This would certainly cover circumstances such as the sale of caskets in connection with the rendering of funeral services, the sale of food in connection with running a restaurant or cafeteria, and the sale of medical equipment in connection with providing services and equipment. In each case, the property has been transferred to a recipient who has obtained full ownership rights in the property. The recipient can use or not use the property as he sees fit, transfer it to others, or otherwise dispose of it.[85]

However, in certain cases, such as those where materials are used and consumed concurrently with the rendition of the service to the customer, the customer acquires nothing more than the service. There is no item over which the customer has any ownership rights or that may be transferred to another. For example, cosmetics used by the personal care specialists, shoe polish used by the bootblack, tires and oil consumed by those who rent trucks and automobiles, and drugs, IV solutions, and other items administered by a doctor are all merged into the service.[86] The customer obtains no item over which he may exercise any rights of ownership.[87]

---

[84] See Gary Black, 38 TC 673 (1962).

[85] See, e.g., Dana Distribs., Inc., 56 TCM 569 (1988), aff'd, 874 F2d 120 (2d Cir. 1989), where the court held that in determining whether certain property was sold it was appropriate to consider (1) whether the seller retained ownership of the property (including implicitly all rights of ownership); (2) whether the asserted purchasers were under an obligation to return the property or were free to sell or otherwise dispose of the property; and (3) whether the asserted seller had an enforceable right to a return of the property. See also Hallmark Cards, Inc., 90 TC 26 (1988), where the court held that no sale occurs until that moment in time when all rights of ownership, including the risk of loss, have passed from the seller to the buyer and that the passing of the rights of ownership constitutes "the very heart of the transaction [of sale and purchase]."

[86] See, e.g., Melvin L. Cochran, D.D.S., Inc., 56 TCM 1433 (1989), where the issue involved the deductibility, as an ordinary and necessary business expense, of gold coins purchased by a dentist who melted them down for use in dental castings and fillings. The court allowed the deduction of purchases with no indication whatever that the gold coins should have been regarded as merchandise inventory rather than as supplies used in rendering services.

[87] See Honeywell, Inc., 64 TCM 437 (1992), where the taxpayer was held not to have sold merchandise when providing replacement parts to its customers. The customers purchased computers from the taxpayer, and the provision of the parts was pursuant to a maintenance agreement. The customers, even though acquiring full ownership of the parts, merely desired to have the computers function properly. See also discussion infra ¶ 6.05[1][g].

[e] Dual-Use Property or Change in Use

Property is sometimes acquired for sale or lease by the taxpayer. In other cases, the property is originally acquired for use in business as equipment but is later sold. Conversely, some property is originally acquired for resale but is subsequently converted to use in the business. The question arises as to how the property is to be treated in these circumstances.

There does not appear to be any case directly on point. However, some guidance is provided by cases pertaining to the issue of whether gain on the sale of this dual-use or changed-use property constitutes capital gain or ordinary income.[88] These cases suggest that as long as the property is offered for both sale and lease, it should be treated as inventory. Thus, the burden would be on the taxpayer to show that in the particular circumstances, the property should not be included in inventory.[89]

Where property has been acquired for purposes other than sale to customers in the ordinary course of business but is thereafter converted to that purpose, the issue is somewhat more difficult. The IRS has taken the position that the property, which is not initially treated as inventory, should not be converted to inventory on the change in character.[90] Nevertheless, inasmuch as this is an area of uncertainty, it may be that the particular circumstances should be viewed carefully and that conversion to inventory treatment will not be unwarranted or inappropriate in all cases.[91]

Where property is acquired for the purpose of resale but is temporarily used for some other purpose, it is generally required to be included in inventory even during the period it is used for the other purpose. For example, automobiles that are purchased for resale but are temporarily used as demonstrators should be included in inventory.[92] Where property is originally acquired for inventory purposes but is subsequently converted to

---

[88] See, e.g., Recordak Corp. v. United States, 325 F2d 460 (Ct. Cl. 1963); American Can Co. v. Comm'r, 317 F2d 604 (2d Cir. 1963), cert. denied, 375 US 993 (1964); Continental Can Co. v. United States, 422 F2d 405 (Ct. Cl. 1970), cert. denied, 400 US 819 (1970).

[89] See, e.g., Honeywell, Inc., 64 TCM 437 (1992) and discussion infra ¶ 6.05[1][g].

[90] See George S. Jephson, 37 BTA 1117 (1938); Massey Motors, Inc. v. United States, 364 US 92 (1960); Priv. Ltr. Rul. 7917004 (Jan. 3, 1979). See also Kermit M. DeHaai, 56 TCM 1549 (1989), involving a determination that property was not merchandise even though some of the property was originally intended to be sold though it was subject to an agreement that was not common in agreements for the sale of goods.

[91] See analysis of court in Grant Oil Tool Co. v. United States, 381 F2d 389 (Ct. Cl. 1967), where inventories were not required for oil well drilling tools manufactured by the taxpayer for lease to drillers even though similar items were sometimes sold on the request of some drilling contractors.

[92] See W.R. Stephens Co., 10 TCM 688 (1951), aff'd, 199 F2d 665 (8th Cir. 1952); Rev. Rul. 75-538, 1975-2 CB 34. See also Albright v. United States, 173 F2d

noninventory use, the property should be removed from the inventory, and it should be treated as used property acquired for trade or business purposes.

[f] Ordinary Course of Business

Assuming items are acquired for sale (and, in fact, are sold), such acquisition and sale must have been in the ordinary course of business for the items to be subject to the requirements governing merchandise inventory. Typically, this means that the acquisition for sale was made with a view toward making a profit and was not an isolated event but part of a regular course of business conduct.

[i] **Profit element.** The profit element is important in characterizing inventory. If items are acquired for sale at either no profit or at a loss, these items may be excluded from inventory. For example, in *Francisco Sugar Co. v. Commissioner*,[93] a sugar manufacturer doing business in Cuba maintained a large supply of tools, building supplies, pipes, and other articles, some of which were sold to its Cuban workers at no profit to promote goodwill. With respect to supplies sold to the workers, the court held that the inventory rules did not apply to those goods "merely because accountants would carry them in an inventory."[94] The court concluded:

> As a whole, it is true that the business was one in which the "production . . . of merchandise was in an income-producing factor." Such goods are "supplies on hand which have been acquired for sale," or they are "finished goods," but we think that "sale," as applicable to this situation, means one which produces some income. . . . In general, sale implies the motive of profit; to extend it to such a case as this is beyond its usual significance.[95]

Although *Francisco Sugar Co.* is but one case and it is not certain if the lack of a profit motive would be determinative in all cases, the case does

---

339 (8th Cir. 1949); Duval Motor Co. v. Comm'r, 264 F2d 548 (5th Cir. 1959), pertaining to automobiles used as demonstrators and by company officials and salesmen for other business use; Rev. Rul. 89-25, 1989-1 CB 79, pertaining to the temporary use of residential homes as models and sales offices.

[93] Francisco Sugar Co. v. Comm'r, 47 F2d 555 (2d Cir. 1931).

[94] Id. at 557.

[95] Id. See also Pierce-Arrow Motor Car Co. v. United States, 9 F. Supp. 577 (Ct. Cl. 1935), where the court found that steel used by an automobile manufacturer was not merchandise, because it was not the type of inventory normally maintained for sale at a profit in the ordinary course of its business. This result applied even though some surplus steel was later offered for sale by the manufacturer.

point out the importance of taxpayer intent.[96] If profit is not intended, it may be incorrect to treat the goods as having been acquired for sale (i.e., as merchandise).[97]

[ii] **Regular business activity.** The proper characterization may also depend on whether the items are acquired and sold in the ordinary course of the business. To the extent items are acquired or sold outside the ordinary course of business, the possibility exists that they may be excluded from merchandise inventory or treated as being separate from the taxpayer's normal inventory. For example, in *United States v. Ingredient Technology Corp.*,[98] the taxpayer, a sugar refiner, sought to characterize items purchased as merchandise to avoid a liquidation of low-basis LIFO inventory.[99] The court held that the purchased raw sugar was not merchandise because the refiner had previously agreed to resell the sugar to the original seller. The court noted that the refiner "would have us give meaning to inventory which was never intended to be used or sold in the regular course of business. In fact, the transaction was designed *not* to earn money. . . ."[100]

Again, a case like this does not establish an unyielding rule that all purchases and sales outside the regular course of business will be excluded from treatment as inventory. Rather, it points out the need for taxpayers to scrutinize carefully any unusual transactions to determine their tax effect.[101]

As a practical matter, if the transaction is one that is unusual but nevertheless intended to enhance the regular business activity of the taxpayer or

---

[96] See United States v. Ingredient Technology Corp., 698 F2d 88 (2d Cir. 1983), cert. denied, 462 US 1131 (1983). See discussion infra ¶ 6.05[1][g] regarding taxpayer intent.

[97] See A. Raymond Jones, 25 TC 1100 (1956), acq. 1958-2 CB 6, rev'd on another issue, 259 F2d 300 (5th Cir. 1958), where goods acquired as accommodation for customer and sold to him at no profit were found not to be inventory.

[98] United States v. Ingredient Technology Corp., 698 F2d 88 (2d Cir. 1983), cert. denied, 462 US 1131 (1983).

[99] See ¶ 7.07 for discussion of the tax consequences resulting from liquidation of LIFO inventory.

[100] United States v. Ingredient Technology Corp., 698 F2d 88, 94 (emphasis by court); accord Illinois Cereal Mills, Inc., 46 TCM 1001, 1018 (1983), aff'd, 789 F2d 1234 (7th Cir. 1986), where taxpayer could not artificially inflate year-end inventory of corn because only property acquired for sale "in the ordinary course of business" or "physically incorporated into finished goods and intended for sale" is properly includable in inventory; Rev. Rul. 79-188, 1979-1 CB 191, where jewelry manufacturer could not treat certain gold as inventory where the gold was purchased near year-end (to prevent a liquidation of LIFO inventories) and then resold to the original supplier.

[101] See Illinois Cereal Mills, Inc., 46 TCM 1001 (1983), aff'd, 789 F2d 1234 (7th Cir. 1986), where the court stated that the taxpayer could not increase its year-end inventory of raw corn by purchasing warehouse receipts near the end of the fiscal year under a contract to reconvey.

to attain legitimate business objectives, its treatment should be in accord with regular treatment. For example, it is not unusual for a taxpayer to acquire and sell some goods at a loss to encourage customers to purchase other items or otherwise to promote its business. The issue in such a case is whether the taxpayer's acquisition and sale should be treated as the purchase and sale of items of merchandise inventory or as promotional activity, the cost of which should be deducted as advertising. Similarly, a taxpayer might accelerate purchases or purchase large quantities of inventory items. The issue here is whether there has been a purchase of inventory (e.g., to ensure a sufficient supply or to protect against anticipated price increases) or the making of an investment unrelated to the reasonable or foreseeable needs of the business for inventory. Even if the intent of the taxpayer is to structure purchase and sale transactions to reduce taxation (e.g., by increasing inventory to avoid liquidations of LIFO inventory), it is appropriate for the IRS to recognize these transactions as true purchases and sales unless other circumstances demonstrate that the transactions are not bona fide.

[g] Taxpayer Intent

An important factor in determining whether there has been a sale of goods or a provision of services is the essential nature of the transaction, including how the parties themselves viewed the transaction. In *Honeywell, Inc.*,[102] an accrual method taxpayer was in the business of selling, maintaining, and servicing computers that were available for both lease or sale to customers. The taxpayer typically entered into maintenance agreements that required it to provide its customers with the parts, materials, and labor needed to repair their computers. The taxpayer charged its customers a fixed fee for the maintenance agreement that was based on a number of factors, including the cost of replacement parts.

The taxpayer treated its inventory of parts as depreciable property and not as a merchandise inventory that had been acquired for sale. The main issue before the court was whether the Commissioner abused her discretion in determining that the taxpayer's inventory of parts should be treated as merchandise. The Commissioner argued, among other things, that the parts were merchandise, because title to the parts was transferred to the customer at the time of installation, the customer obtained all indicia of ownership, and, according to the Commissioner, a sale necessarily occurred. Notwithstanding these circumstances, the taxpayer argued that it was engaged in the business of selling services, not parts, and that its parts inventory was nothing more than an asset used in its business.

In response, the court stated that the parts would be regarded as merchandise within the meaning of the regulations only if they were acquired

---

[102] Honeywell, Inc., 64 TCM 437 (1992).

and held for sale and that for the parts to have been acquired and held for sale, the taxpayer must have intended that they be sold. The court then looked to the essence of the transaction to decide whether the parts had been acquired and held for sale. The court noted that, in effect, the owner of the computer (the taxpayer's customers) had broken or defective computers and sought only to have their computers fixed. The parts, which were delivered by the taxpayer to its customers in connection with the repairs, were, in essence, nothing more than assets or supplies used in providing services. Accordingly, the court concluded that the taxpayer's inventory of parts was not acquired and held for sale and, therefore, was not merchandise within the meaning of the regulations.

Among the factors noted by the court as being influential were (1) the desire of the customer to have its computer repaired; (2) the fact that the price for the maintenance agreement was established prior to the time the taxpayer or the customer would have been in a position to determine what parts, if any, would be needed to repair the computer should it become defective (i.e., the charge for maintenance services could not be tied directly to the cost of the parts that might be used in providing the maintenance services); (3) the charge for the maintenance agreement would be the same whether computers were leased or sold or whether parts would be needed to maintain the computers during the maintenance period; and (4) the fact that the customer generally would be indifferent as to whether parts would be replaced, the customer wanting merely its computer to function properly. Consequently, the court made it clear that in evaluating whether a taxpayer has merchandise, supplies, or depreciable property and whether such property is used in providing services or is sold, all relevant facts and circumstances, including the intent of the parties, must be considered. Moreover, the fact that the tangible property itself, as well as title to that property, is conveyed by the taxpayer to its customer is not determinative.

[2] Supplies Under Section 162

Virtually all taxpayers, whether they sell goods or provide services, maintain and use supplies. Supply items range from paper, pencils, cleaning items, and toiletries used in all businesses to small parts and tools, oil, and lubricants used in the manufacture of merchandise. Key issues regarding supplies include the periods in which their cost is deductible and the extent to which these items are subject to the requirements of Sections 471 and 263A pertaining to merchandise inventory.

The analysis of supplies begins with the applicable regulation under Section 162.[103] This regulation applies to both cash and accrual method taxpayers. It permits them to deduct as an expense (or, as may be required

---

[103] Treas. Reg. § 1.162-3 provides as follows:

by the regulations under Sections 471 and 263A, to take into account as an inventoriable cost) the cost of supplies actually used or consumed during the taxable year.[104] However, if the supplies are incidental, if no record of consumption is maintained, and if physical inventories are not taken, then inventories of supplies are not required, and the total cost of the supplies purchased during the year may be deducted (or taken into account as an inventoriable cost).[105]

[a] Business Expense or Inventoriable Cost

If supplies are not used in the manufacture of inventory for sale to customers in the ordinary course of business, the cost of the supplies may be deducted as an ordinary and necessary business expense. However, if the supplies are used in the manufacture of merchandise, the cost of the supplies is not deductible under Section 162 but is taken into account in determining inventoriable merchandise costs under Section 263A and Treasury Regulation § 1.471-11.[106]

EXAMPLE: Assume an accrual method taxpayer uses pencils in the course of providing services to clients, that it has no pencils at the beginning of the year, purchases 1,000 at $1 per pencil during the year, and has 50 pencils remaining at the end of the year. Since the pencils are not merchandise and are not used in producing merchandise, the cost of the pencils is not treated as an inventoriable cost. The only issue is whether inventories of pencils are required so that the taxpayer's deduction is limited to the cost of the pencils consumed during the year or whether inventories are not required.[107] If inventories are required,

---

Taxpayers carrying materials and supplies on hand should include in expenses the charges for materials and supplies only in the amount that they are actually consumed and used in operation during the taxable year for which the return is made, provided that the cost of such materials and supplies have not been deducted in determining the net income or loss or taxable income for any previous year. If a taxpayer carries incidental materials or supplies on hand for which no record of consumption is kept or of which physical inventories at the beginning and end of the year are not taken, it will be permissible for the taxpayer to include in his expenses and to deduct from gross income the total cost of such supplies and materials as were purchased during the taxable year for which the return is made, provided the taxable income is clearly reflected by this method.

[104] Treas. Reg. § 1.162-3. See discussion infra ¶¶ 6.06[2][c][i], 6.06[2][c][ii], Treas. Reg. § 1.471-11(c)(2)(i)(F), and Temp. Reg. § 1.263A-1T(b)(2)(iii)(F) regarding the treatment of supplies as an inventoriable cost.

[105] Treas. Reg. § 1.162-3. See discussion infra ¶ 6.05[2][c].

[106] See discussion infra ¶¶ 6.06[2][c][i], 6.06[2][c][ii].

[107] See infra ¶¶ 6.05[2][b], 6.05[2][c], regarding the need for supply inventories.

the taxpayer in this example is entitled to a deduction of $950 for the cost of the pencils consumed during the year (beginning inventory of $0 plus cost of supplies purchased $1,000 minus cost of ending inventory $50). If supply inventories are not required, the taxpayer's deduction is $1,000. If the taxpayer uses the cash method, its deduction is limited to that portion of the $1,000 cost actually paid within the year.

Alternatively, if the facts are the same as in the preceding example except that the taxpayer is a manufacturer of merchandise and the supply items are acquired for use in manufacturing merchandise, the same issue exists as to whether supply inventories are required. However, instead of the applicable amount (either $950 or $1,000, depending on whether supply inventories are required) being entirely deductible in the year, that amount is treated as an inventoriable cost and, hence, some portion of the $950 or $1,000 must be allocated to ending merchandise inventory with the balance treated as part of the cost of goods sold.[108] The Treasury's interpretation of the law was well understood and generally accepted by taxpayers for many years. However, doubt as to the Treasury's position has been created by Notice 88-86.[109] This Notice, while seeking to clarify whether the uniform capitalization costing rules apply to taxpayers who provide both goods and services to customers, indicated that where the goods provided to customers are not de minimis in amount, the provisions of Section 263A (regarding property acquired for resale) will apply, notwithstanding the fact that the predominant nature of the taxpayer's business is the rendition of services. This position is consistent with the application of law prior to the 1986 Act. However, the Notice adds that property will in no event be considered de minimis if it would be classified as inventory under Section 471 or the regulations thereunder. Thus, the only property for which the de minimis rule is applicable would be inventories not previously subject to Section 471, i.e., supply inventories. These statements by the Treasury give the impression that all property previously subject to Section 471 is now subject to the uniform capitalization rules (assuming no other exclusion applies) and, more significantly, that the uniform capitalization rules are also applicable to supplies if supplies are acquired for resale. However, if supplies are acquired for resale, the supplies generally will be classified as merchandise. This confusion and circularity of language should be eliminated when final regulations are adopted. If the supplies are not acquired for resale, the supplies should not be subject to the uniform capitalization costing rules, except to the extent they are used in the production of merchandise.[110] In this case, the cost of supplies becomes part of the cost of the merchandise.

---

[108] See discussion infra ¶ 6.06 regarding inventoriable costs.

[109] Notice 88-86, 1988-34 IRB 10 (1988).

[110] See id. at Section VI for the rules regarding expedited changes in methods of accounting under the Notice.

However, the cost of the supplies itself should not be subject to the uniform capitalization costing rules. To the extent the Notice suggests a contrary conclusion, the Notice would appear to be inconsistent with other authorities and incorrect.

[b] Supplies Inventories Required

In the absence of particular circumstances,[111] only the cost of supplies used or consumed during the taxable year may be deducted or treated as an inventoriable cost. To compute the supplies used or consumed, it is anticipated that the taxpayer will maintain inventories of supplies and apply the following formula:

> Beginning inventory of supplies
> + Cost of supplies purchased during the year
> − Ending inventory of supplies
> = Cost of supplies consumed

Except for supplies that became part of the merchandise intended for sale (and, hence, are considered merchandise), supplies inventories themselves are generally not subject to the requirements of Sections 263A, 471, and 472. Thus, supply inventories are not subject to the costing rules of Sections 263A and 471, are not eligible for write-downs (should their market values decline below cost),[112] and are not eligible to elect the LIFO method.[113] (See Chapter 7.)

As a consequence, when supply inventories are required, taxpayers should give consideration to the actual flow of supplies used. Costs may then be assigned to ending supply inventory on a basis consistent with that flow.

As a practical matter, the IRS will accept a first-in, first-out (FIFO) approach in assigning costs to supplies.[114] However, a LIFO approach may be used if goods are actually removed from supply inventories on a LIFO basis. For example, in *Madison Gas & Electric Co.*,[115] the taxpayer's supply inventories included coal. The taxpayer used the coal that was most recently added to its coal pile. The accounting method used by the taxpayer in computing its coal inventory was similar to LIFO. The Commissioner sought

---

[111] See discussion infra ¶ 6.05[2][c].

[112] In Notice 88-86, 1988-34 IRB 10, the Treasury announced that these same rules apply under Section 263A (i.e., supplies used or consumed in producing or acquiring property for resale shall be treated as an inventoriable cost under Section 263A). But see discussion supra ¶ 6.05[2][a].

[113] See infra ¶¶ 6.06 regarding the costing rules of Sections 471 and 263A, 6.09 regarding write-downs from cost to market.

[114] See infra ¶ 6.08 for an illustration of FIFO and LIFO cost-flow assumptions.

[115] Madison Gas & Elec. Co., 72 TC 521 (1979), aff'd, 633 F2d 512 (7th Cir. 1980).

to require the taxpayer to use a FIFO approach. The court rejected the Commissioner's position. The court also rejected the Commissioner's argument that the taxpayer should have filed an application for the adoption and use of LIFO.[116] The court pointed out that the key issue in computing supply inventories is determining the cost of the supplies actually consumed, and the taxpayer's method did this.

[c] Supplies Inventories Not Required

If supplies are "incidental," no record of consumption is maintained, and physical inventories are not taken at the beginning and end of the year, then the total cost of supplies purchased during the year may be deducted (or taken into account as an inventoriable cost), as long as income is clearly reflected. This rule has the effect of accelerating the deduction (or the treatment as an inventoriable cost) of the cost that would otherwise be allocated to the ending supplies inventory. For example, if a taxpayer acquired 100 units of supplies during the year at $1 per unit, the entire $100 would be deducted in the year (or treated as an inventoriable cost of that year). However, if the taxpayer maintained records (or took counts) showing that 20 units were on hand at the end of the year, only $80 could be deducted (or taken into account as an inventoriable cost) in the year.

The rationale behind this provision seems clear. Many taxpayers do not maintain financial accounting records of consumption and do not take physical inventories of the supplies on hand at the beginning and end of the year for business purposes. In these cases, it would be inconsistent with the book conformity requirement of Section 446(a),[117] impractical, and unduly burdensome to require that they undertake such record-keeping responsibilities or make such physical counts solely for tax purposes. However, to protect the Treasury against taxpayers who might avoid undertaking these activities solely for the purpose of obtaining a tax benefit, two protections are afforded. First, the supplies must be incidental and, second, the taxable income so computed must be reflected clearly.

The three issues that typically arise from the application of this special provision of the regulations are whether (1) records of consumption are maintained; (2) supplies inventories are incidental; and (3) income will be reflected clearly. Although these issues are important and often involve substantial amounts of money, surprisingly few cases have focused on them.

[i] **Records of consumption and physical inventories.** If the taxpayer maintains records of consumption or takes physical inventories to determine

---

[116] Taxpayers generally may adopt the LIFO method for merchandise inventories only by filing an appropriate election. See discussion at ¶ 7.03[1].

[117] See ¶ 2.02[1] for discussion of the book conformity requirement.

consumption, it is reasonable for the benefit of that record keeping or accounting to be available to the government in determining the amount of supplies consumed.[118] Correlatively, if a taxpayer does not maintain these records or take physical counts for financial accounting purposes, it would seem unreasonable for these records to be required solely for tax purposes.

Obviously, every taxpayer has some records pertaining to supplies. At a minimum, for example, these consist of invoices and canceled checks. More sophisticated accounting systems may use purchase orders, retain identification numbers, or store other information to facilitate reordering. In addition, it is not unusual for persons outside of the accounting department who are responsible for maintaining physical control over various supply items to establish their own record keeping on an ad hoc basis. For example, they may attempt to maintain a list of items on hand, the number of each, and the persons or departments to whom these items are issued.

In these circumstances, the question arises as to whether such informal information constitutes records of consumption or the taking of physical inventories. Although this issue does not appear to have been addressed by the courts, it is an issue that frequently arises on audit. It would appear that the proper resolution of the issue would be for these records and counts not to be treated as records of consumption or the taking of physical inventories in the sense contemplated by the regulation. This conclusion is based on several factors. First, the records and counts are generally not part of the taxpayer's financial accounting system or practices. Rather, they are ad hoc records whose reliability and accuracy are often in doubt. Second, the records are not used by the taxpayer in computing income for book or financial reporting purposes. To treat the records or counts as part of the bookkeeping system of computing income is erroneous and inconsistent with Section 446(a). Third, as a practical matter, even if the records were accurate, it would not be possible to determine the dollar amount of supplies consumed without the development of additional records.

Of course, each taxpayer's supply records must be evaluated on the basis of the particular facts and circumstances. For example, a taxpayer should not be able to ignore for tax purposes reliable information about its supplies inventory, especially if that information is readily available and used for financial accounting purposes.[119]

[ii] Incidental supplies. Common sense must be used in determining whether supplies are "incidental." Consideration should be given to the

---

[118] Indeed, this is seemingly required under the book conformity requirement of Section 446(a). See discussion at ¶ 2.02[1].

[119] See David Baird & Son, Inc., 2 BTA 901 (1925), where memorandum accounts were found sufficient to be treated as records of consumption, but those memorandum accounts apparently showed the dollar value of the supplies on hand at the end of the year as contrasted with merely representing the physical number of items on hand at such time.

nature of the supplies as well as to the relative dollar values of the items on hand. For example, manufacturing facilities often have thousands of items, such as nuts, bolts, screws, and nails. It would be highly impractical and uneconomical for taxpayers to inventory such items solely for tax purposes.

In addition, "incidental" need not be considered synonymous with immaterial. For example, in *Smith Leasing Co.*,[120] supplies on hand at the end of the year with a value of approximately $20,000 were permitted to be deducted even though they constituted almost 10 percent of the assets to which they related.

The IRS has defined "incidental supplies" to mean supplies of secondary or minor importance. Consequently, it has sought to exclude from the concept of "incidental," items that were essential for the taxpayer's manufacturing process.[121] Again, however, common sense must be exercised.[122] For example, if a certain type of oil is necessary for machinery to work, the absence of the oil may prevent the machinery from working and cause production to stop. In this sense, the oil is essential. On the other hand, if the machinery requires virtually no oil or only a small amount each year, it makes no sense to require the taxpayer to determine the amount of oil on hand at the end of the year.

[iii] **Clear reflection of income.** The clear reflection of income requirement must not be used by the IRS to require supply inventories in all cases. Rather, the requirement should be used by the IRS to guard against taxpayer abuse.[123]

[3] Other Inventories—Ability to Trace Costs

Except for use of a specific identification method of inventory accounting,[124] the use of merchandise inventories involves the aggregation of inventoriable costs and the allocation of those costs between items sold during the year and items remaining on hand at the end of the year (i.e., remaining in ending inventory). An underlying assumption of these aggregation and allocation

---

[120] Smith Leasing Co., 43 TC 37 (1964), acq. 1965-2 CB 6.

[121] See, e.g., Priv. Ltr. Rul. 7936014 (May 23, 1979), where the IRS required supply inventories of perishable tools.

[122] See Rev. Rul. 69-81, 1969-1 CB 137, where an industrial laundry was permitted to expense items with a useful life of one year or less as such items were placed in service. Thus, once placed in service, the items were not required to be included in supplies inventory.

[123] The clear reflection of income requirement is discussed at ¶ 2.02[2].

[124] Treas. Reg. § 1.471-2(d) provides rules for valuing inventories where goods "have been so intermingled that they cannot be identified with specific invoices." This implies that the IRS could require the use of a specific identification method where such method is possible.

rules is that fungible items are involved. However, this is not always the case, and questions have sometimes been raised as to whether unique items, such as real estate and special order merchandise, should be subject to the requirements governing merchandise inventories.

[a] Real Estate

Traditionally, real estate has not been treated as merchandise subject to the requirements of Sections 471 and 446.[125] The exclusion of real property from merchandise inventory prevents real estate dealers from determining the tax basis of real estate on the basis of the lower-of-cost-or-market concept.[126] Thus, declines in value from cost cannot be deducted in the year incurred. The exclusion of real property from merchandise inventory also prevents real estate dealers from using methods of accounting such as FIFO and LIFO in determining the tax basis of their properties.[127]

[b] Special Order Merchandise

Many manufacturers produce custom merchandise pursuant to special order. Frequently, the cost of this merchandise is accounted for separately and, hence, manufacturers are able to match these costs against sales price to determine gain. In these instances, the IRS has required the use of inventories and an accrual method.[128] On the other hand, the IRS has frequently challenged the use of LIFO in these cases, particularly in connec-

---

[125] See OD 848, 4 CB 47 (1921), superseded by Rev. Rul. 69-536, 1969-2 CB 109; see also W.C. & A.N. Miller Dev. Co., 81 TC 619 (1983), where the Tax Court found that the bricks, lumber, mortar, and other items purchased by the taxpayer for the purpose of constructing, remodeling, and selling residential property were not inventories under Section 471, the court stating that real property should not be considered merchandise and pointing out that the term "merchandise" was defined to encompass wares and goods, not realty; Atlantic Coast Realty Co., 11 BTA 416 (1928); Albert F. Keeney, 17 BTA 560 (1929), acq. in result IX-1 CB 29 (1930), each of which refused to treat real property as inventory.

[126] See discussion infra ¶ 6.09. See also Rev. Rul. 86-149, 1986-2 CB 67, where the use of the LIFO method was denied to a real estate developer.

[127] See discussion infra ¶ 6.08[2]. See also Rev. Rul. 86-149, 1986-2 CB 67, where the use of the LIFO method was denied to a real estate developer.

[128] See, e.g., Frank G. Wikstrom & Sons, Inc., 20 TC 359 (1953); Fame Tool & Mfg. Co., Inc. v. United States, 334 F. Supp. 23 (SD Ohio 1971), where such goods were found to be inventory. Such goods are treated as inventoriable goods, the purchases and sales of which must be reported under an accrual method, even if the taxpayer has no (or virtually no) ending inventory because whatever is not used for a specific job is returned to the supplier. See J.P. Sheahan Assocs., Inc., 63 TCM 2842 (1992).

tion with goods produced under long-term contracts, but the IRS has generally been unsuccessful.[129]

¶ 6.06 INVENTORIABLE COSTS

Taxpayers incur many costs in the course of their business activities. To the extent these costs are incurred in connection with the acquisition or production of merchandise inventories, the costs are not deductible in the year incurred; rather, they must be included in the basis of the inventory so acquired or produced. That basis is taken into account for tax purposes in the year in which the inventory is sold or otherwise disposed of.[130] The costs that must be included within the basis of the merchandise inventory are referred to as inventoriable costs.

Costs that are not inventoriable costs are generally deductible as trade or business expenses under Section 162. Consequently, the determination of inventoriable costs is one of the most significant determinations that can be made for inventory tax accounting purposes.

To a large extent, the proper identification and characterization of costs as inventoriable costs depends on the methods, systems, approaches, and procedures adopted by the taxpayer for financial accounting purposes. Thus, the prudent taxpayer must take into account the tax accounting consequences of these financial accounting decisions.

As a result of the 1986 Act, many of the inventory costing rules were changed to include within the ambit of inventoriable costs a number of costs that previously had been treated as period costs. The legislative history of the 1986 Act indicates that these changes are intended to more clearly reflect income by a better matching of revenues and costs than was achieved under prior law.[131] In addition, the 1986 Act requires significantly more uniformity in the identification and characterization of inventory costs than had been the case under prior law. This greater uniformity in treatment is premised on the need and perceived desire for more uniform and equitable treatment of all taxpayers.[132] Notwithstanding these assertions, the changes are widely perceived among taxpayers and their advisors to be based on the congressional desire to make the 1986 Act as revenue neutral as possible. Simply stated,

---

[129] See, e.g., Peninsula Steel Prods. & Equip. Co., 78 TC 1029 (1982); Spang Indus., Inc., 84-2 USTC ¶ 9739 (Ct. Cl. 1984), rev'd, 791 F2d 906 (Fed. Cir. 1986); RECO Indus., Inc., 83 TC 912 (1984).

[130] If the market value of the inventory declines from its cost, the difference may be deducted in the year in which the decline occurs even though the inventory is still on hand. See discussion infra ¶ 6.09.

[131] General Explanation of the Tax Reform Act of 1986, at 508–509 (May 4, 1987).

[132] Id.

changes in inventory costing rules are a complex matter that do not receive a great deal of attention. Consequently, these changes may often be made without significant adverse public reaction. Nevertheless, as taxpayers and their tax and business advisors begin to review the inventory costing requirements of the 1986 Act and integrate them into their accounting systems, it may be expected that substantial issues involving significant amounts of money will arise. Moreover, the complexity of the new rules and the lack of adequate records and record-keeping systems may cause initial compliance with the new rules to be a matter of estimate and guesswork

[1] Wholesalers, Retailers, and Other Nonmanufacturers

Inventories of wholesalers, retailers, and other nonmanufacturers generally must be computed at cost.[133] For this purpose, the items included within the inventory's cost will vary, depending on whether the taxpayer is subject to Section 263A, which was enacted as part of the 1986 Act. For those wholesalers, retailers, and other nonmanufacturers not subject to Section 263A, cost consists of the same items as under pre–1986 Act law. For those subject to Section 263A, cost consists of all pre–1986 Act items plus some new ones.[134]

Prior to the 1986 Act, cost was relatively easy to determine. It consisted of all costs and expenses incurred in acquiring possession of the goods. Thus, it usually consisted of the invoice price of the goods (taking into account applicable discounts) and all applicable transportation costs, handling costs, and other costs incurred in acquiring possession of the goods.[135]

The focus was on costs incurred in acquiring possession of the goods. Costs incurred in storing the goods, insuring the goods, or otherwise in maintaining the goods after acquisition were not part of the cost of the goods.[136] Rather, they were treated as ordinary and necessary business expenses, the deduction of which was controlled by other sections of the Code.

For taxpayers not covered by Section 263A (i.e., those whose average gross receipts do not exceed $10 million), the pre–1986 Act principles still apply. However, for those wholesalers, retailers, and other nonmanufacturers whose average gross receipts exceed $10 million, the costs of their merchan-

---

[133] See infra ¶¶ 6.09 regarding the valuation of inventories at the lower of cost or market, 6.10 regarding special inventory costing rules.

[134] The impact of the 1986 and 1987 Acts is discussed infra ¶ 6.06[1][c].

[135] Treas. Reg. § 1.471-3(b). For financial accounting purposes, "cost" has been defined as "the sum of the applicable expenditures and charges directly or indirectly incurred in bringing an article to its existing condition and location." ARB No. 43, ch. 4, Statement 3 (AICPA 1953).

[136] See, e.g., George C. Peterson Co., 1 BTA 690 (1925), acq. IV-1 CB 3, regarding shipping costs; McIntosh Mills, 9 BTA 301 (1927), acq. VII-1 CB 21, regarding warehouse and drayage costs.

dise inventories are subject to the requirements of Section 263A.[137] However, two items that affect all taxpayers, whether covered by the new rules or not, are discounts and so-called excessive costs. These two items are discussed in the immediately succeeding sections, followed by a discussion of the new Section 263A rules.

Of particular importance is determining whether a taxpayer is a manufacturer or nonmanufacturer. If the taxpayer is a manufacturer, the provisions of Section 263A apply notwithstanding the size of the taxpayer's business.[138] However, if the taxpayer is not a manufacturer, the provisions of Section 263A apply only if the taxpayer's average gross receipts exceed $10 million. In applying the $10 million average gross receipts test, the gross receipts to be taken into account include gross receipts from all sources of revenue, not merely gross receipts from the sale of inventory.[139]

Consequently, a major issue is whether manufacturing activities of a taxpayer, who is principally a nonmanufacturer, will cause the taxpayer to be treated as a manufacturer for purposes of Section 263A. Examples include retailers such as supermarkets who devote a portion of their space to preparing foods for consumption on the premises or for takeout, retailers and wholesalers who assemble some or all of the products they sell, and retailers and wholesalers who install products for their customers.

In Notice 88-86,[140] the Treasury indicated that forthcoming regulations would provide a de minimis rule for retailers, wholesalers, and other nonmanufacturers who engage in some production or manufacturing activities. The rule would allow such taxpayers to use the simplified resale method[141] (i.e., they will not be precluded from use of that method solely by reason of a de minimis amount of production activities). The determination as to whether the amount of production activities is de minimis will be made on the basis of all the facts and circumstances. Appropriate consideration will be given to the relative volumes of the production and resale activities.

Unfortunately, the Notice did not suggest that rules would be provided for determining whether the taxpayer should be characterized as a manufacturer or nonmanufacturer for purposes of applying the Section 263A rules. Hopefully, similar de minimis rules will be provided so that a taxpayer whose average gross receipts or manufacturing activities are quite small will not be subject to Section 263A. However, until such rules are provided, taxpayers who produce or manufacture merchandise must cost such merchandise under Section 263A, notwithstanding the size of their business or the amount of

---

[137] See infra ¶ 6.06[1][c] for discussion of the manner in which these new costing rules affect these wholesalers, retailers, and other nonmanufacturers.

[138] See discussion infra ¶ 6.06[2][c][ii].

[139] See Temp. Reg. § 1.263A-1T(d)(2)(iv)(A); Rev. Rul. 89-26, 1989-1 CB 87 (1989).

[140] Notice 88-86, 1988-2 CB 401 (1988).

[141] The simplified resale method is discussed infra ¶ 6.06[1][c][ii].

such merchandise. In other words, taxpayers who manufacture some merchandise but act as retailers or wholesalers with respect to other merchandise must apply Section 263A to the manufactured merchandise (i.e., all manufacturing inventory), but should not be required to apply Section 263A to the nonmanufactured merchandise (i.e., all other inventory) unless the applicable average gross receipts test of Section 263A(b)(2)(B) is satisfied.

[a] Discounts

Discounts may be of several types. The most common are trade discounts and cash discounts.

[i] **Trade discounts.** Trade discounts are usually considered adjustments to the purchase price and are available to the purchaser without regard to the timeliness of payment. They are frequently available in connection with purchases of a specified quantity of goods or as the result of various incentive programs offered by a seller. Trade discounts should be regarded as reductions in or adjustments to the purchase price. In other words, the cost of the item to the purchaser is the invoice cost less the trade discount.[142]

The question has sometimes been raised as to the precision with which trade discounts must be determined. Precise determinations of trade discounts may not be required where the record-keeping costs would be exorbitant. For example, early cases suggest that adequate and reasonable determinations of trade discounts will be accepted.[143] However, arbitrary determinations will not be permitted.[144]

[ii] **Cash discounts.** Cash discounts generally are reductions in the invoice cost attributable to prompt or early payment. It is typical for vendors to offer a reduction in the purchase price if payment is made within a specified period.

A cash discount may be treated as a reduction in the purchase price or as a miscellaneous item of income.[145] If treated as a reduction in purchase

---

[142] Treas. Reg. § 1.471-3(b).

[143] See, e.g., Blumberg Bros. Co., 12 BTA 1021, 1023 (1928), nonacq. VIII-1 CB 51, where the court approved an inventory adjustment of 5 percent to take the discounts into account based on fact that the adjustment was consistently used and "substantially and to all practical purposes correct"; Trorlicht-Duncker Carpet Co., 22 BTA 466, 473 (1931), acq. X-2 CB 71, where the taxpayer's method of computing discounts was followed for several years under the advice of accountants and found to be "substantially accurate and therefore is satisfactory for the purpose of ascertaining cost."

[144] C.E. Longley Co., 4 BTA 246 (1926).

[145] See Warfield-Pratt-Howell Co., 13 BTA 305 (1928).

price, then any discounts not taken are treated as expenses.[146] If treated as an item of income, the cost of the items purchased is the gross price without regard to the discount.[147]

As with trade discounts, questions sometimes arise as to the precision with which cash discounts must be determined. The IRS construes the applicable regulations to permit only actual discounts to be taken into account,[148] but the courts have taken a more lenient attitude, allowing approximations.[149]

[b] Excessive Costs

Inventory costs may be excessive or above normal in particular circumstances, such as when supplies are limited and premiums have to be paid to acquire the goods. An important issue in these circumstances is whether the premium or excess costs may be deducted in the period to which they relate or must be treated as part of the cost of the acquired inventory. Although sound economic arguments can be made for either position,[150] the Supreme Court indicated in *Thor Power Tool Co.*[151] that the inventory regulations should be construed strictly. In that case, the Court said that these regulations suggest that the full amount of inventoriable costs must be taken into account, even if these costs are abnormally high. Thus, it appears that the more appropriate result for tax purposes is that these costs should be part of the cost of the inventory.

[c] Impact of 1986 Act

Under new Section 263A, retailers and wholesalers must include within their inventoriable costs not only the direct costs of acquiring goods (as

---

[146] Rev. Rul. 73-65, 1973-1 CB 216.

[147] See Rev. Rul. 73-65, 1973-1 CB 216, where it was noted that under the permissable "gross invoices valuation method, the gross invoice prices are charged to purchases and cash discounts are accounted for as income items."

[148] See Treas. Reg. § 1.471-3(b); Rev. Rul. 69-619, 1969-2 CB 111, where taxpayer was not allowed to average cash discounts received as a basis for reducing the invoice price of goods on hand, the IRS noting that Treas. Reg. § 1.471-3(b) "is to be construed literally."

[149] See, e.g., Leedom & Worrall Co., 10 BTA 825, 831 (1928), where the use of average cash discounts was approved despite an IRS argument that the amount claimed was a "mere approximation and the true amount of the discounts should be ascertained"; J.M. Radford Grocery Co., 19 BTA 1023 (1930), nonacq. X-1 CB 90, where the taxpayer's consistent practice of deducting average cash discounts was approved.

[150] For financial accounting purposes, excessive acquisition costs should be treated as period costs. ARB No. 43, ch. 4, Statement 3 (AICPA 1953).

[151] See Thor Power Tool Co. v. Comm'r, 439 US 522 (1979).

described previously),[152] but also a share of the taxpayer's indirect costs of acquiring and holding inventory.[153] However, the new rules do not apply to taxpayers whose average gross receipts are $10 million or less.[154]

In determining whether Section 263A applies, the taxpayer must review its annual gross revenues for the three-taxable-year period ending with the taxable year preceding the current taxable year. In other words, a taxpayer who is in its sixth year of operation will examine gross revenues for the three-year taxable period ending with year 5. Aggregation rules, similar to those specified in Section 448(c), apply to prevent a taxpayer from avoiding the impact of the new rules by dividing its inventory among several taxpayers.[155] For taxpayers whose gross receipts do not exceed the specified limit, Section 263A will not affect their computation of inventoriable costs. For taxpayers whose gross receipts exceed the limit, the temporary regulations provide two methods for determining the indirect costs to be treated as inventoriable costs—the general method and the so-called simplified resale method.[156]

[i] **General method.** Under the general method, which is applicable to taxpayers who do not elect the simplified resale method, retailers, wholesalers, and other nonmanufacturers must inventory the same costs that are required to be inventoried by taxpayers electing the simplified resale method,[157] except that the required allocation must be made with the same degree of specificity required of manufacturers.[158] Although use of the simplified method should reduce record-keeping costs, taxpayers must carefully evaluate whether its use will result in a higher allocation of costs to inventory than would be the case under a more precise allocation. Because the simplified resale method treats various portions of cost as inventoriable costs without regard to the actual relationship of the costs to the inventories, use of the simplified method for some businesses may be disadvantageous.[159]

[ii] **Simplified resale methods.** Under the regulations and announcements provided by Treasury, taxpayers may use either of two simplified resale

---

[152] See discussion supra ¶ 6.06[1].

[153] IRC § 263A(a)(2)(B).

[154] IRC § 263A(b)(2)(B).

[155] IRC § 263A(b)(2)(C); see Temp. Reg. § 1.263A-1T(d)(2) and discussion at ¶ 3.06[1][a]. See also Notice 88-86, 1988-34 IRB 10, where the Treasury announced the rules that would be provided in forthcoming regulations for determining the $10 million threshold. The Treasury stated that, among other rules, the regulations would include aggregation rules, annualization rules, and rules governing entities that were not part of an aggregate group of entities during the applicable three-year period.

[156] Temp. Reg. § 1.263A-1T(d).

[157] See discussion infra ¶ 6.06[1][c][ii].

[158] Temp. Reg. §§ 1.263A-1T(d)(1)(i), 1.263A-1T(d)(1)(ii). See discussion infra ¶ 6.06[2].

[159] See discussion infra ¶ 6.06[1][c][ii].

methods—the regular method and an alternative method. Each is discussed below.

Under the regular simplified resale method, the taxpayer computes its inventories just as under prior law. The additional costs required to be capitalized under Section 263A are then added to these preliminary computations to determine the final inventory amounts.[160] The procedures for determining the amounts to be added are discussed later in this section.

The simplified resale method is applied separately to each of the taxpayer's trades or businesses.[161] For a trade or business that consists of both production activities and resale activities, the simplified resale method may not be used.[162] The only simplified procedures available in that situation are those available to manufacturers.[163]

The simplified resale method requires the following indirect costs to be capitalized:[164]

- Off-site storage or warehousing
- Purchasing
- Handling, processing, assembly, and repackaging
- General and administrative

Off-site storage and warehousing costs. Off-site storage and warehousing costs include the costs attributable to all storage or warehousing facilities that are not physically attached to, and not an integral part of, a retail sales facility, which is a facility where the taxpayer sells merchandise stored at that facility to customers physically present at the facility.[165] Consequently, if the facility operates as a center for shipment of goods to customers who purchase the goods through orders placed over the telephone or by mail, it is an off-site storage facility, because customers do not acquire the goods by being physically present at the facility.[166]

If a facility serves both as an off-site storage facility for some operations and an on-site facility for other operations of the taxpayer, a portion of the cost of the facility must be allocated to off-site storage operation and treated as an inventoriable cost.[167] The portion to be allocated is based on the ratio of gross sales made to persons who are physically present at the facility to

---

[160] Temp. Reg. § 1.263A-1T(d)(3)(i).
[161] Id.
[162] Id.
[163] Id. See discussion infra ¶ 6.06[2][c][ii].
[164] Temp. Reg. § 1.263A-1T(d)(3)(ii).
[165] Temp. Reg. § 1.263A-1T(d)(3)(ii)(A)(1).
[166] Id.
[167] Temp. Reg. § 1.263A-1T(d)(3)(ii)(A)(2).

gross sales made by the facility.[168] For example, if 40 percent of the facility's total sales are made to customers who acquired the goods while physically present at the facility, then 40 percent of the costs attributable to the facility will be treated as on-site costs.[169] The balance of 60 percent will be treated as off-site costs and, hence, as inventoriable costs under Section 263A.[170] If the percentage of total facility sales allocable to on-site sales is 10 percent or less, then all sales are considered off-site; correspondingly, if 90 percent or more of total facility sales are attributable to on-site sales, then all the sales are deemed to be on-site sales.[171] This 10 percent/90 percent rule operates as a de minimis rule for dual function facilities.

Following promulgation of the temporary regulations, commentators raised questions about the manner in which these allocation formulae should take into account items that were stored in dual function facilities for shipment (but not sale) to other facilities of the taxpayer or for the taxpayer's own use. The Treasury has stated that forthcoming regulations will provide that the value of shipped items will be included in the denominator of the ratio for purposes of determining whether the facility is a dual function facility and the percentage of the facility that should be treated as an on-site facility.[172] For this purpose, an arm's-length price must be used to value the shipped but unsold items. Additional rules will be provided regarding items that are stored at the facility for the taxpayer's own use.

As a general rule, the off-site storage costs that must be treated as inventoriable costs under Section 263A include direct and indirect labor costs; occupancy expenses, including rent, depreciation, insurance, security, taxes, utilities, and maintenance; materials and supplies; tools and equipment; and general and administrative costs that directly benefit or are incurred by reason of the storage activities.[173] However, to the extent costs are incurred in the off-site storage facility but are not incurred by reason of the storage functions of the facility, these costs need not be treated as inventoriable costs. For example, the labor costs associated with clerical personnel who receive and process customer orders for goods shipped directly to the customer's location are treated as selling or distribution costs and, hence, are not required to be treated as inventoriable costs.[174] In Notice 88-86,[175] the Treasury made it clear that except as may otherwise be provided with respect to the adoption of the simplified production method or simplified resale method, storage costs

---

[168] Id.

[169] Id.

[170] Id.

[171] Temp. Reg. § 1.263A-1T(d)(3)(ii)(A)(3).

[172] Notice 88-86, 1988-34 IRB 10.

[173] Temp. Reg. § 1.263A-1T(d)(3)(ii)(A)(5).

[174] Temp. Reg. § 1.263A-1T(d)(3)(ii)(A)(4).

[175] Notice 88-86, 1988-34 IRB 10.

are to be treated as inventoriable costs on the basis of all the facts and circumstances. Thus, storage costs associated with raw materials, work-in-process, and finished goods must be taken into account in inventoriable costs without regard to the taxpayer's use of a LIFO or FIFO cost-flow assumption.

Purchasing costs. Inventoriable purchasing costs include the costs associated with a purchasing department and with personnel, such as buyers, assistant buyers, and clerical workers, whose functions relate to the selection of merchandise, maintenance of stock, assortment and volume of stock, placement of purchase orders, establishment and maintenance of vendor contracts, and comparison or testing of merchandise.[176] In determining whether a person is engaged in these purchasing activities, the actual activities of the person must be considered, not the person's particular title.[177] Thus, it will not be appropriate to merely review titles of individuals. Instead, consideration must be given to the actual activities of those individuals.

If a person performs activities that are both included in and excluded from inventoriable costs, an allocation of the labor costs of that person must be made. The simplified resale method provides that if less than one third of the person's activities relate to purchasing, then none of the labor costs is treated as relating to the purchasing function.[178] However, if more than two thirds of the person's activities relate to the purchasing function, then all the costs of that person must be allocated to the purchasing function.[179] In all other cases, an appropriate allocation must be made.

EXAMPLE: Assume that *A*, *B*, and *C* are employees of the taxpayer, that 25 percent of *A*'s activities relate to purchasing, that 70 percent of *B*'s activities relate to purchasing, and that 50 percent of *C*'s activities relate to purchasing. In this case, the taxpayer will treat none of *A*'s cost as allocable to purchasing, all of *B*'s cost as allocable to purchasing, and 50 percent of *C*'s cost as allocable to purchasing.[180]

For some taxpayers, application of this one-third/two-thirds rule might cause so high a percentage of costs to be capitalized that use of the simplified resale method should be rejected. For other taxpayers, application of the rule may have little, if any, adverse effect.

Handling, processing, assembly, and repackaging costs. Handling, processing, assembly, and repackaging costs are treated as inventoriable costs

---

[176] Temp. Reg. § 1.263A-1T(d)(3)(ii)(B)(1).
[177] Temp. Reg. § 1.263A-1T(d)(3)(ii)(B)(2).
[178] Temp. Reg. § 1.263A-1T(d)(3)(ii)(B)(4)(ii)(A).
[179] Temp. Reg. § 1.263A-1T(d)(3)(ii)(B)(4)(ii)(B).
[180] Temp. Reg. § 1.263A-1T(d)(3)(ii)(B)(4)(iii).

under Section 263A.[181] These costs include the costs incurred by the taxpayers in transporting goods (including loading and unloading) from the place of purchase to the taxpayer's storage facility, from storage facility to storage facility, and from a storage facility to the location where the sale occurs.[182] In addition, these costs would include all costs incurred by the taxpayer in preparing the goods for sale as well as, apparently, all installation costs.[183] On the other hand, these costs do not include distribution costs.[184] Distribution costs are the costs of delivering goods directly to the customer.[185] Consequently, the costs of repackaging goods in preparation for shipment or delivery directly to a particular customer are not included in inventoriable costs if the repackaging occurs after the customer has ordered those goods.[186]

An open question relates to goods shipped pursuant to order, but repacked at a staging area prior to ultimate delivery to the customer. For example, the taxpayer may ship goods by rail to point *A* in response to orders. At point *A*, the goods may be broken down into smaller parcels, placed on trucks, and transported from point *A* to different sites. Arguably, the costs incurred at the staging point are distribution costs. This conclusion is consistent with the required treatment of costs incurred in delivering goods

---

[181] Temp. Reg. § 1.263A-1T(d)(3)(ii)(C)(1).

[182] Id. In Notice 88-86, 1988-34 IRB 10, the Treasury announced that forthcoming regulations will provide that labor costs incurred at a retail facility to unload a truck, unpack and handle the goods that were contained in the truck, and mark and tag such goods are not required to be capitalized under Section 263A if, and to the extent that, the goods will be sold in on-site sales to customers at the retail facility. Similarly, the labor cost for clerks and other personnel incurred in displaying the goods and in handling the goods in the course of waiting on customers for the purpose of making on-site sales will not be required to be capitalized. However, the costs of processing, assembling, packaging, and so forth incurred at the retail facility that are not de minimis in amount will be required to be capitalized. Similarly, costs that were required to be treated as inventoriable costs of manufacturing prior to the 1986 Act must continue to be included in inventoriable costs. See, e.g., Rev. Rul. 81-272, 1981-2 CB 116, relating to the cost of assembling merchandise, printing or monogramming property, customizing or altering property, and undertaking similar activities.

[183] See Temp. Reg. § 1.263A-1T(a)(5)(ii), which defines "produce" to include "install" and, in effect, makes such costs inventoriable for all affected taxpayers. Under prior law, preparation and installation costs were not treated as inventoriable costs. See Marcor, Inc., 89 TC 181 (1987).

[184] Temp. Reg. § 1.263A-1T(d)(3)(ii)(C)(3). But see Notice 88-86, 1988-34 IRB 10, where the Treasury announced that forthcoming regulations will provide that the cost of transporting goods from a taxpayer to a related person must be capitalized as part of the cost of the goods being transported. Thus, when a taxpayer sells goods to a related person, the cost of transporting the goods must be included in determining the basis of the goods that are sold, and, hence, the resulting gain or loss from the sale for all purposes of the Code and regulations.

[185] Temp. Reg. § 1.263A-1T(d)(3)(ii)(C)(3).

[186] Temp. Reg. § 1.263A-1T(d)(3)(ii)(C)(2).

ordered by the customer to the store where the sale occurs. If these costs are incurred pursuant to an identifiable order placed by a customer before delivery, the costs may be distribution costs rather than inventoriable handling costs.[187]

Once identified as an inventoriable cost, all handling, processing, assembly, and repackaging costs must be taken into account. This includes all direct and indirect labor, tools, vehicles and equipment, maintenance of vehicles and equipment, rent, depreciation, and insurance of vehicles and equipment, materials and supplies used, and general and administrative costs that directly benefit or are incurred by reason of the handling, processing, assembly, and repackaging activities.[188]

General and administrative costs. In addition to the storage and warehousing costs, purchasing costs, and handling and related costs previously described, the simplified resale method requires that a portion of all direct and indirect administrative costs be treated as inventoriable costs.[189] Accordingly, a portion of the direct and indirect costs incurred by any administrative, service, or support function or department that directly benefits or is incurred by reason of warehousing, purchasing, or handling costs must be treated as an inventoriable cost. In addition, if costs are incurred by an administrative, service, or support function or department in benefiting warehousing, purchasing, or handling activities as well as other activities of the taxpayer (so-called mixed service costs), then a portion of those costs must also be treated as inventoriable costs.[190]

Allocation procedures and other rules governing the regular and alternative simplified resale methods. The precise allocation and other rules governing use of the simplified resale method are provided by the temporary regulations.[191] With respect to allocation of the additional Section 263A costs, the taxpayer first determines its inventory under the pre–1986 Act rules. The additional Section 263A costs are then allocated to inventory based on the ratio of the additional Section 263A costs incurred during the year to the taxpayer's purchases for the year. This is known as the allocation ratio. This ratio is then multiplied by that portion of the taxpayer's ending inventory that is comprised of purchases made during the year.

EXAMPLE: Assume that a taxpayer using the FIFO method incurred

---

[187] See Temp. Reg. § 1.263A-1T(d)(3)(ii)(C)(4).

[188] Temp. Reg. § 1.263A-1T(d)(3)(ii)(C)(5).

[189] Temp. Reg. § 1.263A-1T(d)(3)(ii)(D).

[190] Id.

[191] See Temp. Reg. §§ 1.263A-1T(d)(4) regarding allocation methods, 1.263A-1T(d)(5) regarding the Section 481 adjustment required on the change to the uniform capitalization rules, 1.263A-1T(d)(6) regarding the election to use the simplified resale method.

$500,000 of the Section 263A costs during the year, that its beginning inventory balance (computed without regard to Section 263A) was $2 million, that it made $8 million of purchases during the year, and that its ending inventory (again excluding the Section 263A costs) was $3 million. Under FIFO, the entire $3 million of ending inventory is treated as consisting of purchases made during the year.[192] The ratio of the additional Section 263A costs to purchases made during the year is 6.25 percent ($500,000 ÷ $8 million). The Section 263A costs to be capitalized amount to $187,500 (6.25% x $3 million).[193] If the taxpayer had been on LIFO, only $1 million of the ending inventory would have been treated as purchases of the year,[194] and $62,500 of the additional Section 263A costs would have been capitalized (6.25% x $1 million).[195]

With respect to these allocation procedures, a separate computation must be made to determine what portion of mixed service costs must be treated as additional Section 263A costs. The temporary regulations provide that this amount is determined by multiplying the total amount of mixed service costs incurred during the year by the ratio of (1) the sum of the labor costs allocated to the storage, purchasing, and handling activities to (2) the total of all labor costs incurred in the taxpayer's trade or business (excluding labor costs included in the mixed service costs being allocated).[196]

> EXAMPLE: Assume the taxpayer incurs $1 million in mixed service costs for the year, that its labor costs attributable to purchasing, handling, and off-site storage activities are $5 million, and that the labor costs of its particular trade or business as a whole (but excluding the labor costs contained in the $1 million of mixed service costs) are $25 million. The mixed service costs that must be treated as additional Section 263A costs are $200,000 (($5 million ÷ $25 million) x $1 million).

The regulations provide that a taxpayer who desires to use the simplified resale method in costing inventories must also use that method in computing the Section 481 adjustment that must be made on the change to the uniform costing rules for taxpayers covered by (or who become covered by) Section 263A.[197] The election to use the simplified resale method is to be made separately for each trade or business of the taxpayer. The election must be made on a timely filed return for the taxpayer's first taxable year for which

---

[192] See discussion infra ¶ 6.08[2].

[193] See Temp. Reg. § 1.263A-1T(d)(4)(iv) for additional examples.

[194] See discussion infra ¶ 6.08[2].

[195] See Temp. Reg. § 1.263A-1T(d)(4)(iv).

[196] See Temp. Reg. § 1.263A-1T(d)(4)(iii).

[197] Temp. Reg. § 1.263A-1T(d)(5).

Section 263A is effective. For subsequent taxable years, an election to use, or change from use of, the simplified resale method requires the prior approval of the Commissioner.[198] In response to suggestions by commentators following promulgation of the temporary regulations, the Treasury announced in Notice 88-86[199] that forthcoming regulations will recognize that the two mixed service cost calculations provided in the temporary regulations (one determining the amount of mixed service costs to be considered as additional Section 263A costs and the other determining the portion of the costs that should be capitalized in ending inventory) constitute two different simplified methods. The election of either method may be made independently of the election of the other method. Thus, taxpayers may elect only one of the simplified methods, both of the methods, or neither of the methods.

Moreover, the Notice stated that forthcoming regulations will permit taxpayers to elect to use an alternative-simplified-resale method, under which a taxpayer will calculate a separate allocation ratio for handling and storage costs (and related mixed service costs). This ratio will include both beginning inventory balances and purchases in the denominator of the allocation ratio. The ratio will be multiplied by all amounts included in the taxpayer's ending inventory, including purchases made during the year as well as amounts present in the beginning inventory for the year under the taxpayer's method of accounting.

In addition, the alternative-simplified-resale method will permit a separate allocation ratio to be used for purchasing costs (and related mixed service costs). This ratio will include only purchases in the denominator. The ratio will be multiplied by that portion of the taxpayer's ending inventory that, under the taxpayer's method of accounting, is viewed as consisting of purchases made during the year.

Taxpayers electing to use the alternative-simplified-resale method will separately determine the amount of mixed service costs related to their off-site storage, purchasing, and handling activities. This amount will be computed by multiplying the total amount of mixed service costs incurred in the trade or business for the taxable year by a separate ratio for each particular activity (i.e., storage, purchasing, or handling). The ratio will consist of the labor costs allocable to the particular activity (excluding labor costs included in mixed service costs) to the total of all labor costs incurred in the taxpayer's trade or business (excluding labor costs included in mixed service costs).

The taxpayer may elect to use either the alternative-simplified-resale method or the regular simplified resale method provided in the present temporary regulations. The election may be made for each of the taxpayer's separate trades or business. Should the taxpayer elect to use the alternative-simplified-resale method, the Notice provides the applicable requirements

---

[198] Temp. Reg. § 1.263A-1T(d)(6).

[199] Notice 88-86, 1988-34 IRB 10.

governing an expedited change to that method. In general, the method may be adopted on a federal income tax return using the method for the taxpayer's first taxable year for which Section 263A became or becomes effective, including an amended return filed on or before May 19, 1989, or on a federal income tax return adopting the use of the method for the second year for which Section 263A became effective, including an amended federal income tax return filed on or before May 19, 1989, but, in this latter case, only if the method used for the taxpayer's first taxable year for which Section 263A became effective was a correct method of accounting. This use of the alternative-simplified-resale method is made without restating beginning balances of the year for which the change is made and, hence, without any corresponding Section 481 adjustment. In effect, the entire effect of the change will be taken into account in the year in which the alternative method is first used.

[2] Manufacturers

Manufacturers are subject to complex rules governing the costing of their inventories. However, the initial question to be addressed is whether the taxpayer is a manufacturer or a processor. Proper characterization depends on a consideration of all the facts and circumstances. If the taxpayer owns the goods but contracts to others the responsibility for manufacture or processing, the taxpayer nevertheless will generally be regarded as a manufacturer. Correlatively, if the taxpayer merely provides services with respect to goods owned by another, the taxpayer will not be a manufacturer subject to the inventory requirements.[200]

Similarly, if holding the goods after acquisition is an essential part of bringing the goods to a salable state (e.g., the aging of wine or whiskey), the taxpayer may be a manufacturer, even though no manufacture takes place in the traditional sense.[201]

For manufacturers and processors, inventoriable costs are generally broken down into three categories: (1) direct material costs, which include the cost of raw materials and supplies entering into, or consumed in connection with the manufacture of, the product; (2) direct labor costs; and

---

[200] Rev. Rul. 81-272, 1981-2 CB 116. See discussion infra ¶ 6.06[2][c][ii] regarding the interest capitalization rules.

[201] For pre–1986 Act law, see Van Pickerill & Sons Inc. v. United States, 445 F2d 918 (7th Cir. 1971), where the purchaser of unaged whiskey was allowed to deduct as expenses its monthly storage charges and state taxes despite the government's claim that these costs should have been treated as inventoriable costs and deducted at the time of sale; Heaven Hill Distilleries v. United States, 476 F2d 1327 (Ct. Cl. 1973).

(3) indirect production costs or overhead.[202] These categories have not been changed by the 1986 Act rules,[203] although the particular costs to be included in the categories have been affected.[204]

Although Section 263A and its regulations govern the costing of inventories of a manufacturer (and in that sense take precedence over the rules of the costing regulations under Section 471), some of the costing approaches under the Section 263A regulations are based on (at least in part) continued application of the Section 471 regulations. For this reason both sets of regulations are discussed below.

[a] Direct Material Costs

"Direct material costs" is defined as the cost of materials that become an integral part of the specific product, and materials that are consumed in the ordinary course of manufacture and that can be identified or associated with particular units or groups of units of products.[205] Direct material costs are costed just as other purchased items, that is, invoice cost less applicable discounts plus all transportation and other expenses incurred in acquiring the product. These other acquisition costs include compensation paid to purchasing agents, buyers, and brokers.[206] They might also include the cost of operating a raw materials warehouse, although the IRS has at times suggested that such costs are indirect production costs, and warehousing costs are now identified as indirect costs under Section 263A.[207] Acquisition costs might also include taxes, if the tax is a cost of acquiring goods or bringing them to a salable state rather than a tax on the sale or other distribution of the goods.[208]

[b] Direct Labor Costs

Direct labor costs include the cost of labor that can be identified or associated with particular units or groups of units of a specific product.[209] The elements of direct labor costs include not only basic compensation but also overtime

---

[202] Treas. Reg. §§ 1.471-3(c), 1.471-11.

[203] See Temp. Reg. § 1.263A-1T(b).

[204] See discussion infra ¶ 6.06[2][c][ii].

[205] Treas. Reg. § 1.471-11(b)(2); Temp. Reg. § 1.263A-1T(b)(2)(i).

[206] See, e.g., Rev. Rul. 66-145, 1966-1 CB 98.

[207] See Priv. Ltr. Rul. 8303005 (July 29, 1982). The IRS may be correct in the sense that direct material costs are typically limited to acquisition costs. See discussion infra ¶ 6.06[2][c][ii].

[208] See Childers Distrib. Co., 46 TCM 3 (1983), regarding sales tax. But see discussion infra ¶ 6.06[2][c][ii].

[209] Treas. Reg. § 1.471-11(b)(2); Temp. Reg. § 1.263A-1T(b)(2)(i).

pay, vacation and holiday pay, sick leave pay (other than payments pursuant to a wage continuation plan under Section 105(d)), shift differential, payroll taxes, and payments to a supplemental unemployment benefit plan paid or incurred on behalf of employees engaged in direct labor.[210]

[c] Indirect Production Costs

"Indirect production costs" (also known as manufacturing burden or overhead) has long been defined to include those costs that are incident to and necessary for production or manufacturing operations or processes but that are not direct material costs or direct labor costs.[211] However, under Section 263A, these costs are defined as all costs (other than direct costs) that "benefit or are incurred by reason of the performance of a production or resale activity."[212] Under either definition, it is clear that the category of indirect costs is a residual category, a catchall. It includes both fixed indirect costs (i.e., those that do not vary in amount as production increases or decreases) and variable indirect production costs (i.e., those that do vary with production).[213]

For financial cost accounting purposes, there is considerable debate whether and to what extent each of the categories of cost should be taken into account in costing inventories. Some accountants argue that only direct production costs (i.e., direct materials and direct labor) should be taken into account in costing inventories. This is known as prime costing. Others take the position that all direct costs and only variable indirect costs should be taken into account. This is known as direct costing, variable costing, or marginal costing. Still others believe that all production costs (direct and indirect, fixed and variable) should be taken into account. This is known as full absorption costing.

For federal income tax purposes, the present inventory costing requirements are set forth in the regulations under Sections 471 and 263A.[214] Section 263A is effective for taxable years beginning after December 31, 1986. However, the new rules do not entirely override the prior rules. Indeed, the new rules offer taxpayers the opportunity of continuing to use their prior inventory costing procedures and then adjusting the results obtained under the prior procedures by simplified approaches to comply with the new uniform capitalization rules. Consequently, it is important for taxpayers to consider both the costing rules under Section 471, which adopted a form of full absorption costing, and the costing rules under Section 263A, which are

---

[210] Treas. Reg. § 1.471-11(b)(2); Temp. Reg. § 1.263A-1T(b)(2)(i).

[211] Treas. Reg. § 1.471-11(b)(3).

[212] Temp. Reg. § 1.263A-1T(b)(2)(ii).

[213] Of course, in the long run, all costs are variable.

[214] Treas. Reg. § 1.471-11; Temp. Reg. § 1.263A-1T.

known as the uniform capitalization costing rules. Of course, only the full absorption costing rules are applicable to issues arising from returns filed for years prior to the effective date of Section 263A.

[i] Full absorption costing rules.   The full absorption costing rules are among the most detailed of all tax regulations. Prior to their promulgation in 1973, inventory-costing requirements were in a state of flux. Issues often arose as to whether particular items of overhead were to be included in or excluded from inventoriable costs. The courts addressed many of these issues but the results were not always consistent.[215]

Questions also arose as to whether particular items of expense could be treated as inventoriable costs when their deduction was expressly authorized by other sections of the Code or the regulations. Examples included deductions for repair and maintenance expenses and compensation. The IRS generally argued that these expenses should be included in inventoriable costs to the extent they were associated with the manufacture or processing of inventories, and the courts usually agreed.[216]

In an effort to obtain greater consistency and conformity with appropriate concepts of financial inventory accounting, the Treasury promulgated the so-called full absorption regulations in 1973. These regulations require that all direct costs (raw materials and direct labor) and certain indirect costs be taken into account in computing inventoriable costs. To assist taxpayers in determining which indirect production costs must be included in inventoriable costs, the Treasury established three classifications: (1) costs that must be included in inventoriable costs; (2) costs that need not be included in inventoriable costs; and (3) costs that must be included in or excluded from inventoriable costs, depending on their treatment for financial reporting purposes.[217]

Indirect costs that must be included in inventoriable costs.   Certain indirect production costs were considered so essential to the production of

---

[215] See, e.g., Photo-Sonics, Inc., 42 TC 926 (1964), acq. 1965-2 CB 6, aff'd, 357 F2d 656 (9th Cir. 1966), where the Ninth Circuit indicated that both direct costing and absorption costing may be appropriate for tax purposes in particular circumstances; Geometric Stamping Co., 26 TC 301 (1956), acq. 1958-1 CB 4, which allowed use of a direct costing method; McNeil Mach. & Eng'g Co. v. United States, 1967-7 Stand. Fed. Tax Rep. (CCH) ¶ 8173 (Ct. Cl. 1967), which permitted use of direct costing; All Steel Equip. Inc., 54 TC 1749 (1970), acq. in part in result 1978-2 CB 1, aff'd and rev'd in part per curiam, 467 F2d 1184 (7th Cir. 1972), where the Tax Court and the court of appeals differed on whether repair expenses were inventoriable costs.

[216] See All-Steel Equip. Inc., 54 TC 1749 (1970), acq. in part in result 1978-2 CB 1, aff'd and rev'd in part per curiam, 467 F2d 1184 (7th Cir. 1972), where the taxpayer sought to deduct repair expenses in the year incurred and to exclude those expenses from inventoriable costs. The Tax Court agreed with the taxpayer, but the appeals court reversed. See discussion infra ¶ 6.06[2][c][i].

[217] Treas. Reg. §§ 1.471-11(c)(2)(i)–1.471-11(c)(2)(iii).

merchandise that they were to be treated as inventoriable costs without regard to their treatment in the taxpayer's financial reports. These so-called Category One costs included the following:[218]

- Repair expenses
- Maintenance
- Utilities, such as heat, power, and light
- Rent
- Indirect labor and production supervisory wages, including basic compensation, overtime pay, vacation and holiday pay, sick leave pay (other than payments pursuant to a wage continuation plan under Section 105(d)), shift differential, payroll taxes, and contributions to a supplemental unemployment benefit plan[219]
- Indirect materials and supplies
- Tools and equipment not capitalized
- Cost of quality control and inspection

The amounts of the Category One costs were to be included in inventoriable costs only to the extent that they were incident to and necessary for production or manufacturing operations or processes. In evaluating the relationship of these costs to such operations and processes, considerable deference was paid to engineering studies and cost-accounting analyses undertaken by the taxpayer.

Prior to the enactment of Section 263A, the nature of some of the Category One costs had to be considered carefully by taxpayers and their advisors. For example, careful attention had to be given to whether facilities and equipment should be leased or purchased. Rent was a Category One expense and therefore had to be included in inventoriable costs. If the taxpayer were to purchase equipment or facilities rather than to rent them, the cost of the items would be taken into account for inventory purposes through depreciation, which was both a Category Two cost (to the extent tax depreciation exceeded book depreciation) and a Category Three cost (to the extent tax depreciation did not exceed book depreciation), neither of which was required to be treated as an inventoriable cost. Thus, for tax purposes, a taxpayer sometimes found it more attractive to buy than to lease. Similarly, to the extent that expenditures for repairs and maintenance resulted in the creation of an asset having a life substantially beyond the end of the year, these costs might have been capitalized. As a consequence, the cost of these

---

[218] Treas. Reg. § 1.471-11(c)(2)(i).

[219] In Rev. Rul. 87-84, 1987-2 CB 137, the IRS ruled that cash bonuses paid to production workers on a regular basis, but not pursuant to a contractual requirement, were indirect labor and production supervisory compensation includable in inventoriable costs under Category One and not employee benefits entitled to treatment as Category Three expenditures.

items would be taken into account through depreciation and, hence, would not have to be included in inventoriable costs. The enactment of Section 263A has eliminated much of the flexibility that had existed under the prior full absorption rules.[220]

Indirect costs that need not be included in inventoriable costs. Some costs were not required to be included for tax purposes in the computation of inventoriable costs regardless of their treatment by a taxpayer in its financial reports.[221] These so-called Category Two costs included the following:[222]

- Marketing expenses
- Advertising expenses
- Selling expenses
- Other distribution expenses
- Interest
- Research and experimental expenses including engineering and product development expenses
- Losses under Section 165 and the regulations thereunder
- Percentage depletion in excess of cost depletion
- Depreciation and amortization reported for federal income tax purposes in excess of depreciation reported by the taxpayer in his financial reports
- Income taxes attributable to income received on the sale of inventory
- Pension contributions to the extent that they represent past services cost
- General and administrative expenses incident to and necessary for the taxpayer's activities as a whole rather than to production or manufacturing operations or processes
- Salaries paid to officers attributable to the performance of services that are incident to and necessary for the taxpayer's activities taken as a whole rather than to production or manufacturing operations or processes

Category Two costs consisted almost entirely of expenses related to (1) the disposition of goods rather than to their acquisition and manufacture; (2) expenses of financing; or (3) general administrative expenses, none of which was directly and solely associated with manufacturing. Category Two costs also included product development costs, percentage depletion in excess of cost depletion, and tax depreciation in excess of depreciation for financial purposes.

---

[220] See discussion infra ¶ 6.06[2][c][ii].

[221] Note that this language is permissive, not mandatory. Thus, the inclusion of these costs in inventoriable costs is not incorrect.

[222] Treas. Reg. § 1.471-11(c)(2)(ii).

The scope of product development costs was uncertain. Research and experimental costs were clearly included. Less clear were start-up costs or unusually high costs incurred during initial production.[223] Since nonlisted costs were to be included in (or treated as) Category Two costs if they were more similar to Category Two than to Category One costs,[224] these start-up or unusual initial production costs were sometimes treated as Category Two costs.[225]

The inclusion of the excess of tax depreciation over financial depreciation in Category Two recognized that depreciation for tax purposes was based on many factors other than economic concepts of capital asset utilization. For example, the periods over which plant and equipment were depreciated for tax purposes and the rates of depreciation varied as Congress sought to spur or retard economic growth and investment. For financial purposes, the periods and rates of depreciation were based more on the economic life of the property and the proper matching of related items of revenue and expense. As a consequence, tax depreciation often exceeded book depreciation. To prevent these tax-depreciation methods from distorting inventory values, tax depreciation in excess of financial depreciation did not need to be treated as an inventoriable cost. Of course, to take maximum advantage of this provision, taxpayers could not use accelerated depreciation methods for financial reporting purposes.

Although the regulations made it clear that Category Two costs did not need to be included in inventoriable costs, any change in their treatment (e.g., their inclusion in or exclusion from inventoriable costs) was considered a change in method of accounting subject to the requirements of Sections 446 and 481. As a consequence, taxpayers needed to establish a business purpose for any requested inclusion or exclusion. (See Chapter 8 regarding changes in methods of accounting.)

Inclusion of Category Two costs in inventoriable costs was sometimes helpful to a taxpayer who desired to increase income, perhaps to take advantage of expiring net operating losses or relatively low rates of tax then being imposed. The IRS had ruled that requests to include Category Two costs in inventoriable costs would not be permitted unless, in addition to appropriate business purposes for the change, the taxpayer could establish that the inclusion would reflect income more clearly than continued exclu-

---

[223] These unusually high initial costs must be distinguished from the cost-of-production overruns. See Rev. Rul. 77-228, 1977-2 CB 182; Thor Power Tool Co. v. Comm'r, 439 US 522 (1979).

[224] Treas. Reg. § 1.471-11(c)(2)(iii).

[225] To enhance treatment as noninventoriable costs, taxpayers often excluded these costs from inventoriable costs for financial reporting purposes. If a cost was not similar to a Category One or a Category Two cost, it was treated as a Category Three cost whose inclusion or exclusion from inventoriable costs was based, in part, on whether that cost was so included or excluded for financial accounting purposes.

sion.[226] This was often difficult to establish, particularly with respect to those Category Two costs not related to manufacturing or production. On the other hand, the IRS was fairly liberal in permitting taxpayers to exclude from inventoriable costs those costs whose inclusion was not consistent with GAAP. Of course, as in the case of Category One costs, the enactment of Section 263A has eliminated much of the flexibility that had previously existed.

Indirect costs whose treatment depends on taxpayer's financial reporting. There were certain costs, the so-called Category Three costs, that were to be included in or excluded from inventoriable costs on a basis consistent with their treatment in the taxpayer's financial reports, but only if that treatment was not inconsistent with GAAP. These costs included the following:[227]

- Taxes allowable as a deduction under Section 164 (other than state, local, and foreign income taxes) attributable to assets incident to and necessary for production or manufacturing operations or processes

- Depreciation reported in financial reports and cost depletion on assets incident to and necessary for production or manufacturing operations and processes

- Employee benefits incurred on behalf of labor incident to and necessary for production or manufacturing operations or processes, including pension and profit-sharing contributions representing current service costs otherwise allowable as a deduction under Section 404, workers' compensation expenses, payments under a wage continuation plan described in Section 105(d), amounts of a type that would be includable in the gross income of employees under nonqualified pension, profit-sharing, and stock bonus plans, premiums on life and health insurance, and miscellaneous benefits provided for employees, such as safety, medical treatment, cafeteria, recreational facilities, and membership dues, which are otherwise allowable as deductions[228]

- Costs attributable to rework labor, scrap, and spoilage, which are incident to and necessary for production or manufacturing operations or processes, and costs attributable to strikes incident to production or manufacturing operations or processes

- Factory administrative expenses incident to and necessary for production or manufacturing operations or processes

---

[226] Rev. Rul. 79-25, 1979-1 CB 186.

[227] Treas. Reg. § 1.471-11(c)(2)(iii).

[228] In Rev. Rul. 87-84, 1987-2 CB 137, the IRS ruled that cash bonuses paid to production workers on a regular basis, but not pursuant to a contractual requirement, were not employee benefits entitled to treatment as Category Three expenditures, but instead were indirect labor and production supervisory compensation includable in inventoriable costs under Category One.

- Officers' salaries attributable to services performed incident to and necessary for production or manufacturing operations or processes
- Insurance costs

The rules for Category Three costs permitted significant flexibility to taxpayers. They permitted the financial accounting decisions of taxpayers to be determinative of the proper tax reporting. The natural tension between the desire to report higher earnings for financial purposes and lower income for tax purposes allowed a balance to be struck. It also permitted a practical means for the accumulation and computation of inventoriable costs.

Nevertheless, the flexibility available with respect to Category Three costs was initially perceived by some taxpayers as providing an opportunity for abuse. These taxpayers would first exclude items from inventories for financial accounting purposes and then seek to exclude these same items for tax purposes. Although the exclusion was essentially based on financial reporting conformity, it was evident that the exclusion for financial reporting purposes was acceptable only because of the immateriality of the amount involved when considered in connection with the taxpayer's financial statements taken as a whole. To counter this possible abuse, the IRS ruled that the taxpayer must be able to demonstrate that the exclusion of the item from inventoriable costs was consistent with GAAP when the item was viewed in isolation and materiality was disregarded. In addition, if a change of method was involved, the taxpayer had to demonstrate that the change from includability to excludability was preferable from a financial-accounting standpoint.[229] A change in the taxpayer's treatment of Category Three costs in financial reports, which would otherwise result in a change in his treatment for tax purposes, constituted a change in method of accounting subject to the provisions of Sections 446 and 481.

Other costs. Recognizing that these three categories of indirect costs were not all-inclusive, the regulations provided that if a particular cost was not expressly identified as either a Category One cost or a Category Two cost, the taxpayer had to determine whether the cost was similar to costs in either of those categories. If so, the cost had to be treated as if it were in that category. If the cost was not similar to Category One or Category Two costs, then the cost had to be treated as a Category Three cost.[230]

If a taxpayer's method of accounting for production costs in its financial reports was not comparable to the method required for tax purposes, such as in the case of a taxpayer who used a prime cost or some other nonabsorption method for purposes of its financial reports,[231] then special rules applied under which two categories of cost were established. One category identified all costs that had to be treated as inventoriable costs; the other category

---

[229] See generally Rev. Proc. 75-40, 1975-2 CB 571.

[230] Treas. Reg. § 1.471-11(c)(2)(iii).

[231] See discussion infra ¶ 6.06[2][c].

identified those costs that did not need to be included in inventoriable costs.[232] Nevertheless, considerable discretion and flexibility were still available. For instance, if the taxpayer was in an industry where the usual rules for computing the costs of production were inapplicable, inventoriable costs could be approximated on any reasonable basis in conformity with established trade practice in the particular industry.[233]

Impact of other Code sections. One unresolved issue prior to the 1986 Act involved the relationship of (1) that portion of the full absorption regulations that identified otherwise deductible expenses (such as compensation, supplies, taxes, and depreciation) as inventoriable costs to (2) those Code sections expressly providing for the deduction of those items in the year paid or accrued.[234] In the case of ordinary and necessary business expenses under Section 162, the Treasury expressly provided that the inventory-costing rules took precedence.[235] In other words, the inventory-costing rules would effectively limit the amount that would have been fully deductible in the absence of such rules. An example would be the deduction for compensation paid to factory workers.

However, prior to the promulgation of the present full absorption regulations, the Tax Court had held that expenses deductible under other provisions of the Code were deductible wholly in the year paid or accrued and, hence, were not inventoriable.[236] In September 1973, the full absorption regulations were promulgated and made it clear that the inventory rules were to take precedence over the seemingly inconsistent provision of the various Code sections in question.

Assuming the Section 162 regulation is valid, it would appear reasonable to conclude that the regulations under Sections 471 and 263A would also

---

[232] Treas. Reg. § 1.471-11(c)(3).

[233] Treas. Reg. § 1.471-3(d).

[234] E.g., IRC §§ 162 relating to business expenses, such as compensation, supplies, and rent, 164 relating to taxes, 167 relating to depreciation, 174 relating to research and experimental costs, 404 relating to pension costs.

[235] Treas. Reg. § 1.162-1(a) provides, "No such item [of business expense] shall be included in business expenses, however, to the extent that it is used by the taxpayer in computing the cost of property included in its inventory. . . ."

[236] See All-Steel Equip. Inc., 54 TC 1749, 1759 (1970), acq. in part in result 1978-2 CB 1, aff'd and rev'd in part per curiam, 467 F2d 1184 (7th Cir. 1972), where the Tax Court held:

Deductions for taxes, losses, and research and experiment are expressly authorized in the year the taxes are paid or accrued, the losses are sustained, or the research and experimental expenditures are paid or incurred. Secs. 164, 165, 174. Neither the statutory provisions nor the regulations indicate in any way that such deductions are limited to current expenses as distinguished from capital expenditures for the acquisition of capital assets or inventory. To the contrary, it has been held that deductions expressly granted by statute are not to be deferred even though they relate to inventory or capital items.

control, even though the priority of these regulations is not set forth explicitly. This conclusion appears consistent with the one case that has indirectly addressed this issue.[237]

[ii] Uniform capitalization costing rules. The uniform capitalization costing rules are applicable to all manufacturers of merchandise.[238] Unlike the rules applicable to retailers and wholesalers, there is no exclusion for manufacturers based on the size of their operations.[239] If the taxpayer is not a manufacturer, it is not subject to the uniform capitalization costing rules unless its average gross receipts exceed $10 million.[240]

The uniform capitalization costing rules include within the scope of inventoriable costs many of the costs that had previously been excluded under the full absorption regulations. In addition, the new rules expressly require certain manufacturers to treat interest as an inventoriable cost.

The new rules are quite complex and, because of their extreme departure from GAAP accounting, it may be quite difficult for taxpayers to integrate them into their present accounting systems. Taxpayers may be forced to base application of the new rules on estimates or, alternatively, to spend considerable amounts of money in maintaining dual-bookkeeping and cost-accounting systems or in changing their existing cost-accounting systems to comply with the new rules.

The temporary regulations under Section 263A recognize the complexity of the new rules. Consequently, they allow taxpayers to allocate inventoriable costs to inventory under the pre–1986 Act rules and also provide various alternative, assertedly simplified procedures that taxpayers may adopt to compute and allocate the newly identified inventoriable costs to inventory.[241] The costs that must be inventoried and that may be excluded from inventories under the uniform capitalization costing rules, the treatment of interest under the new rules, the simplified procedures available under the new rules, and the means by which taxpayers may adopt the new rules are discussed in the following sections.

Inventoriable costs. Under the uniform capitalization rules, amounts incurred for the following indirect costs must be capitalized with respect to production activities:[242]

- Repair of equipment or facilities

---

[237] See Comm'r v. Idaho Power Co., 418 US 1 (1974), where the Supreme Court ruled that depreciation incurred during construction had to be capitalized as part of the cost of contruction.

[238] IRC § 263A(b)(1).

[239] See discussion infra ¶ 6.06[1][c].

[240] See discussion supra ¶ 6.06[1].

[241] See discussion infra ¶ 6.07.

[242] Temp. Reg. § 1.263A-1T(b)(2)(iii). Section 10204 of the 1987 Act. These costs must also be capitalized (or treated as inventoriable costs) with respect to resale

- Maintenance of equipment or facilities
- Utilities, such as heat, light, and power, relating to equipment or facilities
- Rent of equipment, facilities, or land
- Indirect labor and contract supervisory wages, including basic compensation, overtime pay, vacation and holiday pay, sick leave pay (other than payments pursuant to a wage continuation plan under Section 105(d) as it existed prior to its repeal in 1983), shift differential, payroll taxes, and contributions to supplemental unemployment benefit plans
- Indirect materials and supplies
- Tools and equipment, the costs of which are not otherwise capitalized
- Quality control and inspection
- Taxes otherwise allowable as a deduction (other than state, local, and foreign income taxes) that relate to labor, materials, supplies, equipment, land, or facilities (other than taxes described in Section 164 that are paid or accrued by a taxpayer in connection with the acquisition of equipment and facilities used in production activities, and that are treated as part of the cost of such property)
- Depreciation, amortization, and cost recovery allowances on equipment and facilities (to the extent allowable as deductions under the Code)
- Depletion (whether or not in excess of cost)[243]
- Administrative costs, whether or not performed on a job site, but not including any cost of selling or any return on capital
- Direct and indirect costs incurred by any administrative, service, or support function or department to the extent those costs are allocable to production activities
- Compensation paid to officers attributable to services performed in connection with production activities (but not including any cost of selling)
- Insurance, such as insurance on plant, machinery, or equipment, or insurance on the subject matter of the activity

---

activities of retailers, wholesalers, and other nonmanufacturers who are subject to Section 263A. See discussion supra ¶ 6.06[1][c].

[243] In response to comments received after promulgation of the temporary regulations, the Treasury has announced that forthcoming regulations will clarify that the capitalization of depletion is applicable in determining the basis of property sold and in determining gain or loss from the sale. However, the producing taxpayer does not capitalize depletion with respect to property sold until the property is in fact sold. In other words, capitalization of depletion is not applicable to property that has been produced but still is on hand (i.e., property that has not been sold). Notice 88-86, 1988-2 CB 401.

- Contributions paid to or under a stock bonus, pension, profit-sharing, or annuity plan, or other plan deferring the receipt of compensation whether or not the plan qualifies under Section 401(a) (except for amounts that represent past service costs for taxable years beginning prior to January 1, 1988),[244] and other employee benefit expenses paid or accrued on behalf of labor, to the extent those contributions or expenses are otherwise allowable as deductions under the Code. "Other employee benefit expenses" include (but are not limited to): workers' compensation; amounts deductible or for whose payment reduction in earnings and profits is allowed under Section 404A and the regulations thereunder; payments pursuant to a wage-contribution plan under Section 105(d) as it existed prior to its repeal in 1983; amounts includable in the gross income of employees under a method or arrangement of employer contributions or compensation which has the effect of a stock bonus, pension, profit-sharing or annuity plan, or other plan deferring receipt of compensation or providing deferred benefits; premiums on life and health insurance; and miscellaneous benefits provided for employees, such as safety, medical treatment, recreational and eating facilities, and membership dues

- Rework labor, scrap, and spoilage

- Bidding expenses incurred in the solicitation of contracts (including contracts pertaining to property acquired for resale) ultimately awarded to the taxpayer. For purposes of Section 263A, the term "bidding expenses" does not include any research and experimental expenses described in Section 174 and the regulations thereunder. The taxpayer must defer all bidding expenses paid or incurred in the solicitation of a particular contract until the contract is awarded. If the contract is awarded to the taxpayer, the bidding costs become part of the indirect costs allocated to the costs of the subject matter of the contract. If the contract is not awarded to the taxpayer, bidding costs become deductible in the taxable year the contract is awarded, in the taxable year the taxpayer is notified in writing that no contract will be awarded and that the contract (or a similar or related contract) will not be re-bid, or in the taxable year that the taxpayer abandons its bid or proposal, whichever occurs first. Abandoning a bid does not include modifying, supplementing, or changing the original bid or proposal. If the taxpayer is awarded only part of the bid (e.g., the taxpayer submitted one bid to build each of two different types of products and the taxpayer was awarded a contract to build only one

---

[244] In Notice 88-86, 1988-2 CB 401, the Treasury announced that forthcoming regulations will permit taxpayers required to include past service pension costs in inventoriable costs beginning January 1, 1988, to include such costs in inventoriable costs beginning in the taxpayer's first taxable year subject to the 1986 Act.

of the two products), the taxpayer must deduct the portion of the bidding expense related to the portion of the bid not awarded to the taxpayer. In the case of a bid or proposal for a multi-unit contract, all the bidding expenses must be included in the costs allocated to the subject matter of the contract awarded to the taxpayer to produce or acquire for resale any of those units (e.g., where the taxpayer submitted one bid to produce three similar turbines and the taxpayer was awarded a contract to produce only two of the three turbines)

- Engineering and design expenses (to the extent that these amounts are not research and experimental expenses as described in Section 174 and the regulations thereunder)

- To the extent not previously described as a direct or indirect cost subject to capitalization, the following items incurred with respect to production or resale activities: (1) storage and warehousing costs; (2) purchasing costs; (3) handling, processing, assembly, and repackaging costs; and (4) a portion of general and administrative costs allocable to these functions[245]

As indicated by the preceding list, there has been a major change in the treatment of depreciation. Prior to Section 263A, not only was depreciation not a required inventoriable cost (i.e., not a Category One cost), but also the excess of tax depreciation over book depreciation did not need to be included in inventoriable costs, even if the amount of tax depreciation equal to book depreciation had to be included in inventoriable costs under Category Three. Under Section 263A, all depreciation allowed for tax purposes is treated as an inventoriable cost.

Prior to Section 263A, a question arose as to whether excise taxes were inventoriable costs. The question arose from the fact that many excise taxes were assessed after production had been completed. Consequently, the issue was whether the tax was really in the nature of a production cost or in the nature of a selling or distribution expense. Although the temporary regulations under Section 263A do not expressly answer the question, the IRS is expected to assert that all excise taxes imposed prior to the point of sale are inventoriable costs. If the tax is imposed at the point of sale (so that there would be no tax in the absence of a sale), a strong argument may be made that the tax should not be treated as an inventoriable cost.

Noninventoriable costs. The following costs are not required to be capitalized under Section 263A with respect to production activities:[246]

---

[245] See discussion infra ¶ 6.06[1][c].

[246] Temp. Reg. § 1.263A-1T(b)(2)(v). Section 10204 of the 1987 Act. These costs also do not need to be capitalized (or treated as inventoriable costs) with respect to retailers, wholesalers, and other nonmanufacturers who are subject to Section 263A. See discussion supra ¶ 6.06[1][c]. In Notice 88-86, 1988-34 IRB 10, the Treasury

- Marketing, selling, advertising, and distribution expenses[247]
- Bidding expenses incurred in the solicitation of contracts not awarded to the taxpayer
- General and administrative expenses (but not including those costs described in the preceding section as inventoriable costs) and compensation paid to officers attributable to the performance of services that do not directly benefit or are not incurred by reason of a particular production activity
- Research and experimental expenses (described in Section 174 and the regulations thereunder)
- Losses under Section 165 and the regulations thereunder
- Depreciation, amortization, and cost-recovery allowances on equipment and facilities that have been placed in service but are temporarily idle (for this purpose, an asset is not considered to be temporarily idle on nonworking days, and an asset used in construction is considered to be idle when it is not enroute to or located at a jobsite)
- Income taxes
- For taxable years beginning before January 1, 1988, contributions paid to or under a pension or annuity plan allowable as a deduction under Section 404 (and Section 404A if applicable) to the extent these contributions represent past service costs as determined under the particular funding method established for the plan for the period in question under the provisions of Section 412
- Costs attributable to strikes
- Repair expenses that do not relate to the manufacture or production of property

A number of points should be considered in connection with the preceding list of noninventoriable costs. First, the temporary regulations identify the listed items as items "which are not required to be capitalized."[248]

---

announced that forthcoming regulations will permit taxpayers to treat period costs as inventoriable costs if such treatment does not result in a material distortion of income. If such a procedure is adopted, it will amount to a method of accounting.

[247] In Notice 88-86, 1988-2 CB 401, the Treasury announced that forthcoming regulations will clarify that accounting and data service operations pertaining to the accounts receivable function are associated with selling activities rather than production or resale activities and, thus, will not be required to be capitalized under Section 263A. However, taxpayers using the simplified service cost method or the simplified resale method or any other alternative simplified method must include such amounts in the total cost of the various functions or departments performing mixed service activities. The Treasury also announced that warranty costs and the costs of obtaining product liability insurance are in the nature of marketing and selling costs and, hence, are not required to be capitalized under Section 263A.

[248] Temp. Reg. § 1.263A-1T(b)(2)(v).

Consequently, it would appear that although there is no requirement that these items be treated as inventoriable costs, their treatment as inventoriable costs would not be incorrect.

Second, although the items identified as noninventoriable costs generally may be deducted as period costs, this is not always the case. A careful analysis must be made of the character of each particular expenditure. For example, many taxpayers routinely deduct as period costs all expenses incurred for marketing, selling, and advertising. However, in Revenue Ruling 89-23,[249] the IRS ruled that certain so-called package design costs incurred after December 31, 1986, must be capitalized under Section 263. In a companion revenue procedure,[250] provision was made to allow taxpayers to elect to amortize over a period of 60 months the expenditures incurred in connection with the development of and design of product packages pursuant to Revenue Ruling 89-23. Subsequently, in Revenue Procedure 90-63,[251] the IRS revoked Revenue Procedure 89-17 and promulgated a new procedure by which taxpayers could obtain the Commissioner's approval to change their method of accounting for package design costs in accordance with Revenue Ruling 89-23. This new procedure provides three alternative approaches. First, taxpayers may capitalize package-design costs with no scheduled amortization. Second, taxpayers may capitalize individual package design costs and amortize them over a period of 60 months. Third, all package designs may be pooled together, capitalized, and amortized over a 48-month period. Taxpayers who do not change to one of these alternatives may be required on audit to change to the first alternative, capitalization without amortization.

Among the general and administrative expenses that will ordinarily not be treated as inventoriable costs are costs associated with functions or departments responsible for the following:[252]

- Overall management or setting overall policy, such as the activities of the board of directors, chief executive, and financial, accounting, and legal officers, provided that no portion of the costs of their activities directly benefits particular production activities
- General business planning
- General financial accounting, such as general budgeting, banking relations, and cash management
- Economic analysis and forecasting
- Internal audit costs

---

[249] Rev. Rul. 89-23, 1989-1 CB 85.

[250] Rev. Proc. 89-17, 1989-1 CB 827; revoked by Rev. Proc. 90-63, 1990-2 CB 664.

[251] Rev. Proc. 90-63, 1990-2 CB 664.

[252] See Temp. Reg. § 1.263A-1T(b)(4)(vii).

- Shareholder, public, and industrial relations
- Tax department
- Other departments or functions that are not responsible for day-to-day operations but are instead responsible for setting policy and establishing procedures

Another interesting item on the noninventoriable cost list is the cost associated with equipment and facilities that are temporarily idle. The temporary regulations indicate that a facility operating two or more shifts each day will not be considered temporarily idle if it cancels one shift, but otherwise continues to operate.[253] To be considered temporarily idle, no work must be done. This means that companies that operate two plants, one in each of two different cities, each operating two shifts, must close one facility completely rather than eliminate one shift at each facility in order to treat the costs associated with the reduced production as noninventoriable costs. This rule is particularly important in that the Treasury's temporary regulations under Section 263A deny use of the practical-capacity concept.[254] In addition, the temporary regulations indicate that the treatment of costs associated with idle capacity as a noninventoriable cost is not available if the closing of the facility was scheduled. In other words, the concept of idle capacity means that the facilities are idle on days that would normally be scheduled work days.[255]

Capitalization of interest. The 1986 Act provides that interest must be treated as an inventoriable cost if the interest is paid or incurred during the production period and is allocable to property produced by the taxpayer having either (1) an estimated production period that exceeds two years or (2) an estimated production period that exceeds one year and costs more than $1 million.[256] On August 9, 1991, the Treasury proposed regulations pertaining to the interest capitalization requirements of Section 263A. In general, these new regulations are proposed to be effective with respect to interest incurred in taxable years beginning after the proposed regulations become final.[257] For periods prior to their effective date, the proposed regulations specify the taxpayers must apply an interpretation of the statute that is reasonable in light of the statute's legislative history and applicable administrative pronouncements.[258] The regulations point out that, for this

---

[253] Temp. Reg. § 1.263A-1T(b)(2)(viii).

[254] See discussion infra ¶ 6.07[3].

[255] Temp. Reg. § 1.263A-1T(b)(2)(viii).

[256] IRC § 263A(f)(1). The interest capitalization rules also apply to the production, development, or construction of real property and to the production of property with a class life of at least 20 years.

[257] Prop. Reg. § 1.263A(f)-9.

[258] Id.

purpose, Notice 88-99[259] will apply to taxable years beginning after August 17, 1988. Consequently, the proposed regulations will not be applied adversely to a taxpayer who took a position that was consistent with a reasonable interpretation of the statute as indicated above.[260]

Interestingly, the provisions of Notice 88-99 apparently will continue to be effective until superseded by final regulations even where the proposed regulations are inconsistent with the rules set forth under Notice 88-99. Consequently, taxpayers who are following approaches or methods that are presently acceptable under Notice 88-99 may have the option of requesting a change from that method to a method specified in the proposed regulations (assuming that the method in the proposed regulations is regarded as an acceptable method consistent with the legislative history and prior administrative pronouncements, although this could be questioned) or continuing on the methods specified under Notice 88-99 until a change is required as a result of the promulgation of final regulations.

Once the regulations become final, taxpayers will have an opportunity to make any required changes in accounting methods automatically and without the need for filing requests for change. In addition, the automatic changes may be available on either a cutoff basis or, at the taxpayer's option, with a Section 481 adjustment.[261] However, in order to take advantage of the provisions for automatic change and for use of the cutoff procedure, the change must be from a method that represents a "reasonable interpretation" of Section 263A, its legislative history, and applicable administrative pronouncements.

Although the interest-capitalization rule described above might suggest that no interest is to be capitalized unless debt is actually incurred in financing the production or holding of inventory, this is not the case. The rule provides that interest on any and all debt of the taxpayer will be taken into account to the extent that interest could have been reduced if production expenditures had been used to repay debt.[262] This is known as the avoided cost method.[263] Under the avoided cost method, debt that can be traced specifically to production activities is allocated first to those activities.[264] Traced debt consists only of debt that is directly attributable to property to which the interest capitalization rules of Section 263A(f) apply.[265]

---

[259] Notice 88-99, 1988-2 CB 422.

[260] Prop. Reg. § 1.263A(f)-9(a).

[261] Prop. Reg. § 1.263A(f)-9(d).

[262] IRC § 263A(f)(2).

[263] Temp. Reg. § 1.263A-1T(b)(2)(iv)(B).

[264] Id. Under Notice 88-99, 1988-2 CB 422, traced debt should be determined and allocated to expenditures in accordance with the rules of Treas. Reg. § 1.163-8T.

[265] Notice 88-99, 1988-36 IRB 29.

Thus, traced debt does not include debt that is attributable to production activities to which Section 263A (but not Section 263A(f)) applies. To the extent that production expenditures exceed the amount of this debt, other debt is treated as allocable to the production activities.[266] The actual interest rate applicable to the specifically traced debt is used in determining the interest subject to the capitalization rules.[267] For other debt, the interest rate to be used is the weighted average of the interest rates on that other debt outstanding during the production period.[268] Notice 88-99[269] allows taxpayers to elect to avoid the tracing requirements and, instead, to treat all of traced debt as avoided cost debt.

Interest is to be capitalized under the interest capitalization rules only if

---

[266] Id.

[267] Id. In Notice 88-99, 1988-2 CB 422, the Treasury announced that traced debt may include accounts payable even though no interest is charged on such accounts payable. However, accounts payable may not be included if their inclusion will result in the avoidance of the interest capitalization rules, such as where the accounts payable were incurred by another person and transferred to the taxpayer or where the taxpayer incurred the accounts payable for goods and services used by another person. In addition, accounts payable to or between related parties were to be excluded if the rate of interest on such debt was less than an adequate interest rate. For this purpose, the rate would be less than adequate if it were less than the applicable federal rate, after taking into account the provisions of all Code sections that may be applicable to such debt (e.g., Sections 482, 483, 1272, 1274, and 7872). See discussion at ¶¶ 11.02, 11.04. On August 9, 1991, the Treasury proposed regulations that would change the treatment of accounts payable. Under the proposed regulations, which will be effective with respect to interest incurred in taxable years beginning after the proposed regulations become final, non-interest-bearing debt to unrelated parties will be excluded from the definition of eligible debt unless the non-interest-bearing debt is "traced debt." Prop. Reg. § 1.263A(f)-2(a)(4)(ii). The "Explanation of Provisions" accompanying the proposed regulations states that the reason for the exception for traced debt is that, in the case of traced debt, any implicit interest reflected in the debt will also be reflected in the production expenditures to which the debt relates and, therefore, the interest rate will not be distorted by treating such debt as eligible debt. This implies that accounts payable for raw materials, labor, and overhead may still be taken into account assuming such debt is traced debt. Despite the proposed change from the rules set forth in Notice 88-99, this change apparently will not be effective until years beginning after the proposed regulations become final. As under Notice 88-99, the proposed regulations exclude from the definition of "eligible debt" amounts borrowed from related parties, if that debt bears a rate of interest less than the applicable federal rate in effect at the date of issuance. Prop. Reg. § 1.263A(f)-2(a)(4)(iii). This provision regarding related party debt is for the purpose of determining the average interest rate. After the average interest rate has been determined, it applies to all debt (in an amount up to the amount of applicable accumulated production expenditures), including debt owed to a related party. Prop. Reg. § 1.263A(f)-2(c)(2).

[268] Notice 88-99, 1988-2 CB 422 provides numerous examples of the manner in which the traced and avoided cost method rules should be applied.

[269] Notice 88-99, 1988-2 CB 422.

the debt to which the interest relates is "eligible debt."[270] Eligible debt consists of all debt of the taxpayer other than the following:[271]

- Debt with respect to which the interest is permanently nondeductible by reason of a disallowance provision within the meaning of Temporary Regulation § 1.163-8T(m)(7)(ii)

- Debt that gives rise to personal interest within the meaning of Section 163(h)(2)

- Debt that gives rise to qualified residence interest within the meaning of Section 162(h)(3)

- Debt incurred by an organization that is exempt from federal income tax under Section 501(a)

- Debt between the taxpayer and a related party or between related parties of the taxpayer, if the effective rate of interest on such debt is less than the applicable federal rate under Section 2674(d)[272]

Eligible debt includes intercompany debt if the rate of interest on the debt is equal to or greater than an adequate interest rate (i.e., the applicable federal rate). This gives rise to the possibility of double counting. For example, a party related to the taxpayer may borrow funds from an independent third party. Those funds, in turn, may be lent to the taxpayer in an intercompany transaction. Apparently, the intercompany transaction and the original loan to the related party will be treated as separate debts for the purpose of computing the total debt with respect to which the interest capitalization rules apply.

For purposes of the interest-capitalization rules, the taxpayer must also take into account interest on debt incurred or continued to finance assets used to produce inventory.[273] If these assets are used for production and other purposes, only the portion allocable to production must be taken into account in determining inventoriable costs.[274] It is anticipated that the Treasury will promulgate regulations preventing taxpayers from avoiding the effect of the interest-capitalization rules by placing debt in related entities or otherwise through the use of related parties.[275]

---

[270] Id.

[271] Id.

[272] For this purpose, persons are related if the relationship is described in Section 267(b) or Section 707(b). Moreover, the rate of interest is determined only after taking into account all provisions that apply to the debt, including, e.g., Sections 482, 483, 1272, 1274, and 7872. See ¶ 11.02[5][a][i], for a discussion of applicable federal rates. See also Prop. Reg. § 1.263A(f)-2(a)(4)(iii).

[273] Temp. Reg. § 1.263A-1T(b)(2)(iv)(D).

[274] Id.

[275] See IRC § 263A(h)(1).

In Notice 88-99,[276] the Treasury announced that forthcoming regulations will provide two methods for handling related party interest: the deferred asset method and the substitute cost method. The deferred asset method must be used unless the substitute cost method is elected.[277]

Under the deferred asset method, the related party determines the amount of interest that would have been deferred had the debt been in the producing taxpayer. The related party then defers its deduction of an equal amount of interest until the year or years in which the producing taxpayer would have benefited from this interest (by means of depreciation or cost of goods sold) had the debt on which the interest was incurred been in the producing taxpayer.

Under the substitute cost method, the producing taxpayer defers the deduction of its deductible, but noninventoriable expenses, in an amount equal to the amount of interest that the related party would not have deducted if the deferred asset method had been employed.

Although the Notice provides these methods only, it is understood that the Treasury might be amenable to other methods. It is understood that the deferred asset and substitute cost methods were accepted only because of their presumed simplicity. It would be appropriate for the Treasury to permit taxpayers to treat related-party interest as if the debt were actually in the manufacturing party. In other words, producing taxpayers should be permitted to treat interest on related-party debt just as if such debt were in the producing taxpayer. Such an alternative has the benefit of making the location of debt irrelevant. The results produced under the present related-party rules can differ depending on the location of debt. Preventing such differences in result depending on location of the debt may be important to manufacturers using the LIFO method of inventory valuation. Under the deferred asset and substitute cost methods, the location of the debt will affect LIFO computations, including determination of inventoriable costs, computation of increments to or decrements in pools, determination of current costs, and the computation of annual or cumulative price indices.

In addition to the foregoing rules, Notice 88-99 contains numerous examples and rules governing so-called flow-through entities. These entities include S corporations and partnerships. Notice 88-99 should be reviewed carefully and taxpayers should be aware of changes from the rules described in the Notice when the regulations are ultimately promulgated.

EXAMPLE: Assume that a taxpayer incurs production expenditures

---

[276] Notice 88-99, 1988-2 CB 422.

[277] The proposed regulations do not address the rules contained in Notice 88-99 with respect to related party interest. Instead, the proposed regulations merely point out that related-party interest will be the subject of a separate regulation to be proposed at a future date. The related-party interest rules set forth in Notice 88-99 will continue to apply unless and until they are superseded. See "Explanation of Provisions" accompanying the proposed regulations; and Prop. Reg. § 1.263A(f)-8.

amounting to $20 million; that $5 million of debt, bearing 10 percent interest, is incurred to finance these expenditures; and that the taxpayer has $25 million of debt, bearing an average interest rate of 12 percent, that was incurred for reasons unrelated to inventory. Since the production expenditures could have been used to repay the other debt, the taxpayer will be deemed to have inventoriable interest of $2,300,000 (10 percent of $5 million specifically traceable debt + 12 percent of $15 million of other debt, the $15 million representing the difference between the $20 million production expenditures and the $5 million of specifically traceable debt). If the nontraceable debt had aggregated only $10 million, then interest of $1,100,000 would have been treated as an inventoriable cost (10 percent of $5 million + 12 percent on $5 million of other debt). As this example shows, there is no imputation of interest for purposes of the interest-capitalization rules.

Interest is treated as an inventoriable cost where the estimated production period of the property exceeds two years, or where the estimated production period exceeds one year and the property costs more than $1 million. In determining whether property has the requisite production period, the production period is deemed to begin on the date that production begins and to end on the date that the property is ready to be placed in service or is ready to be held for sale.[278] This provision should make it clear that the production does not begin with the ordering of raw materials, the receipt of the materials, or the storage of materials for later use, but only on the actual commencement of production activity.[279]

However, in Notice 88-99,[280] the Treasury announced that forthcoming regulations will clarify that the production period of real property generally begins when physical activity is first performed upon the property. This physical activity may consist of the grading or clearing of the land, the excavation of foundations or utility lines, the performance of plumbing or electrical work or other mechanical activities upon a building that is being rehabilitated or improved, or any other work relating to the construction or improvement of the property. In the case of inventory, the production period begins on the date by which the cumulative production expenditures that have been incurred (including planning and design costs) equal or exceed 5 percent of total estimated production expenditures (including planning and design costs) allocable to the property. The production period ends on the date the property is ready to be placed in service or is ready to be held for sale. Until final regulations are promulgated, the obvious uncertainties regarding the above-described rules, together with their apparent inconsistencies, will remain.

---

[278] IRC § 263A(f)(4)(B).

[279] This conclusion seems confirmed by Temp. Reg. § 1.263A-1T(b)(2)(iv)(B).

[280] Notice 88-99, 1988-2 CB 422.

Assuming production has commenced, an unanswered question is whether the requisite period is tolled if production is discontinued. For example, assume that in the midst of production, the plant is closed by reason of a strike, casualty, or other circumstance beyond the taxpayer's control. Alternatively, assume that the taxpayer, for legitimate business reasons (or because of the nature of its product), decides not to continue with production, but to hold the goods in their in-process state. Should the period the goods are so held be counted as part of the production period? In proposed regulations, which were issued on August 9, 1991, the Treasury established rules providing for a suspension of the production period when all but a de minimis amount of production activities have ceased for a period of 12 consecutive months.[281] If the 12-month period of cessation occurs, the capitalization of interest is not required for the period beginning with the thirteenth month of continuous cessation of activity and ending on the date that more than a de minimis amount of production activity resumes. The "Explanation of Provisions" accompanying the proposed regulations points out that while Section 263A(f) does not itself provide for an interruption of interest capitalization, the proposed regulations are consistent with the principles of FASB Statement No. 34, which provides for a temporary cessation of interest capitalization under certain conditions. Reliance on the principles set forth in FASB Statement No. 34 suggests that that document may be influential in determining the manner in which other interest-related questions will be answered. The regulations illustrate the application of the suspension period with the following example:[282]

EXAMPLE: *D*, a calendar-year taxpayer, began production of a residential housing development on January 1, 1990. From January 1, 1990, through December 31, 1990, *D* incurred accumulated production expenditures of $2,000,000 and capitalized interest of $200,000. On January 1, 1991, a prolonged strike began and forestalled all construction activities until July 1, 1992. During the period January 1, 1991, through December 31, 1991, *D* is required to capitalize an additional $220,000 of interest with respect to the accumulated production expenditures of $2,200,000. *D* incurred additional accumulated production expenditures of $3,000,000 for the six-month period ending December 31, 1992. Because the strike caused a complete cessation of production activities for 12 continuous months, *D* may treat the six-month period beginning January 1, 1992, and ending June 30, 1992, as a suspension of the production period. Accordingly, *D* is not required to capitalize any interest during that period with respect to the accumulated production expenditures of $2,420,000. However, *D* is required to capitalize interest during

---

[281] Prop. Reg. § 1.263A(f)-5(g).
[282] Prop. Reg. § 1.263A(f)-5(g)(2).

the final six months of 1992 with respect to the total accumulated production expenditures of $5,420,000.

If the proposed regulations are adopted without change, numerous taxpayers whose normal production periods would not exceed the specified periods for application of the interest capitalization rules might become subject to the rules because of circumstances beyond their control. This result is particularly harsh in the case of taxpayers who become subject to the interest-capitalization rules only because there is no suspension of the production period during the first year of cessation of activity. To illustrate, assume a taxpayer's normal production period is 1.6 years. To the extent business is interrupted due to a strike or for other reasons, which involve negotiations between unrelated parties, the other side to the negotiation would have considerable bargaining power if they understand that a forced delay of only a few additional months may subject the taxpayer to significant additional tax by virtue of the interest-capitalization rules.

Another important question is the manner in which particular construction projects will be defined. In other words, what is the correct "unit of property" for purposes of applying the interest capitalization rules? For example, assume a taxpayer constructs a production line consisting of several components and that while the overall cost of the line will exceed $1 million and require more than a year of construction activity, the line consists of many components, none of which will individually cost more than $1 million or require more than one year of production activity. The proposed regulations adopt the concept of "integrated construction projects" as a single property unit for purposes of interest capitalization.[283] The proposed regulations generally define the applicable unit of property as comprising all components of a single project or asset (produced by the taxpayer and all related parties) that are functionally interdependent. The term "functionally interdependent" is defined to mean that the placing in service of one component is dependent on the placing in service of another component or, in the case of property produced for sale, that the components are customarily sold as a single unit. Special rules are provided for units of real property to ensure that in addition to functionally interdependent components, the unit of real property includes an allocable share of common features, such as streets, sidewalks, playgrounds, club houses, tennis courts, sewer lines, and cables, even though these features do not meet the functionally interdependent test.[284]

As a separate matter, if the taxpayer produces (or is treated as producing) property that is installed on or in other property, the production activity generally will not be aggregated with the installation activity for purposes of determining whether the property is subject to interest capitalization. On the

---

[283] Prop. Reg. § 1.263A(f)-3.

[284] Prop. Reg. § 1.263A(f)-3(b)(3).

other hand, if the taxpayer is treated as producing and installing property for use by the taxpayer itself or by a related party (within the meaning of Section 267(b) or Section 707(b)), or if the taxpayer enters into a contract requiring the taxpayer to install property for use by a customer, the production activity and installation activity are aggregated.[285]

Except as noted above, there is relatively little guidance as to how these questions should be resolved. On one hand, interest is associated with the use of money over time. It does not offend a sense of reason to view the two-year or one-year production period as running without regard to the actual processing of goods throughout the entire period. On the other hand, it seems inappropriate to require these rules to apply to taxpayers whose products do not require a total of one or two years (as appropriate) of actual production activity.

The amount of interest to be treated as an inventoriable cost is the interest on debt equal in amount to the amount of the taxpayer's production expenditures. For this purpose, the term "production expenditures" means the cost required to be capitalized with respect to the property.[286] Thus, all costs of direct materials, direct labor, and overhead items are treated as production expenditures. In addition, the temporary regulations point out that production expenditures include costs required to be capitalized whether or not incurred during the production period.[287] The regulations raise the question of whether, for this purpose, production expenditures include beginning inventory and interest already included in the cost of that inventory.

Another unresolved question is whether production expenditures include only the annual depreciation on plant and equipment used in the production process or whether those expenditures include the entire cost of the plant and equipment. For instance, a taxpayer may have incurred production expenditures (including depreciation) of $1 million and had a remaining basis in its plant and equipment of $3 million. Would the maximum debt on which interest would be capitalized and treated as an inventoriable cost be $1 million or $4 million? Answers to all these questions should be provided when final regulations are issued with respect to these rules. In the meantime, Notice 88-99[288] addresses at least some of these issues. The Notice makes it clear that the interest capitalization rules require the capitalization of interest on debt allocable to property to the extent such property is used to produce qualified property. For this purpose, the property's adjusted basis is the measure of the debt to be taken into account. However, this rule apparently does not apply to all machinery, equipment, and facilities, but only to those items

---

[285] Prop. Reg. § 1.263A(f)-3(d).

[286] IRC § 263A(f)(4)(C).

[287] Temp. Reg. § 1.263A-1T(b)(2)(iv)(B).

[288] Notice 88-99, 1988-2 CB 422.

of machinery, equipment, and facilities that are used in a reasonably proximate manner to produce the qualified property. In effect, the rule requires the adjusted basis of equipment and facilities directly used to produce qualified property or components thereof (e.g., assembly-line property, manufacturing plant, and so forth) to be taken into account. The adjusted basis of machinery, equipment, and facilities that house service departments or are used by service departments may be excluded from the calculation of production expenditures.

Another open question is whether interest will be treated as an indirect cost (i.e., an overhead item) or whether it will be treated in a special fashion. If treated as a traditional item of overhead, the amount of the interest that is capitalized and not deducted as a period cost is the portion that is applicable to work-in-process and finished goods inventory only. No portion should be applicable to raw materials. The anticipated regulations should address this issue also.

If the manufacturer undertakes production for a customer who agrees to make payments during the course of production, or payments in advance of production, the customer will be treated as the manufacturer to the extent of those payments.[289] In addition, the customer is treated as the manufacturer to the extent the actual manufacturer incurs other costs with respect to the property under production. Thus, interest on debt incurred or continued during the production period to finance payments made and costs incurred by the customer must be capitalized by the customer if the property is subject to the interest-capitalization rules.[290] If the actual manufacturer incurs production expenditures that exceed the payments received from the customer, then the manufacturer is subject to the interest-capitalization rules to the extent of this excess.[291]

¶ 6.07 ALLOCATION OF INVENTORIABLE COSTS TO ITEMS PRODUCED

After identifying the inventoriable costs, the next step is to compute these costs and allocate them to the items manufactured. Perhaps no area of tax accounting provides as much discretion to taxpayers in making computations and places as much reliance on financial accounting techniques and procedures as this area of inventory costing. The general inventory regulations under Section 471 recognize that inventory rules cannot be uniform but must give effect to trade customs that come within the scope of the best accounting practice in the particular trade or business. This deference to trade practice

---

[289] Temp. Reg. § 1.263A-1T(b)(2)(iv)(C).

[290] Id.

[291] Id.

and financial accounting ordinarily means conformity to GAAP.[292] This deference also exists with respect to inventory-costing computations.

As a practical matter, manufacturers are not able to determine with precision the exact cost of any single item manufactured. Rather, they must accumulate all the costs associated with the manufacture of inventories (i.e., the inventoriable costs) throughout the taxable year and then allocate these costs to goods produced during the year, including goods whose production has not been completed. Once these costs have been accumulated and allocated to the goods produced during the year, various cost-flow assumptions are used to allocate total costs between the goods sold during the year and the goods remaining in inventory at the end of the year.[293]

In determining the procedure for allocating accumulated inventoriable costs among goods produced during the year, the regulations under Section 471 require only that the inventoriable costs be allocated by the use of a method that "fairly apportions such costs among the various items produced."[294] Acceptable methods include the manufacturing burden rate method and the standard cost method. Other methods are also permitted as long as they result in a "fair apportionment."[295] The temporary regulations under Section 263A continue this flexibility. They provide that any method of allocation may be used as long as that method "results in a reasonable allocation of [the] indirect costs."[296] Moreover, the temporary regulations provide that even if an allocation method does not result in the capitalization of all costs that directly benefit or are incurred by reason of production activities, it nevertheless will be acceptable if, with respect to the taxpayer's production or resale activities as a whole, the amounts capitalized do not differ significantly from the amounts that otherwise would be capitalized.[297] However, this allocation method must be used consistently and must not result in a significantly disproportionate allocation of costs to production or resale activities in such a manner as to avoid the principles of the Section

---

[292] See Treas. Reg. § 1.471-2(b); Thor Power Tool Co. v. Comm'r, 439 US 522 (1979).

[293] See infra ¶ 6.08 for discussion of these cost-flow assumptions.

[294] Treas. Reg. § 1.471-11(d)(1).

[295] The IRS frequently takes the position on audit that any procedure other than a "traditional" burden-rate method or standard cost method should be denied. This position is generally abandoned by the Office of the IRS Regional Director of Appeals.

[296] Temp. Reg. § 1.263A-1T(b)(3)(iii)(A)(1).

[297] Temp. Reg. § 1.263A-1T(b)(3)(iii)(A)(2). In Notice 88-86, 1988-2 CB 401, the Treasury announced that this de minimis provision applies not only to allocation methods used to capitalize indirect costs but also applies to direct costs and interest required to be capitalized under Section 263A. In other words, de minimis differences in results under the taxpayer's procedures and those that might otherwise be required may not be a basis for proposing adjustments.

263A capitalization rules.[298] In other words, the temporary regulations recognize the difficulties inherent in precisely allocating indirect costs. Consequently, they recognize (and, implicitly, authorize) the use of common sense and business expediency in determining how best to apply the new inventory-costing rules as long as there is no obvious violation of the rules or a result that allows the taxpayer effectively to ignore these rules.[299]

Recognizing that the taxpayer's existing allocation procedures may not adequately comply with the new Section 263A requirements, the temporary regulations provide that the taxpayer must change its standard costs, burden rates, or other methods, to increase the indirect costs being capitalized so that the taxpayer will comply with the new capitalization rules.[300] Alternatively, the taxpayer may retain use of its present standard costs, burden rates, or other methods but must then adopt additional methods to ensure that the additional costs required to be capitalized by Section 263A are taken into account.[301]

As a result of this significant flexibility, many allocation methods have been devised. In addition, the temporary regulations authorize various simplified methods of cost allocation.

[1] Manufacturing Burden Rate Method

Under a manufacturing burden rate method, indirect production costs are allocated to goods produced by the use of predetermined rates intended by the taxpayer to approximate its actual indirect production costs incurred.[302] To illustrate how the method works, assume that a taxpayer expects to manufacture 1,000 units of product and to incur $10,000 of overhead. If each unit of product is identical and is manufactured according to the same processes and procedures, it is reasonable for the taxpayer to project an overhead rate of $10 per unit ($10,000 ÷ 1,000 units).

For more complex production activities or where different products are produced, the unit of product basis of allocation described in the preceding paragraph may be inappropriate. It may be that a more appropriate basis of allocation would be direct labor hours, machine hours, or some similar basis that allocates costs on the basis of time spent.[303] Other acceptable approaches may include a percentage of direct labor dollars, a percentage of direct

---

[298] Temp. Reg. § 1.263A-1T(b)(3)(iii)(A)(2).

[299] Id.

[300] Temp. Reg. § 1.263A-1T(b)(3)(iii)(A)(3)(i).

[301] Temp. Reg. § 1.263A-1T(b)(3)(iii)(A)(3)(ii).

[302] See Treas. Reg. § 1.471-11(d)(2); Temp. Reg. § 1 .263A-1T(b)(3)(iii)(C).

[303] See Treas. Reg. § 1.471-11(d)(2)(ii); Temp. Reg. § 1.263A-1T(b)(3)(iii)(C)(2).

materials cost, or even a percentage of selling price.[304] For example, if the amount of direct labor dollars (or other basis of allocation) is expected to be $100,000 and overhead is expected to be $10,000, then 10 percent ($10,000 ÷ $100,000) of the amount of the direct labor dollars (or other basis) is treated as overhead.

In determining the appropriateness of the manufacturing burden rates used, substantial deference is paid to financial accounting. Manufacturing burden rates should be developed in accordance with acceptable accounting principles applied in a reasonable manner. Different manufacturing burden rates may be used for different types of activities or for different types of overhead items.[305] The method used by the taxpayer in financial reports is given great weight in determining whether the method used for tax purposes fairly allocates indirect production costs.

At the end of the year, it is often the case that the aggregate cost applied through use of predetermined manufacturing burden rates differs from the aggregate amount of indirect production costs actually incurred during the year. For example, if certain indirect production costs were projected to be incurred at the rate of $10 per unit and at the end of the year it was determined that 1,000 units were produced at an actual aggregate cost of $1,050, the variance of $50 (or $0.05 per unit) represents the undercosting of inventory that took place during the year. An adjustment (in this case, an increase) to the taxpayer's ending inventory should be made to correct for this undercosting.[306]

However, the regulations provide that if the adjustment or variance is not significant in amount in relation to the taxpayer's total actual indirect production costs for the year, then the adjustment need not be made unless the allocation is made in the taxpayer's financial reports.[307] A taxpayer must treat both positive and negative adjustments consistently.[308]

A change in a particular burden rate based on changes in the applicable facts and circumstances is not a change in method of accounting. However, any change in the concept on which these rates are based does constitute a change in method of accounting.[309] A taxpayer is required to maintain ade-

---

[304] See Treas. Reg. § 1.471-11(d)(2)(ii); Temp. Reg. § 1.263A-1T(b)(3)(iii)(C)(2). See also Lundborg & Co. v. White, 3 F. Supp. 610 (D. Mass. 1933), involving use of percentage of selling price to cost inventories; McNeil Mach. & Eng'g Co. v. United States, 1967-7 Stand. Fed. Tax Rep. (CCH) ¶ 8173 (Ct. Cl. 1967), involving use of percentage of direct labor cost to value a portion of indirect inventoriable costs.

[305] Treas. Reg. § 1.471-11(d)(2)(i); Temp. Reg. § 1.263A-1T(b)(3)(iii)(C)(1).

[306] Treas. Reg. § 1.471-11(d)(2)(iii); Temp. Reg. § 1.263A-1T(b)(3)(iii)(C)(3).

[307] Treas. Reg. § 1.471-11(d)(2)(iii); Temp. Reg. § 1.263A-1T(b)(3)(iii)(C)(3).

[308] Treas. Reg. § 1.471-11(d)(2)(iii); Temp. Reg. § 1.263A-1T(b)(3)(iii)(C)(3).

[309] Treas. Reg. § 1.471-11(d)(2)(i); Temp. Reg. § 1.263A-1T(b)(3)(iii)(C)(1).

quate records and work papers to support all manufacturing burden rate calculations.[310]

[2] Standard Cost Method

In addition to the use of a manufacturing burden rate method, a taxpayer may use a standard cost method.[311] Under a standard cost method, engineering analyses and other costing techniques are used to project the cost for particular items. These projections are generally made for both direct and indirect production costs. To the extent actual costs vary from the standard costs, these variances should be allocated among the goods produced. However, if these variances are not significant in relation to the total indirect production cost for the year, then they need not be allocated unless the allocation is made in the taxpayer's financial reports. All positive and negative variances must be treated consistently.

[3] Practical Capacity

Under the practical-capacity concept, a portion of fixed indirect production costs is treated as a period expense, i.e., one fully deductible in the period incurred.[312] This portion is not allocable to inventory or otherwise treated as an inventoriable cost. Rather, it is deducted entirely in the year incurred. The portion that may be treated in this manner is the portion that is attributable to underutilization of plant capacity.

> EXAMPLE: Assume that a plant is determined to have a practical capacity of 98,000 machine hours within the year. This may be based on either historical experience or an analysis based on theoretical capacity. If the plant actually works 78,400 machine hours during the year, then 80 percent (78,400 ÷ 98,000), of the indirect fixed production costs would be treated as inventoriable costs, and the balance would be treated as a period cost wholly deductible in the particular year.

The rationale for this treatment is that fixed production costs should be treated as inventoriable costs only to the extent of actual production. To the extent they are attributable to underutilization of the plant, they should be treated as period costs, not costs of producing inventory.[313] In effect, the cost

---

[310] Treas. Reg. § 1.471-11(d)(2)(i); Temp. Reg. § 1.263A-1T(b)(3)(iii)(C)(1).

[311] Treas. Reg. § 1.471-11(d)(3); Temp. Reg. § 1.263A-1T(b)(3)(iii)(D).

[312] See Treas. Reg. § 1.471-11(d)(4).

[313] See Waukesha Motor Co. v. United States, 322 F. Supp. 752, 757 (ED Wis. 1971), aff'd sub nom., Bangor Punta Operations, Inc. v. United States, 466 F2d 930 (7th Cir. 1972), where the district court stated:

attributable to this idle capacity, which is the difference between practical capacity and capacity actually used, is treated as the cost of maintaining excess capacity rather than a cost of current production.

The temporary regulations issued under Section 263A expressly prohibit the use of the practical-capacity concept in determining inventoriable costs.[314] In connection with this prohibition, "practical capacity concept" is defined as any procedure under which fixed costs would not be capitalized because of the relationship between the taxpayer's actual production at a particular production facility and the "practical capacity" of that facility. However, this prohibition does not preclude the deduction otherwise available under the regulation for temporarily idle equipment and facilities.[315] Many congressmen have expressed disappointment in the Treasury's decision to deny continued use of the practical-capacity concept.[316] These congressmen have indicated that steps may be taken in the future to make it clear that Congress did not intend this action on the part of the Treasury.

Notwithstanding the position taken by the Treasury in the temporary regulations, since the practical-capacity concept was available in prior years that are still subject to audit, it is important that tax advisors be familiar with it. In determining what portion of the plant's capacity was actually used during a year, the taxpayer first determined the practical capacity of the plant. Practical capacity was that level of production that the plant could reasonably be expected to achieve if operated fully. Practical capacity was measured in terms of tons, pounds, yards, labor hours, machine hours, or any other appropriate unit of production. The maximum production so determined needed to be modified from time to time to reflect changes in operating conditions during the period for which costs were being deter-

---

The practical capacity method of accounting involves a basic concept of business economics which is: unit production costs are substantially affected by changes in production volume. While some costs do not fluctuate with changes in production volume, others do. Therefore, because some costs are fixed, there is an inverse relationship between production volume and unit production costs. As production volume increases, unit costs of production decrease. As production volume decreases, unit costs of production increase. The lowest unit cost of production therefore is achieved at the maximum attainable capacity of a manufacturing operation.

Some accounting theorists believe that the differences in production costs that are attributable to differences in production volume should not be accounted for in the same manner as other production costs. This difference, they contend, represents the cost of idle (excess or unused) plant capacity that should not be carried into inventory but rather charged each year against profits. The method of accounting used to reflect this theory is called the practical capacity method.

[314] Temp. Reg. § 1.263A-1T(b)(2)(vii).

[315] Id. See discussion supra ¶ 6.06[2][c][ii].

[316] See, e.g., Daily Tax Rep. (BNA) No. 141, at G-3 (July 24, 1987), which reported the opposition of several members of the Ways and Means Committee to Treasury's repeal of the practical capacity concept.

mined. These modifications did not constitute a change in accounting method.

Practical capacity was ordinarily based on the historical experience of the taxpayer. It also could be based on the plant's theoretical capacity, adjusted for the estimated inability to achieve maximum production for reasons such as machine breakdown, idle time, and other normal work stoppages.

One important question not explicitly addressed in the earlier regulations was whether, in determining practical capacity, a taxpayer had to take into account anticipated sales. In *Brush Wellman, Inc.,*[317] the Tax Court concluded that practical capacity pertained to the capacity to produce, not the capacity to sell. Therefore, the court held that customer demand did not have to be taken into account. Recognizing that taxpayers have an incentive to reduce the cost allocated to ending inventory as compared with cost of goods sold, it is surprising how few taxpayers used the practical-capacity concept.

[4] Simplified Production Method

Recognizing that many taxpayers may find it inordinately expensive or difficult to make precise computations and allocations among goods produced during the year, the temporary regulations provide a simplified method of dealing with the additional costs required to be treated as inventoriable costs under Section 263A (the so-called additional Section 263A costs). This simplified procedure is known as the simplified production method.[318]

Under the simplified production method, the taxpayer first determines its inventoriable costs just as it did under the full absorption regulations; i.e., the computation is made without regard to the uniform capitalization rules of Section 263A. The taxpayer next determines the ratio of (1) the additional Section 263A costs to be treated as inventoriable costs to (2) the total full absorption costs as just determined. The amount of additional Section 263A costs to be treated as inventoriable costs is then found by multiplying the ratio just determined (i.e., the so-called absorption ratio) by the taxpayer's ending inventory as determined under the full absorption regulations.[319]

EXAMPLE: Assume that a taxpayer incurred $1 million of additional Section 263A costs during the taxable year, that its beginning inventory (determined under the full absorption regulations) was $2 million, that it incurred $10 million of Section 471 costs during the year, and that it had an ending inventory balance under Section 471 of $3 million. The

---

[317] Brush Wellman, Inc., 79 TC 160 (1982), acq. in result 1984-2 CB 1.

[318] See Temp. Reg. § 1.263A-1T(b)(5).

[319] Temp. Reg. § 1.263A-1T(b)(5)(ii).

absorption ratio is 10 percent ($1 million of additional Section 263A costs divided by $10 million of Section 471 costs). Pursuant to the simplified production method, the taxpayer's ending inventory under Section 263A is $3,300,000 ($3 million plus 10 percent of $3 million). For LIFO taxpayers, the approach is the same, except that the absorption ratio is applied only in determining the increment to the LIFO inventory.[320] Therefore, if the taxpayer had been on the LIFO method, its ending inventory would have exceeded its beginning inventory by $1 million and, consequently, 10 percent of the increment of $1 million, or $100,000, would have been capitalized in ending inventory because of the additional Section 263A costs.[321]

For the purpose of making the preceding computations, the Section 471 costs are those costs treated as inventoriable costs by the taxpayer under pre–1986 Act law. Thus, to the extent costs could have been included in inventoriable costs under pre–1986 Act law but the taxpayer did not do so under its method of full absorption accounting, such additional costs will be treated as includable pursuant to Section 263A.[322] In addition, the additional Section 263A costs include all costs that were not included in the taxpayer's method of inventory accounting prior to the 1986 Act, except for interest. In other words, interest is ignored.[323]

The election to use the simplified production method is made separately for each of the taxpayer's trades or businesses. It may be made on a timely filed income tax return for the taxpayer's first taxable year for which Section 263A is effective. Thereafter, a change to or from the method would require the prior approval of the Commissioner.[324]

Originally, the simplified production method was not available to property acquired for resale, property constructed by the taxpayer for use in its trade or business, property produced under a long-term contract, or any other property not described in Section 1221(1). However, in response to comments received after issuance of the temporary regulations, the Treasury decided that certain modifications to the earlier rules were appropriate. In Notice 88-86,[325] the Treasury expanded the availability of the simplified pro-

---

[320] Indeed, all necessary LIFO determinations (including relevant indexes and determinations of increments or decrements) may be determined without regard to the additional Section 263A costs. Temp. Reg. § 1.263A-1T(b)(5)(iv). See discussion at ¶ 7.04.

[321] These and other examples are provided in the temporary regulations. See Temp. Reg. § 1.263A-1T(b)(5)(i)(B).

[322] Temp. Reg. § 1.263A-1T(b)(5)(iii).

[323] Id. See discussion supra ¶ 6.06[2][c][ii] for the uniform capitalization costing rules, including the rules regarding interest.

[324] Temp. Reg. § 1.263A-1T(b)(5)(vi).

[325] Notice 88-86, 1988-34 IRB 10.

duction method to property constructed by a taxpayer for use in its trade or business, if the taxpayer also produces similar property for inclusion in its merchandise inventory, and to property constructed by the taxpayer for use in its trade or business, if the taxpayer produces such property on a routine and repetitive basis. As in the temporary regulations, the election to use the simplified production method may be made separately with respect to each trade or business of the taxpayer. However, the taxpayer may limit its application of the simplified production method to inventory or to property constructed for use in the trade or business.[326]

Although the simplified production method does reduce the difficulty and expense that otherwise would result from determining inventoriable costs under Section 263A, it is not clear whether a taxpayer actually benefits by employing the simplified procedure. It is clear that accounting costs are reduced, but application of the method may result in an increase in the amount of inventoriable costs as compared to what the increase would be under a more precise computation. Because the increase to ending inventory is based on the ratio of additional Section 263A costs incurred during the year to Section 471 costs incurred during that year, for some businesses a significant portion of the additional Section 263A costs would not be associated with goods in ending inventory if precise computations were made. For example, additional Section 263A costs incurred during the year may be 10 percent of total Section 471 costs incurred during the year. Yet, the nature of the additional Section 263A costs may be attributable to producing only a very small portion of items actually in ending inventory. Thus, these additional costs might have only a slight impact on ending inventory under a precise computation. However, under the simplified production method, 10 percent of these additional Section 263A costs will be allocated to ending inventory.

[5] Simplified Method for Allocating Mixed Service Cost

The required inclusion of general and administrative expenses in inventoriable costs also poses difficult issues of computation and allocation. In recognition of this situation, the temporary regulations provide a simplified procedure for allocating so-called mixed service costs, which are administrative, support, and service costs that directly benefit or are incurred by reason of the performance of production activities as well as other activities of the taxpayer.[327] For this purpose, mixed service costs do not include administrative, support, and service costs that directly benefit production activities

---

[326] Id.

[327] Temp. Reg. § 1.263A-1T(b)(6).

only.[328] If a taxpayer uses a simplified production method, then the inventoriable portion of the mixed service costs is allocated under the simplified production method.[329]

Similar to the procedure followed in connection with the simplified production method, the determination of inventoriable mixed service costs is determined by multiplying total mixed service cost by the ratio of (1) total production costs incurred during the year (excluding mixed service costs and interest) to (2) the total of all operating costs incurred during the year (excluding mixed service costs and interest).[330] To illustrate, assume a taxpayer incurs $1,000 of mixed service costs, that its total production costs (excluding mixed service costs and interest) aggregate $10,000, and that its total operating costs (excluding mixed service costs and interest) aggregate $20,000. In these circumstances, the inventoriable mixed service costs are $500 ($1,000 x ($10,000 ÷ $20,000)).[331]

Following promulgation of the temporary regulations, commentators pointed out that the formula set forth in the temporary regulations resulted in the capitalization of too high a percentage of mixed service costs, because the formula included raw material costs in both the numerator and denominator. Commentators suggested that a labor-based formula be permitted as an alternative. In Notice 88-66,[332] the Treasury indicated that forthcoming regulations will permit the use of such a labor-based formula. The numerator will be the sum of all labor costs allocable to the taxpayer's production activities under Section 263A, and the denominator will be the total of all labor costs incurred in the operation of the taxpayer's trade or business. In the case of both the numerator and denominator, labor costs included within the mixed service costs will be excluded.

In computing this ratio, the operating costs of the taxpayer consist of all direct and indirect costs of production as well as all other costs of operations, including salaries, depreciation, research and experimental costs, and selling, marketing, and distribution costs. However, federal, state, local, and foreign income taxes (including other taxes that are based on income) are excluded.[333]

A de minimis rule is also provided.[334] Under this rule, if 10 percent or less of the costs of an activity is allocable to production, then no part of the activity's cost is treated as an inventoriable cost. Similarly, if 90 percent or

---

[328] Id.

[329] See Temp. Reg. § 1.263A-1T(b)(6)(iii). See discussion supra ¶ 6.07[4].

[330] Temp. Reg. § 1.263A-1T(b)(6)(iii).

[331] See Temp. Reg. § 1.263A-1T(b)(6)(iii)(B).

[332] Notice 88-86, 1988-34 IRB 10.

[333] Temp. Reg. § 1.263A-1T(b)(6)(iii)(C).

[334] Temp. Reg. § 1.263A-1T(b)(6)(iv).

more of an activity's cost is related to production, then all the activity's cost is allocated to production.[335]

The election to use the simplified service cost method must be made separately for each trade or business of the taxpayer.[336] For the taxpayer's first taxable year, the election is made merely by using the method on a timely filed return for that year.[337] For subsequent years, a change to or from the simplified method requires the prior approval of the Commissioner.[338]

Following promulgation of the temporary regulations, commentators suggested that the simplified service cost method be made available to property constructed by the taxpayer for use in its trade or business. In response, in Notice 88-86,[339] the Treasury indicated that forthcoming regulations will allow application of the mixed simplified service cost method to property constructed for the taxpayer for use in its trade or business, if similar property is constructed for inclusion in its inventory or if the taxpayer produces such property for use in its trade or business on a routine and repetitive basis during the year. Taxpayers will be able to elect to use the simplified service cost method for all inventory and not for property used within the trade or business, or vice versa. However, taxpayers will not be able to use the simplified service cost method for a portion of the property within a trade or business but not for the other portion within the same category and in the same trade or business.

If the simplified method of allocating mixed service costs is not used, the taxpayer must follow the detailed procedures set forth in the temporary regulations.[340] Among the allocation methods approved by the temporary regulations is the direct reallocation method, under which service costs are allocated only to departments or cost centers engaged in production or resale activities, and the step-allocation method, under which a series of allocations is made to both production or resale departments or cost centers and to other service departments that provide benefits to fewer service departments than the service department whose costs are being allocated.[341] The direct reallocation method ignores the benefits provided by one service department to another, while the step-allocation method allocates the costs of one service department to another, based on a declining number of service departments receiving benefits.

EXAMPLE:　Assume that a taxpayer has five production departments (*A*,

---

[335] Id.

[336] Temp. Reg. § 1.263A-1T(b)(6)(v).

[337] Id.

[338] Id.

[339] Notice 88-86, 1988-34 IRB 10.

[340] See Temp. Reg. § 1.263A-1T(b)(4).

[341] See Temp. Reg. §§ 1.263A-1T(b)(4)(iii)(A), 1.263A-1T(b)(4)(iii)(B).

B, C, D and E), that it has four service departments (W, X, Y, and Z), that W provides benefits to all production and service departments, that X provides benefits to Y and Z and all production departments, that Y provides benefits only to Z and all production departments, and that Z provides benefits only to production departments. Under the direct reallocation method, the costs of W, X, Y, and Z are allocated only to departments A, B, C, and D. These costs are not allocated to any service departments. Under the step-allocation method, the costs of W are allocated first to departments A, B, C, D, E, X, Y, and Z. The costs of X (including its share of costs allocated from W) are next allocated to departments A, B, C, D, E, Y, and Z. The costs of Y (including costs allocated to it from W and X) are then allocated to Z and to all production departments. Finally, the costs of Z (including costs allocated to it from W, X, and Y) are allocated to production departments only.

¶ 6.08 ALLOCATION OF INVENTORIABLE COSTS TO ENDING INVENTORY

After determining what items are subject to inventories, what costs are inventoriable costs, and how these costs should be allocated to goods manufactured, the next primary issue is how these aggregate costs should be allocated between goods purchased or manufactured during the year and goods remaining on hand at the end of the year.[342] If the goods in question are relatively few or sufficiently unique, the taxpayer may be able to determine the cost associated with each particular item without the need to apply assumptions to resolve this issue. For example, a jeweler may record and trace the actual cost of unique pieces of jewelry and thereby know the actual cost of the items sold and the items remaining in inventory. This is a specific identification approach to allocation and is allowed for tax purposes.[343] The actual cost of each item will be assigned specifically to that item.

[1] Cost-Flow Assumptions

Where a large number of essential similar or fungible items are purchased or produced or where it is otherwise impractical to trace the cost of particular items because of the expense involved, the number of items involved, or other practical impediments, assumptions have to be made as to which goods have

---

[342] See discussion supra ¶¶ 6.07[4], 6.07[5], for simplified procedures that also accomplish this objective.

[343] Treas. Reg. § 1.471-2(d).

been sold. (These assumptions are actually used more for the purpose of determining a flow of costs than a flow of goods.)

EXAMPLE: Assume that in its first year of operation, a retailer acquires identical products at the following times and costs:

Date	Number	Unit cost	Total
Jan. 1	10	$1.00	$10.00
Apr. 1	15	1.02	15.30
July 1	15	1.04	15.60
Oct. 1	10	1.06	10.60
	50		$51.50

Assuming that 10 units remain on hand at the end of the year, it is necessary to determine what portion of the $51.50 aggregate cost should be allocated to those 10 units. The balance will be allocated to cost of goods sold. The assumptions used in making these allocations are discussed in the following sections.[344]

[2] FIFO and LIFO

The assumptions generally used for financial accounting purposes are FIFO, LIFO, and any of several forms of average. Under FIFO, it is assumed that the first goods acquired or produced are the first goods sold and that the goods remaining in ending inventory are the last goods acquired or produced. Under FIFO, $10.60 (10 x $1.06) would be allocated to ending inventory in the preceding example. Under LIFO, it is assumed that the last goods acquired or produced are the first goods sold. Under LIFO, $10.00 (10 x $1.00) would be allocated to ending inventory.[345] Under a weighted average approach, $10.30 (10 x ($51.50 ÷ 50)) would be allocated to ending inventory.

For federal income tax purposes, only FIFO and LIFO are expressly permitted. FIFO is authorized by the regulations under Section 471,[346] and LIFO is authorized by Section 472. Although the absence of or reference to average cost methods may suggest that average cost methods may not be

---

[344] See infra ¶¶ 6.08[2], 6.08[3].

[345] As the example shows, during periods of inflation, the LIFO method allocates the current, higher costs to cost of goods sold, thereby reducing gross income (and taxes) as compared to FIFO. The LIFO method is discussed in Chapter 7.

[346] Treas. Reg. § 1.471-2(d) provides as follows:

Goods taken in the inventory which have been so intermingled that they cannot be identified with specific invoices will be deemed to be the goods most recently purchased or produced, and the cost thereof will be the actual cost of the goods purchased or produced during the period in which the quantity of goods in the inventory has been acquired.

used, there is no express regulatory or Code prohibition to the use of these methods.[347]

[a] Record Keeping

The regulations contemplate that the taxpayer will maintain appropriate inventory records and accounts so that the actual cost of the goods may be determined[348] and also that the inventory balances shown in the accounts will be verified by physical inventories at reasonable intervals with any discrepancies between the book figures and the actual physical inventories conformed to the physical inventories. This has the effect of allocating to cost of goods sold the cost of items that are removed from inventory as a result of such events as damage and theft.

A frequent issue that arises in connection with so-called shrinkage in inventory is whether the taxpayer may claim a deduction for the difference between the cost of its inventory as shown on its books at the end of the year and the cost of the inventory as estimated to exist at the end of the year where the most recent physical count occurs before year-end. The question is whether the taxpayer may estimate additional shrinkage for the period between the time of the last physical count and the end of the taxable year. The most frequently cited case on this point is *Altec Corp.*,[349] where the Tax Court disallowed a taxpayer's deduction of such additional shrinkage but did not rule out the possibility of such deductions being appropriate. Instead, the court found that the taxpayer's determination of the amount of shrinkage had not been supported by the evidence presented. Indeed, in determining that the taxpayer's determination was unsupported, the court suggested that a pro rata method of allocating shrinkage might have been appropriate. In this regard, in earlier cases[350] where shrinkage deductions had been claimed in the year of the physical count, which occurred after several years during which there had been no physical counts, the IRS sought to prevent the bunching of the deductions in the year of the physical count. The IRS argued that the deduction for shrinkage should have been allocated pro rata over the current year and the preceding years during which there had been no physical counts. The position of the IRS was upheld.

Under these cases and the government's present position, the taxpayer is in a catch-22 situation. If the taxpayer fails to claim shrinkage for the period from the time of the physical count to the end of the year and, instead, defers any deduction until the later year when the physical count occurs, the

---

[347] See infra ¶ 6.08[3] for discussion of average cost-flow assumptions.

[348] Treas. Reg. §§ 1.471-2(d), 1.471-2(e).

[349] Altec Corp., 36 TCM 1795 (1977).

[350] See, e.g., Rhinelander Paper Co. v. Wilkinson, 35-1 USTC ¶ 9328 (ED Wis. 1935); Swinehart Tire & Rubber Co., 2 BTA 223 (1925), acq., IV-2 CB 4.

government may argue that the shrinkage should be allocated back over the period from the last physical inventory through the most recent physical count. However, if the taxpayer itself seeks to make such an allocation through estimates based on experience, the government may argue that the deduction should not be allowed.

The government generally supports a disallowance of estimated shrinkage by asserting that a taxpayer may not estimate a "future" loss. However, it would appear that the more reasonable view is that indicated by the court in *Altec Corp.*, which, in effect, is not whether a loss has occurred but whether the taxpayer has produced sufficient evidence of a loss that has occurred.

It is generally assumed that the conforming of inventory balances shown in the taxpayer's accounts to actual physical inventories will produce an adjustment to be taken into account in the year of the conforming. However, to the extent that a taxpayer changes its inventory record-keeping system from a perpetual inventory system (with no conforming to physical balances) to a perpetual inventory system (with conforming to physical balances), the change may result in a change in method of accounting for which the prior approval of the IRS is necessary, particularly where the effect of the change is substantial and the prior method was erroneous. For example, in *Wayne Bolt & Nut Co.*,[351] the taxpayer used a perpetual inventory system that contained numerous systemic problems resulting in major inaccuracies. When the taxpayer began a physical count of its inventory, which resulted in a ten-fold increase in inventory, the court found that this was not a change in the nature of a mathematical or posting error but rather a change in method of accounting. (Changes in methods of accounting are discussed in Chapters 8 and 9.

Although the regulations anticipate that taxpayers will maintain accurate records and make physical counts of their inventories, it is often the case that such record keeping and physical counts are impractical. For example, many relatively small businesses acquire literally thousands of different products for resale from hundreds of vendors. Frequently, these taxpayers do not have the accounting capacity or the trained employees necessary to account for the constant inflow and outflow of products. For example, in plumbing supply and hardware businesses, wholesalers may receive and ship daily thousands of small parts, such as washers, bolts, nails, and screws. For convenience, these items are frequently stored in large tubs, boxes, and cartons. It is neither economical nor practical for taxpayers engaged in this type of operation to maintain records showing the number of units on hand or to take physical counts of inventories at the end of the year. Estimates must be made on a practical basis of the number of items on hand each year. Examining agents are familiar with these problems and traditionally have not sought to cause the taxpayer to adopt inappropriately expensive and time-

---

[351] Wayne Bolt & Nut Co., 93 TC 500 (1989).

consuming practices. Instead, the agents have typically allowed taxpayers to adopt practical means of determining the value of their inventories. Thus, although FIFO is specified by regulation (and LIFO available for adoption by statute), it is recognized that many taxpayers may use some method not wholly in accord with FIFO or LIFO.[352]

[b] Proscribed Methods

The regulations expressly forbid the use of the following methods of accounting for inventories:[353]

- Deducting from inventory a reserve for price changes or an estimated depreciation in value
- Valuing inventory at a nominal price
- Omitting portions of the inventory on hand
- Using a constant price or nominal value for a so-called base stock or quantity of goods
- Including inventory, the title to which is not vested in the taxpayer
- Using the direct cost method
- Using a prime cost method

By excluding some but not all inventory procedures, questions may be raised as to the legitimacy of inventory procedures not listed. These nonlisted methods include use of an average cost method or a method that does not conform expressly to the requirements of the regulations.[354]

[3] Average Cost

There are many average cost assumptions for financial accounting purposes. For example, average cost may be based on a simple, unweighted average of costs incurred during the year. It may also be based on a weighted average, which would take into account both the cost and number of goods acquired or produced at that cost during the particular year. Alternatively, these simple or weighted costs may be based on a moving average, which takes into account costs in beginning inventory and aggregates them with costs incurred during the year. This moving average approach has the effect of costing inventories on the basis of both current- and prior-year costs.

EXAMPLE: Assume that a taxpayer's beginning inventory and purchases are as follows:

---

[352] See discussions infra ¶¶ 6.10, 6.11.

[353] Treas. Reg. § 1.471-2(f)

[354] See discussion infra ¶¶ 6.08[3] regarding average cost methods, 6.11 regarding nontraditional methods.

	Units	Per unit cost	Total
Beginning inventory	10	$1.03	$10.30
Purchases	10	1.06	10.60
	20	1.10	22.00
	20	1.11	22.20

If ending inventory consists of 10 units, these units would be valued as follows:

Average method	Allocated cost	Computation
Simple average	$10.90	[($1.06 + 1.10 + 1.11) ÷ 3] x 10
Weighted average	10.96	[($10.60 + 22.00 + 22.20) ÷ 50] x 10
Simple moving average	10.75	[($1.03 + 1.06 + 1.10 +1.11) ÷ 4] x 10
Weighted moving average	10.85	[($10.30 + 10.60 + 22.00 + 22.20) ÷ 60] x 10

For tax purposes, the propriety of average cost methods is uncertain. The regulations indicate that where goods have been so intermingled that they cannot be identified with specific invoices, FIFO should be used unless LIFO has been elected. Thus, the regulations appear to rule out the use of an average cost method. Nevertheless, many taxpayers have used average cost methods for tax purposes, including taxpayers in the tobacco, chemicals, food processing, lumber, natural gas, and oil industries, and several commentators have concluded that an average cost method may be used where FIFO is impractical and LIFO has not been adopted.[355]

[a] IRS Position

The position of the IRS on average costing is set forth in Revenue Ruling 71-234.[356] In this ruling, the IRS focused on a taxpayer whose product

---

[355] Montgomery's Federal Taxes 2.22 (39th ed. 1964) states: "The average cost method is not usually allowed when identification or the first-in, first out method *can be used*." (Emphasis added.) The author thereby suggested that average cost could be acceptable if LIFO were not elected and FIFO were impractical. See also 10 RIA Federal Tax Coordinator G-5112, which states:

Any method which comes within the best accounting practice of the particular trade or business and which clearly reflects income will be acceptable. However, the goods which are intermingled are deemed to be sold on the 'first-in-first-out' basis, and the taxpayer must overcome that presumption to obtain the use of the average cost method. The rule is, however, merely a matter of convenience and can be overcome by competent evidence to the contrary.

See also Ozark Mills, Inc., 6 BTA 1179 (1927), acq. VII-1 CB 24.

[356] Rev. Rul. 71-234, 1971-1 CB 148.

required aging for a period of from one to three years. The taxpayer used a moving average cost method that was described as follows:

> In computing its inventories, materials purchased during a month are added, both as to quantity and cost, to the quantity and cost balance brought forward from the previous month and an average cost to the close of the month is computed by dividing the total quantity into the total money figure. This average is then applied to the quantity of materials used for manufacture during the month and the amount so computed is credited to the material account.[357]

The IRS ruled that this procedure was inappropriate in the circumstances and stated:

> In a business requiring goods to be carried for lengthy periods and where an average cost method of inventory valuation is used [profit will be over or understated unless the market is stable]. The computation of taxable income upon such a basis results in an assignment of income to a year, not upon the basis of the transactions of the year, but upon the basis of transactions parts of which spread over more than a year. An annual accounting period is a fundamental requirement of the Federal income tax law, and every computation of taxable income must be made in conformity therewith. This the average cost inventory method in the instant case failed to do.[358]

The principal problem identified by the IRS was the impact of costs incurred in prior years on the computation of inventory costs in the current year. Assuming that this impact were negligible or nonexistent (e.g., where the average cost employed is based only on costs incurred during the current year), this deficiency in the use of an average cost method would not exist, and it would appear that use of the method should be accepted.[359]

Revenue Ruling 71-234 superseded and restated under the then-current law a position originally taken in 1919.[360] The earlier position also involved a taxpayer whose purchased materials required aging for a period of from one to three years and who employed an average cost method identical to that described in Revenue Ruling 71-234. However, the following comments, which were included in TBR 48, were omitted from Revenue Ruling 71-234:

---

[357] Id. at 148.

[358] Id. at 148–149.

[359] Support for this conclusion may be found in the regulations governing the use of LIFO. For example, taxpayers who use the LIFO inventory method and are faced with valuing increments to the LIFO inventory for a particular year may value increments on the basis of average costs incurred during that particular year. This is an express recognition by the Treasury of the acceptability of an average costing approach where the costs being averaged are costs incurred only during the current year. See discussions at ¶¶ 7.04[2][c], 7.04[3][c].

[360] TBR 48, 1 CB 47 (1919).

[The average cost method was] a well-established custom, which has been adopted by the leading concerns of the trade.[361] When the market is stable the average method will reflect with approximate accuracy the true profits, and in a business in which the turnover is rapid, the effect of such a method upon the computation of annual income is small as compared with a business in which it is necessary to carry goods, such as raw materials, for long periods. In such cases, so long as the annual profits are stated with substantial accuracy, taxpayers should not be required to make inventory changes which are annoying to them and which are without commensurate importance to the Government. The average cost method of inventory may, however, have an important effect upon taxation, and in the cases now under consideration it appears to have a material bearing upon the amount of the tax.[362]

[With respect to taxpayers using such a method, the IRS concluded:] Amended returns should be filed or other proper correction made in the case of returns for the taxable year 1917 or any subsequent year in which the income through the use of such an average cost inventory method is materially larger or smaller than it would be if computed on the basis of an inventory correctly valued.[363]

The omission of these comments from Revenue Ruling 71-234 suggests that the IRS has left open the possibility that, when the omitted circumstances are present, a moving average method might be acceptable. In 1920, the IRS approved the use of a moving average cost method for tobacco companies on the basis that no other method was practical or more nearly approached theoretical accuracy.[364] The following factors were considered most significant:

• The purchase of small lots of varying quality and at widely fluctuating prices

• The necessity of regrading and sorting

• The long period during which the raw material must be held

• The fact that the raw material must be blended in varying proportions to get a uniform product

• The fact that oldest purchases are not and cannot be used, because of the necessity for blending

• The fact that the product must be sold at a uniform price in containers, the size of which is regulated by statute

Although these factors were identified in the context of tobacco inventory, they, or similar factors, may also support the view of a moving average cost method for other goods.

---

[361] Id. at 48.

[362] Id. at 50.

[363] Id. at 51.

[364] ARR 18, 2 CB 50 (1920). In accordance with IRS policy, ARR 18 was subsequently declared obsolete. Rev. Rul. 69-661, 1969-2 CB 265.

In summary, the IRS has been reluctant to approve explicitly the use of an average cost method. However, most requests for that approval have involved the use of rolling or moving averages that take into account the costs incurred in prior years. This aspect of the method may be the stumbling block to its approval. However, the IRS has sometimes indicated to taxpayers that where the use of the average cost method (even a rolling or moving average method) makes sense and is consistent with sound accounting practices, and where it is unreasonable to require a change, then no change in the use of that method will be required.[365]

[b] Judicial Review

The primary judicial authority pertaining to an average cost method is *Ozark Mills, Inc.*[366] *Ozark* involved the proper valuation of a yarn manufacturer's inventories. The yarn was produced from 10 to 40 different types of cotton that were blended during the production process. The Commissioner attempted to use a FIFO method of valuing the raw cotton on the basis of the applicable regulation. The taxpayer argued that the Commissioner's proposed method was inequitable, that it was based on a presumption that the goods on hand were those most recently purchased, and that the facts rebutted any such presumption. The Board of Tax Appeals agreed but refused to permit the taxpayer to use its proposed average cost method. The Board found that while the taxpayer's proposed method was more appropriate than the Commissioner's, it too was arbitrary in the circumstances and not reflective of the actual flow of goods. Accordingly, the Board required inventories of goods in process and finished goods to be valued on the basis of the cost of an equivalent number of pounds of the raw cotton most recently placed in process. In effect, the Board seemed to approve a form of LIFO.[367]

Although there is a dearth of authority pertaining to the use of average cost methods, a few points seem clear. First, the IRS is less likely to challenge the use of an average cost method in circumstances where the method is accepted for financial accounting purposes and reflects a flow of goods consistent with the average cost-flow assumption as opposed to a FIFO cost-flow

---

[365] In Rev. Proc. 88-15, 1988-1 CB 683, which provides an automatic consent to taxpayers changing from a LIFO method to a permissible non-LIFO method, the IRS noted that the average cost method described in Rev. Rul. 71-234, 1971-1 CB 148, which is sometimes also referred to as a rolling average method, is not a permissible method. However, no express requirement was issued that taxpayers now using such an average cost method must change from that method.

[366] Ozark Mills, Inc. 6 BTA 1179 (1927), acq. VII-1 CB 24.

[367] See also Ashtabula Bow Socket Co., 2 BTA 306, 308 (1925), where the Board stated that for the taxpayer's proposed average cost method to be approved, it must be "clearly substantiated in its application to the goods of the taxpayer as a whole, and its propriety in respect of a particular class of its materials is not determinative."

assumption. Second, there would seem to be no sound basis for failing to approve an average cost-flow assumption where the average cost is determined on the basis of costs incurred within the current year and does not include costs from the prior year.

¶ 6.09 INVENTORY WRITE-DOWNS TO MARKET

The previous discussion focuses on the means of determining costs of merchandise inventory and the fact that gain from the sale of merchandise is determined by matching the cost of the inventory against its sales price. However, separate and apart from the gain or loss recognized on the sale of merchandise, taxpayers are permitted in certain circumstances to deduct a decline in value of their merchandise, from its cost to a lower market value, in the year in which the decline occurs even though the goods have not at that time been sold. A basic premise underlying these deductions is the existence of ending inventory.[368] Such so-called inventory write-downs to market are addressed in this section.

The authority for making inventory write-downs is Section 471 and its regulations, which provide that an acceptable inventory method must conform to two tests: "(1) It must conform as nearly as may be to the best accounting practice in the trade or business, and (2) it must clearly reflect the income."[369] The regulations continue that "[t]he bases of valuation most commonly used by business concerns and which meet [these tests] are (1) cost and (2) cost or market, whichever is lower."[370]

[1] Evolution of Rule

The lower-of-cost-or-market concept permits goods to be written down to market values whenever market value is less than cost. For example, if goods are bought at $10 per unit but their market value declines to $6 per unit, then the $6 per unit value is assigned to the goods in ending inventory, and the owner recognizes a loss of $4 per unit. The lower-of-cost-or-market concept is a well-established concept of financial accounting, going back to before the

---

[368] See Kollsman Instruments Corp. v. Comm'r, 870 F2d 89 (2d Cir. 1989), where the court denied the taxpayer's deduction of an inventory write-down in connection with its use of the percentage of completion method of accounting, the court holding that inventory write-downs are inconsistent with the percentage of completion method and that the costs written down were never included in any ending inventory.

[369] Treas. Reg. § 1.471-2(a).

[370] Treas. Reg. § 1.471-2(c).

nineteenth century.[371] One of the reasons for its initial prominence was the early emphasis on the balance sheet as a report to creditors. Creditors tended to emphasize the lower probable conversion value of assets and, thus, a policy of conservatism was adopted with respect to balance sheet valuations.

On the change in emphasis to the income statement, the cost-or-market rule took on a new meaning. Gains were not to be recognized until there was little or no possibility of their being reversed, but losses were to be recognized whenever evidence was available that such losses had occurred. The cost-or-market concept is recognized by the American Institute of Certified Public Accountants as a necessary departure from the cost basis of pricing goods when the utility of the goods is no longer as great as their cost.[372]

Initially, the Treasury did not permit inventories to be valued on the basis of lower of cost or market.[373] However, by 1918, provision had been made in the regulations to permit the use of lower of cost or market.[374]

The present regulations provide for write-downs below cost in the case of so-called abnormal goods and, in certain circumstances, in the case of normal goods.[375] Absent approval of the IRS, it is important to recognize that write-downs are permitted for tax purposes pursuant only to the provisions of these regulations. The mere fact that a write-down may be permitted under GAAP is not controlling.[376]

In addition, where a taxpayer has elected to value inventories under a lower-of-cost-or-market method, the write-downs should be taken in the first year in which they are available. Taxpayers may not claim the deduction in

---

[371] E. Hendriksen, Accounting Theory 215 (1965).

[372] Accounting Research and Terminology Bulletins, Acct. Res. Bull. No. 43, "Restatement and Revision of Accounting Research Bulletins" 30 (final ed. 1961):

> Where there is evidence that the utility of goods, in their disposal in the ordinary course of business, will be less than cost . . . the difference should be recognized as a loss of the current period. This is generally accomplished by stating such goods at a lower level commonly designated as *market*.

[373] TBR 48, 1 CB 47 (1919), superseded by Rev. Rul. 71-234, 1971-1 CB 148.

[374] Regs. 45, Article 1582 (1918).

[375] Treas. Reg. §§ 1.471-2(c), 1.471-4. Although the lower-of-cost-or-market concept has been accepted for federal income tax purposes for taxpayers using various non-LIFO methods of inventory costing, and although the lower-of-cost-or-market principle is used for LIFO inventories for financial accounting purposes, the IRS takes the position that the concept is not available under the LIFO method for tax accounting purposes. See discussion at ¶ 7.03[3].

[376] See Thor Power Tool Co. v. Comm'r, 439 US 522, 532 (1979), where the Court pointed out that conformity to GAAP is only one of the two tests under Section 471. The second test is that the method clearly reflect income. The second test was failed by the taxpayer in *Thor Power Tool Co.* See discussion supra ¶ 6.04[1][a][ii] and infra ¶ 6.09[3][b][iii].

a year subsequent to the first year in which all applicable requirements have been satisfied.[377]

The Treasury regulations governing market write-downs for both abnormal and normal goods are quite important and must be analyzed quite closely. For these reasons, the two following sections discussing abnormal and normal goods begin with a statement of the controlling regulations followed by a discussion of applicable points that must be considered in applying these regulations. Any attempt to paraphrase or otherwise explain the regulatory language without paying particular attention to the precise words of the regulation is fraught with risk.

[2] Abnormal Goods

The regulations provide as follows:

> Any goods in an inventory which are unsalable at normal prices or unusable in the normal way because of damage, imperfections, shop wear, changes of style, odd or broken lots, or similar causes, including second-hand goods taken in exchange, should be valued at bona fide selling prices less direct cost of disposition, whether subparagraph (1) [pertaining to inventory valued at cost] or (2) [pertaining to inventory valued at the lower of cost or market] is used, or if such goods consist of raw materials or partly finished goods held for use or consumption, they shall be valued upon a reasonable basis, taking into consideration the usability and the condition of the goods, but in no case shall such value be less than the scrap value. Bona fide selling price means actual offering of goods during a period ending not later than 30 days after inventory date. The burden of proof will rest upon the taxpayer to show that such exceptional goods as are valued upon such selling basis come within the classifications indicated above, and he shall maintain such records of the disposition of the goods as will enable a verification of the inventory to be made.[378]

Several points must be noted about this provision. First, it literally applies whether the taxpayer uses a cost method or a lower-of-cost-or-market method for valuing inventories.[379] Thus, the question may be raised whether this is a true write-down, a cost adjustment, or a loss permitted to be recognized. Second, to the extent a taxpayer wishes to avail himself of this provision, it is important for him to actually offer goods for sale during the

---

[377] See Treas. Reg. § 1.471-4 and discussion at ¶ 12.02 regarding the annual accounting concept.

[378] Treas. Reg. § 1.471-2(c).

[379] Notwithstanding this, the IRS takes the position that LIFO taxpayers who are not permitted to take market write-downs are prohibited from making these adjustments to cost. See discussion at ¶ 7.03[3].

requisite period and to maintain records thereof.[380] The IRS usually requires that this procedure be followed strictly. Third, for a taxpayer to avail himself of this provision, the goods must be defective in some way. If the goods are salable at normal prices and usable in the normal way, this provision is inapplicable.[381] Moreover, the mere fact that goods are not then being used or sold does not mean they are abnormal. Inactivity does not equal abnormality.[382] Fourth, if a taxpayer seeks to value goods on a "reasonable basis" because of its view that they are in the nature of raw materials, the Commissioner will examine this contention carefully.[383]

[3] Normal Goods

The regulations contain a precise definition of "market" as it applies to normal goods under ordinary circumstances.[384] Paragraph (a) provides the general rule, and paragraph (b) provides exceptions:

(a) Under ordinary circumstances and for normal goods in an inventory, "market" means the current bid price prevailing at the date of the inventory for the particular merchandise in the volume in which usually purchased by the taxpayer, and is applicable in the cases—
      (1) Of goods purchased and on hand, and
      (2) Of basic elements of cost (materials, labor, and burden) in goods in process of manufacture and in finished goods on hand;

---

[380] See Hal Hertz, 12 TCM 370, 372 (1953), where taxpayer did not sustain the burden of bringing himself within the exception contained in the regulations, because (1) there was no actual offering of goods; (2) verification of the inventory was impossible; and (3) "the entire closing inventory was valued by approximation." See also United Hardware Distrib. Co. v. Comm'r, 695 F. Supp. 426 (D. Minn. 1988); The Tog Shop, Inc. v. United States, 721 F. Supp. 300 (MD Ga. 1989).

[381] See Thor Power Tool Co. v. Comm'r, 439 US 522 (1979), where the taxpayer was not permitted to write down its excess inventory under Treas. Reg. § 1.471-2(c) because its excess inventory was both normal and offered for sale at normal prices. See also Payne E. L. Thomas, 92 TC 206 (1989), where this rule was applied to the inventories of a book publisher. Moreover, purported sales of excess inventory at lower market values will be disregarded by the IRS unless all applicable requirements for a bona fide sale are satisfied. See Rev. Rul. 83-59, 1983-1 CB 103; Paccar, Inc., 85 TC 754 (1985), aff'd, 849 F2d 393 (9th Cir. 1988); The Tog Shop, Inc. v. United States, 721 F. Supp. 300 (MD Ga. 1989); Robert Bosch Corp., 58 TCM 921 (1989).

[382] Jostens, Inc., 58 TCM 933 (1989).

[383] See, e.g., Jostens, Inc., 58 TCM 933 (1989), where the court rejected the taxpayer's contention that loose stones manufactured according to the taxpayer's specifications for incorporation into rings were in the nature of raw materials for which the reasonable basis method of valuation would be available. The court also noted that the stones were not "abnormal" merely because they were not actively used or marketed.

[384] Treas. Reg. § 1.471-4.

exclusive, however, of goods on hand or in process of manufacture for delivery upon firm sales contracts (i.e., those not legally subject to cancellation by either party) at fixed prices entered into before the date of the inventory, under which the taxpayer is protected against actual loss, which goods must be inventoried at cost.

(b)　Where no open market exists or where quotations are nominal, due to inactive market conditions, the taxpayer must use such evidence of a fair market price at the date or dates nearest the inventory as may be available, such as specific purchases or sales by the taxpayer or others in reasonable volume and made in good faith, or compensation paid for cancellation of contracts for purchase commitments. Where the taxpayer in the regular course of business has offered for sale such merchandise at prices lower than the current price as above defined, the inventory may be valued at such prices less direct cost of disposition, and the correctness of such prices will be determined by reference to the actual sales of the taxpayer for a reasonable period before and after the date of the inventory. Prices which vary materially from the actual prices so ascertained will not be accepted as reflecting the market.

In effect, paragraphs (a) and (b) of this regulation provide three comparatives for determining the market value of normal goods.

1. Initially, the market value of the inventories is set at the current bid price prevailing at the date of the inventory for the goods or basic elements of cost, as appropriate.[385]

2. However, where no open market exists or where quotations are nominal, the taxpayer must use such other evidence of FMV as may be available.

3. But, where the taxpayer has offered merchandise for sale at prices lower than the prices determined under the "bid price" method, the inventory should be valued at the lower offering prices less direct cost of disposition.

The applicability of this final comparative—use of offering prices—has been recognized for a number of years and appears to have been found inapplicable only where the taxpayer has been unable to supply evidence of its sales prices or where the sales prices used were not confirmed by actual sales.[386] Finally, in comparing cost to market, the regulations provide that the

---

[385] A dispute exists as to whether "bid price" requires use of the cost to produce (reproduction cost) or the cost to replace (replacement cost) where a replacement market exists. The IRS and the Tax Court appear to accept the use of replacement costs where a replacement market is available. The Court of Claims, on the other hand, believes that reproduction cost must be used in all cases. See discussion infra ¶ 6.09[3][b].

[386] Bedford Mills, Inc. v. United States, 59 F2d 263 (Ct. Cl. 1932), cert. denied, 290 US 655 (1933), discussed infra ¶ 6.09[3][b]; Space Controls, Inc. v. Comm'r, 322

comparison must be made on an item-by-item basis.[387] In *The Tog Shop, Inc. v. United States*,[388] the taxpayer estimated the costs and market values for its items. The taxpayer asserted that because it had approximately 100,000 items in inventory, it would be arbitrary and an abuse of discretion for the IRS to require comparisons on an item-by-item basis. The court rejected the taxpayer's contention but pointed out that separate data would not have to be maintained for each and every item. Instead, based on IRS statements, the court concluded that the necessary data would only need to be maintained for each particular type of article so that the relationships between cost and market for representative items of that type could be used for all articles of the same type. Although this position provides some record-keeping relief, it raises numerous questions about the latitude that taxpayers will be afforded in classifying articles as being of the same type.

[a] Definition of "Market for Purchased Goods"

Assuming there is an existing active market for the goods at issue, market for the nonmanufacturer of inventory is the current bid price of the inventory. This requirement has uniformly been interpreted by the courts to mean the price that the taxpayer would have to pay on the open market to purchase the inventory items in question.[389] As a result of the 1986 Act, the Treasury has announced that forthcoming regulations will make it clear that the market price of purchased goods includes all inventoriable costs of wholesalers and retailers.[390] Thus, the market price will consist of the invoice price of the goods and freight-in as well as all the purchasing, handling, storage, and associated general and administrative costs incurred by the taxpayer.

F2d 144 (5th Cir. 1963), discussed infra ¶ 6.09[3][b][ii]. See Contadina Foods, Inc., 21 TCM 602 (1962); Ideal Reversible Hinge Co., 7 BTA 1066 (1927); Abbeville Cotton Mills, 10 BTA 646 (1928), acq. VII-1 CB 1 (1928); Melvin H. Goodman, 30 TCM 970 (1971), and Saul S. Pearl, 36 TCM 1059 (1977), where the court and the Board consistently indicated that the taxpayers' inventories could be valued in accordance with applicable selling prices if the evidentiary requirements are satisfied; see also Rev. Rul. 77-364, 1977-2 CB 183, and Rev. Rul. 71-366, 1971-2 CB 225, where, in disallowing the use of certain proposed methods of determining market value, the IRS made it clear that the benefits of Treas. Reg. § 1.472-4(b) would not have been available because the respective taxpayers had not offered or sold their merchandise at prices below actual or replacement cost; E.W. Bliss Co. v. United States, 351 F2d 449 (6th Cir. 1965), aff'g, 224 F. Supp. 374 (ND Ohio 1963), where the court adopted, with respect to a somewhat different inventory question, a very liberal approach that would permit taxpayers to use consistently applied valuation methods where those methods were in conformity with the best accounting practice in the trade.

[387] Treas. Reg. § 1.471-4(c).

[388] The Tog Shop, Inc. v. United States, 721 F. Supp. 300 (MD Ga. 1989).

[389] See, e.g., Thor Power Tool Co. v. Comm'r, 439 US 522, 534 (1979); Hitachi Sales Corp., 64 TCM 634 (1992); Bloom Brothers, Inc., 10 BTA 710 (1928); Crown Mfg. Co., 12 BTA 37 (1928).

[390] Notice 88-86, 1988-34 IRB 10.

Under the regulations, it would appear that if the goods are not defective or otherwise abnormal and if they are salable at normal prices, then where the sales prices are less than the current bid price, the lower sales price should determine market.[391] However, some cases suggest that the bid price must be used as market even though the taxpayer might actually sell the items at a higher or lower price.[392] These cases did not focus squarely on the issue and, thus, their significance on this point is uncertain. In any event, it would be the rare case where goods that are of normal quality and condition (and are salable at normal prices) have a resale price less than their bid price.

[b] Definition of "Market for Manufactured Goods"

For manufacturers, an initial question is whether "market" for finished goods and goods-in-process should be determined on the basis of reproduction costs or replacement costs. The reproduction cost method is authorized by Treasury Regulation § 1.471-4(a)(2) and uses the current market bid price for the labor, materials, and overhead used in production.[393] Under the replacement cost method, market is determined on the basis of the price at which the taxpayer can replace its inventory through purchase.

The regulations suggest that reproduction cost is the appropriate method. Nevertheless, the IRS has historically preferred replacement cost. In 1931,[394] the IRS took the position that the replacement cost of a manufacturer's finished goods and goods-in-process inventory should be used as the "market" value if the inventory in question were in a salable state. The IRS added that if the inventory were not in such a state, replacement cost in its most recent salable state should be used as the starting point in determining market value.

The IRS position, which has not been withdrawn, superseded, or declared obsolete, concluded that the use of replacement cost achieves the better result.[395] It added that article 104, the predecessor of Treasury Regulation § 1.471-4(a), did not intend to provide for a buildup of theoreti-

---

[391] Treas. Reg. § 1.471-4(b).

[392] See D. Loveman & Son Export Corp., 34 TC 776, 796 (1960), aff'd per curiam, 296 F2d 732 (6th Cir. 1961), cert. denied, 369 US 860 (1962), where the Tax Court stated that "market" "does not mean the price at which such merchandise is resold or offered for resale." See also Morrie Chaitlen, 37 TCM 17 (1978), to the same effect.

[393] In Notice 88-86, 1988-34 IRB 10, the Treasury indicated that forthcoming regulations will make it clear that the applicable overhead costs to be taken into account are those required under Section 263A.

[394] Gen. Couns. Mem. 9401, X-1 CB 102 (1931).

[395] The General Counsel Memorandum addressed the situation of a manufacturer of paper and paper products who had an inventory of wood pulp, part of which it had produced itself and part of which it had purchased. In Gen. Couns. Mem. 38906 (Oct. 6, 1982), the IRS indicated that it still follows Gen. Couns. Mem. 9401.

cal market value to a manufacturer, as distinguished from a trader, or for a distinction between the market value of goods produced by the manufacturer and those purchased by him.[396]

This position was followed by the Board of Tax Appeals in two cases,[397] but was rejected by the Court of Claims in *Bedford Mills, Inc. v. United States,*[398] where the court held that the inventory of finished goods of a manufacturer must be valued at the lower of their actual cost or the current bid price of the raw materials, labor, and overhead attributable to their manufacture.[399] The court rejected the taxpayer's attempt to value its finished goods inventory on the basis of what it would have cost to replace those goods in the open market on the inventory date, as disclosed by expert testimony. In rejecting this alternative, the court discussed and rejected the position of General Counsel Memorandum 9401 as not being justified under the language of the regulations.[400]

This early conflict between the Court of Claims on one hand and the IRS and the Board of Tax Appeals on the other has been noted by both the Tax Court and the Court of Appeals for the Fifth Circuit[401] but has not conclusively been resolved.

---

[396] Gen. Couns. Mem. 9401, X-1 CB 102, 106, which added

that purchased or produced goods in the inventory of a manufacturer in a form salable on the open market on the inventory date should be valued at the current bid prices prevailing in the open market for like goods on that date; and that any such goods which have been moved into process to a further state of manufacture, but which have not reached a form salable on the open market, should be valued at the current bid prices prevailing on the inventory date for goods of the preceding salable form plus the necessary labor and burden attaching up to the state in which the goods are found on the inventory date.

[397] See Ideal Reversible Hinge Co., 7 BTA 1066 (1927); Rialto Mining Corp., 9 BTAM (P-H) ¶ 40,369 (1940).

[398] Bedford Mills, Inc. v. United States, 2 F. Supp. 769 (Ct. Cl. 1933), cert. denied, 290 US 655 (1933).

[399] The court recognized a third alternative of net realizable value to be used in the case where the merchandise had been offered for sale by the taxpayer in the ordinary course of business at a price less than its value as determined under the other two alternatives. The court found that this alternative did not apply, since the inventory had not been offered for sale at that price.

[400] See also Hunt v. United States, 59 F2d 1014 (Ct. Cl. 1932), cert. dismissed, 289 US 764 (1933), where the Court of Claims followed its earlier decision in *Bedford Mills.*

[401] See Ralph Ellstrom, 14 TCM 312, 313, 317 (1955), aff'd per curiam, 235 F2d 181 (6th Cir. 1956), where the court stated, "There are two accepted methods of determining market, in the valuation of a manufacturer's inventory. [Citations omitted.] Respondent contends that under either method of valuation the cost value of Dearborn's closing inventory on December 31, 1946, was less than its market value on that date. We agree."; Space Controls, Inc. v. Comm'r, 322 F2d 144, 151, n.19 (5th Cir. 1963), where the court stated:

In light of the foregoing, the IRS today appears to be neutral on the issue and is willing to allow the use of either reproduction or replacement cost. This latitude could be helpful to taxpayers, since reproduction cost would be expected to be less than replacement cost because it would not include the profit to the seller.

[i] No open market or nominal quotations.   Where an active market does not exist or where quotations are nominal, the taxpayer must use such evidence of FMV as may be available. Thus, where the market is in disarray owing to wartime conditions or other unusual conditions,[402] where the market is simply stagnant owing to economic conditions,[403] and where goods are made under special order for customers who do not take the goods,[404] other approaches are used to determine market value. These other approaches must be based on all the relevant facts and circumstances. They may, for example, be referenced to sales or purchases made by the taxpayer or others, the actual disposition of the goods, and expert opinion.[405] However, write-downs will not be permitted where based on speculation and mere estimates.[406]

The Government's brief referring to this takes a neutral position as to whether § 1.471-4(a)(2) means "replacement or reproduction costs." It does not choose sides in the controversy between the Tax Court (and its predecessor Board) and the Treasury Department, on the one hand, and the Court of Claims on the other.

[402] See Neusteter Suit Co., 8 BTA 477, 481 (1927), acq. VII-1 CB 23, where "the merchandise is not available for reorders and there is no replacement market, the general rule fails to meet the situation and it becomes necessary to seek another basis for measuring market value."

[403] See Willard Mfg. Co. v. Kennedy, 109 F2d 83, 85 (2d Cir. 1940), cert. denied, 311 US 660 (1940), where "market was abnormal or unusually inactive instead of normal or active"; Elder Mfg. Co. v. United States, 10 F. Supp. 125 (Ct. Cl. 1935), where market was stagnant, quoted prices were nominal, and trading that occurred was in quantities less than the volume normally purchased by the taxpayer.

[404] McKay Mach. Co., 28 TC 185 (1957), where (1) initial purchaser of specialized machinery left the country and (2) taxpayer's request for export license to sell machinery to the U.S.S.R. was refused, with appeal orally denied, there was no market as such for the machinery.

[405] See St. James Sugar Coop. Inc. v. United States, 643 F2d 1219 (5th Cir. 1981), where taxpayer was found to produce sufficient objective evidence of reduced market value based on (1) testimony of expert witnesses in tax accounting for cooperatives; (2) offers to purchase; and (3) actual sales; E.W. Bliss Co. v. United States, 224 F. Supp. 374 (ND Ohio 1963), aff'd, 351 F2d 449 (6th Cir. 1965), where taxpayer manufactured unique and unusual presses. The court accepted valuation of incomplete presses based on use of detailed formula adopted 30 years ago at the direction of taxpayer's accountant. Several expert witnesses testified as to the conformity of the method with GAAP.

[406] See Rockwell Int'l Corp., 77 TC 780 (1981), aff'd per curiam, 694 F2d 60 (3rd Cir. 1982). See also Hitachi Sales Corp., 64 TCM 634 (1992), where a write-down to estimated market value was disallowed because of a lack of evidence

[ii] **Goods offered for sale.** The market value of inventory may be determined by selling price less costs of disposition "[w]here the taxpayer in the regular course of business has offered for sale such merchandise at prices lower than the current price as above defined [i.e. reproduction or replacement cost]. . . ."[407] In other words, if the taxpayer actually offers those goods for sale at a price that is less than the price at which other similar goods have actually been sold, the lower offering price may be used as market. To illustrate, if goods cost $10 per unit, have been sold for $8 per unit, and are offered at $6 per unit, the $6 amount may be used as market. However, the regulations add that the validity of the offering prices used will be determined by reference to actual sales during a reasonable period before and after the inventory date. If the offering prices used as market vary materially from actual sales prices, offering prices will not be accepted.[408]

In a few cases, the courts have allowed the use of actual selling prices near the inventory date as determinants of market value without expressly referring to the availability of using offering price as the market price. For example, in *Franklin Mills*,[409] the court, noting that the market was abnormal on the inventory date, valued the taxpayer's finished goods inventory at the price at which those goods had been sold by the taxpayer within 60 days of the inventory date. In *Herbert A. Nieman*,[410] the court valued the taxpayer's inventory of pelts at the price at which identical pelts had been sold for the taxpayer at an auction held 16 days prior to the inventory date. The section of the regulations dealing with determination of market value for inventory purposes was cited, but no mention of the offering price provision was made. In addition, in *Neusteter Suit Co.*,[411] a retailer of women's apparel was allowed to write down items in its inventory no longer available on the wholesale market or replacement market to the price for which they could be sold. The court mentioned both provisions of Treasury Regulation § 1.471-4(b) (relating to selling price and offering price) but did not make clear the basis for this particular write-down. The absence of a greater number of cases suggests that the IRS has applied a reasonable approach on audit. Wholesalers and retailers who wish to avail themselves of the offering price provision should make sure they retain evidence of the applicable prices.

There are relatively few cases applying the offering price rule to

---

substantiating the write-down. The application of certain state consumer laws, which required the taxpayer to retain a supply of inventory for a period longer than the period for which the inventory would have been retained without such laws, was held to be of no consequence.

[407] Treas. Reg. § 1.471-4(b).

[408] Id.

[409] Franklin Mills, 7 BTA 1290 (1927), acq. VII-1 CB 11.

[410] Herbert A. Nieman, 19 TCM 634 (1960).

[411] Neusteter Suit Co., 8 BTA 477 (1927), acq. VII-1 CB 23.

manufacturers. An important case is *Space Controls, Inc. v. Commissioner*,[412] where the Court of Appeals for the Fifth Circuit reviewed the proper methods for determining the market values of raw materials, goods-in-process, and finished goods inventories that consisted of items of a special design for sale to the military pursuant to fixed-price contracts. The items in question were not suitable for commercial or civilian use. The government argued that the term "market" relates to what the manufacturer pays for raw materials, labor, and overhead, not to what it receives on the sale of its product. However, the court held to the contrary. Because of the lack of authorities on this point, the language used by the court is most informative:

> Before discussing the two provisions [of the Treasury regulations] we regard of crucial significance, it will be helpful to point out briefly that, contrary to the Government's thesis that market concerns *purchases for* inventory, not *sales from* it, the Regulations make the sales price significant in a number of instances. See, for example, goods which are "unsalable at normal prices or unusable in the normal way," § 1.471-2(c), and the use of "specific purchases or sales by the taxpayer or others. . . ." as evidence of a fair market price where "no open market exists or quotations are nominal. . . ."[413] Next, paragraph (b) affirmatively prescribes the exceptions to the standard established under paragraph (a) which defines "market" as "the current bid price. . . ." The first situation giving rise to the exception of paragraph (b) is the absence of a reliable, active market. The second situation is covered under the remainder of paragraph (b). It provides: "Where the taxpayer in the regular course of business has offered for sale such *merchandise* at prices lower than the current prices as above defined, the *inventory* may be valued at such prices less direct cost of disposition, and the correctness of such prices will be determined by reference to the actual sales of the taxpayer for a reasonable period before and after the date of the inventory. . . ."[414]

The government had taken the position that the exception provided by the second sentence of paragraph (b) applied only to the "fairly clear situation where the taxpayer is offering merchandise for sale in substantially the same form as it would be purchased in the current market."[415] This position had the objective of making the second sentence of paragraph (b) inapplicable to most work-in-process inventories. However, it was rejected by the court:

> [T]his argument overlooks the purposeful use of the separate terms "merchandise" and "inventory" in § 1.471-4(b). This whole section is

---

[412] Space Controls, Inc. v. Comm'r 322 F2d 144 (5th Cir. 1963), rev'g in part and aff'g in part 21 TCM 295 (1962).

[413] Space Controls, Inc. v. Comm'r, 322 F2d at 150 (emphasis by court).

[414] Id. at 151 (emphasis by court).

[415] Id. at 152.

dealing with finished goods and goods in process. Constructed to meet practical problems, the Regulation certainly did not contemplate that to get the benefit of paragraph (b) the taxpayer must have offered goods in process for sale in their incompleted state at prices lower than cost. The Regulation deliberately used the term "merchandise" which would mean the finished product. But the Regulation did not then proceed to limit the benefit of paragraph (b) to inventory insofar as it was represented in such "merchandise." Rather the Regulation itself states that in such event "the *inventory* may be valued at such [sales] prices less direct cost of disposition." This brings in as highly significant the general definition of inventory found in section 1.471-1 (note 14, *supra*). The term inventory "should include all finished goods or partly finished goods . . ." the latter being, of course, the equivalent of goods in process.[416]

Thus, the court made it clear that the benefit of the second sentence of paragraph (b) would be available to both goods-in-process and finished goods and that the market value of the goods-in-process would be determined by reference to the current sales prices of the finished goods. The court then stated:

And even the much cited Court of Claims decision in Bedford Mills [citation omitted], which as to finished goods adopted the "reproductive" rather than "replacement" test for the market value . . . recognized the applicability of the forerunner of what is now § 1.471-4(b). Following its analysis of the structure of the Regulation and particularly subparagraph (a)(1) and (2), the Court did hold that after (1) determining cost, (2) market should then be ascertained "by applying . . . prices prevailing on the inventory date" for "what it would cost to purchase raw materials," labor, burden, etc. Upon this comparative determination of (1) and (2), the "lower of the two . . . amounts should be used. . . ." But that very sentence went on. Completing the sentence, the Court stated, "[t]he lower of the two foregoing amounts should be used except (3) in the case 'where the taxpayer in the regular course of business has offered for sale such merchandise at prices lower than the current prices above defined, the inventory may be valued at such prices, less proper allowances for selling expense.'" The Court described this as "the third comparative." True, it was not there used, but not because it was inapplicable. Rather, it was because the Court did not "understand that plaintiff contends for the use of the third comparative . . ." which was borne out by the fact that "(there is no evidence that [taxpayer] offered its finished goods at the prices contended for). . . ."[417]

Although dealing with a limited situation—goods sold pursuant to fixed-price contracts—it appears that the court's analysis should be applicable

---

[416] Id. at 152 (emphasis by court).
[417] Id. at 153–154.

to a broad variety of situations and circumstances. Thus, taxpayers who sell goods at a price below reproduction or replacement cost should be able to value all components of their inventory with respect to those prices.

[iii] **Impact of GAAP on market write-downs.** In *Thor Power Tool*,[418] the U.S. Supreme Court addressed the issue of whether a market write-down for excess inventory that was appropriate for and consistent with GAAP was appropriate for tax purposes. The Court made it clear that notwithstanding that the write-downs were consistent with GAAP, they nevertheless would not be sustained for federal income tax purposes unless they conformed to the applicable regulations.[419]

The Court also made it clear that the allowance of write-downs for market is permitted only where there are sufficient evidentiary and practical safeguards as to ensure the IRS that a loss has in fact been realized.[420] Thus, if the requirements of the regulations cannot be satisfied, a write-down will not be permitted even if an economic loss has occurred that would be recognized for financial accounting purposes. As a consequence, taxpayers who wish to avail themselves of write-downs for federal income tax purposes must take care to come within the purview of the existing regulations rather than to rely on approaches that are acceptable for GAAP purposes, but not expressly available for tax purposes.

[iv] **Taxpayer response to *Thor Power Tool*.** Following the U.S. Supreme Court's decision in *Thor Power Tool*,[421] some taxpayers sought to achieve the write-downs denied by the Court by selling their excess inventories to unrelated parties who, in turn, would agree to resell the inventories back to the taxpayer as needed. The IRS announced that such agreements would be carefully scrutinized and would only be allowed if, in fact, bona fide sales and repurchases had occurred.[422] The courts have agreed with the position of the IRS.[423]

---

[418] Thor Power Tool Co. v. Comm'r, 439 US 522 (1979).

[419] See also Clark Equip. Co., 55 TCM 389 (1988), where purported sales of excess inventory to a warehouser of dormant parts and subsequent repurchases of that same inventory were not treated as bona fide sales or purchases for federal income tax purposes because of the control maintained by the taxpayer over the inventory while it was in the hands of the warehouser.

[420] See The Tog Shop, Inc. v. United States, 721 F. Supp. 300 (MD Ga. 1989), where write-downs claimed by the taxpayer were denied because of the taxpayer's inability to demonstrate by appropriate evidence that it had complied with the regulatory requirements.

[421] Thor Power Tool Co. v. Comm'r, 439 US 522 (1979).

[422] Rev. Rul. 83-59, 1983-1 CB 103.

[423] See, e.g., Paccar, Inc., 85 TC 754 (1985), aff'd, 849 F2d 393 (9th Cir. 1988); Clark Equip. Co., 55 TCM 389 (1988); Robert Bosch Corp., 58 TCM 921 (1989). See discussion supra ¶ 6.05[1][d], regarding when a sale is deemed to occur for tax

In *Robert Bosch Corp.*,[424] the Tax Court reaffirmed its position that agreements would be carefully scrutinized to determine whether they amounted to bona fide sales. The court also made it clear that the absence of formal, legally binding agreements, which required a repurchase or limited the discretion of the asserted purchaser, would not be required for the asserted sale to be disregarded so long as the overall arrangement made it clear that there was not a bona fide sale. The court specified four questions to be considered in analyzing each arrangement:

- *What items are taken into inventory?* Does the purchaser have the right to decide what goods to accept or must the purchaser accept whatever goods are offered?

- *Who determines when transferred items are to be scrapped?* Does the purchaser obtain actual control over the items? Does the purchaser get to decide when to dispose of the items, to whom it may dispose of the items, and so forth?

- *Who decides when to sell the items and to whom?* Does the original seller effectively control the asserted purchaser's discretion as to whether to sell property and, if so, to whom?

- *Who has the right to alter inventory?* Does the asserted purchaser have the right to alter the property, repackage it, modify it, or take any actions other than pursuant to permission or direction from the original seller?

Although these points were set out in the context of an excess inventory issue, they may be appropriate criteria of whether a bona fide sale has occurred in any circumstance. The key is the degree of discretion and control that has passed from the seller to the buyer. The extent that such key decisions as what to do with the property after it is acquired, whether to retain the property or dispose of it, the terms for any such retention or disposition, the parties to whom it may be sold or transferred, and so forth, are appropriate indicia of whether a true sale has occurred. Of course, these are difficult issues that may affect a wide variety of factual situations. Each situation must be considered carefully.

¶ 6.10 SPECIAL INVENTORY COSTING RULES

Consistent with the deference paid to financial accounting concepts in the inventory area, the regulations recognize that it may be appropriate to modify the foregoing rules in the case of taxpayers engaged in particular businesses.

---

purposes.

[424] Robert Bosch Corp., 58 TCM 921 (1989).

Accordingly, special rules are provided in the regulations for inventories of dealers in securities, inventories of livestock raisers and other farmers, inventories of miners and manufacturers, inventories of retail merchants, and inventories pertaining to taxpayers who report income on a long-term contract method.[425]

[1] Dealers in Securities

Dealers in securities may value their inventories at (1) cost; (2) the lower of cost or market; or (3) market regardless of the relationship of cost to market.[426]

   Whichever method is used by the taxpayer for tax purposes must also be used for purposes of his books of account. In addition, the taxpayer must include with his return a description of the method used, the method must be used for all inventories of securities, and the method must be continued unless a change in method of accounting is approved by the Commissioner.[427]

   For purposes of this provision of the regulation, a dealer may be an individual, a partnership, or a corporation. The dealer must have an established place of business and must be regularly engaged in the purchase and sale of securities. Securities that are bought for investment are not subject to these inventory valuation rules.[428]

[2] Inventories of Livestock Raisers and Other Farmers

For taxpayers engaged in raising livestock or in farming activities who are required to use inventories, special methods have been provided by the regulations.[429] These methods, either of which may be used, are the farm price method and the unit livestock price method.[430] In Revenue Ruling 88-60,[431] the IRS ruled that a taxpayer adopting the cash method to account for purchases and sales of livestock must determine the cost of any livestock sold on a basis of actual costs and not on the basis of inventory methods.

   Under the farm price method, inventories are valued at market price less

---

[425] See Treas. Reg. § 1.451-3 and Section 263A(c)(4) regarding property produced under long-term contracts.

[426] Treas. Reg. § 1.471-5.

[427] Id.

[428] Id.

[429] Treas. Reg. § 1.471-6.

[430] Treas. Reg. § 1.471-6(c). See also Notice 88-86, 1988-34 IRB 10, where the Treasury announced that forthcoming regulations will clarify that farmers using the unit livestock method are permitted to elect the simplified production method of determining inventoriable costs under Section 263A.

[431] Rev. Rul. 88-60, 1988-2 CB 30.

direct cost of disposition.[432] Under the unit livestock method, the animals are divided into different classes, and each class in inventory is valued at a standard unit price.[433] The classifications selected and the unit prices assigned to the various classes are subject to approval by the IRS on examination of the returns.[434]

Although Section 263A is generally applicable to farmers, the uniform capitalization costing rules are not applicable to plants or animals produced by a taxpayer in a farming business if the plant or animal has a preproductive period of two years or less.[435] However, this exception does not apply to any farming corporation, partnership, or tax shelter required to use an accrual method of accounting under Section 447 or Section 448(a)(3).[436] On the other hand, if the plant or animal has a preproduction period in excess of two years, the taxpayer may nevertheless elect not to have the rules of Section 263A apply, unless the taxpayer is one of the designated farming taxpayers required to use an accrual method.[437]

[3] By-Products

Taxpayers engaged in mining and certain manufacturing activities often produce two or more products (i.e., a principal product and a by-product) through a single process or a series of processes. Frequently, the determination must be made on how to allocate production costs among the products produced. The regulations provide that the allocation should bear a reasonable relationship to the respective selling prices of the different products.[438] However, if the value of the by-product is nominal, its cost may generally be ignored, in which case it would be carried in inventory at a zero cost.

[4] Inventories of Retail Merchants

Under a retail inventory method, the cost of goods is determined by reference to their selling prices. The selling prices are reduced to approximate cost by deducting amounts determined to reflect gross profit.[439] To accomplish this reduction, the aggregate selling prices of goods in ending inventory are multiplied by the ratio of (1) the cost of goods in beginning inventory plus

---

[432] Treas. Reg. § 1.471-6(d).

[433] Treas. Reg. § 1.471-6(e).

[434] Id.

[435] IRC § 263A(d)(1)(A).

[436] IRC § 263A(d)(1)(B).

[437] IRC § 263A(d)(3).

[438] Treas. Reg. § 1.471-7.

[439] Treas. Reg. § 1.471-8.

the cost of purchases to (2) the aggregate selling prices of beginning inventory and purchases.[440] It is noteworthy that this formula, by reference to beginning inventory, incorporates prior-year costs into the costing of current-year inventory.[441]

To make this computation, the retail selling prices of the goods on hand at the end of the year in each department or for each class of goods must be reduced by the projected gross profit of that department or class of goods.[442] In addition, adjustment must be made to reflect all so-called markups and markdowns of selling prices. The regulations make it clear that non-LIFO taxpayers are not required to take markdowns into account in determining the ratio of selling price to cost, but once a practice has begun, it must be continued.[443] LIFO taxpayers must take markdowns into account to ensure that inventories are valued at cost.[444]

EXAMPLE: To illustrate application of the retail method, assume that a taxpayer has one class of goods about which the following information is available:

	Retail	Cost
Beginning inventory	$100,000	$ 60,000
Purchases	400,000	280,000
Net markups	10,000	—
Net markdowns	6,000	—
Sales	380,000	—

This information shows that the total goods available for sale have a retail value of $510,000 ($100,000 beginning inventory + $400 purchases + $10,000 net markups) and a cost of $340,000 ($60,000 beginning inventory + $280,000 purchases). Ending inventory is determined merely by subtracting sales from goods available for sale and multiplying the result by the appropriate cost ratio. Consequently, since sales are $380,000, ending inventory at retail is $86,667 (($510,000 − $380,000) = $130,000; $130,000 x ($340,000 ÷ $510,000) = $86,667). Because net markups were taken into account, but not net markdowns, the resulting inventory of $86,667 represents inventory at the lower of cost or market. If the taxpayer were required to value inventory at cost, the ending inventory would be computed on the same basis, except that goods available for sale would have been $504,000 ($510,000 − $6,000 of net markdowns).

---

[440] As a result of the 1986 Act, adjustments must be made to reflect the impact of the uniform capitalization rules of Section 263A to taxpayers who are affected by those rules.

[441] See discussion supra ¶ 6.08[3][a] regarding IRS disapproval of average costing methods that use this same approach.

[442] Treas. Reg. § 1.471-8(c).

[443] Treas. Reg. §§ 1.471-8(d)–1.471-8(f).

[444] See Treas. Reg. § 1.471-8(g) and discussion at ¶ 7.03[3].

¶ 6.11 NONTRADITIONAL INVENTORY METHODS

Notwithstanding all the technical requirements for the costing of inventories, the courts have recognized over the years that, in particular circumstances, it is inappropriate to require a taxpayer to meet these requirements. In these circumstances, taxpayers have been permitted to use inventory methods that are not wholly consistent with the technical requirements of the regulations but are nonetheless found acceptable as clearly reflecting income.

The cases that have allowed the use of these nonconforming inventory methods demonstrate the willingness of the courts to defer to normal industry practices and to the judgment and expertise of the taxpayer's personnel in valuing unique inventories or inventories whose character is such that it would be unreasonable to require strict adherence to the regulations. This willingness on the part of the courts mirrors the general approach of the IRS, which is to work with taxpayers in developing and using reasonable means for valuing inventories. Taxpayers should not assume, however, that they may substitute arbitrary subjective valuations for objective evidence of cost or market where such objective evidence is reasonably available.

Although some of these cases were decided in the 1920s, they are still exceedingly important. Many revenue agents believe that the level of accounting sophistication and capacity available today (through use of computers) make data accumulation comparatively simple and inexpensive. This perception is not always accurate. There are many businesses that do not have this accounting sophistication or capacity and could not afford to acquire it. For other businesses, adequate systems and capacity may still be unavailable. These businesses are therefore faced with the need to maintain accurate accounting data and to prepare proper tax returns while, at the same time, not spending unreasonable amounts of money to achieve a level of accuracy that is not necessary for nontax purposes. The following cases illustrate the court's efforts to strike an appropriate balance.

In *Heinz Molsen, Jr.,*[445] the taxpayer was a cotton merchant. Under some of its contracts with suppliers, the purchase price would remain open or "on call" until the supplier exercised a call right granted to it under the contract. Generally, the call right would provide for the price of the cotton to be based on market price on a particular date as specified in the call. In accordance with GAAP and industry-wide practice, the taxpayer had historically and consistently determined its cost of goods sold by valuing that portion of its ending inventory subject to these contracts at the price it would have to pay if the call were exercised on the last day of the taxable year and by adding to its cost of purchases the corresponding additional amounts that would have to be paid on such purchases if the calls were then exercised. The Commissioner allowed the valuation of inventory on this basis but denied the additional accrual to the purchases account, asserting that these accruals

---

[445] Heinz Molsen, Jr., 85 TC 485 (1985).

failed to satisfy the all events test of accrual accounting and otherwise failed to result in a clear reflection of income. The court rejected the Commissioner's position and stated that the Commissioner had abused his discretion in requiring a change in reporting. The court based its decision on a number of factors including (1) the government's long-standing acceptance of the use of the market approach in valuing ending inventories; (2) the fact that the taxpayer's method was consistent with GAAP and was a long-standing practice of other taxpayers in the industry; (3) the fact that the approach used by the taxpayer had been recognized as the only practical means of arriving at income; (4) the fact that the cost of goods sold was technically not a deduction subject to the all events test; and (5) the fact that an inconsistency would otherwise result between the valuation of inventory and corresponding purchases. The court was also influenced by the wide variety of inventory valuation methods accepted by the Treasury. The court expressly noted the unit-livestock price method of Treasury Regulation § 1.471-6(f) and the retail method of Treasury Regulation § 1.471-8, pointing out that these methods were sanctioned because of the practical accounting problems that otherwise would have resulted from attempts to apply more technical methods. Moreover, the court added that although such practical methods may entail some degree of estimation, their use results in a clear reflection of income if consistently applied. The court then cited with approval the following statement:

> The practice of disapproving consistent accounting systems of long standing seems to me to be exceeding all reasonable bounds. . . . Methods of keeping records do not spring in glittering perfection from some unchangeable natural law but are devised to aid business men in maintaining sometimes intricate accounts. If reasonably adapted to that use they should not be condemned for some abstruse legal reason, but only when they fail to reflect income. . . .[446]

In *S. Weisbart & Co.*,[447] the taxpayer was in the business of fattening cattle for slaughter. The taxpayer purchased cattle of various ages, types, weights, and classes, and precise identification of animals on hand at any time was extremely impractical. In costing its year-end inventory of cattle, the taxpayer assumed that the lightest weight animals would be held the longest time and, hence, the invoices for these cattle were used as the basis for costing the inventory.

The Commissioner asserted that the taxpayer could not properly identify the animals in its inventory and was therefore required to use a strict FIFO method. The court disagreed, finding the taxpayer's method to be reasonable.

---

[446] Id., at 505, the court citing the observations of Judge Opper in Pac. Grape Prods. Co., 17 TC 1097, 1110 (1952) (Opper, J., dissenting), rev'd, 219 F2d 862 (9th Cir. 1955).

[447] S. Weisbart & Co., 23 TCM 788 (1964).

The court noted that methods of inventory are frequently modified to suit sets of unusual circumstances, and explained that "[w]here experienced persons, well acquainted with market conditions and prices, modify the usual inventory methods, their calculations are often accorded substantial weight in the absence of contradictory indications that these calculations are inaccurate."[448]

This reliance on the judgment and experience of the taxpayer's personnel was also given great weight by the Board of Tax Appeals in *Justus & Parker Co.*,[449] where the taxpayer was in the wholesale automobile equipment and supply business and assertedly used a lower-of-cost-or-market method of valuing inventory. At the end of each year, the taxpayer took a physical inventory at original cost. This inventory was then reviewed by the taxpayer's president and general manager, who analyzed the inventory and evaluated the value of the individual items listed. These individuals were thoroughly familiar with the merchandise, and the values determined by them were the prices at which, in their judgment, the inventory could be sold. The Board found the taxpayer's approach to be reasonable and appropriate in the circumstances.

Similar principles were applied in *E. Rauh & Sons Fertilizer Co.*,[450] where the taxpayer manufactured and sold fertilizer and animal foods. Raw materials and mixed products were stored in piles that were sometimes 35 to 40 feet high. In taking closing inventory, two of the taxpayer's officers took separate physical inventories and valued these inventories according to their experience and personal opinions. The two then met to compare their inventories, discuss differences, and agree on the quantities and the value.

The Board noted that the determination of the quantity of products and raw materials on hand was a complex task due to the impracticability of weighing the piles of materials. The Board also stated that at the inventory date under consideration, market values were almost nonexistent due to extreme market stagnation. It found that the taxpayer had produced "convincing" evidence of the correctness of its method of inventory valuation, and stated that the Code does not in every case limit the inventory to cost, or the lower of cost or market, and that methods of inventorying are frequently modified to suit the circumstances.

Values determined on the basis of the taxpayer's judgment and experience have been accepted even where it was the taxpayer who was challenging the values used. For instance, in *Crown Manufacturing Co.*,[451] the taxpayer was a manufacturer of cotton yarn. It classified its inventory of raw cotton according to various grades or types, waste, yarn in process, and finished

---

[448] Id. at 798.

[449] Justus & Parker Co., 13 BTA 127 (1928), acq. VII-2 CB 21.

[450] E. Rauh & Sons Fertilizer Co., 12 BTA 468 (1928), acq. VII-2 CB 33.

[451] Crown Mfg. Co., 12 BTA 37 (1928), acq. VII-2 CB 10.

yarn. The inventory of raw cotton and waste was valued by the taxpayer's general manager, who purchased almost all its cotton, although he made no purchases during the latter part of the year at issue and was therefore "somewhat out of touch with the market." The Commissioner accepted the taxpayer's inventory as so reported. However, the taxpayer claimed that the inventory was overstated. The Board held for the Commissioner, finding that the valuations originally used by the taxpayer were more reliable than the substitute values proposed by the taxpayer.

Finally, consideration must be given to *Morrie Chaitlen*,[452] where the taxpayer was in the business of purchasing, processing, and selling scrap metal. Because it is a comparatively recent case, it deserves significant attention. In *Morrie Chaitlen*, the scrap metal was stored in piles, separated into grades, and then processed. Although its tax returns stated that inventory was valued at the lower of FIFO cost or market, it was found by the court that the taxpayer actually valued inventory under a method peculiar to the scrap metals industry under which

> a corporate officer would visit the scrap yard, estimate quantities of the various categories of scrap, and determine a price for the scrap after referring to market quotes of trade journals, market conditions, and the processing stage in the inventory. [The taxpayer] did not maintain a perpetual inventory to assist in inventory valuation and compiled no other records reflecting its inventory method.[453]

In March 1970, the stock of the taxpayer was sold to a group of individuals. In September 1970, the new president and vice-president of the taxpayer inspected the scrap yard for purposes of valuing closing inventory and, based on discussions and prices quoted in trade journals, estimated the value at $100,000.

In November 1970, negotiations began for the sale of the taxpayer's assets to another corporation. The prospective purchaser was engaged in the same type of business and maintained an adjoining scrap yard. The president, vice-president, and warehouse superintendent of the prospective purchaser inspected the taxpayer's inventory. They visually inspected the scrap metals on hand and offered the taxpayer $200,000 for its operating assets, allocating $150,000 to the inventory. The parties ultimately agreed on a sales price of $300,000, of which $200,000 was allocated to inventory.

The Commissioner thereafter asserted that a value of $200,000 should be assigned to the inventory. The court noted that the regulations under Section 471 recognized industry customs and accorded great weight to consistency. It stated the issue as "whether petitioners have established that the

---

[452] Morrie Chaitlen, 37 TCM 17 (1978).
[453] Id. at 18.

[company's] inventory valuation method was acceptable in the industry and, if so, whether [the company] properly applied it."[454]

The court found that the inventory valuation practice used was acceptable in the scrap metal industry and had been consistently applied by the taxpayer throughout the years. However, the court found that the persons who had valued the 1970 inventories were not qualified to do so. It noted that the president had no experience in the scrap metal business prior to the March 1970 acquisition of the taxpayer and that the vice-president had only limited experience in dealing with a particular class of scrap metals. The court found that the officers of the acquiring corporation that visited the scrap yard in November 1970 were experts in valuing metals and held that their estimate of the replacement cost of the inventory at $150,000 was the best evidence in the record. It was noted that this figure did not represent a "selling market quote," as contended by the taxpayer, since the inventory was sold for $200,000 and the acquiring corporation was not a retail purchaser of the taxpayer's inventory. The court stated that had the $150,000 figure been offered by a regular customer and the inventory been actually sold for $150,000, the taxpayer's argument would have had greater validity.

There are numerous businesses that are unable to compute inventories with the precision that the IRS would like. Examples abound. Consider the plumbing company that may have literally thousands of items, such as nails, washers, and screws in barrels or tubs. Consider merchants who, as a regular course of their inventory acquisition procedures, negotiate and obtain numerous items for an aggregate price. Operations may be such that it is impossible to allocate the aggregate pay among the items acquired. Frequently, the aggregate may be paid to obtain some but not all the items acquired. Additionally, consider those taxpayers whose employees are not sufficiently trained or educated for the purpose of taking inventories or who are simply not able to take correct inventories, frequently making incorrect counts. For all these reasons, taxpayers must be able to exercise discretion in applying the inventory costing rules to their particular circumstances, and the IRS must exercise reasonable discretion in permitting these varied applications.

_____

[454] Id. at 20.

CHAPTER 7

LIFO

¶ 7.01 Reason for Cost-Flow Assumptions 7-2

¶ 7.02 LIFO Concept 7-3
    [1] Objective 7-4
    [2] History and Development 7-6

¶ 7.03 Requirements for Adoption and Use of LIFO 7-8
    [1] Adoption 7-9
        [a] Application or Other Statement 7-9
        [b] Selective Use of LIFO 7-10
        [c] Subsidiary Elections 7-12
        [d] Commissioner's Discretion in Terminating LIFO 7-13
    [2] Conformity Requirement 7-14
        [a] Rationale for Requirement 7-15
        [b] Application of Requirement 7-16
            [i] Supplementary or explanatory information 7-17
            [ii] Reporting on non-LIFO basis on a balance sheet ... 7-18
            [iii] Internal management reports 7-19
            [iv] Reports covering less than entire taxable year 7-19
            [v] Lower of LIFO cost or market 7-19
            [vi] Use of different costing procedures 7-20
            [vii] Reconciliations 7-22
            [viii] Controlled groups 7-22
            [ix] Financial forecasts and projections 7-23
    [3] Cost Requirement 7-24
        [a] Rationale for Requirement 7-25
        [b] Requirement's Impact on Timing of Adoption of LIFO .. 7-25
        [c] Restored and Prohibited Write-Downs 7-26
        [d] How Restoration Is Made 7-27
    [4] Books and Records 7-27
    [5] Statutory Periods of Limitation 7-29

¶ 7.04 LIFO Systems 7-29
    [1] Essentials 7-30
    [2] Specific Goods LIFO 7-30
        [a] Pooling 7-33
        [b] Quantitative Measure 7-34
        [c] Valuing Increments 7-34

[3] Dollar-Value LIFO 7-35
  [a] Pooling 7-38
    [i] Natural-business-unit pools 7-38
    [ii] Other pools 7-43
    [iii] Single pool for certain small businesses 7-44
  [b] Base Costs and Alternative Measurement Procedures ... 7-44
    [i] Double-extension method 7-45
    [ii] Index method 7-48
    [iii] Link-chain method 7-49
    [iv] Reconstruction techniques 7-50
  [c] Valuing Increments 7-51
  [d] New or Revised Base Year 7-52
  [e] Product Costing Versus Component Costing 7-53
[4] Retail LIFO 7-64
[5] Simplified LIFO Methods 7-64
  [a] Price Index Method 7-65
    [i] Operation of method 7-65
    [ii] Adoption of price index method 7-70
    [iii] Changing to price index method 7-71
  [b] Simplified Dollar-Value LIFO: Section 474 7-72

¶ 7.05 Termination of LIFO 7-73
  [1] Judicial Attitude 7-75
    [a] In General 7-75
    [b] Regarding Proposed Terminations 7-77
  [2] IRS Attitude 7-78

¶ 7.06 Change From LIFO and Readoption of LIFO 7-79
  [1] Change Requiring Consent 7-80
  [2] Change Pursuant to Automatic Consent Provisions 7-80
  [3] Readoption of LIFO 7-82

¶ 7.07 Liquidations of LIFO Inventory 7-82
  [1] The Problem 7-82
  [2] Taxpayer Response 7-83
  [3] Statutory Relief 7-84

¶ 7.08 Acquisition and Transfer of LIFO Inventory 7-85
  [1] Section 351 Transfer 7-85
    [a] Impact on Transferor 7-85
    [b] Impact on Transferee 7-87
  [2] Acquisition at Bargain Price 7-88
  [3] Section 381 Transaction 7-90
    [a] Acquired Business and Acquirer on Same Method 7-90
    [b] Businesses to Remain Separate 7-92
    [c] Businesses to Be Integrated 7-92

¶ 7.09 Adoption of S Corporation Status 7-92

¶ 7.01 REASON FOR COST-FLOW ASSUMPTIONS

When an inventory consists of a relatively small number of items, each with its own identifiable characteristics and cost (as in the case of an inventory of antiques or expensive pieces of jewelry), the actual cost of each item may be readily ascertainable. The use of the actual cost of each item in inventory to determine aggregate inventory cost is known as the specific identification method. This method allows for the precise matching of sales revenue and cost of goods sold.

However, when an inventory consists of a large number of essentially similar or fungible goods, practical problems arise as to how the aggregate cost of these goods should be allocated between goods sold during the year and goods remaining on hand at the end of the year. For financial accounting purposes, these problems are resolved by using assumptions as to which costs should be assigned to goods sold and which costs should be assigned to ending inventory.

Many cost-flow assumptions have gained general acceptance within the accounting community. These assumptions include first-in, first-out (FIFO), an assumption that the cost of the first goods acquired or produced should be assigned to the first goods sold; and last-in, first-out (LIFO), an assumption that the cost of the goods most recently acquired or produced should be assigned to the first goods sold.

Under FIFO, the earliest costs incurred are matched against current revenues. To the extent that current costs exceed earliest costs, gross profit is arguably overstated and distorted because a portion of the gross profit must be used merely to replace the inventory that was sold rather than being available for the payment of operating expenses, repayment of debt, new investment, or distribution to owners. Under LIFO, current costs are matched against current revenue. This matching arguably produces a more accurate measure of income.[1]

This chapter focuses on the LIFO method of inventory accounting and covers the requirements for adoption and use of the method, necessary computations under traditional LIFO systems, the use of simplified LIFO systems, and a number of special problems affecting LIFO inventories.

¶ 7.02 LIFO CONCEPT

The LIFO concept is codified in Section 472, which authorizes the use of the LIFO method for tax purposes.[2] This section provides that under LIFO, (1) the costs assigned to goods sold during any taxable year shall be the cost of the goods most recently acquired or produced and (2) the costs assigned to

---

[1] See, e.g., Fox Chevrolet, Inc., 76 TC 708, 726 (1981), where the court stated, "at the heart of the LIFO method is the principle that income is more clearly reflected by matching current costs with current revenues."

[2] All "IRC" references are to the Internal Revenue Code of 1986, as amended (the Code).

goods in ending inventory shall be, first, the costs assigned to goods in beginning inventory (in the order of their acquisition or production to the extent thereof) and, second, the cost of goods acquired during the year.[3] This manner of assigning costs to ending inventory is known as sequential layering.[4]

EXAMPLE: Assume that a taxpayer with a beginning inventory of 10 units of product at a cost of $1 per unit acquires additional units of product at the following times and costs:

Date	Number	Unit cost	Total
Beg. inv.	10	$1.00	$10.00
April 1	15	1.02	15.30
July 1	15	1.04	15.60
October 1	10	1.06	10.60
	50		$51.50

Assuming that 12 units of product remain on hand at the end of the year, it is necessary to determine what portion of the $51.50 aggregate cost should be allocated to these 12 units. Under LIFO, the ending inventory would be deemed to cost $12.04 (consisting of a layer of 10 units at $1.00 per unit and a layer of 2 units at $1.02 per unit). The balance of $39.46 would be allocated to cost of goods sold. Under FIFO, the ending inventory would be deemed to cost $12.68 ((10 x $ 1.06) + (2 x $1.04)), and the balance of $38.82 would be allocated to cost of goods sold.

[1] Objective

The objective of the LIFO method is to match relatively current costs against current revenues to compute a meaningful gross profit.[5] Use of the LIFO method is predicated on the theory that business operations require a certain level of inventory and that the changing costs associated with maintaining that level of inventory should be expensed during the year incurred.

---

[3] IRC § 472(b).

[4] For a further description of sequential layering, see infra ¶ 7.04.

[5] See, e.g., IRC ¶ 472(b)(1); Comm'r v. Joseph E. Seagram & Sons, Inc., 394 F2d 738, 742 (2d Cir. 1968) ("It is the underlying purpose of the LIFO method of inventory accounting to match current income against *current* costs. . . ."). However, in Hamilton Indus., Inc., 97 TC 120 (1991), which focused on the proper treatment of inventory acquired in a bargain purchase, the Tax Court seemingly relegated this objective of matching current costs against current revenues to a position of somewhat lesser importance than a LIFO objective of including inflation in cost of goods sold, with "inflation" defined in such a way as to prevent the preservation in inventory of the bargain element if, by so doing, income would be clearly reflected. *Hamilton* is discussed further infra ¶¶ 7.08[1][b], 7.08[2].

Under LIFO, the costs associated with changing prices are generally reflected in the cost of goods sold. In effect, these costs are treated as period costs and excluded from income. For instance, in the preceding example, the use of LIFO increased the cost of goods sold by $0.64 (from $38.82 to $39.46). This $0.64 represented the inflation that had occurred during the year in the cost of items that remained on hand at the end of the year ((10 units x increase in price of $.06 per unit) + (2 units x increase in price of $.02 per unit)).

Use of the LIFO method provides a number of benefits. Most obvious is the improvement in cash flow, which results from reduced state and federal income taxes.[6] The taxpayer obtains increased funds for replenishing inventory without having to borrow "profit." In other words, the profit that is reported for financial or tax purposes is true profit, which may be distributed to owners without reducing the level of operations or used to pay debts, to make new investments, or otherwise to expand the business. In this sense, many accountants, business people, and financial analysts believe that LIFO permits a more rational basis than other inventory methods for economic decision making.

Despite its many advantages, use of the LIFO method entails one significant risk even during periods of inflation. To the extent that a taxpayer sells more inventory during the year than it acquires or produces, current revenues will be matched not only against current costs but also against some of the older costs that had been assigned to beginning inventory. If these older costs were incurred many years earlier, when prices were substantially lower, exorbitant taxable profits may arise from the liquidation of this inventory.

EXAMPLE: Assume that a taxpayer began the year with a LIFO inventory of six units that cost $1 per unit but whose current cost was $4 per unit. If the taxpayer purchased 10 units during the year but sold 11 units, its cost of goods sold would be $41 (($10 units x $4 per unit) + (1 unit x $1 per unit)). If it had purchased 11 units and sold 11 units, its cost of goods sold would have been $44. By failing to acquire as many units as it sold, the taxpayer experienced a liquidation of low basis beginning inventory and, as a consequence, had to recognize $3 of so-called inventory profit.[7]

---

[6] The reduction in reported earnings that generally arises from the use of the LIFO method has caused many taxpayers to be reluctant to make the change to LIFO, fearing an adverse reaction on the price of their stock. However, sophisticated investors should recognize the financial benefits associated with LIFO, and it has been reported that a study conducted by Shyam Sunder of the University of Chicago showed that companies switching to LIFO tended to outperform the market. Merjos, "FIFO to LIFO," Barron's 5 (Oct. 21, 1974).

[7] See infra ¶ 7.07 for discussion of LIFO liquidations.

[2] History and Development

The history of financial accounting, including the concept of inventories, can be traced back to before the early fifteenth century.[8] Yet the LIFO concept is of relatively recent origin, owing its creation and development to a number of factors including, principally, the desire of some companies to remove inventory profits from reported earnings and the acceptance of the method in 1938 for federal income tax purposes.[9]

The earliest attempts to remove inventory profits from income arose in the early 1900s with the development of so-called normal stock methods of inventory accounting. These methods included the base stock and reserve methods,[10] which were based on the premise that a certain "normal" quantity of inventory was generally required throughout the life of a business and thus should be valued as a fixed asset rather than on the basis of changing prices over the course of a business cycle.

Interest in normal stock methods abated somewhat in 1919 after the Treasury ruled that they could not be used for federal income tax purposes.[11] The Treasury's position was affirmed by the U.S. Supreme Court in 1930.[12] The Court found that these methods were inconsistent with the annual accounting concept,[13] did not conform to the best accounting methods,[14] and had not been approved by accountants.[15] Despite its rejection for tax purposes, interest in the normal stock concept was revived as a result of price fluctuations during the post–World War I period, the stock market crash, the depression, the increase in corporate income tax rates during the 1930s, and

---

[8] See, e.g., R. Hoffman & H. Gunders, Inventories 146–150 (2d ed. 1970); E. Hendriksen, Accounting Theory 15–21 (1965).

[9] See McAnly, "The Current Status of Lifo," 105 J. of Accountancy 55 (May 1958); Moonitz, "The Case Against Lifo as an Inventory-Pricing Formula," 95 J. of Accountancy 682 (June 1953).

[10] E. Hendriksen, supra note 8, at 260, 270. The base stock method valued the amount of the normal inventory at constant, more or less arbitrary, prices and not necessarily on the basis of actual historical costs. The reserve method accomplished the same result by establishing a reserve on the liability side of the balance sheet equal to the excess of historical costs over a selected normal valuation.

[11] TBR 65, 1 CB 51 (1919).

[12] Lucas v. Kansas City Structural Steel Co., 281 US 264 (1930).

[13] See discussion at ¶ 12.02 regarding the annual accounting concept.

[14] See Section 471 and discussion at ¶ 6.04[1][a][i] regarding the general requirement that inventory methods conform to the best accounting practice in the trade or business.

[15] Lucas v. Kansas City Structural Steel Co., 281 US 264 (1930). The Court also recognized that the quantity labeled "normal" was subjectively, and in some cases arbitrarily, determined, it did not permit adequate comparison among firms within the same industry, it created a balance sheet reflection of inventory based on neither cost nor market, and it generally permitted manipulation in the determination of net income; see also E. Hendriksen, Accounting Theory 270–271 (1965).

the pressures placed on the accounting profession after creation of the Securities and Exchange Commission (SEC).

In 1934, representatives of the petroleum industry recommended the use of the LIFO method for that industry for financial accounting purposes. A Special Committee on Inventories (the Committee) of the American Institute of Accountants (the AIA), the predecessor to the American Institute of Certified Public Accountants (AICPA), collaborated with the American Petroleum Institute on this matter and, in 1936, the AIA concluded that LIFO was an acceptable method of accounting for oil company inventories.[16] Immediately thereafter, the Committee turned its attention to inventory problems in other industries. Its chairman met with representatives of the nonferrous metals and leather industries who were interested in using LIFO for corporate reporting purposes and in obtaining Internal Revenue Bureau approval of the method for income tax purposes.[17]

At first, the Treasury refused to budge from its traditional opposition to the normal stock concept and repeatedly turned down requests by tanners and the producers and processors of nonferrous metals to use the LIFO method.[18] Nevertheless, continuing pressure from these groups caused Congress to permit them to use LIFO for tax purposes beginning in 1938.[19] Soon thereafter, other groups pressured Congress for the right to use the LIFO method. As a result, Congress extended the option of using the LIFO method for tax purposes to all taxpayers in the Revenue Act of 1939.[20] This general codification of the LIFO method has continued through the present without material change.[21]

Although the accounting profession had been instrumental in gaining LIFO's initial acceptance for tax purposes,[22] at the time the option to use the method was extended to all taxpayers, the AIA had not yet officially approved LIFO as an inventory method available to all businesses for financial accounting purposes. Official approval was first published in 1947.[23] Even then, however, considerable debate took place within the accounting

---

[16] R. Hoffman & H. Gunders, supra note 8, at 189.

[17] "The Valuation of Inventory," 65 J. of Accountancy 29 (Jan. 1938).

[18] 83 Cong. Rec. 5043–5044, cited in J. Seidman, Legislative History of Federal Income Tax Laws (1938-1861), 6–7 (1938).

[19] Revenue Act of 1938, § 22(d).

[20] Internal Revenue Code of 1939, § 22(d).

[21] IRC § 472.

[22] The legislative history of the LIFO provision in the Revenue Act of 1938 reflected the fact that in particular industries LIFO was "recognized by the leading accounting authorities as most accurately reflecting income." 83 Cong. Rec. 5043, cited in J. Seidman, Legislative History of Federal Income Tax Laws (1938-1861), 6 (1938).

[23] Acct. Res. Bull. No. 29, "Inventory Pricing" (July 1947).

profession as to the propriety of the LIFO method for financial accounting purposes.[24]

Today, there is virtually no debate among accountants or others as to the propriety of the LIFO method for financial accounting purposes. In fact, many accountants believe LIFO to be a preferable method of inventory accounting, and changes to LIFO are generally justified on the basis that this change minimizes the impact of inflation and produces a more realistic statement of income.[25]

¶ 7.03 REQUIREMENTS FOR ADOPTION AND USE OF LIFO

The initial adoption of LIFO is not conditioned on the prior approval of the Internal Revenue Service. Nevertheless, there are a number of other conditions that must be met before the taxpayer may adopt and use the LIFO method. Failure to satisfy any of these conditions gives the IRS the discretion to terminate the taxpayer's use of LIFO. However, assuming these conditions are satisfied, the LIFO method is available to all taxpayers as a matter of right.[26]

---

[24] See Moonitz, supra note 9; McAnly, "The Case for Lifo: It Realistically States Income and Is Applicable to Any Industry," 95 J. of Accountancy 691 (June 1953); Johnson, "Inventory Valuation: The Accountant's Achilles Heel," 29 Acct. Rev. 15 (Jan. 1954); Husband, "The First-In, Last-Out Method of Inventory Valuation," 15 Acct. Rev. 190 (June 1940); Cotter, "Why Last-In? A Comment on the Husband Article," 15 Acct. Rev. 419 (Sept. 1940); Blough, "Accounting and Auditing Problems: Pooling of LIFO Inventories," 110 J. of Accountancy 61, 62 (July 1960). The author, Carman G. Blough, was then the Director of Research of the AICPA.

[25] See, e.g., Sprouse & Moonitz, "A Tentative Set of Broad Accounting Principles for Business Enterprises," Acct. Res. Study No. 3, 50 (1962), where the authors, in concluding that inventories, in addition to the cost of goods sold, should be measured by the most recently established current values, stated:

> The advantages of measuring cost of goods sold and revenues from sales in consistent current terms have long been stressed as the primary justification for the use of the last-in-first-out-assumption of flow of inventory costs in profit calculations. We have accepted this position in principle and extend it to the inventory items themselves.

[26] See, e.g., John Wanamaker Philadelphia, Inc. v. United States, 359 F2d 437 (Ct. Cl. 1966), where the court stated that taxpayers have "an absolute right" to use the LIFO method, and the Commissioner's discretion, except for proposing necessary or appropriate adjustments, is quite narrow. On the other hand, Treas. Reg. § 1.472-6 implies that consent to readopt LIFO is required if the taxpayer has voluntarily changed from or has been required to change from the use of LIFO, and Rev. Proc. 92-20, 1992-1 CB 685, § 9.04 expressly requires the prior approval of the Commissioner to readopt LIFO where the taxpayer has previously received permission to change from the LIFO method. See discussion infra ¶ 7.06[3]. Similarly, consent may

[1] Adoption

The initial adoption of LIFO by a taxpayer is conditioned on the filing of a proper application with the Commissioner.[27]

[a] Application or Other Statement

The application, which consists of Form 970 and applicable supporting schedules, must be filed with the taxpayer's original federal income tax return for the first year for which the method is used.[28] The regulations do not require that the original return be a timely return in order for the LIFO election to be valid, and the IRS has apparently concluded from this fact that a timely return is not required.[29] In addition, on a showing of good cause by a taxpayer, the Commissioner has the discretion to grant a reasonable extension of time to make the election.[30]

Form 970 notifies the Commissioner of the taxpayer's adoption of LIFO and also provides the means for the taxpayer to make a number of subsidiary elections.[31] For example, the form is used by the taxpayer to specify the particular goods for which the LIFO method is adopted, the number and type of pools into which these goods will be placed, the manner of computing increases or decreases in the inventory pools, the method of valuing increases to the pools, and other aspects of the taxpayer's particular LIFO computations.

Considerable care should be taken in completing Form 970. It should include sufficient information to anticipate and resolve (through the information furnished) potential questions or issues that otherwise might arise on

---

be required if so specified in some earlier ruling or change in method granted the taxpayer.

[27] Section 472(a) provides, "A taxpayer may use the [LIFO] method . . . in inventorying goods specified in an application to use such method filed at such time and in such manner as the Secretary may prescribe." The regulations provide that the election must be made by filing an appropriate statement of election or "in such other manner as may be acceptable to the Commissioner." Treas. Reg. § 1.472-3(a).

[28] Treas. Reg. § 1.472-3(a).

[29] See "LIFO Method of Inventory Valuation," IRS Training Manual No. 3127-01, 1 (1976), where the IRS stated, "It would appear that a taxpayer filing a delinquent return with Form 970 and supporting schedules has made a valid election."

[30] See Rev. Proc. 79-63, 1979-2 CB 578, regarding requests for extensions of time for making elections under Treas. Reg. § 1.9100-1(a), pertaining to the general discretion of the Commissioner; Priv. Ltr. Rul. 8831041 (May 10, 1988), permitting an extension of time for adopting LIFO where the taxpayer had directed its accountants to file a Form 970 LIFO election in connection with a Section 351 transfer of a corporation's LIFO inventory to a new corporation so that the LIFO method could be continued, but where the accountant had failed to carry out these instructions.

[31] See also discussion infra ¶¶ 7.03[1][b], 7.03[1][c].

audit. Many taxpayers provide only a minimal amount of information. Consequently, questions frequently arise on audit as to whether the taxpayer's LIFO system is consistent with the methods and descriptions contained in its Form 970.

Alternatively, a taxpayer may adopt LIFO by filing a statement (in lieu of Form 970) on its timely filed original federal income tax return for the first year for which the method is used, as long as the statement provides all the information that would have been submitted with Form 970.[32] If the taxpayer fails to file Form 970 or an otherwise appropriate statement, or fails to provide all of the information required on or by the currently applicable Form 970, the Commissioner takes the position that the IRS may terminate the taxpayer's use or continued use of LIFO.[33]

As a practical matter, if at all possible, taxpayers should avoid filing a statement in lieu of Form 970. The use of such a statement is atypical and may create a risk of more attention being given to the election by the IRS than otherwise would be the case.

Although other means of adopting LIFO may be acceptable to the Commissioner,[34] none has been announced. Nevertheless, one example of such other means might be where the IRS changes a taxpayer to a LIFO method on audit because of the IRS's dissatisfaction with the taxpayer's prior method or because of the taxpayer's inability to compute inventories practically and correctly on any non-LIFO basis. However, a mere indication on the tax return that the taxpayer is adopting the LIFO method is not sufficient.[35]

A separate Form 970 should be filed for each corporation that is electing the LIFO method, even if those corporations are members of a single affiliated group of corporations that files consolidated tax returns. Taxpayers must not make the mistake of assuming that an adoption of LIFO by the parent corporation automatically constitutes the adoption of LIFO by its subsidiaries.

[b] Selective Use of LIFO

The LIFO method may be adopted for all or some specified portion of the taxpayer's total inventory. Consequently, if the taxpayer's inventory consists of unrelated groups of items (e.g., groups that differ by type or class), LIFO may be adopted for one group but not for another. A manufacturer

---

[32] In Rev. Proc. 74-2, 1974-1 CB 412, the IRS authorized the use of such a statement, but unlike the adoption of LIFO by Form 970, the IRS specified that the return with which the statement is submitted must be timely filed.

[33] See Rev. Proc. 79-23, 1979-1 CB 564 and discussion infra ¶ 7.05.

[34] Treas. Reg. § 1.472-3(a).

[35] Rev. Rul. 78-262, 1978-2 CB 170.

may limit its LIFO election to any one or more of its raw materials (including the raw material content of its work in process and finished goods),[36] but it is not clear whether the election may be limited to labor and overhead. There are no examples expressly authorizing such an approach, although such an approach is computationally possible. Moreover, for a taxpayer that elects LIFO for raw materials only, the associated labor and overhead necessarily must be computed on a FIFO (or other non-LIFO) basis.[37] Since such inventory costs must be accounted for on a non-LIFO basis where LIFO is elected for raw material only, it seems logical to conclude that LIFO may be elected for labor and overhead costs where raw material costs remain on a non-LIFO basis. Otherwise, a taxpayer is denied the opportunity to adopt LIFO for the same items of inventoriable cost for which FIFO is available.[38] A taxpayer may also limit its LIFO election to all inventoriable costs through any production phase from which a saleable product emerges.[39]

Selective use of LIFO can be quite helpful. For example, LIFO may be adopted for those items or groups of items whose prices are increasing due to inflation or other factors, but not for items or groups of items whose prices are stable or declining. A taxpayer may stagger the timing of its adoption of LIFO for different portions of its inventory so as to achieve maximum tax advantage. The adoption of LIFO for a portion of the inventory does not in any way prohibit the taxpayer from adopting LIFO for the remainder of the inventory at a later date. Such later adoption is available at the taxpayer's choice and without the need for the prior approval of the IRS. However, if the taxpayer desires to make changes in its existing LIFO method at the time it adopts LIFO for additional types or classes of goods, the prior approval of the IRS will be necessary.

The LIFO election is available only for goods that are subject to the merchandise inventory rules set forth in Section 471 and the regulations

---

[36] Treas. Reg. §§ 1.472-1(c), 1.472-(j). A taxpayer is apparently also permitted to adopt LIFO for raw materials only (i.e., excluding raw material content in work in process and finished goods), but the issue is not free from doubt. Compare, e.g., Priv. Ltr. Rul. 7807006 (Oct. 27, 1977), where the National Office denied this election, with Priv. Ltr. Rul. 5104241590X (Apr. 24, 1951), where such an election was approved.

[37] Treas. Reg. § 1.472-1(c).

[38] Notwithstanding this analysis, until the appropriateness of the use of so-called LIFO component costing is resolved, the IRS may be expected to challenge the adoption of LIFO for labor or overhead or both while raw material costs remain on FIFO. See discussion of component costing, infra ¶ 7.04[3][e].

[39] Treas. Reg. § 1.472-1(i). The regulations cite the textile industry as an industry for which this option might be attractive. For example, one phase of the production process might result in the production of yarn. Since yarn is generally recognized as a salable product, the LIFO election may be limited to that portion of the overall process that results in the production of yarn. Later portions of the process would be excluded.

thereunder.[40] Consequently, LIFO is available for merchandise produced under long-term contracts,[41] but not for real estate.[42] Care must be taken in specifying the portion of the taxpayer's inventory for which LIFO is being adopted. If there is ambiguity in the election, the courts will examine all the facts and circumstances to determine the scope of the election, and the taxpayer's stated intent (as to the scope of the election) at the time the issue is raised may not be controlling.[43] Of course, in determining the scope of any particular election, it is appropriate to examine both the taxpayer's existing method of accounting for the relevant items and also the amounts it thereafter reports on its returns for these items, and this point is recognized by the IRS.[44]

[c] Subsidiary Elections

When a taxpayer adopts LIFO, it also adopts subsidiary methods of accounting associated with its use of LIFO. The subsidiary elections are made on Form 970 and include methods of pooling, computing increases and decreases in the quantity of the LIFO inventory, and valuing increases (or so-called increments) to inventory.[45]

The subsidiary elections are quite important. Any change in a subsidiary election (such as a change in method of pooling or in LIFO computational procedure) is generally treated as a change in method of accounting and, as a consequence, requires the prior approval of the Commissioner. (See Chapter 8 for discussion of changes in accounting methods.)

However, not all of these changes would require a Section 481 adjustment. For example, applicable Treasury regulations provide that any change in method of pooling under the dollar-value LIFO concept that is required or permitted shall be made pursuant to the principles set forth in the

---

[40] See discussion at ¶ 6.05[1].

[41] Peninsula Steel Prods. & Equip. Co., 78 TC 1029 (1982); Spang Indus., Inc. v. United States, 791 F2d 906 (Fed. Cir. 1986), rev'g 84-2 USTC ¶ 9739 (Ct. Cl. 1984); RECO Indus., Inc., 83 TC 912 (1984). See discussion at ¶ 6.05[1].

[42] W.C. & A.N. Miller Dev. Co., 81 TC 619 (1983); Homes by Ayres, 48 TCM 1050 (1984), aff'd, 795 F2d 832 (9th Cir. 1986). See discussion at ¶ 6.05[3][a].

[43] See First Nat'l Bank of Gainesville, 88 TC 1069 (1987), where the taxpayer stated that its LIFO election did not apply to a significant portion of its inventory, but where the court found that the taxpayer had failed to exclude this portion of the inventory from its adoption of LIFO when filling out the form and that the taxpayer had later indicated in its returns that 100 percent of its inventory was valued on a LIFO basis.

[44] See, e.g., Tech. Adv. Mem. 9132001 (Jan. 9, 1991).

[45] See infra ¶¶ 7.04[2], 7.04[3], regarding the subject matter of these subsidiary elections.

regulations.[46] These regulations require that the LIFO value of the pool or pools at the beginning of the year of change be reallocated to the greater or lesser number of new pools without a Section 481 adjustment. In other words, the taxpayer is not required to adjust its inventory as if it had been under the new method of pooling for all prior years following its adoption of LIFO. This is an appropriate approach. It would be virtually impossible to reconstruct retroactively the results in earlier years under a different method of pooling. In addition, a change in pools is often occasioned by a change in relevant facts and circumstances. For example, a taxpayer's business operations following its election of LIFO may warrant a certain number of LIFO pools. However, due to later changes in management, reorganization of its operations, or similar events, a greater or lesser number of pools may be appropriate in subsequent years. If the IRS were to require a change in pooling based on the then-applicable facts and circumstances, or if a taxpayer were to request a change in pooling because of a change in circumstances, a Section 481 adjustment may well be inappropriate. It suggests that determinations as to appropriate pooling in prior years should be undone even though the new method of pooling may have been inappropriate in such prior years. Similar problems arise in connection with changes to or from an index method, a link chain LIFO method, component costing to product costing, and vice versa.

In addition, a Section 481 adjustment may not be required on changes in LIFO methods or sub-methods because of the taxpayer's circumstances at the time of its application for change in method. Revenue Procedure 92-20[47] provides special rules governing applications for changes in LIFO methods or sub-methods. In certain circumstances, the changes will be made using a so-called cutoff approach, under which no Section 481 adjustment is required. Instead, the effect of the change in method of accounting on that portion of the inventory attributable to years prior to the year of change will be taken into account only as such inventories are liquidated.[48] Except as otherwise provided by regulation, Revenue Procedure 92-20, or other document published by the IRS, a change in LIFO method will require a Section 481 adjustment.[49]

[d] Commissioner's Discretion in Terminating LIFO

In practice, the Commissioner has been fairly restrained in exercising his discretion to terminate the use of LIFO by a taxpayer who has failed to adopt the LIFO method properly. This is not to say that the Commissioner will not

---

[46] Treas. Reg. § 1.472-8(g)(2).

[47] Rev. Proc. 92-20, 1992-1 CB 685.

[48] See Rev. Proc. 92-20, 1992-1 CB 685, § 9; and discussion at ¶ 8.06[3][b][v].

[49] See Rev. Proc. 92-20, 1992-1 CB 685, § 9.01.

terminate the use of LIFO for failure to file Form 970 or other appropriate statement; he will. Nevertheless, these terminations have generally been limited to those involving examinations of the initial year for which LIFO is first adopted.[50]

In cases where the taxpayer has failed to file a fully completed Form 970 or other appropriate statement, but has nevertheless used the LIFO method for many years during which examinations have been made of the taxpayer's LIFO inventory without objection, the Commissioner has generally not sought to terminate the method when the deficiency is discovered. By extension, in circumstances where the Commissioner has, on audit, required a taxpayer to change from its current inventory method to LIFO or to a method that approximates LIFO, it would seem inappropriate for the Commissioner later to assert that the change to the LIFO procedure was improper on the basis of a failure to file Form 970 or other appropriate statement.

[2] Conformity Requirement

A second condition is that LIFO may be used for tax purposes only if it is used for financial reporting purposes. This is known as the financial conformity requirement. It differs from the book conformity requirement of Section 446(a) by focusing on the taxpayer's financial statements rather than its internal books and records.[51]

Section 472(c) provides that LIFO may be used for tax purposes only if it is also used to ascertain

> the income, profit, or loss of the first taxable year for which the method described in subsection (b) [the LIFO method] is to be used, for the purpose of a report or statement covering such taxable year—(1) to shareholders, partners, or other proprietors, or to beneficiaries, or (2) for credit purposes.[52]

This Code provision requires only that the income, profit, or loss reported to equity owners and creditors be based on the same inventory method as that used for tax purposes. It does not prohibit the submission of explanatory or supplementary data. Nevertheless, prudent taxpayers for many years were reluctant to provide gratuitously any such explanatory or supplementary data through either written statements or oral presentations.

---

[50] See discussion infra ¶ 7.05. In particular see authorities cited infra note 208.

[51] See ¶ 2.02[1] for discussion of the book conformity requirement of Section 446(a).

[52] Section 472(e)(2) grants the Commissioner the discretion to require a change of inventory methods if the financial conformity requirement is violated in any subsequent year.

This reluctance was justified, since violation of the conformity requirement gives the Commissioner the opportunity to terminate the taxpayer's use of LIFO and, thereby, to cause the difference between the LIFO value and FIFO value of the inventory (the so-called LIFO reserve) to be included in income.[53] In 1981, the regulations were amended to clarify the LIFO conformity rules and to expand a taxpayer's ability to provide meaningful financial information to creditors, shareholders, and others without risk. Indeed, under the present regulations, LIFO conformity violations are more a matter of how information is provided than of what information is provided.[54]

[a] Rationale for Requirement

When originally enacted in 1938, the LIFO method was available only to a limited group of taxpayers and contained no requirement of financial statement conformity. However, when the method was extended to all taxpayers in 1939, the conformity requirement was imposed.

One of the great mysteries among scholars interested in LIFO is the reason for the conformity requirement. A review of the pertinent legislative history fails to shed any specific light. The committee reports merely set forth the terms of the requirement itself.[55] One LIFO scholar familiar with the legislative history of LIFO and influential in getting LIFO established suggested that the requirement was intended both to deter taxpayers from using LIFO for tax purposes and also to impose an obligation on the accounting profession to conclude that the method was sound for financial accounting purposes.[56]

---

[53] IRC § 472(e).

[54] See discussion infra ¶ 7.03[2][b].

[55] S. Rep. No. 648, 76th Cong., 1st Sess. 6 (1939):

If a taxpayer elects to use the [LIFO] method, he must specify the goods with respect to which the method is to be used. The taxpayer must show that he, for the period the method is to be used for tax purposes, has used no other method for certain business purposes, such as income statements, applications for bank loans, and reports to shareholders.

[56] See Barker, "Practical Aspects of Inventory Problems Under Current Conditions: Lifo, Involuntary Liquidation," 10 NYU Inst. on Fed. Tax'n 511, 512–513 (1952), where the author stated:

Considerable discussion has taken place as to the reason for the outside report requirement in the statute. Certainly, it is the first and only time the revenue laws have been used specifically to control private accounting. Perhaps the best answer is that the outside report requirement was put into the law as a deterrent to the use of the Lifo method of inventory valuation. An influential group in the Treasury believed that Lifo was not an inherently sound accounting method except in certain fungible goods industries like the non-ferrous metal and tanning industries. It was apparently their belief, proved fallacious by subsequent

Considering the accounting climate in the late 1930s,[57] imposition of the conformity requirement may have been reasonable. By imposing a conformity requirement when the LIFO option was extended to all taxpayers, Congress was only requiring that taxpayers (and, in many cases, their independent accountants) take the position that LIFO was an acceptable method of financial inventory accounting.[58] Even before 1939, the Code section governing all inventories had required that inventories be taken on a basis conforming as nearly as possible to the best accounting practice and as most clearly reflecting income.[59] Therefore, it does not seem unreasonable in the circumstances for Congress to have imposed a LIFO conformity requirement.

[b] Application of Requirement

The scope of the LIFO conformity requirement has been a continuing problem for taxpayers. For many years, the IRS provided guidelines through revenue rulings. These rulings were often inadequate, as they addressed particular facts only and did not provide sufficiently broad guidance to most taxpayers. Nevertheless, the issues in most rulings were resolved in accordance with certain general principles that demonstrated the IRS's expansive interpretation of the requirement. For example, although the requirement applies literally only with respect to financial statements furnished to creditors or owners of the taxpayer, the IRS has interpreted the requirement as applying to virtually every recipient of a taxpayer's financial statements.[60] Similarly, although the requirement applies literally to reports covering taxable years, the requirement is deemed applicable to any statement covering a period of one year, even though that period may not be the taxable year, as long as the one-year period begins and ends in a taxable year for which the taxpayer used the LIFO method for tax purposes.[61] The requirement also

---

events, that very few corporate taxpayers would be willing to supply their stockholders and the public with reports in which the inventories were valued on a Lifo basis.

[57] See discussion supra ¶ 7.02[2]. See also J. Butters, Effects of Taxation-Inventory Accounting and Policies 64-66 (Riverside Press 1949).

[58] See Rev. Rul. 74-586, 1974-2 CB 156, declared obsolete by Rev. Rul. 88-21, 1988-1 CB 245, which states, "The legislative history indicates that the purpose of this conformity requirement was to give assurance that with respect to a particular taxpayer the LIFO method clearly reflects income." Id. at 157.

[59] See Section 471 and its predecessors. See also ¶ 6.03 regarding the history of these inventory requirements.

[60] See Rev. Proc. 75-10, 1975-1 CB 651, declared obsolete by Rev. Proc. 88-19, 1988-1 CB 695, regarding reports to security analysts; Priv. Ltr. Rul. 7925128 (Mar. 26, 1979), where the IRS indicated that disclosure of prohibited information, which is, or may in any way become, available to the general public, violates the conformity requirement.

[61] Treas. Reg. § 1.472-2(e)(2). See ¶ 10.02 for discussion of taxable years.

applies to retroactive restatements of prior-year financial statements on a non-LIFO basis.[62]

In 1981, the Treasury made comprehensive revisions to the regulations governing the conformity requirement. These revisions provide substantial guidance as to instances in which the disclosure of non-LIFO information will not violate the LIFO conformity requirement.[63]

[i] Supplementary or explanatory information. The taxpayer does not violate the LIFO conformity requirement where non-LIFO data is used in providing information that supplements or explains the taxpayer's primary presentation of income, which must be on a LIFO basis.[64] The regulations point out that where non-LIFO information accompanies the taxpayer's primary financial income statement, it must not be reported on the face of the primary income statement for the information to be deemed supplementary or explanatory within the scope of the exception. However, the non-LIFO information may be presented in notes to the income statement (which may be on the same page as the income statement) if all notes are presented together and accompany the income statement in a single report.

Where the non-LIFO information does not accompany the primary financial income statement (e.g., where the information is presented in a news release, letter to shareholders, oral statement at a press conference, shareholders' meeting, or section of an annual report independent of the income statement), the information will be considered supplementary to or explanatory of the primary presentation only if (1) that information is clearly identified as a supplement to or explanation of the taxpayer's primary presentation of income as reported on the face of the income statement and (2) the specific item of information being explained or supplemented is included in the supplementary statement. For example, if the taxpayer wishes to report its income on a non-LIFO basis, it may do so without violating the LIFO conformity requirement only if it also reports the LIFO information as

---

[62] See Rev. Proc. 89-10, 1989-1 CB 796, where the IRS ruled that if a taxpayer is required by Opinion No. 20 (APB 20) of the Accounting Principles Board of the AICPA to restate prior-year financial statements because of a change from the LIFO method in the current year, the restatement of the prior-year financial statements will result in a violation of the LIFO conformity requirement. However, the IRS also stated that it would not disallow a taxpayer's use of LIFO in the prior year if the prior-year's restatement is solely because of the application of APB 20.

[63] As a result of these comprehensive regulations, the IRS issued Rev. Rul. 88-21, 1988-1 CB 245, which declared obsolete a number of previously issued revenue rulings; and Rev. Proc. 88-19, 1988-1 CB 695, which declared obsolete a number of previously issued revenue procedures.

[64] Treas. Reg. § 1.472-2(e)(1)(i).

reported in the primary presentation and points out that the non-LIFO information is presented as a supplement to the LIFO information.[65]

Where the non-LIFO information is reported in an appendix or a supplement that is to accompany the income statement in a single report, the supplementary information must clearly be identified as such or as explanatory of the primary presentation as reported on the face of the income statement. The information will be considered sufficiently identified as a supplement to or explanation of the primary presentation if the information is:[66]

- Reported in a form that contains a general statement identifying all such supplementary or explanatory information
- Specifically identified as supplementary or explanatory by a statement preceding or following the non-LIFO information
- Disclosed in the context of making a comparison to corresponding information that is disclosed both on the face of the primary income statement and in the supplement or appendix
- Disclosed by describing the effect of the LIFO method on an item reported on the face of the income statement

The Treasury's primary objectives are for the taxpayer to provide information based on LIFO, to provide the non-LIFO information as a supplement, and to make it clear that the non-LIFO information supplements the LIFO information. The Treasury's position is apparently that a failure to provide the primary data or to make appropriate reference to it will result in a violation of the conformity requirement. The Treasury takes this so far as to provide an example in the regulations of how an officer of a corporation may respond to a question raised by a security analyst as to what the income of the corporation would have been if reported on a non-LIFO basis. The Treasury indicates the proper response is first to report the information on a LIFO basis and then to report what the result would have been if reported on a non-LIFO basis.[67] This example raises the possibility that a failure to make the initial statement could be considered a violation of the conformity requirement.

[ii] **Reporting on non-LIFO basis on a balance sheet.** The taxpayer does not violate the LIFO conformity requirement where a non-LIFO method is used to value the taxpayer's inventory on its balance sheet.[68] However, the taxpayer must make certain that it does not disclose on the balance sheet what the income for the year would have been if such non-LIFO method had

---

[65] Treas. Reg. § 1.472-2(e)(3).

[66] Treas. Reg. § 1.472-2(e)(3)(iii).

[67] Treas. Reg. § 1.472-2(e)(3)(v).

[68] Treas. Reg. § 1.472-2(e)(1)(ii).

been used in computing income. Consequently, a balance sheet that discloses the net worth of the taxpayer on a non-LIFO basis may result in a violation of the conformity requirement. However, this disclosure may be made in a footnote or other supplement to or explanation of the balance sheet or even by a parenthetical disclosure on the face of the balance sheet.[69]

[iii] **Internal management reports.** The taxpayer does not violate the LIFO conformity requirement where a non-LIFO method is used to provide information in an internal management report.[70] The Treasury has not yet promulgated regulations providing details as to how this particular exception will be applied. However, it would seem appropriate for this exception to cover all internal reports that are used for management purposes and received by employees in their capacity as managers of the business (rather than as creditors or owners of the business), so long as such items are not presented to others who receive them (or may receive them) in their capacity as creditors or owners. If the reports may be received by such persons in their capacity as creditors or owners, the reports should be issued only if they satisfy the requirements for the presentation of supplementary or explanatory information.

[iv] **Reports covering less than entire taxable year.** The taxpayer does not violate the LIFO conformity requirement by using a non-LIFO method in a report or a statement covering a period of less than an entire taxable year.[71] However, if a taxpayer issues a series of such non-LIFO interim reports that in the aggregate, may be used or combined to ascertain non-LIFO income for the entire taxable period, the reports will violate the conformity requirement unless some other exception applies. Consequently, taxpayers should not issue interim reports that can be combined in that way.[72]

[v] **Lower of LIFO cost or market.** The taxpayer does not violate the LIFO conformity requirement where inventories are reported for financial reporting purposes on the basis of the lower of LIFO cost or market. However, a taxpayer may not value inventories for financial reporting purposes on the basis of market in lieu of cost.[73]

Although application of this exception to the conformity requirement resolves most issues, some unresolved issues remain. For example, if a taxpayer's application of the lower of LIFO cost or market concept for financial reporting purposes is highly unusual or inconsistent with genrally

---

[69] Treas. Reg. § 1.472-2(e)(4).

[70] Treas. Reg. § 1.472-2(e)(1)(iii).

[71] Treas. Reg. § 1.472-2(e)(1)(iv).

[72] Treas. Reg. § 1.472-2(e)(6).

[73] Treas. Reg. § 1.472-2(e)(1)(v).

accepted accounting principles (GAAP), legitimate questions may be raised as to whether the taxpayer is entitled to the benefits of this particular exception to the LIFO conformity requirement. Nevertheless, in light of the history of this provision, the IRS should not exercise its discretion to seek a termination of LIFO because of an erroneous application of this exception, except in the most egregious cases.

[vi] **Use of different costing procedures.** The taxpayer does not violate the LIFO conformity requirement when it uses the LIFO method for financial reporting purposes but determines the cost of its LIFO inventories for those purposes on a different basis from that used for tax reporting purposes.[74] Accordingly, differences in LIFO values for tax and financial reporting purposes will be deemed not to result in a violation of the LIFO conformity requirement where the difference is attributable to differences in the following:[75]

- Inventoriable costs
- Pools[76]
- Computational procedures (such as the use of double extension, index, or link-chain)
- Price indexes
- Methods of valuing increments
- Classifications of items
- Accounting periods used

---

[74] Treas. Reg. § 1.472-2(e)(1)(vi).

[75] Treas. Reg. § 1.472-2(e)(8). See Priv. Ltr. Rul. 8709019 (Nov. 26, 1986), where the IRS National Office (the National Office) concluded that no violation of the LIFO conformity requirement occurs if the taxpayer uses a single pool, link-chain LIFO method (with increments valued on the basis of latest acquisition costs) for financial reporting purposes, but uses a multiple pool, double extension LIFO system (with increments valued on the basis of earliest acquisition costs) for tax reporting purposes.

[76] In Priv. Ltr. Rul. 9019018 (Feb. 9, 1990), the IRS, citing Treas. Reg. § 1.472-2(e)(8), confirmed that use of a single pool for tax-reporting purposes would not violate the LIFO conformity requirement if the taxpayer were to change to the use of multiple pools, as outlined in Treas. Reg. § 1.472-8(b)(3), for financial reporting purposes. As an aside, the taxpayer represented that the method it would use for financial-reporting purposes would conform to the regulation's rules for multiple pooling. The IRS stated that this representation was subject to review on audit by the District Director. Although this statement suggests that the taxpayer's representation regarding its proposed multiple pooling for financial-reporting purposes would be reviewed closely, any appropriate pooling for financial reporting purposes should be acceptable without regard to whether the financial reporting meets tax-reporting rules. Otherwise, the impression might be created that tax-reporting rules must be followed for financial reporting purposes in order to prevent a violation of the LIFO conformity requirement.

- Cost estimates
- Time when sales and purchases occur
- Allocation procedures when businesses are combined

In addition, differences between financial and tax LIFO inventories that arise from the adoption of LIFO at different times for financial and tax purposes or are attributable to different financial and tax accounting rules governing business acquisitions or other transactions do not result in a violation of the conformity requirement.[77] On the other hand, the application of some financial accounting rules may give rise to a violation of the conformity requirement. For example, in Revenue Procedure 89-10,[78] the IRS addressed APB 20, which was issued in July 1971. That opinion states that when a company changes from the LIFO inventory method to another inventory method, the financial statements of all prior periods, which are included with the company's present financial statements for the current year, must be restated under the new inventory method. In other words, if a company were presenting financial statements for each of two years and discontinued its use of LIFO in the second year, the company would have to restate its financial statements for the first year on the non-LIFO method. Assuming the company also terminated its use of LIFO for tax purposes in the second year, the question arises as to whether the retroactive restatement of the first year's financial statements violates the LIFO conformity requirement for that first year, thereby giving the IRS the opportunity to terminate the taxpayer's use of LIFO in that year. The IRS has now concluded that the retroactive restatement does amount to a violation of the conformity requirement, but the IRS also stated that it would exercise its discretion not to terminate a taxpayer's LIFO election (or require a change from the taxpayer's use of LIFO) in that prior year solely because of the application of APB 20. This revenue procedure puts taxpayers on notice that in other circumstances, any such prior year's restatement would give rise to the possibility of a termination of the taxpayer's use of LIFO.

In effect, these regulations make it clear that the concept of sequential layering,[79] which is inherent in the LIFO method, is the key to satisfying the LIFO conformity requirement. The regulations also make it clear that taxpayers who must use the new costing procedures required under the Tax Reform Act of 1986 (the 1986 Act),[80] but who will not use these procedures for financial reporting purposes, will not violate the LIFO conformity requirement.

---

[77] Treas. Reg. §§ 1.472-2(e)(1)(vii), 1.472-2(e)(1)(viii).

[78] Rev. Proc. 89-10, 1989-1 CB 796.

[79] See discussion supra ¶ 7.02 and infra ¶ 7.04 regarding the sequential-layering concept.

[80] See discussion at ¶¶ 6.06[1][c], 6.06[2][c][ii].

Although this protection against a violation of the LIFO conformity requirement is comforting, taxpayers should not assume that differences between the two methods will be ignored by the IRS for all purposes. For example, if a taxpayer uses a single natural-business-unit pool for tax reporting purposes but multiple natural-business-unit pools for financial reporting purposes, the difference in reporting may cause the IRS to question the appropriateness of the number of pools used by the taxpayer for tax purposes.[81] Consequently, whenever the appropriateness of a LIFO method or sub-method is subject to review on audit, the use of a different LIFO method or sub-method for financial-reporting purposes may be influential.

[vii] **Reconciliations.** The regulations provide that a taxpayer may be required to reconcile differences between the value of inventories computed for credit or financial purposes and the value computed for tax purposes in order to demonstrate that the taxpayer has satisfied the conformity requirement.[82] This requirement is somewhat of a non sequitur in that the results produced under different LIFO methodologies are not necessarily reconcilable. They are merely the results of applying different methodologies to the same basic data and may be reconciled only by showing that the different LIFO results come from the same basic data. Over time, any rigid adherence to this requirement of reconciliation could become quite burdensome.

[viii] **Controlled groups.** In the past, some taxpayers avoided the full impact of the LIFO conformity requirement by placing their LIFO inventories in a subsidiary that filed consolidated financial statements with its parent. The practice was for the subsidiary to report to its shareholder (i.e., its parent corporation) on a LIFO basis. The parent corporation would then take the information provided by the subsidiary, convert it to a non-LIFO basis, include the non-LIFO data in the consolidated financial statements, and submit those statements to its shareholders and creditors.

This practice was initially accepted by the IRS, but the IRS later reversed itself.[83] However, in *Insilco Corp.*,[84] the Tax Court held that this approach did not violate the LIFO conformity requirement.

Congress thereafter enacted Section 472(g) to overturn the decision in

---

[81] See discussion of pooling infra ¶¶ 7.04[2][a], 7.04[3][a].

[82] Treas. Reg. § 1.472-2(e)(9).

[83] See Rev. Rul. 69-17, 1969-1 CB 143, revoked by Rev. Rul. 70-457, 1970-2 CB 109, which, in turn, was declared obsolete by Rev. Rul. 87-49, 1987-1 CB 156, in which the IRS ruled that for tax years beginning before July 19, 1984, the IRS would not litigate the issue of whether the consolidated financial statements of an affiliated group violate the LIFO conformity requirement when they incorporate a conversion of a subsidiary's LIFO inventory method to a different method.

[84] Insilco Corp., 73 TC 589 (1980), nonacq. 1982-1 CB 1, nonacq. withdrawn 1987-2 CB 1, aff'd in unpublished decision, 659 F2d 1059 (2d Cir. 1981).

Insilco Corp. Section 472(g) makes the LIFO conformity rule applicable to a group of financially related corporations by treating all members of the group as if they were one taxpayer. The term "group of financially related corporations" includes (1) any affiliated group within the definition of Section 1504 (except that "50 percent" is substituted for "80 percent" for purposes of determining the requisite ownership) and (2) any other group of corporations that consolidates or combines the financial information of its members for purposes of presenting financial statements. Although all members of a group are treated as if they were one taxpayer, this does not mean that any member of the group using a non-LIFO method must use a LIFO method when its inventories are included in a consolidated financial statement.[85]

This new rule provides an especially difficult problem for subsidiaries whose parent corporations operate in countries that do not permit the use of LIFO for financial-reporting purposes. However, it seems clear that Congress did not intend for this to be a problem. For example, prior to the enactment of Section 472(g), the IRS had ruled in Revenue Ruling 78-246 that the conversion of a subsidiary's LIFO data by a foreign parent whose operating assets in foreign countries were substantial (30 percent or more of the group's operating assets) would not violate the conformity requirement.[86] In the legislative history to Section 472(g), Congress indicated its intent that Revenue Ruling 78-246 continue in effect.[87] Thereafter, in Revenue Ruling 89-41,[88] the IRS ruled that Revenue Ruling 78-246 is still a valid exception to the LIFO conformity requirement for certain foreign parent-subsidiary groups of corporations and to the combined financial statements of certain foreign controlled brother-sister groups of corporations, but the ruling does not apply to U.S.-owned groups of corporations.

[ix] **Financial forecasts and projections.** In Revenue Ruling 88-84,[89] the IRS considered whether the issuance of financial forecasts and projections

---

[85] See Rev. Rul. 88-69, 1988-2 CB 124, where the IRS concluded that Section 472(g) does not require a taxpayer that uses a LIFO inventory method for tax purposes to report the inventories of its subsidiary in consolidated financial statements under the LIFO method if the subsidiary uses a non-LIFO inventory method for federal income tax purposes. The IRS explained that the conformity requirement is applicable to a subsidiary under Section 472(g) only to the extent that such requirement would apply to a separate trade or business of a single taxpayer. In other words, just because a single taxpayer uses the LIFO method for one trade or business, it is not required to use the LIFO method for the inventory of any other trade or business, nor is the taxpayer required to include the non-LIFO inventories of any other trade or business in consolidated financial statements on a LIFO basis in order to satisfy the LIFO conformity requirement.

[86] Rev. Rul. 78-246, 1978-1 CB 146.

[87] Conf. Rep. H.R. No. 861, 98th Cong., 2d Sess. 897 (1984).

[88] Rev. Rul. 89-41, 1989-1 CB 681.

[89] Rev. Rul. 88-84, 1988-2 CB 124.

to stockholders and creditors using a non-LIFO inventory method would violate the LIFO conformity requirement. The IRS concluded that the issuance of such forecasts would not violate the LIFO conformity requirement. The IRS explained that the LIFO conformity requirement is not applicable to speculative reports and projections based on future expectations. The IRS indicated that the conformity requirement only applies to ascertaining income, a profit, or a loss for past operations. This conclusion seems eminently reasonable, but taxpayers should be cautious not to extend their projections and forecasts to include restatements of prior historical data in a manner in which readers are provided with historical data on a non-LIFO basis.

[3] Cost Requirement

A third condition for the use of LIFO is that LIFO inventories must be stated at cost.[90] To the extent that market write-downs of these inventories had been taken in prior years, the amount of those write-downs must be restored to inventories and income as a condition of the adoption and use of LIFO.

To comply with the cost-only rule, the cost of the opening LIFO inventory is determined under the inventory method employed by the taxpayer under regulations applicable to the prior year, and all items in inventory are treated as having been acquired at the same time and at the same unit cost.[91] Thus, the opening LIFO cost of similar items is computed by dividing the aggregate cost of those items by the number of units then on hand.

Questions sometimes arise as to whether inadequacies in the taxpayer's costing method (e.g., a failure to conform to the full absorption costing regulations prior to the 1986 Act or to the uniform capitalization rules enacted as part of the 1986 Act, or a failure to use a traditional FIFO method) must themselves be corrected as part of the change to LIFO. (See Chapter 6 for discussion of applicable inventory costing rules.) Although the IRS sometimes suggests that this correction is necessary,[92] costing and similar issues exist independent of the use of LIFO and, for that reason, should not be treated as part of the adjustment to cost that is required on the adoption

---

[90] Section 472(b)(2) provides that in inventorying the goods for which LIFO is adopted, the taxpayer shall inventory them at cost. Treas. Reg. § 1.472-2(b) adds, "The [LIFO] inventory shall be taken at cost regardless of market value." See ¶ 6.06 for discussion of costs that must be treated as inventoriable costs.

[91] Treas. Reg. § 1.472-2(c).

[92] See Priv. Ltr. Rul. 8043023 (July 25, 1980), where the IRS indicated that a failure to comply with the full absorption rules could be equated with a failure to value LIFO inventories at cost so that the taxpayer's use of LIFO could be terminated.

of LIFO. Of course, any egregious failure in the taxpayer's costing system may, if not corrected, increase the risk of a LIFO termination being proposed on audit.

[a] Rationale for Requirement

The basis for the cost requirement is not articulated in its legislative history.[93] Nevertheless, the requirement is apparently based on the presumed inconsistency between traditional LIFO theory and the concept of lower of cost or market. In the early decades of this century, which were the developing days of the LIFO and so-called normal stock methods of inventory costing, many economists and accountants viewed economic trends in terms of business cycles. Among the advantages claimed for LIFO at the time were (1) a removal from income of unrealized gains and losses resulting from the mere holding of inventory as prices changed over the course of the business cycle; (2) the consequent stabilizing of income over the business cycle; and (3) the matching of current costs against current revenues. These asserted advantages would not be obtained if a lower-of-LIFO-cost-or-market method of inventory costing were permitted, because goods would be valued on LIFO during some periods and on FIFO during others. When prices were rising, the inventory would be valued on the basis of older costs, and the cost of goods sold would reflect current costs. When prices were falling, the ending inventory would reflect current costs, and the cost of goods sold would represent a combination of current costs and older costs (to the extent these older costs were written down to current market). Thus, LIFO would be used when prices rose, and FIFO would be approximated when prices fell. This procedure has sometimes been referred to as highest-in, first-out. Further, the full benefit of matching current costs against current revenues would be lost under a lower-of-LIFO-cost-or-market approach. Unrealized inventory losses would be included in the computation of income whenever replacement costs fell below LIFO costs, while inventory gains would be excluded.

[b] Requirement's Impact on Timing of Adoption of LIFO

When inflation continues over a period of years, the likelihood lessens that replacement or reproduction costs (i.e., market values) will fall below

---

[93] H. Rep. 2330, 75th Cong., 3d Sess. 35 (1938), provided only the following: "In the case of the application of the above rules all inventories of such materials shall be taken at cost, including the inventory as of the close of the preceding taxable year."

LIFO costs for any significant portion of the LIFO inventory.[94] However, this economic reality does not mean that the timing of the adoption of LIFO is insignificant. Price trends in the taxpayer's particular industry must be reviewed and analyzed carefully. To the extent that prices are expected to decline, the full tax benefit of LIFO may be realized only by delaying its adoption until the anticipated decline has been realized and prices are expected to increase. In this way, the taxpayer is able to match the higher FIFO costs against sales (as inventory costs decline) and then match the higher LIFO costs against sales (as inventory costs increase).

[c] Restored and Prohibited Write-Downs

A continuing issue is that of determining which inventory adjustments are market write-downs of the type that must be restored when LIFO is adopted and that are thereafter not permitted. The issue stems from an apparent conflict in the regulations.

On the one hand, the general inventory regulations provide that so-called abnormal goods, which are unsalable at normal prices, may be written down to market (i.e., for this purpose, selling price less the direct cost of disposition) without regard to whether the taxpayer values inventories at cost or the lower of cost or market.[95] Since LIFO is one type of cost method, it would appear that write-downs or cost adjustments may be made under this regulatory provision whenever goods in the LIFO inventory are not salable at normal prices owing to any of the factors mentioned in the regulations. On the other hand, the LIFO regulations specifically provide that "the inventory shall be taken at cost regardless of market value," and that "restoration shall be made with respect to any write-down to market values resulting from the pricing of former inventories."[96] Consequently, a question arises as to whether the write-downs referred to in the LIFO regulations are any write-

---

[94] See ¶ 6.09 for discussion of the lower-of-cost-or-market method of inventory costing.

[95] Treas. Reg. 1.471-2(c) provides:

The bases of valuation most commonly used by business concerns and which meet the requirements of section 471 are (1) cost and (2) cost or market, whichever is lower. . . . Any goods in an inventory which are unsalable at normal prices or unusable in a normal way because of damage, imperfections, shop wear, changes of styles, odd or broken lots, or other similar causes, including secondhand goods taken in exchange, should be valued at bona fide selling prices less direct cost of disposition, whether subparagraph (1) or (2) of this paragraph is used. . . .

See discussion at ¶ 6.09[2].

[96] Treas. Reg. §§ 1.472-2(b), 1.472-2(c).

downs to market or only those write-downs to market that reflect reductions in the prices of normal goods.[97]

The IRS has ruled that write-downs of abnormal goods under Treasury Regulation § 1.471-2(c) are not permitted under LIFO,[98] and that this requirement may not be avoided by excluding abnormal goods from the LIFO election.[99] However, the issue has not yet been litigated. A taxpayer who desires to challenge the IRS interpretation without risk to its use of LIFO should restore all write-downs (or report all LIFO inventories at cost) and then file a claim for refund of the tax attributable to that portion of the restoration (or attributable to the taking of deductions) relating to prior write-downs for abnormal goods. Considering the comparative ease with which this issue could be litigated and the amounts involved, it is surprising that no such litigation has occurred.

[d] How Restoration Is Made

Prior market write-downs must be restored to income ratably over a three-year period beginning with the year for which LIFO is adopted.[100] For taxable years that began before December 31, 1981, the restoration had to be made all at once by filing an amended return that included the full amount of the restoration in the year preceding the year for which LIFO was first adopted.[101] This restoration requirement dissuaded many taxpayers from adopting LIFO because of their financial inability or their unwillingness to pay tax on write-downs previously taken on the inventory for which LIFO would be adopted. The inclusion of the restoration over a period of three years has apparently been sufficient to alleviate the deterrent effect of the restoration rule.

[4] Books and Records

The LIFO method is based on the concept that the last goods acquired are the first goods sold. Accordingly, the earliest goods acquired are treated as the goods remaining in inventory. As a consequence, LIFO computations are often based on data accumulated at the beginning of the year of the adoption of LIFO. It is essential that the taxpayer retain all books, records, work sheets and other material supporting its LIFO computations throughout the

---

[97] Write-downs in the cost of normal goods are permitted under Treas. Reg. ¶ 1.471-4(c). See discussion at ¶ 6.09[3].

[98] See ¶ 6.09[2] for discussion of market write-downs for abnormal goods.

[99] Rev. Rul. 76-282, 1976-2 CB 137. See ¶ 6.09[2] regarding write-downs for abnormal goods.

[100] IRC § 472(d).

[101] See Section 472(d) as then in effect; Rev. Proc. 76-6, 1976-1 CB 545.

period of its adoption and use of LIFO.[102] A taxpayer who fails to maintain this information runs the risk that the IRS may on audit seek to disallow the use of the LIFO method on the basis of the taxpayer's inability to demonstrate the basis for its LIFO computations.[103]

The sophistication of the accounting system needed to support the use of LIFO must be balanced against the taxpayer's right to adopt LIFO. Although the precise degree of accounting and record-keeping sophistication necessary to support the use of the LIFO method has not yet been litigated, the use of LIFO may not be denied to taxpayers who have the data from which appropriate LIFO computations may be made, although that data is not in a readily retrievable form or is not computed on the basis of the most sophisticated accounting means possible. On technical advice, the National Office has indicated that the adequacy of books and records is determined on the basis of the taxpayer's elected LIFO methods and not on the basis of the taxpayer's ability to make computations in accordance with the LIFO methods to which an examining agent might seek to require the taxpayer to change.[104]

In general, the IRS on audit has accepted data and accounting systems that are approved for financial-reporting purposes. In other words, the IRS has traditionally been reluctant to seek a termination of the taxpayer's use of LIFO on the basis of inadequate books and records. However, taxpayers should not assume that it is unnecessary to maintain some minimal amount of record-keeping data. It is often advisable to make certain that the accounting and cost systems can support LIFO computations or that these systems are changed on the adoption of LIFO to be able to produce adequate data.

Inadequacies in books, records, and other supporting data are more serious in connection with the use of LIFO than with the use of FIFO. For instance, under the FIFO method, any errors in computational procedures flow through to cost of goods sold very quickly. However, any errors or other inadequacies inherent in a LIFO system may be perpetuated, and possibly compounded, year after year. This perpetuation of error puts a greater

---

[102] Treas. Reg. § 1.472-2(h) requires the taxpayer to maintain such records as will enable the IRS readily to verify its LIFO computations and its compliance with all requirements for use of LIFO.

[103] See Rev. Proc. 79-23, 1979-1 CB 564. See also discussion infra ¶ 7.05; Tech. Adv. Mem. 8744003 (June 30, 1987), where the parent corporation's use of indexes computed by a subsidiary raised the issue of whether the parent had maintained adequate books and records.

[104] See Tech. Adv. Mem. 8851001 (July 28, 1988), where the National Office rejected an agent's contention that a taxpayer's books and records were inadequate because the taxpayer was unable to compute the value of its LIFO inventory in a manner that the agent considered appropriate, the agent having already acknowledged that the taxpayer's books and records did support the taxpayer's own LIFO computations.

burden on taxpayers in connection with the use of the LIFO method. For example, if a FIFO taxpayer computes its inventory costs on the basis of mere estimates or other inadequate data, any difference between the estimated costs and the correct costs will flow through to cost of goods sold. However, a corresponding adjustment will take place in the succeeding taxable period. This immediate offset in adjustment does not occur in connection with the use of LIFO. Similarly, as FIFO taxpayers improve their cost systems, the benefits of those improvements are almost immediate. The benefits may never fully be realized by LIFO taxpayers, whose inventories contain LIFO layers that predate the improvements in the accounting and cost systems.

[5] Statutory Periods of Limitation

An important, but as yet unresolved, issue is the impact of statutory periods of limitation on the adoption and use of LIFO. For example, if LIFO were adopted in a year that is now closed and if that adoption were improper for any of the reasons mentioned previously,[105] would the IRS remain authorized year after year to terminate the taxpayer's use of LIFO, or would the running of the statutory period applicable to the year of adoption preclude that termination? In practice, the IRS generally has not sought terminations as a result of deficiencies or failures in a closed year.[106] However, these deficiencies ought to be correctable by adjustments of the taxpayer's inventory in an open year. Accordingly, it would be reasonable for the taxpayer to be protected from a termination of its use of LIFO on the basis of an event or a failure in a closed year but for the IRS nevertheless to be able to make all appropriate adjustments in an open year.

¶ 7.04 LIFO SYSTEMS

The premise of the LIFO method is that the most recently incurred costs should be the first costs charged against sales and that ending inventory should be valued on the basis of earliest costs incurred. The computations made under any LIFO systems must be designed to carry out this objective.

Accordingly, a sequential layering approach is used, under which the portion of a company's investment in closing inventory that coincides with its investment in beginning inventory is assigned the same cost as the beginning inventory. To the extent ending inventory exceeds beginning

---

[105] See supra ¶¶ 7.03[1]–7.03[4].

[106] On the other hand, it is not unusual for examining agents to propose LIFO terminations without regard to when the method was first adopted.

inventory, that increase is valued on the basis of costs incurred during the year of the increase. The increase or increment is generally referred to as a new layer of inventory. To the extent ending inventory is less than beginning inventory, that decrease or decrement is reflected by reductions in the most recently added layer of inventory, then in successively lower layers, and finally in the base inventory (i.e., the inventory as of the beginning of the year for which LIFO was first adopted).

The LIFO method has the effect of allocating price level fluctuations to cost of goods sold rather than inventory.

> EXAMPLE: Assume a taxpayer's beginning inventory is valued at $100 but will cost $160 to replace. If the taxpayer sells its entire beginning inventory during the year for $200 but also purchases or produces an equal amount of inventory to maintain its level of operations, it will report a gross profit of $40 under the LIFO method ($200 selling price − $160 of most recent cost). The $60 of inflation in replacement costs ($160 of replacement cost − $100 original cost) will be charged against the $200 of sales rather than being allocated to inventory on hand at the end of the year. Under FIFO, $100 of gross profit would be reported ($200 selling price − $100 of earliest cost), and the $60 of inflation in costs would be reflected in the ending inventory.

[1] Essentials

Although there are several systems for computing the value of a LIFO inventory, each system essentially involves only three determinations: (1) the LIFO inventory must be segmented into groups or "pools" of similar items; (2) the system must determine whether there has been a quantitative change in the inventory of each pool during the particular accounting period; and (3) the system must determine the manner in which increments to (or increases in the quantity of) each pool are to be valued. The effectiveness of any LIFO system in deferring the recognition of inflationary inventory profit for the longest possible time depends on how these subsidiary determinations are made.

There are two basic LIFO computational systems. One is based on specific items or goods. The other, known as dollar-value LIFO, is based on the dollars invested in inventory. Both systems may take any of several forms, but each is essentially designed to make the three determinations previously identified.

[2] Specific Goods LIFO

The specific goods method is the simplest and oldest of LIFO systems. Under this method, items are grouped into pools based on their similarity. Quantitative changes within each pool are then measured in terms of an appropriate unit, such as pounds, feet, pieces, and gallons. Any increments are valued on the basis of costs incurred during the year of the increment, with such "current costs" determined under any of several methods.

Under a specific goods LIFO system, each specific goods pool is treated as if it were a separate inventory. As a consequence, the deferred inventory profit, or LIFO reserve, in a pool that is experiencing reductions in quantity (or liquidations) is not transferable to another pool, which is experiencing increases in quantity. Accordingly, a change in style, demand, and supply, or in any other factor that may alter the mix of items in an overall LIFO inventory, may cause the liquidation of a particular pool and thus the recognition of all or a portion of the deferred inventory profit in that pool.

This aspect of a specific goods LIFO system may be illustrated by the following example in which a taxpayer shifts its product mix from one item (*A*) to two items (*A* and *B*).

> EXAMPLE: Assume that the taxpayer began operations in 1940 with four pounds of item *A* that cost $0.10 per pound. Its total inventory was thus valued at $0.40. If normal operations had required both the purchase and consumption of four pounds of item *A* each year, the LIFO value of the inventory would have remained at $0.40, even though the cost of item *A* may have increased to $0.50 per pound in subsequent years. Assume further that because of technological advances, an equal quantity of item *B* may now be used in lieu of item *A* but that *A* and *B* are not properly includable in the same pool. The taxpayer decides to switch its inventory investment from *A* to *B* because the current cost of *B* is $0.40 per pound, i.e., $0.10 per pound less than *A*. If the taxpayer begins this switch by consuming four pounds of *A* but acquiring two pounds of *A* and two pounds of *B*, the following results will occur under a specific-goods, multiple-pool LIFO system.

> **LIFO Reserve At Beginning Of Year**
>
> | | |
> |---|---:|
> | LIFO value of beginning inventory (4 pounds at $0.10) | $0.40 |
> | Current replacement cost (4 pounds at $0.50) | 2.00 |
> | LIFO reserve | $1.60 |

> **Inventory At Beginning Of Year**
>
> | Pools | Pounds | Cost | Total |
> |---|:---:|:---:|:---:|
> | *A* | 4 | $0.10 | $0.40 |
> | *B* | — | — | — |
> | Total LIFO inventory | | | $0.40 |

Purchases

Pools	Pounds	Cost	Total
A	2	$0.50	$1.00
B	2	0.40	0.80
			$1.80

Cost Of Goods Sold

2 pounds of A at $0.50	$1.00
2 pounds of A at $0.10	0.20
	$1.20

Inventory At End Of Year

Pools	Pounds	Cost	Total
A	2	$0.10	$0.20
B	2	0.40	0.80
Total LIFO inventory			$1.00

LIFO Reserve At End Of Year

LIFO value of ending inventory	$1.00

Current replacement cost:
2 pounds of A at $0.50 = $1.00
2 pounds of B at $0.40 = 0.80

	1.80
LIFO Reserve	$0.80

As the example shows, the taxpayer's cost of goods sold was $1.20. Had the taxpayer purchased only A, its cost of goods sold would have been $2.00.[107] By purchasing two units of B instead of an additional two units of A, the taxpayer's cost of goods sold decreased by $0.80, and, correspondingly, its taxable income increased by $0.80. This difference of $0.80 represents the appreciation that had occurred over the years in the price of A. It is recognized as taxable gain as the A pool is depleted, thereby increasing taxes and reducing cash flow. Thus, even though the current cost of B was less than A, the shift from A to B initially cost more than it saved.

In the specific goods LIFO system illustrated in the preceding example, the LIFO reserve in A was not preserved in inventory as B replaced A but, instead, was reported in current profits. Under a specific goods system, similar results may occur from liquidations due to long-range shifts (from one type of product or raw material to another) or short-term shifts (attributable

---

[107] Beginning inventory (4 pounds of A at $0.10/pound) $0.40
Plus: Purchases (4 pounds of A at $0.50/pound)   2.00
Goods available for sale   2.40
Less: Ending inventory (4 pounds of A at $0.10/pound)   0.40
Cost of goods sold $2.00

to temporary market conditions). As illustrated in the next section, the effect of such liquidations can be minimized if the shift that occurs is among items within the same pool. Thus, determination of the items within each pool is most important.

[a] Pooling

Under the LIFO method, the quantity of goods in beginning inventory is compared each year with the quantity of goods in ending inventory. If the ending inventory exceeds the beginning inventory, the excess is valued in terms of current costs and constitutes a new LIFO layer, and the deduction for cost of goods sold reflects only current costs. On the other hand, if the ending inventory is less than the beginning inventory, the cost of goods sold will consist of both current costs and those historical costs attributable to that portion of the beginning inventory liquidated during the year. Consequently, if a reduction in inventory takes place, the possibility exists for exorbitant profits to be recognized when low historical costs associated with the portion of the beginning inventory that was liquidated are matched against current revenues.

A question that necessarily arises is how the beginning and ending inventories are to be measured to determine whether there has been an increase or a decrease. For companies engaged in the acquisition (or production) and sale of more than one particular type of item, a determination must also be made of which items or groups of items are to be compared at the beginning and end of the year. In the administration of the LIFO method, the proper segregation of items of inventory into particular groups or pools is a matter of great significance. If items are sufficiently similar to be included within the same LIFO pool, the mix of items within the particular pool becomes less significant. Only the aggregate number of units within the pool may be of importance.

To illustrate, assume a taxpayer manufactures red, blue, and green widgets. Assume that all these widgets are used for the same purpose and that the cost of producing these widgets is essentially the same, regardless of color. The initial LIFO calculations will be based on increases and decreases in the total number of widgets. The number of red widgets versus green widgets versus blue widgets within the pool and the changes within the mix of these items are not significant. On the other hand, if the taxpayer produces two dissimilar products, decreases in the number of units of the first product may result in liquidations of the low-basis LIFO inventory, regardless of an offsetting increase in the other product.[108]

Under the specific goods method, similar items of inventory are included in the same pool, and each pool is treated as if it were a separate inventory.

---

[108] This result was illustrated by the example infra ¶ 7.04[2].

At the end of the taxable year, the physical quantity of items in each pool (measured in such terms as pieces, yards, pounds, and feet) is compared with the quantity of items in the beginning inventory of that pool to determine whether there has been an increase or decrease during the year.

Taxpayers are provided little guidance in ascertaining whether items are sufficiently similar to be included in the same pool. The regulations provide that in determining whether raw materials are similar, reference should be made to the character, quality, price, and type of raw material.[109] The use of the items or products, their processing operations, degree of interchangeability, the manner in which they are marketed, and the class of customers to whom they are marketed are all important.[110] Other factors to consider include trends in the taxpayer's industry, the impact of changes in style or technology on the essential nature of the taxpayer's business, and customary business and accounting classifications within the industry. The IRS should give taxpayers sufficient flexibility in determining the composition of their pools to realize the LIFO objective of matching current costs against current revenues.

[b] Quantitative Measure

A common unit of measurement must be used in computing whether there is an increase or a decrease in the inventory of a pool. In specific goods LIFO systems, it is typical for this measurement to be based on such units as pounds, gallons, feet, or pieces.

Although issues rarely arise regarding the chosen unit of measurement, the choice may sometimes be highly significant. For example, assume a taxpayer acquires two products for sale to customers. The products are used for essentially the same purpose, but their cost is different. One product consists of one pound of raw material A in a certain configuration while the other product consists of seven pounds of raw material A in a much different configuration. If the taxpayer measures quantitative changes in the inventory on the basis of pounds, a change in the mix of products within the pool could produce a much different result than would be produced if quantitative changes were based on number of pieces.

[c] Valuing Increments

Under specific goods LIFO, the taxpayer may select any of the following four approaches in valuing increments, as long as the approach selected is based on costs incurred only during the year of the increment:[111]

---

[109] Treas. Reg. § 1.472-1(d).

[110] See, e.g., Treas. Reg. § 1.472-1(e) addressing the cotton textile industry; Treas. Reg. § 1.472-1(f) addressing the pork-packing industry; Treas. Reg. § 1.472-8(b)(3) addressing the use of multiple pools by manufacturers in general.

[111] Treas. Reg. § 1.472-2(d)(1).

- Actual cost of goods most recently purchased or produced
- Actual cost of the earliest goods purchased or produced within the year of the increment
- Average cost of goods purchased or produced during the year
- Any other method that in the opinion of the Commissioner, clearly reflects income

Assuming inflation in costs occurs steadily throughout the year, the maximum LIFO benefit is achieved by selecting an approach that values increments on the basis of the earliest costs incurred during the year. That election also has the advantage of allowing the taxpayer to know early in the year exactly what costs will be used to value increments. This knowledge facilitates planning and computations. On the other hand, if the taxpayer's business is subject to abnormal costs at the beginning of the year or to erratic cost movements throughout the year, one of the other approaches may be more desirable.

Although there is no precise authorization in the regulations, because every separate LIFO pool is, in effect, treated as a separate inventory for purposes of computations, it would appear appropriate for a taxpayer to select different methods of valuing increments should the taxpayer so desire. However, once a method is selected, it constitutes a method of accounting and generally may be changed only with the prior approval of the Commissioner.[112] (For discussion of changes in accounting methods, see Chapter 8.)

[3] Dollar-Value LIFO

Initially, the Treasury and the IRS took a rather narrow view of acceptable LIFO procedures. Even after the Revenue Act of 1939 extended the use of the LIFO method to all taxpayers, regardless of business, the Treasury's position was that LIFO was not appropriate unless the taxpayer's inventory consisted of a few basic commodities that could easily be measured in terms of units, such as yards and pounds. In other words, only the specific goods method was recognized as an acceptable method of computing LIFO inventory.

However, in 1941, Herbert T. McAnly developed a practical means of applying the LIFO concept to any inventory, regardless of its character, by expressing all items in inventory in terms of dollars at a specific price level.[113] A number of merchants then developed the idea of combining this so-called

---

[112] Treas. Reg. § 1.472-2(d)(1)(ii).

[113] Address entitled "A Practical View of the Last-In, First-Out Principles of Inventory Valuations" presented in May 1941 to the Central States Accounting Conference held in Chicago and referred to in McAnly, "The Current Status of Lifo," 105 J. of Accountancy 55, 56 (May 1958).

dollar-value LIFO method with the retail inventory method of pricing retail merchandise inventories.[114] Because the Commissioner opposed the use of the resulting method for department stores, based on the theory that LIFO required the matching of similar goods in beginning and ending inventories, many taxpayers declined to adopt LIFO in its early days.[115] However, in 1947, in *Hutzler Brothers Co.*, the Tax Court rejected the Commissioner's position and upheld a department store's use of the dollar-value method.[116]

Thereafter, the Treasury regulations were amended to permit the use of the dollar-value method by retail stores, provided that suitable statistical procedures were used.[117] In 1948, the regulations were amended to permit the use of the dollar-value method by all taxpayers.[118]

Although IRS acceptance of the dollar-value method moved forward, IRS opposition continued to the concept of a broad pool of dissimilar items, i.e., the very type of pool made feasible by the dollar-value technique. Pooling had not been an issue in *Hutzler Brothers Co.*, and although the 1948 regulatory amendment authorized the use of dollar-value LIFO by retailers, it made no changes in applicable pooling provisions.

In 1954, the IRS began work on revised procedures for use of the dollar-value method. The resulting regulations were ultimately promulgated in 1961 and have remained virtually unchanged.[119]

Under the dollar-value method, the common denominator for measuring items within a pool is not units, such as pounds or yards, but dollars as of a particular date. Thus, a reduction in the number of inventory items within a pool will not reduce the LIFO value of the inventory as long as the total inventory stated in base-year dollars (i.e., the base cost of the inventory) is not reduced. The base cost of an item is generally what the item cost or would have cost at the beginning of the year for which LIFO was first adopted.[120]

The primary benefit of a dollar-value LIFO system is that, since all goods can be expressed in terms of dollars, all items in inventory may be

---

[114] The retail method is described at ¶ 6.10[4].

[115] Humer, Galliher, & Stewart, LIFO: Fundamentals, Pooling and Computations, Tax Mgmt. (BNA) No. 69-4, at A-35 (1986).

[116] Hutzler Bros. Co., 8 TC 14 (1947). The court stated that the Commissioner's position was "supported neither by logic nor by legislative intent." Id. at 28.

[117] TD 5605, 1948-1 CB 16. Also in 1948, the Tax Court held that the dollar-value method was a permissible method of determining LIFO inventories and specifically upheld the taxpayer's computations with respect to his warehouse inventory. Edgar A. Basse, 10 TC 328 (1948).

[118] TD 5756, 1949-2 CB 21.

[119] See Treas. Reg. § 1.472-8.

[120] For a discussion of base cost, see infra ¶ 7.04[3][b].

included in the same LIFO pool, regardless of the dissimilarity of the items. This principle may be illustrated as follows:[121]

EXAMPLE: Assume a taxpayer has an opening inventory of four pounds of item A with a LIFO base cost of $0.10 per pound. The taxpayer normally purchases and consumes four pounds of A each year. The taxpayer begins to switch from use of A to use of B by purchasing two pounds of A at $0.50 per pound and two pounds of B at $0.40 per pound. B also has a base price of $0.10 per pound, and the price of both A and B remain stable during the year. Under these facts, if the manufacturer follows a dollar-value system with a single pool that includes both A and B, its cost of goods sold and ending inventory will be determined as follows:

Dollar-value, single pool

Quantitative change in base cost of inventory:

Beginning inventory at base costs		
(4 pounds of A at $0.10)	$0.40	
(0 pounds of B at $0.10)	0.00	
	$0.40	
Ending inventory at base costs		
(2 pounds of A at $0.10)	$0.20	
(2 pounds of B at $0.10)	0.20	
Increase in inventory at base costs	$0.40	

LIFO value of inventory:

Beginning inventory	$0.40	
Ending inventory	0.40	

Cost of goods sold:

Beginning inventory	$0.40	
Purchases (2 pounds of A at		
$0.50/lb. + 2 pounds of B at $0.40/lb.)	1.80	$2.20
Less: Ending inventory		0.40
Cost of goods sold		$1.80

LIFO reserve at end of year:

LIFO value of ending inventory	$0.40	
Replacement cost:		
2 pounds of A at $0.50 = $1.00		
2 pounds of B at $0.40 = 0.80	1.80	
LIFO reserve	$1.40	

As this example shows, although the LIFO reserve under the specific goods multiple pool system was reduced from $1.60 to $.80,[122] the LIFO reserve would have been more fully maintained had the company been using

---

[121] Assume the same facts set forth in the example supra ¶ 7.04[2].
[122] See example supra ¶ 7.04[2].

a dollar-value system with a single pool. The dollar-value system had the effect of focusing solely on changes in the taxpayer's total inventory investment rather than on the particular mix of items comprising that investment.

The single pool dollar-value system allowed the taxpayer to take full advantage of the current cost of A and B in determining its cost of goods sold. Total inventory investment did not increase in terms of base year dollars. Consequently, rather than matching against current revenue $0.20 of A (the LIFO value associated with the liquidation in the inventory of A), as was the case under the specific goods system,[123] the taxpayer was able to match the full $0.50 cost of A and the full $0.40 cost of B against current revenue. In effect, this permitted a tax-free exchange of A in the opening inventory for B in the closing inventory. This exchange, in turn, helped maintain the LIFO reserve. The reduction in the LIFO reserve (from $1.60 at the beginning of the year to $1.40 at the end of the year) was attributable to the difference in the current costs of A and B.

The preceding example illustrates that use of the dollar-value method with a single pool allows the taxpayer to switch its current inventory investment to goods with a lower current cost without having to incur a tax on past inflation. The example also shows the effects of a shift from one type of purchased product or raw material to another in a single pool. Similar benefits may be realized with respect to shifts in items of labor and overhead, as long as these items are included in the same pool.

In addition to the importance of pooling, the example illustrates the importance of determining base costs.[124] Had a single pool not been available or had the taxpayer not been able to establish a low base cost for B, the results could have been significantly different.

[a] Pooling

[i] **Natural-business-unit pools** *Theory.* In July 1960, prior to the promulgation of the dollar-value regulations in 1961, three distinguished accountants discussed the pooling of LIFO inventories under the dollar-value method.[125] These accountants concluded that the "use of a large number of pools under the dollar-value method may result in a failure to accomplish the LIFO objective of matching

---

[123] Id.

[124] See infra ¶ 7.04[3][b] for discussion of base costs.

[125] Blough, Broad Trueblood, "Pooling of LIFO Inventories by Use of Dollar-Value Method," 110 J. of Accoutancy 77 (July 1960). This statement was jointly authored by Carmen G. Blough, then director of research of the AICPA; Samuel J. Broad, former president of the AICPA and former chairman of the Committee on Accounting Procedure; and Robert M. Trueblood, an accountant who had served in numerous capacities for various accounting organizations.

current costs with current revenues."[126] The accountants then proposed a method of pooling based on what they termed a "natural business unit." They pointed out that in general, the more inclusive the individual pools, the less opportunity exists for manipulation of profits by liquidations and transfers of investment. Moreover, with a smaller number of pools, there is less chance that income or loss would be reflected as a result of temporary, fortuitous, or arbitrary shifting of inventory dollars from one pool to another. They defined "natural business unit" as

> an integrated activity within an enterprise that has all the basic components and characteristics commonly found in competitive operations. In identifying a natural business unit, various criteria may be appropriate. Interchangeability of materials, or common production facilities and processes, or sales into essentially similar markets would each tend to indicate the existence of a natural business unit.[127]

As the accountants pointed out, use of a single pool also provides a more accurate computation of income than under a multiple pool system because use of the single pool prevents mere substitutions in raw materials or changes in manufacturing processes from significantly distorting income. The accountants believed this prevention important because, in their view, procedural shifts or technological changes within a natural business unit do not of themselves cause the realization of income.[128]

Definition. Following the presentation by the accountants,[129] the income tax regulations were amended to permit manufacturers to pool on the basis of natural business units.[130] Wholesalers, retailers, and other nonmanufacturers may pool on the basis of natural business units only with the prior approval of the Commissioner.[131] Where a taxpayer engages in business activity both as a manufacturer and as a wholesaler or retailer, the separate pooling rules apply to the separate activities.[132] This is the case even though the goods are virtually identical and sold in the same business.[133] On the other hand, care must be taken in evaluating whether particular transactions are a part of a wholesaling or retailing activity or a manufacturing activity. For example, the National Office has recognized that the sale of products purchased as an integral part of a manufacturing activity may appropriately

---

[126] Id. at 79.

[127] Id.

[128] Id. But see infra ¶ 7.04[3][e], where the position of the IRS on component costing is, in effect, that technological advance should cause the realization of income.

[129] See supra ¶ 7.04[3][a][i].

[130] Treas. Reg. §§ 1.472-8(b), 1.472-8(h)(10); TD 6539, 1961-1 CB 167.

[131] Treas. Reg. § 1.472-8(c).

[132] Treas. Reg. §§ 1.472-8(b), 1.472-8(c).

[133] Amity Leather Prods. Co., 82 TC 726 (1984).

be included within a manufacturer's specific goods or dollar-value LIFO pools.[134] Similarly, the courts have recognized that not all activity that technically may be wholesaling should be treated as necessitating the establishment of a separate LIFO pool. For example, in *UFE, Inc.*,[135] the Tax Court held that an inventory of finished goods purchased by a taxpayer who was simultaneously purchasing all the assets of an ongoing manufacturing business was properly included in the taxpayer's manufacturing pool. The court distinguished *Amity Leather Products Co.*,[136] on the basis that the taxpayer in *Amity Leather* was engaged in a wholesaling business whereas in *UFE, Inc.*, the taxpayer's single purchase should not cause it to be deemed the trade or business of wholesaling.

The decision in *UFE, Inc.* was followed by the Tax Court in *Hamilton Industries, Inc.*,[137] but with a very significant twist. In *Hamilton*, the inventories were acquired for a bargain price. The court held that the inventories could be included in the manufacturing pool of the acquirer (following *UFE, Inc.*), but the court then held that the price or cost characteristics of the acquired inventory were so different from the inventories then being manufactured at significantly higher prices that the acquired inventory had to be treated as consisting of different items than the subsequently manufactured inventory. This resulted in the bargain element (i.e., the lower costs) being recognized in income, thereby creating the same increase in income that would have resulted had the acquired goods been placed in a separate pool.[138] In this sense, *Hamilton* effectively overrules *UFE, Inc.* in the case of bargain acquisitions.

An interesting question arising from Section 263A is whether activities that were considered wholesaling or retailing prior to the effective date of the 1986 Act will be treated as manufacturing following the effective date of the 1986 Act. For example, the temporary regulations under Section 263A provide with respect to the application of that section that where property is manufactured for the taxpayer by another, the taxpayer is deemed a manufacturer with respect to costs it incurs in connection with that property.[139] This language suggests that a taxpayer may not avoid classification as a manufacturer by contracting with another to manufacture property for the taxpayer. Thus, a taxpayer whose average gross receipts are less than $10 million may nonetheless be required to capitalize costs it incurs with respect to property produced for it, even though it might have been classified as a wholesaler or a retailer prior to the 1986 Act. Notwithstanding this regula-

---

[134] See Priv. Ltr. Ruls. 8807036 (Nov. 20, 1987), 8842061 (July 28, 1988).

[135] UFE, Inc., 92 TC 1314 (1989).

[136] Amity Leather Prods. Co., 82 TC 726 (1984).

[137] Hamilton Indus., Inc., 97 TC 120 (1991).

[138] Hamilton Indus., Inc. is discussed further infra ¶ 7.08[2].

[139] Temp. Reg. § 1.263A-1T(a)(5)(ii).

tion, some revenue agents have sought to deny natural-business-unit pooling to some taxpayers or to deny the inclusion in a natural-business-unit pool to goods manufactured for the taxpayer by another on the basis that the taxpayer was not a manufacturer for LIFO purposes. The ultimate resolution of this issue is uncertain.

The LIFO regulations provide that natural-business-unit pooling must be used by manufacturers with dollar-value LIFO systems unless some other method of pooling is elected.[140] Thus, natural-business-unit pooling is considered the norm.

The regulations specify that a natural-business-unit pool "shall consist of all items entering into the entire inventory investment for a natural business unit of a business enterprise."[141] As this indicates, if the taxpayer adopts the natural-business-unit method of pooling, each natural-business-unit pool must include all items entering into the taxpayer's entire inventory investment for that business. Accordingly, if a taxpayer seeks to exclude any portion of its inventory from its LIFO election, it may be denied the opportunity to use the natural-business-unit method of pooling.

The regulations define "natural business unit" in the following way:[142]

> Whether an enterprise is composed of more than one natural business unit is a matter of fact to be determined from all the circumstances. The natural business divisions adopted by the taxpayer for internal management purposes, the existence of separate and distinct production facilities and processes, and the maintenance of separate profit and loss records with respect to separate operations are important considerations in determining what is a business unit, unless such divisions, facilities, or accounting records are set up merely because of differences in geographical location. In the case of a manufacturer or processor, a natural business unit ordinarily consists of the entire productive activity of the enterprise within one product line or within two or more related product lines including (to the extent engaged in by the enterprise) the obtaining of materials, the processing of materials, and the selling of manufactured or processed goods.

The regulations then provide the following examples of natural business units:

- Manufacture of automatic clothes washers and dryers of both commercial and domestic grades, as well as electric ranges, mangles, and dishwashers
- Manufacture of radio and television sets
- Production and sale of uncoated paper and coated paper

---

[140] Treas. Reg. § 1.472-8(b).

[141] Treas. Reg. § 1.472-8(b)(1).

[142] Treas. Reg. § 1.472-8(b)(2).

These examples appear designed to illustrate what is meant by single product lines (coated and uncoated paper), by related product lines (washers, dryers, ranges, mangles, and dishwashers), and by unrelated product lines (washers and dryers on the one hand and radios and televisions on the other).

The regulations indicate that use of a natural business unit in a LIFO system is premised on the theory that there is no economic realization of gain or loss as a result of a mere shift of inventory dollars from one item to another within a naturally related group of activities. This is a logical extension of the dollar-value theory, which bases LIFO inventory changes on fluctuations in the dollars invested in inventory rather than the quantity levels of particular inventory items.

The regulations also raise the issue of how a so-called supplier unit of a taxpayer should be treated.[143] On one hand, the regulations suggest that where a taxpayer's supplier unit produces a finished product that is both sold to unrelated parties in substantial quantities and also transferred to other units of the taxpayer for manufacture into unrelated products, the supplier unit should be treated as a separate natural business unit. However, where the supplier unit produces a finished product that is sold to outsiders and is also transferred for manufacture into related products, the supplier unit should be included in the same natural-business-unit pool. Some agents take the position that any sales to outsiders by a supplier unit should cause the supplier unit to be treated as a separate natural-business-unit pool. However, this appears inconsistent with the regulatory standards. Instead, the more appropriate interpretation would be that insignificant sales by supplier units may be disregarded in evaluating whether one or more natural-business-unit pools are appropriate and that even substantial sales to outsiders do not require the inclusion of the supplier in a separate pool, if the products of the supplier unit and the transferee unit are related.

The appropriateness of the number and composition of the taxpayer's natural-business-unit pools is to be determined on audit.[144] Considerable variation has occurred in the manner in which revenue agents interpret these pooling requirements. In some cases, agents have accepted broad groupings of items within a single natural business unit. In other cases, agents have asserted that a single pool should be divided into a number of separate pools. Issues raised by the agents are frequently resolved on a satisfactory, practical basis without the need for litigation.

To date, there have been no decisions articulating in a meaningful way the manner in which the definitional requirements of the regulations are to be applied in practice. Perhaps the most instructive decision is that of the Tax Court in *RLC Industries Co.*[145] In that case, one of the issues before the

---

[143] Treas. Reg. §§ 1.472-8(b)(2)(i), 1.472-8(b)(2)(ii).

[144] Treas. Reg. § 1.472-8(d).

[145] RLC Indus. Co., 98 TC 457 (1992).

court was whether a large timber products company would be able to combine its tracts of Oregon and California timber into a single block for purposes of computing depletion. In approaching the issue, the court first recognized that the function of depletion for a timber products company "in a sense resembles an inventory system of allocating costs to goods sold during the year." The court also noted:[146]

> By way of analogy, petitioner points out and we agree, that its method has similarities to the LIFO method. That method has as one of its basic premises the pooling of inventory which allows less room for extreme variation in income and less opportunity to manipulate income. Various experts have seen this feature as more effectively matching income as opposed to a system of specific matching.

The court then analyzed numerous factors associated with the operation of the taxpayer's Oregon and California timber divisions. Among the factors examined were the history of the taxpayer's operations, its management and the evolution of that management over the years, the degree of integration between the operations of the California and Oregon tracts, the geographical areas involved, the accounting used for the different timber blocks, the views of expert accountants experienced in timber industry accounting, and the concept of the term "block," which the court indicated corresponded to the concept of "pool" for LIFO inventory purposes. The court found, among other facts, that the taxpayer had integrated, interdependent operations that were operated under the control of the taxpayer's central management, even though the taxpayer's divisions could also be viewed as autonomous on a day-to-day operational basis. The court ultimately found that use of the single block or pool was proper. The fact that use of the single block permitted the taxpayer to offset current income from sales of low-basis Oregon timber with depletion from high-basis California timber did not cause the court to conclude that a different result was required.

[ii] **Other pools.** A manufacturer is not required to pool on the basis of natural business units. Instead, it may elect to use multiple pools.[147] Ordinarily, each such pool consists of items that are substantially similar. Just as in the case of specific goods LIFO,[148] similarity is to be determined by a consideration of all relevant facts and circumstances, including the types of raw materials used, the manufacturing processes, interchangeability, similarity in the use of the ultimate products, groupings used for internal

---

[146] Id. at 495, n.31.

[147] Treas. Reg. § 1.472-8(b)(3).

[148] See supra ¶ 7.04[2][a] for discussion of pooling in a specific goods LIFO system.

accounting and management purposes, and general practices in the taxpayer's industry.[149]

Wholesalers, retailers, and similar taxpayers are generally required to pool inventory on the basis of major lines, types, or classes of goods. They may use natural-business-unit pools only with the prior approval of the Commissioner.[150] In identifying major lines, types, or classes of goods, important considerations include customary business practices within the trade or industry as well as all other relevant facts and circumstances. As in the case of manufacturers, the determination of the appropriateness of the pooling method is determined on audit by the Commissioner.

[iii] **Single pool for certain small businesses.** During the late 1970s and early 1980s, when inflation persisted at unusually high levels, significant interest developed in amending the LIFO rules to simplify the necessary computations and thereby make the method more attractive to smaller businesses that did not have sophisticated record-keeping capacity. In partial response to this interest, Congress enacted special rules enabling certain small businesses to use one LIFO inventory pool in circumstances where that result would have been prohibited under the normal LIFO pooling rules.[151] As part of the 1986 Act, Congress repealed this special pooling provision and replaced it with a simplified dollar-value LIFO method.[152] However, the 1986 Act permits taxpayers who already had elected to use the special single-pool method of original Section 474 to continue their use of that method.[153] Consequently, the rules of original Section 474, as it existed prior to the 1986 Act, are still relevant and applicable to affected taxpayers.

Under the special single-pool method, any taxpayer whose average gross receipts did not exceed $2 million for the three-taxable-year period ending with the taxable year was eligible to include all the inventory of any single trade or business within a single LIFO inventory pool.[154] With respect to the $2 million limit, the gross receipts of all members of a controlled group of which the taxpayer was a member were aggregated. For this purpose, "controlled group" was defined as all members who would be treated as a single employer under Section 52(b).[155]

[b] Base Costs and Alternative Measurement Procedures

Once items have been grouped into pools, the next step is to determine changes in the quantity of each pool. These changes are determined by

---

[149] See Treas. Reg. § 1.472-8(b)(3), and discussion supra ¶ 7.04[2][a].

[150] Treas. Reg. § 1.472-8(c).

[151] See Section 474, as it existed prior to the 1986 Act.

[152] Section 474, as amended by the 1986 Act. See infra ¶ 7.04[5] for discussion of the new simplified dollar-value LIFO method.

[153] See the 1986 Act, § 802(c)(2).

[154] Sections 474(a), 474(b), as they existed prior to the 1986 Act.

[155] Section 474(c)(1), as it existed prior to the 1986 Act.

comparing the aggregate base cost of the beginning inventory to the aggregate base cost of the ending inventory. The base cost of the inventory is determined by valuing each item in inventory at what it cost (or would have cost) as of the base date. "Base date" is the first day of the first year for which LIFO is adopted.

Under any dollar-value LIFO system, it is necessary to establish a means for determining the base cost of the items in inventory and for comparing the aggregate base cost of the beginning and ending inventories. Generally, the three approaches used are the double extension method, the index method, and the link-chain method.

[i] Double-extension method. Under the double-extension method, quantitative changes in inventory are determined by measuring all items in the beginning and ending inventories at their respective base costs. If there is a reduction in the quantity of the LIFO inventory, an appropriate portion of the LIFO value of the beginning inventory is excluded from ending inventory. If there is an increase in inventory (i.e., if the ending inventory at base cost exceeds the beginning inventory at base costs), the increase or increment to inventory is calculated by multiplying the increase at base cost by the ratio of the current-year cost of the ending inventory to the base cost of the ending inventory.

The double-extension method requires that a base cost be computed for every item in inventory.[156] As new items enter the inventory, the base cost of each item will be the current-year cost of the item, unless the taxpayer is able to reconstruct or otherwise establish what the base cost would have been if the item had been in existence on the base date. If the taxpayer is unable to so reconstruct or otherwise establish a base cost as of the base date, it may use as the base cost the earliest cost that it is otherwise able to reconstruct or establish.

Where a taxpayer's inventory is subject to a continuing influx of new items, the ability to reconstruct or otherwise establish a base cost as of the base date is quite important. If the taxpayer is not able to so reconstruct or otherwise establish such a base cost, it runs the risk of increasing its LIFO inventory (and reducing its LIFO reserve) merely because of inflation that otherwise will exist in the base cost of the new items.

EXAMPLE: If a taxpayer acquires a new item X with a current cost of $2 and a base cost of $1, only $1 will be used in determining whether there is an increase in inventory for any given year. However, if that same taxpayer had not been able to determine that the base cost of the item was $1, it would have been required to use $2 as the base cost and, as a consequence, ending inventory would have had a base cost $1 higher than what it otherwise would have been. The additional $1 would have

---

[156] Treas. Reg. § 1.472-8(e)(2)(iii).

been included in the value of inventory, rather than in cost of goods sold. This, in turn, would have increased taxable income.

To the extent that the taxpayer's objective is to minimize its inventory in order to reduce taxable income, the ability to reconstruct base costs is quite important.

The double-extension method may be illustrated by the following example, which is based on an example in the regulations.[157]

EXAMPLE: A taxpayer elects, beginning with calendar year 1, to compute its inventories by use of the dollar-value LIFO method. The taxpayer creates Pool No. 1 for items A, B, and C. The composition of the inventory for Pool No. 1 at the base date, January 1 of year 1, is as follows:

Items	Units	Unit cost	Total cost
A	1,000	$5	$ 5,000

Items	Units	Unit cost	Total cost
B	2,000	4	8,000
C	500	2	1,000
Total base-year cost at January 1, year 1			$14,000

The closing inventory of Pool No. 1 at December 31, year 1, contains 3,000 units of A, 1,000 units of B, and 500 units of C. The taxpayer computes the current-year cost of the items making up the pool by reference to the actual cost of goods most recently purchased. The most recent purchases of items A, B, and C are as follows:

Item	Purchase date	Quantity purchased	Unit cost
A	December 15, year 1	3,500	$6.00
B	December 10, year 1	2,000	5.00
C	November 1, year 1	500	2.50

The inventory of Pool No. 1 at December 31, year 1, shown at base-year and current-year cost is as follows:

Item	Quantity	Dec. 31, year 1 inventory at Jan. 1, year 1 base-year cost		Dec. 31, year 1 inventory at current-year cost	
		Unit cost	Amount	Unit cost	Amount
A	3,000	$5.00	$15,000	$6.00	$18,000
B	1,000	4.00	4,000	5.00	5,000
C	500	2.00	1,000	2.50	1,250
	Total		$20,000		$24,250

---

[157] Treas. Reg. § 1.472-8(e)(2)(v), Ex. (1).

If the amount of the December 31, year 1, inventory at base-year cost were equal to, or less than, the base-year cost of $14,000 at January 1, year 1, this amount would be the closing LIFO inventory at December 31, year 1. However, since the base-year cost of the closing LIFO inventory at December 31, year 1, amounts to $20,000 and is in excess of the $14,000 base-year cost of the opening inventory for that year, there is a $6,000 increment in Pool No. 1 during the year. This increment must be valued at current-year cost, i.e., the ratio of $24,250 to $20,000, or 121.25 percent. The LIFO value of the inventory at December 31, year 1, is $21,275, computed as follows:

	Dec. 31, year 1 inventory at Jan. 1, year 1 base-year cost	Pool No. 1 Ratio of total current-year cost to total base-year cost	Dec. 31, year 1 Inventory at LIFO value
January 1, year 1 base cost	$14,000	100.00%	$14,000
December 31, year 1 increment	6,000	121.25	7,275
Total	$20,000		$21,275

In this example, all items in ending inventory were purchased or produced during the year. However, if a taxpayer has items in ending inventory that were not purchased or produced during the tax year, the taxpayer will not have an actual current cost for these items. In that case, the question arises as to how the taxpayer should compute its ratio of current-year cost to base cost for purposes of valuing an increment to inventory.

The IRS has ruled in such a situation that the taxpayer has two choices.[158] If the taxpayer is able to determine what the current cost of the item is or would have been, it may use that cost as the current-year cost. If the taxpayer is unable to determine the current-year cost, then for purposes of determining the ratio of current cost to base cost, the particular item should be excluded. In effect, this will attribute to the excluded item a degree of inflation equal to the inflation in items that were in ending inventory and were purchased or produced during the current year. In other words, the increment at base cost will be valued only on the basis of index computed for items purchased or produced during the current year. Thus, to maintain the lowest LIFO value possible, a current-year cost should be reconstructed for items not purchased or produced during the year whenever the inflation arising from such a reconstruction is less than the inflation in items that were purchased or produced during the current year.

---

[158] Rev. Rul. 79-103, 1979-1 CB 192.

[ii] **Index method.** The regulations provide that where use of the double-extension method is impractical because of the extensive variety of items within the inventory, an index method may be used.[159] Under an index method, a representative portion of the inventory in a pool is extended to determine the ratio of current costs to base costs. The portion to be extended may also be determined by using sound and consistent statistical sampling techniques. In effect, under an index method, it is assumed for purposes of valuing increments that the inflation inherent in the entire pool is identical to the inflation in the items on which the index is based. Thus, the selection of the sample is most important. A taxpayer who desires to use an index method must attach to its return for the year for which the method is first used a statement describing the method, and a copy must be filed with the Commissioner.[160]

The sample may be chosen on the basis of a representative portion of the inventory or statistical sampling techniques. Despite the fact that the two methods are regulatory alternatives, agents often prefer the use of statistical sampling techniques as opposed to evaluating whether a truly representative portion of the inventory has been selected. Nevertheless, this is not required. In either case, the taxpayer must be able to demonstrate the appropriateness, suitability, and accuracy of the particular sample or index to the satisfaction of the District Director on audit.

The regulations do not provide examples of an index method. Accordingly, the IRS generally gives substantial deference to financial accounting concepts and GAAP in determining the appropriateness of an index method. A taxpayer that wishes to obtain advance approval of its index method may request such approval from the Commissioner.[161]

Notwithstanding the failure of the IRS to issue definitive guidelines on requisite sampling procedures, certain standards have evolved over time. Many practitioners assume that representative sampling will be acceptable if it is based on at least 50 percent of the items in inventory and 70 percent of the dollars. Statistical sampling is generally assumed to be acceptable where it is based on a confidence level of at least 90 percent to 95 percent with a precision error of no more than plus or minus 2 percent. Some taxpayers also look for guidance to the sampling guidelines previously announced by the Service for application of the installment method to revolving credit sales.[162] However, the Service takes the position that such guidance may not be appropriate for statistical sampling in connection with a LIFO index method.[163]

---

[159] Treas. Reg. § 1.472-8(e)(1).

[160] Id.

[161] Id.

[162] See Rev. Proc. 64-4, 1964-1 CB 644 (part 1). See discussion at ¶ 5.04[2][d][ii].

[163] "LIFO Method of Inventory Valuation," IRS Training Manual No. 3127-01 at A-8 (Rev. 12-87).

Despite any such guidelines, or the lack thereof, the key issue is whether the taxpayer has demonstrated to the satisfaction of the examining agents the appropriateness, suitability, and accuracy of the sample. Moreover, to the extent the taxpayer's sample departs from what the agents would regard as an appropriate sample, the result is generally only modest adjustments, if any, not a discontinuance of the use of the index method.

[iii] Link-chain method. Where use of either an index or a double-extension method is impractical or unsuitable, a taxpayer may use a "link-chain method."[164] Under this method, a ratio of current-year costs to prior-year costs is computed to determine price changes for the particular year. The annual price change is then multiplied by the price change of each prior year to determine a cumulative price change. In practice, the price index of the current year is multiplied against the cumulative price index as of the prior year.

The essential difference between the link-chain method and the pure double-extension method is that the index computed under the link-chain method takes into account changes in the mix of items throughout the years, whereas the index computed under a pure double-extension method ignores the effect of changes in mix (and other circumstances) during the intervening years. In addition, under a link-chain method, it is not necessary to reconstruct the base cost of new items entering the inventory by determining what the new items would have cost on the base date. It is only necessary to determine what the new item would have cost at the end of the prior year. The base cost of the new item will be, in effect, the current-year cost of the item deflated by the product of the current-year index (which included the new item) and the cumulative price index as of the end of the prior year (which, of course, did not include the new item). In effect, the assumption is made that the inflation inherent in the new item from the base date to the end of the prior year is equal to the inflation inherent in the taxpayer's ever-changing inventory of other items throughout that same period. The taxpayer is thereby relieved of much of the difficulty otherwise inherent in reconstructing a base cost for new items entering inventory. If the taxpayer is unable to reconstruct a prior-year cost for new items, the current-year cost will be used as the prior-year cost.

As in the case of an index method, a statement describing the link-chain method must be attached to the return for the first year for which the method is to be used, and the taxpayer may be called on to demonstrate the suitability of the link-chain method to the IRS on audit.[165] Just as in the case of an index method, a taxpayer may request advance approval of its link-chain method.

---

[164] Treas. Reg. § 1.472-8(e)(1).

[165] Id. A copy of the statement must be submitted to the Commissioner.

Taxpayers may also use a combination of index and link-chain methods. In that case, a taxpayer has the opportunity to determine an annual price index on the basis of a representative portion (or statistically determined portion) of its total inventory. This annual price index is then multiplied by the cumulative price index of the prior years to determine cumulative price index of the current year. The current-year cost of all items in inventory may then be deflated to determine the base cost of those items. This total is then compared to the base cost as of the end of the prior year to determine whether there has been an increment. If there has been an increment, the increment is valued on the basis of a ratio of aggregate current costs to aggregate base costs. This ratio will generally be the applicable cumulative price index, although the use of this particular index is not necessary in every case. Other ratios of current cost to base cost may be acceptable.

[iv] **Reconstruction techniques.** The regulations provide some guidance to taxpayers on how to reconstruct the base-year cost (for taxpayers using the double-extension method) and the prior-year cost (for taxpayers using the link-chain method).[166] These regulations provide that if the new item is a product or raw material that was not in existence on the base date, its cost may be reconstructed by using reasonable means to determine what the cost of the item would have been on the base date had the item existed in the base year. If the item was in existence, but was not stocked by the taxpayer, the taxpayer may use available data and records to establish what the item would have cost the taxpayer had he stocked it.

Taxpayers use many approaches in attempting to reconstruct. Sometimes, they seek to obtain data from price lists in their possession, from information still retained by their suppliers, or from other sources. Some taxpayers attempt to use published price indexes to determine what the cost would have been at the base date, and such indexes are often accepted on audit if they are sufficiently demonstrative of the inflation inherent in the new item.

Of course all facts and circumstances should be taken into account. These might include the quantities that normally would have been purchased, any special circumstances existing at the time of purchase, and so forth.

An important question affecting new items, whose creation is the result of technological advance, is whether, for purposes of reconstructing a base cost, the present technology should be deemed to have existed in the base year or, instead, only the actual technology of the base year should be taken into account. Although this question has not been specifically addressed by the courts, it would seem appropriate to assume that the present technology existed in the base year. Such an assumption allows a determination of what

---

[166] Treas. Reg. § 1.472-8(e)(2)(iii), which pertains to the double-extension method.

the *new* item would have cost had it existed in the base year. If the new technology is ignored, then the taxpayer is only determining what the cost of the old item was in the base year.[167]

[c] Valuing Increments

The regulations provide the taxpayer with several means of determining current cost for the purpose of determining the ratio of current cost to base cost.[168] Current costs may be determined on the basis of (1) the most recent purchases or production during the year; (2) the earliest purchases or production during the year; (3) the average cost of all goods purchased or produced during the year; or (4) any other method that in the opinion of the Commissioner clearly reflects income.

It is important to note that each approach is based solely on costs incurred during the year of the increment. Consequently, any averaging approach must be based solely on costs incurred during the year. Rolling averages or moving averages, which are based in part on costs incurred in prior year, generally may not be used.[169]

Generally, taxpayers are allowed significant discretion in making their computations. However, the IRS always has the right to review such procedures to determine whether they clearly reflect income. For example, the IRS has determined that a taxpayer may value the increments to its LIFO inventory by reference to the earliest costs incurred during the year, but that it may not value such an increment by using an index based on quantities and a product mix that is not consistent with the quantities and mix existing as of the end of the year.[170]

Taxpayers have sometimes sought to use dual indexes, i.e., they will use a deflator index based on year-end prices for the purposes of determining base costs but will use a separate, increment valuation index (based on earliest costs incurred) for valuing increments. The use of such indexes is generally accepted by revenue agents on audit, if the taxpayer can demonstrate a proper computation of the index in light of the mix of goods in inventory at year-end.[171] In addition, taxpayers sometimes use shortcut approaches. Such approaches often incorporate inventory turnover computations and assumptions as to how inflation determined for an entire year arises during, or may be

---

[167] See AICPA, "Issues Paper: Identification and Discussion of Certain Financial Accounting and Reporting Issues Concerning LIFO Inventories," 28–34 (Nov. 30, 1984).

[168] Treas. Reg. § 1.472-8(e)(2)(ii).

[169] See Rev. Rul. 77-480, 1977-2 CB 186; Rev. Proc. 88-15, 1985-1 CB 683.

[170] See, e.g., Tech. Adv. Mem. 8749005 (Aug. 12, 1987).

[171] "LIFO Method of Inventory Valuation," IRS Training Manual No. 3127-01 at 11-3–11-5 (Rev. 12-87).

attributable to, earlier months in the year.[172] The IRS is aware of the use of such approaches, but generally requires substantiation of their appropriateness before allowing them.[173]

[d] New or Revised Base Year

In certain circumstances, it may be desirable for a taxpayer to change its base year for purposes of making LIFO computations. An example is where a taxpayer requests permission to change from a specific-goods multiple-pool LIFO system to a dollar-value system based on natural-business-unit pools. Another example is where there is a significant change in the taxpayer's costing system, such as when taxpayers were first required to adopt the full absorption method of inventory costing or to change to the expanded costing requirements required by the 1986 Act.[174]

In effect, the use of a revised base year means only that there has been a change in the costs used in determining whether there has been an increase or a decrease in inventory and, if an increase, in valuing that increase. The change is often desirable where the taxpayer has significantly changed or improved its costing system, has used estimates in the past or, as is the case under the 1986 Act, is required or permitted to use estimates to determine past costs. In these cases, more precise computations of future inventories are possible if measurements are made using revised base costs that themselves are more precise and verifiable than the previously determined base costs.

Where a new base year is used, the LIFO layers attributable to periods prior to the revised base year will have a base cost determined on the basis of the ratio of the new base-year costs to the prior-year costs.

EXAMPLE: Assume that a taxpayer adopted dollar-value LIFO in 1981, using the double-extension method with a single pool. Assume the taxpayer's LIFO inventory at December 31, 1986, had to be revalued as a result of the 1986 Act and that after revaluation, it was as follows:

	Base year costs	Index	LIFO carrying value
Base layer	$17,920	1.00	$17,920
1981 layer	5,120	1.20	6,144
1982 layer	6,400	1.30	8,320
1983 layer	2,560	1.35	3,456
1984 layer	0	1.40	0
1985 layer	5,120	1.50	7,680
1986 layer	6,400	1.60	10,240
Total	$43,520		$53,760

---

[172] Id.

[173] Id.

[174] See, e.g., Temp. Reg. § 1.263A-1T(e)(b).

Under the 1986 Act, the year prior to the year of change (1986) is treated as the new base year for the purpose of determining the index in 1987 and future years.[175] This requires that the index of layers in years prior to the base year be restated in terms of the new base year. In this example the restated inventory would be as follows:

	Restated base year costs	Index	LIFO carrying value
Old base layer	$28,672	0.625	$17,920
1981 layer	8,192	0.75	6,144
1982 layer	10,272	0.81	8,320
1983 layer	4,114	0.84	3,456
1984 layer	0	0.875	0
1985 layer	8,170	0.94	7,680
New base layer (1986)	10,240	1.00	10,240
Total	$69,660		$53,760

Although the example is based on examples provided in the temporary regulations,[176] it is doubtful that the Treasury really consciously intended for 1986 to be the new base year rather than 1987. If 1987 were the new base year, revised costs would be determined as of the first day of the year affected by the 1986 Act. (This would be January 1, 1987, in the example). However, by virtue of the examples contained in the temporary regulations, revised base costs are the 1986 current costs, which would be costs determined as of the beginning of 1986 for taxpayers valuing increments on the basis of earliest costs incurred.[177] It is not yet known whether this result in the temporary regulations was intentional or an apparent oversight that will be corrected.[178]

[e] Product Costing Versus Component Costing

In recent years, the IRS has increased its scrutiny of the various practices and procedures used by taxpayers employing dollar-value LIFO methods. One of the more significant areas of attention by the IRS is the use of so-called component costing by taxpayers (rather than product costing) in applying their dollar-value LIFO methods.

---

[175] See Temp. Reg. § 1.263A-1T(e)(6)(iv)(C).

[176] Id.

[177] See discussion infra ¶ 7.04[3][c].

[178] In Notice 88-86, 1988-34 IRB 10, the Treasury announced that taxpayers using the simplified resale method or simplified production method (see discussion at ¶¶ 6.06[1][c][ii], 6.07[4]) are not required to establish a new base year under the three-year average method. However, taxpayers who desire to establish such a new base year may do so. The Treasury has announced that forthcoming regulations will also permit other taxpayers to establish a new base year.

Both product costing and component costing are concerned with the manner in which beginning and ending inventory quantities are computed so that taxpayers may determine whether there has been an increase or a decrease in the quantity of their inventory during the year. Under product costing, the units of measure are the number of products themselves. Under component costing, the units of measure are based on the various cost components that make up the finished products. For example, the units of measure may be the number of ounces, pounds, gallons, yards, or other unit of measure for raw materials, the number of hours for direct labor, and the number of labor hours, machine hours, labor dollars, or other unit of measure for overhead costs.

EXAMPLE: Assume that a taxpayer produces widgets. At the time LIFO is first adopted, each widget consists of five units each of raw material, labor, and overhead. Each unit of raw material initially costs $1, and, for simplicity, each unit of labor and overhead combined initially costs $1. Assume further that beginning inventory consists of one widget with a total cost of $10 and that because of technological changes experienced during the year, the cost of producing a widget at the end of the year consists of five units of raw material but only of three units of labor, and overhead. For simplicity, assume there has been inflation of 10 percent during the year in the cost of raw materials (RM), labor and overhead (L&OH). In these circumstances, the cost of the widget will be as follows:

Cost of producing widget at beginning of year:
RM: 5 units at $1 per unit = $ 5.00
L&OH: 5 units at $1 per unit =   5.00
                                                 $10.00

Cost of producing widget at end of year:
RM: 5 units at $1.10 per unit = $ 5.50
L&OH: 3 units at $1.10 per unit =   3.30
                                                 $ 8.80

In these circumstances, the LIFO value of the beginning inventory would be $10, under both product costing and component costing. This is the FIFO cost associated with the one unit of product in inventory at the beginning of the first year of which LIFO is adopted.

At the end of the year, the LIFO value of the inventory depends on whether product costing or component costing is used. Under product costing, because there is still one unit of product in beginning inventory, that unit of product will have a LIFO value of $10. Under component costing, the beginning inventory will consist of five units of raw material and five units of labor and overhead, each with a unit cost of $1 for a total beginning LIFO inventory of $10. During the year, the quantity of raw material has remained the same, but the quantity of labor and overhead has declined from five units to three units. Conse-quently, under component costing, a liquidation in the quantity of labor and overhead has occurred and the aggregate LIFO value at the end of the year will be $8, consisting of five units of raw material at $1 per unit and three units of labor and overhead at $1 per unit.

As this simple example illustrates, because of the technological advance that occurred during the year, it was possible for the taxpayer to reduce the quantity of labor and overhead needed to produce its inventory and, as a result, the value of the inventory under component costing was lower than the value of the inventory under product costing. This reduction of $2 in the LIFO value of the inventory under component costing has the effect of correspondingly increasing cost of goods sold by $2. It is this effect that the IRS finds objectionable. (Of course, if the number of units of raw material, labor, or overhead in each product increased during the year, an opposite result could occur.) In effect, the IRS is concerned that the cost of the item sold during the year can exceed the cost of the item most recently produced. The IRS concern fails to recognize that a liquidation may occur in units of cost even though there has been no liquidation in products. Alternatively, the IRS fails to recognize that if the product at the end of the year is different from the product sold during the year, product costing generally would val-ue the end of the year inventory at the same LIFO cost as it would have under component costing. Lastly, the IRS position has the effect of treating production efficiencies or technological advance inherent in year-end inven-tory automatically as creating profit, whereas component costing would defer the recognition of profit associated with such developments until such time as the affected products are sold. This is another way of viewing the end of the year inventory as new items.

The simple issue now under scrutiny by the IRS is whether component costing is acceptable. At the time the dollar-value LIFO regulations were first promulgated in 1961, the use of component costing by manufacturers was widespread. Indeed, for manufacturers with complex inventories that changed rapidly over time due to changes in styles, materials, technological advance, and so on, the use of component costing often was (and often remains) the only practical way of applying a LIFO method. For many taxpayers, it simply was not then possible (nor is it now possible) as a practical matter to determine whether the products in inventory at the end of the year were sufficiently identical to the products in inventory at the beginning of the year so that comparisons of the number of each product adequately and accurately disclosed whether there had been an actual increase or decrease in the taxpayer's investment in inventory. By segregating the products in ending inventory into their cost components and comparing the quantity of these cost components to the same cost components that existed in beginning of the year inventory, quantities could more easily and accurately be computed and LIFO values determined.

The Treasury and IRS were familiar with the use of component costing at the time the 1961 dollar-value LIFO regulations were promulgated. The use of component costing was described in extensive writings, including the writings of Herbert T. McAnly, who is widely acknowledged as the father of dollar-value LIFO, and others including those of a group of tax professionals who worked with the Treasury and the IRS throughout the 1950s on the development of the dollar-value LIFO regulations.[179]

The use of component costing remained widespread after 1961 and was routinely reviewed by the IRS on audit and accepted by it. Indeed, the IRS Training Manual on LIFO, which was issued in 1976, made it clear that a manufacturer's election to use LIFO could be implemented in any of several ways, including the use of component costing.[180] Illustrations of both product costing and component costing were included in this LIFO Training Manual.

During the late 1970s and early 1980s, the National Office had occasion to focus on component costing in a technical advice memorandum (TAM) and a general counsel memorandum (GCM)[181] These documents indicated concern with the use of component costing. The concern was premised on the following assertions:

- That there was no express authorization for the use of component costing in the dollar-value regulations
- That under component costing, the number of products in inventory may not change; yet the LIFO value of the inventory may decline
- That LIFO presupposes a tangible physical product, and component costs are not tangible physical products
- That LIFO presupposes that the items to be quantified in determining whether there has been an increase or a decrease in inventory must be goods or products and not hours or other units of cost components

Following issuance of the TAM and GCM, the IRS nevertheless continued to accept the use of component costing on audit. Moreover, the IRS never issued any official document disallowing the use of component costing. Indeed, the GCM had recommended the publication of a revenue ruling on this matter, but this recommendation apparently was rejected because no such ruling was ever published.

Thereafter, in a more recent version of the LIFO Training Manual,

---

[179] See, e.g., H.T. McAnly, "Origin of the Dollar Value LIFO Method," published in the addresses delivered at Accounting Clinic and the Central States Accounting Conference (May 1941); Blough, Broad & Trueblood, "Pooling of Lifo Inventories by Use of the Dollar-Value Method," J. Accountancy, 77 (July 1960).

[180] "LIFO Method of Inventory Valuation," IRS Training Manual No. 3127-01,60 (1976).

[181] Tech. Adv. Mem. 7920008 (Feb. 12, 1979); GCM 38478 (Aug. 25, 1980).

which has not been made available to the general public, the concerns expressed in the TAM and GCM were incorporated.[182] Nevertheless, use of component costing continues to be used by many taxpayers, questioned and sometimes challenged on the audit of some taxpayers, and ignored on the audit of other taxpayers.

As to the issue itself, the IRS position seems without merit and, if tested in the courts, should not be sustained. This conclusion is suggested by an overwhelming number of factors, including the following:

- The 1961 dollar-value regulations were intended to confirm the appropriateness of the dollar-value concept as that concept had been developed for financial accounting purposes. That concept and the manner in which it was routinely applied for financial accounting purposes often included the use of component costing. This use was well known by the IRS and Treasury, and there was no objection to it. Such a circumstance has sometimes been cited by the courts as compelling the acceptance of the financial accounting technique in question.[183]

- Component costing is the only practical way for determining dollar-value LIFO inventories for many manufacturers and, without it, they would as a practical matter be denied the opportunity of using a traditional LIFO method. Such a practical denial is impermissible.[184]

- Following promulgation of the dollar-value regulations in 1961, all

---

[182] "LIFO Method of Inventory Valuation," IRS Training Manual 3127-01 (Rev. 12-87).

[183] See, e.g., Beneficial Corp. v. United States, 814 F2d 1570 (5th Cir. 1989); Shell Oil Co., 89 TC 3701 (1987); E.W. Bliss Co. v. United States, 224 F. Supp. 374 (ND Ohio 1963), aff'd, 351 F2d 449 (6th Cir. 1965). See, also, RLC Indus. Co., 98 TC 457 (1992), where, in focusing on the importance of industry and accounting experts regarding typical industry practice, the court made it clear that such information was relevant to the issue of whether a method of accounting clearly reflected income and did not need to be supported by the introduction of the practices of other specifically identified taxpayers in order to be relevant.

[184] See, e.g., Fox Chevrolet, Inc., 76 TC 708, 727 (1981); where the court stated "[a]dmittedly dollar-value LIFO was developed in order to effectuate the congressional purpose of making LIFO available to all taxpayers when some might otherwise be excluded due to the practical problems of accounting for complex inventories by matching specific items"; Richardson Invs., Inc., 76 TC 736, 747 (1981), where the court recognized that it would be inappropriate to require particular computational systems where to do so would "create serious practical impediments to its [LIFO's] application"; and Amity Leather Prods., Co., 82 TC 726, 734 (1984), where the court stated, "the method of inventory accounting must be administratively feasible and not unduly burdensome from the standpoint of each of the parties. Within limits of reasonableness, regulations governing LIFO inventory accounting have to be applicable across the board. Whether they achieve the best accounting result in a particular fact situation is not controlling.'

the practitioners who had been working with the Treasury and the IRS considered the matter resolved. Had there been no acceptance of the component costing concept in those regulations or if the practitioners and IRS had thought the regulations did not allow the use of component costing, there would have been an outcry because of the inability of many taxpayers to use LIFO. However, there was no such outcry.

- The dollar-value regulations expressly authorize and illustrate the use of component costing in regulations governing the adoption of LIFO for raw materials and raw material content.[185] These regulatory provisions authorize manufacturers to segregate their inventories into raw material, labor, and overhead costs, and to adopt LIFO for raw material costs only, thereby necessarily requiring that the labor and overhead costs be accounted for separately on a FIFO basis. This *is* component costing. For instance, assume the taxpayer in the example set forth above had adopted LIFO for raw materials and the raw material content of work-in-process and finished goods. If technological advance had reduced the quantity of necessary raw material (but not labor and overhead) from five units to three units, the product in the ending inventory would have been valued at $8.50 consisting of three units of raw material on LIFO at $1 per unit and five units of labor and overhead on FIFO at $1.10 per unit.

- The terms "goods," "products," and "merchandise" contained in Section 472 are also contained in Section 471. Consequently, if the use of these terms in Section 472 cause LIFO to be applicable only to goods or physical items (rather than to the costs of these items), the adoption of LIFO for raw material costs would leave the intangible labor and overhead costs on FIFO. However, under the IRS position, taxpayers apparently would be able to exclude such intangible costs from the requirements of Section 471 and, presumably, Section 263A because these costs are not tangible items or goods. Such a result is absurd; yet it would seemingly be required under the IRS position because it is a fundamental principle of tax law that the same words used in different sections of the code and regulations must be given the same meaning absent an express direction to the contrary.[186]

- LIFO is allowed for the inventories of dealers in securities, even

---

[185] See Treas. Reg. § 1.472-8(b)(3)(ii), for dollar-value LIFO; and Treas. Reg. § 1.472-1(c) for specific-goods LIFO.

[186] See, e.g., Malat v. Riddell, 383 US 569 (1966); Hollywood Baseball Assoc. v. Comm'r, 423 F2d 494 (9th Cir. 1970).

though securities represent only intangible assets and not physical, tangible assets.[187]

- Component costing is accepted for all financial accounting and SEC reporting purposes.[188]

- Only component costing provides the same result as FIFO, assuming there is no inflation. Consequently, component costing may be the most accurate means of eliminating the effects of inflation as required by the courts.[189]

- Component costing is the only practical way for manufacturers to apply LIFO in conjunction with long-term contracts, and the use of LIFO for such taxpayers had expressly been approved.[190]

- If production efficiencies, technological advances, or changes in cost structure cause the product at the end of the year to be a new item, which differs from the product existing at the beginning of the year, then the results produced by product costing and component costing are the same.[191]

- Until amended by the final economic performance regulations, which apply prospectively from April 10, 1992, the applicable Treasury regulations governing the clear reflection of income provided that the taxpayer's method "will be acceptable" if three conditions were satisfied: (1) the method was in accord with GAAP; (2) the method was used consistently from year to year; and (3) the method was consistent with the Treasury regulations.[192] In effect, there should be no question but that the method was in accord with GAAP, the method has been consistently used by many taxpayers, and the method is consistent with the income tax regulations. Certainly, there is no inconsistency between the use of component costing and the Treasury regulations, and this point has been recognized by representatives of the Treasury, who have acknowledged that while (in their view) the

---

[187] See Rev. Rul. 60-321, 1960-2 CB 166, allowing the use of LIFO to dealers in securities; and U.C.C., § 8-102(1)(C), defining a security or intangible property.

[188] See AICPA, "Issues Paper: Identification and Discussion of Certain Financial Accounting and Reporting Issues Concerning LIFO Inventories," (Nov. 30, 1984); Securities Exchange Commission, Staff Acct. Bull. 58, Topic 5-L (Mar. 19, 1985).

[189] See Amity Leather Prods., Co., 82 TC 726 (1984).

[190] See, e.g., Peninsula Steel Prods. & Equip. Co., 78 TC 1029 (1982); Spang Indus., Inc. v. United States, 791 F2d 906 (Fed. Cir. 1986); RECO Indus., 83 TC 912 (1984). The use of LIFO with long-term contracts has since been proscribed. See Treas. Reg. §§ 1.451-3(a)(6), 1.451-3(d)(8); IRC § 460; Notice 89-15, 1989-1 CB 816.

[191] See discussion supra ¶ 7.04[3][e], regarding the effect of technological change on the reconstruction of base costs for new items.

[192] Treas. Reg. § 1.446-1(c)(1)(ii), as it existed prior to its amendment by the final economic performance regulations. See discussion at ¶ 4.04[3].

method has not been explicitly authorized by the regulations, it certainly has not been prohibited. Of course, if there was any such consistency with the regulations, the Commissioner and Chief Counsel could not have stated that the method could not be denied *per se*.[193]

No court has yet been asked to focus directly on the use of component costing. However, the decisions that have been reached suggest that it would be approved. Perhaps the most significant opinion relating to this matter is that in *Amity Leather Products, Co.*[194]

Amity Leather dealt with the application of the dollar-value LIFO method to a manufacturer of billfolds in the United States and Puerto Rico. The principles of the case can be illustrated using the following simplified facts. Assume that the manufacturer in *Amity Leather* produced billfolds domestically at a cost of $10 per billfold and that its beginning inventory consisted of one billfold as follows:

Cost of one billfold in beginning inventory:

5 units of RM at $1 per unit =	$5.00
5 units of L&OH at $1 per unit =	5.00
	$10.00

Assume that the manufacturer then learned that identical billfolds could be produced in Puerto Rico at a lower price, because the processing costs in Puerto Rico (i.e., the costs of labor and overhead) were only $.60 per unit. In other words, the cost of manufacturing the billfold in Puerto Rico would be as follows:

Cost of billfold:

5 units of RM at $1 per unit =	$5.00
5 units of L&OH at $0.60 per unit =	3.00
	$8.00

Based on the cheaper costs, the manufacturer decided to shift its production activities from the United States to Puerto Rico. Assume that its end-of-year inventory consisted of one billfold, which was produced in Puerto Rico.

Under these simplified facts, the issue before the court in *Amity Leather* was whether the end-of-year billfold should be assigned a LIFO value of $10 as asserted by the Commissioner or $8 as asserted by the taxpayer. The Commissioner argued that the billfold in year-end inventory was identical to the billfold in beginning-of-the-year inventory and, hence, that it must be assigned the same cost. In so arguing in favor of a $10 value, the Commis-

---

[193] See discussion accompanying note 203.

[194] Amity Leather Prods., Co., 82 TC 726 (1984).

sioner asserted that: "changes in [the] cost to produce or acquire an item do not create a new item."[195]

The court rejected the Commissioner's position and held for the taxpayer. The court pointed out that the nature of items contained in a pool "must be similar enough to allow a comparison between ending inventory and base-year inventory."[196] However, the court added that "[b]ecause the change in the price of an item determines the price index and the index affects the computation of increments or decrements in the LIFO inventory, the definition and scope of an item are extremely important to the clear reflection of income."[197]

The court then stated: "[I]f factors other than inflation enter into the cost of inventory items, a reliable index cannot be computed."[198] The court recognized that a change in the cost structure of a product must not be allowed to offset inflation in the component costs of producing the product. The court stated:

[I]f a taxpayer's inventory experiences mix changes that result in the substitution of less expensive goods for more expensive goods, the treatment of those goods as a single item increases taxable income. This occurs because any inflation in the cost of an item is offset by the reduction in cost resulting from the shift to less expensive goods.[199]

Based on this analysis, the court decided that the Puerto Rican billfold should be treated as a different item from the domestic billfold. This conclusion was reached even though the products themselves were identical. Simply stated, the court recognized that when there is a change in the cost structure associated with a particular item, that change in cost structure must not be allowed to affect the determination of inflation, and under a more narrow definition of "item," "the impact of inflation is more accurately eliminated, and [the taxpayer's] income is more clearly reflected."[200]

With respect to the Commissioner's position that the reduction in processing costs should be ignored because the term "item" should be viewed as a finished good and the only good in question was a billfold, the court stated:

The first time that we were confronted with this problem [of defining the word 'item'], we held that in the case of a *retailer* of goods, an 'item' refers to a finished product of inventory and not to its individual components. *Wendle Ford Sales, Inc.* . . . We are unaware, however, of

---

[195] Id. at 739.

[196] Id. at 733.

[197] Id.

[198] Id.

[199] Id.

[200] Id. at 740.

any authority that defines that term [item] as it applies to a manufacturer. Our task, therefore, is to view that term in the context of a manufacturing operation in a manner that most closely satisfies the purpose of maintaining inventories, i.e., the clear reflection of income.[201] (Emphasis by court.)

The court noted that the Commissioner's position on the definition of "item":

would lead to an inaccurate measure of any inflation or deflation [and] would result in the assumed or 'constructive' substitution of less expensive goods for more expensive goods in the cost of goods sold computation, and any inflation in the cost of the domestic billfolds would be at least partially offset by the shift to the Puerto Rican billfolds in the LIFO valuation of the inventory.[202]

This last statement is quite significant. The court rejected a result that would offset the inflation in costs comprising a product by a change in the cost structure of that very product. The court thus makes it clear that changes in the cost structure of a product (such as those arising from technological advance) should not be permitted to offset the effects of inflation in properly applying LIFO.

A position denying the validity of component costing is essentially the same as the government's position in *Amity Leather*, except that the asserted reduction in costs in the case of component costing is often due to a decrease in the number of labor hours necessary to produce a product rather than in the labor rate. In other words, assume that the situation is exactly the same as it was in *Amity Leather*, except that the domestic labor was able to produce billfolds with only three units of processing costs because of new technology. In such a case, the cost of producing the billfold domestically and in Puerto Rico would be as follows:

Cost of billfold in United States:

5 units of RM at $1 per unit =	$5.00
3 units of L&OH at $1 per unit =	3.00
	$8.00

Cost of billfold in Puerto Rico:

5 units of RM at $1 per unit. =	$5.00
5 units of L&OH at $0.60 per unit =	3.00
	$8.00

As this table shows, regardless of the place of manufacture, the billfold would cost $8. Yet, the government's position on component costing would reject an $8 valuation and require instead a valuation of $10. Such a position is inconsistent with *Amity Leather* or seeks to distinguish *Amity Leather* on the

---

[201] Id.

[202] Id.

basis that a reduction in the hourly rate of processing costs (which reduces the aggregate processing cost to $3 per product) differs from a corresponding reduction in the quantity of labor. There would seem to be no basis for such a distinction. The change in the cost structure should in either case cause the billfold included in ending inventory to be a new item under product costing, and the cost of a new item is the same under product costing and component costing.

Finally, it should be noted that the consequence of the use of component costing identified by the IRS—a decline in the LIFO value of the inventory when there has been no decline in the number of products—is not unique to component costing. A similar consequence may arise under the use of raw material LIFO and under link-chain dollar-value LIFO with product costing. Simply stated, the persons at the National Office who are interested in this matter are reviewing again particular means of computation that have been in existence for more than 50 years. These computational procedures are often essential elements to the use of dollar-value LIFO by manufacturers, and their elimination would have the practical effect of denying LIFO to these taxpayers. The IRS should accept component cost.[203]

Following *Amity Leather*, the Tax Court had another occasion to determine the effect of a change in costs on the definition of "item". In *Hamilton Industries, Inc.*,[204] an issue was whether goods acquired in a bargain purchase by a manufacturer consisted of the same or different "items" from identical goods thereafter manufactured by the taxpayer. Although the goods were recognized as being the same, the issue was raised because there was a substantial difference between the low "bargain" cost of the acquired goods and the replacement cost of the subsequently produced goods. The change in cost was treated by the court as creating a different item.

This conclusion seems questionable. Unlike the situation where a manufacturer's cost structure changes, the *Hamilton* situation merely involved the purchase of items at a lower price than the then-applicable reproduction cost. To treat the items acquired at a bargain price as constituting different items in this circumstance, merely because the taxpayer obtained them at a low price, effectively denies the taxpayer its right to adopt LIFO for this bargain purchased inventory.

---

[203] In a letter to Mr. Leonard Podolin, Chairman of the AICPA's Tax Executive Committee, the Commissioner and Chief Counsel stated that use of LIFO component costing was not impermissible *per se*. Instead, its availability should depend on whether its application will clearly reflect income. Moreover, the letter made it clear that component costing could be permitted even in cases where the results produced were not identical to the results produced under product costing. Daily Tax Rep. (BNA) No. 152 (Aug. 6, 1992), at L-24.

[204] Hamilton Indus., Inc., 97 TC 120 (1991). See further discussion of *Hamilton* infra ¶ 7.08[2].

[4] Retail LIFO

Taxpayers who cost inventories on the basis of the retail method are expressly authorized to use LIFO in conjunction with that method.[205] Under the retail method, published price indexes prepared by the U.S. Bureau of Labor Statistics (BLS) may be used to reduce the current costs of items to their base costs. Current costs are determined under the retail method, except that an adjustment must be made to exclude from that cost any previously computed write-downs from cost to market.[206] The National Office has held in a private letter ruling that published price indexes may be used to reduce the current cost of the taxpayer's ending inventory even where those current costs have been reduced by a change in the taxpayer's pricing policy.[207]

[5] Simplified LIFO Methods

The LIFO method has always been considered inherently more complex than other methods, and, as a consequence, it has not been used by many taxpayers for whom it might otherwise be beneficial.[208] One of the more complex administrative and record-keeping requirements is that of accumulating the internal data necessary to develop price indexes. Although simplification techniques are available, such as the use of a published price index to convert FIFO values to LIFO, they are available only to specified taxpayers, such as department stores and others eligible to use the retail method of pricing LIFO inventories.[209] Other taxpayers are permitted to use published indexes only where they can demonstrate the accuracy of the use of the index to the satisfaction of the District Director.[210]

In early 1981, the Treasury proposed regulations that allowed taxpayers not eligible to use the retail method to use published government indexes in their dollar-value LIFO calculations.[211] Shortly thereafter, Congress ap-

---

[205] Treas. Reg. § 1.472-1(k); see also Hutzler Bros. Co., 8 TC 14 (1947), where such method was permitted by the Tax Court.

[206] See description of retail method at ¶ 6.10[4].

[207] Priv. Ltr. Rul. 8940082 (July 14, 1989).

[208] H.R. Rep. No. 97-215, 97th Cong., 1st Sess. 226 (1981).

[209] Treas. Reg. § 1.472-8(e)(1). See discussion supra ¶ 7.04[4].

[210] Rev. Rul. 75-181, 1975-1 CB 150, 151 provides:

[E]xcept for department stores meeting the requirements of Rev. Rul. 23, BLS indexes will not be accepted by the Service in connection with the use of the LIFO method unless taxpayers can independently demonstrate the accuracy, reliability, and suitability of the use of such indexes to the satisfaction of the district director. In the absence of such a showing, taxpayers must develop their own indexes based on sound statistical methods using their own specific data on prices and inventory quantities.

[211] See Prop. Reg. § 1.472-8(e)(3), 1981-1 CB 757.

proved this effort by expressly authorizing the Treasury to prescribe regulations allowing taxpayers to use published government indexes in making their dollar-value LIFO computations.[212] On March 16, 1982, final regulations were issued.[213] These regulations, which are applicable to taxable years beginning after December 31, 1981, and to taxpayers other than those already eligible to use price indexes prepared by BLS, authorized the use of published government indexes in pricing dollar-value LIFO inventory.[214]

In addition, as part of the 1986 Act, Congress repealed Section 474 (as it then existed)[215] and replaced it with new rules providing a simplified dollar-value LIFO method to qualifying small businesses. Consequently, as a result of the 1986 Act, taxpayers who seek to use a simplified LIFO procedure may adopt the price index procedure referred to in the preceding paragraph or, if eligible, the new simplified method under Section 474. For taxpayers whose average gross receipts exceed $5 million, only the price index procedures are available as an alternative to regular LIFO methods. For taxpayers whose average gross receipts are $5 million or less, there is a choice of either of the two simplified procedures in addition to the regular LIFO methods. The simplified method of Section 474 may be easier to apply for many taxpayers than the price index method.

[a] Price Index Method

[i] Operation of method

General description. Under the simplified price index method, the taxpayer computes its inventory price index by reference to selected consumer or producer price indexes, using the following steps. First, the inventory items in each pool are classified according to listings in the appropriate tables of the *CPI Detailed Report* or the BLS *Producer Prices and Price Indexes.* Based on these listings, the items are assigned an index category. An appropriate consumer or producer index is then determined for each category.[216] Next, these published indexes are used to calculate the index for each category. Finally, an index is calculated for the specific pool. Once the inventory price index computation method is elected, the taxpayer must use the same method in determining the value for all its inventory.[217]

---

[212] Section 472(f), enacted as part of the Economic Recovery Tax Act of 1981, Pub. L. No. 97-34, 95 Stat. 172 (1981).

[213] Treas. Reg. §1.472-8(e)(3); TD 7814, 1982-1 CB 84.

[214] Treas. Reg. § 1.472-8(e)(3).

[215] Section 474, as it existed prior to the 1986 Act, provided certain small businesses with the opportunity to use one LIFO inventory pool, notwithstanding the normal pooling requirements. See discussion supra ¶ 7.04[3][a][iii].

[216] Treas. Reg. § 1.472-8(e)(3)(iii)(B).

[217] Treas. Reg. § 1.472-8(e)(3)(i).

Selection of index categories. The regulations provide the following procedure for assigning inventory items to index categories:[218]

1. Each specific inventory item that constitutes 10 percent or more of the total inventory value is placed in its own separate index category. The index category selected must be the most detailed index category that includes the item. Any other inventory items of the taxpayer that are also listed in that index category must be included in that category.

2. For remaining items, the taxpayer, beginning with the most detailed index categories, selects the first index category that contains the remaining inventory items. If this category in the aggregate constitutes 10 percent or more of the total inventory value, it becomes a separate index category. This procedure is repeated until all inventory items of the taxpayer are included in an index category, or until the remaining inventory items in the aggregate constitute less than 10 percent of the total inventory value, or until it is determined that an appropriate index category does not exist for the remaining items.

3. If the remaining inventory items constitute less than 10 percent of the total inventory value, the index category selected for these remaining items is the most detailed index category that includes all the items. If an appropriate index category does not exist for the remaining inventory items, they are combined in a miscellaneous index category. The index category selected must not be any less detailed than either the 11 general categories of consumer goods described in Tables 3 and 5 of the *CPI Detailed Report* or the 15 general categories of producer goods described in Table 6 of the *BLS Producer Prices and Price Indexes.*

Selection and calculation of indexes for each category. If an index category is determined under step 1 above, the appropriate index is the published index for that category.[219] If the index category is determined under step 2 or step 3 above, the appropriate index should be a weighted average of the published indexes for the index category items actually present in the particular grouping, weighted according to the appropriate weights published by BLS.[220] For example, if the index category contains numerous items, the appropriate index should be a weighted average of the published indexes for the various index categories actually present, weighted according to the designated factors.

---

[218] Treas. Reg. § 1.472-8(e)(3)(iii)(B); see also Rev. Proc. 8457, 1984-2 CB 496, which details the outlined calculations.

[219] Treas. Reg. § 1.472-8(e)(3)(iii)(B)(4).

[220] Treas. Reg. § 1.472-8(e)(3)(iii)(B)(5).

The use of the weight factors published by BLS is limited, in this context, to the weighted determination of an appropriate index for an index category.[221]

The required use of BLS weights is potentially distorting. BLS weights are based on the percentage weight of each index category reflected in the composite producers price index for "all commodities," a measure of inflation for the economy as a whole. By using such weights, rather than the relative weights of the actual items in the taxpayer's inventory, a potentially distorting and arbitrary result may occur.

Manufacturers, processors, wholesalers, jobbers, and distributors may select indexes only from tables in the *BLS Producer Prices and Price Indexes.*[222] These indexes should be selected from the appropriate month or months for determining the taxpayer's current-year costs or the taxpayer can make a binding election of a representative month.[223] Once the indexes have been selected, the selected index must be converted into a cost price index.[224] Specific instructions are not permitted as to how the conversion to a cost price index is to occur. Although it is generally recognized that the conversion would occur by reducing the published price index by the taxpayer's gross profit margin, the determination of this gross profit margin for this purpose is unstated. Possible alternatives include use of a single gross profit percentage developed for the taxpayer as a whole, use of a single gross profit percentage attributable to each pool, and, assuming the data is readily available, use of a separate gross profit percentage for each category of goods in ending inventory. Of course, use of a cost conversion, in turn, raises questions as to how and whether it should be applied to work-in-process.

The conversion of the price index to a cost index is most important. As a general rule, declining profit margins will increase the effective index whereas increasing profit margins would decrease the resulting index. In determining the level of detail required for purposes of making the cost conversion, taxpayers and tax practitioners should assume that agents will review the computations carefully, but agents should apply reason, common sense, and understanding in determining the acceptability of the cost conversion process. To the extent too much detail is required, the benefits of applying the simplified indexing method will be greatly reduced.

Retailers using the retail inventory method may select indexes from either the *CPI Detailed Report* or the *BLS Producer Prices and Price Indexes,* but if the indexes that could be selected from both reports are equally

---

[221] Id.

[222] Treas. Reg. § 1.472-8(e)(3)(iii)(C).

[223] Id. If the taxpayer uses earliest acquisitions to determine the current-year cost of the inventory pool, a month at the beginning of the year should be used. If latest acquisitions are used, the taxpayer should select a month from the end of the year.

[224] Treas. Reg. § 1.472-8(e)(3)(iii)(C).

appropriate, the *CPI Detailed Report* must be used.[225] Retailers not using the retail inventory method may also select indexes from either publication, but they must select indexes from *BLS Producer Prices and Price Indexes* if both are equally appropriate.[226]

Retailers using the retail inventory method must use the appropriate index for the last month of their taxable year.[227] Where the retail inventory method is not used, taxpayers should select indexes from the month or months most appropriate to their method of determining the inventory's current year costs or make a one-time binding election of an appropriate representative month during the tax year.[228] Generally, once the taxpayer has selected an appropriate representative month, the Commissioner will not consent to a request for a change in the representative month unless the taxpayer can demonstrate that the previously selected month is no longer an appropriate representative month.[229]

Retailers using the retail inventory method must determine the total value of ending inventory at retail selling prices.[230] Taxpayers not using the retail method must determine the value of ending inventory at current-year costs by reference to the actual cost of the most recently purchased goods, the first goods purchased, or the average cost of goods purchased during the year.[231]

When the index categories and corresponding indexes are selected from Table 3 or Table 5 of the *CPI Detailed Report* (pertaining, respectively, to food and nonfood categories), the proper BLS weights are those published in Table 1 of the *Relative Importance of Components in the Consumer Price Indexes.*[232] When a taxpayer selects index categories and corresponding indexes from Table 6 of the *BLS Producer Prices and Price Indexes* (pertaining to commodity groupings and individual items), the proper BLS weights are those published in Table 13 of the *Supplement to Producer Prices and Price Indexes.*[233]

For a retailer not using the retail inventory method who selects an index from the *CPI Detailed Report*, the selected index must be converted to a cost price index because the *CPI Detailed Report* measures changes in retail

---

[225] Id.

[226] Id.

[227] Id. Retailers using the retail method must comply with this rule. See description of retail method at ¶ 6.10[4] and supra ¶ 7.04[4]. All other taxpayers have the option of choosing a representative month.

[228] Id.

[229] See Rev. Rul. 89-29, 1989-1 CB 168.

[230] Rev. Proc. 84-57, 1984-2 CB 496.

[231] Id. at 497.

[232] Id.

[233] Id.

prices, not in wholesale or cost prices.[234] For a retailer using the retail inventory method who selects a price index from the *BLS Producer Prices and Price Indexes*, the selected index must be converted to a retail price index.[235] Revenue Procedure 84-57[236] demonstrates the proper conversion of indexes, based on the changes in the cost complements of the gross margins of the individual index categories.

Determination of inventory pools and pool indexes. After the inventory categories and indexes are determined, they are grouped into a pool or pools according to their respective items. A retailer, wholesaler, jobber, or distributor may establish an inventory pool or pools for any group of goods included within one of the 11 general categories of consumer goods described in the *CPI Detailed Report.*[237] Inventory pools that constitute less than 5 percent of the total inventory value may be combined to form a single miscellaneous inventory pool.[238] If the resulting miscellaneous inventory pool constitutes less than 5 percent of the total inventory value, the pool can be combined with the largest inventory pool.[239]

Manufacturers and processors may establish natural-business-unit pools.[240] A natural-business-unit pool consists of all items entering into the entire inventory investment for a natural business unit of the business enterprise.[241] Substantially similar inventory items may also be grouped into multiple pools in certain circumstances.[242]

If more than one inventory category is included in an inventory pool, the pool index must be the weighted average of all the indexes for the actual categories in the pool.[243] The weighted average is calculated based on the actual costs in ending inventory of the respective categories.[244]

Inventory price index. Under the applicable regulations, only taxpayers who are eligible small businesses, as defined by Section 474(b) (as it existed prior to the 1986 Act) are entitled to use 100 percent of the calculated price

---

[234] Id.

[235] Treas. Reg. § 1.472-8(e)(3)(iii)(C).

[236] Rev. Proc. 84-57, 1984-2 CB 496.

[237] Treas. Reg. § 1.472-8(e)(3)(iv).

[238] Id.

[239] Id.

[240] Rev. Proc. 84-57, 1984-2 CB 496, 499; see also Treas. Reg. §§ 1.472-8(b)–1.472-8(d).

[241] Treas. Reg. § 1.472-8(b). See discussion supra ¶ 7.04[3][a][i].

[242] Rev. Proc. 84-57, 1984-2 CB 496, 499. As this revenue procedure points out, the formation of detailed rules in this area is not feasible. The taxpayer should consult Treas. Reg. § 1.472-8(b). See also discussion supra ¶ 7.04[3][a][ii].

[243] Rev. Proc. 84-57, 1984-2 CB 496, 499.

[244] Id.

index.[245] All other taxpayers must use 80 percent of the calculated price index.[246]

Under old Section 474(b), an "eligible small business" was one whose actual gross receipts for the three-taxable-year period ending with the taxable year did not exceed $2 million. New Section 474(c) defines "eligible small business" for years covered by the 1986 Act as one whose average annual gross receipts for the preceding three taxable years do not exceed $5 million. It is not yet clear whether the Treasury will use the old or new definition for purposes of applying the price index method to years covered by the 1986 Act.

When calculating the final inventory price index, the calculated price index for a specific inventory pool is multiplied by either 80 or 100 percent, as applicable, in order to determine the allowable inventory price index. This calculation is computed on a cumulative basis for changes over several years.[247] In this sense, the approach followed is that of double-extension and not link-chain.

For example, if the selected index for a category of goods increased 10 percent for the period December 1981 to December 1983, the inventory price index will reflect either a 10 percent change for an eligible small business or an 8 percent change (80 percent of 10 percent) for other taxpayers. If the selected index increases 20 percent for the period December 1981 to December 1983, the inventory price index will reflect either a 20 percent change for an eligible small business or a 16 percent change (80 percent of 20 percent) for other taxpayers.

Although intended to simplify the LIFO computations of taxpayers, the simplified indexing method has not had this effect. Most manufacturers, who produce a wide variety of items subject to frequent change, find use of the simplified indexing method much too complicated. The time that would be required in making the necessary determinations under the simplified method often exceeds the time, effort, and cost that would be required in developing internal indexes.

[ii] **Adoption of price index method.**   A taxpayer not on a LIFO method may adopt the price index LIFO method merely by indicating on a completed Form 970, or in such other manner as may be acceptable to the Commissioner, that the method is being adopted and by listing each inventory pool, the type of goods included in each pool, and the consumer or producer price index or indexes selected for each inventory pool.[248] Form

---

[245] Treas. Reg. § 1.472-8(e)(3)(ii).

[246] Id.

[247] Id.

[248] Treas. Reg. § 1.472-8(e)(3)(v).

970 with the relevant data should be attached to the taxpayer's income tax return for the taxable year of the adoption.[249]

The selection of a consumer or producer price index for specific inventory items to calculate an inventory price index is a method of accounting.[250] Accordingly, a taxpayer must obtain the prior approval of the IRS to change a price index.[251] If an existing LIFO taxpayer receives permission to make that change, any already-existing LIFO layers are retained, but the year of change will constitute a new base year for making subsequent LIFO computations.[252]

[iii] Changing to price index method. When a taxpayer already on LIFO wants to change to the price index method or when the prior approval of the IRS is otherwise required, Form 970 and accompanying data should be attached to Form 3115 and filed in accordance with the rules governing changes in accounting methods under Treasury Regulation § 1.446-1(e).[253] (See Chapter 8 regarding changes in methods of accounting.

Where the taxpayer previously used another method to determine the dollar-value LIFO prices of the inventory pool, any layers of inventory increments and their LIFO values should be retained when the taxpayer changes to the simplified LIFO method.[254] However, instead of using the initial LIFO year as the base year, the year of change will thereafter become the base year for determining the LIFO value of the inventory pool for all taxable years. The base-year costs of layers of increments in the pool at the beginning of the year of change should be restated in terms of the new base-year costs, using the year of change as the new base year.[255] This is the same procedure employed when the taxpayer changes its indexes. Despite the regulatory provision that existing LIFO layers will be retained, some agents have asserted on audit that the regulatory provision applies only if the taxpayer demonstrates that its prior LIFO computations were accurate. To the extent the taxpayer is unable to make such a demonstration, agents sometimes propose Section 481 adjustments. Such proposals seem at odds with the objective of the regulatory indexing method. The method is intended to alleviate the complexities of determining internal indexes. Consequently, taxpayers for whom the method may be most attractive would include those who have difficulty in computing internal indexes. Thus, those taxpayers would be the ones expected to receive the benefit of a change to the indexing

---

[249] Id.

[250] Treas. Reg. § 1.472-8(e)(3)(iii)(B).

[251] Id.

[252] Id.

[253] Id.

[254] Treas. Reg. § 1.472-8(e)(3)(vi).

[255] Id.

method without the need for a revaluation of prior layers and computations of a Section 481 adjustment. Indeed, if the taxpayers had the ability to recompute what the prior layers would have been on a precisely computed internal index, there presumably would be no reason for the taxpayers to adopt the simplified indexing method.

[b]　Simplified Dollar-Value LIFO: Section 474

Under the simplified dollar-value LIFO method, which was enacted as part of the 1986 Act, eligible taxpayers are permitted to make their LIFO computations on the basis of published government indexes.[256] Under this method, inventory items are grouped into pools in accordance with the so-called major categories published in the *BLS Producer Price Index* or the *BLS Consumer Price Index*.[257] For the Producer Price Index, the term "major category" means any of the two-digit standard industrial classifications in the *Producer Prices Data Report*. For the Consumer Price Index, the term "major category" means any of the general expenditure categories published in the *CPI Detailed Report*.

The annual price change in inventory costs of the pool is the corresponding change in the major category on which the pool is based. These annual changes are then used to determine LIFO values, just as under a link-chain LIFO method.[258] In other words, taxpayers may rely on published price indexes rather than having to compute their own price indexes.

The simplified dollar-value method is available only to taxpayers whose average annual gross receipts for their three preceding taxable years do not exceed $5 million.[259] In determining the eligibility of a taxpayer for this method, aggregation rules are provided to treat all members of a controlled group as a single taxpayer.[260] For this purpose, all persons are treated as members of a controlled group if those persons are treated as a single employer under Section 52.[261]

The rules governing adoptions and changes to the simplified dollar-value method and changes from that method are generally set forth in Section 474(d).[262] It is anticipated that the Treasury will provide more detailed rules in the future.

In general, non-LIFO taxpayers who wish to adopt the simplified dollar-value method and LIFO taxpayers who wish to change to that method, may

---

[256] IRC § 474.

[257] See IRC § 474(b).

[258] See discussion of link-chain method supra ¶ 7.04[3][b][iii].

[259] IRC § 474(c).

[260] IRC § 474(d)(1)(A).

[261] IRC § 474(d)(1)(B).

[262] See IRC §§ 474(d)(2), 474(d)(4).

do so without the prior approval of the IRS. If the change represents the adoption of a LIFO method by a non-LIFO taxpayer, all the other conditions applicable to the adoption of LIFO must be satisfied.[263] If a LIFO taxpayer changes to that method, the LIFO inventory as of the end of the year prior to the year of change becomes the simplified dollar-value LIFO inventory at the beginning of the year of change, and the year of change represents a new base year.

Once on the simplified dollar-value LIFO method, the prior approval of the IRS will be required for a change from that method as long as the taxpayer remains eligible to use the simplified method.[264] (See Chapter 8 for discussion of changes in accounting methods.)

For taxpayers who must change from the simplified dollar-value method because they cease to remain eligible for that method, no specific rules have been provided. However, the legislative history to the 1986 Act indicates that without the prior approval of the Commissioner, the taxpayer may return to the method from which it changed to the simplified method, or the taxpayer may change to any other method to which it would have been able to change without the prior approval of the Commissioner.[265] To illustrate, an eligible FIFO taxpayer may adopt the simplified dollar-value LIFO method without prior IRS approval assuming all requirements are satisfied.[266] If this taxpayer later becomes ineligible for continued use of the simplified method, the taxpayer may, without the prior approval of the Commissioner, return to its original FIFO method or, because a FIFO taxpayer may adopt LIFO without the prior approval of the IRS, may change to another LIFO method.

¶ 7.05 TERMINATION OF LIFO

Section 472 allows every taxpayer to adopt LIFO as a matter of right.[267] Only three statutory conditions must be satisfied: (1) There must be a valid election

---

[263] See discussion supra ¶ 7.03.

[264] IRC § 474(d)(2)(B)(ii).

[265] See H.R. Rep. No. 99-841, 99th Cong., 2d Sess., Conference Report to accompany H.R. 3838, Vol. II at 291-292 (Sept. 18, 1986).

[266] See discussion supra ¶ 7.03.

[267] See, e.g., John Wanamaker Philadelphia, Inc. v. United States, 359 F2d 437 (Ct. Cl. 1966), where the court stated that taxpayers have "an absolute right" to use the LIFO method of accounting and that the Commissioner's discretion, except for proposing necessary or appropriate adjustments, is quite narrow. But see Hamilton Indus., Inc., 97 TC 120 (1991), where, in requiring goods acquired in a bargain purchase to be treated as different items from identical goods thereafter manufactured, the court effectively denied the taxpayer the right to benefit from an adoption of LIFO for the inventory acquired in the bargain purchase. In effect, the court's decision required the low-basis inventory acquired in the bargain purchase to be flowed

of LIFO; (2) there must be no violation of the LIFO conformity requirement; and (3) LIFO inventories must be valued at cost (i.e., there must be a restoration of prior market write-downs, and subsequent market write-downs are not permitted). Even if a taxpayer fails to satisfy any one or more of these conditions, termination of its use of LIFO does not automatically result. Rather, it is discretionary with the IRS. In fact, the IRS is not required to terminate the use of LIFO even if the taxpayer deliberately violates one of the statutory conditions. Correspondingly, a taxpayer may not effect or force a termination of LIFO by violating one of these conditions.

In addition to the three statutory conditions, the IRS stated a fourth condition in Revenue Procedure 79-23,[268] which stated that LIFO may be terminated if the taxpayer fails to maintain adequate books and records. The adequacy of these records relates to their substantiation of the taxpayer's present LIFO method and computations and not to their ability (or lack thereof) to substantiate the LIFO method or computations preferred or proposed by the IRS on audit.[269]

---

through to cost of goods sold just as if the taxpayer had been on FIFO.

[268] Rev. Proc. 79-23, 1979-1 CB 564. See Tech. Adv. Mem. 8744003 (June 30, 1987), for an illustration of the manner in which the National Office applies Rev. Proc. 79-23 to asserted deficiencies in the taxpayer's LIFO pooling and computations.

[269] In Tech. Adv. Mem. 8851001 (July 28, 1988), the National Office considered an agent's position that a taxpayer's books and records were inadequate because the taxpayer was unable to compute the value of its LIFO inventory in a manner in which the agent considered appropriate. The agent contended that the taxpayer's books and records would not permit it to value its inventory using a proper method. However, the agent also acknowledged that the taxpayer's books and records did support the taxpayer's own LIFO computations. The National Office concluded that a termination for inadequate books and records in these circumstances would not be warranted under Rev. Proc. 79-23, because that revenue procedure contemplated "that the taxpayer's books and records need not substantiate any computation other than the taxpayer's CURRENT method of inventory valuation." This position, if followed consistently, should relieve taxpayers of anxiety over whether their record-keeping systems would be adequate to produce results under methods other than or in addition to the LIFO methods they have selected. This conclusion also necessarily suggests that required adjustments or changes to a taxpayer's LIFO system will have to be worked out in a practical, reasonable manner so as to accommodate the taxpayer's then-existing records.

In Priv. Ltr. Rul. 9010039 (Dec. 11, 1987), a taxpayer was unable to compute its LIFO inventories after it discovered that when it switched to a new computer system, the original inventory cost information had not been copied into the new system and had been destroyed. The taxpayer thereafter sought to change from its use of the LIFO method. The IRS focused on the technical rules governing the procedures to be followed in requesting a change in method of accounting. However, in doing so, the IRS referred to the inability of the taxpayer to compute inventories on a cost basis, one of the termination events set forth in Rev. Proc. 79-23. The IRS made no reference to the inadequacy of the taxpayer's books and records as a result of the destruction of the original cost records. This left open the possibility that the IRS might have excused the destruction and permitted a continuation of LIFO (had the taxpayer

For situations that do not involve any of these four specified circumstances, the IRS has indicated that deficiencies or inadequacies in a taxpayer's LIFO method will not be a basis for termination but, rather, only a basis for making adjustments. Moreover, although the degree of inadequacy in books and records that will sustain a termination of LIFO is uncertain, the overall approach taken by the IRS in the revenue procedure seems reasonable. LIFO terminations should not be proposed except in the clearest of circumstances. For example, in the context of the overall discretion afforded taxpayers with respect to inventory costing and LIFO computational procedures, no single approach is required or possible. The LIFO statute and accompanying regulations illustrate the great flexibility afforded to taxpayers.[270] The regulations provide that the LIFO method is not dependent on the character of the taxpayer's business or the nature of its inventory, and the method may be adopted as of the close of any taxable year.[271] The regulations also make it clear that no particular computational procedure is required. For example, Treasury Regulation § 1.472-1(1) provides:

> If a taxpayer uses consistently the so-called "dollar-value method" of pricing inventories, or any other method of computation established to the satisfaction of the Commissioner as reasonably adaptable to the purpose and intent of section 472 and this section, and if such taxpayer elects under section 472 to use the LIFO inventory method authorized by such section, the taxpayer's opening and closing inventories shall be determined under section 472 by the use of the appropriate adaptation.

In light of the foregoing, the IRS should not propose LIFO terminations in any but the most egregious of circumstances.

[1] Judicial Attitude

[a] In General

The courts have recognized the mandate of Congress to make LIFO available to all taxpayers without any requirements as to the precise manner in which the LIFO calculations are to be made. For example, the Tax Court

---

so requested) if the taxpayer had been able to estimate what its original inventory cost had been. Such a result would be reasonable. It would seem entirely too drastic a result to require a termination of LIFO upon an inadvertent unintentional error such as this. One alternative to termination would be to allow the continued use of the LIFO method but to require the taxpayer to establish a new base date for subsequent computations. Such an action, together with other necessary adjustments, would reasonably ensure accurate computations of LIFO inventories on a prospective basis without requiring a restoration to income of the prior LIFO reserve on account of such an unfortunate error.

[270] IRC § 472(a); Treas. Reg. § 1.472-1(a).

[271] Treas. Reg. § 1.472-1(a).

has indicated that in making LIFO available to all taxpayers at their option, Congress cut back on the Commissioner's almost plenary authority as to changes in accounting methods.[272]

Taking into account the many ways in which computations may be made and information developed by particular taxpayers, the courts have also recognized the need for variety in LIFO calculations. For example, in *Hutzler Brothers Co.*,[273] focusing on the broad statutory authority for the general use of LIFO, the court stated:

> [I]t does not follow . . . that, when the [LIFO] statute was amended to acquire its present all-embracing character, it was designed to cover only the industries which originally sought its enactment. The conclusion is rather to be drawn that, like all revenue legislation, particularly of a relief character, the purpose of the lawmakers was to have it apply in general terms to all those coming within its provisions.[274]

In effect, the court recognized that while there were no specific procedures expressly authorizing the use of a dollar-value LIFO computation, it was clear that the statute was intended to be available to all taxpayers. The issue was therefore whether the dollar-value technique was so inherently wrong that the use of LIFO should be denied. In approving the use of LIFO in that situation, the court stated:

> The computations involved may be somewhat extensive, but they lack neither adequate clarity nor logic, and they cannot be discarded as unduly burdensome in light of the permissive character of the statutory option. We conclude that adaptation of the LIFO theory to inventories maintained . . . by the present petitioner is permissible and proper within the provisions of section 22(d).[275]

The need for the practical approach is also evident in more recent cases in which the courts have generally focused on particular adjustments being proposed by the IRS. For instance, in *Fox Chevrolet, Inc.*,[276] the court stated that dollar-value LIFO was developed to carry out the Congressional purpose of making LIFO available to all taxpayers when some might otherwise be

---

[272] Peninsula Steel Prods. & Equip. Co., 78 TC 1029 (1982). The court added:

Respondent has failed to show us a policy problem so overwhelming as to force us to conclude that the Congress could not have meant what it said. [Citation omitted]. The Congress has enacted its judgment regarding LIFO; we must guard against the efforts of the parties to persuade us to diminish [citation omitted] or expand [citation omitted] what the Congress has chosen to enact.

Id. at 1059.

[273] Hutzler Bros. Co., 8 TC 14 (1947).

[274] Id. at 29.

[275] Id. at 31.

[276] Fox Chevrolet, Inc., 76 TC 708 (1981).

excluded because of the practical problems of accounting for complex inventories by matching specific items.[277]

[b] Regarding Proposed Terminations

Since the adoption of the general LIFO statute in 1939, relatively few cases have been litigated in which the IRS has proposed a termination of LIFO. Of these, most involved a failure to file Form 970 or otherwise to properly elect LIFO.[278] Others involved the use of LIFO in connection with real estate or the completed contract method,[279] or asserted violations of the LIFO financial conformity requirement.[280] Only a few cases involved the propriety of a taxpayer's LIFO computations. Of these latter cases involving computations, most involved the use of a dollar-value method prior to the

---

[277] Id. at 727. See also Richardson Invs., Inc., 76 TC 736 (1981), where the court denied the IRS proposal to require the taxpayer to use a large number of inventory pools in connection with its LIFO computations. Quoting Wendle Ford Sales, Inc., 72 TC 447 (1979), acq. 1980-2 CB 2, the court stated that such a proposal would "create serious practical impediments to its [LIFO's] application." 76 TC at 747; Amity Leather Prods. Co., 82 TC 726 (1984), where the court stated:

> The method of inventory accounting must be administratively feasible and not unduly burdensome from the standpoint of each of the parties. Within limits of reasonableness, regulations governing LIFO inventory accounting have to be applicable across the board. Whether they achieve the best result in a particular fact situation is not controlling.

Id. at 734.

[278] R.H. Macy & Co. v. United States, 255 F2d 884 (2d Cir. 1958, cert. denied, 358 US 880 (1958)); Carson, Pirie, Scott & Co. v. United States, 186 F. Supp. 480 (ND Ill. 1960), aff'd, 286 F2d 772 (7th Cir. 1961); Kaufmann & Baer Co. v. United States, 137 F. Supp. 725 (Ct. Cl. 1956), cert. denied, 352 US 835 (1956); Gimbel Bros. v. United States, 404 F2d 939 (Ct. Cl. 1968); R.H. Macy & Co. v. United States, 202 F. Supp. 206 (SDNY 1961), aff'd per curiam, 311 F2d 575 (2d Cir. 1963); Textile Apron Co., 21 TC 147 (1953), acq. 1954-1 CB 7; H.C. Godman Co. v. Busey, 56-2 USTC ¶ 9856 (SD Ohio 1956), which also involved a violation of the conformity requirement; Fischer Indus., Inc., 87 TC 116 (1986), aff'd per curiam, 843 F2d 224 (6th Cir. 1988).

[279] W.C. & A.N. Miller Dev. Co., 81 TC 619 (1983); Homes by Ayres, 48 TCM 1050 (1984), aff'd, 795 F2d 832 (9th Cir. 1986); Peninsula Steel Prods. & Equip. Co., 78 TC 1029 (1982); Spang Indus., Inc. v. United States, 791 F2d 906 (Fed. Cir. 1986), rev'g 84-2 USTC ¶ 9739 (Ct. Cl. 1984); RECO Indus., 83 TC 912 (1984). See also Rev. Rul. 86-152, 1986-2 CB 72, where the IRS ruled that the LIFO method was not available to compute the adjusted depletion basis of timber for the purpose of computing gain or loss when timber was cut and treated as a sale or exchange under Section 631(a); Rev. Rul. 86-149, 1986-2 CB 67, where the IRS denied use of the LIFO method to a real estate developer.

[280] Insilco Corp., 73 TC 589 (1979), aff'd in unpublished decision, 659 F2d 1059 (2d Cir. 1981); William Powell Co. v. United States, 524 F. Supp. 841 (SD Ohio 1981).

express authorization of that method.[281] In virtually every case involving computations, the court permitted the taxpayer to use LIFO, recognizing that the method's operation had to be practical in application and not overly burdensome. In only one case was a taxpayer actually denied the use of the LIFO on the basis of its LIFO computations.[282] In that case, the computations used by the taxpayer were premised on false and misleading information, which the court found to be fraudulent, and the taxpayer was held liable for fraud.

In no case has a taxpayer's use of LIFO been terminated for an insignificant failure or deficiency, even if the failure was a violation of one of the statutory conditions for use of LIFO. In fact, there is no decided case where such a circumstance has even been suggested by the IRS as warranting a termination of LIFO.[283]

[2] IRS Attitude

Over the years, the IRS has recognized that a flexible approach is appropriate in responding to LIFO issues and that a termination of LIFO should be sought in only the most egregious circumstances. This is indicated by the hundreds of private letter rulings and technical advice memoranda issued by the IRS with respect to the many approaches used by taxpayers in valuing their inventories under LIFO. Yet, it is rare for a termination to be suggested.[284]

---

[281] Hutzler Bros. Co., 8 TC 14 (1947); Edgar A. Basse, 10 TC 328 (1948); Sweeney & Co., 7 TCM 121 (1948).

[282] Miracle Span Corp. v. United States, 82-1 USTC ¶ 9365 (SDNY 1982).

[283] See, e.g., Richardson Invs., Inc., 76 TC 736, 740 (1981), a case pertaining to the pooling method used by the taxpayer, where it was noted that the taxpayer had already conceded an error in its LIFO reserve because of the failure to reflect an inventory write-down. Similarly, the IRS recognizes that the individual facts and circumstances of any particular write-down must be considered in determining whether the circumstances are so egregious as to warrant a termination of LIFO. See, e.g., Priv. Ltr. Rul. 8402015 (Oct. 3, 1983), where the National Office found in the circumstances presented that even deliberate, intentional write-downs by the taxpayer did not warrant a termination of its use of LIFO.

[284] See Rev. Proc. 79-23, 1979-1 CB 564, for circumstances that warrant and do not warrant the consideration of a termination of LIFO. See also discussion supra ¶ 7.05. Notwithstanding the rarity of proposed terminations and the issuance of Rev. Proc. 79-23, some agents continue to propose terminations in circumstances where the revenue procedure states that termination is not warranted. Although this seems wholly inappropriate, agents suggest that they nevertheless have the discretion to ignore the revenue procedure where the taxpayer's computations, pooling arrangements, or other LIFO methods, which are generally thought of as constituting circumstances not warranting a termination of LIFO, are unusual or unfamiliar to the agents. This is a most difficult problem for taxpayers and should not be permitted to continue.

The way that the IRS typically handles these matters is discussed in a private letter ruling[285] in which a LIFO taxpayer requested National Office approval of a new procedure for determining the index to be used in valuing increments to its LIFO inventory. For prior years, the taxpayer had calculated its index on the basis of the ratio of current costs (of raw materials, labor, and overhead) to base costs. The index so computed was then used to determine both the average current cost of inventory items and the taxpayer's cost of goods sold. The current cost of finished goods inventory had not been used in making these calculations because it had not been possible to determine the cost of such goods.

The IRS stated, "This method [the old method] was adopted many years ago because changes in wage rates and material costs made the calculation of current standard costs unwieldy and practically impossible." This is a most telling statement. It demonstrates that the taxpayer had not been denied the use of LIFO even though it had not been possible for the taxpayer to determine the cost of its finished goods. The IRS then stated the taxpayer's request:

> Because of today's computer facilities and techniques, you believe it will now be possible to carry forward cost changes through the many levels of components and sub-assemblies to determine accurate current standard costs which will provide the management with much needed and improved data for purposes of cost control, cost estimation, pricing and decisions on such things as whether to make or buy a component, etc. It will also be possible to double extend a significant portion of the inventory at both base year costs and current year costs to obtain an index.

The National Office approved the taxpayer's request.

¶ 7.06 CHANGE FROM LIFO AND READOPTION OF LIFO

Although LIFO may be adopted by the taxpayer without the need for the prior approval of the Commissioner, a change from the LIFO method to a non-LIFO method of inventory valuation generally may be made only with the prior approval of the Commissioner.[286] However, the IRS has provided procedures for automatic changes from the LIFO method in certain circumstances.[287] In either case (i.e., where the requested change may be made only pursuant to prior approval or pursuant to the automatic consent provision), the taxpayer must file an application for change on Form 3115.[288]

---

[285] Priv. Ltr. Rul. 7106182241B (June 18, 1971).

[286] IRC § 472(e). But see discussion supra ¶ 7.04[5] regarding simplified LIFO methods. See Chapter 8 for a discussion of changes in methods of accounting.

[287] Rev. Proc. 88-15, 1988-1 CB 683.

[288] See discussion at ¶ 8.06.

[1] Change Requiring Consent

If such a change is to be made, the regulations set forth rules governing the particular non-LIFO inventory method to be used by the taxpayer.[289] The regulations provide that if a taxpayer is either authorized or required to change from a LIFO method, it must use the inventory method then being used for goods not previously subject to LIFO. If LIFO had been used for all goods, then the taxpayer must change to the method that was used prior to the adoption of LIFO. Alternatively, the taxpayer may change to whichever method it selects if that method has been approved by the Commissioner. As a practical matter, the ordering rules of the regulations are relevant only where a taxpayer is required to change from the LIFO method. In that case, the taxpayer may choose to follow or be required by the IRS to follow the ordering rules of the regulations. Where the taxpayer requests permission to change from the LIFO method, the taxpayer ordinarily does so pursuant to an application for change that may request that the change be to any method desired by the taxpayer. So long as the application must be approved by the Commissioner, there is no reason to assume that a taxpayer must follow the ordering rules of the regulations.

Generally, a request for change from the LIFO method will be approved if the taxpayer (1) agrees to spread the resulting adjustment, which increases income, over a period of not more than six years; (2) agrees not to reelect LIFO for a period of at least five years, beginning with the year of change, without the prior approval of the Commissioner; (3) states under penalty of perjury that there has been no termination event with respect to the taxpayer's use of LIFO (in which case the maximum spread period would be reduced); and (4) agrees to comply with any other terms and conditions required.[290] Interestingly, where a taxpayer seeks approval to accelerate the recognition of income in circumstances where the acceleration does not itself benefit the taxpayer (such as through offset against an otherwise expiring net operating loss or by causing the amount of the adjustment to be subject to reduced tax rates), the IRS generally still requires the spread.

[2] Change Pursuant to Automatic Consent Provisions

In Revenue Procedure 88-15,[291] the IRS provides means by which certain taxpayers may obtain expeditious consent to discontinue or change from the use of the LIFO method. This new procedure applies to all taxpayers that desire to discontinue the use of the LIFO method and to change to a permitted method as that term is defined in the procedure. Taxpayers eligible

---

[289] Treas. Reg. § 1.472-6.

[290] See Rev. Proc. 92-20, 1992-1 CB 685, discussed at ¶ 8.06[3][b].

[291] Rev. Proc. 88-15, 1988-1 CB 683.

for use of this procedure may not change from the use of the LIFO method under the provisions of Revenue Procedure 92-20.

Revenue Procedure 88-15 applies to all taxpayers seeking to change from LIFO except the following:

- Any taxpayer that has been contacted by the IRS for the purpose of scheduling an examination at the time the Form 3115 is filed, assuming the examination has not been completed. If the taxpayer has been contacted by the IRS, and the examination has not been completed, the new revenue procedure may be used only with an agreement from the IRS examining agent indicating that there is no objection to the proposed change in method.

- Any taxpayer that is before an Appeals Office of the IRS with respect to an examination of its returns for any year or is before any federal court with respect to an income tax issue arising in any year unless (in either case) agreement to the change has been received from the Appeals Officer or counsel for the government, as appropriate.

- Any taxpayer that as of the date of filing Form 3115, is the subject of a criminal investigation concerning its federal tax liability for any year.

- Any taxpayer that failed to properly compute its inventoriable costs for the year preceding the year of change.

- Any taxpayer that as of the date on which Form 3115 is filed, has experienced a termination event (as described in Revenue Procedure 79-23) unless that termination event is the issuance of a nonconforming financial statement in the year for which the change from LIFO is requested.

- Any taxpayer that issued a nonconforming financial statement in violation of Section 472(g), unless the issuance of the nonconforming financial statement occurred in the tax year in which the requested change is filed.

- Any taxpayer that did not properly adopt the LIFO method.

- Any taxpayer that is a cooperative within the meaning of Section 1381(a) and seeks a spread of the Section 481 adjustment over a period of more than one year.

- Any taxpayer that previously filed a request for change from the LIFO method but failed to make the requested change.

A taxpayer seeking to change from the LIFO method pursuant to Revenue Procedure 88-15 must file a copy of Form 3115 with the National Office addressed to Internal Revenue Service, Corporation Tax 4, P.O. Box 7616, Benjamin Franklin Station, Washington, D.C. 20044, within 270 days after the beginning of the year of change. The original Form 3115 must be attached to the taxpayer's timely filed (determined with regard to extensions) return for the year of change. No user fee needs to be paid in connection with this change.

The revenue procedure provides numerous rules, including rules regarding the method to which the taxpayer may change and the period over which the resulting Section 481 adjustment may be spread. Taxpayers and their advisors must evaluate carefully the various requirements of this revenue procedure.

In Notice 88-23,[292] the IRS provided that taxpayers who are required to change their methods of costing inventories pursuant to Section 263A and who are normally required to make the appropriate Section 263A adjustment before any other change in method of accounting will be permitted to change the normal ordering rule and, instead, to treat the change from the LIFO method as occurring before the change in method of accounting for Section 263A costs.

[3] Readoption of LIFO

Revenue Procedure 92-20[293] provides that a taxpayer who has previously received permission from the Commissioner to change from the LIFO method must file an application on Form 3115 in order to readopt (or change back to) the LIFO method.[294] Absent a showing of extraordinary circumstances, the Commissioner will not approve a readoption of the LIFO method unless five taxable years have elapsed since the taxable year the taxpayer changed from the LIFO method.[295]

The five-year waiting period is a reduction from the 10-year waiting period of prior Revenue Procedure 84-74.[296] Taxpayers who previously changed from the LIFO method under Revenue Procedure 84-74 were subject to the 10-year period of that revenue procedure. However, it is understood that in light of the reduced waiting period under Revenue Procedure 92-20, such taxpayers will generally receive permission to readopt LIFO after five years have elapsed notwithstanding the 10-year condition imposed under the prior revenue procedure.

¶ 7.07 LIQUIDATIONS OF LIFO INVENTORY

[1] The Problem

A LIFO liquidation occurs when a taxpayer experiences a decrease in its LIFO inventories. In such a case, the taxpayer risks matching low-basis

---

[292] Notice 88-23, 1988-1 CB 490.

[293] Rev. Proc. 92-20. 1992-1 CB 685.

[294] Id. at § 9.04.

[295] Id.

[296] Rev. Proc. 84-74, 1984-2 CB 736, § 5.10.

beginning inventory against current revenue, thereby producing a higher profit than there would have been if the taxpayer had been able to replace its inventory and avoid the liquidation.[297]

Under a specific-goods, multiple-pool LIFO method or even a dollar-value method, the taxpayer is often faced with the task of maintaining or increasing the quantity of inventory in each pool to prevent a liquidation of inventory.[298] This task exists even though the liquidation in one pool is more than offset by an increase in the quantity of inventory in other pools. If the product mix of the taxpayer's inventory is subject to continuous change due to technological advances or changing consumer demand, this problem can be particularly burdensome.

In many cases, a liquidation of inventory is attributable to normal swings in the business cycle, to a decline in business activity, or to efforts by management to reduce inventory as an economy measure. In other cases, the liquidation is attributable to factors beyond the taxpayer's control and not directly associated with the inherent nature of its particular business activity, such as shortages of raw materials, strikes, delays in receipt of purchases, and losses resulting from fire, flood, or other casualty.

[2] Taxpayer Response

In any case where a liquidation of LIFO inventory is anticipated, the taxpayer must either recognize inflationary profits or take action to avoid the liquidation. To avoid a liquidation, a taxpayer may seek to purchase inventory, to delay sales, or to request a change in its method of pooling.

If the taxpayer attempts to accelerate purchases to avoid a liquidation, it clearly may do so. However, the taxpayer must be certain that its actions are consistent with its method of accounting for purchases. For example, if the taxpayer's method is to recognize purchases on receipt of the goods, which is when risk of loss passes to the taxpayer, the mere ordering of the goods will not increase inventory. Consequently, if there is not sufficient time for the taxpayer to receive the goods or if the taxpayer does not have sufficient space to store the goods even if there were time to receive them, the taxpayer may seek to enter into a new agreement with its suppliers under which risk of loss would pass on shipment or risk of loss would pass on identification and segregation of the goods at the supplier's facility. Assuming compliance with applicable law governing the passage of title, these techniques should be satisfactory. They also should amount to a change in facts, not to a change in accounting method.[299]

Assuming such arrangements are made, it is important that the transactions be bona fide. For example, transactions may be ignored by the IRS and

---

[297] See example supra ¶ 7.04[2] for an illustration of this problem.

[298] Id.

[299] See discussion at ¶ 9.06.

the courts where the taxpayer, as part of the overall transaction, agrees that following year-end, it will sell back to the seller the items assertedly purchased before year-end.[300] Similarly, the taxpayer must make sure that the goods acquired are of a type or kind to permit them to be treated as inventory and included in the desired pool.[301]

A taxpayer may also avoid a LIFO liquidation by delaying sales. This tactic is also subject to the potential issues and questions discussed in connection with accelerated purchases. Moreover, the nontax business and legal risks of delayed sales may pose a problem, particularly if customers need the goods quickly or the taxpayer is under a contractual or other obligation to ship goods promptly.

Of course, the taxpayer should consider adopting or seeking early on a change to the broadest possible pooling method. In other words, the fewer the number of pools, the less the risk of a liquidation.[302]

[3] Statutory Relief

In addition to manageable situations,[303] LIFO liquidations arise from non-manageable events, such as supplier shortages that result in the unavailability of goods at any price, strikes, natural disasters, or other occurrences over which the taxpayer has no control. In the Crude Oil Windfall Profit Tax Act of 1980, Congress enacted Section 473 to provide relief from liquidations arising from some types of uncontrolled events, but not from all. Section 473 permits a taxpayer who has paid tax attributable to a qualified LIFO liquidation to replace the liquidated inventory in a later year and claim a refund of taxes paid in the earlier year on account of the liquidation.

For a liquidation to be covered by Section 473, the liquidation must be one that is caused by (1) a Department of Energy regulation or request with regard to energy supplies or (2) an embargo, international boycott, or other major foreign trade interruption but, in either case, only if that action has made the taxpayer's ability to replace inventory during the year of liquidation difficult or impossible. However, in no event will any such action give rise to a qualified liquidation unless the Secretary of the Treasury publishes a notice to that effect.

---

[300] See, e.g., United States v. Ingredient Technology Corp., 698 F2d 88 (2d Cir. 1983), cert. denied, 462 US 1131 (1983); Illinois Cereal Mills, Inc., 46 TCM 1001 (1983), aff'd, 789 F2d 1234 (7th Cir. 1986), cert. denied, 86-2 USTC ¶ 9808 (1986). See also discussion at ¶ 6.09[3][b][iv], for other circumstances involving whether a sale is bona fide for tax purposes.

[301] In Rev. Rul. 79-188, 1979-1 CB 191, the IRS held that the purchase of raw materials did not increase the taxpayer's LIFO inventory, because the items purchased were not intended for use in the manufacturing process.

[302] See discussion supra ¶¶ 7.04[2], 7.04[3].

[303] See discussion supra ¶ 7.07[2].

The taxpayer must elect to have Section 473 applied. If elected, the taxpayer will have a period of three taxable years following the liquidation year (or a shorter period if so specified by the Secretary in the published notice) within which to replace the liquidated inventory. If the replacement occurs, the taxpayer's income for the liquidation year will be recomputed. It will be decreased or increased, as may be appropriate, by the difference between the cost of the replacement inventory and the cost of the liquidated inventory.

¶ 7.08 ACQUISITION AND TRANSFER OF LIFO INVENTORY

[1] Section 351 Transfer

Three issues generally arise in connection with Section 351 transfers of LIFO inventory: (1) identification of the particular inventory being transferred; (2) determination of the basis of that inventory; and (3) depending on anticipated price trends, determination by the transferee of whether it wishes to adopt FIFO and thereby match the basis of the acquired inventory against sales or, instead, adopt LIFO and preserve that basis in its own ending inventory. These issues must be considered in terms of their impact on transferors and transferees.

[a] Impact on Transferor

No gain or loss is recognized by the transferor on a Section 351 transfer of LIFO inventory.[304] Consequently, in determining the transferor's cost of goods sold for the year of transfer, adjustment must be made to eliminate the cost (or basis) of the inventory transferred in the Section 351 transaction. This adjustment requires that the total basis of goods available for sale during the year (the sum of the transferor's beginning inventory and acquired or manufactured inventories) be allocated between goods sold during the year and goods transferred under Section 351.

There is virtually no direct authority specifying precisely how the basis of LIFO inventory should be allocated between inventory sold and inventory transferred. The problem is especially difficult because of the fact that LIFO inventory computations are generally made only at the close of the year. LIFO computations generally ignore the actual timing of transfers made during the year.

EXAMPLE: Assume a taxpayer's beginning LIFO inventory consists of

---

[304] IRC § 351.

40 units with a LIFO cost of $1 per unit. Assume further that the taxpayer sells all 40 units soon after the beginning of the year and thereafter replaces these 40 units with 40 units that cost $1.25 per unit. Under LIFO, the timing of the foregoing sales and purchases is ignored. The taxpayer's ending inventory of 40 units is valued at $1 per unit, and its cost of goods sold is computed on the basis of $1.25 per unit.

In light of these characteristics of LIFO computations, and depending on the particular facts and circumstances, any of several assumptions may be reasonable in making the necessary allocation of cost between goods sold during the year and goods transferred under Section 351. For example, it may be reasonable for the tax basis of inventory transferred under Section 351 to be based on the LIFO basis of (1) the beginning inventory; (2) the ending inventory; or (3) a combination of beginning inventory and inventory purchased or produced during the year. Assuming the basis selected consists, in whole or in part, of the basis of the transferor's beginning or ending inventory, the further question arises as to whether the transferred cost comes out of the most recently added layers of that inventory (a so-called horizontal slice), the base inventory and oldest layers (another form of horizontal slice), or proportionately from all layers (a so-called vertical slice). If Section 351 transfers occur at varying times throughout the year, the analysis becomes even more complicated.

The IRS has apparently concluded that a pro rata or vertical slice approach should be used. For example, in Revenue Ruling 85-176,[305] a calendar-year taxpayer using a dollar-value LIFO method made a Section 351 transfer in the middle of the year of approximately one half its LIFO inventory. The IRS ruled that the basis of the transferred inventory should be computed in accordance with the principles of Treasury Regulation § 1.472-8(g)(2), using a pro rata (vertical) division of costs in the base year and in all subsequent layers. The IRS stated that any other approach would inappropriately treat the nontaxable transfer as if it were just another sale.[306] Under the regulation, when a LIFO pool is split into two or more pools, the base cost of inventory to be transferred to each new pool is divided by the base cost of the total inventory prior to the split. The resulting percentage is multiplied by the LIFO value of the base layer and each subsequent layer to determine the LIFO cost of the inventory transferred to the new pool.[307]

Despite the suggestion in Revenue Ruling 85-176 that a vertical slice should be used in all Section 351 transfers of LIFO inventory, this may not be the case. For example, in TAM 8331003 (April 21, 1983), this same issue

---

[305] Rev. Rul. 85-176, 1985-2 CB 159.

[306] See also Rev. Rul. 70-564, 1970-2 CB 109; Rev. Rul. 70-565, 1970-2 CB 110; Comm'r v. Joseph E. Seagram & Sons, Inc., 394 F2d 738 (2d Cir. 1968), rev'g 46 TC 698 (1966); Treas. Reg. § 1.472-8(g).

[307] Treas. Reg. § 1.472-8(g)(2)(ii).

was addressed by the National Office, i.e., whether the LIFO inventory transferred under Section 351 should be treated as coming entirely from the most recently added layers or pro rata from the base year and all subsequently added layers. Consideration was also given to whether a specific computation should be made by identifying and tracing the specific dollar-value inventory that was transferred. The National Office concluded that while the third alternative might be the most appropriate, the pro rata (vertical slice) approach was to be preferred if a specific computation could not be made.

On the basis of the published ruling and TAM, taxpayers may expect that a vertical slice approach will be accepted by the IRS on audit and any departure from it will have to be justified. On the other hand, if the circumstances (including, principally, the identity of the particular inventory transferred) make it clear that a vertical slice approach may be distorting (such as when the only inventory transferred is inventory that did not exist in the transferor's base year or early layer years), use of a pro rata approach may be inappropriate.

[b] Impact on Transferee

The effect of a Section 351 transfer of LIFO inventory on the transferee depends (1) on whether the transferee is an already existing or a newly formed corporation and (2) on which inventory method the transferee already uses or intends to adopt. Where the transferee is an existing taxpayer that has used the LIFO method for many years, the base inventory and LIFO layers of the transferred inventory carry over to the transferee.[308]

If LIFO inventories are transferred to a newly formed corporation or an existing corporation that does not use LIFO, the basis of the transferred inventories is carried over to the transferee, but not as individual layers.[309] Instead, the transferred cost of each layer is aggregated, and the transferred goods receive an average cost. The transferee must then decide whether it wants the transferred basis to be matched against sales or preserved in inventory.

To illustrate, under FIFO, the first goods acquired are deemed to be the first goods sold. As a consequence, under FIFO, the basis of the transferred inventory will be matched against sales before the basis of any subsequently purchased inventory is matched against sales. Thus, the adoption of FIFO is most helpful when inventory costs are declining or when the transferee otherwise desires to match the basis of the transferred inventory against sales.

If the transferee receives low-basis inventory from the transferor or

---

[308] See Joseph E. Seagram & Sons, Inc. v. Comm'r, 394 F2d 738 (2d Cir. 1968); Rev. Rul. 70-565, 1970-2 CB 110.

[309] Rev. Rul. 70-564, 1970-2 CB 109.

inventory with a basis that the transferee wants to preserve, the transferee should elect LIFO. If possible, the transferee should also time the transfer so that the newly acquired inventory will be its beginning inventory. If this is not possible (so that the acquisition might be viewed by the IRS as the equivalent of a first purchase of inventory within the year), the transferee should elect to value increments to inventory on the basis of earliest costs incurred. If increments are valued on the basis of earliest costs incurred, then the low basis of the transferred inventory arguably should be included in the transferee's LIFO inventory without regard to whether the transfer is found to be a beginning inventory or a first purchase. However, if increments are valued on the basis of average costs or latest costs, the characterization of the initial transfer as a beginning inventory will be necessary to preserve the low basis of the transferred inventory in the transferee's LIFO inventory.

Although there have been no cases squarely rejecting the conclusions and analysis set forth above, considerable doubt on the practical ability of taxpayers to achieve the foregoing results has been injected by the opinion of the Tax Court in *Hamilton Industries, Inc.*[310] In *Hamilton*, the taxpayer, a manufacturer, had acquired certain inventories in a bargain purchase, with the inventories being acquired at a substantial discount from the then-prevailing cost to reproduce. The government initially sought to require the bargain element to be recognized in income by seeking to have the taxpayer place the acquired inventories in a separate pool from its manufacturing pool. However, this argument was rejected on the basis of the Tax Court's decision in *UFE, Inc.*[311] In an effort to achieve essentially the same result as would be achieved with a separate pool, the government next argued that the acquired items constituted "different" items from those manufactured after the acquisition. The court, in an opinion that seemed to miss the very point of the use of LIFO inventories, accepted the government's position. The court effectively rejected the LIFO objective of matching current costs against current revenues in favor of a LIFO objective of allowing the deduction of inflation, with "inflation" defined so as to preclude the bargain element from being preserved in inventory. As a result of *Hamilton*, the IRS might seek to deny the preservation of low-basis inventory acquired in a Section 351 transaction by a transferee that adopts LIFO on the basis that the items received are different from the same products thereafter acquired or produced. However, in *Hamilton*, the government expressly rejected any parallel, on this point, between a Section 351 transfer and a bargain purchase.

[2] Acquisition at Bargain Price

It is not unusual for a newly formed corporation to acquire its initial inventory by means of a bulk purchase at a bargain price. If the taxpayer

---

[310] Hamilton Indus., Inc., 97 TC 120 (1991).

[311] UFE, Inc., 92 TC 1314 (1989). See discussion supra ¶ 7.04[3][a][i].

desires to preserve the bargain element by adopting LIFO, an issue necessarily arises as to whether that initial acquisition should be treated as a beginning inventory or a first purchase. If treated as a beginning inventory, the bargain element (or low basis) will be preserved except as inventory decrements occur. If the acquisition is treated as a first purchase, beginning inventory is $0, ending inventory is treated as an increment, and the degree of preservation of the low basis of the bargain purchase depends on the taxpayer's method of valuing increments to its LIFO inventory.

The IRS takes the position that an initial purchase of inventory at a bargain price should be treated as a current year's purchase and not as a beginning inventory.[312] Consequently, in order to preserve the low basis inherent in the bargain purchase, the taxpayer should time the purchase to occur just prior to the end of its taxable year. The taxpayer may adopt LIFO effective with the succeeding year and in that way ensure that the bargain purchase in fact becomes a beginning inventory. Alternatively, if the bargain purchase occurs at the beginning of the year, the taxpayer may elect to value increments on the basis of earliest costs incurred and in that way seek to preserve the low basis inherent in the bargain purchase.

Notwithstanding the foregoing, in *Hamilton Industries, Inc.,*[313] the government successfully argued that inventory acquired by a manufacturer in a bargain acquisition constituted items that were different from the same items that were produced by the taxpayer after the acquisition. As a result of this treatment as separate items, the bargain element inherent in the goods acquired in the transaction flowed through cost of goods sold rather than being preserved in ending inventory and having cost of goods sold consist of only recently produced items. The court in *Hamilton* did not foreclose the possibility that the bargain element would not necessarily be lost in all cases, but it stated that the determination of whether the bargain element would be preserved in inventory or recognized in income (as a result of the low basis flowing through cost of goods sold) was to be made on a case-by-case basis depending on whether the recognition of the bargain element in income was necessary in order to reflect income clearly.[314]

---

[312] Rev. Rul. 85-172, 1985-2 CB 151.

[313] Hamilton Indus., Inc., 97 TC 120 (1991).

[314] See Id. at 139 n.6 where the court stated:

We do not mean to suggest that every bargain purchase of inventoriable property will require the creation of new items within the dollar-value LIFO pool, as occasional purchases concluded on advantageous terms are to be expected in the course of normal business activities. Moreover, where a taxpayer uses LIFO, the gain realized upon sale of such goods probably will be recognized within a short time, unless an increase in closing inventory prevents such bargain costs from flowing into costs of goods sold. Consequently, an isolated bargain purchase in the course of an on-going business differs materially from the case where a taxpayer attempts to value its entire base year inventory at bargain cost.

This result is quite troubling. It suggests that the Commissioner will make these case-by-case determinations on audit under the broad umbrella of clear reflection. This could pose an administrative and planning nightmare for many taxpayers. It leaves the matter completely unresolved and places taxpayers at great risk.

Following *Hamilton*, the IRS provided guidance to taxpayers who requested the approval of the Commissioner to voluntarily change their method of accounting for bulk bargain purchases of inventory to a method consistent with that required by the court in *Hamilton*.[315] The IRS concluded that for applications filed on or after November 7, 1991, it would require a Section 481 adjustment to implement the change, and the provisions relating to category B methods of accounting would apply.[316] The IRS pointed out that if the taxpayer's books and records did not contain sufficient information to accurately compute the Section 481 adjustment, the use of reasonable estimation procedures generally would be permitted. This announcement poses serious difficulties for taxpayers who have acquired inventory in bargain purchases. Since the court in *Hamilton* concluded that the preservation of the bargain element depended on whether income was clearly reflected, taxpayers may be faced with new disputes over whether *Hamilton* is applicable. Since the issuance of *Hamilton*, the IRS has stepped up its attack

---

The court then stated:

Creation of a new item for tax accounting purposes on the basis of differences in cost characteristics is required only where necessary to clearly reflect income, and the issue is to be resolved on a case-by-case basis.

Interestingly, following *Hamilton*, the Tax Court decided a somewhat analogous issue dealing with the computation of appropriate timber depletion in RLC Indus., Co., 98 TC 457 (1992). There, the issue was whether the relatively high cost of certain California timber could be merged with the comparatively low cost of previously acquired Oregon timber into a single block or pool so that the taxpayer would benefit by offsetting income from liquidation of the Oregon timber by the high cost of the California timber. The court allowed such a merging of costs, indicating that the merging was appropriate under the applicable regulatory guidelines, which were very similar to the guidelines allowing use of a single natural business unit pool for LIFO taxpayers and notwithstanding the resulting tax benefit. The court expressly referred to the analogy to the LIFO method of inventory accounting and then chastised the Commissioner for seeking to declare that the results produced by application of controlling regulatory principles resulted in a method that did not clearly reflect income. The court stated:

In essence, we are asked by respondent to decide that the regulation may produce results which do not clearly reflect income. We suggest that the Secretary should seek to correct any perceived defects in the regulations under section 611 by appropriate amendment or modification. Id. at 489–490.

The analogies to the LIFO issue in *Hamilton* are striking. It remains to be seen whether *RLC* will be regarded as inconsistent in principle with *Hamilton*.

[315] Ann. 91-173, 1991-47 IRB 29 (Nov. 25, 1991).

[316] See ¶ 8.06 regarding changes in methods of accounting.

on the preservation of bargain elements in bulk acquisitions of LIFO inventory.

[3] Section 381 Transaction

Section 381 provides rules governing the carryover of corporate tax attributes in connection with certain nontaxable corporate reorganizations and complete liquidations of subsidiaries. Inventory methods are included in the attributes governed by the section. Section 381(c)(5) provides that an acquiring corporation must compute inventories on the same basis as computed by the transferor (acquired) corporation unless different methods were used by the acquired and acquiring corporations. The regulations provide the applicable rules where different methods were used.[317] These rules apply to virtually all such nontaxable acquisitions, including those where there is no difference in the inventory methods used by the acquired corporation and the acquirer, where different methods are used by each, but the acquired business is to be operated as a separate trade or business, and where the acquired business will be integrated into the existing business of the acquirer.

[a] Acquired Business and Acquirer on Same Method

If the acquired business and the acquirer use the same inventory methods, then those methods may be continued without regard to whether the acquired business will be operated as a separate business or integrated into the business of the acquirer.[318] For this purpose, if, on the date of transfer, either party's inventory did not include goods of a particular type, then that party is not treated as employing a different method of accounting with respect to goods of that type.[319] Where the acquired business uses LIFO, it is not necessary for the acquirer to file a new Form 970 election to have the acquired business continue its use of LIFO.[320]

In determining whether the acquired business and the acquirer use the same methods, all subsidiary methods of accounting for LIFO inventories must be taken into account. For example, even though the acquired business and the acquirer use LIFO, the methods used will not be treated as being the same if there are differences in their respective methods of pooling, methods of valuing increments, or methods of computing indexes. Where these differences exist, the determination of the particular procedure to be used following the acquisition depends on whether the acquired business will remain separate or will be integrated into the acquirer's business.

---

[317] Treas. Reg. § 1.381(c)(5).

[318] Treas. Reg. § 1.381(c)(5)-1(b)(1)(i).

[319] Treas. Reg. § 1.381(c)(5)-1(b)(4)(i).

[320] Treas. Reg. § 1.381(c)(5)-1(b).

[b] Businesses to Remain Separate

If, following the acquisition, the acquired business is to remain separate and distinct, with its own complete and separate set of books and records, that business must continue its inventory methods as they existed prior to the transfer. For example, if the acquired business used LIFO, there would be no need for the acquirer to renew any LIFO election for the acquired business to continue its use of LIFO.[321]

[c] Businesses to be Integrated

If, following the acquisition, the acquired business is to be integrated into the acquirer's already existing business, then special rules determine which methods of accounting are to be applied. If the method of accounting employed by the acquired business and the acquirer prior to the date of the transfer are the same, that method may be continued. If the methods are different, the so-called principal method must be used.[322] The principal method is determined for each particular type of goods held for sale by the integrated business and is determined on the basis of the relative fair market values (FMVs) of the inventories of the acquired business and the acquirer's business.[323]

Where the principal method is not LIFO but the acquirer desires to use the LIFO method, the use of LIFO must be elected by filing a proper Form 970.[324] Consequently, where one business uses LIFO and another FIFO, and where FIFO was the principal method, a Form 970 LIFO election must be filed to use LIFO for all inventories. The LIFO election should cover all inventories to be governed by LIFO, not merely the inventories previously reported on a FIFO basis.

¶ 7.09 ADOPTION OF S CORPORATION STATUS

Prior to the Revenue Act of 1987 (the 1987 Act), if a C corporation elected S corporation status and, at the time of the election, held assets with a net unrealized built-in gain—assets with an FMV in excess of basis—the built-in gain would be subject to a separate corporate-level tax to the extent that gain

---

[321] Treas. Reg. § 1.381(c)(5)-1(b)(4)(i).

[322] Treas. Reg. § 1.381(c)(5)-1(c)(1).

[323] Treas. Reg. § 1.381(c)(5)-1(c)(2); see also Rev. Proc. 77-12, 1977-1 CB 569, which suggests that for this purpose, values should be determined on the basis of the lower of cost or market.

[324] See discussion supra ¶ 7.03[1].

was realized within 10 years after the election of S corporation status.[325] This built-in gain rule was applicable to LIFO inventories of affected corporations but, as a practical matter, there would be no gain unless, and to the extent, the taxpayer's LIFO inventory (at the time of the election of S corporation status) was liquidated within the following 10-year period.

The 1987 Act amended Section 1363 to require the excess of the FIFO value of the inventory (determined on the basis of lower of FIFO cost or market) over its LIFO value to be included in the income of the taxpayer for its last taxable year as a C corporation.[326] The tax associated with this increase in income is payable in installments over a four-year period beginning with the due date (determined without regard to extensions) of the taxpayer's return for its last taxable year as a C corporation.[327]

This LIFO recapture provision is generally applicable to elections of S corporation status made after December 17, 1987.[328] However, this general rule does not apply in the case of an election made by a corporation after December 17, 1987, and before January 1, 1989, if, on or before December 17, 1987, the board of directors of the corporation had adopted a resolution to elect S corporation status or a ruling request had been filed with the IRS in which the taxpayer's intention to elect S corporation status was expressed.[329]

---

[325] IRC § 1374.

[326] See ¶ 12.05[4][b][v] for discussion of other LIFO recapture provisions. In Ann. 88-60, 1988-15 IRB 47, the IRS stated that a corporation affected by Section 1363 must include the "LIFO recapture amount" in its "other income" on line 10 of Form 1120, for its last tax year as a C corporation. To determine the additional tax due, the corporation must complete lines 1 through 9b of Schedule J of the form based on income that includes the LIFO recapture amount. The corporation must then compute its tax by completing the work sheet based on income that excludes the LIFO recapture amount. The difference between the two amounts of tax is the tax due to the LIFO recapture. This amount is then paid in four equal installments. The first installment is due with the return for the corporation's last year as a C corporation. The remaining three installments must be paid by the due dates of the S corporation returns for the three succeeding years. No interest is paid on these amounts. The Form 1120S instructions for these years should include instructions with respect to the payment of the tax attributable to the LIFO recapture.

[327] IRC § 1363(d)(2), as amended by the 1987 Act.

[328] 1987 Act, § 10227(b)(1).

[329] 1987 Act, § 10227(b)(2). See also Rev. Proc. 92-20, 1992-1 CB 685, § 9.03 for rules governing changes from the LIFO method by a C corporation for which an S election becomes effective either for the year of the change from the LIFO method or for a subsequent year.

CHAPTER 8

Changes in Methods of Accounting

¶ 8.01   Governing Rules   8-3

¶ 8.02   What Constitutes a "Change in Method of Accounting"   8-4

¶ 8.03   Requirement of Prior Approval   8-5

¶ 8.04   Section 481 Adjustment Required   8-7
     [1]   Amount of Adjustment   8-11
     [2]   Limitations on Tax: Spread-Back of Adjustment   8-14
         [a]   Three-Year Allocation   8-14
         [b]   Consecutive Prior Years Allocation   8-15
         [c]   Special Rules   8-16
         [d]   Character of Taxpayer   8-17
     [3]   Spread-Forward of Adjustment   8-18
     [4]   Spread of Adjustment Under Revenue Procedure 84-74   8-23
         [a]   General Rule   8-23
         [b]   Exceptions to General Rule   8-24
             [i]   Prior-year rule   8-24
             [ii]   Disproportionate build-up rule   8-24
             [iii]   Spread period for Category A methods   8-26
             [iv]   Spread period for Category B methods   8-27
     [5]   Acceleration of Adjustment Balance Under Revenue
        Procedure 84-74   8-28
         [a]   Cessation of Trade or Business   8-28
         [b]   Substantial Reduction in Inventory   8-31
         [c]   Change to LIFO Inventory Method   8-32
         [d]   Termination of LIFO Inventory Method   8-33
         [e]   Other Circumstances   8-33
     [6]   Spread of Adjustments Required by 1986 Act   8-33
         [a]   Change From Cash Method   8-34
         [b]   Change From Installment Method for Revolving Credit
             Sales   8-35
         [c]   Inventory Capitalization Rules   8-36
         [d]   Repeal of Reserve Method for Bad Debts   8-37
     [7]   Spread of Adjustment Under Revenue Procedure 92-20   8-38

[8] Cut-off Method for LIFO Changes Under Revenue Procedure
92-20 8-38

¶ 8.05 Earnings and Profits 8-39

¶ 8.06 Application to Change Method of Accounting 8-39
[1] General Rule 8-39
[2] Governing Procedures Under Revenue Procedure 84-74 8-40
[a] IRS Change of Erroneous Method in First Year Method
Used 8-41
[b] Change From Category A Method Following Contact by
IRS 8-41
[i] Definition of "Category A method" 8-41
[ii] Contact by IRS 8-43
[iii] Taxpayers subject to continuous audit 8-44
[c] Return Under Review When Form 3115 Filed 8-44
[d] Proposed LIFO Termination 8-46
[e] Criminal Investigation 8-46
[f] IRS Decision Not to Process Application 8-46
[3] Governing Procedures Under Revenue Procedure 92-20 8-47
[a] Categorization and Definition of "Accounting Methods" 8-47
[i] Definition of "Category A method" 8-48
[ii] Definition of "Designated A method" 8-49
[iii] Definition of "Category B method" 8-50
[iv] Definition of "Designated B method" 8-50
[b] Terms and Conditions of Change 8-50
[i] Taxpayers not under examination (timely, early, and
late applications) 8-52
[ii] Taxpayers under examination 8-57
[iii] Special rules regarding Designated A methods 8-64
[iv] Exceptions to Section 481 adjustment spread
periods 8-67
[v] Special rules for LIFO taxpayers 8-70
[c] General Procedures Under Revenue Procedure 92-20 ... 8-72
[i] IRS discretion not to apply revenue procedure or to
modify other provisions 8-72
[ii] Compliance with provisions 8-72
[iii] Effect of particular facts and circumstances 8-73
[d] Incomplete Forms 3115: Forty-Five-Day Rule 8-74
[e] Two or More Trades or Businesses 8-74
[f] Particular Filing Details 8-75
[i] Where to file 8-75
[ii] Copy to District Director 8-75
[iii] Signature requirements 8-75
[g] Consent Agreement Requirements 8-76
[h] Protection for Years Prior to the Year of Change 8-77
[i] Request for Conference the National Office 8-77
[j] Effect of Revenue Procedure 92-20 on Appeals Office and
Others 8-77
[k] Effective Date 8-78
[4] Year of Change 8-78
[5] Application Pending at Time Return Is Due 8-78

¶ 8.07 Commissioner's Discretion in Approving Request for Change 8-80

[1] Change From One Acceptable Method to Another 8-80
[2] Change From Improper to Proper Method 8-82
    [a] IRS Consent Required on Change From Incorrect
        Method 8-84
    [b] IRS Consent Not Required on Change From Incorrect
        Method 8-85
[3] Automatic Changes and Changes Deemed Approved 8-87

¶ 8.08 Obligation of Taxpayer to Change From Incorrect Method 8-88

¶ 8.09 Imposition of Penalties 8-88

¶ 8.01 GOVERNING RULES

The requirements governing changes in methods of accounting are often among the most confusing and uncertain of all tax law. Yet, because of the large dollar amounts involved in such changes, these requirements are also among the most important of the tax law. Tax practitioners must be familiar with both the applicable general principles and their specific applications.

The statutory requirements pertaining to changes in accounting methods are contained in Sections 446(e) and 481.[1] Section 446(e) sets forth the requirement that except as otherwise provided, once a method of accounting has been adopted for tax purposes, it may not be changed without the prior approval of the Commissioner of the Internal Revenue. The requirements and procedures for obtaining the Commissioner's approval are provided in the regulations under Section 446(e)[2] and in published revenue procedures.[3]

The mechanics of making a change in method that is approved by the Commissioner or is required on audit by the Internal Revenue Service are governed by Section 481. Section 481 provides the adjustment to be made as a result of the change (the Section 481 adjustment), the manner in which the adjustment is to be taken into account in computing income, and the method of computing the tax arising from the adjustment. Section 481 is designed to ensure that items of income and expense are neither duplicated nor omitted in computing taxable income following a change in method of accounting.

The initial adoption of a method of accounting for tax purposes is an act of great significance. Taxpayers generally have considerable discretion in choosing their initial methods of accounting (and methods to which they may request a change)[4] and should make their selections carefully. Once the initial choices have been made (or changes have been made to requested methods),

---

[1] Unless otherwise indicated, all references to "Code" or to "IRC" are to the Internal Revenue Code of 1986, as amended.

[2] Treas. Reg. § 1.446-1(e)(3).

[3] See Rev. Proc. 92-20, 1992-1 CB 685 and discussion infra ¶ 8.06[3].

[4] See Treas. Reg. § 1.446-1(e)(1) and discussion at ¶ 2.03.

most of the discretion to change accounting methods shifts to the Commissioner.

This chapter defines "change in method of accounting." It also covers the adjustments required in connection with a change in method, the discretion of the Commissioner to require a change or to accept or to reject an application for change, the obligation of the taxpayer to request a change from an incorrect method of accounting, and the risks incurred by a taxpayer that fails to request a change from an incorrect method.[5] Chapter 9 covers changes in accounting practices and procedures that do not amount to changes in methods of accounting and the means by which the equivalent of a change in accounting method may be achieved without the prior approval of the IRS.

¶ 8.02 WHAT CONSTITUTES A "CHANGE IN METHOD OF ACCOUNTING"

The Internal Revenue Code (the Code) does not define the phrase "change in method of accounting." However, the regulations under Section 446(e) provide some guidance as to what is and what is not included in the phrase.[6] In general, a "change in method of accounting" includes a change in the overall plan of accounting for gross income or deductions or a change in the treatment of any material item used in that overall plan. However, a change in method of accounting does not include (1) a change in reporting that is occasioned by the correction of a mathematical or a posting error; (2) the recharacterization of an item of income or expense, such as from deductible compensation to nondeductible dividends; (3) a change occasioned by the continued application of a method of accounting to new or changed facts; and (4) certain changes that traditionally are not treated as changes in methods of accounting, such as a change in the useful life of depreciable property or adjustments to a reserve for bad debts.[7]

If a proposed change in accounting practice amounts to a change in method of accounting, three basic conditions apply to the proposed change. First, a taxpayer that desires to make the change generally may do so only with the prior approval of the IRS.[8] Second, the change is subject to the requirements of Section 481, which permits adjustments to be made to ensure that the change does not result in a double inclusion of items of income or

---

[5] See infra ¶¶ 8.07 (regarding the Commissioner's discretion), 8.08 (regarding the taxpayer's obligation to request a change from an incorrect method), and 8.09 (regarding the imposition of penalties with respect to methods of accounting).

[6] Treas. Reg. § 1.446-1(e)(2)(ii).

[7] Treas. Reg. § 1.446-1(e)(2)(ii)(B).

[8] IRC § 446(e); Treas. Reg. § 1.446-1(e)(2)(i).

expense or an omission of such items. Third, as a practical matter, the making of the change and any subsequent review of the change by the IRS are not subject to the running of the applicable statutory periods of limitation; i.e., the Section 481 adjustment will include amounts attributable to years on which the applicable statutory periods of limitations otherwise has run.[9]

If the proposed change does not amount to a change in method of accounting, the foregoing conditions do not apply. Thus, determining whether a particular change in reporting is a change in method of accounting is one of the most important determinations of tax accounting, yet it is also one of the most difficult. Relevant decisions are not consistent, and it is often difficult to discern the legal or factual distinctions between them. Nevertheless, considerable tax savings or tax costs often hinge on these determinations. Consequently, the significance of a favorable characterization cannot be overstressed.

¶ 8.03 REQUIREMENT OF PRIOR APPROVAL

In general, a taxpayer may not change its method of accounting for tax purposes[10] without the prior approval of the Commissioner.[11] The purpose of the prior-approval requirement is to permit the Commissioner to review the proposed change in method in order to make certain that the change will be to a correct method, that no tax abuse will result from the change, and that the change will be made with appropriate adjustments to ensure that no items of income escape taxation and that no items of expense are deducted twice.[12] The requirement also enables the Commissioner to review changes for the protection of the public treasury, to assure taxpayer compliance with the requirement that the method used clearly reflect income, and otherwise to monitor taxpayer conduct.[13] The requirement generally applies even though

---

[9] See, e.g., Graff Chevrolet Co. v. Campbell, 343 F2d 568, 572 (5th Cir. 1965), where the court relied on the legislative history of the statute to conclude that the Section 481 adjustment necessarily affects closed years and that the section would be "virtually useless" if this were not the case.

[10] Section 446(e) provides, "Except as otherwise expressly provided in this chapter, a taxpayer who changes the method of accounting on the basis of which he regularly computes his income in keeping his books shall, before computing his taxable income under the new method, secure the consent of the Secretary."

[11] See discussion at ¶ 2.02[1] regarding the so-called book conformity requirement.

[12] See discussion infra ¶ 8.04.

[13] See, e.g., Wright Contracting Co., 36 TC 620, 634 (1961), acq. 1966-2 CB 7, aff'd, 316 F2d 249 (5th Cir. 1963), cert. denied, 375 US 879 (1963), the requirement "prevent[s] distortions of income which might result in an adverse effect upon the revenues"; Ed Smithback Plumbing, Inc., 76-1 USTC ¶ 9139 (Ct. Cl. Tr. Div. 1975),

the taxpayer may have legitimate reasons for changing its method of accounting and despite the fact that it might be an abuse of discretion for the Commissioner to refuse to permit the change.[14]

On the other hand, there is no tax prohibition to or restriction on the taxpayer changing its method of accounting for financial reporting purposes. Nevertheless, changes in methods of accounting for financial reporting purposes may raise questions as to whether continued use of the original method for tax purposes will clearly reflect income.

The purpose and objective of Section 446(e) are given practical effect in the regulations, which reiterate the statutory requirement[15] and make it applicable to changes from both correct and incorrect methods.[16] These regulations also provide a mechanism for requesting IRS approval for a change in method of accounting. Treasury Regulation § 1.446-1(e)(3) specifies that except as otherwise provided, a taxpayer must file an application for change with the Commissioner within the first 180 days after the beginning of the taxable year in which it desires to make the change. The application is made on Form 3115. The taxpayer must provide all information required by the form and respond to any other questions that might thereafter be asked by the Commissioner.[17] The change will not be granted unless the taxpayer and the Commissioner agree on all terms, conditions, and adjustments under which the change is to be effected. However, the Commissioner's discretion cannot be exercised to impose arbitrary or unduly harsh terms and conditions.[18]

If a taxpayer changes its method of accounting without first obtaining the Commissioner's approval, the Commissioner generally may require the taxpayer to change back to its original method of accounting.[19] The change back to the original method may be made in the year of the taxpayer's unapproved change. This rule applies even where the change is from an erroneous method to a correct method. Simply stated, the Commissioner may require that the change to the correct method be made in the appropriate manner.

---

adopted, 76-1 USTC ¶ 9373 (Ct. Cl. 1976); Chesapeake & Ohio Ry., 64 TC 352 (1975); and Comm'r v. O. Liquidating Co., 292 F2d 225, 230 (3d Cir. 1961), cert. denied, 368 US 898 (1961), "(t)he rationale of the Regulation here involved is that virtually any material change in the method of reporting income or deduction items will result in a distortion of taxable income, and it is the Commissioner's responsibility to insure that the distortion will not be to the detriment of the Government."

[14] See discussion infra ¶ 8.07.

[15] Treas. Reg. § 1.446-1(e)(2)(i).

[16] Id. But see discussions infra ¶ 8.07[2] and at ¶ 9.05 for decisions suggesting that the prior approval of the Commissioner is not always required where the change is from an incorrect method.

[17] For a discussion of the procedures to be followed and factors to be considered in preparing and filing an application for change, see infra ¶ 8.06.

[18] See discussion infra ¶ 8.07[2].

[19] But see discussions infra ¶ 8.07[2] and at ¶ 2.04[3] and ¶ 9.05.

If the year in which the unauthorized change was made is closed by the running of the applicable statutory period of limitations, the result is less certain. On one hand, support exists for making the change back in the earliest year still open and requiring an appropriate Section 481 adjustment on the change back to the original method in order to prevent an omission of income or a duplication of deductions.[20] Otherwise, the taxpayer might derive a tax benefit by violating the rule requiring prior approval.

On the other hand, the discretion of the Commissioner to return the taxpayer to its original method is less clear where the original method is impermissible and the unauthorized change was made in a year on which the statute of limitations has run. In such a circumstance, the new method may be a method from which the taxpayer cannot change without prior approval. In such a case, the Commissioner may not have the discretion to require a change from a proper method to an improper method.

As a practical matter, changes from incorrect to correct methods are sometimes made without the prior approval of the Commissioner.[21] In such cases, it is not unusual for an examining agent to accept the change if the taxpayer has included the appropriate Section 481 adjustment in income in the year of change. Alternatively, making such a change without prior approval exposes the taxpayer to the risk of later adjustments on audit (such as those described in the preceding paragraphs) and even to penalties for failing to follow the regulatory requirements.[22] Such risks increase if the amount involved is large or if the method to which the change is made is a method that is not favored by the IRS.

¶ 8.04   SECTION 481 ADJUSTMENT REQUIRED

Section 481(a) requires adjustments to be made in connection with changes in accounting methods in order to prevent an omission of income or a double deduction.[23] Absent the provisions of Section 481, a change in method of accounting would permit various items of income and expense to escape taxation

---

[20] See, e.g., Handy Andy T.V. & Appliances, Inc., 47 TCM 478 (1983), where an accrual basis retailer changed from a method that included total prepaid income to a method that included prepaid income less estimated costs without securing the prior approval of the Commissioner. The court found that Section 446 authorized the Commissioner to require the taxpayer to revert to its old method of accounting and to make the appropriate Section 481 adjustment in that year.

[21] See discussion at ¶ 9.05[1].

[22] See IRC § 446(f); Rev. Proc. 92-20, 1992-1 CB 685, § 2.07; discussion infra ¶ 8.09.

[23] Section 481(a) provides: "In computing the taxpayer's taxable income for any taxable year (referred to in this section as the 'year of change')—(1) if such computation is under a method of accounting different from the method under which the taxpayer's taxable income for the preceding taxable year was computed, then (2)

or to be taken into account twice, once under the old method and again under the new method. It should be emphasized that the Section 481 adjustment applies only in the case of a change in accounting method. If a particular change in method of reporting does not amount to a change in method of accounting, Section 481 is not applicable, and the opportunity exists for items of income and expense to be omitted from income or included twice.

Section 481 was enacted as part of the original 1954 Code. Prior to that time (as under present law), a taxpayer could not voluntarily change a method of accounting without the prior approval of the Commissioner.[24] However, before Section 481 was enacted, there was no provision requiring adjustments to prevent omissions or duplications of items of income or expense on account of the change in method.[25] Consequently, when a change in method was requested by a taxpayer, the Commissioner would generally condition his approval of the change on the taxpayer's agreement to take into account in the year of change the entire amount of any adjustment necessary to prevent an omission or a duplication of items of income or expense.[26]

When a change was required on audit by the Commissioner, the taxpayer was not compelled to agree to an adjustment to avoid omissions or duplications of income or expense, and the Commissioner did not have the authority to require such an adjustment.[27] The Commissioner could require adjustments only for changes initiated by the taxpayer.

---

there shall be taken into account those adjustments which are determined to be necessary solely by reason of the change in order to prevent amounts from being duplicated or omitted, except there shall not be taken into account any adjustment in respect of any taxable year to which this section does not apply unless the adjustment is attributable to a change in the method of accounting initiated by the taxpayer."

[24] Reg. 118, § 39.41-2(c).

[25] The 1939 Code contained no equivalent of Section 481.

[26] See, e.g., Howard H. Perelman, 41 TC 234 (1963), acq. 1965-2 CB 6, where Section 481 was inapplicable to tax years involved, a Commissioner-initiated change to accrual method of accounting resulted in accounts receivable escaping taxation, since they were technically attributable to earlier years; cf. Fruehauf Trailer Co., 42 TC 83 (1964), acq. 1965-2 CB 5, aff'd, 356 F2d 975 (6th Cir. 1966), cert. denied, 385 US 822 (1966), where change in method of valuing used trailer inventory from $1 per unit to lower of cost or market would result in significant income-escaping tax, the income being attributable to the different values of the inventory as of the beginning of the year of change and there being no Section 481 adjustment. But see, Advance Truck Co., 262 F2d 388 (9th Cir. 1958), where Commissioner initiated a change from cash to accrual method of accounting as of January 1, 1950, amounts received in the year of change attributable to 1949 accounts receivable were included in income on receipt pursuant to the Commissioner's authority under pre-1954 Code law even though a strict accrual analysis would have excluded the sums altogether.

[27] Early decisions held that the Commissioner had such authority. See, e.g., William Hardy, Inc. v. Comm'r, 82 F2d 249, 252 (2d Cir. 1936), where the court held that where the Commissioner initiated a change from the cash method to an accrual method, he was entitled to make adjustments that departed from "strict accrual

To illustrate, if a cash basis taxpayer with accounts receivable of $100 and accounts payable of $20 requested permission to change to an accrual method, the Commissioner would condition his approval of the change on the taxpayer's agreement to recognize $80 of income in the year of change. This $80 represented the income that had not been recognized under the prior cash method, yet absent the taxpayer's agreement, would not be recognized in the future under an accrual method (see discussion in Chapter 4).[28] If the Commissioner required the change to an accrual method, the $80 would escape taxation.

As a result of these rules, both taxpayers and the Commissioner were reluctant to initiate a change in method of accounting. Taxpayers would not request a change voluntarily because of the sizable adjustment that would result.[29] The IRS would not require a change because of the revenue that would be lost. The problem was especially acute where the method in question was erroneous. Such erroneous methods would be continued year after year, and the cumulative difference in reported income between the erroneous method and a correct method would continue to grow.[30] Against this background, Congress enacted Section 481.

Originally, this section provided that in computing a taxpayer's income for a year in which there had been a change in method of accounting, adjustments would be made to prevent amounts from being duplicated or

---

principles" but were "required to put the petitioner on the accrual basis without permitting income to escape from taxation." Later decisions made it clear that the Commissioner had no such authority. See, e.g., Comm'r v. Dwyer, 203 F2d 522, 524–525 (2d Cir. 1953), where the Court of Appeals for the Second Circuit expressly overruled *William Hardy*, stating that even where the Commissioner properly initiated a change in accounting method, "if a taxpayer has not misrepresented or suppressed the facts, the statute of limitations not only prevents any reassessment of the tax after the prescribed period has passed; [but also] the Treasury may not assess a tax for a later year to make up for a credit erroneously allowed, or a charge erroneously omitted, in an earlier year." In effect, the courts were then recognizing the principle that where an adjustment is made as of the end of the taxable year of change, a corresponding adjustment must be made as of the beginning of the year of change in order for income to be reflected clearly during the year of change. See, e.g., Primo Pants Co., 78 TC 705 (1982); Payne E.L. Thomas, 92 TC 206 (1989).

[28] The $80 was not recognized prior to the year of change because the taxpayer had not received payment of the accounts receivable and had not made payment of the accounts payable. Absent adjustment, the $80 would not be recognized under an accrual method in the year of change or thereafter because the applicable tests for accrual would have been satisfied in years prior to the year of change.

[29] Correlatively, if the applicable adjustment would be favorable to the taxpayer, the IRS would neither require nor, if possible, permit the change in method.

[30] See, e.g., Fruehauf Trailer Co., 42 TC 83 (1964), acq. 1965-2 CB 5, aff'd, 356 F2d 975 (6th Cir. 1966), cert. denied, 385 US 822 (1966), where the disparity between the taxpayer's incorrect inventory method and the correct method was large and continued to grow, but the IRS was reluctant to require a change in method because of the then-existing rules.

omitted solely by reason of the change,[31] but items of income and expense attributable to pre–1954 Code years would be excluded from the required adjustment.[32] In other words, the Section 481 adjustment, as computed at any time subsequent to 1953, would be reduced by what the Section 481 adjustment would have been if computed on December 31, 1953. To illustrate, if a taxpayer's Section 481 adjustment was $100 at the end of 1953 but had grown to $140 at the beginning of the year of change, the actual adjustment for the year of change would be limited to $40, i.e., the growth in the adjustment since the end of 1953. The balance (i.e., the portion of the adjustment attributable to the pre-1954 period) was excluded.

These rules applied without regard to whether the taxpayer or the Commissioner initiated the change.[33] Thus, the prior distinction that had developed between taxpayer-requested changes and IRS-required changes was eliminated.

This elimination from the adjustment of items attributable to pre-1954 years enabled taxpayers to change from improper methods of accounting to proper methods without substantial tax cost. Taxpayers were also able to change from one proper method to another and thereby generate tax savings. The IRS was soon inundated with requests for such changes, and it became apparent that this provision of Section 481 would cost the Treasury substantial revenue.[34] Therefore, the IRS sought legislative relief,[35] which resulted in the Technical Amendments Act of 1958. This Act essentially codified case law and administrative practice under the 1939 Code. Thus, the provisions governing the Section 481 adjustment were changed to include pre-1954 amounts when the change was requested by the taxpayer, but to exclude such amounts when the change was required by the Commissioner.[36] These rules remain unchanged.

---

[31] IRC § 481(a).

[32] IRC § 481(a)(2).

[33] See S. Rep. No. 1662, 83d Cong., 2d Sess. 308, *reprinted in* 1954 US Code Cong. & Admin. News 4947, where the legislative history provided that "if the taxpayer changes his method of accounting, voluntarily or involuntarily, adjustments will be made in the year of the change."

[34] Informal estimates of the revenue loss ranged from $400 million to $1,200 million. Yager, "The Dilemma Under Section 481," 16 NYU Inst. on Fed. Tax'n 565, 573 n.27 (1958). In response, the Commissioner decided not to act on requests for such changes in accounting methods. He announced that no applications for change in accounting method affecting pre–1954 Code year items would be considered, pending issuance of regulations under Section 481. Misc. Announcement No. 24, Jan. 3, 1956.

[35] In 1957, the Commissioner announced that no regulations would be issued pending passage of corrective legislation and that no applications would be considered until such legislation had been enacted. Technical Information Release (TIR) 41, Feb. 15, 1957.

[36] IRC § 481(a)(2). See infra ¶ 8.04[1] for a discussion of the issue of who initiated the change.

The questions that typically arise under present Section 481 involve (1) computation of the amount of the Section 481 adjustment; (2) computation of the tax imposed on account of the Section 481 adjustment; (3) determination of the time when the adjustment must be taken into account; (4) consequences of a change in the character of a taxpayer (e.g., a sole proprietor who incorporates his business), or of other significant events, prior to the inclusion of the full adjustment in income; and (5) effect of the adjustment on the computation of earnings and profits.

[1] Amount of Adjustment

As a general rule, the amount of the Section 481 adjustment is computed at the beginning of the year of change. The adjustment represents the aggregate amount of net income or expense that would have been reported in years prior to the year of change if the taxpayer had been on the new method in such prior years.

> EXAMPLE: Assume that a cash method taxpayer reported income of $1,500, $2,000, $2,750, and $4,000 for its first four taxable years, respectively. Assume further that the taxpayer had net accounts receivable (accounts receivable less accounts payable) at the end of these four taxable years of $100, $210, $315, and $425, respectively. Consequently, if the taxpayer had been on an accrual method during these years, it would have reported income of $1,600, $2,110, $2,855, and $4,110, respectively. (See Chapter 3 for a discussion of the cash method and Chapter 4 for a discussion of accrual methods.) For each of these four years, the net accounts receivable, taxable income (as computed under both the cash and accrual methods), cumulative income (as computed under both methods), and Section 481 adjustment (as computed at the end of each year) would have been as follows:

	Net	Taxable income		Cumulative income		Section 481
Year	A/R	Cash	Accrual	Cash	Accrual	adjustment
1	$100	$1,500	$1,600	$ 1,500	$ 1,600	$100
2	210	2,000	2,110	3,500	3,710	210
3	315	2,750	2,855	6,250	6,565	315
4	425	4,000	4,110	10,250	10,675	425

As the chart shows, if a taxpayer were to change to an accrual method at the beginning of year 5, the Section 481 adjustment would be $425. This is the aggregate amount of additional income that the taxpayer would have reported in prior years based on an accrual method in such prior years.

The Section 481 adjustment arising from any particular change in method of accounting may be allocated to years prior to the year of change on the basis of the yearly change in the net balance of all items of income or expense that are affected by the change. Thus, in the preceding example, the items of income and expense affected by the change were composed of only accounts receivable and accounts payable. Based on the yearly change in the net balance of these items, the amount of Section 481 adjustment for year 5, $425, would be allocable $100 to year 1 ($100 −$0), $110 to year 2 ($210 −$100), $105 to year 3 ($315 −$210), and $110 to year 4 ($425 −$315). The amount of the Section 481 adjustment allocable to each year is equal to the difference between the Section 481 adjustments as computed at the beginning and end of each particular prior year.

The amount of the Section 481 adjustment to be taken into account in computing income may be reduced where the change in method is initiated or is required by the IRS. In such a case, the Section 481 adjustment to be taken into account in the year of change is reduced by an amount equal to what the Section 481 adjustment would have been if it had been computed as of December 31, 1953 (the date prior to the effective date of Section 481).[37] For instance, if years 1 through 4 in the preceding example coincided with calendar years 1952 through 1955 and if the IRS required the change in method in 1956, only $215 of the Section 481 adjustment would be includable in income ($425 −$210).

To benefit from this rule, which allows exclusion of the pre-1954 amount from the Section 481 adjustment, the taxpayer must have been in business prior to 1954 or must be subject to rules permitting a carryover of tax attributes to it from another taxpayer that was in business prior to 1954. Where such carryover rules do not apply and the taxpayer itself was not in business prior to 1954, the taxpayer may not benefit from this rule.[38]

Over time, the issue of who initiated a particular change in method has become less significant. Many taxpayers began operations subsequent to 1954 and, hence, would have no pre-1954 amount to exclude if a change were required by the Commissioner. In addition, taxpayers who were in business prior to 1954 may find it difficult to determine the applicable pre-1954 amount or, if able to compute that amount, might find that the cost of establishing the amount outweighs the tax benefit to be realized from the effort. Nevertheless, there are many taxpayers who were in business prior to

---

[37] IRC § 481(a)(2).

[38] See, e.g., Payne E.L. Thomas, 92 TC 206 (1989), where the court denied the benefits of the pre-1954 amount rule to a sole proprietorship, where the sole proprietorship began its existence after 1954 even though it traced its origins to a pre-1954 partnership. See also Estate of Biewer, 41 TC 191 (1963), aff'd, 341 F2d 394 (6th Cir. 1965); Ezo Prods. Co., 37 TC 385 (1961), both of which involved a denial of the benefits of the pre-1954 amount rule where the successor entity's existence arose after 1954 and the successor was treated as a different taxpayer from a predecessor that had operated prior to 1954.

1954 that would benefit from the pre-1954 amount rule if their methods of accounting were changed by the IRS. Moreover, in the case of a business that has not grown over the years or, in fact, has declined in size, the pre-1954 amount might offset all or substantially all the Section 481 adjustment that would otherwise be included in income. For these reasons, it may be helpful to review cases focusing on the issue of whether a particular change in method was initiated by the IRS or the taxpayer.

As a general rule, where a change is made by the taxpayer following a revenue agent's suggestion that the change be made, the change is deemed initiated by the taxpayer.[39] On the other hand, if an agent specifically advises a taxpayer that a change in method is required, the subsequent change is considered initiated by the IRS.[40] Similarly, where the IRS determines a deficiency on audit by recomputing the taxpayer's income under a method other than that used by the taxpayer, any change in method is deemed initiated by the Commissioner.[41] Where an agent's proposed change in method is successfully challenged by the taxpayer, the taxpayer cannot later take the position that its change to that proposed method should be deemed initiated by the IRS.[42] In addition, it has been held that where a change is made by the taxpayer in order to comply with a requirement of the tax law, the taxpayer nevertheless is deemed to have initiated the change.[43] Similarly, where Congress has enacted legislation requiring taxpayers to change their methods,

---

[39] See Irving Falk, 37 TC 1078 (1962), acq. 1965-2 CB 4, aff'd, 332 F2d 922 (5th Cir. 1964), where an agent did not require that a change in method be made but merely suggested that such a change be considered.

[40] See United States v. Lindner, 307 F2d 262, 265 (10th Cir. 1962), where the court stated:

> [Congress] recognized that in many instances, in dealing with taxpayers whose only contact with the Internal Revenue Service was through him, an examining agent could as a practical matter cause a change in accounting method by his insistence that the change be accomplished. In this case the agent emphasized his direction by reliance upon the Treasury Regulations. While the change was not required as a matter of law, it plainly was initiated by the agent, and not by the taxpayer, within the usual definition of the word "initiate."

[41] See Howard H. Perelman, 41 TC 234 (1963), where the agent recomputed income under an accrual method rather than the cash method used by the taxpayer. See also Rev. Rul. 68-98, 1968-1 CB 191, where an adjustment made by the IRS to value inventories at the lower of cost or market rather than on a constant nominal price was found to be a change in method initiated by the Commissioner; Rev. Rul. 68-262, 1968-1 CB 202, where an agent's adjustment of the taxpayer's method of reporting revolving credit sales was ruled a change in method initiated by the Commissioner.

[42] See H.F. Campbell Co., 53 TC 439 (1969), aff'd, 443 F2d 965 (6th Cir. 1971).

[43] See, e.g., Fred P. Pursell, 38 TC 263 (1962), aff'd per curiam, 315 F2d 629 (3d Cir. 1963), and Samuel Swartz, 42 TC 859 (1964), each of which involved a change from the cash method to an accrual method by a taxpayer required to use the accrual method for purchases and sales of inventory.

it is not uncommon for the legislation itself to provide that the changes are to be treated as initiated by the taxpayer.[44] In the absence of such provisions, the initiator of the change is an open question, the answer to which may be dependent on the nature of the change.

[2] Limitations on Tax: Spread-Back of Adjustment

In the absence of an agreement to spread the amount of the Section 481 adjustment over a period of years beginning with the year of change,[45] the adjustment must be taken into account entirely in the year of change.[46] However, because Congress recognized that the inclusion of the entire adjustment in the year of change could pose an especially heavy tax burden, it provided certain limitations on the tax attributable to the Section 481 adjustment where the adjustment would result in an increase in taxable income of more than $3,000.

The limitations take the form of alternative computations of tax liability. Each of the alternative computations is based on (1) allocating the Section 481 adjustment over the year of change and prior years; (2) determining the increase in tax arising in each such year; and (3) limiting the tax attributable to the adjustment to the sum of such increases. These alternatives are means of ameliorating the hardship arising from including the entire adjustment in the year of change.

[a] Three-Year Allocation

Under the first alternative computation, the Section 481 adjustment is spread over the year of change and the two preceding years, one third in each year, with the tax for each such year recomputed. The aggregate increase in tax is then determined. If it is less than the increase in tax resulting from placing the entire adjustment in the year of change, then the taxpayer need pay only the lesser amount.[47]

The three-year alternative computation may be used only if the method being changed was used in the two years immediately preceding the year of

---

[44] See, e.g., IRC § 263A, pertaining to inventory costing rules; and IRC § 448 (d)(7), pertaining to limitations on use of the cash method.

[45] See discussion infra ¶¶ 8.04[3], 8.06[3][b].

[46] IRC § 481(a). See also Capitol Fed. Sav. & Loan Ass'n, 96 TC No. 11 (1991), where the court confirmed this point and pointed out that for it to require a spread of the Section 481 adjustment over a period of years beginning with the year of change without the Commissioner's agreement would be to usurp a function expressly assigned to the Commissioner and therefore outside of the court's jurisdiction.

[47] IRC § 481(b)(1). See Treas. Reg. §§ 1.481-2(a) and 1.481-2(c) for further explanation and rules for computation. See also examples infra ¶ 8.04[2][b].

change. If the taxpayer did not use the method being changed in each of these two preceding years, the taxpayer is not entitled to use this alternative tax computation.

[b] Consecutive Prior Years Allocation

Under this alternative, the taxpayer recomputes its taxable income under the new method of accounting for all consecutive years immediately preceding the year of change for which such computations can be made. To the extent the entire amount of the Section 481 adjustment cannot be allocated to such consecutive prior years, any remaining balance of the Section 481 adjustment is allocated to the year of change.[48] The tax attributable to inclusion of the Section 481 adjustment in the year of change may be no greater than the aggregate increase in tax that would have arisen under such consecutive prior-year allocation.

In effect, this alternative recognizes that the Section 481 adjustment represents the aggregate income that would have been reported in prior years had the taxpayer been using the new method in such prior years. Thus, it is considered appropriate to limit the amount of tax arising from the change to the aggregate amount of additional tax that would have been paid had the new method been used in prior years.

EXAMPLE: To illustrate the foregoing alternatives for allocation, assume that a cash basis taxpayer had net accounts receivable (accounts receivable less accounts payable) at the end of each of its first seven years of operation of $10, $15, $20, $25, $27, $18, and $30. If the taxpayer were to change to an accrual method in year 8, its Section 481 adjustment would be $30, i.e., the aggregate amount of additional income that would have been reported under an accrual method, had the taxpayer been on an accrual method in years prior to year 8.[49]

The $30 would be included in income entirely in the year of change, but the tax attributable to this $30 would be the lowest amount of tax computed under three separate allocations. First, the entire $30 would be allocated to the year of change. Second, under the three-year alternative, the $30 would be allocated $10 to the year of change and $10 to each of the two preceding years. Third, under the consecutive prior-years alternative, the $30 would be allocated $12 to the first preceding year, ($9) to the second preceding year, $2 to the third preceding year, $5 to the fourth preceding year, $5 to the fifth preceding year, $5 to the sixth preceding year, and $10 to the seventh preceding year. If

---

[48] IRC § 481(b)(2). See Treas. Reg. §§ 1.481-2(b) and 1.481-2(c) for further explanation and rules for computation.

[49] See discussion supra ¶ 8.04[1].

the taxpayer were only able to establish records for the first four preceding years, then the allocation to such four preceding years would be the same as in the preceding sentence, with the balance of $20 allocated to the year of change.

[c] Special Rules

In making the alternative computations,[50] two special rules must be considered. The first relates to the effect of net operating losses. The Code requires that the taxpayer make adjustments to take into account any increase or decrease in the tax of any taxable year preceding the year of change to which no portion of the Section 481 adjustment is allocated under one of the specified alternative allocation formulas, if the income of that year was reduced by a loss carry-back or carry-over from a year to which some portion of the Section 481 adjustment is allocated.[51] This complex requirement can best be explained by an example.

EXAMPLE: Assume that a taxpayer using the cash method for its first five years has received permission to change to an accrual method in year 6; (2) that the taxpayer's Section 481 adjustment is $10,000; (3) that its records do not permit it to establish accrual method income for its first two years; and (4) that its records otherwise show the following data for its first five years.

Year	Taxable income under the cash method Before net operating loss carry-back	After net operating loss carry-back	Taxable income under accrual method	Increase (decrease) attributable to change	Changes in taxable income due to changes in net operating loss carry-back
1	$ 2,000	$ 0	—	—	$2,000
2	4,000	1,000	—	—	3,000
3	(5,000)	—	$ 1,000	$ 6,000	—
4	80,000	80,000	77,000	(3,000)	—
5	90,000	90,000	96,000	6,000	—

In this example, the Section 481 adjustment could be allocated entirely to year 6. Alternatively, it could be allocated one third to year 6, one third to year 5, and one third to year 4. If allocated in this alternative manner, no year to which the adjustment is allocated (i.e., years 4, 5, and 6) had a loss that was carried back to a year to which no portion of the Section 481 adjustment is being allocated. Therefore, the special rule

---

[50] See discussion supra ¶¶ 8.04[2][a], 8.04[2][b].
[51] IRC § 481(b)(3)(A).

is not applicable. However, under the consecutive prior-year allocation, the $10,000 adjustment could be allocated $6,000 to year 5, ($3,000) to year 4, and $6,000 to year 3. This allocation results in a net amount of $9,000 of the adjustment being allocated to consecutive prior years. The $1,000 balance of the adjustment would be allocated to year 6. Under this alternative, a portion of the Section 481 adjustment is allocated to a year in which a loss was originally reported, and this loss was carried back to earlier years to which no portion of the Section 481 adjustment is now being allocated. In other words, a portion of the adjustment is allocable to year 3, a year with a loss, but no portion of the adjustment is allocable to year 1 or year 2, years that were affected by the loss carry-back from year 3. In this circumstance, the aggregate reduction in taxable income of $5,000 for years 1 and 2 must be taxed. Thus, the increase in tax under the consecutive prior-year spread-back alternative will include the increase in tax attributable to an increase in income of $2,000 to year 1 and $3,000 to year 2.

The second special rule relates to years on which the statute of limitations has run. It provides that any increase or decrease in tax for any year for which an assessment of a deficiency, or a credit or refund of any overpayment, is prevented must be determined by reference to the tax previously determined for that year.[52] In other words, if the statute of limitations has run on a year involved in the alternative computations, the increase or decrease in tax attributable to that year will be based on the tax previously determined for that year.

[d] Character of Taxpayer

Application of the previously described tax limitation alternatives[53] may be affected by the type of entity making the change.[54] For example, where a change in method of accounting is made by a partnership, the Section 481 adjustment is based on the taxable income of the partnership, but the alternative tax limitation computations are applied at the individual partner level only. Accordingly, each individual partner must satisfy requirements for application of the alternative computation limitations. Thus, the $3,000 requirement is applied at the partner level. On the other hand, it is not necessary for the partner to have been a member of the partnership for any of

---

[52] IRC § 481(b)(3)(B).

[53] See discussion supra ¶¶ 8.04[2][a], 8.04[2][b].

[54] The character of the taxpayer may also affect the application of the spread-forward rules, discussed infra ¶¶ 8.04[5][a], 8.04[7].

the years prior to the year of change in order to get the benefit of either alternative limitation computation.[55]

> EXAMPLE: Assume a cash basis partnership with three equal partners, A, B, and C, is changing to an accrual method in year 5, and the partnership's applicable Section 481 adjustment is $21,000. Assume further that A and B had been equal partners in the four years preceding the year of change and that C became a partner at the beginning of year 5. The Section 481 adjustment would be allocated $7,000 to each of A, B, and C. If A is subject to a 30 percent tax rate in year 5, he would not be able to use the spread-back tax limitation alternatives because the increase in his tax arising from the adjustment is not more than $3,000 (0.30 X $7,000 = $2,100). If B and C are each subject to a 50 percent tax rate, the tax attributable to the Section 481 adjustment will exceed $3,000 (0.50 X $7,000 = $3,500), and each will be able to use the spread-back tax limitation alternative. The fact that C was not a member of the partnership prior to year 5 is irrelevant.

Similarly, with respect to an S corporation, the adjustments required by Section 481 are made at the corporate level, but the tax limitation computations are applied at the individual shareholder level. In addition, although the limitations are available only if the shareholder's taxable income is increased by more than $3,000, it is not necessary for the shareholder to have been an owner of the corporation for any years prior to the year of change.[56]

The foregoing rules suggest interesting tax planning opportunities. For example, it appears that a high tax bracket individual would be able to reduce the effective cost of a proposed change in method of accounting by taking as a partner, or giving shares of stock in an S corporation to, a low tax bracket individual, perhaps a child or other relative. Such a transfer would reduce the cost of the change by transferring a portion of the Section 481 adjustment to persons in a lower tax bracket. Although the regulations suggest just such an opportunity, there appears to be no authority directly on point.

[3] Spread-Forward of Adjustment

In addition to the spread-back procedures described in the preceding section, the Section 481 adjustment may be taken into account by spreading it over the year of change and subsequent years. Authority for spreading the adjustment over such a period of years is found in Section 481(c) and the regulations thereunder, which provide that the Section 481 adjustment may be taken into account in such manner and subject to such conditions as

---

[55] Treas. Reg. § 1.481-2(c)(5)(i).
[56] Treas. Reg. § 1.481-2(c)(5)(ii).

agreed on between the Commissioner and the taxpayer.[57] Unless such an agreement is reached (and assuming the IRS has not otherwise issued applicable procedures specifying acceptable spread periods), the taxpayer has no right to require a spread of a Section 481 adjustment.[58]

The spread-forward of the Section 481 adjustment is intended to serve several purposes. First, it serves as an additional means of avoiding the harsh financial consequences of including the entire adjustment in income in the year of change. Second, the spread permits the taxpayer and the IRS to reduce the distortion of income that would result if the entire adjustment were made in the year of change. Third, and perhaps of greatest significance, the spread may be used by the IRS to encourage taxpayers to apply for changes in accounting methods in order to obtain the favorable benefits of the spread and to avoid the risk of either losing the spread or having it reduced if the change is required on audit.[59]

Use of the spread period will often prove more attractive to taxpayers than including the entire Section 481 adjustment in income in the year of change and limiting the amount of tax under the alternative tax limitation provisions previously described. There are several reasons for this. First, the limitation provisions frequently offer little benefit to corporate taxpayers and others whose effective tax rates may be the same throughout a period of several years. Second, use of the spread period allows payment of the tax to be deferred. Consequently, there is less disruption of a taxpayer's cash flow and less of a need to borrow the funds necessary to pay the tax attributable to the adjustment. Third, with certain limited exceptions, no interest or similar time-related payments are charged by the IRS on the tax attributable to the deferred portion of the Section 481 adjustment.[60] In effect, this amounts to an interest-free loan.

The financial benefits of the spread may easily be illustrated. Assume the present cost of including a Section 481 adjustment of $6 in income entirely in the year of change is the tax on $6. If the $6 is included in income over a period of six years (i.e., $1 due immediately with the balance paid at the rate of $1 per year beginning one year from the initial payment), the

---

[57] Treas. Reg. § 1.481-5. In addition, Treas. Reg. § 1.446-1(e)(3)(i) provides, "Permission to change a taxpayer's method of accounting will not be granted unless the taxpayer and the Commissioner agree to the terms, conditions, and adjustments under which the change will be effected."

[58] Southern Pac. Transp. Co., 82 TC 122 (1984), supplemental opinion to 75 TC 497 (1980). Capitol Fed. Sav. & Loan Ass'n, 96 TC 204 (1991). See also L.R. Gustafson, 55 TCM 250 (1988).

[59] See Rev. Proc. 92-20, 1992-1 CB 685, § 1.

[60] Additional time related charges are imposed on prospective changes from so-called Designated A method of accounting. See Rev. Proc. 92-20, 1992-1 CB 685, § 7.03(4); and infra ¶ 8.06[3][b][iii].

present cost of the change is the tax on only about $4.79, assuming a 10 percent discount rate.

Over the years, the IRS has issued a number of revenue procedures setting forth the basis on which Section 481 adjustments may be taken into account over a period of years.[61] Although it is possible for unique spread periods to be agreed to on a case-by-case basis, spread periods are generally made available only pursuant to such published revenue procedures.

Revenue Procedure 64-16[62] was the initial such revenue procedure. In it, the IRS agreed to permit Section 481 adjustments to be included in income ratably over a 10-year period if the taxpayer would agree to treat the change as a change in method of accounting.[63] The IRS hoped that the availability of such a spread would discourage taxpayers from asserting that changes proposed by the IRS did not involve changes in methods of accounting. Since Section 481 adjustments were required only in the case of changes in accounting methods, application of this procedure was tantamount to an admission by the taxpayer that the change at issue was a change in accounting method. On the other hand, by allowing the adjustment to be spread ratably over a 10-year period beginning with the year of change, the cost of the change to the taxpayer was greatly reduced. To further reduce conflicts, the use of Revenue Procedure 64-16 was made available even where the accounting practice in question was under examination by the IRS.[64]

Under Revenue Procedure 64-16, taxpayers knew that if their accounting practices were challenged on audit, they could request application of the procedure at that time and thereupon obtain a 10-year spread of the adjustment. Since no penalty was imposed on a taxpayer that delayed requesting a change until an issue arose on audit, there was no financial incentive to request a change prior to an IRS challenge.

Between 1964 and 1980, the IRS used slightly modified revenue proce-

---

[61] Treas. Reg. § 1.446-1(e)(3)(ii) provides the following:

[T]he Commissioner may prescribe administrative procedures, subject to such limitations, terms, and conditions as he deems necessary to obtain his consent, to permit taxpayers to change their accounting practices or methods to an acceptable treatment consistent with applicable regulations. Limitations, terms, and conditions, as may be prescribed in such administrative procedures by the Commissioner, shall include those necessary to prevent the omission or duplication of items includable in gross income or deductions.

[62] Rev. Proc. 64-16, 1964-1 (Part I) CB 677.

[63] Rev. Proc. 64-16 did not apply to certain changes, including changes (1) from one overall method of accounting to another, such as from the cash method to an accrual method; (2) from LIFO to FIFO; and (3) from a specific charge-off method to a reserve method of accounting for bad debts.

[64] See Bush and Flannery, "New Accounting-Method-Change Rules Restrict Availability of Ten-Year Adjustment Spread," 54 J. Tax'n 138 (Mar. 1981).

dures, which reduced the spread period in certain circumstances.[65] Nevertheless, taxpayers continued to take advantage of the fact that the applicable procedure could still be used after a challenge of a method on audit. Thus, where an incorrect method deferred the recognition of income, the taxpayer would benefit by continuing such method until its use was challenged by the IRS.

In response to this circumstance, the IRS promulgated Revenue Procedure 80-51 in 1980.[66] Revenue Procedure 80-51 represented a major departure from past practice. It was designed to encourage taxpayers to employ proper accounting methods and to discourage the use of methods proscribed by the Code, regulations, or Supreme Court decisions. To this end, spreads of Section 481 adjustments were denied in some cases and limited in other cases.

Revenue Procedure 80-51 was the first generally applicable procedure to reward a taxpayer that requested a change from an improper to a proper method of accounting prior to any contact by the IRS. If the taxpayer acted quickly to request a change, the taxpayer could be assured of the maximum spread possible. However, if the taxpayer failed to request a change prior to being contacted by the IRS, the taxpayer risked the loss of a forward spread of the Section 481 adjustment.

In 1984, the IRS replaced Revenue Procedure 80-51 with Revenue Procedure 84-74.[67] In summary, Revenue Procedure 84-74 permitted a taxpayer that requested a change in its accounting method to obtain a forward spread of the Section 481 adjustment over a period of up to six years. This maximum spread period of six years was reduced in the following circumstances:[68]

- The method from which the taxpayer was seeking to change was a method that was specifically not permitted by the Code, Treasury regulations, or Supreme Court decisions.
- The method had been used for fewer than six years.
- A specified percentage of the Section 481 adjustment was attributable to a period of one, two, or three years immediately preceding the year of change.

---

[65] See, e.g., Rev. Proc. 70-27, 1970-2 CB 509, which provided that any Section 481 adjustment would be taken into account ratably over an *appropriate* period prescribed by the Commissioner, *generally* 10 years; Rev. Proc. 75-18, 1975-1 CB 687, which (1) set the maximum spread period at the number of years the taxpayer had used its old method of accounting, up to a maximum of 10 years and (2) introduced the "substantial increase rule," which provided that regardless of the number of years the taxpayer had been in existence or had used its prior method of accounting, if a substantial portion of the Section 481 adjustment was attributable to events in a few of the years immediately prior to the year of change, then there would be a reduction in the period over which the Section 481 adjustment could be spread.

[66] Rev. Proc. 80-51, 1980-2 CB 818.

[67] Rev. Proc. 84-74, 1984-2 CB 736. See discussion infra ¶ 8.04[4].

[68] See infra ¶ 8.04[4][b] for a discussion of these circumstances.

• Prior to filing an application for change, the taxpayer was contacted by the IRS for the purpose of scheduling an examination.

Experience with Revenue Procedure 84-74 was not entirely satisfactory. In the view of the IRS, taxpayers continued to delay applying for changes from improper methods. Simply put, the incentives were not sufficient to encourage prompt applications or, stated otherwise, the detriments of failing to file an application for change were not sufficient to encourage the filing. As a result, the IRS replaced Revenue Procedure 84-74 with Revenue Procedure 92-20.[69]

To encourage prompt voluntary applications for change from improper methods, Revenue Procedure 92-20 employs a gradation of incentives. Under this revenue procedure, taxpayers receive considerably more favorable terms and conditions for voluntary changes from improper methods than they do if the application for change is filed after contact by the IRS. Nevertheless, if contact is made by the IRS, the filing of an application immediately thereafter results in more favorable terms and conditions than if the change is not made voluntarily by the taxpayer but, instead, is made by the agents on audit. In addition, the revenue procedure includes provisions designed to ensure that changes from methods of accounting prohibited by amendments to the Code or required by such amendments will not be made on more favorable terms and conditions by a taxpayer who delays making the change than a taxpayer who makes the change immediately under the applicable Code provision. Finally, Revenue Procedure 92-20 simplifies or eliminates many of the more complex rules and requirements of Revenue Procedure 84-74.[70]

As this discussion shows, the IRS was initially slow to act and somewhat naive in the manner in which it exercised its discretion under Section 481. However, in recent years, the IRS has become more sophisticated in exercising its discretion to influence taxpayer conduct regarding accounting methods and practices. Taxpayers should assume that this trend will continue. Accordingly, taxpayers who delay initiating changes to correct accounting methods or practices are substantially more at risk today than they were in prior years. It is no longer prudent to assume that a current incorrect practice may be continued without risk of financial loss or imposition of penalty on the basis that opportunities available prior to audit will also be available after an examination has commenced.[71] They will not.

---

[69] Rev. Proc. 92-20, 1992-1 CB 685.

[70] Rev. Proc. 92-20, 1992-1 CB 685, § 1. For a complete discussion of the terms and conditions associated with changes in methods of accounting pursuant to Rev. Proc. 92-20, see discussion infra ¶ 8.06[3][b].

[71] See discussion infra ¶ 8.09 regarding imposition of penalties.

[4] Spread of Adjustment Under Revenue Procedure 84-74

Although Revenue Procedure 84-74 has been modified and superseded by Revenue Procedure 92-20, it is appropriate to summarize the general rules and exceptions to the spread periods provided under Revenue Procedure 84-74, because such rules and exceptions remain applicable to taxpayers who requested changes under that revenue procedure. The applicable general rules and exceptions governing spread periods available under Revenue Procedure 92-20 are discussed later in this chapter.[72]

[a] General Rule

Subject to a number of exceptions,[73] Revenue Procedure 84-74 permitted the Section 481 adjustment (whether it was positive or negative) to be taken into account ratably over the number of tax years the taxpayer had used the method of accounting from which it was changing. However, in no event could the spread period exceed six tax years. As was the case with corresponding revenue procedures issued in earlier years, Revenue Procedures 84-74 and 92-20 should be interpreted by the courts as recognizing that an abuse of discretion may result if the Commissioner fails to observe self-imposed limits on her discretion, particularly where she has invited reliance upon those limitations.[74] In other words, the Commissioner should follow her revenue procedures, especially when they result in the very conduct she sought to induce.

It must be emphasized that the period over which a Section 481 adjustment was spread consisted of tax years.[75] Consequently, if the tax year was for any reason less than a period of 12 months, a full pro rata portion of the adjustment would be allocated to that short year. For example, if a taxpayer had two tax years within a single period of 12 months and if the spread period were six years, two sixths of the total adjustment would be included within that period of 12 months.

Prior to Revenue Procedure 84-74, the IRS generally permitted a spread period of up to 10 years.[76] The reduction to six tax years may have been at-tributable to a desire on the part of the government to reduce the cost of permitting spread periods. However, the reduction from 10 to six years so reduced the financial advantages to be obtained from the spread that some taxpayers that otherwise would have initiated requests for changes in

---

[72] See discussion infra ¶ 8.06[3][b].

[73] See discussion infra ¶¶ 8.04[4][b], 8.04[5].

[74] See Capitol Fed. Sav. & Loan Ass'n, 96 TC (1991), where the court determined that it had the authority to review the Commissioner's application of Rev. Proc. 80-51 to determine whether an abuse of discretion had occurred.

[75] See discussion at ¶ 10.02 regarding tax years.

[76] See discussion supra ¶ 8.04[3].

accounting methods may have been dissuaded from doing so. For example, with a six-year spread, the present cost of a Section 481 adjustment in the amount of $6 (with $1 recognized immediately and at the end of each of the next five years) would be the tax on $4.79, assuming a 10 percent discount rate. With a 10-year spread (with $0.60 recognized immediately and at the end of each of the next nine years), the present cost would be the tax on $4.06. Thus, the reduction in the spread period from 10 to six years resulted in an increased present cost of about 18 percent.

[b] Exceptions to General Rule

Under the general rule, the spread period available under Revenue Procedure 84-74 was reduced from six years to the number of years the taxpayer had been on the method being changed, if fewer than six.[77] The spread period was also reduced pursuant to any of the four following special rules.

[i] **Prior-year rule.** Where the entire Section 481 adjustment was attributable to the tax year immediately preceding the year of change, Revenue Procedure 84-74 provided that the total adjustment was to be taken into account in the year of change. In other words, no forward spread was permitted.

[ii] **Disproportionate build-up rule.** Where the entire adjustment was not attributable to the year preceding the year of change, but 67 percent or more of the adjustment was attributable to the one-, two-, or three-tax-year period immediately preceding the year of change, Revenue Procedure 84-74 provided that the highest percentage attributable to such one-, two-, or three-year period was to be taken into account ratably over a three-year period beginning with the year of change. Any remaining balance was to be taken into account ratably over a period equal to the remainder of the number of tax years the taxpayer had used the method, not to exceed six. Where the old method of accounting had been used for no more than four years, 75 percent was to be used instead of 67 percent.

EXAMPLE: Assume that a taxpayer had been on the cash method for eight years, that it changed to an accrual method in year 9, and that its net accounts receivable (accounts receivable less accounts payable) at the end of each of its first eight years were as follows:

---

[77] This discussion pertains to exceptions to the general rule under Rev. Proc. 84-74, which governed applications for change filed prior to March 23, 1992. For the terms and conditions governing applications for change filed on or after March 23, 1992, see infra ¶ 8.06[3][b].

Year	Net accounts receivable
1	$10
2	15
3	22
4	26
5	26
6	48
7	74
8	88

As explained in an earlier example,[78] the Section 481 adjustment was equal to the balance of the net accounts receivable as of the year preceding the year of change, and the annual change in the balance of these net accounts receivable represented the portion of the Section 481 adjustment allocable to each year. Thus, the Section 481 adjustment in this example was $88 of which $14 was allocable to year 8 ($88 — $74), $26 to year 7 ($74 — $48), and so on. Under these facts, more than 67 percent of the Section 481 adjustment was attributable to the three-year period consisting of years 6, 7, and 8. Of the total Section 481 adjustment, $14 or 15.9 percent was attributable to year 8 (the one-year period), $40 ($88 — $48) or 45 percent of the adjustment was attributable to the two-year period preceding the year of change, and $62 ($88 — $26) or 70 percent of the adjustment was attributable to the three-year period preceding the year of change. In these circumstances, since $62 or 70 percent represented the highest percentage of the Section 481 adjustment attributable to any of the one-, two-, or three-year periods preceding the year of change, $62 of the total Section 481 adjustment of $88 would have been taken into income ratably over the three-year period beginning with year 9, the year of change. The $26 balance of the adjustment would have been taken into account ratably over the succeeding three-year period, i.e., years 12, 13, and 14. If the net receivables at the end of years 7 and 8 had been $16 and $88, respectively, the Section 481 adjustment would still have been $88; $72 ($88 — $16) or 82 percent would have been attributable to year 8, $40 ($88 — $48) or 45 percent would have been attributable to years 7 and 8, and $62 ($88 — $26) or 70 percent would have been attributable to years 6, 7, and 8. The highest percentage of the one-, two-, and three-year periods preceding the year of change would have been the 82 percent attributable to the one-year period. Accordingly, $72 would have been taken into income ratably in years 9, 10, and 11, with the balance of $16 taken into account ratably in years 12, 13, and 14.

---

[78] See supra ¶ 8.04[1].

In many cases, a taxpayer's books and records may not have been sufficient to permit the taxpayer to compute what the Section 481 adjustment would have been in some or all of the years prior to the year of change. In such circumstances, the taxpayer was permitted to make a good faith estimate of the adjustment for purposes of determining applicability of the 67 percent or the 75 percent test. The taxpayer would submit a statement explaining the reasons for its inability to make the appropriate computations and would also explain the basis on which the estimates had been made. The application was required to contain a statement under penalty of perjury relating to the insufficiency of the books and records and to the conclusion that no more than 67 percent or 75 percent was attributable to the one-, two-, or three-year tax period. If the explanation was satisfactory and the approach used in making the estimates was reasonable, it generally was accepted by the IRS.

[iii] **Spread period for Category A methods.** Under Revenue Procedure 84-74,[79] Category A methods generally consisted of methods of accounting that were expressly not permitted by the Code, Treasury regulations, or Supreme Court decisions.[80] Where the change in method was from a Category A method, the availability of any spread period depended on (1) whether the taxpayer had been contacted by the IRS for the purpose of scheduling an examination that had not yet been completed and (2) whether the adjustment was positive (increased income) or negative (reduced income). If the adjustment was positive and the taxpayer had not been contacted by the IRS, the general spread-period rules applied, except that the maximum spread period could not exceed three tax years.[81] However, if the taxpayer had been contacted by the IRS and the examination had not been completed, no spread period was available.

In addition, no spread was available or required where the change in method resulted in a reduction in income (a "negative" Section 481 adjustment). In that case, the entire amount of the adjustment was to be taken into account in the year of change.[82] This benefitted taxpayers by allowing them to realize the full reduction in income as soon as possible.

Although the special rules for Category A methods were designed to encourage taxpayers to request changes from incorrect methods of accounting prior to audit, at which time the opportunity for a spread would be lost,

---

[79] This discussion pertains to the rules provided by Rev. Proc. 84-74, which governed applications for change filed prior to March 23, 1992. For the terms and conditions governing applications for change filed on or after March 23, 1992, see infra ¶ 8.06[3][b].

[80] Rev. Proc. 84-74, 1984-2 CB 736, § 6.02. See infra ¶ 8.06[2][b] for further discussion of changes from Category A methods under Rev. Proc. 84-74.

[81] Rev. Proc. 84-74, 1984-2 CB 736, § 5.06(1)(d).

[82] Rev. Proc. 84-74, 1984-2 CB 736, § 5.06(1)(c).

the maximum spread period was so short that the perceived incentive to change was often illusory. For example, the present cost of a $6 positive Section 481 adjustment recognized immediately was the tax on $6. The present cost of this same $6 spread over three years ($2 immediately and $2 at the end of each of the next two years) was the tax on $5.47, assuming a 10 percent discount rate. Alternatively, if no request for change was made and the IRS did not require a change until two years after the year for which the taxpayer otherwise would have requested the change, the taxpayer benefitted financially by not seeking a change. For instance, the taxpayer would have forgone a three-year spread starting immediately for no spread but with the change effected two years later. Assuming a 10 percent discount rate, the present cost of $6 due in two years would have been the tax on $4.96. Of course, such a decision by the taxpayer entailed a greater risk of penalties being imposed by the IRS because of the continued use of an improper method.

[iv] **Spread period for Category B methods.**   Under Revenue Procedure 84-74,[83] Section 481 adjustments attributable to changes from Category B methods, which were all methods other than Category A methods,[84] were generally spread over a period of six years or, if fewer, the number of years the taxpayer had been using the method.[85] If regulations were amended to prohibit a particular method, the IRS sometimes provided a period of time during which an application to change from the prohibited method would be deemed a change from a Category B method rather than a change from a Category A method.[86]

However, in some cases, the IRS would specify in a published revenue ruling or revenue procedure that a particular Category B method was inappropriate and was subject to Section 5.12(2) of Revenue Procedure 84-74. If such a designation had been made and if the method being changed involved an issue raised on audit by the IRS, then the maximum spread period otherwise available to the taxpayer would not be more than three tax years. This limitation applied only where the publication date of the ruling

---

[83] This discussion pertains to the general rules provided by Rev. Proc. 84-74, which governed applications for change filed prior to March 23, 1992. For the terms and conditions governing applications for change filed on or after March 23, 1992, see infra ¶ 8.06[3][b].

[84] Rev. Proc. 84-74, 1984-2 CB 736, § 6.03.

[85] Rev. Proc. 84-74, 1984-2 CB 736, § 5.06(1)(e). See discussion infra ¶ 8.06[2][b][i], for the definition of "Category A methods" under Rev. Proc. 84-74.

[86] See, e.g., Ann. 87-65, 1987-28 IRB 38 (July 13, 1987), where the IRS announced a transition period during which a change from a method of accounting for long-term contracts that was not in accordance with the December 30, 1985, amendments to Treas. Reg. § 1.451-3 would be treated as a change from a Category B method. The application for change in method of accounting (Form 3115) had to be filed on or before October 31, 1987.

or the procedure was more than two years prior to the date of the Form 3115.[87] The two-year publication requirement was designed to give the taxpayer an opportunity to determine whether its particular method was subject to the revenue ruling or revenue procedure and, if it was, to file a request for change.

[5] Acceleration of Adjustment Balance Under Revenue Procedure 84-74

In many circumstances, the opportunity to spread the Section 481 adjustment over a period of years raised the possibility of an unintended tax benefit by permitting income to be recognized later than it would have been recognized had there been no change in method of accounting.[88] For example, if a cash basis taxpayer with net receivables of $100 desired to change to an accrual method, the taxpayer ordinarily would have been able to obtain approval for such a change and take the $100 into income ratably over a period of several years. If the change were made just prior to termination of the taxpayer's cash basis operations, the recognition of the net receivables would have been deferred even though all cash collections might occur within a year or two following the year of change.

In order to prevent such an unintended benefit, the IRS began to condition its approval of accounting method changes by requiring that the entire balance of any Section 481 adjustment be included in income on the occurrence of any of several specified circumstances. Several of these circumstances were identified in Revenue Procedure 84-74. They are discussed in the following sections.

[a] Cessation of Trade or Business

If the taxpayer ceased to engage in the trade or business to which the change in method of accounting related, the balance of the Section 481 adjustment was generally required to be recognized in the year of the cessation.[89] Where the business operations terminated completely, application of this rule was straightforward. However, where the business operations were continued either to a slight degree or through a different or a successor organization, application of the cessation rule became more troublesome.

The revenue procedure did not discuss the precise degree of business

---

[87] Rev. Proc. 84-74, 1984-2 CB 736, § 5.12(2).

[88] This discussion pertains to the rules provided by Rev. Proc. 84-74, which governed applications for change filed prior to March 23, 1992. For the terms and conditions governing applications for change filed on or after March 23, 1992, see infra ¶ 8.06[3][b].

[89] Rev. Proc. 84-74, 1984-2 CB 736, § 5.09.

reduction necessary to trigger application of the rule. It may be argued that absent a complete termination, the rule would not apply. However, it seems unlikely that a court would find in favor of a taxpayer who attempted to circumvent the rule by continuing only an insignificant amount of business activity. On the other hand, the taxpayer may have much to gain and little to lose in such a case. Moreover, if continuation of even slight business activity was attributable to reasons other than tax reduction motivations, the court might find in favor of the taxpayer.

When the taxpayer's business was continued through a successor entity, application of the rule depended on the organizational form of the taxpayer.

1. *Corporations.* A corporate taxpayer was considered not to have ceased operation of a trade or business for purposes of accelerating recognition of the Section 481 adjustment under Revenue Procedure 84-74 where the cessation was the result of a transaction governed by Section 381, pertaining to the carryover of tax attributes in certain corporate acquisitions.[90] In such a case, the acquiring corporation was subject to the continued reporting of the Section 481 adjustment just as if it were the acquired corporation that made the change in method. On the other hand, a transfer of the trade or business in Section 351 transaction should have resulted in a cessation that triggers the unamortized balance of the transferor's Section 481 adjustment.

2. *Proprietorships.* If the taxpayer was an individual operating his trade or business as a sole proprietorship, the triggering rule applied to a termination of that trade or business. Incorporation of the trade or business in a transaction governed by Section 351 was treated as a cessation of the trade or business for this purpose.[91]

The taxpayer was not deemed to have ceased to engage in a trade or business when he sold a partial interest in the business, and the business was thereafter continued as a partnership. In this circumstance, the entire balance of the Section 481 adjustment was taken into account by the individual taxpayer as if there had been no change in ownership.[92] The new owner was

---

[90] Rev. Proc. 84-74, 1984-2 CB 736, § 5.09(1).

[91] See Rev. Rul. 77-264, 1977-2 CB 187, where, on incorporation of taxpayer's sole proprietorship, he ceased to be engaged in that particular trade or business for purposes of the Section 481 adjustment and was required to take the balance of the adjustment into account in the year of incorporation; Dean R. Shore, 69 TC 689 (1978), aff'd, 631 F2d 624 (9th Cir. 1980), where taxpayers (husband and wife) who incorporated their sole proprietorship ceased their trade or business and were therefore required to include the balance of the adjustment in income in the year of incorporation rather than over the remainder of the then applicable 10-year spread period.

[92] Rev. Proc. 84-74, 1984-2 CB 736, § 5.09(3). See Rev. Rul. 66-206, 1966-2 CB 206, where taxpayer sold an interest in his business and continued to be actively involved in the subsequent partnership, he was deemed not to have ceased to engage

not required or permitted to take any portion of the remaining Section 481 adjustment into account. Thus, it was not possible for a taxpayer to reduce the tax effect of the change in method by thereafter transferring a portion of his business to a family member who was taxed at lower rates. However, if such a transfer occurred prior to the change in method (and was bona fide), the tax cost of the change was apparently reduced by reason of the lower tax rate of the transferee.

3. *Partnerships.* Although not explicitly covered by Revenue Procedure 84-74, the rules applicable to proprietorships suggested that should a partnership change its accounting method, the resulting Section 481 adjustment would be attributable only to the taxpayers who were partners during the year of change and would not affect the income to be reported by subsequently admitted partners. In other words, it appeared reasonable for the principle applicable to the sale of a portion of a sole proprietorship to be applicable to a sale of, or a change in, a partnership interest. If this principle were not applied, the potential for substantial abuse would arise.

To illustrate, assume that a partnership with two equal partners changed its method of accounting in year 10 and that this change resulted in a Section 481 adjustment of $60, to be taken into account ratably over a period of six years. Thus, each partner would recognize his aggregate share ($30) of the Section 481 adjustment at the rate of $5 per year. This recognition would not be affected by the later admission of new partners.

If a partnership ceased to be engaged in a trade or business, the unamortized balance of the Section 481 adjustment would be recognized in the year of the cessation. In general, each affected partner would take his share of the remaining adjustment into account in that year. The incorporation of the partnership in a transaction governed by Section 351 was treated as a termination that triggered this rule.[93]

4. *S corporations.* S corporations presented difficult issues. On one hand, the incorporation of the trade or business of a proprietorship or a partnership was treated as a termination of that business by the proprietorship or the partnership. Since this was the rule when there was no election of S corporation status, there seemed to be no reason for election of S corporation status to trigger a different result. In either case, the corporation was a separate, distinct entity.

On the other hand, support existed for the proposition that the incorporation of a proprietorship or a partnership followed immediately by the election of S corporation status should be treated as a continuation of the proprietorship or the partnership business for purposes of the Section 481

---

in a trade or business. The outstanding balance of the Section 481 adjustment attributable to the proprietorship was therefore not accelerated but included ratably in the taxpayer's income over the remainder of the spread period.

[93] Rev. Proc. 84-74, 1984-2 CB 736, § 5.09(2). See Rev. Rul. 85-134, 1985-2 CB 160.

adjustment rules.[94] This result seemed reasonable, but only as a matter of equity in a particular circumstance. In other circumstances, treating the S corporation differently than a C corporation posed inequitable hardship. For example, such treatment suggested that the balance of a Section 481 adjustment should be accelerated when a C corporation elected S corporation status. Yet, this result would be inappropriate. Election of S corporation status does not give the S corporation an opportunity to elect new methods of accounting and, correspondingly, should not be treated as the termination of the C corporation's business.[95]

[b] Substantial Reduction in Inventory

If the change in method of accounting under Revenue Procedure 84-74 involved a change in method of inventory valuation, a substantial reduction in inventory would cause the balance of the Section 481 adjustment to be recognized.[96] Under this rule, if, at any time during the spread period the value of the ending inventory was reduced by more than one third of the value of the inventory at the beginning of the spread period, and remained so reduced as of the end of the next succeeding tax year, the balance of the Section 481 adjustment had to be included in income in the succeeding year. The succeeding year rule prevented short-term reductions in inventory from accelerating the balance of the adjustment.

To protect itself, a taxpayer could seek consent of the Commissioner not to have the acceleration rule for inventory reduction apply where the taxpayer was able to demonstrate that the reduction was attributable to strikes, involuntary conversions, or involuntary interruptions in the availability of the goods. However, such consent had to be requested not more than 90 days following the tax year to which the acceleration rule would otherwise apply.

---

[94] See E. Morris Cox, 43 TC 448 (1965), acq. 1965-2 CB 4, where a service business partnership with outstanding receivables elected subchapter S status, the court noted that in light of the underlying purpose of Section 481, an argument that the subchapter S corporation is merely a continuation of the old partnership would have strong appeal; Paul H. Travis, 47 TC 502, 518 (1967), aff'd in part, rev'd in part, 406 F2d 987 (6th Cir. 1969), where a sole proprietorship dance studio elected subchapter S status, the Tax Court stated that for purposes of Section 481, the subchapter S corporation and the proprietorship were a single taxable entity, the Court stating that it was following the approach taken in *E. Morris Cox* and found it "sound in light of the purposes of subchapter S."

[95] See Priv. Ltr. Ruls. 8824012 (Mar. 15, 1988) and 8940035 (July 7, 1989), where the National Office ruled that the adoption of S corporation status does not accelerate the unamortized balance of a Section 481 adjustment arising from a change in accounting method by the corporation prior to the adoption of S corporation status.

[96] Rev. Proc. 84-74, 1984-2 CB 736, § 5.08.

[c] Change to LIFO Inventory Method

Under Revenue Procedure 84-74, special acceleration rules applied to taxpayers that obtained permission to change their inventory methods but, prior to the complete recognition of the Section 481 adjustment, adopted the last-in, first-out (LIFO) method of valuing inventories. (For a discussion of the LIFO method, see Chapter 7.)[97] The special rules were considered necessary to prevent a taxpayer from avoiding the rule that on the adoption of LIFO, all prior market write-downs of inventory must be restored to income (and inventory) ratably over a three-year period beginning with the year of the change to LIFO.[98]

For example, if the original change in method were from a lower-of-cost-or-market method of valuing inventory to a cost-only method, the Section 481 adjustment would have been taken into income ratably over a period of up to six years. This Section 481 adjustment would have been the very same adjustment that otherwise would have been required on the adoption of LIFO. Consequently, unless special rules had been provided, taxpayers might have sought to avoid the three-year LIFO restoration rule by virtue of a previously obtained six-year spread.

To prevent this situation, Revenue Procedure 84-74 provided that on the adoption of LIFO, the unamortized balance of the Section 481 adjustment attributable to a prior change in method would be included in income in an amount equal to the amount that would have been included in income by that particular year if the LIFO method had been adopted at the time of the prior change in method.[99]

EXAMPLE: Assume that a taxpayer had changed from a lower of the cost or market method to a cost-only method in year 8 and that the resulting Section 481 adjustment was $60.[100] Under Revenue Procedure 84-74, the taxpayer would have recognized this adjustment at the rate of $10 per year for each of its years 8 through 13. If the taxpayer had elected LIFO in year 9, the taxpayer would have been required to recognize in the income of year 9 and subsequent years the amount that would have been recognized by that time had LIFO been adopted in year 8. Consequently, because $10 had been recognized in year 8, the balance of $50 would have been recognized at the rate of $30 in year 9 and $20 in year 10.[101]

---

[97] LIFO may be adopted without the prior approval of the Commissioner. IRC § 472.

[98] IRC § 472(d).

[99] Rev. Proc. 84-74, 1984-2 CB 736, § 5.07.

[100] For a discussion of the lower-of-cost-or-market method, see ¶ 6.09.

[101] Rev. Proc. 84-74, 1984-2 CB 736, § 5.07.

[d] Termination of LIFO Inventory Method

Generally, under Revenue Procedure 84-74, the IRS would have approved a taxpayer's request to discontinue its use of the LIFO method if (1) the taxpayer had agreed to take the Section 481 adjustment into income pursuant to the general rules of Revenue Procedure 84-74 and (2) the taxpayer had agreed not to reelect LIFO for a period of 10 taxable years (beginning with the year of change) without the prior approval of the Commissioner.[102] As a practical matter, the Commissioner would not approve a reelection within the 10-year period unless the taxpayer was able to show extraordinary circumstances in support of its request.

[e] Other Circumstances

Other circumstances not specifically identified in Revenue Procedure 84-74 may also have caused the IRS to qualify or reduce the otherwise authorized spread period or to require an acceleration in the recognition of the balance of a Section 481 adjustment. Accordingly, a taxpayer that anticipated that the normal spread period rules would permit it to defer the recognition of income beyond the period the IRS would typically approve may have found the spread period limited to prevent this. Alternatively, the taxpayer may have faced an audit challenge to the approved spread period if the examining agent concluded that the taxpayer's application for change in method failed to disclose all material facts, i.e., facts showing the possibility of such a deferral.[103] The issuance of Revenue Procedure 92-20, with its all encompassing scope, may reduce the likelihood that circumstances not expressly identified in that procedure will be raised by the National Office or by agents to limit or accelerate spread periods otherwise available.[104]

[6] Spread of Adjustments Required by 1986 Act

The Tax Reform Act of 1986 (the 1986 Act) requires a number of changes in methods of accounting. In virtually every case, the required change is subject to three requirements. First, the change is treated as if it were initiated by the taxpayer. This treatment ensures that any pre-1954 balance will not be excluded from the amount of the required Section 481

---

[102] Rev. Proc. 84-74, 1984-2 CB 736, § 5.10.

[103] See Cochran Hatchery, Inc., 39 TCM 210 (1979), discussed infra ¶ 8.07, note 307.

[104] See infra ¶ 8.06[3][b] for the terms and conditions affecting spread periods under Rev. Proc. 92-20.

adjustment.[105] Second, the change may be made without filing a formal application. In other words, the Commissioner is deemed already to have approved the change. Third, apparently in an effort to prevent too much of a revenue loss from Revenue Procedure 84-74's typical six-year spread of the applicable Section 481 adjustment, the 1986 Act generally limits the applicable spread to a period of up to four years, although there are certain exceptions. Some of the more important required changes are discussed in the following sections.

[a] Change From Cash Method

Section 448 provides new limitations on the use of the cash method.[106] Section 448(d)(7) sets forth the rules governing a change from the cash method for those taxpayers who are no longer permitted to use that method. In general, the adjustment required on such a change is to be taken into account over a period of up to four years, although hospitals must take the spread into account over a period of 10 years.[107]

The legislative history indicates that except for hospitals, the particular period over which the Section 481 adjustment must be included in income will be determined in accordance with the provisions of Revenue Procedure 84-74.[108] In addition, the applicable committee report indicates (1) that net operating loss and tax credit carry-overs will be allowed to offset any positive Section 481 adjustment; (2) that for purposes of determining estimated tax payments, the adjustment will be taken into account ratably throughout the year in question; and (3) that negative adjustments will be treated on the same basis as positive adjustments.[109]

The mandatory nature of the provision governing the spread periods for hospitals (combined with the congressional recognition of the principles under Revenue Procedure 84-74) suggests that hospitals are entitled to 10-year spreads without regard to the existence of any of the circumstances in Revenue Procedure 84-74 that otherwise would reduce the spread period. Any Treasury Department desire for a contrary conclusion would probably require new legislation. The temporary regulations provide that the 10-year spread available to hospitals may be reduced where, during the 10-year period, the taxpayer ceases to engage in the trade or business to which the Section 481 adjustment relates.[110] This limitation appears inconsistent with the con-

---

[105] See discussion supra ¶ 8.04[1].

[106] See discussion at ¶ 3.06[1].

[107] See H.R. Rep. No. 99-841, 99th Cong., 2d Sess. (1986) (hereinafter Conference Report), at 11-288.

[108] Id. at 11-289.

[109] Id.

[110] Temp. Reg. § 1.448-1T(g)(3)(iii).

trolling statutory language, which specifies that hospitals are to take the applicable Section 481 adjustment into account over a period of 10 years. Consequently, the validity of this regulatory provision is in doubt.

[b] Change From Installment Method for Revolving Credit Sales

Section 453(j) denied use of the installment method of accounting to revolving credit sales.[111] For taxpayers who had been using the installment method for such sales, Section 812(c)(2) of the 1986 Act provided that the required change from that method be treated as initiated by the taxpayer and as having been made with the consent of the Commissioner. Section 812(c)(2) of the Act also provided that the period for taking into account the applicable Section 481 adjustment should not exceed four years. However, the Conference Report accompanying the 1986 Act provided that where the adjustment was to be taken into account over a four-year period, 15 percent of the adjustment should be taken into account in the first taxable year, 25 percent in the second taxable year, and 30 percent in each of the two succeeding taxable years.[112] The conferees presumably were aware of the potential for spread periods of fewer than four years, because the statutory period was stated to be a period not exceeding four years. The Conference Report thus raised the question of whether a taxpayer entitled to a spread period of fewer than four years would be required to take the adjustment into account proportionately in each year or whether some other allocation procedure should be used. To illustrate, assume that a taxpayer has a maximum spread period of three years. Should the Section 481 adjustment be allocated one third to each year? Alternatively, should the 30 percent that would have been reported in year 4 be allocated to the three years and, if so, on what basis? If the 30 percent that would have been allocated to year 4 were allocated one-third to each of the first three years, the total Section 481 adjustment should arguably have been allocated 25 percent to the first year, 35 percent to the second year, and 40 percent to the final year. However, unless the matter is clarified by legislation, taxpayers should assume that when the spread period is shorter than four years, the total adjustment should be allocated ratably, i.e., one third of the total to each of the three years.

[c] Inventory Capitalization Rules

Section 263A made numerous changes in the rules for the costing of

---

[111] See discussion at ¶ 5.04[2][d][ii]. The Revenue Act of 1987 (the 1987 Act) has repealed the use of the installment method by dealers. See ¶ 5.07 for discussion of this repeal and other changes in installment reporting required by the 1987 Act.

[112] Conference Report, supra note 107, at II-301.

inventories.[113] For taxpayers who must change their inventory costing methods, Section 803(d)(2)(B) of the 1986 Act provides that the period for taking the necessary Section 481 adjustment into account will not exceed four years. The Conference Report provides that the actual spread of the Section 481 adjustment is to be determined under the provisions of Revenue Procedure 84-74; net operating loss and tax credit carry-forwards will be allowed to offset any positive Section 481 adjustment, and, for the purpose of determining estimated tax payments, the Section 481 adjustment will be recognized ratably throughout the taxable year of the adjustment.

In temporary regulations issued in March 1987,[114] the Treasury reiterated these points and also provided certain additional rules.[115] For example, if 75 percent or more of a Section 481 adjustment attributable to the change is attributable to the one-, two-, or three-tax year period immediately preceding the year of change, then the highest percentage attributable to such period is to be taken into account ratably over a three-year taxable period. The remaining balance is to be taken into account in the fourth year.

The temporary regulations also provide that the Commissioner may require additional procedures, including the need to file an application for change in method.[116] However, in an apparent attempt to emphasize the mandatory nature of the required change, the regulations provide that taxpayers who must change their method of accounting but who fail to do so will be deemed to be using an improper method.[117] Reference is then made to Section 446(f), which relates to the imposition of penalties for taxpayers using improper methods.[118] This reference seems to be a clear signal that taxpayers who fail to make the change may be subject to the imposition of penalties.

The temporary regulations also require that taxpayers who change their method of accounting under Section 263A must revalue any deferred gain or loss on sales of inventory in deferred intercompany transactions.[119] In Notice 88-86,[120] the Treasury announced that forthcoming regulations would clarify that the deferred gain or loss will not need to be revalued in circumstances where the purchasing member acquires the goods for use in its trade or business and not for the purpose of holding such goods as inventory.

---

[113] See discussion at ¶¶ 6.06[1][c], 6.06[2][c][ii].

[114] See Temp. Reg. § 1.263A-1T.

[115] Temp. Reg. § 1.263A-1T(e)(3).

[116] Temp. Reg. § 1.263A-1T(e)(11).

[117] Temp. Reg. § 1.263A-1T(e)(11)(iv).

[118] Id. See discussion infra ¶ 8.09.

[119] Temp. Reg. § 1.263A-1T(e)(1)(ii).

[120] Notice 88-86, 1988-34 IRB 10 (1988).

In Notice 88-86, the Treasury also announced that a number of modifications to, and clarifications of, the previously issued temporary regulations would be included in forthcoming regulations. In certain instances, the forthcoming regulations will modify the original regulations with regard to opportunities for changes in methods of accounting. For example, the notice provided that for a taxpayer seeking to make a change in its method of accounting for inventories, the change may be adopted on a federal income tax return for the first year for which Section 263A is effective, including an amended return filed on or before May 19, 1989; or, alternatively, on a federal income tax return adopting the use of the new method for the second year for which Section 263A is effective, including an amended federal income tax return filed on or before May 19, 1989, but, in this case, only if the previous method used by the taxpayer was a correct method under Section 263A and the regulations thereunder. In this instance, no Section 481 adjustment will be required. Instead, the new method will be applied to all costs incurred in the taxable year for which the method is first adopted without restating beginning balances for that year.

[d] Repeal of Reserve Method for Bad Debts

The 1986 Act repealed use of the reserve method of accounting for bad debts. Section 805(d)(2) of the 1986 Act provided that the required change from the reserve method shall be treated as initiated by the taxpayer and made with the consent of the Secretary of the Treasury. However, in a departure from the approach taken with respect to other changes, the Section 481 adjustment was to be taken into account ratably only over a period of four years instead of over a period of *up to* four years. There was no indication that the actual spread period would be subject to the principles set forth in Revenue Procedure 84-74.[121]

The Conference Report provided that the amount to be included in income was the full balance of the reserve account without offset for any anticipated amounts that would not be currently accrued as income under the rules allowing accrual-basis service providers to exclude from income amounts determined not to be collectible.[122] This language suggested that an accrual method service provider could take the adjustment resulting from the repeal of the reserve method into income over four years but could exclude essentially the same amount of income entirely in the year of change under the new exclusionary rule. On the other hand, the

---

[121] On the other hand, the Conference Report refers to the applicable spread period as *generally* four years. Conference Report, supra note 107, at II-315.

[122] Id. at II-315–316. See ¶ 4.03[2][d] regarding the new exclusionary rule for accrual method service providers.

Conference Report indicated the intent that the exclusion from income under this new rule would itself be taken into account over a period of four years.[123] This latter interpretation was followed in the temporary regulations, which provided that the adjustment to the so-called non-accrual-experience method must be taken into account ratably over a period of four taxable years.[124]

The National Office has ruled that where the taxpayer was in the process of deducting its initial reserve balance (arising from a prior change to the reserve method) over a 10-year period, the unamortized portion of the initial reserve, computed on December 31, 1986 should reduce the amount of the December 31, 1986 reserve so that only the net amount is taken into income under Section 805(d)(2) of the 1986 Act.[125]

[7] Spread of Adjustment Under Revenue Procedure 92-20

Revenue Procedure 92-20 provides the various terms and conditions governing a taxpayer's change in method,[126] including the period over which any Section 481 adjustment may be spread. The number of years in the spread period varies depending on the method from which the taxpayer is requesting permission to change, whether the taxpayer is then under examination, and various other circumstances. These terms and conditions are discussed more fully below.[127]

[8] Cut-off Method for LIFO Changes Under Revenue Procedure 92-20

Revenue Procedure 92-20 recognizes that a change in a taxpayer's LIFO method of inventory accounting raises numerous, complex problems. Consequently, for the first time, the IRS has expressly approved a so-called cut-off method for handling these changes. Under the cut-off method, no Section 481 adjustment would be required. The cut-off method is not available in all

---

[123] See Conference Report, supra note 107, at II-288, where the conferees stated:

It is the intent of the conferees that this [four-year spread] apply to all changes resulting from the provision, including any changes necessitated by the rule that certain accrual taxpayers, including taxpayers presently on the accrual method of accounting, need not recognize income on amounts statistically determined not to be collectible.

[124] Temp. Reg. § 1.448-2T(g)(2).

[125] Priv. Ltr. Rul. 8724015 (Mar. 13, 1987).

[126] Rev. Proc. 92-20, 1992-1 CB 685.

[127] See discussion infra ¶ 8.06[3][b].

cases. A full discussion of the special rules governing changes in LIFO methods is set forth below.[128]

¶ 8.05 EARNINGS AND PROFITS

The Section 481 adjustment is to be taken into account for purposes of computing earnings and profits just as it is taken into account for purposes of computing taxable income.[129] Consequently, a taxpayer will want to consider carefully the timing of corporate distributions. For example, accelerating an otherwise planned distribution (or delaying an otherwise planned change in method of accounting) might generate a return of capital rather than a dividend.

¶ 8.06 APPLICATION TO CHANGE METHOD OF ACCOUNTING

[1] General Rule

A taxpayer generally requests consent to a change in method of accounting by filing an application for change with the Commissioner of Internal Revenue in Washington, D.C. within 180 days after the beginning of the first tax year for which the change is requested.[130] The taxpayer must provide all information requested on the application form (Form 3115) and all other information that the Commissioner might thereafter require in order to make a decision on the taxpayer's request.[131] A fee must accompany the application for change. The present fee for an application to change a method of accounting is $600,[132] but this fee is subject to revision, and practitioners and taxpayers should confirm the appropriate fee at the time of the filing of the application. A request for a ruling, including a ruling pertaining to an accounting method (other than one submitted on a Form 3115), must also be accompanied by an appropriate fee, which is currently $3,000.[133]

In addition to filing Form 3115, the Code provides other means for the taxpayer to make particular changes. For example, Section 472 provides for

---

[128] See discussion infra ¶ 8.06[3][b][v].

[129] Rev. Proc. 79-47, 1979-2 CB 528.

[130] See ¶ 2.04[3] for a discussion of how the Commissioner's actions on audit may result in an implied acceptance of accounting method change shown in the return.

[131] Treas. Reg. § 1.446-1(e)(3)(i).

[132] Rev. Proc. 93-23, 1993—CB—.

[133] Id.

an automatic election to adopt or change to the LIFO method of inventory accounting. Section 453 provides the rules governing elections not to use the installment method for deferred payment sales of property by nondealers. Any desired change in accounting method that is not covered by a specific Code section, Treasury regulation, or revenue procedure is subject to the general rule previously described.

The IRS may elaborate on the general rule or amplify the requirements governing particular changes by means of revenue procedures. The present revenue procedure governing most changes in accounting methods is Revenue Procedure 92-20.[134]

Should a particular change in method not qualify for application of Revenue Procedure 92-20 and not be covered by any other expressly applicable Code section, Treasury regulation, or revenue procedure, the taxpayer presumably will be subject to the general rules of Sections 446 and 481. The taxpayer should therefore be able to seek agreement with the IRS on the particular terms and conditions governing the change in method, but the taxpayer will not know in advance whether any unusual terms and conditions will be acceptable to, or required by, the IRS.

Discussed in the following sections are the governing procedures under Revenue Procedures 84-74 and 92-20. Revenue Procedure 84-74 was applicable to applications for change filed before March 23, 1992. Revenue Procedure 92-20 is applicable to applications for change filed on or after March 23, 1992.

[2] Governing Procedures Under Revenue Procedure 84-74

Revenue Procedure 84-74 was a fairly comprehensive document.[135] Its purpose was to set forth the applicable procedures for obtaining the Commissioner's consent to a change in method of accounting and to provide the manner in which any Section 481 adjustment resulting from the change was to be taken into account. The procedure was intended to apply to virtually all changes other than those expressly covered by other published documents.[136] Revenue Procedure 84-74 was modified and superseded by Revenue Procedure 92-20, which is applicable to changes in methods of accounting filed on or after March 23, 1992.[137]

Although Revenue Procedure 84-74 is no longer applicable to applica-

---

[134] See Rev. Proc. 92-20, 1992-1 CB 685 and discussion supra ¶ 8.06[3].

[135] Rev. Proc. 84-74 has been modified and superseded by Rev. Proc. 92-20, 1992-1 CB 685. Revenue Procedure 92-20 is discussed infra ¶ 8.06[3].

[136] Rev. Proc. 84-74, 1984-2 CB 736, 737, § 1, stated that a "change in method of accounting can be made only under the provisions of this revenue procedure except as otherwise specifically provided by published documents."

[137] Rev. Proc. 92-20, 1992-1 CB 685, §§ 13, 14.

tions for change in methods of accounting filed currently, it continues to be important with respect to requests for changes filed prior to March 23, 1992. For this reason, the governing procedures of Revenue Procedure 84-74 remain important.

The first matter of importance was to determine the scope of Revenue Procedure 84-74. It did not apply to the changes identified in the following sections.

[a] IRS Change of Erroneous Method in First Year Method Used

If the year in which an erroneous method was first used was under examination, or if a change in method of accounting was made during that year without the prior approval of the Commissioner, then Revenue Procedure 84-74 was inapplicable.[138] Any change in method required by the IRS had to be made in that year with the full amount of the Section 481 adjustment taken into account in that year. Since the Section 481 adjustment was attributable entirely to a single year, the inclusion of the adjustment in that year did not result in any bunching of income or in any undue financial hardship. Consequently, there was no reason to permit a spread of the resulting adjustment. In fact, any such spread would have produced distortion and an unintended financial benefit to the taxpayer.

[b] Change From Category A Method Following Contact by IRS

Revenue Procedure 84-74 was not applicable to changes from Category A (certain improper) methods if the taxpayer had been contacted by the IRS for the purpose of scheduling an examination of the taxpayer's returns and the examination had not yet been completed.[139]

[i] Definition of "Category A method." "Category A methods" was defined under Revenue Procedure 84-74 as methods that were expressly not permitted by the Code, Treasury regulations, or decisions of the U.S. Supreme Court.[140] Consequently, Category A methods did not automatically include methods that only the lower courts or the IRS itself had determined to be improper. However, under the revenue procedure, the IRS could, or at the taxpayer's request would, treat any other method of accounting as a Category A method if such method was "clearly erroneous." A method would not be considered clearly erroneous if that method (1) had been accepted in a published statement on behalf of the accounting profession; (2) had been accepted under any current accounting

---

[138] Rev. Proc. 84-74, 1984-2 CB 736, § 4.01(1).

[139] Rev. Proc. 84-74, 1984-2 CB 736, § 4.01(2).

[140] Rev. Proc. 84-74, 1984-2 CB 736, § 6.02.

convention or practice recognized within the taxpayer's industry or a related industry or type of business; (3) was acceptable under the materiality doctrine of generally accepted accounting practice; or (4) had been accepted in a published document by the IRS.[141]

The definition of "Category A methods" contained in Revenue Procedure 84-74 gave the IRS significant discretion to treat virtually any method of accounting as a Category A method, unless the taxpayer could affirmatively demonstrate the acceptability of the method under one of the previously stated standards. The wide variety of practices within many businesses and industries made it difficult for this acceptability to be established. Moreover, the alternative of showing acceptability in a published document on behalf of the accounting profession made it difficult for the legitimacy of particular methods to be established solely on the basis of oral testimony by expert accountants, accounting academicians, or others who normally would have been in a position to give such testimony. Reasons such as these resulted in a new definition of Category A methods under Revenue Procedure 92-20.[142]

The revenue procedure provided the following examples of Category A methods: certain methods of inventory valuation identified as incorrect by the applicable regulations,[143] write-downs of inventory on a basis other than those in compliance with the applicable Treasury regulations,[144] use of the cash method in connection with the reporting of inventories,[145] use of a long-term contract method of accounting for nonqualifying activities,[146] failure to comply with the full absorption inventory costing regulations,[147] use of an inappropriate method by a farming corporation,[148] use of a method of accounting that provided for deductions as interest of original issue discount on obligations with a term of one year or less,[149] and use of the LIFO meth-

---

[141] Id.

[142] Rev. Proc. 92-20, 1992-1 CB 685, § 3.06.

[143] See Treas. Reg. §§ 1.471-2(f)(1)–1.471-2(f)(7) and discussion at ¶ 6.08[2][b].

[144] See Treas. Reg. §§ 1.471-2(c), 1.471-4(b); Thor Power Tool Co. v. Comm'r, 439 US 522 (1979).

[145] See Treas. Reg. §§ 1.446-1(c)(2), 1.446-1(e)(2)(iii), Example 1.

[146] See Treas. Reg. § 1.451-3(b). See Ann. 87-65, 1987-28 IRB 38, where the IRS exercised its discretion to treat a change from a long-term contract method of accounting as a change from a Category B method, if (1) the change was required by Treasury's amendment to the December 30, 1985, regulations governing the treatment of long-term contracts under Treas. Reg. § 1.451-3 and (2) the application for change was filed on or before October 31, 1987.

[147] See Treas. Reg. § 1.471-11.

[148] See IRC § 1.471-11.

[149] See Treas. Reg. § 1.163-4.

od of inventory accounting when a termination event had occurred in a year not barred by the statute of limitations.[150]

The Commissioner's characterization of a method as Category A or Category B was, and remains, reviewable by the courts.[151] In one such review, the Tax Court determined that an erroneous interpretation of a regulation does not amount to a specifically prohibited method.[152] Similarly, if the propriety of any method required an evaluation of the taxpayer's interpretation of general principles associated with its use of the method, a Category A method should not be found under Revenue Procedure 84-74 unless the application or interpretation was so inappropriate that it would be found to satisfy the clearly erroneous standard.[153] Typically, taxpayers who are uncertain whether they qualify under particular rules should file applications in accordance with the rules and avoid the risk that the IRS will agree with the taxpayer's position, but then assert that the taxpayer failed to file the necessary forms or otherwise to meet the necessary conditions.[154]

[ii] Contact by IRS. Although the method of accounting in question may be a Category A method, Revenue Procedure 84-74 remained applicable unless the taxpayer had been contacted by the IRS for the purpose of scheduling an examination prior to the filing of a Form 3115 application for change, and the examination had not yet been completed. For this purpose, initial contact could have been in any manner whatever, e.g., by letter or by phone call.

Once the taxpayer had been contacted by the IRS, the inapplicability of Revenue Procedure 84-74 continued until the examination was completed. Any change in method of accounting during the period following contact and before completion of the audit would be made by the District Director. As these rules suggest, if a taxpayer did not disclose the use of the erroneous method, and the IRS did not discover its use during the course of an audit, the revenue procedure would become applicable to a change made after the close of the examination.

The foregoing rules put the taxpayer in a most difficult position. On one

---

[150] See Rev. Proc. 79-23, 1979-1 CB 564.

[151] Capitol Fed. Sav. & Loan Ass'n, 96 TC 204 (1991).

[152] Id.

[153] In Capitol Fed. Sav. & Loan Ass'n, 96 TC 204 (1991), the court focused on the definition of "Category A method" under Rev. Proc. 80-51, which did not include the clearly erroneous basis for defining a method as Category A.

[154] This very circumstance arose in Mulholland v. United States, 92-1 USTC ¶ 50,267 (Cl. Ct. 1992), but in light of the particular facts, including the examining agent's position that the taxpayer did not qualify for the benefits of Rev. Proc. 84-28, the court agreed to review the issue and not to deny application of the revenue procedure merely because of the taxpayer's failure to follow it in light of the agent's position.

hand, the taxpayer was entitled to spread the Section 481 adjustment arising from a change from a Category A method, if such change was requested after the audit was closed. This encouraged the taxpayer to remain silent during the audit, since it would not be entitled to a spread of the adjustment if use of the erroneous method was disclosed during the audit. On the other hand, if the erroneous method was discovered by the IRS during the course of its audit, the IRS could seek to impose penalties for use of the incorrect method. Taxpayers needed to evaluate carefully all these countervailing considerations before deciding what, if any, action to take.

[iii] **Taxpayers subject to continuous audit.**   Some taxpayers are under continuous, or almost continuous, audit. For these taxpayers, Revenue Procedure 84-74 became applicable during the 120-day period following the date that the IRS issued the appropriate letter or report concluding the examination. [155] Where an application to change was filed under the 120-day rule, the application had to be marked, "FILED UNDER PARAGRAPH 4.02(1) OF REV. PROC. 84-74." The 120-day rule did not apply (1) when a Category A method had been included as an item of adjustment in the report of the IRS; (2) when the Category A method issue had been placed in suspense by the IRS; or (3) when the taxpayer had within the 120-day period received notification prior to the filing of Form 3115 that the Category A method would be an issue under consideration on audit.

In addition to the 120-day rule, the revenue procedure contained a special 30-day rule that permitted a taxpayer that had been precluded from filing Form 3115 for at least 18 consecutive months to file Form 3115 during the first 30 days of any tax year following the running of an 18-month period. [156] In order to take advantage of this 30-day rule, the taxpayer must not have received a notice that the change in method of accounting was an issue under consideration in the audit. Any application filed under this provision had to be marked, "FILED UNDER PARAGRAPH 4.02(2) OF REV. PROC. 84-74, 30 DAY WINDOW."

[c] **Return Under Review When Form 3115 Filed**

Revenue Procedure 84-74 was not applicable where, at the time of filing Form 3115, the taxpayer's return (1) was under consideration by an IRS Appeals Office; (2) was before any federal court; or (3) otherwise was under examination by the District Director. [157] However, where the return was before an Appeals Office or before a federal court, the taxpayer would nevertheless be permitted to request a change under Revenue Procedure 84-74

---

[155] Rev. Proc. 84-74, 1984-2 CB 736, § 4.02(1).

[156] Rev. Proc. 84-74, 1984-2 CB 736, § 4.02(2).

[157] Rev. Proc. 84-74, 1984-2 CB 736, § 4.01(3).

if it obtained the consent of the Appeals Office or counsel for the government. Alternatively, if the taxpayer was before an Appeals Office and the method of accounting issue has not been raised by the IRS, the taxpayer could apply the revenue procedure if necessary to comply with the requirements of a revenue ruling or revenue procedure that had been published by the IRS and had designated the method used as inappropriate with specific reference being made to Section 5.12(2) of Revenue Procedure 84-74.

It is important to note that this provision regarding the nonapplicability of Revenue Procedure 84-74, where the taxpayer's return was under examination by the District Director, did not govern Category A methods. Category A methods under examination were subject to the rules previously discussed.[158] This provision on nonapplicability where the return was under examination also did not apply to Category B methods, which were all methods other than Category A methods,[159] if the taxpayer agreed to the following three conditions.

First, if the method being changed involved an issue raised by the IRS during the examination, the taxpayer had to agree that the year of change would be the most recent year then under examination but not later than the most recent year for which a return had been filed at the date the examination began. If the taxpayer's accounting method was not raised as an issue during the examination, the year of change would be the normal year of change. In other words, if the taxpayer was able to file its application within the first 180 days of its tax year, the change would be effective in that year. If the taxpayer was unable to meet that deadline, the taxpayer would request that the change be effected in the next succeeding tax year.

Second, if the method being changed involved an issue raised by the IRS during its examination and the method had been designated as improper (for purposes of Section 5.12(2) of Revenue Procedure 84-74) by a revenue ruling or revenue procedure that had been in effect for more than two years, any resulting positive Section 481 adjustment could not be spread over a period of more than three years.

Third, the taxpayer had to comply with such other terms and conditions as had been prescribed by the Commissioner. These could cover the effect of the adjustment on earnings and profits and net operating losses.[160]

If an accounting method issue was before an appeals officer, the appeals officer had discretion to settle the issue on a basis permitting a spread of the resulting adjustment. It was unclear whether the appeals officer would have had the discretion to allow a spread period of more years than otherwise would have been permitted by Revenue Procedure 84-74. However, absent a clear prohibition, the appeals officer probably had such discretion.

---

[158] See supra ¶ 8.06[2][b].

[159] Rev. Proc. 84-74, 1984-2 CB 736, § 6.03.

[160] See Rev. Proc. 84-74, 1984-2 CB 736, §§ 5.05, 5.15.

[d] Proposed LIFO Termination

If a taxpayer sought to change from the use of the LIFO inventory method (see Chapter 7 for a discussion of the LIFO inventory method), it could generally do so under the procedures of Revenue Procedure 84-74.[161] However, if the reason for the requested termination was that a termination event (as described in Revenue Procedure 79-23)[162] had occurred in an open year (i.e., a year not barred by the statute of limitations), then the change from LIFO would be classified as a change from a Category A method.[163]

On the other hand, the revenue procedure was not applicable to changes from the LIFO method of inventory accounting if the IRS proposed to terminate the taxpayer's use of LIFO on the basis of a termination event that had occurred during a tax year on which the statute of limitations had run.[164] In such a circumstance, the general rule would apply. Accordingly, unless the IRS were willing to agree to a spread of the Section 481 adjustment, the adjustment would be included in income entirely in the year of change.

[e] Criminal Investigation

Revenue Procedure 84-74 did not apply where there was a pending criminal investigation or proceeding concerning (1) an issue relating to the taxpayer's tax liability or (2) the possibility of false or fraudulent statements by the taxpayer with respect to any issue.[165]

[f] IRS Decision Not to Process Application

The IRS reserved the right not to process an application for change in method filed under Revenue Procedure 84-74 if approval of the change was not in the best interest of sound tax administration.[166] It was uncertain how this provision would be applied, but the IRS had stated that the impact of approval of the change on compliance efforts would be an important factor.[167]

---

[161] Rev. Proc. 84-74, 1984-2 CB 736, § 5.10.

[162] Rev. Proc. 79-23, 1979-1 CB 564. See ¶ 7.05 for identification and discussion of termination events.

[163] Rev. Proc. 84-74, 1984-2 CB 736, § 6.02.

[164] Rev. Proc. 84-74, 1984-2 CB 736, § 4.01(4).

[165] Rev. Proc. 84-74, 1984-2 CB 736, § 4.01(5).

[166] Rev. Proc. 84-74, 1984-2 CB 736, § 4.05.

[167] Id. See also Capitol Fed. Sav. & Loan Ass'n, 96 TC 204 (1991), where the Tax Court concluded under Rev. Proc. 80-51, that an IRS decision not to process an application may be appropriate where (1) the taxpayer has been contacted for an examination at the time the application for a Category B accounting method change was submitted; (2) the method to be changed had already been disapproved by the

[3] Governing Procedures Under Revenue Procedure 92-20

Following the issuance of Revenue Procedure 84-74,[168] the IRS began reviewing and evaluating its experience under that procedure. The IRS soon became concerned that taxpayers were not voluntarily requesting changes from erroneous methods of accounting and were continuing to play the audit lottery, i.e., taxpayers would delay requesting changes from improper methods of accounting until such time as issues about the methods were raised on audit. Ultimately, the IRS concluded that modifications were needed to the provisions of Revenue Procedure 84-74 to encourage taxpayers to request changes from erroneous methods at an earlier time. Revenue Procedure 92-20 is the result of that conclusion.

In general, this new revenue procedure provides what the IRS refers to as "a gradation of incentives to encourage prompt voluntary compliance."[169] The revenue procedure is lengthy, complex, and probably will be found by many to be cumbersome to use. In addition to modifying the regulatory rules governing requests for changes in methods of accounting, the procedure sets out numerous specific rules for various situations and allows for greater participation in method changes by the District Director's office, the Appeals office, and government counsel.[170] Taxpayers and their advisors are cautioned to review Revenue Procedure 92-20 carefully in connection with any proposed change in method of accounting or in connection with the taxpayer's exposure to adjustments and, perhaps, penalties as a result of using an erroneous method of accounting.

Despite its length, Revenue Procedure 92-20 in many respects seeks to clarify and simplify some of the procedures and principles carried over from Revenue Procedure 84-74. However, in other respects, it is far more complicated.

[a] Categorization and Definition of "Accounting Methods"

Revenue Procedure 92-20 provides four categories of accounting methods: Category A methods, Designated A methods, Category B methods, and Designated B methods. The rules vary depending on the category in which the taxpayer's method of accounting is placed. Thus, it is incumbent on taxpayers and their advisors to categorize properly the taxpayer's affected method of accounting.

Commissioner in published rulings; and (3) the change was thereafter proposed by the agents during their examination.

[168] Rev. Proc. 84-74, 1984-2 CB 36.

[169] Id., § 1.

[170] See discussion infra ¶ 8.06[3][b].

[i] **Definition of "Category A method."** A "Category A method" is defined as a method specifically not permitted by the Code, the Treasury regulations, or a decision of the U.S. Supreme Court.[171] In addition, a Category A method includes a method of accounting that differs from a method the taxpayer is specifically required to use by the Code, the Treasury regulations, or a decision of the U.S. Supreme Court. Finally, a Category A method also includes a Designated B method, if the taxpayer files a Form 3115 requesting a change from a Designated B method more than two years after the designation occurred. In other words, and as explained more fully below,[172] a method may be categorized initially as a Designated B method and, if the taxpayer fails to take action within the appropriate period of time, that method may ripen into a Category A method.

This definition of "Category A methods" departs from the definition of such methods under Revenue Procedure 84-74 in several respects. First, methods that the IRS believes to be "clearly erroneous" methods will no longer be classified as Category A methods unless they fit one of the other standards for such a classification. This deletion of the clearly erroneous test is a considerable improvement over Revenue Procedure 84-74. Under that procedure, agents would sometimes arbitrarily characterize methods of accounting as Category A methods based on the clearly erroneous standard and then impose on taxpayers the burden of proving that the methods were not clearly erroneous. There was a lack of uniformity in the administration of this classification scheme, and it was sometimes used by examining agents as a threat, bargaining chip, or means of intimidating taxpayers. For example, in some cases examining agents would seek to work out an issue involving a method of accounting on the basis that the method at issue was a Category B method. If the taxpayer ultimately refused to agree to the examining agent's particular proposal, the agent would, in his report, reclassify the taxpayer's method as a Category A method in order to remove the benefits that otherwise would have been available to the taxpayer.

The new definition also adds to the ambit of Category A methods those methods that differ from specifically required methods. In some respects, this addition is logical. It treats specifically prohibited methods and methods that differ from specifically required methods the same. On the other hand, one obviously fertile area of controversy will involve determining whether the method used by the taxpayer is inconsistent with or departs from a method specifically required by the Code, the regulations, or a decision of the U.S. Supreme Court. Some revenue agents already have taken the position under Revenue Procedure 92-20 that any method that fails to clearly reflect income may be defined as a Category A method because the method would be inconsistent with a method specifically required by virtue of the clear reflection

---

[171] Rev. Proc. 92-20, 1992-1 CB 685, § 3.06.
[172] See discussion infra ¶ 8.06[3][a][iv].

standard of Section 446(b). Such a position is obviously incorrect and inappropriate. Under such an approach, every incorrect method could be classified as a Category A method. Such a result is not intended by the revenue procedure as evidenced by the mere fact that a Designated B method, which is an incorrect method in the view of the IRS, does not itself ripen into a Category A method until it has been so designated for a period of more than two years.[173] Moreover, a method should not be classified as a Category A method if its impropriety requires a subjective evaluation and interpretation of general tax principles.[174]

The revenue procedure provides the following examples of Category A methods: certain methods of inventory valuation identified as incorrect by the applicable regulations,[175] write-downs of inventory on a basis not in compliance with the applicable Treasury regulations,[176] the use of the cash method for purchases and sales of merchandise when such merchandise is an income producing factor[177] or where the taxpayer is otherwise prohibited from using the cash method,[178] and use of the LIFO method of inventory accounting when a termination event has occurred in a year not barred by the statute of limitations.[179]

[ii] **Definition of "Designated A method."** A "Designated A method" of accounting is defined as a Category A method that has been designated as a Designated A method in a document published in the Internal Revenue Bulletin.[180] Consequently, taxpayers and their advisors must remain alert to revenue rulings, revenue procedures, or other published documents that may make such designations.

---

[173] Notwithstanding this discussion, taxpayers and their advisors should remain alert to the fact that courts have sometimes suggested that even prohibited methods may be allowed (and found to reflect income clearly) if the results produced under such methods are virtually identical to the results produced under the required method. See discussion at ¶ 2.02[f].

[174] See, e.g., Capitol Fed. Sav. & Loan Ass'n, 96 TC 204 (1991).

[175] See Treas. Reg. §§ 1.471-2(f)(1)–1.471-2(f)(7) and discussion at ¶ 6.08[2][b].

[176] See Treas. Reg. §§ 1.471-2(c), 1.471-4(b); Thor Power Tool Co. v. Comm'r, 439 US 522 (1979), and discussion at ¶ 6.09.

[177] See, e.g., Treas. Reg. § 1.446-1(c)(2)(i).

[178] See, e.g., IRC §§ 447, 448.

[179] See, e.g., Rev. Proc. 79-23, 1979-1 CB 564, for termination events. However, for purposes of Rev. Proc. 92-20, a termination event does not occur if the taxpayer first issues nonconforming financial statements during the taxable year for which the LIFO method is discontinued (the year of change) and the nonconforming financial statements relate either to the year of change or the year preceding the year of change. Rev. Proc. 92-20, 1992-12 IRB 12, § 3.06(7).

[180] Rev. Proc. 92-20, 1992-1 CB 685, § 3.07.

[iii] Definition of "Category B method." Consistent with the definition used in Revenue Procedure 84-74, Revenue Procedure 92-20 defines "Category B method" as all methods other than those determined to be Category A methods, without regard to whether the Category A method is a Designated A method.[181]

[iv] Definition of "Designated B method." A "Designated B method" is a Category B method that has been designated as a Designated B method in a document published by the IRS.[182] Consequently, taxpayers and their advisors must remain alert to the possibility of such designations in revenue rulings, revenue procedures, or other documents published by the IRS.

If a method has been designated as a Designated B method, it may ripen into a Category A method two years after the date of such designation or at such other time as may be provided in the designating document. Consequently, taxpayers filing applications to change from Category B methods, must remain alert to whether the Category B method is a Designated B method and, if so, the time when the designating document was published and the possibility that the designating document provided a special rule for determining the time when the method will ripen into a Category A method.

[b] Terms and Conditions of Change

Revenue Procedure 92-20 provides the various terms and conditions that govern a taxpayer's change in method. These terms and conditions may vary depending on the circumstances. The circumstances include the category of method from which the taxpayer is seeking to change; whether the taxpayer is under audit and, if so, whether an issue has been raised as to the taxpayer's method; and the number of years the taxpayer has been using the method. The particular terms and conditions associated with the change include, principally, the year of change and the period over which the resulting Section 481 adjustment may be spread.

The terms and conditions that will be applied to changes in particular circumstances are summarized in the following table and are discussed more fully in succeeding sections. Nevertheless, taxpayers and their advisors must recognize that the IRS has reserved the right to decline to process any application for change under Revenue Procedure 92-20 whenever the IRS determines that it will not be in the best interest of sound tax administration to permit the requested change.[183] The IRS has specified that a principal issue in exercising its discretion in this manner will be whether the proposed change would clearly and directly frustrate compliance efforts of the IRS in

---

[181] Rev. Proc. 92-20, 1992-1 CB 685, § 3.08.

[182] Rev. Proc. 92-20, 1992-1 CB 685, § 3.09.

[183] Rev. Proc. 92-20, 1992-1 CB 685, § 10.01.

administering the tax laws.[184] Consequently, if a taxpayer believes its application and use of the revenue procedure will produce a benefit that could not reasonably be viewed as intended by the IRS, the taxpayer should be ready for the processing of its application to be denied.

Table of Taxpayer Options Under Rev. Proc. 92-20

(1) Category A Methods: Taxpayer not under examination; or within 120-day window; 30-day window; or 90-day post-affiliation window; or who receives consent from District Director.

Adjustment	Year of Change	Maximum § 481 spread period
positive	regular current year; year in of window period begins; or, for 90-day post-affiliation window (if later), first day of year in which acquired subsidiary is in new consolidated group.	up to 3 years
negative	same as above	no spread

(2) Category A Methods: Taxpayer under examination (90-day window).

Adjustment	Year of Change	Maximum § 481 spread period
positive	earliest open year	up to 3 years
negative	current year	no spread

(3) Designated A Methods: Taxpayer not under examination or within 120-day window; 30-day window; or 90-day post-affiliation window and except as otherwise provided in the designating document.

Adjustment	Year of Change	Maximum § 481 spread period
positive	amended returns or current year	no spread; earliest year of change

(4) Designated A Methods: Taxpayer under examination (90-day window): Application for change not permitted.

---

[184] This issue is discussed further infra ¶ 8.06[3][c][i].

(5) Category B Methods: Taxpayer not under examination or within 120-day window; 30-day window; or 90-day post-affiliation window; or who receives consent from District Director.

Adjustment	Year of Change	Maximum § 481 spread period
positive or negative	same as (1) above	up to 6 years

(6) Category B Methods: Taxpayer under examination (90-day window).

Adjustment	Year of Change	Maximum § 481 spread period
positive	Year for which Form 3115 would be applicable if filed on first day of 90-day window	no spread
negative	same as above	up to 6 years

(7) Changes within LIFO methods: Taxpayer not under examination; or within 120-day window; 30-day window; or 90-day post-affiliation window; or who receives consent from District Director.

Adjustment	Year of Change	Maximum § 481 spread period
N/A (except as otherwise published)	same as (1) above	cut-off (except as otherwise published)

(8) Changes within LIFO methods: Taxpayer under examination (90-day window).

Adjustment	Year of Change	Maximum § 481 spread period
positive (modified year § 481 adjustment based on preceding 10 years only)	earliest taxable	up to 6 years
negative	same as (1) above	cut-off (except as otherwise published)

[i] Taxpayers not under examination (timely, early, and late applications). The terms and conditions governing changes in methods of accounting for taxpayers not under examination generally follow the rules set forth in the applicable Treasury regulations,[185] except that a spread of the Section 481 adjustment may be obtained. In addition, various limitations or

---

[185] See Treas. Reg. § 1.446-1(e).

conditions may be imposed on the taxpayer if it has any of its returns before an appeals office of the IRS or a federal court.

Taxpayer not under examination with no tax year before appeals or in federal court.   In general, Form 3115 (application for change in method of accounting) must be filed within the first 180 days after the year of change or, if earlier, on or before the last day of any short taxable year. The application may nevertheless be considered as timely filed if it is filed after the 180-day period expires but within 270 days assuming the taxpayer can demonstrate good cause and show that the extension of time will not jeopardize the interests of government.[186] For this purpose, the requirements for showing good cause are set forth in Revenue Procedure 79-63, which enumerates that the following factors must be considered in determining whether the applicable requirements are met:[187]

- Due diligence of the taxpayer
- Prompt action by the taxpayer
- Intent of the taxpayer
- Prejudice to the interests of the government
- Consistency with statutory and regulatory objectives

Revenue Procedure 79-63 states that taxpayers seeking extensions must provide information "specifically responsive" to each factor previously identified. The application should include (1) a complete chronology of relevant events leading to the taxpayer's failure to make the application; (2) affidavits from, or a list of, persons having knowledge of these events;[188] and (3) copies of all relevant documents. The revenue procedure specifies that an application for extension should be filed with the IRS, Assistant Commissioner (Technical), 1111 Constitution Avenue, N.W., Washington, D.C. 20224, Attention: T:FP:T.[189] The application must be accompanied by a taxpayer declaration, under penalty of perjury, as to the veracity of the facts presented.[190]

Revenue Procedure 92-20 further provides that accepting an application more than nine months after the beginning of the year of change will be considered to jeopardize the government's interests except in very unusual and compelling circumstances.[191]

Any application filed after the 180-day period for which an extension of time is not sought or, if sought, is denied, will be treated as an application

---

[186] Rev. Proc. 92-20, 1992-12 IRB 10, § 5.01(2)(a).

[187] Rev. Proc. 79-63, 1979-2 CB 578.

[188] The full name and current address of each person should be included.

[189] This assumes the Assistant Commissioner (Technical) has jurisdiction over the matter.

[190] In the case of a corporate taxpayer, the application should be verified by a corporate officer who is aware of the facts and circumstances.

[191] Rev. Proc. 92-20, 1992-1 CB 685, § 5.01(2)(a).

for the succeeding taxable year (assuming the taxpayer so requests in the case of an application for extension that is denied).[192] For the early application to be perfected, the taxpayer must provide all additional information that was not on the application at the time of filing (i.e., the amount of the Section 481 adjustment as of the beginning of the year of change and the gross receipt and taxable income amounts for the year immediately preceding the year of change) within the first 90 days after the beginning of the year of change.

Taxpayers who file an early application must state at the top of Form 3115: "FILED UNDER ¶ 5.01(3) OF REV. PROC. 92-20."

The year of change for taxpayers in this situation will be the year for which Form 3115 is considered timely filed.

The spread period for the Section 481 adjustment arising from the change will depend on the category of method from which the taxpayer is changing and whether the adjustment is positive or negative. If the change is from a Category A method and results in a net positive Section 481 adjustment, the taxpayer must take the adjustment into account ratably over a period of up to three taxable years beginning with the year of change.[193] If the change is from a Category A method and results in a negative Section 481 adjustment, the adjustment must be taken into account entirely in the year of change.[194]

If the change is from a Designated A method, the taxpayer has the option of changing retroactively or prospectively.[195] For taxpayers making the change prospectively, a charge is imposed to approximate the time value of money economic benefit that the taxpayer will derive from changing its method prospectively.[196] In effect, the intent is to provide the least benefit to taxpayers changing from Designated A methods.

If the change is from a Category B method, the revenue procedure specifies that the Section 481 adjustment (whether positive or negative) must be taken into account ratably over a period of up to six taxable years beginning with the year of change. If the change is from a Designated B method and Form 3115 is filed within two years after the date of designation (or such other period as may be provided in the designating document), the change will be treated as a change from a Category B method.[197] If the application is filed more than two years after the date the method is designated as a Category B method (or more than whatever other period is

---

[192] Rev. Proc. 92-20, 1992-1 CB 685, §§ 5.01(2)(b), 5.01(3).

[193] Rev. Proc. 92-20, 1992-1 CB 685, § 5.03(1)(a).

[194] Rev. Proc. 92-20, 1992-1 CB 685, § 5.03(1)(b).

[195] Rev. Proc. 92-20, 1992-1 CB 685, § 7.02(2).

[196] Rev. Proc. 92-20, 1992-1 CB 685, § 7.03.

[197] Rev. Proc. 92-20, 1992-1 CB 685, § 3.09.

otherwise provided in the designating document), the change will be treated as a change from a Category A method.[198]

All the spread periods are subject to certain exceptions.[199] In addition, special rules are provided for LIFO taxpayers. For example, if the change is from one LIFO inventory method or sub-method to another LIFO inventory method or sub-method, the change will be made using a so-called cut-off method whether the change is from a Category A or Category B method.[200]

These rules are fairly straightforward. However, some points should be noted. First, where a taxpayer is changing from a Category B method, which does not clearly reflect income, to an acceptable method and the resulting Section 481 adjustment is negative, the Commissioner may not have the discretion to require the taxpayer to spread the negative Section 481 adjustment over a period of years.[201] Second, as in the case of all method changes, the permitted spread period for a change from a Category A or Category B change may not be attractive to the taxpayer when compared to its other options. Consequently, except in cases where taxpayers and their advisors are concerned about the potential imposition of penalties, taxpayers should consider carefully all options available to them, which generally would include continuing their existing method of accounting (even though it may be an incorrect method) or awaiting IRS audit and imposition of change. Interestingly, as in the case of prior revenue procedures, no attempt is made to impose on the taxpayer an obligation to request a change from an improper method. Instead, the revenue procedure merely identifies the consequences of a taxpayer being changed from an improper method, which of course, may include a consideration of penalties depending on the particular facts and circumstances.

Taxpayer not under examination but who has a tax year before an appeals office. A taxpayer who has a tax year before an appeals office may not request a change in method of accounting under Revenue Procedure 92-20 unless the taxpayer obtains a written agreement from the appeals office that

---

[198] Id.

[199] Rev. Proc. 92-20, 1992-1 CB 685, § 8. See discussion infra ¶ 8.06[3][b][v].

[200] Rev. Proc. 92-20, 1992-1 CB 685, § 5.03(3). See discussion infra ¶ 8.06[3][b][v].

[201] See discussion infra ¶ 8.07[2]. See also Treas. Reg. § 1.446-1(e)(3), which provides procedural rules governing an application for change in method of accounting. Although the Commissioner is granted broad authority to prescribe administrative procedures subject to whatever limitations, terms, and conditions she deems necessary to obtain her consent, it is unclear whether such discretion would allow the Commissioner to ignore the precise rules of otherwise controlling statutory provisions, (e.g., the provisions of Section 481, which provide that the Section 481 adjustment resulting from a change in method of accounting is to be taken into account entirely in the year of change unless other terms are agreed on by the taxpayer and the IRS). See discussion supra ¶ 8.04[3] and infra ¶ 8.07[2].

it does not object to the taxpayer requesting that change in method.[202] The revenue procedure does not purport to limit the discretion of the appeals office in dealing with matters, but does point out that if the requested accounting method change is not an issue under consideration by the appeals office, permission to file the application ordinarily should be given.

This requirement directly involves the appeals office in the procedures governing a change in method of accounting. An important practical concern is whether the appeals office will seek to obtain concessions from the taxpayer as a condition for obtaining its approval of the requested change in method. On one hand, such action would seem clearly inappropriate and inconsistent with the spirit of the revenue procedure. On the other hand, since the revenue procedure merely sets forth the offer of the IRS as to the terms and conditions on which it will accept applications for a change in methods of accounting,[203] the IRS may well have the discretion to allow the appeals office to establish whatever conditions it desires. Alternatively, a taxpayer may take the position that obtaining the consent of the appeals office is not consistent with the provisions of applicable Treasury regulations governing changes in methods of accounting and amounts to an unlawful substantive expansion of the conditions required for filing an application for change. Such a challenge may be successful in circumstances where the taxpayer is seeking permission to change from an incorrect method of accounting to a correct method of accounting or to change from a correct method of accounting to another correct method of accounting for substantial business reasons.

The written agreement of the appeals office pursuant to Revenue Procedure 92-20 should be signed by the appropriate appeals officer and attached to the taxpayer's Form 3115. However, if the period within which Form 3115 must be filed will expire before the likely date on which the appeals officer will agree to the method change, the taxpayer may file Form 3115 prior to obtaining the required agreement, provided the application specifies that the agreement is required, and the agreement is thereafter obtained and submitted to the National Office.

The revenue procedure seems to contemplate that the other terms and conditions associated with any particular change in method will be those provided in the revenue procedure. In other words, it does not appear that the IRS expects appeals officers to attach additional conditions to their approval which would vary the terms and conditions otherwise set forth in Revenue Procedure 92-20. However, this remains to be seen.

Taxpayers not under examination but who have a tax year before a federal court with respect to an income tax issue. In circumstances where the taxpayer is not under an examination but has a tax year before a federal court, which does not include an issue involving the affected method of

---

[202] Rev. Proc. 92-20, 1992-1 CB 685, § 4.02.

[203] See discussion infra ¶¶ 8.04[3], 8.06.

accounting, the taxpayer must obtain agreement from government counsel to the filing of Form 3115 pursuant to Revenue Procedure 92-20.[204] In effect, the situation is the same as that just described except that the consent must come from government counsel rather than an appeals officer.

If the taxpayer has tax years before both an appeals officer and a federal court, consent must be obtained from both the appeals officer and government counsel. This requirement raises the possibility of counsel discussing the matter with appeals, which in turn raises that possibility of further delay, complexity, and risk for the taxpayer.

Pending criminal investigation. If at the time the taxpayer desires to request a change in method of accounting there is a pending criminal investigation or a proceeding concerning (1) the taxpayer's federal tax liability for any year or (2) the possibility of false or fraudulent statements made by the taxpayer with respect to any issue relating to its tax liability for any year, the taxpayer may not change its accounting method under Revenue Procedure 92-20.[205] Notwithstanding this prohibition to filing an application for change under Revenue Procedure 92-20, the taxpayer may still be entitled to an application for change under the applicable Treasury regulations.[206] The regulations contain no express prohibition to the filing of Form 3115 in such circumstances, although the Commissioner is given wide discretion in establishing applicable administrative rules regarding requests for changes in methods of accounting.[207] From a policy standpoint, there would seem to be no reason to prohibit a taxpayer from seeking permission from the IRS to change a method of accounting notwithstanding the fact that the taxpayer is presently under criminal investigation. Nevertheless, such a circumstance would certainly be a factor in determining how the National Office will respond to the application for change.

[ii] Taxpayers under examination. Revenue Procedure 92-20 places more conditions on a taxpayer who is under examination than a taxpayer who is not under examination. Although this may not seem illogical, it does place a heavier burden on taxpayers under continuous examination than it does on others. Yet, these very taxpayers are those most likely to follow applicable rules and regulations because of numerous facts, including the fact that they are under continuous examination. Perhaps the reasons for the additional caution are (1) the fact that this group generally consists of the taxpayers earning larger amounts of income whose adjustments involve more money and (2) the government's desire to make sure that it does not somehow forgo obtaining the appropriate amount of revenue by inadvertently

---

[204] Rev. Proc. 92-20, 1992-1 CB 685, § 4.03.

[205] Rev. Proc. 92-20, 1992-1 CB 685, § 4.04.

[206] Treas. Reg. § 1.446-1(e).

[207] Treas. Reg. § 1.446-1(e)(3)(ii).

agreeing to a change in method of accounting that would be undesirable to the District Director conducting the examination. As a general rule, the revenue procedure adopts the view that with certain exceptions, it is not appropriate to permit a taxpayer to file an application for method of accounting while the taxpayer is under examination unless the taxpayer obtains the consent of the District Director. Nevertheless, there are circumstances where the applicable application may be filed within a designated "window period," and the consent of the District Director will not be required. These window periods are discussed in succeeding sections.[208]

In addition, the revenue procedure adopts the view for taxpayers under examination that they should not obtain more advantageous terms and conditions on a change in method than taxpayers who request a change when not under examination. Thus, in evaluating any peculiar facts and circumstances, taxpayers under examination should always consider whether they will obtain an advantage that would not have been available to taxpayers not under examination. If so, they may have a difficult time obtaining the desired treatment.

Application filed within 90-day window after contact for examination.   Special rules exist for taxpayers who have been contacted for an examination and file Form 3115 within 90 days thereafter.[209] However, the running of the 90-day period ends at any time the taxpayer agrees to adjustments proposed by the IRS (e.g., by signing a Form 4549 or a Form 870). Moreover, the 90-day window period will not be available if a taxpayer is already under examination on different tax years and more than 90 days have passed from the beginning of that examination.

Where a taxpayer files the application within the 90-day window, the particular terms and conditions vary depending on the category of method from which the taxpayer is seeking to change and whether the Section 481 adjustment is positive or negative. If the taxpayer is changing from a Category A method and the Section 481 adjustment is positive, the year of change is the earliest taxable year under examination (or, if later, the first taxable year in which the method is considered impermissible). However, if the change results in a net negative Section 481 adjustment, the year of change is the taxable year for which Form 3115 would be considered timely filed if it were filed on the first day of the 90-day period by a taxpayer who was not under examination. In other words, the IRS will delay the effective date of the change where the adjustment results in a reduction in the taxpayer's taxable income.

---

[208] Rev. Proc. 92-20, 1992-1 CB 685, § 6.01. Although consent of the District Director is not required, notice of the application must be provided to the District Director. § 10.06.

[209] Rev. Proc. 92-20, 1992-1 CB 685, § 6.02.

If the change results in a net positive Section 481 adjustment, the adjustment will be taken into account ratably over a period of up to three years beginning with the year of change. If the Section 481 adjustment is negative, the adjustment will be taken into account entirely in the year of change.[210]

If the change is from a Category B method, the year of change is the taxable year for which Form 3115 would be considered timely filed by a taxpayer not under examination, assuming such taxpayer filed the application on the first day of the 90-day window.[211] If the Section 481 adjustment is positive, the taxpayer must take the entire adjustment into account in the year of change. In other words, by filing after the taxpayer has been contacted for examination rather than before the taxpayer has been contacted for examination, the taxpayer has lost the opportunity to spread the positive Section 481 adjustment. If the Section 481 adjustment is negative, the taxpayer must take the adjustment into account ratably over a period of up to six tax years, just as in the case of a taxpayer not under examination.[212] Again, taxpayers whose Category B methods are improper may be able to avoid the required spread of the favorable (negative) Section 481 adjustment by demanding application of IRC Section 481 and the regulations rather than application of the revenue procedure. However, such a demand is likely to be denied, and litigation may be required for the taxpayer to have any chance of obtaining the benefit of taking the negative adjustment into account entirely in the year of change.

If the requested change in method involves a change from one LIFO inventory method or sub-method to another LIFO inventory method or sub-method, the rules are the same whether the taxpayer is changing from a Category A method or a Category B method. In either case, the year of change is the earliest tax year under examination or, if later, the first taxable year in which the particular LIFO method or sub-method from which the taxpayer is changing is considered impermissible. However, if the resulting Section 481 adjustment is negative, the year of change will be the tax year for which Form 3115 would have been considered timely if filed on the first day of the 90-day window by a taxpayer not under examination.[213]

If the Section 481 adjustment arising from the LIFO change is positive, it will be taken into account ratably over a period of up to six taxable years beginning with the year of change. However, if the adjustment is negative, it will be taken into account using a cut-off method.[214] Again, the effect of the cut-off method would be to delay, or perhaps effectively deny, the benefit of

---

[210] Rev. Proc. 92-20, 1992-1 CB 685, §§ 6.02(2)(a), 6.02(2)(b).

[211] Rev. Proc. 92-20, 1992-1 CB 685, § 6.02(3)(a).

[212] Rev. Proc. 92-20, 1992-1 CB 685, § 6.02(3)(b).

[213] Rev. Proc. 92-20, 1992-1 CB 685, § 6.02(4).

[214] Rev. Proc. 92-20, 1992-1 CB 685, §§ 6.02(4)(b), 9.

the favorable Section 481 adjustment to the taxpayer. The taxpayer may seek to challenge this by filing the application in accordance with Section 481 and the applicable Treasury regulations. Any attempt by the IRS to deny to a taxpayer the benefits of Section 481 would seem inappropriate.

For LIFO taxpayers, the revenue procedure recognizes the difficulty taxpayers may have in computing a full Section 481 adjustment. Consequently, the revenue procedure provides a modified procedure for computing the Section 481 adjustment.[215] Under the modified procedure, only LIFO inventory activity during the ten tax years immediately preceding the year of change will be taken into account. Accordingly, LIFO inventory layers created in taxable years prior to the beginning of this 10-year period need not be revalued in computing the Section 481 adjustment.

It is important to note that these special rules pertaining to a change from a taxpayer's LIFO method apply only to those changes (or those portions of changes) affecting the use of LIFO. These rules would not apply to changes in inventory valuation methods of LIFO taxpayers that are required by reason of Section 471 or Section 263A, which generally are applicable to all taxpayers with inventories.[216]

Application filed within 120-day window after examination has ended. A taxpayer may file an application under special rules within 120 days after an examination has ended even though a subsequent examination may already have commenced.[217] However, this 120-day window will not be available (1) when the method of accounting from which the taxpayer seeks to change has been included as an item of adjustment in the report issued as a result of a prior examination by the IRS; (2) when the method has been placed in suspense by the IRS; or (3) when the taxpayer has received written notice from the examining agent prior to the filing of the Form 3115 specifically citing the method to be changed as an issue that will be under consideration for a taxable year involved in the subsequent examination. The notification may be by examination plan, information document request, notification of proposed adjustments or examination changes, or presumably by any other writing. Any application filed under the 120-day window should state at the top of Form 3115: "FILED UNDER SUBSECTION 6.03 OF REV. PROC. 92-20."[218] For taxpayers filing applications within the 120-day window, the year of change is the taxable year that includes the first day of the 120-day window.[219] Literally, this means that the year of change may be a year that would be earlier than the year for which the change would have

---

[215] Rev. Proc. 92-20, 1992-1 CB 685, §§ 6.02(4)(c), 9.

[216] Rev. Proc. 92-20, 1992-1 CB 685, § 6.02(4)(d).

[217] Rev. Proc. 92-20, 1992-1 CB 685, § 6.03.

[218] Rev. Proc. 92-20, 1992-1 CB 685, § 6.03(1).

[219] Rev. Proc. 92-20, 1992-1 CB 685, § 6.03(2).

been permitted had the application been filed by a taxpayer not then under examination.

If the change is from a Category A method and results in a net positive Section 481 adjustment, the adjustment will be taken into account ratably over a period of up to three taxable years beginning with the year of change. If the Section 481 adjustment is negative, the entire Section 481 adjustment must be taken into account in the year of change.[220]

If the change is from a Category B method, the Section 481 adjustment must be taken into account ratably over a period of up to six taxable years beginning with the year of change, regardless of whether the Section 481 adjustment is positive or negative.[221] Again, as in the case of other circumstances, the taxpayer may be able to demand that the negative Section 481 adjustment be taken into account entirely in the year of change under the applicable Treasury regulations. If the change is from a LIFO method or sub-method to another LIFO method or sub-method, the change will be made under a cut-off procedure, except as otherwise provided by the IRS.[222]

Application filed within 30-day window. A taxpayer under examination may request a change in method of accounting under Revenue Procedure 92-20 during the first 30 days of any taxable year,[223] but only if (1) the taxpayer has been under examination for at least 18 consecutive months prior to this 30-day period and (2) the taxpayer, prior to the filing of the Form 3115, has not received a written notification that the method to be changed will be an issue under consideration.[224] The notification may be by examination plan, information document request, notification of proposed adjustments or examination changes, or presumably by any other writing. An application filed under the 30-day window should have the following placed at the top of Form 3115: "FILED UNDER SUBSECTION 6.04 OF REV. PROC. 92-20."[225]

For changes requested under the 30-day window, the year of change will be the tax year that includes the first day of the 30-day window. If the change is from a Category A method and results in a net positive Section 481 adjustment, the adjustment will be taken into account ratably over a period of up to three taxable years beginning with the year of change.[226] If the Section 481 adjustment is negative, it will be taken into account entirely in the year of change.[227] If the change is from a Category B method, the Section

---

[220] Rev. Proc. 92-20, 1992-1 CB 685, § 6.03(3)(a).

[221] Rev. Proc. 92-20, 1992-1 CB 685, § 6.03(3)(b).

[222] Rev. Proc. 92-20, 1992-1 CB 685, §§ 6.03(3)(c), 9.01.

[223] Rev. Proc. 92-20, 1992-1 CB 685, § 6.04.

[224] Rev. Proc. 92-20, 1992-1 CB 685, § 6.04(1).

[225] Rev. Proc. 92-20, 1992-1 CB 685, § 6.04(1).

[226] Rev. Proc. 92-20, 1992-1 CB 685, § 6.04(3)(a)(i).

[227] Rev. Proc. 92-20, 1992-1 CB 685, § 6.04(3)(a)(ii).

481 adjustment will be taken into account ratably over a period of up to six taxable years beginning with the year of change without regard to whether the adjustment is positive or negative.[228] As in the case of other adjustments under Revenue Procedure 92-20, a taxpayer may challenge any requirement that it take the negative Section 481 adjustment into account over a period of years. If the change is from a LIFO method or sub-method to another LIFO method or sub-method, the change will be made using a cut-off procedure, except as otherwise provided by the IRS.[229]

Application filed under 90-day window for newly affiliated subsidiaries. A special rule is provided to corporations that are newly affiliated with a particular consolidated group.[230] This special rule applies to subsidiaries that, but for the affiliation with the new consolidated group, would not have been considered under examination either by reason of an examination of its own returns or the returns of any consolidated group with which it was formerly affiliated. In such a case, the parent of the new consolidated group may request a change in method of accounting on behalf of the newly-affiliated subsidiary within 90 days after affiliation.[231] For purposes of this rule, the first day of affiliation is to be determined without regard to any of the special elections into or out of the group under the 30-day rules provided in the consolidated return regulations.[232] If the filing of an application within this 90-day period overlaps with the 90-day window provided under Section 6.02 of Revenue Procedure 92-20, the rules affecting the 90-day post-affiliation window control.[233] Applications filed under this special window should be identified at the top of Form 3115 by the words: "FILED UNDER SUBSECTION 6.05 OF REV. PROC. 92-20."[234]

For taxpayers filing an application within this window, the year of change will be the taxable year that includes the first day of the 90-day post-affiliation window or, if later, the taxable year that includes the first day the newly acquired subsidiary is included in the consolidated group after taking into account the effects of the special elections provided under the consolidated return rules.[235] If the change is from a Category A method and results in a positive Section 481 adjustment, the Section 481 adjustment will be taken into account ratably over a period of up to three taxable years beginning with

---

[228] Rev. Proc. 92-20, 1992-1 CB 685, § 6.04(3)(b).

[229] Rev. Proc. 92-20, 1992-1 CB 685, § 9.01.

[230] Rev. Proc. 92-20, 1992-1 CB 685, § 6.05.

[231] Rev. Proc. 92-20, 1992-1 CB 685, § 6.05(1).

[232] See Treas. Reg. §§ 1.1502-76(b)(5)(i), 1.1502-76(b)(5)(ii).

[233] Rev. Proc. 92-20, 1992-1 CB 685, § 6.05(1).

[234] Id.

[235] These special rules are set forth under Treas. Reg. §§ 1.1502-76(b)(5)(i), 1.1502-76(b)(5)(ii). Rev. Proc. 92-20, 1992-1 CB 685, § 6.05(2).

the year of change.[236] However, if the Section 481 adjustment is negative, it must be taken into account entirely in the year of change.[237] If the change is from a Category B method, the Section 481 adjustment, whether positive or negative, must be taken into account ratably over a period of up to six years beginning with the year of change.[238] Again, a taxpayer who desires to avoid a spread of the negative Section 481 adjustment may seek to do so under Section 481 and the applicable regulations, although the IRS is likely to challenge any such attempt. If the change is from a LIFO method or sub-method to another LIFO method or sub-method, the change will be made using the cut-off procedure except as the IRS might otherwise have provided in a published document.[239]

Taxpayer under examination that does not qualify for any of the special window periods. Revenue Procedure 92-20 provides that a taxpayer under examination may not request a change from an impermissible method if the year in which the method was adopted is under examination and the method was impermissible in that year.[240] Similarly, a taxpayer may not request a change from a method to which it changed without permission if the taxpayer is under examination for the year in which the unauthorized change was made.[241] The revenue procedure states that a taxpayer under examination may change its accounting method under the revenue procedure in any other circumstances but only if the taxpayer complies with various terms and conditions of the revenue procedure.

Notwithstanding these limitations, it is important to note that a taxpayer is not prohibited from seeking a change in method of accounting. A taxpayer is prohibited from seeking a change in method of accounting only under the terms of this revenue procedure. Presumably, the taxpayer may still request an application for change under the general Treasury regulations governing applications for change.[242] Of course, the IRS may take the position that taxpayers may change methods of accounting only pursuant to Revenue Procedure 92-20 and, accordingly, may deny any request for change that does not comply with the requirements of this revenue procedure. To the extent a taxpayer seeks to follow procedures that differ from those set forth in Revenue Procedure 92-20, the IRS position may prevail. However, to the extent the taxpayer seeks application of the provisions of Section 481 regarding adjustments arising from changes in methods of accounting and the year in

---

[236] Rev. Proc. 92-20, 1992-1 CB 685, § 6.05(3)(a)(i).

[237] Rev. Proc. 92-20, 1992-1 CB 685, § 6.05(3)(a)(ii).

[238] Rev. Proc. 92-20, 1992-1 CB 685, § 6.05(3)(b).

[239] Rev. Proc. 92-20, 1992-1 CB 685, §§ 6.05(3)(c), 9.01.

[240] Rev. Proc. 92-20, 1992-1 CB 685, § 4.01.

[241] Id.

[242] Treas. Reg. § 1.446-1(e).

which such adjustments are to be taken into account, the ability of the IRS to modify the application of Section 481 is subject to question.

Interestingly, the revenue procedure makes the application of the window periods available to taxpayers in a permissive manner rather than in a mandatory manner. The procedure also provides that any taxpayer under examination may file a request for change of accounting method under the same terms and conditions as taxpayers who are not under examination if the consent of the District Director is obtained.[243] The revenue procedure provides that the District Director will not object to such treatment unless the method of accounting to be changed is of a type that ordinarily would be included as an item of adjustment under the years for which the taxpayer is under examination or for years to which the examination can be extended. Any application filed with the consent of the District Director under these provisions should have at the top of Form 3115 the following identification: "FILED UNDER SUBSECTION 6.06 OF REV. PROC. 92-20."[244] If the District Director properly rejects a request for change, the change in method of accounting may not be made under the revenue procedure.

The revenue procedure provides that if a taxpayer under examination is not eligible to change an accounting method under this particular revenue procedure, the change may be made on audit by the District Director.[245] However, this does not preclude the taxpayer from filing an application under the applicable regulations governing changes in methods of accounting. If a taxpayer were to do so, a question may be raised as to whether it would be considered an abuse of discretion for the Commissioner to reject the application filed in accordance with the revenue procedure in order to permit the District Director to make the change in an earlier year on audit.

Moreover, although the District Director may make the change effective in the earliest year under audit and without a spread of the resulting Section 481 adjustment, such a change is not required. The District Director presumably has the authority to agree with the taxpayer on other terms and conditions for making the change. Such a conclusion appears appropriate and may foster an early resolution of possible disputes over an agent's proposed change in method.

[iii] **Special rules regarding Designated A methods.** Revenue Procedure 92-20 provides the exclusive procedures for taxpayers that have failed to make a timely change from a Designated A method, e.g., a change from the method in the year required by the designating document, which may itself tie into the rules provided in an applicable Code section or other au-

---

[243] Rev. Proc. 92-20, 1992-1 CB 685, § 6.06.

[244] Rev. Proc. 92-20, 1992-1 CB 685, § 6.06.

[245] Rev. Proc. 92-20, 1992-1 CB 685, § 2.02.

thoritative pronouncement.[246] Such exclusive procedures generally remain effective for a period of six years beginning with the first taxable year that a taxpayer adopted a Designated A method or was required to change from a Designated A method. This period of time may be changed by the designating document. After the stated period has expired, the rules governing changes from regular Category A methods will control.

The revenue procedure provides that a taxpayer may not use any other provisions of the revenue procedure, except as expressly authorized, to change from a Designated A method.[247] However, this limitation should not be interpreted as preventing a taxpayer from requesting a change in method in accordance with the regulations, although the manner in which the National Office exercises its discretion may be affected by the taxpayer's failure to follow the rules set forth in this revenue procedure, and such discretion may be appropriate unless it is clearly inconsistent with the requirements of the Code, applicable regulations, or other applicable authority. Moreover, where disputes exist, a taxpayer clearly retains its opportunities of resolving the manner under any terms and conditions as may be agreed on with the appeals office or counsel for the government should the matter be in litigation.

Taxpayers not under examination. A taxpayer not under examination may make a change from a Designated A method by filing an amended return and thereby making the change effective retroactively or by filing an application for a prospective change.

Retroactive change from a Designated A method. If the change is requested retroactively, the year of change will be the earliest tax year open under the statutory period of limitations and will be carried through for each affected succeeding taxable year for which a return has been filed.[248] If the change results in a net positive Section 481 adjustment, the entire adjustment must be taken into account in the amended return for the year of change.[249] Consequently, proceeding in this fashion will give rise to an increase in tax plus associated interest. If the change results in a net negative Section 481 adjustment, the taxpayer is to take the Section 481 adjustment into account ratably over a period of up to three tax years.[250]

Any taxpayer so changing from a Designated A method must complete and file a statement in duplicate notifying the IRS of its change. The original statement must be attached to the taxpayer's amended return for the first taxable year for which the taxpayer is changing from the Designated A method, and a copy must be filed with the National Office. The taxpayer must

---

[246] Rev. Proc. 92-20, 1992-1 CB 685, § 7.01.

[247] Id.

[248] Rev. Proc. 92-20, 1992-1 CB 685, § 7.03(3).

[249] Rev. Proc. 92-20, 1992-1 CB 685, § 7.03(3)(b)(i).

[250] Rev. Proc. 92-20, 1992-1 CB 685, § 7.03(3)(b)(ii).

type at the top of the statement: "NOTIFICATION PROCEDURES UN-
DER SUBSECTION 7.04 OF REV. PROC. 92-20 AND (cite to the
designating document)."[251] The notification statement must include the
taxpayer's name, address, and identifying number, a description of the
taxpayer's Designated A method, a description of the method to which the
taxpayer is changing, and a computation of the Section 481 adjustment. No
user fee is required with the filing of a copy of the notification statement.
Typed at the top of each amended return should be: "AUTOMATIC
CHANGE FILED UNDER SUBSECTION 7.04 OF REV. PROC. 92-20
AND (cite to the designating document)."[252]

Prospective change from a Designated A method. Taxpayers are not
required to file amended returns in order to make a change from a
Designated A method. Taxpayers have the opportunity under the revenue
procedure to make the change prospectively. In such a case, Form 3115 must
be filed under the same rules as those provided to taxpayers requesting a
change in method at a time when they are not under examination.[253] This is
the approach for taxpayers changing from Designated A methods at a time
when they are not under examination. The year of change will be the
applicable year for which Form 3115 is filed.

If the Section 481 adjustment is positive, the adjustment must be taken
into account entirely in the year of change.[254] If the adjustment is negative,
the adjustment must be taken into account ratably over a period of up to
three taxable years beginning with the year of change.[255]

In addition, taking into account the possibility that a taxpayer changing
from a Category A method prospectively may obtain a more favorable result
than a taxpayer that properly and timely changed to the required method,
the revenue procedure requires taxpayers that make prospective changes to
pay an additional amount. The additional amount is designed to place the
taxpayer in the same position it would have been in had it filed amended tax
returns or properly and timely made the required change. The additional
amount is intended to reflect the time value of money, i.e., to reflect the economic benefit the taxpayer derived from its delay in making the change or
that it will derive from making the change prospectively. However, this
additional amount is not to be treated as interest, and it may not be
capitalized or deducted under any provision of the Code.[256] Special rules are
provided for calculating this additional amount. Special rules are also

---

[251] Rev. Proc. 92-20, 1992-1 CB 685, § 7.04(1)(a).

[252] Rev. Proc. 92-20, 1992-1 CB 685, §§ 7.04(1)(a)(i), 7.04(1)(a)(ii), 7.04(1)(b).

[253] Rev. Proc. 92-20, 1992-1 CB 685, § 7.02(2).

[254] Rev. Proc. 92-20, 1992-1 CB 685, § 7.03(4)(b)(i).

[255] Rev. Proc. 92-20, 1992-1 CB 685, § 7.03(4)(b)(ii).

[256] Rev. Proc. 92-20, 1992-1 CB 685, § 7.03(4)(c)(i).

provided regarding the computation of the additional amount for so-called pass-through entities.

A taxpayer filing a request for prospective change from a Designated A method must file Form 3115, state its agreement to all the conditions set forth in Revenue Procedure 92-20 and the document that designated the method as the Designated A method, and state its agreement to take the Section 481 adjustment into account over the appropriate period together with other information required in the revenue procedure.

[iv] **Exceptions to Section 481 adjustment spread periods.**   As was the case under prior Revenue Procedure 84-74, Revenue Procedure 92-20 provides various exceptions to the spread periods that otherwise might be provided. These exceptions pertain to circumstances in which the IRS believes it appropriate to reduce what otherwise would be an inappropriately long spread period.[257] In addition to initially reduced spread periods, circumstances may exist where it is appropriate to terminate the initially provided spread period.[258] If the year of change, or any year during the Section 481 spread period, is a short taxable year, that short taxable year will be treated just as if it were a full taxable year. In other words, a full pro rata share is allocable to that year.[259]

De minimis rule.   In the case of either a positive or a negative Section 481 adjustment that is less than $25,000, the taxpayer may elect to take the adjustment into account entirely in the year of change. The election is for the taxpayer, and it may not be imposed by the IRS. This election by the taxpayer must be stated affirmatively on an attachment to its Form 3115.[260]

Adjustment attributable to immediately preceding taxable year.   If 90 percent or more of the Section 481 adjustment is attributable to the taxable year immediately preceding the year of change, the entire Section 481 adjustment must be taken into account in the year of change.[261] The amount attributable to such preceding year is determined by computing what the Section 481 adjustment would have been if the year of change had been that preceding tax year. Similar to the procedures in Revenue Procedure 84-74, if the taxpayer's books and records are not sufficient to allow the computation of the Section 481 adjustment, the amount may be reasonably estimated with an appropriate statement provided.

Number of taxable years method has been used.   If not otherwise limited, the maximum spread period available to the taxpayer may not exceed

---

[257] Rev. Proc. 92-20, 1992-1 CB 685, § 8.01.

[258] Rev. Proc. 92-20, 1992-1 CB 685, § 8.03.

[259] Rev. Proc. 92-20, 1992-1 CB 685, § 8.02; See Rev. Rul. 78-165, 1978-1 CB 276.

[260] Rev. Proc. 92-20, 1992-1 CB 685, § 8.01(1).

[261] Rev. Proc. 92-20, 1992-1 CB 685, § 8.01(2).

the number of years that the taxpayer has used the method from which it is changing.[262]

Cooperatives. A cooperative generally must take the Section 481 adjustment into account entirely in the year of change.[263]

Reduction in inventory value. Following a principle included in Revenue Procedure 84-74, Revenue Procedure 92-20 requires an acceleration in the recognition of any unamortized Section 481 adjustment if the adjustment stems from a change in the taxpayer's method of inventory valuation and on the last day of any taxable year before complete amortization of the Section 481 adjustment there is a significant liquidation in inventory that is not thereafter restored.[264] The acceleration arises when the value of the ending inventory is reduced by more than one third (33^1/$_3$ percent) from the inventory value at the beginning of the first year of the spread period and remains so reduced by the end of the immediately succeeding taxable year. The acceleration will occur in the succeeding taxable year. In applying this rule, only the specific category of inventory to which the Section 481 adjustment relates is taken into account. Moreover, the revenue procedure allows taxpayers to demonstrate that the triggering liquidation arises from certain circumstances beyond the taxpayer's control and, if that demonstration is made, the acceleration will not occur. The circumstances identified in the revenue procedure are reductions attributable to (1) strikes; (2) involuntary conversions; and (3) involuntary interruptions in the availability of goods. Providing such exceptions is consistent with the intent of the provision to ignore temporary fluctuations and only to have permanent reductions taken into account. It is not known whether the IRS will approve nonpermanent reductions attributable to circumstances other than those mentioned above, e.g., a casualty loss although a casualty arguably may be viewed as one type of involuntary conversion.

Ceasing to engage in the trade or business. If a taxpayer ceases to engage in the trade or business to which the Section 481 adjustment relates before the adjustment has been completely taken into account or if the taxpayer itself terminates its existence, any unamortized balance of the Section 481 adjustment must be taken into account in the year of such cessation or termination.[265] The revenue procedure then provides a nonexclusive list of transactions that will be treated as a cessation of a trade or business. These include:

• The incorporation of the trade or business

---

[262] Rev. Proc. 92-20, 1992-1 CB 685, § 8.01(3).

[263] Rev. Proc. 92-20, 1992-1 CB 685, § 8.01(4); See Rev. Rul. 79-45, 1979-1 CB 284.

[264] Rev. Proc. 92-20, 1992-1 CB 685, § 8.03(1).

[265] Rev. Proc. 92-20, 1992-1 CB 685, § 8.03(2).

- The purchase of the trade or business by another taxpayer in a transaction to which Section 1060 applies
- The termination of a trade or business or its transfer pursuant to a taxable liquidation
- The cessation of operations by a division of the corporation of the trade or business to which the adjustment relates
- A contribution to a partnership of the assets of the trade or business to which the adjustment relates

On the other hand, no acceleration is required when a C corporation elects to be treated as an S corporation or an S corporation terminates its S election and is thereafter treated as a C corporation. However, acceleration is required where a sole proprietor incorporates and immediately elects to be treated as an S corporation.

A taxpayer will not be treated as ceasing to engage in a trade or business if substantially all the assets of the trade or business to which the Section 481 adjustment relates are transferred to another taxpayer in a transfer to which Section 381 applies and for which the accounting method (the change to which gave rise to the Section 481 adjustment) is a tax attribute that is carried over and continued by the acquiring corporation. The acquiring corporation will then be subject to the terms and conditions imposed on the transferor as a result of the transferor's change in method of accounting.[266]

A special rule is provided to members of consolidated groups. A member of such a group will not be treated as having ceased to engage in a trade or business if substantially all its relevant assets are transferred to another member of the same consolidated group in a Section 351 transaction, and the transferee member adopts (and immediately after the transfer uses) the same method of accounting as that to which the transferor member had changed.[267] Such a transaction will be entitled to the benefits of this special rule only if the avoidance of tax was not a principal purpose of the exchange and the original transferor continues to take the Section 481 adjustment into account pursuant to the originally applicable terms and conditions. However, if the transferee member of the group thereafter ceases to engage in the trade or business to which the Section 481 adjustment related, acceleration of the unamortized balance of the adjustment will be required by the transferor member.

In addition, this special rule will not apply (and an acceleration will be required) whenever (1) the original transferor ceases to be a member of the group; (2) the transferee ceases to be a member of the group; or (3) a separate return year arises for the common parent of the group. In any of these cases, the acceleration will be deemed to occur immediately preceding the

---

[266] Rev. Proc. 92-20, 1992-1 CB 685, § 8.03(2)(c).
[267] Rev. Proc. 92-20, 1992-1 CB 685, § 8.03(2)(d).

occurrence of the circumstance. Additional rules are provided to prevent an acceleration if the cessation results from Section 381 transaction and the acquiring corporation is a member of the same group as the original transferor and continues to use the same method of accounting as that to which the original transferor had changed.

Subsequent LIFO elections. Special rules are provided to prevent taxpayers that obtain spreads of Section 481 adjustments arising from changes in their methods of valuing inventories from unduly benefiting by thereafter adopting the LIFO method, which itself gives rise to a three-year spread of any restoration of prior cost write-downs.[268] If the taxpayer elects LIFO before such a Section 481 adjustment has been fully taken into account, the taxpayer must include the unamortized balance of that adjustment in income in the taxable year of the LIFO election in an amount equal to the amount that would have been included in income by that time under the LIFO three-year spread provision if LIFO had been adopted at the time that the prior inventory method was adopted.

To illustrate, assume a taxpayer using the lower of FIFO cost or market receives permission to change to the cost method of valuing inventories and that the change results in a $60 Section 481 adjustment to be taken into account ratably over six years. Had the taxpayer adopted LIFO, the $60 would have been taken into account at the rate of $20 per year over the taxable year of change and the immediately succeeding two years. The taxpayer's six-year spread period will thus be changed to make sure that the taxpayer obtains no benefit beyond what it would have obtained had it adopted LIFO.

[v] **Special rules for LIFO taxpayers.** Revenue Procedure 92-20 provides a number of special rules affecting LIFO taxpayers.[269]

Cut-off method. Unless otherwise required (either by Revenue Procedure 92-20 or by any other published guidance of the IRS), a Section 481 adjustment will not be required on a change from one LIFO method (or sub-method) to another LIFO method (or sub-method).[270] Instead, a cut-off procedure will be used. The particular computations associated with a cut-off procedure are not provided. However, it is presumed that the taxpayer will compute its dollar-value LIFO inventories after the change in method (or sub-method) as if it had received permission to treat the year of change as a new base year with all computations to be made under the new method of accounting. The new base date (the first day of the year of change) would be the base date on which future computations would be based, and appropriate ratios would be established to preserve LIFO values of the orig-

---

[268] Rev. Proc. 92-20, 1992-1 CB 685, § 8.03(3).

[269] Rev. Proc. 92-20, 1992-1 CB 685, § 9.

[270] Rev. Proc. 92-20, 1992-1 CB 685, § 9.01.

inal base year and any subsequent layers of LIFO inventory that arose prior to the year of change. In effect, the Section 481 adjustment is not forgiven but is deferred, to be taken into account as the LIFO inventory prior to the year of change is liquidated.

If a LIFO taxpayer makes a change in its inventory method that is the type of inventory change not limited to LIFO taxpayers, the special cut-off rules will not apply. Such changes would include changes in the costing of inventory under Section 471 or Section 263A.

Section 481 adjustment for LIFO taxpayers. Where a Section 481 adjustment is required as the result of a change in a LIFO method or sub-method, the IRS will permit the taxpayer reasonably to estimate the appropriate adjustment.[271] By this provision, the IRS effectively recognizes the practical difficulties that might otherwise hinder LIFO taxpayers in recomputing their inventories under LIFO methods different from those for which their original procedures were established. It also demonstrates that precision in the use of LIFO, and perhaps, by extension, in other inventory methods, is not essential in all cases.

Discontinuance of LIFO. Unless a LIFO taxpayer is eligible for application of Revenue Procedure 88-15,[272] a change to discontinue the use of LIFO is governed by Revenue Procedure 92-20.[273] Such a change will ordinarily be granted providing the taxpayer agrees not to reelect the LIFO method for a period of at least five taxable years beginning with the year of change, unless consent to an earlier change is granted by the Commissioner. The Commissioner generally will agree to such a change only on a showing of extraordinary circumstances.

To qualify for the change, the taxpayer must provide a statement as to whether there has been a termination event as described in Revenue Procedure 79-23[274] or under any other applicable revenue ruling or revenue procedure during a year that is not barred by the statute of limitations. The revenue procedure points out that a termination event does not occur if the taxpayer first issues nonconforming financial statements during the taxable year for which the LIFO method is discontinued and the nonconforming financial statements relate either to the year of change or to the year preceding the year of change.

If a C corporation meets the conditions of Section 5.05(1)(a) of Revenue Procedure 88-15 and the Commissioner approves the requested discontinuance of the use of LIFO, a condition consistent with section 5.05(1)(b) of that revenue procedure will be applied.[275]

---

[271] Rev. Proc. 92-20, 1992-1 CB 685, § 9.02.

[272] Rev. Proc. 88-15, 1988-1 CB 683. See discussion at ¶ 7.06[2].

[273] Rev. Proc. 92-20, 1992-1 CB 685, § 9.03(1).

[274] Rev. Proc. 79-23, 1979-1 CB 564.

[275] Rev. Proc. 92-20, 1992-1 CB 685, § 9.03(3).

If a C corporation makes an S election that is effective for the taxable year in which it discontinues LIFO, the taxpayer must nevertheless increase its income for the LIFO recapture amount under Section 1363(d) and make the corresponding adjustment to the basis of the taxpayer's inventory as of the end of the preceding year.[276] This basis adjustment will be taken into account in computing the applicable Section 481 adjustment (if any).[277]

[c] General Procedures Under Revenue Procedure 92-20

Notwithstanding the substantial number of specific rules provided in Revenue Procedure 92-20, taxpayers and their advisors must also be alert to the possible application of certain overriding general principles. These general principles set forth IRS warnings that may make the special procedures inapplicable.[278]

[i] **IRS discretion not to apply revenue procedure or to modify other provisions.** The IRS reserves the right not to process any application for change under Revenue Procedure 92-20 whenever it determines that application of the procedure will not be in the best interest of the sound administration of the tax laws.[279] In administering this provision, the IRS will consider whether approval of the change would "clearly and directly frustrate compliance efforts of the Service in administering the income tax laws." In addition, the IRS may determine that it should provide terms and conditions different from those otherwise provided in the revenue procedure. For example, a change in procedures may be required in the following circumstances:

- A cooperative may be required to take the Section 481 adjustment into account over a period of taxable years.
- A taxpayer may be required to accelerate the Section 481 adjustment.
- A taxpayer may be prevented from offsetting a positive Section 481 adjustment with a net operating loss that is expiring in the year of change if the IRS believes utilization of the net operating loss was a principal purpose for making the change.
- A taxpayer may be prevented from offsetting the tax attributable to a Section 481 adjustment if the IRS believes utilization of an expiring credit was a principal purpose for making the change.

[ii] **Compliance with provisions.** A taxpayer will be deemed to have changed a method without the consent of the Commissioner if it changes a

---

[276] See ¶ 7.09 for a discussion of the adjustment required on an S election.

[277] Rev. Proc. 92-20, 1992-1 CB 685, § 9.03(4).

[278] Rev. Proc. 92-20, 1992-1 CB 685, § 10.

[279] Rev. Proc. 92-20, 1992-1 CB 685, § 10.01.

method to which Revenue Procedure 92-20 applies without appropriate authorization or without complying with all provisions of the revenue procedure.[280] In such a circumstance, the IRS may require the taxpayer to make the change in an earlier (or later) taxable year, and the taxpayer may be denied the benefit of spreading the Section 481 adjustment over a period of years.

The potential impact of this rule is most uncertain. Although a taxpayer generally may not change a method of accounting without the prior approval of the IRS,[281] once such a change has been made and the statutory period of limitations has run on the year of change, the Commissioner may not have the authority to require a taxpayer to return to a prior improper method. Such discretion would more clearly exist if the prior method were a proper method.

[iii] Effect of particular facts and circumstances. In determining whether to approve a requested change in method, the IRS will consider all applicable facts and circumstances.[282] Among the facts and circumstances the IRS will consider are:

- Whether the method requested is consistent with the Code, regulations, revenue rulings, revenue procedures, and decisions of the U.S. Supreme Court. Interestingly, the revenue procedure does not cite the decisions of lower courts as a relevant circumstance.

- Whether the present method of accounting clearly reflects income. The IRS has considerably more discretion to deny a request for a change in method from a method that already reflects income clearly.[283]

- The taxpayer's reasons for requesting the change. These reasons are quite important and may be the only basis on which a taxpayer could challenge as an abuse of discretion a denial of an application for change from a method that already clearly reflects income.

- The tax effect of the Section 481 adjustment arising from the change. To the extent the change is from a method that fails to reflect income clearly, the discretion of the IRS to deny the requested change on the basis of its tax effect is doubtful.[284]

- Whether the taxpayer's books, records, and financial statements will conform to the requested method.

- The need for consistency in the area of tax accounting. This factor

---

[280] Rev. Proc. 92-20, 1992-1 CB 685, § 10.02.

[281] See discussion infra ¶ 8.07[2][b].

[282] Rev. Proc. 92-20, 1992-1 CB 685, § 10.03(1).

[283] See discussion infra ¶ 8.07[1].

[284] See discussion infra ¶ 8.07[2].

apparently relates to the possibility of requesting a change in method in order to defer income that otherwise would be recognized under the taxpayer's original method.

- For a taxpayer who previously filed an application for change but then either withdrew it, failed to perfect the change, or failed to make the change after it had been approved, and where the present application is within six years of the prior application, the taxpayer's explanation as to why the prior application was withdrawn, not perfected, or not made will be quite important. In such a case, a copy of the earlier application together with any correspondence from the IRS, must be attached to Form 3115, and an explanation must be furnished stating why the prior application was withdrawn, not perfected, or why the change was not made.

- Where a change is requested by or on behalf of a member of a consolidated group, the effects of the change on the income of the group. The common parent must submit any information necessary to permit the IRS to evaluate the effect of the requested change on the income of the group.[285]

[d] Incomplete Forms 3115: Forty-Five-Day Rule

The IRS will notify the taxpayer if Form 3115 is not properly completed or if supplemental information is needed.[286] The taxpayer will then have 45 days from the date of the notification letter to complete Form 3115 or to provide the requested information. The IRS may impose shorter reply periods if subsequent requests for additional information are made. If the requested information is not timely submitted, Form 3115 will not be processed for the requested year of change. In addition to the period specified above, an additional period of not more than 15 days may be granted to a taxpayer in unusual and compelling circumstances. Any request for an extension of time must be made in writing and submitted within the originally specified reply period.

[e] Two or More Trades or Businesses

Whenever a taxpayer operates separate and distinct trades or businesses for which different methods of accounting are used, a change in method of accounting for one of the trades or business will not be permitted unless the taxpayer demonstrates that the proposed change will not result in the creation or shifting of profits between the trades or businesses and will clearly

---

[285] Rev. Proc. 92-20, 1992-1 CB 685, § 10.08.
[286] Rev. Proc. 92-20, 1992-1 CB 685, § 10.03(2).

reflect income.[287] The taxpayer must fully disclose all applicable facts covering its use of different methods of accounting and must identify all other trades or businesses by name and the method of accounting used by each trade or business for the particular item that is the subject of the requested change in method.

[f] Particular Filing Details

[i] **Where to file.**   Revenue Procedure 92-20 specifies the addresses to which Form 3115 must be sent in particular circumstances.[288] In addition to filing a properly completed Form 3115, the taxpayer must make sure it is using a current Form 3115, must state its agreement to all conditions of Revenue Procedure 92-20, and must state its agreement to take the Section 481 adjustment into account over the applicable period of years.

[ii] **Copy to District Director.**   If a taxpayer files a Form 3115 under any of the window periods specified in the revenue procedure for taxpayers under examination, a copy of the Form 3115 must be sent to the District Director for the district in which the returns are being examined at the same time as the original Form 3115 is filed with the National Office. Moreover, the Form 3115 filed with the National Office must contain the name and telephone number of the examining agent.[289] Taxpayers must anticipate that the National Office technician to whom the application is assigned will consult with the examining agent.

[iii] **Signature requirements.**   The appropriate signature requirements are specified in the revenue procedure.[290] In general, Form 3115 must be signed by or on behalf of the taxpayer requesting the change by an individual with authority to bind the taxpayer in such matters. For example, an officer must sign on behalf of a corporation, a general partner on behalf of a partnership, a trustee on behalf of a trust, and an individual on behalf of a sole proprietorship. Taxpayers and their advisors should consult the applicable signature requirements as set forth in the general instructions attached to the then-current Form 3115. If an agent is authorized to represent the taxpayer before the IRS, an applicable power of attorney must be attached to Form 3115. Without such a power of attorney, no information will be provided to the agent regarding the application.

If the taxpayer is a member of a consolidated group, Form 3115 must be

---

[287] Rev. Proc. 92-20, 1992-1 CB 685, § 10.04.

[288] Rev. Proc. 92-20, 1992-1 CB 685, § 10.05.

[289] Rev. Proc. 92-20, 1992-1 CB 685, § 10.06.

[290] Rev. Proc. 92-20, 1992-1 CB 685, § 10.07.

signed by a duly authorized officer of the common parent.[291] A separate Form 3115 and payment of the applicable user fee must be made for each member of the group for which the change in method is requested. This requirement may result in considerable expense to a group consisting of many members.

[g] Consent Agreement Requirements

The National Office's approval of any requested change in method will be set forth in a ruling letter.[292] The letter will identify the items being changed, the Section 481 adjustment (if any), and the terms and conditions under which the change is to be made. The letter will not require the taxpayer to make the change. The taxpayer will still have the option to decide whether to go forward with the change. If the taxpayer agrees to the terms and conditions contained in the letter, the taxpayer must execute a copy of the letter in the space provided and return the letter to the National Office within 45 days of its issuance. The executed letter will constitute a binding "consent agreement." If the taxpayer does not return the agreement within the appropriate time period, the ruling letter granting permission for the change will be deemed null and void.[293] If the taxpayer decides not to make the change, the taxpayer should so indicate by returning an unsigned copy of the letter with an explanation of why the change will not be made. If the taxpayer disagrees with the terms and conditions, the taxpayer must express such disagreement together with an explanation of its reasons within the 45-day period. The IRS will then consider the reasons for the disagreement and notify the taxpayer whether the original ruling will be modified. If the ruling is not modified, the taxpayer will be so notified and given an additional 15 days from the date of such notification either to accept the original ruling and return an executed consent agreement or to reject the change and return the agreement unsigned. If the taxpayer signs and returns the consent agreement, the taxpayer must implement the change in accordance with the terms and conditions provided in the letter.

Should the taxpayer sign the agreement but not actually make the change, several issues arise. For example, would the IRS require the taxpayer to make the change should it determine on audit that the change has not been made? If such action is not made, will the taxpayer be deemed to be using an improper method by continuing its former method?

---

[291] Rev. Proc. 92-20, 1992-1 CB 685, § 10.08.
[292] Rev. Proc. 92-20, 1992-1 CB 685, § 10.09(1).
[293] Rev. Proc. 92-20, 1992-1 CB 685, § 10.09(3).

[h] Protection for Years Prior to Year of Change

If a taxpayer timely files Form 3115 under Revenue Procedure 92-20, examining agents are thereafter precluded from proposing that the taxpayer make the same change in a year prior to the year required under the revenue procedure.[294] Nevertheless, the computations set forth in Form 3115 are subject to review on audit. Moreover, if the requested change in method is not granted by the National Office or if the taxpayer declines to make the change requested, does not comply with the terms and conditions contained in the ruling letter, or withdraws its request for change, examining agents may propose that the same change be made for a year prior to the year of change as originally set forth. In addition, if a taxpayer is changing a sub-method of accounting that is within another method of accounting, examining agents may propose that a taxpayer change the method (including in appropriate circumstances the sub-method) for a year prior to the year of change under this revenue procedure. For example, an examining agent may propose to terminate the taxpayer's use of the LIFO inventory method during years currently under examination even though those taxable years precede the year of the taxpayer's change from one LIFO inventory method or sub-method to another LIFO inventory method or sub-method.

[i] Request for Conference in National Office

The taxpayer must state in writing at the time Form 3115 is filed whether the taxpayer desires a conference if an adverse response is contemplated by the IRS. If a conference is not so specifically requested in writing at the time the taxpayer files Form 3115 or in a later written communication, the IRS will presume that the taxpayer does not desire such a conference. If requested, the conference will be arranged in the National Office prior to its formal reply to the taxpayer.[295]

[j] Effect of Revenue Procedure 92-20 on Appeals Office and Others

Appropriate representatives of the IRS, including appeals officers with delegated settlement authority, are not precluded by reason of Revenue Procedure 92-20 from settling a particular taxpayer's case involving a method of accounting by agreeing to terms and conditions that differ from those provided in the revenue procedure.[296] Consequently, taxpayers who believe they may be able to resolve accounting method issues at appeals on terms and conditions that will be more favorable than those set forth in Revenue Procedure 92-20 may want to consider this opportunity.

---

[294] Rev. Proc. 92-20, 1992-1 CB 685, § 10.12.

[295] Rev. Proc. 92-20, 1992-1 CB 685, § 10.13.

[296] Rev. Proc. 92-20, 1992-1 CB 685, § 10.14.

[k] Effective Date

Revenue Procedure 92-20 is effective for Forms 3115 filed on or after March 23, 1992.[297]

[4] Year of Change

In the normal case, the year of change will be the year requested in a timely filed Form 3115 application for change in accounting method. Thus, if the taxpayer files its request for change within the first 180 days of the year for which the new method will first be used, that year will be the year of change. Similarly, if a request for change is filed after the first 180 days but is nevertheless considered as timely filed by the IRS, the year of change will be the year requested. If the request for change is filed prior to the year for which the change is requested, the year of change will be the requested year, assuming the taxpayer supplies all additional information as requested in a timely manner.[298]

The present rules governing the applicable year of change are set forth in Revenue Procedure 92-20.[299] For the various situations covered by this revenue procedure, the applicable year of change is summarized in a table and described in preceding sections.[300]

Notwithstanding these provisions, taxpayers and their advisors should remain alert to the possibility of reaching agreement on a different year of change either with revenue agents on audit or appeals officers during further administrative review. Appeals officers clearly have the authority to make such an agreement, and there is no prohibition on the ability of the District Director to do the same on audit.

[5] Application Pending at Time Return Is Due

For many reasons, including the present significance of time value of money concepts, new legislative and regulatory restrictions on accounting methods, and an increased desire of taxpayers to seek method changes that will reduce taxes,[301] the number of applications for change in accounting method has increased over the years. This increase has often caused the processing of

---

[297] Rev. Proc. 92-20, 1992-1 CB 685, § 14.

[298] See discussion supra ¶ 8.06[3][b].

[299] Rev. Proc. 92-20, 1992-1 CB 685.

[300] See supra ¶ 8.06[3][b].

[301] See, e.g., ¶ 3.06[1] regarding limitations on use of the cash method; ¶ 4.04[3] regarding the economic performance test for deductions by accrual method taxpayers; ¶ 6.06 regarding the costing of inventories; ¶¶ 11.02–11.10 regarding time value methods of accounting.

applications for change to be delayed. It may well take the IRS 12 to 18 months or more before it finally concludes whether a particular request for change should be granted. As a consequence, taxpayers frequently must prepare and file returns for the year for which the change is requested before the taxpayer is informed whether the change will be approved. The taxpayer is faced with a choice—preparing and filing returns either (1) on the basis of the old method (knowing that it must duplicate substantial time and effort to prepare returns on the new method, if the change to the new method is approved) or (2) on the basis of the new method without having received prior approval.

In these circumstances, the law makes the choice clear. The taxpayer must continue to report under the existing method until approval to change has been obtained. Accordingly, to comply with this requirement, the taxpayer should prepare the return under the old method.

Despite these requirements, some taxpayers nevertheless prepare the returns on the basis of the requested new method and disclose that fact on the returns. Typically, the taxpayer will explain that the returns are being filed on the basis of the new method in anticipation of the new method being approved. The taxpayer's reasoning is that the requested new method was used in order to reduce administrative costs and burdens that would otherwise occur. The taxpayer generally adds that if the request for change is ultimately denied, the taxpayer will immediately redetermine its income on the basis of its old method.

Although this approach would seem to be reasonable (particularly when the requested change is from an incorrect method to a correct method), it is subject to various risks. First, it is contrary to the rules stated in the controlling regulations and revenue procedures. Second, it may expose the taxpayer to penalties. For example, the IRS has ruled in the context of a request for change in accounting period that penalties may be imposed where a taxpayer failed to make estimated tax payments on the basis of its then-existing taxable year because it had filed a request for change to a different tax year.[302] However, this ruling may be distinguished from other situations in that the taxpayer had not made payments when due.

In the context of a request for change in accounting method, a failure to obtain the approval prior to filing the return may subject the taxpayer to similar penalties for underpayment of tax. However, assuming the taxpayer paid a sufficient amount of tax to cover what its liability would have been under the old method but nevertheless filed on the basis of the new method in order to reduce administrative costs, it would seem unduly harsh for that taxpayer to be subject to penalties.

Nevertheless, the IRS has taken the position in litigation that penalties could be imposed where the taxpayer filed under the requested method after

---

[302] Rev. Rul. 81-259, 1981-2 CB 247.

its application for change from an incorrect method had been denied. The penalties were asserted even though the taxpayer disclosed its method of accounting and stated that it was filing on the requested basis in order to challenge the Commissioner's denial of its request for change on the basis that the denial amounted to an abuse of discretion. The IRS took the position that the taxpayer should have challenged the Commissioner's action by filing on the old method and then filing a claim for refund based on use of the new method. Of course, while this approach may be much safer (in terms of the likely imposition of penalties), it does force the taxpayer to pay the tax due and to have the issue decided in the United States Court of Federal Claims or a federal district court.

Finally, a taxpayer may always call the technician to whom the application has been assigned to discuss what the taxpayer should do. While this may often seem the most prudent approach, technicians are generally reluctant to give unqualified direction as to what course the taxpayer should follow. Nevertheless, to the extent a favorable response is likely to be provided, the technician may be willing to so advise the taxpayer, and the taxpayer may then put this information in a disclosure on its return. On the other hand, taxpayers may find that the matter is too sensitive to raise with the National Office technician. In such a case, the mere raising of the issue in this fashion may cause the technician to advise the taxpayer that a negative reply is likely to be forthcoming, even though that decision has not actually been made.

¶ 8.07 COMMISSIONER'S DISCRETION IN APPROVING REQUEST FOR CHANGE

[1] Change From One Acceptable Method to Another

When a taxpayer requests permission to change from one accounting method that clearly reflects income to another accounting method that also clearly reflects income, the Commissioner has great discretion in determining whether to approve the change.[303] That discretion generally extends to deciding the terms and conditions associated with any such change.

The IRS usually considers the following factors in evaluating such a request:[304]

---

[303] For further discussion of the Commissioner's discretion, see also ¶ 2.04. In particular, see ¶ 2.04[3][d], for a discussion of circumstances in which the agent's action on audit may cause a change in method to have been deemed accepted by the IRS.

[304] See also Rev. Proc. 92-20, 1992-1 CB 685, § 10.04[1].

- The business reasons for the change[305]
- Whether the old method clearly reflected income
- Whether the new method will result in a clearer reflection of income than the old method
- Whether the new method will be used for financial reporting purposes
- The tax consequences of the change
- The precedential impact of approval or denial of the change should other taxpayers make similar requests

The IRS has no published standard as to the weight to be given to each factor. Nor, for that matter, is there any published requirement that each factor be taken into account. In addition, the IRS has sometimes imposed purely discretionary conditions on approval of a change. For example, it has at times required that the requested change also be made for financial statement purposes.[306]

When the IRS relaxes its policies and requirements governing these changes, a taxpayer who desires to make a change in reliance on the relaxed standard should move quickly. Circumstances have arisen in the past where failure to do so has been critical. For example, in the early 1980s, the IRS followed a practice of permitting changes from an accrual method to the cash method without requiring a similar change for financial reporting purposes. The response by taxpayers who sought to make these changes was so overwhelming that the IRS soon discontinued granting such requests.

It is imperative that the taxpayer present a full and complete statement setting forth all the reasons and circumstances associated with the requested change. Too often, taxpayers and their advisors assume that a request is so routine that it will be granted perfunctorily. This is often a mistake. Frequently, the technician at the National Office who is assigned responsibility for reviewing the request will seek additional information from the taxpayer. Alternatively, even after a request may be granted at the National Office level, an agent may review the facts set forth in the application and either challenge the validity of the statements made or assert that an incomplete picture was presented.[307]

---

[305] See, e.g., Gen. Couns. Mem. 38852 (May 17, 1982), revoked for other reasons by Gen. Couns. Mem. 38912 (Oct. 26, 1982).

[306] See Rev. Rul. 68-35, 1968-1 CB 190, and Rev. Rul. 68-83, 1968-1 CB 190, indicating that the book conformity requirement is also discretionary with the IRS.

[307] See, e.g., Cochran Hatchery, Inc., 39 TCM 210 (1979), where the court upheld a retroactive disapproval of a previously approved change from an accrual method to the cash method because of the failure of the taxpayer to provide all relevant facts and circumstances at the time the application for change was made. The retroactive revocation of consent was deemed not to be an abuse of discretion. See also

Should the IRS consider the taxpayer's reasons for requesting the change to be insufficient and deny the change, the taxpayer has virtually no chance of convincing a court that an abuse of discretion has occurred. Thus, the taxpayer may want to consider alternative means of changing methods without the need for prior approval.[308]

Finally, many changes from one acceptable method to another do not depend on IRS approval, but rather on an election being made by the taxpayer. Examples include a change from a non-LIFO inventory method to a LIFO inventory method,[309] and, prior to the 1987 Act, an election of the installment method of reporting by dealers.[310] Although the IRS has the right to make certain that all applicable conditions and requirements are satisfied, it does not have the discretion to deny the change to an otherwise qualified taxpayer.[311] If the taxpayer fails to satisfy all such conditions, the IRS has the discretion to deny the change and require the taxpayer to remake the election in the next available year.[312]

[2] Change From Improper to Proper Method

Where the request for change is from an improper method to a proper method, the Commissioner's discretion is limited. The courts have made it clear that the denial of a request to change from an incorrect to a correct method would constitute an abuse of discretion.[313] Some courts have even held that

---

Tech. Adv. Mem. 8506003 (Nov. 1, 1984), where the taxpayer's failure to disclose that substantially all its business was done with a commonly controlled entity was found an omission of a material fact, and the IRS was allowed to revoke a previously granted change in method of accounting from accrual to cash; Tech. Adv. Mem. 8726003 (Mar. 3, 1987), where the taxpayer's adoption of a proposed change in method one year prior to the year approved by the National Office was found not to justify a revocation of a previously granted change in method of computing LIFO inventories.

[308] See discussion at ¶ 9.08.

[309] IRC § 472(a). See Treas. Reg. § 1.472-1(a).

[310] See Section 453A as in effect prior to the 1987 Act.

[311] See, e.g., Peninsula Steel Co., 78 TC 1029, 1058–1059 (1982), where the Tax Court found that the Commissioner could not deny the use of the LIFO inventory method to a taxpayer who otherwise qualified for that method, the court noting that "the Congress has even cut back on respondent's almost plenary authority as to changes in accounting method in this area." Similarly, the Court of Claims in John Wanamaker Philadelphia, Inc. v. United States, 359 F2d 437 (Ct. Cl. 1966), stated that taxpayers have "an absolute right" to use the LIFO method of accounting and that the Commissioner's discretion in the area, except for proposing necessary or appropriate adjustments, is quite narrow.

[312] See Rev. Rul. 78-237, 1978-1 CB 135.

[313] See, e.g., National Bank of Fort Benning v. United States, 79-2 USTC ¶ 9627 (MD Ga. 1979); Security Benefit Life Ins. Co. v. United States, 517 F. Supp. 740 (D.

the Commissioner's prior consent to a change from an incorrect method is not necessary.[314]

As a consequence of this limited discretion, the Commissioner may not properly deny a request for change from any Category A method or from an improper Category B method. Nevertheless, such denials sometimes occur. The question then arises as to what the taxpayer should do if the Commissioner denies the request or seeks to impose conditions or adjustments other than those expressly required under Section 481.

One seemingly appropriate response would be to report using the desired method. The taxpayer should make full disclosure of the present incorrect method, the failure of the Commissioner to approve the requested change to a correct method, and the fact that the denial amounts to an abuse of discretion and, hence, need not be followed by the taxpayer. Should the IRS decide to challenge the taxpayer's right to make a change in those circumstances,[315] it would do so in connection with the examination of the taxpayer's return. In response, the taxpayer might argue both that approval was not required and that denial of approval amounts to an abuse of discretion. This procedure does have an element of risk, however, since the IRS could take the position that penalties should be imposed on the basis of the taxpayer's action.[316] Although the likelihood of these penalties being sustained is uncertain, the IRS has asserted penalties on audit in such circumstances.

An alternative and less risky procedure would be to report using the present method and then file a claim for refund on the basis of the desired method. The claim would be based on an abuse of discretion by the Commissioner in denying the request for change.

Although either approach may be appropriate, the former has the advantage of having the taxpayer report on the desired method and putting the burden on the Commissioner to go further with a challenge. However, it has the disadvantage of the risk of penalties being asserted. Under the alternative, the taxpayer must continue the incorrect method and force a

---

Kan. 1980); where in each case the court held it was an abuse of discretion for the Commissioner to refuse consent to a change from an incorrect to a correct method of accounting unless the taxpayer acquiesced in adjustments not expressly required by Section 481; Wright Contracting Co., 36 TC 620 (1961), acq. 1966-2 CB 7, aff'd, 316 F2d 249 (5th Cir. 1963), cert. denied, 375 US 879 (1963), where the court indicated that it would amount to an abuse of discretion for the Commissioner to refuse a request for change from an improper to a proper method; Elsie SoRelle, 22 TC 459 (1954), acq. 1955-1 CB 6, and Douthit v. United States, 299 F. Supp. 397 (WD Tenn. 1969), rev'd on other grounds, 432 F2d 83 (6th Cir. 1970), each of which, in the context of other questions, made it clear that the Commissioner could not compel a taxpayer to remain on an improper method of accounting.

[314] See discussion at ¶ 9.05.

[315] A failure to challenge by the IRS may ultimately ripen into an implied acceptance of the new method. See discussion at ¶ 2.04[3].

[316] See discussion infra ¶ 8.09.

dispute in order to resolve the issue. The taxpayer must also pay amounts due under the incorrect method and lose the opportunity of having the issue resolved in the Tax Court.

[a] IRS Consent Required on Change From Incorrect Method

The courts have generally sustained the regulatory requirement that a taxpayer may not change its method of accounting without the prior consent of the Commissioner, even though its present method is not permissible. In *Commissioner v. O. Liquidating Corp.*,[317] an accrual basis taxpayer had consistently but erroneously reduced its insurance expense of each year by an amount representing dividends to be paid by the insurance company in the following year. In 1953, after years of following this practice, the taxpayer accrued no dividends and deducted the full amount of the premiums for that year. The Tax Court held that the method used prior to 1953 was erroneous and that the 1953 change did not constitute a change in method of accounting for which the prior approval of the Commissioner would be required.

On appeal, the Tax Court's determination that the method used prior to 1953 was erroneous was not contested, but the Commissioner contended that a taxpayer could not change even an erroneous method of accounting without the prior consent of the Commissioner. The Court of Appeals for the Third Circuit agreed.[318] The Courts of Appeal for the Second and Fifth Circuits have agreed that consent is necessary in such circumstances.[319]

---

[317] Comm'r v. O. Liquidating Corp., 292 F2d 225 (3d Cir. 1961), cert. denied, 368 US 898 (1961).

[318] The court of appeals held, "It is not dispositive that taxpayer's former consistent method of reporting the insurance dividends in the instant case was not correct under the accrual accounting system since it could not be changed without the Commissioner's prior consent." Id. at 231.

[319] See American Can Co. v. Comm'r, 317 F2d 604 (2d Cir. 1963), cert. denied, 375 US 993 (1964), where the taxpayer, without obtaining the prior consent of the Commissioner, changed its method of accounting for local taxes and vacation pay from the cash method to the accrual method in order to conform its method of accounting for these items to its general method. The court held that the taxpayer had to obtain the prior consent of the Commissioner to change its method of accounting for these items even though the method used was erroneous. See also Wright Contracting Co. v. Comm'r, 316 F2d 249 (5th Cir. 1963), cert. denied, 375 US 879 (1963), where the Court concluded that the taxpayer's method was not erroneous and that the Commissioner's prior consent was required. While the court was not faced with a change from an erroneous method, it indicated approval of Third Circuit's decision in *O. Liquidating Corp.* See also John P. Bongiovanni, 30 TCM 1124 (1971), rev'd on other grounds, 470 F2d 921 (2d Cir. 1972), where a taxpayer attempted to make a change from the cash method to an accrual method without the Commissioner's prior consent. The taxpayer argued that such consent was not required because his use of the cash method was erroneous. The taxpayer operated a construction company that purchased materials, employed labor, and had

[b] IRS Consent Not Required on Change From Incorrect Method

Despite the statutory and regulatory requirements regarding a change in method of accounting, as well as the cases just discussed, some courts have indicated that in particular circumstances, the prior approval of the IRS is not required for a change from an incorrect method.[320] For example, in *Douthit v. United States*,[321] the court held that the requirement of prior approval is not applicable to a change in method that is required by applicable law. The case involved an accrual method partnership that sold customer notes to finance companies on a limited recourse basis. The finance companies withheld a portion of the amount due the partnership as security against customer defaults. As the customer notes were repaid, the finance companies would release to the partnership the amounts withheld as security. These amounts were included in the partnership's income only as received. The Supreme Court had earlier held in *Commissioner v. Hansen*[322] that an accrual method dealer must report such income on the accrual method rather than the cash method. The court in *Douthit* held that this Supreme Court decision required use of the accrual method for this income,[323] that it compelled a change to the accrual method, and that the prior consent of the Commissioner was not required.[324]

In *North Carolina Granite Corp.*,[325] the Tax Court stated that the general requirement of securing prior IRS consent to a change from an incorrect

---

inventories of brick, block, mortar, and steel as well as inventories of work in process. The taxpayer argued that prior approval was not necessary because applicable regulations required use of the accrual method. The Tax Court disagreed, stating, "Even assuming that the cash basis had been improperly used by the petitioner in prior years, the respondent cannot be compelled to accept a change in accounting." 30 TCM at 1127.

[320] See ¶ 2.04[3][d], discussing circumstances in which the Commissioner may be deemed to have accepted a change in method because of the agent's actions on audit.

[321] Douthit v. United States, 299 F. Supp. 397 (WD Tenn. 1969), rev'd on other grounds, 432 F2d 83 (6th Cir. 1970).

[322] Comm'r v. Hansen, 360 US 446 (1959).

[323] Douthit v. United States, 299 F. Supp. 397, 403 (WD Tenn. 1969).

[324] The court explained:

By the decision in *Hansen* the partnership was required to change its method of accounting by reporting dealer reserve income on the accrual basis. By the same token, the Commissioner was required to accept the change and make the appropriate adjustments for the year of the change and any prior years for the partnership and the individual partners. Both the taxpayer and the government were bound by the mandate of the Supreme Court. The first partnership return due after *Hansen* was the one for the fiscal year ending January 31, 1960. The partnership was compelled to include in its income that amount of dealer reserve income which had accrued to the partnership during this fiscal year.

Id.

[325] North Carolina Granite Corp., 43 TC 149 (1964).

method must yield to a more specific command of law. Therefore, Section 446(e) was held inapplicable where the law specifically prescribes or proscribes a method of accounting or computation. This conclusion was plainly dictum, however, since the court had already held that the change made by the taxpayer did not constitute a change in its method of accounting.

In *Woodward Iron Co. v. United States*,[326] the court agreed with the proposition that Section 446(e) is not applicable to a change required by the law, but in this case the court found that the taxpayer was not required by law to change its method. For 1953 and prior tax years, the taxpayer had accrued and deducted state property taxes ratably. In 1954, the taxpayer changed its method from the ratable accrual method to the lump-sum accrual method but did not obtain the consent of the Commissioner to make the change. On audit, the Commissioner disallowed the change to the lump-sum method and returned the taxpayer to the ratable method because the taxpayer had failed to obtain prior consent to making the change. The taxpayer argued that the consent requirement was not applicable, since a change in the law compelled the taxpayer to change to the lump-sum accrual method. Section 461(c), which was enacted in 1954, provides that at the election of an accrual method taxpayer, any real property tax that is related to a definite period may be accrued ratably over that period. The taxpayer contended that since it had not made an election, it was required to use the lump-sum accrual method. However, the court found that the taxpayer was not compelled by the enactment of Section 461(c) to change its method of accounting and, therefore, that the taxpayer erred in failing to obtain the consent of the Commissioner to change.

The prior approval requirement is designed to ensure that (1) appropriate adjustments are made on changes in accounting methods and (2) the IRS has an opportunity to monitor the changes. For this reason, it seems that the better view is that prior IRS approval should be required in all cases, not merely those where the change is from one acceptable method to another acceptable method. Accordingly, if the issue were ever ultimately decided by the U.S. Supreme Court, it is likely that the Court would find in favor of the prior approval requirement. Nevertheless, until the issue is ultimately resolved, the authorities do suggest the possibility of raising an argument that prior IRS approval is not necessary in jurisdictions where the issue has been resolved favorably or has not yet been decided. Taxpayers and their advisors frequently ignore the possibility of making such an argument, often to their detriment.[327]

---

[326] Woodward Iron Co. v. United States, 254 F. Supp. 835 (ND Ala. 1966), aff'd, 396 F2d 552 (5th Cir. 1968).

[327] In Southern Pac. Transp. Co., 75 TC 497, 682 n.208 (1980), supplemental opinion, 82 TC 122 (1984), the Tax Court noted the status of this issue as follows:

[3] Automatic Changes and Changes Deemed Approved

In many cases, taxpayers are permitted to change methods of accounting on their own, without the need for prior IRS approval. In other cases, the IRS has itself issued revenue procedures indicating that approval of certain changes may be assumed by the taxpayer. Examples of the former include changes to LIFO and (prior to the 1987 Act) adoption of the installment method of accounting by dealers. Examples of the latter include changes in a taxpayer's method of depreciation,[328] changes in methods of accounting for bad debts,[329] changes in inventory valuation methods to conform to the *Thor Power Tool* decision,[330] changes in vacation pay plans,[331] changes from the Rule of 78's method of computing interest on installment obligations,[332] and changes from the cash method to an accrual method.[333]

On the question of whether consent is necessary to change from a clearly incorrect accounting method, some Courts of Appeals have adopted a fairly strict approach. See, for example, *Witte v. Commissioner*, 513 F.2d 391 (D.C. Cir. 1975), remanding T.C. Memo 1972-232; *American Can Co. v. Commissioner*, 317 F.2d 604, 606 (2d Cir. 1963), reversed on this point 37 T.C. 198 (1961); *Commissioner v. O. Liquidating Corp.*, 292 F.2d 225, 230 (3rd Cir. 1961), rev'g. TC Memo 1960-29, cert. denied 368 U.S. 898 (1961). In each of the appellate decisions cited above, the Court of Appeals held that the consent of the Commissioner is necessary for a change even where the taxpayer's old method is shown to be wrong. This Court has tended not to require consent in such situations. In addition to the above-cited Tax Court opinions, see *Underhill v. Commissioner*, 45 TC 489, 496-497 (1966). Compare *H.F. Campbell Co. v. Commissioner*, 53 TC 439, 448 (1969), aff'd. 443 F.2d 965 (6th Cir. 1971); *Bongiovanni v. Commissioner*, T.C. Memo 1971-262; and sec. 1.446-1(e)(2)(i), Income Tax Regs.

[328] See IRC §§ 167(e) and 167(j)(2)(C) (as previously in effect) regarding changes from accelerated depreciation methods to the straight-line depreciation method; Rev. Proc. 74-11, 1974-1 CB 420, regarding changes to accelerated depreciation methods and vice versa.

[329] See Rev. Proc. 82-19, 1982-1 CB 463, superseded by Rev. Proc. 85-8, 1985-1 CB 495, pertaining to a change from the specific charge-off method to the reserve method of accounting for bad debts; Rev. Rul. 79-123, 1979-1 CB 215, pertaining to a change from the percentage of loans method to either the percentage of taxable income method or the experience method of accounting for bad debts.

[330] See Rev. Proc. 80-5, 1980-1 CB 582.

[331] See Rev. Proc. 82-32, 1982-1 CB 486, declared obsolete by Rev. Proc. 86-20, 1986-1 CB 560, pertaining to an accrual method taxpayer's change from deducting fully vested vacation pay in the year paid to the year in which it accrues.

[332] Rev. Proc. 84-74, 1984-2 CB 736; Rev. Proc. 84-28, 1984-1 CB 475, 84-30, 1984-1 CB 482. Of course, these rulings and procedures apply only to amounts attributable to a valid indebtedness. See Rev. Rul. 87-140, 1987-2 CB 120.

[333] See Rev. Proc. 85-36, 1985-2 CB 434, which provides expeditious IRS consent to a change from the cash method to an accrual method for taxpayers who are required to use inventories in order to clearly reflect income; Rev. Proc. 85-37, 1985-2 CB 438, which provides similar IRS consent to such changes for most other

¶ 8.08 OBLIGATION OF TAXPAYER TO CHANGE FROM INCORRECT METHOD

In the absence of express requirement,[334] there is no general requirement in the Code or in Treasury regulations and no general principle of taxation that obligates a taxpayer to seek permission to change its method of accounting, even when that method is clearly erroneous. This conclusion has generally been accepted by commentators.[335]

Nevertheless, the IRS may seek to impose penalties on a taxpayer who knowingly continues an obviously incorrect method. [336] Although it may be difficult for the IRS to sustain a proposed imposition of penalties, the enactment of Section 446(f), which is discussed in the following section, indicates congressional recognition of the problem and an intent to make the continued use of erroneous methods more risky.

Moreover, in Revenue Procedure 92-20,[337] the IRS stated that available penalties *may* be imposed if the taxpayer does not timely file a request to change from an incorrect method of accounting.[338] However, no affirmative obligation to make such a change was imposed, and the IRS stated that penalties would not be imposed when a taxpayer changes from an impermissible method by complying with the revenue procedure.

¶ 8.09 IMPOSITION OF PENALTIES

The imposition of penalties based on accounting methods and practices employed by taxpayers has always been an area of great uncertainty. Since

---

taxpayers. These procedures were superseded by Rev. Proc. 92-74, 992-38 IRB 16 and Rev. Proc. 92-75, 1992-38 IRB 22, respectively.

[334] See discussion supra ¶ 8.04[6] for examples of express requirements to change methods of accounting.

[335] According to two experts:

> In the accounting methods area, where the Commissioner issues a pronouncement indicating that a taxpayer's method is erroneous, the present view is that, while a taxpayer may not unilaterally change to the correct method (unless the pronouncement permits or requires him to do so), he is not obligated to request the Commissioner's consent to change his method.

Borini and Dunkle, "Forced Changes in Method of Accounting," 36 NYU Inst. on Fed. Tax'n 481, 489 (1978). Similarly, Diamond & Holman, "Accounting Methods Adoption and Changes," Tax Mgmt. (BNA) 303-4th, A-22 (1987), report that a taxpayer using an erroneous method is generally not obligated to seek to change from that method.

[336] See supra ¶ 8.07[2][b] for discussion of cases that could be used by the IRS to show affirmative obligation to change an erroneous method.

[337] Rev. Proc. 92-20, 1992-1 CB 685.

[338] Rev. Proc. 92-20, 1992-1 CB 685, § 2.07.

taxpayers (1) are prohibited by regulation from changing even an erroneous method of accounting without the prior approval of the Commissioner and (2) generally have no affirmative obligation to seek such changes, any continued application of an erroneous method would seem consistent with the governing requirements. As a consequence, a taxpayer generally should not be penalized for continuing to use an improper method of accounting when there is no affirmative obligation on the taxpayer to change that method and the taxpayer is prohibited from making any change without prior IRS approval.

In order to overcome some of the uncertainty posed by the foregoing circumstance, Congress enacted Section 446(f) in 1984. This provision specifies that if a taxpayer fails to file a request for a change in method of accounting, the absence of consent to the change shall not be taken into account to prevent imposition of a penalty.[339]

Although the congressional intent was intended to overcome the dilemma described above, the provision seems deficient in several respects. First, the provision does not impose an affirmative obligation on the taxpayer to seek a change. Thus, a taxpayer is still under an express requirement that absent approval of a change by the IRS, the taxpayer must continue to use its existing method of accounting even though that method of accounting is erroneous.

Second, the statute does not provide an incentive to taxpayers to seek permission to change methods of accounting. It does not make the filing of an application for change a defense or bar to the imposition of a penalty in connection with the use of the erroneous method. Rather, the statute provides only that if the taxpayer has not filed an application for change in method, the failure of the Commissioner to give consent to a change shall not be taken into account. Although this language suggests that the failure of the Commissioner to grant consent to a change should be taken into account if the application has been filed, the language does not prohibit the imposition of a penalty in such a case.

However, perhaps in recognition of this statutory deficiency, just such a prohibition was included in Revenue Procedure 92-20.[340] After warning taxpayers that penalties may be imposed where incorrect methods of accounting are continued, the revenue procedure specifies that penalties will not be imposed when a taxpayer changes from an impermissible method of accounting in accordance with the provisions of the revenue procedure.

Although it is extremely rare for penalties to be imposed with respect to the use of erroneous accounting methods, their imposition is not pre-

---

[339] IRC § 446(f).
[340] Rev. Proc. 92-20, 1992-1 CB 685, § 2.07.

cluded. For example, in *Boynton v. Pedrick*,[341] a taxpayer in the business of processing and selling sheepskins maintained his books on an accrual basis and took inventories to prepare profit and loss statements. Nevertheless, returns were prepared on a cash basis. This was in direct conflict with the governing statute and regulations.[342] The IRS sought to impose the penalty for intentional disregard of rules and regulations. A jury found that the plaintiff's failure to file returns on the proper basis was due to negligence, and the court of appeals found that the evidence amply supported the jury's finding.

In light of the recent trend of increasing legislative control over methods of accounting, taxpayers should exercise extreme caution in continuing clearly erroneous methods of accounting.[343] Such continuation is fraught with risk. For example, assertedly improper methods of accounting for spare parts by publicly held utility companies have led to criminal investigations.[344]

Taxpayers must also be alert to the recommendations of tax advisors. For example, in *Thomas Nelson, Inc. v. United States*,[345] the government sought to impose a penalty for negligence on a taxpayer that followed a course of action recommended by its national accounting firm. The court found the taxpayer's reliance to preclude imposition of the penalty. However, the mere fact that the government sought imposition of the penalty in the circumstances is significant, and the court hinted that had the law been more certain at the time the accountants proposed their recommended course of action, reliance on their advice might not have been a sufficient defense to the proposed penalty.

Taxpayers may fare somewhat better when the erroneous method has been used for many years and those years have been audited. For example, in *Lynn Haynes*,[346] the court refused to impose a penalty for use of an improper accounting method because the accounting method had been used for many years, the taxpayer's books reflected use of the method, the taxpayer had been examined a number of times, and on at least one occasion the taxpayer inquired specifically of the examining agent whether the method of accounting was appropriate, and no change in method was required.

---

[341] Boynton v. Pedrick, 228 F2d 745 (2d Cir. 1955), aff'g 136 F. Supp. 888 (SDNY 1954), cert. denied, 351 US 938 (1956).

[342] Section 41 of the Internal Revenue Code of 1939; Reg. 111, §§ 29.22(c)-1, 29.41-a.

[343] See discussion supra ¶ 8.04[6][c] regarding Treasury's perceived desire to impose penalties on taxpayers who fail to change their methods of accounting to comply with the new inventory costing rules required by the 1986 Act.

[344] These investigations were reported in the *Wall Street Journal* over the period August and September 1988. See, e.g., Wall St. J., Aug. 31, 1988, § A, at 2; Id., Sept. 1, 1988, § A, at 3.

[345] Thomas Nelson, Inc. v. United States, 88-1 USTC ¶ 9339 (ND Tenn. 1988).

[346] Lynn Haynes, 59 TCM 107 (1990).

CHAPTER 9

Accounting Changes Not Requiring IRS Approval

¶ 9.01	Opportunities for Taxpayers	9-2
	[1] When There Is a Change in Method of Accounting	9-2
	[2] When There Is No Change in Method of Accounting	9-3
	[3] Planning	9-4
¶ 9.02	Definition of "Change in Method of Accounting"	9-6
	[1] What Is Included?	9-6
	[2] What Is Excluded?	9-7
	[3] Factors to Consider	9-8
¶ 9.03	Material Item	9-9
	[1] Development of Regulations	9-9
	[a] 1939 Code Regulations	9-9
	[b] Legislative History	9-9
	[c] Regulatory Definition Evolves	9-10
	[2] Pre-1970 Regulation Cases	9-11
	[a] Absolute Materiality	9-12
	[b] Relative Materiality	9-13
	[i] Material item of gross income	9-13
	[ii] Comparison to gross amount of item, taxable income, or gross income	9-14
	[3] Post-1970 Regulation Cases	9-16
¶ 9.04	Consistent Treatment	9-20
	[1] Adoption of Method in Initial Year	9-21
	[a] Change of Correct Method	9-21
	[b] Change of Incorrect Method	9-22
	[2] Consistent Use of Arbitrary Procedures	9-25
	[a] Problem Confronting Taxpayers	9-25
	[b] Alternatives Available to Taxpayers	9-27
	[i] Treat existing practice as a method of accounting and request change	9-27
	[ii] Elect method not requiring prior approval	9-27
	[iii] Make "do-it-yourself" correction	9-28
	[iv] Continue past practice	9-28

[c] Recommendation 9-29

¶ 9.05 Correction of Errors 9-30
  [1] United States Court of Federal Claims 9-31
  [2] Tax Court 9-33
  [3] Courts of Appeals for Fifth and Tenth Circuits 9-35
  [4] Other Forums 9-37
  [5] Challenging Commissioner's Denial of Change 9-37

¶ 9.06 Change in Underlying Facts 9-38
  [1] Regulations 9-38
  [2] Judicial Development 9-40
    [a] Change in Contract, Business Practice, or Economic
      Consequences 9-40
    [b] Significant Consequences to Parties 9-43
  [3] Importance of Defining "Method" 9-46
  [4] Change in Fact vs. Adoption of Method for New "Item" ... 9-48
  [5] Expansion of Existing Business 9-51

¶ 9.07 Change in Character of the Item 9-52

¶ 9.08 Techniques for Changes Without Prior Approval 9-56
  [1] The Drop-Down 9-57
    [a] Section 351 Transfers 9-58
    [b] Section 368 Reorganizations 9-58
    [c] Section 269 Acquisitions 9-60
  [2] Carryover Tax Attributes in Certain Corporate Acquisitions 9-62
  [3] Transfers of Business Growth 9-64

¶ 9.01 OPPORTUNITIES FOR TAXPAYERS

The Internal Revenue Service defines "change in method of accounting" broadly and generally seeks to have every change in reporting treated as a change in method. This treatment gives the Commissioner of the Internal Revenue the discretion to accept or reject taxpayer applications for a change in method. Chapter 8 discusses the requirements for, and rules governing, these changes.

Significant opportunities to change reporting practices are available to taxpayers, because not every change in the time an item of income or expense is reported for federal income tax purposes is the result of a change in method of accounting. Moreover, in many circumstances, a taxpayer may effect the equivalent of a change in method of accounting without being subject to the normal conditions and requirements governing the change. This chapter covers these two distinct topics.

[1] When There Is a Change in Method of Accounting

One of the most difficult determinations of tax accounting is whether a particular change in reporting is a change in method of accounting (this topic is discussed more fully in Chapter 8). Relevant court decisions and administrative determinations are not always consistent, and it is often difficult to discern the legal or factual distinctions between them. Yet, because of the potential for considerable tax savings or tax costs, these determinations are very significant.

If a particular change in accounting practice amounts to a change in method of accounting, three basic consequences result. First, the change may generally be made only with the prior approval of the IRS.[1] Second, the change is subject to the requirements of Section 481,[2] which permits an adjustment (the "Section 481 adjustment") to be made to ensure that the change does not result in a double inclusion or an omission of items of income or expense.[3] Third, as a practical matter, the making of the change and any subsequent review of the change by the IRS are not subject to the running of the applicable statutory periods of limitation. Consequently, although the running of the applicable periods of limitation may prevent the Section 481 adjustment from being made in a closed year, the adjustment is not, in fact, prohibited; it is simply deferred until the appropriate open year.

[2] When There Is No Change in Method of Accounting

If a change in reporting does not amount to a change in method of accounting, then the change may be made without the prior approval of the IRS. Such a change is also not subject to the requirements of Section 481. Thus, as illustrated in the example that follows, the change may result in an omission of items of income or expense or a double inclusion of such items. In addition, the change is subject to (and, hence, has the protection or bears the risk of) the running of the applicable statutory periods of limitation. Consequently, amounts attributable to years prior to the year of change cannot increase or decrease the amounts of income or expense to be reported in the year of change and subsequent years.[4]

---

[1] In some cases, the equivalent of an accounting method change may be made without the prior approval of the IRS. See discussion infra ¶ 9.08.

[2] Unless otherwise indicated, all IRC references are to the Internal Revenue Code (the Code) of 1986, as amended.

[3] The Section 481 adjustment is, in effect, the aggregate amount of income or expense that would have been reported in years prior to the year of change had the taxpayer been on the new method in the prior years. See ¶ 8.04 for a discussion of the Section 481 adjustment.

[4] Nevertheless, changes that do not amount to changes in methods of accounting are subject to other provisions of the Code that may affect the normal impact of statutory periods of limitation. See, e.g., the mitigation provisions of Sections 1311–1314.

EXAMPLE: Assume that a taxpayer follows a reporting practice that incorrectly defers the recognition of income for a period of one year and that the aggregate amounts of deferred income at the end of years 1, 2, 3, and 4 are $100, $250, $300, and $400, respectively. As a consequence of its incorrect reporting, the taxpayer has deferred an aggregate of $400 as of the end of year 4. If the statutory period of limitations has run on years 1, 2, and 3 and either the taxpayer or the IRS seeks to correct the reporting of items beginning in year 4, substantially different adjustments result, depending on whether the correction amounts to a change in method of accounting.

If the correction amounts to a change in method of accounting, the taxpayer may not correct its incorrect practice without the prior approval of the IRS.[5] In addition, a Section 481 adjustment in the amount of $300 will be required. The $300 represents the aggregate amount that properly reported, would have been recognized in years prior to year 4.[6] The change in method will require the $300 to be included in income in year 4 or to be taken into income ratably over some appropriate period of years beginning with year 4.[7] The $100 increase in the deferred amount during year 4 (the $400 balance at the end of year 4 minus the $300 balance at the beginning of year 4) will be taken into account entirely in year 4.

If the change in reporting practice does not amount to a change in method of accounting, the $300 beginning balance, which should have been reported in years prior to year 4, will escape taxation, since the statutory period of limitations has run on such years.[8] The amount of the $100 increase in the deferred income during year 4 will still be taken into account as income in that year.

[3] Planning

For many years, taxpayers have been cognizant of the tax benefits of deferring the recognition of income or accelerating the recognition of expense. Nevertheless, rarely have they reviewed their existing accounting practices to see if variations or changes in these practices would produce tax

---

[5] Treas. Reg. § 1.446-1(e)(2)(i) states, "Consent must be secured whether or not such method is proper or is permitted under the Internal Revenue Code or the regulations thereunder." See discussion at ¶ 8.03. But see also discussions at ¶ 8.07[2][b], and infra ¶ 9.05 for contrary authority.

[6] See discussion at ¶ 8.04 for description and computation of Section 481 adjustment.

[7] For a discussion of the various periods over which a Section 481 adjustment may be taken into account, see ¶¶ 8.04[3], 8.04[4], 8.04[6], 8.04[7].

[8] However, consider application of mitigation provisions of Sections 1311–1314.

benefits. The failure to pursue such changes may be attributed to one or more of the following factors: (1) ignorance of the opportunities available; (2) a belief that IRS approval of the change must be obtained and that such approval is unlikely; or (3) an expectation that the cost or difficulty of pursuing or effecting the change would outweigh the tax benefits to be gained.

The opportunities for deferring income or accelerating expense exist in most cases. More often than not, even a cursory review of the taxpayer's practices will reveal a number of opportunities for effecting significant tax savings. These savings can often be achieved simply and inexpensively through relatively minor variations in accounting procedures or business practices that would not amount to changes in accounting methods and therefore would not require IRS approval. Such action by the taxpayer avoids the probable reluctance of the IRS to approve a change in method where the taxpayer's present method is proper, and the change would result in a deferral in tax.[9]

As mentioned previously, such a change in practice may result in double deductions or an omission of income. For instance, if the change in the preceding example did not amount to a change in method of accounting, the adjustment arising from the change would have been only $100, the amount attributable to year 4 ($400 − $300). The $300 attributable to years prior to year 4 would escape taxation, assuming the statutory period of limitations had run on such years.

In some cases, similar tax benefits may be achieved without the prior approval of the IRS, even when a change in method of accounting is involved. For example, because each taxpayer has the opportunity of selecting its own methods of accounting, it is possible for the business of an existing taxpayer to be transferred to a newly formed entity. The transferee entity may adopt and use a different method of accounting from the transferor and thereby effect a change in the method of reporting the income and expense of the particular business activity.[10]

For example, assume an accrual basis taxpayer is in the business of providing both goods and services, such as a television dealer who both sells sets and provides repair services. If the taxpayer wishes to convert the reporting of income from the service activity from an accrual method to the cash method, it may be able to achieve this result by forming a new corporation to conduct the service business and having the new corporation elect the cash method.[11]

---

[9] The IRS is not required to approve a change from a method of accounting that is correct and clearly reflects income. See discussion at ¶ 8.07[1].

[10] This opportunity is discussed infra ¶ 9.08.

[11] See, e.g., Jerry Fong, 48 TCM 689 (1984), where grocery store managerial activities were successfully transferred from accrual basis taxpayers to a newly formed cash basis partnership. See discussion infra ¶ 9.08[1]. See ¶ 3.06 regarding availability of cash method.

Taxpayers and their advisors should remain alert to these tax accounting opportunities. The benefits from such opportunities are potentially enormous, yet the cost and complexity of implementation are often insignificant.

While the IRS may take the position that a particular change in reporting does not involve a change in method of accounting (e.g., where that position would result in increased income or lost deductions to the taxpayer), it is rare for the IRS to do so. The IRS knows that in most cases, it benefits by arguing that a change in practice amounts to a change in method. Thus, a position to the contrary in a particular case could, if sustained, cause more of a revenue loss than a revenue gain if such a position were followed in other cases.

¶ 9.02 DEFINITION OF "CHANGE IN METHOD OF ACCOUNTING"

The Internal Revenue Code does not define the phrase "change in method of accounting." However, guidance as to whether a particular change in reporting amounts to a change in method of accounting is provided in two paragraphs of the applicable Treasury regulations, one governing what is included in the concept[12] and the other governing what is excluded.[13]

[1] What Is Included?

Paragraph (a) of the applicable treasury regulations states the following:

> A change in the method of accounting includes a change in the overall plan of accounting for gross income or deductions or a change in the treatment of any material item used in such overall plan. Although a method of accounting may exist under this definition without the necessity of a pattern of consistent treatment of an item, in most instances a method of accounting is not established for an item without such consistent treatment. A material item is any item which involves the proper time for the inclusion of the item in income or the taking of a deduction.[14]

This paragraph makes three points regarding the phrase "change in method of accounting." First, the phrase encompasses a change in an overall plan of accounting. Consequently, any change from the cash method to an accrual method or vice versa is included.

---

[12] Treas. Reg. § 1.446-1(e)(2)(ii)(A).
[13] Treas. Reg. § 1.446-1(e)(2)(ii)(B).
[14] Treas. Reg. § 1.446-1(e)(2)(ii)(A).

Second, a change in method arises only if the item involved in the change is material, even though a method of accounting may exist for any item of income or expense without regard to its materiality.[15] Although materiality is usually thought of in terms of absolute or relative size of dollar amount, the final sentence of the previously quoted regulation defines "material" in terms of the time when an item is reported. As explained later in this chapter,[16] this regulatory definition of material" has not been accepted in all cases.

Third, a method of accounting generally is not established without a pattern of consistent treatment, which is established by using the same method of accounting over a period of consecutive tax years. This requirement of consistent treatment suggests that a taxpayer that has not reported on a consistent basis over a period of years may be able to change to a new method without being subject to the requirements affecting changes in methods of accounting (e.g., the need to obtain IRS approval of the change or to make a Section 481 adjustment). The requirement of consistent treatment raises the question of whether a taxpayer is able to change its method of accounting without the prior approval of the IRS if the initial method has only been used for one or perhaps two years rather than for a period of several consecutive tax years.[17]

[2] What Is Excluded?

Paragraph (b) of the applicable treasury regulations identifies changes that are not changes in methods of accounting.

> A change in method of accounting does not include correction of mathematical or posting errors, or errors in the computation of tax liability (such as errors in computation of the foreign tax credit, net operating loss, percentage depletion or investment credit). Also, a change in method of accounting does not include adjustment of any item of income or deduction which does not involve the proper time for the inclusion of the item of income or the taking of a deduction. For example, corrections of items that are deducted as interest or salary, but that are in fact payments of dividends, and of items that are deducted as business expenses, but that are in fact personal expenses, are not changes in methods of accounting. In addition, a change in the method of accounting does not include an adjustment with respect to the

---

[15] Treas. Reg. § 1.446-1(a)(1) provides, "The term 'method of accounting' includes not only the over-all method of accounting of the taxpayer but also the accounting treatment of any item."

[16] See infra ¶ 9.03 for a full discussion of the definition of "materiality."

[17] See infra ¶ 9.04 for a full discussion of this requirement of consistent treatment.

addition to a reserve for bad debts or an adjustment in the useful life of
a depreciable asset. Although such adjustments may involve the question
of the proper time for the taking of a deduction, such items are
traditionally corrected by adjustments in the current and future years.
For the treatment of the adjustment of the addition to a bad debt reserve,
see the regulations under section 166 of the Code; for the treatment of a
change in the useful life of a depreciable asset, see the regulations under
section 167(b) of the Code. A change in the method of accounting also
does not include a change in treatment resulting from a change in
underlying facts. . . .[18]

[3] Factors to Consider

The two paragraphs of the applicable regulation together demonstrate that
three circumstances must coalesce before a change in accounting method may
be found. First, the item involved in the change must be material. Second,
the accounting practice in question generally must have been applied consistently. Third, the change must not be (1) the correction of an error; (2) a
change in character; (3) a change in underlying fact; or (4) a change
traditionally handled other than as a change in method.

Courts have been faced with a number of countervailing considerations
in attempting to apply the foregoing standards. One of the most important
of these considerations is the administrative cost and convenience versus
potential revenue loss. On the one hand, if a taxpayer is required to request
the prior approval of the IRS for every incidental adjustment it makes that
affects the timing of its recognition of income or expense, both the taxpayer
and the IRS would soon be overwhelmed by the requisite paper work. This
is because the making, filing, and reviewing of applications for changes in
accounting methods would be a never-ending task for many taxpayers. In
addition, the time and cost involved in carrying out such responsibilities
would be wholly out of proportion to the benefits of such required monitor-
ing by the IRS.

On the other hand, the IRS has a sufficient interest in ensuring that
income does not escape taxation to warrant a review of changes in reporting
practices where such changes might cause a significant loss of revenue or
otherwise result in abuse. It is therefore essential that a balance be struck.
Courts have generally sought to strike a balance between these two consider-

---

[18] Treas. Reg. § 1.446-1(e)(2)(ii)(B). Despite the regulatory statement regarding
the traditional way in which adjustments are made to bad debt reserves, the IRS has
ruled that a correction in the base of outstanding loans to include previously excluded
accrued interest is a change in method of accounting. Tech. Adv. Mem. 8741006
(May 21, 1987). See discussion at ¶ 8.04[6][d] regarding the repeal of the reserve
method of accounting for bad debts.

ations. At least some decisions indicate a judicial sensitivity to these competing interests.[19]

¶ 9.03 MATERIAL ITEM

The Treasury regulations provide that a change in method of accounting includes a change in the treatment of any material item. The definition of "material" for this purpose has proven a most perplexing problem for taxpayers and their advisors. In order to evaluate whether a particular item is material, taxpayers must consider the evolution of the regulatory and judicial definition of "materiality" for tax purposes.

[1] Development of Regulations

[a] 1939 Code Regulations

The applicable regulation promulgated under the 1939 Code did not expressly refer to "material items." It provided that "a change in the method of accounting employed in keeping books means any change in the accounting treatment of items of income or deductions. . . ."[20] This regulation, although worded in terms of the plural, "items," and not conditioned on the items' being material, was interpreted by the IRS as applying to a change in the treatment of a single, material item.[21] Consequently, the clear implication was that the requirements governing changes in methods of accounting would not apply to a change in the method of accounting for an immaterial item.

[b] Legislative History

The legislative history of Section 446 also implied that the rules governing changes in methods of accounting were not to be applied to a change in the method of accounting for an immaterial item. For example, the applicable committee report indicated that Section 446(e) was intended to codify existing regulations and that a change in method of accounting was

---

[19] See, e.g., Southern Pac. Transp. Co., 75 TC 497 (1980), quoted infra ¶ 9.03[3], note 64. This decision was supplemented by 82 TC 122 (1984).

[20] Reg. § 29.41-2.

[21] In Rev. Rul. 59-285, 1959-2 CB 458, 459, the IRS stated, "Under the 1939 Code, the prior consent of the Commissioner is required in order for a taxpayer to change his method of accounting with respect to a material item. . . ."

considered to include only a change in material items or changes that were substantial.[22]

[c] Regulatory Definition Evolves

The regulations originally issued under Section 446 did not contain a definition of the term "material item." They simply provided that a "change in the method of accounting includes a change in the overall method of accounting for gross income or deductions, or a change in the treatment of a material item."[23]

Similarly, the regulations promulgated under Section 481 did not contain an explicit definition of "material item." Nevertheless, they implied that the rules affecting a change in method of accounting did not apply to every change in method. For example, at one point reference was made to a change in method of accounting "with regard to one or more material items, such as research and experimental expenditures," "soil and water conservation expenditures," and "exploration expenditures."[24] Some courts have suggested that this language implied that "material items" were intended to encompass entire classes of income or expense.[25] Other courts *have held to the contrary.*[26] These regulations under Section 481 are still applicable and have not been amended.

However, in 1970, the Treasury amended the applicable regulation under Section 446(e) by defining "material item" as "any item which involves

---

[22] Subsection (e) [Requirement Respecting Change of Accounting Method] codifies existing regulations and states that a change in method of accounting "includes a change in the treatment of a material item such as a change in the method of valuing inventory, or a change from an accrual method without estimating expenses to an accrual method with estimated expenses, or vice versa, or a change in the method of depreciating any property." H.R. Rep. No. 1337, 83d Cong., 2d Sess. 4297 (1954). The legislative history also provided that a "change in the method of accounting is a substantial change as distinguished for [sic] each change in the treatment of each item." Id.

[23] Treas. Reg. § 1.446-1(e)(2)(i) (as it read before 1970 amendments).

[24] Treas. Reg. § 1.481-4(g)(3).

[25] See discussion infra ¶ 9.03[3].

[26] Id. The more widely held view is that an "item," whether material or not, may consist not only of an entire class of income or expense but also of a single type of income or expense within a class, or even a portion of such single type of expense or income. See, e.g., Peoples Bank and Trust Co. v. Comm'r, 415 F2d 1341 (7th Cir. 1969), aff'g 50 TC 750 (1968), where the court of appeals concluded that a change in the time for deducting a particular type of interest expense amounted to a change in "method of accounting"; and American Can Co. v. Comm'r, 317 F2d 604 (2d Cir. 1963), rev'g 37 TC 198 (1961), cert. denied, 375 US 993 (1964), where the court of appeals concluded that the taxpayer's change in its method of reporting deductions for property taxes imposed by four states to the method used for reporting similar taxes imposed by other states amounted to a change in "method of accounting."

the proper time for the inclusion of the item in income or the taking of a deduction."[27] By focusing on timing rather than on absolute or relative amount, the Treasury's definition appeared to eliminate the importance of materiality in the traditional sense.

Under the Treasury's definition, since every method of accounting involves the time when an item of income or expense is to be recognized, every change in method of accounting would involve a change in a material item. Consequently, there would be no immaterial items, and the insertion of the word "material" in the first sentence of the regulation would effectively be rendered mere surplus.[28]

The judiciary has not yet concluded whether to accept the Treasury's definition of "material." Yet some post-1970 cases suggest that the regulatory definition will not be accepted in all circumstances.[29] For this reason, the earlier cases remain relevant and must be considered. Nevertheless, as discussed in the following section, even under the earlier cases, it was very rare for the item in question to be found immaterial.

[2] Pre-1970 Regulation Cases

Following the rule that words should be given their ordinary meaning,[30] the courts initially defined a "material item" as one that was substantial in amount or of significant consequence and importance.[31] Thus, before the present regulations were issued in 1970, "materiality" was typically defined by the courts in terms of amount—either absolute or relative. In some cases, courts employed what could be termed the "absolute" test of materiality, determined solely on the basis of the dollar amount of the item at issue.[32] In other words, the amount might have been so large or so small that comparing the relative significance of the amount of the item at issue was unnecessary.

In other cases, courts employed what could be termed the "relative" test, under which materiality was determined only after comparing the

---

[27] Treas. Reg. § 1.446-1(e)(2)(ii)(A).

[28] Some commentators have noted, "[We] cannot readily theorize an instance involving an accounting practice respecting items of income or expense which would not, in turn, involve the proper time for the inclusion of such item in income or the taking of a deduction. Accordingly, virtually any change of a consistent accounting practice, regardless of its monetary consequences, is considered to be a change in accounting method." Diamond & Holman, *Accounting Methods—Definitions, Permissibility*, Tax Mgmt. (BNA) 46-4th, at A-5 (1986).

[29] See discussion infra ¶ 9.03[3].

[30] See, e.g., Malat v. Riddell, 383 US 569 (1966).

[31] See Webster's Third New International Dictionary (G.&C. Merriam Co. 1971), which defined "material" as "being of real importance or great consequence: substantial." See also the discussion infra ¶¶ 9.03[2][a], 9.03[2][b].

[32] See discussion infra ¶ 9.03[2][a].

amount of the item at issue to some other amount.[33] More often than not, the courts considered both tests. Whichever test was employed, however, "materiality" was consistently defined in terms of amount, not time. It was also clear that standards for determining materiality were not precise.

[a] Absolute Materiality

The most significant conclusion to be drawn from the cases that have employed the absolute materiality test is that the amount at issue can be relatively small. An example is *Dorr-Oliver, Inc.*,[34] where the Tax Court found a $25,000 item to be material in both an absolute and relative sense.[35] The court stated that the issue was whether an unauthorized change in method of accounting for accrued vacation pay amounted to "a *substantial* change of a *material* item." (Emphasis by court.)[36] The court first noted, "No clear standards exist for determining materiality."[37] Although the taxpayer argued that $25,000 was not material,[38] the court reasoned, "In our view $25,000 is seldom insubstantial."[39]

The *Dorr-Oliver* decision suggests that any change in method involving approximately $25,000 or more may be found to be material, regardless of the size of the taxpayer's business. From the standpoint of an equitable

---

[33] See discussion infra ¶ 9.03[2][b].

[34] Dorr-Oliver, Inc., 40 TC 50 (1963).

[35] See also Comm'r v. O. Liquidating Corp., 292 F2d 225 (3d Cir. 1961), cert. denied, 368 US 898 (1961), where the taxpayer had consistently accrued dividends to be paid by insurance companies with which the taxpayer maintained employee group insurance policies. In 1953, the taxpayer, without the consent of the Commissioner, did not accrue $114,117.44 in dividends. The Tax Court held for the taxpayer, but the court of appeals reversed, finding that there had been a change in method of accounting for a material item, the court being impressed by "the very sizeable dividend income involved." 292 F2d at 231.

[36] Dorr-Oliver, Inc., 40 TC 50, 54 (1963). Notice that the court used the adjective "substantial" to modify "change," thereby suggesting that an insubstantial change of even a material item would not amount to a change in method of accounting. The court's use of the word "substantial" in this manner was probably unintentional. Once a change in method of accounting has been found, the rules governing those changes should apply without regard to the size or significance of the change.

[37] Dorr-Oliver, Inc., 40 TC 50, 54 (1963).

[38] Id. at 55.

Petitioner contends that $24,908.23 is both absolutely insubstantial and relatively minimal when compared with [the company's] total payroll, gross sales, taxable income, and any other significant standard. It [the petitioner] concludes that the change can be made *ex parte* by the taxpayer unless the item changed is a major source of revenue or deduction of a taxpayer.

Id.

[39] Id. at 54–55.

administration of the tax laws, a finding of materiality in the absolute sense should be based on a relatively small dollar amount in order to keep large businesses from benefiting significantly more than smaller businesses and most individual taxpayers.[40]

Consequently, no taxpayer, regardless of the level of its revenue or expense, should assume that relatively insignificant amounts will be found immaterial for tax purposes. Moreover, as discussed in the next section, amounts substantially below $25,000 have been found material in a relative, if not an absolute, sense.

[b] Relative Materiality

[i] Material item of gross income. A determination of materiality on the basis of relative size often hinges on whether the amount to be considered is the gross amount of the item, the net amount of the item, or the amount of the item to be included within any Section 481 adjustment. This question was addressed by the Tax Court in *William H. Leonhart*,[41] which involved a reinsurance broker who, for years prior to 1960, had reported exclusively on the cash basis, except for commissions accrued from the American Fire and Casualty Co. In 1960, without the prior approval of the Commissioner, the taxpayer used the cash method to report commissions from American Fire. The taxpayer argued that in the context of the rules governing methods of accounting, it is the net effect of any purported change in method that should be focused on. In response, the court stated:

> This argument [of the taxpayer] appears to be predicated on a misconception of the pertinent regulation, which provides that "a change in the method of accounting includes a change in the overall method of accounting for gross income or deductions or the change in treatment of a material item" . . . [citations omitted]. It is obvious that "material item" should be read in context as "material item of gross income or deductions" and should not be construed as meaning "a material item

---

[40] See Southern Pac. Transp. Co., 75 TC 497, 684 (1980), supplemented by 82 TC 122 (1984), where, in the context of a taxpayer with revenues, expenses, and income in the tens of millions and hundreds of millions of dollars, the court stated:

> We do not think the expenditures involved herein can escape classification as a "material item" merely by virtue of their relative insubstantiality. We find it hard to view the claimed deductions of $65,299, $30,531, and $26,429 during the years at issue as immaterial, despite the fact that they may be overshadowed by much larger figures appearing on petitioner's accounting statements. Such amounts must be viewed as material in any context. While the claimed deductions may be small when compared to petitioner's total income and expenditures, the tax dollars involved cannot be considered minimal.

[41] William H. Leonhart, 27 TCM 443 (1968), aff'd, 414 F2d 749 (4th Cir. 1969).

of net income" nor as meaning a material difference between the amount of income computed under one method of accounting and that computed under another method.[42]

The focus of attention on gross amounts rather than net amounts is appropriate. It also is consistent with the normal treatment of offsets.[43]

[ii] Comparison to gross amount of item, taxable income, or gross income. In determining relative materiality, the courts have not been uniform in approach or in the application of any particular standard. Comparisons have been made between the amount at issue and the gross amount of the item itself, taxable income, and gross income.[44]

Despite the application of inconsistent standards, the cases indicate a definite preference for a finding of materiality. Thus, where the amounts of the items affected by the change were compared to the total deductions for those very items, materiality was generally found even though the absolute amounts were quite small.[45] Where comparisons were made to taxable

---

[42] William H. Leonhart, 27 TCM at 466.

[43] The widely followed rule regarding offsets is that when a taxpayer pays to, or receives from, another party a net amount, which reflects the setting off of a smaller amount due from or owing to the other party, the amounts taken into account for tax purposes are the gross amounts, not the net amounts. See, e.g., Bailey v. Comm'r, 103 F2d 448 (5th Cir. 1939); Sidney A. Wells, 26 TCM 719 (1967). See also Colonial Sav. Ass'n. v. Comm'r, 88-2 USTC ¶ 9458 (7th Cir. 1988), where, in affirming the decision of the Tax Court, the appeals court approved the treatment of penalties charged to customers for early withdrawals of deposits as separate items of income and not as offsets to the taxpayer's obligations to its customers; Comm'r v. Hansen, 360 US 446 (1959); Lawyers Title Guar. Fund v. United States, 501 F2d 1 (5th Cir. 1975).

[44] In several cases, the courts found that a change in method of accounting for a "material item" had occurred, but the courts did not indicate clearly the basis for their findings. See, e.g., Woodward Iron Co. v. United States, 254 F. Supp. 835 (ND Ala. 1966), aff'd, 396 F2d 552 (5th Cir. 1968), where a change in reporting state property taxes from a ratable method to a lump-sum method was found material even though the amount involved ($187,476.20) was only about 2 percent of taxable income; Hackensack Water Co. v. United States, 352 F2d 807 (Ct. Cl. 1965), where a change from the cash method to an accrual method for reporting property taxes was found a material change, the amount of taxes in question exceeding $1 million; I. Lewis Corp., 22 TCM 35 (1963), where a change from the cash method to an accrual method of reporting vacation pay was held material, accrued vacation pay representing about 46 percent of amount of vacation pay actually paid in the year.

[45] See Dorr-Oliver, Inc., 40 TC 50 (1963), where a deduction of approximately $25,000 of vacation pay was found material, this amount representing 28 percent of the total deduction for vacation pay and 40 percent of the amount actually paid; George C. Carlson, 26 TCM 537 (1967), where an accrual basis taxpayer, which expensed prepaid vehicle license fees ratably at the end of each month, deducted $20,607.08 on its tax return for its last taxable year. Of this amount, $6,920.04 was the unamortized balance of license fees at the date of liquidation. The IRS disallowed deduction of the $6,920.04 on the ground that it had distorted income and represented

income,[46] or even to gross income,[47] the amounts in question were generally found to be material. However, there are exceptions. For example, where the amounts involved were significantly less than one percent of operating expenses or net income, the Court of Claims found an absence of materiality.[48]

---

a change in the treatment of a material item for which prior approval had not been received. The Tax Court agreed.

> We regard $6,920.04 as "material" under these circumstances, even though we recognize that no definite standards exist as to what constitutes a "material item." Viewed in relation to total license expense [citations omitted] and taxable income [citations omitted], the amount deducted by [the corporation] was about 34 percent of total license expense and about 8.5 percent of its taxable income.

Id. at 540.

[46] See e.g., Broida, Stone & Thomas, Inc. v. United States, 204 F. Supp, 841 (ND W. Va. 1962), aff'd, 309 F2d 486 (4th Cir. 1962), which involved the deduction of personal property taxes by an accrual basis taxpayer with a January 31 fiscal year. For many years, the taxpayer accrued taxes monthly, beginning with the month following the month of assessment. For example, taxes assessed January 1 of one calendar year would be accrued monthly from February of that year through January 31 of the next year. In June 1959, the state legislature changed the assessment date from January 1 to December 31 of the preceding year. On its income tax return for its 1960 taxable year, the taxpayer deducted $6,200 for taxes assessed January 1, 1959, and $6,600, the entire amount assessed on December 31, 1959. The Commissioner disallowed the deduction of this latter sum on the ground that the taxpayer had changed its method of accounting without prior approval. The district court, affirmed by the Court of Appeals for the Fourth Circuit, found that the taxpayer could not change from its former, although incorrect, system of monthly accruals to a lump-sum accrual method without securing the Commissioner's consent. It found that a change in the treatment of a "material item" had occurred:

> Taxpayer's contention that its change in accounting treatment of tax accruals is not a change in the treatment of a material item is also without merit. Taxpayer reported taxable income of $64,711.50 for its fiscal year. The item of $6,660.00 would add more than 10% to taxable income, and must certainly be considered material.

204 F. Supp. at 843.

[47] In William H. Leonhart, 27 TCM 443, 466 (1968), aff'd, 414 F2d 749 (4th Cir. 1969), the Tax Court stated:

> There can be no doubt that the commissions from American Fire constituted a material item of gross income. The total commissions from American Fire were $46,735.35 in 1960 and $33,103.94 in 1961. Commissions from American Fire were material both absolutely and with relation to [taxpayer's] gross income in 1960 of $186,442.92 [25 percent] and in 1961 of $210,990.95 [16 percent].

[48] In Cincinnati, New Orleans & Tex. Pac. Ry. v. United States, 424 F2d 563 (Ct. Cl. 1970), the taxpayer deducted expenses in accordance with an ICC "minimum rule," which required that rail carriers "expense" certain purchases costing less than a stated figure. In 1940, the minimum-rule amount was changed from $100 to $500. The Commissioner disallowed deductions for minimum rule items costing more than $100, in part on the ground that the use of the new $500 rule constituted an unauthorized change in a method of accounting. The Court of Claims held that the use of

Put in perspective, the considerations before the courts in cases decided prior to 1970 seemed rather straightforward. On one hand, the amounts involved in some changes could be of such minor significance, whether viewed in absolute or relative terms, that it would be inappropriate to require a taxpayer to incur the delay in time, incur the cost, and incur the inconvenience of seeking IRS approval of the change. In addition, permitting the change without such prior approval could not be perceived as opening a loophole or permitting an abuse that other taxpayers would seek for themselves. On the other hand, where the amount involved would be large enough that other taxpayers could be expected to seek similar changes in order to obtain the resulting tax benefits, materiality was found and prior IRS approval of the change was required.

When focusing on the dollar amounts of the items at issue, the courts often seemed pressured to disallow most changes for which prior IRS approval had not been obtained. It appeared that the courts believed that judicial approval of the taxpayer's unapproved change would have opened a significant loophole. Such a result seemed particularly likely because the reporting practice for each of several items could constitute a separate method of accounting. If "materiality" were not broadly construed, taxpayers might seek to make a substantial number of changes, any one of which would not be material but all of which, in the aggregate, would be quite substantial. Alternatively, taxpayers might switch accounting methods, depending on which would be most advantageous in a particular year. Considerations such as these apparently gave rise to the amendment of the regulations in 1970.[49]

[3] Post-1970 Regulation Cases

Since the regulations were amended in 1970, the IRS has defined "materiality" in strict accordance with the definition added to the regulation; i.e., a material item includes any item that involves the proper time at which to

---

the $500 minimum rule reflected a change in the underlying facts rather than a change in the taxpayer's method of accounting. The court also stated that "the only change needing the Service's assent is a substantial or material one." Id at 573. It found that the change in question "had only a very slight effect on net income." Id. For the three taxable years at issue, the disallowed expenses represented 6/100 of one percent, 4/100 of one percent, and 1/10 of one percent of the taxpayer's yearly operating expenses, respectively; and amounted to 2/10 of one percent, 1/10 of one percent, and 3/10 of one percent of the taxpayer's net income, respectively. If the taxpayer had reported its income in accordance with the method used by the Commissioner and depreciated the items over a 15-year period, its income for the three years would have been increased by $5,400, $3,149, and $15,971 in each respective year. These figures represented 7/100 of one percent, 3/100 of one percent, and 2/10 of one percent, respectively, more than the income reported by the taxpayer in those years.

[49] TD 7073, 1970-2 CB 98.

recognize income or to take a deduction.[50] For example, assume a taxpayer in a manufacturing business reported all items of income and expense on an accrual method except for interest income, which it reported on a cash basis. If the taxpayer wanted to change its method of reporting that interest income from the year received to the year accrued, the change would involve a change in the time when the item would be recognized and, hence, would invo. ? a change in a "material" item regardless of the relative or absolute dollar amount of the interest.

The courts have not wholly embraced the timing standard, however, and it is unclear how they will ultimately respond to (or apply) the definition in the present regulations. Initially, courts attempted to apply both the new regulation and the former quantitative tests. For example, in *Witte v. Commissioner*,[51] the taxpayer sought to shift from the cost recovery method of recognizing income to the completed transaction method.[52] Focusing on both the amount involved and the regulatory definition, the Court of Appeals for the D.C. Circuit held that the shift would constitute a change in accounting method.[53] By focusing on both, the court indicated some uncertainty that the regulation would of itself, be sufficient. Moreover, the court added in a footnote that there were no definite tests with which to determine what constitutes a material item and that several other courts had relied on "comparable dollar amounts to find materiality."[54]

Similar uncertainty was thereafter indicated by the Tax Court in *Gap Anthracite Co.*,[55] where it stated: "According to [the Commissioner's] regu-

---

[50] The IRS National Office (National Office) has consistently expressed this view in published rulings and technical advice memoranda. See, e.g., Rev. Rul. 77-134, 1977-1 CB 132; and Tech. Adv. Mem. 7924011 (Mar. 7, 1979), 7924008 (Feb. 27, 1979).

[51] Witte v. Comm'r, 513 F2d 391 (DC Cir. 1975).

[52] Under the cost recovery method, payments received by a taxpayer are applied first to a recovery of basis, with only payments in excess of basis reported as gain.

[53] The court stated:

This case involves a "change in the treatment of [a] material item." The Tax Court opinion reveals that gain from payments for the 1962–1964 period totaled more than $88,000.00. Taxpayer's proposed shift to completed transaction treatment "involves the proper time for the inclusion of the item in income" and thereby satisfies the definition of "material item" set forth in the regulation.

Witte v. Comm'r, 513 F2d 391, 393 (DC Cir. 1975).

[54] Id. at 393 n.4.

[55] Gap Anthracite Co., 31 TCM 924 (1972), aff'd without published opinion sub nom. Susquehanna Coal Co. v. Comm'r, 487 F2d 1395 (3d Cir. 1973), cert. denied, 417 US 931 (1974). This case involved a 1961 agreement between Gap and the Susquehanna Coal Company (another taxpayer whose case was consolidated with Gap's) under which Gap operated one of Susquehanna's processing plants, with Susquehanna to reimburse Gap for all its operating costs, including worker's compensation. Both companies reported Gap's worker's compensation claims on the

lations, a material item is *any* item which involves the proper time for the inclusion of the item in income or the taking of a deduction. . . . We need not now decide whether [the Commissioner's] regulations encompassing 'any item should be applied under all circumstances." [56]

In 1980, in *Southern Pacific Transportation Co.*,[57] the Tax Court reiterated that a quantitative analysis may still be appropriate: "In addition to the factors enumerated in the regulations, various courts, including this Court, have considered an inquiry into comparable dollar amounts as pertinent to a determination of the materiality of an expenditure." [58]

The Court of Claims has also seemed unwilling to accept exclusively the broad definition of "materiality" contained in the present regulations. For example, in *Baltimore & Ohio R.R. v. United States* [59] the court determined that the amount at issue was not material, since it constituted less than 2/10 of one percent of the taxpayer's net income. The court gave no indication that such a quantitative analysis was irrelevant in light of the present regulation. In *Korn Industries, Inc. v. United States*,[60] the taxpayer reincluded in its beginning inventories three "cost elements" that for a period of four

---

cash basis; otherwise, both were on the accrual basis. For the taxable year at issue, Gap billed Susquehanna and accrued the entire amount of unpaid workers' compensation claims.

[56] Gap Anthracite Co., 31 TCM at 934–935. The court applied a form of pre-1970 analysis, stating:

The amount involved, i.e., $62,076.48 [total amount accrued], is certainly substantial in absolute terms. Moreover, it is substantial insofar as Susquehanna is concerned in that it represents over 20 percent of its claimed net operating loss for the taxable year in question, or, to put it another way, increases that loss by over 25 percent. With respect to Gap, it represents more than 8 percent of its claimed deductions for such taxable year. Under these circumstances, we hold that the item was "material."

Id.

[57] Southern Pac. Transp. Co., 75 TC 497 (1980), supplemented by 82 TC 122 (1984).

[58] 75 TC 684. See also Wayne Bolt & Nut Co., 93 TC 500 (1989), where the court concluded that a change from an erroneous perpetual inventory system to a physical inventory system amounted to a change in method of accounting because there would be a change in the time when items of income and expense were reported. However, the court distinguished Korn Indus., Inc. v. United States, 532 F2d 1352 (Ct. Cl. 1976), on the basis that it involved omitted items of inventory, which constituted only a small percentage of the overall inventory, but that the taxpayer in *Wayne Bolt & Nut Co.* grossly understated its inventory with the valuation under the new procedure being ten times greater than the valuation under the old procedure. However, in some cases, the Tax Court has seemingly followed the literal language of the regulations. See, e.g., Connors, Inc., 71 TC 913 (1979), regarding a change in reporting bonuses from an accrual method to the cash method.

[59] Baltimore & Ohio R.R. v. United States, 603 F2d 165 (Ct. Cl. 1979).

[60] Korn Indus., Inc. v. United States, 532 F2d 1352 (Ct. Cl. 1976).

years had inadvertently been excluded from inventories and therefore expensed. The issue was whether this reinclusion amounted to a change in method of accounting. The taxpayer argued that the cost elements in question were only individual items of cost. It asserted that the regulations promulgated under Section 481 indicated that "material items," which could be the subject of changes in accounting methods, were limited to "entire classes of cost."[61] The Court of Claims, without coming to any definite conclusion on this point, acknowledged that the regulations cited by the taxpayer did "provide some guidance in delineating a material item."[62] The court then concluded that the taxpayer's inclusion of the previously excluded cost elements seemed more like a correction of a mathematical or posting error than a change in method of accounting.

In Revenue Ruling 77-134,[63] the IRS stated that it would not follow *Korn Industries*. It reasoned that the taxpayer had established a consistent pattern of reporting the cost elements that were excluded from inventories. It argued that, since a change in such treatment involved a change in the proper time for recognizing an item of income or expense, the reinclusion amounted to a change in a method of accounting. Consequently, while the Court of Claims may have injected some doubt as to whether the consistent treatment of particular items within a category of income or expense should be deemed a "method of accounting" in all cases, the IRS takes the position that it should be.

The foregoing cases point up the difficulties facing taxpayers and the IRS. On one hand, the IRS clearly relies on the present Treasury regulations for the proposition that any change affecting the time of reporting items of income or expense is a change in method of accounting that may be

---

[61] Treas. Reg. § 1.481-4(g)(3) referred to changes in "material items such as research and experimental expenditures (section 174), soil and water conservation expenditures (section 175), last-in, first-out inventories (section 472), and exploration expenditures (section 615)." The taxpayer argued that this language was intended to show that the term "item" referred to entire classes of expenditures. Other cases have implied that a change in accounting method does not necessarily include a change in the treatment of a particular item within a class. See, e.g., Monfort of Colorado, Inc. v. United States, 561 F2d 190 (10th Cir. 1977), which involved a taxpayer that participated as a hedger in the grain futures market for purposes of inventory cost protection. In 1965, the taxpayer reported gain on transactions in the futures market as a separate income item. In 1967, it began recording such gains and also losses as adjustments to its closing inventory. The IRS concluded that this amounted to a change in method of accounting without prior approval. The trial court found that the change was so small that it need not be treated as a change in method of accounting. The court of appeals affirmed, quoting with approval the following statement by the trial court: "[I]t seems clear that the kind of change in accounting method requiring the Commissioner's prior consent is a change in the basic method of reporting and not in the treatment of specific items." Id. at 197.

[62] Korn Indus., Inc. v. United States, 532 F2d 1352, 1355 (Ct. Cl. 1976).

[63] Rev. Rul. 77-134, 1977-1 CB 132.

accomplished only with the prior approval of the IRS. On the other hand, it is clear that neither the courts nor, as a practical matter, the IRS wants a flood of requests for a change in method of accounting where the amounts involved are so insubstantial that there is virtually no economic significance to the change.

Nevertheless, any guidelines establishing de minimis limits for methods of accounting will themselves give rise to complexity and the possibility of abuse. Therefore, this may be an area of continuing uncertainty and confusion. In most cases, it may be expected that such matters will be resolved on a practical basis on audit or otherwise through the administrative channels of the IRS.[64]

¶ 9.04 CONSISTENT TREATMENT

The regulations indicate that while it is possible for a method of accounting to exist in the absence of a pattern of consistent treatment, in most instances, a method of accounting is not established without such consistent treatment.[65] Questions necessarily arise as to the circumstances in which consistency is required in order to establish a method of accounting and the circumstances in which it is not. Typically, these questions relate to (1) attempts to change methods of accounting that are adopted in the initial return filed by the taxpayer (or the first return in which the particular item of income or expense is reported) and (2) attempts to change to or to adopt a proper method of accounting following a period of use of inconsistent or arbitrary accounting practices.

For many years, this issue of consistent treatment has been fraught with uncertainty. Little guidance was provided by cases or published positions of the IRS. Thus, in evaluating the circumstances of each particular case, consideration had to be given to all the facts, including the consequences of finding that a method of accounting had been established.[66]

However, in more recent years, the IRS has attempted to bring greater certainty to at least some of the relevant issues; at least greater certainty

---

[64] The problem of a quantitative approach was identified by the Tax Court in Southern Pac. Transp. Co., 75 TC 497, 684 (1980), supplemented by 82 TC 122 (1984), where it stated:

If we were to adopt petitioner's view that the amounts involved herein are not a "material item," then we would be granting the petitioner a license to change back and forth from capitalizing to expensing when to do so would work to its tax advantage. As we point out below, such a practice would not properly reflect income and would impose unacceptable uncertainties in the area of tax administration.

[65] Treas. Reg. § 1.446-1(e)(2)(ii)(A).

[66] See discussion supra ¶ 9.01[1].

regarding its position.[67] Whether its position will be sustained by the courts remains to be seen.

[1] Adoption of Method in Initial Year

The regulations point out that a pattern of consistent use is not always required to establish a method of accounting.[68] Some commentators have concluded that this regulatory exception to the generally required pattern of consistent use is intended to permit a method of accounting to be established on adoption so that the taxpayer will immediately become subject to the rules regarding changes in methods of accounting.[69] This seems to be a reasonable conclusion. Otherwise, a taxpayer who had filed returns for only one or two years might be able to change its methods of accounting without the prior approval of the Commissioner on the basis that the adoption and use of the particular accounting practice for such a limited period did not satisfy the consistent treatment test and, hence, did not cause that accounting practice to ripen into a method of accounting.

As discussed in the following section, the IRS and the courts appear to have accepted this analysis where the method used in the initial return is an acceptable method. However, they have relaxed application of this analysis where the method used in the initial return is improper.

[a] Change of Correct Method

Where the method of accounting adopted and used in the initial return is an acceptable method that is available to the taxpayer, the use of that method constitutes adoption of a method of accounting. The taxpayer is thereupon subject to the rules regarding changes in accounting methods. Consequently, the taxpayer is not permitted to change the method of

---

[67] See Rev. Rul. 90-38, 1990-1 CB 57; Rev. Proc. 92-20, 1992-1 CB 685; and discussion infra ¶ 9.04[1][b].

[68] Treas. Reg. § 1.446-1(e)(2)(ii)(A) provides, "Although a method of accounting may exist . . . without the necessity of a pattern of consistent treatment of an item, in most instances a method of accounting is not established for an item without such consistent treatment."

[69] See, e.g., Diamond & Holman, supra note 27, at A-3, where it states:

In the opinion of the author, random treatment of an item does not constitute an accounting method. Accordingly, the only logical explanation for the above quoted excerpt from the regulations [pertaining to the existence of a method of accounting without a pattern of consistent treatment] is that the Commissioner will generally treat the first permissible treatment of an item as the adoption of a method of accounting with regard to that item, even if such treatment is used only in the taxpayer's first year and is changed thereafter.

accounting used in its initial return without the prior approval of the Commissioner.[70]

This rule apparently applies whether the change is attempted in a subsequent year or by the filing of an amended return for the initial year. The rule seems sound. If there were no such rule, taxpayers would be free to review and make changes in their chosen methods of accounting prior to the running of the applicable statutory periods of limitation. This could result in considerable administrative difficulty and taxpayer abuse. For example, a taxpayer initially on an accrual method could review its level of receivables a year or two later and, if significant, retroactively adopt a cash method.

On the other hand, the Commissioner is not prohibited from accepting a retroactive change from one permissible method to another permissible method. For example, in *Ronnie L. Barber*,[71] the court noted that although neither Section 446(e) nor any other provision of the Code expressly provides the Commissioner with authority to allow a retroactive change in method, no provision of the Code prohibits the Commissioner from permitting such a change. The court then stated that several theories have been advanced for the principle that elections of proper methods are considered binding. These explanations include protection of the Treasury against loss of revenue, prevention of administrative burdens and inconvenience in the administration of the tax laws, and promotion of consistent accounting practice thereby securing uniformity in the collection of taxes.[72] The court then concluded that these purposes can certainly be satisfied in cases where the Commissioner agrees to accept a retroactive change in method.

[b] Change of Incorrect Method

The IRS and the courts have long accepted the proposition that where a taxpayer has chosen an incorrect method in its initial return but thereafter seeks to correct that choice by filing an amended return using a correct method, such a change may be made without prior IRS approval. The question has been whether this right (1) exists so long as the original year and any subsequent years remain open or (2) exists for a shorter period.

---

[70] See, e.g., Ann S. Russo, 68 TC 135 (1977), where the use of a cash method in the initial return precluded subsequent change to accrual method without the prior approval of the Commissioner.

[71] Ronnie L. Barber, 64 TC 314 (1975).

[72] See, e.g., Elmwood Corp. v. United States, 107 F2d 111 (5th Cir. 1939), cert. denied, 309 US 675 (1940), where the Court stated that "[t]o allow change at will from one method of accounting and computation to another would require recomputation and readjustment of tax liability, and would result in confusion, delay, and inconvenience and 'impose burdensome uncertainties upon the administration of the revenue laws.'"

Originally, the IRS and some cases seemed to adopt a rule that the use of an incorrect method on the initial and subsequent returns should not constitute a binding election prior to the running of the statutory period for filing all applicable amended returns.[73] However, if the period for filing any of the amended returns had expired, the taxpayer was deemed to have adopted a method of accounting and to have become subject to the requirements governing changes in methods of accounting.[74]

More recently, however, the IRS and some other cases have limited the period during which the change from an improper method may be made by amended return. In *Diebold, Inc. v. United States*,[75] the court, in a somewhat confusing and inconsistent discussion, concluded that the opportunity for changing a method of accounting by filing an amended return for the original year in which the method is first used should be limited so that the amended return must be filed before an original return is filed for the next succeeding tax year. Thereafter, in early 1990, the IRS issued Revenue Ruling 90-38, in which it reviewed its past practices regarding the filing of amended returns to deduct as current operating expenses various expenditures that had improperly been capitalized under Section 266.[76] In effect, the IRS decided to limit the opportunity of correcting the initial reporting by filing amended returns to situations where the amended return for the initial year of such reporting is filed prior to the filing of an original return for the second year. The IRS revoked earlier inconsistent revenue rulings.

In Revenue Procedure 92-20,[77] the IRS confirmed that a taxpayer may correct its adoption and use of an impermissible method of accounting in its

---

[73] See Rev. Rul. 70-539, 1970-2 CB 70 (later revoked by Rev. Rul. 90-38, 1990-1 CB 57), where the taxpayer was permitted to amend its initial and subsequent returns to deduct previously capitalized expenses; Kentucky Utils. Co. v. Glenn, 394 F2d 631 (6th Cir. 1968), where, reversing the trial court, the court of appeals held that the taxpayer could not retroactively change from a correct method to a different, but also correct method; but the court left open the possibility of a change where the originally chosen method was incorrect or resulted from ignorance or mistake on the part of the taxpayer. See also Silver Queen Motel, 55 TC 1101 (1971).

[74] See Rev. Rul. 75-56, 1975-1 CB 98, where the IRS ruled that "by permitting the period for amending its first return to expire, [the taxpayer had] adopted a method of accounting. . . ." Rev. Rul. 70-539 was distinguished. But see Rev. Rul. 90-38, 1990-1 CB 57, where Rev. Rul. 70-539 was revoked, and Rev. Rul. 75-56 was modified to eliminate any inference that the statute of limitations must expire before a taxpayer will be deemed to have adopted a method of accounting under Section 266. As a consequence, Rev. Rul. 75-56 was then revoked as obsolete. See also opinion of trial judge in Ed Smithback Plumbing, Inc., 76-1 USTC ¶ 9139 (Ct. Cl. 1976), adopted by court 76-1 USTC ¶ 9373 (Ct. Ct. 1976), where filing of amended return to correct erroneous, initially chosen method was found ineffective for that purpose.

[75] Diebold, Inc. v. United States, 89-1 USTC ¶ 9141 (Cl. Ct. 1989).

[76] Rev. Rul. 90-38, 1990-1 CB 57.

[77] Rev. Proc. 92-20, 1992-1 CB 685.

initial return by filing an amended return, but only if the amended return is filed before the incorrect method has been used in a return for the immediately succeeding year.[78]

An interesting issue arises from the present IRS position. Assume that a taxpayer learns during the preparation of its return for the second year that the method of reporting used in the initial year was incorrect. Must the taxpayer actually file an amended return for the initial year prior to the filing of the original return for the second year or, alternatively, may the taxpayer file a correct return for the second year and disclose on that return that an amended return will be filed for the initial year as soon as the necessary information has been obtained? By filing the return for the second year using the correct method and not the incorrect method, the taxpayer may not be precluded from the later filing of an amended return for the initial year. This conclusion would be based on the fact that the return for the second year did not use the same incorrect method that was used in the initial year. Language in Revenue Procedure 92-20 suggests that this latter approach may be acceptable.[79] Nevertheless, absent further clarification of this by the IRS, prudent action may be to file an amended return for the initial year before filing the original return for the second year. The amended return should describe the change from the erroneous treatment to a correct method and disclose the fact that additional information must be accumulated before all corrections to the initial year's return may be made. By following this approach (if time permits), the taxpayer is able to show an examining agent

---

[78] Id. at § 2.01, where the Service stated:

The treatment of a material item in the same way in determining the gross income or deductions in two or more consecutively filed tax returns (without regard to any change in status of the method as permissible or impermissible) represents consistent treatment of that item for purposes of section 1.446-1(e)(2)(ii)(a) of the regulations. If a taxpayer treats an item properly in the first return that reflects the item, however, it is not necessary for the taxpayer to treat the item consistently in two or more consecutive tax returns to have adopted a method of accounting. See Rev. Rul. 90-38, 1990-1 C.B. 57. If a taxpayer has not adopted a method of accounting under these rules, the taxpayer may correct the impermissible treatment of an item by amending its prior income tax return.

Note that the above language does not state that the impermissible treatment of an item is not equivalent to the adoption of a method for that item. Yet earlier in the paragraph, the clear implication is that the filing of a second return is what results in "consistent treatment." This procedure later states that a retroactive change in method, whether from a permissible or impermissible method, is not permitted unless specifically authorized by the Commissioner. Depending on the circumstances, there may be considerable confusion as to whether a particular change is specifically authorized.

[79] See supra note 77, quoting from Rev. Proc. 92-20, 1992-1 CB 685, § 2.01, which implies that the filing of an amended return to correct the adoption of an erroneous method in the initially applicable return is foreclosed only after the erroneous treatment has been followed in two or more consecutively filed returns.

that an amended return for the initial year was filed before the original return for the second year. Depending on the sophistication of the agent, such a change may, as a practical matter, be quite helpful.

Because the regulations provide that the rules regarding methods of accounting apply to all methods of accounting, whether correct or incorrect,[80] any distinctions drawn between correct and incorrect methods are always questionable. Nevertheless, the objective of getting taxpayers on correct methods of accounting is laudatory. Consequently, a reasonable basis for the distinction, and a basis that is consonant with the regulations, would be that the Commissioner has merely exercised his discretion to allow changes from incorrect to correct methods of accounting by the filing of an amended return for an initial year, but has not so exercised that discretion when the initial method is correct.[81] However, there is a dearth of rulings and case authority on this point, and, except by means of an implicit exercise of discretion as previously suggested, it is uncertain how the issue might be resolved in various contexts.

[2] Consistent Use of Arbitrary Procedures

[a] Problem Confronting Taxpayers

Taxpayers sometimes follow certain accounting practices or procedures for a number of years. In many cases, the practice or procedure involves the application of judgment or discretion on the part of the taxpayer. Such judgmental determinations often evolve for reasons of convenience or to avoid other approaches that are either too costly or too impractical to implement. In other cases, the exercise of such judgment takes into account the tax consequences.

These judgmental approaches often arise in the valuation of inventories by taxpayers operating small businesses. Taxpayers either do not have, or do not believe they can afford to establish, inventory accounting systems that meet all applicable requirements, particularly with respect to determining the market value of goods that have declined in value.[82] The result is that the inventories are not valued on a wholly predictable basis. Instead, there are

---

[80] Treas. Reg. § 1.446-1(e)(2)(i).

[81] See Ronnie L. Barber, 64 TC 314 (1975), where the court held that the Commissioner had the discretion to accept a retroactive change from a permissible method or a nonpermissible method and that the exercise of such discretion was not inconsistent with the benefits to be derived from the binding election rule. The court also noted that where a taxpayer files an amended return on or before the due date of the initial return in which a method is first adopted, the taxpayer may effect a change in method on that amended return. See also Rev. Rul. 90-38, 1990-1 CB 57; Rev. Proc. 92-20, 1990-1 CB 685.

[82] See discussion at ¶ 6.09 regarding write-downs of inventory to market value.

judgmental, discretionary, and perhaps arbitrary aspects to the valuation process. These aspects raise the question of whether the taxpayer is using a method of accounting.[83]

A taxpayer who has followed this practice but wishes to adopt or change to a correct method of accounting is faced with at least six questions.[84]

1. Will prior approval of the IRS be required?
2. Is the taxpayer obligated to seek such approval?
3. Will a Section 481 adjustment be required?
4. May the taxpayer begin to use a new method on his own, or, more importantly, is he required to do so?
5. Will any adjustment arising from the change to an acceptable method be subject to the running of the applicable statutory period of limitations (or is the change otherwise subject to application of the mitigation provisions)?
6. Will the taxpayer be subject to the imposition of penalties?

These are difficult questions not only for the taxpayer but also for the IRS. On one hand, if the IRS concludes that the assertedly arbitrary practice does not amount to a method of accounting or to the consistent application of a method of accounting, it may be in a better position to impose penalties on the taxpayer for failing to satisfy various regulatory and statutory requirements. On the other hand, if an asserted penalty is not sustained, the applicable statutory periods of limitation may have run and, as a consequence, tax deficiencies may be lost. Moreover, fostering such an attitude is likely to make taxpayers reluctant to seek (or even fearful of seeking) changes to correct methods of accounting.

To illustrate the problem, assume a taxpayer uses the following accounting practices regarding its inventory. First, a visual inspection (but not necessarily a full, detailed count) is made of the inventory each year. Then, based in large part on judgment, experience, and discretion, as well as whatever inventory records are available, the taxpayer assigns a value to the inventory. Assume this practice has resulted in the value of the beginning inventory of a particular year being $100 less than it should have been under the applicable regulations. If the IRS takes the position that the taxpayer's method of valuing inventory amounts to an arbitrary practice (and not to an accounting method), then the IRS may be in a better position to seek imposition of a penalty. However, if the penalty is not sustained (and if the statutory periods of limitation have run on applicable prior years), the IRS risks losing the chance to include the $100 in income under Section 481.

---

[83] See discussion at ¶ 2.01 regarding the definition of "method of accounting."

[84] See discussions at ¶ 8.08, regarding the taxpayer's obligation to change from an improper method of accounting, and ¶ 8.09, regarding the imposition of penalties.

Moreover, and perhaps more importantly, such a position by the IRS would discourage other taxpayers from requesting changes from incorrect practices.

These situations raise difficult questions that the courts have not yet resolved. Moreover, such situations are not limited to taxpayers operating small businesses. Large businesses face similar issues, particularly in their treatment of supplies, parts, tools, and the like. Taxpayers facing such questions must carefully evaluate the available alternatives.

[b] Alternatives Available to Taxpayers

Taxpayers desiring to change from an arbitrary procedure to a correct method of accounting are generally faced with a number of alternatives.

[i] Treat existing practice as method of accounting and request change. The taxpayer might decide (1) to treat its existing practice as a method of accounting (describing the practice as best it can to achieve this result) and (2) to request permission from the IRS to change to a new method of accounting. Although questions may be raised as to whether the taxpayer's practice actually amounts to a method of accounting, the IRS will almost always approve such applications.

The IRS benefits from this approach by applying the provisions of Section 481,[85] and by having the taxpayer change to a correct method of accounting, thereby encouraging others to change to correct methods. The taxpayer benefits by adopting a proper method of accounting, by obtaining a spread of the Section 481 adjustment resulting from the change (assuming the spread is not denied by reason of the nature of the practice being changed),[86] and by eliminating the uncertainties and risks of audit. The taxpayer also minimizes the risk of a penalty being asserted by the IRS on account of the past practice.[87]

[ii] Elect method not requiring prior approval. A taxpayer may elect a method of accounting whose adoption does not require prior approval of the IRS. For example, a taxpayer that has used an arbitrary method of valuing its inventory may elect the last-in, first-out (LIFO) method or a simplified LIFO method without the prior approval of the IRS.[88] In connection with the requirement that LIFO inventories be valued at cost,[89] the taxpayer may treat the adjustment from the value determined under the old practice as part of the cost restoration requirement, thereby obtaining a spread of that adjustment over three years but without subjecting itself to the

---

[85] See discussion at ¶ 8.04.

[86] See discussion at ¶¶ 8.04[3], 8.04[4].

[87] See discussion at ¶ 8.09.

[88] See IRC § 472 and discussions at ¶¶ 7.03[1], 7.04[5].

[89] See discussion at ¶ 7.03[3].

requirement of prior approval by the IRS.[90] Such an approach may be especially attractive to a taxpayer that believes that a spread of the Section 481 adjustment would otherwise not be available because of the nature of its past practice or that for reasons unrelated to the change, does not wish its tax posture to be brought to the attention of the IRS through an application for change in method. In addition, the change to the new procedure is automatic when specified conditions are satisfied. Therefore, the consequences of this approach are often more certain in ultimate result than an application for change to a new method, which is subject to the review and approval of the IRS.[91]

[iii] Make "do-it-yourself" correction.   In some cases, the Section 481 adjustment arising from a change would be so large (or the potential spread period would be so short) that the taxpayer may desire to correct or adjust its past practice on its own. For example, if the taxpayer's practice has resulted in a substantial undervaluation of inventory as compared to a correct method, the taxpayer may apply its present inventory practice in such a way as to increase the value of its ending inventory to a correct value. If the increase is put into effect over a period of years, the result is comparable to a do-it-yourself correction to a proper basis of valuing inventory.[92] Alternatively, the taxpayer may simply begin reporting on a correct method of accounting, secure in the expectation that it would be highly unlikely for its change to be challenged on audit.[93] Although these alternatives may constitute a less expensive means of changing to a proper method, they may expose the taxpayer to the risk of a penalty being considered by the IRS on audit.[94]

[iv] Continue past practice.   Lastly, the taxpayer may simply continue its past practice on the basis that such practice amounts to a method of accounting from which the taxpayer may not change without prior approval and with respect to which it is not obligated to seek such a change.[95] Unlike the prior approach, the taxpayer would not apply its practice to reach the equivalent of an acceptable method. Rather, the taxpayer would continue its practice on a basis that perpetuates the undervaluation of inventory or the underreporting of income as compared to a correct method. If the taxpayer's practice is later reviewed on audit by the IRS, the taxpayer will request the

---

[90] See IRC § 472(d) and discussion at ¶ 7.03[3].

[91] See discussion infra ¶ 9.08 for additional techniques for effectively changing methods of accounting without the need for prior IRS approval.

[92] See also discussions at ¶ 8.07[2][b] and infra ¶ 9.05.

[93] On the other hand, where the correct reporting results in an immediate tax benefit to the taxpayer, the IRS is much more likely to challenge the unauthorized change.

[94] See discussion at ¶ 8.09.

[95] See discussion at ¶ 8.08.

IRS to treat the existing practice as a method of accounting, make the applicable Section 481 adjustment, allow the adjustment to be spread over some period of years, and not impose a penalty. This alternative is often the most financially attractive one. However, because it involves the knowing, deliberate perpetuation of an erroneous practice, it also bears the greatest risk of a penalty being imposed.[96]

[c] Recommendation

Choosing from the foregoing alternatives is most difficult for both the taxpayer and its advisors. From the standpoint of ensuring compliance with applicable requirements of the Code and regulations, filing an application for change in accounting method is often preferable. It places the imprimatur of the IRS on the change to, and use of, the new method and also generally reduces the risk of penalties being imposed on the taxpayer. Consequently, if the minimization of the risk of penalties is the primary objective, this alternative may be the most appropriate one to pursue.

On the other hand, filing an application for change is often the most expensive alternative for the taxpayer. The elimination of Section 481 spread periods for some changes and the limited spread periods available for other changes often dissuade taxpayers from employing this alternative.[97] Consequently, where there is sufficient justification for the accounting practice at issue that the risk of penalties seems slight or is not of principal concern, one of the other alternatives may be more appropriate.

If the risk of penalty is significant, but the taxpayer desires not to call attention to itself or its past accounting practices, adoption of a method that does not require prior IRS approval is often most beneficial. An example would be the adoption of LIFO for taxpayers whose inventory practices are questionable.

Selecting the best alternative for any particular taxpayer depends on a consideration of several factors in addition to cost. These additional factors include the degree of impropriety of the present method, the current attitudes of the National Office and the local District Office on such matters, and the level of risk with which the taxpayer is comfortable. Of course, the state of the law on the issue at the particular time may prove determinative.[98]

---

[96] See discussion at ¶ 8.09. See Lynn Haynes, TC Memo. 1990-135, where the court refused to impose a penalty because (1) the taxpayer's improper method of accounting had been continued for many years; (2) the method was clearly identified on the taxpayer's books; (3) the taxpayer had been audited several times; and (4) the taxpayer, on at least one occasion, had inquired of the agent whether the use of the method was proper.

[97] See discussion at ¶¶ 8.04[3], 8.04[4].

[98] See also infra ¶ 9.08 for a discussion of techniques for changing methods without the need for prior IRS approval.

¶ 9.05　CORRECTION OF ERRORS

The "correction of an error" does not amount to a change in method of accounting.[99] Examples include mathematical or posting errors and errors in the computation of tax liability, such as errors in computation of the foreign tax credit, net operating loss, percentage depletion, or investment credit.[100] Similarly, application of the deferral and restoration adjustments of the consolidated return regulations, which apply to deferred intercompany transactions, do not constitute a method of accounting.[101] Consequently, an erroneous practice regarding the application of these rules may be corrected without the prior approval of the IRS.

In some cases, where the error is mathematical or is one of posting or computation, its correction generally affects only the amount of income or expense to be taken into account in the particular year, and no issue arises as to whether there has been shifting of income or expenses from one year to another. In effect, the taxpayer is merely seeking to apply correctly its already established accounting method.[102]

In other cases, where the correction affects the reporting of income or expense in more than one year (i.e., where income may be shifted from one year to another), determination of whether the particular correction amounts to a change in method of accounting becomes more difficult. To further complicate the matter, some courts have suggested that the concept of "correction of an error" is broad enough to include not only adjustments to apply correctly an existing method,[103] but also (as discussed in the following sections) adjustments permitting taxpayers to change from an incorrect

---

[99] Treas. Reg. § 1.446-1(e)(2)(ii)(B).

[100] Id. See also First Nat'l City Bank v. United States, 557 F2d 1379 (Ct. Cl. 1977), where correction to require use of proper exchange rate in determining foreign tax credit was not a change in accounting method. But see Tech. Adv. Mem. 8741006 (May 21, 1987), where the IRS ruled that an increase in the taxpayer's loan base for the purpose of computing its bad debt reserve (by including previously excluded accrued interest) constituted a change in method of accounting.

[101] See, e.g., Henry C. Beck Builders, Inc. 41 TC 616 (1964); United Contractors, Inc., 23 TCM 453 (1964), aff'd, 344 F2d 123 (4th Cir. 1965); Vernon C. Neal, Inc., 23 TCM 1338 (1964); Henry C. Beck Co., 52 TC 1 (1969), aff'd, 433 F2d 309 (5th Cir. 1970); Priv. Ltr. Ruls. 9002006 (Sept. 30, 1989), 8204094 (Oct. 28, 1981), 7820024 (Feb. 15, 1978); all pertaining to the application of Treas. Reg. § 1.1502-13 or its predecessors.

[102] See, e.g., Richard M. Evans, 55 TCM 902 (1988), where the court found the prior reporting of bonuses by cash basis taxpayers in the year authorized rather than in the year received did not establish an accrual method of accounting for this item but was only a misapplication of the cash method.

[103] See Richard M. Evans, 55 TCM 902 (1988), where the reporting of bonuses on an accrual method for three years (i.e., in the year authorized) by cash method taxpayers did not prohibit these taxpayers from subsequently reporting the bonuses in the years received.

method to a correct method, a result seemingly at odds with the regulations.[104] These courts appear disinclined to place impediments in the way of a taxpayer desiring to change from an incorrect to a correct method. Although this objective is laudatory, such an approach is analytically inappropriate and increases the practical opportunity for abuse. Thus, it would appear more appropriate for a change from an incorrect method to a correct method to be subject to the rules governing changes in methods, except as might otherwise expressly be provided by the Code, Treasury regulation, or IRS pronouncement.

There are comparatively few authorities to guide taxpayers. Nevertheless, a pattern has emerged in the decided cases suggesting that some forums are more likely than others to find a correction of an error rather than a change in method of accounting. Consequently, a prudent tax advisor must carefully consider the forums available to a client before making a recommendation as to how that client should proceed.

Nevertheless, it must be noted that most jurisdictions will not permit taxpayers unilaterally to change from an incorrect method of accounting to a correct method on the basis of the correction of an error exception. Moreover, it is uncertain whether these changes will be permitted even in jurisdictions that have allowed them in the past. The cases in which these changes were permitted involved unique factual circumstances. Consequently, the scope of such decisions remains uncertain.

[1] United States Court of Federal Claims

The claims court has indicated that an adjustment may be regarded as the correction of an error rather than as a change in method of accounting if it is made to (1) conform the taxpayer's present accounting practice to its established accounting method; (2) properly apply its chosen method; or (3) correct departures from its chosen method. In these circumstances, the court appeared to be most impressed by the fact that the taxpayer already had an established method of accounting from which it had departed for one reason or another. For example, in *Korn Industries, Inc.*,[105] the taxpayer had consistently included 14 elements of cost in valuing its finished goods inventories. Later, it inadvertently excluded three elements of cost in valuing this inventory, and the exclusions continued for a period of four years. The question was whether the reinclusion of these items in the fifth year constituted a change in the taxpayer's method of accounting. The court stated:

At no time did [the taxpayer] change its standard cost method of valuing

---

[104] Treas. Reg. § 1.446-1(e)(2)(i) subjects both correct and incorrect methods of accounting to the rules governing changes in accounting methods.

[105] Korn Indus., Inc. v. United States, 532 F2d 1352 (Ct. Cl. 1976).

inventories. [The taxpayer] did not change its basis of valuation from cost to the lower of cost or market price. It did not neglect to include overhead in valuing its inventories. It did not deduct a percentage of the cost of inventory items in valuing inventory items.... [The taxpayer's] action falls more readily into the category described in Treas. Reg. § 1.446-1(e)(ii)(b), that is "correction of mathematical or posting errors...." It was most assuredly an error analogous to a mathematical or posting error. There has not been a change in method of accounting... but only a correction... of an inventory error.[106]

The court was obviously impressed with the taxpayer's history of reporting, the element of inadvertence, and the taxpayer's overall intent and practice.[107] The court may also have recognized that a contrary decision in *Korn Industries* would have made it difficult and impractical for similarly situated taxpayers to correct unintended departures from proper accounting practices. Potentially more significant is the fact that if the IRS view had prevailed, it necessarily would have meant that unintended changes that go undetected for relatively brief periods ripen into methods of accounting. This

---

[106] Id. at 1355–1356. Compare Dearborn Gage Co, 48 TC 190 (1967), where the initial inclusion of overhead items that were previously excluded was found to be a change in method of accounting. "We think it clear that the exclusion of overhead costs in valuing inventory is an erroneous method of accounting involving a material item." Id. at 197–198.

[107] See also Gimbel Bros. v. United States, 535 F2d 14 (Ct. Cl. 1976), where the Court of Claims held that the taxpayer's change from the accrual method regularly used to the installment method, which had previously been elected, amounted to the correction of an error. Compare Hooker Indus., Inc., 44 TCM 258 (1982), where the court rejected the taxpayer's argument that a change from expensing supplies in the year used to expensing them in the year purchased was a "correction of an error in [its] usual method of accounting." The court stated that the taxpayer "did not believe that it was expensing supplies and suddenly discover in 1974 that its bookkeeper had been 'mistakenly' inventorying them." The court concluded that the change constituted a change in method of accounting requiring the prior approval of the IRS. Id. at 267, 268, and Superior Coach of Fla., Inc., 80 TC 895 (1983), where the Commissioner's revaluation of the taxpayer's inventory because the original figure was inadequately substantiated was found to constitute a change in method of accounting. See also Diebold, Inc. v. United States, 89-1 USTC ¶ 9141 (Cl. Ct. 1989), where the court found a change in the treatment of items—from their characterization as inventory to a characterization as depreciable property—to constitute a change in method of accounting and not the correction of an error; and Wayne Bolt & Nut Co., 93 TC 500 (1989), where the taxpayer's change from a grossly incorrect perpetual inventory system to a physical inventory system was found to constitute a change in method of accounting and not the correction of an error. The court in *Diebold* apparently concluded that its holding was consistent with *Korn Industries*. See 89-1 USTC ¶ 9141 at 87,153, n.9. The court in *Wayne Bolt & Nut Co.* distinguished *Korn Industries, Inc.* on the basis that in *Korn Industries, Inc.*, the items omitted were a small percentage of the total and the omission was a mistake, whereas in *Wayne Bolt & Nut Co.* the erroneous method resulted in a gross understatement of inventory and the inaccuracies in that method stemmed from systemic problems of which the taxpayer was well aware.

could have led to abuse by causing unscrupulous taxpayers to change undesired methods of accounting without prior approval of the IRS and then to defend continued use of the new method on the basis that it is a method of accounting from which there is no obligation to change. Nevertheless, the IRS has announced that in issues before other forums, it will not follow the decision in *Korn Industries*.[108]

Should an incorrect procedure be used for a substantial period or otherwise be used under circumstances that suggest that the taxpayer's change has been accepted by the IRS as a change in method of accounting.[109] a different situation would exist. The departure itself may well have ripened into a method of accounting.[110]

[2] Tax Court

The Tax Court also has suggested that where adjustments are required to apply properly the taxpayer's chosen method of accounting, such adjustments do not cause a change in method and, hence, may be made without the prior approval of the IRS. In *North Carolina Granite*,[111] an accrual method taxpayer adjusted its computation of cost of goods sold to take into account certain changes in inventory but, in computing taxable income for purposes of percentage depletion, the taxpayer did not make these adjustments. The taxpayer contended that it was entitled to recompute its maximum depletion deduction by making appropriate adjustments for the inventory changes. The Commissioner contended that such a change would constitute a change in the taxpayer's method of accounting for which prior IRS approval would be necessary.

The Tax Court held (1) that the taxpayer's method of arriving at the depletion limitation was erroneous; (2) that the error appeared on the face of the tax returns; and (3) that mistakes such as this could be corrected by the taxpayer without prior IRS approval. The Tax Court also said that the fact that the petitioner may have repeated its mistake for a number of years does not transform the mistake into a method of accounting. The court stated that even if the petitioner's method of determining its taxable income from the property (computed without allowance for depletion) were to be considered a method of accounting, it is the kind that the petitioner may change without respondent's consent.[112]

---

[108] Rev. Rul. 77-134, 1977-1 CB 132, discussed supra ¶ 9.03[3].

[109] See discussion at ¶ 2.04[3] regarding the actions of the IRS on audit being treated as the acceptance of a change in method of accounting.

[110] See IRS position in Korn Indus., Inc. v. United States, 532 F2d 1352 (Ct. Cl. 1976); Rev. Rul. 77-134, 1977-1 CB 132.

[111] North Carolina Granite Corp., 43 TC 149 (1964).

[112] Id. at 167–168.

In *Wingate E. Underhill*,[113] the Tax Court considered the issue in the context of a taxpayer who acquired certain negotiable promissory notes at sizable discounts from their face amounts. In the years at issue, the taxpayer treated payments on the notes first as a recovery of cost and only thereafter as income. However, in prior years, the taxpayer had treated a pro rata portion of each payment as income. The Tax Court first held that the taxpayer was not required to report as income a pro rata portion of the payments on such notes. It then held that the taxpayer was not precluded from reporting on the cost recovery basis for the years at issue because of his treatment of similar notes in prior years. The court said that the issue was the extent to which payments received by the taxpayer are taxable or nontaxable, i.e., the character of the payment, not the proper method or the time of reporting an item the character of which is not in question. According to the court, the taxpayer should no more be precluded from reporting his payments on the correct basis than a taxpayer who has previously been reporting nontaxable income as taxable income would be required to continue to do so because of his prior error.[114]

Although relying principally on the "change in character" exception to the treatment of the change as a change in method of accounting, the court also used language appropriate to the "correction of an error" exception. This suggested that an erroneous practice, even if a method of accounting, could be corrected without the prior approval of the IRS. This suggestion was furthered by the Tax Court in *Herbert S. Witte*,[115] where it stated:

> When a taxpayer is required by law to report income in a certain way but instead reports it in a manner inconsistent with the requirements of the statute, absent estoppel, the error in reporting income is not binding on either the taxpayer or respondent, and it is proper that the error be corrected in a subsequent year.[116]

On appeal, the court of appeals reversed the decision, rejecting any suggestion that the requirements of Section 446(e) and the regulations thereunder are not applicable to changes from an improper to a proper method.[117]

---

[113] Wingate E. Underhill, 45 TC 489 (1966).

[114] Id. at 496.

[115] Herbert S. Witte, 31 TCM 1137 (1972), rev'd, 513 F2d 391 (DC Cir. 1975).

[116] Herbert S. Witte, 31 TCM at 1143. See also Thompson-King-Tate, Inc. v. United States, 296 F2d 290, 294 (6th Cir. 1961), where the court stated:

If, under the statutes, income must be reported in a certain way and the taxpayer erroneously reports it in a different way, such treatment is not binding upon either the taxpayer or the Commissioner. The taxpayer made an error, not an election, which error in the absence of estoppel, is subject to correction if timely challenged by either the taxpayer or the Commissioner. . . .

[117] The regulatory requirement has been held not inconsistent with the statute

Nevertheless, the ultimate position of the Tax Court remains uncertain, and language in decisions of the Tax Court continues to cause confusion. For example, in *First National Bank of Gainesville*,[118] the taxpayer argued that its alteration of a LIFO inventory valuation procedure constituted the correction of an error and not a change in method of accounting. The Tax Court held that although the alteration in question may have constituted a correction, it also constituted a change of accounting method pursuant to Section 472(e). Where the correction of an error results in a change in accounting method, the requirements of Section 446(e) are applicable.[119]

[3] Courts of Appeals for Fifth and Tenth Circuits

The Courts of Appeals for the Fifth and Tenth Circuits have also held in particular circumstances that taxpayers may convert from incorrect to correct accounting practices without the prior approval of the IRS. These decisions were based on the correction-of-an-error exception. For example, in *United States v. Catto*[120] and *United States v. Wardlaw*,[121] the taxpayers changed their method of reporting breeding cattle—from including them in inventory to expensing them—on the basis that the Treasury regulation requiring them to be included in inventory was invalid. The court of appeals for the Fifth Circuit agreed that the regulation was invalid and stated: "[W]e think the taxpayers are justified in correcting the error which the regulation imposed ... [and] we do not deem this a change in accounting method. . . ."[122]

The court of appeals for the Tenth Circuit has taken a similar approach.

---

and, hence, should be followed. See Comm'r v. O. Liquidating Corp., 292 F2d 225 (3d Cir. 1961), cert. denied, 368 US 898 (1961).

[118] First Nat'l Bank of Gainesville, 88 TC 1069 (1987).

[119] Id. The Tax Court cited numerous other Tax Court cases in support of this conclusion, but it did not fully evaluate the circumstances of those cases. But see Richard M. Evans, 55 TCM 902 (1988), where the Tax Court allowed a cash basis taxpayer to report bonuses in the year received even though bonuses in prior years had been recognized in income prior to the year of receipt.

[120] United States v. Catto, 344 F2d 227 (5th Cir. 1965), aff'g per curiam 223 F. Supp. 663 (WD Tex. 1963), rev'd on other grounds, 384 US 102 (1966).

[121] United States v. Wardlaw, 344 F2d 225 (5th Cir. 1965), aff'g per curiam 223 F. Supp. 631 (WD Tex. 1963), rev'd on other grounds sub. nom. United States v. Catto, 384 US 102 (1966).

[122] United States v. Wardlaw, 344 F2d at 229. It should be noted that the court's conclusion that the prior approval of the Commissioner was not needed stemmed in part from the consistent refusal of the Commissioner, during the years in question, to approve applications for changes such as these. Absent this circumstance, the court might be less inclined in the future to follow *Catto/Wardlaw* on this issue.

In *Mountain Fuel Supply Co. v. United States*[123] and *Oklahoma Gas & Electric Co. v. United States*,[124] changes in the taxpayers' procedures, from capitalizing to currently deducting certain items, were treated as corrections of errors, not as changes in methods of accounting.[125] In *Beacon Publishing Co. v. Commissioner*,[126] the taxpayer initially reported prepaid subscriptions as income in the year received but subsequently began to defer their recognition. The Tenth Circuit concluded that this deferral was not a change in accounting method requiring the Commissioner's consent because the taxpayer only corrected a past error (by properly applying the accrual method it had previously adopted).[127]

These decisions of the claims court, the Tax Court, and the Courts of Appeals for the Fifth and Tenth Circuits appear to adopt an approach that is not in all cases consistent with either the regulations or the decisions of other circuits. The decisions reflect a desire to eliminate the need to involve the IRS in every correction of an improper accounting practice and have the effect of permitting convenience to be emphasized over potential double counting or exclusion of items of income or expense.

It would appear that the rationale of the foregoing decisions is appropriate in circumstances where a taxpayer has properly adopted and followed a method of accounting and has not received either express or implied permission from the IRS to change its method of accounting. In these circumstances, any departure from, or failure to follow, that method of accounting is incorrect and should not be continued. By permitting the taxpayer to correct this erroneous treatment, the courts are merely permitting the taxpayer to adhere to its existing method of accounting from which it never received approval to change. If the courts were to hold to the contrary, it would suggest that the initial departure itself constituted a change to a method of accounting from which the taxpayer could not therefore change without prior approval. This would not make sense.

On the other hand, in circumstances where the courts have permitted

---

[123] Mountain Fuel Supply Co. v. United States, 449 F2d 816 (10th Cir. 1971), cert. denied, 405 US 989 (1972).

[124] Oklahoma Gas & Electric Co. v. United States, 464 F2d 1188 (10th Cir. 1972).

[125] These decisions should be compared with Electric & Neon, Inc., 56 TC 1324 (1971), acq. 1973-2 CB 1, aff'd, 496 F2d 876 (5th Cir. 1974); William K. Coors, 60 TC 368 (1973), acq. 1974-2 CB 2, aff'd sub. nom. Adolph Coors Co. v. Comm'r, 519 F2d 1280 (10th Cir. 1975), cert. denied, 423 US 1087 (1976); and Alabama Coca-Cola Bottling Co., 28 TCM 635 (1969), where the courts found similar changes to be changes in methods of accounting.

[126] Beacon Publishing Co. v. Comm'r, 218 F2d 697 (10th Cir. 1955).

[127] The court said, "[N]or do we have any doubt but that a taxpayer may, without the consent of the Commissioner, apply the method of accounting which he has adopted, though not theretofore applied to a particular item, when that change will correct errors and clearly reflect his income." Id. at 702.

the taxpayer to change from an erroneous method of accounting or from a practice that the Commissioner has impliedly accepted as a method of accounting, the taxpayer is not merely applying its existing method but is changing to a different, although correct, one. Such changes should be subject to the regulatory provisions governing changes in methods of accounting. The taxpayer should not be allowed to make the change on its own, free of the requirements of Section 481.[128]

[4] Other Forums

Other forums have also treated adjustments to conform to an already-established method as the correction of an error. For example, in *Thompson-King-Tate, Inc. v. United States*,[129] the court of appeals for the Sixth Circuit held that the taxpayer could make an adjustment to report income from a construction contract in the year the contract was finally completed because the taxpayer had previously adopted that method for such contracts.[130] In *Wetherbee Electric Co. v. Jones*,[131] the taxpayer consistently reported income from its wholesale and retail electrical supply business on an accrual basis and income from its electrical contracting business on the completed contract basis. The court held that the taxpayer was not only entitled but required to allocate an equitable portion of its general overhead expenses to both contracts completed during each taxable year and contracts incomplete at the end of each taxable year in order to clearly reflect income. The taxpayer's correction of an oversight in making such allocation did not require the Commissioner's approval because it involved no change in the method of accounting.

[5] Challenging Commissioner's Denial of Change

Should the Commissioner deny a request for change from an incorrect method or seek to impose unacceptable and illogical conditions on the requested change, his actions could be challenged as constituting an abuse of discre-

---

[128] But see discussions at ¶ 8.07[2][b] and supra ¶ 9.05.

[129] Thompson-King-Tate, Inc. v. United States, 296 F2d 290 (6th Cir. 1961).

[130] The court said the following:

[T]he taxpayer had no legal opportunity to choose between reporting the income in 1953 or in 1955. . . . Taxpayer's action in reporting the income under consideration in its 1953 return was accordingly improper and unauthorized and should be corrected. . . . Under these circumstances the taxpayer was required to return its profit from the long-term contract in the year 1955, consistent with the method previously used by it, and it had no election to return it in 1953 instead of in 1955.

The court emphasized that a taxpayer has no election but is required to report income in the year when it is taxable. Id. at 294, 295.

[131] Wetherbee Elec. Co. v. Jones, 73 F. Supp. 765 (WD Okla. 1947).

tion.[132] The taxpayer may then seek to effect a change on its own. To minimize the risk of proceeding in this manner, the taxpayer should file its return under its old, incorrect method and then seek a refund based on use of the new, correct method. Otherwise, the IRS may seek to impose penalties for an asserted intentional disregard of the regulations requiring prior IRS approval of a change in method.

¶ 9.06 CHANGE IN UNDERLYING FACTS

A change in tax reporting generally will be attributable to a "change in underlying facts" and not to a "change in method of accounting," where the taxpayer continues to apply its existing method of accounting to a change in business practices, a change in economic or legal relationships, or an otherwise altered fact situation. However, a change in tax law that causes the taxpayer's accounting method to become incorrect is generally not a change in fact that will allow a change in method without prior approval.[133]

[1] Regulations

The regulations provide two examples of the proper application of this principle regarding a change in underlying facts:

EXAMPLE (3): A taxpayer in the wholesale dry goods business computes its income and expenses on the accrual method of accounting and files its federal income tax returns on such basis. Vacation pay has been deducted in the year in which paid because the taxpayer did not have a completely vested vacation pay plan, and, therefore, the liability for payment did not accrue until that year. Subsequently, the taxpayer adopts a completely vested vacation pay plan that changes its year for accruing the deduction from the year in which payment is made to the

---

[132] See discussions at ¶¶ 2.04, 8.07.

[133] See, e.g., Treas. Reg. § 1.471-11(e) regarding application of full-absorption regulations that caused non-full-absorption methods to be incorrect; Temp. Reg. §§ 1.263A-1T(e)(1), 1.263A-1T(e)(11) regarding application of the uniform capitalization rules for inventory costing; IRC § 461(h), regarding addition of the economic performance test to the test for application of the accrual method of accounting to expenses. In each case, the change to the newly established method was a change in method of accounting subject to rules governing those changes to the extent not otherwise provided in the new regulatory or Code provision. See also Southern Pac. Transp. Co., 75 TC 497 (1980), supplemented by 82 TC 122 (1984), where attempted switch to method approved by court in another case was found to be a change in accounting method. But see ¶ 8.07[2][b] for a discussion of cases holding that a taxpayer may change from an erroneous method without the prior approval of the IRS.

year in which the liability to make the payment now arises. The change for the year of deduction of the vacation pay plan is not a change in method of accounting but results, instead, because the underlying facts (that is, the type of vacation pay plan) have changed.

EXAMPLE (4): From 1968 through 1970, a taxpayer has fairly allocated indirect overhead costs to the value of inventories on a fixed percentage of direct costs. If the ratio of indirect overhead costs to direct costs increases in 1971, a change in the underlying facts has occurred. Accordingly, an increase in the percentage in 1971 to fairly reflect the increase in the relative level of indirect overhead costs is not a change in method of accounting but is a change in treatment resulting from a change in the underlying facts.[134]

In each example, it is clear that the taxpayer has applied its existing method of reporting to a changed fact situation. The different tax consequences arose from a different legal obligation and economic condition, respectively, and not from a change in method of reporting.

The foregoing regulations were promulgated in 1970.[135] There were no comparable provisions in prior regulations. However, the question had arisen as to whether a change in reporting resulted from a change in accounting method or from a change in underlying facts. The 1970 regulations were intended to reflect prior decisions of the IRS and the courts.[136]

---

[134] Treas. Reg. § 1.446-1(e)(2)(iii).

[135] TD 7073, 1970-2 CB 98.

[136] See, e.g., Rev. Rul. 58-340, 1958-2 CB 174, where the IRS dealt with the situation addressed in Example (3) of the present regulations. See also Texaco-Cities Serv. Pipe Line Co. v. United States, 170 F. Supp. 644 (Ct. Cl. 1959), where accrual basis taxpayer who previously deducted vacation pay when paid and who changed from nonvested to vested plan was allowed to deduct, in the year of change, both payments made during the year and payments that accrued at end of such year under the new plan. On the other hand, in Rev. Rul. 59-285, 1959-2 CB 458, the IRS indicated that if an accrual basis taxpayer improperly deducted vacation pay in the year paid rather than the year accrued, the taxpayer would be required to obtain the Commissioner's prior consent before changing the method of accounting. This conclusion is in accord with the consistent position of the IRS that a change from an improper to a proper accounting method also requires the prior consent of the Commissioner. It can be distinguished from the facts in Rev. Rul. 58-340 on the ground that the later ruling did not involve any change in the terms of the vacation plan itself. See also I. Lewis Corp., 22 TCM 35 (1963), where taxpayer could not, on its own, change from the cash method to an accrual method for vacation pay, because the taxpayer did not establish that the applicable labor union contracts required such a change in accounting treatment; Dorr-Oliver Inc., 40 TC 50 (1963), where an unauthorized change from the cash to an accrual method for vacation pay deductions, unaccompanied by change in the vacation pay plan, was disallowed.

[2] Judicial Development

The cases focusing on the change in underlying facts doctrine are few in number but of great significance. For these reasons, they must be considered carefully when evaluating any change, or proposed change, in underlying facts.

[a] Change in Contract, Business Practice, or Economic Consequences

It appears that the change-in-underlying-facts doctrine was first expressly articulated in *Decision, Inc.*,[137] which involved a calendar-year, accrual basis taxpayer that derived the bulk of its income from the sale of advertising. Prior to 1963, the taxpayer used a contract that called for the billing of its customers at the end of one year with the advertising to be published in the following year. The taxpayer reported the income in the year the advertising was published. The IRS successfully contended that the advertising income should have been accrued in the year in which it was billed and contractually due. In response, the taxpayer changed its contracts to provide that no amounts would be billed or would become due and payable until the year the advertising was published. The court noted that this change by the taxpayer stemmed "at least in part because of [the IRS'] disapproval of [the taxpayer's prior] method of deferring income. . . ."[138] The IRS argued that the change in reporting was a change in accounting method for which its prior approval was necessary. The court concluded:

> Although the change had consequences in the annual determination of income, such consequences were not produced by the accounting system. In essence this kind of business policy change was no different from a decision to lower prices or halt production for a year. To sustain this argument [of the Commissioner] would have the effect of denying a business the right to determine the terms of sale of its product without clearing the matter with the Commissioner of Internal Revenue, clearly an odious propagation of the tentacles of the Government anemone. Petitioner merely agreed with its customers not to bill on 1963 orders until 1964. . . ."[139]

While *Decision, Inc.* might be read expansively to stand for the proposition that any change in business policy would be a change in underlying fact, the case should probably not be accorded a meaning that broad.[140] Neverthe-

---

[137] Decision, Inc., 47 TC 58 (1966), acq. 1967-2 CB 2.

[138] Id. at 64.

[139] Id. See Hallmark Cards, Inc., 90 TC 26 (1988), for an affirmation of this same point.

[140] See discussion infra ¶ 9.06[2][b].

less, the case does point out that where a changed business or legal relationship occurs and has consequences to each party to the transaction, the
application of the taxpayer's existing methods of accounting to the changed
circumstances will be respected for tax purposes.[141] This is the case even
though the taxpayer may be able to control the relevant events or unilaterally
change the relevant facts in order to fix the time for the recognition of accrual
basis income and even though the change emanates from tax reduction
motives.[142]

Other cases support the preceding analysis. In *Federated Department
Stores v. Commissioner*,[143] the taxpayer sometimes made sales on credit but
charged a service fee (equivalent to interest) for this. The taxpayer often
borrowed from banks using these accounts receivable (including the unpaid
service fees) as collateral. It reported the service fees in income ratably as
payments were received from customers. In 1964, the taxpayer changed its
business practice and began selling the accounts receivable rather than
borrowing against them. One of the issues before the court was whether the
deferred service fees would have to be included in income at the time the
receivables were sold or whether the fees could continue to be included in
income ratably on the basis of the taxpayer's past practice. The court held
that the reporting of fees could no longer be deferred. This holding resulted
in the additional question of whether the change was a change in accounting
method or a change in underlying facts. Finding that the sale of receivables
created a legal relationship materially different from that involved in borrowing on the receivables, the court held that a change in underlying facts had
occurred.

In *Angelus Funeral Home*[144] an accrual basis taxpayer had sold funeral
plans under a contract providing that the amounts received would be
deposited in a bank or savings and loan association, maintained in trust for
the benefit of the purchaser, and used only for specified purposes consistent
with the trust relationship. In 1961, the taxpayer began using a different form
of contract, which required it to pay interest to the purchaser but permitted
it to use the funds for whatever purpose it desired. The court found that a
change in facts had occurred. It held that while amounts received under the
earlier form of contract did not have to be included in income until used for
the intended purposes, amounts received under the later form of contract had
to be included in income at the time of payment. Similarly, in *Thriftimart*

---

[141] See Priv. Ltr. Rul. 8643029 (July 25, 1986), for an example of a situation in
which this result was accepted by the National Office.

[142] Decision, Inc., 47 TC 58, 64 (1966), acq. 1967-2 CB 2. *Decision, Inc.* was
decided prior to the issuance of Rev. Proc. 71-21, 1971-2 CB 549. See
¶ 4.03[3][e][ii][1] for a discussion of Rev. Proc. 71-21.

[143] Federated Dep't Stores v. Comm'r, 426 F2d 417 (6th Cir. 1970).

[144] Angelus Funeral Home, 47 TC 391 (1967), acq. 1969-2 CB 20, aff'd, 407 F2d
210 (9th Cir. 1969), cert. denied, 396 US 824 (1969).

Inc.,[145] the taxpayer modified a preexisting collective bargaining agreement affecting sick pay to provide that its employees would be entitled to payment for unused sick leave. Without discussion, the court concluded that this change entitled the taxpayer to accrue its liability for unused sick leave pay under its established accounting method.[146]

The preceding cases demonstrate the importance of the legal relationship between a taxpayer and its customers in determining the proper time for reporting income. Where the legal or business relationship changes, continued application of an existing method of accounting may give rise to a change in the time when income or expense is reported.[147] As this suggests, it is often a relatively easy matter for taxpayers to change such factual circumstances so as to derive significant tax benefits.[148]

The ease with which the changes in legal or business relationships may be effected is evidenced by a series of IRS private letter rulings and technical advice memoranda relating to the recognition of income from points, loan fees, and other forms of discounted interest on residential mortgage loans.[149]

---

[145] Thriftimart, Inc., 59 TC 598 (1973), acq. 1973-2 CB 4.

[146] See also Charles B. Schniers, 69 TC 511 (1977), where in order to defer until 1974 the recognition of income from the sale of certain cotton in 1973, the cash basis taxpayer entered into agreements that called for payment by the purchaser in 1974 and made it clear that the taxpayer would have no rights, claim, or action against the purchaser for payment prior to 1974. The court held that the agreement controlled and did not involve a change in accounting method.

[147] Where the rendition of services or the delivery of goods occurs in the same year as the recipient's contractual obligation to pay, a change in the contract to defer the effective time of the contractual obligation may not always have the desired result. Concepts of quantum valebant and quantum meruit may apply to establish at least a portion of the obligation as being fixed in the year the services are rendered or the goods delivered.

[148] Some commentators have stated that a change in underlying fact

suggests great potential for tax planning. Because the time when income must be recognized and expenses deducted is determined by applying the law to factual situations that are, in turn, largely controlled by the taxpayer, different tax accounting results can be obtained through changing the underlying facts.

Diamond & Holman, *Accounting Methods-Adoption and Changes,* Tax Mgmt. (BNA) 303-4th, at A-43 (1987).

[149] In Rev. Rul. 70-540, 1970-2 CB 101, the IRS set forth rules governing the reporting of points, loan fees, and other charges made in connection with residential mortgage loans. In general, the ruling provided that if points or other forms of interest were paid at the closing by the borrower from his own funds, the lender had to recognize as income the entire amount of such interest in the year the loan was closed. However, if the points were discounted from the face amount of the note and financed by the lender, the interest was deferred and recognized ratably over the life of the loan as it was repaid. On the basis of the ruling, many financial institutions have used one form of agreement or another, depending on whether they wanted to accelerate the recognition of income or defer it. See Tech. Adv. Mem. 8707001 (June 30, 1986), for an application of Rev. Rul. 70-540.

In these, the IRS confirmed that changes in loan documents (and the different tax reporting occasioned thereby) would be recognized as changes in underlying facts.[150] Similarly, this same point was effectively recognized by the Tax Court in *Bell Federal Savings & Loan Ass'n.*,[151] which involved the issue of whether the particular agreements entered into between the lender and its borrowers required points to be paid at the time of the loan closing or, instead, required the amount of the points to be discounted from the proceeds of the loan; this factual issue, in turn, determining the proper tax reporting. The nature of the court's opinion made it clear that the taxpayer needed only to specify in its agreements with borrowers whether there was to be a discounting of the points from the proceeds of the loan or a payment of the points by the borrowers at the time of the loan closing. Of course, the change in underlying agreements is not limited to circumstances involving borrowers and lenders. For example, in *Hallmark Cards, Inc.*,[152] the court indicated that a change in the contractual terms under which goods are sold may well result in a change in the time at which sales should be recognized.

[b] Significant Consequences to Parties

Despite the apparent ease of effecting a change in reporting by means of a change in underlying facts, it must be noted that neither the IRS nor the courts will respect a purported change in underlying facts where the change

---

[150] In Priv. Ltr. Rul. 7804028 (Oct. 26, 1977), a cash basis savings and loan association requested a ruling that a change in its loan-closing procedures would not constitute a change in accounting method, even though the change in procedures would generate a substantial deferral in the reporting of taxable income. The association proposed to revise its then-current procedure from one that required the borrower to pay points at the loan-closing out of his own funds to one in which the points would be included in the face amount of the note but a disbursement would be made to the borrower (or on his behalf) equal to the difference between the face amount of the note and the amount of the points. The IRS ruled that the proposed change "involves, in essence, the application of consistent [accounting] treatment to an altered factual situation." Accordingly, it ruled that the change would constitute a change in underlying facts, not a change in accounting method. Accord Priv. Ltr. Rul. 7826025 (Mar. 28, 1978); Priv. Ltr. Rul. 7829028 (Apr. 19, 1978) (accrual basis taxpayer); see e.g., Tech. Adv. Mem. 8135030 (May 29, 1981), 8135015 (May 18, 1981), and 8134014 (Apr. 30, 1981), all recognizing the significance of the loan documents and the parties' intent. The ease with which such favorable changes can be made is not limited to points and fees on residential mortgage loans. See also Priv. Ltr. Rul. 7732006 (Apr. 29, 1977), which involved a modification in a lease agreement; Tech. Adv. Mem. 8146015 (July 24, 1981), which involved a change in method of computing interest on installment loans and which pointed out that a change in facts does not cause an acceleration of the balance of a Section 481 adjustment. See also Priv. Ltr. Ruls. 8643008 (July 9, 1986); 8643029 (July 25, 1986), to the same effect.

[151] Bell Federal Savings & Loan Ass'n, 62 TCM 376 (1991).

[152] Hallmark Cards, Inc., 90 TC 26 (1988).

either has no substantive legal or economic consequences to the parties or no corresponding tax effect to the other party. In that case, the change in reporting will be treated as a change in accounting method and subjected to the rules governing such changes.

For example, in *Gap Anthracite Co.*,[153] Gap operated a processing plant for the Susquehanna Coal Company. Under this agreement, Susquehanna reimbursed Gap for all expenses, including worker's compensations, which was reimbursed and deducted by Susquehanna only as payments were made by Gap. In 1964, Gap suffered a major liability as the result of an accident in which three of its employees were killed. Although actual payments were to be made over a number of years, Gap billed Susquehanna for the total liability. Susquehanna deducted the amount of the billing, while Gap accrued the billing as income and the liability to the workers as a deduction.

The IRS disallowed that portion of Susquehanna's claimed deduction in excess of actual payments on the theory that the taxpayers had changed their methods of accounting without permission. The taxpayers argued that Gap's change in its billing method and Susquehanna's action with respect to that change constituted a modification of the 1961 agreement and therefore was a change in underlying facts rather than a change in accounting method. The Tax Court held for the IRS, apparently because there was no evidence that Susquehanna assented to the change in billing procedure and thereby made itself legally liable for these unpaid amounts.[154] The court also suggested that since the only apparent economic effect of the transaction was a tax benefit to Susquehanna, the transaction should for that reason be classified as a change in method of accounting.[155] The court's analysis implied that the result might have been different had there been a corresponding tax consequence to Gap (e.g., an acceleration in the recognition of income without a simultaneous accrual of the deduction). The case points out the importance

---

[153] Gap Anthracite Co., 31 TCM 924 (1972), aff'd without published opinion sub. nom. Susquehanna Coal Co. v. Comm'r, 487 F2d 1395, (3d Cir. 1973), cert. denied, 417 US 931 (1974).

[154] The court explained:

For aught that appears, Susquehanna still [even after accruing the deduction] did not consider itself liable for the payment until Gap actually made an expenditure on a claim. We are unable to conclude, therefore, that there was such mutuality of assent to a changed procedure as to constitute a change in business policy rather than a change of accounting method.

Gap Anthracite Co., 31 TCM at 934. Unlike the parties in *Decision, Inc.*, discussed supra ¶ 9.06[2][a], the parties here did not formalize the new procedure in a binding agreement that established their legal rights and obligations.

[155] The court also noted that "absent any other explanation, the only reason for the change appears to have been to enable Susquehanna substantially to increase its net operating loss; as far as Gap was concerned, the transaction produced a 'wash,' whichever method was utilized." 31 TCM at 935.

of recording new economic or business relationships in a legally binding manner.

Similarly, in Revenue Ruling 60-243,[156] the IRS focused on a soft drink manufacturer whose agreement with customers required a deposit on bottles. The deposit was to be refunded at the time the bottles were returned. The taxpayer proposed to alter the relevant agreement by "selling" the bottles for an amount equal to the deposit and then reacquiring them for the same amount. Because this change had no economic significance to the parties other than to accelerate deductions by the taxpayer,[157] the IRS held that there was no real change in underlying facts. Thus, the IRS ruled that the change in tax reporting would be regarded as a change in method of accounting, which could not be effected without the prior consent of the Commissioner.[158]

In Revenue Ruling 65-287,[159] the IRS ruled that where an accrual basis public utility changed from a monthly to a bimonthly meter reading and billing cycle, a change in accounting method resulted, and the prior consent of the Commissioner was required. Following the issuance of this ruling, the IRS acquiesced to the holding in *Decision, Inc.* However, the IRS subsequently reaffirmed its position in Revenue Ruling 65-287 by the issuance of Revenue Ruling 71-429,[160] which held that an accrual basis public utility's change from a bimonthly meter reading and billing cycle to a bimonthly meter reading and interim monthly billing cycle would be deemed a change in the utility's method of accounting. Although it appears difficult to distinguish these revenue rulings from the holding in *Decision, Inc.*, one

---

[156] Rev. Rul. 60-243, 1960-2 CB 160.

[157] The acceleration would result from the fact that under the sale-and-repurchase theory, the taxpayer would obtain a large loss on the sale of new bottles because the bottles were sold at a price far below their cost.

[158] See also Advertisers Exch. Inc., 25 TC 1086 (1956), aff'd per curiam, 240 F2d 958 (2d Cir. 1957), where the Tax Court held that a change in method of accounting had occurred because the change in relationship affected only one party. Advertising contracts between the taxpayer and its customers covered a period of 12 months and were for a stated annual amount, payable monthly. More often than not, the 12-month period during which the services were to be performed covered portions of two taxable years. The taxpayer had accrued all income during the month in which the contracts were signed but deducted expenses only as incurred, thus producing a mismatching of income and expense. In 1945, the taxpayer created a deferred income account and unilaterally began deferring income, reporting it over the year or years covered by the contract. The taxpayer argued that it had merely changed its method of selling, but the court held otherwise.

[159] Rev. Rul. 65-287, 1965-2 CB 150. (Note that Section 451(f), added by the Tax Reform Act of 1986 (the 1986 Act), affected the use of cycle meter reading methods by requiring that income not be deferred beyond the year in which the services are rendered.)

[160] Rev. Rul. 71-429, 1971-2 CB 217. (Note that Section 451(f), added by the 1986 Act, affected the use of cycle meter reading methods by requiring that income not be deferred beyond the year in which the services are rendered.)

possible distinction is that in *Decision, Inc.*, billing occurred prior to the rendition of services or the sale of goods. Thus, the underlying event that gave rise to the accrual of income was billing that changed. In the revenue rulings, the event that triggered the accrual of income was the performance of services, which did not undergo any change.[161] Other commentators have not made this distinction and have stated that the two authorities are in direct conflict.[162]

The foregoing cases and rulings demonstrate that while it is comparatively simple for a taxpayer to effect changes in the time when items of income or expense are reported by changing the underlying circumstances, this change in circumstances must be based on a substantive change in economic or legal relationship or, at least, on changed tax consequences to the other parties in the transaction. It is not sufficient to produce a tax benefit to the party effecting the change without any consequences to the other party. Assuming this condition can be satisfied, such changes may be made even though the reason for the change is motivated by tax considerations. In effect, the taxpayer is merely applying its existing method of accounting to the facts before it. It is not changing its method of accounting.

[3] Importance of Defining "Method"

Essential to a determination of whether there has been a change in underlying facts or in method of accounting is a proper identification of the method used. Frequently, the taxpayer's accounting practice is consistent with any of several methods, and the results produced are the same under each of these methods.[163] Thus, when a transaction occurs that would not be accounted for in the same way under any of several methods of accounting, identification of the method used together with the reporting of that transaction may often decide the issue of the taxpayer's method.[164]

---

[161] See Diamond & Holman, supra note 28, at A-15.

[162] See, e.g., Tanenbaum, "Recent Developments in What Constitutes a Change of Accounting Method: Growth of a Business Element; When Does the Change Occur; Who Initiates It," 26 NYU Inst. Fed. Tax'n 505, 523–524 (1968).

[163] For example, if a business has no accounts receivable or payable at the end of its first year, the income recognized for tax purposes may be the same under both the cash and accrual methods.

[164] See ESCO Corp. v. United States, 750 F2d 1466 (9th Cir. 1985), where the taxpayer had deducted its liability for certain workers' compensation claims only as paid. In 1979, it deducted amounts in excess of the amounts paid. The government argued that the taxpayer had changed its method of accounting from cash to accrual without the prior approval of the Commissioner. The court disagreed, concluding that the taxpayer had always been on an accrual method and that prior to 1974, proper application of the accrual method had resulted in deduction of only the claims paid.

For example, in *Cincinnati, New Orleans & Texas Pacific Ry. v. United States*,[165] an accrual method railroad was subject to the supervision of the Interstate Commerce Commission (ICC). For many years prior to 1940, the ICC required that rail carriers expense purchases of certain property costing less than $100. In 1940, the $100 level was raised to $500. For tax purposes, the railroad followed its ICC accounting practice.

The IRS allowed the taxpayer's deductions for items costing less than $100, but contended that use of the $500 minimum constituted a change in accounting method for which consent had not been received. The court disagreed, stating that the increase in the minimum amount resulted from a "change, not in accounting method, but in the underlying facts, i.e., the increase in business occasioned by World War II."[166]

The court apparently defined the taxpayer's method as use of the ICC rule. Consequently, under the court's analysis, the taxpayer continued, and never departed from, its accounting method, i.e., use of the ICC rule. Under this analysis, it was easy for the court to conclude that change in the minimum amount used by the ICC was only a change in fact.

On the other hand, an alternative analysis might have identified or defined the taxpayer's method in terms of the $100 amount itself. For example, the taxpayer's method might have been identified as one that expenses all items costing $100 or less rather than one that follows specifically the ICC rule. If such a definition had been used, then the court most likely would have found a change in method when the taxpayer shifted from expensing all items costing $100 or less to expensing all items costing $500 or less.[167] Naturally, the courts and the IRS will examine carefully all relevant facts and circumstances, including the manner in which items have been reported on relevant tax returns, in defining the method of accounting actually adopted and used by the taxpayer.[168]

Identification issues such as this often arise in connection with methods used for valuing inventory. For example, a taxpayer may consistently have valued its inventory at cost because market value had never fallen below cost. If market does fall below cost, there is a question whether the lower value

---

[165] Cincinnati, New Orleans & Tex. Pac. Ry. v. United States, 424 F2d 563 (Ct. Cl. 1970), a case decided under the 1939 Code.

[166] Id. at 573.

[167] See Baltimore and Ohio Ry. v. United States, 603 F2d 165 (Ct. Cl. 1979), where the court found a change in method of valuing assets for depreciation purposes not to constitute a change in method of accounting, the change in valuation formula perceived as a change in fact.

[168] See First Nat'l Bank of Gainesville, 88 TC 1069 (1987), which involved a taxpayer's adoption to use the LIFO method of accounting; Tech. Adv. Mem. 9132001 (Jan. 9, 1991), where the IRS evaluated applicable facts and circumstances in determining the scope of a taxpayer's election to capitalize interest expense under Section 266.

may be used. The answer often depends on whether the taxpayer defined its method as cost only or as lower of cost or market.[169]

[4] Change in Fact vs. Adoption of Method for New "Item"

Methods of accounting exist with respect to every "item" of income or expense.[170] Consequently, a taxpayer's reporting of a new and different item of income or expense for the first time does not necessarily involve a "change" of accounting method merely because the item is reported on a different basis than that used with respect to existing items.[171]

The foregoing principle has been followed in a number of instances. For example, in *Federated Department Stores, Inc.*,[172] the taxpayer had for many years borrowed against its receivables. In 1964, it sold the receivables. This sale was found to be a new transaction not subject to the prior method of accounting. The Tax Court concluded that the pre-1964 bank transactions were "so materially" different from the 1964 sale that no change in accounting method had been involved. It was found that the earlier transactions, although cast in the form of sales of the taxpayer's accounts receivable, were in substance loans secured by such accounts.[173]

The principle was also applied in *Morris-Poston Coal Co. v.*

---

[169] See St. James Sugar Coop., Inc. v. United States, 79-2 USTC ¶ 9476 (ED La. 1979), aff'd, 643 F2d 1219 (5th Cir. 1981), where taxpayer was allowed to value inventory at net realizable value because its method was found to be the use of market value not to exceed net realizable value.

[170] Treas. Reg. § 1.446-1(a)(1). "The term 'method of accounting' includes not only the over-all method of accounting of the taxpayer but also the accounting treatment of any item." See discussion at ¶¶ 2.01[4], 2.03[1].

[171] However, taxpayers do not have unbridled discretion in choosing methods for new items. The new item must be reported on the basis of a method which clearly reflects income, and the method used for existing items can affect whether income is clearly reflected with respect to the new item. See Treas. Reg. §§ 1.446-1(a)(2), 1.446-1(c)(1)(iv), and discussion at ¶ 2.03[1][b]. See also supra ¶ 9.03, for discussion of "item."

[172] Federated Dep't Stores, Inc., 51 TC 500 (1968), nonacq. 1971-2 CB 4, aff'd, 426 F2d 417 (6th Cir. 1970).

[173] The Tax Court held as follows:

A change of accounting must be with respect to a "material item. . . ." Fundamentally, the item itself must be basically the same as an item previously accounted for with the present method of accounting differing from the prior treatment. Unless the transactions are basically the same, the accounting treatment would not be [a] "change" of accounting but only a new accounting method for a different transaction. Thus, the issue is whether the pre-1964 transactions were in substance the same as the sale of the accounts on February 1, 1964, to [the bank].

Federated Dep't. Stores, Inc., 51 TC at 513–514.

Commissioner,[174] where an accrual method taxpayer discontinued one business (the mining and selling of coal) and thereafter started another business (the leasing of its property) using a cash method. Since *Morris-Poston* is one of the few cases focusing squarely on this issue, it deserves careful consideration. The Commissioner argued that the taxpayer was required to recognize rental income on an accrual method and that the taxpayer could not change to the cash method without prior consent. The Board of Tax Appeals, upheld the Commissioner.[175] The court of appeals for the Sixth Circuit reversed, holding that the taxpayer was not bound in its reporting of rental income by the accounting methods formerly used with respect to revenue derived from coal mining:

> The Commissioner rests his action largely upon his conclusion that this taxpayer, during the year, changed its method of accounting. We think the facts do not support this conclusion. As to all the transactions customary before [the change in business], to the extent that these transactions continued in a modified and winding up way, there was no change in the method of bookkeeping. Then a new kind of business was beginning and a new kind of income was in contemplation. This kind of income had never been handled by the method of bookkeeping in former use, because such type of income had never existed. What the company had formerly received, in exchange for its coal coming out of the ground, had been short-term invoices in relatively small amounts against responsible persons; the debts were subject to no contingencies; and experience showed that there was little delay and little loss. The sales were characteristically not very different from cash sales; and even though they had not been paid, to take them into account at the end of the year as income for the year was natural. The new rental involved a different set of conditions. . . .

A similar result was reached in Anderson-Dougherty-Hargis Co. v. United States, 96 F. Supp. 404 (ND Cal. 1950), which involved the reporting of income under government contracts. In 1943, the taxpayer, which had theretofore used an accrual method except for lump-sum government contracts, entered into a government contract to perform engineering work under a "unit price contract." For this particular project, the taxpayer used its accrual method. The Commissioner contended that use of the accrual method for this contract amounted to a change in method without prior approval of the Commissioner. In analyzing the issue presented, the court first noted: "The present contract was the first of its kind that plaintiff entered into. Bookkeeping methods resorted to would be methods of first instance rather than those of modification." Id. at 406. The court then held that the taxpayer had utilized a consistent method of accounting since it had used the accrual method of accounting for all items, except lump-sum contracts. Since the unit price contract involved was "clearly distinguishable" from a lump-sum contract, the court held that the taxpayer had applied an "old" method to a new type of income. This language suggests that the taxpayer would not have been deemed to have changed its accounting method even if it adopted a "new" method for this item.

[174] Morris-Poston Coal Co. v. Comm'r, 42 F2d 620 (6th Cir. 1930).

[175] 13 BTA 344 (1928).

It seems equally clear that a taxpayer who has customarily employed a combination of cash and accrual methods, classifying his items in accordance with his judgment, does not change his method of bookkeeping . . . merely because, having vitally changed the character of his business and created income of a nature never before entered on the books, he classifies that income, in accordance with his honest judgment and not imprudently as deserving treatment on a cash basis.[176]

The court went on to hold that even if the taxpayer had changed its method of accounting, it was entitled to do so, since its prior business had ended, at which time the taxpayer had engaged in a new business "of a different character, with different prospective income and with different risks and contingencies."[177] The court held that the requirement that the Commissioner consent to changes in accounting methods should not be applied to such a situation.

Although the *Morris-Poston* factual situation may be unique, the language in the decision suggests that when a taxpayer begins to receive income that is of a new and different nature and that is governed by different accounting considerations than existing items of income, it may choose a different method of accounting for the new item without obtaining the Commissioner's prior consent.

The cases previously discussed involve items of income that the courts found were not the same as items previously received by the taxpayer. Thus, the taxpayer was permitted to adopt a method of accounting different from that used with respect to other items.

The courts that have allowed the use of new or different accounting methods in this context have typically focused on the nature of the underlying transactions and the circumstances surrounding the item in order to find that the item was, indeed, "new." Another important factor that distinguishes the adoption of a new method of accounting for a different item of income or expense from a change in method of accounting is that there is no opportunity for an omission of income or expense or a double inclusion of items of income or expense in connection with the reporting of the new item. All income and expense arising from the accounting treatment for existing items will continue to be accounted for in accordance with the existing method of accounting. All income or expense associated with the new item will be taken into account under the method of accounting adopted for the new item. There should be no occasion for income or expense to escape taxation. Thus, there is no need for application of Section 481 in order to prevent omissions or double deductions.

---

[176] Morris-Poston Coal Co. v. Comm'r, 42 F2d 620, 621–622.
[177] Id. at 622.

[5] Expansion of Existing Business

An independent question is whether a taxpayer may adopt a new or different method of accounting for new offices, new products, or other activities that reflect an expansion of its existing business rather than its embarking on a new business. The regulations provide that different methods of accounting may be used for separate and distinct trades or businesses. However, they add that no trade or business will be considered separate and distinct unless (1) a complete and separable set of books and records is kept for it and (2) the use of different methods clearly reflects income.[178]

The regulations provide no further guidance, and there is a dearth of case authority. However, one case on this point is Peterson Produce Co. v. United States.[179] In this case, the taxpayer expanded its feed and hatchery business by adding a broiler operation. The court confirmed the general rule that once a taxpayer "elects a method of accounting, he must abide by it until he either obtains permission from the Commissioner to change or enters into a new, separate and distinct business."[180] The court then required the taxpayer to use its existing method of accounting for the new operation. The court was principally influenced by the degree of integration and interdependence of the various, assertedly separate activities.

Independent of the rules allowing different methods of accounting for separate and distinct trades or businesses[181] are rules permitting a taxpayer to use a combination of methods within a single trade or business.[182] The key to using a combination of methods within a single trade or business is whether all related items of income and expense are reported on the same method. To the extent they are, the use of different methods of accounting for different activities within a single trade or business may be acceptable. For example, a business that provides both goods and services may account for purchases and sales of goods under an accrual method and account for revenues and expenses from the performance of services on the cash method.[183] On the other hand, it generally would be inappropriate to report items of income on one method and corresponding items of expense on another method.[184]

---

[178] Treas. Reg. § 1.446-1(d). See discussion at ¶ 2.03[1][a].

[179] Peterson Produce Co. v. United States, 205 F. Supp. 229 (WD Ark. 1962), aff'd, 313 F2d 609 (8th Cir. 1963). See ¶ 2.03[1][a] for a further discussion of *Peterson Produce* in connection with the principle that a taxpayer may use a different method of accounting for each separate and distinct trade or business.

[180] 205 F. Supp. at 239.

[181] See Treas. Reg. § 1.446-1(d) and discussion at ¶ 2.03[1][a].

[182] See Treas. Reg. § 1.446-1(c)(1)(iv)(A) and discussion at ¶ 2.03[1][b].

[183] See Treas. Reg. § 1.446-1(c)(1)(iv)(A) and discussion at ¶ 3.06[2].

[184] See Treas. Reg. § 1.446-1(c)(1)(iv)(A). However, under the economic performance rules for reporting deductions on an accrual method, deductions for certain

In light of the lack of cases in this area, and the difficulty and potential cost of demonstrating or defending a position that an expansion is sufficiently akin to new business or activity to warrant adoption of a new method of accounting, taxpayers may be better served by forming a new corporation through which they will conduct the new or expanded operations. The new corporation, as a separate taxpayer, may then elect the desired methods of accounting.[185]

¶ 9.07 CHANGE IN CHARACTER OF THE ITEM

The regulations provide that a change in method of accounting does not include

> adjustment of any item of income or deduction which does not involve the proper time for the inclusion of the item of income or the taking of a deduction. For example, corrections of items that are deducted as interest or salary, but which are in fact payments of dividends, and of items that are deducted as business expenses, but which are in fact personal expenses, are not changes in method of accounting.[186]

---

expenses are effectively reported on the cash method. See discussion at ¶ 4.04[3][c][ii].

[185] See discussion infra ¶ 9.08[1][a]. See also Tanenbaum, supra note 162, at 527, where the author concludes:

> In the event the taxpayer's business expands by the addition of a "separate and distinct" line of business activity, a different method of accounting may be used for the other business. The adoption of a different method of accounting for the added business would not be considered a change of accounting method.
>
> While close questions might arise as to whether the additional activity constitutes a "separate and distinct" trade or business, it would not appear that the taxpayer would be "risking" anything if he adopted a different, more acceptable, method of accounting for his new line, provided he did not change the method used in his existing business. If the Commissioner disputed whether the new activity was "separate and distinct," his remedy would be simply to require a recomputation of income on the same method that had been used by the business to which it is considered an adjunct.

[186] Treas. Reg. § 1.446-1(e)(2)(b). See Coulter Elec., Inc., 59 TCM 350 (1990), where the court concluded that no change in method of accounting was involved where the question related to whether the taxpayer's transfer of certain leases constituted sales or pledges for loans. The court noted that this issue did not involve timing as would be contemplated with a change in method of accounting, but rather raised a question of characterization. McPike Inc. v. United States, 90-1 USTC ¶ 50,092 (Cl. Ct. 1988), where the court concluded that no change in method of accounting was at issue where the particular question involved classification and categorization of expenditures to determine whether they should be capitalized as a cost of construction or deductible as a cost in the nature of a maintenance expense. The court pointed out that "an accounting method is not a procedure used to learn the facts about a taxpayer's expense but is the *treatment* of that expense by the taxpayer." (emphasis

Thus, where the character of an item in a particular year is at issue, rather than the year in which the item is to be reported or otherwise taken into account, a change in character does not amount to a change in method of accounting and is not subject to the requirements governing such changes. This rule includes (1) changes in the character of an item of income or expense (such as from salary income to dividend income or from supplies expense to interest expense) and (2) changes in character between includable and nonincludable items or deductible and nondeductible items, including the recharacterization of nonincludable deposits to includable sales or service income and deductible compensation to nondeductible dividends.

The precise scope of the change-in-character exception is uncertain. Only a few cases have attempted to distinguish between a change in character and a change in accounting method. In one of these, *Wingate E. Underhill*,[187] the taxpayer bought second mortgage notes at a discount. Before 1961, he reported the income attributable to the discount on a pro rata basis. Thus, if he paid $80 for a $100 note and thereafter received a $20 payment, he would treat $16 as a return of his investment and $4 as income. In 1961, he changed to a cost recovery approach without requesting the Commissioner's approval. Under this approach, his receipt of another $20 payment on the same note would not constitute income unless and until total aggregate receipts equaled basis.[188] With respect to this change, the court stated:

> The issue before us is the extent to which payments received by petitioner are taxable or non-taxable—i.e., the character of the payment—not the proper method or time of reporting an item the character of which is not in question. Petitioner should no more be precluded from reporting his payments on the correct basis than a taxpayer who has previously been reporting nontaxable income as taxable income would be required to continue to do so because of his prior error.[189]

The court concluded that the payments received in the particular year were to be taken into account for tax purposes entirely in that year and that there was no issue as to whether income would be shifted from one year to another. In effect, the court held that the government should not be

---

supplied.)

[187] Wingate E. Underhill, 45 TC 489 (1966).

[188] As these facts indicate, the issue was the treatment of payments received in 1961 on obligations received prior to 1961 on which payments had been received prior to 1961 and reported on a different basis. The IRS did not challenge the taxpayer's right to determine, in the year of receipt of an obligation, the reporting method (cost recovery or pro rata) to be used for payments received on that obligation. Id. at 496 n.11. Even under the cost recovery method, interest on periodic payments of principal must be reported in accordance with the taxpayer's overall method of accounting, cash or accrual, as may be appropriate. Estate of Harlan O'Leary, 51 TCM 1073 (1986).

[189] Wingate E. Underhill, 45 TC at 496.

permitted to use the method-of-accounting rules to ignore the true character of any particular payment.

For example, if a taxpayer makes regular payments to its officers, which it characterizes as deductible compensation, the taxpayer may not rely on the rules governing methods of accounting to conclude that similar payments made in later years must always be treated as compensation without regard to their true character. If the circumstances of the particular year suggest that the payment is, at least in part, a nondeductible dividend, it must be so characterized. Similarly, if a taxpayer records sales at the time of shipment but concludes that certain shipments are, in fact, not sales but transfers to customers for a period of trial use, such shipments should not be treated as sales even if similar shipments in prior years were erroneously characterized as sales.[190]

A characterization issue similar to that in *Underhill* subsequently arose in *Herbert S. Witte*.[191] In 1956 and 1957, the taxpayer bought real estate, subdivided it, and sold it to various purchasers. The sales contracts called for 10 percent down with the balance, plus interest at 6 percent, to be paid at the rate of one percent of the sales price per month until payment was completed. Such contracts normally sold for a discount of 25 to 50 percent from face value. The particular contracts in question were worth 75 percent of face value. Although the taxpayer initially reported income from these transactions on a cost recovery method, he argued in the Tax Court that this method was erroneous and that the sales should have been reported as completed transactions in the years made. As a consequence, he argued that in the later years that were before the court, only the interest received under the contracts and the applicable pro rata portions of discounts should have been included in income. To illustrate, assume that land with a basis of $60 was sold in 1956 for $10 plus a land contract with a face value of $100 and

---

[190] See Tech. Adv. Mem. 8947004 (Aug. 17, 1989), which involved a partnership's deduction for the cost of producing goods that it distributed in kind to its partners, i.e., the partnership did not sell the goods to the partners. Shortly after the distribution, a corporate partner determined that the appropriate treatment was for the cost of producing these goods not to be deducted by the partnership but, instead, to be treated as the corporation's cost of the goods sold in the year in which the corporate partner sold the goods. The National Office concluded that this change in treatment did not amount to a change in method of accounting, citing Wingate E. Underhill, 45 TC 489 (1966), and stating that "[c]orrecting determinations regarding the taxability or nontaxability of income, including determinations of income character, are not changes in methods of accounting because the determinations do not involve the proper time for the inclusion of an item in income or the taking of a deduction." Compare Diebold, Inc. v. United States, 89-1 USTC ¶ 9141 (Cl. Ct. 1989), where a change in character—from inventory items to depreciable property—was found to involve a change in the time when items of income or expense would be recognized.

[191] Herbert S. Witte, 31 TCM 1137 (1972), rev'd, 513 F2d 391 (DC Cir. 1975).

a fair market value (FMV) of $75. The petitioner argued that he should have reported $25 of gain in the year of sale,[192] with interest plus 25 percent of each payment on the note included in income as received.

The IRS agreed with the petitioner that the sales were completed transactions in the years made. Nevertheless, the IRS argued that since the petitioner had used the cost recovery method in the prior years, he could not change his method for purposes of reporting income in the years before the court without the prior approval of the Commissioner. Purportedly relying on *Underhill*,[193] the Tax Court held for the taxpayer. However, the Tax Court in fact went further than it had in *Underhill* and suggested that the prior approval of the Commissioner was not necessary to change an erroneous method of accounting.[194] On appeal, the Court of Appeals for the D.C. Circuit reversed. However, its reversal was based on its view that even an erroneous method could not be changed without the prior approval of the IRS. The court of appeals distinguished *Underhill*.[195]

Where an item is under no circumstance includable in income or deductible as an expense, the later, proper inclusion or deduction of a related item does not amount to a change in accounting method. For example, in *Schuster's Express Inc.*,[196] the improper deduction of estimated expenses did not amount to a method of accounting. Thus, the later, proper deduction of actual expenses did not amount to a change in method of accounting.[197] This

---

[192] Cash of $10 plus the FMV of the contract of $75 minus basis of $60.

[193] Wingate E. Underhill, 45 TC 489 (1966).

[194] See discussion supra ¶ 9.05[2] and quote cited supra note 116.

[195] The court of appeals in *Witte* also noted that the first sentence of the quote, discussed supra ¶ 9.07, text accompanying note 116, was relied on by the court in Poorbaugh v. United States, 423 F2d 157, 163 (3d Cir. 1970), for the proposition that *Underhill* did not stand for the "proposition that because an erroneous accounting method was adopted by the taxpayer he should not be subject to the tax consequences resulting from that method absent a consent to change it." Herbert S. Witte, 513 F2d 391, 393 n.5 (DC Cir. 1975). But see Crosley Corp. v. United States, 229 F2d 376 (6th Cir. 1956), where the court held that a taxpayer, who had incorrectly expensed particular expenditures in earlier years, could begin capitalizing similar current expenditures, and such change was not a change in accounting method. For discussion of authorities suggesting that an incorrect method may be changed to a correct method without the need for prior approval, see discussions at ¶ 8.07[2][b], and supra ¶ 9.05.

[196] Schuster's Express, Inc., 66 TC 588 (1976), nonacq. 1978-2 CB 4, aff'd per curiam, 562 F2d 39 (2d Cir. 1977).

[197] In Rev. Rul. 81-93, 1981-1 CB 322, the IRS announced that it disagreed with the holding in *Schuster's Express Inc.* and would not follow it. However, this disagreement was not with the principle being addressed. For instance, in Tech. Adv. Mem. 8947004 (Aug. 17, 1989), the National Office concluded that a corporate taxpayer's proper treatment (as nondeductible expenditures) of production costs incurred by a partnership in which it was a partner amounted to a change in character and not to a change in method of accounting.

circumstance must be contrasted with the termination of a practice that would result in a shifting or change in the time when legitimate deductions may be obtained.[198]

Finally, as is often the case in this area of law, the decision of a court may avoid dealing with the issue directly. For instance, in *City Gas Co. of Florida*,[199] the taxpayer obtained "security deposits" for gas, with the deposits to be returned at the time final services were rendered and gas provided. The primary issue was whether the asserted deposits were, in fact, nontaxable deposits or taxable advance payments for goods. The court found that the asserted deposits were advance payments. This conclusion required the court next to determine whether the corrected reporting of the advance payments amounted to a change in method of accounting. Although the court found that such a change occurred, it seemed to base its decision on its finding that the deposit was in fact a prepayment for gas to be sold during the customer's final period of service. Having made this initial determination, it was relatively easy to frame the issue as whether a change in the time for recognizing income for gas sold during the final period (from the final period to the period of prepayment) was a change in method. If the facts had permitted the court to frame the issue only in terms of the character of the initial payment, the conclusion of the court might have been different.

¶ 9.08 TECHNIQUES FOR CHANGES WITHOUT PRIOR APPROVAL

Many taxpayers believe that it is not possible to change from one method of accounting to another without the prior approval of the IRS. Although this belief is certainly supported by the applicable Code provisions and Treasury regulations previously discussed, it is not entirely correct. Techniques do exist that permit taxpayers to effect the equivalent of changes in accounting methods without the need for the prior approval of the Commissioner. The IRS is aware of these techniques and sometimes expresses frustration because of them, but it has not sought regulatory or legislative changes to prevent their use.

The opportunity for using any of these techniques to effect such a change without the need for prior approval is especially helpful where a taxpayer finds that while it is using an acceptable method of accounting, the method is not as beneficial to the taxpayer as another method would be. Similarly, such techniques are quite useful for a taxpayer who would like to change from an improper method but who would prefer (for one reason or another)

---

[198] See Copy Data, Inc., 91 TC 3 (1988). See also Priv. Ltr. Rul. 8643029 (July 25, 1986).

[199] City Gas Co. of Fla., 47 TCM 971 (1984).

to avoid the filing of an application for change.[200] A typical example of the former case is where a service company using an accrual method would like to change to the cash method in order to defer the recognition of income on services rendered until payment is received. In this case, the taxpayer may file an application to change from its present accrual method to the desired cash method, but it is rare for the IRS to approve these changes without substantial business reasons and, as a practical matter, it is doubtful that sufficient business reasons could be demonstrated to the satisfaction of the IRS. An example of the latter case is where a taxpayer wants to change from an improper inventory method but does not want to disclose the use of its method to the National Office. In either case, use of one or more of the following techniques may prove helpful.

[1] The Drop-Down

The drop-down involves the transfer of some portion of the taxpayer's business to a newly formed corporation that under applicable tax law, is permitted to adopt its own methods of accounting in its initial year of operations. The new corporation will thereafter operate the transferred portion of the business using the desired methods of accounting.[201]

The newly formed corporation must be a legitimate, viable entity, not merely a sham corporation that may be disregarded for tax purposes. The principal issues that arise in connection with this technique are whether the initial transfer is tax-free, whether it involves a reorganization under which attributes of the transferor will carry over to the transferee, and whether Section 269 may be used by the Commissioner to disallow the benefits of the new method.[202]

---

[200] Assuming the advantages of the corporate form of organization are not essential, this technique may also be used through transfers from corporations to a newly formed partnership. See, e.g., Jerry Fong, 48 TCM 689 (1984), where grocery store managerial activities were transferred from accrual basis corporations to a newly formed cash basis partnership.

[201] See discussion supra ¶ 9.04[2].

[202] Section 269(a) provides:
IN GENERAL. -If-
(1) any person or persons acquire, or acquired on or after October 8, 1940, directly or indirectly, control of a corporation, or
(2) any corporation acquires, or acquired on or after October 8, 1940, directly or indirectly, property of another corporation, not controlled, directly or indirectly, immediately before such acquisition, by such acquiring corporation or its stockholders, the basis of which property, in the hands of the acquiring corporation, is determined by reference to the basis in the hands of the transferor corporation, and the principal purpose for which such acquisition was made is evasion or avoidance of Federal income tax by securing the benefit of a deduction, credit, or other allowance which such person or corporation would

[a] Section 351 Transfers

Section 351 provides that no gain or loss will be recognized on the transfer of property to a newly formed corporation in exchange for stock or securities in that corporation if the transferors are in control of the corporation following the transfer. The control requirement is met if the transferor owns at least 80 percent of the total combined voting power of all classes of stock entitled to vote and at least 80 percent of the total number of shares of all classes of stock immediately after the exchange.[203] The tax bases of the properties transferred will be carried over to the transferee subsidiary.[204]

Assuming that the Section 351 transfer is handled properly, the newly formed corporation will be entitled to adopt its own methods of accounting with respect to the business it will conduct. Because it is a valid newly formed corporation, it may adopt these methods of accounting on its initial return without the prior approval of the IRS.

There are frequently many sound business reasons for such restructurings in addition to the tax accounting benefits. For example, it may be helpful to decentralize business activities in order to provide better profit center analyses, to give employees associated with a particular operation's activities an opportunity to share in the earnings of those activities alone, or to give those employees an equity interest in the entity itself. Decentralization may also help the business develop a local identity that in turn may enhance its image in the community.[205]

As discussed in the following section, it is generally not possible to transfer a substantial portion of the business at one time. Taxpayers sometimes effect the change in reporting through a series of transfers over a period of years. The period of years over which the series of transfers may be made is often not significantly different from the number of years over which a Section 481 adjustment would have been spread had the transferors applied for a change in method of accounting and then received permission to make the change.

[b] Section 368 Reorganizations

The newly formed corporation will be permitted to adopt the desired method of accounting only if the transfer is not a reorganization under

---

not otherwise enjoy, then the Secretary may disallow such deduction, credit, or other allowance. For purposes of paragraphs (1) and (2), control means the ownership of stock possessing at least 50 percent of the total combined voting power of all classes of stock entitled to vote or at least 50 percent of the total value of shares of all classes of stock of the corporation.

[203] IRC § 368(c).

[204] IRC § 362.

[205] The transfers may possibly be attacked by the IRS if there are no substantial business reasons for the transfers.

Section 368(a)(1)(C), which pertains to a transfer of substantially all of one corporation's assets in exchange solely for voting stock of another corporation.[206] If the transfer does qualify as such a reorganization, a carryover of accounting methods from the transferor to the transferee will be required.[207]

Two obvious means exist for preventing an application of the carryover rules as they would apply to reorganizations under Section 368(a)(1)(C). First, the transferor may arrange the transaction so that it will receive nonvoting stock and debt obligations as well as voting stock. This will take the transfer out of the scope of Section 368(a)(1)(C). The IRS might argue that since the nonvoting stock and debt would be held in the same proportion as the voting stock, there is in reality only one class of stock. The likelihood of an IRS attack along this line is uncertain because of a lack of precedent under Section 368 for treating debt and nonvoting stock as equivalent to voting stock. Even if nonvoting stock and debt obligations are not treated as voting stock, a transfer may be classified as a Section 368(a)(1)(C) reorganization if the voting stock portion of the consideration received has an FMV that is equal to at least 80 percent of FMV of the properties of the transferor.[208] Thus, to avoid application of the carryover of the tax attributes rule, it is prudent to make sure that the aggregate FMV of any nonvoting stock and debt obligations involved in the exchange exceeds 20 percent of the value of the property transferred.[209]

Second, the transferor may limit the amount of property to be transferred so that the newly formed corporation will receive less than substantially all the transferor's assets as required by Section 368(a)(1)(C). If the transferor attempts to avoid the substantially-all condition by making a series of transfers to several newly formed corporations over a period of years, the IRS might argue that the transfers or transferees should be treated collective-

---

[206] IRC § 368(a)(1)(C) defines a "reorganization" to include

the acquisition by one corporation in exchange solely for all or a part of its voting stock (or in exchange solely for all or a part of the voting stock of a corporation which is in control of the acquiring corporation), of substantially all of the properties of another corporation, but in determining whether the exchange is solely for stock the assumption by the acquiring corporation of a liability of the other, or the fact that property acquired is subject to a liability, shall be disregarded.

[207] See infra ¶ 9.08[2] for discussion of Section 381(c)(4) provisions.

[208] IRC § 368(a)(2). This section will not apply if the subsidiaries are not treated collectively as one "transferee." IRC § 368(a)(2)(B)(i).

[209] The drop-down transfers will be subject to the accounting method carryover rule of Section 381(c)(4) if they qualify as reorganizations under Section 368(a)(1)(F), which applies to "a mere change in identity, form, or place of organization, however effected." See Gordon v. Comm'r, 424 F2d 378 (2d Cir. 1970), cert. denied, 400 US 848 (1970), where the court indicated in dictum that transfers similar to the ones previously discussed might qualify as an F reorganization.

ly as one transfer and transferee so that the substantially-all requirement is met. However, there is no case law directly on this point.

[c] Section 269 Acquisitions

Section 269 is another potential impediment to use of the drop-down technique. It provides that if any person[210] acquires control of a corporation,[211] or any corporation acquires property of another corporation,[212] and the principal purpose for that acquisition is tax evasion or avoidance by securing the benefit of a deduction, credit, or other allowance that such person or corporation would not otherwise enjoy, then the Commissioner may disallow such deduction, credit, or other allowance.

To acquire "control" of a corporation under Section 269(a)(1) means to own stock possessing at least 50 percent of the total combined voting power of all classes of stock entitled to vote, or at least 50 percent of the total value of shares of all classes of stock of the corporation.[213] The regulations indicate that a stock acquisition, as well as the organization of one or more new corporations, may be viewed as an "acquisition" for purposes of Section 269(a)(1).[214] Thus, the creation of a separate subsidiary in connection with a proposed Section 351 transfer will satisfy the threshold "acquisition of control" test of Section 269(a)(1).

Whether use of the new method of accounting constitutes the type of otherwise unavailable allowance or tax benefit that may be disallowed under Section 269 will depend on an examination of "the basic purpose or plan which the deduction, credit or other allowance was designed by the Congress to effectuate."[215] In *Rocco, Inc.,*[216] the issue was whether the Commissioner was empowered under Section 269 to require a newly created cash basis farming subsidiary of an accrual basis parent to adopt the accrual method of accounting. The Tax Court observed that the Commissioner's power under Section 269 is not limitless, and that Section 269 had not been applied in situations where corporations were organized to take advantage of provisions that represent a deliberate grant of tax benefits to a specified class of taxpayers.[217] The court indicated that the "privilege consciously granted" to

---

[210] Section 7701(a)(1) indicates that "person" includes a corporation. See also Treas. Reg. § 1.269-1(d).

[211] See IRC § 269(a)(1).

[212] See IRC § 269(a)(2).

[213] See IRC § 269(a)(1).

[214] Treas. Reg. § 1.269-3(b).

[215] Treas. Reg. § 1.269-2(b).

[216] Rocco, Inc., 72 TC 140 (1979).

[217] Id. at 152. It should be noted that although the Commissioner objected to the subsidiary's election of the cash method of accounting, he did not "invoke directly the

farmers to use the cash method of accounting was analogous to the benefits considered beyond the reach of Section 269.[218]

Although the *Rocco* decision is helpful to taxpayers, it is not clear how it will be applied in other circumstances. For instance, the regulations define the term "allowance," as it is used in Section 269, very broadly as referring to "anything in the internal revenue laws which has the effect of diminishing tax liability."[219] Further, the Tax Court in *Rocco* was obviously influenced to some extent by the special accounting treatment provided to farmers. Finally, despite dicta in *Rocco* questioning whether the Commissioner had "overstepped the bounds in applying section 269 in this case," the Tax Court did not in fact actually decide that question. Rather, it ultimately held that the principal purpose of the transaction was not tax avoidance. Thus, it is possible that the tax benefit gained by a taxpayer as a result of its separate incorporation could be found in some circumstances to be the type of benefit that may be disallowed under Section 269.

The critical question under Section 269 is therefore likely to be whether the principal purpose of the acquisition is tax evasion or tax avoidance. This determination is made on the basis of all the facts and circumstances surrounding a given transaction. "Evasion or avoidance" for this purpose is not limited to cases involving criminal or civil fraud penalties.[220] If the tax avoidance purpose "exceeds in importance any other purpose," then it is the principal purpose.[221]

---

various provisions of IRC Sec. 446 which limit a taxpayer's right to adopt or change to various methods of accounting." Id. at 149. Faced with a similar situation in the future, the IRS is likely to assert its authority under both Sections 269 and 446(b). The court did suggest, however, that the Commissioner would not have fared any better had he invoked Section 446 because "[e]ven under section 446 [the Commissioner] could hardly claim that the cash method would not clearly reflect the incomes of [the subsidiaries] if used consistently over the years." Id. at 154. See, e.g., Modern Home Fire & Casualty Ins. Co. v. Comm'r, 54 TC 839 (1970), where incorporation to elect Subchapter S status was immune to a challenge under Section 269; Rev. Rul. 70-238, 1970-1 CB 61, where incorporation to obtain benefits for Western Hemisphere trade corporations was found not to be a tax avoidance purpose. See also Tech. Adv. Mem. 7804006 (Sept. 30, 1977), regarding incorporation of a subsidiary electing domestic international sales corporation status; Achiro v. Comm'r, 77 TC 881 (1981), regarding incorporation to elect certain pension benefits.

[218] In Gold-Pak Meat Co., Inc. v. Comm'r, 522 F2d 1055, 1057 (9th Cir. 1975), the court noted that the regulations give "farmers a favor which comports with the general beneficence given farmers by the Congress and it is not lightly to be taken away. . . ."

[219] Treas. Reg. § 1.269-1(a). Indeed, in *Rocco*, the Tax Court noted, "On its face, the scope of section 269(a) may be broad enough to preclude the adoption of an accounting method by newly created subsidiaries if the requisite tax avoidance purpose is present." Rocco, Inc., 72 TC 140, 152 (1979).

[220] Treas. Reg. § 1.269-1(b).

[221] Treas. Reg. § 1.269-3(a)(2).

In *Rocco*, the court was influenced by the fact that the parent corporation had historically conducted its various activities through separate corporations for reasons unrelated to taxes. Moreover, a minority shareholder had insisted on the separate incorporation and the establishment of a separate corporation limited the group's liability with respect to the operations of the subsidiary. Further, the use of a separate subsidiary for these operations was consistent with the custom in the industry. Finally, the parent corporation did not consult a tax advisor with respect to the advantages of establishing a separate corporation on a cash basis. In short, there was "no convincing evidence" that the principal purpose of the transaction was tax avoidance.[222]

[2] Carryover Tax Attributes in Certain Corporate Acquisitions

Section 381 focuses on various tax attributes that are carried over from one corporation to another in the case of certain corporate acquisitions. These involve the acquisition of assets by one corporation from another in transactions to which Sections 332 and 361 apply. Section 332 relates to liquidations of subsidiaries; Section 361 relates to nonrecognition of gain or loss to corporations in the case of certain reorganizations.

If Section 381 is applicable, then the provisions of Sections 381(c)(4) and 381(c)(5) apply:

(4) *Method of accounting.*—The acquiring corporation shall use the method of accounting used by the distributor or transferor corporation on the date of distribution or transfer unless different methods were used by several distributor or transferor corporations or by a distributor or transferor corporation and the acquiring corporation. If different methods were used, the acquiring corporation shall use the method or a combination of methods of computing taxable income adopted pursuant to regulations prescribed by the Secretary.

(5) *Inventories.*—In any case in which inventories are received by the acquiring corporation, such inventory shall be taken by such corporation (in determining its income) on the same basis on which such inventories were taken by the distributor or transferor corporation,

---

[222] *Rocco* involved a challenge by the Commissioner with respect to the formation of each of two subsidiary corporations. The Commissioner contended, inter alia, that each subsidiary merely *continued* a business previously conducted in the parent corporation and therefore accomplished a change in accounting method without the Commissioner's consent. In fact, the Tax Court found that one of the subsidiaries continued the parent's business where the other subsidiary was engaged in a new business. Moreover, the Tax Court dismissed the significance of the point by stating, "Here [the subsidiaries] were organized and operated as separate corporations and they were entitled to elect the cash method of accounting, regardless of whether their businesses were separate and distinct from [the parent's business]." Rocco, Inc., 72 TC 140, 153–154 (1979).

unless different methods were used by several distributor or transferor corporations or by a distributor or transferor corporation and the acquiring corporation. If different methods were used, the acquiring corporation shall use the method or combination of methods of taking inventory adopted pursuant to regulations prescribed by the Secretary.

The regulations under Section 381 concerning situations where the transferor and transferee corporations are on different methods of accounting provide that if the transferred business is to be continued as a separate business after the transfer, then the methods of accounting employed prior to the transfer shall be continued.[223] If the businesses of the transferor and transferee are integrated after the transfer, the acquiring corporation shall adopt the principal method of accounting as the method of accounting to be followed, assuming that the principal method clearly reflects the income of the acquiring corporation. The appropriate adjustment must be made to reflect the change in method of accounting, but the change may be made without the prior approval of the Commissioner.

The principal method of accounting with respect to the integrated businesses is determined immediately after the transfer by reference to the methods of accounting used by each of the businesses prior to the transfer. The determination of the principal method is based on a comparison of the total of the adjusted bases of the assets immediately preceding the date of transfer and the gross receipts for a representative period (ordinarily the most recent period of 12 consecutive months) of the component trades or businesses that are integrated.

To illustrate application of the foregoing principles, assume that two corporations provide services, that one uses the cash method, and that the other uses an accrual method. If the accrual method corporation acquires the cash method business in a Section 381 transaction and thereafter operates the acquired business as a separate and distinct business, the acquired business may continue to use the cash method.[224] However, if the acquired business is integrated into the acquiring corporation's accrual business, the resulting integrated business must use the method that was the principal method at the time of the Section 381 transaction. Accordingly, if the assets and gross receipts of the accrual method business were greater than those of the cash method business, the integrated business would be required.[225]

---

[223] Treas. Reg. §§ 1.381(c)(4)-1, 1.381(c)(5)-1.

[224] Treas. Reg. § 1.381(c)(4)-1(b)(2).

[225] Treas. Reg. § 1.381(c)(4)-1(c). In circumstances where there is no principal method of accounting or the taxpayer desires not to follow the required principal method, the consent of the Commissioner is necessary to depart from use of the principal method. Treas. Reg. § 1.381(c)(4)-1(d). Care must be taken in pursuing any restructurings to achieve changes in methods of accounting lest the automatic rules not be satisfied. See, e.g., Priv. Ltr. Rul. 8950025 (Sept. 18, 1989), where the Commissioner was able to determine the method to be used following a Section 381

These regulations under Section 381 make it possible for a taxpayer that is on one method of accounting to acquire or form a new business that operates on a different method of accounting. At some point in the future, the two businesses may be merged and integrated, with the principal method to be continued thereafter. Thus, the merger may have the effect of permitting a change in method where the Commissioner might otherwise decline to approve the change.

This integration approach is particularly attractive where taxpayers have, over the years, acquired a number of operating subsidiaries, each of which may have its own particular methods of accounting. The integration or merger of the subsidiaries' various businesses may result in the desired method of accounting being predominant and thereafter continued for the entire business. This approach also affords the opportunity of aggregating several smaller businesses, which are already on the desired method, into a larger business that in turn would thereafter be using the principal method for purposes of subsequent acquisitions.

Although it may take several years for this strategy to accomplish an overall change in methods of accounting, this period may not be a significant burden. For example, if a taxpayer were to receive IRS approval of a change from one method of accounting to another, the change is generally effected with the Section 481 adjustment taken into account over a period of years. Often, the period of years it would take to effect all the previously described transactions is no greater than the Section 481 spread period.[226]

[3] Transfers of Business Growth

Another option that avoids virtually all risks but allows taxpayers to use the desired method of accounting prospectively is the formation of a new corporation to conduct the taxpayer's business in a new geographic area, in a new product line, or in some other manifestation of growth of the business. Business may be developed in that new corporation and reported under the methods of accounting adopted by it. In many cases, management can make decisions that allow much, if not all, of the growth of the entire organization to be realized through that newly formed corporation. Although there is no change in method of accounting for the existing business, this approach permits a substantial amount of the growth of the business to be reported under the new method of accounting.

---

transaction where no method was found to be the principal method. Had the taxpayers in the ruling structured their transactions over a period of years using a combination of Section 351 transfers, purchases and sales, and other techniques, they might have been able to achieve their desired methods of accounting without running afoul of the regulations under Section 381.

[226] See discussion at ¶ 8.04 for such spread periods.

CHAPTER 10

Accounting Periods

¶ 10.01   Need for Accounting Periods 10-3

¶ 10.02   Taxable Year 10-4
     [1]   Annual Accounting Period 10-4
        [a]   General Definition 10-4
        [b]   Significance of Books 10-5
     [2]   52–53 Week Year 10-6
     [3]   Short Periods 10-7
        [a]   Change in Accounting Periods 10-7
           [i]   Change in year requested and approved 10-8
           [ii]   Change in year required—Joining or leaving
              consolidated group 10-8
           [iii]   Change in year required—Joining or leaving
              partnership 10-9
        [b]   Taxpayer in Existence for Less Than Entire Year 10-9
        [c]   Jeopardy Assessments 10-10
     [4]   FSCs and DISCs 10-11

¶ 10.03   Selection of Taxable Year 10-11
     [1]   Business Considerations—Natural Business Year 10-12
     [2]   Tax Considerations 10-13

¶ 10.04   Adoption of Taxable Year 10-14
     [1]   Taxpayer Choice 10-14
     [2]   Time of Adoption 10-15
     [3]   Means of Adoption 10-16
     [4]   Rules Affecting Particular Taxpayers 10-16
        [a]   Individuals 10-16
        [b]   Regular Corporations 10-17
           [i]   General rules 10-17
           [ii]   First taxable year—New corporation 10-17
           [iii]   First taxable year—Successor corporation 10-18
           [iv]   First taxable year—Reactivated dormant
              corporation 10-19
        [c]   Partnerships and Partners 10-19
           [i]   Ordering rules under 1986 Act 10-19
           [ii]   Sufficient business purpose rules 10-20
           [iii]   Required change in year 10-22

[iv] Effect of 1986 Act on business decisions 10-23
[d] S Corporations and Shareholders 10-24
[e] Personal Service Corporations 10-25
[f] Other Entities 10-26
   [i] Trusts and estates 10-26
   [ii] Members of an affiliated group 10-27
   [iii] Real estate investment trusts 10-27
[5] Adoption of 52-53 Week Taxable Year 10-27

¶ 10.05   Change in Taxable Year 10-29
[1] Reasons for Change in Taxable Year 10-29
[2] Requirements for Change in Taxable Year 10-30
[a] Substantial Business Purpose 10-30
[b] Conform to Natural Business Year 10-30
[c] Circumstances Not Amounting to Substantial Business
   Purpose 10-31
[d] Request for Change Within 10 Years of Prior Change ... 10-32
[e] Deferral or Distortion of Income Resulting From
   Change 10-32
[f] Change to Conform to Annual Accounting Period 10-34
[g] Change to or From 52-53 Week Taxable Year 10-34
   [i] Without prior approval 10-34
   [ii] With prior approval 10-35
[3] Applications for Change in Taxable Year 10-36
[a] Form 1128 10-36
[b] Taxpayer Acceptance of IRS Approval 10-37
[c] Return Due Before IRS Determination 10-37
[4] Requests for Change Affected by Nature of Taxpayer 10-38
[a] Individuals 10-38
[b] Corporations 10-39
   [i] Automatic change per regulations 10-39
   [ii] Automatic change per revenue procedure 10-40
   [iii] Special rules 10-42
[c] Partnerships, S Corporations, and Personal Service
   Corporations 10-43
   [i] Deferral of three months or less 10-43
   [ii] Change to natural business year 10-45
   [iii] Corporate partners 10-46
[d] Other Entities 10-46
   [i] Exempt organizations 10-46
   [ii] Taxpayer with no prior accounting period 10-47
[5] Computation of Taxable Income for Short Period 10-47
[a] Normal Annualization 10-48
[b] Alternative Method of Annualization 10-50

¶ 10.06   Special Requirements Affecting 52-53 Week Taxable Years 10-52
[1] General 10-52
[2] Effective Dates 10-52

¶ 10.07   1987 Act: Use of Fiscal Year 10-53
[1] Section 444 Election by Partnerships, S Corporations, and
Personal Service Corporations 10-54
[a] Background 10-54
[b] Conditions for Making Section 444 Election 10-55

[2] Termination of Section 444 Election 10-55
[3] Tiered Structures 10-55
    [a] De Minimis Rules 10-56
    [b] Same-Taxable-Year Exception 10-57
[4] Limitations on Deferral Period 10-57
[5] Section 444 Election Procedures 10-58
    [a] Corporation Electing S Corporation Status 10-58
    [b] Back-Up Section 444 Election 10-59
[6] Required Payment by Partnership or S Corporation 10-59
    [a] Amount of Payment 10-59
        [i] Net base year income 10-60
        [ii] Base year, deferral ratio, and applicable payment . . . 10-60
        [iii] Special rule for base years of less than 12 months . . . 10-61
        [iv] Special rules for certain applicable election years . . . 10-61
    [b] Payment of Required Payments 10-61
    [c] Refunds of Required Payments 10-61
[7] Returns Under Section 7519 10-62
[8] Distributions or Reduced Deductions by Personal Service
Corporations 10-62
    [a] Applicable Amount 10-62
    [b] Minimum Distribution Requirement 10-63
        [i] Preceding-year test 10-63
        [ii] Three-year-average test 10-63
    [c] Adjusted Taxable Income 10-64
    [d] Maximum Deductible Amount 10-64
    [e] Disallowance of Operating Loss Carry-Backs 10-64

¶ 10.01 NEED FOR ACCOUNTING PERIODS

As a general rule, it is not possible to determine aggregate net income or loss on any particular transaction or business activity until the transaction or the activity has been concluded. Nevertheless, for both business and tax purposes, it would be highly impractical to compute income only at this point. Business decision making and government fiscal responsibility require regular, periodic determinations of income and payments of tax.[1]

The period selected for such a determination of income or loss and associated tax liability is called an accounting period. For federal income tax purposes, the accounting period for which income is computed is known as the taxable year.[2]

---

[1] See Burnet v. Sanford & Brooks Co., 282 US 359, 365 (1931), where the Supreme Court stated that the essence of any system of taxation is to produce revenue ascertainable and payable at regular intervals and allow application of practical accounting, assessment, and collection methods. See discussion of the annual accounting concept at ¶ 12.02.

[2] Section 441(a) provides: "Taxable income shall be computed on the basis of the taxpayer's taxable year." All "IRC" or "Code" references are to the Internal Revenue Code of 1986, as amended.

¶ 10.02 TAXABLE YEAR

Although worded in terms of "year," a "taxable year" may be a period ranging from much less than, to slightly more than, 12 consecutive months. Section 441 includes the following within the definition of "taxable year":

- The taxpayer's annual accounting period, whether a calendar year or fiscal year [3]
- The calendar year, if the taxpayer keeps no books, has no annual accounting period, or has an annual accounting period that otherwise does not qualify as a proper fiscal year [4]
- An annual period that varies from 52 to 53 weeks, if that period meets certain specified requirements [5]
- Any period of less than 12 months for which a return must otherwise be made [6]
- In the case of a foreign sales corporation (FSC) or a domestic international sales corporation (DISC), the same taxable year as that of the shareholder (or group of shareholders) having the highest percentage of voting power [7]

In addition, special rules restrict the taxable year available to partners of partnerships, shareholders of S corporations, and personal service corporations (PSCs). [8]

[1] Annual Accounting Period

[a] General Definition

"Annual accounting period" is the annual period on the basis of which the taxpayer regularly computes income in keeping its books. [9] That period may be either a calendar year, which is a period of 12 consecutive months ending December 31, [10] or a "fiscal year," which is defined to include both (1) a period of 12 consecutive months ending on the last day of any month other than December and (2) a 52–53 week year. [11] Except for a proper 52–

---

[3] IRC § 441(b)(1).
[4] IRC §§ 441(b)(2), 441(g).
[5] IRC § 441(f). See discussion infra ¶ 10.02[2].
[6] IRC §§ 441(b)(3), 7701(a)(23).
[7] IRC §§ 441(b)(4), 441(h). See discussion infra ¶ 10.02[4].
[8] See discussion infra ¶¶ 10.04[4][c]–10.04[4][e].
[9] IRC § 441(c).
[10] IRC § 441(d).
[11] IRC § 441(e). See discussion infra ¶ 10.02[2].

53 week year, a taxpayer may not use for its taxable year any annual period ending on a day other than the last day of a month.[12] A taxpayer whose books are maintained on the basis of an annual period not ending on the last day of the month must use the calendar year for tax purposes. [13]

[b] Significance of Books

If no books are kept and no otherwise acceptable annual accounting period exists, the taxpayer's taxable year must be the calendar year. Consequently, if a taxpayer desires a taxable year other than a calendar year, the taxpayer must establish a proper initial accounting period for book purposes. If this is done, the book period will control the accounting period to be used for tax purposes.[14]

The applicable Treasury regulations do not define what constitutes the proper keeping of books.[15] They provide only that records that are sufficient to reflect income adequately and clearly on the basis of an annual accounting period will be regarded as the keeping of books.[16]

Records that do not purport to reflect a computation of income on an annual basis will generally not be sufficient to constitute the keeping of books. For example, records consisting only of check stubs, rent receipts, and dividend statements are not regular books of account, and the maintenance of those records does not constitute the keeping of books.[17] Similarly, the sole

---

[12] See Parks-Chambers, Inc., 46 BTA 144 (1942), aff'd, 131 F2d 65 (5th Cir. 1942), where a year ending on dates between January 22 and 28 was held improper despite returns having been filed on that basis for 10 years; Rev. Rul. 85-22, 1985-1 CB 154, where a year ending exactly 12 months after the beginning of the first year was held improper because the year-end did not coincide with the last day of a month.

[13] IRC § 441(g)(3). Rev. Proc. 85-15, 1985-1 CB 516, provides the procedures by which a taxpayer using an improper taxable year may change to the calendar year. The taxpayer must file Form 1128 (Application for Change in Accounting Period), which is attached to an amended return filed on a calendar year and which specifies at the top of the form that it is filed under Rev. Proc. 85-15.

[14] See Jonas-Cadillac Co. v. Comm'r, 41 F2d 141 (7th Cir. 1930), aff'g without opinion 16 BTA 932 (1929), where use of the calendar year was held improper, since the taxpayer maintained its books and records on the basis of a fiscal year; Horace B. Brown, 1968-2 USTC ¶ 9657 (MD Fla. 1968), where a taxpayer lost its S corporation status by using a fiscal year for tax purposes while keeping its books on the basis of the calendar year.

[15] Treas. Reg. § 1.441-1(g).

[16] Id. The records are not required to be bound.

[17] Max H. Stryker, 36 BTA 326 (1937), acq. 1937-2 CB 27. See also Malcom G. Brooks, 5 TCM 181 (1946), where the court stated that informal records kept in a file together with some summary sheets contained in a binder marked "ledger" did not satisfy the books requirement; Stonegate of Blackburg, Inc., 33 TCM 956 (1974), where the court stated that it had "no need to delve into" whether a file of bills, contracts, invoices, and letters constituted books or records, because no books

act of filing an income tax return does not establish an annual accounting period or constitute the keeping of books.[18]

Where books were established and maintained by a public accountant hired for that purpose, the Tax Court found that the accountant's records, which consisted of a journal and general ledger, constituted the keeping of books for purposes of establishing an annual accounting period.[19] In addition, if a taxpayer keeps books on a particular accounting period, that period controls for tax purposes even though the taxpayer prepares financial statements on the basis of a different annual period.[20]

After a taxpayer establishes and uses the desired year for book purposes, it must thereafter use that book year consistently for tax purposes. However, the taxpayer should be able to adjust or change its book year to any other period desired or required for other, nontax purposes.[21]

[2] 52-53 Week Year

For tax purposes, the 52-53 week taxable year is regarded as a fiscal year that always ends on the same day of the week, which is always the last such day to occur in the same calendar month or the day that occurs nearest to

---

or records were offered in evidence, and the presumption was that no such records existed.

[18] See Ian W. Maclean, 73 TC 1045 (1980), where the petitioner was required to use a calendar year where he asserted that he had complete records but, with the exception of the tax return, failed to introduce such records into evidence. See also Max Freudmann, 10 TC 775 (1948), acq. 1948-2 CB 2, where evidence showed petitioners failed to keep individual books; Albert L. Dougherty, 60 TC 917 (1973), where informational returns and other items did not support use of a fiscal year.

[19] See E M. Godson, 5 TCM 648 (1946), where books were opened and kept by the public accountant who also prepared the petitioner's tax returns.

[20] See Atlas Oil & Ref. Co., 17 TC 733 (1951), acq. 1952-1 CB 1. See also Heinz Molsen, Jr., 85 TC 485 (1985), which involved the taxpayer's determination of cost of goods sold under a procedure that involved adjusting purchases and ending inventories to a specified market value. The government argued that one reason for the taxpayer's adjustment was its use of a calendar year for tax purposes (a time when there were a number of transactions requiring such adjustments) rather than the fiscal year that it used for financial reporting purposes (a time when there were relatively few, if any, such transactions). Nevertheless, there apparently was no adequate basis for the Commissioner to require a change in the taxpayer's tax year. However, in response to the Commissioner's observation, the court stated that there was no evidence that the taxpayer had attempted to manipulate its tax liability by using the calendar year, the court noting that the taxpayer had employed the calendar year for more than 50 years and that its original adoption of the calendar year was apparently to conform the tax year of the business, which was then operated as a partnership, to the taxable year of its partners.

[21] See Atlas Oil & Ref. Co., 17 TC 733 (1951), acq. 1952-1 CB 1.

the last day of the selected calendar month.[22] To illustrate, a taxpayer may select a 52–53 week year ending either on the last Saturday in November or on the Saturday nearest November 30.[23]

If the taxable year selected is one ending on a specified day last occurring in the calendar month, the taxable year will always end within that month. Depending on the day selected, the taxable year may end on the last day of the month or as many as six days before the end of the month.[24] If the taxable year selected is one ending on the same day of the week nearest to the end of the month, the year may end on the last day of the month or as many as three days before or three days after the last day of the month.[25] However, regardless of the month of reference, the 52–53 week taxable year is a fiscal year and, once adopted, must consistently be adhered to in subsequent years.

[3] Short Periods

The taxable year includes any period of less than 12 months for which a return is required.[26] A return for such a so-called short period is required (1) where there is a change in the taxpayer's annual accounting period; (2) when the taxpayer is in existence for only part of its selected taxable year;[27] and (3) when there has been a determination of the need to make a jeopardy assessment of tax under Section 6851.[28] Generally, the dates prescribed for filing the return and paying the tax for a short period are the same as the requirements for filing the return and paying the tax for any period of 12 months that ends on the same day on which the short period ends.[29]

[a] Change in Accounting Periods

Generally, a return for a short period is required whenever there is a change in the taxpayer's accounting period. This change in period may result either from approval of the taxpayer's request for change or from a change required by the Internal Revenue Code or Treasury regulations.

---

[22] IRC § 441(f)(1).

[23] Treas. Reg. § 1.441-2(a).

[24] Id.

[25] Id.

[26] IRC § 441(b)(3).

[27] IRC § 443(a).

[28] Section 6851(a)(1) permits the IRS to assess a tax immediately (i.e., to bypass normal procedural rules for assessing a tax) whenever it finds that a taxpayer intends to leave the country or transfer property out of the country to make the collection of tax more difficult. This assessment is called a "jeopardy assessment." See discussion infra ¶ 10.02[3][c].

[29] Treas. Reg. § 1.443-1(a)(1).

[i] Change in year requested and approved. When a taxpayer changes an annual accounting period, it must file a return for the period that begins on the day after the close of the former taxable year and ends on the day before the first day of the new taxable year.[30] For example, if a taxpayer changes from a calendar year to a fiscal year ending June 30, a return must be filed for the period that begins on January 1 and ends on June 30.

However, no return is required for periods of six days or less, or 359 days or more, resulting from a change to or from a 52–53 week taxable year.[31] A period of 359 days or more is treated as a full taxable year; a period of six days or less is included in the following taxable year.[32] The regulations also do not require a short period return where a change to or from a 52–53 week taxable year does not involve a change in the month on the basis of which the taxable year ends. Otherwise, a change to or from a 52–53 week taxable year does require the filing of a short-period return.

[ii] Change in year required—Joining or leaving consolidated group. When a corporation becomes a member of an affiliated group filing consolidated returns, the new corporate member of the group must adopt the taxable year of the parent and, as a consequence, must file a return for the short period prior to its inclusion within the consolidated group.[33] Similarly, if a corporation leaves a consolidated group, a short-period return is required for that portion of the taxable year during which the corporation is not a member of the group.[34]

EXAMPLE: Assume that corporations P and S are members of an affiliated group filing consolidated returns on the basis of the calendar year. On July 1, P acquires all the stock of a third corporation, X, which is on a September 30 year, and P sells all the stock of X on April 1 of the following year. In these circumstances, X must file a short-period return covering the period from October 1 to June 30 of the year of acquisition. The operations of X from July 1 to December 31 will be included in the consolidated return for the calendar year of P's acquisition of X. The operations of X from January 1 to March 31 of the following year will be included in the consolidated return for that year,

---

[30] IRC § 443(a)(1); Treas. Reg. § 1.443-1(a)(1).

[31] Treas. Reg. §§ 1.443-1(a)(1), 1.441-2(c)(5).

[32] Treas. Reg. §§ 1.443-1(a)(1), 1.441-2(c)(5).

[33] See Treas. Reg. § 1.1502-76(a). Short-period returns will also be required where a parent receives permission to change to the taxable year of its subsidiary. See also Rev. Rul. 55-80, 1955-1 CB 387, where the IRS ruled that where a parent corporation was granted permission to change its accounting period to conform to that of its subsidiaries, a consolidated return was required to be filed for the short period.

[34] Treas. Reg. § 1.1502-76(b)(2).

and X will be required to file a short-period separate return for the period April 1 to December 31 of that year, assuming that X was not sold to a different affiliated group filing consolidated returns. Note that by virtue of its acquisition and later sale, X has been changed from a fiscal year to a calendar year. When X left the consolidated group, X's taxable year did not revert back to its original taxable year.

[iii] **Change in year required—Joining or leaving partnership.** A short-period return is required when a partner changes his taxable year to conform to the partnership's year. For example, in Revenue Ruling 60-268,[35] the Internal Revenue Service (IRS) ruled that where members of a newly formed partnership were to change their taxable years from calendar years to an August 31 fiscal year to conform to the taxable year adopted by the partnership, each would have a short period ending on the last day of the partnership's first taxable year. In other words, their short-period returns would cover the period from January 1 to August 31.

[b] Taxpayer in Existence for Less Than Entire Year

If a taxpayer is not in existence for an entire taxable year, a short-period return must be filed for the taxpayer's period of existence.[36] This requirement applies to both new taxpayers and those taxpayers whose existence is terminated.

For corporate taxpayers whose existence has terminated, the final return is due on or before the fifteenth day of the third month following the month of termination.[37] For tax purposes, a corporation is not in existence after it ceases to do business, dissolves, and retains no assets even though, for purposes of state law, it may thereafter continue in existence for the purpose of winding up its affairs.[38] If the corporation's final return is filed and accepted, the taxable year ends, regardless of the corporation's possible continuance under state law. Under these circumstances, the corporation has effected a de facto dissolution for federal tax purposes.[39] On the other hand, mere inactivity of the corporation is not sufficient to end its tax existence.[40]

---

[35] Rev. Rul. 60-268, 1960-2 CB 206. See discussion infra ¶ 10.05[4][c] regarding these changes.

[36] IRC § 443(a)(2); Treas. Reg. § 1.443-1(a)(2).

[37] Treas. Reg. § 1.6072-2(a). See Rev. Rul. 71-129, 1971-1 CB 397, applying this rule to a corporation that had liquidated and made a de facto dissolution.

[38] See Treas. Reg. § 1.6012-2(a)(2). The regulations list suing and being sued as examples of activity connected with the winding up of a corporation's affairs.

[39] See Rev. Rul. 71-129, 1971-1 CB 397.

[40] See, e.g., American Coast Line v. Comm'r, 159 F2d 665 (2d Cir. 1947), where the court found that payment of its franchise tax prevented the corporation's tax existence from terminating, although there was a long period of no other activity; Rev.

The death of an individual will ordinarily require a return to be filed for the short period ending on the date of death. An exception to this rule exists in the case of the death of a married individual filing a joint return. In that case, the date of death is ignored, and the joint return filed by the surviving spouse is for the same period as if the taxable years of both spouses ended on the last day of the taxable year of the surviving spouse.[41]

Similarly, the formation or termination of a partnership can require the filing of a short-period return. As in the case of a corporation, the termination of a partnership for federal income tax purposes is not necessarily governed by state or local law.[42]

A partnership will terminate for federal income tax purposes when its operations are discontinued, and no part of any business, financial operation, or venture continues to be carried on by any of its partners in a partnership form.[43] In addition, a partnership will terminate if there is a sale or exchange of 50 percent or more in partnership capital and profits within a 12-month period.[44]

The partnership's taxable year will not close as the result of the death of a partner, the entry of a new partner, the liquidation of a partner's entire partnership interest, or the sale or exchange of less than 50 percent of the partnership.[45] Nevertheless, in each of these examples, the taxable year of the partnership will close with respect to that specific partner.[46]

[c] Jeopardy Assessments

Short-period returns are also required whenever the District Director determines that collection of a tax may be jeopardized because the taxpayer is planning to leave the country, transfer property out of the country, or take other action to make ultimate collection of the tax more difficult.[47] In such a case, the IRS may immediately terminate the taxpayer's taxable year and

---

Rul. 56-483, 1956-2 CB 933, where the IRS ruled that where, among other things, a corporation ceased all business operations, had no source of income, but retained a small sum of cash to pay state franchise taxes, it was required to file a tax return.

[41] See IRC § 6013(c); Catherine K. Poorbaugh v. United States, 69-1 USTC ¶ 9134 (WD Pa. 1968), rev'd on other grounds, 423 F2d 157 (3d Cir. 1969), where the decedent was killed July 9, 1962, his surviving widow properly filed joint tax return for herself and him for the entire year ending December 31, 1962. The return included the income of the wife for the full year and the income of the decedent from January 1, 1962 through his date of death.

[42] Treas. Reg. § 1.706.1(c)(1).

[43] See IRC § 708(b)(1)(A); Treas. Reg. § 1.708-1(b)(1)(i).

[44] See IRC § 708(b)(1)(B); Treas. Reg. § 1.708-1(b)(1)(ii).

[45] Id.; IRC § 706(c)(1).

[46] See Treas. Reg. § 1.706-1(c)(2)(i).

[47] IRC § 6851.

require the filing of a short-period return.[48] The short-period return would cover the period from the end of the taxpayer's preceding year to the date the IRS jeopardy assessment is made.[49]

The filing of a short-period return under a jeopardy termination does not relieve the taxpayer of his duty to file a return at the end of his normal taxable year.[50] The taxpayer must file a return for his normal year just as if there had been no jeopardy assessment. However, the taxpayer will be able to credit payments made pursuant to the jeopardy assessment against the tax liability that is otherwise shown on the return for the normal year.[51] Payments of tax pursuant to jeopardy assessments may be avoided by posting a satisfactory bond.[52]

[4] FSCs and DISCs

Special rules apply to FSCs and DISCS. These rules provide that the taxable year of any FSC or DISC must be the same taxable year as that of the shareholder (or group of shareholders) having the highest percentage of voting power.[53] Where more than one shareholder (or group of shareholders) has the same percentage of voting power, then the FSC or DISC may use the year of either such shareholder (or group of shareholders).[54] For this purpose, voting power is determined on the basis of the combined voting power of all classes of stock entitled to vote.[55]

¶ 10.03 SELECTION OF TAXABLE YEAR

Subject to various limitations and restrictions on the availability of particular taxable years,[56] every taxpayer has the right to adopt whichever annual accounting period it desires. By establishing the desired year as its year for computing income in keeping its books, the taxpayer is able to use that year for federal income tax purposes.

The means by which a particular taxable year is adopted and the

---

[48] Treas. Reg. § 1.6851-1(a)(2).

[49] Id.

[50] See Treas. Reg. § 1.6851-1(a)(3).

[51] Id.

[52] See Treas. Reg. § 1.6851-3.

[53] IRC § 411(h)(1).

[54] IRC § 441(h)(2).

[55] IRC § 441(h)(4).

[56] See infra ¶ 10.04[4] for discussion of special rules affecting particular taxpayers.

restrictions on the adoption of a taxable year by various categories of taxpayers are discussed later. In considering whether a taxpayer should adopt a calendar year or a particular fiscal year, the taxpayer and its advisors should take into account all relevant business and tax considerations. Full consideration is necessary because, once a taxable year has been adopted, it may generally be changed only with the prior approval of the IRS.

[1] Business Considerations—Natural Business Year

Virtually every business or industry has its own unique cycle of transactions and activities.[57] Fluctuations in the number of transactions or degree of activity vary with the peculiarities of each. For instance, these fluctuations may be seasonal, as in the case of farmers, who always plant during one period and harvest during another, or retailers whose sales generally peak during the holiday season.

Use of a calendar year by these businesses may distort income by matching the income of one business cycle against the expenses of another. Use of a calendar year may also increase administrative and financial costs and burdens by requiring the closing of the books at the time of greatest activity. Businesses, such as farmers and retailers, that are affected by these circumstances should consider use of a natural business year. "Natural business year" has been defined for financial accounting purposes as "the period of twelve consecutive months which ends when the business activities of the enterprise have reached the lowest point in their annual cycle."[58]

The IRS also recognizes the presence of a natural business year but uses a slightly different definition. The IRS has stated that the existence of a natural business year depends on the type of business and its locality, and that "[w]here a trade or business has a nonpeak period and a peak period of business, the natural business year is generally deemed to end at, or soon after, the close of the peak period of business."[59] In the IRS's view, a business does not have a natural business year if its monthly income is relatively steady throughout the year.

Subtle yet important differences exist in the definition of "natural busi-

---

[57] The Natural Business Year Committee of the American Institute of Accountants (predecessor to the American Institute of Certified Public Accountants) has published suggested fiscal years for various businesses. Although this list was last revised in 1955, it continues to be a valuable guide. Among the manufacturing businesses included are agricultural (Aug., Sept., or Oct.), automobiles (Sept.), building materials and supplies (June), furniture (Dec. or Nov.), and toys (Sept.). Among the wholesalers and retailers included are clothing (Jan.), books (June), and restaurants (June). Other businesses included are hospitals (Sept.), building contractors (Feb.), hotels (June or July), and real estate agencies (Sept.).

[58] Accountants' Handbook 2-2 (4th ed. 1985).

[59] See Rev. Proc. 74-33, 1974-2 CB 489.

ness year" for financial and tax reporting purposes. Financial accounting focuses on levels of least activity, while the IRS focuses on periods following peak activity. Although application of the two approaches often results in the same natural business year, differences may occur. For example, the IRS may conclude that the low point in the annual cycle of activity is not coincident with a natural business year on the basis that it does not follow a period of peak activity. This difference in definition is quite important where a taxpayer must obtain approval of the IRS to change to a natural business year.[60] Moreover, in the case of entities whose income is taxed to others (e.g., partnerships and S corporations), the IRS generally follows a practice of finding a natural business year only if certain mechanical tests are met.[61]

A taxpayer's adoption of the natural business year as its book and tax year often provides many business advantages. First, it facilitates the matching of interrelated items of income and expense and, therefore, may result in a fairer, more meaningful presentation of income. Second, it simplifies and lessens the cost of required year-end closing activities, such as the taking of inventory and the cutting off of purchases, sales, and similar activities. Finally, it generally facilitates and lessens the cost of an audit by the taxpayer's independent accountants.

Adoption of a 52–53 week year may yield additional business benefits. For example, the collection and measurement of accounting data on the basis of uniform weekly periods may result in more reliable and comparative financial data for management purposes. In addition, the adoption of a 52–53 week year may reduce accounting time and expense, since weekly bookkeeping entries are simplified and other accounting procedures may more easily be planned.

[2] Tax Considerations

A taxpayer's choice of the calendar year or a particular fiscal year is often made on the basis of perceived tax advantages. These advantages often arise from the progressive rate structure of the federal tax system and the potential for mismatching interrelated items of income and expense.

To benefit from the progressive rate structure, a taxpayer may choose to establish a fiscal year that is timed to end with the initial recognition of an amount of income that will be taxed at the lowest tax rates.

EXAMPLE: Assume that a taxpayer is subject to a tax rate of 15 percent on its first $50,000 of income and 25 percent on income in excess of $50,000. By choosing a tax year that ends after the recognition of $50,000 of income, the taxpayer obtains the lowest possible tax rate for

---

[60] See discussion infra ¶ 10.05.

[61] See infra ¶¶ 10.04[4][c], 10.04[4][d], 10.05[4][c][ii] for discussion of these tests.

that amount of income as well as for an equal amount of income attributable to the immediately succeeding year. In effect, this is a one-time tax benefit equal in amount to the product of the difference in tax rates and the amount of income subject to the lowest rates. In this example, assuming the taxpayer would have had $75,000 of income if its first tax year had not coincided with the recognition of $50,000, the tax savings would be $2,500.[62]

A business may also seek to benefit from a mismatching of related items of income and expense by choosing a taxable year that does not coincide with the natural business year. Where the business anticipates significant growth in its level of income, continuing benefits may be realized by use of that year.

For instance, a business may have a natural business year with expenses incurred in the fall and revenue realized in the spring. As growth or inflation occurs, the expenses may increase before being offset by increased revenues. If the taxpayer establishes a taxable year that matches the higher expenses against the income of the prior business cycle, the taxpayer will derive a continuing tax benefit.

> EXAMPLE: Assume that a taxpayer with a June 30 natural business year incurs expenses during the fall and receives revenue in the following spring and that revenues are generally 150 percent of expenses. If the taxpayer adopts a June 30 taxable year and incurs expenses of $1,000 in the fall, it will obtain $1,500 of revenue in the spring and report taxable income of $500 in its first taxable year. Assume instead that the taxpayer adopts a calendar year and that expenses and revenues increase 10 percent per year. The taxpayer will now recognize a loss of $1,000 in its first year. In its second year, the taxpayer will have a profit of $400 ($1,500 − $1,100), but this profit will be eliminated by a net operating loss carryover of $400 from the prior year. In its third year, the taxpayer will have a profit of $440 ($1,650 − $1,210), but this profit will be eliminated by a carryover of $440 of the $600 loss still available from year 1. Similar benefits may continue year after year.

¶ 10.04　ADOPTION OF TAXABLE YEAR

[1] Taxpayer Choice

In most cases, a taxpayer may adopt whatever taxable year it desires. However, limitations exist for certain taxable entities. For example, partner-

---

[62] $25,000 X (25% − 15%).

ships, S corporations, and PSCs do not have the same flexibility in selecting a taxable year as do other taxpayers.[63]

[2] Time of Adoption

The time for adopting a taxable year is rather straightforward. Generally, a taxpayer must adopt its taxable year on or before the time prescribed by law (exclusive of extensions) for filing a return for the selected taxable year.[64] This adoption requirement does not mean that the taxpayer must actually file its original return by that date or that the election of the taxable year must be made on the original return. It means only that the adoption itself[65] should occur by the due date of the return (exclusive of extensions).

These rules were followed in Revenue Ruling 68-125,[66] where the taxpayer's books and records were found to have established the adoption of the desired year prior to the due date of the return for that year. The fact that the taxpayer did not file its return within the time prescribed by law did not preclude adoption of the desired year.

The adoption of a taxable year may also be made by filing an amended return within the period in which the original return could have been filed.[67] Similarly, an application for extension of time to file an initial return may itself establish the taxable year.[68] Conversely, the mere statement of a taxable year by a new taxpayer without the filing of an initial return or the taking of other appropriate action does not constitute the adoption of a taxable year.[69]

---

[63] The restrictions on these entities are discussed infra ¶¶ 10.04[4][c]–10.04[4][e], respectively. See discussion infra ¶ 10.07 for impact of the Revenue Act of 1987 (the 1987 Act).

[64] Treas. Reg. § 1.441-1(b)(3).

[65] See infra ¶ 10.04[3].

[66] Rev. Rul. 68-125, 1968-1 CB 189.

[67] See Wilson v. United States, 267 F. Supp. 89 (ED Mo. 1967), where the original return showed the adoption of a March 31 fiscal year. Thereafter, to better match related items of income and expense, the taxpayer filed an amended return on June 14, using a May 31 fiscal year. Since the amended return was filed within the period ending two months and 15 days following the originally selected year, the court allowed the change.

[68] See Rev. Rul. 69-563, 1969-2 CB 104, where executor filed application for extension of time to file a fiduciary return indicating a calendar year, the subsequent filing of return on a fiscal year basis was found improper; Rev. Rul. 57-589, 1957-2 CB 298, where corporation's application for an extension of time to file its income tax return indicated a calendar year, the calendar year was established as the applicable accounting period.

[69] See Rev. Rul. 66-68, 1966-1 CB 197, where statement on S corporation election form that taxpayer would adopt January 31 fiscal year was held not to prevent adoption of September 30 year. (Rev. Rul. 66-68 was subsequently declared obsolete by Rev. Rul. 85-83, 1985-1 CB 291, which required taxpayers to comply with

[3] Means of Adoption

Generally, a taxpayer adopts a desired taxable year by adopting that year for the purpose of computing its book income. If the taxpayer fails to establish such books, a calendar year will be required.[70] These and other special rules applicable to certain taxable entities, including partnerships, members of affiliated groups filing consolidated returns, and real estate investment trusts (REITS), are discussed below.[71]

[4] Rules Affecting Particular Taxpayers

[a] Individuals

There are no special provisions regarding adoption of a taxable year by individual taxpayers. They must only comply with the provisions of Section 441 and the regulations thereunder. Consequently, an individual may, in his or her first return, adopt a calendar year or, if appropriate books are maintained, any fiscal year.[72] The year must be adopted on or before the time prescribed by law (not including extensions) for filing the return.[73]

As a practical matter, individual taxpayers rarely maintain books sufficient to establish a fiscal year. Consequently, they are generally required to adopt the calendar year as their taxable year. Whatever taxable period is adopted, the individual must use the same taxable period for reporting the income and expense of all business activities, regardless of type.[74]

The requirements for individuals are relatively straightforward, but a sometimes confusing matter has been the definition of "new taxpayer" with respect to nonresident aliens. "New taxpayer" is defined by the IRS as one "newly subject to tax."[75] This definition applies in determining whether an individual will be allowed to adopt a taxable year or will be required to request approval of a change from an otherwise imposed taxable year.

---

all terms and conditions of Rev. Proc. 83-25, 1983-1 CB 689, modified and superseded by Rev. Proc. 87-32, 1987-2 CB 396). Rev. Proc. 83-25 is discussed infra ¶¶ 10.04[4][c][i], 10.05[4][c][ii]. See also Rev. Proc. 87-32.

[70] See discussion supra ¶ 10.02[1][b] and infra ¶ 10.04[4][c]–10.04[4][f].

[71] See discussion infra ¶ 10.04[4]. See also Treas. Reg. § 1.441-1(b)(3).

[72] Treas. Reg. § 1.441-1(b)(3).

[73] Id. See discussion supra ¶¶ 10.04[2], 10.04[3].

[74] See Rev. Rul. 57-389, 1957-2 CB 298.

[75] See Rev. Rul. 80-352, 1980-2 CB 160, where a nonresident alien engaged in business in the United States was permitted to adopt a March 31 fiscal year without the Commissioner's approval, even though the alien was on a calendar year in his home country.

[b] Regular Corporations

[i] **General rules.** A regular, or C, corporation may adopt as its taxable year a calendar year or any fiscal year.[76] If a fiscal year is desired, the corporate taxpayer should begin maintaining books on the basis of that year and should confirm adoption of the year on its first return. The corporation should correlate its accounting, financial, and business practices with its fiscal year returns to avoid possible disqualification of its selected fiscal year on the basis of a lack of conformity.[77]

A taxpayer may use only one taxable year for all its businesses Thus for the corporate taxpayer using a fiscal year, the same fiscal year must be used for the corporation's entire business, regardless of the number of separately operated branches or divisions. If different tax years are desired for the different businesses, branches, or divisions, the businesses of each should be separately incorporated. Even then, it must be noted that a parent corporation and its separately incorporated subsidiaries may have different accounting periods and taxable years only if a consolidated return is not filed.[78]

[ii] **First taxable year—New corporation.** A new corporation's taxable year begins on the date when the corporation begins its legal existence, which, in turn, depends on state law.[79] Following the end of its taxable year, every corporation that is subject to taxation and has gross income should file an income tax return, regardless of whether it has taxable income.[80] However, a corporation is not required to file a return where it has received a charter but has not (1) perfected its organization; (2) transacted business, and (3) received income from any source.[81] Under these circumstances, the corporation may be relieved of its duty to file a return on a proper presentation of these facts to the District Director of the IRS.[82] Note that the taxpayer may be excused from filing a return, not from the need to timely adopt a fiscal year if such year is desired.

The fact that a corporation may have a dormant period during which it neither keeps books nor files returns under the exception previously noted

---

[76] IRC § 441(b). In the case of a FSC or DISC filing a return for a period of at least 12 months, the taxable year is defined under Section 441(h) according to the shareholders' percentage of voting power. See discussion supra ¶ 10.02[4]. See also discussion infra ¶ 10.04[4][e] for rules affecting personal service corporations.

[77] See discussion supra ¶ 10.02[1][b].

[78] See discussion infra ¶ 10.04[4][f][ii].

[79] C.F. Smith Co., 13 TCM 607 (1954), where the taxable year began when the articles of incorporation were filed.

[80] Treas. Reg. § 1.6012-2(a)(1).

[81] See Treas. Reg. § 1.6012-2(a)(2).

[82] Id. See Rev. Rul. 84-123, 1984-2 CB 244, which provides guidance on when a corporate taxpayer may be relieved of filing a return following bankruptcy, dissolution, or similar action; Rev. Proc. 84-59, 1984-2 CB 500, which provides procedural rules with respect to the foregoing.

raises the possibility of the corporation being deprived of its choice of taxable year. Since the corporation's first taxable year starts on the date its legal existence commences, unaffected by any exception from the need to file a return, the corporation must take action to elect a fiscal year if such a year is desired. The corporation should establish books and file its returns on the basis of the desired year. A failure to do so may result in the required use of a calendar year.

> **EXAMPLE:** Assume that a corporation is formed March 1 of year 1, no business activity occurs until November of that year, and the corporation desires to adopt a September 30 fiscal year. To adopt that year, the corporation must adopt a September 30 year for purposes of computing income in keeping books and should either prepare a return for year 1 that sets forth the adoption of that year or seek to be relieved of the need to file a return for that particular year. Otherwise, any attempt to adopt a September 30 year as if the first year ended September 30 of year 2 will be improper, by virtue of covering a period in excess of 12 months.[83] These requirements must be kept in mind to prevent a deprivation of the corporate taxpayer's choice of taxable year.

[iii] First taxable year—Successor corporation. A new C corporation is entitled to establish whatever year it desires even though it is a successor to another taxpayer, which had a different taxable year. This rule applies where the new corporation acquires its property through a 351 transfer or in connection with a corporate reorganization that is tax-free and subject to Section 381, which provides for a carry-over of other tax attributes to the new corporation. The only exception to this rule is in the case of an F reorganization, where the new entity results from a mere change in identity, form, or place of organization of the predecessor entity.[84]

The preceding rules provide interesting planning opportunities. Assume a corporate taxpayer seeks a change in its taxable year, but its application for

---

[83] See IRC § 441(g); Treas. Reg. § 1.441-1(b)(2); Calhoun v. United States, 370 F. Supp. 434 (WD Va. 1973), where failure to keep books during dormant period prevented adoption of desired fiscal year.

[84] Section 381(b) provides, "The taxable year of the distributor or transferor corporation shall end on the date of distribution or transfer" except in the case of an F reorganization. A reorganization under Section 368(a)(1)(F) results in a mere change in identity, form, or place of organization of the corporation. Under these circumstances, the part of the taxable year before the reorganization and the part after the reorganization each constitute a single taxable year. For applications of this principle, see Rev. Rul. 57-276, 1957-1 CB 126; Stauffer Estate v. Comm'r, 403 F2d 611 (9th Cir. 1968); Home Constr. Corp. of Am., 311 F. Supp. 830 (SD Ala. 1969), aff'd, 439 F2d 1165 (5th Cir. 1971).

change is denied by the IRS. The taxpayer may nevertheless achieve the desired result by transferring one or more of its businesses or, perhaps, a portion of its sole business to a newly formed corporation. The new corporation may then adopt the desired year. As long as the transfer is not an F reorganization, the adoption of the desired year by the new corporation should be allowed.[85]

[iv] **First taxable year—Reactivated dormant corporation.** A corporation is not in existence for federal tax purposes after it ceases business, dissolves, and retains no assets, whether or not it may be treated under state law as a continuing corporation for limited purposes.[86] These circumstances constitute a de facto dissolution of the corporation for tax purposes.[87] If the corporation is later reactivated, it is considered a new taxpayer and is entitled to select a new taxable year just as any other new taxpayer.[88] However, to satisfy these rules, the "old" corporation must not have carried on activities demonstrating an intent to continue its existence during the dormant period. If it engages in these activities, the corporation may be required to obtain approval of the IRS before changing its taxable year.[89]

[c] Partnerships and Partners

The taxable year of a partnership is determined as though the partnership entity were a separate taxpayer.[90] However, as a result of the Tax Reform Act of 1986 (the 1986 Act), a partnership has very limited discretion in selecting a taxable year. In most cases, a calendar year will be required.[91]

[i] **Ordering rules under 1986 Act.** Under the 1986 Act, for years beginning after December 31, 1986, the taxable year to be used by both newly

---

[85] But see infra ¶ 10.04[4][f][ii] for rules applicable to affiliated groups filing consolidated tax returns.

[86] Treas. Reg. § 1.6012-2(a)(2). See United States v. McDonald & Eide, Inc., 670 F. Supp. 1226 (D. Del. 1987), where the corporation ceased to exist as a taxpayer following (1) the expiration of Delaware's three-year-limited-existence provision for a corporation whose corporate charter is revoked for failure to pay franchise tax and (2) its cessation of all activities.

[87] See Rev. Rul. 71-129, 1971-1 CB 397.

[88] Rev. Rul. 60-51, 1960-1 CB 169.

[89] See, e.g., American Coast Line v. Comm'r, 159 F2d 665 (2d Cir. 1947), where payment of franchise taxes to prevent forfeiture of the corporation's charter was found to evidence an intention to maintain existence, and therefore the corporation was found not to be a new taxpayer on reactivation; Rev. Rul. 56-483, 1956-2 CB 933, where a corporation's retention of cash to pay state franchise tax was held sufficient to require the filing of a return even though all business had ceased.

[90] IRC § 706(b)(1); Treas. Reg. § 1.706-1(b)(1)(i).

[91] See infra ¶ 10.07 for discussion of special fiscal year system under 1987 Act.

formed partnerships and existing partnerships is determined according to the following hierarchy. First, if the same taxable year is used by partners who own a majority (more than 50 percent) interest in the partnership's profits and capital, then this year must be used by the partnership.[92] This is known as the "majority interest rule." It applies only if the taxable year of the partners owning the majority interest has been the same for the three taxable years of the partners ending on or before the taxable year of the partnership.[93]

If the partners owning the majority interest do not use the same tax year, then the partnership must adopt the same year as that used by all its principal partners.[94] This is known as the "principal partner rule." For this purpose, a "principal partner" is defined as a partner having an interest of 5 percent or more in partnership profits or capital.[95]

If all the partnership's principal partners are not on the same taxable year, then the partnership must adopt the calendar year unless, as described in the following section, it is able to use a fiscal year or such other year as may be prescribed in regulations.[96] The Treasury has promulgated regulations to prevent partners and partnerships from avoiding these rules by adopting a 52–53 week taxable year.[97]

[ii] Sufficient business purpose rules. Notwithstanding the ordering rules previously described, a partnership may use a different taxable year if it is able to establish, to the satisfaction of the IRS, a sufficient business purpose for that year.[98] In determining whether a sufficient business purpose exists, the IRS will consider all relevant facts and circumstances, including the federal income tax consequences resulting from the adoption and use of that year.[99]

The regulations in effect prior to the 1986 Act provided that the selection of a tax year to coincide with a partnership's natural business year

---

[92] IRC § 706(b)(1)(B)(i).

[93] IRC § 706(b)(4).

[94] IRC § 706(b)(1)(B)(ii).

[95] IRC § 706(b)(3).

[96] IRC § 706(b)(1)(B)(iii). See infra ¶ 10.05[5] regarding the availability of 52–53 week taxable years. Prior to the 1986 Act, Rev. Proc. 83-76, 1983-2 CB 594, allowed a newly formed partnership to adopt a calendar year without prior approval if (1) it had no principal partners; (2) all its partners were on a calendar year; or (3) all its partners not on a calendar year were concurrently changing to a calendar year. See also C.H. Leavell & Co., 53 TC 426 (1969) (joint venture deemed to be on calendar year, since all coventurers on different accounting periods); Austin Clapp, 36 TC 905 (1961), acq. 1964-1 CB 4 (Part 1), aff'd, 321 F2d 12 (9th Cir. 1963) (failure to obtain prior approval required partnership to use calendar year).

[97] See Temp. Reg. § 1.441-3T.

[98] IRC § 706(b)(1)(C).

[99] Rev. Proc. 72-51, 1972-2 CB 832. See also General Explanation of the Tax Reform Act of 1986 (May 4, 1987) (hereinafter Blue Book), at 537.

would constitute a sufficient business purpose,[100] and there was nothing in the legislative history of the 1986 Act to suggest that this rule would not be continued. However, the legislative history to the 1986 Act added that the Treasury may prescribe tests and standards to be used in determining the existence of a sufficient business purpose, and the legislative history pointed out that the following circumstances would not ordinarily be deemed to satisfy the business purpose requirement:[101]

- Use of a particular year for regulatory or financial accounting purposes
- Hiring patterns of the particular business
- Use of a particular year for administrative purposes, such as the admission of partners and the promotion of staff
- Fact that the business involves the use of price lists, models, or other items that change on an annual basis

In cases where a partnership is permitted to adopt a taxable year different from that of its partners, there will be some deferral in the recognition of partnership income by the partners. This deferral arises from the rule that a partner reports his or her share of the income from a partnership in the partner's taxable year in which the partnership's year ends.[102] For example, if on February 1 of year 4, a calendar year taxpayer becomes a partner in a January 31 fiscal year partnership, the partner will not report any partnership income in his or her calendar year 4 even though 11 months of income may already have been recognized by the partnership and distributed to the partner. The partner will recognize all income from the partnership's taxable year ending January 31 of year 5 in the partner's return for calendar year 5.

These deferrals often troubled the IRS. Nevertheless, prior to the 1986 Act, the IRS generally approved taxable years (or requests for changes in taxable years) where the requested year resulted in a deferral in the recognition of income to partners of three months or less, provided the partnership and the Commissioner could agree on the terms under which the adoption

---

[100] See Treas. Reg. § 1.706-1(b)(4)(iii), which provides the following example:

[P]artnership AB, which is on a calendar year, is engaged in a business which has a natural business year (the annual accounting period encompassing all related income and expenses) ending on September 30. The intention of the partnership to make its tax year coincide with such natural business year constitutes a sufficient business purpose.

[101] Blue Book, supra note 99, at 537. The IRS illustrated the manner in which it will take these circumstances into account in Rev. Rul. 87-57, 1987-2 CB 117, which covers partnerships, S corporations, and personal service corporations. See infra ¶ 10.07 for discussion of fiscal year option under the 1987 Act.

[102] IRC § 706(a).

would be made.[103] The 1986 Act makes it clear that even such limited deferrals will no longer be tolerated absent the existence of a sufficient business purpose for the use of the year that generates the deferral.[104]

In determining whether a taxpayer's requested year was its natural business year (and, hence, whether a change to that year would be deemed a sufficient business purpose), the legislative history of the 1986 Act approved the prior IRS policy of applying to partnerships the principles of Revenue Procedure 83-25, under which a natural business year was deemed to exist for an S corporation whenever 25 percent or more of the corporation's gross receipts for the 12-month period in question was recognized in the last two months of that period and this 25 percent requirement was also satisfied for the two immediately preceding 12-month periods.[105] Thus, any partnership that meets this test should be permitted to continue or to change to the requested year.[106]

[iii] **Required change in year.** As a result of the 1986 Act, many partnerships were required to change their tax years. This change in year was to be treated as initiated by the taxpayer with the consent of the IRS.[107] To ameliorate the effect of requiring the partners to include more than 12 months of income in a single calendar year, the 1986 Act permitted the income for the short tax period to be taken into account ratably over each of the partners' first four years (including the short taxable year) beginning after December 31, 1986, unless the partner elected to include all income in the short year.[108]

EXAMPLE: Assume that a partnership was on a February fiscal year prior to the 1986 Act and that its partners were, and were to remain, on calendar years. Under Section 706(a), each partner would have included in his 1986 calendar-year return his share of the partnership's income for its fiscal year ending February 28, 1986. As a result of the 1986 Act, each individual partner must have included his share of the partnership's 1987 fiscal year income in his 1987 calendar-year return.

---

[103] Rev Proc 72-51, 1972-2 CB 832. See Blue Book, supra note 99, at 533.

[104] IRC § 706(b)(1)(C). See Blue Book, supra note 99, at 536. But see infra ¶ 10 07 for discussion of fiscal year option under the 1987 Act.

[105] Rev Proc. 83-25, 1983-1 CB 689, modified and superseded by Rev. Proc. 87-32, 1987-2 CB 396, which provides further explanation of how the IRS intends to apply the 25 percent test. For further discussion of this test, see infra ¶ 10.05[4][c][ii].

[106] See Blue Book, supra note 99, at 536–537. See also Temp. Reg. § 1.442-2T(c) regarding the 25 percent test; Rev. Proc. 87-32, 1987- 2 CB 396, which provides additional details on how the 25 percent test will be applied.

[107] 1986 Act, § 806(e)(2).

[108] Id. See discussion infra ¶ 10.07 for additional alternative provided by the 1987 Act.

In addition, the partner's share of the partnership's income for the short period from March 1, 1987 (the first year beginning after the 1986 Act) through December 31, 1987 must also have been included in 1987 calendar-year income. Alternatively, in lieu of including 22 months of income in a single year, the partner could take the income for the 10-month short period into account ratably (25 percent in each year) over the years 1987 to 1990. If the partner believed that his effective tax rate would increase significantly in the years 1988, 1989, and 1990, as compared to his rate in 1987, he may have decided to elect to include his entire share of the partnership's income for the short period in his 1987 calendar year.

This rule permitting partners to spread their respective shares of the partnership's short-period income over a period of four years applied without regard to the nature of the entity that was the partner.[109]

[iv] Effect of 1986 Act on business decisions. The 1986 Act changes had the practical effect of requiring most partnerships to change to a calendar year.[110] This was certainly true for virtually all partnerships engaged in the practice of one of the professions such as law, medicine, accounting, and engineering.

Because partnerships were able to continue or adopt a fiscal year if they satisfied the 25 percent test, it was expected that many partnerships (particularly the smaller partnerships where decision making was controlled by only a few individuals) would attempt to time billing and collection so as to satisfy the 25 percent test. Of course, any manipulation in the timing of billing and collection activities could give rise to adjustments on audit (on the basis that the "manipulated" results did not clearly reflect income). Any such adjustments could, if sustained, cause the partnership to fail the 25 percent test and thereby lose use of the fiscal year.

For partnerships that were not able to satisfy the 25 percent test, the factors identified in the legislative history as not indicating a sufficient business purpose for a fiscal year were essentially those factors that generally would be asserted by professional partnerships as a business purpose for a fiscal year. Consequently, there seemed a clear intent on the part of Congress to require these partnerships to change their tax years, thereby preventing the partners from enjoying the deferral in the recognition of income that had previously been available.

For many of the larger partnerships (e.g., those with hundreds of partners), the new rules often required significant changes in business and operating practices. For example, although most partnerships are able to determine their aggregate incomes shortly after the close of their taxable

---

[109] Blue Book, supra note 99, at 538.

[110] But see infra ¶ 10.07 for fiscal year option under the 1987 Act.

years, many need several additional months in which to determine how that income should be allocated among their partners. This time is spent in evaluating the operating results of the partnership's various offices and the performance of each partner within those offices. Use of a fiscal year allowed the partnership sufficient time to make these evaluations before the return of the individual partners would be due. Now that the partnership's year will coincide with the years of the individual partners, the partnership may need to change its evaluation procedures to determine more promptly how its income should be allocated.

In addition, accounting partnerships were expected to face considerable increases in their work loads during the initial tax filing season. This sometimes required significant changes in the number of temporary personnel that were retained and sometimes drastically affected work levels throughout the year as compared to what they were prior to the 1986 Act.

[d] S Corporations and Shareholders

Under the 1986 Act, an S corporation may not adopt, change to, or use as its taxable year any accounting period other than a "permitted year."[111] "Permitted year" is defined as the calendar year or any other accounting period for which the corporation establishes a business purpose to the satisfaction of the Secretary of the Treasury.[112] This rule applies even where the deferral arising from the present or desired year is for a period of three months or less and regardless of when the election to be taxed as an S corporation was filed.[113]

Some of these limitations on the choice of taxable year were originally enacted as part of the Subchapter S Revision Act of 1982, which went into effect for elections made on or after October 20, 1982, and for tax years beginning in 1983.[114] Prior to the 1986 Act, an S corporation whose taxable year included December 31, 1982 (or which was an S corporation owing to an election prior to October 20, 1982) was required to use the permitted year only after a 50 percent shift in ownership.[115]

Generally, under the 1986 Act, the IRS will apply rules similar to the partnership rules in determining whether an S corporation may have a taxable year other than a calendar year.[116] Consequently, any S corporation that received permission to use a fiscal year-end (other than on the basis of the

---

[111] IRC § 1378(a).

[112] IRC § 1378(b).

[113] See IRC § 1378(b); Blue Book, supra note 99, at 535.

[114] Section 1378(c), as it existed prior to 1986 Act.

[115] Id.

[116] See generally Blue Book, supra note 99, at 533. See also Rev. Proc. 87-32, 1987-2 CB 396; discussion infra ¶ 10.07.

resulting deferral in income being three months or less) and any S corporation meeting the 25 percent test described in the preceding section will be permitted to continue its use of that year.[117] Just as in the case of partnerships, the increase in income to the shareholders of an S corporation resulting from the required use of a calendar year could be taken into account ratably over a four-year period beginning with the S corporation's first taxable year beginning after December 31, 1986.[118] The opportunity for this spread was available unless the shareholder elected to forgo the spread, and the opportunity for the spread applied without regard to the type of S corporation shareholder entity.[119]

Prior to the 1986 Act, a request to adopt a taxable year ending other than on December 31 had to be made on Form 2553 when the election to be an S corporation was filed.[120] The Treasury has promulgated new regulations and the IRS has issued new procedures on these matters as a result of the 1986 Act.[121]

As a result of the 1986 Act requirements regarding the tax year of an S corporation, individuals who desire to adopt a fiscal year may be reluctant to elect S corporation status. Although the decision to remain a C corporation will subject the income of the corporation to tax at the corporate level, which may entail higher rates, that decision may be appropriate where the corporation does not anticipate significant taxable income, such as where the salaries paid by the corporation will prevent its generation of significant taxable income, and the use of a fiscal year is very important.[122] Should the income of a corporation thereafter increase, S corporation status may be elected at that time.

[e] Personal Service Corporations

"Personal service corporation" is defined as a corporation whose principal activity is the performance of personal services and whose services are "substantially performed" by employee-owners.[123] Although the substantially performed test is not defined by the statute, the Treasury has taken the position in temporary regulations governing the adoption, retention, or change to or from a 52–53 week year that for purposes of these rules, a corporation will be treated as a PSC if at least 10 percent of the fair market value of the

---

[117] See Rev. Proc. 87-32, 1987-2 CB 396.

[118] 1986 Act, § 806(e)(2).

[119] See Blue Book, supra note 99, at 538.

[120] See Rev. Proc. 83-25, 1983-1 CB 689, modified and superseded by Rev. Proc. 87-32, 1987-2 CB 396.

[121] See Temp. Reg. §§ 1.442-2T, 1.442-3T; Rev. Proc. 87-32, 1987- 2 CB 396.

[122] See discussion infra ¶ 10.07 for impact of the 1987 Act.

[123] IRC §§ 269A(b)(1), 441(i)(2).

stock is owned by employees and the total time spent by employee-owners in rendering services is at least 10 percent of the total time spent by all employees in rendering services.[124]

Prior to the 1986 Act, PSCs generally were permitted to adopt any taxable year, subject only to the requirements applicable to other C corporations. However, the 1986 Act changed the applicable rules to require that a PSC adopt and use the calendar year as its taxable year unless it is able to establish to the satisfaction of the IRS a sufficient business purpose for adopting and using a different tax year.[125]

In effect, PSCs will be subject to the same rules applicable to partnerships and S corporations.[126] The legislative history to the 1986 Act indicates that any corporation that has elected S corporation status is not to be regarded as a PSC.[127] This legislative history also indicates a congressional intent that in the case of a corporation that is a member of an affiliated group filing consolidated returns, all members of the group will be taken into account in determining whether a corporation is a PSC. Thus, a corporation may be a PSC where the owners of the parent are employees of a subsidiary. In determining if the principal activity of a corporation is the provision of personal services, the activities of all members of the group are to be taken into account.[128]

Just as in the case of partnerships and S corporations, a PSC will be able to use a fiscal year if it satisfies the 25 percent test.[129] On the other hand, if a PSC must change to a calendar year as a result of the 1986 Act, the rules providing for a ratable inclusion of the short-period income by partners in a partnership and shareholders in an S corporation are not applicable to a PSC. This is because, unlike those partners or shareholders, the PSC is not required to include in the income of one year more than 12 months of income.[130] Finally, as part of the overall changes by the 1986 Act, Section 267, which defers a deduction for payments made by one taxpayer to a related taxpayer to the year in which the income is recognized, was amended to apply to a corporation and its employee-owners regardless of the amount of the stock owned directly or indirectly by them.[131]

[f] Other Entities

[i] Trusts and estates. Prior to the 1986 Act, estates and trusts were entitled to adopt any taxable year permissible under the Code and regula-

---

[124] Temp. Reg. § 1.441-3T(b).

[125] IRC § 441(i)(1).

[126] See Rev. Proc. 87-32, 1987-2 CB 396, and discussion supra ¶¶ 10.04[4][c], 10.04[4][d], and infra ¶ 10.07.

[127] Blue Book, supra note 99, at 536.

[128] Blue Book, supra note 99, at 536. The Blue Book indicates that a technical correction to the law may be necessary to achieve this objective.

[129] See Rev. Proc. 87-32, 1987-2 CB 396.

[130] Blue Book, supra note 99, at 538.

[131] IRC § 267(a)(2); Blue Book, supra note 99, at 538.

tions. This rule afforded an opportunity for tax deferral to the beneficiaries of the estate or the trust. To prevent this deferral, the 1986 Act changed the law to require all trusts to use the calendar year, except for charitable trusts described in Section 4947(a)(1) and tax-exempt trusts under Section 501(a).[132] A special transition rule permits a trust beneficiary to take the income from the required short period into account ratably over a four-year period beginning with the beneficiary's first taxable year beginning after December 31, 1986.[133] Apparently because estates are usually of shorter duration than trusts, no changes in pre–1986 Act law were made for estates.

[ii] **Members of an affiliated group.** Members of affiliated groups filing consolidated returns are subject to special rules that require use of the same tax year. If a new member joins an affiliated group filing consolidated returns, it must change its taxable year to that of the group.[134] This change does not require the prior approval of the IRS.[135] If the new member of the group is on a 52–53 week year, the conformity requirement is, with the Commissioner's prior approval, deemed satisfied if the taxable years of all members of the group end within the same seven-day period.[136]

[iii] **Real estate investment trusts.** REITS are required to use the calendar year as their taxable year.[137] No exceptions are provided.

[5] Adoption of 52–53 Week Taxable Year

A new taxpayer may adopt a 52–53 week taxable year for its first taxable year if it (1) keeps its books and computes its income on that basis; (2) conforms its books and computes its income on that basis; or (3) conforms

---

[132] IRC § 645.

[133] 1986 Act, § 1403(c)(2). In Notice 88-18, 1988-8 IRB 14, the IRS determined that any trust required to report income on a calendar-year basis for taxable years beginning after December 31, 1986, must annualize income earned during the short taxable year in 1987. The Commissioner's advisory group subsequently urged that this notice be withdrawn because of the significant problems it created for fiduciaries. However, this request was rejected. See Daily Tax Report (BNA) No. 53, at G-2 (Mar. 18, 1988). Thereafter, in Ann. 88-110, 1988-35 IRB 32, the IRS provided instructions for trusts to determine whether returns filed for the short period ending December 31, 1987, and annualizing income were eligible for the benefits provided under Section 443(b)(2). See discussion infra ¶ 10.05[5][b]. The application for such benefits must have been filed no later than April 17, 1989.

[134] Treas. Reg. § 1.1502-76(a)(1).

[135] Id.

[136] Id. Any request for such consent is timely if filed with the Commissioner of Internal Revenue, Washington, DC 20224, not later than the thirtieth day, excluding extensions, before the due date for filing the consolidated return.

[137] IRC § 859.

its books accordingly in closing them.[138] An additional requirement exists for a partnership that adopts a 52–53 week year. Prior to the 1986 Act, the regulations provided that a newly formed partnership could adopt a 52–53 week taxable year without the Commissioner's permission if the selected year ended either with reference to December or to the same month in which ended the taxable years of all its principal partners.[139] The legislative history to the 1986 Act indicated that the Treasury would issue regulations to prevent the avoidance of the new limitations on the tax years of partnerships and S corporations through use of a 52–53 week year. Toward this end, it was anticipated that the Treasury would suspend the operation of the regulations allowing taxpayers to adopt or change to a 52–53 week year in certain cases without the prior approval of the IRS.[140]

Temporary regulations were issued on February 4, 1987.[141] These regulations apply to any partnership, partner, S corporation, S corporation shareholder, PSC, or employee-owner that wants to adopt, retain, or change to or from a 52–53 week taxable year. The regulations also apply to a corporation that wants to adopt S corporation status and, in connection with that, wants to adopt, retain, or change to or from a 52–53 week taxable year.

The temporary regulations suspend the otherwise applicable rules and do not permit the adoption of or change to or from a 52–53 week taxable year if the principal purpose of the change or adoption is the evasion or avoidance of tax. However, taxpayers are permitted to adopt or change to the 52–53 week taxable year if the partners or shareholders, as the case may be, agree to treat the 52–53 week year as if it ended on the last day of the calendar month that ends nearest to the last day of the 52–53 week year. In other words, if a 52–53 week year ended on January 2, the calendar year partner or S corporation shareholder must agree to treat the 52–53 week year as if it ended on December 31. This requirement will prevent the operation of the 52–53 week year from causing a deferral in the recognition of income by the partner or the shareholder. Similar rules apply to PSCs. Although these temporary regulations were applicable for a limited period only,[142] they suggest the form that later, permanent regulations might take.

A new taxpayer adopts a 52–53 week taxable year by filing a statement with the return for its first taxable year. The statement must contain the following information: (1) the calendar month with reference to which the new 52–53 week taxable year ends; (2) the day of the week on which the 52–

---

[138] Treas. Reg. § 1.441-2(c)(1).

[139] Id.

[140] Blue Book, supra note 99, at 539.

[141] Temp. Reg. § 1.441-3T.

[142] With certain exceptions, Temp. Reg. § 1.441-3T was applicable where the return for the first year (or the short year) for which the election to use or retain the 52-53 week year is made was filed after September 29, 1986, and the first taxable year itself ended before January 5, 1987. Temp. Reg. § 1.441-3T(f).

53 week taxable year always will end; and (3) whether the 52–53 week taxable year will always end on (a) the date on which such day of the week falls last in the calendar month or (b) the date on which such day of the week last occurs that is nearest to the last day of the calendar month.[143] Once adopted, the taxpayer must thereafter keep its books and report income on the basis of the 52–53 week taxable year unless the Commissioner approves a change in taxable year.[144]

¶ 10.05 CHANGE IN TAXABLE YEAR

Section 442 provides, "If a taxpayer changes his annual accounting period, the new accounting period shall become the taxpayer's taxable year only if the change is approved by the Secretary." This provision makes it clear that a taxpayer may change its accounting period for nontax purposes without the prior approval of the Commissioner. However, if the change is desired for tax purposes, the Commissioner's prior approval must be obtained, or the change must otherwise be authorized under applicable regulations.[145]

[1] Reasons for Change in Taxable Year

A taxpayer may realize both business and tax benefits from a timely, well-planned change of tax year. The business benefits are most easily illustrated by the case of a taxpayer whose business has a natural business year that differs from its taxable year. A change to the natural business year for tax purposes may have the practical benefits of reducing the cost of taking inventory, increasing the time available to handle year-end matters, and lowering accounting and administrative costs.

Tax benefits might include accelerating the effective date of a favorable change in the tax law, delaying the effective date of an unfavorable change in law, achieving an acceleration in the recognition of expense or a deferral in the recognition of income, or cutting off a year, which may later become unprofitable, to offset the profits already obtained by a net operating loss (NOL) that might otherwise expire. Of course, the opportunity to realize these benefits depends on approval of the change, which may be denied if the request is premised solely on tax benefits. Even if the change is not premised

---

[143] Treas. Reg. § 1.441-2(c)(3).

[144] Treas. Reg. § 1.441-2(c)(1).

[145] Treas. Reg. § 1.442-1(a).

on tax benefits, the IRS may seek to condition its approval of the change on a limitation or denial of associated tax benefits.[146]

A taxpayer considering a change in taxable year must balance its ability to avail itself of potential advantages against potential disadvantages. Since a short year is treated as a full taxable year,[147] a change in taxable years may have a detrimental effect by causing a loss of unused NOL carryovers or other carryovers resulting from capital losses, charitable contributions, and investment credits.

[2] Requirements for Change in Taxable Year

[a] Substantial Business Purpose

The regulations provide that a request for change in tax year will generally be approved only where the taxpayer establishes to the Commissioner's satisfaction a substantial business purpose for the change.[148] The regulations add that in determining whether a substantial business purpose has been established, the Commissioner will consider all the facts and circumstances relating to the change, including the resulting tax consequences,[149] and the effect of the change on the taxpayer's annual cycle of business activity.[150]

However, the regulations themselves do not specify or illustrate what reasons will satisfy the substantial business purpose test. As discussed in the following section, the IRS has ruled that a change to a natural business year will be deemed to satisfy the test, but no other guidance has been provided. Presumably, factors that significantly reduce the costs and burdens associated with the year-end closing of the books should be important. Similarly, changes to years generally used by others in the same business or industry should be important, particularly where the change will facilitate the presentation of comparative data to creditors, shareholders, and government.

[b] Conform to Natural Business Year

The substantial business purpose requirement is deemed satisfied if the desired taxable year coincides with the taxpayer's natural business year.[151]

---

[146] In recognition of this potential for using changes in accounting periods to obtain tax benefits, the Treasury issued temporary regulations to prevent these benefits from being realized in connection with the 1986 Act. See Temp. Reg. § 1.441-3T.

[147] See discussion supra ¶ 10.02[3].

[148] Treas. Reg. § 1.442-1(b)(1).

[149] Id.

[150] Id. The regulation refers to this as a nontax factor to be considered.

[151] See Rev. Proc. 74-33, 1974-2 CB 489.

The IRS defines "natural business year" principally in terms of levels of activity. Although stating that a natural business year depends primarily on the type of business and its locality, where a trade or business has a peak and a nonpeak period of business, the natural business year is generally deemed to end at, or soon after, the close of the peak period of business. A business whose income is steady from month to month is deemed not to have a natural business year.[152]

If a taxpayer requests a change in taxable year to conform to a natural business year, the taxpayer must include in the application for change a statement indicating gross receipts from sales or services and approximate inventory costs for each month of the short period and the three preceding taxable years. Absent substantial distortion of income or other factors showing that the change in tax year is requested only for tax advantages, the Commissioner ordinarily will grant approval of a request for change to a natural business year.[153] For partnerships, S corporations, and PSCs, a requested year will be deemed a natural business year if at least 25 percent of the taxpayer's annual gross receipts are recognized in the last two months of the requested taxable year and the two corresponding preceding 12-month periods.[154]

[c] Circumstances Not Amounting to Substantial Business Purpose

At first glance, the standards and requirements relating to a change in taxable year appear relatively straightforward. However, in practice, the scope of a substantial business purpose or a natural business year becomes more elusive due to the relative absence of specific guidelines and the seeming reluctance of representatives of the IRS National Office (the National Office) to exercise discretion in a manner that favors the taxpayer.

The IRS has issued only a few rulings as substantive guidelines. These guidelines are more indicative of when a substantial business purpose does not exist than when it does. For example, the Commissioner generally will not grant permission for a change in tax year where the requested change is attributable to the business of entities dealing with the taxpayer rather than to the business of the taxpayer. For instance, one taxpayer whose principal source of income was dividends from an S corporation was not granted permission to change from a calendar year to a fiscal year where the change would have coincided with the availability of dividend information from the corporation that in turn, would have enabled the taxpayer to make a more accurate fourth quarter estimated tax payment.[155] Similarly, a corporate

---

[152] Id.

[153] Id.

[154] See Rev. Proc. 83-25, 1983-1 CB 689.

[155] Rev. Rul. 76-407, 1976-2 CB 127.

taxpayer was denied permission to change from a calendar year to a fiscal year where the request was to enable the corporation's former sole shareholder and its new shareholders, who acquired all the former shareholder's stock, to better allocate the taxpayer's income among them.[156] The Commissioner also denied approval of a change to a fiscal year to a partnership where the partnership wanted to make the change to provide information to its partners at a time more convenient for them.[157]

Neither the preservation of a special tax status nor the incentive to claim tax benefits, standing alone, constitutes a sufficient business purpose for making a change in tax year. For example, the preservation of a corporate taxpayer's status as a DISC has been held not to constitute a sufficient business purpose for approval of a change in its tax year.[158] Similarly, an individual taxpayer was denied permission to change from a calendar year to a fiscal year where the purpose of the change was to enable him to benefit from his retirement income credit at an earlier date.[159]

In addition, with respect to partnerships, S corporations, and PSCs, the legislative history of the 1986 Act provides that a substantial business purpose would ordinarily not be found where (1) the requested change is based on a desire to conform the tax year to a changed year for financial or regulatory reporting purposes; (2) hiring patterns of the business follow a particular annual pattern; or (3) the requested year would conform to annual administrative patterns of the business.[160] These statements appear to be more intent on denying requests for change than on establishing guidelines as to the nature of a substantial business purpose.

[d] Request for Change Within 10 Years of Prior Change

Except in unusual circumstances, the Commissioner generally will not approve any request for a change in tax year within 10 taxable years of a previous change.[161] There are no substantive guidelines as to the definition of "unusual circumstances" in this regard or to the rigidity of this articulated guideline. Consequently, taxpayers who desire to make such a change should be prepared to demonstrate the business reasons for the change, why the reasons for the earlier change are not inconsistent with the present reasons, and why the IRS will not suffer any detriment by approving the change.

[e] Deferral or Distortion of Income Resulting From Change

To obtain approval for a change in taxable year, the taxpayer and the Commissioner must agree on the terms, conditions, and adjustments under

---

[156] Rev. Rul. 76-497, 1976-2 CB 128.

[157] Rev. Rul. 60-182, 1960-1 CB 264.

[158] Rev. Rul. 76-30, 1976-1 CB 112.

[159] Rev. Rul. 76-43, 1976-1 CB 113.

[160] Blue Book, supra note 99, at 537. See Rev. Rul. 87-57, 1987-2 CB 117, for illustrations of how these guidelines are being applied by the IRS.

[161] Rev. Proc. 74-33, 1974-2 CB 489.

which the change will be made.[162] This agreement is intended to prevent a substantial distortion in income that might otherwise result from the change.[163] The regulations list the following as examples of changes that would substantially distort income:[164]

- Deferring a substantial portion of income, or shifting a substantial portion of deductions from one year to another, in order to reduce tax liability

- Causing a deferral or shift in the income of any other entity, such as a partner, beneficiary, or shareholder in an S corporation

- Creating a short period in which (1) there will be a substantial NOL or (2) in the case of an S corporation, a substantial portion of distributed amounts will be treated as long-term capital gain

Both the substantial business purpose standard[165] and the requirement of an agreement between the taxpayer and the Commissioner as to any terms, conditions, and adjustments under which the change is made are designed to prevent abuse and tax avoidance through the manipulation of taxable years. Although the regulations indicate that a substantial distortion of income may result from changing a tax year to create a short period with a substantial NOL, Revenue Procedure 85-16[166] permits a change in taxable year if a substantial business purpose exists, regardless of the resulting NOL. If the change is approved, any resulting short-period NOL must be deducted ratably over a six-year period beginning with the first tax year after the short period unless the taxpayer meets one of the following exceptions:

1. If the NOL resulting from the short period is $10,000 or less, the NOL may be carried back or carried over in accordance with Section 172(b).

2. If the NOL resulting from a short period of nine months or longer is greater than $10,000 and less than the NOL for a full 12-month period beginning on the first day of the short period, the NOL may be carried back or carried over in accordance with Section 172(b).[167]

---

[162] Treas. Reg. § 1.442-1(b)(1).

[163] Id.

[164] Id. See also Rev. Rul. 78-96, 1978-1 CB 131, which involved an S corporation that desired to change from a calendar year to a 52–53 week taxable year. The S corporation was a partner in various calendar-year partnerships. To obtain approval of the change, the S corporation had to agree to include its share of the partnerships' income in its taxable year as if it were on a calendar year.

[165] See description supra ¶ 10.05[2][a].

[166] Rev. Proc. 85-16, 1985-1 CB 517.

[167] Id.

[f] Change to Conform to Annual Accounting Period

A change in taxable year to conform to a changed annual accounting period requires the Commissioner's prior approval. However, prior approval is not required where the taxpayer has consistently maintained an annual accounting period based on one year but filed returns on the basis of a different year.[168] This rule regarding periods is different from that applicable to changes in accounting methods. Treasury Regulation § 1.446-1(e)(2)(i) requires prior IRS approval to change a method of accounting, even where the method used is erroneous and the change is to conform the tax method to an unchanged book method.

A change in tax year to conform to an unchanged book year does not result in a short period; instead, there is an overlapping period during the year of change for which an adjustment will be permitted.[169]

> EXAMPLE: Assume that a taxpayer has consistently maintained its books on the basis of a calendar year but has filed returns on the basis of a June 30 fiscal year. Assume further that the taxpayer reported $100,000 of income for its fiscal year ending June 30 of year 5 and that it has $120,000 of income for its fiscal year ending June 30 of year 6, of which $80,000 is attributable to the six-month period from July 1 to December 31 of year 5. The change to the calendar year may be effected by increasing the income of calendar year 5 by $80,000. If it is not possible to determine the actual amount of income allocable to the six-month period, a pro rata amount may be used.[170] For instance, because six months is one half of a full year, $60,000 (or one half of $120,000) would be so allocated.

[g] Change to or From 52–53 Week Taxable Year

[i] **Without prior approval.** A new taxpayer generally may adopt the 52–53 week taxable year for its first taxable year if it keeps its books and computes its income accordingly.[171] As a result of the 1986 Act, additional requirements exist and further requirements are anticipated for partnerships, S corporations, and PSCs so that they will not be able to generate unintended

---

[168] Section 441(b)(1) requires a taxpayer's taxable year to be the same as its annual accounting period. See also Rev. Rul. 58-256, 1958-1 CB 215; Atlas Oil and Ref. Co., 17 TC 733 (1951), acq. 1952-1 CB 1.

[169] American Hide & Leather Co. v. United States, 284 US 343 (1932); Paso Robles Mercantile Co. v. Comm'r, 13 F2d 653 (9th Cir. 1929), cert. denied, 280 US 595 (1929).

[170] Id.

[171] See IRC § 441(f); Treas. Reg. § 1.441-2(c)(1).

deferrals for their partners and shareholders, respectively.[172] Prior to the 1986 Act, all taxpayers, including partnerships, S corporations, and PSCs, could change to a 52–53 week taxable year without the Commissioner's permission if the desired tax year was based on the same calendar month as the former tax year, and the taxpayer kept its books and computed its income on the basis of the 52–53 week year or made adjustments conforming to that year.[173] Once elected, the selected year must be continued unless permission to change is obtained from the Commissioner.[174]

The change to a 52–53 week year may be made by filing a statement of election with the return for the first taxable year for which the election is made.[175] The statement must set forth the following:[176]

- The calendar month with reference to which the new 52–53 week taxable year ends
- The day of the week on which the taxable year will always end
- Whether the taxable year will always end on the date on which the designated day of the week last falls in the calendar month or the date on which the designated day of the week occurs that is nearest to the last day of the month

Additional requirements are applicable to partnerships, S corporations, and PSCs.[177]

[ii] **With prior approval.** Unless a taxpayer meets the requirements previously discussed, any change to a 52–53 week taxable year, any change from a 52–53 week taxable year, or any change in the month on which the 52–53 week is based requires the prior approval of the Commissioner in accordance with Section 442 and the regulations thereunder.[178] However, the IRS has ruled that certain corporations may change from a 52–53 week taxable year without prior approval if they meet the conditions set forth in Treasury Regulation § 1.442-1(c).[179]

Parent corporations and their subsidiaries who file consolidated returns present some complications when adopting 52–53 week taxable years. To

---

[172] See Blue Book, supra note 99, at 539; Temp. Reg. § 1.441-3T. See discussion supra ¶ 10.04[5] and infra ¶ 10.07.

[173] Treas. Reg. § 1.441-2(c)(2).

[174] Id.

[175] See Treas. Reg. § 1.441-2(c); Temp. Reg. § 1.441-3T(e).

[176] Treas. Reg. § 1.441-2(c)(3).

[177] See Temp. Reg. § 1.441-3T(e).

[178] Treas. Reg. § 1.441-2(c)(4).

[179] Rev. Rul. 65-316, 1965-2 CB 149. These conditions are discussed infra ¶ 10.05[4][b][i].

alleviate these complications, the IRS issued Revenue Ruling 72-184,[180] which provides conditions under which an affiliated group may file a consolidated return when some, but not all, members use a 52–53 week taxable year (or where consent is requested for some, but not all, members to adopt a 52–53 week taxable year). Generally, the Commissioner will consent to the use of a 52–53 week taxable year by some members of the affiliated group, while others remain on a calendar or fiscal year, as long as (1) a timely request for consent is made; (2) the taxable years of all members of the group end within the same seven-day period; and (3) it is demonstrated that the use of a 52–53 week taxable year will clearly reflect the consolidated income of the group.[181] Revenue Ruling 72-184 also prescribes rules for the treatment of intercompany transactions in these circumstances.[182]

[3] Applications for Change in Taxable Year

Except for circumstances in which permission to change to a specified taxable year is not required, or where permission for a change is automatic, all changes of taxable years require the Commissioner's prior approval. Generally, approval is requested by the timely filing of Form 1128.[183] An application for change in accounting period must be accompanied by a fee.[184] Tax advisors and taxpayers must confirm the appropriate fee at the time of the filing of the application. A request for a ruling pertaining to an accounting period (other than one submitted on Form 1128 or Form 2553) must also be accompanied by a fee.[185]

[a] Form 1128

A taxpayer formally requests approval of a change in taxable year by filing an application on Form 1128, in triplicate, with the Commissioner of Internal Revenue, Washington, D.C. 20224.[186] Letters requesting a change in

---

[180] Rev. Rul. 72-184, 1972-1 CB 289.

[181] Id.

[182] Id.

[183] But see Jonas-Cadillac Co., 16 BTA 932 (1929), aff'd, 41 F2d 141 (7th Cir. 1930), where a taxpayer maintaining its books and records on the basis of a fiscal year erroneously filed its tax returns on the basis of a calendar year. The IRS determined overassessments and deficiencies on the basis of the returns as filed. These actions of the IRS, together with the acquiescence of the taxpayer, were later held to constitute a request for, and approval of, a change to the calendar year.

[184] Rev. Proc. 93-23, 1993 — CB —.

[185] Id.

[186] Treas. Reg. § 1.442-1(b)(1).

taxable year are not sufficient to request approval; Form 1128 must be filed.[187]

The taxable income (which may be estimated) for the short period must be included in the application.[188] The procedural regulations state that if the application for a change in taxable year is approved, the taxpayer must file its returns and compute its net income on the basis of the new taxable year,[189] but, as discussed in the following section, the IRS does not require this in practice unless the taxpayer accepts the approval of its requested change.

The application should be filed on or before the fifteenth day of the second calendar month following the close of the requested year.[190] This will generally cause the year of change to be a short taxable year.

The taxpayer may be permitted to file a late application for change if good cause is shown and the government's interests are not jeopardized.[191] Absent such a showing, an application for change that is not timely filed will be denied.

[b] Taxpayer Acceptance of IRS Approval

To put an approved change into effect requires the taxpayer to file a return for the resulting short period by the due date of the return, including extensions, or by the thirtieth day after the date of approval, whichever is later. The old taxable year continues in effect if the proper short-period return is not timely filed. As a consequence, even though an application for change is approved, a taxpayer is not required to use the new taxable year. The taxpayer may continue to use its old taxable year merely by not filing the short-period return necessary to effect the change in taxable year. Thus, if a taxpayer believes there may be reasons (business or tax related) for not making the change, it may nevertheless proceed with the filing of the application, secure in the knowledge that it is not bound to accept the approved change. However, taxpayers and tax advisors must remain alert to changes in this IRS practice.

[c] Return Due Before IRS Determination

Typically, a taxpayer that requests permission to change its taxable year will request an extension of time within which to file the necessary short-period return for the requested year. The extension allows the IRS to review

---

[187] Stonegate of Blacksburg, Inc., 33 TCM 956 (1974).

[188] Rev. Rul. 55-111, 1955-1 CB 333.

[189] Treas. Reg. § 601.204(a).

[190] Treas. Reg. § 1.442-1(b)(1).

[191] Treas. Reg. § 1.9100-1(a). See ¶ 8.06[3][d] for discussion of this good cause requirement.

the request for change and to discuss any questions with the taxpayer prior to the time that the taxpayer would actually have to prepare the return.

Unfortunately, the IRS is sometimes delayed in completing its review of the request. When such a delay occurs, the period for filing a return on the basis of the requested year is in danger of expiring. To prevent that expiration, if the request is approved, the taxpayer will have 30 days from the date of approval within which to file the return on the basis of the approved request. However, if the request is not approved, the taxpayer may be faced with filing a late return for its old year. There is no clear answer as to what the taxpayer should do when faced with this situation. One seemingly appropriate approach would be for the taxpayer to request a delay in the filing of the return that otherwise would be due. However, in the absence of approval of such a request (or the failure of the IRS reviewer to suggest other action), the filing of the return on the basis of the old year will be required.

[4] Requests for Change Affected by Nature of Taxpayer

[a] Individuals

An individual who wishes to change his or her taxable year generally must comply with the requirements previously identified.[192] In addition, there are a few special rules applicable to individual taxpayers.

The regulations authorize the Commissioner to permit a husband or wife to change his or her respective taxable year in order to file a joint return, even though a substantial business purpose is not established and the only reason for the change is to obtain the tax advantage of filing a joint return.[193] The regulations also provide that a newly married husband or wife may change his or her taxable year to the year of the other without the prior approval of the Commissioner, if this is done to file a joint return for the first or second taxable year ending after the date of marriage. However, to do this, the newly married husband or wife adopting the taxable year of the other spouse must file a return for the short period resulting from the change on or before the fifteenth day of the fourth month following the close of the resulting short period.[194] If the due date of the short-period return occurs before the date of marriage, the first taxable year of the other spouse ending after the date of marriage cannot be adopted under this method. The short period return should contain a statement indicating that it is filed under the authority of these regulations.

Most individuals have calendar years as their taxable periods. Other than the special provisions for newly married couples and couples wishing to

---

[192] See supra ¶¶ 10.02, 10.03, 10.05.

[193] Treas. Reg. § 1.442-1(b)(1).

[194] Treas. Reg. § 1.442-1(e).

file joint returns, an individual taxpayer must comply with the substantial business purpose requirement for changing the tax year. Revenue Procedure 66-50[195] grants an individual whose income is solely from wages, interest, dividends, capital gains, pensions, annuities, rents, and royalties automatic approval to change to a calendar year if that individual files a timely application. This automatic approval does not apply if the individual receives income from a proprietorship, partnership, trust, estate, or S corporation.[196]

The IRS has privately ruled that it does not believe an individual employee can establish a substantial business purpose for changing from a calendar year to a fiscal year.[197] In light of this private ruling and the general lack of guidelines in this area, an individual taxpayer should be able to change from a fiscal year to a calendar year. However, he or she will undoubtedly encounter significant difficulty changing from a calendar year to a fiscal year. This difficulty should not exist for an individual whose request for change is premised on sound business reasons associated with the individual's operation of a proprietorship.

[b] Corporations

[i] Automatic change per regulations.   Under specified conditions, the regulations permit a corporation to change its taxable year without the Commissioner's prior approval.[198] This change may be made by filing a statement with the District Director with whom the corporation files its returns on or before the time (including any extension) for filing the return for the applicable short period resulting from the change.[199] This statement must specify that the corporation is changing its taxable year under paragraph (c) of Treasury Regulation § 1.442-1 and that the corporation has satisfied the following five conditions:[200]

1. The corporation must not have changed its annual accounting period at any time within the previous 10 calendar years, ending with the calendar year that includes the beginning of the short period required to make the change of taxable year.
2. The short period required to make the change of taxable year must not be a year in which the corporation has an NOL, as defined in Section 172.

---

[195] Rev. Proc. 66-50, 1966-2 CB 1260, modified by Rev. Proc. 81-40, 1981-2 CB 605.

[196] Id.

[197] Priv. Ltr. Rul. 7844042 (Apr. 25, 1978).

[198] Treas. Reg. § 1.442-1(c).

[199] Treas. Reg. § 1.442-1(c)(1).

[200] Treas. Reg. § 1.442-1(c)(2).

3. The corporation's taxable income for the short period required to effect the change, if placed on an annual basis, must be 80 percent or more of the corporation's taxable income for the taxable year immediately preceding the short period.

4. If the corporation had a special status either for the short period or for the taxable year immediately preceding the short period, it must have the same special status for both the short period and the preceding taxable year. (For purposes of this condition, special tax status includes only a personal holding company, a corporation that is an exempt organization, a foreign corporation not engaged in a trade or business within the United States, a Western Hemisphere trade corporation, and a China Trade Act corporation.)

5. The corporation must not make an S corporation election under Section 1372(a) that becomes effective in the taxable year immediately following the short period required to make the change.

Although the above procedure provides for a change in taxable year without the Commissioner's prior approval, adjustments resulting from a subsequent examination of the corporation's returns may cause the corporation to fail to meet the specified conditions. In that circumstance, the statement filed with the District Director will be considered a timely application for permission to change the corporation's taxable year.[201]

[ii] Automatic change per revenue procedure. If a corporation cannot meet the requirements for automatic approval under Treasury Regulation § 1.442-1(c), it nevertheless may qualify for an expedited approval of a request for change in year under Revenue Procedure 84-34.[202] This expedited procedure is available where the corporation cannot satisfy all the regulatory prerequisites. To be eligible to use this procedure, the corporation must satisfy seven conditions. The corporation must not:

1. Have changed its accounting period at any time within the previous 10 calendar years, ending with the calendar year that includes the beginning of the short period required to effect the change of taxable year.

2. Be a member of a partnership, a beneficiary of an estate or trust, or a shareholder of a DISC.

---

[201] Treas. Reg. § 1.442-1(c)(3).

[202] Rev. Proc. 84-34, 1984-1 CB 508, corrected by Ann. 84-84, 1984-35 IRB 8, which corrected Section 5.03 of Rev. Proc. 84-34 to read as follows: "An affiliated group that files consolidated returns may change its annual accounting period without the prior approval of the Commissioner if every member of the affiliated group meets all of the requirements and complies with all the conditions of either section 1.442-1(c) of the regulations or this revenue procedure."

3. Be an S corporation or attempt to make an S corporation election that would become effective for the tax year immediately following the short period.

4. Be a DISC.

5. Be a controlled foreign corporation.

6. Be a foreign corporation satisfying the foreign personal holding company stock-ownership requirements.

7. Be a tax-exempt organization or cooperative.

A corporation satisfying these criteria should file Form 1128 with the Service Center where the corporation files its tax returns on or before the fifteenth day of the second calendar month following the close of the short period for which the return is required to make the change. If the following five prerequisites are satisfied, the corporation may assume that the change will be approved unless it receives a letter to the contrary:[203]

1. The short period required to effect the change must begin with the date following the close of the old tax year and must end with the day preceding the first day of the new tax year.

2. The corporation's books must be closed as of the last day of the new tax year, returns for subsequent years must be made on the basis of a full 12 months or 52–53 week year, and the corporation must compute its income and keep its books and records (including financial reports and statements for credit purposes) on the basis of the new tax year.

3. Short-period taxable income must be annualized and taxes computed in accordance with the provisions of Section 443(b) and Treasury Regulation § 1.443-1(b).

4. If the corporation has a short-period NOL, the NOL must be deducted ratably over a period of six years beginning with the first tax year after the short period unless the corporation meets one of the following exceptions: (1) if the NOL is $10,000 or less, the NOL may be carried back or forward in accordance with Section 172(b) or (2) if the NOL resulting from a short period of nine months or longer is more than $10,000 but less than the NOL for a full 12-month period beginning with the first day of the short period, the NOL may be carried over in accordance with Section 172(b).[204]

5. If there are any unused investment tax credits or other credits for the short period, the corporation must carry them forward. Unused credits from the short period may not be carried back.

---

[203] Unless the taxpayer fails to comply timely with all applicable requirements of Rev. Proc. 84-34, it should not receive a letter of denial.

[204] This principle was restated in Rev. Proc. 85-16, 1985-1 CB 517.

To facilitate the processing of this change in tax year, the taxpayer should type or print the following statement at the top of page 1 of Form 1128: FILED UNDER REV. PROC. 84-34. This revenue procedure is only effective for changes in taxable years where the resulting short period ends on or after April 23, 1984.[205]

[iii] **Special rules.** Special rules exist for certain corporations. One example is a subsidiary corporation, which is required to change its taxable year to that of the members of an affiliated group with which it files a consolidated return. In that instance, the subsidiary corporation does not need to file an application to change its taxable year.[206] In addition, where an affiliated group filing consolidated returns wants to avail itself of the provisions allowing automatic changes, each member of the group must satisfy all applicable criteria in order for the entire group to comply. Thus, if a member of an affiliated group joined the group within the past 10 years and at that time was required to change its year, the group would not be able to satisfy the requirement of no change within the prior 10 years and, hence, would not be able to use the provisions for an automatic change.[207]

Another example is that any corporation that is an S corporation or a DISC during the short period required to effect a change in taxable year must secure prior consent from the Commissioner for any change in taxable year.[208] A corporation that elects to become an S corporation or a DISC immediately following the short period required to effect the change must also obtain the prior approval of the Commissioner.[209]

Controlled foreign corporations and foreign corporations that meet the stock ownership requirements of a foreign personal holding company must also secure the Commissioner's prior consent to a change.[210] The application for approval should be made by one or more of the controlled foreign corporation's U.S. shareholders, by one or more of the individuals who comprise the foreign corporation's U.S. group, or by the respective corporations.[211] Generally, the Commissioner will approve the change where the taxable year is changed to conform to the requirements of foreign law or because of a bona fide foreign business purpose.[212]

Temporary regulations do not permit a corporation to avail itself of the automatic change provisions if it is entitled to elect the possessions tax cred-

---

[205] Rev. Proc. 84-34, 1984-1 CB 508.

[206] Treas. Reg. §§ 1.442-1(d), 1.1502-76.

[207] Rev. Rul. 74-326, 1974-2 CB 142.

[208] Treas. Reg. § 1.442-1(c)(4).

[209] Treas. Reg. § 1.442-1(c)(2)(v).

[210] Treas. Reg. § 1.442-1(c)(5).

[211] Treas. Reg. § 1.442-1(b)(3).

[212] Id.

it under Section 936 (allowing, in certain cases, a credit against income tax for amounts of tax attributable to income earned outside of the United States but within a possession of the United States) or the benefits of Section 934(b) (pertaining to a reduction in tax liability for inhabitants of the Virgin Islands).[213] Therefore, such a taxpayer must obtain the Commissioner's prior approval to a change in taxable year.[214]

[c] Partnerships, S Corporations, and Personal Service Corporations

The income of partnerships and S corporations is taxed to their partners and shareholders, respectively, in the year with which or in which the partnership or S corporation year ends.[215] This rule presents opportunities for tax deferral. As a consequence, the IRS has required partnerships and S corporations to comply with relatively strict procedures in order to change their taxable years. For example, an existing partnership could change its taxable year without securing the Commissioner's prior approval only if all its partners had the same taxable year as that to which the partnership changed or if all its principal partners who did not have such a taxable year were concurrently changing to that year.

An S corporation could change its taxable year only to a permitted year.[216] A "permitted year" was, and remains under the 1986 Act, the calendar year, or any other year for which the S corporation establishes a business purpose to the satisfaction of the IRS.[217] Nevertheless, as discussed in the following section, prior to the 1986 Act, opportunities for deferral still remained.

The 1986 Act has made substantial changes in the taxable years available to partnerships and S corporations and, in addition, to PSCs.[218] As a consequence, except as may be provided in the future, a partnership, S corporation, or PSC may change its taxable year only with the prior approval of the IRS.[219]

[i] Deferral of three months or less.

Where a partnership or S corporation changes to a tax year that is different from that of its partners or owners, respectively, a deferral in the recognition of income becomes avail-

---

[213] Temp. Reg. § 5f.442-1.

[214] Id.

[215] IRC §§ 706(a), 1366(a).

[216] Rev. Proc. 83-25, 1983-1 CB 689, § 3.02, modified and superseded by Rev. Proc. 87-32, 1987-2 CB 396.

[217] Id.

[218] See supra ¶¶ 10.04[4][c], 10.04[4][e]. See also infra ¶ 10.07 for impact of the 1987 Act.

[219] See Rev. Proc. 87-32, 1987-28 IRB 14; Rev. Rul. 87-57, 1987-2 CB 117; discussion infra ¶ 10.07.

able. The 1986 Act has all but eliminated the opportunity for such deferrals by prohibiting partnerships and S corporations from using years different from those of its majority partners or principal partners.[220] The only exception is where the use of a different year comes about from a substantial business purpose.[221]

Nevertheless, in years prior to the 1986 Act, the IRS had routinely permitted automatic changes in taxable years where the resulting deferral was for a period of three months or less. In Revenue Procedure 72-51,[222] the IRS provided that a partnership that desired to change its tax year to one different from that of its principal partners generally would be allowed to do so where the change would result in a deferral of no more than three months. Where such a change was made, the partnership income for the first three months (or shorter period) immediately succeeding the short taxable year was required to be included in the taxable income of the short taxable year. This rule resulted in a double inclusion of income—once in the short period and once in the immediately succeeding year. To offset this double inclusion, the amount of such income was excluded ratably over a period of 10 years beginning with the short taxable year. No adjustment was required where the partnership incurred a loss during the deferral period. Revenue Procedure 72-51 also applied to requests for changes in tax years of S corporations.[223]

In Revenue Procedure 83-25,[224] the IRS outlined further procedures by which an S corporation could automatically adopt, retain, or change to an annual accounting period other than one ending on December 31, if the resulting deferral was for a period of less than three months. It provided that S corporations could change their tax years to a year other than one ending on December 31 if (1) the shareholders holding more than one half of the shares of the corporation's stock (as of the first day of the tax year to which the request related) had the same tax year that the corporation wanted or were concurrently changing to that year or (2) the shareholders holding more than one half of the corporation's shares (as of the first day of the tax year to which the request related) had a tax year or were concurrently changing to a tax year that did not result in deferment of income to any of these shareholders of more than three months.

Paralleling the partnership requirements, an adjustment was required for the resulting short period. The adjustment period began on the first day of the new tax year and ended on the last day of the former tax year of the

---

[220] See discussion supra ¶¶ 10.04[4][c], 10.04[4][d]; see also discussion infra ¶ 10.07 regarding the 1987 Act.

[221] See discussion supra ¶¶ 10.04[4][c], 10.04[4][d]; see also discussion infra ¶ 10.07 regarding the 1987 Act.

[222] Rev. Proc. 72-51, 1972-2 CB 832.

[223] Id.

[224] Rev. Proc. 83-25, 1983-1 CB 689, modified and superseded by Rev. Proc. 87-32, 1987-2 CB 396.

corporation. The period was not to exceed three months from the first day of the new tax year. The income for the deferral period was included in the S corporation's taxable income for the short tax year required to effect the change. The amount of this income was then deducted ratably over a period of 10 years, which consisted of the short tax year and each of the nine succeeding tax years. No adjustment was required where a loss was incurred during the adjustment period.

[ii] **Change to natural business year.** Where a partnership or an S corporation is not entitled to an automatic change in taxable year, it must obtain the Commissioner's prior approval by establishing a substantial business purpose for the change. Revenue Procedure 83-25 provides additional guidelines for an S corporation that desires to adopt a tax year that coincides with its natural business year.[225] The legislative history accompanying the 1986 Act provides that these guidelines will also be applicable to partnerships and personal service corporations.[226]

Under the procedure, an S corporation will be deemed to be changing to a tax year that coincides with its natural business year if the following two calculations for each of the three designated 12-month periods equals or exceeds 25 percent (the 25 percent test):

1. The corporation's gross receipts from sales or services for the first preceding 12-month period (prior to the S corporation election becoming effective and ending with the last month of the requested natural business year) are totaled and divided into the gross receipts from sales or services, respectively, for the last two months of this 12-month period.

2. The same computation as above is made for the two other preceding 12-month periods ending with the last month of the requested natural business year.[227]

With respect to corporations that have not adopted a tax year prior to making the S corporation election, the following three additional rules are applicable:

1. The corporation must be a successor to an organization that had actively conducted its business (1) for at least three years prior to the formation of the successor corporation and (2) for a period that is sufficient to enable the following determinations to be made.

---

[225] See Rev. Proc. 87-32, 1987-2 CB 396, which modifies and supersedes Rev. Proc. 83-25. See also discussion infra ¶ 10.07 for impact of the 1987 Act.

[226] Blue Book, supra note 99, at 536. See also Temp. Reg. § 1.442-2T.

[227] Rev. Proc. 83-25, 1983-1 CB 689, §§ 4.04(2)(a), 4.04(2)(b), modified and superseded by Rev. Proc. 87-32, 1987-2 CB 396.

2. Where the requested natural business year begins with the incorporation of a predecessor organization and ends 12 months thereafter, the
same 12-month period ending on the last month of the requested natural business year of the predecessor organization for the prior three
years is used for purposes of the 25 percent test.

3. Where the requested natural business year does not begin with the
period of incorporation, the first preceding 12-month period for
purposes of the 25 percent test will be the last 12-month period of the
predecessor organization ending on the last month of the requested
natural business year. The next two preceding 12-month periods for
purposes of the 25 percent test will be the two prior 12-month periods
of the predecessor organization ending on the last month of the
requested natural business year.[228]

Where the corporation qualifies under these procedures for more than
one natural business year, the natural business year and the tax year that will
be permitted must end with the two-month period for which the highest
average percentage of gross receipts is achieved.[229] For example, assume that
a taxpayer satisfies the 25 percent test for two two-month periods within the
same calendar year, one ending in July and one ending in September. If the
applicable percentage for the July period is 28 percent and for the September
period is 26 percent, only a change to the July period will be permitted.[230]

[iii] Corporate partners. A corporate partner may change its taxable
year only if it obtains the Commissioner's approval and demonstrates a
substantial business purpose in accordance with the regulations.[231] This rule
applies even though the corporate partner complies with all the prerequisites
for automatic approval of tax years for corporations.[232]

[d] Other Entities

[i] Exempt organizations. Certain exempt organizations may change
their tax years in an expedited manner under the provisions of Revenue Procedure 76-9.[233] A qualified exempt organization may change its accounting
period merely by filing an application on Form 1128 with the Service Center

---

[228] Rev. Proc. 83-25, 1983-1 CB 689, § 4.04(2)(c).

[229] Rev. Proc. 83-25, 1983-1 CB 689, § 4.04(2)(d). See also Temp. Reg. § 1.442-
2T(c).

[230] See Temp. Reg. § 1.442-2T(c)(5).

[231] Treas. Reg. § 1.442-1(b)(2)(ii).

[232] Rev. Rul. 78-179, 1978-1 CB 132.

[233] Rev. Proc. 76-9, 1976-1 CB 547, modified and superseded by Rev. Proc. 85-
58, 1985-2 CB 740.

with which it files its annual Form 990 on or before the fifteenth day of the second calendar month following the close of the short period for which a return is required. Unless a letter is received denying the change, the organization may assume the change has been approved.

This procedure applies to an exempt organization if:

- It does not have an NOL for the short period.
- Its taxable income for the short period, on an annual basis, is 80 percent or more of the taxable income for the previous tax year.
- Its exempt status is maintained for both the short period and the preceding tax year.

These provisions are also applicable to groups of exempt organizations.[234]

[ii] Taxpayer with no prior accounting period. Generally, new taxpayers who adopt taxable years in accordance with Section 441 are not required to obtain the Commissioner's approval under Section 442. However, Section 441(g) provides that if a taxpayer does not keep books, does not have an annual accounting period, or has an accounting period that does not meet the requirements for a fiscal year, its taxable year must be the calendar year. If Section 441(g) applies to a taxpayer, the later adoption of a fiscal year is regarded as a change in its taxable year under Section 442. Accordingly, the prior approval of the Commissioner must be obtained before the taxpayer may adopt a fiscal year. The Commissioner will deny approval unless the taxpayer agrees to establish and maintain accurate records of its taxable income for the short period resulting from the change and the proposed fiscal year.[235]

[5] Computation of Taxable Income for Short Period

Generally, income is not earned ratably throughout the year. As a consequence, inequities may result when a return must be filed for a period of fewer than 12 months. To lessen the potential for these inequities when a short-period return is required, a taxpayer must annualize its short-period income in computing its liability for tax.[236] "Annualization" refers to mechanisms for determining tax liability as if the period in question were a period of 12 months.

The annualization provisions apply only to income. Losses are not

---

[234] Rev. Proc. 76-10, 1976-1 CB 548; see Rev. Proc. 79-3, 1979-1 CB 483, Rev. Proc. 85-58, 1985-2 CB 740.

[235] Treas. Reg. § 1.442-1(a)(2).

[236] IRC § 443(b); Treas. Reg. § 1.443-1(b).

annualized for carry-back or carry-over purposes.[237] Annualization also is not required where the short period occurs because the taxpayer has been in existence for less than an entire taxable year.[238] In computing taxable income and tax for the portion of a year during which the taxpayer was in existence, the taxpayer generally must make the same determinations as would be made for a return covering a full 12-month period. However, the exclusion from any minimum tax on tax preference items should be prorated and allocated to the short period on the basis of the ratio of the number of days in the short period to 365.[239] In addition, any alternative minimum taxable income should be annualized, the tax computed, and the result multiplied by the number of months in the short period divided by 12.[240]

Annualization is not required with respect to the accumulated earnings tax,[241] the personal holding company tax,[242] undistributed foreign personal holding company income,[243] the taxable income of an REIT,[244] and the taxable income of a regulated investment company.[245] In addition, self-employment tax under Section 1401 does not need to be annualized.[246]

[a] Normal Annualization

Under the normal rule, taxable income is annualized by multiplying modified taxable income by 12 and dividing the result by the number of months in the short period.[247] "Modified taxable income" is defined as gross income for the short period minus allowable deductions and adjusted personal exemptions.[248] Once the previous computations have been used to compute annualized income, a tentative tax is computed on that income. This tentative tax is then multiplied by the number of months in the short period and divided by 12 to determine the applicable tax.

EXAMPLE: Assume a corporate taxpayer has modified taxable income of $100,000 for a short period of 10 months. To annualize this income, the $100,000 would be multiplied by $12/10$ for a result of $120,000. If

---

[237] Rev. Rul. 56-463, 1956-2 CB 297.

[238] See IRC § 443(b)(2)(B)(ii).

[239] IRC § 443(d).

[240] Id.

[241] IRC § 536.

[242] IRC § 546.

[243] IRC § 557.

[244] IRC § 857(b)(2)(C).

[245] IRC § 852(b)(2)(E).

[246] See Rev. Rul. 94, 1953-1 CB 84; Rev. Rul. 69-410, 1969-2 CB 167.

[247] IRC § 443(b); Treas. Reg. § 1.443-1(b).

[248] IRC § 443(b)(3).

subject to a tax rate of 30 percent, the tentative tax would be $36,000. Applicable tax would then be determined by multiplying the $36,000 by $10/12$ for a tax of $30,000.

Certain items must be considered separately by an individual who is annualizing income for a short-period return. First, the zero bracket amount must be added to annualized taxable income. Second, an individual may not use the tax tables for calculating tax but must use the tax rate schedules.[249] Third, any deductions for personal exemptions should be reduced to an amount that bears the same ratio to the full amount of the exemptions as the number of months in the short period bears to 12.[250] Fourth, the standard deduction may not be used in computing taxable income.[251]

When the short period results from a change to or from a 52–53 week taxable year, the computation for personal exemptions should be made on a daily basis—the ratio of the number of days in the short period to 365.[252] This method of prorating personal exemptions allowed to individuals (or deductions in lieu of personal exemptions allowed to other taxpayers) is only required when taxable income is annualized under the normal method. It is not allowed when the alternative method, which is described in the following section, is used.

Where the short period resulting from a change to or from a 52–53 week taxable year is more than six days and less than 359 days, taxable income should be annualized by multiplying that income by 365 and dividing the result by the number of days in the short period.[253] Any deductions for personal expenses should be computed on a daily basis. The deduction for personal exemptions also should be reduced to an amount that bears the same ratio to the full deduction as the number of days in the short period bears to 365.[254] Finally, the tax for the short period is in the same proportion to the tax computed on the annualized income as the ratio of the number of days in the short period bears to 365.[255]

Any credit against tax that depends on the amount of any item of income or deduction is computed on the amount of the item annualized separately.[256] The credit is treated as a credit against the tax computed on the annualized taxable income. Where the credit is limited by taxable income, the taxable income should be annualized for this purpose.

When a parent corporation changes its taxable year to conform to that of its subsidiaries and is required to file a short-period return, it may elect to

---

[249] IRC § 3(b)(2); IRS Pub. 538 (Rev. Nov. 1983), at 15.

[250] Treas. Reg. § 1.443-1(b)(1)(v).

[251] Treas. Reg. § 1.443-1(b)(1)(iv).

[252] Treas. Reg. § 1.443-1(b)(1)(v).

[253] Treas. Reg. § 1.441-2(c)(5).

[254] See Treas. Reg. § 1.443-1(b)(1)(v).

[255] Treas. Reg. § 1.441-2(c)(5).

[256] See Treas. Reg. § 1.443-1(b)(1)(vi).

file a consolidated return. Consolidated taxable income for the affiliated group should be annualized.[257] When a corporation changes its annual accounting period to conform to that of the affiliated group that it is entering, it must file a short-period return for the period between the end of its preceding taxable year and its entrance into the consolidated group. Under these circumstances, the corporation is not required to annualize its income for the short period.[258] Where a subsidiary leaves an affiliated group during the taxable year, its income for the period of affiliation with the group must be included in the group's consolidated return, but that income need not be annualized.[259]

[b] Alternative Method of Annualization

Annualization of short-period income under the normal rule may result in inequity to a taxpayer, particularly when the short period includes an unusual fluctuation in business activity, large nonrecurring items of income, or other abnormal increases in income. To mitigate these inequities, an alternative method of annualization is available.[260]

The alternative method allows the tax attributable to the short-period income to be computed under two procedures. The first procedure focuses on a 12-month period, while the second procedure focuses on the actual short period.

Under the first procedure, the tax is computed for a full 12-month period beginning on the first day of the short period. The tax attributable to the short period is determined by multiplying the tax for the 12-month period by a fraction, the numerator of which is short-period income and the denominator of which is income for the full 12-month period. Under the second procedure, the tax for the short period is computed solely on the basis of short-period taxable income.[261] If the lower of the tax computed under either of these procedures is less than the tax imposed under the normal method of annualization, the taxpayer will not be required to pay more than that lower amount. Otherwise, the taxpayer is liable for the tax computed under the normal method.[262]

As previously stated, the 12-month period used in the alternative method is the 12-month period beginning on the first day of the short period.[263] If the taxpayer terminates its existence or substantially disposes of its assets

---

[257] Rev. Rul. 55-80, 1955-1 CB 387.

[258] See Rev. Rul. 70-378, 1970-2 CB 178; Rev. Rul. 67-189, 1967-1 CB 255.

[259] Rev. Rul. 74-585, 1974-2 CB 143.

[260] IRC § 443(b)(2).

[261] Treas. Reg. § 1.443-1(b)(2)(i).

[262] Id.

[263] Treas. Reg. § 1.443-1(b)(2)(ii)

before the end of that 12-month period, then the 12-month period to be used is the period that ends on the last day of the short period.[264] In case of a change from a 52–53 week taxable year, the 12-month period is the period of 52 or 53 weeks beginning on the first day of the short period.[265]

The taxable income for the 12-month period is computed just as if the 12-month period were the taxpayer's actual taxable year.[266] All items that fall within this 12-month period must be included in taxable income, even though they may be extraordinary in amount or of an unusual nature.[267]

If the taxpayer is a member of a partnership, the taxpayer's taxable income for the 12-month period includes its distributive share of partnership income for any taxable year of the partnership ending within that 12-month period. No amounts are included with respect to a taxable year of the partnership ending before or after that period.

If any other item is partially attributable to the 12-month period and partially attributable to another taxable year, the taxpayer, subject to the Commissioner's review, should apportion the item in a manner that would clearly reflect income. The cost of goods sold during the 12-month period is the actual cost of goods sold for the short period and the cost of goods sold for the remaining portion of the 12-month period. With respect to inventory, unless a more exact determination is available, the cost of goods sold during the 12-month period that is also includable in another taxable year is considered to bear the same ratio to sales in the 12-month period as cost of goods bears to sales for the entire taxable year. In this respect, the Commissioner may require, as a condition for granting the change in taxable year, that the taxpayer take a closing inventory on the last day of the 12-month period to obtain the benefits of the alternative method. This inventory may not be used for any other purpose.

The benefits of the alternative method of annualization are available only if the taxpayer makes a timely application to the District Director.[268] Procedurally, the taxpayer first files its short-period return and computes its tax under the normal method of annualization. The taxpayer then files an application in the form of a claim for credit or refund to obtain the benefits of the alternative method. The application should show the computation of taxable income and tax for the 12-month period. It must be filed no later than the time (including extensions) prescribed for filing a return for the taxpayer's first taxable year that ends on or after the day that is 12 months

---

[264] Id. The regulation states that a corporation that has ceased its business and distributed so much of the assets used in its business that it cannot resume its customary operations with the remaining assets will be considered to have disposed of substantially all of its assets.

[265] Treas. Reg. § 1.443-1(b)(2)(ii).

[266] Treas. Reg. § 1.443-1(b)(2)(iii)(A).

[267] Id.

[268] Treas. Reg. § 1.443-1(b)(2)(v)(a).

after the beginning of the short period. Once the District Director determines taxable income for the 12-month period, excess tax will be credited or refunded to the taxpayer in the same manner as any overpayment. At the time the short-period return is filed, the 12-month period is often determinable. For example, this is the case where the taxpayer is not in existence or has been substantially liquidated, and the 12-month period ends on the last day of the short period. If the period is determinable, the tax on the short-period return may be computed under the alternative method at that time. A return covering the 12-month period should be attached, and it will be considered an application for the benefits of the alternative method. If the application is not filed within the time prescribed, the short-period tax is determined on the basis of the normal method of annualization.[269]

¶ 10.06 SPECIAL REQUIREMENTS AFFECTING 52–53 WEEK TAXABLE YEARS

[1] General

All items of income and deduction may be determined on the basis of a 52–53 week taxable year. Alternatively, each item may be determined as though the 52–53 week taxable year were a taxable year consisting of 12 calendar months, if that practice is consistently followed and clearly reflects income.[270] Unless some other practice is consistently followed, depreciation allowances and amortization deductions are to be determined as though the 52–53 week taxable year were a period of 12 calendar months.[271]

In Revenue Ruling 76-482,[272] an accrual method taxpayer elected to use a 52–53 week taxable year. The taxpayer neither treated the year as consisting of 12 calendar months nor did it elect to ratably accrue real property taxes pursuant to Section 461(c)(1). In these circumstances, the taxpayer was allowed to accrue and deduct all property taxes attributable to the 52–53 week taxable year even though this period contained two assessment periods. In other words, since the taxpayer did not elect to treat the 52–53 week year as a 12-month period, general principles of accrual tax accounting prevailed.

[2] Effective Dates

For purposes of filing returns and other documents, paying tax, or performing other acts, a 52–53 week taxable year begins on the first day of the

---

[269] Andrew John Williamson, 22 TC 684 (1954); Visintainer v. Comm'r, 187 F2d 519 (10th Cir. 1951), cert. denied, 342 US 858 (1951).

[270] Treas. Reg. § 1.441-2(d). The regulations point out that the principles of Sections 451, relating to the taxable year for inclusion of items of gross income, and 461, relating to the taxable year for taking deductions, are generally applicable to 52–53 week taxable years.

[271] Treas. Reg. § 1.441-2(d).

[272] Rev. Rul. 76-482, 1976-2 CB 127.

calendar month beginning nearest to the first day of the 52–53 week taxable year and ends on the last day of the calendar month ending nearest to the last day of the 52–53 week taxable year.[273] Under this rule, the taxpayer may determine the effective date or applicability of any provision under the Code that is expressed in terms of taxable years beginning, including, or ending with reference to the first or last day of a specified calendar month.

There is one exception to this rule. If a change in tax rates is effective during a 52–53 week taxable year (other than on the first day of that year), the taxpayer must compute the tax in accordance with Section 15.[274] Under Section 15(a), tentative taxes are computed by applying the rate for the period before the effective date of the change and the rate for the period on and after the effective date to the taxable income for the entire year. The actual tax for the year is based on a weighted average of the tax computed under the two rates. The weighting is based on the number of days in each period to the number of days in the entire taxable year.

¶ 10.07 1987 ACT: USE OF FISCAL YEAR

As a result of intensive lobbying (principally by the AICPA) against the 1986 Act's required use of a calendar year by most partnerships, S corporations, and PSCs,[275] Congress included within the 1987 Act special provisions allowing partnerships, S corporations, and PSCs to elect to retain their fiscal years or to adopt new fiscal years where the deferral in the recognition of income will be no more than three months.[276] However, the electing entity must agree to make payments (in the case of partnerships and S corporations)[277] or to make distributions or reduce deductions for payments to employees-owners (in the case of PSCs)[278] so that there will be no deferral in the payment of tax. In other words, by agreeing to make the specified payments so that there will be no significant tax benefit from the use of the fiscal year, the entity may retain its present fiscal year or adopt any of certain specified new fiscal years.

The controlling Code sections are poorly drafted. As a consequence, taxpayers anticipated that technical corrections or other appropriate action would be taken to correct the statutory deficiencies. These provisions are also lengthy. They contain numerous definitions, various limitations on the use of the election, transition rules, and certain so-called administrative provisions.

---

[273] Treas. Reg. § 1.441-2(b)(1).

[274] Treas. Reg. § 1.441-2(b)(2).

[275] See discussion supra ¶¶ 10.04[4][c]–10.04[4][e], 10.05[4][c].

[276] IRC § 444, as enacted by the 1987 Act.

[277] IRC § 7519, as enacted by the 1987 Act.

[278] IRC § 280H, as enacted by the 1987 Act.

Although the congressional objective in these accounting period provisions is to permit the use of a fiscal year without providing a deferral in the payment of tax, the required payments, distributions, and limitations on deductions, as applicable, will only approximate the tax results that would have occurred if a calendar year had been used. For taxpayers experiencing particular patterns of income growth, use of the election procedure may, in fact, permit a deferral. However, on balance, it appears unlikely that taxpayers will realize any significant federal tax benefit by making the election. On the other hand, it is possible that the election will preserve or create a deferral in the payment of state income taxes.

An interesting issue that remains open is the relationship between the applicable election provision and the general provisions allowing taxpayers to retain, adopt, or change to a fiscal year for substantial business reasons.[279] The National Office may take a position that taxpayers failing to make the election implicitly acknowledge that they do not have substantial business reasons for using a fiscal year. Otherwise, the IRS may argue, the taxpayer would have made the election. Such a position by the IRS would be unfortunate, inappropriate, and inconsistent with the present rules allowing use of a fiscal year for substantial business reasons.

[1] Section 444 Election by Partnerships, S Corporations, and Personal Service Corporations

[a] Background

On May 24, 1988, the Treasury issued temporary regulations under Section 444 relating to the election of a taxable year other than a required year by a partnership, S corporation, or PSC.[280] The temporary regulations are lengthy, complex, and comprehensive. They come with their own table of contents. They cover the election to use a taxable year other than the required taxable year (providing both general rules and limitations), tiered structures, and rules governing the manner and time of making Section 444 elections.

Taxpayers and tax advisors must be familiar with these regulations and any subsequently issued modifications, explanations, and interpretations. The regulations are generally effective for tax years beginning after December 31, 1986.

---

[279] See discussion supra ¶¶ 10.05[2], 10.05[4].

[280] Temp. Reg. § 1.444-0T, et. seq.

[b] Conditions for Making Section 444 Election

A partnership, S corporation, or PSC is eligible to make an Section 444 election to adopt, continue, or use a fiscal year if three conditions are satisfied:

- The entity must not be a member of a tiered structure (with a certain limited exception).
- The entity must not have had an Section 444 election in effect previously.
- Generally, the fiscal year must not have a deferral period of more than three months (i.e., the adopted or continued year must be a September, October, or November fiscal year).[281]

To make a Section 444 election, the entity must file Form 8716.[282]

[2] Termination of Section 444 Election

A Section 444 election generally remains in effect until it is terminated. A Section 444 election is terminated when the entity takes certain actions or when certain events exist, as follows:[283]

- When the entity changes to a required taxable year
- When the entity liquidates, including a deemed liquidation of a partnership under Treasury Regulation § 1.708-1(b)(1)(iv)
- When the entity fails to comply with the requirements of either Section 7519 or Section 280H, whichever is applicable
- When the entity becomes a member of a tiered structure (unless an applicable exception is available)
- When a corporation's S corporation election is terminated
- When a PSC ceases to be a PSC.

In the latter two events, a special rule applies to continue the Section 444 election when a corporation is a PSC immediately after termination of its S corporation status or, conversely, when a PSC ceases to be a PSC because it becomes an S corporation.

[3] Tiered Structures

Generally, a tiered structure exists when an entity owns or is owned by a partnership, an S corporation, a PSC, or a trust. However, for this purpose,

---

[281] There are special rules regarding the deferral period for entities that change or retain their taxable years.

[282] See Temp. Reg. § 1.444-3T.

[283] Temp. Reg. § 1.444-1T(a)(5).

grantor trusts and certain trusts treated like grantor trusts are excluded. The entity that is owned or that owns is referred to as "deferral entity."[284]

If an entity is a member of a tiered structure, the entity cannot make or continue a Section 444 election unless all the entities within the tiered structure have the same taxable year.[285] The date for determining the existence of a tiered structure generally is the last day of the required taxable year ending within the taxable year that would result from a Section 444 election. In other words, if an S corporation with a September 30 taxable year desired to retain that taxable year by making a Section 444 election for its taxable year beginning October 1, 1987, then December 31, 1987, would be the time for determining whether the S corporation is a member of a tiered structure. However, for taxable years beginning in 1987, a special rule provides that an entity will not be a member of the tiered structure if, on the date the entity files its Section 444 election, it is not a member of the tiered structure. Thus, in the above illustration, the S corporation would be considered a member of a tiered structure for its taxable year beginning October 1, 1987, only if the S corporation was a member of a tiered structure on both December 31, 1987, and the date that the S corporation filed its Section 444 election.

[a] De Minimis Rules

The temporary regulations include two de minimis rules allowing an entity to disregard certain deferral entities in determining whether it is a member of a tiered structure. The first de minimis rule (known as the downstream de minimis rule) provides that ownership by the entity of one or more deferral entities will be disregarded if, in the aggregate, all such deferral entities meet either a 5 percent adjusted taxable income test or a 2 percent gross income test.[286] Under the 5 percent test, ownership will be disregarded if all such deferral entities accounted for not more than 5 percent of the partnership's, S corporation's, or PSC's adjusted taxable income for the testing period. "Testing period" means the taxable year that ends immediately prior to the taxable year for which the partnership, S corporation, or PSC desires to make or continue a Section 444 election. Under the 2 percent test, the approach is the same except that the percentage is applied to gross income rather than to adjusted taxable income.

The second de minimis rule (known as the upstream de minimis rule) provides that if an entity is directly owned by one or more deferral entities, such ownership is disregarded if the deferral entities own in the aggregate 5 percent or less of the entity desiring to make or continue a Section 444

---

[284] Temp. Reg. § 1.444-2T.

[285] Temp. Reg. § 1.444-2T(e).

[286] Temp. Reg. § 1.444-2T(c)(2).

election. For this purpose, the 5 percent or less may be of either an interest in the current profits of the partnership or the stock (measured by value) of the S corporation or PSC.

[b] Same-Taxable-Year Exception

A partnership or S corporation may have a Section 444 election, in effect, if the tiered structure consists entirely of partnerships or S corporations (or both), all of which have the same taxable year. Consequently, this exception is generally not available if a PSC is a member of the tiered structure.[287]

[4] Limitations on Deferral Period

In general, a Section 444 election may be made only for a deferral period that is not longer than three months. In other words, an entity may adopt a September, October, or November fiscal year. However, if the entity is changing from a taxable year that has a shorter deferral period (e.g., a taxpayer is changing from an October or November taxable year), then the deferral period elected may not exceed the deferral period of the year from which the taxpayer is changing. To illustrate, a taxpayer with an October taxable year may only change to a November taxable year. It may not change to a September taxable year.

The temporary regulations provided special transition rules. First, if a corporation elected S corporation status after September 18, 1986 and before January 1, 1988 and elected to have a calendar taxable year, then that corporation was allowed to modify the normal deferral period limitations on changing its taxable year. Such a corporation could use the deferral period of its last taxable year prior to electing S corporation status. In order to benefit from this rule, the corporation electing S corporation status must have been in existence prior to electing that status.[288]

A second transition rule provided that an otherwise qualified entity could make a Section 444 election to have a taxable year that was the same as the entity's last taxable year beginning in 1986.[289] Under this rule, the election could only be made for the entity's first taxable year beginning after December 31, 1986.

There seems to be no sound reason or logical basis for limiting the deferral period to three months. Inasmuch as taxpayers are paying for the

---

[287] Temp. Reg. § 1.444-2T(e). See Temp. Reg. § 1.444-2T(e)(5) for the detailed rules governing the interaction of the de minimis rules with the same-taxable-year exception.

[288] Temp. Reg. § 1.444-1T(b)(2)(ii).

[289] See Temp. Reg. § 1.444-1T(b)(3).

privilege of being on a fiscal year,[290] it seems unnecessary to restrict the available fiscal years to September, October, and November. Instead, taxpayers should be able to take into account the circumstances of their particular businesses, the costs incurred in filing applicable tax returns, and other relevant factors. The present rule thus seems somewhat shortsighted on the part of the Treasury.

[5] Section 444 Election Procedures

A Section 444 election is made by filing Form 8716 (Election to Have a Tax Year Other Than a Required Tax Year) with the Service Center indicated in the instructions to the Form. The Form must be filed by the earlier of (1) the fifteenth day of the fifth month following the month that includes the first day of the taxable year for which the election will first be effective or (2) the due date (without regard to extensions) of the income tax return resulting from the Section 444 election.[291]

However, if by reason of the preceding rules, the due date for filing Form 8716 was prior to July 26, 1988, the due date was extended to July 26, 1988.[292] In addition to filing the form with the appropriate Service Center, a copy of Form 8716 must be attached to the income tax return for the taxable year for which the Section 444 election is made.

[a] Corporation Electing S Corporation Status

A corporation electing S corporation status that also desires to make a Section 444 election is required to file Form 8716 in accordance with the general rules. However, the corporation need not file Form 8716 with its Form 2553 (Election by Small Business Corporation).

On the other hand, a corporation electing S corporation status after September 26, 1988, that desires to make a Section 444 election, is required to state its intention to make a Section 444 election on Form 2553, if qualified. Alternatively, it may make a "back-up Section 444 election." If the corporation fails to state either of these intentions, the District Director may at his discretion disregard a subsequent Section 444 election by the entity.

---

[290] See infra ¶¶ 10.07[6], 10.07[8].

[291] Temp. Reg. § 1.444-3T(b). The Commissioner granted an extension of time for filing the requisite Form 8716 in numerous instances where the taxpayer intended to file the form timely and engaged a qualified tax professional for that purpose, but the form was filed late due to an error on the part of the tax professional. See, e.g., Priv. Ltr. Ruls. 9018009 (Jan. 30, 1990), 9018012 (Jan. 30, 1990), 9018014 (Jan. 31, 1990), and 9018021 (Jan. 31, 1990).

[292] Temp. Reg. § 1.444-3T(b).

[b] Back-Up Section 444 Election

If an entity requests permission to use a particular tax year based on business purpose, the entity may file a so-called backup Section 444 election, if otherwise qualified. Then, if the entity's business purpose request is denied by the Commissioner, the entity will be able to activate its backup election for the year.[293]

This opportunity is obviously beneficial but may also be detrimental. On one hand, if the taxpayer believes that its request for a change to a fiscal year may be denied for lack of adequate business reasons, it benefits by having a backup election in place. However, the backup election may only be for a September, October, or November fiscal year, which may be inconsistent with the needs of the business.

On the other hand, the filing of such a backup election, if known to the technician at the National Office to whom the request for change in fiscal year is assigned, may cause that technician to conclude that the taxpayer does not have confidence that its business reasons are sufficient. This, in turn, may cause the technician to conclude that inadequate business reasons have been provided.

[6] Required Payment by Partnership or S Corporation

For each applicable election year, a partnership or an S corporation must make the specified required payment.[294] However, if the required payment for an applicable year is not more than $500 and the partnership or the S corporation was not obligated to make a required payment for a prior year, the partnership or the S corporation need not make a required payment for the applicable election year. Nevertheless, the partnership or S corporation must file a return.

[a] Amount of Payment

The required payment for any election year of a partnership or S corporation is the amount equal to the excess of (1) the highest applicable tax rate plus one percentage point (36 percent for election years beginning in 1987), determined without regard to the effect of the phase-out of the 15 percent rate and personal exemptions, times the entity's net base year income over (2) the cumulative amount of all required payments actually made for all preceding applicable election years. A partnership or an S corporation that is a member of a tiered structure must separately determine the amount

---

[293] See Temp. Reg. § 1.444-3T(b)(4), for the rules and procedures regarding a backup Section 444 election.

[294] IRC § 7519; Temp. Reg. § 1.7519-2T.

of its required payment without regard to the required payment of any other member of the tiered structure.[295]

Under the 1986 Act, certain partners and shareholders were entitled to a four-year spread of the income and expense items from a partnership or an S corporation that was required to change its taxable year. In order to provide a de facto four-year spread, Section 7519(b)(1)(A) multiplied the required payment otherwise required to be made by a partnership or an S corporation by a specified percentage.[296] However, certain entities (e.g., a corporation electing to be an S corporation for a taxable year beginning in 1987) that qualified to make a Section 444 election (and thereby to obtain a de facto four-year spread) may have had partners or shareholders that would not have been entitled to a four-year spread under the 1986 Act. Nevertheless, the temporary regulations provided that the applicable percentage for the first taxable year beginning in 1987 for any partnership or S corporation properly making a Section 444 election was 25 percent.

[i] **Net base year income.** The net base year income of a partnership or an S corporation is the sum of (1) the deferral ratio multiplied by the partnership's or the S corporation's net income for the base year plus (2) the excess (if any) of (a) the deferral ratio multiplied by the aggregate amount of applicable payments made by the partnership or S corporation during the base year over (b) the aggregate amount of such applicable payments made during the deferral period of the base year.

[ii] **Base year, deferral ratio, and applicable payment.** The term "base year" means, with respect to any applicable election year, the taxable year of the partnership or the S corporation immediately preceding the applicable election year. The term "deferral ratio" is defined as the number of months in the deferral period of the applicable election year divided by 12. The term "applicable payment" is defined as any amount deductible in the base year that is includable at any time, directly or indirectly, in the gross income of a taxpayer who is a partner or shareholder during the base year. The term "applicable payment" does not include any guaranteed payment made under Section 707(c). In general, an amount is indirectly includable in the gross income of a partner or a shareholder if the amount is includable in the gross income of a related party.[297]

If an S corporation was a C corporation for the base year, the corporation must be treated as if it were an S corporation for the base year for purposes of determining net base year income, including applicable payments. Consequently, amounts deductible by a C corporation in the base

---

[295] See Temp. Reg. § 1.7519-1T(d), Ex. 3.

[296] IRC § 7519(d)(4).

[297] For this purpose, a related party is determined under Temp. Reg. § 1.7519-1T(b)(5)(iv)(D).

year that are includable in the gross income of a taxpayer who is a shareholder during the base year are treated as if deductible by an S corporation and are within the meaning of the term "applicable payment."

[iii] Special rule for base years of less than 12 months. If the base year is a taxable year of less than 12 months, the net base-year income for this short base year is an amount equal to the excess, if any, of (1) the deferral ratio multiplied by the annualized short base-year income over (2) applicable payments made during the deferral period of the applicable election year following the base year.[298]

[iv] Special rules for certain applicable election years. Special rules are provided for determining the applicable payment for certain applicable election years. If an applicable election year is a partnership's or S corporation's first year in existence, because the partnership or S corporation is newly formed, the required payment is zero. If a partnership or an S corporation makes a Section 444 election and the resulting applicable election year (the first applicable election year) of the partnership or the S corporation ends prior to the last day of the required year, the required payment is also zero.

[b] Payment of Required Payments

For an applicable election year that began in 1987, the required payment was due and payable without assessment and notice on or before the date specified for filing Form 720. The required payment must have been paid by check or money order and sent, together with Form 720, to the Service Center indicated in the instructions. For an applicable election year beginning after 1987, the required payment is due and payable without assessment and notice on or before May 15 of the calendar year following the calendar year in which the applicable election year begins.

[c] Refunds of Required Payments

A partnership or an S corporation is entitled to a refund of all or a portion of required payments previously made if either of two circumstances arise. First, a refund is required if the product of the applicable percentage of the adjusted highest section one rate multiplied by the net base-year income is less than the cumulative amount of the required payments in all preceding applicable election years reduced by cumulative refunds from such years). Second, a refund is also required if the partnership or the S corporation terminates its Section 444 election.[299]

---

[298] See Temp. Reg. § 1.7519-1T(b)(5)(v).

[299] See Temp. Reg. § 1.444-1T(a)(5), regarding terminations of Section 444 elections.

[7] Returns Under Section 7519

Each partnership or S corporation that makes a Section 444 election must include all information required on any return or statement as necessary to carry out the provisions of Section 7519. A partnership or an S corporation must file a return showing the required payment, even if the required payment for the applicable election year is zero. For an applicable election year that began in 1987, the return had to be made on Form 720 (Quarterly Federal Excise Tax Return). For an applicable election year beginning after 1987, the return must be made on Form 720 unless some other form is prescribed by the Commissioner.

Partnerships and S corporations that otherwise would have filed Form 720 for the second quarter of 1988 had to file Form 720 by the normal due date of the form for the second quarter of 1988. Thus, is most cases, these partnerships and S corporations had to file Form 720 on or before July 31, 1988. However, some partnerships or S corporations had to file Form 720 on or before August 31, 1988, for example, those required to pay the windfall profits tax. Partnerships and S corporations making a Section 444 election that otherwise would not file Form 720 for the second quarter of 1988 had to file the form on or before July 31, 1988.[300]

[8] Distributions or Reduced Deductions by Personal Service Corporations

The rules governing the availability of Section 444 elections to PSCs are set forth under Section 280H. For these purposes, the term PSC has the same meaning as it has under Section 441.[301]

If for any applicable election year, a PSC does not satisfy certain minimum distribution requirements,[302] the deduction otherwise allowable will not exceed the maximum deductible amount.[303] Any amount not allowed as a deduction in an applicable election year is allowed as a deduction in the succeeding taxable year. The disallowance of deductions under Section 280H does not apply for purposes of determining whether compensation to employee-owners is reasonable.

[a] Applicable Amount

The term "applicable amount" means, with respect to a taxable year, any amount otherwise deductible by a PSC in such year and includable at

---

[300] Temp. Reg. § 1.444-3T(b)(4)(iii) provides a special rule regarding the due date for filing a return when a partnership or S corporation makes a backup Section 444 election.

[301] Temp. Reg. § 1.441-4T(d).

[302] See discussion infra ¶ 10.07[8][b].

[303] See infra ¶ 10.07[8][d], for discussion of maximum deductible amount.

any time, directly or indirectly, in the gross income of an employee-owner. An amount includable in the gross income of an employee-owner will be considered an applicable amount even though such employee owns no stock of the corporation on the date the employee included the amount in income.[304]

[b] Minimum Distribution Requirement

A PSC meets the minimum distribution requirement for an applicable election year if, during the deferral period of such year, applicable amounts (not including excess applicable amounts carried over from the preceding year) for all employee-owners in the aggregate equal or exceed the lesser of the amount determined under the preceding-year test or the amount determined under the three-year-average test.[305]

Special rules are provided for applying Section 280H to newly organized PSCs and to existing corporations that become PSCs. A newly organized PSC satisfies the preceding year test and the three-year-average test for the first year of the corporation's existence. This satisfaction is deemed to apply without regard to any other facts. If an existing corporation was not a PSC for each of the three years preceding the corporation's first applicable election year, the determination of whether the corporation satisfies the various tests is made by treating the corporation as though it were a PSC for each of these years. If the corporation has not been in existence for three or more years, then the test is applied for as many as the corporation has been in existence.

[i] **Preceding-year test.** The amount determined under the preceding-year test is the product of (1) the applicable amounts during the taxable year preceding the applicable election year divided by the number of months in the preceding taxable year, multiplied by (2) the number of months in the deferral period of the preceding taxable year.

[ii] **Three-year-average test.** The amount determined under the three-year average test is the applicable percentage multiplied by the adjusted taxable income for the deferral period of the applicable election year. The term "applicable percentage" is defined as the percentage (not in excess of 95 percent) determined by dividing (1) applicable amounts during the three taxable years of the corporation immediately preceding the applicable election year by (2) the adjusted taxable income of such corporation for such three taxable years. Again, if the PSC has been in existence for fewer than three

---

[304] An amount is indirectly includable in the gross income of an employee-owner if the amount is includable in the gross income of a related party as determined under Temp. Reg. § 1.280H-1T(b)(4)(ii).

[305] These tests are described in Temp. Reg. § 1.280H-1T(c).

years, the three-year-average test is applied by taking into account only the years that the corporation has been in existence.

[c] Adjusted Taxable Income

The term "adjusted taxable income" is defined as the taxable income determined without regard to applicable amounts. The adjusted taxable income for the deferral period of an applicable election year equals the adjusted taxable income that would have resulted if the PSC had filed an income tax return for the deferral period of the applicable election year under its normal methods of accounting. However, a PSC may make a reasonable estimate of such amount.

For these purposes, any net operating loss carry-over must be reduced by the amount of such carry-over that is attributable to the deduction of applicable amounts. The portion of the carry-over attributable to the deduction of applicable amounts is the difference between the carry-over computed with the deduction of such amounts and the carry-over computed without the deduction of such amounts. Any NOL loss carry-over to the applicable election year is to be allowed first against the income of the deferral period.

[d] Maximum Deductible Amount

The term "maximum deductible amount" means the applicable amounts during the deferral period of the applicable election year, plus the product of (1) such amounts divided by the number of months in the deferral period of the applicable election year times (2) the number of months in the nondeferral period of the applicable election year. The term "nondeferral period" means that portion of the applicable election year that occurs after the portion of such year constituting the deferral period.[306]

[e] Disallowance of Operating Loss Carry-Backs

No net operating loss carry-back is allowed to (or from) any taxable year of a PSC to which a Section 444 election applies.[307]

---

[306] Temp. Reg. § 1.280H-1T(d).

[307] Temp. Reg. § 1.280H-1T(e)(3).

CHAPTER 11

Time Value of Money

¶ 11.01 Definition of "Time Value of Money" 11-3
    [1] The Problem—A Failure to Consider 11-3
        [a] Different Character of Income 11-4
        [b] Different Methods of Accounting 11-5
    [2] Congressional Response 11-5
        [a] Before 1984 Act 11-5
            [i] Original Section 483 11-5
            [ii] Section 163(b) 11-6
            [iii] Early OID provisions 11-7
            [iv] IRS position 11-7
        [b] 1984 Act 11-8

¶ 11.02 Original Issue Discount 11-9
    [1] Debt Instruments 11-11
    [2] Amounts Received for Debt Instruments: Section 1271 11-12
        [a] Effect of Intent to Call Before Maturity 11-13
        [b] Short-Term Obligations 11-15
        [c] Exceptions 11-16
    [3] Current Inclusion of OID: Section 1272 11-16
        [a] Obligations Issued After July 1, 1982 11-17
            [i] Definitions and terms 11-18
            [ii] Exceptions 11-22
            [iii] Subsequent holders of debt obligation 11-24
        [b] Corporate Obligations Issued Before July 2, 1982 11-25
    [4] Amount of OID: Section 1273 11-26
        [a] Stated Redemption Price at Maturity 11-26
            [i] Qualified stated interest 11-26
            [ii] Loans with indefinite maturities 11-28
            [iii] Installment obligations 11-28
            [iv] Puts, calls, and other options 11-31
        [b] Issue Price 11-31
            [i] Publicly offered debt instruments issued for cash ... 11-31
            [ii] Non–publicly offered debt instruments issued for
                cash 11-32
            [iii] Debt instruments issued for property with public
                trading 11-33
            [iv] Investment units; convertible debt 11-34

           [v] Other cases 11-35
        [c] De Minimis Rule 11-35
    [5] Issue Price in Certain Cases Involving Property: Section
        1274 11-37
        [a] Imputation of Interest 11-38
            [i] General rules—applicable federal rates 11-38
            [ii] Potentially abusive situations 11-40
            [iii] Use of special 9 percent discount rate 11-42
            [iv] Sale-leaseback transactions 11-42
        [b] Exceptions 11-42
            [i] Sale of certain farms for $1 million or less 11-42
            [ii] Sale of principal residence 11-43
            [iii] Sale or exchange of property for $250,000 or less ... 11-43
            [iv] Sale of patent 11-43
            [v] Sale or exchange to which Section 483(e) applies ... 11-44
            [vi] Debt instruments due in six months or less 11-44
            [vii] Personal use property 11-44
        [c] Election to Use Cash Method 11-44

¶ 11.03 Contingent Payments 11-45
    [1] Definition 11-46
    [2] Market-Based Contingent Payments 11-47
    [3] Small Issues 11-49
    [4] Other Contingent Debt Instruments 11-51

¶ 11.04 Certain Deferred Payments: Section 483 11-53
    [1] History and Development 11-53
    [2] Application of Section 483 11-55
        [a] Due Dates of Payments 11-55
        [b] Unstated Interest 11-56
            [i] General rules 11-56
            [ii] Special rules on sale of land to related party 11-57
        [c] Periods When Unstated Interest Is Recognized 11-57
        [d] Exceptions to Application of Section 483 11-57

¶ 11.05 Market Discount: Sections 1276–1278 11-58
    [1] Definitions 11-58
    [2] Treatment of Market Discount Income 11-59
    [3] Deferral of Interest Deductions Allocable to Accrued Market
        Discount 11-60

¶ 11.06 Short-Term Obligations: Sections 1281–1283 11-61
    [1] Current Inclusion of Acquisition Discount 11-61
    [2] Deferral of Interest Deduction 11-62

¶ 11.07 Tax Treatment of Stripped Bonds: Section 1286 11-62
    [1] Treatment of Stripper 11-62
    [2] Treatment of Purchaser 11-63

¶ 11.08 Gains on Certain Obligations: Section 1287 11-63

¶ 11.09 OID on Tax-Exempt Obligations: Section 1288 11-64

¶ 11.10 Use of Property or Services: Section 467 11-64
    [1] Section 467 Rental Agreement 11-64
        [a] Deferred Payments of Rent 11-65

　　　　　　[b] Stepped Rents 11-65
　　　　　　[2] Treatment of Section 467 Rental Agreements 11-66
　　　　　　[3] Agreements Pertaining to Deferred Payments for Services ... 11-67

¶ 11.11　Below-Market Loans: Section 7872 11-67
　　　　　　[1] Definition of "Below-Market Loan" 11-68
　　　　　　[2] Below-Market Loans Subject to Section 7872 11-68
　　　　　　[3] Treatment of Below-Market Loans 11-69
　　　　　　　　[a] Demand Loans 11-69
　　　　　　　　[b] Term Loans 11-71
　　　　　　　　[c] Special Rules for Gift Loans 11-72

¶ 11.01 DEFINITION OF "TIME VALUE OF MONEY"

"Time value of money" refers to the economic premise that a dollar received today is worth more than a dollar received tomorrow. The term embraces both the economic benefit of making and the economic cost of receiving a deferred payment, i.e., a payment that is made after the date of the transaction to which it relates. Typical transactions that give rise to deferred payments are loans, seller-financed sales of property, and all other transactions in which one party provides consideration before equivalent consideration is provided by the other party. Parties to these transactions generally take the time value of money into account through charges for interest, which is generally defined as the charge for the use of money or for forbearance from its use.[1]

This chapter describes the more significant time value of money provisions of the Internal Revenue Code,[2] identifies their objectives, and discusses the uncertainties associated with them. Guidance is provided in many instances, but it is incumbent on taxpayers and tax practitioners to remain alert to changing interpretations, new rulings, newly proposed and final regulations, and all other explanatory material.

[1] The Problem—A Failure to Consider

Prior to the Tax Reform Act of 1984 (the 1984 Act), unless the parties to a transaction agreed to a charge for the time value of money, there generally would be none, i.e., no such charge would be imputed. Hence, the tax law essentially ignored the time value of money inherent in deferred payment transactions.[3]

---

[1] Deputy v. DuPont, 308 US 488 (1940); Rev. Rul. 72-458, 1972-2 CB 514.

[2] Unless otherwise indicated, all references to the "Code" or to "IRC" are to the Internal Revenue Code of 1986, as amended.

[3] There were a few exceptions. See, e.g., Sections 483, 163, 1231, 1232A, and 1232B as they existed prior to 1984.

The general failure of the tax law to address time value of money concepts (together with the very high interest rates that prevailed during the late 1970s and early 1980s) gave rise to tax practices that the Treasury and the Internal Revenue Service ultimately deemed to be inappropriate and abusive. These practices were premised on two facets of the U.S. tax system at the time: (1) that different types of income (e.g., ordinary and capital) were subject to different rates of tax and (2) that the different parties to the same transaction could recognize corresponding items of income and expense in different tax years, depending on their particular methods of accounting.

[a] Different Character of Income

The effect of taxing different types of income at different rates is demonstrated in the following situation.

EXAMPLE: Assume that a capital asset with a basis of $10 and a fair market value (FMV) of $100 was sold in 1983 under a deferred payment arrangement calling for a payment of $100 one year from the date of the sale. Assume further that applicable interest rates at the time were 10 percent. Under the then-applicable bifurcated structure of our tax system, the gain on the sale would have been taxed at capital gain rates while interest would have been taxed at ordinary rates. Hence, if 10 percent interest had been charged, the seller would have been subject to a maximum capital gains tax of $18 [20% × ($100 selling price − $10 basis)] and a maximum ordinary income tax of $5 (50% × $10 interest). The total tax would have been $23 ($18 + $5).

In light of the foregoing result, the seller would have been better off to take the time value of money into account by charging a higher price for the property instead of charging interest. Thus, if the seller had sold the property for $110 payable one year from the date of sale and had not charged any specified interest, the seller's maximum aggregate tax liability would have been $20 [20% × ($110 selling price − $10 basis)]. Recharacterizing the $10 of interest as additional selling price would have saved the seller $3 ($23 − $20).

Although it was possible that the purchaser would not consent to such a recharacterization of deductible interest to additional purchase price, generally that was not the case. The purchaser was often less concerned than the seller by the character of payments because the purchase price of depreciable property was deductible by means of depreciation. Although depreciation would spread total deductions over a period of years, whereas interest is often deductible entirely in the year to which it relates, the difference in timing could be insignificant or, if significant, the parties could negotiate a sharing of the tax benefits arising from the recharacterization. In this way, both the seller and purchaser would benefit, and only the government would lose.

[b] Different Methods of Accounting

The time value of money also provided tax benefits when it was taken into account in connection with transactions between parties using different methods of accounting. The benefits arose because of the different principles for recognizing income and expense under different methods of accounting. For example, under an accrual method, taxpayers are required to recognize income in the year in which the so-called all events test is satisfied even though the accrued income may not be received for a substantial period of time and even though interest is not charged on the deferred payments. Correlatively, accrual method taxpayers may deduct expenses prior to payment, without regard to whether interest is owed on the deferred payment. See Chapter 4 for a discussion of accrual methods of accounting. Under the cash receipts and disbursements method (the cash method), income is recognized when actually or constructively received, and expenses are deducted when paid. See Chapter 3 for discussion of the cash method.

Application of these rules to a transaction between a purchaser on an accrual method and a seller on the cash method generated the following benefit. The cash method seller would charge interest on deferred payments but would not recognize interest income until the payments were received. The accrual method purchaser would accrue and deduct the interest currently, although payments would not be made until later. Similarly, an accrual method borrower could obtain a loan from a cash method lender. The borrower would obtain current deductions for accrued but unpaid interest, while the lender deferred the recognition of income until payment was received. In each case, there would be a mismatching of the time when corresponding sides of the same transaction would be reported. Although the tax reporting just described was proper, the Treasury viewed it as an abuse that resulted in revenue-escaping taxation.

[2] Congressional Response

[a] Before 1984 Act

Prior to the 1984 Act, congressional responses to the time value of money problems described in the preceding section were minimal. Essentially, they consisted of the enactment of Sections 483 and 163(b), and the original issue discount (OID) provisions of Sections 1232, 1232A, and 1232B.

[i] Original Section 483.   Section 483, as originally enacted, provided for a recharacterization of principal as interest on certain deferred payment sales of property where the applicable agreement called for no interest or provided for interest at less than a specified rate. If the specified rate of interest was itself below the then-applicable market rate (as it often was), taxpayers could charge interest at the specified rate and recharacterize

additional economic interest as principal with no practical risk of challenge by the IRS. For example, if the specified rate of interest were 9 percent and the then-prevailing market rate were 18 percent, the parties to a transaction calling for a one-year deferral in payment might agree to charge 9 percent interest and to increase the selling price by an appropriate corresponding percent, secure in the knowledge that the IRS would not, as a practical matter, seek to recharacterize the additional selling price as interest.[4]

[ii] **Section 163(b).** Section 163(b) is a rather limited provision. It provides that in the case of personal property or educational services that are purchased under a contract calling for installment payments and requiring separately stated carrying charges that do not permit the interest charge to be ascertained, the installment payments are deemed to include interest of 6 percent on the average unpaid balance. For this purpose, the average unpaid balance is the sum of the unpaid balance outstanding on the first day of each month beginning during the taxable year divided by 12.[5] However, in no event may the amount treated as interest in any year exceed the aggregate carrying charges attributable to that year.[6]

EXAMPLE: Assume that on January 10 of year 1, the taxpayer purchases a television set for $375 plus a stated carrying charge of $25. Assume further that of the $400 total, $50 is paid at the time of sale and the balance is payable in 14 consecutive monthly installments of $25, each installment due on the tenth day of each month beginning with February. If all payments are timely made, the unpaid balance at the beginning of each month for year 1 will be as follows:

First date of	Unpaid balance
January	$ 0
February	$ 350
March	$ 325
April	$ 300
May	$ 275
June	$ 250
July	$ 225
August	$ 200
September	$ 175
October	$ 150
November	$ 125
December	$ 100
	$2,475

---

[4] For example, a 9 percent return on $108.26 invested for one year produces $9.74. This amount when added to an increased selling price of $108.26 would produce a total recovery of $118. See infra ¶ 11.04 for discussion of present Section 483.

[5] IRC § 163(b)(1).

[6] IRC § 163(b)(2).

To determine the deemed interest in this transaction, the sum of the unpaid balances ($2,475) is divided by 12. This results in an average balance of $206.25. Multiplying this amount by 6 percent results in $12.38 of deemed interest. Since this amount is less than the stated carrying charge of $25, the full amount of the $12.38 is treated as interest.[7]

[iii] Early OID provisions. The original OID provision did nothing more than make it clear that OID was to be characterized as interest.[8] It did not affect the time when the OID would be included in income or deducted as an expense. In 1969, the OID rules were amended to require OID to be reported ratably over the period between the issue date and the maturity date of the obligation. For example, if the taxpayer borrowed $100,000, agreeing to repay $133,100 in three years, $11,033 of the $33,100 of OID would be allocated to each of the three years. This ratable allocation provided larger amounts of income and expense in earlier years than would have been provided if a constant interest rate had been applied to the initial borrowing. If a constant interest rate had been applied, compounded annually, the allocation would have been as follows:

Year	Interest	Computation
1	$10,000	.10 × $100,000
2	11,000	.10 × 110,000
3	12,100	.10 × 121,000
	$33,100	

If the lender were a tax-exempt entity, use of the straight-line approach was especially desirable because it would benefit the borrower and be of no adverse tax consequence to the lender. In 1982, the OID provisions were changed to require the allocation of OID using a constant interest rate. This change effectively incorporated economic accrual concepts by applying the interest rate to the sum of unpaid principal and unpaid interest, as opposed to merely allocating equal amounts of interest to each period of equal length, i.e., the straight-line concept.[9] Nevertheless, the OID rules continued to be inapplicable to a number of obligations, including those issued by individuals, those maturing in less than one year, those that were tax-exempt, those that were issued for rent or services, and those that were not themselves traded on a market and were issued for property that was not traded on a market.

[iv] IRS position. Although each of the provisions previously discussed (Sections 483, 163(b), 1232, 1232A, and 1232B) was intended to recast

---

[7] See Treas. Reg. § 1.163-2(d).

[8] IRC § 1232, repealed by the 1984 Act.

[9] IRC §§ 1232A (repealed by 1984 Act), 163(e) (prior to amendment by 1984 Act).

deferred payment transactions as if interest had been taken into account, their coverage was limited in scope. Moreover, because of the significant inflation and corresponding high interest rates during the late 1970s and early 1980s, great interest was rekindled in enacting legislation to guard against time value of money abuses.

Although legislative responses to the time value of money problems were minimal throughout this period, the IRS was not passive. It often attacked time value of money abuses through the exercise of its discretion under the congressional mandate that the taxpayer must use methods of accounting that clearly reflect income.[10] For example, the taking of a particular deduction was often challenged by the IRS on the basis that in light of a lengthy delay in payment or the probability that payment would not be made, the taking of the deduction would violate the clear reflection of income standard.[11] However, the position of the IRS met with relatively little success.[12] In other contexts, e.g., the making of a no-interest or low-interest loan to a relative, the IRS asserted that a taxable gift had been made to the borrower. At first, the IRS position met with little success,[13] but it ultimately prevailed.[14] Nevertheless, the IRS concluded that success in combating perceived time value of money abuse would be limited unless new legislation were enacted.

[b] 1984 Act

The time value of money rules enacted as part of the 1984 Act are among the most comprehensive rules within the Code. They also are among the most aggressive at seeking to incorporate various principles of economic theory into the Code.

These rules are also among the most complicated in the history of our income tax system. To some extent, they became an embarrassment to the Treasury in that many taxpayers, tax practitioners, and revenue agents did not understand them and were often unable to apply them to transactions. In 1986, more than 100 pages of regulations were proposed in an attempt to

---

[10] See IRC § 446(b) and discussion at ¶¶ 2.02[2], and 4.04[3]. See Don P. Setliff, 53 TCM 1295 (1987), where the court, in finding that the Rule of 78's method of allocating interest did not clearly reflect income in that case, expressly declined to rule whether that method would fail to reflect income clearly per se. In fact, the court used language suggesting that the Rule of 78's method of apportioning interest might be upheld in appropriate circumstances.

[11] See IRC § 446(b) and discussion at ¶¶ 2.02[2], and 4.04[3].

[12] See, e.g., Harrold v. Comm'r, 192 F2d 1002 (4th Cir. 1951); Denise Coal Co. v. Comm'r, 271 F2d 930 (3d Cir. 1959); Ohio River Collieries Co., 77 TC 1369 (1981). But see Mooney Aircraft, Inc. v. United States, 420 F2d 400 (5th Cir. 1969).

[13] Crown v. Comm'r, 585 F2d 234 (7th Cir. 1978).

[14] Dickman v. Comm'r, 465 US 330 (1984), reh'g denied, 466 US 945 (1984).

clarify and explain just some of the time-value provisions.[15] These 1986 proposed regulations were later amended four times in 1989 and 1991.[16] Then, on December 22, 1992, the IRS issued completely revised regulations, albeit still in proposed form.[17] Then, in January 1993, the IRS released a new set of proposed regulations concerning contingent payment debt instruments, but those rules were withdrawn before ever being published in the *Federal Register* and, as of June 1993, still have not been officially issued in any form.[18]

The new proposed regulations are proposed to be effective for debt instruments issued on or after the date that is 60 days after the date the regulations are finalized.[19] The IRS has indicated, however, that it intends to treat the 1986 proposed regulations as authority under Section 6662 for debt instruments issued (and for lending transactions, and sales and exchanges that occurred) prior to withdrawal of the 1986 proposed regulations.[20] Thus, tax practitioners may need to be aware of many of the technical nuances of a set of proposed regulations that were never finalized, especially on points where they prescribe a result somewhat different from the newly proposed regulations or the regulations that ultimately are adopted in final form.

The remainder of this chapter describes the more significant of the Code's time value of money provisions.[21] References to the proposed regulations are to the newly proposed regulations, unless otherwise indicated.

¶ 11.02 ORIGINAL ISSUE DISCOUNT

OID refers to the difference between the consideration received on the issuance of a debt obligation and the amount that will be paid at the maturity of that debt obligation. In effect, it is intended to represent all or some portion of the time value of money.

> **EXAMPLE:** Assume a taxpayer sells property that is traded on an

---

[15] See Prop. Regs. §§ 1.1271–1.1275, as originally proposed April 8, 1986.

[16] 54 Fed. Reg. 37,125 (1989); 56 Fed. Reg. 8308 (1991); 56 Fed. Reg. 21,112 (1991); 56 Fed. Reg. 887 (1991).

[17] 57 Fed. Reg. 60,750 (1992).

[18] See Daily Tax Rep. (BNA) No. 12, at L-9 (Jan. 21, 1993) (release of revised Prop. Reg. § 1.1275-4; Daily Tax Rep. (BNA) No. 14, at G-4 (Jan. 25, 1993) (withdrawal of Prop. Reg. § 1.1275-4 and other regulations projects pending approval by an appointee of President Clinton).

[19] 57 Fed. Reg. 6754 (1992) (preamble to proposed regulations). The rules for "qualified reopenings" of Treasury securities are proposed to be effective for reopenings on or after March 25, 1992.

[20] 57 Fed. Reg. 6754 (1992) (preamble to proposed regulations).

[21] See ¶ 4.04[3] for discussion of economic performance.

established market with a present FMV of $100 in exchange for the purchaser's promise to pay $110 one year later. The OID is $10, the difference between the consideration received on issuance of the debt obligation and the ultimate amount to be paid at maturity of the debt obligation. Had the same property been sold for $121 to be paid two years later, the OID would have been $21. In these two examples, the OID represented the full charge for the time value of money. If the property had been sold under the same terms but with a specified interest charge of 5 percent, then the OID plus the specified interest would have represented the full charge for the time value of money.[22]

The basic issues that arise with respect to OID are simple to state:

- What is a debt instrument for purposes of OID?
- Does the transaction involve OID and, if so, how much?
- In what periods should the OID be recognized by each of the parties to the transaction?
- What happens if the holder of the obligation disposes of it prior to maturity?

Before the 1984 Act, the time value of money provisions governing OID were sufficiently narrow in scope that their applicability was not a problem for many taxpayers and tax practitioners. Generally, those taxpayers whose transactions were covered knew it and were able to retain sufficient technical assistance to respond to the requirements of the OID rules. Those taxpayers and practitioners who did not know much about the OID rules often did not need to know about them because they did not participate in, or advise on, covered transactions. However, such ignorance of the OID rules is no longer defensible on the basis of the rules' limited scope. The 1984 Act so broadens the applicability of the OID rules that virtually all deferred payment transactions may now be covered and, hence, virtually all tax practitioners must be familiar with them.

To accomplish its objective of reducing abuse, the 1984 Act repealed the old OID rules and replaced them with a broad assortment of new rules. In addition, substantial modifications were made to Section 483, and a number of related provisions were added to cover special issues.

The OID rules are spread over a host of Code sections. Sections 1271 through 1275 contain the basic OID rules. Section 1271 pertains to the

---

[22] As discussed infra ¶¶ 11.02[4][b], 11.02[5], the amount received on issuance of the debt obligation in this example is considered to be the $100 value of the property sold only because that property is traded on an established market. See IRC § 1273(b)(3). If the property sold in the example were nontraded property, Section 1274 generally would determine the issue price of the debt instrument (and thus the amount of OID) by discounting the $110 payment to be received, not by reference to the FMV of the property sold.

treatment of amounts received on a retirement, sale, or exchange of debt instruments. Section 1272 provides rules governing the manner in which OID should be allocated to taxable periods. Section 1273 provides rules governing the determination of OID. Section 1274 provides rules governing an imputation of interest where a debt obligation is issued for property and either no interest or inadequate interest is provided. Section 1275 provides various definitions and special rules.

Special rules governing market discount bonds are provided in Sections 1276 through 1278. Separate rules governing short-term obligations are covered in Sections 1281 through 1283. Additional rules governing OID and tax-exempt obligations are provided in Section 1288.

Following a brief discussion of the debt instruments to which the OID rules apply, these various Code provisions are discussed in the sections that follow. For convenience to the reader, they are generally discussed in the order in which they are presented in the Code.

In addition, rules focusing on certain below-market loans are provided in Section 7872. These rules must be considered in all cases that might involve a lack of arm's-length bargaining. Typical situations to which Section 7872 might apply are loans between relatives where an element of gift is likely to be present and loans between a corporation and its owner-employees or key employees where an element of compensation or dividends is present.

[1] Debt Instruments

The OID rules apply to debt instruments. Accordingly, as an initial matter, it is most important that the scope of the term "debt instrument" be defined. The applicable Code section and proposed Treasury regulations provide a very expansive definition. Section 1275(a)(1) provides that except for certain annuity contracts,[23] the term "debt instrument" means a "bond, debenture, note, or certificate or other evidence of indebtedness." The proposed regulations provide that the term debt instrument means "any instrument or contractual arrangement that constitutes indebtedness under Federal income tax law."[24] As a consequence of the breadth of this definition, the term "debt instrument" may include oral promises to pay, obligations arising from the present use of property, and other transactions where the application of the

---

[23] See Section 1275(a)(1)(B), which provides that the term "debt instrument" does not apply to an annuity contract to which Section 72 applies and that depends (in whole or substantial part) on the life expectancy of one or more individuals or is issued by a life insurance company (1) in a transaction in which there is no consideration other than cash or another annuity contract for which this exception is applicable; (2) pursuant to the exercise of an election under an insurance contract by the beneficiary of the contract on the death of the insured party; or (3) in a transaction involving a qualified pension or an employee benefit plan.

[24] Prop. Reg. § 1.1275-1(d).

OID rules might be surprising. On the other hand, debt instruments should not include agreements for the mutual provision of consideration in the future. In other words, a debt instrument for purposes of the OID rules should be one where one party provides consideration currently, with the other party to provide the corresponding consideration later. If each party to the transaction agrees to provide the required consideration at the same time in the future, there is no deferral and the agreement should not be regarded as creating a debt instrument for purposes of the OID rules.

Notwithstanding the breadth of the foregoing definition, particular debt instruments or debt instruments with particular terms may be excluded from the OID rules. These exceptions are identified in the subsequent discussions of particular OID rules.[25] It is important for taxpayers and their tax advisors to be alert to the exceptions and to be prepared to apply the OID rules in their absence.

[2] Amounts Received for Debt Instruments: Section 1271

Section 1271 is a characterization rule. It provides that amounts received on the retirement, sale, or exchange of a debt instrument are to be treated as amounts realized on the sale or exchange of a capital asset. Thus, this provision treats a retirement as the equivalent of a sale or exchange.[26] Consequently, the difference between the amount realized on the retirement, sale, or exchange and the holder's adjusted basis in the debt instrument is recognized as capital gain.[27]

> EXAMPLE: Assume a taxpayer acquires a debt instrument for $860 at the time of its original issue, that the instrument has a face amount of $1,000, and that it matures in 15 years. OID exists in the amount of $140 ($1,000 − $860). Assume further that as of a certain point, this taxpayer has been required to recognize $30 of OID in accordance with the provisions of Section 1272.[28] The amount of OID so recognized increases the taxpayer's basis in the obligation.[29] Thus, after the recognition of $30 of OID, the taxpayer's basis in the obligation is $890 ($860 + $30). If the obligation is then sold for $900, there will be a gain of $10. If the debt is a capital asset in the hands of the taxpayer, this gain on the sale will be capital gain.

---

[25] See discussions infra ¶¶ 11.02[2][c], 11.02[3][a][ii], 11.02[4][c], 11.02[5][b].

[26] The Supreme Court had previously held that gain on the retirement of a debt instrument was ordinary income. Fairbanks v. United States, 306 US 436 (1939).

[27] IRC § 1001(a).

[28] See infra ¶ 11.02[3] for discussion of IRC § 1272.

[29] IRC § 1272(d)(2).

A different rule may apply to the sale, exchange, or retirement of a contingent payment debt instrument.[30] Under the January 1993 regulations that were withdrawn prior to their official publication, a holder's gain on the disposition of such a debt instrument would be treated as interest income.[31] The IRS apparently believes such a rule is necessary in order to prevent changes in value that are properly attributable to the resolution of a contingency, which changes usually are taxed in whole or in part as ordinary income, from being treated like value fluctuations attributable to general market conditions or the creditworthiness of the issuer, which generally receive capital gain treatment under Section 1271.[32] Nevertheless, this rule would represent a departure from both the statute and the 1986 proposed regulations and, therefore, should not govern dispositions prior to its being proposed and becoming effective.

Section 1271 also provides various modifications and exceptions to the general rules of that section. These modifications and exceptions are described in the immediately following sections.

[a] Effect of Intent to Call Before Maturity

Application of the general rules described in the preceding section can result in the conversion of ordinary interest income into capital gain in certain circumstances.

> EXAMPLE: Assume a debt instrument with a face amount of $1,000 payable in 10 years is acquired at original issue for $800 and that the instrument is a capital asset. The $200 of OID will be taken into income over a period of 10 years in accordance with Section 1272.[33] If the debt instrument is called for $1,000 after only five years have run, only a portion of the total OID ($94.43) will have been recognized at the time of sale. Therefore, at the time of call, the holder's basis in the instrument will be $894.43 and capital gain on the call will be $105.57 ($1,000 − $894.43). If the issuer originally had intended to call the obligation after five years (and had provided for a five-year term), all $200 of OID would have been recognized after five years, and there would have been no capital gain on payment of the obligation at maturity.

In other words, when an instrument is called before maturity, less OID will have been recognized at the time of call than would have been recognized had the actual term been the original term. The longer the instrument's stated period to maturity and the earlier the call, the more ordinary income is converted into capital gain.

---

[30] See infra ¶ 11.03 for discussion of contingent payment debt instruments.

[31] Prop. Reg. § 1.1275-4(f), as it would read under the January 1993 release.

[32] See Daily Tax Rep. (BNA) No. 12, at L-12, (Jan. 21, 1993).

[33] See infra ¶ 11.02[3] for discussion of IRC § 1272.

Section 1271(a)(2) prevents this conversion where, at the time of original issue of the debt instrument, there is an intent to call the instrument before maturity. If this intent exists, any gain realized on the sale or exchange of the debt instrument that does not exceed the unaccrued OID is treated as ordinary income.[34] Unaccrued OID for this purpose is the total OID on the debt instrument reduced by the portion previously includable in the gross income of any holder (unreduced by any acquisition premium any holder may have paid).[35] Thus, in the preceding example, if the parties had intended that the debt instrument be called after only five years, the holder's gain of $105.57 would be ordinary income. Section 1272(a)(2) recognizes the economic fact that when a call is intended, the difference between the call price and the holder's adjusted basis is more in the nature of an agreed-on return to the holder (i.e., interest) than capital gain.

Because this rule applies only where, at the time of issuance, there is an intent to call the debt instrument prior to maturity, determination of this intent is quite important. An "intention to call a debt instrument before maturity" means a written or oral agreement or understanding, not provided for in the debt instrument, between the issuer and the original holder of the debt instrument that the issuer will redeem the debt instrument before maturity.[36] This intention can exist even if it is conditional (e.g., the issuer's decision to call depends on its financial condition on the potential call date) or is not legally binding.[37] A mandatory sinking-fund provision, call option, or other similar device that is provided in the debt instrument is not evidence of an intention to call under these rules.[38] Thus, the intention to call before maturity should be limited to fact patterns involving an unwritten plan to avoid taxes, i.e., to minimize current accruals of OID and to convert ordinary income into capital gain.

The rules governing the computation of gain on the sale or exchange of a debt instrument where there is an intention to call before maturity do not apply to tax-exempt obligations or to any holder who purchased the debt instrument at a premium.[39] The rules also do not apply to debt instruments that are publicly offered or to which Section 1272(a)(6) applies (relating to certain interests in or mortgages held by a real estate mortgage investment conduit (REMIC) and certain other debt instruments with payments subject to acceleration).[40]

Note that the purpose of Section 1271(a)(2) is to recharacterize as

---

[34] IRC § 1272(a)(2)(A).

[35] Id.

[36] Prop. Reg. § 1.1271-1(a)(1).

[37] Id.

[38] 57 Fed. Reg. 60,751 (1992) (preamble to proposed regulations).

[39] IRC § 1271(a)(2)(B).

[40] Prop. Reg. § 1.1271-1(a)(2).

ordinary income what might otherwise be reported as capital gain. Consequently, the characterization provisions of Section 1271 are significant whenever there is a difference in the effective tax rates on ordinary income and capital gains and, of course, with regard to matching capital gains and capital losses.

In contrast to Section 1271, Treasury Regulation § 1.61-7(d) provides for the proceeds of a sale to be allocated first to accrued interest and then only the balance to be treated as the amount realized on the sale. To illustrate, if a $10,000 bond were sold for $10,500 after $400 of interest had accrued, $400 of the $10,500 would be treated as a payment of the interest and the balance of $10,100 would be the amount realized on the sale. If the bond were sold for $10,200, $400 would still be a payment of interest even though a loss was realized on the sale.[41]

[b] Short-Term Obligations

Section 1271 also prevents the conversion of ordinary income into capital gain in the case of any government or nongovernment obligation (excluding any tax-exempt obligation) that has a fixed maturity date of one year or less from the date of issue.[42] This rule, which is illustrated later in this section, is similar to that described in the preceding section in that it compares the gain on the sale or exchange of that obligation to an amount that is regarded as ordinary income in the nature of OID. Capital gain is then limited to the excess of gain on the transaction over the amount treated as ordinary income.

A taxpayer may choose either of two options in determining the portion of the gain that must be treated as ordinary income. Under the first option, the acquisition discount (i.e., the difference between the acquisition price and the price to be paid at maturity on a government obligation) or the OID (on a nongovernment obligation) is allocated pro rata on a daily basis.[43] Alternatively, the taxpayer may elect to apportion the discount on an economic yield or so-called constant rate basis with daily compounding.[44] The election is made merely by using one method or the other in reporting the transaction in the return for the year of the transaction.[45] For example, if the constant rate method is desired, the taxpayer elects that method merely by using it. Once made, the election is irrevocable.[46]

---

[41] See also Prop. Reg. § 1.1275-2(a), which generally provides that payments are allocated to accrued OID before being allocated to principal.

[42] IRC §§ 1271(a)(3), 1271(a)(4).

[43] IRC §§ 1271(a)(3)(C), 1271(a)(3)(D), 1271(a)(4)(C).

[44] IRC §§ 1271(a)(3)(C), 1271(a)(3)(E), 1271(a)(4)(D).

[45] Prop. Reg. § 1.1271-1(b)(2).

[46] IRC §§ 1271(a)(3)(E), 1271(a)(4)(D); Prop. Reg. § 1.1271-1(b)(2).

EXAMPLE: Assume that a taxpayer purchases a one-year $10,000 Treasury bill on January 1 for $9,200 and then sells this instrument on August 1 for $9,700. Under the pro rata method, $466.67 of the $500 gain is treated as ordinary income. (Number of days from January 1 through August 1 = 210, 210 ÷ by 360 = 58.333%, 58.333 x $800 = $466.67.) The balance of $33.33 is treated as capital gain.[47]

Less OID may be recognized under the constant rate method than under the pro rata method, despite the fact that the total amount of interest to be allocated is the same under each method. This is because the constant rate method assigns more interest to each succeeding day, which has the effect of deferring interest. Therefore, if the constant rate method of computing interest has been used in the preceding example, $800 ($10,000 −$9,200) would still have been subject to allocation, but, as contrasted with the pro rata method, a smaller amount would have been treated as ordinary income, and a larger amount would have been treated as capital gain.

[c] Exceptions

The Section 1271 rules do not apply to any obligations issued by a natural person.[48] If an entity is a primary obligor under a debt instrument, the debt instrument is considered to have been issued by the entity and not by a natural person, even if a natural person is a comaker and is jointly liable for the debt. A debt instrument issued by a partnership is also not considered to be issued by a natural person, even if the partnership is composed entirely of natural persons.[49] The Section 1271 rules also do not apply to obligations issued before July 2, 1982, by issuers other than (1) corporations and (2) governments or political subdivisions thereof.[50]

[3] Current Inclusion of OID: Section 1272

Section 1272 provides the rules governing the manner and taxable years in which OID is taken into account by both the issuer and holder of the debt obligation.[51] Section 1272, by itself, does not determine whether there is OID

---

[47] See Prop. Reg. § 1.1271-3(c), Ex. (1).

[48] IRC § 1271(b)(1). But see United States v. Midland-Ross Corp., 381 US 54 (1965), where, in the case of the sale or exchange of a debt instrument by a natural person, the Supreme Court indicated that recognition of OID as interest is not dependent on a statutory basis.

[49] Prop. Reg. § 1.1275-1(h).

[50] IRC § 1271(b)(2).

[51] Income is covered by Section 1272(a)(1). The corresponding deductions are covered by Section 163(e), which incorporates the definitions and computational procedures applicable to Section 1272.

or the amount of OID. These determinations are made by Sections 1273 and 1274.[52]

The manner in which OID is recognized depends on when the debt obligation was issued and on the identity of the issuer. For debt obligations issued after July 1, 1982, OID is allocated on a constant interest rate (or so-called economic yield) basis. For debt instruments issued prior to July 2, 1982, OID is allocated on a ratable basis.

[a] Obligations Issued After July 1, 1982

For obligations issued after July 1, 1982, which are not otherwise excepted from application of the OID rules,[53] OID is allocated as if a constant rate of interest were applicable to the acquisition price of the debt instrument. The precise interest rate to be applied is the rate that will cause the issue price plus the accumulated OID to equal the redemption price at the date of maturity.

EXAMPLE: Assume that a debt instrument is issued on January 1 for $1 million and that $1,340,096 will be paid three years later at maturity. The $340,096 difference between the issue price and the redemption price at maturity represents OID. The $340,096 is allocated among the applicable periods by applying the constant rate of interest to the $1 million, which, compounded semiannually, will produce a total of $1,340,096 to be paid at the end of the period.[54]

Based on applicable present value tables, the $1 million would increase to $1,340,096 at the end of three years through application of an annual interest rate of 10 percent, compounded semiannually. The computations are as follows:

$$\$1,000,000 \times 10\% \times \tfrac{1}{2} \text{ year} = \$50,000$$
$$\$1,050,000 \times 10\% \times \tfrac{1}{2} \text{ year} = \$52,500$$
$$\$1,102,500 \times 10\% \times \tfrac{1}{2} \text{ year} = \$55,125$$
$$\$1,157,625 \times 10\% \times \tfrac{1}{2} \text{ year} = \$57,881$$
$$\$1,215,506 \times 10\% \times \tfrac{1}{2} \text{ year} = \$60,776$$
$$\$1,276,282 \times 10\% \times \tfrac{1}{2} \text{ year} = \$63,814$$

Based on these computations, the $340,096 of OID must be allocated $102,500 to year 1 ($50,000 + $52,500); $113,006 to year 2 ($55,125 + $57,881); and $124,590 ($60,726 + $63,814) to year 3.

---

[52] See discussions infra ¶¶ 11.02[4], 11.02[5].

[53] See discussion infra ¶ 11.02[3][a][ii].

[54] Section 1272(a)(5) provides that the compounding period, referred to as the accrual period, is a period of six months except as otherwise provided in the regulations. See infra ¶ 11.02[3][a][i] for discussion of the accrual period and the proposed regulations that eliminate the presumption in favor of semiannual compounding.

The OID allocated to the final accrual period is always the excess of the stated redemption price at maturity over the adjusted issue price at the beginning of the last accrual period.[55] This rule has the effect of ensuring that all OID is taken into account. Thus, any rounding or similar adjustments are taken into account in the final accrual period.

[i] **Definitions and terms.** Although the allocation of OID illustrated in the preceding section is relatively simple, for precision, Section 1272 defines the allocation in terms of "yield to maturity," "accrual period," "daily portions," and "adjusted issue price." The proposed regulations use these terms to take taxpayers through a four-step process to determine the amount of OID includable in the holder's income for any taxable year:

1. Taxpayers must determine the debt instrument's yield to maturity.
2. Taxpayers then determine the debt instrument's accrual periods.
3. The amount of OID allocable to each accrual period is computed, using the yield to maturity.
4. OID is allocated to each day in an accrual period.

The holder of the debt instrument includes in income the daily portions of OID for each day during the taxable year on which the holder held the debt instrument.[56]

Yield to maturity. "Yield to maturity" is the interest rate that will cause the original issue price of the debt instrument to grow to the redemption price when applied to that issue price. Stated in other words, the yield to maturity is the interest rate that, when used to compute the present value of all payments of principal and interest due under the debt instrument, produces an amount equal to the issue price. The yield must be constant over the entire term of the debt and, when expressed as a percentage, must be calculated to at least two decimal places.[57] Moreover, the yield to maturity is determined on the basis of compounding, usually at the end of each accrual period (as defined in the next section). Thus, in the preceding example, the yield to maturity would be expressed as an annual interest rate of 10.00 percent, compounded semiannually.

If a loan calls for a fixed rate of interest over the entire term of the debt instrument (including loans with indefinite maturities, such as loans payable on demand) compounded at periodic intervals of one year or less, then the applicable yield to maturity is the stated interest rate.[58] For example, if *A* issued a debt instrument for $100,000 payable on demand, bearing interest

[55] Prop. Reg. § 1.1272-1(c)(2).
[56] Prop. Reg. § 1.1272-1(b)(1).
[57] Prop. Reg. § 1.1272-1(b)(1)(i).
[58] See Prop. Reg. § 1.1272-1(d)(5).

at 12.00 percent compounded semiannually, all interest to be added to principal and payable at maturity, the yield of this loan would be 12.00 percent compounded semiannually. Thus, this yield would be used in computing the amount of OID to be recognized in each accrual period.

It is not unusual for the issuer of a debt instrument to have the right to call the instrument before maturity. In other words, the issuer of the instrument may have the right to prepay the instrument at a specified price. Similarly, the holder of the instrument may have the right to put the instrument back to the issuer, i.e., to require the issuer to prepay the instrument.

For purposes of determining the yield to maturity, the proposed regulations provide that the exercise of a call will be presumed if it lowers the issuer's yield to maturity. Correspondingly, the exercise of a put will be presumed if it increases the holder's yield to maturity.[59] In other words, since it makes sense for an issuer to reduce the cost of its deferred payment and for the holder to increase the benefits from the deferred payment, this action will be presumed.

> EXAMPLE: Assume that a calendar-year taxpayer acquires for $70,000 a debt instrument with a face amount of $100,000, that the instrument matures in 15 years, and that the instrument provides interest at an annual rate of 8 percent, payable semiannually ($4,000 semiannually). Assume further that the taxpayer has the right to put the bond to the issuer at the end of 10 years at a price of $85,000. Under these facts, if the put is not exercised, the yield to maturity is 12.47 percent, compounded semiannually. If the put is exercised, the yield to maturity is 12.56 percent, compounded semiannually. Accordingly, under the proposed regulations, the yield to maturity is deemed to be 12.56 percent. Since the yield to maturity will be higher if the put is exercised, for purposes of the OID rules it is assumed that the put will be exercised. Thus, all calculations assume a yield to maturity of 12.56 percent, a term of 10 years, and a stated redemption price at maturity of $85,000. If the put is, in fact, not exercised, then the instrument will be treated as if it were retired on the presumed exercise date (i.e., at the end of year 10), and the issuer will be treated as having issued a new debt instrument to the taxpayer at an issue price equal to the put price on that date ($85,000). This new debt instrument will be treated as maturing five years later at a stated redemption price of $100,000, providing for interest at 8 percent compounded semiannually and, hence, bearing a yield to maturity of 12.08 percent.

Of course, the reality of the presumptions is itself an assumption that is embodied in the proposed regulations. There may be many circumstances

---

[59] Prop. Reg. § 1.1272-1(d)(3).

where it is unreasonable to assume that such a call or a put will be exercised. For example, in many cases, the holder of the debt instrument may prefer to maintain the present yield of the instrument it holds rather than to increase the yield in the short term by exercising the put, especially if the holder will not be able to reinvest the proceeds of the put in other investments yielding similar or higher rates. To illustrate, the holder of a 10 percent 10-year instrument may not want to call the instrument in year 6 in order to increase the yield from 10 to 10 1/2 percent if, on the exercise of that put, the proceeds could only be reinvested in comparable instruments bearing 8 percent. Appropriate adjustments are made if the presumptions prove incorrect when the time comes.[60] For purposes of Section 1274 pertaining to the imputation of interest, a slightly different version of the rule is used, one based on presumptions as to whether there will be an increase or decrease, respectively, of the testing rate against which the debt instrument is compared.[61]

Accrual period. "Accrual period" is the applicable period of compounding. Section 1272 provides that except as may otherwise be provided in the regulations, "accrual period" is a period of six months (or shorter period from the date of original issue), which ends on a day of the year that corresponds to the maturity date of the debt instrument or the date six months before that maturity date.[62] For example, under this statutory definition, if a debt instrument is issued on January 1 of year 1 and is to mature on September 30 of year 4, then the applicable accrual period is the six-month period ending each September 30 and each March 31 as well as the initial three-month period from January 1 to March 31 of year 1.

The proposed regulations offer a great deal more flexibility than the statute in determining accrual periods. "Accrual period" is defined simply as an interval of time with respect to which the accrual of OID is measured. Under the proposed regulations, an accrual period may be of any length and may vary in length during the term of the debt instrument, provided that each accrual period is no longer than a year and each scheduled payment occurs at the end of an accrual period.[63] The computation of OID generally will be easiest if accrual periods correspond to the intervals between payment dates. Any reasonable counting convention (e.g., 30-day months and a 360-day year) can be used in computing the length of accrual periods.[64]

EXAMPLE: *A* pays $90,000 at original issue for Corporation *B*'s ten-year, $100,000 note. The note calls for semiannual interest payments of

---

[60] Prop. Reg. § 1.1272-1(d)(4).

[61] Prop. Reg. § 1.1274-2(c)(3). See generally the discussion infra ¶ 11.02[5].

[62] IRC § 1272(a)(5).

[63] Prop. Reg. § 1.1272-1(b)(1)(ii).

[64] Id.

$3,000; all principal and the last interest payment are due at maturity. The yield of this debt instrument is approximately 7.44 percent, compounded semiannually. In computing the accrual of the $10,000 of OID on this note, the simplest approach is for A to use semiannual accrual periods. Assuming 30-day months and a 360-day year, the amount of OID for the first semiannual accrual period would be $345.78, determined by multiplying the issue price ($90,000) times the yield to maturity adjusted for the length of the accrual period (7.44% ÷ 2), minus the $3,000 "qualified stated interest" payment.[65] Alternatively, A could choose to use monthly accrual periods. If monthly compounding were used, the yield to maturity of the debt instrument would be approximately 7.32 percent.[66] The $3,000 semiannual interest payment would be treated as if it were payable $500 per month.[67] The amount of OID for the first monthly accrual period would be $49.18, or $90,000 times 7.32 percent divided by 12, minus $500.[68] If this example were extended, the amount of OID accruing in the first six monthly accrual periods would equal the $345.78 that accrues over the same period using semiannual accrual periods.

It is quite common for the interval from the date of original issue of a debt instrument to the first payment date to differ from the intervals between subsequent payment dates. For example, a note calling for semiannual interest payments on March 31 and September 30 might be issued on January 15. The holder of this note can use semiannual accrual periods ending on each payment date and a short initial accrual period ending on March 31 after the issue date. In these circumstances, the computation of OID for the first initial accrual period can be made using any reasonable method.[69]

Daily portion. "Daily portion" is each day's ratable share of OID applicable to an accrual period.[70] The daily portion may be computed merely by dividing the OID allocable to the accrual period by the number of days

---

[65] The definition of "qualified stated interest" is discussed infra ¶ 11.02[4][a][i]. As in the examples in the proposed regulations, although the yield to maturity is rounded to two decimal places, the computations in the example do not reflect any such rounding. See Prop. Reg. § 1.1272-1(j).

[66] Prop. Reg. § 1.1272-1(j), Ex. 1, provides a mathematical formula for determining equivalent yields for different compounding intervals.

[67] Prop. Reg. § 1.1272-1(c)(1).

[68] Prop. Reg. § 1.1272-1(j), Ex. 2. The computations reflect the actual yields, not the rounded percentages stated in the example.

[69] Prop. Reg. § 1.1272-1(c)(3). See Prop. Reg. § 1.1272-1(j), Ex. 3 for an example of a reasonable method of calculating the OID for the initial short accrual period.

[70] IRC § 1272(a)(3).

in the accrual period.[71] For example, if an accrual period consists of 90 days and if $90,000 of OID is allocable to this period, the daily portion is $1,000 ($90,000 ÷ 90).

The holder of a debt instrument includes in income the daily portions of OID for every day on which the instrument is held.[72] Since OID is allocated among accrual periods on a constant yield basis but to days within each accrual period on a ratable basis, the selection of accrual period by the holder can have a small effect on the allocation of OID among taxable years. To illustrate, continuing the previous example of a 10-year $100,000 note acquired at original issue for $90,000, assume the holder is a calendar year taxpayer and the note is issued on November 30. If semiannual accrual periods are used, one sixth of the $345.78 of OID allocable to the first accrual period, or $57.63, is recognized by the taxpayer in the year of issuance. If monthly accrual periods are used, only $49.18 is recognized in the first year. If the taxpayer holds the instrument to maturity, the $8.45 difference will be made up in the OID accruals in later years.

Adjusted issue price.   "Adjusted issue price" is the original issue price of the debt instrument increased by the amount of OID previously includable in the income of any holder and decreased by any payment previously made other than a payment of "qualified stated interest."[73] The adjusted issue price at the beginning of an accrual period is used to determine the OID allocable to that accrual period.[74]

Thus, in the 10-year note example with semiannual accrual periods, the adjusted issue price at the beginning of the second accrual period is $90,345.78. This figure is then multiplied by the yield to maturity, compounded semiannually and divided by two to adjust for the length of the accrual period, and the excess of the resulting product over the $3,000 qualified stated interest payable at the end of the second accrual period is the OID that accrues during that accrual period.

[ii] Exceptions.   Even though OID might be present in a debt instrument, it is not reported as income under the rules of Section 1272 (or deducted as expense under Section 163(e)(1)) in the case of the following obligations or circumstances:[75]

---

[71] See Prop. Reg. § 1.1272-1(b)(1)(ii), which allows the use of actual days or any reasonable accounting convention.

[72] Prop. Reg. § 1.1272-1(b)(1)(iv).

[73] Prop. Reg. § 1.1275-1(b); see IRC § 1272(a)(3).

[74] Prop. Reg. § 1.1272-1(b)(1)(iii); see IRC § 1272(a)(3).

[75] IRC § 1.1272(a)(2). Prop. Reg. § 1.1272-1(a)(2). Life insurance companies and holders of debt instruments issued before 1985 in whose hands the instrument is not a capital asset are also excluded from application of the Section 1272 rules. IRC § 1272(c)(2); Tax Reform Act of 1984, Pub. L. No. 98-369, § 44(g) (1984), as amended by the Tax Reform Act of 1986, Pub. L. No. 99-514, § 1803(b)(5) (1986).

- Any tax-exempt obligation
- Any U.S. savings bond
- Any debt instrument that has a fixed maturity date not more than one year from the date of issue (so-called short-term obligations)
- Any obligation issued by a natural person before March 2, 1984
- Any loan between natural persons (a husband and wife being treated as one person, except where they lived apart at all times during the year in which the loan was made),[76] if that loan is not made in the course of a trade or business of the lender, does not exceed $10,000, and does not have as one of its principal purposes the avoidance of federal tax

For purposes of the exclusion from application of Section 1272, tax-exempt obligations include only those obligations where the interest is not includable in income under Section 103 or the interest is exempt from tax (without regard to the identity of the holder) under any other provision of law.[77]

With respect to short-term obligations, although Section 1272 does not apply, the amount of the OID may have to be accrued under other provisions. For example, taxpayers using an accrual method of reporting income and expense may have to report the same amounts of income as would have been reported under Section 1272. (See Chapter 4 for discussion of accrual methods of accounting.) Moreover, Sections 1281 through 1283 provide additional rules for the recognition of income on short-term obligations.[78] Cash method taxpayers who are not subject to the application of these other provisions are permitted to report OID in the year in which payments are made or received.[79]

With respect to loans between natural persons, the proposed regulations provide that the excepted loans do not include stripped bonds or stripped coupons within the meaning of Section 1286(e).[80] To determine whether the loan amount exceeds the $10,000 limitation, all loans between the parties are taken into account, regardless of the time when the loans were made, the character of the loans, and the purpose of the loans. For this purpose, a husband and wife are treated as one person with respect to loans made by either of them to a third person or to a spouse of that third person.[81]

---

[76] Prop. Reg. § 1.1272-1(a)(2) points out that this treatment of a husband and wife as one person does not apply to loans between the spouses.

[77] IRC § 1275(a)(3); Prop. Reg. § 1.1275-1(d).

[78] See discussion infra ¶ 11.06.

[79] See Prop. Reg. § 1.446-2(a)(1).

[80] See Prop. Reg. § 1.1272-1(a)(2); IRC § 1286(e); see also infra ¶ 11.07 for discussion of stripped bonds.

[81] IRC § 1272(a)(2)(E)(iii); Prop. Reg. § 1.1272-1(a)(2).

However, this treatment does not apply if the husband and wife have lived apart at all times during the taxable year in which the loan is made.[82]

[iii] Subsequent holders of debt obligation. A taxpayer may acquire a debt obligation at a point in time between the obligation's issue date and its maturity date. In that case, the taxpayer may pay an amount equal to, less than, or more than the adjusted issue price of the obligation at the time of transfer. The variance between the amount paid and the adjusted issue price may arise from a number of factors, including (1) fluctuations in the difference between the original yield on the obligation and the prevailing market rate of interest on similar instruments at the time of transfer and (2) changes in the degree of risk associated with the instrument.

If the taxpayer-transferee pays an amount that is more than the redemption price at maturity of the instrument, there will be no OID for the taxpayer to recognize.[83] The excess of the purchase price over the stated price at maturity may be deducted over the remaining life of the bond instrument.[84] If the taxpayer pays an amount that is less than the stated redemption at maturity but in excess of the adjusted issue price of the instrument, then the amount of OID to be reported by the taxpayer-transferee is reduced to take into account the "acquisition premium" that was paid. Consequently, the acquisition premium offsets the amount of OID to be recognized by the taxpayer-transferee.[85]

> EXAMPLE: Assume that a debt instrument paying $100,000 at maturity was originally issued for $80,000 and that at the time of the initial holder's transfer to the taxpayer, $8,000 of OID has been recognized by the initial holder. Consequently, the adjusted issue price of the obligation was $88,000 at the time of transfer. If the transferee paid $90,000 for the instrument, the $2,000 difference between the $90,000 price and the holder's $88,000 basis would represent an acquisition premium paid by the transferee.

The OID to be recognized by the taxpayer-transferee is the original remaining OID reduced by the acquisition premium. The amount of the reduction in OID is based on the ratio of the acquisition premium paid to the remaining OID to be recognized. For instance, in the preceding example, the remaining OID is $12,000 ($100,000 due at maturity less the adjusted basis to the transferor of $88,000), and the acquisition premium is $2,000. The ratio of acquisition premium to remaining OID is $2,000 divided by $12,000, or 16.67

---

[82] IRC § 1272(a)(2)(E)(iii).

[83] IRC § 1272(c)(1); Prop. Reg. § 1.1272-2(a).

[84] IRC § 171.

[85] IRC § 1272(a)(7); Prop. Reg. § 1.1272-2(a).

percent. Consequently, the new holder reports as OID 83.33 percent (100% − 16.67%) of the OID that otherwise would have been reported.[86]

If the purchase price is less than the adjusted issue price at the time of purchase, the new holder has market discount in addition to the remaining OID. Under Sections 1276(a) and 1271(a), market discount is generally treated as ordinary income, but it need not be recognized until the debt instrument is sold, exchanged, or retired.[87]

[b] Corporate Obligations Issued Before July 2, 1982

The OID in debt instruments issued by a corporation after May 27, 1969, and before July 2, 1982, is allocated over the period from issuance to maturity on a pro rata basis.[88] This allocation procedure ignores the effects of compounding. Consequently, more OID is allocated to early years and less to later years than would occur if the allocation were made on an economic yield or a constant-rate basis.

Total OID is first allocated ratably to the number of complete months between the date of original issue and the date of maturity.[89] For this purpose, a complete month commences with the date of issue and the corresponding date of each succeeding month.[90] For example, if the obligation was issued June 17, then the periods of complete months would begin on June 17 and the seventeenth of each succeeding month.

If the obligation is transferred within a given monthly period, the ratable monthly OID is allocated between the transferor and transferee on the basis of the relative number of days held by each.[91] Thus, if an instrument issued on June 17 was transferred on June 30, 13/30 of the monthly OID is allocated to the transferor and 17/30 to the transferee.

If a premium is paid by the transferee, then the OID to be recognized by it is reduced proportionately.[92] The total acquisition premium is allocated over the remaining months to redemption by dividing the number of complete months plus any fractional part of a month into the total amount of premium.[93] For example, if there were $12,000 of acquisition premium and 12 months remaining to maturity, the amount of OID to be recognized each month would be reduced by $1,000.

---

[86] Alternatively, the purchaser of the debt instrument may elect to recompute OID remaining on the instrument as if the purchase were an acquisition of a new instrument at original issue. Prop. Reg. § 1.1272-2(b)(5).

[87] See discussion infra ¶ 11.05.

[88] IRC § 1272(b).

[89] IRC §§ 1272(b)(1), 1272(b)(2).

[90] IRC § 1272(b)(3)(A).

[91] IRC § 1272(b)(3)(B).

[92] IRC § 1272(b)(4).

[93] IRC § 1272(b)(4)(B).

[4] Amount of OID: Section 1273

Section 1273 provides rules for determining the amount of OID. For this purpose, "OID" is defined as the excess, if any, of the stated redemption price at maturity over the issue price.[94] If there is no OID, then none of the OID rules apply.[95]

[a] Stated Redemption Price at Maturity

"Stated redemption price at maturity" is defined as the amount fixed by the last modification of the agreement pursuant to which the debt obligation was acquired.[96] This amount includes interest and, subject to the exception stated in the next sentence, all other amounts payable at maturity.[97] The stated redemption price at maturity does not include interest based on a fixed rate and payable unconditionally at fixed periodic intervals of one year or less during the entire term of the debt instrument (so-called qualified stated interest).[98]

[i] Qualified stated interest. The term "qualified stated interest" means stated interest that is unconditionally payable in cash or in property (other than debt instruments of the issuer) at least annually at a single fixed rate.[99] Interest is payable at a single fixed rate only if the rate appropriately takes into account the length of time between payments.[100]

Interest rate. To illustrate the meaning of the term "qualified stated interest" described in the preceding paragraph, assume that an obligation is issued in the amount of $10,000, bearing interest at 10 percent payable annually. The $1,000 interest payable annually is "qualified stated interest". The term also generally includes payments made pursuant to application of a variable rate of interest, if that variable rate is tied to current values of either (1) a single qualified floating rate or (2) a single objective rate.[101] A variable interest rate is a qualified floating rate (e.g. a bank's prime rate) if

---

[94] IRC § 1273(a)(1).

[95] If there is only de minimis OID within the meaning of Section 1273(a)(3), OID is treated as zero, but the proposed regulations nevertheless contain rules for the holder's treatment of de minimis OID. See discussion infra ¶ 11.02[4][c].

[96] IRC § 1273(a)(2).

[97] Id.

[98] Id.; Prop. Reg. § 1.1275-1(b).

[99] Prop. Reg. § 1.1273-1(c)(1).

[100] Id.

[101] Prop. Reg. §§ 1.1275-5(e), 1.1275-5(a)(3), 1.1275-5(a)(4). "Current value" is the value of the rate on any day occurring during the interval that begins three months prior to the first day on which that value is in effect under the debt instrument and ends one year following that day. Prop. Reg. § 1.1275-5(a)(4).

variations in that rate can reasonably be expected to measure contemporaneous variations in the cost of newly borrowed funds.[102]

"Objective rate" is an interest rate (other than a qualified floating rate) that is based on the price of property that is actively traded or on an index of the prices of such property.[103] An objective rate is also one based on one or more qualified floating rates but one that is not itself a qualified floating rate, such as a multiple of a bank's prime rate.[104]

Qualified stated interest can also include stated interest at a single qualified floating rate followed by a second qualified floating rate or a single fixed rate followed by a single qualified floating rate, but special rules may treat a portion of the interest on such instruments as either "accelerated interest" or "deferred interest" rather than qualified stated interest.[105]

Any stated interest on a debt instrument in excess the qualified stated interest is included in the instrument's stated redemption price at maturity.[106] However, no payments will be treated as qualified stated interest in the case of any so-called short-term obligation (i.e., a debt instrument that has a fixed maturity date of not more than one year from the date of issue).[107]

Unconditionally payable. Interest is considered payable unconditionally only if the failure to pay the interest timely (or at all) results in consequences to the borrower that are typical in normal lending transactions.[108] In other words, the failure to pay must result in consequences such as an acceleration of all amounts due under the debt instrument, the imposition of a higher penalty rate of interest, or similar burdens. Interest is not considered payable unconditionally if the obligation to pay is subject to the occurrence of a contingency, such as the existence of profits.

Rationale for rule. The exclusion of qualified stated interest from stated redemption price at maturity makes sense in light of the overall purpose of the OID provisions, which is to cause the taxpayer to report interest as it economically accrues. Since qualified stated interest payments are generally reported in the desired periods, there is no reason to include them as part of the stated redemption price. If these payments were treated as part of the stated redemption price, the difference between stated redemption price at maturity and issue price would increase, and there would be more OID to allocate. For accrual method holders, this additional OID

---

[102] Prop. Reg. § 1.1275-5(b)(1). A cap or a floor on a variable rate generally does not affect whether it will be a qualified floating rate, unless, as of the issue date, the cap or the floor is "very likely" to come into play. Prop. Reg. § 1.1275(b)(2).

[103] Prop. Reg. § 1.1275-5(c)(1). Again, caps and floors are generally ignored. Prop. Reg. § 1.1275-5(c)(2)(i).

[104] Prop. Reg. § 1.1275-5(c)(1).

[105] Prop. Reg. § 1.1275-5(e), 1.1275-5(f).

[106] Prop. Reg. § 1.1273-1(c)(3).

[107] Prop. Reg. § 1.1273-1(c)(4).

[108] Prop. Reg. § 1.1273-1(c)(1).

would be reported in the same periods that the qualified stated interest payments are already to be reported. For cash method holders, the small timing differences between the recognition of qualified stated interest under the cash method and the economic accrual of qualified stated interest if it were treated as OID are minimal and do not warrant any additional complexity.

[ii] **Loans with indefinite maturities.** It is not possible at the time of issuance to determine the amount of OID on a loan with an indefinite maturity date, including loans payable on demand. Nevertheless, certain rules have been proposed to determine how much OID should be taken into account with such loans.

The proposed regulations specify that if the issue price is equal to the stated principal amount of a debt instrument (including an instrument with an indefinite maturity, such as a loan payable on demand) and if that instrument calls for a fixed rate of interest over its entire term compounded at periodic intervals of one year or less, then the yield of the instrument is its stated interest rate.[109]

EXAMPLE: Assume that a debt instrument is issued on March 1 of year 1 for $100,000, payable on demand. Assume further that the instrument calls for interest to accrue at an annual rate of 11 percent, compounded quarterly, all principal and accrued interest to be paid on demand. The holder of the note does not have the option to demand partial payment or payment of interest only, only the right to demand full payment of the principal and all accrued interest.

Assume that the holder of the debt instrument elects to treat the quarterly periods ending May 31, August 31, November 30, and February 28 of each calendar year as the accural period.[110] The yield of the debt instrument, therefore, is 11 percent, compounded quarterly.

Assuming that the debt instrument is not called at any time during calendar year 1, the amount of OID for the first accrual period would be $2,750 ($100,000 × 11% ÷ 4). The adjusted issue price at the beginning of the second accrual period is $102,750 ($100,000 + $2,750). The OID allocable to the second accrual period is $2,825.63 ($102,750 x 11% ÷ 4). OID for subsequent accrual periods is calculated in the same manner.

[iii] **Installment obligations.** For purposes of Section 1273, "installment obligation" is defined to mean any debt instrument providing for a payment (other than a payment of qualified stated interest) before the final

---

[109] Prop. Reg. § 1.1272-1(d)(5).

[110] See discussion supra ¶ 11.02[3][a][i] regarding accrual periods.

maturity date.[111] Only one such payment before maturity is all that is necessary to turn the instrument into an installment obligation.

As for other debt instruments, the stated redemption price at maturity of an installment obligation is the total of all payments due under the obligation other than qualified stated interest payments.[112]

> EXAMPLE: Assume that a debt instrument with a face amount of $100,000 is issued for $80,000 and that the $100,000 is payable $50,000 at the end of year 3 and $50,000 at the end of year 4. The obligation is an installment obligation, and the stated redemption price at maturity of the obligation is $100,000.

Some installment obligations are so-called self-amortizing installment obligations. These obligations call for equal payments, which are composed of principal and interest, at least annually during the entire term of the obligation, with no significant additional payment required at maturity.[113] The stated redemption price at maturity of these self-amortizing installment obligations also is the sum of all payments made under the instrument other than qualified stated interest payments.

> EXAMPLE: Assume a debt instrument with a term of five years and a stated principal amount of $500,000 is issued on January 1 of year 1 and that the recipient is to receive annual payments of $145,641.77 for each of five years. This would be the amount necessary to pay off the entire loan, assuming interest at 14 percent compounded annually on the unpaid principal balance. The payment schedule for this obligation and the composition of the required payments are as follows:

Year	Principal	Interest	Total payments
1	$ 75,641.77	$ 70,000.00	$145,641.77
2	86,231.62	59,410.15	145,641.77
3	98,304.05	47,337.72	145,641.77
4	112,066.62	33,575.15	145,641.77
5	127,755.94	17,885.83	145,641.77
	$500,000.00	$228,208.85	$728,208.85

Payments of interest qualify as qualified stated interest payments and are excluded from the definition of "stated redemption price at maturity." The stated redemption price at maturity is equal to $500,000, the sum of all payments made other than qualified stated interest payments.

---

[111] Prop. Reg. § 1.1273-1(e)(1).
[112] Prop. Reg. § 1.1273-1(b).
[113] Prop. Reg. § 1.1273-1(e)(2).

If the obligation in the preceding example had been acquired at a price of $500,000, there would have been no OID. However, if it had been acquired at a price less than $500,000, OID would have existed in the amount of the difference between the stated redemption price and the lower purchase price.

EXAMPLE: Assume that a debt instrument with a face amount of $100,000, bearing 8 percent annual interest, compounded semiannually, is payable in six equal semiannual payments of $19,076.19, and that the instrument is issued for $93,803.81. The payment schedule for this obligation and the composition of the required payments are as follows:

Semiannual accrual period	Unpaid principal before payment	Payment		
		Principal	Interest	Total
1	$100,000.00	$ 15,076.19	$4,000.00	$19,076.19
2	84,923.81	15,679.24	3,396.95	19,076.19
3	69,244.57	16,306.41	2,769.78	19,076.19
4	52,938.16	16,958.66	2,117.53	19,076.19
5	35,979.50	17,637.01	1,439.18	19,076.19
6	18,342.49	18,342.49	733.70	19,076.19
		$100,000.00		

The interest shown above represents 4 percent (an annual rate of 8 percent for a period of six months) multiplied by the then-outstanding principal balance. However, since the purchaser acquired the instrument for $93,803.81, there is a total of $6,196.19 ($100,000 − $93,803.81) of OID to be recognized. Based on this acquisition price, the yield to maturity is 12 percent.[114] The allocation of the OID among the six semiannual accrual periods is made by multiplying the yield to maturity by the acquisition price and subtracting out the qualified stated interest payment for that accrual period. The initial computations are set forth in the following table:

Semiannual accrual period	Beginning of period-adjusted issue price	Multiplied by 6 percent	Qualified stated interest payments	OID
1	$93,803.81	$5,628.23	$4,000.00	$1,628.23
2	80,305.85	4,821.35	3,396.95	1,424.40
3	66,101.01	3,966.06	2,769.78	1,196.28
4	50,990.89	3,059.45	2,117.53	941.92
5	34,974.15	2,098.45	1,439.18	659.27
6	17,996.41	1,079.78	733.70	346.08

---

[114] See supra ¶ 11.02[3][a][i] for discussion of yield to maturity.

	Adjusted issue price	Less payment of principal	Plus OID	Adjusted issue price
1	$93,803.81	$15,076.19	$1,628.23	$80,355.85
2	80,355.85	15,679.24	1,424.40	66,101.01
3	66,101.01	16,306.41	1,196.28	50,990.89
4	50,990.89	16,958.66	941.92	34,974.15
5	34,974.15	17,637.01	659.27	17,996.41
6	17,996.41	18,342.49	346.08	0.00

Although the principles involved are relatively simple, these computations are somewhat complicated. For this reason, care must be taken in evaluating transactions so as to make certain that they comply with all applicable rules.

[iv] **Puts, calls, and other options.** When determining stated redemption price at maturity, yield to maturity, and related items, the proposed regulations require that all puts, calls, or other options be presumed exercised if an exercise is in the economic interest of the person holding the option. Consequently, it is presumed that an obligation will be called at the time and in the amount of the call price by the issuer if that call would lower the issuer's yield to maturity.[115] Correspondingly, if the holder of the obligation would increase its yield to maturity by exercising a put or other option, the exercise will be presumed.[116] The regulations contain a number of examples illustrating these rules.[117]

[b] Issue Price

The precise definition of "issue price" varies depending on whether the debt instrument is issued publicly or privately and whether it is issued for money or for property.[118] (For this purpose, property includes services and the right to use property.[119]) However, as a general rule, the issue price is the consideration received on issuance of the debt instrument.

[i] **Publicly offered debt instruments issued for cash.** A debt instrument is considered publicly offered if it is registered with the Securities and Exchange Commission or would be required to be registered but for an exemption from registration (1) under Section 3 of the Securities Act of 1933 (1993 Act), (2) under section 2 or section 4 of the 1933 Act because of the identity of the issuer or the nature of the security, or (3) because the issue is

---

[115] Prop. Reg. § 1.1272-1(d)(3).

[116] Id.

[117] See Prop. Reg. § 1.1272-1(j), Ex. (5)–(7).

[118] IRC § 1273(b).

[119] IRC § 1273(b)(5).

intended for distribution to non-U.S. persons.[120] For publicly offered debt instruments (other than Treasury securities), which are issued for cash, the issue price is the initial offering price to the public (excluding bond houses, brokers, and similar persons or organizations acting in the capacity of an underwriter or wholesaler), as long as a substantial dollar amount of the debt instruments is sold at that price.[121] As a result of this rule, the issue price will be the same for all instruments in a debt issue even though some individual instruments in the overall issue might be sold at different times and at different prices.[122] For example, if a substantial portion of a debt issue is sold for $1,000 per unit, $1,000 per unit is the issue price for all portions even though some units might later be sold for an amount that is higher or lower than $1,000. In the case of Treasury securities, the issue price is the average price of the debt instruments that are sold.[123]

[ii] **Non–publicly offered debt instruments issued for cash.** In the case of debt instruments that are not publicly offered but are issued for cash, "issue price" is the price paid by the first buyer of the particular debt instrument.[124] This rule covers typical cash-lending transactions. Unlike the case of publicly offered debt instruments, non–publicly offered instruments do not have a common issue price. Consequently, the issue price may vary for each instrument that is sold.

Any payment from the borrower to the lender at the time the loan is made, other than a payment for services provided by the lender, such as commitment fees or loan-processing costs, reduces the issue price. Thus, if a borrower is obligated to pay two points (2 percent of the loan) to the lender at the time of acquiring a $100,000 loan, the issue price is deemed to be $98,000 ($100,000 face amount less $2,000 of points).[125] However, the points are deductible by the borrower and, with respect to the borrower, do not reduce the issue price if (1) the points are paid in connection with the purchase or improvement of (and the loan is secured by) the taxpayer's principal residence, (2) the charging of those points is an established business practice in the area in which the indebtedness is incurred, and (3) the amount of payment for points does not exceed the amount generally charged in that area.[126] But the treatment of the lender in this case is not symmetrical. Under the current proposed regulations, points that are deductible by the borrower

---

[120] Prop. Reg. § 1.1273-2(a)(2).

[121] IRC § 1273(b)(1); Prop. Reg. § 1.1273-2(a)(1).

[122] Prop. Reg. § 1.1273-2(a)(1).

[123] Prop. Reg. § 1.1273-2(a)(3).

[124] IRC § 1273(b)(2); Prop. Reg. § 1.1273-1(b)(1).

[125] Prop. Reg. § 1.1273-2(j)(2).

[126] Id. See IRC § 461(j).

under Section 461(g)(2) are not income to the lender but rather reduce issue price under the general rule.[127]

If the points are paid by a person other than the borrower (e.g., the seller of the property), the treatment of the points depends on the substance of the transaction.[128] Depending on the circumstances, the third party's payment of points may be treated as a payment to the borrower followed by the borrower's payment to the lender, a reduction in the amount due from the borrower to the third party, or an amount paid by the third party to the borrower.

> EXAMPLE: Assume that A sells property to B for $500,000, and B makes a cash down payment of $100,000 and borrows the remaining $400,000 from L. B's obligation to L is to be repaid over a period of 15 years at an annual interest rate of 9 percent. As part of the lending transaction, A is required to pay $8,000 to L to facilitate its loan to B. In this situation, B will be treated as having made a direct payment of $8,000 to L and a down payment of only $92,000 to A. The payment to L reduces the issue price of B's debt instrument to $392,000, the amount that in substance L has lent to B. B's basis in the property acquired from A is $492,000, $500,000 less the $8,000 payment made by A on B's behalf.[129]

[iii] **Debt instruments issued for property with public trading.** Where (1) the debt instrument is issued for property other than cash and (2) there is public trading of either the debt instrument or the consideration received for it, then the issue price is the price established by the public trading. This rule is set out more precisely in the Code as follows. In the case of debt instruments issued for consideration other than cash, where the debt instrument itself is traded on an established securities market or is issued for stock, securities, or, to the extent provided in the regulations, other property that is traded on the established market, the issue price is the FMV.[130] Although the Code bases the issue price in these circumstances on the FMV of the property received as consideration, the proposed regulations specify that if the debt instrument is part of an issue that is traded on an established market, the issue price of the debt instrument is its FMV determined as of the issue date.[131]

Property or a debt instrument will be treated as traded on an established market if, at any time during a 60-day period ending 30 days after the debt

---

[127] Prop. Reg. § 1.1273-2(f)(2). This represents a change from the 1986 proposed regulations. See former Prop. Reg. § 1.446-2(e).

[128] Prop. Reg. § 1.1273-2(j)(4).

[129] See Prop. Reg. § 1.1273-2(j)(5) for this and other examples.

[130] IRC § 1273(b)(3).

[131] Prop. Reg. § 1.1273-2(c)(1).

instrument's issue date, it meets any of several alternative tests set forth in the proposed regulations.[132] A debt instrument not traded on an established securities market under these rules is not treated as so traded just because it is convertible into property that is so traded.[133]

[iv] Investment units; convertible debt. Debt instruments frequently are issued in connection with property rights, such as options or warrants to acquire shares of stock in the issuer or a related party at a specified price. The issue price of such an "investment unit" must be allocated between the debt instrument and the property right or rights based on their relative FMV.[134]

> EXAMPLE: If A, a venture capital firm, loans corporation B $1 million in exchange for B's interest-bearing $1 million note and warrants to acquire 50,000 shares of common stock in B for $0.10 per share, the issue price of the investment unit is $1 million.[135] This overall issue price must be allocated between the note and the warrants in proportion to their relative FMV. Assume that this allocation results in an issue price for the note of $800,000 and a basis in the warrants of $200,000. If the interest payments under the note are qualified stated interest, the note has OID of $200,000, which is includable by A and deductible by B under Sections 1272 and 163.

Importantly, the proposed regulations provide that the issuer's allocation of the issue price of an investment unit will be binding on the holder, unless the holder discloses on its tax return that it is taking a different position.[136] In a private lending transaction, the allocation of issue price thus should be a negotiated term of the deal.

In contrast to the treatment of investment units, the issue price of a debt instrument that is convertible into stock or another debt instrument of either the issuer or a related party includes any value allocable to the conversion privilege.[137] Under the proposed regulations, this rule holds even if the privilege may be satisfied or exercised for the cash value of the stock or the debt into which it is convertible (a so-called cash settlement option).[138] Thus, if A had loaned B $1 million in exchange for a note convertible into 50,000 shares of B common stock instead of the above-described package of a note and warrants, the issue price of the note would have been $1 million, and,

---

[132] Prop. Reg. § 1.1273-2(d).

[133] Prop. Reg. § 1.1273-2(d)(7).

[134] IRC § 1273(c)(2); Prop. Reg. § 1.1273-2(f)(1).

[135] See IRC §§ 1273(c)(2), 1273(b)(2).

[136] Prop. Reg. § 1.1273-2(f)(2).

[137] Prop. Reg. § 1.1273-2(g).

[138] Id.

assuming the stated redemption price at maturity of the note was also $1 million, there would have been no OID.[139]

[v] **Other cases.**   Where the debt instrument is issued for non–publicly traded property, the issue price is determined under Section 1274. In all other cases, the issue price will be treated as the stated redemption price.[140] In other words, where the issue price is not determined under Sections 1273(b)(1) through 1273(b)(3) or Section 1274, there will be no OID.

[c] De Minimis Rule

If the excess of the stated redemption price at maturity over the issue price is less than one quarter of one percent of the stated redemption price multiplied by the number of complete years to maturity, then, as illustrated in the following example, the amount of OID is treated as if it were zero.[141] In the case of an installment obligation, the same formula is used except that the weighted average maturity of the debt instrument is used instead of the number of complete years to maturity.[142] For this purpose, the weighted average maturity of an installment obligation is the sum of the amounts obtained by multiplying the amount of each payment (other than a payment of qualified stated interest) by a fraction, the numerator of which is the number of complete years from the issue date until the date of the payment and the denominator of which is the stated redemption price at maturity.[143] Moreover, if an installment obligation calls for payments of principal no more rapidly than would be made under a self-amortizing installment obligation, one sixth of one percent may be substituted for one quarter of one percent.[144]

EXAMPLE: Assume a debt instrument providing for a principal payment after 10 years of $100 and annual interest payments of $10 per year is issued for $98. There is actual OID of $2. However, the OID is considered to be zero because $2 is less than $2.50, which is one quarter of one percent of the stated redemption price at maturity multiplied by the number of full years to maturity (0.0025 × $100 × 10). If the debt instrument had been issued for $97.50 or less, the OID would not have been considered to be zero. Nor would the actual OID have been reduced by $2.50.

---

[139] Of course, the packages are economically different. The exercise of a conversion privilege involves surrender of the debt instrument. The exercise of warrants, on the other hand, generally does not affect the holder's rights under the debt instrument.

[140] IRC § 1273(b)(4).

[141] IRC § 1273(a)(3).

[142] Prop. Reg. § 1.1273-1(d)(3).

[143] Prop. Reg. § 1.1273-1(e)(3).

[144] Prop. Reg. § 1.1273-1(d)(3).

EXAMPLE: Assume that a debt instrument in the principal amount of $1,500 is payable at a rate of $100 a year for each of nine years with a payment of $600 in the year 10. Also assume that the instrument bears interest at an annual rate of 10 percent on the unpaid principal balance and that the instrument is issued for $1,475. The actual OID is $25 ($1,500 −$1,475). However, under the de minimis rule previously referred to, the instrument is treated as having no OID because the actual OID is less than $26.25, which is the amount computed under the stated de minimis rule, as follows. The stated redemption price at maturity of $1,500 is multiplied by 0.0025 (one quarter of one percent) multiplied by the weighted average maturity of the debt instrument. The definition of the weighted average maturity of the debt instrument provided by the proposed regulations can be restated more logically as the sum of the products of the number of full years until each principal payment is made multiplied by a fraction, the numerator of which is the amount of the principal payment and the denominator of which is the stated redemption price at maturity (SRPM). In this example, the various multiplications, their products, and the sum of their products are as follows:

Year to payment	Ratio of payment to SRPM	Product
1	100 ÷ 1,500	0.067
2	100 ÷ 1,500	0.133
3	100 ÷ 1,500	0.20
4	100 ÷ 1,500	0.267
5	100 ÷ 1,500	0.333
6	100 ÷ 1,500	0.4
7	100 ÷ 1,500	0.467
8	100 ÷ 1,500	0.533
9	100 ÷ 1,500	0.6
10	600 ÷ 1,500	0.4
		7.0

Using the weighted average maturity of seven years, the de minimis amount of $26.25 is computed as follows: one quarter of one percent (0.0025) × stated redemption price ($1,500) × 7 =$26.25.

Many debt instruments are structured with low-interest or no-interest terms for an initial time period followed by a market (or higher) rate of interest. The initial "teaser rate" or "interest holiday" in general will cause the debt instrument to have OID, since the interest payments called for under the note will no longer meet the definition of "qualified stated interest." The proposed regulations provide a special test for determining whether the amount of OID on such debt instruments might be considered de minimis. In essence, this test measures the amount of interest forgone during the period of the teaser rate or interest holiday, and if that amount is less than the de minimis threshold, the instrument will be treated as not having any OID.[145]

The de minimis rule generally applies only to the holder of the debt instrument. The issuer of a debt instrument with de minimis OID must nevertheless deduct that amount of OID over the life of the debt.[146]

The holder of a debt instrument with de minimis OID in effect is exempt from the current accrual of the discount inherent in that instrument. The proposed regulations take the position that the holder must recognize a proportionate amount of any de minimis OID as stated principal payments are made under the instrument.[147] Any amounts included in income under this rule are treated as amounts received in retirement of the debt instrument under Section 1271 and, therefore, will likely be treated as capital gain.[148]

[5] Issue Price in Certain Cases Involving Property: Section 1274

Section 1274 is nominally limited to a determination of the issue price for non–publicly traded debt instruments issued for non–publicly traded property. However, Section 1274 actually goes far beyond that.[149] It provides for an imputation of interest where the sum of actual OID and all stated interest payments is less than a specified amount of interest.

In other words, Section 1274 represents a congressional codification of the economic proposition that covered transactions must be treated as if the parties had provided for interest at rates that are equal to or greater than certain specified rates that are intended to reflect an appropriate market rate of interest on similar deferred payment transactions. To accomplish this result, Section 1274 provides for the recharacterization of principal as interest. In effect, Section 1274 has assumed much of the responsibility that previously had been borne by Section 483 as it existed prior to the 1984 Act.[150]

---

[145] Prop. Reg. § 1.1273-1(d)(5). For an example applying this special rule, see Prop. Reg. § 1.1273-1(f), Ex. 3.

[146] IRC § 163(e)(2)(B); Prop. Reg. § 1.163-7(b). In general, de minimis OID is accrued using the constant yield method, but an election is available to use straight-line accrual. Prop. Reg. § 1.163-7(b)(3).

[147] Prop. Reg. § 1.1273-1(d)(6).

[148] Id. See discussion supra ¶ 11.02[2].

[149] See Priv. Ltr. Rul. 8829067 (Apr. 27, 1988) for an illustration of the applicability of Section 1274 to circumstances where the trading price of publicly traded property failed to reflect adequately the property's market value and, consequently, Section 1274 was applicable for purposes of determining the issue price. The difference in value was attributable to a control premium, blockage discounts, and other substantial contractual and regulatory restrictions affecting the value of the property.

[150] See infra ¶ 11.04 for discussion of Section 483.

[a] Imputation of Interest

Section 1274(a) provides that when a debt instrument has adequate stated interest, the issue price is the principal amount stated in the debt instrument. When the debt instrument does not have adequate stated interest, the issue price is the so-called imputed principal amount. Section 1274(b), which is discussed in the next section, provides the rules for determining the imputed principal amount.

[i] General rules—applicable federal rates. The imputed principal amount is the present value of all payments due under the particular debt instrument as determined by specified discount rates.[151] The specified discount rates are based on the so-called applicable federal rates. The applicable federal rates differ according to the terms of the debt instruments. For instruments with a term of three years or less, the applicable federal rate is the federal short-term rate. For instruments with a term of more than three years but not more than nine years, the applicable federal rate is the federal midterm rate. For instruments with a term of more than nine years, the applicable federal rate is the federal long-term rate.[152]

Determining applicable federal rates. The applicable federal rates are based on outstanding marketable obligations of the United States.[153] Each month, the IRS announces by revenue ruling the rates that will be applicable during the immediately succeeding month.[154] In certain circumstances, debt instruments having a qualified floating rate that resets at least every six months may qualify for a lower testing rate based on a comparable Treasury index rate.[155]

In determining the particular rate applicable to a sale or to an exchange, the applicable federal rate is the lowest of the rates determined for the three-calendar-month period ending with the first calendar month in which there is a binding written contract for the sale or exchange.[156] In other words, if a sale is consummated in June pursuant to a binding contract executed in April, the rate applicable to that sale would be the lowest of the rates determined for February, March, and April of that year.

In determining the term of a debt instrument for purposes of selecting the applicable federal rate, options to renew or extend the debt instrument must be taken into account.[157] If the exercise of the option is in the economic interest of the holder of the option (e.g., if the holder of the debt instrument

---

[151] IRC § 1274(b)(1).

[152] IRC § 1274(d)(1).

[153] IRC § 1274(d)(1)(C).

[154] IRC § 1274(d)(1)(B); Prop. Reg. § 1.1274-4(b).

[155] Prop. Reg. § 1.1274-4(d); see IRC § 1274(d)(1)(D).

[156] IRC § 1274(d)(2); Prop. Reg. § 1.1274-4(g).

[157] IRC § 1274(d)(3).

would have a higher yield, or the issuer of the instrument would have a reduced yield), exercise of the option is presumed.[158]

Determining adequate stated interest. To determine whether there is adequate stated interest, the present value of the payments due under the obligation is computed using the applicable federal rate. The result is compared to the instrument's stated principal amount (i.e., all amounts due under the instrument other than stated interest), and the issue price is whichever figure is lower. In effect, application of this rule means that adequate stated interest will exist only when the effective interest rate under the agreement is equal to or greater than the applicable federal rate.

The proposed regulations reflect these concepts and provide a safe harbor that is easily deduced from these principles. If a debt instrument has a single stated rate of interest that is paid or compounded at least annually, and that rate equals or exceeds the applicable federal rate, then the debt instrument has adequate stated interest.[159]

> **EXAMPLE:** Assume that a debt instrument issued for non–publicly traded property calls for the payment of $1 million at the end of 10 years, with 20 semiannual interest payments of $60,000 each. If the applicable test rate is 12 percent compounded semiannually, the debt instrument provides for adequate stated interest because it provides for interest equal to the test rate. On the other hand, if the test rate were 12 percent and the agreement provided for payments of $50,000 semiannually, inadequate stated interest would exist and the issue price would be the imputed principal amount of $885,295, which is the present value, at 12 percent compounded semiannually, of 20 semiannual payments of $50,000 and one $1 million payment due in 10 years.[160]

Testing for adequate stated interest for a debt instrument with a variable interest rate is problematic, since the amounts of future interest payments, and thus the present value of those payments, are uncertain. In the case of a variable rate debt instrument that provides for stated interest at a qualified floating rate, the proposed regulations solve this problem by treating the instrument as providing for a fixed interest rate equal to the value of the qualified floating rate as of the date of the sale or exchange (or, if earlier, the contract date).[161] For example, if a debt instrument is issued in exchange for non–publicly traded property and provides for quarterly interest payments equal to a bank's prime rate plus two percentage points, the instrument will

---

[158] See Prop. Reg. § 1.1274-2(c)(3).

[159] Prop. Reg. § 1.1274-2(c)(1).

[160] See Prop. Reg. § 1.1274-3(b)(3) for additional examples.

[161] Prop. Reg. § 1.1274-2(d)(1)(i). Caps and floors generally are ignored unless they will significantly affect the expected yield of the debt instrument. Prop. Reg. § 1.1274-2(d)(1)(ii).

have adequate stated interest if the applicable federal rate does not exceed the initial value of this variable rate.

Special rules also apply in Section 1274 transactions to debt instruments that provide for contingent payments. Under the recently revised proposed regulations, the stated principal amount of a debt instrument that provides for contingent payments is the maximum amount of the contingent and noncontingent payments, excluding any amount of stated interest (whether or not contingent). The imputed principal amount of such a debt instrument is the sum of the present values of the noncontingent payments (discounted at the applicable federal rate) and the FMV of the contingent payments determined as of the issue date.[162] If the contingent payments cannot be valued apart from the noncontingent payments, the imputed principal amount of the debt instrument is its FMV. In the IRS's view, the FMV of the instrument will not be reasonably ascertainable only in "rare and extraordinary cases."[163]

In business acquisitions, debt instruments frequently are issued that provide for future payments that are contingent on the performance of the acquired enterprise. For example, a debt instrument may be issued to the sole shareholder of a corporation in exchange for the shareholder's stock; the instrument provides for five annual payments of $1 million, plus noncontingent interest of 8 percent, plus contingent interest equal to 10 percent of the corporation's annual profits in excess of a specified amount. Under a special rule applicable to such earn-out provisions, such a debt instrument will be considered to have adequate stated interest if (1) it would be considered to have adequate stated interest if tested at a rate equal to 80 percent of the applicable federal rate and (2) it is reasonable to expect that contingent interest payments will raise the total yield on the debt instrument to at least the applicable federal rate.[164] Thus, in this example, if the applicable federal rate is 10 percent and future profits can reasonably be expected to increase the interest payments to 10 percent or more, the debt instrument will have adequate stated interest.[165]

[ii] **Potentially abusive situations.** Special rules are provided in so-called potentially abusive situations. "Potentially abusive situations" is defined to mean (1) a tax shelter as defined in Section 6662(d)(2)(C)(ii) and (2) any other situation that by reason of recent sales transactions, nonrecourse financing, financing with a term in excess of the economic life of the property, or other circumstances, is of a type that the Treasury concludes has the

---

[162] Prop. Reg. § 1.1274-2(e)(1). See discussion infra ¶ 11.03.

[163] Id. See also discussion at ¶ 5.05[15][b].

[164] Prop. Reg. § 1.1274-2(e)(2).

[165] See discussion infra ¶ 11.03 for additional rules applicable to contingent payment debt instruments.

potential for tax avoidance.[166] The proposed regulations also classify the use of a debt instrument with clearly excessive interest as a potentially abusive situation.[167] Interest is clearly excessive if, considering the terms of the debt and the creditworthiness of the borrower, it is "clearly greater" than the arm's-length amount of interest that would have been charged in a cash-lending transaction between the same two parties.[168]

In the case of a potentially abusive situation, the imputed principal amount is the FMV of the property for which the debt instrument is issued, taking into account any other consideration involved in the transaction.[169] For example, if a taxpayer pays $1 million down and issues a nonrecourse note for $6 million, payable in 10 years to acquire property worth $4 million, the imputed principal amount is $3 million ($4 million FMV less $1 million cash paid). Note that the imputed principal amount that is in a potentially abusive situation is the issue price even if the note provides for interest in excess of the applicable federal rate and even if the imputed principal amount exceeds the stated principal amount.[170]

Not all transactions involving nonrecourse financing will be potentially abusive situations. A sale or an exchange of any interest (other than an interest solely as a creditor) in real property financed by a nonrecourse debt instrument will not be considered to involve a potentially abusive situation if, in addition to the nonrecourse debt instrument, the purchaser makes a down payment equal to at least 20 percent of the total stated purchase price.[171] Moreover, the issuance of a nonrecourse debt instrument for an outstanding recourse or nonrecourse debt instrument is not a potentially abusive situation.[172] In either of these circumstances, the imputed principal amount of the nonrecourse debt is determined under the general rules by discounting the payments due under the debt at the applicable federal rate, and the issue price will be the lower of the imputed or stated principal amount.

The issuer's determination that a debt instrument is or is not issued in a potentially abusive situation is binding on all holders of the debt instrument.[173] A holder may take a different position only if it explicitly discloses the inconsistency on its tax return.[174]

---

[166] IRC § 1274(b)(3)(B).

[167] Prop. Reg. § 1.1274-3(a)(2)(iv).

[168] Prop. Reg. § 1.1274-3(b)(3).

[169] IRC § 1274(b)(3)(A); Prop. Reg. § 1.1274-2(b)(3).

[170] Prop. Reg. § 1.1274-2(b)(3).

[171] Prop. Reg. § 1.1274-3(b)(2).

[172] Prop. Reg. § 1.1274-3(b)(1).

[173] Prop. Reg. § 1.1274-3(d).

[174] Id.

[iii] **Use of special 9 percent discount rate.** In the case of debt instruments with a stated principal amount of $2.8 million or less that are given in consideration for the sale or exchange of any property (other than new Section 38 property within the meaning of Section 48(b)), the discount rate for purposes of Section 1274 is not to exceed 9 percent, compounded semiannually.[175] For debt instruments arising out of sales or exchanges during any calendar year after 1989, the $2.8 million amount referred to previously is increased by an appropriate inflation adjustment.[176] In Revenue Ruling 90-68,[177] the IRS issued its first ruling setting forth the new principal amounts. The $2.8 million amount was increased to $2,933,200. Taxpayers must keep abreast of corresponding adjustments in succeeding years.

[iv] **Sale-leaseback transactions.** If a debt instrument is issued as consideration for the sale or exchange of property pursuant to a plan under which the transferor of the property, or any person related to the transferor, leases a portion of the property after the transfer, then the discount rate for purposes of determining the issue price is to be 110 percent of the applicable federal rate, compounded semiannually.[178] In addition, Section 1274A, pertaining to debt instruments with a stated principal amount of $2.8 million or less,[179] will not apply to any instrument issued in connection with such a sale-leaseback transaction.[180]

[b] Exceptions

A number of transactions that otherwise would be covered by Section 1274 are expressly excluded from application of the section.

[i] **Sale of certain farms for $1 million or less.** If a debt instrument is issued in connection with the sale or exchange of a farm by an individual, estate, testamentary trust, corporation (which, at the date of the sale or exchange, is a small business corporation as defined in Section 1244(c)(3)), or partnership that meets certain conditions similar to those of IRC Section 1244(c)(3), then Section 1274 does not apply.[181] Although Section 1274 itself does not apply in this situation, this means only that there will be no potential imputation of interest under that section. Section 1274 does not, of itself,

---

[175] IRC §§ 1274A(a), 1274A(b). The phrase "new Section 38 property within the meaning of Section 48(b)" refers to property of the type that would have been eligible for the investment credit prior to the credit's repeal in the 1986 Act.

[176] IRC § 1274A(d)(2).

[177] Rev. Rul. 90-68, 1990-2 CB 200.

[178] IRC § 1274(e).

[179] See IRC § 1274A. See also discussion supra ¶ 11.02[5][a][iii].

[180] IRC § 1274(e)(2).

[181] IRC § 1274(c)(3)(A). See Prop. Reg. § 1.1274-1(b)(2)(ii)(A).

remove the transaction from the OID rules, and it also does not prevent application of Section 483.[182]

For purposes of this special rule, "farm" is defined to include "stock, dairy, poultry, fruit, fur-bearing animal, and truck farms, plantations, ranches, nurseries, ranges, greenhouses or other similar structures used primarily for the raising of agricultural or horticultural commodities, and orchards."[183] A corporation is considered a small business if the aggregate amount of money and other property received by the corporation as a contribution to capital and paid in surplus for its stock does not exceed $1 million as of the time of the issuance of the stock, taking into account all amounts received for that stock and any stock previously issued.[184] A partnership must meet the same requirements except as modified to be applicable to partnerships.[185] Aggregation rules are provided with respect to the $1 million limit. All related sales or exchanges are treated as one sale or exchange.[186]

[ii] Sale of principal residence. Section 1274 does not apply to any instrument arising from the sale or exchange by an individual of his principal residence.[187] For this purpose, "principal residence" is defined to have the same meaning as it has for purposes of Section 1034, which pertains to the rollover of gain on the sale of a principal residence.[188]

[iii] Sale or exchange of property for $250,000 or less. Section 1274 does not apply to any debt instrument that arises from the sale or exchange of property if all consideration for the sale (taking into account all payments to be made under the debt instrument, principal and interest, all other debt instruments arising from that same transaction, and all other consideration) does not exceed $250,000.[189] For this purpose, consideration other than a debt instrument is taken into account at its FMV and all transactions that are a part of the same transaction or part of a series of related transactions are treated as a single sale or exchange.[190]

[iv] Sale of patent. Section 1274 does not apply to any transfer described in Section 1235(a) (pertaining to the sale or exchange of patents)

---

[182] See discussion infra ¶ 11.04.

[183] IRC §§ 6420(c)(2), 1274(c)(3)(A)(i).

[184] IRC §§ 1244(c)(3), 1274(c)(3)(A)(i)(II).

[185] IRC § 1274(c)(3)(A)(i)(III).

[186] IRC § 1274(c)(3)(A)(ii).

[187] IRC § 1274(c)(3)(B).

[188] Id.

[189] IRC § 1274(c)(3)(C). See Prop. Reg. § 1.1274-1(b)(2)(ii)(B).

[190] IRC § 1274(c)(3)(C).

to the extent the amounts received for the sale are contingent on the productivity, use, or disposition of the property transferred.[191] Correlatively, to the extent the consideration received for the transfer is fixed, and thus not contingent, Section 1274 does apply.

[v] **Sale or exchange to which Section 483(e) applies.** Section 1274 does not apply to any debt instrument to the extent that Section 483(e) applies to that instrument. Section 483(e) pertains to a sale or exchange of land by an individual to a member of that individual's family to the extent that the price does not exceed $500,000.

[vi] **Debt instruments due in six months or less.** Section 1274 does not apply to any debt instrument given in consideration for the sale or exchange of property if no payments are due under the debt instrument more than six months after the date of the sale or exchange.[192] Such debt instruments, however, may be subject to other short-term obligation rules, such as Section 1281.[193]

[vii] **Personal use property.** Section 1274 does not apply to any debt instrument given in consideration for the sale or exchange of personal use property.[194] The term "personal use property" means any property, substantially all the use of which by the taxpayer is not in connection with a trade or business or an activity described in Section 212.[195] Moreover, if a debt instrument issued in connection with the acquisition or carrying of personal use property has OID and the issuer is a cash method taxpayer, the OID on such instrument is deductible only when paid.[196]

[c] **Election to Use Cash Method**

If a debt instrument that is issued for property has a stated principal amount of $2 million or less and is issued to a seller/lender who does not use the accrual method and is not a dealer in the property sold, and if Section 1274 would otherwise apply, an election may be made by both the borrower and the lender pursuant to which interest on the debt instrument may be taken into account by each under the cash method of accounting.[197]

Since the election to use the cash method focuses on the principal

---

[191] IRC § 1274(c)(3)(E).

[192] IRC § 1274(c)(1)(B); Prop. Reg. § 1.1274-1(b)(2)(i).

[193] See discussion infra ¶ 11.06.

[194] IRC § 1275(b)(1).

[195] IRC § 1275(b)(3).

[196] IRC § 1275(b)(2).

[197] IRC § 1274A(c); Prop. Reg. § 1.1274A-1(c).

amount of the debt instrument, other consideration may be issued for the property that makes the total amount involved in the transaction much greater than $2 million. On the other hand, contingent principal payments must be taken into account in determining whether the $2 million amount is exceeded.[198] The rigidity of the $2 million limitation is lessened somewhat by the fact that it will be indexed for inflation beginning in 1990.[199] In Revenue Ruling 90-68,[200] the IRS issued its first ruling adjusting the $2 million for inflation. This initial adjustment increased the $2 million amount to $2,095,100. Taxpayers must be alert for corresponding adjustments in succeeding years.

The buyer and seller make the election by attaching a statement of election to their respective returns.[201] The election binds all successors of the buyer, but only qualifying successors of the seller. If the instrument is transferred to an accrual method taxpayer, the election terminates.[202]

¶ 11.03 CONTINGENT PAYMENTS

The broad scope of the OID rules makes it virtually impossible for the statutory provisions to provide guidance on all situations that arise. One case is that of contingent obligations. Section 1275(d) provides the Treasury with the authority to promulgate regulations governing the treatment of contingent payments.

The government has attempted to write rules governing contingent payment debt obligations at least four times. The 1986 version took a wait-and-see approach to the tax treatment of such instruments, usually ignoring the contingent payment features until the contingencies were resolved. The February 1991 amendments would have bifurcated certain contingent payment instruments and taxed the contingent pieces as options or something else, i.e., something other than debt. The December 1992 proposed regulations, the current version generally described in this chapter, purport to retain the prior rules concerning contingent-payment debt instruments but change the computation of issue price for such instruments. The result is that the currently outstanding proposed regulations contain provisions that are internally inconsistent in the tax treatment of contingent payment obligations.

Some harmony would have been brought to this chaos by the January

---

[198] Prop. Reg. § 1.1274A-1(b)(2).

[199] IRC § 1274A(d)(2); Prop. Reg. § 1.1274A-1(b)(4).

[200] Rev. Rul. 90-68, 1990-2 CB 200.

[201] See Prop. Reg. § 1.1274A-1(c)(1) for the information to be included in the statement.

[202] Prop. Reg. § 1.1274A-1(c)(2).

1993 proposed regulations that were released and then withdrawn without ever being officially published. These rules apparently were withdrawn not because of any concerns relating to their substantive provisions, but rather as part of a general freeze on a number of regulatory projects throughout government that were in the pipeline at the time of the change in the presidential administrations.[203] Although these rules still have not been published as of June 1993, it is anticipated that they ultimately will be issued in substantially their January 1993 form.

The rules described below are these January 1993 rules that might be described as "withdrawn but anticipated." Practitioners are cautioned, however, that the rules ultimately promulgated may differ from those described below and that the current proposed regulations should be consulted with respect to any transaction not clearly subject to the revised regulations only, whenever issued.

The current proposed rules completely replace these prior proposed rules. In general, they divide the universe of contingent payment debt instruments into three categories: (1) those calling for "market-based contingent payments"; (2) certain "small issue" debt instruments; and (3) all other contingent payment obligations.

[1] Definition

There is no explicit definition of "contingent payment" in the statute or the proposed regulations. Rather, the proposed regulations provide certain exclusions from what might otherwise be included in the concept. Under these rules, a payment is not contingent merely because of the possibility of impairment by insolvency, default, or similar circumstances.[204] Further, a debt instrument does not provide for contingent payments as a result of being convertible into stock of the issuer or a related party, even if the conversion right may be satisfied in cash.[205] Exceptions also are provided for variable rate debt instruments, debt instruments whose only contingencies relate to the acceleration or deferral of fixed payments,[206] debt instruments subject to

---

[203] See 58 Fed. Reg. 6074 (1993).

[204] Prop. Reg. § 1.1275-4(a)(3), as it would read under the January 1993 release.

[205] Prop. Reg. § 1.1275-4(a)(4), as it would read under the January 1993 release.

[206] The rules of Prop. Reg. § 1.1272-1(d) provide that the yield and maturity of a debt instrument are determined according to the instrument's stated payment schedule, even if the debt instrument provides for a contingency that could result in the acceleration or the deferral of one or more payments that is fixed in amount as of the issue date. If the contingency is more likely than not to occur, the proposed regulations assume it will occur.

IRC Section 988 (relating to certain foreign currency transactions), and tax-exempt obligations.[207]

In determining whether or not a payment is contingent, the IRS may disregard remote and incidental contingencies.[208] Otherwise, such contingencies would provide unintended results that could lead to tax avoidance.

[2] Market-Based Contingent Payments

The centerpiece of the January 1993 contingent payment rules are those dealing with market-based contingent payments. A market-based contingent payment, as the name suggests, is any payment that is based on the price or yield of personal property that is actively traded (within the meaning of Section 1092(d)(1)), such as actively traded stock, commodities, and options, or on an index of the prices or yields of such property. The term also encompasses any payment the variations of which can be substantially hedged through the use of property that is actively traded. Finally, a market-based contingent payment also is a payment based on one or more qualified floating rates (i.e., a floating interest rate whose variations can reasonably be expected to measure variations in the cost of newly borrowed funds).[209]

The proposed regulations require the holder and the issuer of a debt instrument that provides for market-based contingent payments (but no other substantial contingent payments) to accrue interest based on a reasonable estimate of the yield at the time the instrument is issued or acquired or on a reasonable estimate of the performance of the contingencies each year. The accrued amount is recognized whether or not the contingent payments become fixed as to amount during the taxable year.[210]

Taxpayers may choose among five methods to determine the amount of interest accruing each year with respect to a debt instrument with market-based contingent payments, and the holder and the issuer need not choose the same method.[211] Two of the methods, the yield adjustment method and the noncontingent bond method, may be used for any such debt instrument. The other three methods are more specialized.[212] The goal of all five methods, however, is the same—to provide for current interest accruals that reflect the instrument's underlying economics.

---

[207] Prop. Reg. § 1.1275-4(a)(2), as it would read under the January 1993 release.

[208] Prop. Reg. § 1.1275-4(a)(6), as it would read under the January 1993 release.

[209] Prop. Reg. § 1.1275-4(a)(7), as it would read under the January 1993 release.

[210] Prop. Reg. § 1.1275-4(b)(2)(i), as it would read under the January 1993 release.

[211] Prop. Reg. § 1.1275-4(b)(2)(ii), as it would read under the January 1993 release.

[212] The market yield method, the variable yield method, and the spot price method are described in Prop. Reg. § 1.1275-4(b)(5), 1.1275-4(b)(6), and 1.1275-4(b)(7), respectively, as they would read under the January 1993 release.

The yield adjustment method provides for interest accruals based on an annual estimate of the expected contingent payments. A schedule of all prior and expected payments is constructed at the end of each taxable year, and the interest accruing during the year is computed on the basis of that schedule.[213]

EXAMPLE: On January 1, 1994, *B*, a calendar-year taxpayer, pays $1 million at original issue for *X*'s debt instrument, which entitles the holder to receive on December 31, 1998, $1 million plus interest equal to the then-market price of 1,000 ounces of gold. Under the yield adjustment method, on December 31, 1994, the end of *B*'s first taxable year, *B* constructs an estimated payment schedule. Based on the forward price as of that date for the payment of 1,000 ounces of gold four years later, the estimated payment schedule consists of a single payment at maturity of $1.4 million. The yield to maturity of a five-year debt instrument with an issue price of $1 million and a stated redemption price at maturity of $1.4 million is approximately 6.96 percent, compounded annually. *B* uses this yield to accrue $69,610 of interest income in 1994.

B computes a new payment schedule at the end of each subsequent year. Assume that the anticipated payment as of December 31, 1995, is only $1.3 million. The yield to maturity of a five-year note with an issue price of $1 million and a stated redemption price at maturity of $1.3 million is approximately 5.39 percent, compounded annually. The accrual of interest on such a note for the first two years would total $110,650. *B* accrues as interest income for 1995 the excess of this total over its interest accrual for 1994, or $41,040.[214]

If the price of gold in this example continues to fall, the holder or the issuer of the instrument may find itself at the end of a taxable year in the position of having accrued more interest in its prior taxable years than its revised estimated yield indicates it should have accrued through the current year. This situation creates a "negative adjustment." Any negative adjustment first reduces the interest accrual for the period in which the negative adjustment occurs, then gives rise to ordinary loss (in the case of the holder) or ordinary income (to the issuer) to the extent of prior years' accruals, and then creates a carry-forward negative adjustment to the extent of any excess.[215]

In contrast to the yield adjustment method, the noncontingent bond method reflects an assumed reasonable rate of return that is based on an

---

[213] Prop. Reg. § 1.1275-4(b)(3), as it would read under the January 1993 release.

[214] Prop. Reg. § 1.1274-4(b)(12), Ex. 1, as it would read under the January 1993 release.

[215] Prop. Reg. § 1.1275-4(b)(8), as it would read under the January 1993 release.

estimate, as of the issue date, of the amount of the contingent payments. Interest accruals are based on this estimated yield, with appropriate adjustments made when the amount of a contingent payment becomes fixed.[216]

> EXAMPLE: Assume B acquires X's debt instrument on January 1, 1994, at original issue for $1 million. The instrument provides for annual payments on December 31 equal to the market price of 400 units of an actively traded commodity as of the payment date and a payment at maturity, December 31, 1998, of $800,000. Assume that a reasonable estimated payment schedule, determined as of the issue date, calls for payments of $100,000, $115,000, $125,000, $140,000, and $950,000 at the end of each year. The yield to maturity of such an instrument would be approximately 9.04 percent, compounded annually. The interest accruing during the first year at this estimated yield would be $90,450. To the extent that the amount of the payment that is actually made on December 31, 1994, is greater than or less than the $100,000 estimated amount, there is either additional interest or a negative adjustment for 1994.[217]

The determination of whether a debt instrument is subject to the market-based contingent payment rules is made by the issuer and is binding on the holder, unless the holder discloses a contrary position on its return.[218] The choice of which method to use to compute the annual interest accruals, on the other hand, is made independently by the issuer and the holder. Subsequent unrelated holders are also free to choose any of the computational methods prescribed by the proposed regulations, unless the instrument was acquired in a transaction described in Section 381(a) or otherwise is acquired with a carry-over basis from the prior holder.[219]

[3] Small Issues

While the January 1993 rules governing market-based contingent payments are elaborate and detailed, the guidance offered for other instruments with contingent payments is much briefer. Such instruments are segregated into those that are part of a small issue and those that are not.

A debt instrument that is issued for cash or publicly traded property, or

---

[216] Prop. Reg. § 1.1275-4(b)(4), as it would read under the January 1993 release.

[217] Prop. Reg. § 1.1275-4(b)(12), Ex. 2, and Prop. Reg. § 1.1275-4(b)(4)(iv), as they would read under the January 1993 release.

[218] Prop. Reg. § 1.1275-4(b)(1)(ii), as it would read under the January 1993 release.

[219] Prop. Reg. § 1.1275-4(b)(9), as it would read under the January 1993 release.

which itself is part of a publicly traded issue, is part of a small issue if the aggregate issue price of all debt instruments in the issue is $250,000 or less.[220] Debt instruments with similar credit and payment terms issued as part of a common plan of marketing (whether or not sold at substantially the same time) will be considered part of the same issue.[221] If a debt instrument is issued for non–publicly traded property or has its issue price determined under Section 1273(b)(4), it is part of a small issue if its issue price is $2 million or less.[222]

If a debt instrument is part of a small issue and does not provide for any market-based contingent payments other than payments at a single qualified floating rate paid or compounding at least annually, the noncontingent payments are separated from the contingent payments.[223] The noncontingent payments are treated as a separate debt instrument with an issue price equal to the lesser of the issue price for the overall debt instrument or the sum of the noncontingent payments. All interest on this noncontingent debt instrument is treated as OID.[224]

If the sum of the noncontingent payments is equal to or greater than the instrument's issue price, then each contingent payment is treated entirely as interest and is taken into account when the amount of the payment is fixed.[225] If the contingent payment is not paid within six months of the date it becomes fixed, however, a special rule treats the issuer as issuing another debt instrument on the date the payment became fixed, and the amount taken into account on that date is the issue price of this new obligation (i.e., the present value of the future contingent payment that has become fixed).[226]

If the issue price of the debt instrument exceeds the sum of the noncontingent payments, the contingent payments are treated first as principal to the extent of this excess. Payments are then treated entirely as interest

---

[220] Prop. Reg. § 1.1275-4(a)(7)(ii)(A), as it would read under the January 1993 release.

[221] Id.

[222] Prop. Reg. § 1.1275-4(a)(7)(ii)(B), as it would read under the January 1993 release. If the debt instrument is subject to Section 483, the concept analogous to issue price under Section 1274 (generally, the sum of the present values of the deferred payments and the present values of any stated interest payments) is substituted for issue price in applying this rule. See Prop. Reg. § 1.483-2(a)(1).

[223] Prop. Reg. § 1.1275-4(c)(1), as it would read under the January 1993 release.

[224] Prop. Reg. § 1.1275-4(c)(2), as it would read under the January 1993 release. See Prop. Reg. § 1.1274-2(e) and discussion supra ¶ 11.02[5][a][i] for rules governing the determination of issue price when a contingent payment obligation is issued for nonpublicly traded property.

[225] Prop. Reg. § 1.1275-4(c)(3)(i), as it would read under the January 1993 release.

[226] Prop. Reg. § 1.1275-4(e), as it would read under the January 1993 release.

and accrue when the amount of the payment becomes fixed, subject to the same deferred payment rule just described.[227]

> EXAMPLE: Assume *B* sells *X* non–publicly traded property in exchange for *X*'s debt instrument with a stated principal amount of $1 million. In all events, this full amount must be repaid at maturity, which is in five years. The instrument also provides for annual payments on December 31 equal to 2 percent of *X*'s gross receipts for the preceding twelve months. Assume that the debt instrument has an issue price of $1 million under Proposed Regulation § 1.1274-2. Since the noncontingent payment at maturity is equal to the issue price of the debt instrument, the issue price of the noncontingent portion is also $1 million, and there is no OID or interest to accrue on that noncontingent debt instrument. All annual contingent payments are treated entirely as interest.[228]

> EXAMPLE: *C* pays *Y* $100,000 at original issue for a five-year note paying $8,000 in interest at the end of each year, $55,000 in principal at maturity, plus a payment at maturity equal to one percent of *Y*'s gross receipts for the preceding twelve months. The sum of the noncontingent payments is $95,000, which is the issue price of the noncontingent debt instrument. The yield on the noncontingent debt instrument is zero, and no interest accrues on the noncontingent debt instrument. If the amount of the contingent payment paid at maturity is $15,000, $5,000 is treated as principal and the remaining $10,000 as interest.[229]

[4] Other Contingent Debt Instruments

All debt instruments with contingent payments that are not governed by the market-based or small issue rules fall into the "other" category—large debt instruments that provide for substantial nonmarket-based contingent payments. Again, the debt instrument is separated into its contingent and noncontingent components.[230] The issue price of the noncontingent component is the present value of the noncontingent payments determined by using a discount rate equal to the greater of the debt instrument's yield to maturi-

---

[227] Prop. Reg. § 1.1275-4(c)(3)(ii), as it would read under the January 1993 release.

[228] Prop. Reg. § 1.1275-4(c)(4), Ex. 1, as it would read under the January 1993 release.

[229] Prop. Reg. § 1.1275-4(c)(4), Ex. 2, as it would read under the January 1993 release.

[230] Prop. Reg. § 1.1275-4(d)(1), as it would read under the January 1993 release.

ty, disregarding all contingent payments, or the applicable federal rate.[231] All interest on the noncontingent debt instrument is treated as OID.[232]

The issue price of the contingent component of the debt instrument is the issue price of the overall debt instrument less the issue price allocated to the noncontingent portion. Interest accrues on the contingent component at the same rate used to compute the issue price of the noncontingent debt instrument, but such interest is taken into account by the issuer and the holder only when the amount of the payment becomes fixed.[233] Contingent payments that are fixed prior to maturity of the debt instrument are treated first as interest to the extent interest is accrued but unpaid, then as a reduction of issue price, and finally again as interest.[234] The total payments at maturity are allocated first to basis, and any excess is interest.[235] Any loss at maturity is treated as ordinary to the extent of the issue price originally allocated to the contingent component plus interest previously included in income on the contingent component.[236]

EXAMPLE: On January 1, 1994, D pays Z $10 million for Z's note maturing December 31, 1998. The full principal is payable at maturity. Annual interest is payable each December 31 equal to 3 percent of Z's gross receipts for the preceding twelve months. The applicable federal rate is 8 percent, compounded annually. The noncontingent component consists of the $10 million payment at maturity and has an issue price of $6,805,832, determined by discounting at the applicable federal rate (since the yield ignoring the contingent payments was less, i.e., zero). OID accrues with respect to this noncontingent debt instrument under the rules of Section 1272. The issue price of the contingent component is $3,194,168. The amount of each contingent payment treated as interest is determined by multiplying the 8 percent imputed interest rate times the adjusted issue price of this contingent component (i.e., its issue price minus contingent payments treated as principal). Thus, if the first contingent payment that becomes fixed and is paid is $1 million, the first $255,533 is a payment of accrued but previously unpaid interest (8 percent × $3,194,168) and is taken into account as such. The balance of the payment, $744,467, reduces the adjusted issue price of the contingent component. This allocation method continues for future contingent payments until more than $3,194,168 has been allocated to

---

[231] Prop. Reg. § 1.1275-4(d)(2)(i), 1.1275-4(d)(7), as it would read under the January 1993 release.

[232] Prop. Reg. § 1.1275-4(c)(2)(i), as it would read under the January 1993 release.

[233] Prop. Reg. § 1.1275-4(d)(3), as it would read under the January 1993 release.

[234] Prop. Reg. § 1.1275-4(d)(4), as it would read under the January 1993 release.

[235] Prop. Reg. § 1.1275-4(d)(5), as it would read under the January 1993 release.

[236] Prop. Reg. § 1.1275-4(d)(6), as it would read under the January 1993 release.

issue price, in which case all additional payments are interest, or the note matures before the $3,194,168 of basis in the contingent component has been recovered, in which case D recognizes an ordinary loss.[237]

¶ 11.04 CERTAIN DEFERRED PAYMENTS: SECTION 483

Section 483 is a recharacterization provision. It is intended to recharacterize payments of principal as payments of interest. Section 483 applies to transactions in property where no or inadequate interest has been provided and the OID provisions do not apply. In other words, if a taxpayer engages in the purchase or sale of property in a transaction that is not covered by the OID provisions, the taxpayer may nevertheless be subject to the provisions of Section 483.

Unlike the OID provisions, Section 483 does not affect the time when interest is reported. Thus, the amounts recharacterized as interest are recognized in the year that is otherwise appropriate under the method of accounting employed by the taxpayer.[238] These amounts are not subject to the provisions of Sections 1272 and 1273.

[1] History and Development

Section 483 was first enacted in 1964. It was designed to recharacterize as interest those amounts that had been characterized by the parties to the transaction as principal. Congress deemed that the amounts so recharacterized were, as a matter of economic reality, a charge for the use or forbearance from the use of money.

Section 483 did not change the taxpayer's method of accounting. Instead, its scope was limited to changing the character of amounts that were reported under the taxpayer's method of accounting. Thus, a cash method seller would recharacterize amounts as interest in the year of actual or constructive receipt, and a cash method buyer would recharacterize amounts as interest in the year of actual payment.[239]

An accrual method taxpayer would recharacterize amounts as interest in the year in which the payment being recharacterized was due. This latter point was quite significant. In effect, it recharacterized a portion of a principal payment as interest but required that the interest so recharacterized be reported in the year in which the principal payment was due, not in the year in which interest would normally have accrued.

---

[237] Prop. Reg. §§ 1.1275-4(d)(8), Ex. 1, 1.1275-4(d)(6), as it would read under the January 1993 release.

[238] Prop. Reg. § 1.483-1(a)(2)(ii).

[239] See discussion of these cash method rules at ¶¶ 3.03, 3.04.

Initially, Section 483 compared the interest rate stated in the agreement to a test rate. If the stated rate did not produce interest in an amount at least equal to the amount produced by using the test rate, the section required a recharacterization of principal as interest. In other words, interest would be imputed. The amount of interest to be imputed was based on a rate that was one percentage point higher than the test rate. The Treasury had the authority to change the applicable test rate, but, as a practical matter, these changes were not made on a regular basis, and they generally failed to keep pace with changes in the market.

Original Section 483 created four major problems for the Treasury and opportunities for taxpayers almost from enactment. The first of these was the failure of the test rate and the imputation rate to keep pace with market interest rates. During the periods of high inflation and high interest in the late 1970s and early 1980s, the test and imputation rates were generally far below the market rate of interest. Consequently, transactions governed by Section 483 still permitted portions of the current market interest to be recharacterized as principal. In fact, the section encouraged it because use of the test rate of interest generally precluded a challenge to the characterizations used by the parties, regardless of the facts.

Second, imputed interest was allocated among payments of principal on a pro rata basis. The compounding feature of interest was ignored, thereby providing further opportunities for tax savings by taxpayers. To illustrate, assume property with an FMV of $100,000 was sold for $200,000, $100,000 of which would be paid one year after the date of sale, with the remaining $100,000 to be paid 10 years after the date of sale. The $100,000 of imputed interest would be allocated half to the first payment and half to the second payment. This allocation afforded the purchaser a much larger interest deduction than would have been the case if principles of economic accrual had been used.[240]

Third, use of a single test and imputing rate for all transactions ignored the impact of different market rates for different types of obligations, regardless of maturity. Congress desired that different rates be used, depending on the different terms of the loans.

Finally, since interest was taken into account in the year in which the payment was due by an accrual method taxpayer, those taxpayers could use the imputed interest rules to defer or accelerate the time for the recognition of interest as compared to when interest would otherwise have been recog-

---

[240] In Lloyd Williams, Jr., 94 TC No. 27 (1990), the court held that the interest deduction provided by Section 483 during the years at issue was to be determined on a pro rata basis, even though that computation provided a larger deduction than would have been provided under an economic accrual basis. Moreover, the court emphasized that neither Section 446(b) nor Section 461(g) provided the Commissioner with discretion to limit the interest deduction to the amount of interest that had economically accrued. See also Thomas O. Weis, 94 TC 473 (1990), to the same effect.

nized under an accrual method. Thus, accrual method sellers who wanted to defer the reporting of interest on deferred payment sales effectively used Section 483 for this purpose.

> EXAMPLE: Assume an accrual method seller wanted to sell property with a FMV of $100 for a $100 note to be paid in eight years with interest at 9 percent. If the note provided for 9 percent, then interest would be recognized each year as it accrued. However, if the note provided for a payment of $200 at maturity with no interest stated, $100 of the $200 payment would be recharacterized as interest, but the interest would not be recognized until year 8.

For all of these reasons, Congress determined that the problems with Section 483 should be corrected, that Section 483 was inadequate, and that its rules needed to be revised. Therefore, Congress broadened the scope of the OID rules and changed the nature of the Section 483 rules.[241] Today, although the Section 483 rules are much narrower in scope than in the past (as a result of the broadening of the OID rules), the IRC Section 483 rules must nevertheless be taken into account.

[2] Application of Section 483

Section 483 applies to payments, if the following conditions are satisfied:

- Payment must be made on account of a sale or exchange of property.
- Payment must purportedly represent part or all of the sales price for the property.
- Payment must be due more than six months after the date of sale or exchange.
- Payment must be made pursuant to a contract under which some or all of the payments are due more than one year after the date of the sale or exchange.
- There must be total unstated interest.

Most of the preceding conditions are easily understood, while others require some explanation.

[a] Due Dates of Payments

Section 483 applies to any payment that satisfies two conditions. First, the payment itself must be due more than six months after the date of the sale or exchange. Second, there must be at least one payment under the

---

[241] The OID rules are discussed supra ¶¶ 11.02, 11.03.

contract that is due more than one year after that date.[242] Thus, a payment due seven months after the date of sale under a contract that provides for all payments to be made prior to one year following the date of sale would not be covered by the section. Similarly, a payment due five months after the date of sale will not be subject to the section even though other payments under the contract may be covered. For example, if a contract calls for payments 4 months, 8 months, and 13 months after the date of sale, both the second and third payments will be covered. If the contract had called for payments 4 months, 8 months, and 12 months after the date of sale, none of the payments would have been covered.

[b] Unstated Interest

[i] General rules. Section 483 is applicable if there is unstated interest. To determine whether there is unstated interest, the sum of all payments to which the section applies is compared to the sum of the present value of these payments plus the present value of any interest payments under the contract. For the purpose of determining this present value, taxpayers must use the applicable federal rate specified by the OID provisions.[243] The excess of the total payments to which the section applies over the present value of the sum of those payments plus interest due under the contract is treated as unstated interest.[244]

> EXAMPLE: Assume that property is sold on January 1 of year 1 under a contract calling for the purchaser to pay $100,000 plus interest at 6 percent compounded annually. The total of $179,084.77 ($100,000 + 6 percent compounded annually) is to be paid January 1 of year 10. Assuming that the imputing rate is 9 percent compounded semiannually, the present value of the total payments due under the contract is $74,273.23 (the present value of a deferred payment of $100,000 plus the present value of the deferred payment of interest of $79,084.77). The contract contains unstated interest of $25,726.77 ($100,000 deferred payment − $74,273.23 present value of all payments due under the contract).[245]

In general, a contract does not have unstated interest if it provides for a stated interest rate at least equal to the applicable federal rate and the interest is paid or compounded at least annually.[246] If unstated interest exists, it is

---

[242] IRC § 483(c)(1).

[243] IRC § 483(b). See discussion supra ¶ 11.02[5][a][i].

[244] Prop. Reg. § 1.483-2(a).

[245] See Prop. Reg. § 1.483-2(c) for additional examples.

[246] Prop. Reg. § 1.483-1(a)(1).

allocated to payments in a manner consistent with the manner of computing and allocating interest under the OID provisions of Section 1272(a).[247] In other words, an economic yield basis is used rather than a straight proration method based on relative principal amounts.

[ii] Special rules on sale of land to related party. Special rules limit the maximum rate at which interest may be imputed in particular cases. For instance, in the case of a sale or exchange of land by an individual to a member of his family, the discount rate used is not to exceed 6 percent, compounded semiannually, to the extent that the sales price does not exceed $500,000.[248]

[c] Periods When Unstated Interest Is Recognized

Section 483 provides that any unstated interest is to be allocated to payments in a manner consistent with Section 1272(a).[249] Thus, interest is to be recognized in the year in which the payment is received or due (depending on the taxpayer's method of accounting), but the amount of interest to be recognized is based on the compounding rules of the OID provisions as opposed to the pro rata rules of the former Section 483 provisions.

[d] Exceptions to Application of Section 483

The Section 483 rules do not apply to the following:[250]

- Any debt instrument for which an issue price is determined under Sections 1273(b) (other than paragraph (4) of that section) and 1274
- Payments on account of sales or exchanges where the sales price cannot exceed $3,000
- Amounts that are deemed to include interest under Section 163(b)
- Transfers described in Section 1235(a), which relates to a sale or exchange of patents

Other exceptions to and limitations on the application of Section 483 apply in the case of transfers incident to divorce, sales of personal use property, certain below-market loans described in Section 7872, annuity contracts, and payments under an option to buy or sell property.[251]

---

[247] IRC § 483(a).

[248] IRC § 483(e). See Prop. Reg. § 1.483-3(b).

[249] IRC § 483(a).

[250] IRC § 483(d).

[251] Prop. Reg. § 1.483-1(c).

¶ 11.05 MARKET DISCOUNT: SECTIONS 1276–1278

After a bond or other evidence of indebtedness is issued, a change in the market rate of interest for obligations of that type will affect the value of the originally issued obligation.

> EXAMPLE: Assume a bond is issued with a face amount of $100. If the bond bore interest at 10 percent per annum and the market rate of interest at that time was also 10 percent, the FMV of the bond would have been $100, the face amount. Thereafter, if the interest rate for bonds of that type fell below 10 percent, holders would only be willing to sell the previously issued bond at an amount in excess of $100. The amount of this excess (or premium) is the amount necessary to ensure that the 10 percent interest rate on the bond (in combination with the payment due at maturity) provides the purchaser with a yield to maturity equal to the then-prevailing market rate.
>
> Correlatively, if interest rates increased, an investor would only be willing to purchase the previously issued bond at some amount below its face amount in order for the investor to get a return on his investment equal to the then-applicable market interest rate.

In the former case, the amount paid in excess of face is known as "bond premium."[252] In the latter case, the difference between the face amount of the bond and the lower amount actually paid is known as market discount. The treatment of market discount is the subject of Sections 1276, 1277, and 1278.

[1] Definitions

For purposes of these market discount provisions, "bond" is defined to mean any bond, debenture, note, certificate, or other evidence of indebtedness.[253] "Market discount" on any such bond is defined to be the excess of the stated redemption price of the bond at maturity over the basis of the bond immediately after its acquisition by a taxpayer.[254] If a bond has OID, the stated redemption price at maturity is the sum of the original issue price of the bond plus all amounts of OID includable in the income of prior holders of the bond for all periods prior to the acquisition of the bond by the taxpayer, i.e., the bond's adjusted issue price at the time of acquisition.[255]

Notwithstanding the foregoing, even if a bond is acquired at a market

---

[252] See discussion supra ¶ 11.02[3][a][iii].

[253] IRC § 1278(a)(3).

[254] IRC § 1278(a)(2)(A).

[255] IRC § 1278(a)(2)(B).

discount, the bond is not treated as a market discount bond if any of the following circumstances apply:[256]

- The bond has a maturity date that does not exceed one year from the date of issue.
- The bond is tax-exempt.
- The bond is a U.S. savings bond.
- The bond is an installment obligation to which Section 453B applies.
- The bond is acquired by the taxpayer at its original issue, unless the taxpayer's basis in the bond is determined under Section 1012 and that basis is less than the issue price, or the bond is issued pursuant to a plan of reorganization in exchange for another bond having market discount. Thus, for example, if a bond is part of a public offering whose issue price is determined under Section 1273(b)(1) and the bond is acquired by the first holder for an amount less than the issue price, this exception is inapplicable and the market discount rules will apply.

Prior to the 1984 Act, market discount on any obligation that was issued by a corporation or governmental unit and held for more than one year was generally treated as capital gain. In addition, it was often possible for taxpayers to borrow funds to acquire market discount bonds and then deduct the interest as an ordinary expense even though the discount itself would be treated as capital gain and, in many cases, would not be recognized until a later year when received.[257]

Congress determined as part of the 1984 Act that market discount should be treated as ordinary income because it played essentially the same role as OID. In addition, Congress did not want to foster continued use of tax shelter transactions predicated on the favorable tax treatment previously afforded market discount bonds. The revised rules are intended to achieve this objective.

These rules are divided into three sections. Section 1276 pertains to the treatment of income arising from market discount. Section 1277 pertains to the treatment of interest expense on debt incurred to acquire market discount bonds. Section 1278 provides various definitions and special rules.

[2] Treatment of Market Discount Income

On a sale or other disposition of a market discount bond, that portion of the gain equal to "accrued market discount" is treated as ordinary income.[258] In

---

[256] IRC §§ 1278(a)(1)(B), 1278(a)(1)(C).

[257] General explanation of the Revenue Provisions of the Deficit Reduction Act of 1984 (Dec. 31, 1984) (hereinafter Blue Book), at 93.

[258] IRC § 1276(a)(1).

the case of a disposition other than a sale, the gain is determined on the basis of the FMV of the bond at the time of the disposition.[259]

Accrued market discount is determined by allocating total market discount from the date of acquisition to the date of maturity and dividing it by the number of days in that period.[260] In other words, accrued market discount is allocated on a straight-line basis.

For example, assume that a taxpayer acquires a bond with no OID and a stated redemption price at maturity of $100 for $80 and that the bond will mature in 200 days. The $20 will be allocated ratably over the 200 days. If the taxpayer then sold the bond for $91 at the end of 100 days, $10 of the gain would be ordinary income and $1 would be capital gain.

The taxpayer may elect to accrue market discount on an economic yield basis as under Section 1272(a) in lieu of using the pro rata approach.[261] It should be noted that these rules do not provide for a recognition of interest in each year the bond is held. Rather, the sole function of the provision is recharacterization.

To the extent the taxpayer wishes to reduce the total amount to be recharacterized as interest, the taxpayer will need to evaluate the two allocation approaches carefully. In general, it would appear that the election of the economic yield basis will reduce the total amount of market discount to accrue as compared with the straight-line basis.

[3] Deferral of Interest Deductions Allocable to Accrued Market Discount

Since market discount, unlike OID, is not accrued over the term of the bond, rules were adopted in Section 1277 to defer a portion of the interest expense on indebtedness used to purchase or carry a market discount bond. In effect, the rules defer the deduction in any year of the taxpayer's net interest expense on the transaction (i.e., interest expense on the indebtedness in excess of interest income on the bond) to the extent of market discount accruing during that year.[262] Any interest expense deferred under this rule will later be taken into account either on a disposition of the market discount bond or, if the holder elects, in a subsequent year to the extent that the interest income on the market discount bond exceeds the interest expense with respect to such bond.[263]

---

[259] IRC § 1276(a)(2).

[260] IRC § 1276(b)(1).

[261] IRC § 1276(b)(2).

[262] IRC §§ 1277(a), 1277(c).

[263] IRC § 1277(b).

¶ 11.06 SHORT-TERM OBLIGATIONS: SECTIONS 1281–1283

Prior to the 1984 Act, it was possible for taxpayers to incur indebtedness to purchase Treasury bills or other obligations with a maturity not exceeding one year. Interest on the debt could be deducted in one year, with a corresponding amount of income reported in the later year. This deferral resulted in a significant tax advantage. In addition, it was possible for some of the gain on disposition of the acquired obligation to be capital gain.

The 1984 Act sought to curtail this practice through a series of sections pertaining to the discount on short-term obligations. These new sections are Section 1281, which pertains to the inclusion in income of the discount on certain short-term obligations; Section 1282, which pertains to the deferral of interest deductions allocable to accrued discount; and IRC Section 1283, which provides special rules and definitions.

[1] Current Inclusion of Acquisition Discount

Under the new rules, certain holders of short-term obligations must accrue within each taxable year a portion of the acquisition discount associated with that obligation.[264] "Acquisition discount" is the excess of the stated redemption price at maturity over the holder's basis in the obligation.[265] The amount to be accrued can be determined either under a pro rata approach or through use of an economic accrual approach based on application of a constant interest rate.[266]

Short-term obligations covered by the new rules include any bond, debenture, note, certificate, or other evidence of indebtedness (other than a tax-exempt obligation) that has a fixed maturity date of one year or less from the date of issue.[267] However, Section 1281 is applicable only if the short-term obligation is held by one of the following:[268]

- An accrual method taxpayer
- A taxpayer holding the obligation primarily for sale to customers in the ordinary course of the taxpayer's trade or business
- A bank
- A regulated investment company or common trust fund
- A taxpayer identifying the obligation as part of a hedging transaction
- A taxpayer who holds a short-term obligation that is a stripped bond or stripped coupon and who stripped the bond or coupon

---

[264] IRC § 1281(a).

[265] IRC § 1283(a)(2).

[266] IRC § 1283(b).

[267] IRC § 1283(a)(1).

[268] IRC § 1281(b)(1).

In addition, certain pass-through entities (e.g., partnerships, S corporations, trusts) in which a taxpayer listed above has an ownership interest may be subject to Section 1281.[269] A special rule applies in the case of short-term nongovernmental obligations. For these obligations, the provisions of the inclusion section and deferral section (Sections 1281 and 1282, respectively) are applied by taking into account OID in lieu of acquisition discount and by making various other adjustments.[270]

[2] Deferral of Interest Deduction

Where Section 1281 does not require a current inclusion of acquisition discount (or, in the case of short-term nongovernmental obligations, of OID), Section 1282 defers the deduction of net direct interest expense except to the extent that the amount of that interest exceeds the daily portions of acquisition discount for the period. This deferral rule thus generally applies to holders other than those enumerated in IRC Section 1281(b). Deferred interest deductions will be taken into account in later years under rules similar to those applicable to market discount bonds.[271]

¶ 11.07 TAX TREATMENT OF STRIPPED BONDS: SECTION 1286

Many debt instruments evidence the obligation to pay interest in coupons that are physically attached to the bond. The holder of the obligation is expected to remove each coupon as it comes due and exchange it for the interest that is due. Where the coupons have been removed from the debt obligation itself, the bond is referred to as a stripped bond. In other words, the interest coupons have been stripped from the bond. Section 1286 covers the tax treatment of stripped bonds.

[1] Treatment of Stripper

If any person strips one or more coupons from the bond and disposes of the bond or any coupon after July 1, 1982, then that person must include in income an amount equal to the interest accrued on the bond during the period the bond was held plus any accrued market discount on the bond

---

[269] IRC § 1281(b)(2).

[270] IRC § 1283(c).

[271] IRC § 1282(c). See discussion supra ¶ 11.06[3].

determined as of the time of the disposition of the bond or coupon.[272] The amount of income so reported will increase the basis of the bond and coupons.[273]

Once the stripping has occurred, the obligation representing the principal and the obligations representing the interest are treated as separate debt obligations. Basis is allocated between the principal and interest obligations on the basis of their relative FMV at the time of the strip. OID is then reported on the items in accordance with the normal rules.

[2] Treatment of Purchaser

Any person who purchases a stripped bond or stripped coupon must treat such bond or coupon as a bond originally issued on the purchase date. This debt instrument will have OID equal to any excess of the bond's stated redemption price at maturity (or, in the case of a coupon, the amount payable on the due date of the coupon) over the bond's or coupon's ratable share of the purchase price. The ratable shares of the purchase price are determined according to the relative FMVs of the bond and coupon on the date of purchase.[274] OID on the stripped bond or stripped coupon is allocated over the period from the purchase date to the relevant due date using a constant interest method in accordance with Section 1272.

¶ 11.08 GAINS ON CERTAIN OBLIGATIONS: SECTION 1287

Section 1287 provides a special rule denying capital gain treatment to gain on the disposition of certain obligations. The obligations to which the section applies are so-called registration-required obligations. Registration-required obligations include all obligations (including those issued by a governmental entity) other than an obligation that (1) is issued by a natural person; (2) is not of the type offered to the public; or (3) has a maturity date at issuance of not more than one year.[275]

Section 1287 does not apply if the obligation was subject to the excise tax provided by Section 4701, which imposes a tax on the issuer of a registration-required obligation, which is not in registered form, equal to one percent of the principal amount of the obligation multiplied by the number of calendar years (or portions thereof) from date of original issue to maturity.

---

[272] IRC § 1286(b)(1). The inclusion of accrued market discount applies only to obligations acquired after October 22, 1986.

[273] IRC § 1286(b).

[274] IRC § 1286(a).

[275] IRC §§ 1287(b)(1), 163(f)(2).

¶ 11.09 OID ON TAX-EXEMPT OBLIGATIONS: SECTION 1288

Although interest earned on tax-exempt obligations is not subject to tax, gain or loss on a sale, retirement, or other disposition of a tax-exempt obligation is subject to tax under the normal rules. As a consequence, it remains necessary to determine the amount of OID on a tax-exempt obligation in order to determine the appropriate basis of that obligation when it is disposed.

Section 1288 makes it clear that OID on tax-exempt obligations is determined in the manner provided by Section 1272(a) (without regard to paragraph 6 of that subsection). For purposes of determining the adjusted basis of the instrument to the holder, OID is calculated in the manner provided by Section 1272(a) determined with regard to paragraph 6. The exception in the general rules for de minimis OID is ignored, so that the holder's basis is properly adjusted regardless of the amount of discount.

¶ 11.10 USE OF PROPERTY OR SERVICES: SECTION 467

Prior to the 1984 Act, lessors and lessees of property could arrange their lease transactions to generate significant tax benefits. For example, an accrual method lessee could agree to pay rent to a cash method lessor only at the end of the lease term. The lessee would benefit by deducting its rent obligations annually. The lessor would benefit by deferring the recognition of income until the year in which the lease terminated and payment was received.

In some cases, similar benefits were achieved by leasing property from tax-exempt entities. Lessees could accrue deductions for rent without causing any adverse tax consequences to the tax-exempt lessor. Similarly, terms for leases extending over a period of years could be arranged so that lower rates were paid in the earlier years with higher rates paid in later years.

In response to the perceived abuses caused by these agreements, Congress ultimately enacted Section 467.[276] This section is designed to require lessors and lessees to report rental income on an accrual basis, regardless of their overall methods of accounting, and to take the time value of money into account by recharacterizing applicable portions of the agreements as interest in appropriate cases.

[1] Section 467 Rental Agreement

Section 467 applies to any so-called Section 467 rental agreement.[277] A Section 467 rental agreement means any rental agreement for the use of

---

[276] See Blue book, supra note 257, at 284–286.
[277] IRC § 467(a).

tangible property calling for aggregate payments in excess of $250,000 and under which (1) there is at least one amount that will be paid more than one year after the year in which the rent accrues or (2) there are increases in the amounts to be paid as rent under the agreement. In other words, payments of at least some rent must be deferred for more than one year following the close of the year in which the rent accrues, or there must be stepped rents.[278] In determining whether the payments for the use of property exceed $250,000, all payments received as consideration for the use of property and the aggregate value of any other consideration received for the use of property must be taken into account.[279]

[a] Deferred Payments of Rent

If there is at least one payment of rent allocable to the use of property during a given calendar year that is to be paid after the close of the following year, then the arrangement is a Section 467 rental agreement.[280] In effect, this means that rent may be paid in the year following the year of use without causing the agreement to be a Section 467 rental agreement.

EXAMPLE: Assume that property is leased for three years at a rate of $300,000 per year, with rent to be paid six months after the end of the year of lease. In other words, the lease provides for $300,000 per year rent for years 1, 2, and 3, with the rent for year 1 to be paid June 30 of year 2, the rent for year 2 to be paid June 30 of year 3, and the rent for year 3 to be paid June 30 of year 4. The agreement is not a Section 467 rental agreement. However, if the agreement provided for all the rent to be paid on June 30 of year 4, the agreement would be a Section 467 rental agreement because the rent due for years 1 and 2 will be paid in year 4, which is more than one year after the year of use.

[b] Stepped Rents

Even if an agreement does not provide for deferred payments that satisfy the requirements for a Section 467 rental agreement, the agreement may be so classified if it provides for increases in the amount to be paid as rent.[281]

This provision leaves open numerous questions. First, should there be a de minimis rule? In other words, will any increase in rent from period to period trigger application of the Section 467 rules? Arguably, the answer should be no. However, this is an open question.

---

[278] IRC § 467(d).

[279] IRC § 467(d)(2).

[280] IRC § 467(d)(1)(A).

[281] IRC § 467(d)(1)(B).

Similarly, should the rule apply only to increases in the aggregate rents for a particular period, such as a year, or to any increases in rent, such as an increase from month to month. To illustrate, assume that $50,000 is paid at the end of six months, with $100,000 paid at the end of the next six months. If each succeeding year calls for $50,000 on June 30 and $100,000 at the end of the year, technically there are increases in rent. However, there are no increases in rent from year to year.

Under Section 467(f), the Treasury has the authority to promulgate regulations that would treat agreements that provide for decreasing rental payments as Section 467 rental agreements. No such regulations have yet been prescribed.

[2] Treatment of Section 467 Rental Agreements

The lessor and the lessee under a Section 467 rental agreement are required to take into account for any taxable year both the rentals accruing during such taxable year and interest for the year on the rentals accrued in prior taxable years that remain unpaid.[282] The amount of the rent accruing during a taxable year depends upon whether the Section 467 rental agreement involves either a leaseback or a lease of property for a term in excess of 75 percent of the property's statutory recovery period used for depreciation purposes. If the agreement does not fall into either of these categories, then the determination of the amount of rent that accrues during any taxable year is made by allocating rents in accordance with the Section 467 rental agreement, appropriately discounting payments to be made in the future that are allocable to that year.[283] In other words, both the lessor and the lessee are placed on an accrual method with respect to the lease agreement, and the amounts accrued are the present value of the rentals that the agreement allocates to that year plus interest for that year on prior years' accrued but unpaid amounts.

A slightly different rule applies to determine the amount of rent accrued during any taxable year if the Section 467 rental agreement either (1) is silent as to the allocation of rents over the lease period or (2) is part of a leaseback transaction or is for a term in excess of 75 percent of the property's statutory recovery period, provides for increasing rents, and has a tax-avoidance principal purpose. In either of those cases, the amount of rent accruing during any taxable year is the "constant rental amount" for that year.[284] The constant rental amount is the amount that if paid as of the close of each lease period under the agreement, would result in an aggregate present value equal

---

[282] IRC § 467(a).

[283] IRC § 467(b)(1).

[284] IRC §§ 467(b)(2)–467(b)(4). The statute provides some guidance on application of the tax-avoidance-purpose test in Section 467(b)(5).

to the present value of the aggregate payments required under the agreement.[285] If a Section 467 rental agreement is subject to this rule, therefore, not only are the lessor and lessee both put on an accrual method, but the allocation of rental payments is leveled on a present value basis.

If a Section 467 rental agreement that involves a leaseback or a long-term lease passes the tax-avoidance test and thus avoids this rent-leveling rule, any gain realized by the lessor on a disposition of the property during the term of the rental agreement is subject to a recapture provision. Such gain is treated as ordinary income to the extent of the excess of the amount that would have been taken into account by the lessor if the rents had been reported under the leveling rule over the amount actually taken into income by the lessor under the general matching provision.[286]

All present value and interest computations under these rules use a rate equal to 110 percent of the applicable federal rate in effect at the time the Section 467 rental agreement is entered into for debt instruments having a maturity equal to the term of the agreement.[287]

[3] Agreements Pertaining to Deferred Payments for Services

Under Section 467(g), the Treasury is authorized to prescribe similar rules governing the case of deferred payments for services. However, this rule will not apply to amounts covered by Section 404 or Section 404A. No regulations have yet been promulgated.

¶ 11.11 BELOW-MARKET LOANS: SECTION 7872

A debt instrument issued in a private, cash lending transaction frequently will not contain any OID under Section 1273. The issue price generally will be the amount loaned.[288] If all the interest under the debt instrument is qualified stated interest, the stated redemption price at maturity generally will equal the issue price, and there will be no OID.[289] This is true regardless of the interest rate specified by the parties.

Unrelated parties dealing at arm's length generally will not enter into zero-interest- or below-market-rate cash loans. Rather, these transactions typically arise between parties that have some relationship with each other besides that of debtor and creditor. Section 7872 deals with these situations

---

[285] IRC § 467(e)(1).

[286] IRC § 467(c).

[287] IRC § 467(e)(4).

[288] IRC § 1273(b)(2).

[289] See discussion supra ¶ 11.02[4].

and in general recharacterizes the time value of money that the parties omit from, but that is inherent in, their arrangement in accordance with the substance of the parties' relationship. It applies to term loans made after, and demand loans outstanding after, June 6, 1984. Notwithstanding this effective date, the principles underlying Section 7872 may well be applicable to older term loans as well.[290]

[1] Definition of "Below-Market Loan"

A loan is potentially subject to Section 7872 if it is a below-market loan. A below-market loan may be either a "demand loan" or a "term loan." "Demand loan" is any loan that is payable in full at any time on the demand of the lender. Further, if the benefits of the interest arrangements of a loan are not transferable and are conditioned on the future performance of substantial services by an individual, the loan generally will be considered a demand loan.[291] If a loan is not a demand loan, it is by definition a "term loan."[292]

A demand loan is a below-market loan if interest is payable on the loan at a rate less than the applicable federal rate.[293] A term loan will be a below-market loan if the amount loaned exceeds the present value of all payments due under the loan discounted at a rate equal to the applicable federal rate.[294] The applicable federal rate used for term loans (and for loans conditioned on future services that otherwise are treated as demand loans) is determined under Section 1274(d) as of the day on which the loan is made.[295] In the case of demand loans, the applicable federal rate used is the short-term rate in effect for the period for which the "forgone interest" is being determined, compounded semiannually.[296]

[2] Below-Market Loans Subject to Section 7872

As discussed previously, the below-market loan rules are designed to impute interest in certain cash-lending transactions between parties where a link

---

[290] See Dickman v. Comm'r, 465 US 330 (1984) (time value of money inherent in interest-free demand loans from parents to child subject to gift tax under Sections 2501 and 2511).

[291] IRC § 7872(e)(5); Prop. Reg. §§ 1.7872-10(a)(1), 1.7872-10(a)(5).

[292] IRC § 7872(e)(6). See Prop. Reg. § 1.7872-10(a)(2).

[293] IRC § 7872(e)(1)(A).

[294] IRC §§ 7872(e)(1)(B), 7872(f)(1).

[295] IRC § 7872(f)(2)(A). See discussion infra ¶ 11.02[5][a][i].

[296] IRC § 7872(f)(2)(B). See infra ¶ 11.11[3] for definition and discussion of "forgone interest."

might be found that suggests that the economic arrangement embodies something other than arm's-length bargaining over the cost of the use of funds. The three most likely scenarios identified by the statute are situations involving a gift element, loans between an employer and an employee (or independent contractor), and loans between a corporation and one of its shareholders. These circumstances are referred to as gift loans, compensation-related loans, and corporation-shareholder loans.[297]

De minimis exceptions are applicable to these types of loans. A gift loan between individuals is not subject to Section 7872 for any day on which the aggregate amount of loans outstanding between such individuals does not exceed $10,000, but this exception does not apply if the loan is directly attributable to the purchase or carrying of income-producing assets.[298] Similarly, compensation-related loans and corporation-shareholder loans are not subject to Section 7872 on any day on which the aggregate outstanding amount of loans between the borrower and the lender does not exceed $10,000, unless tax avoidance was a principal purpose for the below-market interest terms.[299]

[3] Treatment of Below-Market Loans

[a] Demand Loans

The tax treatment of a below-market demand loan generally must take into account the fact that there is a transfer of value in the form of forgone interest for every time period the loan remains outstanding. The forgone interest for each such period is treated as transferred from the lender to the borrower, and retransferred from the borrower to the lender, on each December 31.[300] For the year the loan is repaid, the transfers are deemed to take place on the date of repayment.[301]

"Forgone interest" for any period is the excess of the amount of interest

---

[297] IRC §§ 7872(c)(1), 7872(f)(3); Prop. Reg. §§ 1.7872-4(b)–1.7872-4(d). The statute also covers below-market loans, one of the principal purposes of which is tax avoidance, and loans the interest arrangements of which have a significant effect on either the borrower's or the lender's tax liability, but the scope of the rules on "significant-effect" loans is unclear. IRC §§ 7872(c)(1)(D), 7872(c)(1)(E); Temp. Reg. § 1.7872-5T(c)(3) (listing some factors to consider in determining whether loan is significant-effect loan); Prop. Reg. §§ 1.7872-4(e), 1.7872-4(f) (reserving guidance on significant-effect loans). Special rules also are provided for loans to qualified continuing care facilities pursuant to continuing care contracts. IRC §§ 7872(c)(1)(F), 7872(c)(g).

[298] IRC § 7872(c)(2).

[299] IRC § 7872(c)(3).

[300] IRC § 7872(a); Prop. Reg. § 1.7872-6.

[301] Prop. Reg. § 1.7872-6(b)(5). An analogous rule applies to the death, termination, or liquidation of the borrower. Prop. Reg. § 1.7872-6(b)(4).

that would have been payable on the loan for the period if interest had accrued on the loan at the applicable federal rate and were payable annually on the day of the deemed transfers, over any interest payable on the loan properly allocable to such period.[302] In other words, it is the amount by which the interest the parties actually charged on the loan falls short of the minimum amount of interest the statute considers to represent what parties dealing at arm's length would have charged.

Whereas the statute states that the deemed transfer from the borrower to the lender is a payment of interest, the deemed transfer from the lender to the borrower is characterized in accordance with the relationship between the parties.[303]

> **EXAMPLE:** On January 1, Corporation X loans A, an employee, $25,000 at 3 percent interest, payable each December 31, with the principal repayable on demand. Assume that the amount of forgone interest for the first year is $1,750; i.e., the amount of interest that would have accrued at the applicable federal rate ($2,500 assuming an applicable federal rate of 10 percent) over the interest actually allocable to the first year ($750). Since this is a loan from an employer to an employee, the $1,750 is treated as additional compensation paid by the employer to the employee and as interest paid by the employee to the employer. A similar computation would be made for each year the loan remains outstanding.

Note that the below-market loan in this example should be a wash to the employer. It has a compensation deduction offset by interest income. The employee, on the other hand, has compensation income and interest expense, but the interest expense appears to be nondeductible personal interest.[304] Similar characterization problems confront taxpayers in nearly every below-market loan. For example, a below-market demand loan from a corporation to one of its shareholders will result in imputed interest income to the corporation and nondeductible deemed dividends to the shareholder.

The amount of forgone interest on a demand loan can be computed every month, since the applicable federal rates are determined monthly. For convenience, taxpayers are permitted to compute the applicable federal rate for semiannual periods beginning each January 1 and July 1.[305] Thus, if a demand loan provides for a variable rate of interest that adjusts either monthly or every January and July to a rate at least equal to the applicable

---

[302] IRC § 7872(e)(2).

[303] Prop. Reg. § 1.7872-4.

[304] IRC § 163(h).

[305] Prop. Reg. § 1.7872-3(b).

federal rate, there will be no forgone interest, and Section 7872 will not apply.[306]

For loans that are treated as demand loans because the interest terms are conditioned on the future performance of services, the applicable federal rate used is the rate in effect on the day of the loan.[307]

[b] Term Loans

In the case of a below-market term loan, there is no need to redetermine periodically the amount of forgone interest, as in the demand loan situation. The parties to a term loan have defined their economic relationship for the time period the loan is to remain outstanding, and the value of the interest arrangement for the entire term of the loan can be determined at inception using present-value concepts.

Thus, the lender in a below-market term loan is treated as having made a transfer to the borrower on the date the loan is made in an amount equal to the excess of the amount loaned over the present value of all payments due under the loan.[308] The amount of such excess is then treated as OID on the loan.[309]

> EXAMPLE: On January 1, Corporation X loans A, its employee, $25,000 at 3 percent interest. The interest is payable each December 31, and the full amount of the loan is due in five years. Assume that the midterm applicable federal rate is 10 percent, compounded annually. The present value of all payments due under the loan, discounted at 10 percent compounded annually, is $18,366. Therefore, X is treated as having paid, and A is treated as having received, compensation in the amount of $6,634 (i.e., $25,000 − $18,366) on the date the loan is made. The $6,634 is then treated as OID on the loan and is includable by X and should be deductible by A over the term of the loan.[310]

It appears that the same character issues that arise in demand loans cannot be avoided by the parties instead using a term loan. For example, in the analogous example above of the employee who received a below-market demand loan, the employee each year had compensation income and a corresponding interest expense, but the interest was nondeductible personal

---

[306] See Prop. Reg. § 1.7872-3(e)(2)(i).

[307] IRC § 7872(f)(5); Prop. Reg. § 1.7872-3(b)(4).

[308] IRC § 7872(b)(1).

[309] IRC § 7872(b)(2).

[310] IRC §§ 1272, 163(e). The loan can be thought of as having an issue price of $18,366 and a stated redemption price at maturity of $25,000. The actual annual interest payments would be qualified stated interest. See discussion supra ¶¶ 11.02[3], 11.02[4].

interest. If a term loan is used, the employee has compensation income in the first year and OID expense over the term of the loan. The OID expense under Section 163(e) on the term loan, like the forgone interest expense under Section 163(a) on the demand loan, should still be subject to the personal interest limitations in Section 163(h).

A variable rate term loan generally will have sufficient interest and escape application of Section 7872 if the initial value of the variable rate is at least equal to the applicable federal rate.[311]

[c] Special Rules for Gift Loans

A below-market gift loan (e.g., a zero-interest loan from a father to his daughter) that is a demand loan is generally treated in the same manner described above for other demand loans. However, gift loans that are term loans are subjected to a hybrid treatment. For gift tax purposes, the amount of the gift from the lender to the borrower at the time of the loan is determined under the rules generally applicable to term loans, but the income tax treatment of the arrangement is determined under the demand loan rules.[312]

> EXAMPLE:　A father loans his daughter $200,000 in exchange for the daughter's note agreeing to repay the $200,000 in 10 years. No interest is to be paid. The long-term applicable federal rate is 8 percent, compounded semiannually. For gift tax purposes, the father has made a gift to the daughter of $108,723, the excess of the amount loaned over the present value of the payment due under the note. For income tax purposes, however, the loan is treated as a demand loan. The amount of the daughter's annual deemed interest payments to her father is that year's forgone interest.

Congress provided some relief for the lender in a gift loan directly between individuals for any day on which the aggregate amount of loans outstanding between such persons does not exceed $100,000. The amount of forgone interest treated as transferred by the borrower to the lender at the close of any year will not exceed the borrower's net investment income for such year.[313] "Net investment income" is defined in Section 163(d)(4), except that it includes all amounts that would accrue on any deferred payment

---

[311] Prop. Reg. § 1.7872-3(e)(1).

[312] IRC §§ 7872(a), 7872(d)(2).

[313] IRC § 7872(c)(1).

obligation if Section 1272 were applicable to such obligation.[314] If the borrower's net investment income is $1,000 or less, it is treated as zero.[315]

Thus, in the preceding example, if the father had loaned only $100,000 to his daughter (and there were no other loans outstanding between them), the father's annual interest accruals would be limited to no more than the daughter's net investment income for that year. The amount of the gift at the loan's inception, however, would still be determined under the general rules and could give rise to a gift tax liability.

---

[314] IRC § 7872(c)(1)(E).
[315] IRC § 7872(c)(1)(E)(ii).

Annual Accounting and Transactional Concepts

¶ 12.01   Goal of Tax Accounting   12-2

¶ 12.02   Annual Accounting Concept   12-3
     [1]   Codification of Concept   12-5
     [2]   Application of Concept   12-5
         [a]   Deduction Proper in Year Claimed   12-5
         [b]   Deduction Improper in Year Claimed   12-6
         [c]   Deduction Not Taken in Year Originally Available   12-6
         [d]   Income Erroneously Reported Before Proper Year   12-8
         [e]   Income Not Reported in Proper Year   12-9
         [f]   Influential Events After Year of Reporting   12-9
             [i]   Change in law   12-10
             [ii]   Additional income   12-11
             [iii]   Tax retroactively imposed   12-11
             [iv]   Taxpayer attempts to change facts retroactively   12-12
             [v]   State court attempts to alter nature of earlier
                payments   12-12
     [3]   Legislative and Judicial Ameliorations of Annual Accounting
         Concept   12-13

¶ 12.03   Claim-of-Right doctrine   12-14
     [1]   Origin   12-14
     [2]   Requirements for Application   12-16
         [a]   Receipt of Income   12-16
         [b]   Unlimited Control   12-17
         [c]   Asserted Claim of Right   12-19
     [3]   Prevailing Issues Under Claim-Of-Right Doctrine   12-19
         [a]   Characterization of Receipts as Income   12-19
             [i]   Prepaid income   12-20
             [ii]   Illegal income   12-21
             [iii]   Amounts received under mistaken claim   12-22
             [iv]   Agreements to refund   12-22
             [v]   Conduits and trustees   12-23
             [vi]   Deposits   12-24

              [b]   Availability of Deduction for Repaid Amounts 12-26
      [4]   Statutory Relief: Section 1341 12-26
              [a]   General Requirements 12-26
              [b]   Unrestricted Right vs. Claim of Right 12-27
              [c]   Connection Between Receipt and Repayment 12-27

¶ 12.04   *Arrowsmith* Doctrine 12-28
      [1]   Scope 12-29
      [2]   Applications 12-31
              [a]   Initial Gain—Later Loss 12-32
              [b]   Initial Loss—Later Gain 12-33
              [c]   Initial Gain—Later Gain 12-33
              [d]   Initial Loss—Later Loss 12-34
      [3]   Inapplicability of Doctrine 12-35
      [4]   Statutory Relief: Section 1341 12-35

¶ 12.05   Tax Benefit Rule 12-36
      [1]   History and Rationale 12-36
      [2]   Definition of "Recovery" 12-38
      [3]   Amount of Recovery 12-39
      [4]   Established Applications of Rule 12-40
              [a]   Judicial Applications 12-40
                  [i]   Previously expensed items 12-40
                  [ii]   Charitable contributions returned 12-41
                  [iii]   Casualty losses 12-42
                  [iv]   Reimbursed losses 12-42
                  [v]   Unpaid accrued expenses 12-43
                  [vi]   Accrued liabilities abandoned by creditor 12-43
                  [vii]   Bad debt reserves 12-43
                  [viii]   Transfer of accounts receivable or other assets to
                        controlled corporation 12-44
                  [ix]   Corporate liquidations 12-45
                  [x]   Contributions to capital 12-47
                  [xi]   Cancellation of indebtedness 12-48
               [b]   Legislative Applications 12-48
                  [i]   Section 111 12-48
                  [ii]   Depreciation recapture including ACRS 12-49
                  [iii]   Damage recoveries 12-49
                  [iv]   Foreign expropriation losses 12-50
                  [v]   LIFO recapture provisions 12-51
              [c]   Exceptions to Tax Benefit Rule 12-52
                  [i]   Erroneous deductions 12-52
                  [ii]   Absence of "deduction" 12-54

¶ 12.01   GOAL OF TAX ACCOUNTING

The primary goal of tax accounting is to determine when items of income and expense should be recognized. The answer depends on the interplay between a taxpayer's method or methods of accounting and its particular taxable year. This interplay produces an allocation of income and expense to specific periods, which is necessary for practical reasons. The primary reason is the government's need for a regular flow of revenue.

As a consequence, taxable income is determined on the basis of periodic intervals, taking into account all of the events occurring within each taxable period. This focus of attention on the events and circumstances of each particular period is generally referred to as the annual accounting concept, which is the most fundamental concept of tax accounting.

However, application of the annual accounting concept does not mean that the events and circumstances of earlier or later periods are to be ignored. Congress and the courts have developed various principles and doctrines to ameliorate the inequities that otherwise would result from a strict application of the annual accounting concept. As a result, the events of an earlier year may be considered in determining how the events of a particular later year are to be taken into account for tax purposes (e.g., whether income or loss should be characterized as capital or ordinary), but not in determining when such later events are to be taken into account. In effect, items of income or expense properly reported in one year remain properly reported, notwithstanding the related later events. Later events are to be taken into account in the year in which they occur, not in an earlier year by filing an amended return for that year.

This chapter focuses on the annual accounting concept and the principal ameliorating concepts, doctrines, and principles that have evolved in response to it. Such concepts, doctrines, and principles must be taken into account by taxpayers and their advisors in considering the ultimate tax consequences of any particular transaction or series of related transactions.

¶ 12.02 ANNUAL ACCOUNTING CONCEPT

The definition and purpose of the annual accounting concept was provided by the U.S. Supreme Court in its landmark decision in *Burnet v. Sanford & Brooks Co.*[1] In this case, the taxpayer incurred $176,271.88 of aggregate net losses from 1913 through 1916 while performing dredging work for the United States. The dredging project was finally abandoned, and in 1916, the taxpayer initiated litigation against the government. The taxpayer was ultimately awarded $176,271.88 in expenses plus $16,305.71 in interest, and this total judgment was paid in 1920. In 1920, the taxpayer reported as taxable income only the $16,305.71 of interest, treating the remaining $176,271.88 as a nontaxable recovery of its prior losses, i.e., a return of capital.

The Commissioner of Internal Revenue asserted that the full payment should have been included in income in 1920. The taxpayer responded that except for the interest, it obviously had realized no income from the dredging project.

---

[1] Burnet v. Sanford & Brooks Co., 282 US 359 (1931).

The Supreme Court acknowledged that the overall transaction did not result in a profit. Nevertheless, the Court held for the government, explaining that the tax system was predicated on the basis of annual tax periods, not on the basis of transactions. The Court stated that tax had to be imposed on the net result of all events occurring within each particular taxable period, even though related events producing a different aggregate result might occur in a later year.[2] The Court explained that the essence of any tax system is to produce revenue at regular intervals on a practicable, easily administrable basis and that while a different system based on the results of particular transactions might have been devised, there is still the practical need to compute tax on the basis of regularly recurring taxable periods.[3]

The problem experienced by the taxpayer in *Burnet v. Sanford & Brooks Co.* was due to the lack of a congressional safeguard to ameliorate the inequity arising from application of the annual accounting requirement. Congress thereafter enacted provisions for net operating loss carry-forwards and carry-backs to mitigate these problems.[4]

The annual accounting concept has not remained unchanged, either in definition or application. Its entire history and evolution present a study in the emergence of similar inequities or problems and the corresponding legislative, regulatory, or judicial solutions. Although the concept has existed from the beginning of our income tax system, this evolutionary process may be expected to continue as long as taxpayers are subject in different years to

---

[2] The Court stated the following:

All of the revenue acts which have been enacted since the adoption of the 16th Amendment have uniformly assessed the tax on the basis of annual returns showing the net result of all the taxpayer's transactions during a fixed accounting period, either the calendar year, or, at the option of the taxpayer, the particular fiscal year which he may adopt.

A taxpayer may be in receipt of net income in one year and not in another. The net result of the two years, if combined in a single taxable period, might still be a loss; but it has never been supposed that that fact would relieve him from a tax on the first, or that it affords any reason for postponing the assessment of the tax until the end of a lifetime, or for some other indefinite period, to ascertain more precisely whether the final outcome of the period, or of a given transaction, will be a gain or a loss.

Id. at 363, 364–365.

[3] Id. at 365–366. See also Security Flour Mills Co., 321 US 281 (1944), where the Court stated:

This legal principle [of annual accounting] has often been stated and applied. The uniform result has been denial both to Government and to taxpayer of the privilege of allocating income or outgo to a year other than the year of actual receipt of payment, or, applying the accrual basis, the year in which the right to receive, or the obligation to pay, has become final and definite in amount.

Id. at 286.

[4] See present Section 172 and its predecessors.

different (1) levels of income; (2) tax rates; and (3) tax laws. Accordingly, taxpayers and their tax advisors must remain alert to the consequences of reporting in different tax years separate parts of the same overall transaction.

[1] Codification of Concept

The annual accounting concept has been incorporated in several provisions of the Internal Revenue Code (the Code).[5] For example, Section 441(a) provides that taxable income "shall be computed on the basis of the taxpayer's taxable year." (See Chapter 10 for a discussion of taxable years.) Similarly, Section 451(a) provides that all items of income received in a taxable year are to be included in the income of that year unless the method of accounting used to compute taxable income requires the item to be accounted for in a different period, and Section 461(a) provides that all deductions or credits are to be taken in the particular taxable year that is the proper taxable year under the method of accounting used in computing income.[6]

[2] Application of Concept

The annual accounting concept has numerous applications. In each case (and absent specific statutory or regulatory authorization to the contrary), the objective is to preserve the integrity of the annual accounting system.

[a] Deduction Proper in Year Claimed

A deduction that is proper in the year claimed is not to be reduced by reason of later events. If the later events are of tax significance, they are to be taken into account only in the later year in which they occur. For example, in *Grace M. Barnett*,[7] the issue was the validity of certain regulations that allowed a specified deduction for mineral depletion. The regulations also provided that if the mining operation were abandoned before removal of the amount of mineral corresponding to the earlier deduction for depletion, the deduction would not be changed, but the excess of the deduction over the actual depletion would be treated as income in the year of abandonment. The

---

[5] Unless otherwise indicated, all references to IRC or the Code are to the Internal Revenue Code of 1986, as amended.

[6] On the other hand, see ¶ 4.04[3][f] for a discussion of the recurring item exception to the economic performance requirement for accrual method taxpayers. Under the rules governing the application of this exception, taxpayers are given an option to retroactively determine in certain circumstances the year in which to claim a deduction.

[7] Grace M. Barnett, 39 BTA 864 (1939).

Board of Tax Appeals (the Board) held that the regulation was valid on the basis of the annual accounting concept.[8]

The Supreme Court later affirmed the validity of this regulation in *Douglas v. Commissioner*,[9] recognizing that the annual accounting concept prevented adjustment of the deduction in the year claimed. With respect to the regulatory provision that required the excess of the initial deduction over actual depletion to be included in income, the Court concluded that the power delegated to the Commissioner to make regulations for depletion necessarily included the power to provide for situations where the anticipated depletion did not occur.[10]

[b] Deduction Improper in Year Claimed

Where the initial deduction is erroneous in the year claimed, the taxpayer may not rely on the annual accounting concept to prevent correction in that year. For example, in *Hart Furniture Co.*,[11] the taxpayer inadvertently overpaid a federal employment tax in 1945 and obtained a refund in the next year. The taxpayer maintained that deduction of the larger amount in 1945 could not be reduced, and that the 1946 refund would be income in 1946. The court disagreed, holding that the initial deduction was erroneous and, hence, could be corrected. The annual accounting concept did not require a contrary result because the initial deduction was not proper.[12]

[c] Deduction Not Taken in Year Originally Available

The annual accounting concept serves as an independent basis for denying deductions in a year other than the year in which the deduction should be taken under the taxpayer's method of accounting.[13] In other words, a taxpayer may indisputably be entitled to a deduction under Section 162 for

---

[8] In discussing the specified deduction for mineral depletion, the Board said: "Income tax liability must be determined for annual periods on the basis of facts as they existed in each period. *Burnet v. Sanford & Brooks Co.* [citation omitted]. When some event occurs which is inconsistent with a deduction taken in a prior year, adjustment may have to be made by reporting a balancing item in income for the year in which the change occurs." Id. at 867.

[9] Douglas v. Comm'r, 322 US 275 (1944).

[10] Id. at 285.

[11] Hart Furniture Co., 12 TC 1103 (1949), rev'd on other grounds, 188 F2d 968 (5th Cir. 1950).

[12] If the initial deduction had been proper or based upon administrative interpretation later held to be in error, the taxpayer's position might have been correct. See Baltimore Transfer Co., 8 TC 1 (1947), acq. 1947-2 CB 1, discussed infra ¶ 12.02[3][f][i].

[13] See IRC §§ 451 and 461, which specify the year in which items of income and expense are to be recognized.

an ordinary and necessary business expense. However, unless the deduction is taken in the proper year, it may be disallowed because it violates the annual accounting concept.

The hardships imposed on accrual method taxpayers by the application of the annual accounting concept is illustrated by several cases involving deductions for state taxes and similar assessments. For example, in *H.E. Harman Coal Co.*,[14] an accrual method taxpayer was notified in 1941 that state tax deficiencies were owed for the years 1938 and 1939. The tax deficiencies were then paid without protest, but the corresponding deductions were claimed on the taxpayer's return for 1941. Consistent with the annual accounting concept, the Tax Court held that deductions were not available in 1941 but, under the accrual method, only in the earlier years to which the tax deficiencies related. The taxpayer failed to file an amended return for such year and, as a consequence, lost the deductions.[15]

Similarly, in *Keller-Dorian Corp. v. Commissioner*,[16] an importer tried to deduct in the year of payment additional custom duties attributable to an uncontested reappraisal of items imported in earlier years. The deduction was rejected by the court. Thus, the taxpayer could properly have claimed the additional deductions only by filing amended returns for the applicable open earlier years.

As these cases indicate, under applicable rules of accrual tax accounting, if a later asserted state tax deficiency is not contested,[17] deduction of the additional amount is permitted for federal tax purposes only in the year to which it relates, not in the year in which the deficiency is asserted or agreed to. Consequently, in order to obtain the deduction, an amended return must be filed. If the statutory period for filing that amended return or claim for refund has expired or if the taxpayer is unable or unwilling to obtain an

---

[14] H.E. Harman Coal Co., 16 TC 787 (1951), aff'd in part, rev'd in part, 200 F2d 415 (4th Cir. 1952).

[15] The court stated:

The rule is well established that for deduction purposes taxes accrue when all events have transpired which determine the amount of the tax and the taxpayer's liability therefor. E.g., *United States v. Anderson*, 269 U.S. 422; *Standard Paving Co.*, 13 T.C. 425, 447; *Oregon Pulp and Paper Co.*, 47 B.T.A. 772, 780; *Haverty Furniture Co.*, 20 B.T.A. 644. Here all of the events had occurred prior to 1941 which fixed the amount and the liability to pay. Petitioner's erroneous report of its proper tax would not alter the correct amount of that tax nor petitioner's liability for it. The subsequent discovery and correction of the error related back to the taxable year in which the mistake occurred.

H.E. Harman Coal Co., 16 TC at 803–804. See ¶ 4.04[1][c][ii] for the time when an asserted but contested liability becomes fixed.

[16] Keller-Dorian Corp. v. Comm'r, 153 F2d 1006 (2d Cir. 1946).

[17] See ¶ 4.04[1][c] for rules governing contested liabilities.

extension of the applicable statutory period prior to its expiration, the deduction for the additional amount may be lost.[18]

[d] Income Erroneously Reported Before Proper Year

The annual accounting concept requires items of income and expense to be reported in the proper year, even if those same items had been reported incorrectly in an earlier year. If the statute of limitations has not run, the erroneous prior inclusion may be corrected by an amended return or by adjustment on audit. However, if the statute of limitations has run, the rule requires that the item of income or expense be reported in the correct year, even though such reporting results in a double inclusion of income or a double deduction of expense.[19]

An example of such a double inclusion is illustrated by *Chatham & Phenix National Bank*,[20] where, in 1917, a bank reported as income discounts on loans made in that year. For example, if a customer borrowed $900 and signed a two-year note for $1,100, the bank would include the $200 difference in income in the year of the closing of the loan. In 1918, the bank switched to a proper accrual method of reporting interest (based on interest earned) and reported all interest earned during 1918 except for the amounts attributable to discounts on 1917 loans, all of which had been reported in 1917. The Commissioner asserted a deficiency for 1918, and his position was upheld by the Board, despite the fact that these same amounts had erroneously been reported in 1917.[21]

A somewhat similar circumstance occurred in *Paul Irvin Redcay*,[22] except the taxpayer attempted to correct the improper inclusion in the earlier year by taking offsetting deductions in the later year. The taxpayer had lost his position as a school principal, but contested his dismissal. During the period of dispute, the taxpayer accrued the amount of his salary as income. When he realized that he would not get his job back and that he would not receive any back pay, he claimed deductions equal to the salary previously

---

[18] Although a contest of the additionally asserted liability will delay the appropriate time for deduction of the additional amount until the year in which the contest is resolved, the contest must be bona fide. A mere assertion of contest will not be sufficient to trigger rules for deferral of the deduction. See discussion at ¶ 4.04[c].

[19] But consider the mitigation provisions of Sections 1311–1314.

[20] Chatham & Phenix Nat'l Bank, 1 BTA 460 (1925), acq. IV-2 CB 2.

[21] The Board stated that the "amount was not income within the year 1917, and the fact that a tax was paid thereon for that year will not excuse [the taxpayer] from paying the tax in the year in which it is properly to be accounted for as income." Chatham & Phenix Nat'l Bank, 1 BTA at 466.

[22] Paul Irvin Redcay, 12 TC 806 (1949).

reported. The Commissioner found the deductions improper, and the court agreed.[23]

[e] Income Not Reported in Proper Year

The annual accounting concept also prevents income from being reported in a later year if it should have been reported in an earlier year. For example, in *Policy Holders Agency, Inc.*,[24] an insurance agency received dividends from mutual insurance companies on behalf of policyholders. For those policyholders it could locate, it either remitted the dividends or reduced their premiums by the amount of the dividends. For policyholders who could not be located, the agency treated the dividends as its own, but it did not report these amounts in income. Later, in 1958, the amount of the dividends was transferred to a surplus account on the taxpayer's books. At that time, the taxpayer filed amended returns for earlier open years, reporting such dividends as income in the years it actually received the dividends. Since the applicable statutory periods of limitation on some earlier years had run, the taxpayer's approach resulted in the amounts received in closed years escaping tax. The Commissioner argued that all amounts transferred to surplus were income in the year of the transfer. The court disagreed, finding that income properly attributable to prior years could not be taxed in later years.

[f] Influential Events After Year of Reporting

Numerous events may occur after the initial year of recognition that bring the earlier reporting into question. The new events generally are not anticipated in the earlier year. The issue in these circumstances is whether

---

[23] See also MacMillan Co., 4 BTA 251, 253 (1926), acq. V-2 CB 2, where the Board stated that each tax year must stand by itself and

> [t]he fact that a taxpayer has paid lower taxes for prior years than those which were rightfully due, because of erroneous computations of taxable income, and that the statute of limitations now bars the assessment and collection of any deficiency for those years, does not justify an erroneous computation of its tax liability for any subsequent years . . .

Farmers & Merchants Nat'l Bank, 8 BTA 58 (1927), acq. VII-1 CB 10, where a bank was denied a deduction in 1920 for amounts that it had erroneously included in income in 1919; Gould Paper Co., 26 BTA 560 (1932), modified, 72 F2d 698 (2d Cir. 1934), where an accrual basis taxpayer was denied a deduction in 1918 for repayments of interest erroneously reported in 1916 and 1917, the Board reasoning that any reported interest income was improperly accrued in the earlier years and the returns for those years should be amended; Herman Paster, 20 TCM 1239 (1961), where the taxpayer was denied a deduction in 1952 for dividend amounts that belonged to another and that were paid over to the rightful owner by the taxpayer in 1952, but which the taxpayer erroneously included in income in 1951.

[24] Policy Holders Agency, Inc., 41 TC 44 (1963), acq. 1964-2 CB 7.

the return for the earlier year should be amended or whether the new events should be taken into account only in the later year in which they occur.

[i] **Change in law.** The impact on earlier reporting of a later change in law or in the validity or interpretation of the law has been the subject of numerous cases. An example is *Freihofer Baking Co. v. Commissioner*,[25] where the taxpayer X purchased flour in 1935 at a price that included a processing tax. The taxpayer properly accrued and deducted this tax in the year of purchase. The tax was thereafter declared unconstitutional and, in 1936, the flour mill refunded the amount of processing tax to the taxpayer. The taxpayer sought to account for this later event by filing an amended return for 1935. The Tax Court found the filing of the amended return to be improper, holding that the refund should have been reported as income in the year of its receipt.

A similar result was reached where the change was in the interpretation rather than the validity of a law. In *Baltimore Transfer Co.*,[26] an accrual basis taxpayer accrued and deducted in 1943 its liability for workmen's unemployment compensation. In 1944, the taxpayer received a refund because of the state's redetermination of its contribution rate under the applicable statute. The taxpayer included the refund in its income for 1944. The Commissioner argued that the amount of refund should have reduced the 1943 deduction. The Tax Court disagreed, holding that the accrual of tax in 1943 was certain enough to justify the deduction, since the taxpayer had not contested the rate and had no reason prior to 1944 to suspect it would receive a refund.[27]

Following this same pattern is *Electric Tachometer Corp.*,[28] where an

---

[25] Freihofer Baking Co. v. Comm'r, 151 F2d 383 (3d Cir. 1945). See also Security Flour Mills Co. v. Comm'r, 321 US 281 (1944), and Bartlett v. Delaney, 173 F2d 535 (1st Cir. 1949), cert. denied, 338 US 817 (1949), where cash basis taxpayers paid and deducted in 1942 interest on a contested tax deficiency. The taxpayers ultimately won the dispute and received a refund of interest in 1943. The taxpayers attempted to reduce the 1942 deduction by the refund, but the court required the refund to be included in income in 1943.

[26] Baltimore Transfer Co., 8 TC 1 (1947), acq. 1947-2 CB 1.

[27] The court stated: "The propriety of the accruals must be judged by the facts which petitioner knew or would reasonably be expected to know at the closing of its books for the taxable year, and under the circumstances here we think that the accruals must be regarded as proper." Id. at 7.

The Commissioner argued that since the statute was in effect in 1943 and all operative facts leading to the reduced rate were available in 1943, the taxpayer should have known it was only required to pay a lower rate. The court considered any such possible knowledge as too remote to effect different tax carry-overs, indicating that a businessman cannot wait for a final legal clarification in order to determine the date of income or expense. The court concluded that "changes in law and in official interpretation of law, particularly if not reasonably expectable, must under the cases . . . be regarded as independent operative facts for accounting purposes." Id. at 9.

[28] Electric Tachometer Corp., 37 TC 158 (1961), acq. 1962-2 CB 4.

accrual basis taxpayer, whose property had been condemned by the state, was required to move its business. The taxpayer deducted the moving expenses it incurred in 1955 and 1956 and then sued for reimbursement. The taxpayer was successful and included the reimbursement in income in the year received. The Commissioner argued that the taxpayer's right to reimbursement existed as soon as the moving expenses were incurred and accrued and, as a consequence, that the deduction should not have been taken in the earlier year. The court rejected this position, holding that neither the right to reimbursement nor the amount of any reimbursement was so certain as to require accrual in the year of the move.

[ii] **Additional income.** Another example of how the reporting of later events is affected by earlier events is where the taxpayer receives additional compensation for services rendered in prior years. For example, in *United States v. Delta Airlines, Inc.*,[29] an airline that reported on an accrual basis received an additional payment in 1942 for mail carried in 1940. The additional payment was ordered by the Civil Aeronautics Board following its review of the reasonableness of the amount originally paid. Delta initially reported this as income in 1942, but thereafter amended its 1940 return to include the additional payments in the income of that year. The Fifth Circuit rejected the filing of the amended return, holding that, since neither the amount of the additional income nor Delta's right to it was fixed until 1942, the additional income could only be reported properly in that year.

[iii] **Tax retroactively imposed.** Where a state imposes a tax on events of an earlier year through retroactively applicable legislation, the accrual or payment of the tax does not entitle the taxpayer to a deduction in the year to which the tax relates. Instead, the tax is deductible only in the year of accrual or payment, as may be appropriate under the taxpayer's method of accounting. For example, in *Van Norman Co. v. Welch*,[30] the Commissioner tried to require an accrual basis taxpayer to take a deduction in 1935 for payments made in 1936 under a Massachusetts excise tax that was increased in 1936 with respect to tax year 1935. The court rejected the position of the Commissioner, noting the requirement of annual accounting.[31]

---

[29] United States v. Delta Airlines, Inc., 255 F2d 501 (5th Cir. 1958), cert. denied, 358 US 882 (1958).

[30] Van Norman Co. v. Welch, 141 F2d 99 (1st Cir. 1944).

[31] Citing Fawcus Mach. Co. v. United States, 282 US 375 (1931), the *Van Norman* court distinguished the situation where the retroactive tax was anticipated and passed in "ample time" to allow the taxpayer to take it into account in preparing the return for the year to which the retroactive tax related. See also James Bliss Coombs, 17 BTA 279 (1929), where a state income tax was enacted in 1919 covering the first seven months of 1918. The Board upheld the position of the government that the amount was deductible by the accrual basis taxpayer only in 1919; Union

[iv] Taxpayer attempts to change facts retroactively. Where a taxpayer takes action in one year in an attempt to alter the tax consequences of events that occurred in earlier years, his action will not affect the earlier years but will be taken into account for tax purposes, if at all, only in the year the action is taken.[32] For example, in *Noble v. Commissioner*,[33] a corporation was loaned money by its sole shareholder. The corporation paid interest on the loan. It also paid various personal expenses for the shareholder and took a deduction for these as business expenses. Just as the Internal Revenue Service was to begin an audit of the corporation, the shareholder adopted a resolution retroactively designating the payment of personal expenses as payment on the corporation's debt. Although this recharacterization was not intended to make the payments deductible, the shareholder hoped that it would avoid the characterization of the payments as income. The IRS asserted that the recharacterization was of no consequence and, hence, that the payment of personal expenses amounted to a constructive dividend. The shareholder responded that the resolution effectively changed the nature of the payment. The court rejected the shareholder's argument, noting that the federal income tax system is based on annual reporting, under which a taxpayer's income tax return is supposed to reflect all income activity of one reporting year. The court pointed out that if one year's income could be changed by events occurring in subsequent years, there would never be any finality in the system. Returns could be reopened and altered, resulting in confusion in fiscal policy and revenue collection.[34]

The result in *Noble* must be distinguished from actions that are taken in a later year to confirm facts that occurred in the earlier year. For instance, as a practical matter, if the corporate borrower in *Noble* had actually intended its payments of personal expenses on behalf of the shareholder to be treated as repayments of the principal debt owed (and if no inconsistent facts had occurred in that year), the later resolution to confirm the earlier actions as representing payments of principal might well have been influential. In effect, the later events would not be new facts creating a change in earlier reporting but would be confirmations of a correct earlier reporting.

[v] State court attempts to alter nature of earlier payments. The mere fact that a recharacterization of payments made in an earlier year is approved by a court for state law purposes does not mean that the earlier reporting was

---

Bleachery v. Comm'r, 97 F2d 226 (4th Cir. 1938), holding that a 1921 South Carolina tax enacted in 1922 was deductible by the accrual basis taxpayer in 1922.

[32] But see ¶ 4.04[3][f] for a discussion of a contrary result apparently provided to accrual method taxpayers under the recurring item exception when they desire to increase the allowable deductions of an earlier year merely by filing an amended return for that year.

[33] Noble v. Comm'r, 368 F2d 439 (9th Cir. 1966).

[34] Id. at 444.

incorrect for federal tax purposes. For example, in *Arthur Z. Gordon*,[35] the taxpayer was initially required to pay alimony, fixed child support, and variable child support. The variable support element was later contested by the taxpayer, and the state court found that it should be considered alimony. The taxpayer thereupon argued that these amounts were deductible for tax purposes just as alimony is deductible. The Tax Court rejected this contention, finding that the federal tax treatment of the payment would not be subject to such a recharacterization by a state court.

On the other hand, in *Blema Newman*,[36] certain periodic payments ordered in a divorce decree were extended retroactively so that they would cover a period of 10 years (the minimum period then required by federal law for the payments to be deductible). The Tax Court found that the order merely stated what the record of the initial divorce hearing showed to be the original intention of the court. Thus, the characterization at issue was found to be a clarification of what had always been intended rather than a change in character.

[3] Legislative and Judicial Ameliorations of Annual Accounting Concept

Over time, Congress and the courts have recognized many of the hardships created from a strict application of the annual accounting concept. Congress has ameliorated some of these hardships by enacting special provisions of the Code. Examples of these include Section 172, pertaining to the carry-over or carry-back of net operating losses, Section 302(b)(3), providing that a redemption of all of a shareholder's stock may be treated as a purchase of the stock (and not a dividend) so long as the redeemed shareholder does not acquire an interest in the corporation within 10 years from the date of the distribution in redemption;[37] Section 1341, pertaining to repayment of amounts received under a claim of right; and Section 111, pertaining to a

---

[35] Arthur Z. Gordon, 70 TC 525 (1978).

[36] Blema Newman, 68 TC 494 (1977).

[37] Similar provisions under the pre-1954 Code law included Section 3806 of the Internal Revenue Code of 1939, pertaining to repayment of amounts previously received under cost-plus contracts with the government; Section 611 of the Revenue Act of 1951, requiring mail carriers who received retroactive rewards from the Interstate Commerce Commission to attribute the income to the year in which the efforts that resulted in the income were made regardless of the time when their work was paid, and the Technical Amendments Act of 1958, Pub. L. No. 85-866, 72 Stat. 1606, 1673, which allowed owners of motor carriers to treat amounts received in settlement of claims against the United States as income for the years in which the carrier was under government control without regard to the year of the receipt of the claim or settlement of the claim.

recovery of previously deducted items.[38] Principal judicial ameliorations include the *Arrowsmith* doctrine and the tax benefit rule.[39]

¶ 12.03 CLAIM-OF-RIGHT DOCTRINE

The claim-of-right doctrine involves a particular manifestation of the annual accounting concept. The doctrine evolved from the tension resulting between (1) the necessity of collecting taxes at regular intervals based on events occurring within each interval and (2) the general approach of the tax law to defer the recognition of income until all contingencies regarding the taxpayer's right to the income are resolved.[40]

Under the claim-of-right doctrine, if a taxpayer receives income under a "claim of right and without restriction as to its disposition," the taxpayer must report the income in the year of receipt regardless of its method of accounting.[41] This rule applies even though the taxpayer may be required in a later tax year to refund the amount received.[42]

A taxpayer who later refunds (or becomes obligated to refund) the amount initially received generally will be entitled to a deduction in the year of repayment.[43] However, because tax rates may differ between the year of receipt and the year of deduction, the tax benefit of the deduction may be more or less than the tax cost of the initial receipt. Where the tax benefit is less than the tax cost, the taxpayer may seek relief under Section 1341, which allows a taxpayer to reduce its tax liability in the year of repayment by the amount of the tax increase that resulted from the initial inclusion.[44]

[1] Origin

The claim-of-right doctrine is most often traced to the Supreme Court's 1932 decision in *North American Oil Consolidated v. Burnet.*[45] This case arose from

---

[38] Section 1341 is discussed infra ¶ 12.03[4]. Section 111 is discussed infra ¶ 12.05[4][b][i].

[39] The *Arrowsmith* doctrine is discussed infra ¶ 12.04. The tax benefit rule is discussed infra ¶ 12.05.

[40] See Burnet v. Logan, 283 US 404, 412 (1931), where the Supreme Court stated: "The liability for income tax ultimately can be fairly determined without resort to mere estimates, assumptions and speculation."

[41] North Am. Oil Consol. v. Burnet, 286 US 417, 424 (1932).

[42] Id.

[43] See discussion infra ¶ 12.03[3][b]. The actual year of deduction depends on whether the taxpayer is on the cash method or an accrual method.

[44] Section 1341 is discussed infra ¶ 12.03[4].

[45] North Am. Oil Consol. v. Burnet, 286 US 417 (1932). Actually, it was the Sixth Circuit that first used the phrase "claim of right" one year before *North Amer-*

earlier litigation between the taxpayer and the government over income attributable to the operation of certain oil lands in 1916. The taxpayer had been in possession of the land, but the government instituted an action to gain possession. While this action was pending, a court-appointed receiver operated the property and held all income. In 1917, a district court dismissed the government's action, and the receiver distributed the income to the taxpayer, including the income earned in 1916. In 1920, the Court of Appeals for the Ninth Circuit affirmed the decision of the district court, and a further appeal to the Supreme Court was dismissed in 1922.

The issue in the subsequent tax litigation was the proper year for reporting the income attributable to 1916. The choice was among three years: (1) 1916, when the income was earned; (2) 1917, when the district court ruled in favor of the taxpayer and the income was received by the taxpayer; and (3) 1922, when the dispute was finally resolved.

The Supreme Court first held that the profits were not income to the taxpayer in 1916 because "the company was not required in 1916 to report as income an amount which it might never receive."[46] This holding was consistent with the so-called all events test, under which income is not recognized by an accrual method taxpayer until all events occur that fix the taxpayer's right to receive the income.[47] However, the Court further held that even though the taxpayer's right to the income did not become fixed until 1922, the proper year for reporting the income was 1917, when the income was paid to the taxpayer. The Court picked 1917 because the funds "became income of the Company in 1917, when it first became entitled to them and when it actually received them." The heart of the decision was contained in the following frequently cited excerpt:

> If a taxpayer receives earnings under a claim of right and without restriction as to its disposition, he has received income which he is required to return, even though it may still be claimed that he is not entitled to retain the money, and even though he may still be adjudged liable to restore its equivalent. [Citations omitted.] If in 1922 the Government had prevailed, and the company had been obliged to refund the profits received in 1917, it would have been entitled to a deduction from the profits of 1922, not from those of any earlier year.[48]

Despite the Supreme Court's definition of the claim-of-right doctrine in *North American Oil*, the decision has spawned a number of questions. For example, does the doctrine apply only in determining the time to report income or may it also be used to identify receipts as income? What limits

---

ican Oil was decided. See Board v. Comm'r, 51 F2d 73 (6th Cir. 1931), cert. denied, 284 US 658 (1931).

[46] North Am. Oil Consol. v. Burnet, 286 US 417, 423 (1932).

[47] See discussion of accrual methods at ¶¶ 4.03[1], 4.04.

[48] North Am. Oil Consol. v. Burnet, 286 US 417, 424 (1932).

should be established in applying the doctrine? How should the opinion affect tax accounting practices? Finally, what should be the tax effect of a repayment in a later year of the amount originally reported in income? These questions are addressed below following a discussion of the necessary elements for application of the doctrine.

[2] Requirements for Application

Four elements must be present before the claim-of-right doctrine may be applied:

1. The taxpayer must receive cash or property.
2. The cash or property must constitute income.
3. The taxpayer must have unlimited control over the use and disposition of this income.
4. The taxpayer must hold the income under an asserted claim of right.

[a] Receipt of Income

An initial requirement for application of the doctrine is receipt. Following *North American Oil*, decisions have indicated that this requirement is to be applied on a basis consistent with the taxpayer's applicable method of accounting. Thus, in the case of a cash method taxpayer, the income in question must actually or constructively be received before the doctrine may be applied.[49] In the case of an accrual method taxpayer, the doctrine operates in tandem with the normal tax accrual rules.[50] Thus, once all events have

---

[49] See, e.g., Brooklyn Union Gas Co. v. Comm'r, 62 F2d 505 (2d Cir. 1933), where the State of New York had charged the petitioner utility company with exceeding the statutory rate prescribed by the Public Service Commission (PSC). The "excess monies" were impounded pending the outcome of litigation that finally ended in 1922. In 1920, however, the utility obtained an interlocutory order declaring the PSC's regulations confiscatory. The order also awarded the utility the right to receive the impounded income without restriction on its use, provided that the utility filed security bonds. The utility did not withdraw all of the funds before the litigation ended in 1922. The Court, with Judge Learned Hand dissenting, held that even those funds not withdrawn were taxable in 1920 under the claim of right doctrine, since the conditional right to the funds constituted a constructive receipt of them. Judge Hand, who dissented in part, felt that the condition on the right of the utility to withdraw the impounded funds—the requirement that the utility deposit securities of its own or the bonds of a security company—was so substantial that the impounded funds should not be considered immediately available to the utility. Id. at 507. See also ¶ 3.03[2] for a discussion of the constructive receipt doctrine.

[50] See discussion at ¶¶ 4.03, 4.04.

occurred that fix the taxpayer's right to the income, it must be recognized even though the right might be extinguished by subsequent events.[51]

The claim-of-right doctrine is not applicable unless the item received is income.[52] Despite the requirement that income be received, a number of courts have seemingly used the doctrine for the purpose of characterizing a receipt as income.[53] Although the receipt of certain items clearly does not constitute a receipt of income subject to the claim-of-right doctrine,[54] other receipts cannot be so easily characterized.[55]

[b] Unlimited Control

The claim-of-right doctrine does not apply unless the taxpayer receives the income without restriction as to its disposition.[56] Subsequent cases have interpreted this requirement to mean that any restrictions on the taxpayer's use of the funds must not be so substantial that they effectively deprive the taxpayer of the economic benefit of possessing the funds.[57] For example,

---

[51] See e.g., Brown v. Helvering, 291 US 193 (1934), where accrued insurance commissions were required to be included in income even though the right to those commissions could be lost if the insurance were later canceled; Barker v. McGruder, 95 F2d 122 (D.C. Cir. 1938), where accrued interest was required to be recognized even though it could later be lost. See also the discussion at ¶ 4.03[3] for circumstances where accrual method taxpayers must recognize prepaid income in the year of receipt even though the all events test has not at that time been satisfied. Just as in the case of a cash method taxpayer, this recognition of income is not prevented on the basis that the receipt might have to be refunded.

[52] See Section 61 for items included within the concept of "income."

[53] See, e.g., Automobile Club of Mich. v. Comm'r, 353 US 180 (1957), holding, in effect, that prepaid income is includable in gross income; James v. United States, 366 US 213 (1961), holding that illegal receipts are taxable income even though the taxpayer had no bona fide claim to the receipts. The *James* Court declined to hold whether the claim of right doctrine could be used to determine whether a receipt was income. Id. at 216 n.7.

[54] See, e.g., North Pa. R.R., 47 TCM 549 (1983), finding that there was no taxable receipt under the claim of right doctrine where the receipt was in the nature of a bona fide loan; M.L. Rose Co, 13 TCM 213 (1954), repayment of loan is not income; Section 1001, recovery of cost is not income; Section 102, receipt of gifts is not income; Warren Serv. Corp. v. Comm'r, 110 F2d 723 (2d Cir. 1940), where the court held that a security deposit was taxable only on default by the tenant.

[55] See discussion infra ¶ 12.03[3][a].

[56] North Am. Oil Consol. v. Burnet, 286 US 417, 424 (1932).

[57] This is consistent with Corliss v. Bowers, 281 US 376, 378 (1930), where the Supreme Court noted that "taxation is not so much concerned with the refinements of title as it is actual command over the property taxed—the actual benefit for which the tax is paid." See Frederic A. Collins, 31 TCM 835 (1972), where funds were not taxed in the year received because the income had to be deposited in a special bank account while the IRS served a Notice of Levy. See also Priv. Ltr. Rul. 8738018 (Sept. 28, 1987), where a transfer of the actuarially determined amount from a state-

sufficient control was not present where the approval of another was needed to obtain the funds, where the funds were in an account beyond the taxpayer's control,[58] or where use of the funds was restricted until the restriction was lifted by a third party.[59] On the other hand, where the asserted restrictions did not prevent the taxpayer from using the funds for its own benefit, the requisite control was found.[60]

---

administered black lung benefits fund to a newly created Section 501(c)(21) trust was not includable in gross income under the claim of right doctrine because of the substantial restrictions imposed on the taxpayer.

[58] In Sara R. Preston, 35 BTA 312 (1937), acq. 1937-2 CB 22, two attorneys received a check payable to both for services rendered, but the two could not agree on their respective shares of the payment. The payment was thereupon placed in a special account pending resolution of the dispute. The court found that access to the funds was sufficiently restricted to prevent a finding of control. See also Frederic A. Collins, 31 TCM 835 (1972), taxpayer did not have unlimited control of funds deposited in a restricted bank account pending the outcome of litigation.

[59] See Mutual Tel. Co. v. United States, 204 F2d 160 (9th Cir. 1953), where a regulated utility, which had received permission from a state agency for a rate increase, was required to account separately for funds received pursuant to the increase until final approval was obtained. The taxpayers did not have to include these receipts in income because of the restrictions on their use. See also Consolidated-Hammer Dry Plate & Film Co. v. Comm'r, 317 F2d 829 (7th Cir. 1963), where a manufacturer's right to partial payments under a sales contract were conditioned on a customer's acceptance, payments received by the manufacturer prior to acceptance by the customer were not includable in income in the year of receipt under the claim of right doctrine; Max E. Cohen, 24 TCM 728 (1965), advances for costs to be incurred by an attorney were not income until credited to the attorney's fee for services; and Anthony D. Miele, 72 TC 284, 290 (1979), prepaid legal fees required to be put into a restricted account pursuant to a state code of professional responsibility were not under the taxpayer's control.

[60] See, e.g., Angelus Funeral Home, 47 TC 391 (1967), acq. 1969-1 CB 20, aff'd, 407 F2d 210 (9th Cir. 1969), cert. denied, 396 US 824 (1969), where the taxpayer received payments from customers to be applied to the cost of their funerals. Under the contract, the taxpayer had the right to use the payments for capital improvements. The court concluded that while these funds seemed to be received in trust, the taxpayer's immediate right to use them for capital improvement satisfied the unlimited control requirement. The mere fact that the taxpayer's use of the funds was limited to capital improvements was not a restriction sufficient to preclude taxability. See also North Am. Oil Consol. v. Burnet, 286 US 417, 424 (1932), control present when funds received without restriction as to disposition even though right to funds conditioned on outcome of pending litigation; Paul C. Nordberg, 79 TC 655 (1982), aff'd without published opinion, 720 F2d 658 (1st Cir. 1983), control present even though receipt conditioned on a contractual provision; Town Park Hotel Corp. v. Comm'r, 446 F2d 878 (6th Cir. 1971), cert. denied, 404 US 1039 (1972), funds withdrawn from deposits with court pursuant to a state condemnation proceeding are includable in income even though the amount actually due the taxpayer not determined until a later year; Healy v. Comm'r, 345 US 278, 283 (1953), taxpayers had to recognize income even though they were subject to transferee liability and might be required to pay the funds over to others.

[c] Asserted Claim of Right

The taxpayer must possess the funds under a "claim of right," which means that the taxpayer must receive and treat the funds as its own. Receipt of funds under a claim of right is typically demonstrated by the taxpayer's appropriation of the item of income without renouncing ownership of it.[61] (i.e., the taxpayer received funds "lawfully or unlawfully, without the consensual recognition, express or implied, of an obligation to repay. . . ."[62]) The obligation to repay must itself not be contingent or otherwise subject to conditions precedent.[63]

[3] Prevailing Issues Under Claim-of-Right Doctrine

[a] Characterization of Receipts as Income

One of the most important issues left unanswered by *North American Oil* is whether the claim-of-right doctrine is merely a rule of tax accounting that determines *when* income is to be recognized for tax purposes or whether it is a substantive tax rule that may be used to determine *whether* a particular receipt is income. The case did not address this question because only timing was at issue, and the item received was unquestionably income. Nevertheless, since *North American Oil*, some courts and commentators have concluded that the doctrine may be used for the purpose of determining the character of receipts as income as well as indicating when such income should

---

[61] This situation should be contrasted with one where the taxpayer merely possesses income, which it admits belongs to someone else and which the taxpayer intends to give to its proper owner. See e.g., United States v. Merrill, 211 F2d 297 (9th Cir. 1954), where the court held that where, in the year of receipt, the taxpayer renounces his rights to the funds and recognizes his obligation to repay them, such receipts will not be included in gross income under the claim of right doctrine.

[62] James v. United States, 366 US 213, 219 (1961) (citing North Am. Oil Consol. v. Burnet, 286 US 417, 424 (1932)).

[63] See, e.g., Continental Ill. Corp., 58 TCM 790 (1989), where the court focused on a loan agreement requiring the borrower to pay interest based on a floating rate but providing the borrower with an opportunity to obtain a partial rebate of interest at the maturity of the loan if the aggregate interest paid on the basis of the floating rate exceeded the interest that would have been paid under a specified fixed rate. The lender attempted to limit its accrual of interest income to the lower of the interest calculated under the floating rate and the specified fixed rate. The court held that the lender should accrue the amount determined under the floating rate, even though any interest in excess of the amount computed on the fixed rate was reported on the books of the lender as a liability. The court based its decision on the fact that the lender's obligation to repay was subject to various conditions precedent.

be reported.[64] The Supreme Court has not yet ruled on the issue,[65] but as discussed in the following section, the Court has implied that the doctrine should not be applied to characterize receipts as income.

[i] **Prepaid income.** The effect of the claim-of-right doctrine on income received in advance of the delivery of goods or the performance of services has been a continuing question. Typically, such payments are received without restriction as to their use, and the taxpayer does not recognize any obligation to repay. The issue is whether the prepayments should be included in the income of an accrual method taxpayer in the year of receipt or the year when the goods are delivered or the services are rendered.[66]

In *Automobile Club of Michigan v. Commissioner,*[67] the Supreme Court focused on the tax accounting treatment of prepaid membership dues entitling members to specified car repair and maintenance services over the period covered by the dues. The Court did not expressly affirm the government's argument that the prepayments were taxable in the year of receipt under the claim-of-right doctrine. Rather, it upheld the government's position on the basis of the requirement that income be clearly reflected. However, four dissenting Justices focused squarely on the issue and concluded that the claim-of-right doctrine was intended only to determine:

> whether the treatment of an item of income should be influenced by the fact that the right to receive or keep it is in dispute; it does not relate to the entirely different question whether items that admittedly belong to the taxpayer may be attributed to a taxable year other than that of receipt in accordance with the principles of accrual accounting.[68]

In later cases, the Supreme Court refused to require the inclusion of

---

[64] See B. Bittker, Federal Taxation of Income, Estates and Gifts, ¶ 6.3.1, at 6-11 (Warren, Gorham & Lamont 1981), where the author states: "*North American Oil Consolidated* is not confined to timing, since it does not point to the proper year for reporting income that the taxpayer will have to report in one year or another over the long haul, but instead determines that the receipt *is* income."

[65] In James v. United States, 366 US 213 (1961), the Supreme Court noted as follows:

> The Government contends that the adoption in *Wilcox* of a claim of right test as a touchstone of taxability had no support in the prior cases of this Court; that the claim of right test was a doctrine invoked by the Court in aid of the concept of annual accounting, to determine *when*, not *whether*, receipts constituted income. [Citations omitted.] In view of our reasoning set forth below, we need not pass on this contention.

Id. at 216 n.7 (emphasis by Court).

[66] See discussion at ¶ 4.03[3].

[67] Automobile Club of Mich. v. Comm'r, 353 US 180 (1957). See discussion at ¶ 4.03[3].

[68] Id. at 191–192 (Harlan, J., dissenting).

prepaid income in the year of receipt on the basis of the claim-of-right doctrine.[69] Instead, the Court stressed the discretion of the IRS under Section 446(b) to require taxpayers to use an accounting method that clearly reflects income.[70]

[ii] Illegal income.   In *Commissioner v. Wilcox*,[71] decided in 1946, the Supreme Court held that embezzled funds did not constitute taxable income. As support for its conclusion, the Court cited *North American Oil* for the proposition that "without some bona fide legal or equitable claim, even though it be contingent or contested in nature, the taxpayer cannot be said to have received any gain or profit within the reach of [the income tax laws]."[72] In other words, the Court appeared to conclude that the claim-of-right doctrine could be applied in determining not only when income should be recognized, but also whether the particular item could properly be characterized as income.

However, this implication was seemingly rejected 15 years later when the Supreme Court overruled *Wilcox* in *James v. United States*.[73] In *James*, the Court held that embezzled funds constituted taxable income when received. The Court emphasized the recipient's control over the funds, not any claim of right to them.[74] The Court stated:

> When a taxpayer acquires earnings, lawfully or unlawfully, without the consensual recognition, express or implied, of an obligation to repay and without restriction as to their disposition, "he has received income

---

[69] See, e.g., Schlude v. Comm'r, 372 US 128, 134–136 (1963), where the Court required inclusion of prepaid tuitions in year of receipt on ground that this was required in order to reflect income clearly; American Auto. Ass'n v. United States, 367 US 687, 691 (1961), where the court focused on the "artificiality" of the taxpayer's current method of accounting. See also Tech. Adv. Mem. 8642001 (June 19, 1986), where the IRS stated that "the claim of right doctrine applies only in the context of concededly earned income and does not apply to cases involving the propriety of the deferral of prepaid receipts held without restriction as to use other than the liability to perform services or sell goods in the future."

[70] See ¶ 2.02[2] for a discussion of the clear reflection of income requirement.

[71] Comm'r v. Wilcox, 327 US 404 (1946), overruled by James v. United States, 366 US 213 (1961). The *Wilcox* Court's opinion noted that since the embezzler in *Wilcox* was under an absolute legal duty to return the funds, he had no genuine claim to them. The Court compared the situation in *Wilcox* to that in a debtor-creditor relationship, holding that the embezzled funds did not constitute taxable income. 327 US at 408–409.

[72] Id. at 408.

[73] James v. United States, 366 US 213 (1961).

[74] Id. at 219. Actually, the "control test" had been adopted by the Supreme Court in Rutkin v. United States, 343 US 130 (1952), reh'g denied, 343 US 952 (1952), decided nine years before *James*. *Rutkin*, however, failed to overrule *Wilcox*. *Rutkin* merely limited *Wilcox* to its facts.

which he is required to return, even though it may still be claimed that he is not entitled to retain the money, and even though he may still be adjudged to restore its equivalent."[75]

Thus, the Court focused on the lack of a consensual recognition to repay rather than any asserted claim of right.

[iii] Amounts received under mistaken claim. The claim-of-right doctrine applies even where the amount initially received is later found to have been paid in error. For example, in *United States v. Lewis*,[76] the taxpayer received a bonus from his employer in 1944. The employer later claimed the bonus had been computed incorrectly, and in 1946, the employee was required to repay a portion of the bonus. The taxpayer wanted to take the correction into account by amending his 1944 return. On the basis of the claim-of-right doctrine, the Supreme Court held that the taxpayer could not file an amended return for 1944, but had to take a deduction in 1946. The court recognized that this prevented the taxpayer from offsetting the tax paid for 1944, since in the earlier year he was subject to a higher tax rate.

[iv] Agreements to refund. If a taxpayer discovers in the year of receipt that a payment was made to him in error, a rejection of the payment or at least an acknowledgement of an obligation to repay prevents the need for recognition. For example, in *United States v. Merrill*,[77] a cash basis taxpayer received an executor's fee of $7,500. Later in the year, he discovered that this was an error. He then made appropriate entries in his and the estate's books to account for the error. The Supreme Court refused to apply the claim-of-right doctrine, stating that there was no reason to apply the doctrine where a taxpayer renounces the receipt and recognizes his obligation to repay it in the year of receipt.[78]

The *"Merrill* rule" does not apply where the taxpayer is not under any legal obligation to repay the income.[79] Further, the *Merrill* rule applies only

---

[75] James v. United States, 366 US 213, 219 (1961) (citing North Am. Oil Consol. v. Burnet, 286 US 417, 424 (1932)).

[76] United States v. Lewis, 340 US 590 (1951).

[77] United States v. Merrill, 211 F2d 297 (9th Cir. 1954).

[78] See also Gilbert v. Comm'r, 552 F2d 478 (2d Cir. 1977), where the court treated a receipt of funds accompanied at the same time by an acknowledgement of an obligation to repay as more like a loan than an amount received under a claim of right. In Paul C. Nordberg, 79 TC 655 (1982), aff'd without published opinion, 720 F2d 658 (1st Cir. 1983), the court indicated that in order to avoid application of the claim of right doctrine, the taxpayer must, in the year of receipt, recognize an existing and fixed obligation to repay and make provision for the repayment.

[79] Hope v. Comm'r, 471 F2d 738 (3d Cir. 1973), aff'g 55 TC 1020 (1971), cert. denied, 414 US 824 (1973). The court stated that the taxpayer was never under any liability to rescind the transaction. The condition precedent to rescission was entirely under his control and imposed no restriction on his use of the funds. Id. at 742.

to funds received by mistake and not to funds acquired through illegal means, such as embezzlement.[80] Finally, the Seventh Circuit has not applied the *Merrill* rule, on the ground that *Merrill* addresses a problem already dealt with by Section 1341,[81] which provides relief to taxpayers in certain situations where a strict application of the claim-of-right doctrine would otherwise impose inequitable hardship.[82]

[v] **Conduits and trustees.** The claim-of-right doctrine does not apply to amounts received by the taxpayer as an agent or trustee for another person or as a conduit for the passage of funds to another. For example, in *Seven-Up Co.*,[83] the taxpayer, a manufacturer of soft drink syrup, received funds from bottling companies to finance a national advertising campaign. The funds received by the taxpayer were passed on to the advertising agency. The Tax Court held that the amounts received by the taxpayer did not constitute taxable income. The court likened the taxpayer to a trustee handling the bottlers' money. The court also noted that the commingling of the unspent portions of the bottlers' money with the taxpayer's own funds did not destroy their identity as trust funds because the bottlers could prohibit the taxpayer from using the funds for any purpose other than advertising.

Similarly, in *Broadcast Measurement Bureau, Inc.*,[84] a club received funds from members to undertake a study. The Tax Court held that the excess of the amounts paid by the members over the cost of the study was not income to the taxpayer because the excess was required to be refunded to the members and, as a consequence, was held in trust for them. On the other hand, this principle has not been applied to constructive trusts.[85]

---

[80] See Buff v. Comm'r, 496 F2d 847 (2d Cir. 1974), where the court found that the taxpayer did not exhibit a bona fide intent to repay the money he had embezzled from his employer; see also United States v. Hauff, 461 F2d 1061 (7th Cir. 1972), cert. denied, 409 US 873 (1972), involving fraud.

[81] See, e.g., Quinn v. Comm'r, 524 F2d 617, 625 (7th Cir. 1975).

[82] See infra ¶ 12.03[4] for a discussion of Section 1341.

[83] Seven-Up Co., 14 TC 965 (1950), acq. 1974-2 CB 4.

[84] Broadcast Measurement Bureau, Inc., 16 TC 988 (1951), acq. 1951-2 CB 2 (withdrawn), nonacq. 1974-2 CB 4. See Rev. Rul. 74-318, 1974-2 CB 14, where amounts received by an organization of franchised automobile dealers from its members constituted income in year of receipt because the sums could be used at its sole discretion to serve the best interests of its members. See also Priv. Ltr. Rul. 8746013 (Aug. 13, 1987), where the National Office recognized that amounts received by a C corporation, which was formed as a nonprofit association to perform administrative and communication services for its members, was not taxable on income collected on behalf of its members.

[85] See Healy v. Comm'r, 345 US 278, 282–283 (1953), where the Supreme Court stated:

A constructive trust is a fiction imposed as an equitable device for achieving justice. It lacks the attributes of a true trust and is not based on any intention of the parties. Even though it has a retroactive existence in legal fiction, fiction

[vi] Deposits. The claim-of-right doctrine may not be used to convert nontaxable receipts, such as loans or customer deposits, into taxable income. However, this does not mean that all such receipts may not be taxable under other theories.[86]

The courts have not been consistent in characterizing deposits as taxable or nontaxable. For example, the Court of Appeals for the Eleventh Circuit has held that if the primary purpose of a deposit is to secure income producing covenants of the customer, the deposit may be treated as an advance payment of income.[87] On the other hand, the Tax Court has decided that the Eleventh Circuit's test is too narrow and that the proper test is whether the primary purpose of the deposit is to serve as an advance payment or as security.[88] The Tax Court stated that all facts and circumstances must be considered. Among the factors that suggest that a payment is a nontaxable deposit are the intent of the parties,[89] a payee's obligation to pay interest on the funds,[90] a payee's duty to keep the payments in a segregated account,[91]

---

cannot change the 'readily reliable economic value' and practical 'use and benefit' which these taxpayers enjoyed during a prior annual accounting period, antecedent to the declaration of constructive trust.

[86] See, e.g., Iowa S. Utils. Co. v. United States, 841 F2d 1108 (Fed. Cir. 1988), which involved permitted surcharges in some years to be offset by negative surcharges in later years. The court found the surcharges and negative surcharges were merely price adjustments, not (1) nontaxable loans or (2) taxable loans accompanied by presently deductible fixed obligations to repay such amounts in the future. See also Dana Distribs., Inc., 56 TCM 569 (1988), aff'd, 874 F2d 120 (2d Cir. 1989), which involved the receipt of refundable deposits on beverage containers. The court concluded that the deposits had to be included in the taxpayer's income because the circumstances indicated that the containers were sold with the beverage and there was no obligation on the part of the purchaser to return the container.

[87] See e.g., City Gas Co. of Fla. v. Comm'r, 689 F2d 943 (11th Cir. 1982), rev'g 74 TC 386 (1980), where the Court held such a principle applicable in characterizing customer deposits received by taxpayer gas utility. But see Indianapolis Power and Light Co. v. Commissioner, 90-1 USTC ¶ 50,007 (1990), where the Supreme Court rejected this principle.

[88] Indianapolis Power & Light Co., 88 TC 964 (1987), aff'd, 857 F2d 1162 (7th Cir. 1988), aff'd, 90-1 USTC 50,007 (1990). See also American Tel. & Tel. Co., 55 TCM 16 (1988). The government intended to appeal the decision in *American Telephone & Telegraph*, but filed its notice of appeal one day late.

[89] See Clinton Hotel Realty Corp. v. Comm'r, 128 F2d 968 (5th Cir. 1942), where the Fifth Circuit held that a deposit paid to secure a tenant's performance under a lease (the deposit to be credited to tenant's last month's rent) was not income to the accrual basis landlord until actually applied to the tenant's liability for rent.

[90] See Gilken Corp., 10 TC 445, 452 (1948), aff'd, 176 F2d 141 (6th Cir. 1949), where the Tax Court recognized that the presence of interest would suggest a nontaxable deposit; however, the court found no evidence of interest in the financial arrangement at issue; J.&E. Enters., 26 TCM 944, 946 (1967), where the court held that certain payments were prepaid rent instead of nontaxable security deposits, because, among other factors, the lessor was not required to pay interest.

[91] See Gilken Corp. v. Comm'r, 176 F2d 141, 144 (6th Cir. 1949), where the

and the possibility that the money may be returned to the payor.[92] However, if the payee is given unrestricted use of the funds or is given sole discretion in deciding whether to repay the funds or to apply them against future obligations, the payment is generally considered to be taxable.[93]

In *Indianapolis Power and Light Co.*,[94] the Supreme Court resolved the issue as to the proper test to be applied. The Court adopted the facts-and-circumstances test, rejecting the primary purpose test that had been adopted by the Court of Appeals for the Eleventh Circuit in *City Gas Co. of Florida v. Commissioner*.[95] An important factor, of course, is whether the obligation to return the deposit is fixed rather than contingent.[96] However, the key facts and circumstances are those affecting the parties' rights and obligations at the time the asserted deposits are made.[97] The questions to ask include whether the taxpayer (1) has a fixed obligation to repay the amounts in question; (2) has complete dominion over the amounts received by it; and (3) will be entitled to keep the amounts received, assuming only that it ful-jfills its own contractual obligations. Other facts and circumstances, although relevant, may be of less significance than these key facts and circumstances.[98]

Sixth Circuit indicated that, had a lessor been required to hold the lessee's "security deposit" in trust or to set it apart as a separate fund, the payment would be more in the nature of a nontaxable deposit; see also Hirsch Improvement Co. v. Comm'r, 143 F2d 912, 915 (2d Cir. 1944), cert denied, 323 US 750 (1944), where the court stated: "If the taxpayer had been required to segregate the payment, then it would not have been income for the taxable year."

[92] See Hirsch Improvement Co. v. Comm'r, 143 F2d 912, 915 (2d Cir. 1944), cert. denied, 323 US 750 (1944), where the court's decision to tax a lessor on an amount received as "security" for payment of rent was strongly influenced by the extremely narrow circumstances under which the lessor would have to make a refund to the lessee. The court stated that "the sum received was to be repaid, in whole or part, under circumstances which might never occur and of a kind so limited as to be insufficient to require that sum to be categorized as primarily not intended as rent."

[93] See J.&E. Enters., 26 TCM 944, 946 (1967), holding that the complete lack of restrictions on the lessor's use of a "security deposit" required it to be taxable in the year of receipt.

[94] Indianapolis Power & Light Co., 90-1 USTC ¶ 50,007 (1990).

[95] City Gas Co. of Florida v. Comm'r, 689 F2d 943 (11th Cir. 1982).

[96] Compare Illinois Power Co. v. Comm'r, 792 F2d 683 (7th Cir. 1986), where the court refused to apply the claim of right doctrine in circumstances where the taxpayer was ordered by the state regulatory commission to raise rates for certain customers in circumstances where the amount of the increase was required to be repaid, with Continental Ill. Corp., 58 TCM 790 (1989), where certain amounts were found to be subject to a claim of right because the taxpayer had only a contingent obligation to repay the amounts in subsequent years.

[97] Oak Indus., Inc., 95 TC No. 20 (1991).

[98] Id.

[b] Availability of Deduction for Repaid Amounts

If amounts included in income under the claim-of-right doctrine are later repaid, the taxpayer is entitled to a deduction for the amount repaid.[99] The amount and character of the deduction are determined on a basis consistent with the *Arrowsmith* doctrine and the tax benefit rule.[100] The year of the deduction will be determined on the basis of the taxpayer's method of accounting.

[4] Statutory Relief: Section 1341

[a] General Requirements

In *United States v. Lewis*,[101] application of the claim-of-right doctrine resulted in the taxpayer including certain amounts in income in one year but deducting in a later year the amount refunded. Due to a reduction in effective tax rates, the taxpayer incurred a net tax loss. Congress enacted Section 1341 to provide relief from this occasionally harsh effect of the claim-of-right doctrine on taxpayers who are later required to repay all or a portion of the amount previously received.

Under Section 1341, the reduction in tax liability attributable to the repayment is to be the greater of the amounts calculated under two approaches. Under the first approach, the taxpayer merely computes the tax for the year of repayment after having deducted the amount of the repayment. Under the second approach, the tax is computed for the year of repayment without deduction, but with a reduction in tax liability equal to the reduction in tax that would have occurred in the year of receipt had the amount of the repayment been excluded from income.[102]

---

[99] See, e.g., United States v. Lewis, 340 US 590 (1951), discussed supra ¶ 12.03[3][a][iii], and North Am. Oil Consol. v. Burnet, 286 US 417 (1932), where the taxpayer was required to report an amount received in 1917 as income for that year even though its right to retain these funds was not unequivocally settled until 1922. Because the taxpayer ultimately prevailed in its claim to the disputed amount, the Supreme Court did not have to consider the effect of a repayment. However, the Court noted that had the taxpayer been required to refund the 1917 receipts, it could have deducted the amount refunded: "If in 1922 the Government had prevailed and the company had been obliged to refund the profits received in 1917, it would have been entitled to a deduction from the profits of 1922, not from those of any earlier year." Id. at 424.

[100] The *Arrowsmith* doctrine is discussed infra ¶ 12.04, and the tax benefit rule is discussed infra ¶ 12.05.

[101] United States v. Lewis, 340 US 590 (1951). See discussion supra ¶ 12.03[3][a][iii].

[102] IRC §§ 1341(a)(4), 1341(a)(5). If the reduction in tax under the second approach is greater than the tax liability for the year, the excess is refunded or

There are three requirements for application of Section 1341. First, a receipt must have been included in the taxpayer's gross income for a prior year because it appeared that the taxpayer had an unrestricted right to that receipt.[103] Second, a deduction must be available in a later year because it was established after the year of receipt that the taxpayer did not have an unrestricted right to the receipt.[104] In other words, there must be a sufficient nexus between the original receipt and the later repayment. Third, the amount of the allowable deduction must exceed $3,000.[105]

The provisions of Section 1341 apply without regard to whether the taxpayer is on the cash or accrual method of accounting.[106] Most of the issues that have arisen under this Code section have involved the first two requirements.

[b] Unrestricted Right vs. Claim of Right

Section 1341 requires that a taxpayer "appear" to have an "unrestricted right" rather than a "claim of right." In determining whether a refund of a payment received during litigation qualified for Section 1341 relief, the IRS has ruled that the term "appeared" requires only a semblance of an unrestricted right.[107]

The IRS also ruled that neither having an "absolute right" at one end of the spectrum, nor having "no semblance of entitlement" at the other, will qualify a taxpayer for relief under Section 1341.[108] Thus, a repayment of embezzled funds was not covered by the section.[109] Similarly, bad debt deductions are not entitled to relief under Section 1341 because even though the debt is uncollectible, the taxpayer's right to payment is unchallengeable.[110]

[c] Connection Between Receipt and Repayment

In order for Section 1341 to apply, there must be a sufficient nexus between the receipt and the later repayment. For example, in *Albert J.*

---

credited just as any overpayment of tax. IRC § 1341(b)(1).

[103] IRC § 1341(a)(1). The item received must not have arisen from a sale or other disposition of property held primarily for sale in the ordinary course of business. IRC § 1341(b)(2). See discussion infra ¶ 12.03[4][b]. See Maier Brewing Co., 54 TCM 46 (1987).

[104] IRC § 1341(a)(2).

[105] IRC § 1341(a)(3).

[106] Treas. Reg. § 1.1341-1(e).

[107] Rev. Rul. 68-153, 1968-1 CB 371, 373.

[108] Id.

[109] Rev. Rul. 65-254, 1965-2 CB 50, 51.

[110] Treas. Reg. § 1.1341-1(g).

Uhlenbrock,[111] the executor of an estate used his own funds to pay a portion of a late filing penalty owed by the estate. The executor sought to deduct this payment under Section 1341 as if it were a repayment of a portion of his previously reported executor's commission. The court held that while payment of the late filing penalty related to the taxpayer's general duties as executor, it was not repayment of commissions. Similarly, the regulations under Section 1341 do not permit payments of legal fees and other expenses incurred in contesting the taxpayer's right to amounts previously included in income to qualify for Section 1341 relief.[112]

¶ 12.04 *ARROWSMITH* DOCTRINE

The "*Arrowsmith* doctrine," which derives its name from the Supreme Court's decision in *Arrowsmith v. Commissioner*,[113] is another amelioration of the impact of the annual accounting concept. This doctrine allows the character of a gain or loss on a transaction to be determined by the character of the gain or loss recognized on a related transaction in a prior taxable year.

In *Arrowsmith*, the Supreme Court resolved a conflict that had arisen between the Courts of Appeals for the Second and Third Circuits regarding the character of amounts paid by shareholders of a liquidated corporation to creditors of the corporation. In each case, the shareholders of a corporation had reported a long-term capital gain on the liquidation. In a later year, a judgment was obtained against the corporation, and the shareholders were required to make payment to the corporation's creditors.

The issue was whether the payment made by the shareholders was deductible as an ordinary loss or a capital loss. The Court of Appeals for the Second Circuit held in *Arrowsmith* that the shareholders could only deduct their payments as a long-term capital loss, since these liabilities represented the diminution of the capital gain received on the prior liquidating distributions. The court determined that the annual accounting concept did not prevent such a conclusion. On the other hand, in *Commissioner v. Switlik*,[114] under substantially identical facts, the Court of Appeals for the Third Circuit held that the repayments were not capital losses but ordinary expenses. The court concluded that the shareholders' payments did not represent losses from the sale or exchange of capital assets, regardless of the fact that the liability of the shareholders as transferees resulted from the liquidating distributions that had been reported as capital gain.

In *Arrowsmith*, the Supreme Court held that the payments by the

---

[111] Albert J. Uhlenbrock, 67 TC 818 (1977).

[112] Treas. Reg. § 1.1341-1(h).

[113] Arrowsmith v. Comm'r, 344 US 6, aff'g 193 F2d 734 (2d Cir. 1952).

[114] Comm'r v. Switlik, 184 F2d 299 (3d Cir. 1950).

shareholders were so integrally associated with the prior capital gains that they must be treated as falling within the definition of "capital losses." The Court stated that it was "plain that their [the shareholders'] liability as transferees was not based on any ordinary business transaction of theirs apart from the liquidation proceedings."[115] If the losses had been incurred in the year of the distributions, they would have reduced the amount of capital gains to the shareholders. The Court stated that although the annual accounting concept requires that each taxable year be treated as a separate unit for tax accounting purposes, this principle does not prevent the events in one year from being characterized on the basis of events that occurred in earlier years. Such an approach does not violate the annual accounting principle because it does not reopen or change the prior tax returns, an action that would be inconsistent with the principle.[116]

Despite this analysis, it should be noted that in *Burnet v. Sanford & Brooks Co.*,[117] where the Supreme Court first articulated the annual accounting concept, application of the concept had the effect of denying the taxpayer's attempt to characterize the receipts of one year as nontaxable returns of capital on the basis of losses incurred in prior years. As this suggests, application of the doctrine may depend on the ingenuity of the taxpayers or the courts in showing the equity of applying the doctrine. In any event, taxpayers should not automatically assume that the doctrine will be applied in novel circumstances where there is a lack of directly applicable precedent.

[1] Scope

Pursuant to the principle enunciated in *Arrowsmith*, where a sale or exchange in one year is followed by a return of all or some portion of the amount received in the earlier transaction, the character of the gain or loss on the return transaction will be based on the character of the gain or loss on the earlier transaction. Therefore, despite the annual accounting concept, events in one year may determine the character of gain or loss in a later year where the later gain or loss is attributable to events that are integrally related to the events of the earlier year. The exact parameters of this doctrine have posed troublesome questions, and there are relatively few cases.

A broad reading was given to *Arrowsmith* in *United States v. Skelly Oil Co.*,[118] where a natural gas producer made refunds to its customers for excess charges received in prior years. In its returns for the prior years, the taxpayer

---

[115] Arrowsmith v. Comm'r, 344 US 6, 8 (1952).

[116] Id. at 8–9.

[117] Burnet v. Sanford & Brooks Co., 282 US 359 (1931). See discussion supra ¶ 12.02.

[118] United States v. Skelly Oil Co., 394 US 678 (1969).

had included these excess amounts in income and had calculated its oil and gas depletion allowance accordingly. In the year of the refunds, the taxpayer deducted the total amount refunded without an adjustment for the prior effect of the depletion allowance. The IRS sought to reduce the amount of the deduction for refunds by the related depletion allowance taken in the prior returns. The Supreme Court upheld the IRS. Despite the annual accounting concept, the Court agreed to limit the taxpayer's deduction in the subsequent period based on the favorable tax treatment accorded the receipts in the earlier years. The Court stated:

> [T]he annual accounting concept does not require us to close our eyes to what happened in prior years. For instance, it is well settled that the prior year may be examined to determine whether the repayment gives rise to a regular loss or a capital loss. *Arrowsmith v. Commissioner*, 344 U.S. 6 (1952). The rationale for the Arrowsmith rule is easy to see; if money was taxed at a special lower rate when received, the taxpayer would be accorded an unfair tax windfall if repayments were generally deductible from receipts taxable at the higher rate applicable to ordinary income.[119]

The language of *Skelly Oil* is quite broad. Nevertheless, proper application of the *Arrowsmith* principle is often a most difficult determination. Most of the difficulty relates to whether the relationship between the transactions in the earlier and later periods is sufficiently close to warrant application of the doctrine. There are no specified conditions that must be satisfied in order to establish the requisite relationship. Instead, the relationship is often dependent on the flexibility of the courts to achieve the result they seek.

This process is well illustrated by decisions involving a taxpayer's deduction for payments required by reason of violations of Section 16(b) of the Securities Exchange Act of 1934, which prohibits the buying and selling of a corporation's stock by an insider within a six-month period. In *Mitchell v. Commissioner*,[120] the taxpayer, a vice-president of General Motors Corporation, sold shares of General Motors common stock and reported long-term capital gain. The taxpayer subsequently repurchased a significant portion of the same type of shares under a restricted stock option. General Motors advised the taxpayer that in its opinion, the taxpayer's actions were in violation of Section 16(b) and, as a consequence, required him to pay the profit to the corporation. Although not admitting liability, the taxpayer remitted the profit to the corporation in settlement of his alleged violation. The taxpayer claimed an ordinary and necessary business expense deduction for the amount of his payment.

---

[119] Id. at 685.

[120] Mitchell v. Comm'r, 428 F2d 259 (6th Cir. 1970), rev'g 52 TC 170 (1969), cert. denied, 401 US 909 (1971).

The IRS recharacterized the deduction as a long-term capital loss. The Tax Court held to the contrary, stating that the payment was deductible as a business expense, since it was made to avoid (1) injury to the taxpayer's business reputation; (2) embarrassment to General Motors and himself; and (3) the expense of possible future litigation.[121] The Tax Court rejected the Commissioner's argument that the *Arrowsmith* doctrine limited the taxpayer to a capital loss deduction. The Tax Court stated that "the underlying element in the *Arrowsmith* line of case law is the existence of an integral relationship between two taxable transactions in separate years, so the characterization of the latter transaction by the earlier one is necessary in order to reflect the true income of the taxpayer."[122] The Tax Court concluded that this requisite integral relationship was lacking.

On appeal, the Court of Appeals for the Sixth Circuit reversed. The appeals court noted that the decision of the Tax Court did not cite *Skelly Oil*, which had just been decided. The appeals court concluded that if the Tax Court had considered *Skelly Oil* it would have applied the *Arrowsmith* doctrine and held that the amount paid by the taxpayer should have been treated as a capital loss.

Nevertheless, in *James E. Anderson*,[123] the Tax Court was later faced with a substantially identical issue involving another Section 16(b) violation. The Court held that *Arrowsmith* was not applicable and that the taxpayer was entitled to an ordinary and necessary business expense deduction. The court stated that

> *Arrowsmith* and *Skelly Oil* are both distinguishable, because the payment in *James E. Anderson* was not directly and integrally related to the earlier sale transaction which gave rise to the capital gain and because the status of petitioner in making the payment differed from that which he had at the time such gain was realized.[124]

On appeal, the Tax Court was again reversed; the court of appeals holding that application of the *Arrowsmith* doctrine did not require that the purpose of the taxpayer's payment "be rooted in the exclusively identical capacity in which the profit was realized. . . ."[125] The decisions of the appeals courts in these cases suggest that taxpayer motivations for the later transaction are not determinative. On the other hand, they certainly may be relevant.

[2] Applications

The *Arrowsmith* doctrine is not restricted to a factual scenario where the earlier transaction involved a gain and the later one a loss. The doctrine also

---

[121] Mitchell v. Comm'r, 52 TC 170 (1969).

[122] Id. at 175.

[123] James E. Anderson, 56 TC 1370 (1971), rev'd, 480 F2d 1304 (7th Cir. 1973).

[124] James E. Anderson, 56 TC at 1375.

[125] James E. Anderson, 480 F2d at 1308.

may be applied where a loss is followed by a gain or where both transactions involve gain or loss. In other words, the doctrine may be applied in any case where a sufficient nexus is found between the assertedly related transactions.

[a] Initial Gain—Later Loss

The majority of cases that have applied the *Arrowsmith* doctrine have involved a taxable or tax-free gain in one year with a related loss in a subsequent year. The circumstances associated with the related transactions have been quite varied. They have included (1) a tax-free exchange of property followed by the transferor's payment of a judgment for misrepresenting the condition of the property;[126] (2) a sale of property followed by an acceptance of a lower sales price, but at an earlier date than originally agreed;[127] (3) the return of a portion of the selling price because of the failure of the property sold to produce specified levels of income;[128] and (4) payments to settle suits brought against the taxpayer on account of sales made by him in earlier years.[129]

---

[126] See Rees Blow Pipe Mfg. Co., 41 TC 598 (1964), aff'd per curiam, 342 F2d 990 (9th Cir. 1965), where the taxpayer entered into an agreement with two other corporations for a three-way exchange of properties. The taxpayer was subsequently sued for misrepresentation regarding the condition of the property it had transferred and was required to pay a judgment of $20,000. The taxpayer claimed an ordinary deduction for this payment. The IRS contended that the payment was capital in nature and should be added to the adjusted basis of the property received in the exchange, but the Tax Court held that the payment was a capital loss under the *Arrowsmith* rationale. See also John E. Turco, 52 TC 631 (1969), where the taxpayer sold property at a capital gain. The taxpayer later made payments to correct certain defects in the property it had sold. The court held that the later payments had to be treated as capital losses under *Arrowsmith*.

[127] See Joe M. Smith, 48 TC 872 (1967), aff'd in part, rev'd in part, 424 F2d 219 (9th Cir. 1970), where the taxpayer's corporation reported a long-term capital gain on a sale of timberland. Under the terms of the sale, the purchaser had an option to prepay the balance due at an 18 percent discount. The purchaser exercised the option, and the corporation claimed the discount as an ordinary expense. The Commissioner argued that the discount was deductible only as a capital loss, and the court agreed.

[128] See Federal Bulk Carriers, Inc., 66 TC 283 (1976), aff'd, 558 F2d 128 (2d Cir. 1977), where the taxpayer sold stock in a corporation whose future earnings were guaranteed by the taxpayer. The earnings of the corporation failed to reach the guaranteed level, and the taxpayer sustained a loss equal to the difference between actual earnings and guaranteed earnings. The court held that the loss represented an adjustment to the sales price and had to be treated as a capital loss under *Arrowsmith*.

[129] See George Eisler, 59 TC 634 (1973), acq. 1973-2 CB 1, where a portion of a payment made by the taxpayer to settle a suit was found to relate to stock that the taxpayer had previously sold at a capital gain. The court held that a proportionate amount of the settlement payment and related legal fees had to be treated as a capital loss. In Paul H. Smith, 67 TC 570 (1976), the taxpayer sold unregistered stock and reported a long-term capital gain. Subsequently, a class action was brought against

[b] Initial Loss—Later Gain

The *Arrowsmith* doctrine is equally applicable to a taxpayer who realizes a loss in one year followed by a related gain in a subsequent year.[130] For example, it has been applied (1) to determine the character of gain on a sale of loans previously deducted as worthless;[131] (2) to a recovery of a debt previously deducted as worthless;[132] and (3) to a recovery in settlement of an antitrust action following a loss on the sale of business property.[133] In effect, the courts have concluded that determination of the appropriate tax treatment of the later transaction must be made on the basis of all the circumstances affecting the earlier, related transaction. As the Tax Court has said, it is "immaterial whether such a result favors the taxpayer or the government."[134]

[c] Initial Gain—Later Gain

It is relatively rare for a taxpayer to recognize gain on a closed transaction and then, in a related transaction in a later year, receive additional gain that should be characterized under the *Arrowsmith* doctrine. Nevertheless, to the extent such circumstances have been the subject of litigation, the *Arrowsmith* doctrine has been applied.

---

the taxpayer for alleged violations of the securities laws. Payments made in settlement of the suits were deducted by the taxpayer as ordinary losses. The Commissioner disallowed the ordinary losses, arguing that they were long-term capital losses. The court agreed because the settlement payments were directly related to the prior sale of stock.

[130] Justice Jackson, in his dissent in *Arrowsmith*, observed this very point:

Suppose that subsequent to liquidation it is found that a corporation has undisclosed claims instead of liabilities and that under applicable state law they must be prosecuted for the benefit of the stockholders. The logic of the Court's decision here, if adhered to, would result in a lesser return to the government than if the recoveries were considered ordinary income.

Arrowsmith v. Comm'r, 344 US 6, 11–12 (1952).

[131] Merchants Nat'l Bank v. Comm'r, 199 F2d 657 (5th Cir. 1952).

[132] See Carroll L. Deely, 73 TC 1081 (1980), where the taxpayer suffered a loss from a nonbusiness bad debt and reported a short-term capital loss. When the debt was subsequently paid, the court ruled it should be reported by the taxpayer as a short-term capital gain, since that was the converse of the earlier reporting.

[133] See David Bresler, 65 TC 182 (1975), acq. 1976-2 CB 1, where the taxpayer reported an ordinary loss incurred on the sale of property used in his trade or business. The taxpayer subsequently received $150,000 in settlement of an antitrust proceeding against a competitor for alleged violations of various federal antitrust provisions. The Tax Court held that the recovery was ordinary income on the basis of *Arrowsmith*.

[134] Id. at 186–187. See also Rev. Rul. 79-278, 1979-2 CB 302, where the taxpayer incurred a short-term capital loss on the sale of stock. The taxpayer then sued the issuer of the stock for violations of federal securities laws and was awarded a partial recovery. The recovery was taxed as a short-term capital gain.

For example, in *Alvin B. Lowe*,[135] a taxpayer sold shares of stock at a gain to a purchaser who made a down payment and issued a promissory note for the balance of the purchase price. The taxpayer retained the stock as security. The purchaser subsequently defaulted. Following negotiations between the two, the taxpayer retained the stock and $22,500 of the amount that had been paid on the purchase price. The IRS contended that this amount should have been reported as ordinary income. However, the Tax Court held on the basis of the *Arrowsmith* doctrine that the gain was capital. The opposite conclusion has been reached where the initial transaction did not amount to a completed sale. In *Harold S. Smith*,[136] the taxpayers entered into a contract to sell shares of stock in a gambling casino. A deposit was put into escrow by the buyer. The buyer subsequently defaulted, the taxpayers retained the deposit, and the buyer sued to recover it. The parties subsequently settled the case, and the taxpayers retained a portion of the deposit. The Tax Court held that the amount received by the taxpayers under the settlement was taxable as ordinary income and not as capital gain from a sale of capital assets. The court distinguished *Alvin B. Lowe* on the basis that that case involved a completed sale, whereas in *Smith*, there was no completed sale but only an executory contract.[137]

[d] Initial Loss—Later Loss

The *Arrowsmith* doctrine is also applicable where a taxpayer who has realized a loss in one year incurs a related loss in a subsequent year. For example, in *Commissioner v. Adam, Meldrum & Anderson Co.*,[138] the taxpayer owned stock in a bank. The stock became worthless, and the taxpayer claimed a capital loss. Certain statutory liability was subsequently imposed on all holders of the bank's stock. The taxpayer reported as an ordinary loss the sums paid in settlement of its liability. The court held that the payments made on account of the statutory liability should be treated as an additional cost of the stock and, hence, as an additional capital loss. Similarly, in *Wener v. Commissioner*,[139] the taxpayers, who were members of a limited partnership, sold their interests in the partnership to the remaining partners, with

---

[135] Alvin B. Lowe, 44 TC 363, 374 (1965), acq. 1966-1 CB 2, where the Court stated "although this is the first case in which we have considered a gain rather than a loss, we found nothing in *Arrowsmith* to make the principle enumerated therein inapplicable to a gain."

[136] Harold S. Smith, 50 TC 273 (1968), aff'd per curiam, 418 F2d 573 (9th Cir. 1969).

[137] See also Ralph A. Boatman, 32 TC 1188 (1959); Binns v. United States, 385 F2d 159 (6th Cir. 1967), to the same effect.

[138] Comm'r v. Adam, Meldrum & Anderson Co., 215 F2d 163 (2d Cir. 1954), cert. denied, 348 US 913 (1955).

[139] Wener v. Comm'r, 242 F2d 938 (9th Cir. 1957).

the purchase price to be paid in installments. The taxpayers reported a capital loss. The purchasing partners later agreed with the taxpayers to pay them a lesser amount in lieu of the installments still owed. The taxpayers claimed the difference between the balance due and the lesser amount as an ordinary loss. Based on the *Arrowsmith* doctrine, the court held that the difference was a long-term capital loss because it was integrally related to the original sale and, in effect, was a reduction in the original price.

[3] Inapplicability of Doctrine

The *Arrowsmith* doctrine is generally applicable only where there is an integral relationship between the transactions at issue. The requisite relationship has been found not to exist in a number of situations, including the treatment of an employer's reimbursement of his employee's loss on an investment recommended by the employer,[140] the payment of legal fees from the proceeds of a sale of stock,[141] the government's attempt to reallocate the consideration received upon a sale of related properties,[142] and the taxpayer's transfer to the seller of property originally acquired from the seller.[143]

[4] Statutory Relief: Section 1341

Section 1341 was enacted to provide relief in a situation where the taxpayer's deduction in a later year does not reduce its tax liability by the same amount

---

[140] See Avery R. Schiller, 43 BTA 594 (1941), where the Tax Court held that the recovery constituted ordinary income, since the payment was not made in consideration for the transfer of title to the stock.

[141] Estate of A.P. Steckel, 26 TC 600 (1956), aff'd, 253 F2d 267 (6th Cir. 1958).

[142] See Arthur F. Brook, 28 TCM 1240 (1969), where the taxpayer sold rights under two contracts. The taxpayer elected the installment method of reporting and, in 1955, received $20,000, which he reported as long-term capital gain. The taxpayer should have reported $4,000 as long-term capital gain and the $16,000 as short-term capital gain. Correction of this error was subsequently barred by the statute of limitations. In later years, the Commissioner attempted to correct the error by reallocating the purchase price between the respective contracts on the basis of the *Arrowsmith* doctrine. The court held for the taxpayer, stating that the *Arrowsmith* doctrine related to situations where a taxpayer reports an item in one year and, subsequently, as the result of later events, must take further action with respect to that same item. The instant case was found to involve only one event, i.e., the sale of the two contracts.

[143] See Bertram H. Slater, 64 TC 571 (1975), where in order to be released from a covenant not to compete, a taxpayer transferred to his former employer certain rights and stock that he had acquired at a bargain price from that employer. The taxpayer attempted to claim an ordinary loss on his transfer on the basis that he had reported the bargain element of his acquisition as ordinary income. The court found that the taxpayer's loss was not integrally related to the circumstances under which he had acquired the stock, and, as a consequence, there was no basis for applying the *Arrowsmith* doctrine.

that its tax liability was increased in the earlier year, when a related amount was included in income.[144] The benefits of Section 1341 are also available to repayments subject to application of the *Arrowsmith* doctrine.[145]

¶ 12.05 TAX BENEFIT RULE

The tax benefit rule is another response to inequities arising from strict application of the annual accounting concept. Although codified in Section 111, the rule is essentially one of judicial origin and development, which the courts and the IRS continue to apply and interpret in new factual circumstances.

The tax benefit rule provides that where an item deducted in one year is subsequently recovered, that recovery must be included in income except to the extent that no tax benefit resulted from the prior deduction.[146] Accordingly, the rule is one of both inclusion and exclusion.[147] It benefits the government by including amounts in income that otherwise might be excluded. It benefits the taxpayer by limiting the inclusion to the amount of deduction for which the taxpayer obtained a prior tax benefit.

[1] History and Rationale

The tax benefit rule first appeared in a Treasury regulation as early as 1914.[148] It was later accepted by the courts, apparently on the basis of its inherent equity.[149] The courts quickly accepted the reasonableness of the rule without

---

[144] See supra ¶ 12.03[4] for a discussion of Section 1341.

[145] "This section [Section 1341] will apply to cases of transferee liability such as *Arrowsmith v. Commissioner* (344 US 6 (1952)). Thus, while the deduction in the current year is capital in nature, the taxpayer is not the deprived of all relief because his tax is reduced at least to the extent of the tax attributable to the prior inclusion." H.R. Rep. No. 1337, 83d Cong., 2d Sess. A294 (1954).

[146] Section 111(a) provides: "Gross income does not include income attributable to the recovery during the taxable year of any amount deducted in any prior taxable year to the extent such amount did not reduce the amount of tax imposed by this chapter."

[147] See Putoma Corp., 66 TC 652, 664 n.10 (1976), aff'd, 601 F2d 734 (5th Cir. 1978), where the court stated that since the enactment of Section 111, the tax benefit rule has been "both a rule of inclusion and exclusion: recovery of an item previously deducted must be *included* in income; that portion of the recovery not resulting in a prior tax benefit is *excluded*." (Emphasis by court.)

[148] See Reg. § 33, art. 125 (1914), relating to recovery of bad debts.

[149] See Excelsior Printing Co., 16 BTA 886 (1929); and Putnam Nat'l Bank v. Comm'r, 50 F2d 158 (5th Cir. 1931), where the court stated that the rule "seems to be taken for granted, as indeed it must be."

articulating a consistent rationale for it. They often explained their application of the rule with conclusory remarks (such as that it is a principle "taken for granted") or espoused theories that varied from case to case, depending on the facts.[150]

The Tax Court has stated that in its true character, the rule serves as a necessary counterweight to the annual accounting concept.[151] Under the annual accounting concept, the flow of economic activity is divided into segments for tax purposes. It is recognized that such segmentation is artificial and that inequities may result. The tax benefit rule addresses one such inequity: that which arises when a deduction is taken in one taxable period and then later events suggest that that deduction would not have been taken if all facts relevant to the transaction had been known at the time of the deduction.[152]

Thus, the tax benefit rule is necessary to ensure that taxpayers do not unduly profit from the annual accounting principle. Deductions taken in earlier years must be restored to income if and when the deducted amount is recovered. In theory, the recovery in the later year stands in the place of that portion of the gross income that was not taxed in the earlier year.[153] Application of the rule is limited to cases in which the deduction and recovery are so interrelated that they are considered integral parts of essentially one transaction.[154]

---

[150] See, e.g., National Bank of Commerce of Seattle v. Comm'r, 115 F2d 875 (9th Cir. 1940), prior deduction converts repayment of debt to income although usually a return of capital; repayment stands in place of previously untaxed income; Grace M. Barnett, 39 BTA 864 (1939), espousing "balancing item" theory—recovery taxed to bring taxpayer's income over a period in balance with actual income for the period; Philadelphia Nat'l Bank v. Rothensies, 43 F. Supp. 923 (ED Pa. 1942), estoppel or waiver theory—prior deduction imports "implied consent" to be taxed on future recovery.

[151] Estate of David B. Munter, 63 TC 663 (1975) (Tannenwald, J., concurring).

[152] In his concurring opinion in the *Munter* case, Judge Tannenwald stated:

> The need to assess and collect taxes at fixed and relatively short intervals underpins the principle of taxation that transactions which may possibly be subject to further developments substantially altering their character for tax purposes should nevertheless be treated as final and closed so that their tax consequences can be determined. [Citations omitted.] On the other hand, a taxpayer should not be permitted to take advantage of this governmental exigency to establish a distorted picture of his income for tax purposes. It is this countervailing consideration which spawned the tax benefit rule. [Citations omitted.] The most common, and most nearly accurate, explanation of the rule is that it recognizes the 'recovery' in the current year of taxable income earned in an earlier year but offset by the item deducted.

Id. at 678.

[153] See Dobson v. Comm'r, 320 US 489 (1943).

[154] Merton E. Farr, 11 TC 552 (1948), aff'd sub nom. Sloane v. Comm'r, 188 F2d 254 (6th Cir. 1951).

[2] Definition of "Recovery"

Application of the tax benefit rule is premised on a recovery of a previously deducted item. Over the years, a conflict emerged between jurisdictions that required an actual recovery of cash or other property and jurisdictions that defined "recovery" to include not only an actual recovery but also an event that was inconsistent with the earlier deduction.[155]

This dispute was resolved by the Supreme Court in *Hillsboro National Bank v. Commissioner*,[156] where the Court made it clear that the taxpayer need not recover any actual cash or property for the tax benefit rule to apply. Rather, the rule will apply whenever there has been a later event that is "fundamentally inconsistent" with an earlier deduction.[157] The Court emphasized that the purpose of the tax benefit rule is "to approximate the results produced by a tax system based on transactional rather than annual accounting,"[158] and in so doing "to protect the Government and the taxpayer from the adverse effects of reporting a transaction on the basis of assumptions that an [unforeseen] event in a subsequent year proves to have been erroneous."[159] However, the Court noted that not every unforeseen event would require application of the rule. Rather, the tax benefit rule will cancel out the earlier deduction only when the later event is shown to be fundamentally inconsistent with the premise on which the deduction was initially based. In other words, if the later event had occurred within the same taxable year as the initial event, would it have foreclosed the deduction?[160]

The Court then provided two examples of unforeseen events that generated a tax benefit, but noted that only one was fundamentally inconsistent with the earlier deduction. In each example, a calendar-year taxpayer made a rental payment on December 15 for a 30-day lease deductible in the current year under Section 162(a)(3). In the first situation, the leased premises were destroyed by fire on January 10, an event not fundamentally inconsistent with the prior deduction, according to the Court, because the

---

[155] Compare, e.g., Tennessee Carolina Transp., Inc. v. Comm'r, 582 F2d 378 (6th Cir. 1978), aff'g 65 TC 440 (1975), cert. denied, 440 US 909 (1979), where an actual recovery was not required, with Comm'r v. South Lake Farms, 324 F2d 837 (9th Cir. 1963), aff'g 36 TC 1027 (1961), where an actual recovery was required.

[156] Hillsboro Nat'l Bank v. Comm'r, 460 US 370 (1983).

[157] *Hillsboro Nat'l Bank*'s "fundamentally inconsistent" standard is seemingly consistent with standards applied by some courts almost 50 years earlier. See, e.g., Estate of William H. Block, 39 BTA 338, 341 (1939), aff'd sub nom. Union Trust Co. v. Comm'r, 111 F2d 60 (7th Cir. 1940), cert. denied, 311 US 658 (1940): "When recovery or some other event which is inconsistent with what has been done in the past occurs, adjustment must be made in reporting income for the year in which the change occurs."

[158] Hillsboro Nat'l Bank v. Comm'r, 460 US 370, 381 (1983).

[159] Id. at 383.

[160] Id. at 383–384.

loss was attributable to the business. In the second situation, the leased premises were converted to personal use. The Court stated that this was an event fundamentally inconsistent with the prior deduction. Similarly, in the first situation, if some provision in the lease allowed the taxpayer a refund of his rental payment, then retaining the benefits of the deduction would be fundamentally inconsistent. Thus, as the Court emphasized, "A court must consider the facts and circumstances of each case in the light of the purpose and function of the provisions granting the deductions."[161]

An interesting question arose in *Hudspeth v. Commissioner*,[162] where shareholders of an S corporation reduced their bases in stock and bonds as a result of their share of the S corporation's loss. However, the shareholders did not receive the full benefit of this loss in either the year it was incurred by the S corporation or in succeeding years. Thereafter, when the S corporation's bonds were redeemed, the taxpayers sought to benefit from the tax benefit rule by increasing the basis of their debt to the extent they had not received a prior benefit from their share of the S corporation's losses. The court rejected the taxpayer's position. The court explained that the later redemption was not fundamentally inconsistent with the prior reductions in the basis of the debt. The court also noted that the taxpayer's position would result in an effective carry-forward of the loss beyond the periods then specified in Section 172, and the adjustments required in the bases of the stock and debt were expressly required under Section 1376.

[3] Amount of Recovery

Originally, the tax benefit rule required that the full amount of all recoveries be included in taxable income.[163] Taxpayers nevertheless argued that a recovery should be taxed only if the deduction actually reduced tax liability in the earlier year, but not otherwise. This argument was eventually accepted by Congress in 1942 by enacting the predecessor to present Section 111, which excludes from gross income the recovery of previously deducted items if the deduction did not result in a reduction of the taxpayer's tax in the applicable prior year.[164] Although Section 111 originally accorded this treatment explicitly to only a recovery of previously deducted bad debts, taxes, and delinquency amounts, the tax benefit rule had been applied in this manner by the courts and regulations to virtually all items,[165] and the statute

---

[161] Id. at 385.

[162] Hudspeth v. Comm'r, 914 F2d 1207 (9th Cir. 1990).

[163] See Lake View Trust & Sav. Bank, 27 BTA 290 (1932), where the Board held that the recovery of debts, which were previously charged off as worthless, was taxable even though the prior deduction did not reduce tax.

[164] IRC § 111.

[165] See Dobson v. Comm'r, 320 US 489, 506 (1943); Treas. Reg. § 1.111-1(a).

was amended for amounts recovered after December 31, 1983, to apply broadly to all items.[166]

Limiting the amount of the recovery to the amount of the deduction that reduced the earlier liability for tax does not provide complete equity. If tax rates change from the year of deduction to the year of recovery, or if they stay the same but the taxpayer's tax bracket is different in the two years, the overall transaction will produce either a taxable gain or loss to the taxpayer even though there has been no substantive transactional gain or loss. For example, assume a bad debt of $100 is deducted in a year in which the taxpayer's effective tax rate is 40 percent but is recovered and taxed in a year in which his effective rate is 50 percent (either because he has more taxable income or because tax rates have increased). The rate change will cost the taxpayer $10 as a result of the transaction ($40 reduction in tax offset by $50 increase in tax) even though the taxpayer actually suffered no net gain or loss from the transaction.[167]

[4] Established Applications of Rule

The tax benefit rule potentially applies to any fact situation in which a taxpayer claims a deduction from income. Nevertheless, certain recurring fact patterns have given rise to established judicial applications of the rule, and Congress has codified the tax benefit rule, initially as it applied to specific items of income and deduction and later to all items.

[a] Judicial Applications

[i] Previously expensed items. The most common judicial application of the rule is to items expensed in one year and actually recovered in a subsequent year. For example, the courts have held that (1) a refund of prepaid interest was income in the year of receipt when the taxpayer had taken an interest deduction in a prior year;[168] (2) an amount received by a flight engineer from his employer in a grievance settlement (relating to per diem expenses already deducted by the engineer) was includable in income when received;[169] (3) a return to a corporate employer of bonuses previously

---

[166] IRC § 111(a).

[167] The Court of Claims initially held that the rule required the taxpayer merely to repay the taxes previously saved—in effect, a true transactional approach—but the court subsequently overruled this prior decision on the ground that statutory authority for it was lacking. Perry v. United States, 160 F. Supp. 270 (Ct. Cl. 1958), overruled by Alice Phelan Sullivan Corp. v. United States, 381 F2d 399 (Ct. Cl. 1967).

[168] Allen D. Unvert, 72 TC 807 (1979), aff'd, 656 F2d 483 (9th Cir. 1981), cert. denied, 456 US 961 (1982).

[169] John C. Giordano, 36 TCM 430 (1977).

paid and deducted (the return being part of the recovery in a shareholders' derivative suit) had to be recognized as income under the tax benefit rule;[170] and (4) proceeds from a sale of previously expensed items had to be included in income.[171] Consequently, whenever the taxpayer recovers an amount that was previously expensed or receives a direct economic benefit on a distribution of items previously deducted, the tax benefit rule may be applicable.[172]

[ii] Charitable contributions returned. Courts have consistently applied the tax benefit rule in instances where property donated is later returned. The rule requires that the amount of a charitable contribution deduction taken for property donated in the earlier year be included in the donor's income in the year in which the donee returns the property.[173] This rule applies if (1) the donee simply reconveys the property to the donor;[174] (2) the property is returned to the donor consistent with a clause in the original transfer that requires the return of the property if not used for a particular purpose;[175] or (3) the property is transferred by the donee to a third party at the request of the donor.[176]

One way the taxpayer can offset the recognition of income is by redonating the property to another charity. In this situation, the IRS has ruled that the taxpayer must report the income received under the tax benefit rule but may concurrently deduct the new contribution just as it would any charitable contribution.[177] The IRS would not allow the taxpayer to

---

[170] Larchfield Corp., 373 F2d 159 (2d Cir. 1966).

[171] Estate of David B. Munter, 63 TC 663 (1975). See Byrd v. Comm'r, 829 F2d 119 (4th Cir. 1987), where the court applied the tax benefit rule to include in the income of former S corporation shareholders the value of previously expensed plants following a sale of the shareholders' stock to a partnership that immediately liquidated the corporation and distributed its assets.

[172] But see James A. Allan, 86 TC 655 (1986), where the taxpayer accrued and deducted his obligation for real estate taxes and interest relating to certain property. The mortgagee advanced funds to cover these liabilities and increased loan principal by the amount of the advances. Ultimately, the mortgagee obtained a deed in lieu of foreclosure. The taxpayer reported the excess of the loan obligation over adjusted basis as capital gain pursuant to Comm'r v. Tufts, 461 US 300 (1983). The IRS wanted that portion of the excess representing previously deducted interest and taxes to be ordinary income under the tax benefit rule. The court held for the taxpayer, explaining that the entire loan obligation represents the amount realized on the sale or exchange and that no part of this amount was subject to bifurcation in order to apply the tax benefit rule.

[173] Alice Phelan Sullivan Corp. v. United States, 381 F2d 399 (Ct. Cl. 1967).

[174] Rosen v. Comm'r, 611 F2d 942 (1st Cir. 1980).

[175] Alice Phelan Sullivan Corp. v. United States, 381 F2d 399 (Ct. Cl. 1967).

[176] Rev. Rul. 54-566, 54-2 CB 96.

[177] Rev. Rul. 76-150, 76-1 CB 38, cash donations to a charitable organization over a period of years that are repaid to the taxpayer and redonated to another

simply roll over the original contribution. Thus, if the taxpayer's effective tax rate changes from the time of the original deduction to the later deduction, the two transactions may not cancel out, and the taxpayer may realize a net taxable benefit or detriment.

[iii] **Casualty losses.** The tax benefit rule also applies to a recovery of casualty and other losses. Generally, such losses are deductible only if and to the extent that they are not compensated by insurance or otherwise.[178] If the right to compensation is unknown, contested, or otherwise doubtful during the taxable year of damage, the taxpayer is entitled to deduct the loss when it occurs but must include any subsequent recovery in income.[179] Thus, the amount of a special disaster relief condemnation award for the value of a home that had been destroyed by flood was held includable in income to the extent of the tax benefit realized from casualty loss deductions previously taken.[180] The court held that this result was required even though the taxpayers had satisfied all requirements to defer gain on an involuntary conversion under Section 1033. In effect, the court held that the tax benefit rule overrode the nonrecognition provision of Section 1033 and, hence, that only the gain in excess of the prior deductions could be deferred under Section 1033. The IRS has issued numerous rulings applying these principles to particular disasters and relief mechanisms.[181]

[iv] **Reimbursed losses.** To the extent a loss deduction provides a tax benefit when taken, recoupment of the loss by way of repayment, suit, or settlement is taxable in the year of recovery. Thus, where taxpayers claimed loss deductions resulting from stock sales, contract overruns, bank stock assessments, worthlessness of oil ventures and partnership interests, and insurance subrogation, the tax benefit rule required the recovery of the loss to

---

charitable organization in the same year are, to the extent a tax benefit was derived from deductions claimed in prior years, includable in gross income in the year of recovery; however, the repaid funds donated to the other organizations are considered a charitable contribution.

[178] IRC § 165(a).

[179] Paul Birnbaum, 37 TCM 1775 (1978); Herman E. Londagin, 61 TC 117 (1973); Lee R. Chronister, 32 TCM 1108 (1973); John E. Montgomery, 65 TC 511 (1976).

[180] Mager v. United States, 499 F. Supp. 37 (MD Pa. 1980), aff'd in unpublished opinion, (3d Cir. 1981).

[181] See, e.g., Rev. Rul. 75-28, 75-1 CB 68, special grant following deduction of loss from flood; Rev. Rul. 74-206, 74-1 CB 198, condemnation award following deduction of loss from flood; Rev. Rul. 73-408 73-2 CB 15, canceled portion of emergency loan to farmer; Rev. Rul. 71-161, 71-1 CB 76, reimbursement of cost of debris removal following casualty; Rev. Rul. 71-160, 71-1 CB 75, canceled portion of a so-called disaster loan.

be included in income to the extent the loss had produced a tax benefit when taken.[182]

[v] **Unpaid accrued expenses.** If an accrual basis taxpayer properly deducts an item when accrued but never actually pays the expense giving rise to the deduction, the taxpayer must restore the amount deducted to income when the obligation to pay the expense is extinguished. In this case, the recovery that is subject to the rule is analogous to income arising from the cancellation of an indebtedness. This principle has been applied to a producer of natural gas who received tax benefits from the deduction of rate refunds ordered by the Federal Power Commission (FPC). The court held that the producer had taxable income in the year in which the FPC rescinded its order and the producer's liability to make refunds terminated.[183] The tax benefit rule has also been applied to the cancellation or other termination of an obligation to pay previously accrued interest[184] and taxes.[185]

[vi] **Accrued liabilities abandoned by creditor.** After issuing and deducting checks for such business expenses as wages, supplies, and customer overcharges, taxpayers often find that some checks are returned because the creditor cannot be found or because they are not cashed by the payee. Unless subject to a local escheat law, these unclaimed or abandoned amounts must be restored to income under the tax benefit rule.[186]

[vii] **Bad debt reserves.** A bad debt reserve reflects accumulated prior deductions. Therefore, the courts have required taxpayers to take the reserve

---

[182] Burnet v. Sanford & Brooks Co., 282 US 359 (1931), contract; Dobson v. Comm'r, 320 US 489 (1943), stock sales; Estate of Harriet A. Watson, 3 TCM 164 (1944), bank stock assessment; William T. Morris, 3 TCM 1 (1944), partnership interest; Lloyd H. Faidley, 8 TC 1170 (1947), oil venture; American Fin. Corp., 72 TC 506 (1979), insurance subrogation. But see Allstate Ins. Co. v. United States, 90-1 USTC ¶ 50,241 (1990), where the court distinguished *American Financial Corp.* on the basis that the parties in *American Financial Corp.* had stipulated that the amounts recovered were sufficiently related to the earlier deductions for which no tax benefit was claimed. The court found that no such relationship had been established by the plaintiff in *Allstate Insurance Co.* The court was also influenced by the fact that the tax benefit rule generally serves as a corrective measure for inconsistent and unexpected events. The court found the subrogation recoveries in *Allstate Insurance Co.* to have been foreseen and, therefore, not fundamentally inconsistent events.

[183] Mayfair Minerals, Inc., 456 F2d 622 (5th Cir. 1972).

[184] Rev. Rul. 58-546, 58-2 CB 143, tax benefit rule applicable to interest canceled on exchange of bonds in a recapitalization; Rev. Rul. 67-200, 67-1 CB 15, unpaid accrued interest that is canceled is subject to tax benefit rule and exclusionary rules of Section 108 regarding solvency of debtor. But see Putoma Corp., 601 F2d 734 (5th Cir. 1979), where shareholder's cancellation of corporation's obligation to pay interest, which it previously accrued and deducted, was a nontaxable capital contribution.

[185] 1180 E. 63rd St. Bldg. Corp., 12 TC 437 (1949).

[186] Roxy Custom Clothes Corp. v. United States, 171 F. Supp. 851 (Ct. Cl. 1959), income when accounts payable credited to eliminate liability; Lime Cola Co.,

into income if and when the reserve becomes unnecessary.[187] For example, if the taxpayer sells the related receivables, changes from the reserve method to a direct charge-off method, or changes its overall accounting method from accrual to cash, the balance of its bad debt reserve must be restored to income.[188] Consistently, as a result of the repeal of the reserve method of accounting for bad debts in the Tax Reform Act of 1986 (the 1986 Act), taxpayers were required to restore the amount of their reserves to income.[189]

[viii] Transfer of accounts receivable or other assets to controlled corporation.   As previously discussed, the balance of a bad debt reserve must be taken into income if and when the receivables to which the reserve relates are sold or otherwise disposed of. During the 1960s, a dispute arose whether this rule should be applied to a taxpayer who transferred accounts receivable to a controlled corporation in a transaction covered by Section 351. The IRS issued rulings requiring this result, and this view enjoyed some initial success in the courts.[190]

However, taxpayers were ultimately successful in persuading the courts that in applying the tax benefit rule, the net value of the receivables is the key factor. Thus, in *Estate of Schmidt*,[191] the court of appeals, reversing the lower court and agreeing with the taxpayer, held that the normal rule regarding bad debt reserves should not apply in a Section 351 transaction because such application ignores economic realities. The court explained that in a Section 351 exchange, the stock received represents the net value of the transferred assets, not the gross value; thus, there is no recovery, in an economic sense, of prior deductions. In its 1970 decision in *Nash v. United States*,[192] the Supreme Court adopted the Ninth Circuit's reasoning in *Estate of Schmidt*.

The *Nash* case established that the corporate organization and liquida-

---

22 TC 593 (1954), acq. 1955-2 CB 7, income when amount credited to surplus; G.M. Standifer Constr. Co., 30 BTA 184 (1934), acq. XIII-1 CB 15, income in year of settlement.

[187] The reserve method of accounting for bad debts was repealed as part of the 1986 Act. See Section 805(a) of that Act and discussion at ¶ 8.04[6][d].

[188] Arcadia Sav. & Loan Ass'n v. Comm'r, 300 F2d 247 (9th Cir. 1962), sale of business; S. Rossin & Sons, Inc. v. Comm'r, 113 F2d 652 (2d Cir. 1940), shift to specific charge-off method; see also Geyer, Cornell & Newell, Inc., 6 TC 96 (1946), acq. 1946-1 CB 2, abandonment of business; Robert F. Haynesworth, 68 TC 703 (1977), aff'd in unpublished opinion, (5th Cir. 1979), closing of subdivider's reserve for development expenses.

[189] See Section 805(a) of the 1986 Act and discussion at ¶ 8.04[6][d].

[190] See Rev. Rul. 62-128, 1962-2 CB 139, revoked by Rev. Rul. 78-280, 1978-2 CB 139; Estate of Schmidt, 42 TC 1130 (1964), rev'd, 355 F2d 111 (9th Cir. 1966); Max Schuster, 50 TC 98 (1968); Nash v. United States, 414 F2d 627 (5th Cir. 1969), rev'd, 398 US 1 (1970).

[191] Estate of Schmidt, 355 F2d 111 (9th Cir. 1966).

[192] Nash v. United States, 398 US 1 (1970).

tion nonrecognition provisions did not preclude application of the tax benefit rule. However, the Supreme Court limited its holding in *Nash* to situations
in which the value of the stock received equals the adjusted basis of the property transferred. In such a case, there is no net economic benefit or recovery
to the taxpayer. However, if the value of the stock exceeds the adjusted basis
of the property or other previously deducted items transferred in exchange
for the stock, both the courts and the IRS have held that the tax benefit rule
will apply to tax the recovery.[193] For example, if stock is issued for the full
value of receivables without regard to the associated bad debt reserve, or if
stock is issued in exchange for previously expensed items, the tax benefit rule
applies.

> EXAMPLE: Assume a business has $1 million in receivables and a cor-
> responding reserve for bad debts (prior to the repeal of the reserve meth-
> od) of $50,000. An exchange of the receivables for $950,000 of stock (or
> less) will result in no recovery; an exchange for $975,000 of stock will
> result in a $25,000 recovery; and an exchange for $1 million or more of
> stock will result in a $50,000 recovery.

[ix] **Corporate liquidations.**   Prior to the 1986 Act, the Tax Court had
held, in *D.B. Anders*,[194] that the tax benefit rule could not apply to override
the clear and unambiguous nonrecognition rule of Section 337 for preliquidation sales of property. However, the Tenth Circuit reversed the Tax Court,
holding that Section 337 (as it existed prior to the 1986 Act) did not bar
application of the tax benefit rule to tax the receipt of cash for items
previously expensed.[195] The IRS also prevailed on this issue in decisions
rendered by the Third Circuit, the Court of Claims, and certain district
courts.[196] The Tax Court finally accepted this result in *Estate of David B.
Munter*,[197] and held the tax benefit rule applicable to tax the consideration
received for expensed items in a preliquidation sale under then applicable
Section 337.[198]

---

[193] See Citizens Acceptance Corp. v. United States, 320 F. Supp. 798 (D. Del.
1970), rev'd on other grounds, 462 F2d 751 (3d Cir. 1972), following *Nash*, the excess
of consideration received over net value of receivables required to be taken into
income under tax benefit rule; and Rev. Rul. 78-280, 1978-2 CB 139, to the same
effect.

[194] D.B. Anders, 48 TC 815 (1967).

[195] D.B. Anders, 414 F2d 1283 (10th Cir. 1969), cert. denied, 396 US 958 (1969).

[196] Connery v. United States, 460 F2d 1130 (3d Cir. 1972); Anders v. United
States, 462 F2d 1147 (Ct. Cl. 1972), cert. denied, 409 US 1064 (1972); Evans v. United
States, 317 F. Supp. 423 (WD Ark. 1970); Krajeck v. United States, 75-1 USTC
¶ 9492 (DND 1975).

[197] Estate of David B. Munter, 63 TC 663 (1975).

[198] See also Altec Corp., 36 TCM 1795 (1977), for same result.

In Revenue Ruling 78-278,[199] the IRS applied the same rule to distributions in kind in subsidiary liquidations governed by then applicable Sections 336, 332, and 334(b)(2). Although extension of the *Nash* principle to a Section 337 transaction was relatively easy because that type of transaction involved a sale, extension of this same principle to a Section 331 or Section 332 liquidation was more difficult because Section 336 protected the liquidating corporation from recognizing gain or loss on a distribution of its assets.

In *South Lake Farms*,[200] the IRS failed in its first attempt to apply the tax benefit rule to a transaction covered by Section 336. A subsidiary distributed assets to its parent in a Section 332 liquidation in which basis was determined under then-applicable Section 334(b)(2). Some of the assets distributed had been expensed in prior years. Pursuant to Sections 332 and 334(b)(2), the parent reported no tax and took a basis in the assets equal to the part of the price that it paid for the subsidiary's stock. The government argued that the price of the stock depended, in part, on the value of these assets and that consequently, the subsidiary had "received an amount equivalent to, and sufficient to offset, the expenses it had incurred, and hence was no longer entitled to the 'tax benefit' of the deduction of these expenses."[201] The court rejected this contention, stating that a corporation and its shareholders are two distinct taxable entities. It considered any recovery to be received by the shareholder parent corporation, not by the subsidiary that had taken the earlier deduction. Therefore, the tax benefit rule did not apply. In effect, the court accepted the taxpayer's argument that only an actual recovery triggers the tax benefit rule; mere inconsistent events do not.

Fifteen years later, the IRS tried again and won. In *Tennessee Carolina Transportation, Inc.*,[202] the facts were almost identical to those in *South Lake Farms*. A subsidiary distributed expensed assets to its parent in a Section 332/334(b)(2) liquidation. The Tax Court adopted the IRS position, holding that the subsidiary had income to the extent of the lessor of (1) the fair market value of the expensed property distributed or (2) the portion of the cost of the property attributable to its remaining useful life on the date of distribution. The Sixth Circuit affirmed.

The Supreme Court ultimately resolved the issue in *Hillsboro National Bank v. Commissioner*,[203] where it held that the tax benefit rule not only applies where there is an actual recovery but also applies where there is an event that is fundamentally inconsistent with the prior deduction. The Court recognized that the purpose of the rule is not merely to tax recoveries but

---

[199] Rev. Rul. 78-278, 1978-2 CB 134.

[200] South Lake Farms, 324 F2d 837 (9th Cir. 1963), aff'g 36 TC 1027 (1961).

[201] South Lake Farms, 324 F2d at 839.

[202] Tennessee Carolina Transp., Inc., 582 F2d 378 (6th Cir. 1978), aff'g 65 TC 440 (1975), cert. denied, 404 US 909 (1979).

[203] Hillsboro Nat'l Bank v. Comm'r, 460 US 370 (1983).

also to achieve rough parity with transactional accounting and, hence, to correct deficiencies that otherwise would result from a strict application of the annual accounting concept. The Court explained that a fundamentally inconsistent event is one that is inconsistent with the basis of a deduction, not one that is merely unexpected or unanticipated. For example, if prepaid rent on business premises is deducted in one year, but the property is converted to personal use in the following year during this rental period, there is a tax benefit recovery. On the other hand, if the premises are destroyed by fire, there is a loss of use that is inconsistent with the initially anticipated use, but the tax benefit rule does not apply unless the fire allows the lessee to recover some portion of the rent from the lessor.[204]

[x] **Contributions to capital.** Courts have generally not applied the tax benefit rule to override statutory nonrecognition provisions afforded contributions to capital. For example, in *Hartland Associates*,[205] the Tax Court rejected the Commissioner's attempt to apply the rule to override the nonrecognition provisions of Section 118 on a shareholder's contribution to a corporation of accrued but unpaid interest that had previously been deducted by the corporation.[206] The corporation owed interest to its sole shareholder and the shareholder gratuitously canceled the obligation to improve the corporation's deteriorating financial position. The court relied on prior decisions for the proposition that a gratuitous forgiveness of an indebtedness is a gift that is not income to the debtor regardless of the prior deduction of the interest component.[207] In the case of forgiveness by a shareholder, the transaction is regarded as a capital contribution to the corporation that is excluded from the corporation's income under Section 118.[208] The Tax Court refused to apply the tax benefit rule to change this result.

---

[204] See Carlton L. Byrd, 87 TC 830 (1986), aff'd per curiam, 829 F2d 1119 (4th Cir. 1987), for a post–*Hillsboro Bank* application of the tax benefit rule to the liquidation of an S Corporation. See also Dorothy S. Rojas, 90 TC 1090 (1988), where a divided Tax Court held that the tax benefit rule did not require the cost of seeds, fertilizers, and associated expenses incurred in producing crops to be included in income at the time the crops were distributed by the liquidating corporation. The court concluded that the previously deducted expenses had been consumed. It rejected the government's argument that the tax benefit rule ought to apply in any case where the cost of already deducted materials and services is consumed in the production of a product that itself has not yet been sold.

[205] Hartland Assocs., 54 TC 1580 (1970).

[206] But see Comm'r v. Fender Sales, Inc., 338 F2d 924 (9th Cir. 1964), cert. denied, 382 US 813 (1965), where the IRS succeeded in taxing the shareholder on his receipt of stock equal in value to a forgiven debt, which was for accrued salary.

[207] See, e.g., Helvering v. American Dental Co., 318 US 322 (1943).

[208] Treas. Reg. § 1.61-12(a).

In *Putoma Corp.*,[209] both the Tax Court and the Fifth Circuit again refused to apply the rule to override Section 118. However, both courts criticized the rule and stated that history, not logic, required the result. As part of the Bankruptcy Tax Act of 1980, Congress enacted provisions to deal with capital contributions. Section 108(e) now provides that shareholder forgiveness will not be governed by the capital contribution rule of Section 118. Instead, the corporation will be treated as having satisfied the debt with an amount of money equal to the shareholder's adjusted basis in the debt. Thus, the debtor corporation will recognize gain to the extent the shareholder's basis in the debt is less than the amount of the debt, including interest that was previously deducted. Consequently, taxpayers may no longer rely on the earlier principle that the gratuitous forgiveness of corporate debt avoids tax to the corporation.

[xi] Cancellation of indebtedness. It has long been established that a canceled debt gives rise to income to the debtor, whether or not the debt gave rise to a deduction when incurred.[210] However, the tax benefit rule has been applied to mitigate the consequences of this principle. For example, if the creditor forgives a liability that would have given rise to a deduction when paid, no income is realized by the debtor.[211]

[b] Legislative Applications

[i] Section 111. Section 111 applies broadly to virtually any recovery to the extent the recovery is of a previously deducted amount that resulted in a tax reduction.[212] The predecessor to Section 111 applied only to bad debts, taxes, and delinquency amounts. Section 111, as it then existed, provided that gross income did not include income attributable to the recovery of bad debts, prior taxes, or delinquency amounts to the extent the item did not produce a tax benefit when deducted. Although the section merely stated the exclusionary aspect of the rule, its clear implication was that the listed items constituted income when recovered. Thus, the collection of a debt previously deducted as worthless was income to the extent that the deduction produced a tax benefit when taken.[213] The rule applied whether the

---

[209] Putoma Corp., 66 TC 652 (1976), aff'd, 601 F2d 734 (5th Cir. 1979).

[210] United States v. Kirby Lumber Co., 284 US 1 (1931); IRC §§ 61(12), 108.

[211] IRC § 108(e)(2). In addition, the Bankruptcy Tax Act of 1980 established new rules regarding income from the cancellation of indebtedness that involve tax benefit principles.

[212] IRC § 111(a).

[213] See Cosmopolitan Credit Corp., 31 TCM 404 (1972), aff'd per curiam, 474 F2d 1344 (5th Cir. 1973); Bear Mill Mfg. Co., Inc., 15 TC 703 (1950), acq. 151-1 CB 1; Merchants Nat'l Bank 57-1 USTC ¶ 9380 (D. Kan. 1956).

prior deduction was based on complete or partial worthlessness.[214] However, except as noted previously,[215] the rule did not apply to debts charged to a reserve.[216]

Refunds of taxes (including interest or other payments for delays or failures in filing returns or paying taxes) that were previously deducted were also covered by old Section 111. In Revenue Ruling 79-15,[217] the IRS adopted the following general rules: (1) If a taxpayer does not itemize deductions in the year the state tax is paid, no part of the refund is includable in income; (2) if the taxpayer does itemize and the itemized deductions (other than state taxes) exceed the applicable zero bracket amount, then the entire refund is income when received;[218] and (3) if the state tax deduction caused the taxpayer to itemize, then either part or none of the refund may be taxable. If the refund is credited against future state tax, the taxpayer is treated as having constructively received the refund.[219]

The broadening of the statutory language for amounts recovered after December 31, 1983, makes the statutory rule commensurate with the scope of prior judicial applications.

[ii] **Depreciation recapture including ACRS.** Generally, Sections 1245 and 1250 require that on a disposition of depreciable personal property or depreciable real property, respectively, taxpayers must recognize as ordinary income the portion of the gain realized that is equal to a specified portion of depreciation taken in earlier years. This type of recovery is also applicable to most tangible depreciable property placed in service after 1980, the cost of which had to be recovered using the accelerated cost recovery system (ACRS), which permitted the cost of various assets to be recovered over specified periods. As a result of the 1986 Act, the significance of the depreciation recapture provisions has been considerably reduced.

[iii] **Damage recoveries.** Section 186 states a special rule applicable to damages recovered for injuries attributable to antitrust violations, patent infringements, and breaches of contract or fiduciary obligations. These dam-

---

[214] Section 111(b)(1), as it governed specified recoveries prior to December 1, 1983.

[215] See discussion supra ¶ 12.05[4][a][vii].

[216] Treas. Reg. § 1.111-1(a)(1); R. Gsell & Co., 34 TC 41 (1960), acq. 1960-2 CB 5, rev'd on other grounds, 294 F2d 321 (2d Cir. 1961).

[217] Rev. Rul. 79-15, 1979-1 CB 80. See Tech. Adv. Mem. 8749007 (1987) for an illustration of the manner in which the IRS applies these rules to a taxpayer who is liable for the alternative minimum tax in the year of the tax refund.

[218] See Lela M. Brownlee, 55 TCM 293 (1988), allowing taxpayer to exclude tax refund from income to extent she did not realize a prior tax benefit because of the applicable zero bracket amount.

[219] Ralph H. Schulz, 79-1 USTC ¶ 9199 (DDC 1979), aff'd without published opinion, 624 F2d 1103 (7th Cir. 1979).

ages are income when received. Nevertheless, inspired by tax benefit principles, the section allows taxpayers a corresponding deduction in an amount equal to the lesser of the damages or the taxpayer's "unrecovered losses"— those net operating losses attributable to the injury that have not been deducted in any carryover year. Section 186 thus differs from other tax benefit provisions in that the tax benefit realized by the taxpayer does not result from a deduction, but from reduced income. Only when the loss of income generates a net operating loss that produces a tax benefit is the recovery taxed. If the injury compensated by the damages does not generate a net operating loss, the damages are fully excludable from income, presumably under the view that the damage recovery represents a nontaxable return of capital. Thus, these kinds of damage recoveries are income when received, but to the extent no tax benefit was obtained from the underlying loss, the amounts are in turn deducted from income. This is wholly consistent with the logic of the tax benefit rule. The principal contribution of Section 186 is its simplified method of determining whether the taxpayer received a tax benefit in prior years for the subsequently compensated injury.[220] By focusing on the taxpayer's net operating loss, Section 186 makes it unnecessary to associate the damages with any specific deductions.[221]

[iv] **Foreign expropriation losses.** Section 1351 provides that a domestic corporation receiving money or property with respect to a foreign expropriation loss may elect to exclude the recovery from gross income to the extent of the loss deductions allowed in prior years. The corporation may elect to pay an additional tax, which is determined by subtracting the actual tax liability for the year of the loss from the tax liability that would have resulted if the loss had been reduced by the amount of the subsequent recovery. This treatment results in a tax liability comparable to the amount that would have been due if the recovery had been received when the expropriation occurred and had been applied to reduce or eliminate the deductible loss, except that tax rates prevailing in the recovery year are used rather than those in effect in the loss years. If the recovery exceeds the prior deductions, the excess is treated as gain from an involuntary conversion that qualifies for nonrecognition if the conditions of Section 1033 are met. If the taxpayer does not elect Section 1351, normal tax benefit rules should apply. Thus, the taxpayer may choose between (1) excluding the recovery to the extent the prior deductions provided no tax benefit and (2) excluding the entire recovery but giving back the prior deductions as well. Further, if

---

[220] Cf. Ralph L. Brutsche, 65 TC 1034 (1976), remanded, 585 F2d 436 (10th Cir. 1978) (taxpayer denied use of exclusionary aspect of rule because recovery not tied to specific loss, but rather affected net operating losses).

[221] Cf. United States v. Rexach, 482 F2d 10 (1st Cir. 1973), cert. denied, 414 US 1039 (1973), exclusionary aspect of rule not applicable when contract claim settled, because "no deduction" originally taken to match income.

Section 1351 is not elected, Section 80 may apply. Under Section 80, securities that were deducted as worthless because of a foreign expropriation must be included in income if their value is restored in whole or in part, up to the prior deductions resulting in a tax benefit.[222] Affected taxpayers should compute the result under all alternatives before deciding which course of action to follow.

[v] **LIFO recapture provisions.** The Code formerly provided that when a corporation distributed inventory assets to its shareholders in a partial or complete liquidation pursuant to plans of liquidation adopted before January 1, 1982, the distribution did not constitute a taxable transaction.[223] Similarly, where a liquidating corporation made a bulk sale of its inventory assets within 12 months before its complete liquidation, no gain or loss was recognized on that sale.[224]

During the 1970s, the IRS considered whether these principles of nonrecognition should apply to distributions and sales of last-in, first-out (LIFO) inventory assets in the same fashion as they applied to inventories computed under any other acceptable method of accounting and to other assets having a cost basis that was less than market value. (See Chapter 7 for a discussion of the LIFO inventory method.) Specifically, the IRS considered the question of whether the tax benefit rule should apply to a sale of LIFO inventory under then-applicable Section 337 of the Code. After analyzing the nature of the LIFO method as contrasted with (1) deductions (or write-downs) from ending inventory and (2) deductions from gross income under Section 162, the IRS ruled:

> The LIFO method of inventory accounting, however, is a technique for sequencing the flow of costs through inventory in a manner that expels the most recent costs incurred into cost of goods sold and retains the earliest costs in inventory. . . . It does not create a deduction that can be recovered.[225]

Consequently, there has been no requirement that the amount of the so-called LIFO reserve—generally, the amount by which the value of inventories determined on a lower of first-in, first-out (FIFO) cost or market basis

---

[222] But see Rev. Rul. 76-41, 1976-1 CB 52 (no worthless security loss for securities pledged to and seized by a foreign government if domestic parent can regain expropriated securities through judicial proceedings in the United States); Rev. Rul. 75-501, 1975-2 CB 69 (expropriation of operating assets of domestic corporation's wholly owned domestic subsidiary, which owns a bank account in the United States and whose securities are located here, does not render the securities worthless).

[223] IRC § 336.

[224] IRC § 337.

[225] Rev. Rul. 74-431, 1974-2 CB 107, 108.

exceeds the value determined under the LIFO method—be included in the income of a liquidating corporation.

However, effective with respect to distributions and dispositions pursuant to plans of liquidation adopted after December 31, 1982, Section 403(b) of the Crude Oil Windfall Profit Tax Act of 1980 amended prior law to require that if any corporation using the LIFO method distributed inventory assets in a partial or complete liquidation or made a bulk sale of inventory under then-applicable Section 337, the amount by which the inventory value as determined under the FIFO method exceeded the inventory value as determined under the LIFO method would be recognized as ordinary income to the corporation. The amount to be so included in income was designated as the "LIFO recapture amount." These requirements were contained in then-applicable Sections 336(b) and 337(f). This treatment was an exception to the then-applicable Section 336 general rule of nonrecognition of gain or loss in a corporate liquidation, but it was not applicable to any liquidation under Section 332, where the basis of the inventory was carried over to the acquirer under Section 334(b)(1). As a result of the 1986 Act, these LIFO recapture provisions are principally of historical interest, except to the extent that issues may be raised on examination of pre–1986 Act years.

Of more immediate interest is the LIFO recapture provision enacted as part of the Revenue Act of 1987 (the 1987 Act). Section 10227 of the 1987 Act requires that the LIFO reserve of a C corporation be included in the income of the corporation upon its adoption of S corporation status. The LIFO reserve is included in the income of the corporation for its last year as a C corporation. The tax attributable to the increase in income may be paid in four installments.[226]

[c] Exceptions to Tax Benefit Rule

Exceptions to the tax benefit rule have been established. These exceptions generally provide that the taxpayer will not have to include a recovery in income even though a tax benefit was received on the earlier deduction.

[i] **Erroneous deductions.** The tax benefit rule does not apply to tax the recovery of an item whose prior deduction was erroneous. In such a case, the government's sole remedy is to assess a deficiency for the year of deduction. If the statute of limitations has run on that year, the IRS may not recoup its loss by including the subsequent recovery in income under the tax benefit rule. The leading case in this area is *Streckfus Steamers, Inc.*,[227] in which an accrual basis taxpayer erroneously accrued and deducted a con-

---

[226] See ¶ 7.09 for discussion of the new LIFO recapture provision.
[227] Streckfus Steamers, Inc., 19 TC 1 (1952).

tested Illinois sales tax.[228] An Illinois court found in favor of the taxpayer and refunded the tax, and the IRS sought to include the amount of the admittedly improper deduction in income. The court disagreed, holding that an improper deduction taken in a prior year may not be treated as income in a later year. The court intimated that the IRS had its chance to challenge the deduction but did not.

In *Adolph B. Canelo*,[229] a cash basis law firm consistently deducted advances for litigation costs in the years it made the advances. If and when it recovered any part of an advance, it included the recovery in income. The IRS contended the advances were not deductible because they were really loans, deductible only when a case was closed without recovery. The IRS made adjustments to the taxpayer's returns for the years in issue and argued that the tax benefit rule required the taxpayers to include subsequent recoveries on advances made in earlier years in income when received. The earlier years were closed by the statute of limitations. The taxpayer argued that the repaid advances were repaid loans under the IRS's view and, therefore, were not includable in income. The court held for the taxpayers. Although the taxpayers received a windfall, the court would not let the IRS overcome the running of the statute of limitations by means of the tax benefit rule.

Subsequent decisions suggest that the erroneous deduction exception applies only if the improper deduction is apparent from the face of the return. Thus, the exception may not apply if the earlier return was either deliberately or inadvertently misleading or if the IRS had no reason to know that the deduction was erroneous.[230] In *Southern Pacific Transportation Co.*,[231] the taxpayer took deductions to which it was not entitled and subsequently recovered the amounts deducted. The court stated that neither the duty of consistency nor anything else was applicable to negate the exception because both the IRS and the taxpayer knew all the pertinent facts when the original deduction was taken. The court added that this is particularly true whenever the erroneous deductions are due to a mutual mistake of law. The court

---

[228] In Dixie Pine Prods. Co., 320 US 516 (1944), the Supreme Court held that a contested liability is not accruable until year in which the dispute is resolved.

[229] Adolph B. Canelo, 53 TC 217, aff'd, 447 F2d 484 (9th Cir. 1971).

[230] See Mayfair Minerals, Inc., 56 TC 82 (1971), aff'd, 456 F2d 622 (5th Cir. 1972) (contested liabilities accrued and deducted; IRS was not aware liability contested and allowed statute to run). Similarly, in Allen D. Unvert, 72 TC 807, 814 (1975), aff'd, 656 F2d 483 (9th Cir. 1981), cert. denied, 456 US 961 (1982), the Tax Court held the exception inapplicable to a taxpayer who claimed that previously deducted interest was actually a deposit and, hence, that its return should not be subject to the tax benefit rule. The court stated:

> The duty of consistency [or quasi-estoppel] precludes a taxpayer who has received a tax benefit due to his treatment of an item in a year barred by the statute of limitations from claiming that the original treatment was incorrect and thus obtaining a tax advantage in a later year.

[231] Southern Pac. Transp. Co., 75 TC 497 (1980).

distinguished the "duty of consistency" cases by stating, "In those cases, either the Commissioner was not apprised of the actual facts at the time of the deduction or the taxpayer in the year of recovery attempted to change the controlling facts and shift his position."[232] In the absence of these facts, the duty of consistency cannot undo the exception and "the question to be resolved is simply whether [the taxpayer] made a legal error in taking the deductions and [the IRS] made a legal error in allowing the deductions."[233]

[ii] **Absence of "deduction."** The tax benefit rule does not apply to a recovery of items that were not deducted for federal income tax purposes, such as the refund of a nondeductible federal income tax or fraud penalty.[234] Although this principle seems obvious, it has been extended to situations that are not so clear. Thus, this principle has been applied to the recovery of an amount that was not deductible when paid because the taxpayer was an exempt organization at the time.[235] Further, in *Boehm v. Commissioner*,[236] the Second Circuit held that an amount received in settlement of a derivative stockholder's action was not includable in gross income by a taxpayer whose stock could have been, but was not, deducted as worthless in an earlier year. The taxpayer had actually claimed a loss in the earlier year, but the IRS disallowed it. Nevertheless, the opinion may be broad enough to exclude a recovery from income if a taxpayer fails to claim the related deduction.

---

[232] Id. at 561.

[233] Id.

[234] Fred W. Staudt, 12 TCM 1417 (1953), aff'd, 216 F2d 610 (4th Cir. 1954).

[235] California and Hawaiian Sugar Ref. Corp. v. United States, 311 F2d 235 (Ct. Cl. 1962), no income under tax benefit rule unless taxpayer derived tax benefit from prior payment; since taxpayer was tax-exempt, no tax benefit arose from prior payment and no income arises on recovery; Home Sav. & Loan Co., 39 TC 368 (1962), acq. in result 1965-2 CB 5.

[236] Boehm v. Comm'r, 146 F2d 553 (2d Cir.), aff'd, 326 US 287 (1945).

Table of IRC Sections

[Text references are to paragraphs (¶) within Chapters; footnote references are to Chapters (boldface numbers) and notes (n.)]

IRC §

IRC §	
3(b)(2)	**10** n.249
15	10.06[2]
15(a)	10.06[2]
22(c)	**6** n.20
22(d)	2.04[3][d]; **3** ns. 266; 7.05[1][a]; **7** n.20
38	11.02[5][a][iii] & n.175
41	2.02[2][j][ii]; **3** n.17; **4** ns. 101, 102; **8** n.341
42	**4** ns. 101, 102
44	**5** n.237
48(b)	11.02[5][a][iii] & n.175
52	7.04[5][b]
52(a)	3.06[1][a]
52(b)	3.06[1][a]; 7.04[3][a][iii]
55	**5** n.16
56(a)(6)	5.07[5]; **5** ns. 16, 23
61	2.02[2][j][ii]; 3.03[1][a]; 3.06[2]; 6.02[1]; **12** n.52
61(a)	6.02[1]
72	5.05[12][e] & n.284; **11** n.23
80	12.05[4][b][iv]
83	**3** n.101
102	**12** n.54
103	11.02[3][a][ii]
105(d)	6.06[2][b]; 6.06[2][c][i]; 6.06[2][c][ii]
108	**12** n.184
108(e)	12.05[4][a][x]
108(e)(2)	**12** n.211
111	12.02[3]; 12.05 & n.147; 12.05[3] & n.164; 12.05[4][a][vii]; 12.05[4][b][i]
111(a)	**12** ns. 146, 166, 212
111(b)(1)	**12** n.214
118	12.05[4][a][x]
162	4.04[3][c][ii]; 5.05[8][b]; 6.04; 6.04[2]; 6.05[2]; 6.05[2][a]; 6.06; 6.06[2][c][i] & n.234; 12.02[2][c]; 12.05[4][b][v]

IRC §	
162(a)(3)	12.05[2]
163	11.02[4][b][iv]; **11** n.3
163(a)	11.11[3][b]
163(b)	11.01[2][a]; 11.01[2][a][ii]; 11.01[2][a][iv]; 11.04[2][d]
163(b)(1)	**11** n.5
163(b)(2)	**11** n.6
163(d)(4)	11.11[3][c]
163(e)	11.11[3][b] & n.310; **11** ns. 9, 51
163(e)(1)	11.02[3][a][ii]
163(e)(2)(B)	**11** n.146
163(f)(2)	**11** n.275
163(h)	11.11[3][b]; **11** n.304
163(h)(2)	6.06[2][c][ii]
163(h)(3)	6.06[2][c][ii]
163(h)(3)(B)(ii)	3.04[5][a]
164	**3** n.173; 6.06[2][c][i] & ns. 234, 236; 6.06[2][c][ii]
165	3.04[1]; **4** n.248; 6.06[2][c][i] & n.236; 6.06[2][c][ii]
165(a)	**12** n.178
166	9.02[2]
166(c)	**4** n.248
166(f)	**4** n.248
167	3.04[1]; 6.05; **6** n.234
167(b)	9.02[2]
167(e)	**8** n.238
167(j)(2)(c)	**8** n.238
170	**4** n.248
171	**11** n.84
172	10.05[4][b][i]; 12.02[3]; 12.05[2]
172(b)	10.05[2][e]; 10.05[4][b][ii]
174	6.06[2][c][ii]; **6** ns. 234, 236; **9** n.61
175	**9** n.61
179	5.05[9]
186	12.05[4][b][iii]
192	**4** n.248

*[Text references are to paragraphs (¶) within Chapters; footnote references are to
Chapters (boldface numbers) and notes (n.)]*

IRC §

194A **4** n.248
195 .... 4.04[3][e]
212 .... 11.02[5][b][vii]
222(2)(a)(ii) **3** n.91
263 .... **3** n.176
263A .... **1** ns. 8, 17; **2** n.102; **4** n.292;
5.04[3]; **5** n.110; 6.01[2]; 6.03;
6.04; 6.04[2]; 6.05; 6.05[1][c];
6.05[2]; 6.05[2][a]; 6.05[2][b] &
ns. 112, 113; 6.06[1]; 6.06[1][c];
6.06[1][c][ii] & n.182; 6.06[2];
6.06[2][a]; 6.06[2][c]; 6.06[2][c][i];
6.06[2][c][ii] & ns. 242, 246, 247;
6.07 & n.297; 6.07[3]; 6.07[4] &
n.320; 6.07[5]; 6.10[2] & n.430; **6**
ns. 38, 52, 393, 440; 7.04[3][a][i];
7.04[3][e]; 7.06[2]; 8.04[6][c];
8.06[3][b][ii]; 8.06[3][b][v]; **8** n.44
263A(a)(2) **6** n.39
263A(a)(2)(B) **6** n.153
263A(b) **6** n.37
263A(b)(1) **6** n.238
263A(b)(2)(B) ...... 6.06[1]; **6** ns. 38,
154
263A(b)(2)(C) **6** n.155
263A(c)(4) **6** n.425
263A(d)(1)(A) **6** n.435
263A(d)(1)(B) **6** n.436
263A(d)(3) **6** n.437
263A(e)(4) .... 3.06[1][c]
263A(e)(5) .... 3.06[1][c]
263A(f) .... 6.06[2][c][ii]
263A(f)(1) **6** n.256
263A(f)(2) **6** n.262
263A(f)(4)(B) **6** n.278
263A(f)(4)(C) **6** n.286
263A(h) **6** n.40
263A(h)(1) **6** n.275
266 ..... **2** n.173; 9.04[1][b] & n.74; **9**
n.168
267 .... **3** n.122; 10.04[4][e]
267(a)(2) **10** n.131
267(b) ...... 5.05[11][b][i] & n.257; **5**
n.246; 6.06[2][c][ii] & n.272
269 .... 9.08[1]; 9.08[1][c] & n.217
269(a) **9** n.202
269(a)(1) .... 9.08[1][c] & ns. 211, 213
269(a)(2) **9** n.212
269A(b)(1) **10** n.123

IRC §

280H .... 10.07[2]; 10.07[8];
10.07[8][b]; **10** n.278
302(b)(3) .... 12.02[3]
318(a) .... 5.05[11][b][i] & n.255
331 .... 5.05[7][d]; 5.05[11][a];
12.05[4][a][ix]
332 .... 5.06[3][b]; 9.08[2];
12.05[4][a][ix]; 12.05[4][b][v]
334(b)(1) .... 5.06[3][b]; 12.05[4][b][v]
334(b)(2) .... 12.05[4][a][ix]
336 .... 12.05[4][a][ix]; 12.05[4][b][v]
& n.223
336(b) .... 12.05[4][b][v]
337 .... 5.05[7][d]; 5.05[11];
5.05[11][a] & n.243; 5.06[3][b];
12.05[4][a][ix]; 12.05[4][b][v] &
n.224
337(b)(2)(B) **5** n.244
337(f) .... 12.05[4][b][v]
341(f) .... 5.06[3][b]
351 .... 3.02[1][a]; 5.06[3][a]; 7.08[1];
7.08[1][a] & n.304; 7.08[1][b]; **7**
n.30; 8.04[5][a]; 8.06[3][b][iv];
9.08[1][a]; 9.08[1][c]; **9** n.225;
10.04[4][b][iii]; 12.05[4][a][viii]
354–368 .... 3.02[1][a]; 3.02[1][c]
361 .... 5.06[3][a]; 9.08[2]
356(a) .... 5.05[5]
362 .... **9** n.204
368 .... 9.08[1][b]
368(a)(1)(C) ...... 9.08[1][b] & n.206
368(a)(1)(F) **9** n.209; **10** n.84
368(a)(2) **9** n.208
368(a)(2)(B)(i) **9** n.208
368(c) **9** n.203
381 ...... **4** n.147; 7.08[3]; 8.04[5][a];
8.06[3][b][iv]; 9.08[2] & n.225;
10.04[4][b][iii]
381(a) .... 4.03[3][e][ii]; 11.03[2]
381(b) **10** n.84
381(c)(4) ... 9.08[2]; **9** ns. 207, 209
381(c)(5) .... 7.08[3] & n.317; 9.08[2]
381(l) .... 4.03[3][e][ii]
401(a) .... 3.06[1][b][ii]; 6.06[2][c][ii]
404 .... **4** n.248; 6.06[2][c][i] & n.234;
6.06[2][c][ii]; 11.10[3]
404A .... **4** n.248; 6.06[2][c][ii];
11.10[3]
412 .... 6.06[2][c][ii]

[Text references are to paragraphs (¶) within Chapters; footnote references are to Chapters (boldface numbers) and notes (n.)]

IRC §

414(m) .... 3.06[1][a]
414(o) .... 3.06[1][a]
419 .... **4** n.248
441 .... 10.02; 10.04[4][a];
  10.05[4][d][ii]; 10.07[8]
441(a) .... **10** n.2; 12.02[1]
441(b) **10** n.76
441(b)(1) .... **10** ns. 3, 168
441(b)(2) **10** n.4
441(b)(3) .... **10** ns. 6, 26
441(b)(4) **10** n.7
441(c) **10** n.9
441(d) **10** n.10
441(e) **10** n.11
441(f) .... **10** ns. 5, 171
441(f)(1) **10** n.22
441(g) .... 10.05[4][d][ii]; **10** ns. 4, 83
441(g)(3) **10** n.13
441(h) .... **10** ns. 7, 76
441(h)(1) **10** n.53
441(h)(2) **10** n.54
441(h)(4) **10** n.55
441(i)(1) **10** n.125
441(i)(2) **10** n.123
442 .... 10.05; 10.05[2][g][ii];
  10.05[4][d][ii]
443(a) **10** n.27
443(a)(1) **10** n.30
443(a)(2) **10** n.36
443(b) ..... 10.05[4][b][ii]; **10** ns. 236,
  247
443(b)(2) .... **10** ns. 133, 260
443(b)(2)(B)(ii) **10** n.238
443(b)(3) **10** n.248
443(d) .... **10** ns. 239, 240
444 .... 10.07[1]; 10.07[1][a];
  10.07[1][b]; 10.07[2]; 10.07[3];
  10.07[3][a]; 10.07[3][b]; 10.07[4];
  10.07[5]; 10.07[5][a]; 10.07[5][b]
  & n.293; 10.07[6][a];
  10.07[6][a][iv]; 10.07[6][c] &
  n.299; 10.07[7] & n.300; 10.07[8];
  10.07[8][e]; **10** n.276
446 .... **1** n.9; 2.02; 2.02[1]; 2.02[2][c];
  2.02[2][j][i]; 2.02[2][j][ii]; 2.04; **2**
  n.100; 3.03[1][a]; 3.03[1][b]; **3** ns.
  197, 266; 4.03[3][e][ii]; 4.04[3][e];
  6.04[2]; 6.05[1][c]; 6.05[3][a];
  6.06[2][c][i]; **8** n.20; 8.06[1];
  9.03[1][b]; 9.03[1][c]; **9** n.217

IRC §

446(a) ..... 2.02[1] & n.11; 2.02[1][b];
  2.02[1][c]; 2.02[1][e]; 2.03; **2** ns.
  12, 15, 29; 3.02; 3.02[1];
  3.02[1][a]; 3.06; 3.07; 3.08[2];
  3.08[7]; **3** n.265; **4** n.101;
  6.05[2][c]; 6.05[2][c][i] & n.118;
  7.03[2] & n.51
446(b) ..... 2.02[2]; 2.02[2][d]; 2.04 &
  n.196; **2** ns. 13, 87, 129; 3.02;
  3.08[5]; 3.08[6]; 6.04[1][a][ii];
  8.06[3][a][i]; 8.06[6][a][i]; **9** n.217;
  11 ns. 10, 11, 240; 12.03[3][a][i]
446(c) .... 2.02[2][f]; 2.03[1];
  2.03[1][b]; **2** ns. 8, 9; 4.01
446(d) .... 2.03[1][a] & n.184
446(e) .... 2.02[1][e]; **2** ns. 11, 14;
  8.01; 8.02 & n.8; 8.03 & n.10;
  8.07[2][b]; 9.03[1][b]; 9.03[1][c];
  9.04[1][a]; 9.05[2]
446(f) .... 8.04[6][c]; 8.08; 8.09 &
  n.339; **8** n.22
447 .... 2.02[2]; **3** n.260; **4** n.13;
  6.10[2]; **8** ns. 148, 178
447(d)(2) **4** n.13
447(d)(2)(A) **3** n.260
448 .... 2.02[2]; **2** n.96; 3.02 & ns. 22,
  23; 3.02[3] & n.35; 3.06 & ns. 196,
  197; 3.06[1]; 3.06[1][d]; 3.08;
  3.08[1]; **3** ns. 6, 229, 253, 254; **4**
  n.79; 8.04[6][a]; **8** n.178
448(a) .... 3.05[2][a]; **3** n.201
448(a)(3) .... 6.10[2]
448(b) **3** n.201
448(b)(2) **3** n.211
448(b)(2)(A) **3** n.212
448(b)(3) **4** n.11
448(c) .... **4** n.11; 6.06[1][c]
448(c)(1) **3** n.204
448(c)(2) **3** n.207
448(c)(3)(C) **3** n.205
448(d)(1) **3** n.229
448(d)(1)(B) **3** n.230
448(d)(2)(A) **3** n.212
448(d)(2)(B) **3** n.221
448(d)(5) .... 4.03[2][d] & n.81; **4**
  n.68
448(d)(6) **3** n.202
448(d)(7) ..... 3.06[1][d]; 8.04[6][a]; **8**
  n.44

[Text references are to paragraphs (¶) within Chapters; footnote references are to Chapters (boldface numbers) and notes (n.)]

IRC §

448(d)(7)(C)(ii) 3 n.254
451 .... 3.03; 3.03[1][b]; 4.03; 4 n.101;
            10 ns. 270, 271; 12 n.13
451(a) .... 12.02[1]
451(d) 3 n.116
451(e) 3 n.117
451(f) .... 4 n.31; 9 ns. 159, 160
452 .... 3 ns. 19, 24; 4.02[3];
        4.03[3][a]; 4.03[3][b]; 4.03[3][e][i];
                    4.04[1][b]; 4 n.118
453 .... 2 n.97; 3.02[1][a];
            3.03[1][d][ii]; 3.03[1][d][iv];
        4.01[2]; 5.01[3] & ns. 10, 11; 5.05
            & n.137; 5.05[2]; 5.05[7][b];
        5.05[12][e]; 5 ns. 130, 237; 8.06[1]
453(a) ..... 5.05[2]; 5.05[8][c]; 5 ns. 7,
                        138, 237
453(b) .... 5.04; 5 ns. 138, 150
453(b)(1) .... 5 ns. 91, 159, 196
453(b)(1)(B) 5 n.144
453(b)(2) .... 5 ns. 158, 160, 224
453(b)(2)(A) .... 5.07[1] & n.347
453(c) 5 n.165
453(c)(2) .... 5.04[1] & n.36
453(d) .... 5.04[4]; 5 ns. 130, 157
453(d)(1) .... 5.04[4]
453(d)(2) .... 5.04[4]
453(d)(5) 5 n.328
453(e) 5 n.249
453(e)(2)(A) 5 n.260
453(e)(2)(B) 5 n.261
453(e)(3) 5 n.259
453(e)(6) 5 n.263
453(e)(7) 5 n.263
453(e)(8) 5 n.265
453(f) 5 n.256
453(f)(1) .... 5.06[2]; 5 n.254
453(f)(2) 5 n.253
453(f)(3) .... 5 ns. 173–175, 206
453(f)(3) 5 n.175
453(f)(4) .... 5 ns. 175, 206
453(f)(5) .... 5 ns. 175, 207
453(f)(5)(A) 5 n.208
453(f)(6) 5 n.176
453(f)(6)(C) 5 n.177
453(g) 5 n.266
453(h) ...... 5.05[7][d]; 5.05[11][a] &
                        n.245
453(h)(1)(B) 5 n.201

IRC §

453(h)(1)(C) .... 5 ns. 202, 246
453(h)(1)(C)(ii) 5 n.247
453(h)(1)(D) .... 5 ns. 202, 250
453(h)(1)(E) 5 n.202
453(i) .... 5 ns. 225, 226
453(j) .... 5 n.268; 8.04[6][b]
453(k) .... 3 n.118; 5 ns. 76, 100, 154,
                        160, 163
453(k)(1) 5 n.154
453(k)(2) .... 5 ns. 154, 252, 258
453(l) 5 n.350
453(l)(1) .... 5.04[2][a]; 5 n.24
453(l)(1)(A) 5 n.49
453(l)(1)(B) 5 n.50
453(l)(2) 5 n.352
453(l)(2)(A) 5 n.25
453(l)(2)(B) 5 n.26
453(l)(3) 5 n.352
453A–453C 1 n.8
453A .... 3.02[1][a]; 3 n.235; 5.01[3]
        & ns. 11; 5.04[1]; 5.04[2][a];
        5.04[2][c]; 5.04[6]; 5.05 & n.137;
        5.07[1]; 5.07[3] & n.360; 5 ns. 9,
            12, 53, 79, 160, 224; 8 n.309
453A(b) 5 n.361
453A(b)(1) .... 5 ns. 169, 361
453A(b)(2) 5 n.361
453A(b)(3) 5 n.362
453A(b)(4) 5 n.362
453A(d) .... 5.07[4]
453A(d)(1) .... 5 ns. 168–170
453A(1) 5 n.29
453B .... 5.01[3] & n.11; 5.04[4];
        5.04[6]; 5.05[12][e]; 5.06 & n.307;
                    5 n.327; 11.05[1]
453B(a) 5 n.124
453B(b) .... 5.04[4]; 5 n.306
453B(c) 5 n.310
453B(d) 5 n.325
453B(d)(1) 5 n.311
453B(d)(2) .... 5 ns. 326, 327
453B(e) 5 n.329
453B(f) .... 5 ns. 317, 319
453B(f)(2) 5 n.324
453B(g) 5 n.308
453C .... 5.01 & n.10; 5.05[6];
            5.07[2]; 5 ns. 154, 172
453C(b)(2) 5 n.189
453C(b)(3)(A) 5 n.190

[Text references are to paragraphs (¶) within Chapters; footnote references are to Chapters (boldface numbers) and notes (n.)]

IRC §

453C(b)(4) **5** n.191
453C(e)(1)(A) **5** n.181
453C(e)(1)(A)(ii) **5** n.180
453C(e)(1)(B) **5** n.186
453C(e)(4) **5** n.187
455 .... 4.03[3][e][i]
456 .... 4.03[3][e][i]
460 .... **7** n.190
461 ..... 2.02[2]; 3.04[1]; 4.04[3][a] &
   n.248; **6** n.9; **10** ns. 270, 272; **12**
   n.13
461(a) .... 4.04; 12.02[1]
461(c) ...... 4.04[3][c][ii]; **4** ns. 160,
   303; 8.07[2][b]
461(c)(1) .... 10.06[1]
461(c)(3) **3** n.203
461(f) .... 4.04[1][c][i] & n.218; **4**
   n.198
461(g) ..... **2** n.87; 3.04[5][a]; **3** n.178;
   11 n.240
461(g)(2) .... 3.04[5][a] & n.152;
   11.02[4][b][ii] & n.126
461(h) .... **1** ns. 2, 10; **3** n.28; 4.04;
   4.04[1][c][i]; 4.04[3]; 4.04[3][a] &
   ns. 242, 248; 4.04[3][b] & n.252;
   4.04[3][b][iv]; 4.04[3][c][ii];
   4.04[3][e]; **4** ns. 3, 303; 6.01[2]; **9**
   n.133
461(h)(1) .... 4.04[3][e]
461(h)(2) **1** n.13; **3** n.189; **4** n.251
461(h)(2)(A)–461(h)(2)(D)
   .... **4** n.251
461(h)(2)(A) **4** n.257
461(h)(2)(A)(iii) **4** n.278
461(h)(2)(B) .... 4.04[3][c][ii]; **4** n.263
461(h)(2)(C) **4** n.268
461(h)(2)(D) **4** n.274
461(h)(3) ..... 4.04[3][f]; 4.04[3][f][i];
   4.04[3][f][iii]
461(h)(3)(A) **4** n.325
461(h)(3)(A)(ii) .... 4.04[3][f][i]
461(h)(3)(A)(iii) .... 4.04[3][f][ii]
461(h)(3)(B) .... 4.04[3][f][iii]
461(h)(3)(C) **4** n.324
461(h)(5) **4** n.248
461(i) ...... 3.05[2][a] & ns. 188, 189;
   3.05[2][b]
461(i)(2) **3** n.190
461(i)(2)(B) **3** n.191

IRC §

461(i)(2)(B)(ii) **3** n.191
461(i)(2)(C) **3** n.192
461(i)(2)(D) **3** n.193
462 ...... **3** n.24; 4.02[3]; 4.03[3][a];
   4.03[3][b]; 4.03[3][e][i]; 4.04[1][b];
   4 n.118
463 .... **4** n.248
464 .... **2** n.100
466 .... **4** n.248
467 ... **1** n.3; **3** ns. 2, 111, 139; 11.10;
   11.10[1]; 11.10[1][a]; 11.10[1][b];
   11.10[2]
467(a) .... **11** ns. 277, 282
467(b)(1) **11** n.283
467(b)(2) **11** n.284
467(b)(3) **11** n.284
467(b)(4) **11** n.284
467(b)(5) **11** n.284
467(c) **11** n.286
467(d) **11** n.269
467(d)(1)(A) **11** n.280
467(d)(1)(B) **11** n.281
467(d)(2) **11** n.279
467(e)(1) **11** n.285
467(f) .... 11.10[1][b]
467(g) .... **1** n.12; 11.10[3]
468 .... **4** n.248
468A **4** n.248
471 ..... **1** n.9; 2.02[2][c]; 2.02[2][j][i]
   & n.152; 2.04; **2** n.129; 3.06[2]; **3**
   n.277; 5.04[3]; **5** n.110; 6.01[2];
   6.02[3]; 6.04; 6.04[1][a]; 6.04[2];
   6.05[1][c]; 6.05[2]; 6.05[2][a];
   6.05[2][b] & n.113; 6.05[3][a] &
   n.125; 6.06[2]; 6.06[2][c];
   6.06[2][c][i]; 6.07; 6.07[4]; 6.08[2];
   6.09; 6.11; **6** ns. 20, 376;
   7.03[1][b]; 7.04[3][e]; **7** ns. 14, 56,
   95; 8.06[3][b][ii]; 8.06[3][b][v]
472 ..... 2.02[1][e]; **3** n.277; 5.04[3]; **5**
   n.110; 6.05[2][b]; 6.08[2]; 7.02;
   7.04[3][e]; 7.05; **7** n.21; 8.06[1]; **8**
   n.97; **9** ns. 61, 88
472(a) .... **7** ns. 27, 270; **8** n.309
472(b) **7** n.3
472(b)(1) **7** n.5
472(b)(2) **7** n.90
472(c) ..... 2.02[1][e]; **3** n.266; 7.03[2]

[Text references are to paragraphs (¶) within Chapters; footnote references are to Chapters (boldface numbers) and notes (n.)]

IRC §

472(d) ...... 7 ns. 100, 101; **8** n.98; **9** n.90
472(e) .... 7 ns. 53, 286; 9.05[2]
472(e)(2) **7** n.52
472(f) **6** n.23; **7** n.212
472(g) .... 7.03[2][b][iii] & n.85; 7.03[2][b][viii]; 7.06[2]
473 .... 7.07[3]
474 ...... **6** n.23; 7.04[3][a][iii] & ns. 151, 152; 7.04[5] & n.215; **7** n.256
474(a) **7** n.154
474(b) .... 7.04[5][a][i]; 7 ns. 154, 257
474(c) .... 7.04[5][a][i]; **7** n.259
474(c)(1) **7** n.155
474(d) .... 7.04[5][b]
474(d)(1)(A) **7** n.260
474(d)(1)(B) **7** n.261
474(d)(2) **7** n.262
474(d)(2)(B)(ii) **7** n.264
474(d)(4) **7** n.262
481 ...... **2** n.76; 3.06[1][d]; 3.06[3] & n.248; 4.03[3][e][ii]; 4.04[3][c][ii]; 4.04[3][f][iv]; 5.07[2]; **5** ns. 100, 357; 6.06[1][c][ii] & n.191; 6.06[2][c][i]; 6.06[2][c][ii]; 7.03[1][c]; 7.04[5][a][iii]; 7.06[2]; 7.08[2]; 8.01; 8.02; 8.03 & n.20; 8.04 & ns. 25, 26, 34; 8.04[1]; 8.04[2]; 8.04[2][a]; 8.04[2][b]; 8.04[2][c]; 8.04[2][d]; 8.04[3] & n.65; 8.04[4][a]; 8.04[4][b][i]; 8.04[4][b][ii]; 8.04[4][b][iii]; 8.04[4][b][iv]; 8.04[5]; 8.04[5][a] & ns. 92, 94; 8.04[5][b]; 8.04[5][c]; 8.04[5][d]; 8.04[5][e]; 8.04[6]; 8.04[6][a]; 8.04[6][b]; 8.04[6][c]; 8.04[6][d]; 8.04[8]; 8.05; 8.06[1]; 8.06[2]; 8.06[2][a]; 8.06[2][b][ii]; 8.06[2][c]; 8.06[2][d]; 8.06[3][b]; 8.06[3][b][i]; 8.06[3][b][ii]; 8.06[3][b][iii]; 8.06[3][b][iv]; 8.06[3][b][v]; 8.06[3][c][i]; 8.06[3][c][ii]; 8.06[3][c][iii]; 8.06[3][f][i]; 8.06[3][g]; 8.07[2] & n.313; **8** ns. 9, 201; 9.01[1] & n.3; 9.01[2] & ns. 6, 7; 9.02[1]; 9.03[1][c]; 9.03[2]; 9.03[2][b][i]; 9.04[2][a]; 9.04[2][b][i];

IRC §

9.04[2][b][ii]; 9.04[2][b][iii]; 9.04[2][b][iv]; 9.04[2][c]; 9.05[3]; 9.08[1][a]; 9.08[2]; **9** n.150
481(a) ..... 8.04 & ns. 23, 31; 8.04[2] n.46
481(a)(2) .... **8** ns. 32, 36, 37
481(b)(1) **8** n.47
481(b)(2) **8** n.48
481(c) .... 8.04[3]
482 .... **4** n.143; **6** ns. 267, 272
483 .... **2** n.87; 3.03[1][d][ii]; 3.03[3][a] & n.78; **3** ns. 2, 139, 178, 260; 5.05[15][a]; **6** ns. 267, 272; 11.01[2][a]; 11.01[2][a][i]; 11.02[5] & n.150; 11.02[5][b][i]; 11.04; 11.04[1] & n.240; 11.04[2]; 11.04[2][a]; 11.04[2][b][i]; 11.04[2][c]; 11.04[2][d]; **11** ns. 3, 4, 222
483(a) .... **11** ns. 247, 249
483(b) **11** n.243
483(d) **11** n.250
483(e) .... 11.02[5][b][v]; **11** n.248
501(a) .... 3.06[1][b][ii]; 6.06[2][c][ii]; 10.04[4][f][i]
501(c)(21) **12** n.57
511(b) **3** n.202
512(l)(1) .... 5.04[2][c][i]
513(a) .... 5.04[2][c][i]
536 .... **10** n.241
546 .... **10** n.242
557 .... **10** n.243
611 .... 3.04[1]
614(d)(1) .... 5.06[3][b]
615 .... **9** n.61
617(d)(1) .... 5.06[3][b]
631(a) **7** n.279
645 .... **10** n.132
691 .... 5.06[1] & n.316
691(a)(2) .... **5** ns. 314, 315
691(a)(3) **5** n.312
691(a)(4) .... **5** ns. 312, 314
706(a) ..... 10.04[4][c][iii]; **10** ns. 102, 215
706(b)(1) **10** n.90
706(b)(1)(B)(i) **10** n.92
706(b)(1)(B)(ii) **10** n.94
706(b)(1)(B)(iii) **10** n.96
706(b)(1)(C) .... **10** ns. 98, 104

[Text references are to paragraphs (¶) within Chapters; footnote references are to Chapters (boldface numbers) and notes (n.)]

IRC §

706(b)(3) 10 n.95
706(b)(4) 10 n.93
706(c)(1) 10 n.45
707(b) .... 6.06[2][c][ii] & n.272
707(c) .... 10.07[6][a][ii]
708(b)(1)(A) 10 n.43
708(b)(1)(B) .... 10 ns. 44, 45
721 .... 5.06[3][a]
731 .... 5.06[3][a]
736 .... 5.06[3][a]
751 .... 5.06[3][a]
803(d)(2)(B) .... 8.04[6][c]
805(d)(2) .... 8.04[6][d]
812(c)(2) .... 8.04[6][b]
852(b)(2)(E) 10 n.245
857(b)(2)(C) 10 n.244
859 .... 10 n.137
934(b) .... 10.05[4][b][iii]
936 .... 10.05[4][b][iii]
988 .... 11.03[1]
1001 .... 3.03[1][b]; 3.03[1][d][ii];
        3.03[1][d][iii]; 4.03[1][b];
        5.05[12][e]; 5 n.1; 12 n.54
1001(a) .... 3.03[1][d][iii]; 11 n.27
1001(b) .... 3.03[1][d][iii]; 4 n.62
1011 .... 5.05[8]
1012 .... 11.05[1]
1013 .... 6.02[3]
1031 .... 3.02[1][c]; 5.05[13]
1031(b) .... 5.05[5]; 5 n.287
1033 .... 5.05[11][b][iii];
        12.05[4][a][iii]; 12.05[4][b][iv]
1034 .... 11.02[5][b][ii]
1038 .... 5.05[14]
1038(e) 5 n.291
1060 .... 8.06[3][b][iv]
1092(d)(1) .... 11.03[2]
1221(1) .... 6.07[4]
1231 .... 11 n.3
1232 .... 11.01[2][a]; 11.01[2][a][iv];
                        11 n.8
1232A .... 11.01[2][a]; 11.01[2][a][iv];
                        11 ns. 3, 9
1232B .... 11.01[2][a]; 11.01[2][a][iv];
                        11 n.3
1235(a) .... 11.02[5][b][iv];
                    11.04[2][d]
1239 .... 5.05[11][c]
1239(b) .... 5.05[11][a] & n.246

IRC §

1244(c)(3) .... 11.02[5][b][i]; 11 n.184
1245 .... 5.05[9]; 12.05[4][b][ii]
1245(a) .... 5.06[3][b]
1250 .... 5.05[9]; 12.05[4][b][ii]
1250(a) .... 5.06[3][b]
1252(a) .... 5.06[3][b]
1254(a) .... 5.06[3][b]
1271–1274 .... 3 n.2
1271–1275 .... 1 ns. 3, 8; 11.02
1271 ..... 11.02; 11.02[2]; 11.02[2][a];
            11.02[2][b]; 11.02[2][c];
                        11.02[4][c]
1271(a) .... 11.02[3][a][iii]
1271(a)(2) .... 11.02[2][a]
1271(a)(2)(B) 11 n.39
1271(a)(3) 11 n.42
1271(a)(3)(C) .... 11 ns. 43, 44
1271(a)(3)(D) 11 n.43
1271(a)(3)(E) .... 11 ns. 44, 46
1271(a)(4) 11 n.42
1271(a)(4)(C) 11 n.43
1271(a)(4)(D) .... 11 ns. 44, 46
1271(b)(1) 11 n.48
1271(b)(2) 11 n.50
1272–1274 .... 3.03[3][a] & n.78;
                3.03[3][e]; 3 n.139
1272 ..... 3 ns. 84, 85; 6 ns. 267, 272;
    11.02; 11.02[2] & n.28; 11.02[2][a]
            & n.38; 11.02[3] & n.51;
    11.02[3][a][i]; 11.02[3][a][ii] &
        n.75; 11.02[4][b][iv]; 11.03[4];
    11.04; 11.07[2]; 11 ns. 44, 46, 310
1272(a) .... 11.04[2][b][i]; 11.04[2][c];
                    11.05[2]; 11.09
1272(a)(1) 11 n.51
1272(a)(2) .... 11.02[2][a]; 11 n.75
1272(a)(2)(A) .... 11 ns. 34, 35
1272(a)(2)(E)(iii) .... 11 ns. 81, 82
1272(a)(3) .... 11 ns. 70, 73, 74
1272(a)(5) .... 11 ns. 54, 62
1272(a)(6) .... 11.02[2][a]
1272(a)(7) 11 n.85
1272(b) 11 n.88
1272(b)(1) 11 n.89
1272(b)(2) 11 n.89
1272(b)(3)(A) 11 n.90
1272(b)(3)(B) 11 n.91
1272(b)(4) 11 n.92
1272(b)(4)(B) 11 n.93

[Text references are to paragraphs (¶) within Chapters; footnote references are to Chapters (boldface numbers) and notes (n.)]

IRC §

1272(c)(1)	**11** n.83
1272(c)(2)	**11** n.75
1272(d)(2)	**11** n.29
1273	11.02; 11.02[3]; 11.02[4]; 11.02[4][a][iii]; 11.04; 11.11
1273(a)	11.09
1273(a)(1)	**11** n.94
1273(a)(2)	**11** ns. 96–98
1273(a)(3)	**11** ns. 95, 140
1273(b)	11.04[2][d]; **11** n.118
1273(b)(1)	11.02[4][b][v]; 11.05[1]; **11** n.121
1273(b)(2)	11.02[4][b][v]; **11** ns. 124, 135, 288
1273(b)(3)	11.02[4][b][v]; **11** ns. 22, 130
1273(b)(4)	11.03[3]; **11** n.140
1273(b)(5)	**11** n.119
1273(c)(2)	**11** ns. 134, 135
1274	3.03[1][d][ii]; **6** ns. 267, 272; 11.02; 11.02[3]; 11.02[4][b][v]; 11.02[5] & n.149; 11.02[5][a][i]; 11.02[5][a][iii]; 11.02[5][b]; 11.02[5][b][i]; 11.02[5][b][ii]; 11.02[5][b][iii]; 11.02[5][b][iv]; 11.02[5][b][v]; 11.02[5][b][vii]; 11.02[5][c]; 11.04[2][d]; **11** ns. 22, 222
1274(a)	11.02[5][a]
1274(b)	11.02[5][a]
1274(b)(1)	**11** n.151
1274(b)(3)(A)	**11** n.169
1274(b)(3)(B)	**11** n.166
1274(c)(1)(B)	**11** n.192
1274(c)(3)(A)	**11** n.181
1274(c)(3)(A)(i)	**11** n.183
1274(c)(3)(A)(i)(II)	**11** n.184
1274(c)(3)(A)(i)(III)	**11** n.185
1274(c)(3)(A)(ii)	**5** n.182; **11** n.186
1274(c)(3)(B)	**11** ns. 187, 198
1274(c)(3)(C)	**11** ns. 189, 190
1274(c)(3)(E)	**11** n.191
1274(d)	11.11[1]
1274(d)(1)	**11** n.152
1274(d)(1)(B)	**11** n.154
1274(d)(1)(C)	**11** n.153
1274(d)(1)(D)	**11** n.155
1274(d)(2)	**11** n.156

IRC §

1274(d)(3)	**11** n.157
1274(e)	**11** n.178
1274(e)(2)	**11** n.180
1274A	11.02[5][a][iv] & n.179
1274A(a)	**11** n.175
1274A(b)	**11** n.175
1274A(c)	**11** n.197
1274A(d)(2)	**11** ns. 176, 199
1275	11.02
1275(a)(1)	11.02[1]
1275(a)(1)(B)	**11** n.23
1275(a)(3)	**11** n.77
1275(b)(1)	**11** n.194
1274(b)(2)	**11** n.196
1275(b)(3)	5.05[6]; **11** n.195
1275(d)	11.03
1276–1278	11.02; 11.04[2][d]
1276	11.05; 11.05[1]
1276(a)	11.02[3][a][iii]
1275(a)(1)	**11** n.258
1276(a)(2)	**11** n.259
1276(b)(1)	**11** n.260
1276(b)(2)	**11** n.261
1277	11.05; 11.05[1]; 11.05[3]
1277(a)	**11** n.262
1277(b)	**11** n.263
1277(c)	**11** n.262
1278	11.05; 11.05[1]
1278(a)(1)(B)	**11** n.256
1278(a)(1)(C)	**11** n.256
1278(a)(2)(A)	**11** n.254
1278(a)(2)(B)	**11** n.255
1278(a)(3)	**11** n.253
1281–1283	11.02; 11.02[3][a][ii]; 11.06
1281	11.02[5][b][iv]; 11.06; 11.06[1]
1281(a)	**11** n.264
1281(b)	11.06[2]
1281(b)(1)	**11** n.268
1281(b)(2)	**11** n.269
1282	11.06; 11.06[1]; 11.06[2]
1282(c)	**11** n.271
1283	11.06
1283(a)(1)	**11** n.267
1283(a)(2)	**11** n.265
1283(b)	**11** n.266
1283(c)	**11** n.270
1286	11.07

[Text references are to paragraphs (¶) within Chapters; footnote references are to Chapters (boldface numbers) and notes (n.)]

IRC §		IRC §	
1286(a)	**11** n.274	4947(a)(1)	10.04[4][f][i]
1286(b)	**11** n.273	6013(c)	**10** n.41
1286(b)(1)	**11** n.272	6081	**4** n.326
1286(e)	11.02[3][a][ii] & n.80	6420(c)(2)	**11** n.183
1287	11.08	6661(b)(2)(C)(ii)	**3** n.191;
1287(b)(1)	**11** n.275		11.02[5][a][ii]
1288	11.02; 11.09	6661(b)(2)(C)(iii)	**3** n.188
1311–1314	**3** n.61; **9** ns. 4, 8	6662	11.01[2][b]
1341	12.02[3] & n.38; 12.03 &	6662(d)(2)(C)(ii)	11.02[5][a][ii]
	n.44; 12.03[3][a][iv] & n.82;	6851	10.02[3]; **10** n.47
	12.03[4]; 12.03[4][a]; 12.03[4][b];	6851(a)(1)	**10** n.28
	12.03[4][c];	7519	10.07[2]; 10.07[7]; **10** ns.
	12.04[4] & n.144		277, 294
1341(a)(1)	**12** n.103	7519(b)(1)(A)	10.07[6][a]
1341(a)(2)	**12** n.104	7519(d)(4)	**10** n.296
1341(a)(3)	**12** n.105	7701(a)(1)	**9** n.210
1341(a)(5)	**12** n.102	7701(a)(23)	**10** n.6
1341(b)(1)	**12** n.102	7805(b)	4.04[3][e]
1341(b)(2)	**12** n.103	7872	**6** ns. 267, 272; 11.02;
1351	12.05[4][b][iv]		11.04[2][d]; 11.11; 11.11[1];
1363	7.09 & n.326		11.11[2]; 11.11[3][a]; 11.11[3][b]
1363(d)	8.06[3][b][v]	7872(a)	**11** ns. 300, 312
1363(d)(2)	**7** n.327	7872(b)(1)	**11** n.308
1366(a)	**10** n.215	7872(b)(2)	**11** n.309
1372(a)	10.05[4][b][i]	7872(c)(1)	**11** ns. 297, 313
1374	**7** n.325	7872(c)(1)(D)	**11** n.297
1376	12.05[2]	7872(c)(1)(E)	**11** ns. 297, 314
1378(a)	**10** n.111	7872(c)(1)(E)(ii)	**11** n.315
1378(b)	**10** ns. 112, 113	7872(c)(1)(F)	**11** n.297
1378(c)	**10** ns. 114, 115	7872(c)(2)	**11** n.298
1381(a)	7.06[2]	7872(c)(3)	**11** n.299
1401	10.05[5]	7872(d)(2)	**11** n.312
1504	7.03[2][b][viii]	7872(e)(1)(A)	**11** n.293
1504(a)	**5** n.180	7872(e)(1)(B)	**11** n.294
1504(b)	**5** n.180	7872(e)(2)	**11** n.302
2031(a)	**5** n.311	7872(e)(5)	**11** n.291
2032A(e)(4)	5.05[6]; **5** n.351	7872(e)(6)	**11** n.292
2032A(e)(5)	5.05[6]; **5** n.351	7872(f)(1)	**11** n.294
2501	**11** n.290	7872(f)(2)(A)	**11** n.295
2511	**11** n.290	7872(f)(2)(B)	**11** n.296
2674(d)	6.06[2][c][ii]	7872(f)(3)	**11** n.297
3806	**12** n.37	7872(f)(5)	**11** n.307
4701	11.08	7872(g)	**11** n.297

Table of Treasury Regulations

[Text references are to paragraphs (¶) within Chapters; footnote references are to Chapters (boldface numbers) and notes (n.)]

TREAS. REG. §

1.61-1(a)	**3** n.39
1.61-2(d)(4)	**3** n.43
1.61-3	**6** n.10
1.61-3(b)	**3** n.113
1.61-4(a)	**3** n.228
1.61-7(d)	**11**.02[2][a]
1.61-8(b)	**3** n.113; **4** ns. 37, 102
1.61-12(a)	**12** n.208
1.111-1(a)	**12** n.165
1.111-1(a)(1)	**12** n.216
1.162-1(a)	**6** n.235
1.163-2(d)	**11** n.7
1.162-3	3.05[1][b]; **3** n.236; **6** ns. 28, 103–105
1.163-4	**8** n.149
1.163-8T	**6** n.264
1.164-6(d)(4)	**3** n.174
1.166-2(d)	**4** n.76
1.263(a)(2)(a)	**3** n.176
1.269-1(a)	**9** n.219
1.269-1(b)	**9** n.220
1.269-1(d)	**9** n.210
1.269-2(b)	**9** n.215
1.269-3(a)(2)	**9** n.221
1.269-3(b)	**9** n.214
1.301-1(b)	**3** n.96; **4** n.37
1.381(c)(4)-1	**9** n.223
1.381(c)(4)-1(b)(2)	**9** n.224
1.381(c)(4)-1(c)	**9** n.225
1.381(c)(4)-1(d)	**9** n.225
1.381(c)(5)	**7** n.317
1.381(c)(5)-1	**9** n.223
1.381(c)(5)-1(b)	**7** n.320
1.381(c)(5)-1(b)(1)(i)	**7** n.318
1.381(c)(5)-1(b)(4)(i)	**7** ns. 319, 321
1.381(c)(5)-1(c)(1)	**7** n.322

TREAS. REG. §

1.381(c)(5)-1(c)(2)	**7** n.323
1.441-1(b)(2)	**10** n.83
1.441-1(b)(3)	**10** ns. 64, 71–73
1.441-1(g)	**10** ns. 15, 16
1.441-2(a)	**10** ns. 23–25
1.441-2(b)(1)	**10** n.273
1.441-2(b)(2)	**10** n.274
1.441-2(c)	**10** n.175
1.441-2(c)(1)	**10** ns. 138, 139, 144, 171
1.441-2(c)(2)	**10** ns. 173, 174
1.441-2(c)(3)	**10** ns. 143, 176
1.441-2(c)(4)	**10** n.178
1.441-2(c)(5)	**10** ns. 31, 32, 253, 255
1.441-2(d)	**10** ns. 270, 271
1.442-1	**10**.05[4][b][i]
1.442-1(a)	**10** n.145
1.442-1(a)(2)	**10** n.235
1.442-1(b)(1)	**10** ns. 148–150, 162–164, 186, 190, 193
1.442-1(b)(2)(ii)	**10** n.231
1.442-1(b)(3)	**10** ns. 211, 212
1.442-1(c)	**10**.05[2][g][ii]; 10.05[4][b][ii]; **10** n.198
1.442-1(c)(1)	**10** n.199
1.442-1(c)(2)	**10** n.200
1.442-1(c)(2)(v)	**10** n.209
1.442-1(c)(3)	**10** n.201
1.442-1(c)(4)	**10** n.208
1.442-1(c)(5)	**10** n.210
1.442-1(d)	**10** n.206
1.442-1(e)	**10** n.194
1.443-1(a)(1)	**10** ns. 29–32
1.443-1(a)(2)	**10** n.36
1.443-1(b)	10.05[4][b][ii]; **10** ns. 236, 247

[Text references are to paragraphs (¶) within Chapters; footnote references are to Chapters (boldface numbers) and notes (n.)]

TREAS. REG. §

1.443-1(b)(1)(iv) **10** n.251
1.443-1(b)(1)(v) ..... **10** ns. 250, 252, 254
1.443-1(b)(1)(vi) **10** n.256
1.443-1(b)(2)(i) ...... **10** ns. 261, 262
1.443-1(b)(2)(ii) ...... **10** ns. 263–265
1.443-1(b)(2)(iii)(a) ...... **10** ns. 266, 267
1.443-1(b)(2)(v)(a) **10** n.268
1.446-1 .... **2** n.197
1.446-1(a)(1) .... **2** ns. 8, 15; **9** ns. 15, 170
1.446-1(a)(2) .... **2** ns. 79, 103; **9** n.171
1.446-1(a)(4) **2** n.49
1.446-1(a)(4)(i) **6** n.41
1.446-1(b)(2) **2** n.16
1.446-1(c)(1)(i) .... **3** ns. 1, 36–38
1.446-1(c)(1)(ii) ..... 4.04[3][c][ii]; **4** ns. 2, 3; **6** ns. 58, 60
1.446-1(c)(1)(ii)(B) .... **4** ns. 318, 319
1.446-1(c)(1)(ii)(C) ..... **2** ns. 79, 103; **4** n.8
1.446-1(c)(1)(iv) **2** n.189; **9** n.171
1.446-1(c)(1)(iv)(a) ..... **3** n.243; **9** ns. 182–184
1.446-1(c)(2) **8** n.144
1.446-1(c)(2)(i) ..... **2** ns. 81, 96; **3** ns. 5, 234, 242, 286; **4** n.12; **5** n.35; **6** ns. 13, 47; **8** n.177
1.446-1(d) ...... **2** n.181; **6** n.73; **9** ns. 178, 181
1.446-1(d)(1) .... **2** ns. 174, 176; **3** n.244
1.446-1(d)(2) **2** n.175
1.446-1(d)(3) **2** n.175
1.446-1(e) .... 7.04[5][a][iii]; **8** ns. 185, 206, 242
1.446-1(e)(ii)(b) ...... 9.05[1]; **9** n.186
1.446-1(e)(1) **8** n.4
1.446-1(e)(2)(i) .... **2** n.17; **8** ns. 8, 15, 16; **9** ns. 5, 23, 80, 104; 10.05[2][f]
1.446-1(e)(2)(ii) **8** n.6
1.446-1(e)(2)(ii)(a) .... 9.02[1] & n.14; **9** ns. 12, 27, 65, 68
1.446-1(e)(2)(ii)(b) ..... **8** n.7; 9.02[2] & n.18; **9** ns. 13, 99, 100
1.446-1(e)(2)(iii) **8** n.145; **9** n.134
1.446-1(e)(2)(b) **9** n.186

TREAS. REG. §

1.446-1(e)(3) **4** n.303; 8.03; **8** n.2, 201
1.446-1(e)(3)(i) .... **8** ns. 57, 131
1.446-1(e)(3)(ii) .... **2** ns. 72, 75; **8** ns. 61, 207
1.451-1(a) .... **3** ns. 36, 39; 4.03[1][b] & n.55; **4** ns. 2, 33, 235
1.451-1(c) **3** n.115
1.451-2 .... **8** n.145
1.451-2(a) .... **3** ns. 57, 79, 80, 86
1.451-2(a)(2) **3** n.87
1.451-2(b) .... **3** ns. 80, 84, 85, 99
1.451-3 .... **4** n.149; **6** n.425; **8** ns. 86, 146
1.451-3(a)(6) **7** n.190
1.451-3(b) **8** n.146
1.451-3(d)(8) **7** n.190
1.451-5 .... 4.03[3][e][ii] & n.150
1.451-5(a)(2) **4** n.150
1.451-5(a)(3) **4** n.150
1.451-5(b)(1) **4** n.152
1.451-5(b)(4) **4** n.153
1.451-5(c) **4** n.154
1.451-5(c)(3) **4** n.155
1.451-5(c)(4) **4** n.157
1.451-6 .... **3** n.116
1.453-1(a)(1) **5** n.78
1.453-1(b) **5** n.214
1.453-1(b)(1) **5** n.110
1.453-1(d) **5** n.126
1.453-2(a) .... **5** ns. 46, 57, 80
1.453-2(b) **5** n.81
1.453-2(b)(1) .... 5.04[6]; **5** n.83
1.453-2(c) **5** n.109
1.453-2(c)(1) **5** n.117
1.453-2(c)(2) **5** n.111
1.453-2(c)(3) **5** n.112
1.453-2(d) **5** n.102
1.453-2(d)(3) **5** n.105
1.453-2(d)(3)(i) **5** n.104
1.453-2(d)(3)(ii) **5** n.104
1.453-2(d)(4) **5** n.105
1.453-9(c)(2) .... **5** ns. 321, 322
1.453-9(c)(3) **5** n.323
1.455-3 .... **4** n.136
1.461-1(a)(1) **3** n.119
1.461-1(a)(2) **4** n.3
1.461-1(a)(2)(i) **4** n.160
1.461-1(a)(2)(ii) .... **4** ns. 224, 227

[Text references are to paragraphs (¶) within Chapters; footnote references are to Chapters (boldface numbers) and notes (n.)]

TREAS. REG. §

1.461-1(a)(2)(iii) ...... **4** ns. 159, 248
1.461-1(a)(2)(iii)(A) **4** n.63
1.461-1(a)(3) ..... **4** ns. 159, 225, 235
1.461-1(c)(3)(ii) **4** n.303
1.461-1(c)(3)(iv) **4** n.303
1.461-1(e)(3) **4** n.303
1.461-2(b)(2) **4** n.205
1.461-2(c)(1)(ii) **4** n.219
1.461-2(e) **4** n.218
1.461-2(f) **4** n.222
1.461-4 ..... **4** ns. 241, 261, 266, 271, 276, 281
1.461-4(d)(2)(ii) **4** n.283
1.461-4(d)(3) **4** n.286
1.461-4(d)(4) **4** n.291
1.461-4(d)(4)(ii) **4** n.293
1.461-4(d)(5) **4** n.310
1.461-4(d)(5)(ii) .... **4** ns. 245, 311
1.461-4(d)(6)(i) **4** n.282
1.461-4(d)(6)(ii) **4** n.284
1.461-4(d)(6)(iii) **4** n.287
1.461-4(d)(6)(iv) **4** n.290
1.451-4(d)(7) **4** n.292
1.461-4(g) .... **4** n.
1.461-4(g)(1) .... **4** ns. 304, 305
1.461-4(g)(1)(ii)(A) **4** n.306
1.461-4(g)(1)(ii)(B) .... **4** ns. 307, 308
1.461-4(g)(1)(ii)(C) **4** n.310
1.461-4(g)(1)(ii)(C)(2) **4** n.311
1.461-4(g)(1)(ii)(C)(3) **4** n.312
1.461-4(g)(2) **4** n.295
1.461-4(g)(2)(i) **4** n.296
1.461-4(g)(2)(ii) **4** n.297
1.461-4(g)(3) **4** n.299
1.461-4(g)(4) **4** n.300
1.461-4(g)(5) .... **4** ns. 269, 301
1.461-4(g)(6) **4** n.302
1.461-4(g)(6)(iii) **4** n.303
1.461-4(g)(7) .... **4** ns. 255, 256, 294
1.461-4(k)(1) **4** n.313
1.461-4(k)(2) **4** n.314
1.461-5 .... **4** n.325
1.461-5(b)(1)(ii) **4** n.327
1.461-5(b)(2) .... **4** ns. 328, 329
1.461-5(b)(3) .... **4** ns. 329, 332
1.461-5(b)(4) **4** n.339
1.461-5(b)(4)(i) **4** n.333
1.461-5(b)(4)(ii) **4** n.334
1.461-5(b)(4)(iii) **4** n.335

TREAS. REG. §

1.461-5(b)(5) **4** n.340
1.461-5(c) **4** n.298
1.461-5(d) **4** n.342
1.461 6 .... **4** n.305
1.471-1–1.471-11 .... **2** n.111
1.471-1 ...... 6.09[3][b][ii]; **6** ns. 12, 41–43, 53, 54, 56, 64
1.471-2 .... **2** n.152
1.471-2(a) **6** n.369
1.471-2(b) ...... **2** n.111; **6** ns. 32, 292
1.471-2(c) .... 6.09[3][b][ii]; **6** ns. 370, 375, 378, 381; 7.03[3][c] & n.95; **8** ns. 144, 176
1.471-2(d) ... **6** ns. 124, 343, 346, 348
1.471-2(e) **6** n.348
1.471-2(f) **6** n.353
1.471-2(f)(1)–1.471-2(f)(7) ..... **8** ns. 143, 175
1.471-3(b) .... **6** ns. 135, 142, 148
1.471-3(c) **6** n.202
1.471-3(d) **6** n.233
1.471-4 .... **6** ns. 375, 377, 384
1.471-4(a) .... 6.09[3][b]
1.471-4(a)(2) ...... 6.09[3][b] & n.401
1.471-4(b) .... 6.09[3][b][ii] & ns. 407, 408; **6** n.391; **8** ns. 143, 175
1.471-4(c) **6** n.387; **7** n.97
1.471-5 .... **6** ns. 426–428
1.471-6 .... **6** n.429
1.471-6(c) **6** n.430
1.471-6(d) **6** n.432
1.471-6(e) .... **6** ns. 433, 434
1.471-6(f) 6.11
1.471-7 .... **6** n.438
1.471-8 .... 6.11; **6** n.438
1.471-8(c) **6** n.442
1.471-8(d)–1.471-8(f) **6** n.443
1.471-8(g) **6** n.444
1.471-11 ...... 6.05[2][a]; **6** ns. 6, 24, 202, 214; **8** n.146
1.471-11(b)(2) .... **6** ns. 205, 209, 210
1.471-11(b)(3) **6** n.211
1.471-11(c)(2)(i) .... **6** ns. 217, 218
1.471-11(c)(2)(i)(f) ...... **6** ns. 28, 44, 104, 105
1.471-11(c)(2)(ii) ...... **6** ns. 217, 222
1.471-11(c)(2)(iii) .... **2** n.67; **6** ns. 217, 224, 227, 230
1.471-11(c)(3) **6** n.232

[Text references are to paragraphs (¶) within Chapters; footnote references are to Chapters (boldface numbers) and notes (n.)]

TREAS. REG. §

1.471-11(d)(1) 6 n.294
1.471-11(d)(2) 6 n.302
1.471-11(d)(2)(i) ...... 6 ns. 305, 309, 310
1.471-11(d)(2)(ii) ...... 6 ns. 303, 304
1.471-11(d)(2)(iii) ..... 6 ns. 306–308
1.471-11(d)(3) 6 n.311
1.471-11(d)(4) 6 n.312
1.471-11(e) 9 n.133
1.472-1(a) ..... 7 ns. 270, 271; 8 n.309
1.472-1(c) .... 7 ns. 36, 37, 185
1.472-1(d) 7 n.109
1.472-1(e) 7 n.110
1.472-1(f) 7 n.110
1.472-1(i) 7 n.39
1.472-1(j) 7 n.36
1.472-1(k) 7 n.205
1.472-1(l) 7.05
1.472-2(b) .... 7 ns. 90, 96
1.472-2(c) .... 7 ns. 91, 96
1.472-2(d)(1) 7 n.111
1.472-2(d)(1)(ii) 7 n.112
1.472-2(e)(1)(i) 7 n.64
1.472-2(e)(1)(ii) 7 n.68
1.472-2(e)(1)(iii) 7 n.70
1.472-2(e)(1)(iv) 7 n.71
1.472-2(e)(1)(v) 7 n.73
1.472-2(e)(1)(vi) 7 n.74
1.472-2(e)(1)(vii) 7 n.77
1.472-2(e)(1)(viii) 7 n.77
1.472-2(e)(2) 7 n.61
1.472-2(e)(3) 7 n.65
1.472-2(e)(3)(iii) 7 n.66
1.472-2(e)(3)(v) 7 n.67
1.472-2(e)(4) 7 n.69
1.472-2(e)(6) 7 n.72
1.472-2(e)(8) .... 7 ns. 75, 76
1.472-2(e)(9) 7 n.82
1.472-2(h) 7 n.102
1.472-3(a) .... 7 ns. 27, 28, 34
1.472-4(b) 6 n.386
1.472-6 .... 7 ns. 26, 289
1.472-8 .... 7 n.119
1.472-8(b) .... 7 ns. 130, 132, 140, 240–242
1.472-8(b)(1) 7 n.141
1.472-8(b)(2) 7 n.142
1.472-8(b)(2)(i) 7 n.143
1.472-8(b)(2)(ii) 7 n.143

TREAS. REG. §

1.472-8(b)(3) .... 7 ns. 76, 110, 147, 149
1.472-8(b)(3)(ii) 7 n.185
1.472-8(c) .... 7 ns. 131, 132, 150, 240
1.472-8(d) .... 7 ns. 144, 240
1.472-8(e)(1) .... 7 ns. 159–161, 164, 165, 209
1.472-8(e)(2)(ii) 7 n.168
1.472-8(e)(2)(iii) .... 7 ns. 156, 166
1.472-8(e)(2)(v) 7 n.157
1.472-8(e)(3) .... 7 ns. 213, 214
1.472-8(e)(3)(i) 7 n.217
1.472-8(e)(3)(ii) .... 7 ns. 245–247
1.472-8(e)(3)(iii)(B) .... 7 ns. 216, 218, 250–253
1.472-8(e)(3)(iii)(B)(4) 7 n.219
1.472-8(e)(3)(iii)(B)(5) ..... 7 ns. 220, 221
1.472-8(e)(3)(iii)(C) .... 7 ns. 222–228, 235
1.472-8(e)(3)(iv) .... 7 ns. 237–239
1.472-8(e)(3)(v) .... 7 ns. 248, 249
1.472-8(e)(3)(vi) .... 7 ns. 254, 255
1.472-8(g) 7 n.306
1.472-8(g)(2) .... 7.08[1][a]; 7 n.46
1.472-8(g)(2)(ii) 7 n.307
1.472-8(h)(10) 7 n.130
1.481-2(a) 8 n.47
1.481-2(c) 8 n.47
1.481-2(c)(5)(i) 8 n.55
1.481-2(c)(5)(ii) 8 n.56
1.481-4(g)(3) .... 9 ns. 24, 61
1.481-5 .... 8 n.57
1.482-1(a) 4 n.143
1.513-1(c)(1) 5 n.63
1.664-1(c)(2)(i) 3 n.5
1.706-1(b)(1)(i) 10 n.90
1.706-1(b)(4)(iii) 10 n.100
1.706-1(c)(1) 10 n.42
1.706-1(c)(2)(i) 10 n.46
1.708-1(b)(1)(i) 10 n.43
1.708-1(b)(1)(ii) .... 10 ns. 44, 45
1.708-1(b)(1)(iv) .... 10.07[2]
1.1341-1(e) 12 n.106
1.1341-1(g) 12 n.110
1.1341-1(h) 12 n.112
1.1502-3(e) 5 n.123
1.1502-13 .... 3 n.283; 5.04[6]; 9 n.101
1.1502-13(a) 5 n.128
1.1502-13(c) 5 n.129

[Text references are to paragraphs (¶) within Chapters; footnote references are to Chapters (boldface numbers) and notes (n.)]

Treas. Reg. §

1.1502-13(e)	**5** n.130
1.1502-13(h)	**5** n.131
1.1502-17	**3** n.283
1.1502-76	**10** n.206
1.1502-76(a)	**10** n.33
1.1502-76(a)(1)	**10** ns. 134–136
1.1502-76(b)(2)	**10** n.34
1.1502-76(b)(5)(i)	**8** ns. 232, 235
1.1502-76(b)(5)(ii)	**8** ns. 232, 235
1.6012-2(a)(1)	**10** n.80
1.6012-2(a)(2)	**10** ns. 38, 81, 82, 86
1.6072-2(a)	**10** n.37
1.6851-1(a)(2)	**10** ns. 48, 49
1.6851-1(a)(3)	**10** ns. 50, 51
1.6851-3	**10** n.52
1.9100-1(a)	**7** n.30; **10** n.191
15A.453-1(d)(2)(i)	**3** n.54
29.22(c)-1	**8** n.342
29.41-a	**8** n.342
29.41-2	**2** n.158; **9** n.20
39.41-2(c)	**8** n.24
481-2(b)	**8** n.48
481-2(c)	**8** n.48
601.204(a)	**10** n.189

PROPOSED REGULATIONS

Prop. Reg. §

453A-3(d)	**5** n.38
1.163-7(b)	**11** n.146
1.163-7(b)(3)	**11** n.146
1.263A(f)-2(a)(4)(ii)	**6** n.267
1.263A(f)-2(a)(4)(iii)	**6** ns. 267, 272
1.263A(f)-2(c)(2)	**6** n.267
1.263A(f)-3	**6** n.283
1.263A(f)-3(b)(3)	**6** n.284
1.263A(f)-3(d)	**6** n.285
1.263A(f)-5(g)	**6** n.281
1.263A(f)-5(g)(2)	**6** n.282
1.263A(f)-8	**6** n.277
1.263A(f)-9	**6** ns. 257, 258
1.263A(f)-9(a)	**6** n.260
1.263A(f)-9(d)	**6** n.261
1.446-2	**3** n.78; **11** n.79
1.446-2(a)(1)	**11** n.79
1.446-2(e)	**11** n.127
1.453-1(f)	**5** n.289
1.453A-3	**5** n.135
1.453A-3(d)	**5** n.35

Prop. Reg. §

1.461-4	**4** ns. 240, 253, 260, 265, 270, 275, 321
1.461-4(g)(6)	4.04[3][c]; **4** n.303
1.461-5(d)	**4** n.341
1.472-8(e)(3)	**7** n.211
1.483-1(a)(1)	**11** n.246
1.483-1(a)(2)(ii)	**11** n.238
1.483-1(c)	**11** n.251
1.483-2(a)	**11** n.244
1.483-2(a)(1)	**11** n.222
1.483-2(c)	**11** n.245
1.483-3(b)	**11** n.248
1.1271–1.1275	**11** n.15
1.1271-1(a)(1)	**11** ns. 36, 37
1.1271-1(a)(2)	**11** n.40
1.1271-1(b)(2)	**11** ns. 45, 46
1.1271-1(b)(1)	**11** n.56
1.1271-3(c)	**11** n.47
1.1272-1(a)(2)	**11** ns. 75, 76, 80, 81
1.1272-1(b)(1)	**11** n.56
1.1272-1(b)(1)(i)	**11** n.57
1.1272-1(b)(1)(ii)	**11** ns. 63, 64, 71
1.1272-1(b)(1)(iii)	**11** n.74
1.1272-1(b)(1)(iv)	**11** n.72
1.1272-1(c)(1)	**11** n.67
1.1272-1(c)(2)	**11** n.55
1.1272-1(c)(3)	**11** n.69
1.1272-1(d)	**11** n.206
1.1272-1(d)(3)	**11** ns. 59, 115, 116
1.1272-1(d)(4)	**11** n.60
1.1272-1(d)(5)	**11** ns. 58, 109
1.1272-1(j)	**11** ns. 65, 66, 68, 69, 117
1.1272-2(a)	**11** ns. 83, 85
1.1272-2(b)(5)	**11** n.86
1.1273-1(b)	**11** n.112
1.1273-1(b)(1)	**11** n.124
1.1273-1(c)(1)	**11** ns. 99, 100, 108
1.1273-1(c)(3)	**11** n.106
1.1273-1(c)(4)	**11** n.107
1.1273-1(d)(3)	**11** ns. 142, 144
1.1273-1(d)(5)	**11** n.145
1.1273-1(d)(6)	**11** ns. 147, 148
1.1273-1(e)(1)	**11** n.111
1.1273-1(e)(2)	**11** n.113
1.1273-1(e)(3)	**11** n.143
1.1273-1(f)	**11** n.145
1.1273-2(a)(1)	**11** ns. 121, 122
1.1273-2(a)(2)	**11** n.120
1.1273-2(a)(3)	**11** n.123

[Text references are to paragraphs (¶) within Chapters; footnote references are to Chapters (boldface numbers) and notes (n.)]

PROP. REG. §

1.1273-2(c)(1) **11** n.131
1.1273-2(d) **11** n.132
1.1273-2(d)(7) **11** n.133
1.1273-2(f)(1) **11** n.134
1.1273-2(f)(2) **11** n.136
1.1273-2(g) .... **11** ns. 137, 138
1.1273-2(j)(2) .... **11** ns. 125, 127
1.1273-2(j)(4) **11** n.128
1.1273-2(j)(5) **11** n.129
1.1274-1(b)(2)(i) **11** n.192
1.1274-1(b)(2)(ii)(A) **11** n.181
1.1274-1(b)(2)(ii)(B) **11** n.189
1.1274-2(b)(3) ...... **11** ns. 169, 170
1.1274-2(c)(1) **11** n.159
1.1274-2(c)(3) .... **11** ns. 61, 158
1.1274-2(d)(1)(i) **11** n.161
1.1274-2(d)(1)(ii) **11** n.161
1.1274-2(e) **11** n.224
1.1274-2(e)(1) .... **11** ns. 162, 163
1.1274-2(e)(2) **11** n.164
1.1274-3(a)(2)(iv) **11** n.167
1.1274-3(b)(1) **11** n.172
1.1274-3(b)(2) **11** n.171
1.1274-3(b)(3) .... **11** ns. 160, 168
1.1274-3(d) .... **11** ns. 173, 174
1.1274-4(b) **11** n.154
1.1274-4(b)(12) **11** n.214
1.1274-4(d) **11** n.155
1.1274-4(g) **11** n.156
1.1274A-1(b)(2) **11** n.198
1.1274A-1(b)(4) **11** n.199
1.1274A-1(c) **11** n.197
1.1274A-1(c)(1) **11** n.201
1.1274A-1(c)(2) **11** n.202
1.1275-1(b) .... **11** ns. 73, 98
1.1275-1(d) .... **11** ns. 24, 77
1.1275-1(h) **11** n.49
1.1275-2(a) **11** n.41
1.1275-4 .... **11** n.18
1.1275-4(a)(2) **11** n.207
1.1275-4(a)(3) **11** n.204
1.1275-4(a)(4) **11** n.205
1.1275-4(a)(6) **11** n.208
1.1275-4(a)(7) **11** n.209
1.1275-4(a)(7)(ii)(A) **11**ns.220,221
1.1275-4(a)(7)(ii)(B) **11** n.222
1.1275-4(b)(1)(ii) **11** n.218
1.1275-4(b)(2)(i) **11** n.210
1.1275-4(b)(2)(ii) **11** n.211

PROP. REG. §

1.1275-4(b)(3) **11** n.213
1.1275-4(b)(4) **11** n.216
1.1275-4(b)(4)(iv) **11** n.217
1.1275-4(b)(5) **11** n.212
1.1275-4(b)(6) **11** n.212
1.1275-4(b)(7) **11** n.212
1.1275-4(b)(8) **11** n.215
1.1275-4(b)(9) **11** n.219
1.1275-4(b)(12) **11** n.217
1.1275-4(c)(1) **11** n.223
1.1275-4(c)(2) **11** n.224
1.1275-4(c)(2)(i) **11** n.232
1.1275-4(c)(3)(i) **11** n.225
1.1275-4(c)(3)(ii) **11** n.227
1.1275-4(c)(4) .... **11** ns. 228, 229
1.1275-4(d)(1) **11** n.230
1.1275-4(d)(2)(i) **11** n.231
1.1275-4(d)(7) **11** n.231
1.1275-4(d)(3) **11** n.233
1.1275-4(d)(4) **11** n.234
1.1275-4(d)(5) **11** n.235
1.1275-4(d)(6) ...... **11** ns. 236, 237
1.1275-4(d)(8) **11** n.237
1.1275-4(e) **11** n.226
1.1275-4(f) .... **11** ns. 31, 32
1.1275-5(a)(3) **11** n.101
1.1275-5(a)(4) **11** n.101
1.1275-5(b)(1) **11** n.102
1.1275-5(b)(2) **11** n.102
1.1275-5(c)(1) .... **11** ns. 103, 104
1.1275-5(c)(2)(i) **11** n.103
1.1275-5(e) .... **11** ns. 101, 105
1.1275-5(f) **11** n.105
1.7872-3(b) **11** n.305
1.7872-3(b)(4) **11** n.307
1.7872-3(e)(1) **11** n.311
1.7872-3(e)(2)(i) **11** n.306
1.7872-4 .... **11** n.303
1.7872-4(b) **11** n.297
1.7872-4(c) **11** n.297
1.7872-4(d) **11** n.297
1.7872-4(e) **11** n.297
1.7872-4(f) **11** n.297
1.7872-6 .... **11** n.300
1.7872-6(b)(4) **11** n.301
1.7872-6(b)(5) **11** n.301
1.7872-10(a)(1) **11** n.291
1.7872-10(a)(2) **11** n.292
1.7872-10(a)(5) **11** n.291

[Text references are to paragraphs (¶) within Chapters; footnote references are to Chapters (boldface numbers) and notes (n.)]

TEMPORARY REGULATIONS

TEMP. REG. §

1.163-8T(m)(7)(ii)	6.06[2][c][ii]
1.263A-1T	**1** n.11; **6** n.214; **8** n.115
1.263A-1T(a)(5)(ii)	**6** n.183; **7** n.139
1.263A-1T(b)	**6** n.203
1.263A-1T(b)(2)(i)	**6** ns. 205, 209, 210
1.263A-1T(b)(2)(ii)	**6** n.212
1.263A-1T(b)(2)(iii)	**6** n.242
1.263A-1T(b)(2)(iii)(F)	**6** ns. 28, 44, 104, 105
1.263A-1T(b)(2)(iv)(B)	**6** ns. 263, 264, 279, 287
1.263A-1T(b)(2)(iv)(C)	**6** ns. 289–291
1.263A-1T(b)(2)(iv)(D)	**6** ns. 273, 274
1.263A-1T(b)(2)(v)	**6** ns. 246, 248
1.263A-1T(b)(2)(vii)	**6** ns. 314, 315
1.263A-1T(b)(2)(viii)	**6** ns. 253, 255
1.263A-1T(b)(3)(iii)(A)(1)	**6** n.296
1.263A-1T(b)(3)(iii)(A)(2)	**6** ns. 297–299
1.263A-1T(b)(3)(iii)(A)(3)(i)	**6** n.300
1.263A-1T(b)(3)(iii)(A)(3)(ii)	**6** n.301
1.263A-1T(b)(3)(iii)(C)	**6** n.302
1.263A-1T(b)(3)(iii)(C)(1)	**6** ns. 305, 309, 310
1.263A-1T(b)(3)(iii)(C)(2)	**6** ns. 303, 304
1.263A-1T(b)(3)(iii)(C)(3)	**6** ns. 306–308
1.263A-1T(b)(3)(iii)(D)	**6** n.311
1.263A-1T(b)(4)	**6** n.340
1.263A-1T(b)(4)(iii)(A)	**6** n.341
1.263A-1T(b)(4)(iii)(B)	**6** n.341
1.263A-1T(b)(4)(vii)	**6** n.252
1.263A-1T(b)(5)	**6** n.318
1.263A-1T(b)(5)(i)(B)	**6** n.321
1.263A-1T(b)(5)(ii)	**6** n.319
1.263A-1T(b)(5)(iii)	**6** ns. 322, 323
1.263A-1T(b)(5)(iv)	**6** n.320
1.263A-1T(b)(5)(vi)	**6** n.324

TEMP. REG. §

1.263A-1T(b)(6)	**6** ns. 327, 328
1.263A-1T(b)(6)(iii)	**6** ns. 329, 330
1.263A-1T(b)(6)(iii)(B)	**6** n.331
1.263A-1T(b)(6)(iii)(C)	**6** n.333
1.263A-1T(b)(6)(iv)	**6** ns. 334, 335
1.263A-1T(b)(6)(v)	**6** ns. 336–338
1.263A-1T(d)	**6** n.156
1.263A-1T(d)(1)(i)	**6** n.158
1.263A-1T(d)(1)(ii)	**6** n.158
1.263A-1T(d)(2)	**6** n.155
1.263A-1T(d)(2)(iv)(A)	**6** n.139
1.263A-1T(d)(3)(i)	**6** ns. 160–163
1.263A-1T(d)(3)(ii)	**6** n.164
1.263A-1T(d)(3)(ii)(A)(1)	**6** ns. 165, 166
1.263A-1T(d)(3)(ii)(A)(2)	**6** ns. 167–170
1.263A-1T(d)(3)(ii)(A)(3)	**6** n.171
1.263A-1T(d)(3)(ii)(A)(4)	**6** n.174
1.263A-1T(d)(3)(ii)(A)(5)	**6** n.173
1.263A-1T(d)(3)(ii)(B)(1)	**6** n.176
1.263A-1T(d)(3)(ii)(B)(2)	**6** n.177
1.263A-1T(d)(3)(ii)(B)(4)(ii)(A)	**6** n.178
1.263A-1T(d)(3)(ii)(B)(4)(ii)(B)	**6** n.179
1.263A-1T(d)(3)(ii)(B)(4)(iii)	**6** n.180
1.263A-1T(d)(3)(ii)(C)(1)	**6** ns. 181, 182
1.263A-1T(d)(3)(ii)(C)(2)	**6** n.186
1.263A-1T(d)(3)(ii)(C)(3)	**6** ns. 184, 185
1.263A-1T(d)(3)(ii)(C)(4)	**6** n.187
1.263A-1T(d)(3)(ii)(C)(5)	**6** n.188
1.263A-1T(d)(3)(ii)(D)	**6** ns. 189, 190
1.263A-1T(d)(4)	**6** n.191
1.263A-1T(d)(4)(iii)	**6** n.196
1.263A-1T(d)(4)(iv)	**6** ns. 193, 195
1.263A-1T(d)(5)	**6** ns. 191, 197
1.263A-1T(d)(6)	**6** ns. 191, 198
1.263A-1T(e)(1)	**9** n.133
1.263A-1T(e)(1)(ii)	**8** n.119
1.263A-1T(e)(3)	**8** n.115
1.263A-1T(e)(6)(iv)(C)	**7** ns. 175, 176

[Text references are to paragraphs (¶) within Chapters; footnote references are to Chapters (boldface numbers) and notes (n.)]

TEMP. REG. §

1.263A-1T(e)(11) **8** n.116; **9** n.133
1.263A-1T(e)(11)(iv) .... **8** ns. 117, 118
1.280H-1T(b)(4)(ii) **10** n.304
1.280H-1T(c) **10** n.305
1.280H-1T(d) **10** n.306
1.280H-1T(e)(3) **10** n.307
1.441-3T ...... **1** n.11; **10** ns. 97, 141, 142, 146, 172
1.441-3T(b) **10** n.124
1.441-3T(e) .... **10** ns. 175, 177
1.441-4T(d) **10** n.301
1.442-2T ...... **1** n.11; **10** ns. 121, 226
1.442-2T(c) .... **10** ns. 106, 229
1.442-2T(c)(5) **10** n.230
1.442-3T **1** n.11; **10** n.121
1.444-0T **10** n.280
1.444-1T(a)(5) .... **10** ns. 283, 299
1.444-1T(b)(2)(ii) **10** n.288
1.444-1T(b)(3) **10** n.289
1.444-2T **10** n.284
1.444-2T(c)(2) **10** n.286
1.444-2T(e) .... **10** ns. 285, 287
1.444-2T(e)(5) **10** n.287
1.444-3T **10** n.282
1.444-3T(b) .... **10** ns. 291, 292
1.444-3T(b)(4) **10** n.293
1.444-3T(b)(4)(iii) **10** n.300
1.448-1T **1** n.11; **3** n.201
1.448-1T(b) **3** n.203
1.448-1T(c) **3** n.196
1.448-1T(e)(4)(i) **3** n.213
1.448-1T(e)(4)(ii) **3** n.214
1.448-1T(e)(4)(iii) ..... **3** ns. 216, 217
1.448-1T(e)(4)(iv) **3** n.218
1.448-1T(e)(4)(iv)(A) **3** n.219
1.448-1T(e)(4)(iv)(B) **3** n.220
1.448-1T(e)(5) **3** n.222
1.448-1T(e)(5)(ii) **3** n.223
1.448-1T(e)(5)(iv) **3** n.224
1.448-1T(e)(5)(v) **3** n.225
1.448-1T(e)(5)(vi) **3** n.226
1.448-1T(e)(5)(vii) **3** n.227
1.448-1T(f) **3** n.204
1.448-1T(f)(2)(i) **3** n.208
1.448-1T(f)(2)(ii) **3** n.207

TEMP. REG. §

1.448-1T(f)(2)(iii) **3** n.209
1.448-1T(g)(3)(iii) **8** n.110
1.448-2T .... **1** n.18; **4** ns. 68, 80
1.448-2T(a) **4** n.83
1.448-2T(c)(1) **4** n.82
1.448-2T(d) **4** n.84
1.448-2T(e)(1) **4** n.87
1.448-2T(e)(2) **4** n.86
1.448-2T(e)(2)(ii) **4** n.88
1.448-2T(e)(2)(iii) **4** n.89
1.448-2T(e)(3) **4** n.90
1.448-2T(e)(4) **4** n.91
1.448-2T(g)(2) **8** n.124
1.453e-10T .... **5** ns. 27, 353, 354
1.461-3T .... **4** ns. 162, 242
1.461-7T .... 4.04[3][c][ii]; 4.04[3][f][iv]; **4** ns. 162, 242
1.7519-1T(b)(5)(iv)(D) **10** n.297
1.7519-1T(b)(5)(v) **10** n.298
1.7519-1T(d) **10** n.295
1.7519-2T **10** n.294
1.7872-5T(c)(3) **11** n.297
5f.442-1 .... **10** ns. 213, 214
15a.453-1(b)(2)(ii) **5** n.209
15a.453-1(b)(2)(iv) ..... **5** ns. 200, 233
15a.453-1(b)(2)(v) **5** n.211
15a.453-1(b)(3)(i) ..... **5** ns. 166, 204, 205, 211
15a.453-1(b)(3)(ii) **5** n.236
15a.453-1(c) .... **5** ns. 18, 269
15a.453-1(c)(2) **5** n.270
15a.453-1(c)(2)(ii) **5** n.210
15a.453-1(c)(2)(iii) **5** n.210
15a.453-1(c)(3) **5** n.271
15a.453-1(c)(4) .... **5** ns. 274, 275
15a.453-1(c)(6) **5** n.276
15a.453-1(c)(7) **5** n.277
15a.453-1(c)(7)(ii) ..... **5** ns. 278–280
15a.453-1(d) **5** n.293
15a.453-1(d)(2)(i) **5** n.301
15a.453-1(d)(2)(ii) **5** n.304
15a.453-1(d)(2)(iii) **5** n.305
15a.453-1(d)(3)(i) **5** n.294
15a.453-1(d)(3)(ii) ..... **5** ns. 297–299
15a.453-1(d)(4) **5** n.300

Table of Revenue Rulings

[Text references are to paragraphs (¶) within Chapters; footnote references are to Chapters (boldface numbers) and notes (n.)]

REV. RUL.

23	7 n.210
94(1953)	10 n.246
267(1953)	5 n.318
54-566	12 n.176
55-5	5 n.330
55-79	5 ns. 222, 223
55-80	10 ns. 33, 257
55-111	10 n.188
55-317	3 n.76
56-463	10 n.237
56-483	10 ns. 40, 89
57-276	10 n.84
57-389	10 n.74
57-589	10 n.68
58-256	10 n.168
58-340	9 n.136
58-546	12 n.184
59-285	9 ns. 21, 136
59-343	5 n.37
60-31	3 n.103
60-51	10 n.88
60-53	5 n.113
60-182	10 n.157
60-237	4 n.41
60-243	9.06[2][b] & n.156
60-268	10.02[3][a][iii] & n.35
60-321	7 n.187
62-128	12 n.190
63-57	3 ns. 91, 141
64-215	3 n.83
65-95	3 n.90
65-185	5 n.342
65-254	12 n.109
65-287	9.06[2][b] & n.159
65-316	10 n.179
66-68	10 n.69
66-145	6 n.206
66-206	8 n.92
67-12	3 n.249
67-147	2 n.48

REV. RUL.

67-189	10 n.258
67-200	12 n.184
68-13	5 ns. 222, 223
68-35	2 n.48; 3 n.268; 8 n.306
68-83	2 ns. 48, 68; 3 n.268; 8 n.305
68-98	8 n.41
68-125	10.04[2] & n.66
68-153	12 ns. 107, 108
68-163	5 n.113
68-262	8 n.41
68-419	5 n.331
68-575	5 n.123
68-674	5 n.143
69-6	5 n.243
69-17	7 n.83
69-74	5 n.284
69-81	6 n.122
69-410	10 n.246
69-462	5 ns. 98, 99, 142
69-536	6 n.125
69-563	10 n.68
69-619	6 n.148
69-661	6 n.364
70-68	4 n.40; 6 n.63
70-139	5 n.127
70-238	9 n.217
70-367	4 n.347
70-378	10 n.258
70-413	3 n.168
70-457	7 n.83
70-539	9 ns. 73, 74
70-540	3 ns. 90, 153; 9 n.149
70-564	7 ns. 306, 309
70-565	7 ns. 306, 308
70-647	3 n.147
71-129	10 ns. 37, 39, 87
71-160	12 n.181
71-161	12 n.181
71-190	3 n.169

[Text references are to paragraphs (¶) within Chapters; footnote references are to Chapters (boldface numbers) and notes (n.)]

REV. RUL.

71-234	6.08[3] & ns. 356–358; 6.08[3][a] & n.365; **6** n.373
71-366	**6** n.386
71-429	9.06[2][b] & n.160
71-595	5.04[2][c][iii] & n.72; 5.04[2][d][i] & n.99; **5** ns. 68, 142
72-34	**4** ns. 175, 347
72-100	**3** n.94
72-184	10.05[2][g][ii] & ns. 180, 181, 192
72-317	**3** n.69
72-570	**5** n.338
73-5	5.04[2][a] & n.48
73-65	**6** ns. 146, 147
73-99	**3** n.132
73-369	**5** n.194
73-385	**4** n.41
73-408	**12** n.181
73-424	**5** n.64
73-436	**5** n.52
73-437	**5** n.52
73-438	**5** n.52
73-485	**6** n.78
74-127	**4** ns. 184, 185
74-157	**5** n.332
74-206	**12** n.181
74-270	**2** n.185
74-279	**6** n.78
74-280	**2** n.185
74-318	**12** n.84
74-326	**10** n.207
74-383	**2** ns. 48, 68; **3** n.268
74-384	**5** n.216
74-431	**12** n.225
74-585	**10** n.259
74-586	**7** n.58
74-607	**3** n.90; **4** ns. 37, 117, 145
75-28	**12** n.181
75-56	**9** n.74
75-96	**6** n.63
75-181	**7** n.210
75-195	**4** n.117
75-200	**5** n.64
75-457	**5** n.333
75-501	**12** n.222
75-538	**6** n.92
76-30	**10** n.158
76-41	**12** n.222
76-43	**10** n.159

REV. RUL.

76-100	**5** n.318
76-135	**3** ns. 56, 136
76-150	**12** n.177
76-282	**7** n.99
76-345	**4** n.175
76-407	**10** n.155
76-482	10.06[1] & n.272
76-497	**10** n.156
77-56	**5** n.267
77-134	9.03[3] & n.63; **9** ns. 50, 108, 110
77-228	**6** n.223
77-257	**3** n.135
77-264	**8** n.91
77-266	**4** n.347
77-364	**6** n.386
77-480	**7** n.169
78-30	**3** n.127
78-38	**3** ns. 127, 128
78-39	**3** ns. 127, 128
78-96	**10** n.164
78-103	**3** n.172
78-117	**3** n.96
78-165	**8** n.259
78-173	**3** n.127
78-179	**10** n.232
78-237	**8** n.312
78-246	7.03[2][b][viii] & n.86
78-262	**7** n.35
78-278	12.05[4][a][ix] & n.199
78-280	**12** ns. 190, 193
79-15	12.05[4][b][i] & n.217
79-25	**6** n.226
79-45	**8** n.263
79-72	**3** n.87
79-103	**7** n.158
79-123	**8** n.329
79-188	**6** n.100; **7** n.301
79-196	**5** ns. 113, 114
79-229	**2** n.100; **3** n.184
79-278	**12** n.134
79-292	**4** n.62; **5** n.3
79-339	**3** n.184
80-157	**3** n.88
80-308	**4** n.117
80-352	**10** n.75
80-361	**4** n.76
81-93	**9** n.197
81-259	**8** n.302

[Text references are to paragraphs (¶) within Chapters; footnote references are to Chapters (boldface numbers) and notes (n.)]

REV. RUL.

81-272 . . . . 6 ns. 182, 200
82-122 . . . . 5 n.333
82-188 . . . . 5.06[4] & n.337
82-208 . . . . 3 ns. 170, 180
83-12 . . . . 3 n.107
83-59 . . . . 6 ns. 83, 381, 422
83-66 . . . . 3 n.166
83-84 . . . . 3 n.94; 4 n.280
83-106 . . . . 4 n.117
84-31 . . . . 4 n.117
84-123 . . . . 10 n.82
85-22 . . . . 10 n.12
85-83 . . . . 10 n.69
85-133 . . . . . 5.04[6] & n.132; 5 ns. 53, 66; 10 n.69
85-134 . . . . 8 n.93
85-172 . . . . 7 n.312
85-176 . . . . 7.08[1][a] & n.305
86-72 . . . . 5 ns. 286, 319
86-149 . . . . 6 ns. 126, 127; 7 n.279
86-152 . . . . 7 n.279
87-22 . . . . 3 n.153
87-29 . . . . 5 n.88
87-30 . . . . 5 n.89
87-48 . . . . 5 ns. 86, 87
87-49 . . . . 7 n.83
87-57 . . . . 10 ns. 101, 160, 219
87-84 . . . . 6 ns. 219, 228
87-140 . . . . 8 n.332
88-21 . . . . 7 ns. 58, 63
88-60 . . . . . . 3 n.228; 4 n.13; 6.10[2] & n.431
88-69 . . . . 7 n.85
88-84 . . . . 7.03[2][b][ix] & n.89
89-23 . . . . . . 6.06[2][c]; 6.06[2][c][ii] & n.249
89-25 . . . . 6 n.92
89-26 . . . . 6 n.139
89-29 . . . . 7 n.229
89-41 . . . . 7.03[2][b][viii] & n.88
90-38 . . . . . 9.04[1][b] & ns. 73, 74, 78, 81
90-68 . . . . . . 9 n.67; 11.02[5][a][iii] & n.177; 11.02[5][c] & n.200
91-30 . . . . 3 n.215

REVENUE PROCEDURES

REV. PROC.

64-4 . . . . 5 n.103; 7 n.162

REV. PROC.

64-16 . . . . 8.04[3] & ns. 62, 63
65-5 . . . . 5 n.103
66-50 . . . . . 10.05[4][a] & ns. 195, 196
70-21 . . . . 4 ns. 139, 140
70-27 . . . . 2.02[1][e] & n.76; 8 n.65
70-63 . . . . 8 n.187
71-21 . . . . 3 n.102; 4.03[3][e][ii] & ns. 140, 143–145, 148; 9 n.142
72-51 . . . . 10.05[4][c][i]; 10 ns. 99, 103
74-2 . . . . 7 n.32
74-11 . . . . 8 n.328
74-33 . . . . 10 ns. 59, 151–153, 161
75-10 . . . . 7 n.60
75-18 . . . . 8 n.65
75-25 . . . . 4.04[3][e] & n.320
75-40 . . . . 6 n.229
76-6 . . . . 7 n.101
76-9 . . . . 10.05[4][d][i]
76-10 . . . . 10 n.234
77-12 . . . . 7 n.323
79-3 . . . . 10 n.234
79-23 . . . . . . 7.05 & ns. 268, 269; 7 ns. 33, 103, 284; 8.06[2][c] & n.162; 8.06[2][d]; 8.06[3][b][v] & n.274; 8 ns. 150, 179
79-47 . . . . 8 n.129
79-63 . . . . 7 n.30; 8.06[3][d][i]; 8 n.187
79-123 . . . . 8 n.329
79-195 . . . . 4 n.117
80-5 . . . . 8 n.330
80-51 . . . . . . 8.04[3] & n.66; 8 ns. 74, 153, 167
81-40 . . . . 10 ns. 195, 196
82-19 . . . . 8 n.329
82-32 . . . . 8 n.331
83-25 . . . . 10.04[4][c][ii]; 10.05[4][c][i]; 10.05[4][c][ii] & ns. 225, 227–229; 10 ns. 69, 120, 154, 216
83-40 . . . . 3 n.94
83-76 . . . . 10 n.96
83-77 . . . . 4 n.303
84-27–84-30 . . . . 3 n.94
84-28 . . . . 8 ns. 154, 332
84-30 . . . . 8 n.332
84-34 . . . . 10.05[4][b][ii] & ns. 202, 203
84-57 . . . . 7.04[4][a][i]; 7 ns. 218, 230–234, 236, 240, 242–244

[Text references are to paragraphs (¶) within Chapters; footnote references are to Chapters (boldface numbers) and notes (n.)]

REV. PROC.

84-59 .... **10** n.82
84-74 .... 3.04[3]; 3.06 & n.197; 3.06[1][d] & n.232; **3** n.228; 4.04[3][c][ii]; 5.07[2] & n.357; 7.06[2]; 7.06[3] & n.296; **7** n.290; 8.04[3] & n.67; 8.04[4]; 8.04[4][a]; 8.04[4][b] & n.77; 8.04[4][b][i]; 8.04[4][b][ii]; 8.04[4][b][iii] & ns. 79–82; 8.04[4][b][iv] & ns. 83–85, 87; 8.04[5] & n.88; 8.04[5][a] & ns. 89, 90, 92, 93; 8.04[5][b] & n.96; 8.04[5][c] & ns. 99, 101; 8.04[5][d] & n.102; 8.04[5][e]; 8.04[6]; 8.04[6][a]; 8.04[6][c]; 8.04[6][d]; 8.06[1]; 8.06[2] & ns. 135, 136; 8.06[2][a] & n.138; 8.06[2][b] n.139; 8.06[2][b][i] & ns. 140, 141; 8.06[2][b][ii]; 8.06[2][b][iii] & ns. 155, 156; 8.06[2][c] & ns. 157–160; 8.06[2][d] & ns. 161, 163, 164; 8.06[2][e] & n.165; 8.06[2][f] & ns. 166, 167; 8.06[3] & ns. 168, 169; 8.06[3][a][i]; 8.06[3][a][iii]; 8.06[3][b][iv]; **8** n.332
85-8 .... **8** n.329
85-15 .... **10** n.13
85-16 ..... 10.05[2][e] & ns. 166, 167; **10** n.204
85-36 .... **8** n.333
85-37 .... **8** n.333
85-58 .... **10** ns. 233, 234
86-20 .... **8** n.331
87-15 .... **3** n.153
87-29 .... **5** n.88
87-30 .... **5** n.89
87-32 .... **10** ns. 69, 105, 106, 116, 117, 120, 121, 126, 129, 216, 217, 219, 224, 225, 227
87-74 .... 3.06[1][d]

REV. PROC.

88-15 ..... **6** n.365; 7.06[2] & n.291; **7** ns. 169, 287; 8.06[3][b][v] & n.272
88-19 .... **7** ns. 60, 63
89-10 .... 7.03[2][b][vi] & n.78; **7** n.62
89-17 .... 6.06[2][c]; **6** n.250
90-63 .... 6.06[2][c][ii] & ns. 250, 251
92-12 .... **3** n.156
92-20 ..... 3.06 & n.198; 7.03[1][c] & ns. 47–49; 7.06[1]; 7.06[3] & ns. 293–295; **7** ns. 26, 290; 8.04[3] ns. 58–60, 70; 8.04[4]; 8.04[4][a]; 8.04[5][e] & n.104; 8.04[7] & n.126; 8.04[8]; 8.06[1] & n.134; 8.06[2] & n.135, 137; 8.06[2][b][i] & n.142; 8.06[3]; 8.06[3][a]; 8.06[3][a][i] & ns. 171, 179; 8.06[3][a][iii] & n.181; 8.06[3][b] & n.183; 8.06[3][b][i] & ns. 186, 191–200, 202, 204, 205; 8.06[3][b][ii] & ns. 208–231, 233, 234, 236–241, 243–245; 8.06[3][b][iii] & ns. 246–256; 8.06[3][b][iv] & ns. 257–268; 8.06[3][b][v] & ns. 269–272, 275, 277; 8.06[3][c] & n.278; 8.06[3][c][i] & n.279; 8.06[3][c][ii] & n.280; 8.06[3][f][i] & n.288; 8.06[3][h] & n.294; 8.06[3][j] & n.296; 8.06[3][k] & n.297; 8.06[4] & n.299; 8.08 & ns. 337, 338; 8.09 & n.340; **8** ns. 3, 22, 180, 182, 282, 285–287, 289–293, 295, 304; 9.04[1][b] & ns. 77–79, 81; **9** n.67
92-28 .... **4** n.303
92-29 .... **4** n.323
92-74 .... **8** n.333
92-75 .... **8** n.333
93-23 ..... **8** ns. 132, 133; **10** ns. 184, 185

Table of Cases

[Text references are to paragraphs (¶) within Chapters; footnote references are to Chapters (boldface numbers) and notes (n.)]

A

Abbeville Cotton Mills **6** n.386
Achiro v. Comm'r **9** n.217
Adam, Meldrum & Anderson Co.,
  Comm'r v. ..... 12.04[2][d] & n.138
Adams, Cecil O. **3** n.96
ADKCO Indus. Inc. v. Comm'r
  .... **4** n.348
Adolph Coors Co. v. Comm'r
  .... **2** n.113; **9** n.125
Advance Aluminum Castings Corp.
  v. Harrison **5** n.323
Advance Truck Co. **8** n.26
Advertisers Exch. Inc. **2** n.206; **9**
                                    n.158
A. Finkenberg's Sons, Inc. **5** n.115
Akin, U.S. v. **3** n.176
Alabama Coca-Cola Bottling Co.
  .... **9** n.125
Albright v. U.S. **6** n.92
Alexander H. Kerr & Co. v. U.S.
  .... **2** n.218
Allan, James A. **12** n.172
Alleghany Corp. **4** n.183
Allied Fidelity Corp. **4** n.119
Allstate Ins. Co. v. U.S. **12** n.182
All Steel Equip. Inc. .... **6** ns. 215,
                                216, 236
Altec Corp. .... 6.08[2][a] & n.349; **12**
                                    n.198
Amalgamated Hous. Corp. **4** n.168
Amalgamated Sugar Co., U.S. v.
  .... **6** n.57
American Auto. Ass'n v. U.S.
  ...... **2** n.200; **3** n.26; **4**.03[3] & n.98;
      4.03[3][b] & ns. 111, 112; **4** n.120;
                                    12 n.69
American Can Co. v. Comm'r
  .... **6** n.88; **8** ns. 319, 327; **9** n.26

American Coast Line v. Comm'r
  .... **10** ns. 40, 89
American Dental Co., Helvering v.
  .... **12** n.207
American Dispenser Co. v. Comm'r
  .... **3** n.176
American Fin. Corp. **12** n.182
American Fletcher Corp. v. U.S.
  ...... **2** ns. 91, 106, 129, 144; **3** n.251
American Hide & Leather Co. v.
  U.S. **10** n.169
American Tel. & Tel. Co. **12** n.88
Amity Leather Prods. Co.
  .... 7.04[3][a][i] & ns. 133, 136;
      7.04[3][d]; 7.04[3][e] & ns. 184,
                    189, 194–202; **7** n.277
Anders, D.B. (10th Cir.) **12** n.195
Anders, D.B. (TC) .... 12.05[4][a][ix]
                                    & n.194
Anders v. U.S. .... 12.05[4][a][ix]
                                    n.196
Anderson, James E. ...... 12.04[1] &
                                ns. 123–125
Anderson, U.S. v. ..... **2** n.26; 4.02[2]
      & ns. 22–25; 4.03 & n.32;
      4.04[1][b] & ns. 196, 199; **12** n.15
Anderson-Dougherty-Hargis Co. v.
  U.S. **9** n.173
Andrews, Curtis R. **4** n.108
Angelus Funeral Home **4** n.119;
      9.06[2][a] & n.144; **12** n.60
Applied Communications, Inc.
  .... 2.02[2] & n.88; **2** ns. 129, 146,
      204; 3.08[4] & n.271; **3** ns. 239,
                    253, 260, 269
Arcadia Sav. & Loan Ass'n v.
  Comm'r **12** n.188
Arkansas Best Corp. v. Comm'r
  .... **6** n.55
Arrowsmith v. Comm'r ..... 12.02[3]
      & n.39; 12.03[3][b] & n.100; 12.04

[Text references are to paragraphs (¶) within Chapters; footnote references are to Chapters (boldface numbers) and notes (n.)]

& ns. 113, 115, 116; 12.04[1]; 12.04[2]; 12.04[2][b] & ns. 130, 133, 134; 12.04[2][c] & n.135; 12.04[2][d]; 12.04[3] & n.142; 12.04[4] & ns. 143, 145; **12** ns. 126, 128

Artnell Co. v. Comm'r ..... 4.03[3][c] & ns. 121–124; 4.03[3][d]; 4.03[3][e][ii]

Ashtabula Bow Socket Co. **6** n.367

Asphalt Prods. Co. v. Comm'r .... **2** ns. 168, 201; **3** n.245

Atlantic Coast Realty Co. **6** n.125

Atlas Oil & Ref. Co. .... **10** ns. 20, 21, 168

Automated Mktg. Sys., Inc. v. U.S. .... 4.03[3][d] & n.133

Automobile Ass'n v. U.S. **4** n.110

Automobile Club of Mich. v. Comm'r..... **2** n.200; 4.03[3] & n.97; 4.03[3][b] & ns. 105, 107; **4** n.120; 12.03[3][a][i] & ns. 67–69; **12** n.53

Auburn Packing Co. .... **2** ns. 138, 139

Avery v. Comm'r **3** n.95

B
_____

Bailey v. Comm'r **9** n.43

Baltimore & Ohio R.R. v. U.S. .... 9.03[3] & n.59; **9** n.167

Baltimore Baseball Club, Inc. v. U.S. **5** n.142

Baltimore Transfer Co. ...... **4** n.165; 12.02[2][f][i] & ns. 26, 27; **12** n.12

Bangor Punta Operations, Inc. v. U.S. **6** n.313

Barber, Ronnie L. ..... **2** ns. 172, 208; 9.04[1][a] & n.71; **9** n.81

Barker v. McGruder **12** n.51

Barnett, Grace M. ..... 12.02 [2][a] & n.7; **12** n.150

Barnsley, Harry L. ...... **3** ns. 43, 113

Bartles-Scott Oil Co. **2** n.41

Bartlett v. Delaney **12** n.25

Basila, Basil F. **3** n.72

Basse, Edgar A. .... **7** ns. 117, 281

Bates, Elizabeth W. **3** n.83

Battelstein v. IRS **3** n.137

Baxter v. Comm'r **3** n.64

Bayard, Theodore R. **3** n.81

Bay Ridge Operating Co. **3** n.96

Beacon Publishing Co. v. Comm'r .... 4.03[3][a] & ns. 100, 102; 4.03[3][b] ns. 108, 113, 114; 4.03[3][c] & n.120; 4.03[3][d] & n.134; **4** ns. 29, 199; 9.05[3] & n.126

Bear Film Co. **4** n.208

Bear Mill Mfg. Co. **12** n.213

Bedford Mills, Inc. v. U.S. .. 6.09[3][b] & ns. 398, 400; 6.09[3][b][ii]; **6** n.386

Beek v. Comm'r **3** n.151

Bell Elec. Co. **4** n.193

Bell Fed. Sav. & Loan Ass'n ..... 2.02[2][f] & n.132; **3** ns. 90, 153; **4** ns. 38, 51; 9.06[2][b] & n.151

Bellevue Mfg. Co. **3** n.251

Beneficial Corp. v. U.S. **7** n.183

Benes, Elmer J. .... **3** ns. 68, 105

Bennett Properties Co. **2** n.185

Bien, V.T.H. .... 2.02[2][i] & ns. 143, 144

Biewer, Estate of **8** n.38

Bilar Tool & Die Corp. v. Comm'r **3** n.176

Binns v. U.S. **12** n.137

Birch Ranch & Oil Co. .... 2.03[1][b] & n.190

Birnbaum, Paul **12** n.179

BKW Sys., Inc., In re .... **2** ns. 89, 129; **3** ns. 253, 271

Black, Gary **6** n.84

Blair v. First Trust & Sav. Bank **3** n.89

Block, William H., Estate of **12** n.157

Bloom Bros., Inc. **6** n.389

Blum v. Higgins **3** n.75

Blumberg Bros. Co. **6** n.143

Blum's Inc., Appeal of ..... 5.04[3][b] & ns. 118, 119; 5.04[3][c]; **5** n.33

Board v. Comm'r **12** n.45

Boatman, Ralph A. **12** n.137

Boca Ceiga Dev. Co. **2** n.40

Boehm v. Comm'r ..... 12.05[4][c][ii] & n.236

Boise Cascade Corp. v. U.S. ...... 4.03[3][c] & n.125; 4.03[3][d]

Bonaire Dev. Co. v. Comm'r .. **3** n.186

Bones, Walter I. **3** n.64

[Text references are to paragraphs (¶) within Chapters; footnote references are to Chapters (boldface numbers) and notes (n.)]

Bongiovanni, John P. **8** n.319
Bongiovanni v. Comm'r **8** n.327
Boston & Providence R.R., U.S. v.
.... **3** n.112
Bowen, Robert R. **5** n.240
Boylston Mkt. Ass'n, Comm'r v.
.... **3** ns. 167, 179
Boynton v. Pedrick **2** n.163; **8**.09
                              & n.341
Bradford v. U.S. **5** n.195
Bradley, Comm'r v. **3** n.133
Bradshaw v. U.S. **5** n.242
Brander, John A. .... **3** n 63
Branham, Joe D. **5** n.342
Bratton v. Comm'r **3** n.58
Braxton, Mary M. .... **3** n 96
Breeze Corps. v. U.S. .... **4** ns. 41, 42
Bresler, David ...... **12** ns. 133, 134
Bressner Radio Inc. v. Comm'r
.... **4**.03[3][b] & n.109
Briarcliff Candy Corp. v. Comm'r
.... **3** n.176
Briffin, Brooks **3** n.134
Briggs, Thomas W. **2** n.41
Bright v. U.S. ...... **3**.03[1][d][iii] &
                         n.53; **3** n.65
Broadcast Measurement Bureau,
Inc. .... **12**.03[3][a][v] & n.84
Broida, Stone & Thomas, Inc. v.
U.S. **9** n.46
Brook, Arthur F. **12** n.142
Brooklyn Union Gas Co. v. Comm'r
.... **12** n.49
Brooks, Malcom G. **10** n.17
Brooks-Massey Dodge, Inc.
.... **2**.04[3][c] & ns. 232, 233
Brown, Horace B. **10** n.14
Brown v. Helvering (US 1963)
.... **2** n.138
Brown v. Helvering (US 1934)
.... **2** n.200; **3** ns. 27, 108; **4** n.202; **12**
                                  n.51
Brownlee, Lela M. **12** n.218
Brush Wellman, Inc. **6** n.317
Brutsche, Ralph L. **12** n.220
Buckeye Int'l. Inc. .... **2**.02[2] & n.85
Buff v. Comm'r **12** n.80
Bullock's Dept. Store, Inc. ...... **3** ns.
                                  70, 71
Burgess Poultry Mkt. Inc. v. U.S.
.... **2**.03[1][a] & n.179

Burlington N. R.R. **4** n.189
Burnet, Eckert v. **3** n.135
Burnet v. Logan **3** n.52; **12** n.40
Burnet v. S&L Bldg. Corp.
.... **5**.05[8][c] & ns. 218, 221
Burnet v. Sanford & Brooks
..... **10** n.1; **12**.02 & ns. 1–3; **12**.04 &
                         n.117; **12** n 182
Burnett, North Am. Oil Consol. v.
..... **3** n.25; **4** ns. 38, 103; **12**.03[1] &
        ns. 45, 46, 48, 56; **12**.03[1][a];
   12.03[3][a]; **12**.03[3][a][ii] & n.75;
        12 ns. 41, 42, 60, 62, 64, 99
Burnham Corp. .. **4** ns 183, 226, 353
Burrell Groves, Inc. .... **5**.06[4] &
                                  n.336
Busey, H.C. Godman Co. v. ... **7** n.278
Busey, Huntington Sec. Corp. v.
.... **2**.02[2][j][i] & ns. 153, 172
Byrd, Carlton L. **12** n.204
Byrd v. Comm'r **12** n.171

C

C.A. Hunt Eng'g Co. ..... **2**.02[2][j][i]
                          & ns. 155, 156
Caldwell v. Comm'r ..... **2**.02[2][j][ii]
   & ns. 157, 160, 163; **2**.02[2][k]; **2**
      ns. 126, 128, 163, 167, 207, 229
Calhoun v. U.S. **10** n.83
California & Hawaiian Sugar Ref.
Corp. v. U.S.............. **12** n.235
Cal-Maine Foods, Inc. ..... **2**.02[2] &
                    n.86; **3** n.260; **4** n.13
Camilla Cotton Oil Co. **4** n.50
Campbell, Graff Chevrolet Co. v.
.... **8** n.9
Campbell v. U.S. ..... **3**.03[1][d][iii] &
                                  n.51
Canelo, Adolph B. ..... **12**.05[4][c][i]
                          & n.229
Capitol Fed. Sav. & Loan Ass'n
.... **2** ns. 137, 211; **3** ns. 82, 271; **8** ns.
        46, 58, 74, 151–153, 167, 174
Cappel House Furnishing Co. v.
U.S. **5** n.52
Carlson, George C. **9** n.45
Carson, Pirie, Scott & Co. v. U.S.
.... **7** n.278

[*Text references are to paragraphs (¶) within Chapters; footnote references are to Chapters (boldface numbers) and notes (n.)*]

Carter, Susan J. .... **3** ns. 246, 248, 250

Catto, U.S. v. (US) ... **2** n.200; **9** n.121

Catto, U.S. v. (5th Cir.) .... **9**.05[3] & ns. 120, 122

Cedar Rapids Eng'g Co. **2** n.151

C.E. Longley Co. **6** n.144

Central Republic Trust, Comm'r v.
.... **3** n.90

C.F. Smith Co. **10** n.79

Chaitlen, Morrie .... **6**.11 & ns. 452–454; **6** n.392

Challenge Publications, Inc. v.
Comm'r ...... **2** n.15; **4** ns. 193, 194

Champion Spark Plug Co., Comm'r
v. **4** n.167

Chatham & Phenix Nat'l Bank
.... **12**.02[2][d] & ns. 20, 21

Chesapeake & Ohio Ry. **8** n.13

Chesapeake Fin. Corp. **4** n.119

Childers Distrib. Co. **6** n.208

C.H. Leavell & Co. **10** n.96

Chronister, Lee R. **12** n.179

Cincinnati, New Orleans & Tex Pac.
Ry. v. U.S. .... **9**.06[3] & ns. 165, 166; **9** n.48

Circle K Corp. v. U.S. **6** n.55

Citizens Acceptance Corp. v. U.S.
.... **12** n.193

City Gas Co. of Fla. ..... **4**.03[3][e][ii] & ns. 151, 158; **9**.07 & n.199

City Gas Co. of Fla. v. Comm'r
.... **12**.03[3][a] & n.95; **12** n.87

City Stores Co. v. Smith **5** n.37

Clapp, Austin **10** n.96

Clark v. Woodward Constr. Co.
.... **4** n.175

Clark Brown Grain Co. .... **2**.04[3][b] & ns. 226, 227

Clark Equip. Co. ...... **6** ns. 419, 423

Clay Sewer Pipe Ass'n v. Comm'r
.... **4** n.108

Cleaver v. Comm'r **3** n.148

Cleveland Woolen Mills **6** n.65

Clifford, Helvering v. **6** n.83

Clifton Mfg. Co. v. Comm'r
.... **4** ns. 66, 76, 77

Clinton Hotel Realty Corp. v.
Comm'r **12** n.89

Coastal Expanded Metal Co. ... **6** n.12

Cochran, D.D.S., Inc., Melvin L.
.... **6** n.86

Cochran Hatchery, Inc. .... **8** ns. 103, 307

Cohen, Max E. **12** n.59

Cohen, Theodore H. **3** n.75

Cold Metal Process Co. **4** n.41

Cole, James V. **2** n.115; **3** n.278

Collegiate Cap & Gown Co.
.... **4** ns. 124, 131

Collins, Frederic A. ..... **12** ns. 57, 58

Colonial Sav. Assoc. v. Comm'r
.... **9** n.43

Colorado Springs Nat'l Bank v. U.S.
.... **3** n.176

Commercial Sec. Bank ..... **3** ns. 127, 249, 250

Commercial Solvents Corp. **4** n.66

Connery v. U.S. **12** n.196

Connors, Inc. **9** n.58

Consolidated Edison Co. of N.Y.,
U.S. (US) v. .. **3** n.130; **4** ns. 198, 217

Consolidated Edison Co. of N.Y. v.
U.S. (Ct. Cl.) **4** n.198

Consolidated Foods Corp. **4** n.183

Consolidated-Hammer Dry Plate &
Film Co. v. Comm'r **6** n.57; **12** n.59

Consumers Power Co. **4** n.31

Contadina Foods, Inc. **6** n.386

Continental Can Co. v. U.S. **6** n.88

Continental Ill. Corp. .... **4**.03[1][a][i] & n.47; **4** ns. 144, 150; **12** ns. 63, 96

Continental Tie & Lumber Co. v.
U.S. .... **4** ns. 41, 56

Continental Vending Mach. Corp.,
In re **4** n.350

Cook, John F. **2** n.41

Coombs, James Bliss **12** n.31

Coors, William K. **2** n.113; **9** n.125

Copy Data, Inc. **9** n.198

Corliss v. Bowers **12** n.57

Corn Exch. Bank v. U.S. .... **4** ns. 67, 69, 76, 78

Corn Prods. Ref. Co. v. Comm'r
.... **6** n.55

Cosmopolitan Bank & Mortgage
Co. .... **2**.02[1][b] & ns. 30, 31

Cosmopolitan Bond & Mortgage
Co. **3** n.262

Cosmopolitan Credit Corp. ... **12** n.213

[Text references are to paragraphs (¶) within Chapters; footnote references are to Chapters (boldface numbers) and notes (n.)]

Coulter Elecs., Inc. **9** n.186
Cowden v. Comm'r ..... 3.03[1][d][i]
　　& ns. 42, 44; 3.03[1][d][ii];
　　3.03[1][d][iii]; 3.03[1][d][v]
Cox, E. Morris **4** ns.118,142; **8** n.94
Crain v. Comm'r **3** n.126
Crane v. Comm'r .... 5.05[10][b]
Credit Life Ins. Co. v. U.S. **4** n.76
Crescent Wharf & Warehouse Co.
　v. Comm'r .... **4** ns. 161, 231
Crile v. Comm'r **3** n.113
Crosley Corp. v. U.S. **9** n.195
Crown v. Comm'r **11** n.13
Crown Mfg. Co. .... **6** ns. 389, 451
Cuba R.R. **4** n.72
Cuddihy, Robert J., Estate of .. **5** n.59
Cunningham, John I. **5** n.335
Cyrus W. Scott Mfg. Co. **2** n.236

D

Daily Record Co. **2** n.31
Dana Distribs., Inc. .... **4** n.193; **6** ns.
　　57, 85; **12** n.86
Davenport Mach. & Foundry Co.
　.................. **5** ns. 66, 67, 96
David Baird & Son, Inc. **6** n.119
Dawkins v. Comm'r **3** n.100
Dearborn Gage Co. **9** n.106
Decision, Inc. .... 4.03[1][a][iii] &
　　n.52; **4** n.141; **5** n.75; 9.06[2][a] &
　　ns. 137–139, 142; 9.06[2][b] &
　　n.154
Deely, Carroll L. **12** n.132
DeHaai, Kermit M. ...... **6** ns. 70, 90
Delta Airlines, Inc., U.S. v.
　.............. 12.02[2][f][ii] & n.29
Denise Coal Co. v. Comm'r
　.......... **4** ns. 169, 352; **11** n.12
Deputy v. Dupont **11** n.1
Desert Palace Inc. v. Comm'r ... **4** n.36
Dial, Robert J. **3** n.56
Dickman v. Comm'r .... **11** ns. 14, 290
Diebold, Inc. v. U.S. **2** n.206;
　9.04[1][b] & n.75; **9** ns. 107, 190
Dixie Pine Prods. Co. v. Comm'r
　........ 4.04[1][c] & ns. 204, 207; **4**
　　n.229; **12** n.228

D. Loveman & Son Export Corp.
　.......................... **6** n.392
Dobson v. Comm'r .... **12** ns. 153,
　　165, 182
Dorr-Oliver, Inc. ..... 9.03[2][a] & ns.
　　34, 36–39; **9** ns. 45, 136
Dougherty, Albert L. **10** n.18
Douglas v. Comm'r .... 12.02[2][a] &
　　ns. 9, 10
Douthit v. U.S. .... 8.07[2][b] &
　　n.321; **8** n.313
Dravo Corp. v. U.S. ..... 4.04[1][b] &
　　ns. 199, 200; 4.04[1][c] & n.207
Drazen, Michael ..... 2.02[1][b] & ns.
　　33, 34, 35; 2.04[3][c] & n.231; **2**
　　n.116; **3** ns. 238, 262, 267, 276; **6**
　　n.77
Dupont, Deputy v. **11** n.1
Duval Motor Co. v. Comm'r **6** n.92
Dwyer, Comm'r v. **8** n.27

E

Eakins v. U.S. **3** n.109
Eastman Kodak Co. v. U.S.
　........ 4.04[1][a][ii] & ns. 188, 189
Eboli, Saverio .... **3** ns. 123, 144
Eckert v. Burnet **3** n.135
Ed Smithback Plumbing, Inc.
　............. **2** n.217; **8** n.13; **9** n.74
Ed Smithback Plumbing, Inc. v.
　U.S. **2** n.217
Eisler, George **12** n.129
Elder Mfg. Co. v. U.S. **6** n.403
Electric & Neon, Inc. ...... **2** ns. 165,
　　216; **9** n.125
Electric Tachometer Corp. ... **4** n.183;
　　12.02[2][f][i] & n.28
Ellstrom, Ralph **6** n.401
Elmwood Corp. v. U.S. **9** n.72
E. Morris Co. **4** n.126
England, Jr., James W. ..... **3** ns. 140,
　　147, 251
Epic Metals Corp. ...... 3.08[6] & ns.
　　284, 286; **6** ns. 48, 68
E. Rauh & Sons Fertilizer Co.
　.................... 6.11 & n.450
Ertegun v. Comm'r **6** n.66
ESCO Corp. v. U.S. ..... 4.04[2][a] &
　　ns. 232, 233; **9** n.164

[Text references are to paragraphs (¶) within Chapters; footnote references are to Chapters (boldface numbers) and notes (n.)]

European Am. Bank & Trust Co. v. U.S. .... **4** ns. 66, 70, 75

Evans, Hiram W. **2** n.41

Evans, Richard M. .... **3** ns. 67, 71; **9** ns. 102, 103, 119

Evans v. U.S. **12** n.196

E.W. Bliss Co. v. U.S. ..... **6** ns. 386, 405; **7** n.183

Excelsior Printing Co. **12** n.149

Ezo Prods. Co. **2** n.234; **3** n.238; **6** n.77; **8** n.38

F

Fahs, Estate of Witt v. **3** n.132

Fahs v. Martin .... **4** ns. 344, 350

Faidley, Lloyd H. **12** n.182

Fairbanks v. U.S. **11** n.26

Falk, Irving **8** n.39

Fall River Gas Appliance Co. v. Comm'r **3** n.176

Fame Tool & Mfg. Co. v. U.S. **6** n.128

Farmer & Merchants Nat'l Bank **12** n.23

Farp, Merton E. **12** n.154

Fawcus Mach. Co. v. U.S. **12** n.31

Federal Bulk Carriers, Inc. .. **12** n.128

Federated Dep't Stores v. Comm'r .... 9.06[2][a] & n.143

Federated Dep't Stores, Inc. .... 9.06[4] & ns. 172, 173

Fender Sales, Inc., Comm'r v. **12** n.206

Ferenc, John B. **3** n.92; **4** n.352

Fetzer Refrigerator Co. v. U.S. .... **3** ns. 59, 60, 69

Field, Gabriel **3** n.133

Fifth Ave. Coach Lines, Inc., Comm'r v. **4** n.223

50 East 75th St. Corp. **5** n.73

50 East 75th St. Corp. v. Comm'r **5** n.47

Fink, Lorraine T. **5** n.240

First Fed. Sav. & Loan Ass'n v. U.S. .... **2** ns. 15, 27

First Nat'l Bank of Gainesville .... **2** n.172; **7** n.43; 9.05[2] & ns. 118, 119; **9** n.168

First Nat'l Bank of Mobile v. Comm'r **3** n.180

First Nat'l City Bank v. U.S. **9** n.100

First Savs. & Loan Ass'n **4** n.61

First Trust & Sav. Bank, Blair v. **3** n.89

Fischer Indus., Inc. **7** n.278

Fischer, L.M. .... **3** ns. 64, 67, 134

Flamingo Resort, Inc. v. U.S. .. **4** n.36

Fletcher v. U.S. **5** n.195

Florence Mills, Inc. **4** n.40

Floyd v. Scofield **3** n.246

Fogle, Nathan **3** n.64

Fong, Jerry (TCM 1987) **2** n.167

Fong, Jerry (TCM 1984) .... **2** n.167; **9** ns. 11, 200

Fong Venture Capital Corp. .. **4** n.164

Fort Howard Paper Co. .... 2.02[2][h] & ns. 141, 142; **2** ns. 112, 165

Fountain, C.D. **3** n.69

Fourth Fin. Corp. ...... **4** ns. 48, 191

Fowler Bros. & Cox, Inc. v. Comm'r ...... 2.04[3][b] & ns. 221, 223; **2** ns. 217, 218

Fox v. Comm'r **4** n.210

Fox Chevrolet, Inc. ..... 7.05[1][a] & ns. 276, 277; **7** ns. 1, 184

Francisco Sugar Co. v. Comm'r .... 6.05[1][f][i] & ns. 93–95

Frank G. Wikstrom & Sons, Inc. **6** n.128

Franklin Mills .... 6.09[3][b][ii] & n.409

Frank Lyon Co. v. U.S. **6** n.83

Freihofer Baking Co. v. Comm'r .... 12.02[2][f][i] & n.25

Freudmann, Max **10** n.18

Frost Lumber Indus. Inc. v. Comm'r **4** n.60

Fruehauf Trailer Co. .... 2.04[3][c] & n.237; **8** ns. 26, 30

G

Ganahl Lumber Co. **2** n.244

Gap Anthracite Co. .... 9.03[3] & ns. 55, 56; **9** ns. 153–155

Garth, W.P. .... **2** ns. 137, 139

[Text references are to paragraphs (¶) within Chapters; footnote references are to Chapters (boldface numbers) and notes (n.)]

General Baking Co. **3** n.77
General Dynamics Corp., U.S. v.
.... **4** ns. 191, 193
Geo. K. Herman Chevrolet, Inc.
.... **4** n.183
Geometric Stamping Co. .... 2.02[1][d]
& ns. 59, 60; 2.04[3][d] & ns. 240,
241; **2** n.111; **6** n.215
George C. Peterson Co. **6** n.136
Georgia School-Book Depository,
Inc. **4** n.71
Geyer, Cornell & Newell, Inc.
.... **12** n.188
Gibson, Joseph H. .... 2.03[3] &
n.194; **2** n.193; **5** ns. 147, 149
Gilbert v. Comm'r **12** n.78
Gilken Corp. .... **12** ns. 90, 91
Gillis v. U.S. .... 4.04[1][a] & ns.
170–172; 4.04[1][c] & ns.
213–216; **4** ns. 118, 264
Gimbel Bros. v. U.S. (Ct. Cl. 1976)
.... **9** n.107
Gimbel Bros. v. U.S. (Ct. Cl. 1968)
.... **7** n.278
Giordano, John C. **12** n.169
Glenn v. Kentucky Color & Chem.
Co. .... **2** ns. 41, 151
Globe Corp. v. Comm'r **4** n.58
G.M. Standifer Constr. Co. ... **12** n.186
Godson, E.M. **10** n.19
Gold-Pak Meat Co. **2** n.182
Gold-Pak Meat Co. v. Comm'r
.... **9** n.218
Goodman, Melvin H. **6** n.386
Goodman, William J. **5** n.232
Gordon, Arthur Z. ..... 12.02[2][f][v]
& n.35
Gordon, Harry **4** n.208
Gordon v. Comm'r **9** n.209
Gould Paper Co. **12** n.23
Graff Chevrolet Co. v. Campbell
.... **8** n.9
Gralapp v. U.S. **5** n.267
Granan, William J. .... **3** ns. 125, 126
Grant Oil Tool Co. v. U.S. **6** n.91
Great Bear Spring Co. **2** n.31
Great S. Life Ins. Co. **3** n.90
Greenspon, Louis .... **5** ns. 66, 67, 96
Greenwood, E.P. **5** n.73
Gullett, C.E. **3** n.72
Gus Blass Co. .... 2.04[3][e] & ns.
248, 250

Gustafson, L.R. ... **2** ns. 7, 113; **8** n.58

H

Hackensack Water Co. v. U.S.
.... **2** n.206; **9** n.44
Hagelin, Edward **3** n.170
Hagen Advertising Displays, Inc. v.
Comm'r .... **4** ns. 118, 156
Hallmark Cards, Inc. .... **2** ns. 95, 99;
4 n.40; **6** n.85; 9.06[2][a] & ns.
139, 152
Hamilton Indus., Inc. .... 7.04[3][a][i]
& ns. 137, 138; 7.04[3][d] &
n.204; 7.08[1][b] & n.310; 7.08[2]
& ns. 313–315; **7** ns. 5, 267
Handy Andy T.V. & Appliances,
Inc. **4** n.131; **8** n.20
Hansen, Comm'r v. **2** n.200;
8.07[2][b] & ns. 322, 324; **9** n.43
Hansen, Paul, Estate of .... 2.02[1][b]
& n.36; **3** n.262
Hardy, William, Inc. v. Comm'r
.... **8** n.27
Harmont Plaza, Inc. **4** n.69
Harrisburg Steel Corp. v. U.S. .. **4** n.49
Harrison, Advance Aluminum
Castings Corp. v. **5** n.323
Harrold v. Comm'r .... **4** ns. 161, 169;
11 n.12
Hart Furniture Co. ..... 12.02[2][b] &
n.11
Hartland Assocs. **12** n.205
Hauff, U.S. v. **12** n.80
Haverty Furniture Co. **12** n.15
Haynes, James F. **2** n.109
Haynes, Lynn .... **2** n.220; 8.09 &
n.346; **9** n.96
Haynesworth, Robert F. **12** n.188
H.B. Ives Co., Comm'r v. **4** n.167
H.C. Godman Co. v. Busey   **7** n.278
Healy v. Comm'r .... **12** ns. 60, 85
Heaven Hill Distilleries v. U.S.
.... **6** n.201
H.E. Harman Coal Co. .... 12.02[2][c]
& ns. 14, 15
Helvering v. American Dental Co.
.... **12** n.207

[Text references are to paragraphs (¶) within Chapters; footnote references are to Chapters (boldface numbers) and notes (n.)]

Helvering, Brown v. (US 1963)
.... **2** n.138
Helvering, Brown v. (US 1934)
.... **2** n.200; **3** ns. 27, 108; **4** n.202; **12** n.51
Helvering v. Clifford **6** n.83
Helvering v. Martin Stubblefield, Inc. **3** n.90
Helvering v. Price **3** n.135
Helvering v. Russian Fin. & Constr. Corp. .... 4.04[1][a][ii] & ns. 179–182; **4** ns. 199, 345
Helvering v. Stockholms Enskilda Bank **5** n.59
Helvering v. Winmill **2** n.125
Henry C. Beck Builders, Inc. .. **9** n.101
Henry C. Beck Co. **9** n.101
Herberger, George **4** n.45
Herberger v. Comm'r **2** n.160
Hertz, Hal **6** n.380
Hess, Henry, Co. **4** n.59
H.F. Campbell Co. **8** n.42
H.F. Campbell Co. v. Comm'r . **8** n.327
Hillsboro Nat'l Bank v. Comm'r
.... 3.05[a][b] & n.182; 12.05[2] & ns. 156–161; 12.05[4][a][ix] & ns. 203, 204
Hirsch Improvement Co. v. Comm'r
.... **12** ns. 91, 92
Hitachi Sales Corp. .... **4** ns. 164, 206; **6** ns. 389, 406
HJH, Inc. SEC v. **4** n.346
H. Liebes & Co. v. Comm'r **4** n.42
Hodge, Raymond W. **4** n.352
Hollingsworth v. U.S. ... **4** ns. 190, 208
Hollywood Baseball Assoc. v. Comm'r **7** n.186
Holt Co. v. U.S. .... **2** ns. 5, 216
Home Constr. Corp. of Am. ... **10** n.84
Home Ice Cream & Ice Co. .. **2** n.244
Home Sav. & Loan Co. **12** n.235
Homes by Ayres .... **7** ns. 42, 279
Honeywell, Inc. ..... **6** ns. 51, 70, 71, 75, 77, 87, 89, 102
Hooker Indus., Inc. **9** n.107
Hoopengarner, Herschel H. .. **3** n.183
Hope v. Comm'r **12** n.79
Hopkins, Walter L. ...... **3** ns. 67, 73
Horneff, J. Carl ...... 5.05[8][c] & ns. 219, 220
Howard, John B. **3** n.135

Hradesky v. Comm'r **3** n.172
Hubbell's Estate **3** n.134
Hudspeth v. Comm'r ..... 12.05[2] & n.162
Hughes Properties, Inc., U.S. v.
.... 4.04[1][a][i] & ns. 175, 176; 4.04[1][a][ii] & ns. 183, 186, 189; **4** ns. 164, 191
Hunt, D.A. **5** n.231
Hunt v. U.S. **6** n.400
Huntington Sec. Corp. v. Busey
.. 2.02[2][j][i] & ns. 153, 154; **2** n.172
Huntsman, James Richard
.... 3.04[5][a] & n.154
Huntsman v. Comm'r .. **3** ns. 155, 157
Huston, Northwestern States Portland Cement Co. v. **4** n.202
Hutchison, Frank ..... **5** ns. 231, 232
Hutzler Bros. Co. ...... 7.04[3] & ns. 116, 205; 7.05[1][a] & ns. 273–275; **7** ns. 205, 281
Hyde Park Realty, Inc. **3** n.113
Hyland v. Comm'r ...... **3** ns. 60, 62, 71, 106
Hyman, Benjamin D. **5** n.53

I

Idaho Power Co., Comm'r v. .. **6** n.237
Ideal Reversible Hinge Co.
.... **6** ns. 386, 397
I. Lewis Corp. .... **9** ns. 44, 136
Illinois Cereal Mills, Inc. ...... **6** ns. 100, 101; **7** n.300
Illinois Power Co. v. Comm'r
.... **4** n.178; **12** n.96
Indianapolis Power & Light Co.
..... 12.03[3][a] & n.94; **12** ns. 87, 88
Ingredient Technology Corp., U.S. v. ..... 6.05[1][f][ii] & ns. 98, 100; **6** n.96; **7** n.300
Insilco Corp. .... 7.03[2][b][viii] & n.84; **7** n.280
International Cigar Mach. Co. .. **2** n.151
Iowa Guar. Mortgage Co. **5** n.53
Iowa S. Utils. Co. v. U.S.
...... 4.04[1][a][i] & n.177; **12** n.86
Irby, Jr., H.G. **2** n.116; **3** n.276

[Text references are to paragraphs (¶) within Chapters; footnote references are to Chapters (boldface numbers) and notes (n.)]

J

Jack's Cookie Co. v. U.S. **3** n.176
Jacobus v. U.S. **3** n.105
James v. U.S. .... 12.03[3][a][ii] & ns. 71–75; **12** ns. 53, 62, 65
James Sugar Coop. v. U.S. **9** n.169
J.E. Enters. .... **12** ns. 90, 93
Jennings & Co. v. Comm'r ... **3** n.113
Jephson, George S. **6** n.90
Jerpe, J.P. **5** n.338
J.F. Stevenhagen Co. .... 2.03[1][a] & n.187
J.J. Little & Ives Co. **4** n.45; **6** n.66
J.M. Radford Grocery Co. ... **6** n.149
Johnson, George W. **3** n.67
John Wanamaker Philadelphia . **5** n.69
John Wanamaker Philadelphia, Inc. v. U.S. .... **7** ns. 26, 267; **8** n.311
Jonas-Cadillac Co. v. Comm'r .... **2** n.228; **10** ns. 14, 183
Jones, A. Raymond **2** n.219; **6** n.97
Jones v. Comm'r **2** n.219
Jones, Wetherbee Elec. Co. v. .. 9.05[4] & n.131
Jones Lumber Co. **5** n.52
Jones Lumber Co. v. Comm'r ... **4** n.70
Joseph E. Seagram & Sons, Comm'r v. .... **7** ns. 5, 306, 308
Jostens, Inc. .... **6** ns. 382, 383
J.P. Sheahan Assocs., Inc. ...... **6** ns. 49, 74, 128
Jud Plumbing & Heating, Inc. .. **3** n.246
Juniata Farmers Coop. Ass'n .. **4** n.193
Justus & Parker Co. .... 6.11 & n.449

K

Kahler, Charles F. **3** n.64
Kaiser Steel Corp. v. U.S. **4** n.231
Kauai Terminal, Ltd. **3** n.167
Kaufmann & Baer Co. v. U.S. . **7** n.278
Kay-Jones Furniture Co. **5** n.121
Keebey's Inc. v. Paschal .... **4** ns. 175, 344
Keeney, Albert F. **6** n.125
Keller-Dorian Corp. v. Comm'r .... 12.02[2][c] & n.16
Kennedy, Roy C. **3** n.289

Kentucky Utils. Co. v. Glenn **2** n.173; **9** n.73
Kial, Robert J. **3** n.56
Kirby Lumber Co., U.S. v. .. **12** n.210
Kirschenmann v. U.S. ..... 5.05[8][b] & n.215
Kleberg, Alice G.K. **3** n.43
Klein Chocolate Co. (TC 1961) .... 2.04[3][d] & ns. 242, 244
Klein Chocolate Co. (TC 1959) **2** n.243
Klein, Zola **5** n.21
Knight-Ridder Newspaper, Inc. v. U.S. .... **2** ns. 126, 207; 6.05[1][d] & n.76
Koebig & Koebig, Inc. ..... 2.02[2][f] & ns. 117, 118; 2.04[3][e] & ns. 253, 254; **2** ns. 111, 151; **3** n.275
Koehring Co. v. U.S. **4** n.71
Kollsman Instruments Corp. v. Comm'r **4** n.55; **6** n.368
Kolowich, George J. ..... **3** ns. 70, 74
Korn Indus., Inc. ...... 9.05[1] & ns. 105, 106
Korn Indus., Inc. v. U.S. .... **2** n.219; 9.03[3] & ns. 58, 60, 62; **9** ns. 105–107, 110
Korstad, William B. **5** n.342
Krajeck v. U.S. **12** n.196
Kuckenberg, Comm'r v. **3** n.246
Kunze v. Comm'r **3** n.98
Kutsunai, Akira **5** n.340

L

Lacy Contracting Co. .. **3** ns. 63, 66, 71
Lake View Trust & Sav. Bank **12** n.163
Lamberth, E.P., Estate of **5** n.237
Larchfield Corp. **12** n.170
La Rue, Joseph W. **4** n.249
Lavery v. Comm'r **3** n.64
Lawyers' Title Guar. Fund v. U.S. **4** n.183; **9** n.43
Leedom & Worrall Co. **6** n.149
Leonard, W.C. v. U.S. .... **3** ns. 59, 69
Leonhart, William H. .... 9.03[2][b][i] & ns. 41, 42; **9** n.47
Levy, Allen J. .... 3.04[5][a] & n.164; **4** n.280

[Text references are to paragraphs (¶) within Chapters; footnote references are to Chapters (boldface numbers) and notes (n.)]

Lewis, U.S. v. ...... 12.03[3][a][iii] & n.76; 12.03[4][a] & n.101; **12** n.99
Lime Cola Co. **12** n.186
Lincoln Sav. & Loan Ass'n, Comm'r v. .... **3** ns. 167, 179
Lindner v. U.S. **2** n.217
Lindner, U.S. v. **8** n.40
Livingston, Story v. **3** n.142
Logan, Burnet v. **12** n.40
Londagin, Herman E. **12** n.179
Lord, Richard D. **3** n.129
Lowe, Alvin B. ... 12.04[2][c] & n.135
Lowenstein, Aaron, Estate of . **3** n.180
Lucas v. American Code Co. .. **2** n.200
Lucas v. Kansas City Structural Steel Co. .... **7** ns. 12, 15
Lucas, Osterloh v. ..... 2.02[2][j][i] & ns. 147, 149–151, 160, 163, 167
Lukens Steel Co. v. Comm'r .. **4** n.175
Lundborg & Co. v. White **6** n.304
Lustgarten, Paul G. **5** n.239
Lutz v. Comm'r .... **4** ns. 207, 208

M

Maclean, Ian W. **10** n.18
MacMillan Co. **12** n.23
Madison Gas & Elec. Co. ... 6.05[2][b] & n.115
Mager v. U.S. **12** n.180
Magnon, Rayman D. **2** n.145
Maier Brewing Co. **12** n.103
Malat v. Riddell **7** n.186; **9** n.30
Mallory, L.W., Estate of **2** n.41
Maloney v. Hammond ..... **2** ns. 137, 246, 247
Mamula v. U.S. **2** n.193; **5** n.147
Marcor, Inc. .... 2.02[2][f] & n.120; **2** ns. 95, 102; **5** ns. 108, 110, 114–116; **6** n.183
Marquardt Corp. **2** n.16; **3** n.275
Marshall Bros. Lumber Co. .... **5** ns. 66, 67, 96
Martin, Karl R. **5** n.195
Martin, Fahs v. .... **4** ns. 344, 350
Martin-Stubblefield, Inc., Helvering v. **3** n.90
Maryland Casualty Co. v. U.S. . **3** n.14

Mass. Mutual Life Ins. Co. v. U.S. **2** n.125
Massey Motors, Inc. v. U.S. ... **6** n.90
Mayer & Co. ...... 5.04[3][b] & n.120
Mayfair Minerals, Inc. .... **12** ns. 183, 230
McAdams v. Comm'r **3** n.126
McDonald & Eide, Inc., U.S. v. **10** n.86
McGowan, Williams v. .... **5** ns. 222, 223
McGruder, Barker v. **12** n.51
McIntosh Mills **6** n.136
McKay Mach. Co. **6** n.404
McNeil Mach. & Eng'g Co. v. U.S. .... **6** ns. 215, 304
McPike Inc. v. U.S. **2** n.241; **9** n.186
Mellinger v. U.S. **3** n.56
Merchants Nat'l Bank **12** n.213
Merchants Nat'l Bank v. Comm'r **12** n.131
Merrill, Ted F. **5** n.195
Merrill, U.S. v. ..... 12.03[3][a][iv] & n.77; **12** n.61
Midland-Ross Corp., U.S. v. **11** n.48
Midwest Motor Express, Inc. **4** n.183
Miele, Anthony D. **12** n.59
Mifflin, Charles D. .... **2** ns. 210, 230
Miller v. Usry **5** n.320
Miller & Vidor Lumber Co. v. Comm'r **4** n.199
Milwaukee & Suburban Transp. Corp. v. Comm'r. **4** n.231
Miracle Span Corp. v. U.S. ... **7** n.282
Mitchell, Lewis **3** n.169
Mitchell v. Comm'r (6th Cir.) .... 12.04[1] & n.120
Mitchell v. Comm'r (TC) ...... **12** ns. 121, 122
M.L. Rose Co. **12** n.54
Modernaire Interiors, Inc. **4** n.119
Modern Home Fire & Casualty Ins. Co. v. Comm'r **9** n.217
Molsen, Heinz, Jr. .... 6.11 & ns. 445, 446; **6** n.9; **10** n.20
Monfort of Colo., Inc. v. U.S. .. **9** n.61
Monroe Cotton Mills **6** n.65
Montgomery, John E. **12** n.179

[Text references are to paragraphs (¶) within Chapters; footnote references are to Chapters (boldface numbers) and notes (n.)]

Mooney Aircraft, Inc. v. U.S. (5th
    Cir. 1970) **2** n.123; **3** n.252
Mooney Aircraft, Inc. v. U.S. (5th
    Cir. 1969) ..... **1** n.14; 4.04[4] & ns.
            351, 353; **4** n.128; **11** n.12
Moore, Jerry C. **4** n.73
Moran v. Comm'r **3** n.61
Morgan Guar. Trust Co. v. U.S.
    .... 4.03[3][c] & n.127
Morris, William T. **12** n.182
Morrison Woolen Co. **6** n.65
Morris-Poston Coal Co. v. Comm'r
    ...... **2** n.172; **3** n.112; 9.06[4] & ns.
                        174, 176, 177
Moss, Estate of **5** n.320
Mountain Fuel Supply Co. v. U.S.
    .... 9.05[3] & n.123
Mulholland v. U.S. ...... 2.02; 2.04 &
        n.205; 3.04[5][a] & n.162; **4** n.280
Munter, David B., Estate of
    ...... 12.05[4][a][ix] & n.197; **12** ns.
                        151, 152, 171
Musgrove, Floyd L. **6** n.64
Mutual Tel. Co. v. U.S. **4** n.43; **12**
                                n.59

                        N

Nash v. U.S. (US) .... 12.05[4][a][viii]
                        & ns. 192, 193
Nash v. U.S. (5th Cir.) **12** n.190
National Airlines .... 2.02[1][d] & n.61
National Bank of Commerce of
    Seattle v. Comm'r **12** n.150
National Bank of Fort Benning v.
    U.S. **8** n.313
National Bread Wrapping Mach.
    Co. **4** n.168
National Muffler Dealers Ass'n v.
    U.S. **5** n.58
Nelson Bros., Inc. **2** n.245
Nesbitt, Abram **3** n.97
Nestle Holdings, Inc. .... 4.03[1][b] &
                        ns. 62, 64
Neusteter Suit Co. .... 6.09[3][b][ii] &
                        n.411; **6** n.402
Newman, Blema .. 12.02[2][f][v] & n.36
Nibley-Mimnaugh Lumber Co. . **2** n.41
Nieman, Herbert A. .... 6.09[3][b][ii]
                        & n.410

Noble v. Comm'r .... 12.02[2][f][iv] &
                        ns. 33, 34
Nordberg, Paul C. (1st Cir.) .. **12** n.78
Nordberg, Paul C. (TC) **12** n.60
North Am. Oil Consol v. Burnett
    .... **3** n.25; **4** ns. 38, 103; 12.03[1] &
                ns. 45, 46, 48; 12.03[2][a];
            12.03[3][a] & n.64; 12.03[3][a][ii]
            & n.75; **12** ns. 41, 56, 60, 62, 99
North Carolina Granite Corp.
    ..... 8.07[2][b] & n.325; 9.05[2] & ns.
                            111, 112
North Pa. R.R. **12** n.54
Northwestern States Portland
    Cement Co. v. Huston **4** n.202
Nye v. U.S. **5** n.240

                        O

Oak Indus., Inc. .... **12** ns. 97, 98
Ocean Accident & Guar. Co.
    ...... 2.02[1][b] & ns. 38–40; **3** n.267
Odom, Fitzhugh L. **3** n.171
Ohio River Collieries Co. **1** n.14;
            4 ns. 161, 169; **11** n.12
Ohmer Register Co. v. Comm'r
    .... 4.04[1][b] & ns. 197, 198; **4** n.160
Oklahoma Gas & Elec. Co. v. U.S.
    .... 9.05[3] & n.124
O'Leary, Harlan, Estate of ...... **9** ns.
                            188, 189
O. Liquidating Corp., Comm'r v.
    ... **2** n.206; 8.07[2][a] & ns. 317–319;
            8 ns. 13, 327; **9** ns. 35, 117
Oliver v. U.S. **3** n.67
Olympic Radio & Television, Inc.,
    U.S. v. **5** n.59
Omholt, Ray E. **3** n.56
1180 E. 63rd St. Bldg. Corp.
    .... **12** n.185
Oregon Pulp & Paper Co. **12** n.15
Osterloh v. Lucas ...... 2.02[2][j][i] &
        ns. 147, 149–151; 2.02[2][j][ii] &
                n.160; 2.02[2][k]
Ostheimer, William J. **4** n.168
Ozark Mills, Inc. .... 6.08[3][b]&
                    n.366; **6** n.355

                        P

Paccar, Inc. .... **6** ns. 381, 423

[Text references are to paragraphs (¶) within Chapters; footnote references are to Chapters (boldface numbers) and notes (n.)]

Pacific Coast Music Jobbers, Inc.
.... **5** n.195
Pacific Grape Prods. Co. v. Comm'r
..... **4** ns. 161, 198, 264; **6** ns. 57, 446
Pacific Nat'l Co. v. Welch **2** n.195
Parker, Loyd L. .... 2.03[1][a] & n.186
Parks-Chambers, Inc. **10** n.12
Paschal, Keebey's Inc. v. .... **4** ns.
175, 344
Paso Robles Mercantile Co. v.
Comm'r .... **10** ns. 169, 170
Paster, Herman **12** n.23
Patchen, Joseph C. **2** n.46
Patchen v. Comm'r ...... 2.02[1][c] &
ns. 45, 47, 70; **3** n.265
Pearl, Saul S. **6** n.386
Peninsula Steel Co. **8** n.311
Peninsula Steel Prods. & Equip. Co.
...... **6** n.129; **7** ns. 41, 190, 272, 279
Peoples Bank & Trust Co. v.
Comm'r **9** n.26
Perelman, Howard H. .... **8** ns. 26, 41
Perfumers Mfg. Corp. **3** n.112
Perkins, James W. **3** n.145; **4**
n.218
Perry, Leon W. **2** n.230
Perry v. U.S. **12** n.167
Peterson Produce Co. v. U.S. (8th
Cir.) .... 2.03[1][a] & n.178; **2** n.165;
9.06[5] & n.179
Peterson Produce Co. v. U.S. (WD
Ark.) ..... 2.03[1][a] & ns. 178, 180,
182–184; **2** n.165
Petroleum Heat & Power Co. v.
U.S. **4** n.132
Philadelphia Nat'l Bank v.
Rothensies **12** n.150
Photo-Sonics, Inc. **2** n.113; **6**
n.215
Pierce-Arrow Motor Car Co. v. U.S.
.... **6** n.95
Pityo, William D. **5** n.240
Poirier & McLane Corp. **4** n.220
Policy Holders Agency, Inc.
.... 12.02[2][e] & n.24
Poorbaugh v. U.S. **9** n.195
Poorbaugh, Catherine K. v. U.S.
.... **10** n.41
Pope, W.W. **5** n.52
Post, James H., Estate of **2** n.151
Potter, Walter H. **2** n.5

Powell, William, Co. v. U.S. .. **7** n.280
Prabel, Bruce A. .... 3.04[5][a] &
n.163; **4** n.280
Pratt, Estate of **3** n.68
Preble, Wallace **4** n.218
Prendergast, Thomas F. .... **5** ns. 5, 58
Preston, Sara R. **12** n.58
Price, Helvering v. ..... **3** ns. 135, 146
Primo Pants Co. **8** n.27
Professional Equities Inc. .... **5** ns.
229, 230, 237
Pursell, Fred P. **8** n.43
Putnam Nat'l Bank v. Comm'r
.... **12** n.149
Putoma Corp. .... 12.05[4][a][x] &
n.209; **12** ns. 147, 184
Putoma Corp. v. Comm'r **4** n.348

Q

Quinn v. Comm'r **12** n.81

R

Radom & Neidorff Inc. v. U.S.
.... **3** ns. 70, 74
Raleigh v. U.S. .... **3** ns. 69, 72
Ralston Dev. Corp. v. U.S.
.... 2.02[2][f] & n.130; **2** ns. 113, 234
Ray, Joe S. **3** n.112
RCA Corp. v. U.S. .... 2.04 & ns.
202, 203; **4** ns. 129, 130
Readers' Publishing Corp. v. U.S.
.... **4** n.202
RECO Indus., Inc. ..... **6** n.129; **7** ns.
41, 190, 279
Recordak Corp. v. U.S. **6** n.88
Rector, Lawrence L. **2** n.225
Redcay, Paul Irvin ..... 12.02[2][d] &
n.22
Reed v. Comm'r **3** n.58
Reed's Jewelers, Inc. v. U.S. **5** n.37
Rees Blow Pipe Mfg. Co. **12** n.126
Republic Petroleum Corp. v. U.S.
.... **5** n.232
Resale Mobile Homes, Inc.
.... **4** ns. 39, 57
Reubel, Henry **3** n.18

[Text references are to paragraphs (¶) within Chapters; footnote references are to Chapters (boldface numbers) and notes (n.)]

Rexach, U.S. v. **12** n.221
Reynolds Cattle Co. ..... 2.04[3][e] & ns. 251, 252
Reynolds Metals, Inc. **4** n.352
R.G. Bent Co. .. 2.02[1][d] & ns. 63, 64
R. Gsell & Co. **12** n.216
Rhinelander Paper Co. v. Wilkinson **6** n.350
R.H. Macy & Co. v. U.S. (2d Cir. 1963) **7** n.278
R.H. Macy & Co. v. U.S. (2d Cir. 1958) **7** n.278
Rialto Mining Corp. **6** n.397
Richardson Invs., Inc. **7** n.184, 277, 283
Riddell, Malat v. **7** n.186; **9** n.30
Ringmaster, Inc. **4** n.40; **6** n.65
RLC Industries Co. ..... 2.02[2][k] & ns. 169–171; **2** ns. 90, 102, 119, 131, 166; **3** ns. 272–274, 278; 7.04[3][a][i] & ns. 145, 146; **7** ns. 183, 314
Roanoke Gas Co. v. U.S. **4** n.178
Robert Bosch Corp. .... 6.09[3][b][iv] & ns. 423, 424; **6** n.381
Roberts, William M. **3** n.137
Rocco, Inc. ..... **2** n.184; 9.08[1][c] & ns. 216, 217, 219, 222
Rockwell Int'l Corp. **6** n.406
Rojas, Dorothy S. **12** n.204
Rosen v. Comm'r **12** n.174
Rosenberg v. U.S. .... **3** ns. 59, 73
Rosenthal, Daniel **4** n.43
Rosenthal v. U.S. **4** n.220
Ross v. Comm'r **3** n.61
Ross B. Hammond, Inc. v. Comm'r .... 2.04[3][c] & ns. 235, 236
Rothensies, Philadelphia Nat'l Bank v. **12** n.150
Rotolo, Louis S. **2** n.127; **6** n.11
Rowe, M.D. **2** n.40
Roxy Custom Clothes Corp. v. U.S. **12** n.186
Royster, W.R. **5** n.148
Rubnitz, Alan A. **3** n.137
Rushing, W.B. **5** n.240
Russian Fin. & Constr. Corp., Helvering v. ..... 4.04[1][a][ii] & ns. 179–182; **4** ns. 199, 345
Russo, Ann S. **9** n.70
Rutkin v. U.S. **12** n.74

Ryan, Thomas A. **4** n.42

S

Safety Car Heating & Lighting Co., U.S. v. **4** n.42
St. James Sugar Coop. Inc. v. U.S. **6** n.405; **9** n.170
St. Luke's Hosp. ..... 2.02[1][c] & ns. 54, 55; **3** n.265; 6.05[1][d] & ns. 79–81
Sam W. Emerson Co. **2** n.80
S&L Build. Corp., Burnet v. .... 5.05[8][c] & ns. 218, 221
Sanford & Brooks, Burnet v. ..... **10** n.1; 12.02 & ns. 1–3; 12.04 & n.117; **12** ns. 8, 182
Schiller, Avery R. **12** n.140
Schlude v. Comm'r ..... **2** n.200; **3** n.26; 4.03[3] & n.99; 4.03[3][b] & ns. 108, 115; **4** n.118; **12** n.69
Schmidt, Estate of .... 12.05[4][a][viii] & ns. 190, 191
Schniers, Charles B. **9** n.146
Schram v. U.S. **2** n.41
Schuessler v. Comm'r .... 4.03[3][a] & n.104; 4.03[3][b] & ns. 108, 113, 114; 4.03[3][c]; 4.03[3][d] & n.134
Schultz, George L. **3** n.171
Schulz, Ralph H. **12** n.219
Schuster, Max **12** n.190
Schuster's Express, Inc. .... 9.07 & ns. 196, 197
Scofield, Floyd v. **3** n.246
Scott Paper Co. .... **4** ns. 184, 185
Seas Shipping Co. **2** n.144
SEC v. HJH, Inc. **4** n.346
Security Benefit Life Ins. Co. v. U.S. **8** n.312
Security Flour Mills Co. **12** n.3
Security Flour Mills Co. v. Comm'r **12** n.25
Setliff, Don P. .... 3.04[5][a] & n.161; **4** n.280; **11** ns. 10, 11
Seven-Up Co. .... 12.03[3][a][v] & n.83
Shelby Salesbook Co. v. U.S. .... **4** ns. 160, 197
Shelley, Guy M. **3** n.246
Shell Oil Co. **7** n.183

[Text references are to paragraphs (¶) within Chapters; footnote references are to Chapters (boldface numbers) and notes (n.)]

Shore, Dean R. 8 n.91
Sierracin Corp. .... 2 ns. 109, 213
Silberman, William J. 2 n.122;
          3.08[5] & ns. 280, 281
Silver Queen Motel 9 n.67
Simon, Maurice W. .... 2 ns. 119,
          162; 3 n.276
Simon v. Comm'r 6 n.67
Simplified Tax Records, Inc.
          .... 4.04[1][a][iii] & n.192
Skelly Oil Co., U.S. v. ..... 12.04[1] &
          ns. 118, 119
Slater, Bertram H. 12 n.143
Slaughter, W.W. 3 n.66
Sloane v. Comm'r 12 n.154
Smith, Harold S. .. 12.04[2][c] & n.136
Smith, Joe M. 12 n.127
Smith, Paul H. 12 n.129
Smith, City Stores Co. v. 5 n.37
Smith Leasing Co. .... 6.05[2][c][ii] &
          n.120
Smucker, Welker J. 3 n.109
Snyder Air Prods. 4 n.42
SoRelle, Elsie 8 n.313
Sorrell, Gordon S. 3 n.183
South Dade Farms v. Comm'r
          .... 4 n.108
South Lake Farms .... 12.05[4][a][ix]
          & ns. 200, 201
South Lake Farms, Comm'r v.
          .... 12 n.155
South Tex. Lumber Co., Comm'r v.
          .... 5 n.5
Southern Cal. Sav. & Loan Ass'n
          .... 2 ns. 95, 99
Southern Pac. Transp. Co. (TC
          1984) .... 8 ns. 58, 327
Southern Pac. Transp. Co. (TC
          1980) .... 9.03[3] & ns. 57, 58, 64; 9
          ns. 19, 40, 133; 12.05[4][c][i] &
          ns. 231–233
Space Controls, Inc. v. Comm'r
          .... 6.09[3][b][ii] & ns. 412–417; 6 ns.
          386, 401
Spang Indus., Inc. 6 n.129
Spang Indus., Inc. v. U.S. ...... 7 ns.
          41, 190, 279
Spencer, White & Prentis, Inc. v.
          Comm'r 4 n.168
Spiegel, Modie J., Estate .. 3 n.132, 133
Sprague v. U.S. 5 n.342

Spring City Foundry Co. v. Comm'r
          .... 4 n.35
Spring City Foundry Co. v. U.S.
          .... 4.03[2][b] & ns. 74, 76
S. Rossin & Sons v. Comm'r
          .... 2 n.244; 12 n.188
Standard Paving Co. v. Comm'r
          .... 2 n.209; 3 n.246; 12 n.15
Standard Television Tube Corp.
          .... 4 ns. 119, 148
Standing, James J. 2 n.41
Staudt, Fred W. 12 n.234
Stauffer Estate v. Comm'r 10 n.84
Steckel, A.P., Estate of 12 n.141
Steen, In re 5 n.267
Stern, Joseph 2 n.185
Stewart Perry ...... 5 ns. 21, 23, 146,
          292, 296
Stewart, Robert E. 3 n.148
Stewart v. U.S. .... 5 ns. 240, 273
Stockholms Enskilda Bank,
          Helvering v. 5 n.59
Stonecrest Corp. 5 n.231
Stonegate of Blacksburg, Inc.
          .... 10 ns. 17, 187
Story v. Livingston 3 n.142
Streckfus Steamers, Inc.
          .... 12.05[4][c][i] & n.227
Stryker, Max H. 10 n.17
Suffolk County Patrolmen's
          Benevolent Ass'n 5 n.65
Sullivan, Alice Phelan, Corp. v. U.S.
          .... 12 ns. 167, 173, 175
Sullivan, Cornelius J. 6 n.74
Sunnen, Comm'r v. 6 n.83
Superior Coach of Fla., Inc. ... 9 n.107
Susquehanna Coal Co. v. Comm'r
          .... 9 ns. 55, 56, 153, 154
Swartz, Samuel 8 n.43
Sweeney & Co. 7 n.281
S. Weisbart & Co. .... 2 n.154; 6.11 &
          ns. 447, 448
Swinehart Tire & Rubber Co. .. 6 n.350
Switlik, Comm'r v. .... 12.04 & n.114

T

Tampa & Gulf Coast R.R. v.
          Comm'r ..... 4.04[4] & ns. 349, 350

[Text references are to paragraphs (¶) within Chapters; footnote references are to Chapters (boldface numbers) and notes (n.)]

Tampa Tribune Publishing Co. v.
Tomlinson .... 2.04[3][b] & ns. 223–225
Tandy Corp. v. U.S. .... **4** ns. 184, 185
10-42 Corp. **5** n.141
Tennessee Carolina Transp. Inc. v.
Comm'r .... 12.04[4][a][ix] & n.202; **12** n.155
Texaco-Cities Serv. Pipe Line Co. v.
U.S. **9** n.136
Texas Mexican Ry., U.S. v. ... **4** n.187
Textile Apron Co. **7** n.278
T.F.H. Publications, Inc. **4** n.119
Thomas, Payne E.L. .... **2** ns. 192, 238; **6** n.381; **8** ns. 27, 38
Thomas Nelson, Inc. v. U.S.
.... **3** ns. 284, 286; **6** ns. 47, 68; 8.09 & n.345
Thompson-King-Tate, Inc. v. U.S.
..... 9.05[4] & ns. 129, 130; **9** n.116
Thor Power Tool Co. v. Comm'r
.... 2.02[2][c] & ns. 104, 105; 2.02[2][k]; 2.04 & n.199; **2** ns. 101, 150; **3** ns. 19, 24; 4.02[4] & ns. 26, 28; **4** n.6; 6.04[1][a][ii]; 6.06[1][b] & n.151; 6.09[3][b][iii] & n.418; 6.09[3][b][iv] & n.421; **6** ns. 30, 31, 33, 223, 292, 376, 381, 389; 8.07[3]; **8** ns. 144, 176
Thriftimart, Inc. ... 9.06[2][a] & n.145
Tillman, Walter, Estate of **5** n.122
Tog Shop, Inc. v. U.S. .. **2** n.238; 6.09[3] & n.388; **6** ns. 380, 381, 420
Tomlinson, Tampa Tribune
Publishing Co. v. ...... 2.04[3][b] & ns. 223, 224
Towers Warehouses, Inc. **2** n.151
Town & Country Food Co.
.... **5** ns. 52, 342
Town Park Hotel Corp. v. Comm'r
.... **12** n.60
Transwestern Pipeline Co. v. U.S.
.... **6** n.72
Travis, Paul H. **8** n.94
Travis v. Comm'r **2** n.229
Trorlicht-Duncker Carpet Co. .. **6** n.143
TSI, Inc. v. U.S. **3** n.124
Tufts, Comm'r v. **12** n.172
Turco, John E. **12** n.126

U

UFE, Inc. ...... 7.04[3][a][i] & n.135; 7.08[1][b] & n.311
Uhlenbrock, Albert J. ..... 12.03[4][c] & n.111
Underhill, Wingate E. ..... 9.07 & ns. 187–190, 193, 195; **9** ns. 113, 114
Underhill v. Comm'r **8** n.327
Unger, U.S. **3** n.58
Union Bleachery v. Comm'r ... **12** n.31
Union Trust Co. v. Comm'r .. **12** n.157
United Contractors, Inc. **9** n.101
United Control Corp. .. **4** ns. 175, 345
United Hardware Distrib. Co. v.
Comm'r **6** n.380
United Pac. Corp. **5** n.231
U.S. Cartridge Co. v. U.S. **4** n.59
United Surgical Steel Co. **5** n.342
Unvert, Allen D. ..... **12** ns. 168, 230
Usry, Miller v. **5** n.320

V

Vander Poel, Francis & Co. .. **3** n.121
Van Norman Co. v. Welch
.... 12.02[2][f][iii] & ns. 30, 31
Van Pickerill & Sons Inc. v. U.S.
.... **6** n.201
Van Raden, Kenneth H. (9th Cir. 1982) .... 2.02[2][b] & n.99
Van Raden, Kenneth H. (9th Cir. 1981) **3** n.276
Van Raden, Kenneth H. (TC)
..... 2.02[2][d] & n.108; **2** ns. 99, 101
Vernon C. Neal, Inc. **9** n.101
Visintainer v. Comm'r **10** n.269
Voight, Floyd J. **5** n.232

W

Wacker, Orville C. **5** n.232
Waldheim Realty & Inv. Co. v.
Comm'r .... **3** ns. 167, 176, 179
Waldrep, R.A. .... **5** ns. 231, 232
Wardlaw, U.S. v. ...... 9.05[3] & ns. 121, 122

[Text references are to paragraphs (¶) within Chapters; footnote references are to Chapters (boldface numbers) and notes (n.)]

Warfield-Pratt-Howell Co. . . . **6** n.145

Warren Jones Co. v. Comm'r
. . . . 3.03[1][d][ii] & n.47;
3.03[1][d][iii]; 3.03[1][d][iv];
3.03[1][d][v]; **5** n.299

Warren Serv. Corp. v. Comm'r
. . . . **12** n.54

Washington Post Co. v. U.S.
. . . . 4.04[1][a][i] & ns. 173–175

Watson v. Comm'r . . . . . 3.03[1][d][iii]
& ns. 49, 50

Watson, Harriet A., Estate of . . **12** n.182

Waukesha Malleable Iron Co. v.
Comm'r **5** n.194

Waukesha Motor Co. v. U.S. . . **6** n.313

Wayne Bolt & Nut Co. . . . . . 6.08[2][a]
& n.351; **9** ns. 58, 107

W.C. & A.N. Miller Dev. Co.
. . . . **6** n.125; **7** ns. 42, 279

Weaver, James H. **5** n.240

Webb, Vincent E. . . . . . . **5** ns. 229, 237

Webb Press Co. Ltd. **4** n.40

Weber, Joseph C. **3** n.131

Weis, Thomas O. **11** n.240

Welch v. DeBlois **2** n.151

Welch, Pacific Nat'l Co. v. . . . **2** n.195

Wells, Sidney A. **9** n.43

Wendle Ford Sales, Inc. . . . . 7.04[3][e];
7 n.277

Wener v. Comm'r . . 12.04[2][d] & n.139

Western Oaks Bldg. Corp. **4** n.61

Westrom, John F. **5** n.194

West Shore Fuel, Inc. v. U.S. . **5** n.241

Wetherbee Elec. Co. v. Jones
. . . . 9.05[4] & n.131

White, Robert B. **3** n.69

White, William H. **2** n.133;
3.08[1] & ns. 255, 256

White, Sr., William J. **2** n.151

Wien Consol. Airlines v. Comm'r
. . . . **4** n.231

Wierschem, Cornelius **5** n.295

Wilcox, Comm'r v. . . . . 12.03[3][a][ii]
& ns. 71, 72, 74; **12** n.65

Wilkinson, Rhinelander Paper Co.
v. **6** n.350

Wilkinson-Beane, Inc. v. Comm'r
. . . . **2** ns. 126, 163, 207, 209; **3** n.245;
6.05[1][d] & n.76; **6** n.69

Willard Mfg. Co. v. Kennedy . . **6** n.403

Willcuts v. Gradwohl **3** n.4

Williams, George V. **3** n.251

Williams, Jay A. **3** n.56

Williams, Lloyd, Jr. **2** n.87; **3**
n.260; **11** n.240

Williams v. McGowan . . . **5** ns. 222, 223

Williamson, Andrew John . . . **10** n.269

Williamson, Harry W. **3** n.186

Williamson v. U.S. . . . . . **3** ns. 246–248

Wilson v. U.S. **10** n.67

Witt, Estate of v. Fahs **3** n.132

Witte, Herbert S. (DC Cir.) . . . **9** n.195

Witte, Herbert S. (TCM) . . 9.05[2] & ns.
115, 116; 9.07 & ns. 191, 195

Witte v. Comm'r . . . . . **8** n.327; 9.03[3]
& ns. 51, 53, 54

Wolder v. Comm'r **3** n.68

Wolf Bakery & Cafeteria Co.
. . . 2.02[1][e] & n.69; **2** n.151; **3** n.267

Woodbury, Leo A. **3** n.58

Woodmont Terrace, Inc. v. U.S.
. . . . 4.04[1][c] & ns. 209, 211, 212

Woodward Constr. Co., Clark v.
. . . . **4** n.175

Woodward Iron Co. v. U.S.
. . . . **2** n.206; 8.07[2][b] & n.326; **9**
n.44

Wrenn, Philip W. **5** n.239

Wright Contracting Co. . . . . **8** ns. 13, 313

Wright Contracting Co. v. Comm'r
. . . . **8** n.319

W.R. Stephens Co. **6** n.92

W.W. Enters. **2** n.190

Y

Yancy Bros. Co. v. U.S. **5** n.342

Yates v. U.S. . . . . 2.02[1][c] & ns.
51–53; **2** n.210

Z

Zaninovich v. Comm'r . . . . . 3.05[1][b]
& ns. 181, 183

Zidanic, Joseph A. **3** n.150

Zimmerman Steel Co. v. Comm'r
. . . . **4** n.344

Index

A

Abandoned liabilities, 12.05[4][a][vi]

Ability to pay, 3.02[1][c]

Ability to trace costs, 6.05[3]

Abnormal goods, 6.09[2], 7.03[3][c]

Absorption costing, 6.06[2][c]

Absorption ratio, 6.07[4]

Abuse of method, 2.02[2][d], 3.02[2], 4.01[5], 5.05[11][b], 6.06[2][c][i], 11.01[1], 11.02

Abusive situations, potential, 5.05[10][d], 11.02[5][a][ii]

Accelerated Cost Recovery System (ACRS), 12.05[4][b][ii]

Acceptance, goods sold subject to, 6.05[1][b]

Accounting methods. *See* Method of accounting

Accounting partnership, 10.04[4][c][iv]

Accounting period, 1.02[6]
  See also Taxable year
  annual accounting concept, 10.02, 12.02
  change in, 10.02[3][a]
  definition, 10.01
  52–53 week year, 10.02, 10.06
  need for, 10.01
  short-period return, 10.02[4][c]

Accounting records, definition, 2.02[1][c]

Accounts receivable, 2.02[1][e], 2.02[2][j][i], 4.03[2][d]
  combined sale and service, 4.03[3]

Accrual information of cash basis taxpayer, 3.08[2]

Accrual method, 1.01[3], 1.02[2], 1.03[2], 2.01[1], 3.02, 5.01, 6.01[2]

acceptance, 4.02[2]

advantages, 4.03[1][a][iii]

characteristics, 4.01[5]

collection previously doubtful, 4.03[2][c]

constructive receipt, 3.03[2][a]

definition, 4.01

development, 4.02

dominant elements, 4.04[1][b]

escrow amounts, 4.04[1][c][i]

expenses, 4.01[1]
  all events test, 4.04
  amount reasonably determinable, 4.04[2]
  "as provided" requirements, 4.04[3][c]
  conditions precedent, 4.04[1][a][iii]
  conditions subsequent, 4.04[1][a][ii]
  contested liabilities, 4.04[1][c]
  economic performance, 4.04[3]
  fixed liability, 4.04[1]
  identification of creditor, 4.04[1][a][i]
  identification of liability, 4.04[1][a]
  impact of economic performance, 4.04[3][e]
  likelihood of performance, 4.04[1][a][ii]
  matching principle, 4.04[1][b]
  payment doubtful, 4.04[4]
  proof of economic performance, 4.04[3][d]
  property provided by taxpayer, 4.04[3][b][ii]
  property provided to taxpayer, 4.04[3][b][i]
  recurring item exception, 4.04[3][f]
  services rendered by taxpayer, 4.04[3][b][ii]
  services rendered to taxpayer, 4.04[3][b][i]

Accrual method *(cont'd)*
  expenses *(cont'd)*
    tort liability, 4.04[3][b][iii]
    workers' compensation,
      4.04[3][b][iii]
  financial accrual
  accounting, 4.01[2], 4.01[3], 4.02[2]
  history, 4.02
    acceptance of financial accounting
      rules, 4.02[2]
    departure from financial accounting
      rules, 4.02[3]
    Thor Power Tool Co., 4.02[4]
  income, 4.01[1], 4.03
    advance payments for goods,
      4.04[3][e][ii]
    advance payments for services,
      4.04[3][e][ii]
    all events test, 4.03
    amount reasonably determinable,
      4.03[1][b]
    conditions precedent, 4.03[1][a][i]
    conditions subsequent, 4.03[1][a][i]
    contests, 4.03[1][a][i]
    deferral in recognition, 4.03[3][d],
      4.03[3][e]
    disputes, 4.03[1][a][i]
    fixed right to receive, 4.03[1][a]
    flexibility in determining right to
      receive, 4.03[1][a][iii]
    items no longer of doubtful
      collectibility, 4.03[2][c]
    items of doubtful collectibility,
      4.03[2]
    knowledge of right to receive,
      4.03[1][a]
    nonaccrual of service income,
      4.03[2][d]
    prepaid income, 4.03[3]
    Supreme Court trilogy, 4.03[3][b]
  IRS view, 4.01[3]
  not required, 4.03[1][b], 4.03[2]
  requirements, 4.01[1], 4.03[1]
  sale, time for accrual, 4.03[1][a]
  tax accounting, 4.01[2], 4.01[3],
    4.01[5]
  users, 4.01[4]
Accrual period for OID, definition,
  11.02[3][a][i]
Accrued market discount, 11.05[2]

Accuracy standard of clear reflection,
  2.02[2][j][ii]
Acquired for sale, goods, 6.05[1][c]
Acquisition
  carryover for tax
  attributes, 9.08[2]
  costs
    definition, 6.06[2][a]
    discount, 11.02[2][b]
    nontaxable, 7.08[3]
    premium, 11.02[3][a][iii]
    tax avoidance, 9.08[1][c]
ACRS. *See* Accelerated Cost Recovery
  System
Adjusted issue price, definition,
  11.02[3][a][i]
Administrative expenses, 6.06[1][c][ii],
  6.06[2][c][i]
Advance commissions, 4.04[1][b]
Advance payment
  by customer, 6.06[2][c][ii]
  for goods, 4.03[3][e][ii]
  for services, 4.03[3][e][ii]
Advertising expenses, 6.06[2][c][ii]
Affiliated group
  availability of cash method, 3.06[1][a],
    3.06[1][b][ii]
  clear reflection of income, 3.08[6]
  LIFO adoption, 7.03[1][a]
  LIFO conformity, 7.03[2][b][viii]
  LIFO pooling, 7.04[3][a][iii]
  members, 10.04[4][f][ii]
  simplified LIFO, 7.04[5][b]
  taxable year, 10.02[3][a][ii],
    10.04[4][f][ii], 10.05[2][g][ii],
    10.05[4][b][iii], 10.05[5][a]
Agent
  See also Conduit
  payment by, 3.04[3][a]
  payment to, 3.04[3][b], 3.04[5][c]
  received by, 3.03[3][a]
Aggregation
  activities, 4.04[3][f][iii]
  cash method rules, 3.06[1][a]
  inventory, 6.06[1][c]
  LIFO, 7.04[5][b]
Aging product, 6.08[3][a]
AIA. *See* American Institute of
  Accountants

[References are to paragraphs (¶)]

AICPA. *See* American Institute of
    Certified Public Accountants
All events test, 4.03, 4.03[3], 4.03[3][b],
    4.03[3][c], 4.04, 11.01[1][b],
    12.03[1]
    definition, 4.03[1]
Allocation procedures for inventory,
    6.06[1][c][ii]
Allowance under Section 269,
    definition9.08[1][c]
Alternative LIFO measurement
    procedures, 7.04[3][b]
Alternative minimum tax, 5.02[7]
American Institute of Accountants
    (AIA), 7.02[2]
American Institute of Certified Public
    Accountants (AICPA), 6.09[1],
    7.02[2]
American Petroleum Institute, 7.02[2]
Amortization, 6.06[2][c][ii]
Annual accounting concept, 12.02
    See also Arrowsmith doctrine;
        claim-of-right doctrine; tax
        benefit rule
    application, 12.02[2]
        deduction improper in year
            claimed, 12.02[2][b]
        deduction not taken, 12.02[2][c]
        deduction proper in year claimed,
            12.02[2][a]
        income erroneously reported early,
            12.02[2][d]
        income not reported in proper year,
            12.02[2][e]
    codification, 12.02[1]
    influential events, 12.02[2][f]
        additional income, 12.02[2][f][ii]
        change in law, 12.02[2][f][i]
        retroactive change in facts,
            12.02[2][f][iv]
        retroactive change in law,
            12.02[2][f][i], 12.02[2][f][iii]
        retroactive tax, 12.02[2][f][iii]
        state court action, 12.02[2][f][v]
    legislative and judicial amelioration,
        12.02[3]
Annual accounting period, 1.02[8],
    10.02[1]
    change, 10.05

definition, 10.02[1][a]
    taxable year change to conform to,
        10.05[2][f]
Annualization, 3.06[1][a], 10.05[5]
    alternative method, 10.05[5][b]
    normal, 10.05[5][a]
Annual price change, 7.04[3][b][iii]
Annuity, 4.04[3][b][iii]
    contributions, 6.06[2][c][ii]
    private, 5.05[12][e]
Antitrust violation, 12.05[4][b][iii]
Applicable installment obligations,
    5.05[6]
Approval, goods sold on, 6.05[1][b]
Arbitrary accounting procedures,
    2.01[2], 2.01[3], 9.04[2]
    alternatives available, 9.04[2][b]
    problem confronting taxpayer,
        9.04[2][a]
Arrowsmith doctrine, 1.02[8], 12.04
    adjustments to sales price, 12.04[2][a]
    applications, 12.04[2]
        initial gain—later gain, 12.04[2][c]
        initial gain—later loss, 12.04[2][a]
        initial loss—later gain, 12.04[2][b]
        initial loss—later loss, 12.04[2][d]
    inapplicability, 12.04[3]
    scope, 12.04[1]
    statutory relief, 12.04[4]
Asset sale, 3.06[3]
Assignment of income doctrine, 3.06[3]
Assumption
    of mortgage, 5.05[10][b]
    of seller's qualifying indebtedness,
        5.05[7][c]
Athletes, 3.06[1][b][i]
Authority
    reconciliation of, for clear reflection
        test, 2.02[2][k]
    statutory and regulatory, 1.04
Authorization by Code or regulations,
    2.02[2][b]
Automatic installment reporting,
    3.03[1][d][iv]
Auxiliary records, 2.02[1][b]
Average cost methods, 6.08[3]
    IRS position, 6.08[3][a]
    judicial review, 6.08[3][b]

[References are to paragraphs (¶)]

Avoided cost method, 6.06[2][c][ii]

B

Bad debt, 5.04[5], 12.03[4][b], 12.05[4][b][i]

Bad debt reserve, 12.05[4][a][vii]

Bad debt reserve method, repeal of, 1.01[3], 4.03[2][d], 5.04[5], 8.04[6][d], 12.05[4][a][vii]

Balance sheet non-LIFO reporting, 7.03[2][b][ii]

Bankruptcy, 5.05[11][b][iii]

Bankruptcy Tax Act of 1980, 12.05[4][a][x]

Base costs, 7.04[3][b]

Base stock method of inventory accounting, 7.02[2]

Below market loans, 11.11

Bidding expenses, 6.06[2][c][ii]

Bid price, 6.09[3]

Binding election rule, 2.03[3]

BLS. *See* United States Bureau of Labor Statistics
  BLS Consumer Price Index, 7.04[5][b]
  BLS Consumer Price Index Detailed Report, 7.04[5][b]
  BLS Producer Prices and Price Indexes, 7.04[5][a][i], 7.04[5][b]
  BLS Producer Prices Data Report, 7.04[5][b]

Bond
  definition, 11.05[1]
  premium, 11.05
  stripped, 11.07
  treatment of original purchaser, 11.07[1]

Book conformity requirement, 2.02, 3.06, 3.08[7], 7.03[2]
  book-tax reconciliations, 2.02[1][c]
  vs. consistency, 2.02[1][d]
  departures from overall method, 2.03[1][a]
  vs. financial statement conformity, 2.02[1][e]
  form of information, 2.02[1][b]

information on different bases, 2.02[1][b]
  intent of taxpayer, 2.02[1][b]
  origin of requirement, 2.02[1][a]
  reconciling workpapers, 2.02[1][c]

Book methods of conformity, 2.02[1]
  divergence from tax accounting, 4.02[3], 4.02[4]

Books. *See* Business, recordkeeping systems

Book year, 10.02[1][b]

Borrowed funds, payment with, 3.04[3][a]

Breach of contract or fiduciary obligation, 12.05[4][b][iii]

Bulk sale, 5.04[2][c], 5.05[7][d], 5.05[11][a]

Business
  beginning a, 2.02[1]
  expense, 6.05[2][a], 6.06
  rapid growth, 3.08[1]
  record-keeping systems, 1.03[3], 10.02[1][b]
  size, 2.02[2][d], 2.02[2][g], 3.08
  termination
    accrual method, 3.06[3]
    cash method, 4.01[4]
    method of accounting, 8.04[5][a]
    taxable year, 10.02[3][b], 10.04[4][b][iv]

By-products, 6.10[3]

C

Caldwell standard of clear reflection, 2.02[2][j][ii]

Calendar year, 10.03[1]
  definition, 10.02[1][a]

Call, 11.02[4][a][iv]
  definition, 11.02[3][a][i]

Canceled debt, 12.05[4][a][xi]

Capital gain, 11.02[2]
  conversion to, 11.02[2][a], 11.02[2][b]

Capitalization, 6.07
  costing, 6.06[2][c][ii]
  doctrine, 3.08[5]
  uniform rules, 1.03[3], 6.07[4]

[*References are to paragraphs (¶)*]

Carryover of tax attributes, 9.08[1][b], 9.08[2]
Cash basis, 3.05[2][b][i]
Cash equivalence, 3.03[1], 5.05[15]
  definition, 3.03[1]
  fair market value of property, 3.03[1][d][ii]
  installment sale election out, 5.05[15]
  position of Treasury, 3.03[1][d][iv]
  present status, 3.03[1][d][v]
  traditional view, 3.03[1][d][i]
Cash flow
  improvement, 7.02[1]
  increase, 5.02[2]
  principles, 3.02[1]
Cash method, 1.02[2], 1.03[2], 2.01[1], 2.02[2][f], 5.01
  ability to pay, 3.02[1][c]
  availability, 3.06
    on behalf of taxpayer, 3.04[1]
  benefits, 3.02[2]
  cash equivalence, 3.03[1], 5.05[15]
  cash-flow principles, 3.02[1]
  change from, required, 3.06[1][d], 8.04[6][a]
  characteristics, 3.01[1]
  clear reflection of income, 3.08
    accrual basis book information, 3.08[2]
    accrual basis financial reporting, 3.08[3]
    consolidation returns, 3.08[6]
    GAAP, 3.08[4]
    mismatching of income and expense, 3.08[5]
    size of deferral, 3.08[1]
  constructive payment, 3.04[2]
  constructive receipt, 3.03[2]
    accrual method taxpayer, 3.03[2][a]
    purpose of rule, 3.03[2][a]
    restrictions and limitations, 3.03[2][b]
  definition, 2.02[1][a], 3.01
  development, 3.02
  effective date of change, 3.06[1][d]
  election to use, 11.02[5][c]
  expense, 3.04
    insurance, 3.04[5][b]
    interest, 3.04[5][a]
    taxes, 3.04[5][c]

  farmers, use by, 9.08[1][c]
  history, 3.02
  income, 3.03
    compensation, 3.03[3][c]
    dividends, 3.03[3][b]
    interest, 3.03[3][a]
    rent, 3.03[3][d]
    royalty, 3.03[3][d]
  intangible property, 3.03[1][c]
  IRS difficulty with, 3.08[7], 3.02[3]
  issues, 3.01[3]
  limitations on use, 1.01[3], 2.02[2][g], 3.01[2], 3.02[3], 3.05[2][a], 3.06, 6.01[2], 8.04[6][a]
  1986 Act limitations, 3.06[1]
    effective dates, 3.06[1][d]
    farming business, 3.06[1][c]
    gross receipts test, 3.06[1][a]
    qualified personal service corporation, 3.06[1][b]
  payment, 3.04
    borrowed funds, 3.04[3][a]
    by check, note, of other, 3.04[4][a], 3.04[4][b]
    constructive, 3.04[2]
  prepayment, 3.05
    capitalization and one-year rule, 3.05[1][b]
    tax shelters, 3.05[2]
  purchases and sales of inventory, 3.06[2]
  required use, 3.02, 3.07
  sales agent, 6.05[1][b]
    on termination of business, 3.06[3]
  transactions, 6.02[3]
  transition rules, 3.06[1][d]
  use by large business, 2.02[2][g]
  users, 3.01[2]
Cash settlement option, 11.02[4][b][iv]
Casualty losses recovered, 12.05[4][a][iii]
Category A methods, 8.04[4][b][iii], 8.06[2][b], 8.06[2][c], 8.06[2][d], 8.06[4], 8.07[2]
  change from, following contract by IRS, 8.06[2][b]
  definition, 8.06[2][b][i]
  IRS discretion to define, 8.06[2][b][i]
Category B methods, 8.04[4][b][iv], 8.06[2][c], 8.06[3][b], 8.06[4], 8.07[2]

[References are to paragraphs (¶)]

Category One cost, 6.06[2][c][i]

Category Three cost, 6.06[2][c][i]

Category Two cost, 6.06[2][c][i]

C corporation (Regular corporation),
    3.02[3], 3.06[1], 4.01[4], 5.05[11][c],
    8.04[5][a], 10.04[4][b][i],
    10.04[4][b][iii], 10.04[4][d],
    10.04[4][e]

Certainty of method, 2.01[3]

Certificate of deposit, interest on,
    3.03[3][a]

Change in character of item, 9.07

Change in law, 12.02[2][f][i]

Change in method of accounting,
    1.02[5], 2.01[4], 2.02[1], 2.02[2][a],
    9.01[1]
  See also Form 3115; Revenue
      Procedure 84-74 adjustment
      spread; Section 481 adjustment
  adjustment requirement, 8.04
  amended return, by, 9.04[1][b]
  application for, 8.06
    early, 8.06[3][c]
    failure to file, 8.06[2][b][i]
    general rule, 8.06[1]
    governing procedures, 8.06[2]
    IRS decision not to process,
        8.06[2][f]
    late, 8.06[3][d]
    pending when return due, 8.06[5]
    taxpayer alternatives if late,
        8.06[3][d][iii]
  approval deemed, 8.07[3]
  arbitrary practices, change from,
      9.04[2]
    alternatives, 9.04[2][b]
  automatic, 8.07[3]
  book confirmity, to achieve, 2.02[1][d]
  category A method, 8.06[2][b]
  category B method, 8.06[2]
  correction of method by amended
      return, 9.04[1][b]
  correct method, 9.04[1][a]
  deferred intercompany transaction,
      9.05[1]
  defined, 8.02, 9.02
    exclusions, 9.02[2]
    inclusions, 9.02[1]
  denial of change by Commissioner,
      8.07
    alternatives to, 9.04[2][b], 9.08
    challenging denial by
        Commissioner, 9.05[5]
  designated A method, 8.06[3][a][ii]
  designated B method, 8.06[3][a][iv]
  directed by Commissioner, 2.04[e]
  discretion of Commissioner, 8.07
    acceptable method to acceptable
        method, 8.07[1]
    automatic approval, 8.07[3]
    consent deemed approved, 8.07[3]
    consent not required, 8.07[2][b]
    consent required, 8.07[2][a]
    incorrect method to correct
        method, 8.07[2]
  earnings and profits, effect on, 8.05
  erroneous method changed in first
      year, 8.06[2][a]
  exclusions from concept, 9.02[2]
  expansion of business, 9.06[5]
  factors to consider, 9.02[3]
  fees, 8.06[1], 10.05[3]
  from improper to proper method,
      8.07[2]
  from one acceptable method to
      another, 8.07[1]
  impact of materiality, 9.03
    absolute materiality, 9.03[2][a]
    comparisons to be made,
        9.03[2][b][i], 9.03[2][b][ii]
    relative materiality, 9.03[2][b]
  imposition of penalties, 8.09
  improper method, from
    IRS consent required, 8.07[2][a]
    IRS consent not required,
        8.07[2][b], 9.04[1][b]
    taxpayer obligation, 8.08
  inclusions in concept, 9.02[1]
  initiated by Commissioner, 8.04[1]
  initiated by IRS, 8.04[1]
  initiated by taxpayer, 8.04[1]
  IRS decision not to process, 8.06[2][f]
  LIFO changes, 7.06, 7.06[1], 7.06[2]
  no change in method, 9.01[2]
    adoption of method for new item,
        9.06[4]
    arbitrary practice, 9.04[2]
    change in business practices,
        9.06[2][a]

[References are to paragraphs (¶)]

change in character of item, 9.07
change in contract terms, 9.06[2][a]
change in economic consequences,
  9.06[2][a]
change in facts, 9.06
correction of error, 9.05
lack of consistency, 9.04
lack of material item, 9.03
significant consequences to parties,
  9.06[2][b]
obligation to change incorrect
  method, 8.08
penalties, 8.09
pending criminal investigation,
  8.06[2][e]
prior approval required, 8.03
procedures, 8.06[3]
recommendation, 9.04[2][c]
required by 1987 Act, 5.07
  repeal of installment method,
    5.07[1]
  repeal of proportionate
    disallowance rule, 5.07[2]
required by 1986 Act, 8.04[6]
  change from cash method,
    8.04[6][a]
  change from installment method,
    8.04[6][b]
  change to uniform capitalization
    rules, 8.04[6][c]
  repeal of bad debt reserve method,
    8.04[6][d]
retroactive change, 8.06[3][b][iii]
Section 481 adjustment, 8.04
taxpayer initiated, 8.04[1]
taxpayer obligation to change
  method, 8.08
taxpayer under continuous audit,
  8.06[2][b][iii]
techniques for, 8.06, 9.08
  application to change, 8.06
  carryover of attribute rules, 9.08[2]
  do-it-yourself approach,
    9.04[2][b][iii]
  drop down, 9.08[1]
  elect method not requiring
    approval, 9.04[2][b][ii]
  Section 351 transfers, 9.08[1][a]
  Section 368 reorganization,
    9.08[1][b]
  transfers of business growth,
    9.08[3]
  year of change, 8.06[4]
Change in method without prior
  approval, 9.08
Change in reporting not a change in
  method of accounting, 9.01[2]
  See also Change in method of
    accounting, no change in method
Changes in tax rates and laws, 5.02[7]
Characterization rules, 1.01[3], 11.02[2]
  exceptions, 11.02[2][c]
Character of items, 1.01
Character of taxpayer affecting Section
  481 adjustment, 8.04[2][d]
Charitable contribution returned,
  12.05[4][a][ii]
Charitable transfers, 5.05[11][b][iii]
Check as payment, 3.04[4][a]
China Trade Act Corporation,
  10.05[4][b][i]
Claim-of-right doctrine, 1.02[8],
  3.02[1][a], 4.03[3][a], 4.03[3][b],
  12.03
  amounts received under mistaken
    claim, 12.03[3][a][iii]
  application requirements, 12.03[2]
  asserted, 12.03[2][c]
  availability of deduction for repaid
    amounts, 12.03[3][b]
  conduits, 12.03[3][a][v]
  deposits, 12.03[3][a][vi]
  illegal "income," 12.03[3][a][ii]
  mitigation of results, 12.03[4]
  origin, 12.03[1]
  prepaid income, 12.03[3][a][i]
  prevailing issues, 12.03[3]
    availability of deduction,
      12.03[3][b]
    characterization of receipt as
      income, 12.03[3][a]
  refund agreement, 12.03[3][a][iv]
  requirements for application, 12.03[2]
    asserted claim, 12.03[2][c]
    receipt of income, 12.03[2][a]
    unlimited control, 12.03[2][b]
  statutory relief, 12.03[4]
  trustees, 12.03[3][a][v]
  unlimited control, 12.03[2][b]

[References are to paragraphs (¶)]

Claim-of-right doctrine *(cont'd)*
  use to characterize receipts as income,
      12.03[3][a]
Clear Reflection of Income
      Requirement, 2.02[2]
  authorization of method by Code or
      regulation, 2.02[2][b]
  consistent use of method, 2.02[2][b]
  correct application of method,
      2.02[2][a]
  GAAP, 2.02[2][c]
  judicial standards of, 2.02[2][j]
  manipulation and abuse, 3.08[5]
  mismatching of income and expense,
      2.02[2][f]
  to more clearly reflect income,
      2.02[2][h]
  nature of business, 2.02[2][d]
  relative merits of methods of
      accounting, 2.02[2][f]
  size of business, 2.02[2][g]
  subsequent legislation, effect of,
      2.02[2]
  substantial identity test, 2.02[2][f]
  use of method by others, 2.02[2][i]
  virtual identity test, 2.02[2][f]
Code. *See* Internal Revenue Code
COD sales, 6.05[1][b]
Collapsible corporations, 5.06[3][b]
Collateral, effect on installment sale,
      5.06[5]
Commission under cash method,
      3.03[3][c]
Commissioner of Internal Revenue
      challenging Commissioner's
      decision, 9.05[5]
  change in method approved or
      directed by, 2.04[3][e], 8.04
  consent to change method, implied,
      2.04[3][b]
  discretion, 1.02[1], 1.02[5], 1.03[1],
      2.02[1][e], 2.02[2], 2.03, 2.04,
      6.04[1][a][ii], 7.03, 7.05, 8.01,
      8.03, 8.04[3], 8.06[3][d], 8.07,
      9.01, 9.08[1][c]
    abuse of, 2.02[1][d], 2.02[2][d],
        2.04[1], 2.04[2], 4.03[3][c],
        8.03, 8.07[1], 8.07[2], 9.05[5]
    impact of IRS actions on, 2.04[3]

not required, 7.04[5][b], 7.06,
    8.07[2][b], 9.06[4], 9.08[2],
    10.05[2][f]
required, 2.02[1], 6.07[4], 6.07[5],
    7.04[3][a][i], 7.06, 8.01, 8.03,
    8.07[2][a], 10.05
Commissions on installment sale,
    5.05[8][b]
Community property laws and cash
    method, 3.06[1][b][ii]
Compensation, 3.03[3][c]
  obligation to repay, 3.03[3][c]
Component costing, 7.04[3][e]
Computers, use of, 2.02[1][a], 2.02[1][b]
Conduit, 12.03[3][a][v]
Conformity
  basis for change in method, 2.02[1][d]
  book, 2.02, 3.06, 3.08[7]
  financial reporting, 2.02[1][e],
      6.06[2][c][i]
Congress
  increasing legislative activity, 1.01[3]
  political, fiscal, economic
      considerations, 1.03[2]
Consent agreement, 8.06[3][a]
Consigned goods, 6.05[1][b]
Consolidated group. *See* Affiliated
    group
Consolidated return group, 5.04[6]
Consolidated return regulations, 5.04[6]
Constant interest rate basis, 4.04[3][c],
    11.02[2][b]
Constructive payment, 1.03[2], 3.04[2]
Constructive receipt doctrine, 1.03[2],
    3.03[1][b], 3.03[2], 3.03[3], 3.08[5],
    12.05[4][b][i]
  See also Cash method
  annual method taxpayer, 3.03[2][a]
  practical considerations, 3.03[2][b]
  purpose, 3.03[2][a]
  restrictions and limitations, 3.03[2][b],
      3.03[3][a]
Consulting services, 3.06[1][b][i]
Contested liability
  definition, 4.04[1][c]
  escrow amounts, 4.04[1][c][i]

income on escrowed amounts, 4.04[1][c][i]
payment, 4.04[1][c][i]
resolution of, 4.04[1][c][ii]

Contingent payment obligation
definition, 11.03[1]
installment sale, 5.05[15][b]
original issue discount, 11.03
treatment, 11.03[2]

Contingent price installment sale rules, 5.05[12], 5.06[4]
alternative basis recovery rules, 5.05[12][d][ii]
fixed payment period, 5.05[12][b]
maximum price stated, 5.05[12][a]
private annuity, 5.05[12][e]
selling price and payment period indefinite, 5.05[12][c]

Contingent services, 4.03[3][e][ii]

Continuous audit, taxpayer under, 8.06[2][b][iii]

Continuous budget accounts, 5.04[2][d][ii]

Contract award, 6.06[2][c][ii]

Contract price, 5.04[3][a]

Contract price rule, 5.05[8][c]

Control under Section 269, 9.08[1][c]

Controlled corporation, 3.02[1][a]
transfers to, 5.05[11][b][iii], 9.08[1][a]

Controlled entity, depreciable proprety sales to, 5.05[11][c]

Controlled foreign corporation, 10.05[4][b][ii], 10.05[4][b][iii]

Controlled group. *See* Affiliated group

Conversion workpapers, 2.02[1][c]

Convertible debt, 11.02[4][b][iv]

Corn Products doctrine, 6.05[1][a]

Corporate obligations issued before July 2, 1982, 11.02[3][b]

Corporation, 6.10[1], 8.04[5][a], 10.05[4][b]
See also C corporation; Personal service corporation; S corporation

Correction of error, 9.05
deferred intercompany transaction, 9.05[1]

Cost-flow assumptions, 6.08[1]
reason for, 7.01

Costing rules, uniform, 6.06[1][c][ii]

Cost of goods sold, 6.02[2], 6.02[3], 6.08[2][a], 6.10[4]

Cost only LIFO rule, 7.03[3]

Cost or market. *See* Lower of cost or market

Cost recovery allowance, 6.06[2][c][ii]

Cost recovery method, 3.03[1][d][iii], 5.05[1][a], 5.05[15], 9.03[3], 9.07

Courts' attitude toward tax accounting, 1.03[1]

Cowden standard of cash equivalence, 3.03[1][d][ii], 3.03[1][d][iii]
CPI Detailed Report, 7.04[5][a][i]

Criminal investigation, 8.06[2][e]

Crop insurance proceeds, 3.03[3][e]

Crude Oil Windfall Profit Tax Act of 1980 (Windfall Profit Tax Act), 7.07[3], 12.05[4][b][v]

Cumulative price change, 7.04[3][b][iii]

Current costs, 7.04[2], 7.04[3][b][i], 7.04[3][b][iii], 7.04[3][c], 7.04[4]

Cycle budget accounts, 5.04[2][d][ii]

D

Daily portion of OID, definition, 11.02[3][a][i]

Damaged inventory, 6.08[2][a]

Damage recovery, 12.05[4][b][iii]

Dealer, 1.02[3]
installment computation by, 5.04[3]
installment method availability, 5.04
personal property
definition, 5.03, 5.04, 5.04[2][a]
installment sales, 5.05[2], 5.05[6]

Death affecting installment obligation, 5.06[1]

Debt instrument
amount received for, 11.02[2]
as payment, 3.04[3]
definition, 11.02[1]
noncontingent payments
less than issue price, 11.03[2][b]

Debt instrument *(cont'd)*
  noncontingent payments *(cont'd)*
    not less than issue price, 11.03[2][a]
  nonpublicly offered, 11.02[4][b][ii]
  nonpublicly traded, 11.02[4][b][iv]
  publicly offered, 11.02[4][b][i]
  publicly traded, 11.02[4][b][iii]

Deduction, 3.04[1], 3.04[3], 3.04[4][a],
  3.04[4][b], 3.04[5], 3.05, 4.04,
  5.04[5], 6.01[2], 6.05[2][c], 12.03,
  12.04[4], 12.05
  absence of, 12.05[4][c][ii]
  deferral of, 3.08[5]
  erroneous, 12.05[4][c][i]
  improper in year claimed, 12.02[2][b]
  not taken in year originally available,
    12.02[2][c]
  other than current, 4.04[3][e]
  proper in year claimed, 12.02[2][a]

Default, 5.04[5], 5.05[14]

Deferral in reporting income allowed by
  Treasury and IRS, 4.03[3][e][ii]
  amount of, 3.08[1]
  gain, 5.02[1]
  length of, 4.03[3][d]
  provisions permitting, 4.03[3][e]

Deferral or distortion of income
  resulting from change of taxable
  year, 10.05[2][e]

Deferred intercompany transaction,
  definition, 5.04[6]
  not accounting method, 9.05[1]

Deferred payment
  compensation, 3.03[3][c]
  IRS position on, 11.01[2][a][iv]

Defining method, importance of, 9.06[3]

Definitions generally, 2.02[2][j][i]

Depletion, 6.06[2][c][ii]

Deposit
  forfeiture of, 12.04[2][c]
  receipt of, 12.03[3][a][vi]

Depreciation, 6.06[2][c][i], 6.06[2][c][ii],
  6.07[5]
  recapture, 5.05[9], 12.05[4][b][ii]

Designated rulings, 8.04[4][b][iv]

Direct costing, 6.06[2][c], 6.08[2][b]

Direct labor costs, 6.06[2][b]

Direct material costs, definition,
  6.06[2][a]

Direct reallocation of inventory costs,
  6.07[5]

DISC, 10.02[4], 10.05[2][c],
  10.05[4][b][ii], 10.05[4][b][iii]

Discount, 6.06[1][a]
  cash, 6.06[1][a][ii]
  interest, 3.03[3][a]
  market, 11.02[3][a][iii], 11.05
  trade, 6.06[1][a][i]

Discount on short-term obligations,
  11.06
  deferral of interest deductions,
    11.06[2]
  obligations covered, 11.06[1]

Discretion
  abuse of, 2.04[2]
  appeals officer, 8.06[2][c]
  Commissioner of Internal
    Revenue/Internal Revenue
    Service, 1.02[1], 1.02[5], 2.02[2],
    2.03[2], 2.04, 3.06[2], 4.03[3][b],
    6.04[1][a][ii], 7.03, 7.05, 8.01,
    8.03, 8.04[3], 8.06[2][b][i],
    8.06[3][d], 8.07, 9.01
  exercise of, 2.04[1]
  Secretary of the Treasury, 6.04[1][a]
  taxpayer, 1.02[1], 2.03, 6.02[2][c][i],
    6.07, 6.11, 7.05

Dishonored check, 3.04[4][a]

Disproportionate disallowance rule,
  1.02[3]

Dissolution. *See* Business, termination

Distribution costs, 6.07[5]
  definition, 6.06[1][c][ii]

Distribution expenses, 6.06[2][c][ii]

Distributor, 7.04[5][a][i]

Dividends, 3.03[3][b]

"Do-it-yourself" correction of
  method, 9.04[2][b][iii]

Dollar-value LIFO, 7.04[3], 7.04[5],
  7.05[1][a], 7.07[1]

Dormant corporation
  effect on taxable year, 10.04[4][b][ii]
  reactivated, 10.04[4][b][iv]

Double extension LIFO method,
  7.04[3][b][i], 7.04[3][b][iii]

[References are to paragraphs (¶)]

Double tax installment reporting, 5.04[1]

Drilling costs, 3.05[2][b][ii]

Drop-down, change in method by, 9.08[1]

Dual-use property, 6.05[1][e]

Dues income, prepaid, 4.03[3][e][i]

Expense items, 1.02[2], 2.02[1], 3.02[1][b], 3.03[3][e], 3.04, 6.05[2][a]
accelerated recognition, 9.01[3]
doubtful of payment, 1.03[2], 4.04[4]
liability fixed, 4.04[1]
reporting, 3.04, 4.04
selling, 5.05[8][b]

E

Economic considerations, 1.03[2]

Economic performance test, 1.02[2], 3.02[1][b], 3.05[2][a], 3.05[2][b], 4.04, 4.04[1][b], 4.04[1][c][i], 4.04[3]
"as provided" requirement, 4.04[3][c]
cash method principle, 3.02[1][b]
proof of compliance, 4.04[3][d]
reasonable period, 4.04[3][f][i]
recurring item exception, 4.04[3][a], 4.04[3][f]
time of, 4.04[3][b]

Economic yield, 11.02[2][b], 11.02[3]
eight-and-one-half-month period, 4.04[3][f][i]

Employee benefits, 6.06[2][c][i]

Employee-owner, 10.04[4][e], 10.04[5]

Employee tips, 3.03[3][e]

Ending inventory, 6.08

Engineering and design expense, 6.06[2][c][ii]

Engineering services, 3.06[1][d]

Error correction, 9.05

Escrow amounts, 4.04[1][c][i], 5.05[7][e]

Estate, 4.04[3][f][iii], 5.06[1], 10.04[4][f][i]

Estimated expenses, 4.02[3]

Excess inventory, 6.09[3][b][iii]

Exchange
like-kind, 5.05[13]
tax-free, 3.02[1][c]

Excise tax, 6.06[2][c][ii]

Excise Tax Act of 1909, 3.02, 6.03

Expansion of business, 9.06[5]

F

Factory administrative espenses, 6.06[2][c][i]

Fair and honest reporting standard of clear reflection, 2.02[2][j][i]

Fair market value, 3.03[1][b], 3.03[1][d], 5.05[15], 6.09[3]

Farm, definition, 11.02[5][b][i]

Farmers inventory costing, 6.10[2]

Farming business, 3.06[1], 4.01[4], 8.06[2][b][i]
definition, 3.06[1][c]

Farming taxpayers, designated, 6.10[2]

Farm land, 5.06[3][b]

Farm price method, 6.10[2]

Farm sale, 11.02[5][b][i]

FIFO. *See* First-in, first-out

52–53 week year, 10.03[1], 10.04[5], 10.06
adoption, 10.04[5]
change to or from, 10.05[2][g]
definition, 10.02[2]
effective date, 10.06[2]
general, 10.06[1]
special requirements, 10.06

Films, motion picture and television, 5.05[12][d][i]

Financial accounting principles, 1.03[1], 2.01[1], 2.02[2][c], 7.04[3][b][ii]

Financial reporting, 2.02[1][a], 3.01[1], 3.02[3]
accrual basis, 3.08[3]
conformity, 2.02[1][e], 6.06[2][c][i]

Financial statement, 2.02[1][e]
conformity requirement, 2.02[1][e], 7.03[2]

Finished goods market value, 6.09[3][b]

First-in, first-out (FIFO), 2.02[2][e],
  3.06[2], 6.05[3][a], 6.08[2], 6.08[3],
  6.11, 7.01, 7.03[3], 7.03[4],
  7.08[1][b]
First taxable year, 10.04[4][b][ii],
  10.04[4][b][iii], 10.04[4][b][iv]
Fiscal considerations affecting tax
  accounting, 1.03[2]
Fiscal year, 1.02[6]
  See also Taxable year, definition,
    10.02[1][a]
  $5 million gross receipts test
  cash method, 3.06[1][a], 3.06[1][b][i]
  LIFO, 7.04[5][a][i], 7.04[5][b]
Fixed amount obligation, installment
  reporting, 5.05[15][a]
Fixed right to receive, 4.03[1][a]
  conditions and disputes, 4.03[1][a][i]
  flexibility to determine, 4.03[1][a][iii]
  IRS position, 4.03[1][a]
  taxpayer's knowledge, 4.03[1][a][ii]
Flexible budget accounts, 5.04[2][d][ii]
Foreclosure, 5.05[11][b][iii]
Foreign currency, 11.03[1]
Foreign expropriation losses,
  12.05[4][b][iv]
Form 970, 7.03[1][a], 7.03[1][d],
  7.04[5][a][ii], 7.04[5][a][iii],
  7.05[1][b], 7.08[3][a]
Form 1128, 10.05[3][a], 10.05[4][b][ii]
Form 3115, 7.04[5][a][iii], 8.04[4][b][iv],
  8.06[1], 8.06[2][b][ii], 8.06[2][b][iii],
  8.06[2][c], 8.06[4]
  application to
    District Director, 8.06[3][b]
    National Office, 8.06[3][a]
Form of payment under cash method,
  3.04[3]
Form of records, 2.02[1][b]
F reorganization, 10.04[4][b][iii]
FSC, 10.02[4]
Full absorption costing rules, 2.02[1][e],
  6.06[2][c][i], 6.06[2][c][ii], 6.07[4],
  8.06[2][b][i]

G

GAAP. *See* Generally accepted
  accounting principles

Gain, recognition of installment, 5.01,
  5.05[5]
  deferral, 5.02[1], 5.06
  flexibility in timing, 5.02[4]
Gain or loss
  definition, 3.03[1][b]
  determination, 5.06
  recognition, 6.05[1][b]
Gas property, 5.06[3][b]
General expenses, 6.06[1][c][ii]
Generally accepted accounting
  principles (GAAP)
  accrual method, 4.01[2], 4.02[4],
    4.04[1][b], 4.04[3][f][iii]
  book conformity requirement,
    2.02[1][a], 2.02[1][e]
  cash method, 3.01[1], 3.02[3], 3.08[4]
  clear reflection of income
    requirement, 2.02[2][c]
  inventory methods, 6.04[1][a][i],
    6.04[1][a][ii], 6.06[2][c][i],
    6.06[2][c][ii], 6.09[1],
    6.09[3][b][iii]
  LIFO, 7.04[3][b][ii]
  Geometric Stamping principle,
    2.04[3][d]
Geothermal property, 5.06[3][b]
Gift as disposition of installment
  obligation, 5.06[2]
Gift transfers, 5.05[11][b][iii]
Goods-in-process, market value of,
  6.09[3][b]
Goods offered for sale, market value of,
  6.09[3][b][ii]
Gross income, 3.03, 4.03[1][a], 12.05[3],
  12.05[4][b][i], 12.05[4][b]iv]
  definition, 3.06[2], 6.02[1]
  determination, 6.02[1]
  material item, 9.03[2][b]
Gross profit on installment sale
  calculation, 5.04[3][a], 5.04[3][b],
    5.04[3][c]
  definition, 5.05[8]
Gross profit ratio, 5.05[8], 5.05[9]
Gross receipts test under cash method,
  3.06[1][a]
Growth, transfer of, 9.08[3]
Guarantee. *See* Warranty reserve

H

Health services, use of cash method for, 3.06[1][b][i]

HIFO (highest-in, first-out) procedure, 7.03[3][a]

History of
  accrual method, 4.02
  annual accounting concept, 12.02
  Arrowsmith doctrine, 12.04
  cash method, 3.02
  claim-of-right doctrine, 12.03[1]
  installment method, 5.04[1], 5.05[1]
  inventory requirements, 6.03
  LIFO, 7.02[2]
  material item, 9.03
  tax benefit rule, 12.05

Horizontal slice on transfer of LIFO inventory, 7.08[1][a]

Hospitals
  change from cash method, 8.04[6][a]
  use of cash method, 3.06[1][d]

Hybrid method. *See* Method of accounting, combination

I

Idle equipment and facilities. *See* Temporarily idle equipment and facilities

Illegal income, 12.03[3][a][ii]

Imputed principal amount, 11.02[5][a]

Incidental supplies, 6.05[2][c][ii]
  IRS definition, 6.05[2][c][ii]

Income, 1.02[2]
  additional, 12.02[2][f][ii]
  annualization, 10.05[5]
  application of annual accounting concept, 12.02[2][d], 12.02[2][e], 12.02[2][f][i], 12.02[2][f][ii]
  character of, 11.01[1][a]
  claim-of-right doctrine, effect of, 12.03
  clear reflection of, 1.02[2], 2.01[4], 2.02[2], 3.02, 3.08, 6.04[1][a][ii], 6.05[2][c][iii]
  judicial application, 2.02[2][j]

  standards, 2.02[2][j]
  compensation, 3.03[3][c]
  constructive receipt, 1.03[2], 3.03[1][b], 3.03[2], 3.03[3], 12.05[4][b][i]
  deferred, 2.01[1], 10.04[4][c][ii]
  determination of amount, 4.03[1][b]
  dividends, 3.03[3][b]
  erroneously reported early, 12.02[2][d]
  interest, 3.03[3][a]
  items, 2.02[1], 3.02[1][a], 3.03[1][a], 3.03[3]
    of doubtful collectibility, 1.03[2], 4.03[2]
  net, definition, 3.02
  not reported in proper year, 12.02[2][e]
  realized, 3.03[1][c]
  receipt, 12.03[2][a]
  recognition, 3.03[1][b], 3.03[1][c]
    deferred, 9.01[3]
  rent, 3.03[3][d]
  reporting, 1.02[3], 3.03, 4.03
  royalties, 3.03[3][d]
  taxable, modified, definition, 10.05[5][a]
  tax benefit rule, 12.05
  verifiability, 2.02[1][a]

Income forecast method, 5.05[12][d][i]

Indefinite maturity, effect on OID, 11.02[4][a][ii]

Index LIFO method, 7.04[3][b][ii], 7.04[3][b][iii]

Indirect production costs, 6.06[2][c]

Individual, taxable year, 6.10[1], 10.02[3][b], 10.04[4][a], 10.05[4][a]

Inflation, effect on tax accounting, 1.01[1], 1.01[2]

Installment costs, 6.06[1][c]

Installment method, 1.01[3], 3.03[1][d][ii], 3.03[1][d][iv], 3.03[1][d][v], 4.01[5]
  See also Installment sale
  availability, 5.04[2][b]
    dealers, personal property, 5.04, 5.05, 5.07[1]
    dealers, real property, 5.05, 5.07[1]
    nondealers, 5.05, 5.07[1]

Installment method *(cont'd)*
benefits, 5.02
burdens, 5.02
computations by dealers, 5.04[3], 5.07
  by type of goods, 5.04[3][c]
  by type of sale, 5.04[3][b]
  by year, 5.04[3][a]
conditions for use, 5.03, 5.05[1][c],
  5.07
contingent price sales, 5.05[12]
contract price, 5.05[8][c]
dealers, 5.04
defaults, repossessions, 5.05[14]
defaults, repossessions—dealers,
  5.04[5]
definition, 5.01, 5.05[3]
deposit, 5.05[7][a]
election, 5.04[7], 5.05[1][a]
election out, 3.03[1][d][iv], 5.05[15]
history, 5.04[1], 5.05[1]
  $1,000 test, 5.05[1][a]
  30 percent test, 5.05[1][a]
  two payment rule, 5.05[1][a]
income computation, 5.05[8]
  recapture under Sections 1245,
    1250, 5.05[a]
ineligible sales, 5.05[2]
issues, 5.04[2]
limitations on use, 5.05[1][d],
  8.04[6][b]
mandatory reporting, 5.01, 5.05,
  5.05[2]
  1987 Act, 5.07
marketable securities, 5.05[2],
multiple asset sale, 5.05[8][d]
$1,000 test, 5.05[1][a]
option payment, 5.05[7][a]
payment
  assumption of seller's debt,
    5.05[7][c]
  contingent payment rules, 5.05[12]
  defined, 5.05[4], 5.05[5]
  issues, 5.05[7]
  letter of credit, 5.05[7][e]
  payment on demand, 5.05[7][f]
  purchaser note, 5.05[7][f]
  readily tradable obligation,
    5.05[7][f]
  right to prepay, 5.05[7][b]
  third-party guarantee, 5.05[7][e]
  third-party indebtedness, 5.05[7][d]

perceived inadequacy, 5.05[1][b]
personal property sales, 5.04[2][b]
  continuous versus periodic sales,
    5.04[2][c][iii]
  personal property defined,
    5.04[2][b]
  portion of total sales, 5.04[2][c][ii]
  regularly made, 5.04[2][c]
prior conditions, 5.05[1][a]
proportionate disallowance rule,
  5.05[6]
  repeal, 5.07[2]
publicly treated property, 5.05[2]
qualifying indebtedness, 5.05[7][c]
recapture under Sections 1245, 1250,
  5.05[a]
related-party sales, 5.05[11]
  controlled entity, to, 5.05[11][c]
  corporate liquidations, 5.05[11][a]
  defined, 5.05[11][b]
  depreciable property, 5.05[11][b][ii]
  exceptions, 5.05[11][b][iii]
  marketable securities, 5.05[b][i]
  nondepreciable property,
    5.05[11][b][ii]
  statute of limitations, 5.05[11][b][iv]
  two-year rule, 5.05[11][b][ii]
repeal, 5.07
requirements for use, 5.03, 5.05[2],
  5.07[1]
risk of loss, 5.02[6]
sale of multiple assets, 5.05[8][d]
selling expenses, 5.05[8][b]
selling price, 5.05[8][a]
statutory format, 5.05[1][b]
Installment obligation, 11.02[4][a][iii],
  11.02[4][c]
cancellation, 5.06[2]
disposition, 5.04[4], 5.04[6], 5.06
  dealer obligation, 5.04[4], 5.06
  death, 5.06[1]
  to life insurance companies,
    5.06[3][c]
  in liquidation, 5.06[3][b]
  to member of affiliated group,
    5.04[6]
  transfer to controlled entity,
    5.06[3][a]
made unenforceable, 5.06[2]
modification, 5.06[4]

[References are to paragraphs (¶)]

received in corporate liquidation,
 5.05[11][a]
self-amortizing, 11.02[4][a][iii]
substitution of collateral, 5.06[4]
transfer to
  controlled entity, 5.06[3][a]
  life insurance company, 5.06[3][c]
use as collateral, 5.06[5]
wraparound mortgage, 5.05[10]
  benefits, 5.05[a], 5.05[d]
  pre–1980 Act law, 5.05[10][b]
Installment plans
revolving credit, 5.04[2][d][ii], 5.07[1]
traditional, 5.04[2][d][i]
  dollar amount of payments,
   5.04[2][d][i]
  number of payments, 5.04[2][d][i]
  two-year rule, 5.04[2][d][i]
Installment receivables, sale of, 5.04[1]
Installment reporting, automatic,
 3.03[1][d][iv]
Installment sale, 5.04[2][d], 5.05[2],
 5.05[5]
See also Installment method
dealers, 5.05
definition, 5.05[2]
contingent payment obligation,
 5.05[15][b]
contingent price rules, 5.05[12]
  alternatives to, 5.05[12][d]
  contemplating proposed legislation,
   5.02[4]
  fixed payment period, 5.05[12][b]
  income forecast method,
   5.05[12][d][i]
  maximum price stated, 5.05[12][a]
  no maximum price, no fixed period,
   5.05[12][b]
  private annuities, 5.05[12][e]
  substantial and inappropriate
   deferral, 5.05[12][d][ii]
continuous, 5.04[2][c][iii]
fixed amount obligation, 5.05[15][a]
multiple assets, 5.05[8][d]
periodic, 5.04[2][c][iii]
portion of total sales, 5.04[2][c][ii]
prepayment right, 5.05[7][b]
property other than inventory, 5.05
"regularly" defined, 5.04[2][c][i]
"regularly" requirement, 5.04[2][c]

unenforceable, 5.06[2]
Installment Sales Revision Act of 1980
 (1980 Act), 3.03[1][d][iv], 5.04[1],
 5.04[2][d][i], 5.05[1][a], 5.05[1][b],
 5.05[1][c], 5.05[1][d], 5.05[7][c],
 5.05[8][b], 5.05[10][b], 5.05[10][c],
 5.05[11], 5.05[12], 5.06[1], 5.06[2],
 5.06[3][c]
potential benefit from new
  regulations, 5.05[10][d]
regulations under, 5.05[10][c],
 5.05[10][d]
Insurance
costs, 6.06[2][c][i], 6.06[2][c][ii]
premiums, 3.04[5][b], 4.04[3][b][iii]
Intangible property, 3.03[1][c]
Integration of acquired business, 9.08[2]
Intent-to-call, effect on OID, 11.02[2][a]
Interest, 1.01[1], 1.01[2], 1.01[3],
 3.03[3][a], 3.04[5][a], 3.05[1][b]
capitalization rules, 6.06[2][c][ii]
  advance customer payments,
   6.06[2][c][ii]
  production expenditure,
   6.06[2][c][ii]
  property to which applicable,
   6.06[2][c][ii]
certificate of deposit, 3.03[3][a]
commission as, 3.03[3][a]
deemed, 11.01[2][a][ii]
definition, 11.01
discount, 3.03[3][a]
imputed, 11.02[5][a], 11.04[1]
  general rules, 11.02[5][a][i]
loan origination fee as, 3.03[3][a]
points as, 3.03[3][a]
qualified periodic payment,
 11.02[4][a][i]
unconditionally payable, 11.02[4][a][i]
unstated, 11.04[2][b], 11.04[2][c]
  general rules, 11.04[2][b][i]
  recognition periods, 11.04[2][c]
  special rules on related party land
   sale, 11.04[2][b][ii]
Interest-free loan, 8.04[3]
Interest holiday, 11.02[4][c]
Interest on certain deferred payments,
 11.04
See also Section 483

[References are to paragraphs (¶)]

Internal management reports, effect on
    LIFO, 7.03[2][b][iii]
Internal Revenue Service
    See also Commissioner of Internal
        Revenue
    acceptance of change, 2.04[3][a],
        2.04[3][b], 2.04[3][d]
    as acceptance of change of accounting
        method, 2.04[3][a], 2.04[3][b]
    as affecting clear reflection of income
        requirement, 3.08[3], 3.08[5]
    agent's actions, 2.04[3][c], 2.04[3][d],
        3.08[3], 3.08[5]
    attitude toward accrual methods,
        4.01[3]
    attitude toward cash method, 3.02[3]
    audit practices regarding clear
        reflection of income requirement,
        2.02[2][d]
    contact by, effect on change in
        accounting method, 8.06[2][b][ii]
    deferral of prepaid income, position
        on, 4.03[3][e][ii], 11.01[2][a][iv]
    difficulty with cash method, 3.08[7]
    discretion, 1.02[1], 1.02[5], 2.02[2],
        2.03[2], 2.04, 4.03[3][b],
        6.04[1][a][ii], 7.03, 7.05, 8.01,
        8.03, 8.04[3], 8.06[2][b][i],
        8.06[3][d], 8.07, 9.01
    prior approval requirement for change
        in method of accounting
        LIFO, 7.04[5][a][ii], 7.04[5][a][iii],
            7.04[5][b]
        methods of accounting generally,
            8.03, 9.01[2], 9.01[3]
    responsibility, 4.02[4]
Inventoriable costs, 6.04[1][b],
    6.05[2][a], 6.05[2][c], 6.06, 6.07
    See also Inventory
    allocation methods, 6.06, 6.07, 6.08
    assembly costs, 6.06[1][c][ii],
        6.06[2][c][ii]
    discounts, 6.06[1][a]
        cash, 6.06[1][a][ii]
        trade, 6.06[1][a][i]
    excessive, 6.06[1][b]
    general method, 6.06[1][c][i]
    handling costs, 6.06[1][c][ii],
        6.06[2][c][ii]
    indirect costs, 6.06[2][c][i],
        6.06[2][c][ii]

manufacturers, 6.06[2]
    customer advance payments,
        6.06[2][c][ii]
    direct labor costs, 6.06[2][b]
    direct material costs, 6.06[2][a]
    full absorption costing, 6.06[2][c][i]
    idle capacity, 6.06[2][c][ii]
    indirect inventoriable costs not
        required, 6.06[2][c][i],
        6.06[2][c][ii]
    indirect inventoriable costs
        required, 6.06[2][c][i],
        6.06[2][c][ii]
    indirect production costs, 6.06[2][c]
    indirect capitalization rules,
        6.06[2][c][ii]
    manufacturing burden rate method,
        6.07[1]
    practical capacity, 6.07[3]
    simplified mixed service cost
        method, 6.07[5]
    simplified production cost method,
        6.07[4]
    standard cost method, 6.07[2]
    uniform capitalization rules,
        6.02[2][c][ii]
1986 Act impact, 6.06[1][c]
processing costs, 6.06[1][c][ii],
    6.06[2][c][ii]
repackaging costs, 6.06[1][c][ii],
    6.06[2][c][ii]
retailers, 6.06[1], 7.04[3][a][i],
    7.04[5][a][i]
simplified resale method, 6.06[1][c][ii]
wholesalers, retailers,
    nonmanufacturers, 6.06[1]
    administrative expenses,
        6.06[1][c][ii]
    allocation procedures, 6.06[1][c][ii]
    general expenses, 6.06[1][c][ii]
    general method, 6.06[1][c][i]
    handling, processing, assembly,
        repackaging, 6.06[1][c][ii]
    off-site storage costs, 6.06[1][c][ii]
    on-site storage costs, 6.06[1][c][ii]
    purchasing costs, 6.06[1][c][ii]
    simplified resale method,
        6.06[1][c][ii]

[References are to paragraphs (¶)]

Inventory, 1.02[4], 3.06[2]
See also Inventoriable costs;
    Inventory accounting; LIFO;
    Merchandise inventory; Supply
    inventory
ability to trace costs, 6.05[3]
accrual method, 6.02[3]
arbitrary methods, 9.04[2]
arbitrary valuations, 9.04[2]
average cost methods, 6.08[3]
   IRS position, 6.08[3][a]
   judicial position, 6.08[3][b]
bargain price acquisition, 7.08[2]
base stock, 7.02[2]
basic requirements, 6.04
   regulatory, 6.04[2]
   statutory, 6.04[1]
best accounting practice, 6.04[1][a][i]
bulk sale, 5.05[11][a]
by-products, 6.10[3]
capitalization rules, 8.04[6][c]
change in use, to or from, 6.05[1][e]
consequences of having, 6.01[2]
cost-flow assumptions, 6.08[1]
costing, 1.03[2], 1.03[3], 2.02[1][e],
   2.02[2][e], 2.04[3][d], 6.01[2],
   6.06, 8.04[6][c]
   special rules, 6.10
deferred payment dispositions, 5.05[2]
definition, 6.05[1][a]
   Corn Products doctrine, 6.05[1][a]
dual use property, 6.05[1][e]
farmers and livestock raisers, 6.10[2]
FIFO, 6.08[2]
history, 6.03
installment costs, 6.06[1][c]
interest capitalization rules, 6.06[2][c]
issues, primary, 6.01[1]
LIFO, 6.08[2]
manufacturers, 6.06[2]
merchandise, 6.05
   acquired for sale, 6.05[1][c]
   definition, 6.05[1][a]
   ordinary course of business,
     6.05[1][f]
   ownership, 6.05[1][b]
mixed goods and services, 6.05[1][d]
most clearly reflecting income,
   6.04[1][a][ii]
moving average, 6.08[3]
need for, 6.02

nonmanufacturers, 6.06[1]
nontraditional methods, 6.11
normal stock, 7.02[2], 7.03[3][a]
physical, 6.08[2][a]
primary issues, 6.01[1]
promotional goods, 6.05[1][f]
proscribed methods, 6.08[2][b]
purchase and sale of, 2.02[2][g]
real property, 6.05[3][a]
reason for, 6.02
record keeping, 6.08[2][a]
reduction, 8.04[5][b]
regulatory and statutory provisions,
   6.04[1], 6.04[2]
retailers, 6.06[1]
retail method, 6.10[4]
securities dealers, 6.10[1]
shrinkage, 6.08[2][a]
special order property, 6.05[3][b]
specific identification, 6.08[1]
supplies, 6.05, 6.05[2]
   business expense, 6.05[2][a]
   clear reflection of income,
     6.05[2][c][ii]
   incidental, 6.05[2][c][ii]
   inventoriable cost, 6.05[2][a]
   inventories not required, 6.05[7][c]
   inventories required, 6.05[2][b]
uniform capitalization rules,
   6.06[2][c][ii]
unrelated groups, 7.03[1][b]
variances, 6.07[1]
wholesalers, 6.06[1]
work-in-process, 6.09[3][b][ii]
write-down to market, 2.02[2][c], 6.09

Inventory accounting
arbitrary valuation methods, 9.04[2]
base stock method, 7.02[2]
normal stock method, 7.02[2]
reserve method, 7.02[2]

Inventory price index, 7.04[5][a][i]

Inventory profit, 7.02[1], 7.02[2]

Investment of deferred tax liability,
   5.02[5]

Investment units, 11.02[4][b][iv]

IRS. *See* Internal Revenue Service

Issue price for OID, 11.02[5]
   definition, 11.02[4][b]

J

Jeopardy assessment, effect on taxable
  years, 10.02[3][c]
Jobber, 7.04[5][a][i]
Joint tenancy, effect on disposition of
  installment obligation, 5.06[1]

L

Labor costs, direct, 6.06[2][b]
Last-in, first-out (LIFO), 2.02[1][e],
  3.06[2], 6.03, 6.05[3][a], 6.05[3][b],
  6.08[2], 6.08[3]
  acquisition and transfer, 7.08
  adoption, 7.03[1]
  adoption, by affiliated group,
    7.03[1][a]
  application, 7.03[1][a]
    selective use, 7.03[1][b]
    subsidiary elections, 7.03[1][c]
  balance sheet non-LIFO reporting,
    7.03[2][b][ii]
  bargain purchase, 7.04[3][a][i], 7.08[2]
  base costs, 7.04[3][b]
    effect of technological advance,
      7.04[3][b][iv]
    reconstructed, 7.04[3][b][iv]
    revised, 7.04[3][d]
  base date, 7.04[3][b]
  benefits, 7.02[1], 7.04[2][c], 7.04[3]
  books and records, 7.03[4]
    deficiencies and inadequacies, 7.05
  change from, 7.06, 8.06[2][d],
    8.06[3][b][iv]
  change in LIFO method, 7.06,
    7.06[1], 7.06[2], 8.06[3][b][v]
  component costing, 7.04[3][e]
  concept, 7.02
  conformity requirement, 7.03[2],
    7.05[1][a]
    balance sheet, 7.03[2][b][ii]
    controlled groups, 7.03[2][b][viii]
    different costing and computational
      procedures, 7.03[2][b][vi]
    explanatory or supplementary
      information, 7.03[2][b][i]
    forecasts and projections,
      7.03[2][b][ix]
  foreign parents or subsidiaries,
    7.03[2][b][viii]
  internal management reports,
    7.03[2][b][iii]
  market value, 7.03[2][b][v]
  reconciliations, 7.03[2][b][vii]
  retroactive violation, 7.03[2][b][vi]
  scope, 7.03[2][b]
  short-year reports, 7.03[3][b][iv]
  supplementary or explanatory
    information, 7.03[2][b][i]
  cost requirement, 7.03[3]
    impact on LIFO adoption timing,
      7.03[3][b]
    rationale, 7.03[3][a]
    restoration of write-down,
      7.03[3][c], 7.03[3][d]
  current cost of goods not purchased
    or produced, 7.04[3][a][i]
  development, 7.02[2]
  deficiencies and inadequacies, 7.05
  dollar-value LIFO, 7.04[3]
    base costs, 7.04[3][b]
    double-extension method,
      7.04[3][b][i]
    increments, 7.04[3][c]
    index method, 7.04[3][b][ii]
    link-chain method, 7.04[3][b][iii]
    natural business-unit pool,
      7.04[3][a][i]
    new base year, 7.04[3][d]
    pooling, 7.04[3][a]
    revised base year, 7.04[3][d]
    simplified dollar-value method,
      7.04[5][b]
    single small business pool,
      7.04[3][a][iii]
  election, 7.03[1][a], 7.03[1][b]
  Form 970, 7.03[1][a], 7.03[1][d],
    7.04[5][a][ii], 7.04[5][a][iii],
    7.05[1][b], 7.08[3][a]
  history, 7.02[2], 7.03[2][a]
  increment valuation, 7.04[2][c],
    7.04[3][c]
  inventory costing, 2.02[2][e], 6.10[4],
    8.04[5][c], 8.04[5][d]
  items, 7.04[2][b], 7.04[3][a]
  judicial attitude, 7.05[1]
    general, 7.05[1][a]
    regarding proposed terminations,
      7.05[1][b]

[References are to paragraphs (¶)]

liquidations of LIFO, 7.07
  problem arising from, 7.07[1]
  S corporation status, election, 7.09
  statutory relief provisions, 7.07[3]
  taxpayer alternatives, 7.07[2]
objective, 7.02[1]
pool index, 7.04[5][a][i]
pooling, 7.04[2][a], 7.04[3]
product costing, 7.04[3][e]
raw material and raw material
    content, 7.03[1][b]
readoption of LIFO, 7.06[3]
recapture, 7.07, 7.09, 12.05[4][b][v]
reconciling different methodologies,
    7.03[2][b][vii]
reconstruction techniques,
    7.04[3][b][iv]
requirements for adoption and use,
    7.03
  application, 7.03[2][b]
  books and records, 7.03[4]
  conformity, 7.03[2]
  cost, 7.03[3]
  deliberate violation, 7.05
  rationale, 7.03[2][a]
S corporation status, election of, 7.09
Section 481 adjustment, 7.03[1][c]
selective use, 7.03[1][b]
sequential layering, 7.03[2][b][iv],
    7.04[1]
simplified LIFO methods, 7.04[5]
  adoption, 7.04[5][a][ii], 7.04[5][b]
  operation, 7.04[5][a][i], 7.04[5][b]
  price index method, 7.04[5][a]
  selection of price indexes,
      7.04[5][a][i]
  simplified dollar-value, 7.04[5][b]
specific goods LIFO, 7.04[2]
  pooling, 7.04[2][a]
  quantity measures, 7.04[2][b]
  valuing increments, 7.04[2][c]
staggered elections, 7.03[1][b]
statute of limitations, 7.03[5]
subsidiary elections, 7.03[1][c]
systems, 7.04
  essentials, 7.04[1]
tax accounting authority, 7.02
technological advance, 7.04[3][b][iv],
    7.04[3][e]
termination of, 7.03[1][d], 7.05,
    8.04[5][d], 8.06[2][b][i]

Commissioner's discretion,
    7.03[1][d]
  IRS attitude, 7.05[2]
  judicial attitude, 7.05[1]
  proposed, 8.06[2][d]
  S corporation status, election of,
      7.09

Legislative reenactment doctrine,
    2.02[2][f]

Level of uncertainty, of collection, effect
    on accrual, 4.03[2][a]

Liability, deduction under accrual
    method
  adjustment, 4.04[2][b]
  amount certainty, 4.04[2][a]
  amount determination, 4.04[2]
  conditional, 4.04[1][a][iii]
  contested, 4.04[1][c]
  fixed, 4.04[1]
  identification, 4.04[1][a]
  services and property, for,
      4.04[3][b][i], 4.04[3][b][ii]

LIFO. *See* Last-in, first-out

LIFO inventory, 6.05[1][b], 6.05[1][f][ii],
    7.02[1], 7.04[2], 7.07, 7.08[3]
  See also Last-in, first-out
  acquisition and transfer, 7.08
    acquired business to be integrated,
        7.08[3][c]
    acquired business to be separate,
        7.08[3][b]
    impact on transferee, 7.08[1][b]
    impact on transferor, 7.08[1][a]
    Section 351 transactions, 7.08[1]
    Section 381 transactions, 7.08[3]
  bargain price, acquisition at, 7.08[2]
  problem, 7.07[1]
  statutory relief, 7.07[3]
  taxpayer response, 7.07[2]

LIFO recapture, 7.07, 7.09,
    12.05[4][b][v]

LIFO reserve, 7.03[2], 7.04[2], 7.04[3],
    12.05[4][b][vi]

Like-kind exchange under installment
    method, 3.02[1][a], 5.05[5],
    5.05[11][b][iii], 5.05[13]

Link-chain LIFO method, 7.04[3][b][iii]

[References are to paragraphs (¶)]

Liquidation
Arrowsmith doctrine, applicable to, 12.04
effect on cash method use, 3.06[3]
installment reporting, 5.05[11], 5.06[3][b]
tax benefit rule, applicable to, 12.05[4][a][ix], 12.05[4][b][v]

Livestock raisers inventory costing, 6.10[2]

Livestock, sales due to draught, 3.03[3][e]

Lowering effective tax rate, effect on installment reporting, 5.02[3]

Lower of cost or market, 6.05[3][a], 6.09[1]

Lower of LIFO cost or market, 7.03[2][b][v], 7.03[3][a]

M

Majority interest rule, affecting partnership taxable year, 10.04[c][i]

Manipulation of method, 2.02[2][d], 3.02[2], 3.08[5], 4.01[5]

Manufactured goods, market value, 6.09[3][b]

Manufacturer, 7.04[5][a][i]
See also Inventoriable costs; Inventory; Last-in, first-out
by-product inventory costing, 6.10[3]
definition, 6.06[2]

Manufacturing burden rate, 6.07[1]

Manufacturing overhead, 6.06[2][c]

Marginal costing, 6.06[2][c]

Marketable security
definition, 5.05[11][b][i]
property other than, 5.05[11][b][ii]
sale of, 3.03[3][e], 5.05[1][d]
"Market," definition, 6.09[3]

Market discount bond, 11.02, 11.05[1], 11.05[2], 11.06[2]

Market discount on bonds, 11.02[3][a][iii], 11.05
definition, 11.05[1]
treatment of income, 11.05[2]

Marketing expenses, 6.06[2][c][ii], 6.07[5]

Market write-down. *See* Write-down, market

Matching income and expense, 2.02[2][f], 4.04, 4.04[1][b], 4.04[3][f][iii], 6.02[3]

Material costs, direct, definition, 6.06[2][a]

Material item, 9.03
net or gross amount, 9.03[2][b]

Materiality
accrual method recurring item exception, 4.04[3][f][iii]

Materiality of item
absolute, 9.03[2][a]
definition, 9.02[1], 9.03
relative, 9.03[2][b]
comparisons, 9.03[2][b][ii]

McAnly, Herbert T., 7.04[3]

Memorandum accounts, 2.02[1][b]

Merchandise inventory, 3.06[2], 6.04[1][b], 6.04[2], 6.05, 6.06
See also Inventory, merchandise
accrual method required, 6.05
definition, 6.04, 6.05[1][a]
ownership, 6.05[1][b]
regulatory provisions, 6.04[2]
rules, 6.04[1][a], 7.03[1][b]
special order, 6.05[3][b]
unique items, 6.05[3]

Merrill rule, as affecting claim of right doctrine, 12.03[3][a][iv]

Method of accounting, 1.02[1]
See also Change in method of accounting
adoption, 9.04[1][a], 9.06[4]
initial year, 9.04[1]
arbitrary procedures, 2.01[3], 9.04[2]
binding election rule, 2.03[3]
book conformity, 2.02[1]
Category A, 8.04[4][b][iii], 8.06[2][b], 8.06[2][c], 8.06[2][d], 8.06[4], 8.07[2]
Category B, 8.04[4][b][iv], 8.06[2][c], 8.06[3][b], 8.06[4], 8.07[2]
changes that are not changes in method, 9.01[2], 9.02[2]

[References are to paragraphs (¶)]

clear reflection of income
    requirement, 2.02[2]
choice of method, 2.03
combination (hybrid), 2.02[1][b],
    2.03[1], 2.03[1][b], 3.06[2]
consistency in, 2.01[2], 2.02[1][b],
    2.02[1][d], 2.02[2][e], 3.08[6],
    9.02[1], 9.04
correct application, 2.02[2][a]
cost recovery, 3.03[1][d][ii], 5.05[12],
    5.05[15], 5.05[15][b], 9.07
definition, 2.01
    certainty and predictability, 2.01[3]
    consistency, 2.01[2]
    importance of defining method,
        9.06[3]
discretion in choice of, 2.03, 3.08[6]
discretion of Commissioner, 2.04
    abuse of discretion, 2.04[2]
    acceptance of returns, 2.04[3][a],
        2.04[3][b]
    actions of agent, 2.04[3][c],
        2.04[3][d]
    impact of use, 2.04[3]
    proper use of discretion, 2.02[1]
discretion of taxpayer, 2.03
    incorrect choice, 2.03[2]
    multiple methods chosen, 2.03[1]
erroneous, 8.06[2][b][ii]
GAAP, use of, 2.02[2][c]
hybrid, 2.02[1][b], 2.03[1], 2.03[1][b],
    3.06[2]
identification of, 9.06[3]
income forecast method, 5.05[12][d][i]
inconsistent methods of accounting,
    9.04
incorrect initial choice, 2.03[2]
individual items, 2.01[4]
Internal Revenue Code requirements,
    2.01[4], 2.02, 2.03[1][a]
limitations on, 2.02[2][b]
new item, 9.06[4]
nonbook, 2.02[1]
overall, 2.01[4]
penalties imposed, 8.09
principal, 7.08[3][c], 9.08[2]
Mineral properties, 5.05[12][d][i]
Mining
    by-product inventory costing, 6.10[3]
    property, 5.06[3][b]

Mismatching income and expense,
    2.02[2][f], 3.08, 4.04, 4.04[1][b],
    6.02[3], 10.03[2]
Mixed service costs, 6.06[1][c][ii],
    6.07[5]
Moving average, 6.08[3], 7.04[3][c]
Multiple assets installment sale,
    5.05[8][d]
Multiple methods of accounting,
    2.02[1][a]
Multiple pool LIFO method,
    7.04[3][a][ii], 7.07[1]

N

National Office. *See* Internal Revenue
    Service
Natural business unit, 7.04[3][a][i]
Natural business-unit pool, 7.04[5][a][i]
Natural business year, 10.03[1],
    10.04[4][c][ii], 10.05[1], 10.05[2][b],
    10.05[4][c][ii]
    IRS definition, 10.03[1]
Natural persons
    loan between, 11.02[3][a][ii]
    obligation issued by, 11.02[2][c]
Nature of transaction affecting clear
    reflection of income, 2.02[2][d]
Net direct interest expense, short term
    obligations, 11.06[2]
Net operating loss (NOL), 10.05[2][e],
    10.05[4][b][i], 10.05[4][b][ii],
    12.02[3]
    S corporation, 12.05[2]
    tax benefit rule, 12.05[2]
New corporation tax year,
    10.04[4][b][ii], 10.04[4][b][iii]
New or revised base year, 7.04[3][d]
New taxpayer tax year, 10.04[4][a],
    10.04[5], 10.05[4][d][ii]
    effect on change in taxable year,
        10.05[4][b]
    effect on Section 481 spread back,
        8.04[2][c]
    tax benefit rule, as affecting,
        12.05[4][b][iii]

[References are to paragraphs (¶)]

9 percent discount rate for OID, 11.02[5][a][iii]

1909 Act. *See* Excise Tax Act of 1909

1913 Act, 3.02
See also Revenue Act of 1913

1918 Act. *See* Revenue Act of 1918

1926 Act. *See* Revenue Act of 1926

1980 Act. *See* Installment Sales Revision Act of 1980

1984 Act. *See* Tax Reform Act of 1984

1986 Act. *See* Tax Reform Act of 1986

1987 Act. *See* Revenue Act of 1987

90-day exception for prepaid expenses of tax shelters, 3.05[2][b]

Nominal price inventory method, 6.08[2][b]

Nominal quotation affecting market value, 6.09[3][b][i]

Nonaccrual-experience method, 4.03[2][d], 8.04[6][d]
periodic system, 4.03[2][d]

Noninventoriable costs, 6.06[2][c][ii]
See also Inventoriable costs

Nonmanageable events affecting LIFO liquidation, 7.07[3]

Nonmanufacturers
inventoriable costs, 6.06[1]
LIFO natural business unit pooling, 7.04[3][a][i]

Nonresident alien taxable year, 10.04[4][a]

No open market, affecting market value, 6.09[3][b][i]

Normal stock concept, 7.02[2]

Notes, acceptance of returns constituting, 2.04[3][b]

Notes as payment under cash method, 3.04[4][b]

O

Obligations issued after July 1, 1982, 11.02[3][a]

Obligations issued before July 2, 1982.
See Corporate obligations issued before July 2, 1982

Offering price, affecting market value, 6.09[3]

Officers' salaries, 6.06[2][c][i]

Offsets, 9.03[2][b]

Off-site storage facility, definition, 6.06[1][c][ii]

OID. *See* Original issue discount

Oil property, 5.06[3][b]
120-day rule on change in accounting method, 8.06[2][b][iii]

One-year rule for cash basis deductions, 3.05[1][b]

Open transaction method, 3.03[1][d][ii], 9.07

Operating costs, 6.07[5]

Opportunities for taxpayers
change in accounting methods, 9.01
change in taxable year, 10.04[4][b][iii]

Option, effect on OID, 11.02[3][[a][i], 11.02[4][a][iv]

Ordering rules for taxable year, 10.04[4][c][i]

Ordinary course of business, 6.05[1][f]

Original issue discount (OID), 1.02[7], 1.03[3], 8.06[2][b][i], 11.02, 11.03[2], 11.04[1], 11.09
amount of, 11.02[4]
applicable to prepayments, 11.02[1]
below-market loans, 11.11
cash settlement option, 11.02[4][b][iv]
contingent payments, 11.03
definition, 11.03[1]
market-based contingent payments, 11.03[3]
other contingent debt instruments, 11.03[4]
small issues, 11.03[3]
convertible debt, 11.02[4][b][iv]
debt instruments, 11.02[1]
de minimis rule, 11.02[4][c]
interest holiday, 11.02[4][c]
teaser rate, 11.02[4][c]
early provisions, 11.01[2][a][iii]
exceptions, 11.02[2][c], 11.02[3][a][ii], 11.02[5][b]
intent to call before maturity, 11.02[2][a]
interest holiday, 11.02[4][c]

[References are to paragraphs (¶)]

investment units, 11.02[4][b][iv]
issue price, 11.02[4][b]
  applicable federal rates,
    11.02[5][a][i]
  convertible debt, 11.02[4][b][iv]
  debt due six months or less,
    11.02[5][b][vi]
  debt for personal use property,
    11.02[5][b][vii]
  debt instruments for property with
    public trading, 11.02[4][b][iii]
  de minimis rule, 11.02[4][c]
  exceptions, 11.02[5][b]
  imputation of interest, 11.02[5][a]
  investment units, 11.02[4][b][iv]
  nonpublicly offered instruments for
    cash, 11.02[4][b][ii]
  non–publicly offered instruments
    for property, 11.02[5]
  other cases, 11.02[4][b][iv]
  potentially abusive situations,
    11.02[5][a][ii]
  publicly offered instruments for
    cash, 11.02[4][b][i]
  sale-leaseback transactions,
    11.02[5][a][iv]
  sale of farm, 11.02[5][b][i]
  sale of patent, 11.02[5][b][iv]
  sale of principal residence,
    11.02[5][b][ii]
  sale of property at $250,000,
    11.02[5][b][iii]
  special 9 percent rate,
    11.02[5][a][iii]
loans with indefinite maturities,
  11.02[4][a][ii]
obligations issued after July 1, 1982,
  11.02[3][a]
obligations issued before July 2, 1982,
  11.02[3][b]
obligations not in registered form,
  11.08
payment in foreign currency, 11.03[1]
puts, calls, options, 11.02[3][a][i],
  11.02[4][a][iv]
retirements, sales, exchanges,
  11.02[2][a]
stated redemption price at maturity,
  11.02[4][a]
  installment obligations,
    11.02[4][a][iii]

loans with indefinite maturities,
  11.02[4][a][ii]
puts, calls, options, 11.03[3][a][i],
  11.02[4][a][iv]
qualified periodic interest payment,
  11.02[4][a][i]
tax-exempt obligations, 11.09
teaser rate, 11.02[4][c]
Osterloh standard of clear reflection,
  2.02[2][j][i]

P

Package design costs, 6.06[2][c][i]
Paragraph (b)(1) installment plan,
  5.04[2][d][i]
Paragraph (b)(2) installment plan,
  5.04[2][d][i]
Partnership, 1.02[6]
  accounting, 10.04[4][c][iv]
  accrual method, 4.04[3][f][iii]
  cash method, 3.02, 3.02[3],
    3.05[2][b][i], 3.06[1], 3.08[5]
  change in method, 8.04[2][d],
    8.04[5][a]
  installment method, 5.05[11][c]
  taxable year, 10.02[3][a][iii],
    10.02[3][b], 10.03[1], 10.04[1],
    10.04[4][c], 10.04[5], 10.05[2][b],
    10.05[2][g][i], 10.05[4][c],
    10.05[5][b]
  transfers to, 5.05[11][b][iii]
Parts
  arbitrary method of accounting,
    9.04[2]
Patent infringement, 12.05[4][b][iii]
Patent sale, 11.02[5][b][iv]
Payee
  cash method deduction affected by,
    3.04[3][b]
  identification for accrual deduction,
    4.04[1][a][i]
Paying agent, 3.04[3][a]
Payment
  definition, 5.05[4]
    exclusions from, 5.05[5]
  issues, 5.05[7]
  prior to year of sale, 5.05[7][a]

[References are to paragraphs (¶)]

Payment *(cont'd)*
under protest, 3.04[3][b]

Penalty for late payment, 4.03[2][d]

Penalty for method of accounting, 8.09

Pension contributions, 6.06[2][c][i],
6.06[2][c][ii]

Performance, likelihood of, 4.04[1][a][ii]

Performing arts services, 3.06[1][b][i]

Periodic system, 4.03[2][d]

Personal holding company taxable year,
10.05[4][b][i], 10.05[5]
foreign, 10.05[4][b][ii], 10.05[4][b][iii],
10.05[5]

Personal property
casual sales, 5.04[2][d][i], 5.05[1][a],
5.05[6], 5.05[8][b]
dealers, 5.04, 5.05[2], 5.05[6]

Personal service corporation, 1.02[6]
qualified for cash method, 3.02,
3.06[1]
function test, 3.06[1][b][i]
ownership test, 3.06[1][b][ii]
taxable year, 10.04[1], 10.04[4][e],
10.04[5], 10.05[2][b],
10.05[2][g][i], 10.05[4][c]

Physical inventories, 6.05[2][c][i]

Points, 3.03[3][a], 3.04[5][a], 3.05[1][b],
11.02[4][b][ii]

Points, prepayment, 3.04[5][b]

Political considerations affecting tax
accounting, 1.03[2]

Pool index, 7.04[5][a][i]

Pooling, 7.04[2][a], 7.04[3]

Possessions tax credit, 10.05[4][b][iii]

Post-trilogy decisions, prepayment cases,
4.03[3][c]

Potentially abusive situations
See also Abuse
installment sales, 5.05[10][d]
OID, 11.02[5][a][ii]

Practical capacity concept, 6.06[2][c][ii],
6.07[3]

Predictability of accounting practice,
2.01[3]

Premium, bond, 11.05

Pre–1984 Act law on OID, 11.01[1],
11.01[2][a], 11.02, 11.05[1], 11.06,
11.10
See also Tax Reform Act of 1984

Prepaid income, 1.02[2], 3.02[1][a],
4.02[3], 4.03[3], 12.03[3][a][i]
See also Claim of right
deferral, 4.03[3][d]
dues, 4.03[3][e][i]
subscription, 4.03[3][a], 4.03[3][e][i]

Prepaid interest, 3.04[5][b]

Prepaid photographic processing,
4.03[3][e][ii]

Prepaid points, 3.04[5][b]

Prepaid supplies, 3.05[1][b]

Prepayment, 3.05
capitalization, 3.05[1], 3.05[1][b]
character, 3.05[1], 3.05[1][a]
goods, for, 4.03[3][e][ii]
insurance, 3.05[1][b]
interest, 3.04[5][a], 3.05[1][b]
issues, 3.05[1]
right to, 5.05[7][b]
services, for, 4.03[3][e][ii]
taxes, 3.05[1][b]
tax shelter expenses, 3.05[2]

President's Task Force, 4.03[3][e][i],
4.03[3][e][ii]

Pretrilogy treatment, prepayment cases,
4.03[3][a]

Price index category, 7.04[5][a][i]

Price indexes, 7.04[4], 7.04[5]

Price index LIFO method, 7.04[5][a]
adoption of, 7.04[5][a][ii]
changing to, 7.04[5][a][iii]

Primary records, 2.02[1][b]

Prime costing, 6.06[2][c], 6.08[2][b]

Principal partner rule for taxble year,
10.04[4][c][i]

Private annuities, 5.05[12][e]

Processor, 7.04[5][a][i]
definition, 6.06[2]

Product costing, 7.04[3][e]

Product development cost, 6.06[2][c][i]

Production costs, 6.07[5]

Production expenditure, 6.06[2][c][ii]

[References are to paragraphs (¶)]

Production period, 6.06[2][c][ii]

Profit motive in defining merchandise, 6.05[1][f][i]

Profit-sharing contributions, 6.06[2][c][i], 6.06[2][c][ii]

Promissory note, 3.03[1][d][i]

Promotional goods, 6.05[1][f]

Proof of compliance, 4.04[3][d]

Property
change in use, 6.05[1][e]
dual-use, 6.05[1][e]
sale or exchange, 1.02[3], 5.01, 11.02[5][b][iii]

Proportionate disallowance rule, 5.05[1][d], 5.05[4], 5.05[6]

Proprietorship, 8.04[5][a]

Protective application for change in method, 8.06[3][d]

Purchased goods market definition, 6.09[3][a]

Purchaser debt payable on demand, 5.05[7][f]

Purchasing
costs, 6.06[2][c][ii]
definition, 6.06[1][c][ii]

Purpose of information as affecting book conformity, 2.02[1][b]

Put, 11.02[4][a][iv]
definition, 11.02[3][a][i]

Q

Qualified periodic interest payment, 11.02[4][a][i]

Qualified personal service corporation. *See* Personal service corporation, qualified

Qualifying indebtedness, 5.05[7][c], 5.05[8][c]

Quantitative measures for specific goods LIFO, 7.04[2][b]

R

Real estate
installment sales, 5.05

as inventory, 6.05[3][a]

Real estate investment trust, 10.04[4][f][iii], 10.05[5]

Real estate taxes, 3.04[5][c]

Real property, casual sales of, 5.04[2][d][i]

Real property, dealer sales of, 5.05[2], 5.05[6]

Recapture
installment sales, 5.06[3][b], 5.05[9]
LIFO, 7.05, 7.07, 7.09
tax benefit rule, 12.05[4][b][ii], 12.05[4][b][v]

Recent legislative activity, 1.01[3]

Recharacterization
annual accounting concept, 12.02[2][f][iv], 12.02[2][f][v]
not change in accounting method, 8.02, 9.07
of principal as interest, 11.01[1][a], 11.01[2][a][i], 11.02[5], 11.04, 11.05[2]

Recognition of gain. *See* Gain, recognition of

Reconciling different methods
book conformity requirement, 2.02[1][c]
LIFO conformity requirement, 7.03[2][b][vii]

Records of consumption, 6.05[2][c][i]

Recovery, definition for tax benefit rule, 12.05[2]

Recurring item exception, 4.04[3][a], 4.04[3][f]

Redemption price at maturity, stated, 11.05[1]
definition, 11.02[4][a]

Refund of tax, 12.05[4][b][i]

Registration-required obligation, 11.08

Regular business activity, 6.05[1][f][ii]

Reimbursed loss, 12.05[4][a][iv]

REIT. *See* Real estate investment trust

Related parties
definition, 5.05[11][b][i], 5.05[11][c]
installment transactions, 5.05[2]
rules, 5.05[11][b]
sales, 5.05[11], 11.04[2][b][ii]

[References are to paragraphs (¶)]

Related parties *(cont'd)*
  sales *(cont'd)*
    exceptions, 5.05[11][b][iii]
    statute of limitations extension,
      5.05[11][b][iv]
  second disposition by, 5.05[11][a],
    5.05[11][b][iii]
  transactions, 3.06[1][d], 4.04[4]
  *Relative Importance of Components in
    the Consumer Price Indexes,*
    7.04[5][a][i]
Rent, 3.03[3][d], 6.06[2][c][ii]
  stepped, 11.10[1][b]
Rental agreement, 11.10[1]
Reorganization
  corporate, 3.02[1][a]
  nontaxable, 7.08[3]
Repair, 6.06[2][c][ii]
Replacement cost, 6.09[3][b]
Reports covering less than entire taxable
  year, 7.03[2][b][iv]
Repossession after installment sale,
  5.04[5], 5.05[14]
Reproduction cost, 6.09[3][b]
Request for change in year within 10
  years of prior change, 10.05[2][d]
Research and experimental expenses,
  6.06[2][c][ii], 6.07[5]
Reserve for guarantee, etc. *See*
  Warranty reserve
Reserve method of inventory
  accounting, 7.02[2]
Residence, principal, sale, 11.02[5][b][ii]
Restructuring techniques
  business, 1.02[5]
  corporate, 1.02[5]
Retailers, 6.06[1], 7.04[3][a][i]
Retail inventory method, 7.04[5][a][i]
Retail LIFO, 7.04[4]
Retail merchants inventory costing,
  6.10[4]
Retail sales facility, definition,
  6.06[1][c][ii]
Return under review when Form 3115
  filed, 8.06[2][c]
Revenue Act of 1913, 3.02

Revenue Act of 1916, 2.02[1][a], 3.02
Revenue Act of 1918, 2.02[1][a], 3.02,
  6.03
Revenue Act of 1921, 5.04[1]
Revenue Act of 1926, 5.04[1], 5.05[1][a]
Revenue Act of 1928, 2.02[1][d],
  5.05[1][a]
Revenue Act of 1939, 7.02[2], 7.04[3]
Revenue Act of 1987, 5.05[1][e], 5.07,
  7.09, 10.07
Revenue neutral, definition, 1.03[2]
Revenue Procedure 84-74 adjustment
  spread, 8.04[4], 8.06[2]
  See also Section 481 adjustment
  Category A methods spread,
    8.04[4][b][iii]
  Category B methods spread,
    8.04[4][b][iv]
  disproportionate build-up rule,
    8.04[4][b][ii]
  exceptions to general rule, 8.04[4][b]
  general rule, 8.04[4][a]
  governing procedures, 8.06[2]
  negative adjustment, 8.04[4][b][iii]
  positive adjustment, 8.04[4][b][iii]
  prior-year rule, 8.04[4][b][i]
Revolving credit sales, 5.04[1],
  5.04[2][d], 5.04[2][d][ii], 5.07,
  8.04[6][b]
Rework labor, 6.06[2][c][i], 6.06[2][c][ii]
Rolling averages, 6.08[3][a], 7.04[3][c]
Rotables, 6.05
Royalty income, 3.03[3][d]
Rule of 78's, 3.03[3][a], 3.04[5][a]

S

Safe haven installment sale provisions,
  5.05[11][b]
Salary, 3.03[3][c], 6.07[5]
Sale, bona fide, 6.09[3][b][iv], 7.07[2]
Sale, COD, 6.05[1][b]
Sale-leaseback transaction,
  11.02[5][a][iv]
Sale of depreciable property to
  controlled entity, 5.05[11][c]

[References are to paragraphs (¶)]

Sale of farm, patent, property, or residence, 11.02[5][b]

Sale of goods and services combined, 4.03[3], 6.05[1][d]

Sale of marketable securities, 3.03[3][e], 5.05[1][d]

Sale of multiple assets, 5.05[8][d]

Sale on approval, 6.05[1][b], 12.03[2][c]

Sale on consignment, 6.05[1][b]

Sale or return contract, 6.05[1][b]

Sales agent, 6.05[1][b]

Sales price adjustment, 12.04[2][a]

Sale, time for accrual, 4.03[1][a], 5.05[7][a], 6.05[1][b]

S corporation
   accrual method, 4.04[3][f][iii]
   cash method, 3.02, 3.02[3], 3.06[1][a]
   change in method of accounting, 8.04[2][d], 8.04[5][a]
   installment sale, 5.05[11][c]
   taxable year, 10.03[1], 10.04[1], 10.04[4][c][ii], 10.04[4][d], 10.04[4][e], 10.04[5], 10.05[2][b], 10.05[2][c], 10.05[2][g][i], 10.05[4][b][i], 10.05[4][b][ii], 10.05[4][b][iii], 10.05[4][c]
   tax benefit rule, 12.05[2]

Scrap, 6.06[2][c][i], 6.06[2][c][ii]

SEC. *See* Securities and Exchange Commission

Secretary of the Treasury, discretionary power, 6.04[1][a]
   See also Treasury Department

Section 111 income exclusionary rule, 12.05[4][b][i]

Section 163(b) deemed interest, 11.01[2][a][ii]

Section 269 acquisition, 9.08[1][c]

Section 351 transfer, 7.08[1], 9.08[1][a]
   impact on transferee, 7.08[1][b]
   impact on transferor, 7.08[1][a]

Section 368 reorganization, 9.08[1][b]

Section 381 transaction, 7.08[3]
   acquired business and acquirer on same method, 7.08[3][a]
   businesses to integrate, 7.08[3][c]

   businesses to remain separate, 7.08[3][b]

Section 444 election
   adjusted taxable income, 10.07[8][c]
   amount of required payment, 10.07[6][a]
   applicable amount, 10.07[8][a]
   applicable payment, 10.07[6][a][ii]
   background, 10.07[1][a]
   back-up election, 10.07[5][b]
   base year, 10.07[6][a][ii]
   base year of less than twelve months, 10.07[6][a][iii]
   by electing S corporation, 10.07[5][a]
   condition for making, 10.07[1][b]
   deferral period limitations, 10.07[4]
   deferral ratio, 10.07[6][a][ii]
   de minimis rules, 10.07[3][a]
   disallowance of NOL carryback, 10.07[8][e]
   election procedures, 10.07[5]
   maximum deductible amount, 10.07[8][d]
   minimum distribution requirement, 10.07[8][b]
   net base year income, 10.07[6][a][i]
   payment of required payment, 10.07[6][a][i]
   preceding year test, 10.07[8][b][i]
   PSC distribution, 10.07[8]
   PSC reduced deductions, 10.07[8]
   refunds of required payments, 10.07[6][c[
   required S corporation or PSC payment, 10.07[6]
   return under Section 7519, 10.07[7]
   same taxable year exception, 10.07[3][b]
   special rules, 10.07[6][a][iii], 10.07[6][a][iv]
   termination of election, 10.07[2]
   three-year average test, 10.07[8][b][ii]
   tiered structures, 10.07[3]

Section 467
   deferred payment agreements, 11.10[2]
   deferred rent, 11.10[1][a]
   rental agreement, 11.10[1]
   use of property or services, 11.10

Section 481 adjustment, 8.04, 8.05, 8.06[2], 8.06[3][b], 8.06[3][c], 9.04[2][b][iii]

[References are to paragraphs (¶)]

Section 481 adjustment *(cont'd)*
See also Revenue Procedure 84-74
  adjustment spread
acceleration of balance, 8.04[5]
  cessation of trade or business,
    8.04[5][a]
  change to LIFO method, 8.04[5][c]
  miscellaneous reasons for, 8.05[e]
  substantial reduction in inventory,
    8.05[b]
  termination of LIFO method,
    8.05[d]
amount, 8.04[1]
cessation of trade or business,
  8.04[5][a]
character of taxpayer, 8.04[2][d]
consecutive prior years allocation,
  8.04[2][b]
earnings and profits, 8.05
history of pre-1954 law, 8.04
Revenue Ruling 84-74 rules, 8.04
special rules, 8.04[2][c]
spread-forward, 8.04[3]
  history, 8.04[3]
  limitation on required spread, 8.04,
    8.06
  negative adjustment, 8.04, 8.06
  purpose, 8.04[3]
  unique spread periods, 8.04[3]
spread required by 1986 Act, 8.04[6]
subsidiary LIFO elections, 7.03[1][c]
tax spread-back limitations, 8.04[2]
three-year allocation, 8.04[2][a]

Section 483 recharacterization,
  11.01[2][a][i]
application, 11.04[2]
certain deferred payments, 11.04
due dates of payments, 11.04[2][a]
exceptions, 11.04[2][d]
unstated interest, 11.04[2][b]
  period of recognition, 11.04[2][c]
  sale of land to related party,
    11.04[2][b][ii]

Section 1271 characterization, 11.02[2]

Section 1272: current inclusion of OID,
  11.02[3]
definitions and terms, 11.02[3][a][i]
exceptions, 11.02[3][a][ii]
subsequent holders, 11.02[3][a][iii]

Section 1273: amount of OID, 11.02[4]

Section 1274 determination of issue
  price, 11.02[5]
exceptions, 11.02[5][b]
sales or exchanges to which Section
  483(e) applies, 11.02[5][b][v]

Section 1282 deferral, 11.06[2]

Section 1287 capital gains denial, 11.08

Section 1341 statutory relief, 12.03[4],
  12.04[4]
connection between receipt and
  payment, 12.03[4][c]
general requirements, 12.03[4][a]

Securities
bought for investment, 6.10[1]
dealers, inventory costing, 6.10[1]
deferred payment dispositions, 5.05[2]

Securities and Exchange Commission,
  7.02[2]

Segregation of sales/service charges,
  4.03[2][d]

Self-amortizing installment obligation,
  11.02[4][a][iii]

Selling expenses, 5.05[8][b],
  6.06[2][c][ii], 6.07[5]

Selling price, definition, 5.05[8][a]

Separate businesses, 2.03[1][a]

Sequential layering under LIFO, 7.02,
  7.04

Service contract. See Warranty reserve

Service income nonaccrual, 4.03[2][d]

Service provider, accrual method,
  8.04[6][d]

Shareholders, taxable year, 10.04[4][d],
  10.05[2][c]

Short period, 10.02[3]
  taxable income computation, 10.05[5]

Short term obligation, 11.02, 11.06
  covered by new rules, 11.06[1]

Short year, 8.04[4][a]

Shrinkage, 6.08[2][a]

Simplified allocation method, 6.07[5]
  de minimis rule, 6.07[5]

Simplified dollar-value LIFO method,
  7.04[5][b]

Simplified LIFO method, 7.04[5]

Simplified mixed service cost method, 6.07[5]

Simplified one-third/two-thirds method, 6.06[1][c][ii]

Simplified production method, 6.07[4]

Simplified resale method, 6.06[1][c][ii]

Simplified 10 percent method, 6.07[5]

Single pool, 7.04[3][a][iii]

Size of business. *See* Business

Small business
   corporation, 11.02[5][b][i]
   eligible, 7.04[5][a][i]

Special Committee on Inventories, 7.02[2]

Special order merchandise, 6.05[3][b]

Special single pool, 7.04[3][a][iii]

Specific goods LIFO, 7.04[2], 7.07[1]

Specific identification approach, 6.08

Spoilage, 6.06[2][c][i], 6.06[2][c][ii]

Standard cost method, 6.07[2]

Standby letter of credit, 5.05[7][e]

State court attempts to alter nature of earlier payments, 12.02[2][f][v]

Stated redemption price at maturity, 11.02[4][a]

State tax deficiencies, 4.04[1][c], 12.02[2][c]

Statute of limitations
   change in method, 8.02, 8.04[2][c], 9.01[1], 9.01[2]
   installment method, 5.05[11][b][iv]
   LIFO, 7.03[5]
   tax benefit rule, 12.05[4][c][i]

Step-allocation method, 6.07[5]

Stepped rent, 11.10[1][b]

Stock, deferred payment dispositions, 5.05[2]

Storage costs, 6.06[2][c][ii]

Straight-line interest recognition concept, 11.01[2][a][iii]

Strike costs, 6.06[2][c][i]

Stripped bonds, 11.07

Structured settlement, 4.04[3]

Subchapter S Revision Act of 1982, 10.04[4][d]

Subject-to mortgage, 5.05[10][b]

Subscription income, prepaid, 4.03[3][a], 4.03[3][e][i]

Subsidiary corporation taxable year, 10.05[4][b][iii]

Substantial business purpose for taxable year, 10.05[2][a]
   circumstances not amounting to, 10.05[2][c]

Substantial identity of methods test, 2.02[2][f]

Successor business, 4.03[2][d], 8.04[5][a], 10.04[4][b][iii]

Sufficient business purpose rules, 10.04[4][c][ii]

Supplementary records, 2.02[1][b]
Supplement to Producer Prices and Price Indexes, 7.04[5][a][i]

Supplies, 6.05[1][c], 6.05[2]
   incidental, 6.05[2][c]
   IRS definition of, 6.05[2][c][ii]

Supply inventory, 3.06[2], 6.04[1][b], 6.04[2], 6.05
See also Inventory, supplies
   arbitrary method of accounting, 9.04[2]
   definition, 6.03
   FIFO costing, 6.05[2][b]
   LIFO costing, 6.05[2][b]
   regulatory provisions, 6.04[2]
   required, 6.05[2][b]

Symmetry of accounting rules, lack of, 1.03[2]

T

Targeted jobs credit, 3.06[1][a]

Taxable year, 1.02[6], 10.02, 10.03, 10.04, 10.05
See also Section 444 election
   adoption, 10.04
      by amended return, 10.04[2]
      corporations, 10.04[4][b]
      DISCs, 10.02[4]
      estates, 10.04[4][f][i]
      FSCs, 10.02[4]
      individuals, 10.04[4][a]

[References are to paragraphs (¶)]

Taxable year *(cont'd)*
  adoption *(cont'd)*
    means of, 10.04[3]
    members of affiliated group,
      10.04[4][f][ii]
    partnerships, 10.04[4][c]
    personal service corporations,
      10.04[4][e]
    REITs, 10.04[4][f][iii]
    rules, 10.04[4]
    S corporations, 10.04[4][d]
    time of, 10.04[2]
    trusts, 10.04[f][i]
  annual accounting concept, 10.02,
    12.02
  annualization of income, 10.05[5]
    alternative method of, 10.05[5][b]
    normal method of, 10.05[5][a]
  business considerations, 10.03[1]
  change, 10.05
    application fees, 8.06[1], 10.05[3]
    application for, 10.05[3]
    automatic, 10.05[4][b][i],
      10.05[4][b][ii]
    change within prior 10 years,
      10.05[2][d]
    conform to annual accounting
      period, 10.05[2][f]
    conform to natural business year,
      10.05[2][b]
    consolidated group, joining and
      leaving, 10.02[3][a][ii]
    convenience to taxpayer or others,
      10.05[2][c]
    corporate partner, 10.05[4][c][iii]
    corporations, 10.05[4][b]
    death of individual, 10.02[3][b]
    deferral in income affecting,
      10.05[2][e]
    distortion in income affecting,
      10.05[2][e]
    exempt organizations, 10.05[4][d][i]
    fees, 8.06[1], 10.05[3]
    implied approval of change,
      2.04[3][b]
    individuals, 10.05[4][a]
    for nontax purposes, 10.02[1][b],
      10.05
    no substantial business purpose,
      10.05[2][c]

    partnership, 10.02[3][a], 10.04[4][c],
      10.05[4][c]
    personal service corporations,
      10.04[4][e], 10.05[4][c]
    preservation of tax status,
      10.05[2][c]
    reason, 10.05[1]
    request affected by nature of
      taxpayer, 10.05[4]
    requirements for, 10.05[2]
    return due before IRS
      determination, 10.05[3][c]
    S corporation, 10.04[4][d],
      10.05[4][c]
    special rules, 10.05[4][b][iii]
    substantial business purpose,
      10.05[2][a]
    tax benefit of, 10.05[1]
    taxpayer acceptance of IRS
      approval, 10.05[3][b]
    without prior approval, 10.05[3]
  definition, 10.01, 10.02
  52–53 week year, 10.02
    adoption, 10.04[5]
    change to or from, 10.05[2][g]
    special requirements, 10.06
  financial statement year vs. book
    year, 10.02[1][b]
  first, 10.04[4][b][ii], 10.04[4][b][iii],
    10.04[4][b][iv]
  Form 1128, 10.05[3][a]
  jeopardy assessments, 10.02[3][c]
  joint return, 10.02[3][b]
  natural business year, 10.03[1]
  new taxpayer, 10.04[4][a]
  1986 Act rules, 10.04[4][c],
    10.04[4][d], 10.04[4][e]
  no books or records, 10.02[1][b]
  sample natural business years,
    10.03[1]
  selection of, 10.03
  short periods, 10.02[3]
    adoption of year, 10.02[3][b]
    after change in year, 10.02[3][a]
    jeopardy assessments, 10.02[3][c]
  tax considerations, 10.03[2]
  taxpayer choice, 10.04[1]
  taxpayer in existence for less than full
    year, 10.02[3][b]
  termination of partnership,
    10.02[3][b]

[References are to paragraphs (¶)]

termination of year for parties,
10.02[3][b]
three-month income deferral,
10.05[4][c][i]
Tax accounting
defined, 1.01
goal, 12.01
issues, 1.01, 1.03, 1.04
legislative activity, 1.03[3]
political, economic, fiscal
considerations, 1.03[2]
principles, 1.03[1], 2.01[1], 2.01[2]
divergence from book accounting,
4.02[3], 4.02[4]
rules
application, 1.03[3]
changing, 1.01[3], 1.04, 5.02[7]
complexity, 1.03[1]
compliance, 1.03[3]
difficulties with, 1.03
topics, 1.02
Tax benefit rule, 1.02[8], 4.04[4], 12.05
accrued liabilities abandoned,
12.05[4][a][vi]
amount of recovery, 12.05[3]
application, 12.05[4]
judicial, 12.05[4][a]
legislative, 12.05[4][b]
bad debts, 12.05[4][b][i]
bad debt recoveries, 12.05[4][a][vii]
cancellation of indebtedness,
12.05[4][a][xi]
casualty loss, 12.05[4][a][iii]
charitable contribution returned,
12.05[4][a][ii]
contributions to capital, 12.05[4][a][x]
corporate liquidations, 12.05[4][a][ix]
definition of recovery, 12.05[2]
damage recoveries, 12.05[4][b][iii]
delinquency amounts, 12.05[4][b][i]
depreciation recapture, 12.05[4][b][ii]
exceptions, 12.05[4][c]
absence of deduction, 12.05[4][c][ii]
erroneous deduction, 12.05[4][c][i]
foreign expropriation losses,
12.05[4][b][iv]
history, 12.05[1]
LIFO recapture, 12.05[4][b][v]
previously expensed items,
12.05[4][a][i]

rationale, 12.05[1]
reimbursed expenses, 12.05[4][a][i]
reimbursed losses, 12.05[4][a][iv]
S corporations, 12.05[2]
taxes, 12.05[4][b][i]
transfer of accounts receivable or
other assets to controlled
corporation, 12.05[4][a][viii]
unpaid accrued expenses,
12.05[4][a][v]

Taxes, 3.04[5][c], 6.06[2][c][i],
6.06[2][c][ii]
on sales, 5.04[3][a]

Tax-exempt obligation, 11.02, 11.06[1],
11.09

Tax-free exchange, 3.02[1][c]

Tax-free transfer, 5.05[11][b][iii],
5.06[3][c]

Tax methods, 2.02[1]

Taxpayer attempts to change facts
retroactively, 12.02[2][f][iv]

Taxpayer in existence for less than an
entire year, 10.02[3][b]

Tax Reform Act of 1984
See also Pre-1984 Act law
accrual method, 4.04[2][c]
impact on tax accounting, 1.01[3],
1.02[2], 1.02[7], 1.04
installment method, 5.05[9]
original issue discount, 11.01[2][b],
11.02, 11.05[1], 11.06

Tax Reform Act of 1986
See also Pre-1986 Act law
accrual method, 4.03[2]
cash method, 3.01[2], 3.02, 3.05[2][a],
3.06, 3.08[1], 3.08[7]
changes in method of accounting,
8.04[6]
impact on tax accounting, 1.01[3],
1.02[2], 1.02[3], 1.02[4], 1.02[6],
1.03[2], 1.04
installment method, 5.04[1],
5.04[2][d], 5.04[2][d][ii], 5.04[5],
5.05[1][d], 5.05[2], 5.05[4],
5.05[6], 5.05[11][a], 5.05[11][b],
5.05[11][c], 5.06[3][b]
inventory, 6.01[2], 6.03, 6.04[1][b],
6.06

[References are to paragraphs (¶)]

Tax Reform Act of 1986 *(cont'd)*
  LIFO, 7.03[2][b][vi], 7.04[3][a][iii],
    7.04[3][d], 7.04[5], 7.04[5][a][i],
    7.04[5][b]
  method of accounting, 2.02[1][c],
    2.02[2][g]
  taxable year, 10.04[4][c], 10.04[4][d],
    10.04[4][e], 10.04[4][f][i],
    10.04[5], 10.05[2][c],
    10.05[2][g][i], 10.05[4][c]
  tax benefit rule, 12.05[4][a][vii],
    12.05[4][b][ii], 12.05[4][b][v]
Tax reporting, change in underlying
    facts, 9.06
Tax retroactively imposed,
    12.02[2][f][iii]
Tax shelters, cash method, 3.05[2],
    3.06[1]
Teaser rate, 11.02[4][c]
Technical Amendments Act of 1958,
    8.04
Techniques for changes without prior
    approval, 9.08
Temporarily idle equipment and
    facilities, 6.06[2][c][ii], 6.07[3]
Termination of business. *See* Business
Theft, 6.08[2][a]
Theoretical market value, 6.09[3][b]
Third-party guarantee, 5.05[7][e]
Third-party indebtedness, 5.05[7][d]
Third-party obligation, 3.04[3][a],
    5.06[4]
Thor Power Tool Co. case, 4.02[4]
Tickets, transportation, 4.03[3][e][ii]
Time of uncertainty, 4.03[2][b]
Time value of money, 1.01[2], 1.02[7],
    4.04[3], 11.01
  congressional action, 11.01[2]
    early response, 11.01[2][a]
    1984 Act, 11.01[2][b]
  definition, 11.01
  different character of income,
    11.01[1][a]
  different methods of accounting,
    11.01[1][b]
  discount on short-term obligations,
    11.06

interest on certain deferred payments,
    11.04
market discount on bonds, 11.05
original issue discount, 11.02
payments for use of property, 11.10
  deferred payments of rent,
    11.10[2][b]
  Section 467 rental agreement,
    11.10[2]
  stepped rents, 11.10[2][c]
payment for use of service, 11.10,
    11.10[3]
problem, 11.01[1]
  character of income, 11.01[1][a]
  method of accounting, 11.01[1][b]
stripped bonds, 11.07
Timing, 1.01, 2.01[1], 3.03[1][b],
    4.04[2][c], 9.03[1][c], 9.03[3]
  corporate distributions, 8.05
Tokens, bus or streetcar, 4.03[3][e][ii]
Tools, 6.06[2][c][ii]
  arbitrary method of accounting,
    9.04[2]
Tort liabilities, 4.04[3][b][iii]
Traditional installment plans,
    5.04[2][d][i]
Transactional concepts, 1.02[8], 12.01
Transition rules, cash method,
    3.06[1][d]
Treasury Department, 1.03[1], 2.01,
    2.02[1][a], 3.02, 4.04[1][b], 5.01,
    5.04[2][d][i], 5.04[3][b], 5.05[10][b],
    5.05[12][e], 5.05[15], 6.06[2][c][i],
    6.07[3], 6.09[1], 7.02[2], 7.03[2][b],
    7.04[3], 11.01[2][b]
  See also Secretary of the Treasury
  cash method, position on,
    3.03[1][d][iv]
  deferral, position on, 4.03[3][e][ii]
  liability, position on, 4.04[3]
Trilogy (prepayment cases), 4.03[3][b]
Trust, 4.04[3][f][iii], 10.04[4][f][i]
  charitable, 10.04[4][f][i]
  REIT, 10.04[4][f][iii], 10.05[5]
  tax-exempt, 10.04[4][f][i]
Trustee, 12.03[3][a][v]
  25 percent test, 10.04[4][c][ii],
    10.04[4][c][iv], 10.05[2][b],
    10.05[4][c][ii], 10.04[4][e]

[References are to paragraphs (¶)]

Twice as fast rule, 5.05[12][d][ii]
Two-payment rule, 5.04[2][d][i],
　5.05[1][a]
Two-taxable-year rule, 5.04[2][d][i]
Two-year limitation rule, 4.04[3][e][ii]
Two-year safe haven, 5.05[11][b][ii]

U

Underlying facts, change in, 9.06
　change in contract, business practice,
　　or economic consequences,
　　9.06[2][a]
　judicial development, 9.06[2]
　regulations, 9.06[1]
　significant consequences to parties,
　　9.06[2][b]
Uniform capitalization rules, 1.03[3],
　6.06[1][c], 6.06[2][c][ii], 6.07[4]
Uniform Commercial Code, 6.05[1][b]
Uniform costing rules, 6.06[1][c],
　6.06[2][c][ii], 6.07[4]
Unintended tax benefit, 8.04[5]
U.S. Bureau of Labor Statistics, 7.04[4],
　7.04[5][a][i]
U.S. savings bond, 11.02[3][a][ii]
Unit livestock price method, 6.10[2]
Unrecovered loss, 12.05[4][b][iii]
Unrelated business taxable income,
　5.04[2][c][i]
Unrestricted right, 12.03[4][b]
Use of different costing procedures,
　7.03[2][b][vi]
User fees, 8.06[1], 10.05[3]
Utilities, 6.06[2][c][ii]
Utility rate adjustments, 4.04[1][a][i],
　12.03[3][a][vi]

V

Valuing increments, 7.04[2][c],
　7.04[3][c]
Variable costing, 6.06[2][c]
Variance, 6.07[1]

Vertical slice, 7.08[1][a]
Virgin Islands inhabitants,
　10.05[4][b][iii]
Virtual identity of methods test,
　2.02[2][f]

W

Warehousing costs, 6.06[2][a],
　6.06[2][c][ii]
Warranty reserve, 4.03[3][a], 4.03[3][b],
　4.04[3][b][ii]
　See also Advance payment, for
　　services
Western Hemisphere trade corporation,
　10.05[4][b][i]
Wholesalers, 6.06[1], 7.04[3][a][i],
　7.04[5][a][i]
Windfall Profit Tax Act. *See* Crude Oil
　Windfall Profit Tax Act of 1980
Workers' compensation, 4.04[3][b][iii]
Wraparound mortgage, 5.05[10], 5.06[5]
　reasons for use, 5.05[10][a]
Write-down, market, 6.09, 7.03[3],
　8.06[2][b][i]
　abnormal goods, 6.09[2]
　evolution of rule, 6.09[1]
　excess inventory, 6.03[3][b][iii]
　GAAP impact on, 6.09[3][b][iii]
　goods offered for sale, 6.09[3][b][ii]
　market for manufacturers, 6.09[3][b]
　market for nonmanufacturers,
　　6.09[3][a]
　nominal quotations, 6.09[3][b][i]
　no open market, 6.09[3][b][i]
　normal goods, 6.09[3]
　restoration, 7.03[3][d]
　restored and prohibited, 7.03[3][c]

Y

Year
　See also Taxable year
　book, 10.02[1][b], 10.03[1]
　business considerations, 10.03[1]
　calendar, definition, 10.02[1][a]
　change in

[References are to paragraphs (¶)]

Year *(cont'd)*
  change in *(cont'd)*
    requested and approved,
      10.02[3][a][i]
    required, 10.02[3][a][ii],
      10.02[3][a][iii], 10.04[4][c][iii]
  52–53 week
    adoption, 10.04[5]

  definition, 10.02[2]
  fiscal, definition, 10.02[1][a]
  permitted, definition, 10.04[4][d],
    10.05[4][c]
  sale, determining, 5.05[7][a]

Yield to maturity, definition,
  11.02[3][a][i]